OUTDOORS

W9-BHX-334

FLORIDA CAMPING

MARILYN MOORE

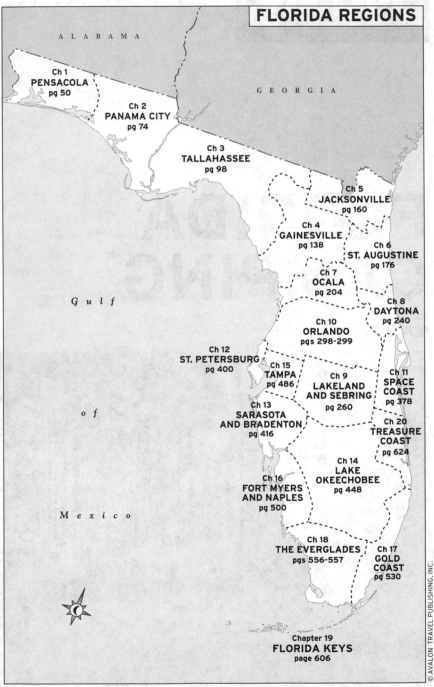

FLORIDA REGIONS

ALABAMA

GEORGIA

Ch 1
PENSACOLA
pg 50

Ch 2
PANAMA CITY
pg 74

Ch 3
TALLAHASSEE
pg 98

Ch 5
JACKSONVILLE
pg 160

Ch 4
GAINESVILLE
pg 138

Ch 6
ST. AUGUSTINE
pg 176

Ch 7
OCALA
pg 204

Ch 8
DAYTONA
pg 240

Gulf

Ch 10
ORLANDO
pgs 298-299

Ch 12
ST. PETERSBURG
pg 400

Ch 15
TAMPA
pg 486

Ch 9
LAKELAND
AND SEBRING
pg 260

Ch 11
SPACE
COAST
pg 378

of

Ch 13
SARASOTA
AND BRADENTON
pg 416

Ch 20
TREASURE
COAST
pg 624

Ch 14
LAKE
OKEECHOBEE
pg 448

Ch 16
FORT MYERS
AND NAPLES
pg 500

Mexico

Ch 18
THE EVERGLADES
pgs 556-557

Ch 17
GOLD
COAST
pg 530

Chapter 19
FLORIDA KEYS
page 606

Contents

How to Use This Book. 8

Introduction. 11

Author's Note. 12

Florida's Best Campgrounds. 14

Best Beachfront Campgrounds   Best Natural Springs
Best for Biking   Most Luxurious
Best for Families   Most Unusual
Best Island Retreats

Camping Tips. 17

Florida Trends. 17

Things You Should Know About Camping in Florida. 19

When To Go   Pets
Reservations   Children
Snowbirds   Age Restrictions
State Parks   Rates
Tents   Using the Facilities
RV Restrictions   The Florida Effect

Climate and Weather Protection. 25

Cold   Sun
Heat   Hypothermia
Rain   Lightning and Severe Weather

Bugs, Beasts, and Toxic Plants. 31

Alligators   Mosquitoes
Poisonous Toads   Roaches
Snakes   Ticks
Raccoons   Ants and Scorpions
Bears   Chiggers
Wild Hogs   Poison Ivy and Other Plant Pests
Bees, Wasps, and Yellow Jackets

Backcountry Camping (Plus a Few Hints for Car Campers). 40

Food
Utensils and Dishes
Stoves

Water
Clothing
Compass, Map, and GPS

Chapter 1 **Pensacola**. 47

Including:
Bear Lake
Bear Lake Recreation Area
Big Lagoon State Park
Blackwater River State Forest
Blackwater River State Park
Choctawhatchee River
Coldwater Recreation Area
Escambia River
Fort Walton Beach
Fred Gannon Rocky Bayou State Park

Gulf Islands National Seashore
Henderson Beach State Park
Hurricane Lake Recreation Area
Juniper Lake
Karick Lake
Kings Lake
Krul Recreation Area
Perdido Key
Santa Rosa Beach
Santa Rosa Island
Topsail Hill State Preserve

Chapter 2 **Panama City**. 71

Including:
Apalachicola River
Chattahoochee River
Choctawhatchee River
Falling Waters State Park
Florida Caverns State Park
Grayton Beach State Park
Mexico Beach

Panama City Beach
Pine Log State Forest
St. Andrews State Park
Three Rivers State Park
T. H. Stone Memorial St. Joseph
   Peninsula State Park
Upper Chipola River

Chapter 3 **Tallahassee**. 95

Including:
Apalachee Bay
Apalachicola National Forest
Camel Lake
Dr. Julian G. Bruce St. George Island
   State Park
Gulf of Mexico
Hitchcock Lake
Lafayette Blue Springs State Park
Lake Seminole
Lake Talquin
Lake Talquin State Forest

Madison Blue Springs State Park
Ochlockonee River
Ochlockonee River State Park
Porter Lake
St. Marks National Wildlife Refuge
Suwannee River
Suwannee River State Park
Torreya State Park
Whitehead Lake
Withlacoochee River
Wood Lake
Wright Lake

Chapter 4 **Gainesville**.......................... 135

Including:

Cedar Key
Crystal River
Lochloosa Wildlife Conservation Area

Manatee Springs State Park
O'Leno State Park
Paynes Prairie Preserve State Park
Shell Mound County Park

Chapter 5 **Jacksonville**......................... 157

Including:

Atlantic Beach
Cary State Forest
Fort Clinch State Park

Little Talbot Island State Park
Ocean Pond
Osceola National Forest
Ralph E. Simmons Memorial State Forest

Chapter 6 **St. Augustine**..................... 173

Including:

Anastasia State Park
Faver-Dykes State Park
Gamble Rogers Memorial State
   Recreation Area
Jennings State Forest

Lake George Conservation Area
Mike Roess Gold Head Branch State Park
Rodman Reservoir
St. Augustine Beach
St. Johns River

Chapter 7 **Ocala**.................................. 201

Including:

Clearwater Lake Recreation Area
Crystal River
Emeralda Marsh Conservation Area
Fore Lake
Juniper Springs Recreation Area
Lake Bryant
Lake Eaton

Ocala National Forest
Ocklawaha River
Orange Lake
Rainbow Springs State Park
Salt Springs Recreation Area
Silver River State Park
St. Johns River

Chapter 8 **Daytona**.............................. 237

Including:

Blue Spring State Park

Hontoon Island State Park
Lake Woodruff National Wildlife Refuge

Chapter 9 **Lakeland and Sebring**........... 257

Including:

Bull Creek Wildlife Management Area
Highlands Hammock State Park
KICCO Wildlife Management Area

Lake Garfield
Lake Jackson
Lake Juliana
Lake Kissimmee State Park

Lakeland RV Resort

Lake Marian

Lake Pierce

Lake Wales

Three Lakes Wildlife Management Area

Chapter 10 **Orlando**............................ 295

Including:

Florida National Scenic Trail/Chuluota

Fort Cooper State Park

Lady Lake

Lake Griffin State Park

Lake Jesup Conservation Area

Mullet Lake

Mutual Mine Recreation Area

Trail's End Camp

Wekiva River

Wekiwa Springs State Park

Withlacoochee State Forest

Withlacoochee State Forest Citrus Tract

Chapter 11 **Space Coast**....................... 375

Including:

Buck Lake Conservation Area

Canaveral National Seashore

Indian River

River Lakes Conservation Area

Sebastian Inlet State Park

Seminole Ranch Conservation Area

Three Forks Marsh Conservation Area

Chapter 12 **St. Petersburg**.................... 397

Including:

Anclote Key State Preserve

Caladesi Island State Park

Lake Manatee State Park

Myakka River State Park

Myakka State Forest

Oscar Scherer State Park

Peace River

Chapter 13 **Sarasota and Bradenton**........ 413

Including:

Caloosahatchee River

Kissimmee River

Chapter 14 **Lake Okeechobee**............... 445

Including:

Big Cypress Seminole Indian
   Reservation

J. W. Corbett Wildlife Management Area

Lake Okeechobee

Chapter 15 **Tampa**............................. 483

Including:

Hillsborough River State Park

Little Manatee River State Park

Chapter 16 **Fort Myers and Naples**........497

Including:
Cayo Costa Island
Cayo Costa State Park
Fred C. Babcock/Cecil M. Webb Wildlife
    Management Area
Koreshan State Historic Site
Webb Lake

Chapter 17 **Gold Coast**...........................527

Including:
Boca Chita Key
Elliott Key

Chapter 18 **The Everglades**....................551

Including:
Big Cypress National Preserve
Chatham River
Chokoloskee Island
Everglades National Park
Joe River
North River
Ten Thousand Islands

Chapter 19 **Florida Keys**......................603

Including:
Bahia Honda State Park
Big Pine Key
Curry Hammock State Park
Dry Tortugas National Park
Grassy Key
John Pennekamp Coral Reef State Park
Key Largo
Long Key State Park
Ohio Key
Stock Island
Sugarloaf Key

Chapter 20 **Treasure Coast**..................621

Including:
Blue Cypress Conservation Area
Blue Cypress Lake
Fort Drum March Conservation Area
St. Lucie Lock Recreation Area
The Savannas Recreational Area

Resources...........................639

Index..............................647

How to Use This Book

ABOUT THE CAMPGROUND PROFILES

The campgrounds are listed in a consistent, easy-to-read format to help you choose the ideal camping spot. If you already know the name of the specific campground you want to visit, or the name of the surrounding geological area or nearby feature (town, national or state park, forest, mountain, lake, river, etc.), look it up in the index and turn to the corresponding page. Here is a sample profile:

Campground name and number →

General location of the campground in relation to the nearest major town or landmark

Map the campground can be found on and page number the map can be found on

Icons noting activities and facilities at or nearby the campground

Rating of scenic beauty on a scale of 1-10 with 10 the highest rating

Symbol indicating that the campground is listed among the author's top picks

■ SOMEWHERE USA CAMPGROUND

Scenic rating: 10

south of Somewhere USA Lake

See map, page 4   BEST (

Each campground in this book begins with a brief overview of its setting. The description typically covers ambience, information about the attractions, and activities popular at the campground.

Campsites, facilities: This section notes the number of campsites for tents and RVs and indicates whether hookups are available. Facilities such as restrooms, picnic areas, recreation areas, laundry, and dump stations will be addressed, as well as the availability of piped water, showers, playgrounds, stores, and other amenities. The campground's pet policy and wheelchair accessibility is also mentioned here.

Reservations, fees: This section notes whether reservations are accepted and provides rates for tent sites and RV sites. If there are additional fees for parking or pets, or discounted weekly or seasonal rates, they will also be noted here.

Directions: This section provides mile-by-mile driving directions to the campground from the nearest major town or highway.

Contact: This section provides an address, phone number, and website, if available, for the campground.

ABOUT THE ICONS

The icons in this book are designed to provide at-a-glance information on activities, facilities, and services available on-site or within walking distance of each campground.

- 🏃 Hiking trails
- 🚲 Biking trails
- 🏊 Swimming
- 🎣 Fishing
- 🚤 Boating
- ⛲ Natural Springs
- 🛶 Canoeing and/or kayaking

- ❄ Winter sports
- 🐾 Pets permitted
- 🎠 Playground
- ♿ Wheelchair accessible
- 🚍 RV sites
- ⛺ Tent sites

ABOUT THE SCENIC RATING

Each campground profile employs a scenic rating on a scale of 1 to 10, with 1 being the least scenic and 10 being the most scenic. A scenic rating measures only the overall beauty of the campground and environs; it does not take into account noise level, facilities, maintenance, recreation options, or campground management. The setting of a campground with a lower scenic rating may simply not be as picturesque that of as a higher rated campground, however other factors that can influence a trip, such as noise or recreation access, can still affect or enhance your camping trip. Consider both the scenic rating and the profile description before deciding which campground is perfect for you.

MAP SYMBOLS

══════ Expressway	🛡80 Interstate Freeway	✈ Airfield
══════ Primary Road	🛡101 U.S. Highway	✈ Airport
══════ Secondary Road	29 State Highway	○ City/Town
- - - - - - - Unpaved Road	66 County Highway	▲ Mountain
·············· Ferry	⬤ Lake	⬧ Park
─ · ─ · ─ National Border	⬡ Dry Lake	⑴ Pass
─ · · ─ State Border	⬡ Seasonal Lake	⊙ State Capital

INTRODUCTION

Author's Note

If camping is your favorite vacation, or if you simply like to travel, this book is for you. Florida is home to some of the finest campgrounds in the nation. Add the Sunshine State's fabled appeal as a tourism destination, and you've got a winning combination for a trip to remember.

Many of us have discovered camping is the perfect escape from the pressures of modern life. It's a way to spend quality time with your family or mate, make new friends, rediscover the soul-restoring qualities of nature, or learn new skills. You can use a camping park as your home base for anything that satisfies you—from active sports like mountain biking and canoeing to more quiet pursuits like antiquing and bird-watching.

You can camp as a cheap way to travel to Disney World or tour the state. Florida is also a favored destination for RVers escaping the winter winds and seeking social and leisure lifestyles. Driving vacations are less hassle: No airport security, no delayed flights, and no expensive restaurant bills, plus you get to bring your own pillow (and whatever other personal belongings you wouldn't bring on a plane).

RV industry associations and RV manufacturers say that more and more people are discovering the joys of camping and the moving lifestyle, particularly since air travel and fears about foreign travel press upon us now. Thankfully, there are many places to go. Since the first edition of this book was published in 1998, dozens of new campgrounds have opened, and thousands of acres of wilderness have been made publicly accessible. The state of Florida makes continuing efforts to acquire and preserve new lands for the public; for example, through the Save Our Rivers program and others.

At the same time, many commercial parks have closed, fallen victim to the developer's bulldozer, or been converted to housing subdivisions or shopping centers. Some older private parks have simply filled to capacity, and many of their sites are now occupied by fulltime RVers in retirement. Even newly built parks are filling up quickly, as they sell the Great American Dream of second-home ownership: a patch of land on which to park your rig that you can rent out to itinerant travelers when you've gone back home to Canada, northern states, or elsewhere. Others were destroyed by the active hurricane seasons of 2004 and 2005.

But one thing hasn't changed: Every camper in Florida is different. One person's idea of the perfect vacation is traveling in a fully equipped, modern RV complete with microwave and satellite dish. Another would scoff at such luxuries, preferring a tent in the woods and cooking over a backpacker's stove. One camper's notion of heaven is hearing the bellow of an alligator deep in a cypress swamp; another would consider wading in waist-deep swamp water something akin to living out a horror movie. Some campgrounds are as luxurious as country clubs, whereas others are little more than a clearing in the forest.

Campers in Florida approach the experience with vastly divergent goals and expectations: to get out of the cold for the winter; to visit friends and family; to tour theme parks; to explore the state's natural wonders; to snorkel, canoe, hike, fish, ride horses, and bicycle off-road; or to scuba dive in a below-ground cavern or bubbling spring. Still others may plan to do a little of everything.

But Florida is a big state. It's a hard day's drive from the state line to South Florida, and it takes six hours to traverse the state from east to west. Even if you've decided where you're going, where will you stay on the way? What will you find when you get there?

This book will answer those questions—whether you're piloting a huge motorcoach or crammed into a tiny Toyota with a tarp and a sleeping bag; whether you need a place to plug in the TV or level ground to pitch a tent; whether you want shade trees to ward off the broiling sun or wide-open space to park a long, long trailer.

Maybe you need a convenient stop on the highway as you travel toward Florida's vast wilderness areas. Perhaps you just want to hunker down for the winter in a deluxe resort with like-minded people. Possibly, you're only interested in finding a cheap place to stay while you visit tourist attractions.

Six million campers explore the Sunshine State each year, according to the Florida Association of RV Parks and Campgrounds. Most of you will find the kind of campground that suits you best in *Florida Camping*. Why? Because this book is the only guide that includes almost every campsite in the state—more than 116,000 of them. They're part of more than 900 campgrounds, RV parks, and backcountry sites stretching from Pensacola to Key West.

If you're a wilderness lover heading for the Everglades by car from the northern state line, you have a lot of mileage to cover. You don't want to waste time on the way, but who wants to sleep in a parking lot? Tent-friendly, wooded campgrounds are noted in these pages.

If you've got your pop-top trailer in tow and the kids in the backseat, Disney World beckons (and Universal Studios, and myriad other tourist attractions clustered around the Big Mouse). Where can you stop? This book helps direct you to family-friendly spots.

If you're a retired couple heading for warmer climes, do you know which RV parks welcome folks for the winter season? This book will tell you.

Other details will help you make your choice, too. Are the mosquitoes worse by the lake? Is it hard to back a trailer into the spots at Campground A? Will you have to pitch your tent and sleep on gravel at Campground B? Are there showers with hot or cold water? Are there outhouses or restrooms? Is electricity available? (In Florida, even die-hard tent campers often use box fans on summer nights.)

This book should give you all the insights you need to choose a campground where you and your companions will be happy.

Ready? Let's hit the road. Fire up the ignition on the Class A motorcoach. Hitch up the fifth wheel, or whatever trailer suits your appetite. Throw the cooler in the back of the car. Snatch up your propane bottles or your backpack, and strap on the bike racks. You'll see Florida in the very best way.

FLORIDA'S BEST CAMPGROUNDS

Can't decide where to camp this weekend? Check out these picks for best of the state in a range of categories:

◖ Best Beachfront Campgrounds

Henderson Beach State Park, Pensacola, page 69
Grayton Beach State Park, Panama City, page 85
St. Andrews State Park, Panama City, page 90
T. H. Stone Memorial St. Joseph Peninsula State Park, Panama City, page 93
Anastasia State Park, St. Augustine, page 182
Fort de Soto Park Campground, St. Petersburg, page 412
Gulf Beach Campground, Sarasota and Bradenton, page 433
Long Key State Park, Florida Keys, page 610
Curry Hammock State Park, Florida Keys, page 612
Bahia Honda State Park, Florida Keys, page 614

◖ Best for Biking

Pine Log State Forest, Panama City, page 83
Suwannee River State Park, Tallahassee, page 111
Stephen Foster Folk Culture Center State Park, Tallahassee, page 113
Wright Lake, Tallahassee, page 120
O'Leno State Park, Gainesville, page 145
Paynes Prairie Preserve State Park, Gainesville, page 147
Trimble Park, Orlando, page 313
Silver Lake Campground, Orlando, page 332
Alafia River State Park, Tampa, page 493
Collier Seminole State Park, The Everglades, page 558
Long Pine Key Campground, The Everglades, page 566

◖ Best for Families

Emerald Coast RV Beach Resort, Panama City, page 87
Suwannee Valley Campground, Tallahassee, page 114
Kathryn Abbey Hanna Park,, Jacksonville, page 166
Sunshine Holiday Daytona RV Resort, Daytona, page 241
River Ranch RV Resort, Lakeland and Sebring, page 281
Peace River Preserve, Lakeland and Sebring, page 286
Disney's Fort Wilderness Campground, Orlando, page 363
Arcadia's Peace River Campground, Sarasota and Bradenton, page 429
Lion Country Safari KOA, Gold Coast, page 534
Markham Park, Gold Coast, page 543

❰ Best Island Retreats

Little Talbot Island State Park, Jacksonville, page 164
Hontoon Island State Park, Daytona, page 246
Canaveral National Seashore Beach, Space Coast, page 379
Long Point Park, Space Coast, page 394
Anclote Key State Preserve Boat-In Sites, St. Petersburg, page 404
Fort de Soto Park Campground, St. Petersburg, page 412
Cayo Costa State Park Boat-In Sites, Fort Myers and Naples, page 507
Peanut Island, Gold Coast, page 532
Boca Chita Key Boat-In Sites, Gold Coast, page 549
Dry Tortugas National Park/Fort Jefferson Boat-In or Fly-In Sites, Florida Keys,
    page 619

❰ Best Natural Springs

Vortex Spring RV Park, Panama City, page 77
Ellie Ray's River Landing, Gainesville, page 142
Ginnie Springs Resort, Gainesville, page 144
Hart Springs Gilchrist County Park, Gainesville, page 151
Manatee Springs State Park, Gainesville, page 151
Otter Springs RV Resort, Gainesville, page 152
Salt Springs Recreation Area, Ocala, page 208
Rainbow Springs State Park, Ocala, page 225
Kelly Park, Orlando, page 318
Wekiwa Springs State Park, Orlando, page 320

❰ Most Luxurious

Roughing it? Not here. These parks can't be called campgrounds, really. They're more
like resort hotels.

Destin RV Beach Resort, Pensacola, page 68
Topsail Hill State Preserve, Pensacola, page 70
Emerald Coast RV Beach Resort, Panama City, page 87
Grand Lake RV and Golf Resort, Ocala, page 205
River Ranch RV Resort, Lakeland and Sebring, page 281
Disney's Fort Wilderness Campground, Orlando, page 363
Deer Creek RV Golf Resort, Orlando, page 371
Seasons in the Sun Motorcoach Resort, Space Coast, page 381
Outdoor Resorts Melbourne Beach, Space Coast, page 391
Bluewater Key RV Park, Florida Keys, page 617

❰ Most Unusual

Camping on the Gulf Holiday Travel Park, Pensacola, page 69, has an indoor
    swimming pool.
Falling Waters State Park, Panama City, page 78, has Florida's only waterfall.
Florida Caverns State Park, Panama City, page 80 has beautiful caves.

Torreya State Park, Tallahassee, page 99, has mountains. Well, OK, steep hills.

Suwannee Valley Campground, Tallahassee, page 114, has a dog activity area.

Miller's Marine Campground, Tallahassee, page 133, rents houseboats from which you can go upstream from the Gulf of Mexico on the Suwannee River.

Tresca Memorial Park/Advent Christian Village, Gainesville, page 139, is oriented to Bible study and a Christian lifestyle.

O'Leno State Park, Gainesville, page 145, has a river that goes underground and reappears three miles later.

Mike Roess Gold Head Branch State Park, St. Augustine, page 178, has a mini-canyon.

Rock Crusher Canyon RV and Music Park, Ocala, page 233, has a big-time concert venue. Top-name artists like Willie Nelson and others perform here in an amphitheater. It's also popular as a quick getaway zone when a hurricane threatens Southern and Central Florida.

Buttgenbach Mine Campground, Orlando, page 331, is nirvana for motorcyclists, dirt bikers, and all-terrain vehicles (ATVs).

Wallaby Ranch Flight Park, Orlando, page 369, is for hang gliders.

Manatee Hammock, Space Coast, page 384, is one the closest campgrounds from which to watch space shuttle launches at Kennedy Space Center; several others also make that claim in the Space Coast chapter. The truth is you can see the shuttle take flight from campgrounds as far away as Kissimmee. It just depends on how good a view you want to get.

Pioneer Park of Hardee County, Lake Okeechobee, page 449, has a small wildlife refuge, including bears and a cougar.

Kissimmee Billie Swamp Safari, Lake Okeechobee, page 482, offers a taste of how the Seminole Indians once lived. Sleep in a chickee hut, or take a swamp buggy ride into the wilderness, and you may see American bison, panthers, and antelopes.

Lion Country Safari KOA, Gold Coast, page 534, has a wildlife zoo with lions.

Quiet Waters Park, Gold Coast, page 536, has a "rent-a-camp" package that includes permanent tents mounted on wooden platforms, plus wakeboarding (the national championships were held here in 2006) and boatless water-skiing (skiers are pulled by cable across a lake).

Campgrounds with technical mountain biking trails include **Alafia River State Park,** Tampa, page 493; **Quiet Waters Park,** Gold Coast, page 536; and **Markham Park,** Gold Coast, page 543.

Seven nudist campgrounds will give you the chance to get an all-over suntan: **Riviera Naturist Resort,** Pensacola, page 59; **Hidden River Resort,** Jacksonville, page 171; **Sunny Sands Nudist Resort,** Daytona, page 241; **Lake Como Club,** Orlando, page 353; **Sunsport Gardens,** Gold Coast, page 533; **Seminole Health Club,** Gold Coast, page 544: and **Sunnier Palms Nudist Campground,** Treasure Coast, page 631.

Camping Tips

FLORIDA TRENDS

Things move quickly in Florida, a state that always seems to be on the cutting edge of national trends. This fourth edition of *Florida Camping* will bring you up to date. Consider the following:

• The Internet has changed the way people camp. New RVs now come equipped with desk areas for computers. Some campgrounds have installed wireless Internet networks that are more or less accessible throughout the property. Others place Web-accessible computers in their recreation halls, so travelers can check email and keep in touch with home. State parks, national parks, and public agencies that administer public lands post maps on their websites that you can download for general orientation and other details. On the negative side, countless gigabytes in commercial cyberspace are devoted to pseudo-RV directories. Use these online directories at your risk; they are often totally out of date. Once the sites are posted, the owners make minimal effort to recheck the information on a regular basis.

• Full-time camping has become a reality for many people. Recessionary times, early retirement bonuses and layoffs, or just plain old wanderlust have converted many a former working stiff into a roadmaster. The full-time camping lifestyle (estimated at about $2,000 a month in expenses, not counting fuel) is more economical than ever. The only drawback is the volatile cost of gasoline.

• Middle-class parents, perhaps recalling the long drive-across-America trips they enjoyed as children, see camping as a budget-stretching way to take their own kids on Disney World vacations or to Florida beaches. The kids themselves, toughened by outdoors Scouting activities and the rage for extreme sports, are happy to go, at least until they reach the age

Curry Hammock State Park in the Florida Keys offers beachside camping.

TIN CAN CAMPERS

Ever since the Model T, Florida has been a camping mecca, drawing thousands of people seeking adventure and sunshine.

As early as 1916, the first "snowbirds" packed up homemade house cars or trailers and headed south for the winter. Experts estimated that half of the 50,000 trailers on the road in the United States were hauled to Florida during one winter in the 1930s. Sunshine State hoteliers and boardinghouse owners howled that their business would drop. But the hotels remained crowded, and trailer parks began to spring up all over the state to accommodate RVs. It helped that the campers' money was as green as everyone else's.

Those early campers formed their own version of the Good Sam Club, calling themselves the Tin Can Tourists of the World. Founded in a Tampa campground in 1919, the group grew to 30,000 members by 1938. Its goals were to provide members with "safe and clean camping areas, wholesome entertainment, and high moral values," according to Florida state archives. Their official emblem? A tin can soldered to the radiator cap of a member's car.

The origin of the tin can moniker isn't clear. It may have referred to their preference for canned foodstuffs (forget the freeze-dried food – it hadn't been invented). Or it could have been a reference to the Tin Lizzie, as Model T Fords were called.

The Tin Can Tourists gathered at parks around the state, usually in Tampa, Sarasota, Ocala, and Eustis. During the summer, they met at a campground in Michigan. Their favored Florida migration route: Dade City (Pasco County) at Thanksgiving and Arcadia (DeSoto County) for Christmas, where they celebrated with a community Christmas tree and Santa Claus for the children, according to *The WPA Guide to Florida*, a book written during the Great Depression.

In 1931, the city of Sarasota opened a municipal trailer park that quickly became

where they no longer want to go anywhere with their parents.

• Our fast-paced modern lives have ignited a thirst for getting out of the city and into a more natural setting. The RV industry has noticed and is now producing both bigger, fancier RVs for affluent retirees and smaller, lighter, more efficient trailers and pop-tops for family campers.

• Older people are no longer "senior citizens." They're "active retirees searching for an active lifestyle." Many RV parks now have tennis courts, golf courses, exercise rooms, and full-time activities directors. Of course, the heated swimming pool and spa, shuffleboard courts, and stocked fishing ponds are still ubiquitous, as is the recreation hall

with bingo, potluck suppers, and ice-cream socials. These parks have become the wintertime home address for both affluent RVers and penny-pinching retirees.

• Florida state parks previously banned pets, making these award-winning natural beauties inaccessible to many travelers. Now most parks allow you to bring dogs, provided they have proof of vaccination against rabies and behave on a leash. Tip: If you travel with a pet, you should carry proof of rabies vaccination. State parks also are now under a convenient, systemwide reservation system, relieving the uncertainty of being greeted with the equivalent of a No Vacancy sign.

• Some RV parks are getting more luxurious—and falling under the ownership of corporate winter headquarters for the Tin Can Tourists. During its first season, 1,500 people in 600 trailers set up camp. Five years later, the population had grown to 7,460 people and nearly 3,000 cars, as noted in *So This Is Florida* (written by Frank Parker Stockbridge and John Holliday Perry, published in 1938).

The Sarasota Tourist Park was located on 30 acres wooded with Australian pines at a railroad crossing and Ringling Boulevard. The park even hosted the Tin Canners' annual convention, featuring a parade of new models and equipment – basically, a 1930s-style RV show.

Ocala and Arcadia had municipal trailer parks in the 1930s, but the millionaire's city of Palm Beach allowed trailers to park for one hour only.

Conveniences at a park in Bartow in Polk County sound much the same as today's: water, electricity, hot and cold showers, laundry facilities, a recreation hall, shuffleboard courts, and horseshoe pits. The price? Stockbridge and Perry tell us that camping cost $1.30 by the week for two people, plus 25 cents for each additional person. (Campground owners got that extra-person charge started early, didn't they?) Fees at other parks ranged from $1 to $5.

Camping in those days presented much the same spectacle as today. You would have seen dusty cars and trailers with license plates from all over the United States. Campers caught up with old acquaintances and made new friends. They played shuffleboard and cards, or they congregated in the recreation hall. They cooked in the open and hung laundry out to dry. And when dusk came, they lounged outdoors to watch the sun set.

So take a moment tonight, after your tent is pitched or the RV is leveled, and think back to the Tin Can Campers. Americans have been enjoying the great outdoors of Florida in their own individual style for a long, long time.

chains. A handful of RV parks are selling not just resort-style living or condominium lots, but "RV ports"—luxury garages for the vehicle, with attached housing. Several parks now offer "super" sites with spas, patio furniture, and barbecue grills. The jury is still out on this feature.

THINGS YOU SHOULD KNOW ABOUT CAMPING IN FLORIDA

Here are some personal insights derived from many years of camping in Florida.

When To Go

You *can* camp in Florida at any time—the weather's fine most of the year. On the other hand, when you *should* camp depends on what kind of experience you're looking for.

When are parks least crowded? For the purposes of most out-of-state visitors, Florida has two seasons. North Florida, particularly along the Gulf Coast in the Panhandle, sees its "high" season in the summer months, when school is out. South and Central Florida campgrounds are busiest in the winter months, mainly mid-December through April.

Most campgrounds are open 12 months of the year. However, some that are oriented to snowbird visitors, usually retirees, do close down in the long, hot Florida summer, generally May through October. Even if they don't close, that would be the "slow" season for this type of park.

Reservations

Most private campgrounds recommend that you make reservations, as noted in the listings. Often, they require a nonrefundable deposit ranging from $25 to $100 or more, depending on the length of your stay.

Overnighters, beware: Don't make reservations for an overnight stop unless you are absolutely certain you wish to stay in a particular place.

On a scorching-hot summer weekend years ago, we made reservations at a private campground in the Florida Keys. We drove south, chose a site as instructed by the office, unhitched the trailer, and plugged in the electric cord. Then we switched on the air-conditioning. Nothing. We jiggled the circuit breaker. Nope. We took the air conditioner apart trying to find a short circuit. Nada. Now the sweat was rolling down our hot little faces. It was 90 degrees in the shade, and there really was no shade to speak of. After an hour of trying, it was clear there was to be no air-conditioning—and that we were not going to stay. We departed, but our $25 deposit was lost.

If you're just traveling through, many private campgrounds will squeeze you in overnight, even without a reservation. Just call ahead and tell them how big your rig is—although using this method may not get you the choicest spot. One private campground near Sarasota put us in a utility right-of-way under the telephone and electric poles. Our view was of the back of some mobile homes, the perimeter fence, and the dumpster. But hey, we were there for only one night and just passing through on the way to someplace nicer.

For state parks and many public lands, definitely make a reservation. Reservations are now handled by ReserveAmerica; call 800/326-3521 or visit www.reserveamerica.com.

Snowbirds

You're the exception to the rule on reservations. If you're coming to Florida to stay for the winter or for several weeks, make a reservation early. Parks fill up fast during their busy season. Many visitors return to the same park year after year, and this is the best way to guarantee you'll get the site you want.

If it's your first time in the area, you might scout for a park where you'd like to stay next winter. Try a few days at several places to get a feel for the crowd, the activities, and things to do in the area. Then make your reservation for the following year. Many parks accept reservations as early as the preceding spring, so you'll have to act quickly.

State Parks

Most of the best campgrounds in Florida are in state parks, where demand is high on weekends and holidays. It's easy to make reservations, especially at the more popular places. You can even book a specific site.

Under the new system, state parks now accept reservations 11 months in advance of your stay. Again, call ReserveAmerica at 800/326-3521 or visit www.reserveamerica.com.

Tents

Roughly 80 percent of the private campgrounds in Florida prohibit tent campers. It seems unfair at first glance, but it's just basic free-market economics. Consider that the bread and butter of most private parks is the retired, long-staying RVer who has invested thousands of dollars in a rig and wants to mix with like-minded folks. Other parks set aside a separate tenting area, which may make you feel like a second-class citizen. An optimist would tell you to consider yourself lucky. You won't be bothered by the hum of loud air conditioners, generators, or TV sets from the RV section.

An alternative for the tenting crowd is to look beyond the private campgrounds. This book lists plenty of out-of-the-way backcountry

CAMPING ETIQUETTE

Miss Manners would have a field day if she ever deigned to visit some campgrounds. While most parks have published rules against noise, some managers are unable or unwilling to enforce them. Don't be inconsiderate of others. It boils down to respecting the rights of others:

Keep radios turned down. Your taste in music does not appeal to everyone. If you have visitors, especially after dark, be attuned to other campers' rights to peace and quiet. Unnecessary noise is everyone's pet peeve. Observe quiet times and curfews.

Children should be supervised at all times. It's also safe practice against harm.

Don't molest, tease, or feed wildlife. Never, ever give food to alligators; it's against the law in Florida. Furthermore, it makes them associate humans with food, and they can turn dangerous.

Don't take shortcuts across occupied campsites. It's rude.

Share the park. Tent campers have no walls. Noisy generators and air conditioners can be bothersome; most parks separate RVs from tent campers, where possible.

In the bathhouse, conserve hot water for others. Don't take long showers or leave faucets running. If you see an open faucet, shut it off. Let the management know if supplies are running low, or if bathrooms are unclean. Wear flip-flops or sandals. Try to avoid tracking dirt or mud into the bathhouse.

Don't tie anything to trees or shrubs. Clotheslines are an eyesore, if sometimes necessary. Bring in towels and bathing suits when they are dry.

Wash dishes in the appropriate place. Most campgrounds frown on dish-washing in the bathhouses.

Most publicly owned campgrounds, including state parks, prohibit alcohol, firearms, and BB guns.

Put garbage in the correct bins; throw cans and plastic bottles into recycling containers. Don't leave household trash outside; it attracts animals and bugs.

Check the rules before doing mechanical repairs, oil changes, and heavy auto maintenance.

In the laundry facilities, don't leave your clothes in dryers or washers after the cycle ends. Fold clothes at your site or at the table provided in the laundry.

Pets should be on a leash at all times. Don't tie your dog up to your car or RV and leave it behind. Barking dogs and aggressive behavior are explicitly prohibited at most places; they can be grounds for eviction.

When you walk your pet, clean up after it. Use the dog-walk area if one is provided.

Park extra vehicles in the designated area. Store away toys and tools when not in use.

Use the dump station when needed. Avoid spilling gray water on the ground.

Where fires are permitted, use existing fire rings or grills. When leaving, put out the fire completely, pack out all trash from the fire ring, and scatter the ashes away from the site. Ground fires *can* be started by campfires that are not properly dismantled.

Scour your campsite for even the tiniest piece of trash and any other evidence of your stay. Never litter.

© MARILYN MOORE

KEEP IT WILD TIP: CAMP WITH CARE

For the safest and most responsible wilderness experience, follow these basic rules of thumb:
- Choose a preexisting, legal campsite. In pristine areas, choose a site on a durable surface that won't be damaged by your stay.
- Camp at least 75 steps (200 feet) from lakes, streams, and trails.
- Don't harm an area by marking trees or trails, moving rocks or fallen logs, digging, or building structures.

wonders where you'll feel well removed from the settled world that greets most RV campers. Florida's award-winning state parks all accept tents, as do many county parks.

You can also try the water management districts and wildlife management areas for the quiet, secluded tent camping of your dreams. One friend treasures his winter trips to the Three Lakes Wildlife Management Area in Central Florida. On a casual visit, he was astounded to see three wild turkeys scampering out of an oak hammock to take cover in tall blond grasses, and a bobcat dashing into saw palmetto thickets. Understandably, many people consider tent camping the only way to go.

I am particularly fond of state parks, which seek to maintain a setting as it looked when the first Europeans arrived in Florida the century after Columbus. But if you really want to get away from city lights, check out the little-known state forests and water management districts, as well as the primitive areas offered by the national parks and national or Florida state forests. Some county parks are real gems, too.

Rugged types who don't mind giving up niceties such as electricity and running water can also consider the hunter domains overseen by the Florida Fish and Wildlife Conservation Commission. Even if you're not a hunter, you're likely to see wild animals in these public areas. The hunting season generally starts in the late fall through early winter and lasts for short intervals. Keep in mind that the starting and ending dates vary from year to year. Check www.floridaconservation.org for exact dates.

RV Restrictions

If you think the only rules limiting RVs are the length of your rig and the size of the available site, think again. A few Florida RV parks don't allow pop-top campers, truck campers, vans, converted school buses, or RVs more than 20 years old. Some now restrict visitors to Class A motorhomes, or recreational vehicles more than 36 feet long.

Pets

Many Florida state parks now allow pets in their campgrounds. You no longer have to show proof of the pet's rabies vaccination, but generally speaking, it's a good idea to carry it with you for other parks. Pets must be kept on a leash at all times and must be well-behaved.

A few state parks, particularly those near beaches, may allow your pet in the campground, but never on the beach.

Pets are allowed in most private parks, national forests, many county-run campgrounds, Florida Fish and Wildlife Conservation Commission campsites, many water management district sites, and U.S. Army Corps of Engineers sites.

In a few fish camps and remote areas, dogs don't need to be leashed, but leashes are the rule just about everywhere else.

Some places charge an extra fee of $2 or so per day per pet. Many RV parks restrict the size and weight of the pets they will allow (under 20 pounds, for example). Others prohibit specific breeds, such as pit bulls, Rottweilers or Great Danes. One campground in the Panhandle told me pets are allowed, except for potbellied pigs.

Most parks have other requirements, such as walking your dog in a special area. It's fair to say that nearly all require you to clean up after your dog. They may even put all the pet owners in a special section. Of course, do not leave your pet unattended or tie him or her up to your RV while you tee up on the golf course or run down to the grocery store.

Which leads to another point: Never leave your pet locked in your car. Even with the windows cracked, the temperature inside a car can quickly reach fatal levels in hot Florida.

Children

At many private RV parks, children are not welcome. This book's campground listings note when this is the case.

Some parks are willing to bend the rules if you look like a reasonable person and promise not to let your kids go unsupervised in the common areas, such as the swimming pool or restrooms. Others, even those strictly targeted to retirees, allow grandchildren to visit for, say, two weeks during the course of a year.

Then there are those parks that say they allow children, but give you the third degree, starting with: "How big are the kids?" Some places frown on babies or small children, perhaps because they cry at night. Others are OK with little ones but dislike teenagers. Said one campground manager in Panama City: "Kids are OK, as long as they're not Spring Breakers."

Sometimes, it's clear that the rules are intended to keep out the working poor. There's a touch of elitism in a regulation that allows retirees to stay as long as they can pay, but wants no school-age children on the grounds for more than two weeks.

But like irresponsible pet owners who have made it difficult for everyone else, some lax parents have made it tough for other families. I was shocked when one campground owner near North Port cautioned us, "We allow kids, as long as you don't go off and leave them here alone for days." Huh?

Age Restrictions

You've reached voting age, so you're an adult, right? Not necessarily. You may not be old enough. Not only do some campgrounds ban children, but there may be other complicated rules as well. Some require at least one camper to be over the age of 55; others say all visitors must be over 65. Yes, in Florida, a trailer park is not always a trailer park; it's a "retirement community," an "over-55 park," or an "adult resort."

KEEP IT WILD TIP:
PLAN AHEAD AND PREPARE

For the safest and most responsible wilderness experience, follow these basic rules of thumb:
• Find out about any regulations or environmental issues concerning the area you plan to visit ahead of time.
• Obtain all the necessary permits.
• Pack food in reusable containers to reduce waste.
• Avoid heavy-use areas, which put strain on the land and its resources.

Rates

Let's start with the free places and work upward. Florida Fish and Wildlife Conservation Commission sites, spots along the Florida National Scenic Trail, and water management district sites do not charge campers, or only charge fees as small as $5 per carload. Also, primitive camping within national forests is free. Check the listings for details.

The least expensive parks are national and state forests, state parks, and county parks. State parks charge more for beachfront campgrounds.

Most private RV parks charge competitive rates, usually around $30 to $35 per night for two people. At deluxe resorts, charges can go as high as $85. In most places, cable TV service and sewer hookups are included in the base rate.

Then there are add-ons. Private parks usually charge a fee for each additional person, normally $3 to $5 each. Sometimes, discounts are given for children under 12. Extra people can cost as much as $8 to $15 in a handful of places. Also, some private operators charge extra for use of air-conditioning, electric heaters, and washers or dryers (usually $2 daily).

More desirable sites (closest to the beach, for example) go for a higher rate. And rates "in season" will be higher than those in slow times of the year. Finally, some campgrounds charge even more when there's a special festival or other crowd-drawing attraction, such as Bikefest in Daytona Beach.

On the other hand, national parks, county parks and others offer discounted rates to folks over 65 or the disabled. You'll be required to provide proof of age or disability.

Rates do not include sales tax, which vary from county to county.

Snowbirds who store their RVs on-site after the season ends can save money. After the sixth month, they do not pay the local tourist tax, which varies by location but can be as high as 11 percent. In addition, most parks charge only nominal fees for storing a rig during the summer.

Just FYI: If you don't mind traffic noise, you can also camp for free in some Wal-Mart parking lots and lots at the Cracker Barrel restaurant chain. You'll need to ask the manager for permission to stay overnight. Some Moose lodges also allow RVs to hook up in their parking areas. Campground owners, naturally, don't like this trend, considering it competition. Frankly, for my money, Florida offers too many pretty places for me to consider staying in a parking lot.

Using the Facilities

If you're not in a self-contained RV, you're going to have to face the communal restrooms and showers. Many parks brag that their facilities are sparkling clean. That may be, but I've found plenty that gave me pause. The drains don't drain, the hot water runs out, or you're forced to listen helplessly to endless palaver from your neighbors. Bring soap, shampoo, toothbrush and toothpaste, and other niceties in a separate bag; sometimes a flashlight is needed for the walk. Don't forget a towel and a change of clothes. Most campgrounds perform a daily cleaning routine about 11 A.M., and that's it for the day. If you must take a shower at night, you'll likely find you have to wait your turn, and by then, things aren't so sparkling, or the water is tepid. Mornings are quieter, and you're more likely to have hot water. Get up early.

The Florida Effect

Things change here. From the time Henry Flagler's railroad came marching down the east coast, change has been a constant in Florida. Hurricanes and wildfires roar through, eradicating buildings, washing out streets, and even eliminating big sections of forest.

Mobile-home parks on the city/suburb edge get supplanted by subdivisions, sometimes in a matter of weeks. One example is the All-Star Resort in Perdido Key, near

Pensacola. Just two years after it opened with brand-new sparkling facilities, winning the highest ranking of 10, it was torn down, reportedly for a condominium. Well, it was right on the beach—the most valuable property in Florida.

Another example is the campground at Fort Pickens in the Gulf Islands National Seashore, which was destroyed in a hurricane in 2004. One of the nicest campgrounds in the state, it remained closed at this writing, and there are doubts as to if or when it will be rebuilt.

All this and much more can affect whether the information in this book is up to date. Although I've made every effort to ensure the data is current and accurate, allow some wiggle room to account for the "Florida Effect."

CLIMATE AND WEATHER PROTECTION

Camping in Florida rewards you with many surprises: Sunsets over the Gulf of Mexico, watching the golden orb drop into the horizon with a refreshing iced tea in your hand and a gentle sea breeze rustling your hair. Snorkeling in the Florida Keys just 20 steps from your beachfront tent. A herd of deer snooping around your campsite in the woods. Hiking in a shady pine forest, canoeing down the Peace River, casting a line into the surf, going to sleep on an island so secluded that you can only get there by boat. Mountain biking on lonely forest roads where you suddenly come across an abandoned homestead from the 1920s.

It can also be a shock—with sudden downpours that Floridians call "palmetto pounders"; gale-force winds that rock your trailer and blow down your tent; mosquitoes, gnats, no-see-ums, spiders, and roaches; or broiling-hot days with sticky humid nights.

Cold

When most folks think of Florida, they see warm weather and sunny skies. (We'll get to

that soon.) The truth is that Florida's climate is amazingly diverse—and subject to dramatic change. Even people who've lived in Florida a long time sometimes overlook this fact.

One spring break several years ago, we set out from Miami on a weeklong camping trip. In Miami, the temperature was near the 80s during the day and in the mid-70s at night, and we thought we'd packed all the personal gear we could possibly need—shorts, T-shirts, swimsuits, and sunglasses. By the time we reached Lake City in northern Florida at the end of that first day, the skies had turned cloudy and then stormy, as the leading edge of a cold front dipped south. Dinnertime in the campground was uncomfortable. Temperatures had dropped into the 60s, and the wind had picked up.

It sounds ridiculous to think about wind-chill factors when there's no snow on the ground, but we had no long pants and no long-sleeved shirts, and we were cold! That Arctic front never traveled south of Orlando, but tell that to our shivering kids as we bundled them up into the car and headed for the nearest Kmart to buy blue jeans and sweatshirts.

Yes, Florida is hot in the summertime. But from October through May, the weather can vary significantly, depending on your location. North Florida—from the Panhandle east to Jacksonville—even has changing seasons.

By most people's standards outside of Florida, though, winters are mild, offset by an occasional cold front that may bring freezing or near freezing weather. And those fronts last for just a couple of days. Many visitors don't seem to mind them, and they don't let the weather interrupt their outdoors pursuits. We've seen Canadians and Europeans accustomed to colder climes basking on the beach in 50-degree weather—giving truth to the old saying that you can tell who the tourists are, because they have tans in the winter.

Even without a weather report, you can often tell what's going to happen. A cold front usually sweeps south in a broad band. As the cold collides with the warm air, cloudy skies and swift winds are formed, sometimes accompanied by rain. As the front continues south, the skies often clear. You'll see crisp, sunny days and clear, starlit skies at night. Keep an ear on the radio weather reports throughout the year.

On any outing in the winter, bring at least a long-sleeved shirt and a pair of long pants. A heavy jacket or windbreaker is also a good idea, even if you just leave it in the car. On one trip, when the mercury dipped into the 20s at night in O'Leno State Park near High Springs, we appreciated having saved our down jackets from long-ago mountaineering days out West.

Watch the weather reports and read the weather maps before you leave. If a cold front is a possibility, bring enough warm clothing to last for a couple of days. And don't forget to pack for everyone in your party, particularly children. When they get cold and miserable, it's hard for anyone to have a good time.

Heat

Yes, it's hot here. But as you can see from the temperature chart, it's often cooler in the hottest summer months than in many places, say, in the landlocked Midwest. Ocean breezes and frequent rains provide extra relief, and you can always jump into the nearest pool or river to cool off. If you're really desperate to get out of the heat, you can stop at a movie theater or a mall.

Still, it's nice to have air-conditioning during summer, both in your car and in your RV. Tenters can buy an inexpensive box fan to stir the air on hot, still nights. (I've actually seen tent campers with window air-conditioners; they set them up on concrete blocks and poke the business end through an opening!) Backpackers, of course, have to make do.

Which brings up the dangers of heat. You need to be concerned about three things (listed here in order of seriousness): heat cramps, heat exhaustion, and heatstroke. The key to preventing all three is to drink plenty of liquids, limit exercise in the hottest part of the day, wear a hat, and look for shade. (After you've been in Florida for a while, you'll instinctively cross the street to walk on the shady side.) Wear lightweight, light-colored clothing that reflects sunlight. Avoid getting sunburned, which makes you feel hotter and impedes your body's thermostat.

Heat cramps, usually painful spasms in the leg or abdominal muscles, are the first symptom that you're not handling your environment properly. It means that you lack salt, probably caused by losing more water (through sweat) than you're gaining. Stop exercising, get out of the sun, and drink salted water (one teaspoon of salt to a quart of water). Do NOT drink caffeine or alcohol, because they make

FLORIDA'S AVERAGE DAILY MAXIMUM TEMPERATURES

	Jan.	March	May	July	Sept.	Nov.
Daytona Beach	68	75	84	90	87	76
Miami	75	79	85	89	88	80
Orlando	71	78	88	92	90	78
Pensacola	60	69	83	90	86	70
Tampa	70	77	87	90	89	78

Source: National Weather Service. Temperatures are in °F.

symptoms worse and are dehydrating. Massage the cramps gently.

Heat exhaustion comes on when your personal cooling system starts to shut down, usually after prolonged activity in hot, humid weather. Your skin may become cold, pale, and clammy. You may become weak or even vomit, but your body temperature will be normal or slightly lower. At these signs, lie down in the shade. Remove any restrictive clothing, and raise your legs above your head to encourage blood flow. Drink salted water.

Heatstroke, also called sunstroke, is really dangerous. Usually, your skin feels hot and dry. You will not sweat, but your internal body temperature may be 106 degrees or higher. Dizziness, vomiting, diarrhea, and confusion are also symptoms. If any of these symptoms occur, call 911 or go to a hospital without delay. If you are in the backcountry (or on the way to the hospital), remove your clothing. Lower your body temperature with cool water or sponges, fans, or air-conditioners. Do NOT give heat-stroke sufferers any liquids.

Rain

Be prepared for drenching downpours. Raingear is essential year-round. Summer (May through October) is officially the rainy season, but thunderstorms and heavy rain are possible at all times of year. Can you imagine 18 inches of rain in 24 hours in the middle of October? How about March? I've seen it happen.

Florida rains are rarely the gentle drizzling kind that last all day. They burst upon you with an intensity that may surprise people who have no experience with the subtropics. Fortunately, the skies often clear within a couple of hours—but by then, several inches of rain may have drenched you to the skin. Driving is dangerous in these conditions, as is the possibility of flash flooding.

Make sure everyone in your party brings a poncho, available at discount stores for less than $5. Or bring a nylon jacket purchased at a discount store, or even something as elabo-rate as Gore-Tex rain pants and jackets from an outdoors shop. The pricier (but hotter) rain pants are worth considering. Lightweight, fast-drying nylon expedition pants are helpful. A friend wore expedition pants while chest-deep in the Everglades and found that they dried quickly after climbing back into the canoe. Inexpensive shorts are practical in most cases. For other helpful gear tips, see *Backcountry Camping*.

In addition to personal raingear, your camping equipment should be up to snuff for storms. Not all tents are created equal. If the rain fly on your model isn't big enough to keep water off the walls, then consider buying a large waterproof tarp to use as a second, backup rain fly. To keep dew, dampness, or rain out, it also helps to lay a ground tarp, which could be something as simple as a poncho or a shower curtain, under the tent.

Examine the seams of your tent for potential leaky points. Find any? Use a seam sealant—usually a polyurethane glue that plugs tiny seam holes. Keep a patch kit in your tent sack. Both items are available at camp stores or large discount retailers.

You don't have to be confined to a tent or RV during a storm. In a summer rain, it's extremely warm to sit inside, and the humidity makes it feel even warmer. Even worse is having to retreat to your car when it's pouring.

Here's something that works in all but the most blustery weather: a plastic tarp rigged with lines and poles. Put it over the picnic table, and you can still sit outside, cook dinner, read a book, or play board games. We once used poles fashioned from metal electrical conduit, but you can buy a shade tent or screen tent house as well.

Sun

Many private campgrounds in Florida don't have tree canopies; in others, you may be assigned to a site as leafless as the desert. After you've spent all day swimming or hiking in the

THE DANGERS OF DEHYDRATION

Dehydration doesn't just mean that your body is in need of water. It also means that you're in danger of a rising body temperature, nausea, and – in hot weather – suffering from heat-related illness. The solution? Replace your body fluids by drinking lots of water: At least 8-10 cups per day, and up to one gallon if the weather is warm or if you're really active.

If you feel thirsty, you are mildly dehydrated. But if you experience headaches and dry mouth – and your urine output is under two cups over a 24-hour period – chances are your case is serious. Replace electrolytes (salt, potassium, and bicarbonate) by drinking fruit juice or an energy drink, such as Gatorade. If these drinks or purified water are not available, then drink whatever liquid is at hand. That's right: Even if the water may be contaminated, avoiding or treating serious cases of dehydration is worth the risk.

Although physicians used to recommend that hikers take salt pills, they now believe that a regular diet, including the dehydrated food that campers often consume, provides enough salts without supplements.

hot sun, you'll crave a chance to get into the shade. Fortunately, you can bring your own.

A sunroom or screen tent comes in handy for keeping the broiling sun at bay. These 8-by 10-foot rooms go up just like a tent; some are big enough to slip over the campground picnic table. They cost anywhere from $50 to $200 at sporting goods or RV supply stores. The kind with screens around them also keep out bugs.

Too much sunshine is a real health concern in Florida. Studies say that native Floridians with fair complexions and light-colored eyes run an extremely high risk of skin cancer. But no matter where you were born or what you look like, sunscreen is a must to prevent sunburn, which can cause problems later in life. In addition to skin cancer, excess exposure to sun can lead to cataracts, premature aging, and even damage to your immune system. Be especially careful with children, who will resist secondary applications of sunscreen after the first dip in the water. Plus, they often lose (or won't wear) hats.

You can buy sunscreen almost everywhere in Florida, from grocery stores to gas stations. Purchase the highest-rated sunscreen you can find—SPF 15 is considered the minimum recommended protection. On a prolonged outdoors trip, SPF 15 is not adequate for kids unless you want to be reapply it every hour or two.

Unfortunately, not even sunscreen may be enough to prevent melanoma, the most malignant and deadly form of skin cancer. Many dermatologists today recommend use of sunscreens in combination with two other caveats: Limit sun exposure, particularly between 11 A.M. and 1 P.M., and wear protective clothing, such as hats, long sleeves, and long pants.

Even on rare days when the skies are overcast, you can still get a harmful sunburn. Ultraviolet rays are particularly dangerous when you're in a boat or at the beach; they reflect off the water or the sand, doubling their impact.

Most people are uncomfortable without sunglasses. If you forgot to bring a pair, cheap sunglasses ($10–20) are readily available in convenience stores, gas stations, drugstores, and even rest stops on the Florida Turnpike. But be forewarned: Unless the glasses promise 100 percent UV protection, they may do more harm than good, in some cases doubling the amount of UVA rays your eyes would experience without sunglasses. You can spring for a better pair from sunglass kiosks in shopping malls. Don't forget to get a pair for the kids, and be prepared to replace them often.

You'll also want to invest in several tubes of lip protection balm. Some brands have sunscreen in their formulas. Soothe painful, sunscorched lips with Bag Balm or Vaseline. (I've seen Bag Balm cure horrible swollen lip damage within hours.)

For backpackers, it's best to limit hikes to mornings or late afternoons, when you're most likely to see wildlife, anyway. Bring plenty of water—one gallon per person per day, if practical.

Boaters, canoeists, and kayakers should wear wide-brimmed hats, available at Army-Navy surplus stores or outdoors shops. Backpackers might make do with baseball caps, but remember to use sunblock, particularly on your ears and neck. Bicyclists must wear helmets, but helmets don't provide sufficient sun protection. Slather on sunscreen repeatedly, especially on your neck under the chin and areas you don't normally think will get burned. Look for a sunscreen that resists sweat, or you'll end up with the double whammy of irritated eyes from sweat plus sunscreen. Use a bandana or sweatband under your bike helmet for a little control.

Hypothermia

Being exposed to wet, cold weather for an extended period can be fatal—even at 50 degrees. In fact, cases of hypothermia are a lot more common than you would expect in the Sunshine State. In part, that's because Florida's sunny reputation makes some campers blasé. A few years ago, rugged Army Rangers training in the Panhandle were severely stricken; some even died. They spent 10 wet hours in air that did not dip below 50 degrees.

So, the first line of defense against hypothermia is the expectation that it could happen. Remember that being cold and wet at the

same time can be deadly. Keep your clothes dry at all costs, and stay out of the wind. In short, remain warm and dry.

If you start to shiver, you could be on the way to hypothermia. Never ignore shivering. Get warm and dry however you can. Make a fire. Go into a building, if one is available. Get out of the wind and into dry clothes.

The second wave of symptoms may include uncontrollable shivering, slow or slurred speech, incoherence, uncoordinated movements, stumbling, exhaustion, and drowsiness.

If a person has entered this second stage of hypothermia, some exercise will help by burning calories and raising the internal body temperature. But remember, as those calories are burned, they must be replaced. A good choice is warm soup (not hot, because blazing temperatures can shock a cold body and cause a heart attack). Another good choice is a snack with quick energy release, such as candy or an energy bar.

Do not let anyone with such symptoms go to sleep! Get the person out of the wind and rain, take off all his or her wet clothes (no need

DIALING FOR WEATHER REPORTS

If you don't have ready access to radio, TV, or the Internet, you can call the National Weather Service for recorded weather information, including local forecasts, tropical (hurricane) outlook, and marine conditions.

Jacksonville: 904/741-4370
Key West: 305/295-1316
Melbourne (Space Coast Area):
321/255-2900
Miami: 305/229-4550
(English and Spanish)
Tallahassee: 850/422-1212
Tampa Bay: 813/645-2506

HURRICANE SHELTER TIPS

If a hurricane approaches, and you are unable to drive out of the area or find lodging in a motel, you may be forced to go to a public shelter. These are usually located in schools, government buildings, or even stadiums. Please note that most shelters do not allow pets, and that comforts are few. Here's what you should bring, according to the National Weather Service:

- First-aid kit
- Medicine
- Baby food and diapers
- Cards, games, books, etc.
- Toiletries
- Battery-powered radio (or television)

- Flashlight (one per person)
- Extra batteries
- Blankets or sleeping bags
- Identification
- Valuable papers and documents, such as insurance
- Cash

to be shy when a person may be dying), and put on dry clothes. Administer warm drinks. Dry clothes and a warm sleeping bag are best until the victim recovers.

If the sufferer is only semiconscious, leave his or her clothes stripped off, and get him or her into a sleeping bag with another naked person. The best treatment then is skin-to-skin contact. In no case should the victim be left in wet clothing, because it tends to wick heat away from the body.

Lightning and Severe Weather

Florida is home to some of the most extreme thunderstorms in the country, so you'll want to keep a close eye on the weather. In 2004, I experienced a storm so severe that the tent blew down during the middle of the night. Luckily, my companion and I were camped in a developed RV park and were able to take shelter for the rest of the night, first in the restroom and later in the park recreation hall.

If you have a cell phone, you can call the National Weather Service for recorded weather information, including local forecasts, tropical (hurricane) outlook, and marine conditions, among others. (See *Dialing for Weather Reports*).

You also can buy a special NOAA Weather Radio. (NOAA is the National Oceanic and Atmospheric Administration, which runs the National Weather Service.) For as little as about $40, you get access to continuous-loop weather reports that are updated throughout the day—weather on demand.

The radios are permanently tuned to the free NOAA service, and the only investment is the initial cost. Advisories are continuous, and bad weather alerts are broadcast as soon as they are issued. The information is immediate, more complete, and thoroughly detailed, unlike the intermittent and brief weather reports on local radio stations. Weather radios are sold at Radio Shack, electronics and sporting goods stores, marine shops, and outdoors stores.

For up to $200, you can also get weather radios that, even when left in inactive mode, will chirp to life and let you know when a weather alert has been issued in your area. These devices are particularly important if you're bound for a boat-in backcountry campsite.

A weather radio can provide good service even if you're camping in more urban conditions. Several years ago, a line of tornadoes rolled across Central Florida, flattening a campground near Kissimmee. Much was made of the fact that campers didn't have warning.

There was talk of installing tornado warning sirens to alert folks that they should leave their RVs and take cover in a secure building on the grounds. The talk has come to little, so you are responsible for monitoring severe weather.

You're more likely to experience lightning than tornadoes. Lightning strikes more than 1,000 people a year in the United States, often in Florida. In fact, Florida is considered the lightning capital of the nation. Most victims are standing when they are hit. The electricity enters the head first, knocking the person unconscious. Nerves and blood vessels speed the electricity through the body.

The good news is that you have some warning, or at least an inkling that something is up. People who are struck often see lightning or hear thunder in the distance and try to squeeze in one more hole of golf or hook another fish. When you hear thunder, take precautions immediately. If you're in a field or on open water, make for cover right away. Do not stand under a solitary tree or clump of trees. Nor should you stand near a fence or metallic objects. Ideally, you will find shelter in a building or car. If you're outdoors away from civilization, try to head for a forest. Do not stand under the tallest tree, but rather seek out the shortest. If you are caught in the middle of a field, lie down far away from objects that might attract lightning.

BUGS, BEASTS, AND TOXIC PLANTS

I don't want to scare anyone. You're not likely to encounter many of these critters, but you ought to be aware that they are out there.

Alligators

Alligators are unlikely to hurt you, with a few important exceptions.

The myth of dangerous alligators is largely just that—a myth. Think about the reports you've heard of alligators attacking people. You hear, what, maybe one every couple of years? The very fact that these encounters make such big news is a sign of their rarity. In Florida, far more people are killed by lightning than by alligators.

Don't feed or disturb alligators, which are common in all freshwater rivers and lakes.

© MARILYN MOORE

One of my friends once waded through alligator-infested, chest-deep waters for long stretches on two consecutive days. It makes for a great story, but in reality, he was largely unconcerned. The reason? He was in the middle of the Everglades, where gators have precious little contact with humans. And when Clyde Butcher, the famous photographic chronicler of Florida's outdoors, lowers his burly body into the water to shoot his stunning black-and-white photos, he says he doesn't worry one bit about alligators snapping at his bare legs or any other part of him.

Of course, there are exceptions. With hundreds of people moving to Florida every day, more and more of the alligator's territory is being invaded. This is not usually a problem—at least from the human point of view—until people start feeding them. A fed gator is a dangerous gator. It's as simple as that. Under normal circumstances, an alligator does not view an adult human as food. Once the marshmallows start flying, all bets are off.

So, if you suspect an alligator has been fed—if he starts edging toward you, for instance, indicating he has lost his natural shyness—get the heck out of there.

Also: Old, sick alligators may go after a person, particularly a child. Because of their size, children make better targets. Alligators six feet or longer present the greatest danger to kids. Those under four feet generally are not a problem. When you swim in freshwater in Florida, keep an eye out for large gators. Also, avoid swimming at dusk or at night, when they often feed. They might not recognize you as a human until it's too late.

Don't let your pets near any body of freshwater in Florida. Pets, also because of their size and posture, may be viewed as eligible fare for the dinner hour. A child splashing in the water with his dog can be a lethal mix.

Poisonous Toads

The nasty little South American import known as *bufo marinus* secretes a toxic substance and is chiefly a threat to pets. If you handle a greenish-gray toad with brown bumps that look like a bad case of warts, be sure to wash your hands thoroughly afterward. Don't let children or pets play with them. A dog who has handled a *bufo* in his mouth may foam at the lip, cough, and gag. Try to get a hose or water bottle to wash out the dog's mouth.

Snakes

Most snakes in Florida are not poisonous. Like alligators, they are a largely overblown menace in the backcountry, especially when you consider how few people are killed by them. Still, a snakebite is serious. At the very least, it will ruin your camping trip. As a rule, stay away from all snakes. Even a nonpoisonous snake can strike and break the skin.

Bear in mind that snakes, poisonous and nonpoisonous, are more scared of you than you are of them. Be careful where you plant your feet and hands when you are outdoors, and never, ever reach into a pile of wood. To gather firewood, use a downed branch to move individual pieces of wood to where you can see them and confirm they are not harboring a snake (or a scorpion or a spider, for that matter).

When bitten, forget the old wisdom of scratching an X on the spot and sucking out the venom. Doctors have found the sucking method to be ineffective, impractical, and messy, as well as potentially dangerous for the good Samaritan sucking the venom. The new wisdom: Stay calm and get medical help as soon as possible. Realize that most bites turn out to be dry bites, meaning no venom was injected.

If you're near your drive-up campsite when the bite occurs, simply get in the car and travel calmly to an emergency physician. If you're in the backcountry, walk out slowly; don't run, because the venom may spread through your bloodstream more quickly. Better yet, sit down and get medical help to come to you. The U.S. Army advises soldiers to lie quietly, move no more than necessary, and not to smoke, eat, or drink any fluids. Remove any jewelry from the bitten extremity, because rings, bracelets, and the like may become a tourniquet if swelling occurs. If a limb was bitten, don't elevate it—keep the extremity level with the body. If you don't know what type of snake struck, try to remember what the reptile looked like so you can describe it to a doctor.

You may fashion a splint out of a tent stake or something similar while you wait for help. Loosely tie it with a sock, T-shirt, or other piece of clothing. It should be tight enough to stop the flow of blood near the skin, the Army advises. But don't tie it tight enough that it becomes a tourniquet—or you'll risk losing the limb. If swelling occurs quickly, place an inch-wide constricting band about two inches above the bite, suggests the Cooperative Extension Service of Mississippi State University. Remember: Make it loose enough that you can slip a finger underneath. Don't place a constricting band on a joint.

There are four types of poisonous snakes to worry about:

RATTLESNAKES

Florida is home to several species of rattlesnakes, including the Eastern diamondback, which can grow up to eight feet long. Usually found in woodpiles and in the ubiquitous clusters of saw palmetto that dot Florida woodlands, they are an excellent reason to stay on hiking trails and watch your step around downed wood.

One time in the Big Cypress Swamp, a troop of about 25 Boy Scouts was hiking along a trail that was blocked by a fallen log. The guys and their scoutmasters all stepped over the log—until the 22nd or 23rd boy noticed a rattlesnake wedged under it. The laggards chose an alternate path.

WATER MOCCASINS

Also known as cottonmouths, these snakes are mottled brown-and-black pit vipers with cotton-white coloring on the inside of their mouths. If you're lucky, though, you'll never see the inside of one's mouth. That's a sign of warning! These snakes are usually found in or near the water. If you're swimming in freshwater, stay away from clumps of vegetation, particularly if enough of it is growing above the water's surface for a snake to hide. And watch where you are stepping when you're at the shoreline.

As a boy, one of my friends was swimming in front of a dock on Lake Placid when his father commanded him to get out of the water

© BOB RACE

The Eastern diamondback rattler can grow to eight feet long.

immediately. Ignoring his father's objections, he swam around to where he could use the ladder at dockside—right next to a clump of vegetation where two big, fat cottonmouths were sunning themselves. He still remembers that cotton-white color.

CORAL SNAKES

These snakes have smaller injectors and inject less poison than the aforementioned pit vipers, but their venom packs more punch and rapidly affects the nervous system. Fortunately, they are not very aggressive. They're usually found under rocks or debris on the ground.

Coral snakes have black snouts, and their bodies are ringed entirely with red, yellow or off-white, and black bands. Several nonpoisonous snakes, such as the scarlet king or the milk snake, look like coral snakes. Remember that coral snakes have a black nose; the imitators have a yellow or red nose. Although other nonpoisonous snakes have the same coloring, on the coral snake, the red ring always touches the yellow ring. (Here's an old saying: "Red touch black, venom lack; red touch yellow, bad for fellow.")

COPPERHEADS

These snakes are pit vipers without rattles that live in dry upland areas in the Panhandle and grow up to four feet long. You can recognize them by their copper-colored heads and the reddish hourglass on their bodies. Their venom is not as potent as a rattler's.

© BOB RACE

Raccoons are experts at opening unsecured coolers.

Raccoons

We know raccoons look cute. Heck, late Florida governor Lawton Chiles even compared himself with an old "he-coon" in a close-fought election campaign—but you should stay away from these masked marauders, because some carry rabies.

And don't feed them. We've been invaded on more than one picnic by raccoons rampaging across the table expecting a handout. It's tough to scare off the little buggers once they know people have food. Also take precautions against raccoons stealing food while you sleep. It's best to store food and water in your car or RV. If you're roughing it in the backcountry, you may want to keep food in the tent with you. Or, if you have a hard-sided cooler, store food and water inside and secure it with numerous loops of rope, tied tight. You need the rope, because raccoons are clever enough to open some coolers. Use thick rope, not twine, so they can't chew their way through.

KEEP IT WILD TIP: RESPECT NATURE

For the safest and most responsible wilderness experience, follow these basic rules of thumb:
- Treat our natural environment with respect. Leave plants, rocks, and historical artifacts where you find them.
- Observe wildlife from a distance. Never feed animals, and always keep food in critter-proof containers or dispose of it properly.
- Let nature's sound prevail. Avoid loud voices and noises. Keep radios at a low volume.
- Control pets at all times.

Bears

Although they once roamed most of the state, black bears in Florida now number fewer than 1,500 and are confined to scattered pockets. The biggest pockets are in the Big Cypress National Preserve and Osceola, Ocala, and Apalachicola National Forests, as well as the surrounding areas.

Bears are so rare today that state biologists have to put electronic collars on the animals and drive 150 miles in a single day at times to find them. Females typically range 10 miles or so in a day, while the larger, 250- to 350-pound adult males will go farther.

These secretive, shy, little-seen mammals come out mostly at night and tend to be found around thick clumps of trees and underbrush. The tender shoots of saw palmetto thickets are a bear's answer to ice cream. You're extremely unlikely to encounter these officially designated "threatened" animals. The worst possibility is unexpectedly coming up against a protective mama bear and her cubs, usually in the summer or fall.

If you're camping where bears are likely to be, place all food inside backpacks or nylon stuff sacks and hang the bags from a tree limb. Here's the process: Look for a sturdy tree limb that extends at least eight feet from the trunk of a tree. Throw a length of rope over the limb. Tie one end of the rope to a sack of food. Pull on the other end of the rope to haul the bag, pulley-style, into the air so the bag hangs 10 feet or higher above the ground. Then wrap the other end of the rope a few times around the tree trunk and tie it tightly.

Wild Hogs

Descended from domestic pigs that escaped from early settlers, wild hogs are a major nuisance. They root around in the ground, leaving big plowlike ruts in their wake, destroying natural areas. They can be very dangerous when cornered. In many designated hunting areas, they are the only animal for which there is no bag limit. (Spareribs all around, I say!)

A friend's family was confronted with a wild hog in the campground at Myakka River State Park. The animal was rooting around for food underneath the picnic table when they returned to camp. Feeling cornered (the picnic table was next to a wet marshy area), the hog grew agitated. Clearly, trouble was on the way. The family was lucky, because they climbed onto the picnic table and the hog soon ran off.

If you see a wild hog, head the other way immediately and start looking for an escape route. Climb a tree, get into a car, or head inside a building. Merely backing away will usually defuse the situation. In any case, do not knowingly approach a hog. It will feel threatened and could charge.

Bees, Wasps, and Yellow Jackets

These insects can be a serious problem—even a fatal one for susceptible people. Obviously, you should never disturb their nests on purpose. Remember when you're walking in the woods that these insects strive to keep their nests dry—so don't poke your hand into a hollow log (good advice for numerous reasons) or places where nests could be hidden.

Yellow jackets may be the most aggressive of the three, followed by wasps, then bees. Unlike bees, which lose their stinger after one piercing, wasps and yellow jackets can return to sting you repeatedly.

If you are being attacked, run! If you are stung, watch for signs of allergic reaction: swelling, wooziness, shortness of breath, fainting, cramps, or shock. Should any of these symptoms seem to occur, head for the nearest emergency room.

As a stopgap measure, consider treating stings with a semi-liquid mixture of water and baking soda. If you know you are allergic to such stings, be sure to bring along an antidote when you go camping.

Mosquitoes

Well, what would Florida be without mosquitoes? A lot more pleasant. But that's impossible and, besides, it wouldn't be the same mosaic of ecosystems that we've come to enjoy. That's right—skeeters have their place in the ecological web.

Think of a camping trip without the soothing croaks of mosquito-eating frogs. What would the Florida outdoors be like without skeeter-munching dragonflies darting across hiking trails? And mosquito larvae are a major food for fish.

Mosquitoes are drawn by carbon dioxide—what we all exhale—so you can't very well avoid them altogether. Mosquitoes are worst in summer, of course, and generally more of a problem in southern Florida than northern Florida. Most, but not all, mosquitoes prefer to bite at dusk. Some also swarm at night. All avoid direct sunlight, though, because it dries them out and kills them.

With rare exception, mosquitoes are merely pests. The exception is when they transmit disease. Although malaria has been wiped out (except in some developing countries), you can contract encephalitis, which causes brain inflammation, through mosquito bites. The potentially fatal West Nile virus is also spread by mosquitoes. These serious illnesses are uncommon, but it makes sense to avoid mosquito bites as much as possible.

In urban areas, so-called sentinel chickens are deliberately put out to be bitten by mosquitoes, then tested to see if the disease-carrying insects have done the deed. For years, little evidence of disease transmission existed, but in recent years a few outbreaks have been reported.

What do we do to protect ourselves? We rub poison all over our bodies! Sad to say, but insecticides are the most effective way to keep skeeters away. I prefer formulations containing DEET—particularly when facing the 47 types of mosquitoes in Everglades National Park. Avon's Skin So Soft can be helpful, although it is not marketed as an insecticide, and hence has not been tested as one. (Some people assume it's safer than DEET.) The standard advice is to wear long sleeves and long pants, although this is fairly hot and uncomfortable in summer, when mosquitoes are most numerous.

Make sure to cover any exposed skin with insecticide. Mosquitoes are particularly attracted to the ankles, arms, neck, and—while you sleep, if you're careless enough to let one into your tent or RV—the face.

If possible, escape to your tent or RV at dusk. Another possibility is a dining fly enclosed by mosquito netting, although this is impractical for backpackers and canoeists. Mosquitoes also tend to avoid smoke and heat, another great argument for having a campfire. Make a big, hot, smoky one, then sit back and enjoy.

Roaches

I hate roaches, but they are as much a part of the Florida landscape as the air. You'll find roaches in five-star hotels, luxury homes, and even cars. Folks here call them "palmetto bugs."

There's not much you can do about roaches if you're tent camping, except push them out of your way. In an RV, clean up Florida-style after every meal: Sweep the floor, wipe the counters, and get rid of crumbs. And please, don't spray the campsite with Raid. We were in a county park near Tampa having dinner at the picnic table when our neighbors decided to declare chemical war on bugs. Not very neighborly when the wind is blowing.

Ticks

Ticks are one of the more serious insect threats, because they can spread Lyme disease. A vaccine is now available if you're really worried about Lyme disease or expect to be regularly exposed to ticks.

You'll tend to find ticks on your body if you've been in the deep woods, although they can appear in standard commercial campgrounds, too. You're most likely to encounter them if you're crashing through little-disturbed, low-lying brush during a hike. Stay on the trail to minimize this threat.

Get into the practice of surveying your skin

anytime you've been in the deep woods. If possible, have a camping mate look over your back, neck, and scalp. Don't forget to check under your clothes—I've discovered ticks in unmentionable areas. If you find a tick, it will look like a brown wart. What happens is that the tick has been sucking on you all day, with its head burrowed in your flesh, and its body has become engorged with your blood.

Don't take the advice of guides that prescribe covering the little bugger with gas, Vaseline, or another toxic substance. The theory is that the tick will come out because it's short on oxygen. Another bird-brained idea is to burn the tick out by touching its back end with a cigarette. These solutions generally don't work. Usually the tick dies ,and you're left with a dead tick partially burrowed into your flesh.

One effective remedy: Take a pair of tweezers and very carefully—as if you were a surgeon—burrow down around the tick's head, which is embedded in your flesh. Give a gentle pull, or two or three, until the tick comes out. You'll have to yank it out. The primary danger is crushing the tick's head or body. This can release its body fluids and the nasties they carry, so try hard not to let it happen. If you screw up, and the tick's head remains embedded in you, go in again with the tweezers (after washing them in alcohol) and try to get it out. Check to see if the mouthparts broke off in the wound, and if so, seek medical attention. No matter what happens, wash the area thoroughly with alcohol. If the area becomes infected or a welt develops, consult a doctor. You can buy a tick removal kit at many camping stores.

More on Lyme disease: A few days or weeks after a bite, you may suffer flu-like symptoms, headaches, a stiff neck, fever, aching muscles, and malaise. A rash usually develops at about the same time. The rash generally looks like an expanding red ring with a clear center (a kind of bull's-eye), but it can vary from a blotchy appearance to red throughout. See a doctor if you're suffering symptoms. A blood test will help determine if you have Lyme disease, in-stead of just an allergic reaction to tick saliva. If you start taking antibiotics soon, the disease can be cured. If you don't get medical help, possible complications may spell trouble later: recurring acute arthritis (usually of the knees, hips, or ankles), heart palpitations, tingling in the extremities, and lethargy.

It should go without saying, but don't forget to check children and pets for ticks after spending any time in the woods.

Ants and Scorpions

The worst ants are fire ants, imported from South America. In northern and central Florida, you'll see the big piles they make as their homes. Just stay away from them. Red ants also inhabit southern Florida, and although their piles are not as obvious, you can avoid them if you're careful.

If you get bitten, wash the affected area with soap and water or rubbing alcohol. Do not scratch open the white-headed blister that may form, because you risk an infection. If you are bitten numerous times, consult a doctor or go to an emergency room.

Scorpions are rare and not a life-threatening problem in Florida. Ditto for centipedes. You're most likely to find them in woodpiles, but they've been known to turn up in tents. Check your shoes before putting them on in the morning; shoes are a favorite hiding place. If you are stung, it will hurt, but won't kill you. Wash the wound, then see a doctor.

Chiggers

"Chigger" is a common term used to describe the larval stage of parasitic mites. These minuscule insects can ruin an otherwise perfect camping trip. Much like a mite, they are impossible to see. But you'll know if you have them, because they will start burrowing into your skin—usually your softest skin, often in private areas—and you will experience an incredible itching and small, red welts.

The best remedy for chiggers can be obtained from a doctor, although a good soap-and-water treatment may suffice. Another

Spanish moss is pretty, but don't touch it because it harbors mites or "chiggers."

remedy is to seal the skin from contact with air: You can use home remedies, such as nail polish, calamine lotion, Vaseline, cold cream, or baby oil. But you'll get more relief by using something that includes antihistamines, such as Caladryl, or hydrocortisone salves and creams, according to Iowa State University's Entomology Department. Or ask a pharmacist to suggest a local anesthetic or analgesic.

To avoid chiggers, stay away from Spanish moss. This gray-green moss commonly hangs in long intertwined curly strands from the branches of old oaks in Central and North Florida. It sways elegantly in the breeze until

CAMPING IN THE EVERGLADES

Nautical Charts

You'll need nautical charts to help you access boat and canoe sites within Everglades National Park. Obtain them from the Marina Store near the Flamingo Visitor Center, Everglades National Park Boat Tours at the Gulf Coast Ranger Station, or at area bait shops and boating stores. Helpful materials can also be ordered online from the Florida Parks and Monuments Association (10 Parachute Key #51, Homestead, FL 33034, 305/247-1216, www.nps.gov/archive/ever/fnpma/fnpma5.htm).

If you don't have your own boat, canoe, or kayak, several outfitters rent them. Call 305/242-7700 and ask an Everglades National Park ranger to mail you a current list of outfitters, along with a free backcountry trip planner.

EVERGLADES FIELD GUIDE

Solitude and star-studded night skies are the main draw to Everglades National Park, but observant campers are also sure to see alligators and long-legged wading birds during their stay. Everglades is the first U.S. National Park preserved primarily for its variety and abundance of wildlife. Here's what to look for each month:

January

Lumbering manatees swimming in the boat basin at Flamingo Marina. Plentiful wading birds at Mrazek Pond. Alligators sunbathing.

February

Manatees on cool mornings at Flamingo Marina. Red-shouldered hawks starting to nest. At Eco Pond, nesting moorhens.

March

Hundreds of roseate spoonbills and their young at Eco Pond.

April

The bellow of alligators (it's mating time).

it falls in clumps onto the ground. So don't roll around on the forest floor. (Darn! That's my favorite part.)

Poison Ivy and Other Plant Pests

Poison ivy is the bane of adventuresome Florida campers. It can be such an innocent mistake to stumble into one of these itch machines. Stay away from any plant with which you are not familiar, particularly because Florida's version doesn't look identical to the poison ivy Northern visitors know.

Locally, poison ivy comes in many forms—bush, ground cover, and vine. It has a special affinity for sabal palms. Remember: "Leaves of three, let it be." The leaves are a forest green, or perhaps a little lighter, and vaguely heart- or arrow-shaped. You can usually see beads of the poison, which often have hardened into little, black, wartlike eruptions on the leaves themselves. You may see white berries accompanying poison ivy—or you may not, depending on whether the plant is in bloom.

Keep your dog on the hiking trails. Otherwise, the next time you snuggle up to your four-legged buddy after his or her romp in the woods, you may find yourself scratching because the itchy sap has been transferred to you.

Many other plants in Florida are irritants

May
Deer fawns with their mothers. Brown pelican chicks.

June
Barn swallows swarming to eat dragonflies.

July
Six-inch baby alligators in ponds. Turtles nesting along road's edge. Snook and tarpon in the Florida Bay flats.

August
Loggerhead turtles hatching from eggs.

September
White-crowned pigeons flying south from here to the tropics.

October
Wintering ducks, peregrine falcons, shorebirds, and turkey vultures starting to rise in numbers.

November
Bald eagles building nests. Manatees swimming on the freshwater side of Flamingo Marina.

December
Recently hatched Great Southern white butterflies. Increasing numbers of ducks in ponds and on Florida Bay.

Source: Everglades National Park

at best, poisonous at worst. Among them are periwinkle, yellow allamanda, crape jasmine, oleander, crown of thorns, lantana, pencil tree, Brazilian pepper, and poinsettia. Even lime or mango trees can lead to problems; oil from the lime peel and mango skin and tree sap sometimes causes blistering and reddening.

BACKCOUNTRY CAMPING (PLUS A FEW HINTS FOR CAR CAMPERS)

Most of Everglades National Park is waterlogged, and many visitors see less than 10 percent of the park, because they stick to the windshield tour and maybe stroll on a few boardwalks. A few, though, venture through the former Indian canoe trails, bootlegger hangouts, and lovely bays, inlets, and sawgrass plains, where a sunset is a spiritual experience.

The hale and hearty can try some overnight trips into Florida's backcountry, either by canoeing, kayaking, or backpacking. Or, if you're a little less fit, some remote spots can be reached by motorboat. By heading into the backcountry, you can see some of the most jaw-droppingly beautiful parts of Florida. An added benefit is that you can usually do it with little or no company in the nation's fourth most populous state.

Friends are particularly fond of Everglades National Park for canoeing trips, although many fine adventures are possible elsewhere, from the Panhandle to Southwest Florida.

For backpacking, your best bet is often the Florida National Scenic Trail, which covers 1,400 linear miles from the Gulf Islands National Seashore near Pensacola to the Big Cypress National Preserve east of Naples. This book lists some of the special camping spots along the way.

The Florida Trail Association is a dedicated group of volunteers who maintain the trail and are usually in the process of building a new leg of it somewhere. It's worthwhile and satisfying work. Their headquarters are in Gainesville (352/378-8823 or 877/HIKE-FLA, www .floridatrail.org). Some fine backpacking is also available on spur trails in state parks and national forests.

Whether you're hoofing it, paddling, or motorboating, you'll need specialized equipment.

Food

If you're in a pop-top camper or even a motorcoach, your menu is pretty much whatever you wish. My friends and family like spaghetti, hamburgers, salad, and soup, just like at home. But if you're going on an overnighter by canoe or motorboat, you're not really in that different a situation than someone tenting in a commercial campground. You could bring along a bulky Coleman stove, a cooler, hot dogs, water jug—the works. But if you're strapping on a 40-pound backpack or going out for an extended stay, you'll want to plan your menus carefully. You can buy the freeze-dried offerings sold in camping stores, but they're fairly expensive.

To save money, at least on some meals, don't neglect the light, easy-to-make stuff you can get right off the supermarket shelf. Consider ramen noodle soup, Lipton Cup-a-Soup, instant oatmeal in single-serving pouches, macaroni and cheese, and small cans of tuna, clams, and the like that go great on top of crackers. Fresh fruits and vegetables generally keep well, too. Some coffee or tea bags come in handy. Whole books have been written about meals for the trail, and I won't try to replicate them here.

Plan ahead, bearing in mind that you may be caught unexpectedly without a fire for some reason, and bring extra food. Surplus food is crucial if you get lost or hurt and have to stay out extra days.

A tasty, easy-to-make concoction is trail mix, or gorp. Buy granola or another oat-based cereal. Lots of breakfast cereals can be substituted, but stick to the granola-type ones;

DO-IT-YOURSELF JERKY

Try making your own beef jerky before you leave home. It's delicious, fairly cheap, lightweight, and compact. It's also easy. Here's the method recommended by camping experts Sally Deneen and Robert McClure:

Buy lean steak (flank steak works best) and remove all fat and gristle. Cutting across the grain, slice it into pieces about 0.25-inch thick. Marinate it in whatever you like. We use a healthy dose of Worcestershire sauce, a somewhat smaller amount of soy sauce, and a little sesame oil (just a splash for flavoring; you can substitute browned sesame seeds if you like). Add red pepper flakes or Tabasco, and some Mrs. Dash or other seasonings. We're garlic freaks, so we always include some of that. Marinate the beef 12–24 hours – the longer you marinate it, the tastier it will be.

Then just plop the strips onto a cookie sheet, leaving at least an inch between each strip. Bake at 125–150°F, if your oven thermometer goes that low; if not, just set it on low. Leave the door cracked. You are not so much cooking the meat as you are drying it out. That's the point – to get rid of all the moisture. As with the marinating process, this will often take 12 hours or more.

Keep checking the strips every half hour or so after about eight hours. It's ready when all the moisture is gone, yet the meat is still chewy. If the ends start to get so dry that they break off in crystal-like pieces, you've overcooked the jerky. Don't worry, though: Some of the thicker pieces are probably still OK. This is one reason to cut one or two extremely thin pieces; they're sort of like the canaries in the coal mine, warning you that it's time to pull the rest of the batch out.

Cocoa Puffs will not suffice. Then add a few things: dried fruit (raisins are traditional, but there's no law), nuts, and small pieces of candy. Chocolate chips are traditional, although I've seen gorp made with all kinds of things, including M&M's and Hershey's Kisses. Mix it all up and divide it into sandwich bags. Gorp is eaten by the handful during rest breaks along a hiking trail or bike ride. The candy provides quick energy. The nuts provide fat, which you will burn slowly. And the oats give your body that midrange energy burn you'll need to keep going. The fruit? It tastes good.

Some people travel light, like the ranger I met at Olympic National Park who carried a Tupperware container of chocolate bars and graham crackers in his daypack. Some people travel cheap, like the pair of hiking retirees I met on their latest of several trips to the bottom of the Grand Canyon, who said they buy all their food at the supermarket (and are sure to include dessert).

Utensils and Dishes

Although I once shared a camp with a guy who lugged along a miniature espresso-maker, you don't really need a lot of kitchen accessories. Bring only what you'll use. A mess kit folds down for compact, lightweight carrying, along with a similar small saucepan apparatus and perhaps a pot holder. Plus, you'll need silverware, maybe a spatula, and a large metal mug you can set on the stove for fast cups of tea (it doubles as a soup bowl).

And what about the washing up? Susan Windrem, one of my best friends from car-camping days, swears by a few drops of ammonia in a bucket or bowl. She even washes her hands in it before starting to cook or handle food. The little bit of ammonia presumably kills germs in the water and caked-on food. It's not a bad idea, if you can stand the smell. Just don't use a lot, and bring some hand lotion for afterward.

Stoves

In most backcountry locations, you'll need a camper's stove, which can be purchased at outdoors shops and through catalogs. Even at campsites where ground fires are allowed, you'll still want to bring along a stove. There's little fun in waiting half an hour or longer while you make a fire and boil water for a cup of tea or some soup when you first reach camp and you're tired, cold, and hungry. Florida's unpredictable downpours can render dead, downed wood useless. Plus, campfires make for notoriously messy cleanup when the meal is done.

Some campers spend hours debating the merits of various lightweight, collapsible stoves. From that, I will refrain. I prefer the MSR Whisperlite, burning white gas, because it's light and folds down to a small size. I know someone who traveled to China and other far-flung points with the MSR Internationale, so he could use all types of fuel he might encounter.

To find the perfect stove for your needs, turn to consumer guides, such as the annual gear-rating edition of *Backpacker* magazine. But the important thing is to find your own favorite stove and make sure you know how to use it before you hit the trail. Always try

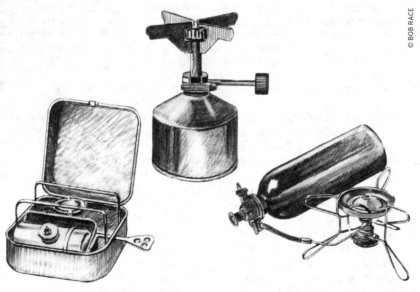

© BOB RACE

Stoves are available in many styles and burn a variety of fuels. These are three typical examples. Left: **White gas stoves** are the most popular because they are inexpensive and easy to find; they do require priming and can be explosive. Middle: **Gas canister stoves** burn propane, butane, isobutane, and mixtures of the three. These are the easiest to use but have two disadvantages: 1) Because the fuel is bottled, determining how much fuel is left can be difficult. 2) The fuel is limited to above-freezing conditions. Right: **Liquid fuel stoves** burn Coleman fuel, denatured alcohol, kerosene, and even gasoline; these fuels are economical and have a high heat output, but most must be primed.

out the stove before you leave home—even if it worked on previous adventures—if it's been in storage for more than, say, a week. You don't want to find out the hard way that your stove no longer works.

Some campers still use white gas for their stoves. Do so with extreme caution. It is highly flammable and even explosive under the wrong conditions. Butane has its adherents. It lights easily, but the canisters are not readily available outside of camp stores. Avoid kerosene. Aside from being smelly, it is hard to find in some places. Remember that these fuels are not interchangeable. Carefully read the instructions that come with your stove.

For car camping, the hardy Coleman stove with propane can't be beat. A two-burner stove can handle the demands of a pasta dinner, or side dishes when you're cooking meat on a grill. Tabletop grills, also powered by propane, are available for as little as $50. Trouble is, once you get all that heating equipment on the picnic table, will you have space to eat? It's all in the organization and planning.

Water

I don't worry about water quality in most campgrounds, because it's city water. But much of the water in natural Florida is just plain nasty. It's not dangerous, but it contains a lot of gunk, usually humus or some other by-product of rotting matter. So, try to bring along all the water you'll need. If you're canoeing or traveling in a motorboat, this should not be much of a problem. (Carry water in a raccoon-proof container, though, if you're in brackish or salt water. Raccoons in these places are perpetually thirsty—and clever. They will gnaw through anything that is not thick enough, including those gallon jugs of water you buy at the supermarket. It's best to store water and food in a hard-sided cooler that is tied shut with numerous loops of rope.)

Backpackers can try to carry enough water for a day or two, but you won't want to skimp on liquids if you're trudging around in

Florida's heat. This calls for a water purifier, which also can be purchased at outdoors shops and through catalogs. Again, some backcountry campers spend hours debating the merits of various models. Just make sure you know how to use the purifier before your trip, and check to make sure it's still in working order before you leave home. I used a water purifier during a bike-packing trip around Lake Okeechobee; frankly, the water

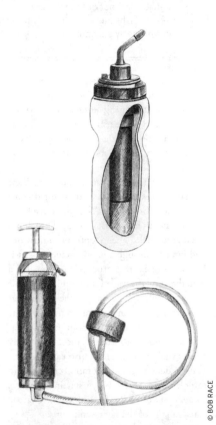

© BOB RACE

Water filters are a wise investment since all wilderness water should be considered contaminated. Make sure the filter can be easily cleaned or has a replaceable cartridge. The filter pores must be 0.4 microns or less to remove bacteria.

KEEP IT WILD TIP: CAMPFIRES

For the safest and most responsible wilderness experience, follow these basic rules of thumb:
- Fire use can scar the backcountry, so take extreme precaution when preparing to build and maintain a fire.
- Where fires are permitted, use existing fire rings. If a fire ring isn't available, then use a lightweight stove for cooking.
- For fuel, gather sticks from the ground that are no thicker than the diameter of your wrist. Don't break branches off live, dead, or downed trees, because this could cause personal injury and scar the natural setting.
- When leaving, put out the fire completely, pack out all trash from the fire ring, and scatter the ashes away from the site. Forest fires *can* be started by campfires that are not properly dismantled.

quality may have been OK, but the taste was not. Blame it on the lake, not the purifier.

It's prudent to bring along an extra filter, in case the one you're using gets clogged. One note of caution: Purifiers do not turn saltwater into fresh, nor do most of them remove industrial pollutants.

What if you have no water? And no purifier? In many places in Florida, you can dig down a few feet and find water. After you dig a hole, let the water sit for at least an hour. This allows the dirt to settle. Then scoop out some water and pour it through a handkerchief to sift it further. Repeat this process until you fill a pan, then boil the water for four minutes. This treatment will eliminate any of the nasties that may send your stomach cramping and your body running to the bathroom. Cryptosporidium, a single-cell parasite, most commonly causes watery diarrhea but also can bring on nausea, dehydration, abdominal cramps, and fever lasting for several days, starting two days to nearly two weeks after infection. Giardia causes many of the same symptoms.

In a real pinch, you can purify water with iodine tablets—no backpack is complete without them. But your first taste of this "water" will remind you why you should invest in a good purifier. Iodine will not kill all illness-causing microorganisms, and too much of it can be dangerous to your health. The effectiveness of the tablets depends on how long you let the water sit—sometimes up to half an hour—and the temperature and organic content of the water.

Clothing

You shouldn't wear cotton, because when it gets wet, it can be deadly. Of course, many people do camp in blue jeans. Opt for nylon expedition pants and a waterproof shell. If you insist on cotton, make sure you always have at least one dry pair of pants and extra shirts in a waterproof bag. That way, if you're forced to make camp early because of inclement weather, you can change into dry duds.

When it's cold, layer your clothes. Usually a T-shirt, overshirt, and light jacket will be enough. But in North Florida and even the southern part of the state in the winter, you'll sometimes want to give yourself four or more layers, including a decent jacket or even a winter coat. Don't forget a knit cap or other hat; some people say that much of your body heat is lost through your head.

In an RV, where you have closets, bringing

extra clothes is not as much of a space issue as when you're on the trail. The important thing is to be prepared for any kind of weather, and be sure that you've considered everyone in your party. And don't count on a campfire to keep warm—most counties have outlawed ground fires because of the risk of starting a conflagration you didn't intend. In wintertime, forest areas are tinder-dry, and forest fires are a danger. (And don't light a fire on top of your picnic table, as I saw in one Florida Keys campground.)

If you're going to canoe or hike in cold weather, consider a layer of underwear made of synthetic fabrics that wick moisture away from the body. On top of that, you'll want an insulating layer. Good choices are down jackets, woolen pants, or more synthetics. On top of that, use a waterproof shell layer to keep your other clothes dry.

About the materials: Down-filled gear is great, until it gets wet. Then it's almost useless. Cotton is even worse—being naked may be preferable in some cases, because at least you're dry. Wool retains some of its insulating properties even when wet. Synthetics offer some of the best combinations but are generally pricey.

For warmer times of year, go ahead and pack that bathing suit. You never know when you might want it.

Raingear

Words to live by: Bring it. Use it.

Bring a poncho, because it also can function as a tarp, a ground cover, and probably a dozen other uses. Also consider some kind of waterproof jacket or shell. Used in combination with rain pants and a poncho, this can help you stay pretty dry in Florida.

You can skip expensive rain pants in favor of nylon expedition pants. They're light enough for a hot Florida afternoon but afford reasonable protection against the wind when wet.

Also, they dry out quickly once you're out of the rain.

Boots

It is hard to underestimate the importance of good boots to a backpacker. Choose them carefully, break them in before you reach the trailhead, and cushion your feet with a good pair of backpacking socks—which often cost about $10. Lightweight silk sock liners, also available at outdoors shops, can prevent blisters from forming.

Remember that your boots and socks are a team; make sure they fit together well. The fit should be snug, but not overly tight. Also make sure the boots support your ankles adequately. If these precautions fail and blisters develop, pull out the moleskin. Cut it into pieces big enough to cover your blisters, so you can slip on dry socks and continue your hike in relative comfort. Moleskin is available at drugstores.

There's nothing wrong with bringing high-ankle hiking boots to an RV park or more nature-oriented campground. They'll keep your feet dry and warm, and you'll generally avoid twisted ankles on uneven terrain. If you have to trek to the restrooms in the middle of the night, they provide ease of mind as you walk through piles of leaves.

Compass, Map, and GPS

Some people bring along a global positioning system (GPS) in the backcountry, and one friend of mine wishes to heaven he had had one during three days lost in the Everglades. GPS is a nice insurance policy for a few hundred bucks. You'll need to spend some time learning to use it first, though—don't just throw it in the rucksack and take off. Also, remember that a GPS is no substitute for a working compass, detailed maps or charts, and a firm grounding in the art of orienteering.

CAMPING GEAR CHECKLIST

Personal Items

Bathing suit
Feminine hygiene products
Hat with a broad brim to keep sun off your face, ears, and neck
Hiking boots or sneakers
Insect repellent
Long pants (airy weave in summer, thicker in winter)
Long-sleeved shirt (airy weave in summer, thicker in winter)
Personal prescription medicine
Raingear: jacket, poncho, rain pants
Sandals, water shoes, or flip-flops
Shorts
Soap
Sunglasses
Sunscreen
Toiletries
Towels

Camping Gear for Backpackers

Bandana or handkerchief
Camping knife
Can opener
Compass
Dishes and silverware
Dish soap (preferably biodegradable)
First aid kit
Flashlight
Food
Fuel
Ground cloth
Hatchet

Matches in waterproof container
Plastic bags for organizing clothes and other items
Sleeping bag (40°F bags will do, particularly if you'll be north of Orlando, unless you plan to do much winter camping)
Stove
Tarp or screen-room tent
Tent
Toilet paper
Whistle

Nice to Have, When Appropriate

Bag for dirty clothes
Bicycles
Board games, deck of cards
Books, magazines
Camera, with flash and extra film or memory cards
Canoe or inflatable boat
Citronella candles or mosquito-repelling coils
Clothespins
Extra propane or stove fuel
Fishing rod and tackle
Folding chairs
Lantern
Laundry detergent
Mosquito netting
Portable folding grill
Rope or clothesline
Tool kit for the car, RV, and other needs

PENSACOLA

© VISIT FLORIDA

BEST CAMPGROUNDS

❰ Beachfront Campgrounds
Henderson Beach State Park, **page 69**

❰ Most Luxurious
Destin RV Beach Resort, **page 68**
Topsail Hill State Preserve, **page 70**

❰ Most Unusual
Riviera Naturist Resort, **page 59**
Camping on the Gulf Holiday Travel Park,
    page 69

The Pensacola area offers loads of nature-oriented recreation and some of the best "Old Florida" scenery of pine, oak, and scrub woods for hiking, backpacking, bicycling, horseback riding, and canoeing. It also offers some of Florida's prettiest beaches, perfect for sunbathing, fishing, and boating.

Often overlooked as a destination by out-of-state visitors, this is one of the most beautiful areas in Florida. It has also been mostly disregarded by real-estate developers, so much of it remains heavily forested, with tall pines stretching from the northern state line to the south.

Vast tracts of wildlife preservation areas, state parks, state forests, and even acreage owned by the U.S. military are available for exploration. A typical example is the Garcon Point Peninsula, a stretch of wild land where bird-watching, hiking, beach-walking, surf-fishing, and nature study are popular. Farther north, you'll find natural camping in the woods, as well as canoeing and hiking around the Blackwater River. The river, favored for kayaking and canoeing, flows gently under a canopy of trees, its water stained by bark to the shade of weak coffee. The dark water contrasts sharply with the white river banks.

Dotted with small towns that are little more than crossroads, the wooded country is divided by I-10, which runs east to west. You'll find plenty of pretty overnight spots right off the highway if you're in a hurry, but it would be a shame not to stop and visit Pensacola, which has an interesting history. Spanish explorers happened on this area in the 1500s, long before the founding of St. Augustine, America's oldest city. A total of five flags have flown over Pensacola: Spain, France, England, the United States, and the Confederacy.

The urban area is bracketed by Escambia Bay and the Gulf of Mexico, where the sand is blindingly white, thanks to years of wave action working its magic on crystals of quartz and silicon dioxide. Several campgrounds offer easy access to the beach and the Gulf of Mexico. Boating opportunities are everywhere, and both saltwater and freshwater fishing are popular pursuits.

One of these small towns, Destin, bills itself as "the world's luckiest fishing village." Each year, anglers catch more billfish in Destin than in all of the other gulf ports combined; they also hook king mackerel, cobia, and other game fish.

Unlike the rest of the state, the most popular times to visit are during the summer, basically April through August. Crowds thin out in the cooler off-season, which is roughly between August and March.

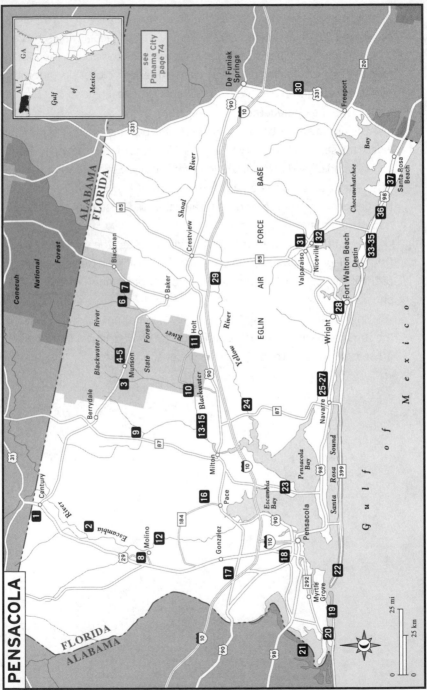

PENSACOLA

see Panama City page 74

© AVALON TRAVEL PUBLISHING, INC.

1 LAKE STONE CAMPGROUND

Scenic rating: 4

in Century, just south of the Alabama border

Large, grassy sites are set on a peninsula extending into an irregularly shaped artificial lake. The shimmering waters of Lake Stone (sometimes called Stone Lake) encircle this quiet, family-style campground favored by all ages, locals, and visitors from as far away as Canada. Some campsites slope down to the water, and guests can fish from their sites—when there's no drought, that is. A nearby boat ramp is part of the county-run park. Activities include walking, fishing, playing cards and dominoes, and attending club meetings; the park also holds dances, potluck dinners, and concerts.

Campsites, facilities: All 77 RV and tent sites have water, 20/30/50-amp electrical hookups, picnic tables, and fire rings. Some sites are waterfront, and 40-foot-long RVs and slideouts can be accommodated. Restrooms, showers, a playground, two dump stations, and a boat ramp are provided. A camp store sells ice, snacks, and limited groceries. Most areas are wheelchair-accessible. Groceries and restaurants are within three miles. Malls are 35 miles away, and the nearest hospital is eight miles away. Children are welcome. Leashed pets are permitted.

Reservations, fees: Reservations are not accepted. Sites are $10 per night for eight people. Credit cards are not accepted. Maximum stay is 30 days.

Directions: From U.S. 29 on the south end of Century, turn west on State Road 4 (across from the courthouse). Drive 1.5 miles to the park, on the left. The entrance is the second driveway.

Contact: Lake Stone Campground, 801 West State Road 4, Century, FL 32535, 850/256-5555.

2 MYSTIC SPRINGS COVE AIRSTREAM PARK

Scenic rating: 6

north of Molino and just south of McDavid, off U.S. 29

Attention, campers: You'll need an Airstream trailer to camp here. Reservations are a must on rally weekends 13 times a year, when the park fills up. This wooded, 10-acre park on the banks of the Escambia River is shaded by old oaks laden with Spanish moss. With the closing of Land Yacht Harbor near Melbourne in 2001, this is one of only two Airstream parks in Florida; the other one is near Christmas, Florida (see *Christmas Airstream Park* in the *Orlando* chapter).

Campsites, facilities: There are 56 sites with full hookups and minimum 30-amp electrical service. Four are pull-through, 11 have 50-amp service. A recreation pavilion and communal kitchen are available. A convenience store is within one mile, and groceries are eight miles away in Century. Most areas are wheelchair-accessible. Children are welcome. Leashed pets are permitted.

Reservations, fees: Reservations are required during rally weekends; the rest of the time, they are not necessary. Sites are $9–11 per night. Credit cards are not accepted.

Directions: From I-10, take Exit 10B onto U.S. 29 northbound. Drive about 23 miles north. Turn right on Mystic Springs Road and drive 0.7 mile.

Contact: Mystic Springs Cove Airstream Park, 591 Mystic Springs Road, McDavid, FL 32568, 850/256-3280, www.geocities.com/mystic-springs.

3 COLDWATER RECREATION AREA

🚶 🌊 🛥 🐎 🚐 ⛺

Scenic rating: 9

in Blackwater River State Forest, west of Munson

Hankering for a trail ride amid oak, juniper, and soaring pine trees? This campground is restricted to horseback riders and to groups needing four or more campsites. Four horse-back-riding trails diverge from Jernigan Bridge near the campground. There's also a swimming area and canoe launch at the bridge. This area is sometimes used for major bird dog field trials. As many as 132 horses can be accommodated in paddocks. Horses are not allowed in the creek.

Campsites, facilities: There are 69 RV and tent sites with water, 30-amp electricity, picnic tables, and fire rings. A maximum of two tents or one RV is permitted on each site. Restrooms, showers, a dump station, two corrals, stables, and outside paddocks are on the property. Kennels for 124 dogs and a dining hall/pavilion accommodating 110 people are available for an extra charge. Children are welcome. Leashed pets are permitted. Proof of a current negative Coggins test is required for each horse.

Reservations, fees: Reservations are required. Sites are $13 per night for five people, or $5 for people 65 and over or people who are disabled. Proof of age or 100 percent disability is required for the discount. Credit cards are not accepted. The maximum stay is 14 days.

Directions: From Milton, drive 15 miles north on State Road 191. At Hardy Road, turn west and drive 5.5 miles to the park.

Contact: Blackwater Forestry Center, 11650 Munson Highway, Milton, FL 32570, 850/957-6140, fax 850/957-6143, www.fl-dof .com/state_forests/blackwater_river.html.

4 KRUL RECREATION AREA

🚶 🌊 ♿ 🚐 ⛺

Scenic rating: 9

in Blackwater River State Forest, west of Bear Lake and east of Munson

A hiking trail begins at the campground and ends at Bear Lake. The Sweetwater Trail (leading to a wheelchair-accessible 2,900-foot boardwalk and a suspended bridge) is accessible by wheelchair for 0.5 mile. The campground also has a seven-acre swimming lake.

Campsites, facilities: There are 45 sites with water and 30-amp electricity, and five primitive tent sites. A maximum of two tents or one RV is permitted on each site. Restrooms, showers, picnic tables, fire rings, and a dump station are available. Children are welcome. Pets are not permitted.

Reservations, fees: Reservations are not accepted. Sites are $13 per night for five people, or $5 for people 65 and over or people who are 100 percent disabled. Proof of age or disability is required. Credit cards are not accepted. The maximum stay is 14 days.

Directions: From Munson, drive 0.75 mile east on State Road 4. The campground entrance is on the north side of the road.

Contact: Blackwater Forestry Center, 11650 Munson Highway, Milton, FL 32570, 850/957-6140, fax 850/957-6143, www.fl-dof .com/state_forests/blackwater_river.html.

5 BEAR LAKE RECREATION AREA

🚶 🚴 🌊 🐎 🚐 ⛺

Scenic rating: 9

in Blackwater River State Forest, east of Munson

Located just east of the Krul Recreation Area (see previous campground), this spot is set on the shores of Bear Lake. Anglers can enjoy the 107-acre lake, but only boats with electric trolling motors are allowed. The fishing pier is wheelchair-accessible. Mountain bikers can use a six-mile-long dirt trail. The Sweetwater hiking trail connects to the four-mile Bear Lake Loop Trail, then to the 21-mile Jackson Trail. The closest stores for supplies are in Munson, 2.5 miles west of the campground.

Campsites, facilities: There are 32 RV sites with water, of which 20 have 30-amp electricity. An additional eight sites with water are for tents only. Three sites are pull-through; RVs as long as 35 feet can be accommodated. A maximum of two tents or one RV is permitted on each site. Restrooms, showers, picnic tables, fire rings, a dump station, and a boat ramp are provided. Children are welcome. Leashed pets are permitted.

Reservations, fees: Reservations are not accepted. Sites are $13 per night for five people, or $5 for people 65 and over or people who are 100 percent disabled. Proof of age or disability is required. Credit cards are not accepted. The maximum stay is 14 days.

Directions: From Munson, drive 2.5 miles east on State Road 4. The campground entrance is on the north side of the road.

Contact: Blackwater Forestry Center, 11650 Munson Highway, Milton, FL 32570, 850/957-6140, fax 850/957-6143, www.fl-dof.com/state_forests/blackwater_river.html.

6 HURRICANE LAKE RECREATION AREA

🏃 🛶 🐕 🚐 ⛺

Scenic rating: 9

in Blackwater River State Forest, north of Baker

Campsites overlook Hurricane Lake, a 318-acre impoundment that is popular for fishing. Half the sites are on the north side; the others are on the south. Boats with electric trolling motors are permitted on the lake, but you may not use outboard motors. A canoe launch with access to the Blackwater River and a six-mile hiking trail are near the campground. Blackwater River State Forest is known for its longleaf pine/wire grass ecosystem, which once covered 60 million acres in the southeast. Don't be alarmed if you see scorched areas: State foresters use fire to control hardwoods and to promote the flowering of wire grass. Fire also helps protect the habitat of the endangered red-cockaded woodpecker. Look for bogs of carnivorous pitcher plants. Throughout the forest, you'll find unpaved roads good for mountain biking. Horse trails are threaded through the western portion of the forest.

Campsites, facilities: There are two campgrounds here: one on the north side, and one on the south. The north side has 13 campsites with water and 30-amp electricity, plus five sites with water only. RVs longer than 35 feet cannot be accommodated; none of the sites is pull-through. A maximum of two tents or one RV is permitted on each site. Restrooms, showers, picnic tables, fire rings, a dump station, and a boat ramp are on-site. The south campground has 18 primitive sites with restrooms only. Children are welcome. Leashed pets are permitted.

Reservations, fees: Reservations are not accepted. Sites are $13 per night for five people, or $5 for people 65 and over or people who are 100 percent disabled. Proof of age or disability is required. Credit cards are not accepted. The maximum stay is 14 days.

Directions: From Baker, drive six miles west on State Road 4. Turn north on Beaver Creek Road and proceed about 8.5 miles. At Bullard Church Road, turn east and follow the signs to the campground.

Contact: Blackwater Forestry Center, 11650 Munson Highway, Milton, FL 32570, 850/957-6140, fax 850/957-6143, www.fl-dof.com/state_forests/blackwater_river.html.

7 KARICK LAKE

Scenic rating: 9

in the far eastern part of Blackwater River
State Forest, north of Baker

Take a refreshing dip or cast your line for fish
in 65-acre Karick Lake. Boats with electric
trolling motors are allowed. The fishing pier
is wheelchair-accessible. One major attraction
is the campground's location at the eastern terminus of the 21-mile-long Jackson Trail, which
meanders through the state forest, crossing the
Blackwater River at Peaden Bridge. The campground, set in a hardwood forest, is actually
two in one; half the sites sit on one side of the
lake, and half on the other.

Campsites, facilities: There are 30 sites with
water and 30-amp electricity, 15 in the northern section and 15 in the southern section. A
maximum of two tents or one RV is permitted
on each site. Restrooms, showers, picnic tables,
fire rings, a dump station, and a boat ramp
are provided. Children are welcome. Leashed
pets are permitted.

Reservations, fees: Reservations are not accepted. Sites are $13 per night for five people,
or $5 for people 65 and over or people who are
100 percent disabled. Proof of age or disability
is required. Credit cards are not accepted. The
maximum stay is 14 days.

Directions: From Baker, drive eight miles
north on County Road 189 to the campground
entrance on the east side of the road.

Contact: Blackwater Forestry Center, 11650
Munson Highway, Milton, FL 32570,
850/957-6140, fax 850/957-6143, www.fl-dof
.com/state_forests/blackwater_river.html.

8 LAKESIDE AT BARTH

Scenic rating: 4

on U.S. 29 north of Pensacola near Molino

Frequented mostly by locals and families,
this place offers country camping near the
city. The area north of the paper mill town of
Cantonment is off the well-worn tourist track
in an area of rolling hills of pine forests and
tiny communities that are little more than
crossroads. Nestled on 80 wooded acres, the
campground has grassy sites with some shade.
About 20 percent of the park is occupied year-
round. The swimming lake is 0.5 acre in size;
the fishing lakes are five and eight acres. Favorite catches are bream, bass, and catfish. A
large Winn-Dixie grocery store is 11 miles
away near I-10, though a local grocery three
miles away is recommended for "the best meat
around."

Campsites, facilities: All 28 full-hookup
sites have 30-amp electrical service. Sites are
narrow and long, but large enough at 60 feet
deep to accommodate big rigs and slideouts.
Restrooms, showers, a playground, a covered
pavilion, two manmade fishing lakes, and one
swimming lake are available. Children are welcome. Leashed pets are permitted.

Reservations, fees: Reservations are not necessary. Sites are $15 per night for two people,
plus $3 for each additional person. Credit
cards are not accepted.

Directions: From I-10 at Pensacola, take Exit
10B heading north on U.S. 29 and drive 16
miles. After you cross State Road 97, continue
two miles to Barth Road. Turn east (right) and
drive one mile to the campground.

Contact: Lakeside at Barth, 855 Barth Road,
Molino, FL 32577, 850/587-2322.

9 ADVENTURES UNLIMITED OUTDOOR CENTER

Scenic rating: 9

north of Milton

Billing itself as a getaway from city life, this privately run resort/canoe concessionaire overlooks the confluence of Wolfe Creek and Coldwater Creek at Tomahawk Landing. It's a sprawling, 88-acre, canoeing-oriented complex with large cabins for groups, a small inn, small cottages, "camping cabins," and group activities for family reunions, birthday parties, and youth retreats. Canoeing and tubing package trips and hayrides are available, as are challenge rope courses for team-building. On the property, you'll find an old dam and millpond, a historic cemetery, and two riverside beaches. Adventures Unlimited also arranges one- to three-day-long canoe trips. Canoes equipped with camping equipment are available (with reservations).

Campsites, facilities: There are eight shady, grassy RV sites with water and 30-amp electricity; and 10 primitive sites for tents, pop-ups, or small, self-contained units. The maximum length of RV is 38 feet, though slideouts can be accommodated. Restrooms, showers, picnic tables, and fire rings are provided. A game field, a volleyball court, a limited store, a small playground, rental cabins, canoes, and inner tubes (for tubing on the river) are available. A camp store sells ice, camping supplies, a few groceries, snacks, souvenirs, fishing tackle, and bait. The four-room Schoolhouse Inn was once a school that served a tiny community nearby. The store and office are wheelchair-accessible. Groceries, restaurants, and hospitals are 15 miles away. Families and groups are welcome. Pets are not permitted.

Reservations, fees: Reservations are recommended. Sites are $20 per night for four people, plus $3 for each additional person. Credit cards are accepted. Long-term rates are available from November through February only; the high season here is the warmer time of the year.

Directions: From Milton, drive 12 miles north on State Road 87. Turn east at the Adventures Unlimited sign. Drive four miles to the campground, which is just south of the confluence of Coldwater Creek and Wolfe Creek.

Contact: Adventures Unlimited Outdoor Center, 8974 Tomahawk Landing Road, Milton, FL 32570, 850/623-6197 or 800/BE-YOUNG (800/239-6864), fax 850/626-3124, www.adventuresunlimited.com.

10 BLACKWATER RIVER STATE PARK

Scenic rating: 10

in Blackwater River State Forest

With just 30 sites, this campground fills up fast in the busy summer months and on most weekends throughout the year, but it's worth planning ahead to stay here. The 590-acre state park is located on the south side of Blackwater River State Forest, the largest state forest in Florida at more than 200,000 acres. The tea-colored river, popular for canoeing and kayaking, flows through the park. Don't expect rough water; the river is quite shallow in places, and the bottom is sandy. It's one of the few rivers in the country with spectacular white-sand beaches. Canoe, kayak, and inner-tube concessions are located nearby. The closest is Blackwater Canoe Rental in Milton, located on the state park access road (10274 Pond Road, 850/623-0235 or 800/967-6789, www.blackwatercanoe.com). Prices range $19–25 daily for canoe, kayak, and tube rentals. The big sandbars on each bend in the river are strikingly white in contrast to the darkness of the water; stop now and then to swim or soak up some rays on the broad ivory banks. In the summer, you may glimpse a Mississippi kite, a graceful, hawklike bird with gray underparts and a pale head, winging overhead. At other times, look for river otters, deer, turkey, and bobcats as you drift lazily downstream.

Campsites, facilities: There are 30 campsites for tents and RVs with water, 30-amp electricity, picnic tables, and fire rings. Sites vary in size, as they do in most state parks, where natural geographic contours are followed in the design of the park. Rigs up to 35 feet can be accommodated, as well as slideouts. Canoe, tube, and kayak rentals, restrooms, showers, souvenirs, guided walks, and nature programs are available. The bathhouse and office are wheelchair-accessible. Children are welcome. Pets are allowed with proof of vaccination.

Reservations, fees: Reservations are recommended; contact ReserveAmerica at 800/336-3521 or reserveamerica.com. Sites are $14 per night for eight people. Credit cards are accepted. The maximum stay is 14 days.

Directions: From I-10 at Milton, use Exit 31 on State Road 87 northbound. Travel 0.5 mile, then turn east on U.S. 90. Drive five more miles to Harold and turn north on the state park access road. The campground is three miles along.

Contact: Blackwater River State Park, 7720 Deaton Bridge Road, Holt, FL 32564, 850/983-5363, fax 850/983-5364, www.floridastateparks.org.

11 EAGLE'S LANDING RV PARK

Scenic rating: 7

near Holt, east of Milton

The owners describe this all-ages, sunny park with huge lots as the perfect overnight stop for campers. It's certainly close to the interstate, at 0.5 mile off the road, and convenient to shopping and outdoor recreation throughout the area. Clean, quiet, and well-maintained, this 10-acre park has 60 large, grassy sites, 24 of which are available for seasonal stays. A few sites are occupied by year-round residents.

Campsites, facilities: There are 60 pull-through RV sites with full hookups, electricity, and picnic tables. Sites are a whopping 85 feet long and 35 feet wide, and some have 50-amp service. The biggest RVs on the market can be accommodated here, including multiple slideouts. There's a wireless Internet network accessible in many parts of the park. Satellite dishes are no problem. Restrooms, showers, laundry facilities, a recreation room, a dog-walk area, and telephone service are available. Planned activities are held during the winter months by repeat visitors who value the peace and quiet here. Children are welcome. Leashed pets are permitted.

Reservations, fees: Reservations are recommended. Sites are $19–21 per night for two people, plus $2 per extra person over age four. Credit cards are not accepted. Long-term rates are available.

Directions: From I-10, take Exit 45 and go north 0.25 mile to the park entrance on the left.

Contact: Eagle's Landing RV Park, 4504 Log Lake Road, Holt, FL 32564, 850/537-9657, fax 850/537-9625, www.campingand campgrounds.com/eagle.htm.

12 ESCAMBIA RIVER WATER MANAGEMENT AREA

Scenic rating: 8

along the Escambia River

Locals like to hop in a boat and head out here for a few days, picking camping spots atop the natural levees created by rivers and streams. Covering a whopping 53 square miles and hugging the banks of the Escambia River for approximately 30 miles, this beautiful flood-plain is packed with hardwoods such as shaggy-limbed cypress, gums, and oaks, as well as stands of Atlantic white cedar and willow oak. (The timber was logged in the past but has substantially regrown.) Because the area is so

wheelchair-accessible. Children are welcome. Leashed pets are permitted.

Reservations, fees: Reservations are recommended. Sites are $23–25 per night for two people, plus $2 for each additional person. There is a charge of $2 per night for using 50-amp electrical service. Credit cards are not accepted. Long-term stays are allowed.

Directions: From U.S. 90 in Milton (Exit 28 off I-10), drive four miles north on State Road 87. The park is on the east side of the road.

Contact: Cedar Pines Campground, 6436 Robie Road, Milton, FL 32570, 850/623-8869, fax 850/623-1520, www.cedarpines.com.

16 RIVIERA NATURIST RESORT

Scenic rating: 5

northwest of Pace and Milton

BEST (

Set on 16 shady, wooded acres, this family-oriented resort offers a haven for those who like to camp in the buff. Nudity is required—weather permitting. Guests are clothed when practical (in cold weather); nude when possible (other times). Identification is required, because management doesn't want to encourage curiosity-seekers. Cameras are not allowed without permission.

Campsites, facilities: This nudist campground has 29 grassy RV spaces, 10 with full hookups and electricity available for vacationers. A large grassy area dotted with tall pine trees accommodates an indeterminate number of tent campers for primitive camping. A dial-up Internet connection is available in the clubhouse. The resort has picnic tables, restrooms, showers, a swimming pool and whirlpool tub, a volleyball field, horseshoes, *pétanque* (a French game similar to cricket), and a 0.5-mile nature trail. An area is set aside for suntanning. Children are welcome with parents. Leashed pets are permitted.

Reservations, fees: Reservations are recommended. Sites are $23–28 per night. Credit cards are accepted. The maximum stay is one month during the summer and three to five months during the winter.

Directions: From I-10 at Pensacola, take Exit 17. Turn east on U.S. 90. Drive 6.5 miles to County Road 197A/Woodbine Road. Turn north on Woodbine Road and go two miles, then turn east on Guernsey Road. The park is 0.4 mile away, on the north side of the road.

Contact: Riviera Naturist Resort, 5000 Guernsey Road, Pace, FL 32571, 850/994-3665, fax 850/994-1906, www.riviera-resort.com.

17 TALL OAKS CAMPGROUND

Scenic rating: 2

on the west side of Pensacola

This five-acre campground caters to overnight travelers, as well as long-term visitors. A shopping center 0.25 mile away offers citified essentials—groceries, a hair salon, and a restaurant, for instance. Within a five-minute drive are golf courses, a hospital, and the Five Flags Speedway. The urban location is convenient to Pensacola attractions. Visitors here include tourists and families, although half the park is occupied year-round by locals.

Campsites, facilities: About 20 to 30 of the park's 75 grassy RV spaces are available for overnighters. They have full hookups and 30-amp electrical service. Fifteen have 50-amp electricity. Picnic tables are provided at about half the sites. The biggest RVs and slideouts can be accommodated. You'll have no trouble setting up your satellite dish here. Amenities include wheelchair-accessible restrooms, showers, laundry facilities, vending machines, a pay phone, and a dump station. Groceries and restaurants are within 0.5 mile, and malls and hospitals are four miles away. Children are welcome. Leashed pets are permitted.

Reservations, fees: Reservations are not

necessary. Sites are $22 per night for two people, plus $5 per extra person. Credit cards are accepted. Long-term rates are available. **Directions:** From I-10 eastbound, take Exit 5 onto Alternate U.S. 90/Nine Mile Road. Drive one mile east, then turn south on Pine Forest Road and continue to the park on your right. From I-10 westbound, take Exit 7 onto State Road 297/Pine Forest Road. Drive north for 0.5 mile to the entrance. **Contact:** Tall Oaks Campground, 9301 Pine Forest Road, Pensacola, FL 32534, 850/479-3212.

18 MAYFAIR MOTEL AND RV PARK

Scenic rating: 2

in west Pensacola

Shopping and restaurants are on hand, and you can swim in the motel's pool (next door). The park's urban location is convenient to Pensacola's historical and tourist attractions; the beach is within a 15-minute drive.

Campsites, facilities: There are 24 RV sites with full hookups and 30-amp electricity; however, just a few are available for overnighters. Management says that big RVs can be accommodated. Restrooms, showers, a dump station, and laundry facilities are provided. Children are welcome. Leashed pets are permitted.

Reservations, fees: Reservations are recommended. Sites are $25 per night. Credit cards are accepted. Long-term rates are available. **Directions:** From I-10, exit on State Road 297/ Pine Forest Road and drive 3.5 miles south to U.S. 90/Mobile Highway. Turn east on U.S. 90 and look for the campground/motel complex. **Contact:** Mayfair Motel and RV Park, 4540 Mobile Highway, Pensacola, FL 32506, 850/455-8561, fax 850/455-0090.

19 BIG LAGOON STATE PARK

Scenic rating: 10

on Perdido Key, southwest of Pensacola

The campground at this 698-acre state park is located along a series of sandy ridges. Birdwatchers will be delighted here, because the wind-whipped sand pine scrub, gnarled slash pines, and swampy salt marshes harbor loons, grebes, cormorants, great blue herons, and many other species seen daily. During the fall, this is one of the last resting places for birds migrating south across the Gulf of Mexico. You may also see gray foxes, raccoons, skunks, and opossums. Hikers can improve their chances of spotting these animals by walking the one-mile boardwalk; there's also the 3.5-mile "Girl Scout Cookie" hiking trail looping through the park. Two swimming areas are on Big Lagoon, near the Intracoastal Waterway. Boating, canoeing, windsurfing, and fishing opportunities are abundant, because the park is encircled almost completely by water. If you're hankering for seaside fun on the Gulf of Mexico, registered campers are permitted to use the white-sand beach at Perdido Key State Park, located five miles west, at no additional charge. Special events are held here throughout the year, including a bluegrass festival in May, concerts on holiday weekends, and Christmas and Halloween celebrations. You can even rent the amphitheater for weddings.

Campsites, facilities: The state park campground has 49 sites with water and electricity. Twenty-five sites have 50-amp electrical service; the rest have 30-amp. None are drivethrough. RVs up to 40 feet long and slideouts can be accommodated; sites vary in size. Picnic tables, grills, restrooms, showers, a playground, and a dump station are provided. The park also has a boat ramp, three nature trails, an amphitheater, and two swimming areas. Campsites 8 and 9 are wheelchair-accessible, as are the restrooms, boardwalks, and some picnic pavilions. Beach wheelchairs are available upon request. Children are welcome. Pets are allowed in the campground with proof of vaccination.

Reservations, fees: Reservations are recommended; contact ReserveAmerica at 800/336-3521 or reserveamerica.com. From March 1 through August 31, sites are $16 per night for up to eight people. Credit cards are accepted. The maximum stay is 14 days.

Directions: From Pensacola, drive 12 miles west on State Road 292 to Perdido Key. Turn east on State Road 292A/Gulf Beach Highway and drive 0.5 mile to the park entrance.

Contact: Big Lagoon State Park, 12301 Gulf Beach Highway, Pensacola, FL 32507, 850/492-1595, fax 850/492-4380, www.floridastateparks.org.

20 PLAYA DEL RIO RV PARK

Scenic rating: 10

on Perdido Key

This resort-style park's location on Perdido Key and the white-sand Gulf of Mexico beaches can't be beat, no matter where you wind up parking your rig. Fronting on the Ole River with a view of Ono Island, this park offers boat dockage for campground guests' boats—and even a free paddleboat and kayak for their use. Bird-watching and various boating tours are available, and the beach is across the street via a short path. Fish off the dock or try your hand at catching crabs from the dock. The Wharf, a huge shopping and entertainment attraction with an amphitheater for concerts and a marina, opened in 2006, is less than a mile away, just across the state line in Orange Beach, Alabama.

Campsites, facilities: There are 30 RV sites for rigs up to 45 feet. Some sites have concrete pads; all have full hookups, 30/50-amp electrical outlets, cable TV, and phone availability. Restrooms, showers, a dump station,

laundry facilities, a fishing dock, a community room, barbecue grills, and a picnic area are on-site. A wireless Internet network is accessible throughout the park. The restrooms, laundry, community room, and boat docks are wheelchair-accessible. Children are welcome. Leashed pets are permitted.

Reservations, fees: Reservations are recommended. Sites are $31–59 (highest rates March 1–September 15) per night for two people, plus $3 per extra person. Credit cards are accepted. Long-term stays are allowed.

Directions: From I-10 westbound, take Exit 7 south onto Route 297 (Pine Forest Road) for 1.5 miles. At Blue Angel Parkway, turn right and head south 5.5 miles on Sorrento Road (Highway 292), which changes to Perdido Key Drive after the Intracoastal Bridge. The resort is 5.7 miles on the right. From I-10 eastbound, take Alabama State Road 59 south through the Alabama towns of Foley and Gulf Shores. At Alabama State Road 182, turn left and continue east. The road name changes to Florida Highway 292, then to Perdido Key Drive.

Contact: Playa del Rio RV Park, 16990 Perdido Key Drive, Perdido Key, FL 32507, 850/492-0904 or 888/200-0904, fax 850/492-4471, www.playadelrio.com.

21 PENSACOLA/ PERDIDO BAY KOA

Scenic rating: 6

west of Perdido Key

Despite its name, this campground is actually in Alabama, across Perdido Bay from Florida. It's less than a mile from the Florida state line and might be an option if the other parks are full. The owners call it "snowbird heaven."

Campsites, facilities: There are 50 full-hookup sites with 30-amp and 50-amp electrical service available for overnighters and seasonal visitors. Sites accommodate both tents and RVs. Restrooms, showers, a dump station, laundry facilities, and telephone service are available. On the premises are a heated pool (open March 14–October 1), a boat dock, a clubhouse, shuffleboard courts, a dog-walk area, and boat access to Perdido Bay and the Gulf of Mexico. Children are welcome. Leashed pets are permitted.

Reservations, fees: Reservations are recommended. Sites are $22–35 per night for two people, plus $3 per extra person and $2.75 for cable TV. Credit cards are accepted. Long-term rates are available.

Directions: From Perdido Key, drive west on U.S. 98 and cross the bridge to Alabama. Turn left (south) on State Route 99 to the park.

Contact: Pensacola/Perdido Bay KOA, 33951 Spinnaker Drive, Lillian, AL 36549, 251/961-1717, www.koa.com/where/al/01102.htm.

22 FORT PICKENS CAMPGROUND

🧍🚴🏊🛶🏕🐕🎣♿🚐🏕

Scenic rating: 10

within Gulf Islands National Seashore, on the western end of Santa Rosa Island

This once gorgeous campground was still closed as of early 2007, in spite of promises to reopen by that time. Hurricanes in 2005 destroyed the road to the campground, although the park is open for day use. The campground will require repairs after the road is rebuilt to new stormproof construction standards. Call the park or check the website for updates.

Campsites, facilities: This National Park Service campground offered 168 sites with water and electricity.

Reservations, fees: Once reopened, the campground will accept reservations through the National Park Service reservations system; call 800/365-2267 or visit www.reservations.nps.gov.

Directions: At the dead end of U.S. 98 in Pensacola Beach, drive west on Fort Pickens Road/State Road 399 for eight miles to the park entrance.

Contact: Gulf Islands National Seashore Park Headquarters, 1801 Gulf Breeze Parkway, Gulf Breeze, FL 32561, 850/934-2600, 850/934-2621, or 800/365-2267 (reservations), www.nps.gov/guis.

23 PELICAN PALMS RV PARK

🏊🐕🚐🏕

Scenic rating: 5

southeast of Milton

A good base for exploring the canoeing, cycling, hiking, and fishing opportunities nearby, this park is three miles from a PGA golf course and other courses. It's also a convenient overnight stop from the interstate. Sites are level and grassy. About 20 percent of the park is occupied year-round.

Campsites, facilities: Thirty-six sites are available; 23 are pull-through, and all have full hookups. Six sites have 50-amp service, 29 have 30-amp, and 10 have picnic tables. Tents can be accommodated on 16 campsites; 10 are primitive with no hookups. Restrooms, showers, a dump station, laundry facilities, a recreation room (but no planned activities), and a pool are on-site. A wireless Internet network, a small store, and a book exchange were added in 2005. A camp store sells ice, camping supplies, snacks, souvenirs, and propane. Children are welcome. Leashed pets are permitted.

Nearby is the Garcon Point Peninsula (850/484-5125), where bird-watching, hiking, beach-walking, surf-fishing, and nature study are popular pursuits. This is one of several places in the state where you can see carnivorous vegetation—pitcher plants that lure passing insects with a display that looks like a blossom, and then, chomp! Also, if you head to Garcon Point in the spring or summer, you're likely to see rainbow-colored displays of wildflowers. The point separates Escambia Bay from East Bay. Animals of interest here include the marsh rabbit and southeastern kestrel, along with deer and wading birds. Swamps, wet prairies, and pine and hardwood forests make up most of the landscape, rounded out by beachfront and salt marshes. Head south from Avalon Beach on County Road 281 or County Road 191 to reach Garcon Point.

Reservations, fees: Reservations are not usually necessary. Sites are $19–25 per night for two people, plus $2 per extra person and $2 for 50-amp service. Credit cards are accepted. Stay as long as you like; long-term rates are available.

Directions: From I-10, take Exit 26 and drive south on County Road 191 for 0.1 mile. The park is on the east side of the road.

Contact: Pelican Palms RV Park, 3700 Garcon Point Road, Milton, FL 32583, 850/623-0576, www.pelicanpalmsrvpark.com.

24 YELLOW RIVER WILDLIFE MANAGEMENT AREA

🎣 🚐 🎍 🏕️

Scenic rating: 8

along the Yellow River, off I-10

Sandwiched between I-10 and the northern boundary of Eglin Air Force Base (see campground in this chapter), this is a place where, if you're lucky, you might see a secretive, nocturnal Florida black bear. Look for mountain laurel and, in spring, the showy blossoms of the spider lily. Realistically, the only way to get around the area is by boat or canoe. The landscape is quite varied: With 18 types of habitat ranging from tidal marsh to high, dry xeric uplands, it is one of Northwestern Florida's most varied parcels of land.

Campsites, facilities: Primitive camping is allowed throughout the area, but there are no designated campsites and no facilities except for eight boat ramps. Bring water, food, and camping supplies. Pack out trash. Children and pets are permitted.

Reservations, fees: Reservations are not necessary. Camping is free.

Directions: There are numerous boat ramps on the river. One of the easiest to reach is the Sigler Lake ramp off I-10. From I-10 at Holt, take Exit 11 and head south on County Road 189. It will become a dirt road that ends at the river. Another boat ramp is accessible by exiting I-10 at State Road 87 (Exit 31) and heading south. Cross the river and look for the Broxson boat ramp on your left.

Contact: Northwest Florida Water Management District, 81 Water Management Drive, Havana, FL 32333, 850/539-5999, www.nwfwmd.state.fl.us. A map can be found online at http://myfwc.com/recreation/cooperative/yellow_river.asp#Camping.

25 EMERALD BEACH RV PARK

🏊 🛶 🚐 🎍 ♿ 🚗

Scenic rating: 10

on U.S. 98, between Fort Walton Beach and Pensacola

This all-ages park slopes gently down to the water and a 300-foot sandy white beach. This area is marketed by local tourist councils as the "Emerald Coast," a reference to the emerald-green waters offshore. Although you won't find much shade here, especially after the 2004–2005 hurricanes, some lucky RVers can overlook the waters of Santa Rosa Sound. Post-storm building has energized the area, and the community is much busier than it was before. Everyone is parked close together, but campers in big rigs don't seem to mind; they are more interested in fishing, boating, swimming, and visiting the nearby Naval Aviation museum. The location of the park is central to Fort Walton Beach (14 miles east) and to Pensacola (18 miles west).

Campsites, facilities: There are 71 RV slots with full hookups and 30/50-amp electrical service; 36 are pull-through. Some sites are waterfront. Rigs up to 50 feet long and slide-outs can be accommodated. Sites range 26–27 feet wide and 45–60 feet deep. A wireless Internet network, restrooms, showers, picnic tables, concrete patios, a dump station, a pool, rental cabins, a camp store with ice, snacks and limited groceries, and shuffleboard courts are available. Big grocery stores and restaurants are within two miles; malls and hospitals are within 15 miles. Most areas are wheelchair-accessible. Streets are paved. Children are welcome. Leashed pets are permitted.

Reservations, fees: Reservations are recommended. Sites are $42–52 per night for two people, plus $3 per extra person. Credit cards are accepted. Long-term rates are available.

Directions: From Navarre, drive 1.5 miles east on U.S. 98. The park is on the south side of the road.

Contact: Emerald Beach RV Park, 8885 Navarre Parkway, Navarre, FL 32566, 850/939-3431, www.emeraldbeachrvpark.com.

26 NAVARRE BEACH CAMPGROUND

Scenic rating: 10

on U.S. 98, between Fort Walton Beach and Pensacola

Palm trees give a tropical atmosphere to this manicured, resort-style family campground that boasts its own small beach and a fishing pier on Santa Rosa Sound. Services are terrific: There's a computer room with PCs and high-speed access, and park employees will escort you to your site. The property, which is a long and narrow rectangle with the highway on one end and the beach on the other, is gated at all times. Children under 12 must be accompanied by an adult, and all kids swimming in the pool must be supervised by a grown-up. Favorite things to do: fish and go to the beach. This oasis is set against a backdrop of development sprawling along the U.S. 98 corridor, with shopping centers, fast-food eateries, and other accoutrements of modern life rapidly moving in.

Campsites, facilities: All 137 sites have full hookups, 30-amp or 50-amp electrical service, concrete patios, picnic tables, and cable TV. Rigs up to 50 feet long and slideouts can be accommodated. The most desirable sites are beachfront "ultra" sites with their own decks. If you are planning to stay long-term and your RV is more than 10 years old, it must be preapproved by management. There's a wireless Internet network in the office and clubhouse. Restrooms, showers, two laundry facilities, a dump station, a game room, a fishing pier, a pool, a hot tub, horseshoe pits, shuffleboard and basketball courts, a store, cabin rentals, and a playground are available. Campfires are permitted at a communal fire pit. A camp store sells ice, camping supplies, groceries, snacks, and souvenirs. During the winter, planned activities are available. All areas are wheelchair-accessible. Children are welcome. Small pets are permitted at the discretion of management; barking dogs, for example, are frowned upon, and campers are encouraged to report errant behavior to the office.

Reservations, fees: Reservations are recommended. Sites are $39–69 per night for two people, plus $3 for each additional person. Credit cards are accepted. Long-term rates are available.

Directions: From the Navarre Beach Bridge, drive one mile east on U.S. 98.

Contact: Navarre Beach Campground, 9201 Navarre Parkway, Navarre, FL 32566, 850/939-2188, fax 850/939-4712, www.navbeach.com.

27 MAGNOLIA BEACH CAMPGROUND

Scenic rating: 10

east of Navarre

Swim off of the park's sandy, 400-foot-long beach or cast a line for a seafood dinner from the long pier. Some sites overlook Santa Rosa Sound, which gets less boat traffic here than in other locations. From this five-acre park, you can combine your seaside experience with the wilderness. Just drive up State Road 87 toward Blackwater River State Park and the surrounding state forest for canoeing and other adventures.

Campsites, facilities: This campground has 50 RV sites with full hookups and 30-amp electricity. Restrooms, showers, laundry facilities, and a 600-foot-long fishing pier are provided. You can tie your boat up to the pier to load or unload passengers or gear, but the boat cannot be left there longer than that. The water around the pier is somewhat shallow, and jumping and diving are not permitted. Children are welcome, but those under 12 must be supervised at all times. Pets under 15 pounds are permitted on a leash; management can suggest several kennels nearby if your dog is larger.

Reservations, fees: Reservations are suggested. Sites are $27.50–35 per night for two people, plus $2 per extra person. Credit cards are not accepted. Long-term rates are available.

Directions: From Navarre, drive three miles east on U.S. 98. The park is on the south side.

Contact: Magnolia Beach Campground, 9807 Navarre Parkway, Navarre, FL 32566, 850/939-2717 or 877/375-4600, www.magnoliabeach.com.

28 PLAYGROUND RV PARK

Scenic rating: 2

on the north side of Fort Walton Beach

Although located beside a busy highway with strip shopping centers and heavy commercial activity, this park is nearly always full. It's convenient to Eglin Air Force Base, and beaches are only four miles away. Most overnighters or vacationers are here for the beach or to visit relatives nearby.

Campsites, facilities: This mobile-home community and apartment complex has a total of 65 RV sites with full hookups, 30/50-amp electrical service, and cable TV. Nine pull-through sites are generally available for short-term visitors. Restrooms, showers, laundry facilities, and a dump station are available. Children are welcome. Small, leashed pets are permitted.

Reservations, fees: Reservations are accepted. Sites are $30 per night for two people, plus $2 for each additional person over the age of six. Credit cards are accepted. Long-term rates are available.

Directions: From the junction of U.S. 98 and State Road 189 in Fort Walton Beach, drive north on State Road 189 for four miles. The park is on the east (right) side of the road.

Contact: Playground RV Park, 777 Beal Parkway, Fort Walton Beach, FL 32547, 850/862-3513, playgroundrvpark@aol.com.

29 RIVER'S EDGE RV CAMPGROUND

Scenic rating: 9

south of Holt

Sprawling across 144 acres on the banks of the Yellow River, this campground is heavily wooded and peaceful, suitable as a destination park or as an overnight spot. Even the biggest rigs can be accommodated on the extra-large pull-through sites. The campground provides 24-hour security. While you're here, fish from the river's edge or on nearby Log Lake and hike the one-mile nature trail. A quaint bridge built in the 1920s once spanned the Yellow River; now it sits on the riverbank as a bit of a historical interest. Blackwater River State Forest is close by. Supplies are available in Crestview, about 10 miles east of the park.

Campsites, facilities: Of the 110 RV sites, most have full hookups and 30-amp and 50-amp electrical service. Twenty primitive tent spots are set apart from the travel trailers. Picnic tables, fire pits, restrooms, showers, laundry facilities, a dump station, a boat launch, a playground, a clubhouse, a pavilion, and a camp circle are on the grounds. Children are welcome. Leashed pets are permitted.

Reservations, fees: Reservations are recommended. Sites are $18–20 per night for two adults, plus $2 for each additional person. No credit cards are accepted. Long-term stays are OK.

Directions: From I-10 near Holt, take Exit 45 and drive south on State Road 189 for 1.5 miles to the park.

Contact: River's Edge RV Campground, 4001 Log Lake Road, Holt, FL 32564, 850/537-2267.

30 LAZY DAYS RV PARK

Scenic rating: 2

east of Niceville in Freeport

This 8.5-acre roadside park usually attracts snowbirds in the winter and a few travelers passing through otherwise. Lately, almost the entire park (98 percent) has been occupied year-round, most recently by workers helping with many construction developments going up in the area. The beach is 10 miles away. Points of interest in the area include Eden State Gardens, Seaside, Grayton Beach, and Destin.

Campsites, facilities: There are 30 full-hookup RV sites with 30/50-amp electrical service, concrete patios, and optional cable TV and telephone service. Only around two sites are normally available for overnighters. RVs as long as 45 feet and slideouts can be accommodated. An Internet connection is available in the office. Picnic tables, restrooms, showers, a dump station, laundry facilities, propane, ice, a game room where potluck dinners are held in the winter months, and horseshoe pits are available. Groceries and restaurants are

within two miles. Children are welcome. Pets are allowed on a leash. Pop-top trailers are not allowed.

Reservations, fees: Reservations are recommended. Sites are $30 per night for two people, plus $3 for each additional person over age five. Credit cards are accepted. Long-term rates are available.

Directions: From I-10 at De Funiak Springs, take Exit 85 and head south on U.S. 331 for 17 miles. Or, from U.S. 98 west of Panama City, drive seven miles north on U.S. 331 to the park.

Contact: Lazy Days RV Park, 18655 U.S. 331 South, Freeport, FL 32439, 850/835-4606.

31 EGLIN AIR FORCE BASE

Scenic rating: 8

south of I-10, between Pensacola and De Funiak Springs

One of the largest swaths of wilderness in Florida is controlled by the Department of Defense (DoD). Although most people don't think of the military as being in the wildwoods business, the DoD has been an admirable caretaker of the grounds in recent years. For instance, the military went so far as to take special steps to save endangered red-cockaded woodpeckers by planting trees and protecting the rare birds' homes from fire.

What this base lacks in amenities, you get back in an astounding variety of natural settings for camping. They include sites on the Choctawhatchee and East Bays, which may be favored by saltwater anglers; six sites on ponds suitable for freshwater fishing; one on Metts Bluff overlooking the Yellow River; one at Gin Hole Landing, where boaters can launch onto the Yellow River; and others beside small creeks or bayous. Swimmers can take a plunge in the Gulf of Mexico, only a short drive away.

Wild animals you might spot include deer,

coyote, wild turkey, wild hog, quail, rabbit, or, if you're exceptionally lucky, the secretive black bear. But also remember that hunting is allowed. The general gun season, when you'll want to be sure to wear orange-blaze vests and hats (or avoid the area altogether), varies from year to year but usually occurs on specific weekends between Thanksgiving and mid-January. Call ahead for dates. Seasons for small-game and turkey hunters follow, but these present less of a threat to campers. Still, ask about hunting dates and bring along the orange-blaze outerwear. Also, if you come at these times, don't be surprised if you're sharing a campsite with hunters. Some areas of the base are closed to hunting, and others are designated for hunting only by bow and arrow. During certain periods, the base lands may be closed to the public for defense reasons; call 850/882-0007 for current status 24/7.

Campsites, facilities: Primitive campsites are scattered across about 446,000 acres square miles. There's an improved campsite with water and electricity at Postl Point; however, only persons affiliated with the Department of Defense may stay here (call 850/882-3569 if you qualify). For the general public, primitive campsites for self-contained RVs are scattered across about 446,000 acres square miles. Children are welcome. Pets are also permitted, but they must be restrained and kept at least 50 yards outside your campsite. Supplies and restaurants are available in Niceville and Valparaiso, on the base's southern boundary.

Reservations, fees: Permits are required. They may be obtained in two ways: 1. At least three weeks before your stay, write to Eglin Air Force Base Natural Resources Branch, 107 Highway 85 North, Niceville, FL 32578. Include a photocopy of a valid driver's license for the main person in your camping party, as well as updated address information and phone number if different from that on the driver's license. Specify that you want a camping permit, which costs $5 for five consecutive days and is payable only by check or money order payable to DFAS-DE DSSN 3801; or 2.

Drop by the office at the address above. It's open 7 A.M.–4:30 P.M. Monday–Thursday, 7 A.M.–6 P.M. Friday, and 7:30 A.M.–12:30 P.M. Saturday, closed Sundays and holidays. The permit is valid for five consecutive nights for up to 10 people.

Directions: From I-10 near Crestview, take Exit 56 and head south on State Road 85 for about 15 miles to the base's Jackson Guard in Niceville.

Contact: Eglin Air Force Base, Natural Resources Division/Jackson Guard, 107 Highway 85 North, Niceville, FL 32578, 850/882-4164, www.eglin.af.mil/newcomers/leisure.htm.

32 FRED GANNON ROCKY BAYOU STATE PARK

🚶 ⛵ 🛶 🎣 🐎 ♿ 🚗 ⛺

Scenic rating: 9

near Niceville

This park on the edge of the Eglin Air Force Base territory has another military link: It was named after a colonel who helped develop the 357-acre parcel of land after the state acquired it from the U.S. Forest Service. Most visitors to the area focus on the beach, even though it's fairly narrow and not your typical postcard bathing beach. There are plenty of other water-oriented delights here in a forest setting of tall sand pines, some of which are 300 years old. Swimmers, boaters, canoeists, and anglers can explore the treasures of Rocky Bayou, which opens into Choctawhatchee Bay; there's also a freshwater lake on the property. (You'll need the appropriate fishing license depending on whether you try your hand at fresh or saltwater fishing.) Ten campsites overlook the bayou. In 2005, several improvements were made to the park, including a new heated bathhouse, a bridge crossing Puddin Head Lake, and 50-amp electrical service at about one-fourth of the campsites. It'll take you about 25 minutes to explore each of the three nature trails. If you choose only one, pick the Sand Pine

Trail, which leads along Puddin Head Lake and through the woods. Incidentally, the town of Niceville was once named Boggy, but folks didn't think that sounded too appealing.

Campsites, facilities: There are 42 campsites in this state park, offering water and electricity (31 are 30-amp, and 11 have 50-amp service), picnic tables, grills, and fire rings. Restrooms, showers, a dump station, a boat ramp, a pavilion, and a playground are available. RVs up to 45 feet long and slideouts are permitted. Groceries and restaurants are within 0.5 mile. Two campsites, the bathhouse, office, store, and the boat ramp are wheelchair-accessible. Streets are paved. Children are welcome. Pets with proof of rabies vaccination are allowed.

Reservations, fees: Reservations are recommended; contact ReserveAmerica at 800/336-3521 or reserveamerica.com. Sites are $12 per night for eight people. Credit cards are accepted. The maximum stay is 14 days.

Directions: From I-10 near Crestview, take Exit 56 and drive south on State Road 85 for 15 miles. Turn east onto State Road 20 in Niceville and drive nine miles to the park.

Contact: Fred Gannon Rocky Bayou State Park, 4281 Highway 20, Niceville, FL 32578, 850/833-9144, www.floridastateparks.org.

33 BAYVIEW RV RESORT
🏊 🚐 🐕 🚍

Scenic rating: 3

in Destin

Located across from Destin's main boat launch, this park offers boat storage for guests and is set in a quiet neighborhood. Long-term visitors are preferred, and usually only a few sites are available. You'll notice the park's lighthouse at the entrance.

Campsites, facilities: This tiny park has 12 RV sites with full hookups; call to see if any sites are available. Restrooms, showers, and laundry facilities are available. Children are welcome. Leashed pets are permitted.

Reservations, fees: Reservations are recommended. Sites are $25 per night for two people, plus $2 per extra person. Credit cards are accepted. Long-term rates are available.

Directions: From the U.S. 98 bridge in Destin, drive east 1.6 miles. Turn north on Beach Drive and continue 1.3 miles to the park on the left.

Contact: Bayview RV Resort, 749 Beach Drive, Destin, FL 32541, 850/837-5085, www.bayviewdestin.com.

34 DESTIN RV BEACH RESORT
🏊 🐕 ♿ 🚐

Scenic rating: 10

east of Destin

BEST (

This beachside motorcoach resort, opened in 2001, offers luxury sites with private beach access, fancy landscaping and lighting, brick pavers instead of an asphalt road, and an intimate setting of just 36 sites. With this much investment, you can expect that upscale RVers are most welcome. Only Class A, B, and C motor homes, fifth wheels, and travel trailers are allowed; they must be at least 22 feet long and no more than 10 years old. Pop-ups, truck campers, and other hybrid travel trailers are prohibited.

Campsites, facilities: There are 36 full-hookup sites with 30/50-amp electrical service, concrete patios, professional landscaping, and cable TV. Lots are 30 feet wide by 60 feet deep, and they can accommodate RVs up to 45 feet long and slideouts. Wireless Internet service is available for an additional charge. Restrooms, showers, laundry facilities, and telephone service are available. On the premises are a heated pool, two luxury rental units above the office building, brick-paved driveways, and a path to the beach. The bathhouse, office, and pool area are wheelchair-accessible. Children are welcome. Leashed pets are permitted.

Reservations, fees: Reservations are recom-

mended. Sites are $79 per night for a family of six (two adults and four children age 16 or under), plus $10 for each additional adult. Only six people are allowed per site. Long-term rates are available.

Directions: From U.S. 98 and MidBay Bridge Road (Highway 293), drive east on U.S. 98 about five miles. Turn right on Miramar Beach Drive to the park at the beach.

Contact: Destin RV Beach Resort, 362 Miramar Beach Drive, Destin, FL 32550, 850/837-3529, www.destinrvresort.com.

35 HENDERSON BEACH STATE PARK

🚶 🚴 🏊 ⛵ 🛶 🎣 🏕️ ♿ 🚐 ⛺

Scenic rating: 10

in Destin

BEST (

Opened in March 2000, this is one of the newer campgrounds in Florida's award-winning state park system. Since opening, Henderson Beach State Park has doubled the size of its campground with the addition of another loop along the Gulf of Mexico. The park has 6,000 feet of white-sand shoreline (with a boardwalk from the campground to the beach) and 208 acres of sand pine, scrub oak, and other vegetation. Why is the sand so white? It's composed of quartz and silicon dioxide polished by countless years of wave action. You can scuba dive just one mile offshore, or swim in the gulf, or cast a line from the surf to while away the day. Restaurants and shopping are within one mile, and there's a Wal-Mart across the street. The campground has its own beach area separate from the day users' beach. On weekends, rangers host interpretive programs, and the park is the site of festivals, such as a national surf-casting fishing event.

Campsites, facilities: Sixty sites have water, 30-amp electricity, picnic tables, and grills. Twenty-two sites are pull-through; 36 sites have 50-amp service. Big RVs and slideouts are permitted. Restrooms, showers, and a

dump station are available. Ice and souvenirs are for sale. Most areas are wheelchair-accessible. Children are welcome. Leashed pets are permitted.

Reservations, fees: Reservations are recommended; contact ReserveAmerica at 800/336-3521 or reserveamerica.com. Sites are $23 for up to eight people. Credit cards are accepted. The maximum stay is 14 days.

Directions: From the intersection of US 98 and Midway Bridge Road in Destin, drive west on U.S. 98 one mile to the park entrance.

Contact: Henderson Beach State Park, 17000 Emerald Coast Parkway, Destin, FL 32541, 850/837-7550, fax 850/650-0290, www.floridastateparks.org.

36 CAMPING ON THE GULF HOLIDAY TRAVEL PARK

🏊 ⛵ 🎣 🏕️ ♿ 🚐

Scenic rating: 10

east of Destin

BEST (

If you've come to Florida to visit the beach, you'll love this family park, where you can book a site directly on the fabled white sands of the Gulf of Mexico. As the owners say, "You can't get much closer than this!" Beachfront spots, naturally, are the most dear, but shady, grassy sites and sites with concrete pads are convenient to the water and the oceanfront walkway. The campground "beach patrol" will help you park your rig, and the management offers "express check-in" for many reserved visitors.

Campsites, facilities: There are 221 RV sites with full hookups, 30/50-amp electrical service, cable TV, concrete patios, and picnic tables; some have telephone service. Twenty-one sites are pull-through. The average lot size of 30 feet wide by 70 feet deep accommodates RVs up to 45 feet long and slideouts. Restrooms, showers, laundry facilities, a dump station, a heated pool, a gift shop, rental cabins, a 3,500-square-foot activity center with planned activities, a fishing guide, and a playground are provided. A wireless Internet connection is available in the clubhouse. The camp store sells ice, snacks, limited groceries, souvenirs, and propane. Groceries, restaurants, malls, and hospitals are within two miles. All areas are wheelchair-accessible. Children are welcome. Leashed pets are permitted, though not on the beachfront campsites.

Reservations, fees: Reservations are recommended. Sites are $41–101 per night for five people, plus $5 per extra person. Rates are higher on holiday weekends. Credit cards are accepted. Six-month stays are OK September–May.

Directions: From the U.S. 98 bridge in Destin, drive east for 10 miles to the park on the south side of the road.

Contact: Camping on the Gulf Holiday Travel Park, 10005 West Emerald Coast Parkway, Destin, FL 32541, 850/837-6334 or 877/226-7485 (reservations), fax 850/654-5048, www.campgulf.com.

⒊⒎ TOPSAIL HILL STATE PRESERVE

🚶 🚴 ⛵ 🛶 🎣 🏠 ♿ 🚐

Scenic rating: 10

in Santa Rosa Beach

BEST (

If you own a large RV, this 140-acre private-campground-turned-state-preserve is where you'll want to be. One of the most deluxe RV parks in Florida, Topsail has resort-style amenities such as a heated swimming pool, fishing lakes, professional landscaping, oversized lots, and immaculate grounds. Even the restrooms are heated and air-conditioned, according to season. The park is tucked into a pine forest near sandy beaches and upscale shopping centers. Free shuttle service is available to the beach.

Longtimers remember this park as Emerald Coast RV Resort, but the neighboring 1,639-acre state preserve—Topsail, home to one of the world's last remaining populations of the endangered Choctawhatchee beach mouse—took it over, and it is now part of the state park system. Tiny wildflowers bloom most months at the preserve, which features wispy savannas, cypress domes, coastal dune lakes, and, of course, the feature from which it derives its name, a 25-foot-high lakeside dune.

Campsites, facilities: All 156 RV sites have sewer hookups, 30/50-amp electricity, cable TV, and optional telephone service. Internet access is available. Picnic tables, grills, restrooms, showers, laundry facilities, a dump station, a heated pool, a recreation center, tennis courts, a lake, boat and canoe rentals, rental cabins, a driving range, horseshoe pits, and shuffleboard courts are on-site. The restrooms, office, and beach boardwalk are wheelchair-accessible. Children and leashed pets are welcome.

Reservations, fees: Reservations are recommended; contact ReserveAmerica at 800/336-3521 or reserveamerica.com. Sites are $38 per night. Credit cards are accepted. Long-term stays are OK.

Directions: From I-10 at De Funiak Springs, take Exit 85 and head south on U.S. 331 for 26 miles to U.S. 98. Turn west (right) and drive five miles to County Road 30A. Turn south (left) and drive 0.2 mile to the park entrance on your right.

Contact: Topsail Hill State Preserve, 7525 West Scenic Highway 30A, Santa Rosa Beach, FL 32459, 850/267-0299, fax 850/267-9014, www.floridastateparks.org.

PANAMA CITY

© FLORIDA STATE PARKS

BEST CAMPGROUNDS

❰ Beachfront Campgrounds
Grayton Beach State Park, page 85
St. Andrews State Park, page 90
T. H. Stone Memorial St. Joseph Peninsula State
   Park, page 93

❰ Biking
Pine Log State Forest, page 83

❰ Families
Emerald Coast RV Beach Resort, page 87

❰ Best Natural Springs
Vortex Spring RV Park, page 77

❰ Most Luxurious
Emerald Coast RV Beach Resort, page 87

❰ Most Unusual
Falling Waters State Park, page 78
Florida Caverns State Park, page 80

Imagine dazzling white sandy expanses offset

by brilliant emerald-green waters and gorgeous picture-postcard vistas. These sugary, textured beaches are so beautiful that a university professor who styles himself as "Dr. Beach" has officially designated them as the best in the world. The sand on the beaches of Panama City and its surrounding areas is so white that it resembles snow.

Little wonder then that beachside camping is the major attraction for visitors fond of sunbathing, sea kayaking, and wading in the surf. Saltwater anglers say the fishing is excellent as well.

This stretch of the Gulf Coast attracts thousands of visitors from the Florida Panhandle and surrounding Southern states of Alabama, Mississippi, and Georgia. This holds especially true during the summer months, a reverse of the traditional "winter season" busyness that befalls most of the state of Florida. Fancier RV parks tend to be clustered along Panama City's beachfront entertainment area, while more nature-oriented campgrounds are scattered across the more remote inland woods and river regions.

You'll find vast acres of forest, as well as natural springs, including one associated with the fabled "fountain of youth." For decades, pitchmen have exploited the legend of Spanish explorer Juan Ponce de Leon, who discovered Florida in 1513. He was hunting for hidden riches, not just a fountain, but his name has been attached ever since to Florida's myriad springs – natural wonders with supposedly curative powers.

Local springs are famous for snorkeling and cave-diving (certified divers only). It sounds strange to think of caves in Florida, but stalactites and stalagmites are found in Florida Caverns State Park. It's the only aboveground cave system in the state that can be toured by the public, and the campground in the park is lovely.

While many campers will focus on the beaches, more outdoorsy types will find the rest of the region to their liking. For example, back-country campers, boaters, and hunters can explore the Choctawhatchee River, once a vital waterway linking antebellum plantations at the Alabama border to the docks downstream at Choctawhatchee Bay on the Gulf of Mexico. Today, it's a scenic waterway fringed by cypress, tupelo, gum, ash, and hickory trees.

Mountain bikers head for the Pine Log State Forest, where single-track trails snake through pine woods and oak trees. Horse trails and several miles of hiking trails, including an eight-mile section of the Florida National Scenic Trail, are also available.

Freshwater anglers have several options, including Juniper Lake. Locals believe that its waters will someday yield the world-record large-mouth bass.

This region is also noteworthy for being home to the highest point in Florida – 345 feet above sea level. It's just an imperceptible bump flagged with a sign and a granite marker, but you can say you bagged another peak.

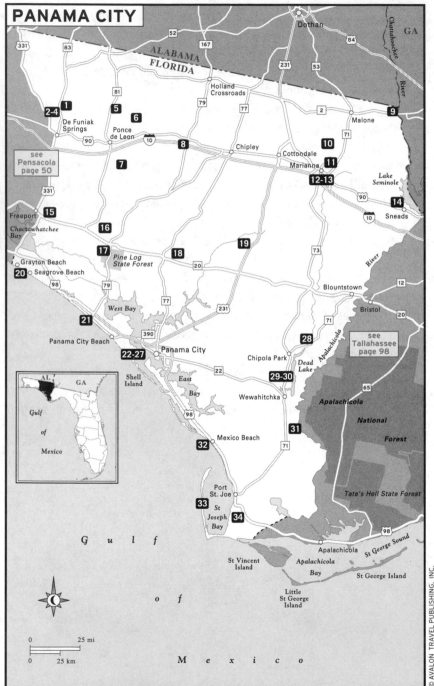

1 SUNSET KING LAKE RESORT

🚴 🏊 🎣 🚤 🐕 🤸 ♿ 🚐 ⛺

Scenic rating: 8

north of De Funiak Springs, on Kings Lake

Set on 580-acre Kings Lake, this park caters to anglers and campers who like lots of on-site amenities, such as miniature golf, croquet, basketball, volleyball, and badminton. It's close enough to I-10 to work as a good stay-over option. Kids can play in the fenced playground, swim in the lakeview pool, or fish off the 75-foot lighted pier. The lake is stocked regularly with black bass, shellcracker, crappie, and bream; in 1987, it yielded a record-breaking bass weighing in at more than 17 pounds. Sites are sunny, with a few trees interspersed. A hired activities director organizes the fun stuff. Lots are for sale as well. These people are really into technology: If you want to check the views online, the park has dock-mounted and pool area Web cameras.

Campsites, facilities: Tenters are welcome in this RV resort for stays of up to one week at 10 grassy sites with water and electricity. The rest of the park has 123 large (40-foot-by-90-foot) full-hookup RV sites with 50-amp electrical service and cable TV, plus another 70 or so sites occupied by long-term visitors. Rigs up to 45 feet long and slideouts can be accommodated. A wireless Internet connection is available throughout the park. Cable TV, picnic tables, grills, restrooms, showers, a dump station, a clubhouse, a pavilion, a pool, a boat ramp, boat docks, a playground, a game room, miniature golf, horseshoe pits, outdoor movie screen, a store, and laundry facilities are on-site. A restaurant is open Wednesday–Sunday. The clubhouse and bathhouse are wheelchair-accessible. Children and pets are welcome. Memberships are for sale, so you may see lots of repeat visitors.

Reservations, fees: Reservations are not necessary, but peak season at the park is February–March and November–December. Sites are $27–45 per night for two people, plus $2 per extra person. Credit cards are accepted. Long-term rates are available.

Directions: If traveling westbound: From I-10 west of De Funiak Springs, take Exit 70 and drive north on State Road 285 for 0.4 mile. Turn right onto U.S. 90 and drive 8.5 miles east. When you reach Kings Lake Road, turn north and follow the signs to the park. If traveling eastbound: Take I-10 Exit 85 and turn right on Highway 331. Drive two miles to U.S. 90 and turn left. Continue five miles on U.S. 90 until you reach Kings Lake Road. Roads leading to the park are paved.

Contact: Sunset King Lake Resort, 366 Paradise Island Drive, De Funiak Springs, FL 32433, 850/892-7229 or 800/747-5454, fax 850/892-7998, www.sunsetking.com.

2 LONG LEAF RV PARK

🏠 🐕 ♿ 🚐

Scenic rating: 3

near De Funiak Springs

Weary travelers on I-10 will find this park convenient, though it offers no pool or recreation room. It has long pull-through spaces on gravel roads just 3.5 miles south of the interstate. Overnighters are welcome. Shopping and restaurants are close by. Among your fellow campers will be European and American touring bicyclists there for the open country and easy roads.

Campsites, facilities: There are 24 partially shaded RV sites, all with water and electricity. Nineteen sites have full hookups with 30- or 50-amp electricity. All have picnic tables. Restrooms, showers, laundry facilities, and telephone service are available. Most areas are wheelchair-accessible, although the streets are gravel. A dog-walk area is on the premises. Children are welcome. Leashed pets are permitted.

Reservations, fees: Reservations are recommended. Sites are $20–22 per night for two people, plus $2 per extra person. Credit cards are not accepted. Long-term rates are available.

Directions: From I-10, take Exit 85 onto U.S. 331 and drive 3.5 miles south.

Contact: Long Leaf RV Park, 5687 U.S. 331 South, De Funiak Springs, FL 32435, 850/892-7261.

❸ BASS HAVEN CAMPGROUND

Scenic rating: 5

north of De Funiak Springs, on Juniper Lake

Rigs up to 40 feet long can be accommodated in this 1.5-acre park on Juniper Lake, which is famed for its bass fishing. But there's more to do around here than fish: Take a 15-minute drive to Vortex Spring or explore the city of De Funiak Springs, which has dozens of spectacular Victorian homes that circle a spring-fed lake; it's said to be one of two perfectly round lakes in the world. Around the turn of the 20th century, this town was famous as the home of the Winter Chautauqua, a cultural and philosophical movement that brought lecturers and speech makers here to the still-standing Chautauqua Auditorium. Also nearby is the Chautauqua Winery (850/892-5887), the largest winery in Florida; tours are available. If you're feeling really energetic, take a drive north to the highest point in Florida—345 feet above sea level. It's just an imperceptible bump flagged with a sign and a granite marker, but you can say you bagged another peak. From De Funiak Springs, drive north on U.S. 331/State Road 285 about 20 miles until State Road 285 forks off to the northeast. Continue on State Road 285 about two miles; the marker is in a pine woods with a small picnic area.

Campsites, facilities: The campground has 19 RV sites, most with sewer hookups and 30-amp electrical service, and six tent sites set apart from the RVs. Two pull-through sites have 50-amp, but no sewer. On the premises are picnic tables, restrooms, showers, a dump station, a boat ramp, boat docks, boat rentals, horseshoe pits, a volleyball field, a store, and laundry facilities. Groceries and restaurants are within five miles. The bathrooms and "sleeping room," a rental suite attached to the clubhouse, are wheelchair-accessible. Children and pets are welcome.

Reservations, fees: Reservations are not necessary. Sites are $20 per night for a family of four, plus $2 per extra person and $1 for cable TV. Credit cards are not accepted. The maximum stay is six months.

Directions: From I-10 at De Funiak Springs, take Exit 85 and drive north on U.S. 331 for two miles, then turn east onto U.S. 90 and go several blocks through town. At State Road 83, turn left and drive 2.5 miles north. At Juniper Lake Road, turn west (left) and follow the signs to the park.

Contact: Bass Haven Campground, 350 Bass Haven Drive, De Funiak Springs, FL 32433, 850/892-4043.

❹ JUNIPER LAKE CAMPGROUND

Scenic rating: 5

north of De Funiak Springs, on Juniper Lake

Juniper Lake is considered one of the area's finest fishing lakes for bass. In fact, those in the know are so confident that they believe a world-record largemouth bass will be pulled from here someday. Will you be the lucky angler? Stay a few days at one of the campsites right on the lakeshore of this 4.5-acre park and give it a try. The lake is 667 acres, and very "fishy."

Campsites, facilities: This park has 18 RV sites with full hookups and cable TV and 15 spots for tenters. Overnighters are welcome, and 50-amp service is available. On the premises are picnic tables, restrooms, showers, a picnic area, a clubhouse, covered boat slips with electricity, johnboats for rent ($30 per day), three docks, and laundry facilities. Children are welcome. Leashed pets are OK.

Reservations, fees: Reservations are suggested. Sites are $18 per night. Credit cards are not accepted. Long-term rates are available.

Directions: From I-10 at De Funiak Springs, take Exit 85 and drive north on U.S. 331 for two miles, then turn east onto U.S. 90 and go several blocks through town. At State Road 83, turn north and drive 2.5 miles. At Juniper Lake Road, turn west and follow the signs to the park.

Contact: Juniper Lake Campground, 363 Black Bass Boulevard, De Funiak Springs, FL 32433, 850/892-3445, fax 850/892-9136.

5 VORTEX SPRING RV PARK

Scenic rating: 10

in Ponce de Leon

BEST (

The family-run Vortex Spring camping resort, on the outskirts of the city of Ponce de Leon, capitalizes on scuba diving and underwater caving. The centerpiece of this 480-acre private campground is a spring and underwater cavern that spews 28 million gallons of water daily at a constant temperature of 68°F. The spring basin, crystal clear and 48 feet deep, is shared by catfish, freshwater eels, rare shadow bass, Japanese koi fish and a vegetarian piranha named Paco. The limestone cavern, restricted to cave-certified divers, meanders farther for 100 yards to a depth of 115 feet. Diving lessons are available. On the surface, the spring spills into Blue Creek, which is good for snorkeling, canoeing, or a paddleboat ride. The swimming area has a small waterslide, a nine-foot diving platform, a slide for small children, and an old-fashioned rope swing. The campsites are grassy and semi-shaded; wood for campfires is sold at the store, along with other supplies.

Near the campground is 443-acre Ponce de Leon Springs State Park, on State Road 181A, 0.5 mile south of U.S. 90. Two springs are surrounded by a wall built in 1926, when the waters were a "fountain of youth" attraction; they produce 14 million gallons daily that flow into the Choctawhatchee River. No camping is permitted, but there's a swimming beach with a bathhouse, a picnic area, and a couple of nature trails. Admission is $2 per car. For more information, call 850/836-4281.

Campsites, facilities: This park has 22 RV sites and 26 tent sites. Seven have full hookups and are pull-through; all have water and electricity. Additional sites are primitive. Each developed site has a picnic table, a grill, and a fire ring. On the premises are restrooms, showers, scuba-diving facilities, a campground store, and a spring for swimming. Snorkel gear, paddleboat, canoe, kayak, and inner-tube rentals are available. A go-cart park is a mile from the campsites. Children are welcome. Pets are not allowed, except with overnighters passing through.

Reservations, fees: Reservations are recommended, particularly during holidays. Sites are $28 per night for two people, plus $6 for each additional person. Credit cards are accepted.

Directions: From I-10 east of De Funiak Springs, take Exit 96 to State Road 81 and drive five miles north to the park at right. Turn right at the sign and drive 0.5 mile to the campground.

Contact: Vortex Spring RV Park, 1517 Vortex Spring Lane, Ponce de Leon, FL 32455, 850/836-4979 or 800/342-0640, fax 850/836-4557, www.vortexspring.com.

6 CHOCTAWHATCHEE RIVER WATER MANAGEMENT AREA BOAT-IN SITES

Scenic rating: 7

near Caryville, along the Choctawhatchee River

The Choctawhatchee River is a scenic waterway that flows to the Gulf of Mexico. The riverbanks are tall and heavily wooded, with large sandbars that make good camping spots.

Bring a johnboat with a small motor, launch at the boat ramp, then travel downriver—passing cypress, tupelo, gum, ash, and hickory trees along the way—to scope out the banks for a good place to pitch a tent. When the river is high, it's hard to find dry campsites. The east side of the river, off State Road 179, is laced with a hiking trail and dirt roads open to backpackers and horseback riders. The river and several lakes are open to boaters and anglers. Wear bright orange clothing during the hunting season, November through early March, lest you be mistaken for a deer or wild hog.

Note: It's not advisable to bring a canoe, because the river here flows swiftly.

Campsites, facilities: Boaters can access an indeterminate number of primitive tent camping areas with no facilities or drinking water. Trash must be packed out. Children and pets are permitted.

Reservations, fees: Reservations are not necessary. Camping is free.

Directions: From I-10 east of Ponce de Leon, take Exit 104 and proceed north on County Road 279 to Caryville. Turn left onto U.S. 90 and travel about two miles west, then turn right onto State Road 179A. Go about five miles north to the crossroads of Cerrogordo (if you hit the hamlet of Baker Settlement, you've gone too far) and turn right onto the unnamed road leading to Cerrogordo Landing. The boat ramp is about one mile ahead.

Contact: Northwest Florida Water Management District, 81 Water Management Drive, Havana, FL 32333, 850/539-5999, www .nwfwmd.state.fl.us/recreation.html.

7 CHOCTAWHATCHEE RIVER WATER MANAGEMENT AREA HIKE-IN SITES

🚶 🏊 ⛵ 🛶 🐕 ⛺

Scenic rating: 4

south of Caryville

This is rustic with a capital R, so only adventurers need read on. Backpacking is possible

in the eastern part of the property near State Road 284, an area loaded with wildlife. This river floodplain is likely to be inundated with water at times, so check ahead on conditions. Wear bright orange during hunting season, November through early March. Boats and canoes are best launched on the west side of the river.

Campsites, facilities: Backpackers can camp along the Choctawhatchee River. There are no facilities. Children and pets are permitted.

Reservations, fees: Reservations are not necessary. Camping is free.

Directions: From I-10 east of Ponce de Leon, take Exit 104 and drive south on County Road 279. Continue south on State Road 280 and drive about five miles to the intersection of County Road 284 at Hinson's Crossroads. A dirt road into the preserve is on the west side of County Road 284, about four miles south of Hinson's Crossroads. For boat and canoe launching: From I-10 at Ponce de Leon, take Exit 96 and drive south on State Road 81. Turn east on the dirt road extension of County Road 183 and drive to the river.

Contact: Northwest Florida Water Management District, 81 Water Management Drive, Havana, FL 32333, 850/539-5999, www .nwfwmd.state.fl.us/recreation.html.

8 FALLING WATERS STATE PARK

🚶 🏊 ⛵ 🛶 ♿ 🚐 ⛺

Scenic rating: 10

near Chipley

BEST (

This 171-acre park is a fine overnight camping spot with a unique attraction: Florida's only waterfall. Sure, it's no Niagara, plunging just 67 feet into a cylindrical sinkhole where it vanishes into the limestone. The site, though, has a prehistoric feel, lush with ferns and ancient hardwoods. Slash pines shade the campground, and there's a trail leading to the swimming lake (swimming in the waterfall is not permitted). The trail continues past the site of an oil well drilled by wildcatters in 1919. It produced a dribble of crude and was capped three years later. Just above the falls, a whiskey still produced spirits for frontier railroad crews in the 1800s. The waterfall itself powered a gristmill for several years. Timbers from the old mill are on display.

Campsites, facilities: This state park has seven campsites for RVs and 17 for tents with water, 30-amp electricity, picnic tables, grills, and fire rings; seven are pull-through sites. There are restrooms, showers, a dump station, a swimming lake, and a playground. Firewood is not provided, but you are welcome to bring your own. Children are welcome. Pets are permitted with up-to-date vaccination records. The picnic area is wheelchair-accessible.

Reservations, fees: Reservations are recommended; contact ReserveAmerica at 800/336-3521 or reserveamerica.com. The fee is $15 for eight people. Credit cards are accepted.

Directions: From I-10 at Chipley, take Exit 120 onto State Road 77 and drive south for three miles to the park.

Contact: Falling Waters State Park, 1130 State Park Road, Chipley, FL 32428, 850/638-6130, fax 850/638-6273, www.floridastateparks.org.

9 NEAL'S LANDING

🎣 ⛵ 🐕 🚐 ⛺

Scenic rating: 4

on the Chattahoochee River, near the Georgia border

Sites are shady and spaced far apart from each other in this rustic county campground. Visitors have access to a boat ramp on the Chattahoochee River but will find that it's typically very busy, attracting boaters and anglers from three states: Georgia is across the river to the east, and Alabama is just a hop, skip, and jump to the north. (Note that bathroom facilities serve both the campground and the boat launch, and that the campground is not staffed.)

Campsites, facilities: There are 11 sites for RVs or tents, about half with a picnic table, a grill, and a lantern hanger. There is no electricity or water hookups at the campsites. Restrooms, showers, a dump station, and a boat ramp are available. Children and leashed pets are welcome.

Reservations, fees: Reservations are not accepted. Sites are free. Credit cards are not accepted. Maximum stay is 14 days.

Directions: From the west side of Sneads at the junction of State Road 271 and U.S. 90, drive 22 miles north on State Road 271. At County Road 164, turn right (northeast) and drive 1.3 miles. At State Road 2, turn right (eastbound) and drive 0.9 mile. The campground is on the south side of the road, just before the bridge and the Georgia state line.

Contact: Jackson County Community Development Department, 4487 Lafayette Street, Marianna, FL 32446, 850/718-0437.

10 UPPER CHIPOLA RIVER WATER MANAGEMENT AREA

🎣 ⛵ 🚐 🐕 ⛺

Scenic rating: 7

along the banks of the Upper Chipola River

If you're into primitive camping, you'll want to come here for solitude, instead of heading to more popular Florida Caverns State Park (see next listing). Just remember that there are no facilities. These 7,374 acres span 18 miles along the Chipola River, so the area is subject to flooding. A trail runs alongside much of the river. Trees in the area include iris, basswood, and Florida maple. In some places, little shade is available right next to the water. You might catch sight of deer in the forested lands set farther back from the river if you're up early or out in the evening at twilight. Also keep your eyes peeled for southern brown bats flitting about at dusk, and the occasional Barbour's map turtle lumbering around the shoreline. In the spring, you can feast on the succulent purple-black boysenberries that grow in briar patches here. In November and December, you may encounter deer hunters, so wear bright orange clothing if you are hiking. Turkey hunters show up in March and April. The best access is by boat.

Campsites, facilities: Primitive camping is available in some 7,400 acres stretching from the Alabama border to Florida Caverns State Park. There are no official campsites, but you'll find no shortage of places to set up housekeeping for up to 14 days. No facilities are provided. Bring water and camping supplies. Pack out trash. Children and pets are permitted.

Reservations, fees: Reservations are not necessary. Camping is free.

Directions: There are only a few places to launch a boat here. My suggestion: Head north on Highway 71 from Marianna and turn left at the small settlement of Greenwood (by the Junior Food Store) onto County Road 162/Fort Road. When you pass the bridge over the Chipola River, double back on the dirt road to the river. For more information, contact the water management district.

Contact: Northwest Florida Water Management District, 81 Water Management Drive, Havana, FL 32333, 850/539-5999, www.nwfwmd.state.fl.us/recreation.html.

11 FLORIDA CAVERNS STATE PARK

Scenic rating: 10

north of Marianna

BEST (

Caves in Florida? You bet. Be sure to take the 45-minute ranger-led tour to see the stalactites, stalagmites, columns, flowstones, and draperies formed tens of thousands of years ago. Although not as large as Kentucky's Mammoth Cave, the Florida Caverns are arguably just as interesting; there's even a "wedding cake" formation in one chamber, where some couples

have celebrated their nuptials. The state park and the caverns were developed in the 1930s by the Civilian Conservation Corps, which built trails and passages and installed lighting to make the caverns accessible to the public. This is the only cave in Florida that the public can enter without a scientific research permit. However, you are not permitted to explore the caverns at whim. Tours are first-come, first-served; if your only reason for coming is to see the caves, go directly there to buy your ticket ($2.50–5), because they sell out fast. The rest of the 1,300-acre park has much to offer: a swimming area at Blue Hole, a boat ramp on the Chipola River, canoe rentals, hiking and equestrian trails, and forests of American beech, southern magnolia, spruce pine, white oak, and some plants more typical of the Appalachian Mountains.

Another feature that makes this park special: It was constructed by the Civilian Conservation Corps during the late 1930s. The CCC, formed by President Roosevelt to provide employment during the Depression, built several parks in Florida, using local rock to create charming buildings. At Florida Caverns, the Corps enlarged the caverns and installed lighting. In much earlier days, the caves were used by Native Americans and as a hiding place during the Civil War.

Campsites, facilities: There are 35 shady, gravel tent/RV sites, all with water and 30-amp electricity, picnic tables, grills, and fire rings. The campground has plenty of trees, but RVers will also find spots suitable for raising a satellite dish. Rigs as long as 40 feet can be accommodated. Restrooms, showers, a dump station, a boat ramp, a playground, a museum, and a snack bar are provided. The bathhouse and visitors center are wheelchair-accessible. Children are welcome. Pets are permitted with proof of vaccination.

Reservations, fees: Reservations are recommended; contact ReserveAmerica at 800/336-3521 or reserveamerica.com. Sites are $17 per night for eight people. Credit cards are accepted. Maximum length of stay is 14 days.

Many state parks have horse trails. Here, Florida Caverns State Park.

Directions: From I-10 at Marianna, take Exit 142 and onto State Road 71 North for 5.8 miles. Turn right on State Road 166/Jefferson Street. That road becomes Caverns Road; keep going for 2.7 miles to the park entrance.

Contact: Florida Caverns State Park, 3345 Caverns Road, Marianna, FL 32446, 850/482-9598, www.floridastateparks.org.

12 ARROWHEAD CAMPSITES

Scenic rating: 5

in Marianna, on U.S. 90

Arrowhead Campground borders on Mill Pond, a spring-fed, seven-mile-long lake where one angler caught a world-record shellcracker. It also overlooks the main drag into town, but situated as it is on a hill, the ambience is superior to sniffing highway exhaust. The campground has tall pines and elms and plenty of stuff for kids, including a swimming pool, a playground, and a game room. A whopping 180 sites are pull-through, which, since they're

located on a slope, is a very good thing for backup-impaired drivers like me. There's an RV dealership and service center on-site, handy in this remote area.

Campsites, facilities: There are 244 tent and RV sites with full hookups, cable TV, and picnic tables. Restrooms, showers, laundry facilities, a dump station, a game room, a pool, a playground, a boat ramp, boat docks, canoe rentals, and five cabins are available. An RV supplies store is on-site. Children are welcome. Leashed pets are permitted.

Reservations, fees: Reservations are recommended. Sites are $16 per night for four people, plus $2 for each additional person. Major credit cards are accepted. Long-term stays are OK.

Directions: From I-10 at Marianna, take Exit 142 heading north on State Road 71 for 1.8 miles. At U.S. 90, turn left and drive 0.2 mile west. The park is on the right, on the lake.

Contact: Arrowhead Campsites, 4820 U.S. 90 East, Marianna, FL 32446, 850/482-5583 or 800/643-9166, fax 850/482-4713, www.arrowheadcamp.com.

13 DOVE REST RV PARK

Scenic rating: 4

south of Marianna

With many pull-through sites near the highway, this lushly wooded 26-acre campground offers easy on-and-off access for even the weariest interstate traveler. It's convenient to Florida Caverns State Park, restaurants, and shopping. The park is divided into two sections: One is sunny, and the other is shaded by some of the park's 300 trees. About a third of the park is occupied by year-round residents or permanently placed units that are for rent. A Wal-Mart is 0.5 mile away.

Campsites, facilities: All 110 pull-through RV sites have full hookups, 30- and 50-amp electrical service, cable TV, and concrete pads. There's plenty of elbow room between sites, and the biggest rigs can be accommodated. Primitive tent camping is permitted throughout the park's 26 acres. Restrooms, showers, laundry facilities, a dump station, a basketball court, a recreation hall, and horseshoe pits are on-site. Restaurants are 0.5 mile away. Children are welcome. Leashed pets are permitted.

Reservations, fees: Reservations usually are not necessary. Sites are $25 per night for two people, plus $2 for each additional person. Credit cards are not accepted. Long-term rates are available.

Directions: From I-10 at Marianna, take Exit 142 and drive south on State Road 71 for 0.5 mile.

Contact: Dove Rest RV Park, 1973 Dove Rest Drive, Marianna, FL 32448, 850/482-5313.

14 THREE RIVERS STATE PARK
🏃 🏊 ⛴ 🏠 🐕 🚐 ⛺

Scenic rating: 9

north of Sneads

Camping here is a lakeside affair in a forest of pines and hardwood trees—but most visitors come to fish, not explore the forest. Three Rivers State Park is so named because of its at the junction of the Chattahoochee and Flint Rivers, which merge to form the Apalachicola River, and Lake Seminole. The 683-acre park fronts two miles of shoreline on Lake Seminole, a popular place for catching largemouth and smallmouth bass, catfish, and bluegill. Alligators and alligator snapping turtles are commonly seen around the lake; in the woods, you may encounter white-tailed deer. A shady, two-mile-long nature trail loop winds along the lakeshore. The fishing pier is 100 feet long, so don't worry if you don't have a boat or choose not to rent one from one of the nearby marinas.

Campsites, facilities: There are 30 shady and semi-shaded sites for RVs or tents with water, 30-amp electricity, picnic tables, grills,

and fire rings. Firewood is available for sale in the park; however, you are not allowed to gather your own wood. Restrooms, showers, a dump station, a boat ramp, and a fishing pier are available. Children are welcome. Leashed pets are accepted with proof of rabies vaccination.

Reservations, fees: Reservations are recommended; contact ReserveAmerica at 800/336-3521 or reserveamerica.com. The fee is $12 per night for eight people. Credit cards are accepted. The maximum stay is 14 days.

Directions: From the west side of Sneads at the junction of State Road 271 and U.S. 90, drive two miles north on State Road 271. Turn north (right) at the sign for the state park.

Contact: Three Rivers State Park, Route 1, P.O. Box 15-A, Sneads, FL 32460, 850/482-9006, www.floridastateparks.org.

15 THE OUTPOST RV PARK
🏊 ⛴ 🐕 🚐

Scenic rating: 2

east of Freeport

Located on Black Creek near the Choctawhatchee Bay, this small rural store has 10 sites available for anglers, hunters, and overnighters. A boat ramp makes water access easy, and bait and tackle are available at the store.

Campsites, facilities: Ten RV sites with full hookups and 50-amp service are available. There are no restrooms or showers. A store, a boat ramp, a dock, and canoe rentals are available. Children are welcome. Small leashed pets are permitted.

Reservations, fees: Reservations are recommended. Sites are $18 per night for two people, plus $2 per extra person. Credit cards are not accepted. Long-term stays are permitted.

Directions: From the intersection of State Road 331 and County Road 3280 in Freeport, drive east five miles on County Road 3280. Look for the store on the right side of the road.

Contact: The Outpost RV Park, 4576 County

Road 3280 East, Freeport, FL 32439, 850/835-2779, fax 850/835-2628.

16 CHOCTAWHATCHEE RIVER WATER MANAGEMENT AREA SOUTHERN BOAT-IN SITES

Scenic rating: 8

along the Choctawhatchee and East Rivers, south of Caryville

This pristine, wildlife-packed area features some of the best fishing in Florida for bass, bream, and catfish. It's also popular for hunting deer, squirrels, and raccoons. It can be difficult to find dry ground where you can pitch a tent when the rivers run high, so contact the water district or the Florida Fish and Wildlife Conservation Commission (850/265-3676) to check conditions. Sometimes you can sleep on ancient beach dunes where water filters quickly through the sand, leaving a dry, shady hammock atop a rise—a nice place to pitch a tent.

Campsites, facilities: There are no established campsites, but primitive camping is allowed throughout the area. Aside from several boat ramps, there are no facilities. Bring water, food, and camping supplies. Pack out trash. Children and pets are permitted.

Reservations, fees: Reservations are not necessary. Camping is free.

Directions: There are seven boat ramps in and around this property. Probably the easiest to reach is where U.S. 20 crosses the Choctawhatchee River, just west of Pine Log State Forest and the tiny town of Ebro. The water management area stretches along the Choctawhatchee and East Rivers from U.S. 20 to just east of Choctawhatchee Bay.

Contact: Northwest Florida Water Management District, 81 Water Management Drive, Havana, FL 32333, 850/539-5999, www.nwfwmd.state.fl.us/recreation.html.

17 PINE LOG STATE FOREST

Scenic rating: 10

south of Ebro

BEST (

Grassy, wooded sites form a half circle around a five-acre swimming lake fringed with slash pines and hardwoods. If the weather is clear, you'll see spectacular sunsets over the water. Swimming is allowed (at your own risk) in the eastern lake only; signs warn of submerged objects. You can fish on all lakes and streams in the forest, but only carry-in boats and electric motors are permitted in the two lakes near the campground. A ranger's residence is within view, which makes for a secure feeling when there are few other campers about. Pine Log is the only developed campground in the 6,911-acre state forest, one of Florida's first. Acquired in the 1930s, it was clear-cut at that time, but replanting has created an enchanting place, thick with slash, longleaf, and sand pines, as well as oak, cypress, red maple, sweet gum, juniper, and magnolia trees. Horse trails and several miles of hiking trails, including an eight-mile section of the Florida National Scenic Trail, are nearby, and the forest roads are good for mountain bikes. Although the Florida trail is open only to foot traffic, the Crooked Creek Trail welcomes mountain bikers. It's a nine-mile, single-track, figure-eight loop (you can also do just 4.5 miles) opened by the division of forestry in conjunction with the Panama City Flyers Bicycle Club. The trail is closed during the first nine days of hunting season. For the exact dates, call ahead or see the kiosk at the parking area located on State Road 79. At other times during the hunting season, cyclists should wear fluorescent orange and use extreme caution. This campground is a bit off the beaten path, so it gets use from locals, as well as tourists from Florida, Alabama, and Georgia. However, as seems to be the rule in Florida, rather than the exception, the area surrounding the park is beginning to come under development.

Campsites, facilities: Twenty campsites have 50-amp electricity, water, picnic tables, grills, and fire rings. They are grassy and level, with shady spots overlooking the water. Rigs as long as 40 feet can be accommodated. Restrooms, showers, a dump station, and two lakes are on-site. Children are welcome. Leashed pets are permitted.

Reservations, fees: Reservations are not taken. Sites are $13 per night for five people. There's a self-pay station at the campground entrance. Credit cards are not accepted. The maximum stay is 14 days within one month.

Directions: From the intersection of U.S. 20 and State Road 79 in the town of Ebro, drive south on State Road 79 for 1.3 miles. Use the second state forest entrance, marked Environmental Road, and watch for signs indicating camping. Turn west on the dirt road and travel about 0.5 mile to the campground.

Contact: Florida Division of Forestry, 715 West 15th Street, Panama City, FL 32401, 850/872-4175, fax 850/872-4879, www.fl<!->dof.com/stateforests/pine_log.htm. Trail information is available from the Pine Log State Forest Field Office, 5583-A Longleaf Road, Ebro, FL 32437, 850/535-2888. For hunting and fishing information, contact the Florida Fish and Wildlife Conservation Commission, 3911 Highway 2321, Panama City, FL 32409, 850/265-3677 or 800/955-8771, www.floridaconservation.org.

18 ECONFINA CREEK WATER MANAGEMENT AREA

🏃 🚴 🛶 🐕 ⛺

Scenic rating: 9

west of Fountain, along Econfina Creek

Wow! It's hard to find this place—"middle of nowhere" doesn't do justice to the remoteness—but it's well worth the drive for its scenic springs, limestone bluffs, ravines, and lots of wild animals. The ground is made of limestone deposited aeons ago by dying sea creatures when this part of Florida was under an ancient ocean. Today, that limestone is easily eaten away by the tannic acids that flow from dead leaves and other vegetation. The process creates huge sinkholes, solution holes, and other paths that allow water to seep through the ground to the Floridan Aquifer, the source of northwest Florida's drinking water.

Look for unusual plants, such as oak leaf hydrangea, ash, pyramid magnolia, St. John's wort, and liverwort. Resident animals include rare snails, brightly colored summer tanager birds, alligator snapping turtles, gopher tortoises, endangered fox squirrels, and a large population of warblers.

The Econfina Creek Canoe Trail begins at Scotts Bridge in northern Bay County and follows the river south to Walsingham Park, the Econfina Creek Canoe Livery, a canoe launch at Highway 20, and last to the Highway 388 bridge. To obtain a rental canoe or learn about water conditions, call the Econfina Creek Canoe Livery (850/722-9032). The Northwest River Water Management District says you can paddle for 26 miles; contact the district for a map, or get information from the canoe livery listed here. By the way, Econfina is pronounced "ee-con-fine-ah."

Horseback riding and bicycling also are permitted on the trails. Hunters head to these parts from mid-November to about January 1, so wear bright orange hats or vests.

Campsites, facilities: Ten primitive camping areas have no facilities. Three areas are designated for groups of 10 campers. Trash must be packed out. Children and pets are welcome.

Reservations, fees: Reservations are not necessary. Camping is free.

Directions: One drive-in camping area, Walsingham, and two hike-in areas, Anise and Ashe, are accessible off a dirt road heading east and then south from Porter Lake Road in southeast Washington County. Two drive-in sites, Bluff and Longleaf, and two other hike-in sites, Devil's Hole and Sea Shell, are located off a network of roads leading north from Highway 20 about two miles east of Econfina Creek. (The hiking distance required is quite short, less than 0.25 mile.) To find a canoe launch, head north from the hamlet of Fountain on US 231 and turn left (west) onto Scott's Bridge Road. You'll see the launch site when you reach Econfina Creek. Call the water district for good maps. Also consider purchasing a U.S. Geological Survey topographic map.

Contact: Northwest Florida Water Management District, 81 Water Management Drive, Havana, FL 32333, 850/539-5999, www .nwfwmd.state.fl.us/recreation.html.

19 PINE LAKE RV PARK

🎣 🐕 🚐

Scenic rating: 5

north of Fountain

This 45-acre, all-ages rural park caters to anglers and countryside-lovers with its two fishing lakes: the stocked seven-acre fishing pond on the property and nearby 150-acre Compass Lake. Feed the fish and the ducks, cast a line for dinner, or watch movies on the big-screen TV in the rec hall. Music is also popular. Some pickers live on-site, and country music jamborees are held frequently. Most sites are pull-through, and the staff is proud to offer easy, safe access for any size RV. About 25 percent of the park is occupied year-round. Visitors come from the northern states, and people working locally stop in also. Their favorite things to do? Fish, relax, and join in the planned activities. Park models are for sale in an adjacent area under development.

Campsites, facilities: There are 100 RV sites with full hookups and picnic tables. One site has 100-amp electricity, 30 have 50-amp, and 39 have 30-amp. Sites average 30 feet wide by 60 feet deep and are semi-shaded by tall pines. Pop-up campers are not allowed. An Internet connection is available in the office. Planned activities include music-making, potluck dinners, exercise classes, games, movies, and fishing tournaments. Restrooms, showers, laundry facilities, a dump station, and horseshoe pits are available. Groceries, restaurants, malls, and hospitals are 14 miles away. Families are welcome, and leashed pets are permitted.

Reservations, fees: Reservations are recommended but usually not necessary. Sites are $25–30 per night for two people, plus $2 for each additional person. Credit cards are accepted. Long-term rates are available.

Directions: From I-10 west of Marianna, take Exit 130 onto U.S. 231. Drive south for 15 miles. The park is just south of the intersection with State Road 167 on the east side of the road.

Contact: Pine Lake RV Park, 21036 U.S. 231, Fountain, FL 32438, 850/722-1401, fax 850/722-1403, www.pinelakerv.com.

20 GRAYTON BEACH STATE PARK

🚶 🚲 🏊 🎣 🚣 ♿ 🚐 ⛺

Scenic rating: 10

east of Destin

BEST (

Set on a stretch of coastline with spectacular beaches, this park is a notch above the rest. The beach is on a peninsula ringed with marshes and the emerald waters of the Gulf of Mexico, and is protected by barrier dunes covered with sea oats. The sand is so white that it resembles snow. Use lots of sunscreen at the swimming beach, because the white sand reflects ultraviolet rays and increases the chance of sunburn. Saltwater and ocean breezes have fashioned the trees into bonsai-like shapes; you may see mature sand pines that resemble bushes. The intimate little campground is slipped into a pine scrub woods near a lake. Both freshwater and saltwater fishing are possible, and the boat ramp is in protected waters on Western Lake. Buy supplies before you arrive; there's not much around here except for Seaside, a planned resort community famed for its architecture. Just two miles east of the state park, Seaside's new Victorian-style buildings are often photographed for magazine advertisements or used as movie backdrops. They're a bit Disneyesque in their perfection.

Campsites, facilities: There are 37 gravel RV/tent sites with water, 30-amp electricity, picnic tables, fire rings, and grills. Lots vary in size; a few are waterfront. Some sites accommodate rigs up to 40 feet long and slide-outs. You can also use a satellite dish at some of the sunnier sites that are not blocked by trees. Restrooms, showers, a dump station, and a boat ramp are available. Canoes and cabins may be rented. There's also a boat ramp for small boats entering a lake. Rangers give nature talks in the summer (remember, in the Panhandle, the tourist season is more summer-oriented than in southern parts of Florida). The bathhouse is wheelchair-accessible. Groceries are five miles away, and restaurants are within one mile. Malls and hospitals are 20 and 10 miles away, respectively. Children are welcome. Pets are prohibited.

Reservations, fees: Reservations are recommended; contact ReserveAmerica at 800/336-3521 or reserveamerica.com. Sites are $19 per night for eight people. Credit cards are accepted. The maximum stay is 14 days.

Directions: From I-10 at De Funiak Springs, take Exit 85 and go south on U.S. 331 for 26 miles. At U.S. 98, turn left and drive two miles east to County Road 283. Turn south and drive three miles. At County Road 30-A, turn eastbound and go 0.5 mile to the park.

Contact: Grayton Beach State Park, 357 Main Park Road, Santa Rosa Beach, FL 32549, 850/231-4210, www.floridastateparks.org.

21 PEACH CREEK RV PARK
🚲 ⚓ 🛶 🏕 🐕 ♿ 🚐

Scenic rating: 6

east of Destin

Set in a wooded area, this park is located on Peach Creek, with access to the Choctawhatchee Bay and River, and is only two miles from Eden State Park. Grayton Beach State Park is just five miles away.

Campsites, facilities: There are 14 full-hookup RV sites, with half available for overnighters. All have 50-amp service and picnic tables. Restrooms, showers, a dump station, laundry facilities, and telephone service are available. On the premises are a boat ramp, a campground store, propane sales, canoe and boat rentals, a dog-walk area, and a nature trail. Most areas are wheelchair-accessible. Children are welcome. Leashed pets are permitted.

Reservations, fees: Reservations are recommended. Sites are $20 per night for two people. Credit cards are accepted. Long-term stays are OK.

Directions: From the intersection of U.S. 98 and Highway 331, drive east four miles. The campground is located one mile east of the intersection with County Road 395.

Contact: Peach Creek RV Park, 4401 Highway 98 East, Santa Rosa Beach, FL 32459, 850/231-1948.

22 PINEGLEN MOTORCOACH AND RV PARK
🚲 🏊 🛶 🛥 🏕 ♿ 🚐

Scenic rating: 9

in Panama City Beach

Nicely secluded from the hurly-burly atmosphere of the beachfront, this modern but nature-blessed park boasts a covered gazebo for picnics along one of the three stocked fishing lakes. Tall pines shade the campground, which is close to the beaches, amusement parks, shopping, and restaurants. Families, take note: Children ages 11–17 are not welcome.

Campsites, facilities: This park offers 60 RV sites with full hookups or water and 30-amp electricity, picnic tables, grills, and cable TV. Sixteen sites are pull-through, and 30 have 50-amp service. Restrooms, showers, a dump station, laundry facilities, and telephone service are available. On the premises are a screened-in pool, a clubhouse, a dog-walk area, and three stocked fishing lakes. The bathhouses, laundry room, and pool area are wheelchair-accessible. Children under age 11 are welcome. Leashed pets are permitted.

Reservations, fees: Reservations are recommended. Sites are $29–39 per night for a family of two adults and four children up to age 10, plus $2 per extra adult. Children ages 11–17 are not permitted. Major credit cards are accepted. Long-term (up to six months) or seasonal stays are allowed.

Directions: From U.S. 98 at the intersection of State Road 79, drive east on U.S. 98 about four miles. The park is on the north side across from a large furniture store.

Contact: Pineglen Motorcoach and RV Park, 11930 Panama City Parkway, Panama City Beach, FL 32407, 850/230-8535, fax 850/230-2554, www.pineglenpark.com.

23 EMERALD COAST RV BEACH RESORT

Scenic rating: 10

west of Panama City Beach

BEST (

Manicured to near perfection, this updated and modernized big-rig resort caters to families and snowbirds who want a beachside destination vacation near shopping and entertainment. Palms and pines cast shade over the paved roads and sites. The managers describe it as "upscale," and the park has won awards for its cleanliness and neatness. All campsites are lighted. Even the restrooms are heated or air-conditioned. About 10 percent of the lots are occupied by full-time residents. Management plans more improvements in the coming years, including premium "fire and water" sites on the lakefront, a pavilion, a basketball court, a spa, and a sauna. From May through September, the park provides free shuttle service to the beach.

Campsites, facilities: There are 138 full-hookup RV-only sites with 50-amp electrical service, concrete pads, picnic tables, and cable TV. All sites have wireless Internet access, though you can also go to the office to connect. Thirty-three sites are drive-through. Sites are paved and level, ranging in size from 20 by 39 feet to 20 by 111 feet. Big rigs and slideouts are welcome. Sites 52–73 are closest to the pool, putting green, and clubhouse. Restrooms, showers, laundry facilities, and telephone service are available. On the premises are a heated pool, a turtle pond, a nature path, a clubhouse, horseshoe pits, shuffleboard courts, three dog-walk areas, a store (selling ice, propane, snacks, souvenirs, and camping supplies), miniature golf, paddleboat rentals, and park model rentals. Movies, pancakes, cookouts, bingo, cards, arts and crafts, and local tours provide entertainment. Malls are within three miles. The clubhouse, office, store, pool area and paved streets are wheelchair-accessible. Children are welcome. Leashed pets are permitted, but not German shepherds, Doberman pinschers, Rottweilers, or pit bulls.

Reservations, fees: Reservations are recommended. Sites are $44–70 per night for two people, plus $3 per extra person and $2 for cable TV and use of the wireless Internet. The rate varies according to the season and whether the site is back-in or pull-through. Credit cards are accepted. Long-term rates are available.

Directions: From I-10, take Exit 17 southbound on State Road 79 about 35 miles to the junction with U.S. 98. At U.S. 98, go east 6.6 miles. Turn right on Allison Avenue (Exit A) and drive one block to the park. From Panama City at the bridge, head west on Alternate 98 for 1.5 miles and follow the directions above.

Contact: Emerald Coast RV Beach Resort, 1957 Allison Avenue, Panama City Beach FL 32407, 850/235-0924 or 800/232-2478, fax 850/235-9609, www.rvresort.com.

24 RACCOON RIVER CAMP RESORT

🏊 🎣 🏠 👫 ♿ 🚐 ⛺

Scenic rating: 5

in Panama City Beach

Set centrally near the beach, this clean RV park backs onto a pretty lake. This is a not a mobile-home park; only one percent of the sites are occupied by year-round residents. It's favored by families and seasonal, repeat visitors from 48 states. From September through February, you'll find bingo, potlucks, cookouts, and horseshoe tournaments, but year-round entertainment can be had at a nearby water park, "goofy golf," the beach, and many festivals. Note: This area has seen a lot of condominium development in recent years.

Campsites, facilities: There are 135 full-hookup RV sites with 30-amp electricity and five sites with 50-amp. Forty-four sites are drive-through. Tenters can be accommodated at 18 sites with water and electricity, or can camp primitive-style in an open field. Campsites have picnic tables, cable TV, and concrete pads. Rigs up to 45 feet long and slide-outs can be accommodated. The grassy, level lots vary in size, with a mix of sunny and shady views. Restrooms, showers, laundry facilities, and telephone service are available. Internet access is available in the office. On the premises are two heated pools, a fenced-in playground, a clubhouse, a store, and a recreation hall. Ice, camping supplies, snacks, and souvenirs are available in the store; groceries and restaurants are within 0.5 mile. The bathhouse, clubhouse, office, store, and pool area are wheelchair-accessible, and the streets are paved. Children are welcome. Leashed pets under 20 pounds are permitted.

Reservations, fees: Reservations are recommended. Sites are $35–45 per night for two people, plus $5 per extra person. Major credit cards are accepted. The maximum stay is six months. Long-term rates are available.

Directions: From Panama City Beach at the bridge over St. Andrews Bay, head west on U.S. 98A for about one mile. Turn right at County Road 392A/Hutchison Boulevard and continue west about 0.5 mile to the park on your left.

Contact: Raccoon River Camp Resort, 12209 Hutchison Boulevard, Panama City Beach, FL 32407, 850/234-0181, fax 850/234-1090.

25 CAMPER'S INN

🏊 🎣 🏠 👫 ♿ 🚐 ⛺

Scenic rating: 4

in Panama City Beach

Set in the most commercial part of Panama City Beach, this park is across the street and about a block's walk from beaches and the Gulf of Mexico, although there's not much of a view. T-shirt and souvenir shops, amusement parks, bumper cars, a dog track, bars, and strip clubs are the milieu, as well as the condominium developments cropping up all around. But there's plenty to do without leaving the campground, from playing ball to swimming in the two pools. Small children and non-swimmers must be supervised in the pool areas. Camping supplies, gifts, toys, groceries, and rental bikes are available. About 10 percent of the park is occupied year-round, and there is an adjacent mobile-home section. It's a popular spot for families, seasonal visitors, anglers, and working people.

Campsites, facilities: Grassy and paved sites with concrete patios and picnic tables are available for 115 RVs in this 240-space mobile-home and RV park, which also allows tenters. All sites have 30/50-amp electrical service, full hookups, and wireless Internet access. Seventeen lots are pull-through. The sunny sites allow for satellite dish setup, and they vary in size from 30 to 50 feet wide and 40 to 80 feet long. Cable TV, restrooms, showers, picnic tables, laundry facilities, and a dump station are available. Also on-site are two pools, a recreation hall, a playground, a volleyball area, basketball and shuffleboard courts, several stores, cabins for rent, propane, a fishing guide, and a gasoline station. Planned activities include potluck dinners, karaoke, dances, cards, and bingo. Streets are paved, and the bathhouse, clubhouse, office, store, and pool area are wheelchair-accessible. Groceries, restaurants, and shopping are within one mile. Children are welcome. Leashed pets are permitted.

Reservations, fees: Reservations are recommended. Sites are $18–50 per night for two people, plus $5 for each additional person over the age of 12 and $3 for cable TV. Credit cards are accepted. Long-term rates are available. The maximum length of stay is six months.

Directions: From the intersection of U.S. 98 and County Road 3033/Beckrich Road in Panama City Beach, drive south on County Road 3033. Turn east on County Road 392 and drive 0.7 mile. Continue for two miles on Thomas Drive to the park.

Contact: Camper's Inn, 8800 Thomas Drive, Panama City Beach, FL 32408, 850/234-5731 or 866/872-2267, http://pcbchcampersinn.com.

26 PANAMA CITY BEACH RV RESORT

≈ 🐕 ♿ 🚐

Scenic rating: 9

in Panama City Beach

Located just outside St. Andrews State Park, this is a deluxe way to be near that park's marvelous beaches. The park caters to motor coaches, fifth wheels, and other big rigs. Three condo apartments are for rent above the park office. Only modern RVs at least 22 feet long and less than 10 years old are accepted; there is no space for pop-ups, hybrid travel trailers, truck campers, or converted horse trailers—and no tents. The park is popular with families, seasonal visitors, and over-age-55 tourists from Florida, Georgia, Alabama, and Tennessee. What do they come for? The beach.

Campsites, facilities: There are 69 large, paved, full-hookup RV-only sites with professional landscaping to accommodate even the biggest vehicles. All sites have 30/50-amp electrical service, cable TV, and concrete patios. With lots ranging in size from 30 by 60 feet (back-in) to 30 by 80 feet (pull-through), there's plenty of room for slide-outs and rigs up to 45 feet long. Instead of concrete walkways, all driveways and paths are covered with pretty paver blocks. Palms, magnolias, wax myrtles, and oaks have been planted, and the lighting is designed to accent the greenery.

Restrooms, showers, laundry facilities, and telephone service are available. On the premises are a heated pool, an exercise room, a recreation hall, snacks, walking paths, beach access, and three luxury condo rental units. Lots are for sale. Groceries and restaurants are within two miles. All areas are wheelchair-accessible. Children are welcome. Leashed pets are permitted.

Reservations, fees: Reservations are recommended. Sites are $59–69 per night for two people and four children under age 16. Each additional adult is charged $10. The maximum number of people per site is six. Prices are subject to change. Credit cards are accepted. Long-term rates are available.

Directions: From the intersection of U.S. 98 and County Road 3033/Beckrich Road in Panama City Beach, drive south on County Road 3033. Turn east on County Road 392 and drive 0.7 mile. Continue for 2.5 miles on Thomas Drive to the park.

Contact: Panama City Beach RV Resort, 4702 Thomas Drive, Panama City Beach, FL 32408, 866/637-3529, www.panamacityrvresort.com.

27 ST. ANDREWS STATE PARK

Scenic rating: 10

east of Panama City Beach

BEST (

Famed internationally for its clear waters and blinding white-sand beaches, this 1,260-acre state park gets hard use from tourists and locals, especially during the summer. Camping is split between the Pine Grove and Lagoon Campgrounds; both overlook Grand Lagoon, a narrow body of water separating the park from the rest of the barrier island. Some sites are directly on the water, and slash pines offer shade. The best swimming is on the gulf side of the park, where big rolling sand dunes separate the road from the beach. You can snorkel there or in a protected pool behind a rock jetty. Fishing is from the jetty, the beach, two piers, or by boat; among the fish caught here are dolphin, bluefish, flounder, Spanish mackerel, sea trout, redfish, and bonito.

Two short nature trails give hikers an opportunity to see alligators and birds in a salt marsh. Also in the park is a turpentine still that shows how early settlers derived the solvent from pine trees, a practice that became a major industry at the turn of the 20th century. World War II–era circular cannon platforms still stand in the park, which was used as a military reservation at the time. Across from the park is Shell Island, which is reachable by park shuttle in spring and summer or by boat year-round; it's a 700-acre oasis that remains almost untouched by development. Unfortunately, this park is so close to major tourist areas and the urban area that it can get crowded.

Campsites, facilities: There are 176 sites with water, electricity, picnic tables, and grills. Restrooms, showers, a dump station, two fishing piers, a boat ramp, a store, picnic areas, and swimming beaches are available. Children are welcome, but pets are not allowed.

Reservations, fees: Reservations are recommended; contact ReserveAmerica at 800/336-3521 or reserveamerica.com. From October 1 through February 28, sites are $10 per night for four people, plus $2 for electricity and $2 for a waterfront location. March 1–September 30, sites are $17 per night, plus the extra charges mentioned. Major credit cards are accepted. The maximum stay is 14 days.

Directions: From the intersection of U.S. 98 and County Road 3031/Thomas Drive in Panama City Beach, turn south on County Road 3031. Drive five miles to the dead end at the beach and turn left. The park entrance is just ahead.

Contact: St. Andrews State Park, 4415 Thomas Drive, Panama City, FL 32408, 850/233-5140.

28 SCOTTS FERRY GENERAL STORE AND CAMPGROUND

Scenic rating: 5

south of Blountstown

Nearly hidden under the highway bridge over the Chipola River, this canoeing-oriented campground is slipped into a hardwood forest sloping down to a little boat dock. It's a shady spot with an open-air pavilion, but you may hear road noise from the bridge. The campground rents canoes and has a boat launch; the affiliated store sells hunting and camping supplies, bait, and gasoline. For a fee, you can rent covered picnic tables, some of which are large enough to accommodate a group.

Campsites, facilities: The 25 campsites have water, 50-amp electric hookups, and picnic tables. Restrooms, showers, a boat ramp, a pavilion, rental cabins, and a store are on-site. The store sells bait and tackle, groceries, hardware, ice, and gasoline. Children are welcome. Leashed pets are permitted.

Reservations, fees: Reservations are not necessary. Sites are $18 per night. Credit cards are accepted. Long-term stays are OK.

Directions: From Blountstown, drive south on State Road 71 for 11 miles. The park is on the west (right) side of the road, just before you cross the bridge.

Contact: Scotts Ferry General Store and Campground, 6648 State Route 715, Blountstown, FL 32424, 850/674-2900.

29 PARKER FARM CAMPGROUND

Scenic rating: 1

northwest side of Wewahitchka

Little more than an open, grassy field in the countryside, this no-frills campground is located next to the North Florida Motor Speedway, which claims to be the fastest dirt track in the nation. It also adjoins a field for flying remote-control airplanes. A model airplane show is held the second week of October. Restaurants and groceries are available within one mile. About a third of the park is occupied by full-time residents. The park also draws hunters and anglers because of its proximity to the Chipola and Apalachicola Rivers.

Campsites, facilities: All 16 grassy, sunny sites have full hookups, 30-amp electrical service, and 2 of the sites have optional telephone service. Big rigs and slideouts are welcome. A dump station can be used for a $2 fee. There are no showers or restrooms. Alcoholic beverages are prohibited. Children are welcome. Leashed pets are permitted, but they must be kept inside your rig. The owner says that all areas of the park are wheelchair-accessible.

Reservations, fees: Reservations are not necessary except during special events. Sites are $15 per night. Credit cards are not accepted. Long-term stays are OK.

Directions: From the junction of State Roads 71 and 22 in Wewahitchka, drive west on State Road 22 for 0.3 mile. Turn north on County Road 22A and drive three miles to the park.

Contact: Parker Farm Campground, 440 Parker Farm Road, Wewahitchka, FL 32465, 850/639-5204.

30 DEAD LAKES PARK

Scenic rating: 9

north of Wewahitchka

Completely renovated in 2006, this county park has an eerie beauty. Its name stems from the thousands of bleached tree trunks rooted in the lake water. The trees drowned when a sandbar formed in the Apalachicola River, blocking the mouth of the Chipola River and flooding 12,000 acres of swamp. Before this event, there were twin lakes that the Indians called "water eyes," or Wewahitchka, a name that was adopted by the nearby town. Two other ponds in the park were dug in 1936 and held a fish hatchery until 1951. Half a century ago, turpentine was tapped from the pines, and honey, harvested by bees from the hardwood tupelo trees, was barreled for medicinal purposes. Spanish moss that draped the trees was a commodity used for packing and furniture stuffing. Such commerce is history today, and the Dead Lakes area is primarily a recreational retreat surrounded by swamp and flat-wood forests. These vistas made the silver screen in Peter Fonda's 1997 movie, *Ulee's Gold,* a critically acclaimed drama in which Fonda played a beekeeper. The bees in this area really do produce a succulent honey called Tupelo Gold. The park is popular with hikers, anglers, bird-watchers, and boaters.

The campsites, which were renovated in 2006, are shaded by native longleaf pines and carpeted with wire grass. There's are two nature trails for viewing wildlife, and the boat ramp provides access to the Dead Lakes and the Chipola River. The tree trunks create an obstacle course for those in canoes and fishing boats. You can hook bass, bream, and carp in the old hatching ponds as well as in the lakes, where the drowned forest makes casting a real challenge.

Campsites, facilities: There are 22 sites for RVs up to 50 feet long, all of which have water and 30-amp electricity. Each site has a picnic table, a grill, and a fire pit. New or renovated facilities include a playground, bike trail, picnic gazebos, fishing pier, boat docks, dump station, and restrooms. Children are welcome. Pets are allowed with proof of vaccination.

Reservations, fees: Reservations are not necessary. Sites cost $10 per night, plus $2 for electricity. The maximum stay is 14 days.

Directions: From Port St. Joe, take State Road 71 north for 24 miles to Wewahitchka. Drive one mile north of town and turn east on Gary Rowell Road. Continue 0.5 mile to the park. From Panama City, take State Road 22 east for 25 miles to State Road 71 and turn north. Go one mile to Gary Rowell Road, turn east, and proceed to the park.

Contact: For information about Dead Lakes Park, contact the Gulf County Tourism Development Council at 850/229-7800, info@ visitgulf.com. The park is located at 510 Gary Rowell Road, Wewahitchka, 850/639-2238 6:30 A.M.–3 P.M. or 850/227-6036 after 3 P.M.

31 APALACHICOLA RIVER WATER MANAGEMENT AREA

Scenic rating: 6

along the Apalachicola River

When Florida was a backwater, the Apalachicola River was the equivalent of a superhighway. Water was the means by which folks got around the Sunshine State before the advent of railroads and automobiles. Today, these 35,000 or so acres along the river are virtually deserted. The isolated upland islands of this large alluvial floodplain are considered unique. River flows are variable and are controlled by the U.S. Army Corps of Engineers at the Jim Woodruff Dam, a two-hour drive north of here. Nevertheless, the Apalachicola is navigable and is a favorite with powerboaters and fishers. Canoeists are less enthusiastic because of the open water and traffic.

Bird-watching is good, with 99 species known to swoop into the area. Hawks, swallow-tailed kites, and Mississippi kites all can be seen soaring high overhead, particularly in the spring. Bald eagles and alligator snapping turtles are common. If you're really lucky, you'll see a Florida black bear. Horseback riding and hiking are popular in the section between the Florida and Apalachicola Rivers—the part most accessible by car—which is known as Florida River Island. The place is loaded with wild animals, including deer, turkey, rabbit, and bobcat, which become targets for hunters starting in mid-November and lasting until late April. Particularly during the general gun seasons—around Thanksgiving and mid-December–mid-February—wear bright orange clothing when hiking or horseback riding.

Campsites, facilities: Three primitive camping areas with no facilities lie at the northern end of this tract. There are 17 boat ramps and a network of dirt roads and hiking trails. Pack in water, food, and camping supplies; pack out trash. Children are welcome. Pets are permitted.

Reservations, fees: Reservations are not necessary. Camping is free.

Directions: Numerous boat ramps are located off dirt roads leading west from State Road 379 or east from State Roads 71 and 22A. For camping, take State Road 379 north from Sumatra and make a left onto Forest Service Road 188, which leads to a network of dirt roads. At the northern edge of the water management area, on the Florida River, is an unnamed primitive campsite. Farther south, not far from a horse-trailer parking area, is the Greenback Lake site. Even farther south, near the Florida River, is the Acorn Lake site. Touring this remote country requires a compass and good maps, such as those available from the U.S. Geological Survey or from the Florida Fish and Wildlife Conservation Commission.

Contact: Northwest Florida Water Management District, 81 Water Management Drive, Havana, FL 32333, 850/539-5999, www. nwfwmd.state.fl.us/recreation.html. Florida Fish and Wildlife Conservation Commission, 3911 Highway 2321, Panama City, FL 32409, 850/265-3676, www.floridaconservation.org/recreation/apalachicola_river/default.asp.

32 EL GOVERNOR RV CAMPGROUND

Scenic rating: 2

in Mexico Beach

Set in the center of Mexico Beach, a family-oriented community of vacation homes and waterfront motels on the Gulf of Mexico, this RV park has a small creek and a good location across the street from the water. Don't expect much shade, greenery, or water views, which are blocked by the motels. Charter boat services, fishing guides, and boat storage and dockage are available in town. There is a similar campground in the area: Rustic Sands Resort, on 15th Street, north of U.S. 98.

Campsites, facilities: This campground has 59 RV sites (10 pull-through) with sewer hookups, 30-amp electrical service, and cable TV. Restrooms, showers, picnic tables, laundry facilities, and a dump station are on-site. Children and leashed pets are permitted.

Reservations, fees: Reservations are recommended. Sites are $31 per night for four people, plus $2 for each additional person. Credit cards are not accepted. Stays up to six months are allowed.

Directions: Drive through Mexico Beach on U.S. 98. The park is in the middle of town at the corner of 17th Street, across from the big El Governor Motel.

Contact: El Governor RV Campground, 1700 Highway 98, Mexico Beach, FL 32410, 850/648-5432.

33 T. H. STONE MEMORIAL ST. JOSEPH PENINSULA STATE PARK

Scenic rating: 10

near Port St. Joe

BEST (

Surrounded by water on three sides, this secluded, woodsy state park boasts one of the best beaches in Florida, with broad expanses of sugar-white sand, dunes studded with sea oats and struggling grasses, and trees twisted by the wind. Year after year, "Dr. Beach," a university professor who rates these things, has named this America's No. 1 beach. You can swim in either the Gulf of Mexico or St. Joseph Bay. The water is clear enough for snorkeling; be sure to use a dive flag. On the bay side, you may see bay scallops, octopus, and three types of crabs (hermit, fiddler, and horseshoe). Canoes are available for rent.

When you can tear yourself away from the water, try hiking on nine miles of heavily forested trails. Bike riders will find paved roads with little traffic inside and outside the park. Supplies in the community of vacation homes on the peninsula are limited, so stock up in Port St. Joe, 22 miles away. Sprawling over 2,516 acres, the park dominates the northern tip of the peninsula, which was used by the Army for training during World War II. More than 200 species of birds have been seen here. In fall, campers may see hawks heading south or monarch butterflies flying to their winter home in Mexico. There's plenty of other wildlife; even a black bear has been spotted—look in the campground office for a photo of the creature.

Campsites, facilities: The state park has two campground loops for RVs and tents: Gulf Breeze, which has larger sites for big rigs, and Shady Pines, which is wooded and more secluded. There are a total of 119 campsites with 30-amp electrical service and 15 with 50-amp. Two sites are drive-through. Rigs up to 38 feet and slide-outs can be accommodated. Each site has water, a picnic table, a grill, and a fire ring. On the premises are restrooms, showers, a dump station, a boat ramp and basin, docks, beaches, a playground, and rental cabins. All areas are wheelchair-accessible. Children are welcome. Pets are not allowed except for guide dogs.

Reservations, fees: Reservations are recommended; contact ReserveAmerica at 800/336-3521 or reserveamerica.com. Sites are $22 per night for eight people. Credit cards are accepted. The maximum stay is 14 days.

Directions: From Port St. Joe, travel east on U.S. 98 to State Road 30. At the fork, veer right and proceed south on State Road C-30 for six miles, then turn right onto State Road 30-E and drive eight miles west to the park.

Contact: T. H. Stone Memorial St. Joseph Peninsula State Park, 8899 Cape San Blas Road, Port St. Joe, FL 32456, 850/227-1327, fax 850/227-1488, www.floridastateparks .org.

sweeping views of St. Joseph Bay and St. Joseph Peninsula. Fishing guides, boat rentals, and charter services are available at the marina. You can swim in the bay, but the clear water is shallow and there's no real beach—just grass flats frequented by wading birds. An 18-hole golf course is located 0.25 mile away.

Campsites, facilities: All 22 RV sites have water and electricity. On the premises are restrooms, showers, a boat ramp, a limited store, rental trailers, bait and tackle, boat rentals, and a small play area. Children are welcome. Leashed pets are permitted.

Reservations, fees: Reservations are required in July and August and recommended the rest of the year. Sites are $25 per night for four people, plus $2 for each additional person. Credit cards are accepted. Long-term stays are OK.

Directions: From Port St. Joe, drive one mile east on U.S. 98 to County Road 30-A. At the fork, veer right and proceed south on County Road 30-A (aka C30-A) for 2.1 miles to the park.

Contact: Presnell's Bayside Marina and RV Resort, 2115 County Road 30-A, Port St. Joe, FL 32456, 850/229-2710, www.presnells .com.

34 PRESNELL'S BAYSIDE MARINA AND RV RESORT

Scenic rating: 8

south of Port St. Joe

All sites in this 7.5-acre, boating-oriented campground are on the waterfront, with

TALLAHASSEE

© MARILYN MOORE

BEST CAMPGROUNDS

◖ Biking
Suwannee River State Park, **page 111**
Stephen Foster Folk Culture Center State Park,
    page 113
Wright Lake, **page 120**

◖ Families
Suwannee Valley Campground, **page 114**

◖ Most Unusual
Torreya State Park, **page 99**
Suwannee Valley Campground, **page 114**
Miller's Marine Campground, **page 133**

Tallahassee holds center billing in one of Florida's

most interesting regions for outdoors enthusiasts. A widely diverse area that encompasses beachside haunts and fishing villages along the Gulf of Mexico, Tallahassee includes the sprawling Apalachicola National Forest, many fishing lakes, the marshy Big Bend area, sparkling natural springs, and the mouth of the fabled Suwannee River.

Mostly rural and mostly undeveloped, the region holds some of Florida's finest natural attractions. Highlights include bicycle trails, freshwater fishing, game-filled forests, and rivers that beckon canoeists and kayakers.

The vast Apalachicola National Forest dominates camping options. It stretches 54 miles from Tallahassee and covers 631,260 acres of pineland, hardwood forest, hammocks, savanna, and dry ridges. The wildlife is as varied as the landscape: 190 species of birds, nine kinds of bats, coral snakes, various rattlers, alligators, flying squirrels, marsh rabbits, red and gray foxes, weasels, mink, otters, skunks, bobcats, deer, feral hogs, and, occasionally, a black bear.

This makes the forest popular with hunters, but hunting season is limited to a few weeks in fall and winter. Crisscrossed by forest roads, the national forest is an ideal place to go canoeing, backpacking, or bicycling. Numerous campgrounds dot the forest; however, you are not limited to designated sites.

For campers who prefer a less hardy experience, there are lots of public parks with more amenities. One example is the state park on St. George Island, home to one of the finest beaches in Florida. After being damaged by hurricanes in 2005, the campground has reopened with completely renovated facilities.

The eastern edge of the region is bounded by the intriguing Suwannee River, which flows south to the Gulf of Mexico. All along the river are places to launch a canoe and paddle along white sand bluffs under a thick wooden canopy of stately oak trees hung with Spanish moss. The Suwannee River area is popular with bicyclists.

Dotted throughout this region are some of the largest and deepest springs in the world, designated as "first-magnitude" (read: really big). The limestone ground – laid down eons ago, when this area was covered by an ancient sea – is pockmarked today with sinkholes and other depressions bubbling with pristine, clear water.

In the northwest corner is Chattahoochee, the access point for Lake Seminole, a 37,500-acre reservoir formed by damming the confluence of the Chattahoochee and Flint Rivers upstream of the Jim Woodruff Lock and Dam. Boating, fishing, water-skiing, and swimming are the things to do here. Anglers may hook lunker, largemouth, scrappy hybrid, striped, and white bass, or catfish, crappie, and bream. Canada geese spend the winter in the area.

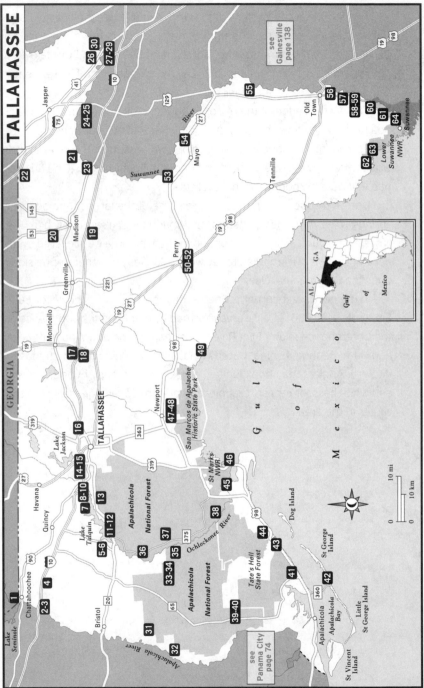

TALLAHASSEE

GEORGIA

Jasper

Madison

Greenville

Monticello

Tallahassee

Quincy

Havana

Chattahoochee

Bristol

Lake Seminole

Apalachicola River

Apalachicola National Forest

Lake Talquin

Lake Jackson

Newport

Perry

Mayo

Old Town

Tennille

Suwannee River

Suwannee

Lower Suwannee NWR

San Marcos de Apalache Historic State Park

St Marks NWR

Tate's Hell State Forest

Ochlockonee River

Dog Island

St George Island

Little St George Island

Apalachicola

Apalachicola Bay

St Vincent Island

Gulf of Mexico

see Gainesville page 138

see Panama City page 74

0   10 mi

0   10 km

AL GA

Gulf of Mexico

© AVALON TRAVEL PUBLISHING, INC.

1 EAST BANK CAMPGROUND, LAKE SEMINOLE

🏊 🏕 🚐 🐕 ♿ 🚙 ⛺

Scenic rating: 8

on Lake Seminole, north of Chattahoochee

This park is actually in Georgia, but the easiest way to reach it is from Chattahoochee, Florida, and its boundary is only a couple of blocks north of the Sunshine State. An engineer's eye for detail is evident: Each neatly kept campsite has a special metal post for hanging camp lanterns, and one site (number 9) was designed for campers in wheelchairs. Sites are laid out in several pods on a gentle slope overlooking Lake Seminole, a 37,500-acre reservoir formed by damming the confluence of the Chattahoochee and Flint Rivers upstream of the Jim Woodruff Lock and Dam. Boating, fishing, water-skiing, and swimming are the things to do here; check the website listed in the contact information to verify whether current water levels are too low at the boat launch for your craft. Anglers may hook lunker, largemouth, scrappy hybrid, striped, and white bass, or catfish, crappie, and bream. Canada geese spending the winter in the area paddle around the edge of the lake near the campground.

Campsites, facilities: There are 68 gravel sites for RVs and 10 improved campsites for tents in this U.S. Army Corps of Engineers campground on Lake Seminole. Forty-one sites have 50-amp electrical service; the rest have 30-amp. Five sites are drive-through, and some are waterfront. Big rigs and slideouts can be accommodated. Two additional primitive sites are set aside for tent camping only. An Internet connection, picnic tables, grills, fire rings, restrooms, showers, a dump station, laundry facilities, a boat ramp, shuffleboard, and horseshoe pits are on the grounds. The bathhouse and office are wheelchair-accessible. Streets are paved. Children are welcome. Leashed pets are permitted.

Reservations, fees: Reserve your spot at least four days in advance of your arrival by contacting 877/444-6777 or www.reserveusa.com. Rangers say, however, that there are almost always spots available, so reservations are not strictly necessary. Sites are $12–16 per night for up to eight people. Credit cards are accepted by the reservation system. The maximum stay is two weeks, although you may request a two-week extension.

Directions: In Chattahoochee, from the junction of U.S. 90 and State Road 269, drive four blocks west on U.S. 90 to Bolivar Street and look for the campground sign. Drive north on Bolivar Street for 1.4 miles to the campground entrance.

Contact: U.S. Army Corps of Engineers, Resource Management Office, Lake Seminole, P.O. Box 96, 2382 Booster Club Road, Chattahoochee, FL 32324, 229/662-2001, www.sam.usace.army.mil. The campground may be reached at 229/662-9273.

2 TORREYA STATE PARK

🚶 🚴 ♿ 🚙 ⛺

Scenic rating: 10

north of Bristol

BEST (

Hiking is the favorite activity here. Perched atop 150-foot bluffs above the Apalachicola River, Torreya (pronounced "tory-ah") State Park is unique in Florida. In addition to its unusual terrain of deep ravines and hills, the park is noteworthy because it supports trees and plants normally seen in Georgia's Appalachian Mountains. Wildlife and birds are plentiful, and the hardwood forest puts on a brilliant autumnal display. It's also one of just a few places in the world where the rare Torreya tree grows. Once common across the river bluffs, the Torreya is nearly extinct today, because it is prone to at least 30 pathogens that attack just before it goes to seed.

Also in the park is the Gregory House, an 1849 plantation home originally built across the river. (You can see a few specimens of the Torreya tree on either side of the entryway to the house.) The Civilian Conservation Corps, which built the park in the 1930s, moved the house—a feat that will boggle your mind. They dismantled the building, floated it across the river, and rebuilt it here. Earlier in history, the river bluffs were home to a Civil War gun battery, and archaeologists have found evidence of many Indian settlements.

The main campground is on top of one of the bluffs, and a few sites offer sweeping views of the valleys beyond. Several short trails lead down to wooded ravines, good spots for exploring and picking up dead branches for your campfire. Take only fallen and dead limbs from the ground.

Torreya State Park is a great place to limber up for hiking in more hilly terrain out of state. Break in those boots on 15 miles of trails; Florida flatlanders will be startled by how steep those slopes are. Hike for 45 minutes, or make a day out of it.

Campsites, facilities: There are 30 RV/tent sites, half with 30-amp electricity and half with 50-amp. Each site has a picnic table, grill, and fire ring. Rigs up to 40 feet long can be accommodated. Park facilities include restrooms, showers, a dump station, hiking trails, and a museum. You can also rent a five-person yurt (a type of circular tent) with air-conditioning and heating. The bathhouse and picnic area are wheelchair-accessible. Children are welcome. Pets are prohibited.

Reservations, fees: Reservations are recommended; call ReserveAmerica at 800/326-3521. Sites are $12 per night for up to eight people. Credit cards are accepted. The maximum stay is 14 days.

Directions: From I-10 west of Quincy, take Exit 174 and head west on State Road 12 for about 11 miles. At County Road 1641, turn north and drive seven miles to the park. Or, from U.S. 20 in Bristol, drive north on State Road 12 for eight miles, turn left on County Road 1641, and drive seven miles west to the park. The route is well-marked, with signs pointing the way.

Contact: Torreya State Park, 2576 North-

west Torreya Park Road, Bristol, FL 32321, 850/643-2674, www.floridastateparks.org.

🎒 TORREYA STATE PARK BACKPACKING SITES
🥾 ⛺

Scenic rating: 9

in Torreya State Park

If you're warming up for a trek on the Appalachian Trail or some other more mountainous locale, this is a great place for a shakedown trip. Backpackers can hike as many as 15 miles of steep hills and ravines to the Rock Bluff and Rock Creek campsites. Not up to it? The Rock Creek site is just 0.8 mile into the woods. Hardier campers can take the long way around (seven miles) to get there. The preferred site is Rock Bluff, just 1.25 miles in. Along the way, you may hear the sharp trill of bald eagles or glimpse deer, foxes, bobcats, raccoons, and all kinds of snakes.

Some caveats: You must stick strictly to the trail and camp only at designated sites. Hunters are common in the lands adjacent to the park, and much of the property is not fenced. During the hunting season (usually November–January), wear brightly colored clothing.

Campsites, facilities: Rock Bluff and Rock Creek are two primitive backpacking areas with ground grills, a few benches, and outhouses. Each area can accommodate 12 people on four sites. Water is available in nearby streams, but it must be treated before drinking; better to bring your own. Pack out all garbage. Children are welcome. Pets are prohibited.

Reservations, fees: You must register with the park ranger at least one hour before sunset. If you can't find a ranger, go to the pay phone at the workshop; a personal phone number is listed there. If you still cannot make contact with a ranger, then the only place you are allowed to stay is at the main campground.

Backpacking costs $3 for adults and $2 for those under age 17.

Directions: From I-10 west of Quincy, take Exit 174 and head west on State Road 12 for about 11 miles. At County Road 1641, turn north and drive seven miles to the park. Or, from U.S. 20 in Bristol, drive north on State Road 12 for eight miles, turn left on County Road 1641, and drive seven miles west to the park. The route is well-marked, with signs pointing the way.

Contact: Torreya State Park, HC 2, Box 70, Bristol, FL 32321, 850/643-2674, www.floridastateparks.org.

4 CHATTAHOOCHEE/ TALLAHASSEE WEST KOA

Scenic rating: 7

off I-10, south of Chattahoochee

Convenient for overnight travelers and located just 35 miles west of Florida State University's football stadium, this wooded and shady KOA could serve as a base camp for exploring nearby attractions in Chattahoochee, such as Lake Seminole. Three Spanish missions were built here in the 1600s, and Native Americans were present as far back as 1450. Andrew Jackson was in command at a federal arsenal here during the Indian wars. That fortification later became a prison, then a mental institution—the Florida State Hospital is still a major employer. East of here is the town of Havana, Florida, with antique shops that draw hundreds of tourists every weekend. Note that the campground pool is open April 1– October 1. Firewood is offered for free.

Campsites, facilities: There are 46 RV sites with water and 30-amp or 50-amp electric hookups, picnic tables, and grills. Six of the 10 tent sites have electricity. Drive-through sites are as long as 75 feet. A modem is available for dialup Internet access. Restrooms, showers, laundry facilities, a dump station, a conve-

nience store, a pool, a playground, a horseshoe pitch area, and cabins are available. The main building, pavilion, and restrooms (except showers) are wheelchair-accessible. Children are welcome. Leashed pets are permitted.

Reservations, fees: Reservations are recommended. Sites are $23–29 per night for two people, plus $2 for each additional child or $3 per adult, and $3 for electricity. Credit cards are accepted. Long-term rates are available.

Directions: From I-10 at Chattahoochee, take Exit 166 southbound on County Road 270A and drive one mile to the park entrance on the east side of the road.

Contact: Chattahoochee/Tallahassee West KOA, 2309 Flat Creek Road, Chattahoochee, FL 32324, 850/442-6657 or 800/KOA-2153 (800-562-2153), www.koa.com.

5 WHIPPOORWILL SPORTSMAN'S LODGE

Scenic rating: 4

on Lake Talquin, south of Quincy

This tiny campground is part of a fishing- and hunting-oriented motel on Lake Talquin. Sites are shady and can accommodate rigs up to 40 feet long. Launch your fishing boat from the paved boat ramp; you can tie it up at the covered docks after your trip. Unpaved roads for exploring by bicycle surround the park. Pick up groceries in Quincy, 15 miles away; limited supplies are available at the lodge. The restaurant hosts a shrimp boil every Friday night.

Campsites, facilities: There are seven RV sites with full hookups, electricity, and picnic tables. Restrooms, showers, laundry facilities, horseshoe pits, a boat ramp, boat and canoe rentals, cottage rentals, covered boat slips, a fishing pier, a convenience store, and a restaurant/waterfront pub are on site. The fishing pier, stores, and restrooms are wheelchair-accessible. Children are welcome. Leashed pets are permitted.

Reservations, fees: Reservations are recommended. Sites are $20 per night for two people, plus $5 for each additional person. Credit cards are accepted. The maximum stay is three months.

Directions: From I-10 at Quincy, take Exit 181 southbound on State Road 267 for eight miles. Turn east at Cook's Landing Road and drive three miles until the road dead-ends.

Contact: Whippoorwill Sportsman's Lodge, 3129 Cook's Landing Road, Quincy, FL 32351, 850/875-2605, fax 850/875-3345, fishtalquin@aol.com.

6 PAT THOMAS PARK

Scenic rating: 7

on Lake Talquin, south of Quincy

Tailored to overnight and short-term campers, this peaceful park is located on an oak-shaded hill sloping down to Lake Talquin, which surrounds it on three sides. Launch your fishing boat or canoe from the boat ramp near the campground. A full-time park ranger lives on the premises. Restaurants, supermarkets, and laundry facilities are available 10 miles north in Quincy. Bait, tackle, and limited groceries can be found within one mile. The park is a popular daytime spot for locals all week long; they fish for the day at the piers, or hold family reunions and other gatherings in the new picnic pavilion.

Campsites, facilities: This two-acre county park has 15 RV sites with full hookups and 30-amp electrical service and 15 tent-only sites with water and electricity. Lots vary in size, but big rigs can be accommodated. Three spots are drive-through. On the premises are showers, restrooms, picnic tables, grills, fishing piers, a dump station, a boat ramp, and a playground. Groceries and restaurants are five miles away. Most areas are wheelchair-accessible. Children are welcome. Dogs are prohibited.

Reservations, fees: Reservations are recommended. Sites are $10 to $15 per night for two people, plus $1 extra for each additional person (small children are free). Credit cards are not accepted. The maximum stay is 14 days.

Directions: From I-10 at Quincy, take Exit 181 southbound on State Road 267 for nine miles. Turn east at the sign for Hopkins Landing and drive one mile until the road dead-ends at the park.

Contact: Pat Thomas Park, 949 Hopkins Landing Road, Quincy, FL 32351, 850/875-4544 or 850/875-8699.

7 INGRAM'S MARINA

Scenic rating: 4

on Lake Talquin, south of Quincy

If you're hooked on fishing, you'll appreciate this angler-oriented camp, which has sprawled over a hill on the edge of Lake Talquin for the past three decades. Interior roads are unpaved and uneven, but plenty of oak trees provide shade. Some boats can be docked in covered slips on a protected inlet. Bait and tackle and limited groceries are available here. It's near popular hunting areas.

Campsites, facilities: This fish camp has five RV sites available with 30-amp electricity, water, and sewer hookups. The 50 other sites are occupied by full-time residents or people who leave their trailers year-round. On the premises are showers, restrooms, cabin and boat rentals, a boat ramp, docks, groceries, bait and tackle, and laundry facilities. All areas of the park are said to be wheelchair-accessible. Children are welcome. Leashed pets are permitted.

Reservations, fees: Reservations are recommended. Sites are $15 per night for two people, plus $1 for each additional person. Credit cards are accepted. Long-term stays are permitted.

Directions: From I-10 at Quincy, take Exit 181 southbound on State Road 267 for eight miles. Turn east at Cook's Landing Road and drive three miles until the road dead-ends at the park.

Contact: Ingram's Marina, 354 Lois Lane, Quincy, FL 32351, 850/627-2241.

8 HIGH BLUFF CAMPGROUND (FORMERLY JOE BUDD)

Scenic rating: 8

on Lake Talquin, south of Quincy

High Bluff Campground is located near one of Florida's premier deer-hunting spots in the Joe Budd Wildlife Management Area, within Lake Talquin State Forest. Hunters and anglers tend to dominate the sole camping area—a mowed pine- and oak-dotted field on the shore of Lake Talquin. The campground has been improved with the addition of vault restrooms, potable water, and 32 designated campsites. It is open year-round, not just during hunting season.

Joe Budd Wildlife Management Area is distinguished by plentiful deer, as well as the rolling hills and creek bottoms that contrast with much of flat Florida. Boaters will notice less development surrounding the upper portion of 12-mile-long Lake Talquin, compared with more evidence of humans around the lower lake. As one of only two sizable reservoirs in Florida, 8,850-acre Lake Talquin offers rewards: largemouth and white bass, speckled perch, and bream. But watch out, or your fishing line or boat motor—not the fish—may be what gets snagged. Dead standing trees jut hazardously from the water. The trees are remnants from when the Jackson Bluff Dam was built on the Ochlockonee River in 1927.

Campsites, facilities: A clearing by the lake with a fishing pier accommodates 32 self-contained camping units or tents. Grills, fire rings, and picnic tables are provided. A county-run boat ramp is nearby. Dogs are permitted on a leash.

Reservations, fees: Reservations are not accepted. Camping permits are not needed, but hunting requires a permit. Sites are $5 each. The maximum stay is 14 days in a 30-day period.

Directions: From I-10 west of Tallahassee, take Exit 192 and go west on U.S. 90 for 2.1 miles, then turn left at State Road 268. Travel 2.4 miles, passing Central Road and veering left onto Peters Road. After the pavement ends (in less than one mile), turn left at High Bluff Road. Continue 2.5 miles to the campground.

Contact: Lake Talquin State Forest, 856 Geddie Road, Tallahassee, FL 32304, 850/488-1871, fax 850/922-2107, www.fl-dof.com.

9 BEAR CREEK TRACT

Scenic rating: 6

in Lake Talquin State Forest, south of Quincy

A primitive campground provides a base for backpacking, hiking and bicycling in Lake Talquin State Forest. This area is closed to hunters year-round, so you can go about your fun with a relaxed mind. A series of nature trails threads through the Bear Creek Tract, and the campground is nestled below tall pines on a small creek. You'll have to hike in about 2.5 miles (no bicycles allowed) from the parking area. The hike is described as moderately strenuous, with narrow footing along steep inclines in some areas. For the less athletically inclined, a "Living Forest" nature trail at the parking area provides educational and interpretive information from "talking trees."

It's worth noting that about two miles south of the main Bear Creek parking area, cyclists will find the Lines Tract Off-Road Bicycle Trail. The main trail, about seven miles long, is for beginning to intermediate-level riders. You'll find low-clearance obstacles, logs, and tight turns around trees. The trail is for two-way traffic, but a counterclockwise direction is recommended. Off the main trail are several more technical loops. To get to the Lines Tract, continue south from the Bear Creek Tract on State Route 267 and turn west on Cooks Landing Road to the parking area. In the rest of the forest, bicycles are allowed on open forest roads, but not on hiking trails.

Campsites, facilities: There are sites for 10 two-person tents with fire rings. Sites are designated by white bands on the trees. A four-person or family sized tent is equivalent to two two-person tents. No water or electricity is available. Human waste must be buried six inches deep at least 100 feet away from the camping area and water sources, and out of sight of the trail. No alcohol is allowed. Children are welcome. Leashed pets are permitted.

Reservations, fees: A state forest use permit is required in advance of your stay. Sites are $5 per night. The maximum stay is 14 days.

Directions: From I-10, take Exit 181 south on State Route 267 for about four miles. The parking area for Bear Creek is on your left.

Contact: Lake Talquin State Forest, 856 Geddie Road, Tallahassee, FL 32304, 850/488-1871, fax 850/922-2107, www.fl-dof.com.

10 FORT BRADEN TRACT

Scenic rating: 6

in Lake Talquin State Forest, west of Tallahassee

Closed to hunters year-round, this area is for hikers and horseback riders. Set within Lake Talquin State Forest on the south side of the lake, this primitive area has an 11-mile circuit hiking loop and a separate 11-mile loop for equestrians. A primitive group camp is located about 0.5 mile from the main parking lot, and two primitive campsites are on the lakefront. You'll have to hike in to all these sites, but the views of the lake are worth the effort.

Campsites, facilities: If you're not traveling with a group, you'll want to choose from the two primitive sites on the lake, about two miles from the parking area. There are sites for three two-person tents with fire rings. Sites are designated by white bands on the trees. A four-person or family-sized tent is equivalent to two two-person tents. No water or electricity is available. Human waste must be buried six inches deep at least 100 feet away from the camping area and water sources, and out of sight of the trail. No alcohol is allowed. Children are welcome. Leashed pets are permitted.

Reservations, fees: A state forest use permit is required in advance of your stay. Sites are $5 per night. The maximum stay is 14 days.

Directions: From Tallahassee, take State Road 263 to the intersection of State Road 20, then follow State Road 20 west for seven miles. Pass the intersection with Coe Landing Road and continue about 0.5 mile to the parking area on the north side of the road.

Contact: Lake Talquin State Forest, 856 Geddie Road, Tallahassee, FL 32304, 850/488-1871, fax 850/922-2107, www.fl-dof.com.

11 HALL'S LANDING

Scenic rating: 6

on Lake Talquin, near Tallahassee

Here's a tent-only, primitive campground with hot showers. Offering a large sodded area for tents, this roomy spot has a long boardwalk along the lake with three observation areas.

Campsites, facilities: There are 10 tent sites with drinking water, but no electricity. Facilities include restrooms, showers, a cooking grill, and a campfire pit. The day-use area has five picnic shelters, a wheelchair-accessible lakeside boardwalk, a picnic area and pier, two fishing piers and boat docks, a fish-cleaning station, and a boat ramp. Children are welcome. Leashed pets are permitted.

Reservations, fees: Reservations are not accepted. Tent sites are $10 for four people, plus $2 per extra person. RVs are not permitted. The maximum stay is 10 consecutive days, or 30 days total in a calendar year.

Directions: From Tallahassee, take State Road 263 to the intersection of State Road 20, then follow State Road 20 west for 14 miles. The park is on the north side of the road, on Lake Talquin.

Contact: Leon County Parks & Recreation Department, 2280 Miccosukee Road, Tallahassee, FL 32308, 850/488-0221, www.co.leon.fl.us/parks/camping.asp.

12 WILLIAM'S LANDING

Scenic rating: 6

on Lake Talquin, near Tallahassee

Located four miles west of Coe's Landing (see next listing), this campground is slightly larger than that facility and has a recreation field. It's popular with large groups of picnickers. There's no dump station or electricity.

Campsites, facilities: There are 10 campsites for RVs and six for tents. Drinking water is available, but there are no hookups. Facilities include restrooms, two picnic shelters, two fishing piers and boat docks, two fish-cleaning stations, and a boat ramp. Children are welcome. Leashed pets are permitted.

Reservations, fees: Reservations are not accepted. Fees are $10 per night for four people, plus $2 per extra person. The maximum stay is 10 days or 30 days in a calendar year.

Directions: From Tallahassee, take State Road 263 to the intersection of State Road 20, then follow State Road 20 west for 11 miles. The park is at 951 William's Landing Road on the north side of the road, on Lake Talquin.

Contact: Leon County Parks & Recreation Department, 2280 Miccosukee Road, Tallahassee, FL 32308, 850/606-1470, fax 850/606-1471, www.co.leon.fl.us/parks/camping.asp.

13 COE'S LANDING

Scenic rating: 7

on Lake Talquin, near Tallahassee

This is one of two RV campgrounds operated by Leon County along Lake Talquin, a haven for anglers just north of Apalachicola National Forest. (It's the only county park that accepts reservations, and park managers brag that each campsite is located so that everyone has a view of the lake.) Most of the lakeshore is publicly owned and open to hikers. Talquin, which covers 8,850 acres, was formed by damming the Ochlockonee River in 1927. The dam broke once, in 1957, and was rebuilt. The lake is managed by the Florida Fish and Wildlife Conservation Commission, which stocks it with largemouth and striped bass, bluegill, and crappie. Swimming is prohibited.

Nearby is the northern starting point of the Tallahassee–St. Marks Historic Railroad State Trail, a 16-mile paved route for bicycling, inline skating, horseback riding, and hiking. The trail follows an abandoned rail bed that was used to transport timber, cotton, and passengers to the Gulf of Mexico for 140 years. It begins at a parking lot at the intersection of U.S. 319 and State Road 363, and ends in St. Marks at the edge of the St. Marks National Wildlife Refuge in Wakulla County. For bicyclists seeking a more rigorous challenge, turn off on a spur about 1.25 miles south of the Tallahassee end to the Munson Hills Off-Road Bicycle Trail through the Apalachicola Forest.

The Munson Hills are rolling sand dunes left from the shoreline one million years ago and now are rooted with longleaf pine forest. The sometimes muddy bike trail dips through wetland hammocks of oak, cherry, and sassafras trees that are home to gopher tortoises, salamanders, deer, and the endangered eastern indigo snake. Bicyclists have two options: the 7.5-mile Munson Hills Loop or the Tall Pine Shortcut, which cuts the loop to 4.25 miles.

Campsites, facilities: There are 17 sites for RVs only with electricity and water in this four-acre park. Facilities include restrooms, showers, a dump station, two picnic shelters, two fishing piers and boat docks, a fish-cleaning station, and a boat ramp. Children are welcome. Leashed pets are permitted.

Reservations, fees: Reservations are accepted; call 850/350-9560 or 866/350-9560. Camping is $24 per night for four people, plus $4 for each additional person. The maximum stay is 10 consecutive days, or 30 days total in a calendar year.

Directions: From Tallahassee, take State Road 263 to the intersection of State Road 20, then follow State Road 20 west for seven miles. The park is at 1208 Coe Landing Road on the north side of the road.

Contact: Leon County Parks & Recreation Department, 2280 Miccosukee Road, Tallahassee, FL 32308, 850/606-1470, fax 850/606-1471, www.co.leon.fl.us/parks/camping.asp.

14 BIG OAK RV PARK

Scenic rating: 4

in Tallahassee

"Very convenient," the management says of Big Oak. Indeed, this RV park puts you just 10 minutes from the governor's mansion and the nerve center of state government. Tallahassee is dotted with RV parks for this very reason—since the state has a part-time legislature, don't be surprised if your neighbor with the big, flashy rig is a senator on official business, or a high-powered lobbyist.

Like most of Tallahassee, Big Oak is shaded by large trees, and it has the feel of bygone motor courts, which were popular before the advent of motel chains. From here, it's a short hike—across a busy highway—to fast-food restaurants, a couple of supermarkets, and an ATM. Just minutes away are a major shopping

mall, movie theaters, and all the cultural fare and political intrigue of the Sunshine State's capital. The city has three marked scenic routes directing motorists along canopied roads and country lanes to museums and historic sites: the Native Trail, which takes about four hours, and the Cotton and Quail Trails, which take 3–3.5 hours each. For information and maps, call the Tallahassee Area Convention and Visitors Bureau at 800/628-2866.

Campsites, facilities: There are 72 RV sites with full hookups, 30/50-amp electricity, and cable TV; 12 are pull-through. A wireless Internet connection is available throughout the park. On the premises are restrooms, showers, laundry facilities, shuffleboard courts, and a horseshoe pit. Children are welcome. Leashed pets are permitted.

Reservations, fees: Reservations are accepted. Sites are $25 per night for two people, plus $2 for each additional person. Credit cards are accepted. Long-term rates are available.

Directions: From I-10 in Tallahassee, take Exit 199 onto U.S. 27 and drive 2.5 miles north to the park, on the west side of the road.

Contact: Big Oak RV Park, 4024 North Monroe Street, Tallahassee, FL 32303, 850/562-4660, www.bigoakrvpark.com.

15 LAKESIDE TRAVEL PARK AND CAMPGROUND

Scenic rating: 2

in Tallahassee

A laid-back spot on the western outskirts of Tallahassee, this 10-acre campground offers a small pond and oak-shaded sites. It's located near good fishing on Lake Talquin and the campuses of Florida State University and Florida Agricultural and Mechanical University. It's also within 0.5 mile of Wal-Mart, fast-food restaurants, and, among other businesses, a car lot. The park has a split personality;

permanent guests reside in one area, while overnighters sleep in another. Plenty of open sites are usually available, except on big football weekends when the Florida State Seminoles play at home against their Gainesville rivals, the University of Florida Gators. About half the sites are occupied by full-timers.

Campsites, facilities: There are 58 RV sites with full hookups and a choice of 30-amp or 50-amp electrical service; 22 are pull-through. Overnighters are welcome at 20 sites. The park has restrooms, showers, laundry facilities, a dump station, and a fishing lake. A wireless Internet connection is available. Within 0.5 mile are a grocery store and restaurants. Children and leashed pets are welcome.

Reservations, fees: Reservations are taken. Sites are $28 to $34 per night for two people, plus $2 per extra person. Credit cards are accepted. Long-term rates are available.

Directions: From I-10 at Tallahassee, take Exit 196 onto State Road 263 (Capital Circle) and drive 1.5 miles south to U.S. 90. Turn west and drive one mile to the park. Alternatively, take I-10 Exit 192, then go east four miles on U.S. 90 to the park on the right.

Contact: Lakeside Travel Park and Campground, 6401 West Tennessee Street, Tallahassee, FL 32304, 850/574-5998.

16 TALLAHASSEE RV PARK

Scenic rating: 4

east of Tallahassee

This park on the east side of Tallahassee offers easy access to the interstate and the city. Its lighted, paved interior roads and big, grassy sites are comfortable for parking even the largest RVs. The park is shaded with large pines, magnolia, and dogwood, and is neatly landscaped with flowers and shrubs. Across the street are a nine-hole golf course and driving range. Visitors come from all over for the

Florida Capitol, antique shops, football games, and fishing on the coast. About 30 percent of the park is occupied year-round.

South of the park, off U.S. 319, are Apalachicola National Forest and an attraction for Civil War history buffs: the Natural Bridge State Historic Site, where a five-day battle raged in the final weeks of the war. It ended with a rebel victory when a militia of old men and boys defeated seasoned Union troops, giving Tallahassee the distinction of being the only Confederate capital never to fall into Yankee hands. To get to the site, take U.S. 319 to State Road 363 and turn south. Continue four miles to Woodville, then turn east on Natural Bridge Road and drive six miles to the park. It's a great spot for picnics and for seeing Natural Bridge, where the St. Marks River disappears into a cavern and runs underground for 150 feet before resurfacing.

Campsites, facilities: This park has 66 gravel, drive-through RV sites with electricity, sewer, water, cable TV, and picnic tables; 23 have 30-amp electrical service, and 43 have 50-amp. Big rigs are welcome, as are slideouts. Wireless Internet service is available throughout the park, including the campsites. On the premises are restrooms, showers, a dump station, a large recreation hall, and a pool. Groceries and restaurants are within 0.25 mile. Management says all areas are wheelchair-accessible. Children are welcome. Leashed pets are permitted.

Reservations, fees: Reservations are recommended. Sites are $29 to $32 per night. Credit cards are accepted. Long-term rates are available.

Directions: From I-10 at Tallahassee, take Exit 209A onto U.S. 90 and drive 0.5 mile west to the park.

Contact: Tallahassee RV Park, 6504 Mahan Drive, Tallahassee, FL 32308, 850/878-7641, and fax 850/878-7082, www.tallahassee rvpark.com.

17 A CAMPER'S WORLD

🏊 🐕 � 🚐

Scenic rating: 3

near Monticello, off I-10

Campers on the move will appreciate the easy interstate access this five-acre park offers. The sites are spacious, shaded by tall pines, and landscaped with flowers and shrubs. It's far enough away from the highway to cut the traffic noise a few decibels. Also, the exit is not as congested as those closer to nearby Tallahassee and Lake City.

Campsites, facilities: There are 29 RV sites with full hookups (30-amp and 50-amp service) and picnic tables; most are pull-through. Big rigs and slideouts are welcome. On the premises are restrooms, showers, laundry facilities, a dump station, a pool, a playground, and a pay-phone modem hookup for laptop computers. Children are welcome. Leashed pets are permitted.

Reservations, fees: Reservations are accepted. Sites are $25 to $28 per night for two people, plus $2.50 per additional person. Credit cards are accepted. Long-term rates are available.

Directions: From I-10, take Exit 225 north onto U.S. 19 and drive 0.2 mile to the park entrance on the west side of the road.

Contact: A Camper's World, 397 Campground Road, Lamont, FL 32336, 850/997-3300, acampersworld@aol.com.

18 TALLAHASSEE EAST KOA

🏊 🛶 🎣 � 🚐 ⛺

Scenic rating: 6

south of Monticello, off I-10

This wooded campground is convenient for travelers, who are welcomed with free cookies on arrival and continental breakfast in the morning. Parking and hooking up are no hassle, because nearly all the sites are pull-through. There's plenty of space for the kids to play, a pond for tossing in a fishing line,

rings to build campfires, and a game room with a fireplace. About 30 percent of the park is occupied by year-round residents. Fishing and firewood are free.

Campsites, facilities: There are 75 pull-through RV sites with water and electric hookups, and 65 of them have sewer connections. About two-thirds of the campsites have 30-amp electrical service, while 25 sites have 50-amp. Tents are welcome at several spots. Picnic tables and grills are provided. A wireless Internet connection is available in the clubhouse. Facilities include restrooms, showers, a laundry room, a dump station, a convenience/country crafts store, a pool, a fishing pond, a game and meeting room, a playground, and rental cabins. Firewood, mini-storage, and propane are available. The pool is available April 1–November 1. Children are welcome. Leashed pets are permitted.

Reservations, fees: Reservations are taken. Sites are $17–34 per night for two adults, plus $2.50 for extra adults. Credit cards are accepted. Long-term rates are available.

Directions: From I-10 near Monticello, take Exit 225 onto U.S. 19 and head south for 0.25 mile. Turn right on County Road 158B (Nash Road) and drive 2.4 miles, then turn north on County Road 259 and drive 0.25 mile to the park.

Contact: Tallahassee East KOA, Route 5, Box 5160, Monticello, FL 32344, 850/997-3890 or 800/KOA-3890 (800-562-3890), fax 850/997-1509, www.koa.com.

19 MADISON CAMPGROUND

🏊 🐕 🚶 🚐 ⛺

Scenic rating: 5

near Madison

Set in a wooded area near the Suwannee River, this campground is part of the Deerwood Inn motel complex, which has a pool with a luau hut, a floodlit miniature golf course, one tennis court, and a game room with pool tables and video games. You're likely not to be crowded by other campers, the owners say, and the park's location near the interstate makes it an ideal stopover. Nearby is historic Madison, the county seat, where pre–Civil War cotton plantations once flourished. Madison County remains a quiet agricultural community. A favorite part activity is swimming in the pool.

Campsites, facilities: This park has 80 pull-through RV sites (39 with full hookups) and 10 tent-only sites set apart from the RVs. Water and 30/50-amp electricity are available at all spots. You'll find restrooms, showers, picnic tables, grills, some fire rings, a dump station, and laundry facilities. A recreation room, a pool, a playground, a game room, a miniature golf course, a tennis court, horseshoe pits, shuffleboard courts, and a volleyball area are available. Children are welcome. Leashed pets are permitted for a $2 fee.

Reservations, fees: Reservations are not necessary, unless you need 50-amp service. Sites are $20 to $25 per night per site, plus $2 for sewer hookups. Credit cards are accepted. Long-term rates are available.

Directions: From I-10 east of Madison, take Exit 258 and head south on State Road 53 for 0.2 mile to the park.

Contact: Madison Campground, 155 Southwest Old Saint Augustine Road, Madison, FL 32340, 850/973-2504, fax 850/973-3805.

20 YOGI BEAR'S JELLYSTONE PARK CAMP-RESORT

Scenic rating: 8

near Madison

Opened in 2000, this popular campground targets overnighters and destination travelers. It's a fun place for kids, with lots for them to enjoy, including a 60-foot-high circular water slide that speeds them down to a lake surrounded by a white-sand beach. The surroundings are wooded and natural, as befits this beautiful area of Florida. Giving new meaning to "planned activities," this park holds paintball contests, concerts, and the like.

Campsites, facilities: Campers in tents or RVs can choose from 100 sites with full hookups, 30/50-amp electricity, picnic tables, and grills. Sixty-five sites are pull-through. Restrooms, showers, a dump station, laundry facilities, and telephone service are available. There's an Internet connection in the clubhouse. On the premises are three lakes, a pool, a playground, a campground store, a nature trail, a snack bar, boat rentals, a clubhouse, putt-putt golf, and a dog-walk area. Most areas are wheelchair-accessible. Children are welcome. Leashed pets are permitted.

Reservations, fees: Reservations are recommended. Sites are $28–38 per night for two adults and two children, plus $6 per extra person and $6 for using 50-amp electricity. Credit cards are accepted. Long-term rates are available.

Directions: From I-10, take Exit 258 and drive south on State Road 53 about 150 yards. Turn right on Southwest Old Saint Augustine Road. Pass the Deerwood Inn; look for the Jellystone campground signs on the left.

Contact: Yogi Bear's Jellystone Camp Resorts, 1151 Southwest Old St. Augustine Road, Madison, FL 32340, 850/973-8269 or 850/973-8546, fax 850/973-4114, www.yogicampingflorida.com.

21 MADISON BLUE SPRINGS STATE PARK

Scenic rating: 8

east of Madison and north of Lee, on the Withlacoochee River

This fantastic park is undergoing changes. It was closed in 2002 and has been developed into a state park for day use only. Call ahead to see if the park has opened for camping—it will be worth the wait.

Several camping areas in Florida share the name Blue Springs, but here the water really is blue, almost turquoise. Nature trails wind along the unspoiled riverbanks, and the woods are laced with horseback-riding trails. The 67-acre wooded park is a popular destination for scuba divers and snorkelers who explored the first-magnitude spring or nearby caverns along the Withlacoochee River. A swimming beach lets non-divers get their feet wet. Divers travel from as far away as Australia to explore the 6.5 miles of caves. Cave divers have to be fully certified; an open-water basin with an underwater platform is great for checkout dives. Solo diving is not allowed. Only 26 springs nationwide pump more than 100 million gallons of freshwater per day—and this is one of them.

Campsites, facilities: Before the park's 2002 closure, there were 15 RV sites with water and electric hookups in two separate areas. About 50 tents could be accommodated on primitive, wooded sites overlooking the Withlacoochee River. Restrooms, showers, picnic tables, and some fire rings were provided.

Reservations, fees: Call for updated information.

Directions: From I-10 east of Madison, take Exit 262 northbound on County Road 255 about five miles. Drive through the town of Lee. At State Road 6 on the north side of town, turn east (right). Go about five miles to the park.

Contact: Check www.floridastateparks.org for updates. The park is located at 8300 Northeast State Road 6, Lee, FL 32059, 850/971-5003.

22 JENNINGS OUTDOOR RESORT

🏊 ⛷ 🛶 🐴 🚴 🚐

Scenic rating: 3

off the northernmost exit in Florida, on I-75

Jennings is a rural park with paved sites set among some oaks, convenient to the interstate. There is a fishing pond on-site (catch-and-release, no license required), and you can take out paddleboats and canoes. Most campers spend a night or two at this 30-acre park, although some stay for months. Drive just 10 miles, and you can take a dip at Madison Blue Springs State Park (see listing in this chapter), one of the super-fun, super-cool, refreshing places in North Florida where clear water bubbles up from the earth. You also can reach the dark, mysterious Okefenokee Swamp in an hour or so. Stephen Foster Folk Culture Center State Park is about a half-hour away. The biggest town nearby is Lake City, about 40 miles to the south. Osceola National Forest near Lake City is another place to explore. But the real buzz is about the roller coasters found three highway exits north at the animal-oriented theme park Wild Adventures in Valdosta, Georgia. For hours, call 229/219-7080.

Campsites, facilities: This park has 102 pull-through RV sites with full hookups and 30/50-amp electrical service. On the premises are showers, restrooms, picnic tables, a dump station, a pool, a fishing pond, boat/canoe rentals, paddleboats, a recreation hall, a playground, horseshoes, shuffleboard, limited groceries, RV supplies, propane, and laundry facilities. Dialup service in available in the laundry facilities. Restaurants are close by. Children are allowed, but the rules remind parents that "it is your responsibility to entertain and discipline your children. If you disagree, choose another campground." Leashed pets are permitted.

Reservations, fees: Reservations are normally not necessary. Sites are $24 per night for two people, plus $2 for each additional person over age four and $2 for cable TV. Credit cards are accepted. Long-term rates are available.

Directions: From Valdosta, Georgia, travel 18 miles south on I-75. If you are coming from the south, it's the last exit in Florida (Exit 467) onto State Road 143. The campground is right off the highway.

Contact: Jennings Outdoor Resort, 2039 Hamilton Avenue, Jennings, FL 32053, 386/938-3321, fax 386/938-3322, jor@alltel.net.

23 SUWANNEE RIVER STATE PARK

🏃 🏊 🐕 👨‍👩‍👧 🚐 ⛺

Scenic rating: 10

northwest of the town of Live Oak, at
the confluence of the Suwannee and
Withlacoochee Rivers

BEST (

One feature of this 1,800-acre park is an
overlook that offers a panoramic view of the
Suwannee and Withlacoochee Rivers and the
surrounding wooded uplands. When the water
is low, springs can be seen bubbling up from
the riverbanks. Today, the river is sentried by
canoeists—the park is the starting point for
the Suwannee River Canoe Trail, which flows
to the Gulf of Mexico. Catfish, bass, and pan
fish can be pulled from the river. The campground is set in a densely wooded forest of
slash pines, and at night, the only sound you
may hear is the lonesome wail of a freight train
headed to the big city.

Established in 1936, Suwannee River State
Park was one of the first parks in the state
system, and it is steeped in American history.

A short hike from the ranger station brings you
to the ruins of earthworks built by Confederate soldiers to protect the railroad bridge over
the river and trainloads of beef, salt, and sugar
headed to rebels based in Georgia.

Later, paddlewheel ferries plied these waters when the Suwannee was a commerce
route, a highway to Gulf ports for a prosper-
ing logging industry. The pioneer village of
Columbus here contained little more than
the railroad bridge, a ferry landing, and a
sawmill. All that's left of the settlement is the
old Columbus Cemetery, which is accessible
from a trail in the park. The disproportion-
ate number of infants buried there is silent
testimony to how tough it was to survive in
the wilds of Florida.

Campsites, facilities: There are 30 campsites
with 30-amp electricity and water, picnic tables, grills, and fire rings. A boat ramp, canoe
rentals, a playground, and several short hiking
trails are in the park. Children are welcome.
Pets are permitted.

Reservations, fees: Reservations are recommended; call ReserveAmerica at 800/326-
3521. Sites are $15 per night for up to eight

© MARILYN MOORE

the legendary Suwannee River

people. Credit cards are accepted. The maximum stay is 14 days.

Directions: From I-10 west of Live Oak, take Exit 275 northbound and drive six miles on U.S. 90 to the park, on the right side of the road.

Contact: Suwannee River State Park, 20185 County Road 132, Live Oak, FL 32060, 386/362-2746, www.floridastateparks.org.

24 SPIRIT OF THE SUWANNEE MUSIC PARK

Scenic rating: 8

north of Live Oak, on the Suwannee River

This music-oriented campground is nestled on 800 acres of forest draped in Spanish moss. Among the things that make this place special are the three pickin' sheds used for impromptu jam sessions, and the grassy meadow that becomes a stage for weekend rock 'n' roll, blues, and bluegrass festivals, plus special activities for Halloween, Thanksgiving, and other holidays. A horse camping area is available, and there are 22 miles of trails for equestrians. The park is open to the public, but management is now selling memberships that include free camping and use of the park, park models, and wedding packages. Because it's so large and off the usual path for hurricanes, the park has served as a Red Cross evacuation center when storms threaten, once accommodating around 8,000 people.

An on-site concession rents bicycles and outfits canoeists for day trips or overnight paddling expeditions. Also available are about 18 miles of walking and bicycling trails along the Suwannee River, Rees Lake, and through the Bay Swamp. The restaurant features a Southern-style menu and holiday dinner specials. Square dancing, bingo, card playing, and Sunday church services are held in the common areas.

Campsites, facilities: This unusual campground has full-hookup sites for 700 RVs (100 more are set aside for members), plus primitive tent camping areas that can accommodate more than 2,000 tents. Cable TV, picnic tables, grills, a pool, a river beach, a fishing dock, a game room, a boat ramp, a restaurant, an amphitheater, a music hall, an open-air concert stage, cabins, rental trailers, stables, canoe rentals, horseshoes, miniature golf, and nature trails are on site. A horse camping area has 68 water and electric sites, with easy access to rental stalls, stables, and pens. Children are welcome and are kept busy with crafts and other activities programs. Up to two pets per site under 20 pounds are allowed; they must be kept on a six-foot leash and are prohibited in concert areas.

Reservations, fees: Reservations are recommended two weeks in advance on holiday weekends and are accepted one year ahead for big events. Sites normally run $15 per night for four people, plus $2 per extra person. Camping rates rise during special events. Pets are prohibited in the campground. during special events. Credit cards are accepted. Maximum stay is six months.

Directions: From I-75 north of Live Oak, take Exit 451 and drive 4.7 miles south on U.S. 129 to the park. Or, from I-10 at Live Oak, take Exit 283 and head 4.9 miles north on U.S. 129.

Contact: Spirit of the Suwannee Music Park, 3076 95th Drive, Live Oak, FL 32060, 386/364-1683 or 800/428-4147, fax 386/364-2998, www.musicliveshere.com.

25 HOLTON CREEK CONSERVATION AREA

Scenic rating: 9

southwest of Jasper and northwest of Live Oak, on the Suwannee River

The biggest draw along these three miles or so of riverfront acreage is Holton Creek, which boils up from one of North Florida's famous "first-magnitude" (read: really big) springs. The limestone ground—laid down eons ago, when this area was covered by an ancient sea— is pockmarked today with sinkholes and other depressions. The property contains a variety of habitats, although the three most common are sandhills, upland forests, and frequently flooded bottomland forests.

Two of the biggest cypress trees in the state are located here, along with the largest collection of old-growth bottomland forest remaining in the area. The juxtaposition of high uplands and undisturbed wetlands is hard to find anywhere else, even way out in the backwoods of North Florida. This diversity is one of the reasons why the Suwannee River Water Management District bought the land.

Campsites, facilities: This is primitive camping along the Suwannee River. There are no designated campsites, but you can find your own spot, often on a sandbars or the riverbanks. No facilities are provided. You are only allowed to camp here if you are canoeing or boating on the Suwannee River or hiking on the Florida National Scenic Trail. Trash and all other waste must be packed out. Leashed pets are permitted, as are children.

Reservations, fees: If you'll be arriving by canoe or boat, you need to obtain a permit, also known as a Special Use License, from the Suwannee River Water Management District. Camping is free.

Directions: The closest upstream canoe launch is at Gibson Park, at the intersection of Highway 751 and Highway 249. From Live Oak, follow Highway 249 north about 12 miles to the boat launch. There are several hiking entry points; download a map from the website of the water management district.

Contact: Suwannee River Water Management District, Public Use Land Coordinator, 9925 County Road 49, Live Oak, FL 32060, 386/326-1001 or 800/226-1066 (within Florida), www.srwmd.state.fl.us.

26 STEPHEN FOSTER FOLK CULTURE CENTER STATE PARK

Scenic rating: 9

in White Springs, on U.S. 41 by the Suwannee River

BEST (

This is one of the state's most unusual parks, combining outdoor recreation, American history, and cultural arts programs. A tribute to composer Stephen Foster, the state park has the feel of a well-manicured antebellum plantation. A museum displays memorabilia of Foster's life, antique pianos, and mechanical dioramas depicting the themes of his works, like "Way Down Upon the Suwannee River" and "Oh Susanna." A tube-bell carillon—touted as the world's largest—regularly chimes a repertoire of Foster favorites and echoes through the campground several times a day.

You'll find lots of shade under moss-draped oaks, and a bit of peace alongside the meandering Suwannee. Fishing is popular from the steep banks of the river, and a canoe launch allows easy access from within the park. Hiking is available along a 4.5-mile nature trail and a 4.5-mile section of the Florida National Scenic Trail that runs alongside the river. Mountain bikers enjoy the nature trail, but are not allowed on the Florida Trail, which is reserved for hikers. Nearby are 33 miles of trails in the Big Shoals Public Lands. Big Shoals is a 3,700-acre preserve along the Suwannee River that features the only white-water rapids in the state. However, water levels fluctuate, and during the winter, the water is too low for white water.

Campsites, facilities: The campground has 45 gravel campsites with water, 30-amp electricity, fire rings, grills, and picnic tables. Three sites have 50-amp plugs. Fourteen sites accommodate big rigs in pull-through sites. Restrooms, showers, laundry facilities, rental cabins, a canoe ramp, and a playground are available. Concession stands with snacks and souvenirs, craft shops, a museum, a carillon bell tower, and an amphitheater for musical events are situated within the park. Entry to the museum, carillon tower, and craft square is free for registered campers. Most areas are wheelchair-accessible. Streets are paved. Groceries are four miles away, and restaurants are within two miles. Children are welcome. Pets are permitted.

Reservations, fees: Reservations are recommended; call ReserveAmerica at 800/326-3521. The campground is open Memorial Day weekend for participants in the Florida Folk Festival only. Sites are $16 per night for up to eight people. Credit cards are accepted. The maximum stay is 14 days. Walk-in campers are accepted for a maximum two-day stay.

Directions: From Lake City, head north on U.S. 41 about 18 miles to White Springs. You'll see the entrance to the state park and culture center after you pass two traffic lights. From I-75, take Exit 439 eastbound on State Road 136. Travel three miles to U.S. 41 and turn north (left). The park is just ahead on the left. From I-10, take Exit 301 and drive north on U.S. 41 about nine miles to the park entrance on the left.

Contact: Stephen Foster Folk Culture Center State Park, P.O. Drawer G, White Springs, FL 32096, 386/397-2733 or 386/397-4331, www .floridastateparks.org.

27 SWIFT CREEK CONSERVATION AREA
🏃 🛶 🚐 🐴 ⛺

Scenic rating: 5

south of White Springs, on the Suwannee River

This timberland is quite convenient for those who don't want to hike or canoe very far. By wilderness standards, though, it's pretty puny at 269 acres, and it's situated right next to the town of White Springs. The water

district purchased the land to buffer the river from the town in an effort to preserve high water quality.

Campsites, facilities: This is primitive camping along the Suwannee River. There are no designated campsites, but you can find your own spot, often on a sandbar or the riverbanks. No facilities are provided. You are only allowed to camp here if you are canoeing or boating on the Suwannee River or hiking on the Florida National Scenic Trail. Trash and all other waste must be packed out. Leashed pets are permitted, as are children.

Reservations, fees: If you'll be arriving by canoe or boat, you need to obtain a permit, also known as a Special Use License, from the Suwannee River Water Management District. Camping is free.

Directions: One boat ramp where you can launch a canoe is at Highway 41 Bridge Park in White Springs, on the right side of U.S. 41, just north of the river. It's immediately adjacent to the conservation area. This is also where you can pick up the Florida National Scenic Trail into the conservation area. Upstream from here is a boat ramp at Turner Bridge Park, about 25 miles east of Jasper. From Jasper, take County Road 6 east to the river.

Contact: Suwannee River Water Management District, Public Use Land Coordinator, 9925 County Road 49, Live Oak, FL 32060, 386/326-1001 or 800/226-1066 (within Florida), www.srwmd.state.fl.us.

28 SUWANNEE VALLEY CAMPGROUND
🏃 🚴 🛶 🛶 🚤 🏊 🐴 🛶 ♿ 🚐 ⛺

Scenic rating: 10

on the Suwannee River, in White Springs

BEST (

This is a favored destination for RV caravans, camping clubs, and family groups that take advantage of the spacious pull-through sites and a large recreation center for group activities. The campground is located on 36 oak-shaded acres on the banks of the Suwannee River and appeals to all age groups and types of campers. Off-road bicycling, canoeing, and hiking are nearby, and the Florida National Scenic Trail skirts the campground. There's a playground and wading pool for kids, and the laundry room is equipped with many washers and dryers. A dog activity area allows you to let your pet off-leash to run and play. Steak and chicken cookouts are held every Saturday night.

Campsites, facilities: The campground has 119 pull-through sites with full hookups and grills. There's a separate tent area in a pretty meadow with 40 sites (primitive camping only). RV sites have 30-amp electrical service, wireless Internet access, and "instant-on" telephone service that allows you to make toll-free and local calls. Other sites have 50-amp service and are suitable for big rigs. Restrooms, showers, a recreation hall, swimming and kiddie pools, horseshoe pits, basketball and shuffleboard courts, laundry facilities, canoe and kayak rentals, a dog activity area, rental cabins, and a convenience store are provided. The clubhouse is wheelchair-accessible. Children are welcome, as are leashed pets.

Reservations, fees: Reservations are recommended. Sites are $12–25 per night for two adults and two children, plus $2 per extra person. Credit cards are accepted. Long-term rates are available.

Directions: From I-75, take Exit 439 and travel 2.5 miles east on State Road 136. Turn right just before a bridge onto White Springs Road. Go 0.1 mile, then turn left onto Stephen Foster Road and drive 0.5 mile to the park. Or, from I-10, take Exit 301 and drive eight miles north on U.S. 41. Turn left on State Road 136. Turn left after the bridge onto White Springs Road. Go 0.1 mile, turn onto Stephen Foster Road, and drive 0.5 mile.

Contact: Suwannee Valley Campground, 786 Northwest Stephen Foster Drive, White Springs, FL 32096, 386/397-1667

or 866/397-1667, fax 386/397-1560, www .suwanneevalleycampground.com.

29 BIG SHOALS CONSERVATION AREA

Scenic rating: 9

east of White Springs, on the Suwannee River

Florida's only real white-water rapids are found on the Suwannee River next to this land, which is owned by the Suwannee River Water Management District. Both the water district tract and the adjacent state forest are named for the Big Shoals rapids. Canoeists should portage around them. The shoals, limestone deposited millions of years ago when this area was covered by vast oceans, can almost provide a bridge across the river in periods of low water. The terrain in the adjacent conservation area and state forest is quite varied, ranging from dry, high ground that supports an ecosystem of longleaf pine and wire grass to dark, low cypress swamps. In the spring, wild azaleas, dogwood, and wild tupelo provide a riot of color. Ticks can be a problem. This is one of the least developed stretches of the Suwannee. Hiking is available in the conservation area and the state forest next door.

Campsites, facilities: This is primitive camping along the Suwannee River. There are no designated campsites, but you can find your own spot, often on a sandbar or the riverbanks. No facilities are provided. You are only allowed to camp here if you are canoeing or boating on the Suwannee River. Trash and human waste must be packed out. Leashed pets are permitted, as are children.

Reservations, fees: If you'll be arriving by canoe or boat, you need to obtain a permit, also known as a Special Use License, from the Suwannee River Water Management District. Camping is free.

Directions: To reach the nearest canoe launch, take Highway 135 north from White Springs.

© MARILYN MOORE

trailhead at Big Shoals

Turn right on Godwin Bridge Road, the first paved road after you cross Four Mile Branch, about 3.5 miles outside town. Follow that road about one mile to the end, where you can launch your canoe into the river. You'll have to portage around Big Shoals about one mile downriver.

Contact: Suwannee River Water Management District, Public Use Land Coordinator, 9925 County Road 49, Live Oak, FL 32060, 386/326-1001 or 800/226-1066 (within Florida), www.srwmd.state.fl.us.

30 KELLY'S RV PARK

Scenic rating: 6

near White Springs

This adults-preferred campground is tidy, with paved streets and spacious, wooded sites on 20 acres. Visitors with pets in tow will find an area set aside for dog-walking. A nature trail hooks up with the state's Gar Pond and Shoal Trails, which are excellent for hiking and off-road biking. A public boat ramp is within 0.5 mile of the campground. The clubhouse has a fire ring for communal use. Visitors come from all over the United States and Canada to rest and relax.

Campsites, facilities: This park offers 56 RV sites with full hookups, 30/50-amp electrical service, concrete patios, and picnic tables. Thirteen sites are drive-through. Wireless Internet service is available at each campsite. RVs as long as 45 feet and slideouts can be accommodated. On the premises are restrooms, showers, laundry facilities, a nature trail, horseshoe pits, and a clubhouse. The bathhouse, clubhouse, and office are wheelchair-accessible. Groceries and restaurants are within two miles; malls and hospitals are 11 miles away. Children are welcome only for short-term visits or special occasions. Leashed pets (no attack breeds) are permitted.

Reservations, fees: Reservations are recommended November–March. Sites are $25 per night for two people, plus $2 for each additional person and $2 for use of electricity when the temperature is above 84 degrees. Credit cards are accepted. Long-term rates are available.

Directions: From I-75, take Exit 439 and proceed east on State Road 136 into White Springs, then turn south on U.S. 41. The park is 1.5 miles down the road. Or, from I-10, take Exit 301 and drive 5.5 miles north on U.S. 41.

Contact: Kelly's RV Park, 142 Northwest Kelly Lane, White Springs, FL 32096, 386/397-2616, www.kellysrvpark.com.

31 CAMEL LAKE

Scenic rating: 7

south of Bristol, in Apalachicola National Forest

Camping at the remote northwestern corner of Apalachicola National Forest is a great destination or starting point for backpackers, because this spot offers a trailhead for the Florida National Scenic Trail, which meanders east from here through the forest for about 60 miles. The site is in a grassy, open area dotted with longleaf pines, and slopes down to Camel Lake, which has a swimming area. Small boats without motors are permitted.

Campsites, facilities: Ten campsites with grills, picnic tables, and fire rings are available for tents or self-contained RVs. There are no electrical or water hookups. Facilities include restrooms with flush toilets, hot showers, drinking water, a swimming beach with outdoor showers, a boat ramp, and a picnic area. Children are welcome. Pets must be leashed in the camping area.

Reservations, fees: Reservations are not accepted. Camping is $8 per night. Stays are limited to 14 days per month.

Directions: From Bristol, take State Road 12 south for 11 miles. Turn left on Forest Service Road 105 and drive two miles east to the park.

Contact: Apalachicola National Forest, Apalachicola Ranger District, P.O. Box 579, Highway 20, Bristol, FL 32321, 850/643-2282, www.fs.fed.us/r8/florida/recreation/index_apa.shtml.

32 COTTON LANDING

Scenic rating: 6

west of Sumatra, in Apalachicola National Forest

This campground offers a more rustic alternative to nearby Wright Lake, with fishing and boating on Kennedy Creek, which feeds into the Apalachicola River. See the trip notes for Wright Lake and Hickory Landing (listings in this chapter) for a description of the area. Campers, be advised: There's no drinking water at Cotton Landing. Canoeing is not recommended, because of the boat traffic on the Apalachicola River.

Campsites, facilities: This rustic camping area has room for about 10 tents or RVs. Camping is primitive; no drinking water or hookups are available. There are chemical toilets and a boat ramp. Children are welcome. Pets must be leashed in the camping area.

Reservations, fees: Reservations are not accepted. Camping is free. Stays are limited to 14 days per month.

Directions: From Sumatra, take County Road 379 northwest for 3.2 miles. Turn west on Forest Service Road 123 and continue 2.8 miles. Turn west on Forest Service Road 123B and drive 0.7 mile to the campground.

Contact: Apalachicola National Forest, Apalachicola Ranger District, P.O. Box 579, Highway 20, Bristol, FL 32321, 850/643-2282, www.fs.fed.us/r8/florida/recreation/index_apa.shtml.

33 PORTER LAKE

Scenic rating: 7

south of Telogia, in Apalachicola National Forest

Porter Lake is a good stop for canoeists on the Ochlocknee River. It's on a short branch about 10 miles downstream from Pine Creek Landing (see listing in this chapter) on the west side of the river. This is also a trailhead for the Florida National Scenic Trail, which meanders through the national forest.

Campsites, facilities: The primitive camping area has room for about four tents and RVs. A hand pump for spring-fed drinking water and a non-flush vault toilet is provided. Children are welcome. Pets must be leashed in the camping area. Camping is not allowed during hunting season.

Reservations, fees: Reservations are not accepted. Camping is $3 per night. Stays are limited to 14 days per month.

Directions: From Telogia, drive south on County Road 67 for 16 miles, then turn east on Forest Service Road 13 and drive three miles to the campground.

Contact: Apalachicola National Forest, Apalachicola Ranger District, P.O. Box 579, Highway 20, Bristol, FL 32321, 850/643-2282, www.fs.fed.us/r8/florida/recreation/index_apa.shtml.

34 WHITEHEAD LAKE

Scenic rating: 6

south of Telogia, in Apalachicola National Forest

This is one of the larger primitive campgrounds on the Ochlockonee River's west bank, a good spot for fishing and launching boats, with no horsepower limit on boat motors. For campers traveling the river, it is

14 miles downstream from Pine Creek Landing and provides an alternative to making camp at Porter Lake, a few miles upriver.

Campsites, facilities: This primitive camping area has room for 10 tents or RVs. Sites have picnic tables and fire rings. Hand-pumped drinking water, chemical toilets, and a boat ramp are available. Children are welcome. Pets must be leashed in the camping area.

Reservations, fees: Reservations are accepted. Camping is $3 per night. Stays are limited to 14 days per month.

Directions: From Telogia, drive 16 miles south on County Road 67. Turn east on Forest Service Road 13 and drive 1.5 miles. Turn south on Forest Service Road 186 and drive 1.5 miles to the campground.

Contact: Apalachicola National Forest, Apalachicola Ranger District, P.O. Box 579, Highway 20, Bristol, FL 32321, 850/643-2282, www.fs.fed.us/r8/florida/recreation/index_apa.shtml.

35 HITCHCOCK LAKE

Scenic rating: 6

south of Telogia, in Apalachicola National Forest

This campground is touted for its excellent fishing and boating on the Ochlockonee River. For canoe campers paddling downstream, it is located on the west side of the river, 27 miles from Pine Creek Landing, roughly across from Mack Landing on the east side.

Campsites, facilities: There are 10 primitive sites with no hookups or drinking water. The campground has a boat ramp. Children are welcome. Pets must be leashed in the camping area.

Reservations, fees: Reservations are not accepted. Camping is free. Stays are limited to 14 days per month.

Directions: From Telogia, drive south on County Road 67 for 23 miles, then turn east on Forest Service Road 184 and drive 1.5 miles to the campground.

Contact: Apalachicola National Forest, Apalachicola Ranger District, P.O. Box 579, Highway 20, Bristol, FL 32321, 850/643-2282, www.fs.fed.us/r8/florida/recreation/index_apa.shtml.

36 PINE CREEK LANDING
🥾 🚴 🛶 🚤 🐕 🚐 ⛺

Scenic rating: 5

in Apalachicola National Forest, on the Ochlockonee River

This rugged camping spot is set at the end of a dirt road, with no drinking water—not even a communal spigot. The camp is popular with local hunters, who leave their trailers behind upon returning to the workaday world. Surrounding it are miles of logging trails for hiking and mountain biking in relative solitude, except during the November–January hunting season, when camping is also not allowed. Some campsites are waterfront. The big plus of Pine Creek Landing is its boat ramp on the Ochlockonee River—a prime portal for canoeing to Ochlockonee River State Park through 50 miles of the vast Apalachicola National Forest. Most people here are locals.

From Pine Creek Landing, you can meander downstream with the river current pushing your canoe at two to three miles per hour, and wind up at Ochlockonee River State Park in two or three days without trying too hard. Possible obstructions include floating logs. Occasionally, the river is low in spots, requiring a portage. The best time for canoeing is February–May, when the weather is cool and not too buggy. Camping is available at five established sites south of Pine Creek Landing, with two tucked away on creeks along the eastern riverbank. Both are usually marked on the river and easily accessible from highways in Wakulla County. The other three sites are on the west bank, accessible from Liberty County.

Campsites, facilities: There are 10 primitive sites for tents and self-contained RVs up to 35 feet long or those with slideout units. Bring water, food, and supplies. No facilities are available, except for the boat ramp. Children are welcome. Pets should be leashed in the camping area.

Reservations, fees: Reservations are not accepted. Camping is free. Each site accommodates up to six people. The maximum stay is 14 days per month.

Directions: From Tallahassee, drive 18 miles west on State Road 20. At Bloxham, turn left on State Road 375 and go south for 12 miles. Head west on Forest Service Road 335/Piney Creek Road and drive 0.5 mile to the campground. The boat ramp is one mile west of the camp.

Contact: Apalachicola National Forest, Wakulla Ranger District, 57 Taft Drive, Crawfordville, FL 32327, 850/926-3561, fax 850/926-1904, www.fs.fed.us/r8/florida/recreation/index_apa.shtml.

37 MACK LANDING
🛶 🚤 🐕 🚐 ⛺

Scenic rating: 9

in Apalachicola National Forest, near Sopchoppy

Mack Landing sits on a bluff in a hardwood forest about 27 miles downstream from Pine Creek Landing (see previous listing) and is popular with anglers. A steep, paved boat ramp leads to a creek that feeds into the Ochlockonee River, and space is available to tie boats to trees on the riverbank. The sites are casually laid-out and spacious.

Campsites, facilities: The 10 primitive sites will accommodate tents or self-contained RVs up to 45 feet long and those with slideouts. Each site has a picnic table and fire ring, but no electricity. There are vault (non-flush) toilets, a communal water spigot, and a boat ramp. Groceries are 40 miles away; malls and hospitals are within 70 miles. Children are welcome. Pets should be leashed in the camping area.

Reservations, fees: Reservations are not accepted. Camping is $3 daily. The maximum stay is 14 days per month.

Directions: From Sopchoppy, drive west and then north on State Road 375 for 10 miles. Turn left on Forest Service Road 336/Mack Landing Road and drive one mile west to the camp.

Contact: Apalachicola National Forest, Wakulla Ranger District, 57 Taft Drive, Crawfordville, FL 32327, 850/926-3561, fax 850/926-1904, www.fs.fed.us/r8/florida/recreation/index_apa.shtml.

38 WOOD LAKE

Scenic rating: 6

in Apalachicola National Forest, near Sopchoppy

This small campground, located about 12 miles downstream from Mack Landing (see previous listing), provides anglers and boaters with a gently sloping ramp for launching into a creek that runs into one of the most interesting stretches, in terms of wildlife, of the Ochlockonee River, as it twists through Liberty and Franklin Counties, passing Ochlockonee River State Park some 10 miles downstream. Fishing is the favorite activity, and most campers here are locals or visitors from other parts of Florida.

Campsites, facilities: These primitive sites will accommodate self-contained RVs up to 35 feet long, as well as slideout campers. There are no amenities, electricity or water, but a vault toilet is provided. The boat ramp may be unusable in low-water conditions. Groceries and restaurants are 20 miles away; hospitals and malls are 70 miles away. Children are welcome. Pets should be leashed in the camping area.

Reservations, fees: Reservations are not accepted. Camping is free. The maximum stay is 14 days per month.

Directions: From Sopchoppy, take U.S. 319 south for four miles. Turn west and then north on County Road 299 and drive three miles. Turn west onto Forest Service Road 338 and drive two miles to the camp.

Contact: Apalachicola National Forest, Wakulla Ranger District, 57 Taft Drive, Crawfordville, FL 32327, 850/926-3561, fax 850/926-1904, www.fs.fed.us/r8/florida/recreation/index_apa.shtml.

39 WRIGHT LAKE

Scenic rating: 8

near Sumatra, in Apalachicola National Forest

BEST (

Set in tall pines on the west side of Apalachicola National Forest, this secluded park offers spacious campsites beside a spring-fed lake lined with moss-draped cypress and live oak. Staffers consider it the KOA of the Apalachicola forest, thanks to its amenities compared with the typical primitive camps elsewhere in the forest. There's a beach for swimming and fishing, a lakeside picnic area, and an interpretive trail for hiking. The camping area is along the 31.5-mile Apalachee Savannahs Scenic Byway, which you can pick up in Sumatra by heading north on State Road 379. The highway, suitable for bicycling, is a showcase of flat and rolling terrain and wet lowlands abundant with magnolia, cypress swamps, and stands of native longleaf pine. Grassy savannas are speckled with wildflowers such as orchids, pitcher plants, and sundews. Stop often, keeping an eye out for red-cockaded woodpeckers, wild turkeys, bobcats, alligators, and possibly a black bear.

South of Wright Lake, off of State Road 65 on Forest Service Road 129, is the Fort Gadsden Historic Site, overlooking the immense Apalachicola River, a waterway once plied by steamboats, ferries, and barges linking Georgia and Alabama to Gulf ports. The fort is a nice stop for a picnic beside oaks covered with resurrection ferns. Interpretive exhibits help resurrect the site's gruesome military history.

Campsites, facilities: There are 18 sites with water, electricity, and fire pits for RVs or tents. Each site has a pad for an RV and a cleared area for a tent. The park has restrooms (with flush toilets), hot showers, a dump station, picnic tables, grills, and a swimming lake. A boat ramp is nearby at Hickory Landing. Children are welcome. Pets should be leashed in the park but may run free in the forest.

Reservations, fees: Reservations are not taken, but you can call the ranger district to see if a spot is available. The fee is $8 nightly. Credit cards are not accepted. The maximum stay is 14 days per month.

Directions: From Sumatra, take State Road 65 south for two miles. Turn west on Forest Service Road 101 and drive two miles. Turn north at the sign for the park and proceed 0.25 mile.

Contact: Apalachicola National Forest, Apalachicola Ranger District, P.O. Box 579, Highway 20, Bristol, FL 32321, 850/643-2282, www.fs.fed.us/r8/florida/recreation/index_apa.shtml.

40 HICKORY LANDING

Scenic rating: 8

near Sumatra, in Apalachicola National Forest

Hickory Landing is the no-frills neighbor of the Wright Lake campground, with secluded sites nestled in hickory trees and oaks. The landing has a mineral spring (by the boat ramp) but no showers, swimming, or electricity. The boat ramp opens onto Owl Creek, which feeds into the Apalachicola River. It's fine for power-boating and fishing, but not so great for canoeing, because of the boat traffic.

Campsites, facilities: There are 10 primitive sites for tents and self-contained RVs. Drinking water is available, as are chemical toilets, picnic tables, grills, and a boat ramp. Children are welcome. Pets should be leashed in the camping area but can run free in the forest.

Reservations, fees: Reservations are not accepted. Camping is $3 per vehicle. The maximum stay is 14 days each month.

Directions: From Sumatra, take State Road 65 south for two miles. Turn west on Forest Service Road 101 and drive 1.5 miles, then turn south on Forest Service Road 101B and drive one mile to the landing.

Contact: Apalachicola National Forest, Apalachicola Ranger District, P.O. Box 579, Highway 20, Bristol, FL 32321, 850/643-2282, www.fs.fed.us/r8/florida/recreation/index_apa.shtml.

41 GULF VIEW CAMPGROUND

Scenic rating: 8

near Eastpoint

The name says it all: Gulf View is a restful spot with a fabulous vista of St. George Island and the water. Its grassy campsites are shaded by towering slash pines on a gentle hill sloping down to the highway, and you can swim or fish from the seawall across U.S. 98 (although relatively few people do). The eight-acre park also is convenient to the resort community on St. George Island. Snowbirds dominate in winter, when license plates often hail from Ohio, Michigan, Indiana, New York, and Canada. About 30 percent of the park is occupied year-round, and there are some mobile homes on the site.

Campsites, facilities: Of the 45 RV and tent sites with full hookups, about 30 are available for overnighters and seasonal visitors; most sites have picnic tables. Some have 20-amp electrical service; others have 30-amp. Restrooms, showers, and laundry facilities are available. Children are welcome. Leashed pets are permitted.

Reservations, fees: Reservations are suggested in winter. Sites are $22 per night for two adults and two children under age 12, plus $1 per additional person. Credit cards are not accepted. Long-term rates are available.

Directions: From Apalachicola, take U.S. 98 east for eight miles to the park.

Contact: Gulf View Campground, 897 U.S. 98, Eastpoint, FL 32328, 850/670-8970, fax 850/670-8857.

42 DR. JULIAN G. BRUCE ST. GEORGE ISLAND STATE PARK

🚶 🚴 🏊 ⛵ 🛶 🐴 🚐 ⛺

Scenic rating: 10

on St. George Island

Again and again, this barrier island makes it onto lists of the finest beaches in the United States. That's a big reason why the campground here is extremely popular and a jewel of the Florida state park system—there are nine miles of beaches and sand dunes with the texture of powdered sugar. Five miles of beachfront are accessible only by foot, guaranteeing hardier pedestrians a near solitary island experience. The 1,962-acre park, a combination of beachfront, sandy dunes, salt marsh, and pine and oak forests, was acquired by the state in 1963 and opened for recreation in 1980. It's a haven for wildlife, with osprey nesting atop dead pines, and ghost crabs, salt-marsh snakes, and diamondback terrapin turtles residing on the bay. Migratory birds rest here in the fall and spring; the feathered guests include snowy plover, tern, black skimmer, and willet. Anglers reel in flounder, redfish, sea trout, whiting, and an occasional Spanish mackerel. (A saltwater fishing license is required.) The park facilities were completely renovated after they were damaged by hurricanes in 2004 and 2005.

Campsites, facilities: Sixty campsites have water and 30/50-amp electricity, picnic tables, and campfire rings. The park has restrooms, showers, a dump station, two boat ramps, a boardwalk, a playground, and beaches. Children are welcome. Alcohol is not permitted. Pets are allowed with proof of vaccination.

Reservations, fees: Reservations are recommended; call ReserveAmerica at 800/326-3521. Sites are $19 per night for eight people. Credit cards are accepted. The maximum stay is 14 days.

Directions: From Apalachicola, take U.S. 98 east for six miles, then turn south on the St. George Island toll bridge. Drive eight miles to the island traffic circle, then turn east on East Gulf Beach Drive. The park is located at the end of the road.

Contact: Dr. Julian G. Bruce St. George Island State Park, 1900 E. Gulf Beach Drive, St. George Island, FL 32328, 850/927-2111, fax 850/927-2500, www.floridastateparks.org.

43 CARRABELLE PALMS RV PARK

🏊 🚶 🐴 🚐

Scenic rating: 7

in Carrabelle

Gulf breezes kiss this sunny campground, which was completely renovated in 2005 with the addition of a new swimming pool, buildings, screened-in porch and convenience store. Across the road is a public beach for fishing and swimming in the gulf waters. The views and beach access are incomparable; however, the park is popular and your neighbors may be parked quite close.

Campsites, facilities: RVs only are accepted at these 97 full-hookup sites with picnic tables and 30/50-amp electricity. Restrooms, showers, a dump station, a small store, a wireless Internet network, and a recreation hall are available. A public beach is located across the street. Children are welcome. Leashed pets are permitted.

Reservations, fees: Reservations are recommended. Sites are $30 per night for two people, plus $3 per additional person. Credit cards are accepted. Long-term rates are available.

Directions: From Apalachicola, take U.S. 98 east for about 20 miles to Carrabelle Beach, then look for the park across from the beach.

Contact: Carrabelle Palms RV Park, 1843 Highway 98 West, Carrabelle, FL 32322, 850/697-2638, www.carrabellepalmsrvpark .com.

44 HO-HUM RV PARK

Scenic rating: 7

east of Carrabelle

For beachfront living, this three-acre park welcomes older RVers who can relax in their lawn chairs and gaze out over the water. The sites are numbered and laid out in rows on hard-as-a-rock shell roads along 400 feet of beachfront. All sites enjoy spectacular views of the Gulf and are swept by sea breezes. The farthest your site can be is 250 feet from water's edge, while some sites are just 15 feet away. Snowbirds come in winter to play cards and bingo; in summer, the crowd turns to anglers. This adults-only park tends to be peopled by a few overnighters and mostly seasonal visitors, who stay for a week or two or the entire winter. The proprietors report that their place is becoming increasingly popular among birders; migratory birds swoop onto

an island one mile offshore. Campers pull their boats up on the sand, which also is fun for wading and shelling. At night, hook up the cable TV, if you must, but keep the volume low enough to hear the surf breaking on the shore.

Campsites, facilities: All 50 sites have full hookups with 30-amp electrical service and cable TV, and some have picnic tables. On the premises are restrooms, showers, a recreation room, a 250-foot fishing pier, and a wireless Internet network. Children are not allowed. Leashed pets are permitted.

Reservations, fees: Reservations are recommended. Sites are $26–29 per night for two people, plus $2 for each additional person. Credit cards are accepted. Seasonal rates are available.

Directions: From Apalachicola, take U.S. 98 east for 22 miles to Carrabelle. The park is four miles east of Carrabelle, on the gulf side.

Contact: Ho-Hum RV Park, 2132 Highway 98E, Carrabelle, FL 32322, 850/697-3926 or 888/88-HO-HUM (888-884-6486), www .hohumrvpark.com.

45 OCHLOCKONEE RIVER STATE PARK

Scenic rating: 9

south of Sopchoppy

Nestled between Apalachicola National Forest and the St. Marks National Wildlife Refuge, this remote, 392-acre state park is an ideal base camp for exploring the vast northwest Florida wilderness on foot or via canoe. Bring plenty of bug repellent in summer; beware of ticks, chiggers, and wasp hives in low-hanging oak branches, and think twice about refilling your water tanks from the park's spigots—the well water, while potable, had a straw-colored tinge when I camped here (hence the park's Indian name: Yellow Water).

The place is teeming with wildlife, including deer, fox squirrels, bobcat, and overly friendly raccoons. It's not unusual to see endangered red-cockaded woodpeckers, which nest in the upper cavities of old pines suffering from heart rot. The woods are periodically cleaned by controlled burning, which produces a bonus for nature-lovers: explosions of wildflowers in summer months. The park also sports small grassy ponds, dense swampy bay heads, and oak thickets. From the park boat ramp, mariners can launch saltwater fishing trips to Ochlockonee Bay and the Gulf of Mexico, which are five miles downstream, or ply the Ochlockonee and Dead Rivers and Tide Creek in search of largemouth bass, bream, catfish, and speckled perch. (State fishing licenses are required.) For canoeists, the park marks the end of the Ochlockonee River Lower Canoe Trail, a 50-mile route along the Wakulla County line through Apalachicola National Forest.

Campsites, facilities: There are 30 tent/RV campsites, all with water, picnic tables, fire rings, grills, and 30-amp electricity. Two have 50-amp service. Three sites are pull-through. Facilities include restrooms (wheelchair-accessible), showers, a dump station, canoe rentals, and a boat ramp. Groceries and restaurants are within five miles. Malls and hospitals are 42 miles away. Children are welcome. Leashed pets are permitted with proof of rabies vaccination.

Reservations, fees: Reservations are recommended; call ReserveAmerica at 800/326-3521. Sites are $16 per night for eight people. Credit cards are accepted. The maximum length of stay is 14 days.

Directions: From Tallahassee, take U.S. 319 south for 40 miles to Sopchoppy. Continue four miles south on U.S. 319 to the park, which is on the east side of the road.

Contact: Ochlockonee River State Park, P.O. Box 5, 429 State Park Road, Sopchoppy, FL 32358, 850/962-2771, fax 850/962-2403.

46 HOLIDAY PARK AND CAMPGROUND

Scenic rating: 6

in Panacea

This seaside resort is a straight shot from Tallahassee, with plenty of space for big RVs, including five pull-through sites. The park sports oak trees, waterfront sites, and fantastic views of the Gulf of Mexico and the Panacea bridge. An open-air pavilion and hefty barbecue pit are available for parties. You can walk to nearby seafood restaurants. There's a nice, quiet beach and a long pier jutting into Ochlockonee Bay, where you can watch the sun set; a public boat ramp is nearby, and Wakulla Springs is a convenient drive away.

Campsites, facilities: This campground has 77 RV sites with full hookups, 30/50-amp electrical service, picnic tables, and cable TV. Six grassy sites with water and electricity are available for tents. Fifty spots are usually available for overnighters and short-term visitors. The clubhouse has a dialup Internet connection. Facilities include restrooms, showers, a laundry room, a gift shop, a pool, a beach, a fishing pier, a recreation room, a playground, horseshoe pits, and shuffleboard and volleyball courts. All areas are said to be wheelchair-accessible. Children are welcome. Leashed pets are permitted.

Reservations, fees: Reservations are accepted. Sites are $27–33 per night for two people, plus $3 for each additional person. Credit cards are accepted. Long-term rates are available.

Directions: From Tallahassee, take U.S. 319 south for 25 miles to the intersection with U.S. 98 in Panacea. Take U.S. 98 west for nine miles to the park.

Contact: Holiday Park and Campground, 14 Coastal Highway, Panacea, FL 32346, 850/984-5757, fax 850/984-5757, www.holidaycampground.com.

47 NEWPORT RECREATION PARK

Scenic rating: 7

in Newport, south of Tallahassee

Located off the beaten path, this no-frills campground serves as a base for exploring the St. Marks River, spectacular Wakulla Springs, and the St. Marks National Wildlife Refuge, a 64,248-acre preserve that sprawls along 40 miles of Apalachee Bay and stretches from the Ochlockonee River (pronounced "o'clock-nee") on the west to the Aucilla River on the east. Its salt marshes, hardwood and pine forests, and palm and live oak hammocks are popular for hiking, fishing, canoeing, mountain biking, and hunting. The park provides a camping destination for backpackers and bicyclists coming from Tallahassee. It is a few miles from the terminus of the Tallahassee–St. Marks Historic Railroad State Trail, a 16-mile paved route. For information, call trail headquarters at 850/922-6007.

Downriver, where the St. Marks joins the Wakulla River, lies the San Marcos de Apalache State Historic Site, hallowed ground steeped in military lore. Another nearby point of interest is Wakulla Springs, a three-acre wonder touted as one of the world's largest and deepest freshwater springs, with as much as a billion gallons a day flowing out. It's located in Edward Ball Wakulla Springs State Park, about 20 miles west of Newport, and can be viewed from glass-bottomed boats. The spring is teeming with fish, and the mouth of a cavern yawns 100 feet below—complete with a few fossilized mastodon bones. The remains of nine other Ice Age mammals have been discovered as far as 1,200 feet into the cave. Wakulla Springs has no camping facilities, but it's especially worth a side trip for bird-lovers. During the winter, the park attracts thousands of migrating waterfowl, including American wigeon, hooded merganser, and American coot. Feathered locals include limpkin, purple gallinule, anhinga, and bald eagles. For more information, contact Wakulla Springs State Park (550 Wakulla Park Drive, Wakulla Springs, FL 32305, 850/224-5950).

Campsites, facilities: There are 41 campsites, 15 suitable for self-contained RVs. Each site has a fire ring. Some sites have electricity and water. Park facilities include restrooms, showers, a dump station, and a boat ramp. All areas of this county park are said to be wheelchair-accessible. Canoes and boats can be rented nearby. Children are welcome. Pets are permitted.

Reservations, fees: Reservations are recommended. Sites are $10 to $15 per night for up to five people. Credit cards are not accepted. Stays are limited to two weeks.

Directions: From Tallahassee, take State Road 363 south for 12 miles, then turn east on U.S. 98/319. Drive through Newport to the park.

Contact: Wakulla County Parks and Recreation Department, 79 Recreation Drive, Crawfordville, FL 32327, 850/926-7227, fax 850/926-5251. The park telephone is 850/925-4530.

48 ST. MARKS NATIONAL WILDLIFE REFUGE

Scenic rating: 8

in southern Wakulla County, between U.S. 98 and Apalachee Bay/Gulf of Mexico

This is strictly for hard-core backpackers. Camping is allowed only along a section of the Florida National Scenic Trail that passes through the scenic refuge, which is alive with the sounds of chirping birds. Only hikers who plan to complete the entire 35-mile route through the refuge are allowed to camp along it. The refuge is run by the U.S. Fish and Wildlife Service, which generally does not permit camping on its Florida lands, but does so in this case to accommodate through-hikers on the trail.

Although the route is quite flat, you'll find it challenging for one very important reason: When you reach the St. Marks River, a refuge official said, there is no bridge, but you must cross the river. Most backpackers flag down a passing boat and persuade the boater to provide ferry service. One suggestion is to call Shield's Marina (850/925-5612) ahead of time and make arrangements for pickup. The marina is across the river and sees a lot of boat traffic. The other alternative is to swim, but no one recommends that. The trail passes through varied terrain—sunny pine flatwoods dotted by fan-shaped saw palmetto; pine uplands studded with turkey oaks; dark, shady bottomland hardwood areas filled with trees such as gum and maple; sun-washed freshwater marsh; and mixed areas of pines, hardwoods, and cabbage palms. It's not uncommon to see deer and turkey. Lucky hikers might spot a Florida black bear or a bobcat. Hundreds of species of birds either live in or pass through the refuge.

Campsites, facilities: There are five primitive hike-in campsites along the Florida National Scenic Trail. No facilities are provided. Bring water, food, and camping gear. Children are allowed. Pets are prohibited.

Reservations, fees: Campers must obtain a permit from the wildlife refuge. You should apply as far ahead as possible by phone, mail or fax. However, you may also be granted a permit at the wildlife refuge office, about a third of the way through your hike. There is rarely competition for these campsites. Sites are $1 per night per person. Credit cards are not accepted.

Directions: The eastern trailhead is at the point where U.S. 98 crosses the Aucilla River. The western trailhead is near Medart on State Road 319. Refuge officials provide more specific directions when they issue the camping permit.

Contact: St. Marks National Wildlife Refuge, 1255 Lighthouse Road, P.O. Box 68, St. Marks, FL 32355, 850/925-6121, www.fws .gov/saintmarks/.

49 ECONFINA RIVER RESORT

Scenic rating: 4

south of Lamont, on the Gulf of Mexico

This private campground is next to the 3,377-acre Econfina River State Park's boat ramp and rents canoes so campers can explore it. About half the park is occupied by RVs used on weekends by their owners, chiefly anglers from southern Georgia. Overnighters stay in another area, sleeping beside two ponds. A six-unit motel and store are in the 27-acre park, but there's not much else around. In the state park, you'll find hiking and horseback trails, pine and oak forests, and a salt marsh. Upstream, the river, which flows almost two miles to the Gulf, offers challenging canoeing waters on the stretch between Lamont and the County Road 257 bridge. Gnats can be a problem in this area, so come prepared. The park has a swimming pool open year-round, but the main attraction is fishing.

Campsites, facilities: There are 82 full-hookup gravel RV sites with a choice of 30-amp or 50-amp electrical service and 20 to 30 primitive tent sites. All have picnic tables and fire rings. Restrooms, showers, a pool, a clubhouse, horseshoes, volleyball, a small playground, a store that sells ice, beer, fishing tackle and limited groceries; canoe rentals, and a boat ramp are available. Children are welcome. Leashed pets are permitted.

Reservations, fees: Reservations are recommended. Full-hookup sites are $25 per rig for two people, plus $10 per extra person. Children under 12 camp for free. Credit cards are accepted. Long-term rates are available.

Directions: From Perry, drive west on U.S. Alternate 27, crossing U.S. 19/98, at which point the highway becomes U.S. 98. Head 22 miles west to County Road 14, turn south and go six miles until it ends at the park.

Contact: Econfina River Resort, 4705 Econfina River Road, Lamont, FL 32336, 850/584-2135, fax 850/838-2164.

50 PERRY KOA

Scenic rating: 5

south of Perry

Formerly known as Southern Oaks RV Park, this KOA campground is a good base camp for exploring the undiscovered Big Bend area, one of the few places in Florida without a convenient interstate highway. The major road that runs through this area is U.S. 19/98, going roughly east–west through Taylor, Dixie, and Levy Counties. Here in Perry, you'll be less than an hour's drive from the beach, freshwater and saltwater fishing, hunting grounds, and wilderness areas, as well as many historic and archaeological sites. Unspoiled rivers, many of them great for canoeing or houseboating, run south toward the Gulf.

Begin your exploration of the area in Perry, known as the "forest capital of Florida." More than 90 percent of the land in Taylor County is owned by the timber industry. Stop by the Forest Capital State Museum (850/584-3227) for a better understanding of the business and modern forest management practices; there's also a "cracker" homestead typical of those where early settlers lived. (Crackers were so-called because they cracked whips to drive their cattle.)

Campsites, facilities: All 97 RV campsites have full hookups, 30/50-amp electrical service, wireless Internet connections, and optional cable TV and telephone service. Twenty grassy, shady tent sites have water and electricity. About 67 sites are available for overnighters. On the premises are picnic tables, restrooms, showers, a dump station, horseshoe pits, fire rings, laundry facilities, a pool, and a whirlpool tub with room for 12 people. The bathhouse, laundry room, clubhouse, and store are wheelchair-accessible. Park models are for sale. Children are welcome. Leashed pets are permitted.

Reservations, fees: Reservations are recommended. Sites are $29–32 per night for two people, plus $5 for each additional person. Credit cards are accepted. Long-term rates are available.

Directions: From I-10 at Greenville, take Exit 241 and drive south on U.S. 221 for 23 miles to Perry. Continue south through Perry on U.S. 19/98 to the park.

Contact: Perry KOA, 3641 Highway 19 South, Perry, FL 32347, 850/584-3221 or 800/562-9864 (reservations only), www.perry-koa.com or www.koa.com.

51 TOWN AND COUNTRY CAMPER LODGE

Scenic rating: 3

south of Perry

Groceries and restaurants are available within one mile of this trailer park, which mostly attracts people visiting friends and family in Perry and visitors passing through. The campsites are grassy and have concrete patios. The Gulf of Mexico is 20 miles to the south. About half the park is occupied year-round.

Campsites, facilities: There are 25 RV/tents sites in this park, which also has 29 mobile homes. All sites have full hookups, 30-amp electricity, cable TV, and telephone service; two additional tent sites have water and electricity only. About 11 sites are available for overnight visitors. On the premises are picnic tables, restrooms, showers, rental trailers, and laundry facilities. The bathhouse and laundry room are wheelchair-accessible. Leashed pets and children are welcome.

Reservations, fees: Reservations are not necessary. Sites are $13 per night for two people, plus $2 for each additional adult and $1 per child. Credit cards are not accepted. Long-term rates are available.

Directions: From the intersection of U.S. 19/98 and U.S. 27 in Perry, drive south on U.S. 19/98 for 2.5 miles to the park.

Contact: Town and Country Camper Lodge,

2785 Highway 19 South, Perry, FL 32348, 850/584-3095.

52 WESTGATE MOTEL CAMPGROUND

Scenic rating: 2

in Perry

Campers stay on pine-shaded acreage behind the motel, located in the town of Perry. Shopping is close by, and the motel pool and other facilities are available to guests of the RV park.

Campsites, facilities: The 60 RV sites have full hookups, electricity, cable TV, and picnic tables. Restrooms and showers are located in the motel building, as is a computer with Internet access. A pool, laundry facilities, a dump station, and RV supplies are available. Children are welcome. Leashed pets are permitted.

Reservations, fees: Reservations are not necessary. Sites are $21 per night for two people, plus $2 for each additional person and $2 for cable TV. Credit cards are accepted. Long-term rates are available.

Directions: From the intersection of U.S. 19/98 and U.S. 27 in Perry, drive south on U.S. 19/98 for one mile.

Contact: Westgate Motel Campground, 1627 South Byron Butler Parkway, Perry, FL 32348, 850/584-5235 or 888/703-7287, fax 850/584-3037, www.westgateusa.com.

53 LAFAYETTE BLUE SPRINGS STATE PARK

Scenic rating: 8

west of Mayo

Set on a bluff on the Suwannee River, this 200-acre park is popular with locals on hot summer days, when the cool waters of the spring are most refreshing. Nearby is yet another spring, Yana Springs. Sites in the wooded, no-frills campground are for walk-in visitors only. Canoes can be launched from the boat ramp, but it's a bit steep for bigger boats. During the rainy season, the campsites and boat ramp may be flooded and unavailable to the public. There's also an extensive underground cave system suitable for exploration by scuba divers.

Campsites, facilities: The state park system acquired this property from the county and reopened the campground in 2006 to walk-in tent campers only. The park is also accessible by boat. A public bathhouse with showers and flush toilets requires an approximately 0.25-mile walk or bicycle ride to the main park, but portable toilets are provided in the camping area. A boat ramp and a playground are also on site. Children are welcome. Leashed pets are permitted in the campground but not in the springs.

Reservations, fees: Sites are first-come, first-served. Fees are $10 nightly. All fees are subject to change. Credit cards are not accepted. Maximum stay is 14 days.

Directions: From the town of Mayo, drive west on U.S. 27 for 4.8 miles. At County Road 251B, turn right (north) and proceed 2.1 miles. Turn right (east) on a dirt road at the sign for the park.

Contact: Lafayette Blue Springs State Park, 799 Northwest Blue Spring Road, Mayo, FL 32066, 386/294-3667, www.floridastateparks.org.

54 THE RIVER RENDEZVOUS

Scenic rating: 8

east of Mayo

A spectacular canopy of old-growth oaks hung with lacy Spanish moss greets guests at The River Rendezvous, which caters to all kinds of campers and nature enthusiasts. Under new ownership since 2005, the park is being improved, with new full-hookup sites, a swimming pool, recreation room, and synagogue. Sites overlook the Suwannee River, which rings with the sounds of paddlers enjoying themselves on sunny weekends. Nearby are half a dozen springs and caverns suitable for experienced cave divers; Peacock Springs State Park is six miles north of Mayo.

Campsites, facilities: Forty RV sites are available with water, sewer hookups, and 30-amp electricity. Several primitive tent spots are set apart from the RVs. On the premises are showers, restrooms, fire rings, a game room, a sauna and steam room, cabins, motel rooms, one hot tub, a boat ramp, boat and canoe rentals, a playground, horseshoes, volleyball, pavilions, pool tables, a restaurant, a spring for fishing and swimming, and laundry facilities. Children and leashed pets are welcome.

Reservations, fees: Reservations are recommended. Sites are $17 per night for two people, plus $2 per extra person. Credit cards are accepted. Long-term rates are available.

Directions: From Mayo, drive south on U.S. 27 for three miles. Turn left on Convict Springs Road. When the road turns to graded dirt (in about one mile), continue another mile to the park. Alternatively, from Branford, drive north on U.S. 27 for 12.7 miles. Turn right on Convict Springs Road. Proceed two miles to the park.

Contact: The River Rendezvous, 828 Northeast Primrose Road, Mayo, FL 32066, 386/294-2510 or 800/533-5276, fax 386/294-1133.

55 GORNTO SPRINGS PARK

Scenic rating: 6

north of Old Town

Tucked on a rise of oak trees and saw palmetto, this out-of-the-way campground is one of three Dixie County–operated parks on the west side of the Suwannee River. These parks are suitable for canoeists and people who want to get far away from city life. You can swim in the river or launch your canoe and paddle all the way to the Gulf of Mexico. Yes, there is a spring next to the riverbank at Gornto (sometimes spelled Guaranto), and swimmers appreciate the cool water in the hot summer months. The campground is not attended by any managers living on-site.

Campsites, facilities: This small, riverside county park has 24 campsites, some picnic tables, flush toilets (no showers), and a boat ramp. Electricity is available at 10 sites. Bring your own water. Children are welcome. Pets are prohibited, as are alcoholic beverages and firearms.

Reservations, fees: Reservations are not accepted. Sites are $12 per night. An attendant picks up the fee once a day. Credit cards are not accepted. The maximum stay is 14 days.

Directions: From U.S. 19/98 in Old Town, drive north on County Road 349 for 12 miles. Turn east on County Road 353, drive 0.5 mile past Rock Sink Baptist Church, make a sharp right, and follow the pavement until it ends. Continue on the limerock road about two miles to the park.

Contact: Dixie County Commissioner's Office, P.O. Box 2600, Cross City, FL 32628, 352/498-1239.

56 ORIGINAL SUWANNEE RIVER CAMPGROUND

Scenic rating: 8

east of Old Town

Tall oaks cast shade on this waterfront park, which is set on a small peninsula with canal access to the Suwannee River. Boats can be tied up near the campsites in protected waters; boat ramps are nearby. You can fish in the canal from the campground dock or toss in a line all around the 12.5-acre, horseshoe-shaped campground; it's nearly surrounded by water. Twenty sites are pull-through. The park offers plenty of space, so you won't feel crowded next to your neighbor. Favorite things to do include fishing and enjoying the retirement years.

Campsites, facilities: Seventy sites with full hookups accommodate RVs, of which 20 sites are open for overnighters; the rest belong to year-round residents and snowbirds. Both 30-amp and 50-amp electrical service are available. Sites have picnic tables and fire rings, and some have grills. Dialup Internet access is available in the office. Restrooms, showers, laundry facilities, a dump station, boat docks, and a clubhouse are available. Children are welcome. Small, leashed pets (no attack breeds) are permitted.

Reservations, fees: Reservations are recommended. RV sites are $21 per night for two people, plus $2 for each additional person. Kids under age six stay free. Credit cards are accepted. Long-term rates are available.

Directions: From Old Town, drive three miles south on U.S. 19/98. See the park just before you cross the river.

Contact: Original Suwannee River Campground, 28872 Southeast Highway 19, Old Town, FL 32680, 352/542-7680, fax 352/542-0046.

57 OLD TOWN CAMPGROUND 'N' RETREAT
Scenic rating: 6

south of Old Town

Owners Linda and Joe Navatto have made improvements to this oak- and pine-tree-shaded park that welcomes adult vacationers. Since purchasing the property in 1999, they have built two new bathhouses, added a miniature golf area and volleyball field, and upgraded the grounds. If a camper has a sudden health problem, Joe—an emergency medical technician—may be available to assist. The park is situated just three miles from the Suwannee River. Favorite things to do include enjoying the country quiet and sitting around a campfire. Most visitors come from Michigan, Ohio, and Canada.

Campsites, facilities: There are 35 RV grassy sites with 30-amp electrical service, water, fire rings, and picnic tables. Fifteen have sewer hook ups. Sites averaging 40 feet by 100 feet accommodate the largest RVs and slideouts on the market. About 20 tents can be accommodated in a separate area. Restrooms, showers, laundry facilities, cable TV, telephone service, a pavilion, miniature golf, a volleyball field, rental cabins, and horseshoe pits are available. Most areas are wheelchair-accessible. Children under age 16 are not welcome. Leashed pets are permitted.

Reservations, fees: Reservations are recommended. Sites are $15–18 per night for two people, plus $3 per extra person over the age of 5. Credit cards are not accepted. Seasonal stays are allowed. Long-term rates are available.

Directions: From U.S. 19/98 in Old Town, drive about two miles south on County Road 349 to the campground on the east side.

Contact: Old Town Campground 'n' Retreat, 2241 Southeast Highway 349, Old Town, FL 32680, 352/542-9500 or 888/950-2267, fax 352/542-9914, www.oldtowncampground .com.

58 HINTON LANDING
Scenic rating: 7

south of Old Town

Hinton Landing is the nicest of the three Dixie County parks west of the Suwannee. The river flows past your doorstep, perfect for canoeing, and the setting is wooded and peaceful. There's an open-air pavilion with three picnic tables on the high riverbank, a parking area for boat trailers, and two docks, including one that is wheelchair-accessible. Don't expect fancy restrooms, though.

Campsites, facilities: This Dixie County park has 10 sites with non-potable water, picnic tables, and flush toilets (no showers). Some sites have electricity. Most of the park can be used by someone in a wheelchair, including the floating dock, county officials say. Children are welcome. Bring drinking water. Pets are prohibited, as are alcoholic beverages and firearms.

Reservations, fees: Reservations are not accepted. Sites are $12 per night. An attendant picks up the fee once a day. Credit cards are not accepted. Maximum stay is 14 days.

Directions: From U.S. 19/98 in Old Town, drive three miles south on County Road 349. Turn east on County Road 346A and go two miles. Turn south on County Road 317 and drive 0.25 mile to the park.

Contact: Dixie County Commissioner's Office, P.O. Box 2600, Cross City, FL 32628, 352/498-1239.

59 SUWANNEE RIVER HIDEAWAY CAMPGROUND

Scenic rating: 8

south of Old Town

A 1,500-foot boardwalk that meanders through the wetlands and ends at the Suwannee River is the centerpiece of this park on 108 wooded acres. It's the perfect choice for campers who need more developed amenities than Hinton Landing (see previous listing), but seek the tranquility and peace of being near the river and in the woods. A new clubhouse offers space for socializing. Most visitors hail from Michigan, New England, and the Southern states. Favorite things to do are bike riding, bird-watching, and fishing.

Campsites, facilities: There are 50 RV sites with full hookups, including 30-amp and 50-amp electrical service and cable TV. Fourteen primitive sites are set aside for tents. Rigs up to 50 feet long and slideouts can be accommodated. Some sites have concrete patios and picnic tables. Restrooms, showers, laundry facilities, and telephone service are available. On the premises is a picturesque 1920s-style general store that sells ice, camping supplies, and souvenirs. The bathhouse and new clubhouse are wheelchair-accessible. Grocery stores and restaurants are located within three miles. Children are welcome. Leashed pets are permitted.

Reservations, fees: Reservations are recommended. Sites are $15 to $26 per night for two people, plus $2 per extra person over age 10. Fifty-amp service costs an additional $2. Credit cards are accepted. Long-term rates are available.

Directions: From U.S. 19/98 in Old Town, drive three miles south on County Road 349. Turn east on County Road 346A and go one mile to the park entrance on the right.

Contact: Suwannee River Hideaway Campground, P.O. Box 1135, Old Town, FL 32680, 352/542-7800, www.riverhideaway.com.

60 NEW PINE LANDING

Scenic rating: 4

south of Old Town

These tiny sites are clustered around a boat ramp on the Suwannee River in a wooded residential neighborhood of stilt homes. This park's single RV site is too small for most trailers; a county spokesperson figures that the maximum length might be 24 feet. Come well-stocked; groceries can be purchased about 15 miles to the northwest in Cross City or in Chiefland, 25 miles to the northeast. An attendant lives one block away.

Campsites, facilities: There are five sites for tents and one for a small RV, with electricity, picnic tables, and grills. Bring drinking water. Restrooms (no showers) and a boat ramp are available. Children are welcome. Pets are prohibited, as are alcoholic beverages and firearms.

Reservations, fees: Reservations are not accepted. Sites are $12 per night. An attendant picks up the fee once a day. Credit cards are not accepted. Maximum stay is 14 days.

Directions: From U.S. 19/98 in Old Town, drive five miles south on County Road 349. Turn east on New Pine Landing Road (just south of Old Pine Landing Road) and drive 1.5 miles to the campground.

Contact: Dixie County Commissioner's Office, P.O. Box 2600, Cross City, FL 32628, 352/498-1239.

61 YELLOW JACKET CAMPGROUND

Scenic rating: 10

south of Old Town

This enchanting 40-acre campground has been completely renovated since new owners came in a few years ago. They call it an "oasis." Standing on the banks of the Suwannee in this shady, secluded campground, you'll see little but wilderness up and down the river for about a mile in either direction. You can fish for bass or bream in several private ponds or on the river; there are also 85,000 acres of public hunting lands adjacent to the park. But the natural setting doesn't mean you go without amenities—the pool and spa are heated. Launch your boat from the park's own ramp, which is set along 1,300 feet of riverfront. Campers tend to be families, and some bring bicycles to tool around the place. Sites 1–24 overlook the river. While long-term

rates are available, no permanent residents are parked here.

Campsites, facilities: The park offers 66 sites with sewer, water, and 20/30/50-amp electricity, as well as primitive tent camping. Twenty sites are drive-through. Picnic tables, fire pits, restrooms, showers, cottages, a remodeled clubhouse, laundry facilities, a playground, boat and canoe rentals, waterfront decks, and a boat ramp are available. Sites have cable TV, and there is a modem available in the clubhouse. The bathhouse, office, pool areas, and boat docks are wheelchair-accessible. Groceries and restaurants are 10 miles away; malls and hospitals are within 40 miles. Children are welcome. Leashed pets of any size are permitted.

Reservations, fees: Reservations are recommended. Sites are $27 to $37 per night for two people, plus $6 for each additional person. Credit cards are accepted. Long-term rates are available.

Directions: From U.S. 19/98 in Old Town, drive south on County Road 349 for 9.1 miles. Turn left (east) at the sign and drive one mile to the park.

Contact: Yellow Jacket Campground, 55 Southeast 503rd Avenue, Old Town, FL 32680, 352/542-8365, www.yellowjacket-campground.com.

62 HORSESHOE BEACH PARK

Scenic rating: 9

on the Gulf of Mexico, south of Cross City

Campsites are clustered around a sunny circular gravel drive overlooking the Gulf of Mexico in the little fishing community of Horseshoe Beach. Mudflats covered with old oyster shells make swimming difficult, but you'll have great views of the water and several uninhabited spoil islands (sandbars or oyster beds that are visible at low tide). One restaurant is in town; watch the shrimp boats head home every afternoon with their catch.

Campsites, facilities: All 14 RV sites and five tent sites in this Dixie County park have city water and electricity; a few have picnic tables. Restrooms with showers are available. Children are welcome. Pets are prohibited, as are alcoholic beverages and firearms.

Reservations, fees: Reservations are not accepted. Sites are $12 per night. An attendant picks up the fee once a day. Credit cards are not accepted. Maximum stay is 14 days.

Directions: From Cross City, drive south on County Road 351 for 15 miles. Turn right on 8th Avenue in Horseshoe Beach and continue to the park, which is also called Butler Douglas Memorial Park.

Contact: Dixie County Commissioner's Office, P.O. Box 2600, Cross City, FL 32628, 352/498-1239.

63 SHIRED ISLAND PARK

🏊 ♿ 🚐 ⛺

Scenic rating: 9

on the Gulf of Mexico, south of Cross City

Although not an island in the traditional sense of the word, Shired Island (pronounced "shirred") is surrounded by swamps and wetlands. At these prices, it offers one of the best deals in Florida for an island camping experience. The water vistas are spectacular; all around you are the marshy islands of the Lower Suwannee National Wildlife Refuge. Swim in the warm, shallow waters of the Gulf of Mexico, but don't expect white-sand beaches; the sand is more coarse and dark along this stretch of the Big Bend. Many campers set up near one of the six covered picnic pavilions at this county park and use them as outdoor living rooms. A boat ramp is nearby. Bring

everything you need, because stores are 20 miles away in Cross City.

Campsites, facilities: There are 17 RV sites and five tent sites with non-potable water, electricity, picnic tables, and grills. Restrooms with wheelchair-accessible concrete floors are available, but not showers. Bring drinking water. Children are welcome. Pets are prohibited, as are alcoholic beverages and firearms.

Reservations, fees: Reservations are not accepted. Sites are $12 per night. An attendant picks up the fee once a day. Credit cards are not accepted. Maximum stay is 14 days.

Directions: From Cross City, drive south on County Road 351 for seven miles. At County Road 357, turn left (south) and go 11 miles to the park. Don't turn at the boat ramp.

Contact: Dixie County Commissioner's Office, P.O. Box 2600, Cross City, FL 32628, 352/498-1239.

64 MILLER'S MARINE CAMPGROUND

🏊 🚐 🐕 🚐

Scenic rating: 8

in Suwannee

BEST (

There's an RV park here, but the real emphasis is on fishing and houseboating. Miller's Marine rents these floating homes (at least 44 feet long), so you can explore the marshes at the mouth of the Suwannee River where it empties into the Gulf of Mexico. Or travel upstream 70 miles to get a glimpse of what it may have been like when stern-wheelers cruised north at the turn of the century. Fishing boats are also available; anglers catch drum, redfish, sea trout, and tarpon near East Pass. The campsites, which are barely large enough to accommodate a big rig, overlook a river marsh and a canal leading to the Suwannee. Covered boat docks are available at this 16-acre complex, but you are not permitted to park your boat trailer at your site. Most of the park's original 34 camping lots have been converted to condominium ownership.

Campsites, facilities: Eight sunny, grassy, drive-through sites are available with full hookups, 30-amp electricity and cable TV. Restrooms, showers, a dump station, a marina, a boat ramp, cabins, houseboats, picnic tables, docks, fishing guide service, and boat rentals are available. A camp store sells ice, camping supplies, propane, snacks, souvenirs, and bait and tackle. Limited groceries are located within 1.5 miles. The office and store are wheelchair-accessible. Streets are paved. Children are welcome. Leashed pets are permitted.

Reservations, fees: Reservations are recommended. Sites are $30 per night. Credit cards are accepted. Long-term rates are available.

Directions: From U.S. 19/98 in Old Town, drive south on County Road 349 for 23 miles to the park. Turn left at the bridge in Suwannee and follow the sign to Miller's Marine on Big Bradford Road.

Contact: Miller's Marine Campground, P.O. Box 280, Suwannee, FL 32692, 352/542-7349 or 800/458-2628, fax 352/542-3200, www .suwanneehouseboats.com.

GAINESVILLE

© MARILYN MOORE

BEST CAMPGROUNDS

☾ **Biking**
O'Leno State Park, **page 145**
Paynes Prairie Preserve State Park, **page 147**

☾ **Natural Springs**
Ellie Ray's River Landing, **page 142**
Ginnie Springs Resort, **page 144**
Hart Springs Gilchrist County Park, **page 151**
Manatee Springs State Park, **page 151**
Otter Springs RV Resort, **page 152**

☾ **Most Unusual**
Tresca Memorial Park/Advent Christian Village,
  page 139
O'Leno State Park, **page 145**

For campers not in a hurry to get to points south, the Gainesville area is worth a stop. There's much to explore, such as the Suwannee River, historic Cedar Key, several first-rate natural springs, and dozens of great places for viewing wildlife.

On the north side of Gainesville, Devil's Millhopper State Geological Site is a must-see, with its 120-foot-deep sinkhole. Visitors can view plants and animals similar to those in the Appalachian Mountains while following the stairway to the bottom of the hole.

Just south of Gainesville, near Micanopy, is Paynes Prairie State Park. Once called the "great Alachua Savannah," its 22,000 acres hold some roaming bison, but more commonly observed wildlife include sandhill cranes, hawks, and wading birds. You can spend the night in the state park's campground, or there's an overlook at a rest stop on I-75 for those just passing through.

Long before I-75, the oldest federal highway or road in Florida passed near High Springs. The interstate was built in 1824 on the route taken by Franciscan missionaries in the 1590s. It was also one of the major north–south trails used by Florida Indians; Hernando de Soto became the first European to set foot on it, back in 1539.

Ginnie Springs, just east of High Springs, covers 200 acres of wilderness along a two-mile stretch of the lazy Santa Fe River and includes seven bubbling crystal springs. The park hosts one of Florida's most attractive private campgrounds, Ginnie Springs Resort, offering everything from mountain biking to canoeing, kayaking, and diving. The black water of the

Santa Fe continues through Ginnie Springs to nearby O'Leno State Park, meanders through the forest, then actually retreats underground at the "river sink," reappearing three miles later. Many nature trails follow the spot where it disappears.

For those more interested in riding the river than following it, Ichetucknee Springs State Park farther north is a center for the leisurely sport of river tubing, an endeavor that requires little in the way of skill, energy, or equipment – just an old inner tube or float for lounging.

Off the beaten path is the east side of Suwannee River, which flows from north to south into the gulf. Fishing is good along the riverbank for trout, bass, bream, and catfish. Along the river's edge, you may see alligators, turtles, herons, and the occasional manatee. You're more likely to see the elusive sea cow at Manatee Springs State Park, which also provides a fantastic swimming and snorkeling hole. The crystal-clear water bubbles to the surface here, before entering a 1,000-foot run to the Suwannee and the Gulf of Mexico, 23 miles downstream.

At the southern tip of the Gainesville area is Cedar Key, sometimes known as Margaritaville North. Reminiscent of Key West, quaint Cedar Key is home to a colony of artists and fishermen, as well as a history museum and plenty of seafood restaurants, art galleries, and the ubiquitous tourist shops.

If you're too weary to explore the Gainesville area, Lake City is a popular layover off I-75 and I-10 for travelers in a hurry to refuel, restock supplies, and reenergize before hitting the highway again in the morning.

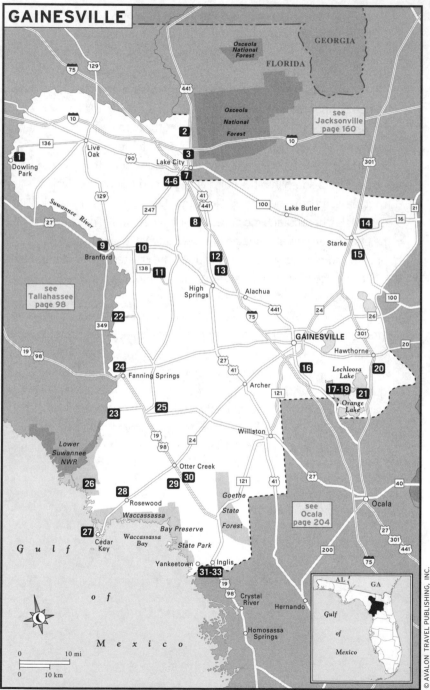

GAINESVILLE

GEORGIA

Osceola National Forest

FLORIDA

Osceola National Forest

75 129

441

10

see Jacksonville page 160

10

1 Dowling Park

136 Live Oak

90 Lake City

2

3

4-6 **7**

41 441

8

100 Lake Butler

301

21

16

14

Starke

15

Suwannee River

129

247

27

9 Branford

10

138 **11**

High Springs

Alachua

441

12

13

24

26

100

see Tallahassee page 98

349

22

75

27

41

GAINESVILLE

301

Hawthorne

20

19 98

24 Fanning Springs

Archer

121

16

Lochloosa Lake

20

17-19

21

Orange Lake

23

25

Williston

19 98

24

see Ocala page 204

27

40

Ocala

Lower Suwannee NWR

Otter Creek

30

121 41

27

301

441

26

28 Rosewood

29

Goethe State Forest

200

75

27 Cedar Key

Waccassassa Bay

Waccassassa Bay Preserve State Park

Yankeetown

Inglis

31-33

19

98 Crystal River

Hernando

G u l f

o f

M e x i c o

Homosassa Springs

0   10 mi

0   10 km

AL   GA

Gulf of Mexico

© AVALON TRAVEL PUBLISHING, INC.

1 TRESCA MEMORIAL PARK/ADVENT CHRISTIAN VILLAGE

🧍 🚴 🏊 🦢 🛶 🐎 🏕 🚐 ⛰️

Scenic rating: 6

southwest of Live Oak

BEST (

The RV park here is part of Advent Christian Village, a 1,000-acre nondenominational retirement community set on the serene Suwannee River. But it is not strictly for seniors—there's also a church youth camp, and children are welcome in the campground. Outdoor recreation amenities abound, including hiking, fishing, and canoeing. There's also exercise equipment in the fitness center. The campground is oriented toward churchgoers, with conference facilities available for conventions, family celebrations, and personal retreats; alcoholic beverages are prohibited. Pastoral and counseling staff are on call. Each year, the village hosts a cultural series featuring theater, music, and dance. Most people staying in the park are building homes in the area.

Campsites, facilities: A retirement community, a youth-oriented church camp, and an RV campground all in one, this park offers 15 RV sites and limited tent-only sites. Eleven pull-through RV sites have full hookups (both 30-amp and 50-amp are available) and cable TV; telephone service can be arranged. On the premises are restrooms, showers, a dump station, two pools, a boat ramp, a dock, canoe rentals, a playground, exercise equipment, horseshoe pits, shuffleboard and tennis courts, a volleyball area, a hiking trail, laundry facilities, and a medical clinic. A grocery store, a post office, a barbershop, and a beauty salon are on the property. Twenty-four-hour security is provided. Children are welcome in the RV park. Pets are permitted.

Reservations, fees: Reservations are not usually necessary, but you can be assured of a spot by calling 800/371-8341. Sites are $19 per night for full hookups, $14 for dry camping. Long-term rates are available.

Directions: From I-10 west of Live Oak, take Exit 258 southbound on State Road 53 for 17 miles to State Road 250. Turn east and drive three miles to the park.

Contact: Tresca Memorial Park/Advent Christian Village, P.O. Box 4320, Dowling Park, FL 32064, 386/658-5200 or 800/371-8341, fax 386/658-5279, www.acvillage.net.

2 LAKE CITY CAMPGROUND

🏊 🏕 🧍 🚐 ⛰️

Scenic rating: 3

in northwest Lake City, off I-10

Located on the outskirts of Osceola National Forest, this 20-acre park is grassy and mostly shaded. Still, it's convenient to the interstate, and you'll find free coffee in the morning. Additional features include a pool and two small ponds, where campers fish or feed ducks. The dirt interior roads lead to grassy sites which are named for native American tribes. It's about 3.5 miles to shopping and restaurants on U.S. 90 in Lake City.

Campsites, facilities: Twelve grassy tent sites have water, electricity, and picnic tables under covered shelters. For RVs, there are 24 sites for overnighters and 15 for seasonal visitors. Most sites have full hookups and 50-amp electrical service; the rest have water and 30-amp electricity. All sites have picnic tables. Cable TV and wireless Internet access are available. On the premises are restrooms, showers, laundry facilities, a pool, a playground, shuffleboard, volleyball, basketball, firewood, propane, and rental cabins. A dial-up Internet connection is available in the clubhouse. The swimming pool is open March 1–October 31. Children are welcome. Leashed pets are permitted.

Reservations, fees: Reservations are recommended for full-hookup sites with cable TV.

Sites are $28–34 per night for two people, plus $2 per additional person over age three. Credit cards are accepted. Long-term rates are available.

Directions: From I-10, take Exit 301 onto northbound U.S. 441, then drive one mile to the park.

Contact: Lake City Campground, 4743 North U.S. Highway 441, Lake City, FL 32055, 386/752-9131 or 866/773-CAMP, fax 386/529-9414, www.lakecitycampground.com.

3 INN AND OUT CAMPGROUND
♒ 🐕 🚐 ⛺

Scenic rating: 2

in Lake City off I-75

Lake City is a popular layover for traveling campers in a hurry to refuel, restock supplies, and reenergize before hitting the highway again in the morning. This park sits atop a hill overlooking the bustling intersection of I-75 and U.S. 90—convenient to restaurants, a large Wal-Mart shopping center, RV repair services, and even a bowling alley and movie theater. Two more perks are that Inn and Out has its own gas station and convenience store on the premises. For late-night arrivals, an attendant is on duty 24 hours. Grassy sites sit aside paved interior roads.

Campsites, facilities: There are 95 campsites with full hookups, 30-amp and 50-amp electrical service, and cable TV. Seventy-eight sites are pull-through. Restrooms, showers, laundry facilities, a dump station, a pool, a gas station, and a 24-hour convenience store are available. Children are welcome. Leashed pets are permitted.

Reservations, fees: Reservations are recommended but not always necessary. Sites are $25 per night. Credit cards are accepted. Long-term rates are available.

Directions: From I-75, take Exit 427 and head east on U.S. 90 for 0.25 mile, then turn south into the park.

Contact: Inn and Out Campground, 3010 U.S. 90 West, Lake City, FL 32055, 386/752-1648.

4 WAYNE'S RV RESORT
♒ 🐕 🚼 ♿ 🚐 ⛺

Scenic rating: 2

in western Lake City, off I-75

This 40-acre park is convenient to the interstate, as well as restaurants and suburban shopping centers on U.S. 90. If you dally on your way down the road, dip into the two swimming pools (one is a kiddie pool), let the kids burn off steam in the campground, and do your laundry. An "adult lounge" keeps non-parents secluded from the kids. About 80 percent of the sites are occupied year-round by local workers.

Campsites, facilities: Most of the 100 campsites have full hookups, 30-amp electrical service, cable TV, and are pull-through. The park has a pool, a playground, volleyball, picnic tables, laundry facilities, limited groceries, propane, a dump station, restrooms, and showers. The restrooms, store, and pool area are wheelchair-accessible. Children are welcome. Leashed pets are permitted.

Reservations, fees: Reservations are recommended. Sites are $22 per night for two people, plus $3 for each additional person and $3 for using air-conditioning or electric heaters. Credit cards are accepted. Long-term rates are available.

Directions: From I-75, take Exit 427 and head west on U.S. 90 for 0.2 mile to the third stoplight. Turn south on County Road 252B.

Contact: Wayne's RV Resort, Inc., 427 Southwest County Road 252B, Lake City, FL 32024, 386/752-5721, fax 386/754-3864.

5 SLOW AND EASY LIVING RV PARK

🏊 🐕 👫 ♿ 🚐

Scenic rating: 2

southwest of Lake City, off I-75

This small RV park offers "country living" within 15 minutes of shopping malls. Convenience to nearby state parks, rivers, and walking trails is another selling factor. Generally, visitors come from all over the United States and Canada to take part in Friday-night cookouts, potluck dinners, and domino games.

Campsites, facilities: Sixteen of the 20 full-hookup sites are drive-through. Ten sites have 30-amp electrical service, and six have 50-amp. Lots are 25 feet wide by 175 feet deep, accommodating large rigs. An Internet connection is available in the clubhouse. Picnic tables, restrooms, showers, and an animal run are on-site. All areas are wheelchair-accessible. Children are welcome. Leashed pets are permitted.

Reservations, fees: Reservations are recommended. Sites are $18 per night for two people, plus $2 per extra person. Credit cards are not accepted. Long-term rates are available.

Directions: From I-75, take Exit 423 onto State Road 47 and drive southwest two miles. Turn left (south) on Southwest Walter Avenue and drive 2.75 miles (the road name changes to Southwest Old Wire Road). If your rig weighs more than eight tons, continue on State Road 47 to Highway 240. Turn left and drive one mile. Turn right on Old Wire Road and proceed 0.75 mile.

Contact: Slow and Easy Living RV Park, 929 Southwest Old Wire Road, Lake City, FL 32024, 386/755-4945 or 877/203-4125, fax 386/719-4446, halw38@aol.com.

6 CASEY JONES CAMPGROUND

🐕 👫 🚐 ⛺

Scenic rating: 2

south of Lake City, off I-75

This well-kept, grassy park offers quick access to I-75. Restrooms are kept clean and stocked, and the proprietors are friendly and helpful. Overnighters may find this spot appealing because it's easy to get in and out of, but a remarkable number of snowbirds have decided to spend winters here on a sunny hill above the interstate. Asked why, one RVer in a new fifth-wheel explained he'd had a heart attack on his last stay here, and spent a month in a hospital in nearby Lake City. After enduring another winter in the Northeast, his wife told him, "Let's just go back to Casey Jones."

Campsites, facilities: The campground has a few tent-only spots and 69 pull-through campsites with full hookups, 30-amp and 50-amp electrical service, cable TV, and a picnic table. Facilities include restrooms, showers, a laundry room, a dump station, and a recreation room. Restaurants and a convenience store are within 0.1 mile. Children are welcome, but the park tends to draw retirees. Leashed pets are permitted.

Reservations, fees: Reservations are recommended, but not required. Sites are $20 per night. Credit cards are accepted. Long-term rates are available.

Directions: From I-75, take Exit 423 onto State Road 47 heading east for 0.1 mile. Turn north at the stoplight and travel 0.2 mile to the park.

Contact: Casey Jones Campground, 185 Southwest Arrowhead Terrace, Lake City, FL 32024, 386/755-0471 or 800/226-5559.

7 LAKE CITY RV PARK

Scenic rating: 1

south of Lake City off I-75

This one-acre park provides a shady layover for interstate travelers, but there are no restrooms or showers. Groceries, restaurants, and laundry facilities are available off the interstate within two miles of the campground. About half the park is occupied year-round.

Campsites, facilities: Ten sites have full hookups, 50-amp electrical service, and cable TV. A dump station is available, but there are no restrooms or showers, so campers must be self-contained. Children are welcome. Leashed pets are permitted.

Reservations, fees: Reservations are not necessary. Sites are $17 per night. Credit cards are not accepted.

Directions: From I-75, take Exit 427 and head east on U.S. 90 to U.S. 41. Drive two miles south to the campground.

Contact: Lake City RV Park, 2463 Southwest Main Boulevard, Lake City, FL 32025, 386/755-0110.

8 E-Z STOP RV PARK

Scenic rating: 1

south of Lake City off I-75

Guests at this pine- and oak-shaded park enjoy some easy pull-through sites big enough to accommodate 42-foot rigs, as well as convenient access to gas stations and restaurants. Lots of overnighters stay here, but long-term campers toss horseshoes, play basketball, use the grill, or browse the aisles of antiques at the shops next door. About half the occupants live here year-round.

Campsites, facilities: Twelve of these 25 RV sites are pull-through, full-hookup spots with 30-amp and 50-amp; the rest have water and electricity only. Lots are about 70 feet deep. Restrooms, showers, picnic tables, horseshoes, basketball, a barbecue area, and a dump station are available. Need a haircut? A barbershop and beauty salon are on the premises. Children are welcome. Leashed pets are permitted.

Reservations, fees: Reservations are not necessary. Sites are $17–20 per night for two people, plus $2 per additional person. Credit cards are not accepted. Long-term rates are available.

Directions: From I-75, take Exit 414 southbound onto U.S. 41 for 0.1 mile, then turn west on Howell Street and proceed 500 feet to the park.

Contact: E-Z Stop RV Park, 181 Southwest Howell Street, Lake City, FL 32024, 386/752-2279.

9 ELLIE RAY'S RIVER LANDING

Scenic rating: 9

west of High Springs

BEST (

Set on the banks of the Santa Fe River, this nature-oriented campground is popular with families, hunters, and canoeists. It's close to Ichetucknee Springs (see next listing), which is famed for tubing trips, and convenient to antique stores in High Springs. Also nearby is the Waccasassa Plantation, a commercial hunting and shooting attraction (www.wplantation.com). Perhaps the most notable feature of Ellie Ray's is the spring-fed swimming area, which is surrounded by tall trees. The banks are shallow enough for child swimmers.

Campsites, facilities: Ten tents can be accommodated in a shady grassy area with no hookups. The tent area is set apart from the 99 RV sites, which have full hookups and 30/50-amp electrical service. Each RV site has patios, and most campsites are shady. On the premises are restrooms, showers, a riverside swimming area, a floating boat dock, a horseshoe pit, a board-

© MARILYN MOORE

paddling along the Santa Fe River

walk, and laundry facilities. Only two people are allowed per tent. Children are welcome. Leashed pets are permitted; however, barking will not be tolerated, and all pets must have proof of vaccination.

Reservations, fees: Reservations are recommended, especially on holiday weekends. Sites are $27 per night for two adults and two children under the age of 12, plus $10 for each additional person. Rates are subject to change.

Directions: From the north, take I-75 to Exit 427 in Lake City and drive west on U.S. 90 for 0.4 mile. Turn south onto Country Road 252B and drive 2.2 miles. At State Road 247, turn west. Drive 14.5 miles to County Road 49/Highway 129 and turn south. Proceed seven miles to the park, which is just across the Santa Fe River bridge. If traveling from the south, take I-75 to Exit 399. Drive northwest on U.S. 441 for 5.5 miles. At State Road 41 (Main Street), turn west and drive 0.2 mile to the first traffic light. At U.S. 27, turn northwest and proceed 19.6 miles, driving through the towns of High Springs and Fort White. At Highway 129, turn south and travel 3.8 miles to the park.

Contact: Ellie Ray's River Landing, 3349 Northwest 110th Street, Branford, FL 32008, 386/935-9518, fax 386/935-4190.

10 ICHETUCKNEE SPRINGS CAMPGROUND

Scenic rating: 9

near Fort White, off I-75

Rustic, forested Ichetucknee Springs Campground covers 20 acres, complete with a tavern serving up pizza, nachos, and other munchies. The emphasis is on family fun; there's even an annual New Year's Eve party. Groups can rent the entire campground during off-season, and some visitors stay here while their homes are being built nearby. But the main attraction is next door: Ichetucknee Springs State Park, a hot spot for the leisurely sport of river tubing. Deepwater springs pump 233 million gallons a day into the Ichetucknee River, creating a gin-clear waterway so remarkable that the main spring was declared a National Natural Landmark in 1972. The waters draw thousands to the state park each year for tubing, an endeavor that requires little in the way of skill, energy, or equipment—just an old inner tube or float for lounging. You'll drift 3.5 miles past limestone outcrops under a canopy of oak and cypress. Occasionally, an alligator or snake can be spotted, and caution is advised. Tubing is permitted from 8 A.M. until sunset.

Launch at one of three drop sites: at the north entrance, the south entrance, or a midpoint drop-off open only during peak periods. From the south entrance, the river ride lasts 60–90 minutes. A free shuttle tram, which operates May–September, returns tubers to the starting point. The ride from the north entrance is the longest-lasting—from two to three hours—and so popular that the park limits the trip to 750 tubers a day. Return shuttle service also is available. Inner tubes can be rented at the campground and dropped off at the end of the ride.

A few pointers: Start early to avoid the crowds. Stick together because it's easy to get separated. Children and non-swimmers should wear flotation vests. Bring along a pair of old sneakers or other footwear for the walk to the shuttle trams. A few rules: Food, drink, alcohol, tobacco, and disposable items are prohibited on the river. Climbing and jumping from riverbanks, trees, and docks are strictly forbidden. Respect the environment and your fellow tubers—avoid stirring up the river bottom with swim fins.

Campsites, facilities: There are 17 sites with 30-amp electricity and water in this 20-acre wooded park. Five sites are drive-through. Some of the 30 tent-only sites are large enough to accommodate several tents. Restrooms, showers, a dump station, a tavern, two game rooms, a volleyball field, a basketball court, and horseshoe pits are on-site. The campsites, bathrooms, showers, and tavern/restaurant are wheelchair-accessible. Canoes, inner tubes, and snorkeling equipment may be rented. Groceries and stores are 15 miles away. Children are welcome. Leashed pets are permitted.

Reservations, fees: Reservations are recommended. Sites are $10 per night for two people, plus $4 for each extra adult, $2 for each child, and $5 for electricity. Credit cards are not accepted.

Directions: From I-75 southbound, take Exit 423 onto State Road 47 and drive south for 14 miles to Elim Church Road/County Road 238. Turn west and drive 3.5 miles to Breckenridge Lane. Turn right at the park. From I-75 northbound, take Exit 399 onto U.S. 441, then merge with U.S. 27 North for 2.5 miles and go west on Elim Church Road. Go west for 3.5 miles to Breckenridge Lane, and look for the park sign on your right.

Contact: Ichetucknee Springs Campground, 245 Southwest Breckenridge Lane, Fort White, FL 32038, 386/497-2285.

11 GINNIE SPRINGS RESORT

🥾 🚴 🏊 🎣 🛶 🤿 💆 🚐 ⛰️

Scenic rating: 10

near High Springs

BEST (

For active campers, this is one of Florida's most attractive campgrounds, offering everything from mountain biking to canoeing, kayaking, and diving. The park covers 200 acres of wilderness along a two-mile stretch of the lazy Santa Fe River and includes seven crystal springs, all bubbling away at a constant water temperature of 72°F. Rent or bring your own rubber raft (get free air refills here) for a refreshing hour-long float down the Santa Fe on a hot summer day. For really adventurous visitors, the park offers instruction in underwater cavern and cave exploration.

Campsites, facilities: In addition to nearly 300 tent sites (which have spigots), there are 92 RV sites with water and electricity. Half have 50-amp service. All sites have picnic tables and grills. Some are set in the woods or have water views. Rigs up to 40 feet long can be accommodated. Group sites are available. Restrooms, showers, laundry facilities, a restaurant, two rental cottages, five covered picnic pavilions each located next to a spring, beach-style volleyball courts, a playground, firewood, and a country store are located on the premises. The bathhouses are heated during the winter. Also available is a full complement of recreational sports services, including scuba diving and underwater cave exploration for certified divers. Canoes, kayaks, inner tubes, and diving equipment can be rented here. Groceries and restaurants are eight miles away. Children are welcome. Pets are not permitted.

Reservations, fees: Reservations are highly recommended. Sites are $32 per night for two people and $16 for each additional person. Younger children camp for free. Electricity costs an additional $6 per site. Credit cards are accepted.

Directions: From I-75, take Exit 399 onto U.S. 441, then go five miles north to the town of High Springs. At the first stoplight in High Springs (at the Hardee's), turn left. Continue through the next stoplight, at the center of town, and go approximately 0.5 mile to the turnoff for County Road 340/NE 182nd Avenue. (You will see a sign on top of a pole indicating that this is the turnoff for Ginnie, Blue, and Poe Springs.) Turn right onto

County Road 340 and go approximately 6.5 miles, to the sign indicating the turnoff to Ginnie Springs (NE 60th Avenue). Turn right and drive approximately one mile to the Ginnie Springs entrance.

Contact: Ginnie Springs Resort, 7300 Northeast Ginnie Springs Road, High Springs, FL 32643, 386/454-7188, fax 386/454-2085, www.ginniespringsoutdoors.com.

12 O'LENO STATE PARK

Scenic rating: 10

north of High Springs, off I-75

BEST (

Always magical, this place is especially so in the cooler months, when it's quiet and uncrowded. The park encompasses 6,400 acres of hardwood forest flush with deer and other wildlife, miles of service roads great for mountain biking, and a historic wooden suspension bridge built by the Civilian Conservation Corps in the 1930s. The blackwater Santa Fe River meanders through the forest, then actually goes underground at the "river sink" and reappears three miles later. Hike along one of the many nature trails to the spot where it disappears, but don't expect drama; the water gathers in a wide lake and seeps into the ground so slowly that algae grows across the top.

You can swim or canoe on the river, a tributary of the Suwannee; canoes are available for rent. Rangers say the river is an unpredictable fishing spot, but you may see alligators and turtles while trying your luck. Campsites are split between two areas: the Dogwood Camp and the Magnolia Camp. The heart of the park is an assortment of 1930s-era buildings and newer cabins at the point where the bridge crosses the river. Near this spot in the mid-1800s stood a lumber town perhaps called Keno (as in the game of chance), and later known as Old Leno. All that remains is a mill dam and an old road. Groceries, laundry facilities, and restaurants are available six miles from the park.

Campsites, facilities: This state park campground has 61 sites with water, 30/50-amp electricity, picnic tables, grills, and fire rings. Restrooms, showers, a dump station, a playground, and hiking and horseback-riding trails are available. Children are welcome. Pets are prohibited.

Reservations, fees: Reservations are accepted. Sites are $15 per night for up to eight people. Credit cards are accepted. Maximum stay is 14 days.

© MARILYN MOORE

the old hanging bridge at O'Leno State Park

Directions: From I-75 southbound, take Exit 414 onto U.S. 441 and drive five miles south to the park. From I-75 northbound, take Exit 399 onto U.S. 441 and drive 15 miles west and north to the park.

Contact: O'Leno State Park, Route 2, P.O. Box 1010, High Springs, FL 32643, 386/454-1853, www.floridastateparks.org.

13 HIGH SPRINGS CAMPGROUND

Scenic rating: 9

east of High Springs, near I-75

With tall oaks, a natural setting, and a secluded location, this place will remind you more of a state park than a privately operated campground. Sites are shaded and thoughtfully laid out; 18 are pull-through, and even big rigs can be accommodated. About a third of the park is occupied by year-round residents. This makes a good overnight spot for I-75 travelers—indeed, most guests are overnighters—but it's also a good base for exploring High Springs' antiques shops, the museums of Gainesville 17 miles to the south, and the O'Leno, Ichetucknee Springs, and Paynes Prairie State Parks. Groceries and restaurants are located within four miles. The campground is located on the oldest federal highway or road in Florida, built in 1824 on the route taken by Franciscan missionaries in the 1590s. (Three of the missions they built were within 15 miles of this campground.) It was also one of the major north–south trails used by Florida Indians; Hernando de Soto became the first European to set foot on it, back in 1539.

Campsites, facilities: There are 45 RV sites with full hookups and 30-amp electrical service, plus five tent areas. Most sites have concrete picnic tables and fire rings. Restrooms, showers, laundry facilities, a dump station, a pool, and a playground are available. All areas are said to be wheelchair-accessible. Streets are paved. Children are welcome. Leashed pets are permitted.

Reservations, fees: Reservations are not necessary. Sites are $22 per night for four people, plus $2 for each additional person. Credit cards are not accepted. Long-term rates are available.

Directions: From I-75 north of Alachua, take Exit 404 and drive west on County Road 236 for 0.1 mile. Turn north onto Old Bellamy Road and drive 1,000 feet to the campground, on the left.

Contact: High Springs Campground, 24004 Northwest Old Bellamy Road, High Springs, FL 32643, 386/454-1688, www.highsprings-campground.com.

14 BRADFORD MOTEL AND CAMPGROUND

Scenic rating: 2

north of Starke

This urban park is set in a partially wooded area behind a motel and near restaurants and shops; about half the sites are occupied year-round. Just north of the campground is the little burg of Lawtey. Drive slowly, because it's known as a speed trap. Starke is a good starting point for exploring this off-the-tourist-track area, which is famous for extra-sweet strawberries, timber (half of Bradford County is heavily forested), lake fishing, hunting, and agriculture. Outside Florida, Starke may be more familiar as a newspaper dateline when there's an execution at the Florida State Prison in Raiford. On execution days, reporters and protesters pour into Starke, the nearest big town.

Campsites, facilities: There are 33 shady full-hookup campsites, including 8 that are drive-through and two for tents. RVs up to 35 feet long can be accommodated; about 12 sites are available for overnighters. Restrooms, showers, a laundry room, and a dump station are on the grounds. Restaurants and shops are within 0.5 mile. The bathhouse is wheelchair-accessible. Children and leashed pets are welcome.

Reservations, fees: Reservations are recommended. Sites are $20 per night for two people, plus $3 for each additional person. Credit cards are accepted. Long-term rates are available.

Directions: From I-75, take Exit 414 northbound on U.S. 441 for 0.25 mile. Turn east on State Road 238 and drive 13 miles to the town of Lake Butler. Continue east on State Road 100 for 15 miles into Starke. Turn north on U.S. 301; the park is on the north side of town.

Contact: Bradford Motel and Campground, 1757 North Temple Avenue, Starke, FL 32091, 904/964-5332, fax 904/964-2026.

15 STARKE KOA

Scenic rating: 6

south of Starke

This KOA offers easy access to several fishing lakes nearby, and to Gainesville, Jacksonville, and Kingsley Lake. The owners, the four-generation Steffen family, have a full schedule of activities planned for their guests, including bingo, potluck dinners, Sunday-morning breakfasts, and hobo-stew dinner around the campfire. Nearly 75 people came for turkey and all the trimmings on one recent Thanksgiving Day. Note that the pool is not open January–March. The Starke golf course is nearby, but the favorite things to do are going to the local flea markets and out to eat. Restaurants are within less than a mile.

Campsites, facilities: There are 136 sites, plus a separate camping area with fire rings, electricity and water accommodating 10 tents.

The RV section has full hookups, 30-amp and 50-amp electrical service, cable TV, and picnic tables. About 25 percent of the sites are occupied year-round. RVs up to 48 feet long and slideouts can be accommodated. Restrooms, showers, laundry facilities, a pool, a recreation hall, and a store are available. An Internet connection is available in the office. The clubhouse, restrooms, and recreation hall are wheelchair-accessible. Children are welcome. Leashed pets are permitted.

Reservations, fees: Reservations are recommended. Sites are $30–40 per night for two people, plus $3 for each additional person. Rates are likely to be higher during the annual Gatornational drag races in March. Credit cards are accepted. Long-term rates are available.

Directions: From the intersection of U.S. 301 and State Road 100 in Starke, drive south on U.S. 301 for 1.5 miles to the campground.

Contact: Starke KOA, 1475 South Walnut Street, Starke, FL 32091, 904/964-8484 or 800/KOA-8498 (800/562-8498), www .starkekoa.com.

16 PAYNES PRAIRIE PRESERVE STATE PARK

Scenic rating: 10

near Micanopy, south of Gainesville

BEST (

Would you ever expect to see bison in Florida? At Paynes Prairie, wild bison still roam this 22,000-acre park, once called the "great Alachua Savannah." More commonly observed wildlife includes sandhill cranes, hawks, and wading birds. Hook up with a ranger-led nature walk, or venture out on one of the many trails. Foot traffic only is allowed on the 2.5-mile La Chua Trail and the short (0.3-mile) Wacahoota Trail. Hikers, mountain bikers, and horseback riders share the path as they travel through 6.5 miles of shady hammock, pine flat woods, and old fields on the Chacala Trail. At Cone's Dike, hikers and mountain bikers have access to the 8.24-mile trail that heads out into the marsh; wear a hat, because there is no shade. Cyclists can also use the paved park road from the campground to the visitors center, where an observation tower provides views of the vast prairie.

Anglers and canoeists have access to Lake Wauberg at a boat ramp near the camping area. Common catches are bream, bass, and speckled perch. On the north side of the park at the Boulware Springs Trailhead is the terminus for the 17-mile Gainesville-to-Hawthorne walking, biking, and horseback-riding trail. The campground is 10 miles south of Gainesville, home to the University of Florida and the Florida Museum of Natural History. Don't miss seeing Devil's Millhopper State Geological Site on the north side of town. There's a 120-foot-deep sinkhole with a stairway to the bottom; on the way down, you'll see plants and animals similar to those in the Appalachian Mountains.

Campsites, facilities: There are 35 RV sites and 15 tent sites, all with water and 30-amp electricity. Picnic tables, lantern posts, grills, fire rings, a dump station, a boat ramp, a visitors center with an observatory, and 25 miles of hiking, horseback-riding, and bicycling trails are in the park. The campground and visitors center are wheelchair-accessible. Children are welcome. Pets are prohibited.

Reservations, fees: Reservations are recommended; contact ReserveAmerica at 800/336-3521 or reserveamerica.com. Sites are $15 per night for up to eight people. Credit cards are accepted. The maximum stay is 14 days.

Directions: From I-75, take Exit 374 eastbound for 0.5 mile to U.S. 441 in Micanopy. Turn north on U.S. 441 and drive 0.6 mile to the park.

Contact: Paynes Prairie Preserve State Park, 100 Savannah Boulevard, Micanopy, FL 32667, 352/466-3397, fax 352/466-4297, www.floridastateparks.org.

17 RANCH MOTEL AND CAMPGROUND

Scenic rating: 2

in Hawthorne

"Close to everything and friendly" is how the owners of this motel/RV park complex describe their property. The motel has only 12 rooms, so the RV park is a dominant feature, not an afterthought. With 15 fishing lakes within three miles, the park attracts anglers and seasonal visitors.

Campsites, facilities: There are 30 RV sites (12 pull-through) with full hookups and 5 tent sites with water. All have 30-amp electricity and picnic tables. Restrooms, showers, laundry facilities, cable TV, and telephone service are available. Most areas are wheelchair-accessible. Children are welcome. Leashed pets are permitted.

Reservations, fees: Reservations are recommended. Sites are $18 per night. Credit cards are accepted. Long-term rates are available.

Directions: From the intersection of U.S. 301 and State Road 20 in Hawthorne, drive 0.75 mile south on U.S. 301 to the park.

Contact: Ranch Motel and Campground, P.O. Box 806, 8010 Southeast U.S. Highway 301, Hawthorne, FL 32640, 352/481-3851, fax 352/481-3562.

18 LOCHLOOSA HARBOR RV PARK

Scenic rating: 7

south of Hawthorne

Fishing and boating are the names of the game at this campground, which has a boat ramp (open 24 hours, seven days a week) and marina with access to Lochloosa Lake. The 6,000-acre lake, connected to Orange Lake via Cross Creek, is considered one of the best fishing spots in Florida. Lucky anglers will hook shellcracker, bass, bream, or crappie. Watch for alligators; you won't want to swim here. The park has a bait and tackle shop and convenience store with limited groceries.

Campsites, facilities: Of the 35 RV sites, 10 full-hookup spots with satellite TV service are available for overnighters. Ten grassy tent sites have water and electricity. On the premises are restrooms, showers, a dump station, a boat ramp, boat slips, a dock, boat rentals, laundry facilities, cabin rentals, and a store. Children are welcome. Pets are permitted.

Reservations, fees: Reservations are recommended. Sites are $22 per night for two people, plus $10 for each additional person. Long-term rates are available.

Directions: From the intersection of U.S. 301 and State Road 20 in Hawthorne, drive 8.5 miles south on U.S. 301 to the park.

Contact: Lochloosa Harbor RV Park, 15008 Southeast U.S. 301, Hawthorne, FL 32640, 352/481-2114, www.lochloosaharbor.com.

19 TWIN LAKES FISH CAMP
🐕 ♿ 🚐 ⛺

Scenic rating: 4

Just north of Cross Creek, halfway between Gainesville and Ocala

Located on Cross Creek, which flows into Lake Lochloosa and Orange Lake, the campground attracts anglers interested in catching bass or crappie. You also can photograph an eagle on the wing or watch a sunset over the water. Cross Creek is famous as the home of Marjorie Kinnan Rawlings, Pulitzer Prize–winning author of *The Yearling*. You can tour the home at the Marjorie Kinnan Rawlings State Historic Site, 1.5 miles from the campground. The Cracker-style house comprises three separate structures connected by screen porches and open verandas, all designed to take advantage of cooling breezes. The house is closed to the public on Mondays, Tuesdays,

and Wednesdays and during August and September. Restaurants are nearby, and the Yearling Restaurant, which is 0.5 mile from the park, offers a variety of dishes from seafood to venison. The park is near the rails-to-trails bike path and Micanopy's fall antiques and arts-and-crafts festivals.

Campsites, facilities: The 15 RV sites have full hookups and 30-amp electricity; five grassy tent sites come with water and electricity. RVs up to 36 feet long and slideouts can be accommodated, but overnight spaces are limited. Picnic tables, restrooms, showers, a dump station, laundry facilities, cabins, and snacks are available. All areas of the park are said to be wheelchair-accessible. Children are welcome. Leashed pets are permitted.

Reservations, fees: Reservations are recommended. Sites are $18 per night for two people, plus $2 for each additional person. Credit cards are not accepted. Long-term rates are available. The campground is closed Christmas Day, Easter weekend, and Thanksgiving Day.

Directions: From I-75, take Exit 374 eastbound for 0.5 mile on County Road 346 into Micanopy. Continue east for five miles until County Road 346 dead-ends at County Road 325. Turn south and drive three miles. The campground is one mile north of the hamlet of Cross Creek.

Contact: Twin Lakes Fish Camp, 17105 South County Road 325, Hawthorne, FL 32640, 352/466-3194.

20 ELITE RESORTS AT LITTLE ORANGE LAKE
🚴 🏊 🐟 🛶 🐕 🚐 ⛺

Scenic rating: 6

south of Hawthorne

Set on 800-acre Little Orange Lake, this resort boasts a 130-foot fishing pier and water sports. Formerly the Gator Landing Golf Club and Campground, the park was acquired in 2005 by the Elite Resorts chain, and improvements are planned. The park was closed as of May 2006 but is due to reopen; call ahead for updated information.

Campsites, facilities: All sites have water and electricity, and some have full hookups. Oversized sites are 40 by 70 feet. Restrooms, showers, a dump station, a pool, a dock, a lake, a dog-walk area, and a boat ramp are on the premises. Children are welcome. Leashed pets up to about 50 pounds are permitted; no Rottweilers, Doberman pinschers, or pit bulls are allowed.

Reservations, fees: Reservations are recommended. Sites are $14–20 per night for two people, plus $1 per extra person and $1 for 50-amp service. Rates are subject to change. Credit cards are not accepted. Long-term stays are allowed.

Directions: From the intersection of U.S. 301 and State Road 20, drive south on U.S. 301 across the railroad tracks. Take the first left and go 1.3 miles on Holden Park Road.

Contact: Elite Resorts at Little Orange Lake, 8815 Holden Park Road, Hawthorne, FL 32640, 352/481-5547 or 352/685-1900, www.eliteresorts.com.

21 LOCHLOOSA WILDLIFE CONSERVATION AREA

Scenic rating: 7

surrounding Lochloosa Lake, southwest of Hawthorne

Not too long a drive from author Marjorie Kinnan Rawlings' historic home/museum at Cross Creek, this 27,327-acre conservation area offers rustic camping on the shore of Lochloosa Lake. More than 20 miles of meandering trails can be used for hiking, bicycling, or horseback riding. Along the way, you might spy some of the rare or endangered resident critters, such as black bear, sandhill cranes, wood storks, and fox squirrels, among others. Seasonal hunting is allowed in nearly half the area. Much of this land was owned by Georgia-Pacific Corp. until 1995, when the St. Johns River Water Management District bought it to protect the environmentally sensitive watershed and preserve the shoreline. A fishing pier was built after the property changed hands. After all, this is all part of the Orange Lake basin, and nearby angler haven Orange Lake (to the west, on the other side of Cross Creek) was deemed an Outstanding Florida Water site by the state in 1987. Don't be too surprised if you see some forestry work going on in this conservation area; through the sales agreement, Georgia-Pacific is allowed to continue operating here, although with some restrictions.

Campsites, facilities: Tents only are permitted at this primitive camping area. An observation deck is provided, and four boat ramps here or nearby provide access to the area. There are no restrooms or other facilities. Bring food, water, mosquito repellent, and everything you'll need. Children are welcome. Leashed pets are permitted. Camping is not allowed during hunting season.

Reservations, fees: Sites are first-come, first-served. Camping is free. If your party has at least seven people, get a free permit and reserve at least one week ahead at 386/329-4883. Maximum stay for all campers is seven days.

Directions: From Hawthorne, go south on US 301 to the entrance at right. The entrance is less than two miles north of Highway 325 and a little more than eight miles south of the Gainesville-Hawthorne State Trail. Alternatively, if you're arriving from the town of Cross Creek, drive nearly six miles southeast on County Road 325, turn north (left) onto US 301, and continue less than two miles to the entrance at left.

Contact: St. Johns River Water Management District, Division of Land Management, P.O. Box 1429, Palatka, FL 32178-1429; tel. 386/329-4500 or 800/451-7106, www.sjrwmd.com.

22 HART SPRINGS GILCHRIST COUNTY PARK

🚶 🏊 ⚓ 🚣 🏕 🐕 🧑‍🦽 🚐 ⛺

Scenic rating: 9

near Trenton

BEST (

Bordering this sprawling 400-acre park is the Suwannee River, a beautiful spot with bubbling springs and a beach for swimming and snorkeling. Fishing is good along the riverbank for bass, bream, and catfish; there's also a boat ramp. A 0.5-mile-long, wheelchair-accessible boardwalk meanders along the river's edge for a view of alligators, turtles, herons, and the occasional manatee. The campground is nestled under spreading oaks. The park is staffed around the clock by an attendant who lives here.

Campsites, facilities: There are 70 full-hookup RV sites with 30/50-amp electricity and 50 grassy tent sites. Restrooms, showers, volleyball courts, a boat ramp, a snack bar, playground, and both open-air and closed pavilions for group activities are available. Most areas are wheelchair-accessible. Children are welcome. Pets are allowed. Alcohol is prohibited.

Reservations, fees: Reservations are not necessary. Sites are $20 per night for four people, plus $2 for each additional person. Credit cards are not accepted. Long-term rates are available.

Directions: From I-75 north of Gainesville, take Exit 387 onto State Road 26 and drive west for 32 miles, through Trenton, then turn right on County Road 232 and head north for 4 miles. Turn left (west) on County Road 344 for 0.7 mile to the park.

Contact: Hart Springs Gilchrist County Park, 4240 Southwest 86th Avenue, Bell, FL 32619, 352/463-3444, www.hartsprings.com.

23 MANATEE SPRINGS STATE PARK

🚶 🚴 🏊 🚣 🚤 🎿 🏕 🐕 🧑‍🦽 🚐 ⛺

Scenic rating: 10

near Chiefland, west of U.S. 19/98

BEST (

One of the gems of Florida's state park network, Manatee Springs encompasses 2,373 acres of heavily wooded hammock dressed in Spanish moss beside the lower Suwannee River. A nature trail and boardwalk lead to the scenic, meandering waterway; at the end is a boat dock, a launch pad for canoeing and fishing expeditions. And more natural wonders await within the park's boundaries: Manatee Springs is a fantastic swimming and snorkeling hole, where 117 million gallons of crystal-clear water bubble to the surface every day, then wash down a thousand-foot run to the Suwannee and the Gulf of Mexico, 23 miles downstream. Occasionally, manatees can be seen from the banks, especially during the winter months. Certified divers can explore underground caverns that link a series of sinkholes. Divers must register at the ranger station. More than eight miles of trails for hikers and mountain bikers wind through the park. Keep on the lookout for red-shouldered hawks, and keep an ear cocked at night for the eerie hoots of barred owls. Just one word of warning about this pretty place: Ticks and chiggers can be a nuisance during the summer months. First aid is available at the ranger station.

Campsites, facilities: The park has 94 sites with water, 30-amp electricity, fire grills, and picnic tables. Two of the sites are 50-amp. RVs up to 35 feet long can be accommodated. On the premises are showers, restrooms, a dump station, playgrounds, a snack bar, a canoe rental concession, nature trails, horseshoe pits, and volleyball courts. The docks, bathhouse, office, and store are wheelchair-accessible. Golf, groceries, restaurants, and laundry facilities are located within six miles. Children are welcome. Pets are allowed with proof of vaccination.

Reservations, fees: Reservations are recommended; contact ReserveAmerica at 800/336-3521 or reserveamerica.com. Sites are $16 per night for up to eight people. Credit cards are accepted. The maximum stay is 14 days.

Directions: From U.S. 19/98 in Chiefland, turn west on State Road 320 and drive six miles to the park.

Contact: Manatee Springs State Park, 11650 Northwest 115th Street, Chiefland, FL 32626, 352/493-6072, fax 352/493-6089, www .floridastateparks.org. Additional information can be obtained from Suwannee Basin GEOpark, 11650 Northwest 115th Street, Chiefland, FL 32626, 352/493-6072.

24 OTTER SPRINGS RV RESORT

Scenic rating: 10

northwest of Fanning Springs

BEST (

Otter Springs is a lovely place that boasts one mile of frontage on the east bank of the Suwannee River and two natural springs. These 820 acres of woods have access to the Suwannee River for boating, canoeing, bird-watching, and fishing. One spring empties into the Suwannee after a mile-long run through the park; the other is about 30 yards in size. New owners have made vast improvements; the park had been closed for more than five years and reopened in 2005. The word is not out yet, so you can be among the first to tell your friends. The park is equestrian-friendly, and the owners allow people to ride their horses on the trails.

Campsites, facilities: There are 110 drive-through campsites with sewer hookups, water, and 50-amp electricity, of which 10 only have water and electric. Most have fire rings and picnic tables. Even the largest RVs can be accommodated. You can access the Internet in the office. There are restrooms, showers, laundry facilities, a pool, a lodge with a wrap-around porch, cabin rentals, a boat launch, and a dock for small boats, canoes, or kayaks. A store that sells ice and limited supplies, a game room, a screened picnic pavilion, a pool, a playground, and canoe rentals are on-site. The lodge and the pool area are wheelchair-accessible. A church is on the premises; management requests "proper attire and conduct." Groceries are 10 miles away in Chiefland, and restaurants are within four miles in Fanning Springs. Children are welcome. Leashed pets (but no attack dogs) are permitted.

Reservations, fees: Reservations are not necessary. Sites are $20 per night for a family of four people, plus $3 for electricity and $4 for each additional person. Rates are subject to change. Credit cards are not accepted. Long-term rates are available.

Directions: From the intersection of U.S. 19/98 in Fanning Springs, drive east one mile on State Road 26. At State Road 232, turn left on Southwest 70th Street and continue about one to the entrance.

Contact: Otter Springs RV Resort, 6470 Southwest 80th Avenue, Trenton, FL 32693, 352/463-0800 or 800/883-9107, fax 352/463-0575, www.ottersprings.com.

25 BREEZY ACRES CAMPGROUND

Scenic rating: 4

near Chiefland, on Alternate U.S. 27

This tranquil, sunny park in the countryside caters to seniors, with coffee-and-doughnut socials on Saturday mornings and cozy pot-luck dinners on Wednesday nights. Other favorite things to do are enjoying the peace and quiet.

Campsites, facilities: You'll be out in the country sleeping at one of the park's 50 large, grassy RV sites with full hookups. Eight sites have 50-amp electrical service, and the rest have 30-amp. On the premises are showers, restrooms, laundry facilities, a dump station, a recreation room, horseshoe pits, and shuffleboard courts. The bathhouse, clubhouse, and office are wheelchair-accessible. Children are permitted for short visits. Leashed pets are allowed.

Reservations, fees: Reservations are recommended. Sites are $14 per night for four people, plus $1 for each additional person and $1 for using air conditioners. Credit cards are not accepted. Long-term rates are available.

Directions: From U.S. 19/98 in Chiefland, turn east on Alternate U.S. 27 and drive seven miles to the park.

Contact: Breezy Acres Campground, 10050 Northeast 20th Avenue, Chiefland, FL 32626, 352/493-7602.

26 SHELL MOUND COUNTY PARK

Scenic rating: 9

outside Cedar Key

This little treasure is a favorite for locals, but often overlooked by travelers exploring nearby Cedar Key. Here you can camp beneath gnarled oaks in the heart of the Lower Suwannee River National Wildlife Refuge, a 52,000-acre parcel of dry scrub, bottomland hardwoods, cypress swamp, and coastal marshes that teems with more than 250 species of birds, reptiles, and mammals, including American bald eagles, eastern indigo snakes, Atlantic Ripley turtles, gopher tortoises, bobcats, red foxes, and white-tailed deer. The refuge stretches for 26 miles along the Gulf of Mexico and offers plenty of paved roadways, scenic overlooks, and trails for animal lovers who want to observe wildlife. For more information, contact the refuge manager at 352/493-0238 or see detailed maps and trail guides at http://lowersuwannee.fws.gov. Adjacent to the nine-acre campground is a prehistoric Indian mound. Throughout the park, you'll find spectacular views of the gulf and marshes.

Campsites, facilities: Eight RV sites and six tent sites have water, electricity, picnic tables, and campfire rings. Restrooms, showers, a boat ramp, and a dump station are available. Children are welcome. Leashed pets are permitted. Alcohol is forbidden.

Reservations, fees: Sites are first-come, first-served. The fee is $5 per night for two people, plus $1 for each additional person. Credit cards are not accepted. Stays are limited to seven days.

Directions: From U.S. 19/98 at Otter Creek, turn southwest on State Road 24, drive 22 miles to County Road 347, and turn right. Drive 2.3 miles north to County Road 326 and turn left, then proceed 3.2 miles west to the campground. The park address is 17650 SW 78th Place, Cedar Key, FL 32625.

Contact: Levy County Parks and Recreation Department, P.O. Box 248, Bronson, FL 32621, 352/486-5127.

27 CEDAR KEY SUNSET ISLE PARK

Scenic rating: 6

in Cedar Key

Shady sites and beguiling sunsets on a marsh at the edge of the Gulf of Mexico are featured at this campground behind the Sunset Isle Motel. It's just 1.3 miles from the center of Cedar Key, so you could cycle, walk, or take a street-worthy golf cart into town. This might make a good base camp to explore the Cedar Keys National Wildlife Refuge, which is accessible only by boat and has a dozen islands that host a seabird rookery and an 1850s lighthouse. Rental boats are available at the downtown marina. To the south, the 30,000-acre Waccasassa Bay State Preserve, also accessible only by boat, offers more opportunities for fresh- and saltwater fishing, bird-watching, and canoeing—or for simply savoring unspoiled vistas of windswept black rush marsh and cypress hammocks. For information, call 352/543-5567.

Campsites, facilities: There are 53 RV sites with full hookups, 30-amp and 50-amp electrical service, concrete patios, and picnic tables, plus around six grassy tent spots. RVs up to 52 feet long can be accommodated. Lots are long and narrow, at 100 by 20 feet. Three sites are pull-through. Restrooms, showers, a recreation room, and a pool are available, as are motel rooms. You can fish from five docks, or watch the sunset; one dock even has a fireplace. Children are welcome. Leashed pets are permitted.

Reservations, fees: Reservations are recommended. Sites are $16–35 per night for two people, plus $5 for each additional person. Credit cards are accepted. Long-term rates are available.

Directions: From U.S. 19/98 at Otter Creek, turn west on State Road 24 and drive 24 miles. The park, which is part of a motel facility, is on the north side of State Road 24 as you enter Cedar Key.

Contact: Cedar Key Sunset Isle Park, P.O. Box 150, Cedar Key, FL 32625, 352/543-6124, www.cedarkeyrv.com.

28 RAINBOW RV CAMPGROUND

🛥️ 🚐 🏠 ♿ 🚐 ⛺

Scenic rating: 7

in Sumner, off U.S. 19/98

You'll find a mix of sunny and shaded sites at this family-oriented campground, which is located just five miles from the beaches, docks, restaurants, and shopping in the historic village of Cedar Key. Next door are an antiques shop, bait, tackle, and groceries. Perched on the edge of expansive wildlife preserves, this is a perfect spot for artists and shutterbugs whose favored subjects are panoramas of marshland dotted with palms. About 20 percent of the

park is occupied by year-round residents. Favorite things to do are fishing, hunting, shelling, shopping, and relaxing.

Campsites, facilities: This park has 62 campsites for RVs or tents, 42 with full hookups. Ten sites have 50-amp electrical service, and the rest have 30-amp. Each site has a concrete patio, a fire ring, and a picnic table. RVs up to 45 feet long and slideouts can be accommodated. On the premises are showers, restrooms, a dump station, laundry facilities, limited groceries, rental campers, a community kitchen with potluck dinners, a game room, a recreation room, boccie ball (lawn bowling), horseshoes, and basketball hoops. The bathhouse, clubhouse, office, and store are wheelchair-accessible. Children are welcome. Leashed pets are permitted.

Reservations, fees: Reservations are recommended. Sites are $19 per night for two people, plus $2 for each additional person. Kids under three are free. Credit cards are accepted. Long-term stays are allowed.

Directions: From U.S. 19/98 at Otter Creek, turn southwest on State Road 24 and drive 14 miles to the campground.

Contact: Rainbow RV Campground, 11951 Southwest Shiloh Road, Cedar Key, FL 32625, 352/543-6268, www.rainbowcampground.com.

29 SHADY OAKS CAMPGROUND

🏠 🚐

Scenic rating: 2

south of Otter Creek off U.S. 19/98

Shady Oaks is described as "edge of woods quiet," which aptly sums up this place on the road to Cedar Key. The campground is wooded and grassy, with deer and wild turkeys occasionally wandering through. Like the critters, you are on your own: Select a site, slip $10 in the self-service payment box, hook up your rig, and kick back. "Just holler" across the fence if you want to meet owner Wayne Fouts. There are no restrooms, so your unit must be self-contained.

Campsites, facilities: The 13 RV sites have full hookups and picnic tables. There are no restrooms or showers. The closest groceries and restaurants are 13 miles north in Chiefland. Children are welcome. Leashed pets are permitted.

Reservations, fees: Reservations are not necessary. Sites are $15 per night. Credit cards are not accepted. Long-term rates are available.

Directions: From U.S. 19/98 in Otter Creek, turn west on State Road 24 and drive 0.75 mile to the campground.

Contact: Shady Oaks Campground, 440 Southwest 3rd Street/P.O. Box 184, Otter Creek, FL 32683, 352/486-3236.

30 VILLAGE PINES CAMPGROUND

Scenic rating: 5

on U.S. 19/98, north of Inglis

Snowbirds flock to this park each winter to find peace and shade under the pines. Close to the Gulf Hammock Wildlife Management Area and Goethe State Forest, this 48,000-acre tract of longleaf pine flat woods is laced with roads and trails for hiking and horseback riding. For state forest information, call 352/447-2202. Groceries and restaurants are available seven miles away in Inglis.

Campsites, facilities: There are 32 RV sites with full hookups, electricity, and picnic tables; half are pull-through. Four grassy tent sites have water and electricity. On the premises are restrooms, showers, laundry facilities, a dump station, a recreation room, horseshoe pits, and shuffleboard courts. Children are allowed. Leashed pets are permitted.

Reservations, fees: Reservations are not necessary. Sites are $12 per night for two people, plus $3 for each additional person and $2 for using air conditioners or electric heaters.

Credit cards are not accepted. Long-term rates are available.

Directions: From Inglis, on U.S. 19/98, drive seven miles north to the campground. Look for the covered wagon out front.

Contact: Village Pines Campground, 8053 Southeast 140th Lane, Inglis, FL 34449, 352/447-2777.

31 BIG OAKS RIVER RESORT AND CAMPGROUND

Scenic rating: 7

between Inglis and Crystal River

These wooded three acres in this campground offer direct access to the Withlacoochee River for canoeing, fishing, and just enjoying the view. Saltwater fishing is just 7.5 miles downstream at the Gulf of Mexico.

Campsites, facilities: There are 21 full-hookup RV sites with water and electricity for overnighters and seasonal visitors. A tent area accommodating five tents is set apart from the recreational vehicles; it offers water, electricity, and a common fire pit. Restrooms, showers, laundry facilities, and cable TV are available. On the premises are a pool, a boat ramp, a dock, canoe rentals, cabins, and a dog-walk area. Kayaks, bicycles, pontoon boats, inner tubes, and johnboats are available for rent. A recreation hall offers darts, games, TV, and other entertainment. Children are welcome. Leashed pets are permitted.

Reservations, fees: Reservations are recommended. Sites are $25 per night for two people, plus $1.50 per extra person. Credit cards are accepted. Long-term rates are available.

Directions: From Inglis, drive south on U.S. 19 to the outskirts of town. Turn west on West River Road to the park entrance.

Contact: Big Oaks River Resort and Campground, 14035 West River Road, Inglis, FL 34449, 352/447-5333, fax 352/447-4125, www.bigoaksriverresort.com.

32 B'S MARINA AND CAMPGROUND

🛶 🚐 🐕 🚙 ⛰ 🛶

Scenic rating: 5

west of Yankeetown

The only campground in Yankeetown that fronts on the Withlacoochee River, this park is just three miles from the Gulf of Mexico. With an emphasis on kayaking and fishing, this campground is decidedly water-oriented. Fishing guides and charters are available. "We want you to come back and tell us some good fish tales," say the owners.

Campsites, facilities: There are 15 RV sites for overnighters and 15 for seasonal visitors. All have full hookups and a choice of 30-amp or 50-amp electrical service. Five tent sites have water and electricity. Restrooms, showers, laundry facilities, a boat ramp, a dock, kayak and pontoon boat rentals, and a dog-walk area are provided. Children are welcome. Leashed pets ("good dogs only") are permitted.

Reservations, fees: Reservations are recommended. Sites are $25 per night for two people, plus $2.50 per extra person. Credit cards are not accepted. Long-term rates are available.

Directions: From Yankeetown, drive west on County Road 40 to 66th Street, where you'll see a sign for the park. Turn left on 66th Street and continue to Riverside Drive. Turn right and go one block to the park entrance on the river.

Contact: B's Marina and Campground, 6621 Riverside Drive, Yankeetown, FL 34498, 352/447-5888, fax 352/447-3177, www.bmarinacampground.net.

33 CATTAIL CREEK RV PARK

🛶 🛶 🚐 🐕 ♿ 🚙 ⛰

Scenic rating: 8

in Yankeetown

This friendly, well-kept campground has plenty of shade and paved roads great for little kids on skates and bikes. The pool is the social center of the park, although every now and then, the party shifts to the recreation hall for a "wingding" potluck supper and dance. Fishing is a favorite pastime; a nearby county boat ramp and several marinas provide access to the Gulf of Mexico and estuaries in the Gulf Hammock Wildlife Management Area, havens for redfish, sea trout, flounder, and drum. The campground has fish-cleaning tables set aside for successful anglers and holds "fish lie-fabrication classes" for those who come back empty-handed. The management also sponsors community fish fries and contests.

Campsites, facilities: About 18 tents can be set up in a large open area with one water spigot. Additionally, there are 72 developed campsites with full hookups, picnic tables, and cable TV (long-term only). Both 30-amp and 50-amp electrical sites are available. On the premises are restrooms, showers, laundry facilities, a dump station, a pool, and a recreation hall. An Internet connection is available in the office (broadband) and clubhouse (dial-up). The restrooms are wheelchair-accessible. Children and leashed pets are welcome.

Reservations, fees: Reservations are recommended. Sites are $25 per night for two adults and children, plus $5 for each extra adult. Credit cards are not accepted. Long-term rates are available.

Directions: From U.S. 19/98 in Inglis, turn west on County Road 40 and drive three miles to the campground.

Contact: Cattail Creek RV Park, 41 Cattail Lane, Yankeetown, FL 34498, 352/447-3050.

JACKSONVILLE

BEST CAMPGROUNDS

❰ Families
Kathryn Abbey Hanna Park, **page 166**

❰ Island Retreats
Little Talbot Island State Park, **page 164**

❰ Most Unusual
Hidden River Resort, **page 171**

Jacksonville boasts unspoiled forests and great beaches, city attractions, full-service RV parks, and rustic campgrounds in beautiful settings. For most visitors to Florida, this is the first stop after crossing the state line, and it's worthy of exploration.

Rich in history, this part of Florida was first settled by Europeans in 1513. A few years later, the French built the first Protestant colony in America at Fort Caroline. There, about 140 French colonists were killed when Spanish soldiers swept down on their fort in 1565. It was the first decisive battle fought by Europeans for American soil and set into motion a chain of events that left Florida in Spanish hands for years. Today, a replica of the fort, with French flags flying above cannons, stands on the banks of the St. Johns River.

If you want to camp near the beach, head for Huguenot Memorial Park, surrounded by three bodies of water: Fort George Inlet, the St. Johns River, and the Atlantic Ocean. From the beach, you're likely to see huge ships headed to Mayport Naval Air Station, where ship tours are available most weekends. The base is the third largest in the country. North of Jacksonville Beach is Fort Clinch, named for a commander who fought in the Second Seminole War in the 1840s.

You may be sorry if you don't leave time to explore the five-square-mile Talbot Islands State Parks, especially Big Talbot Island State Park, where huge, bleached fallen tree trunks give the shore a spooky feel. Nearby attractions include the George Crady Bridge Fishing Pier and the historic Ribault Club (newly restored in 2005) at Fort George Island Cultural State Park. Don't miss a visit to Florida's oldest plantation – the former home of Zephaniah Kingsley, a slave trader who freed and married one of his African slaves, Anna Madgigine Jai Kingsley. The plantation is part of the National Park Service's 46,000-acre Timucuan Ecological and Historic Preserve.

Inland from the beach and coastline developments, the dominant landscape is pine forest. The vastness of this forest is breathtaking; it's hard to believe there is still this much undeveloped land in the Sunshine State. Much of the forest land is commercial and privately owned. A notable exception is the 200,000-acre Osceola National Forest, where the campground at Ocean Pond is highly recommended. It overlooks a large fishing lake, with sites right on the water.

The Battle of Olustee, Florida's only major battle during the Civil War, was fought in this forest where some 3,000 soldiers lost their lives. Confederate soldiers headed off a Sherman-style invasion of Florida, which served as the Confederacy's breadbasket. Each February, on the second weekend of the month, reenactors dressed in Union and Confederate garb come here to light cannons, ride cavalry horses, and the like.

For a special side trip, cross the St. Marys River to get to the Cumberland Island National Seashore in Georgia. Wild horses roam the northern stretches of the island, and a couple of old mansions can still be viewed along its beaches.

This area has a decided Southern accent, giving truth to the notion that the farther north you roam when in Florida, the more you are in the South.

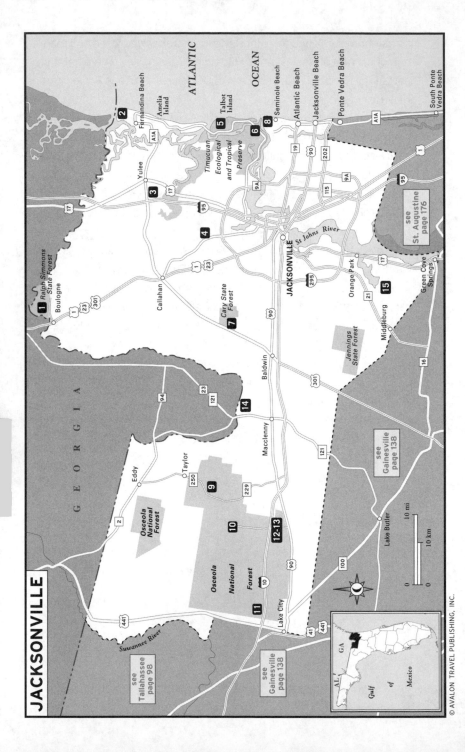

© AVALON TRAVEL PUBLISHING, INC.

◼ RALPH E. SIMMONS MEMORIAL STATE FOREST

🏕 🏊 🏖 🚣 🐕 🚐 ⛺

Scenic rating: 8

north of Hilliard on the St. Marys River, just
south of Georgia

One great thing about camping here is that
you're likely to be very much alone, except
possibly during hunting season. Part of this
3,630-acre state forest (formerly known as St.
Marys State Forest) borders a six-mile stretch
of the St. Marys River, the watery line between
Florida and Georgia. The vehicle-accessible
site is simply an oak-shaded area where the
palmettos and scrub oaks have been cleared
out, along with the rest of the underbrush—so
expect little privacy from neighbors. The oak
hammock is just off the St. Marys River and
Pigeon Creek, a rivulet that empties into the
St. Marys. A county-maintained boat ramp
is less than 0.25 mile away, and right next to
that is a popular summer swimming spot on
the St. Marys. The forest is a largely ignored,
out-of-the-way spot where nature lovers who
don't mind skipping a shower or two will have
a blast. Look for deer, wild turkeys, and the
once-endangered fox squirrel, which is now
making a comeback. Early in the day, keep
your eye out for otters alongside the river or
the creek. That's also a good time for freshwater anglers to try their hand at the river. The
forest contains some increasingly rare natural areas, such as seepage slopes and longleaf
wire grass sand hills. Horseback camping is
available, as are trails for horseback riding and
day hikes.

Canoeists can use any of three designated
primitive campsites along the St. Marys. If
you need to rent a canoe, contact local liveries such as Canoeport in St. George, Georgia
(912/843-2688), or Outdoor Adventures in
Jacksonville (904/393-9030).

Only hunters are welcome to camp in the
forest during hunting seasons, which are periods of no more than two weeks—usually just
four days or so—scattered across the calendar
from late September to late February. Hunters
go after deer, hogs, wild turkeys, and small
game then. However, unlike many places
frequented by hunters, this stretch of natural
Florida has been reserved for non-hunters in
significant periods during the cooler winter
months, which is dandy news for primitive
campers.

Campsites, facilities: One primitive camping
area is accessible by car, and four primitive
sites are accessible by canoe or boat on the St.
Marys River. The site accessible by car offers
a vault toilet and is near a boat ramp on the
river. No showers, dump stations, restrooms,
or other facilities are provided. Groceries and
other supplies can be purchased about five
miles away in Hilliard or in Folkston, Georgia.
Children and leashed pets are welcome.

Reservations, fees: For the drive-in site, contact either the Florida Division of Forestry
or the St. Johns River Water Management
District ahead of time to learn the combination for the lock that controls an access gate.
Canoeists and other boaters on the St. Marys
should contact the water management district
to see if space is available. Campsites are first-
come, first-served. Camping is free.

Directions: From Hilliard, drive seven miles
north on U.S. 1 to the town of Boulogne, then
turn right onto Lake Hampton Road/State
Road 121. Look for an entrance less than
one mile ahead on the left, just past Pigeon
Creek.

Contact: Florida Division of Forestry, 3742
Clint Drive, Hilliard, FL 32046, 904/845-
3597. Additional information is available from
the St. Johns River Water Management District, Division of Land Management, P.O. Box
1429, Palatka, FL 32178-1429, 386/329-4500
or 800/451-7106, www.sjrwmd.com.

2 FORT CLINCH STATE PARK

🥾 🏊 🛶 🎣 🏕 🐕 🚶 🚐 ⛺

Scenic rating: 10

on the Atlantic Ocean, at Florida's
northeastern tip

You can fall asleep to the sound of ocean waves
crashing near your sandy campsite. The ride
to the park is a study in contrasts, as you pass
neat shops and Victorian homes in old-town
Fernandina Beach, as well as huge power
plants. But the key attraction is the park.

The campground is set where the St.
Marys and Amelia Rivers come together to
form Cumberland Sound, the border between
Florida and Georgia. You have a choice of two
camping areas: 21 unshaded, sandy sites are
near the ocean, and 41 others are in a shady
coastal hammock of big, beautiful oaks and
cedars on the Amelia River. Both are outstanding in their own way. Fireflies might
flicker like Christmas lights at dusk in the
shady "river campground," where you will feel
more sheltered from other campers, thanks to
at least some native brush providing a screen.
At the beach sites, you'll be closer to other
campers. But it's hard to beat waking up to
feel the sea breeze and see the pink fingers
of dawn reaching over the Atlantic and the
nearby dunes. Raccoons can be an irksome
but manageable problem at the river sites (tip:
Keep food and coolers in the car).

Anglers use a fishing pier to catch whiting,
red bass, and sheepshead, while windsurfers
take to the Amelia River, also known as the
Intracoastal Waterway. The beach is popular
among sunbathers and swimmers. Nearby
in town are rental canoes and kayaks, a boat
ramp, tennis and volleyball courts, and saltwater fishing charters. At the park, nature
lovers have two hiking trails to choose from:
a loop that leads through a wooded area and
around manmade Willow Pond, or a shorter
path near the park's namesake fort that passes
through a hammock en route to the Intracoastal Waterway.

Even if you have a passing interest in history,
don't miss the centerpiece of the two-square-
mile park—the fort. Named for a commander
who fought in the Second Seminole War in
the 1840s, Fort Clinch was only partially
finished when the Civil War commenced in
1861. Because no Yankee troops were around,
the Confederates quickly took over the place.
By early the following year, though, with the
coastal islands to the north in Federal hands,
the Confederates abandoned the fort as in-
defensible, and Union troops moved in soon
thereafter. The fort never was completed because construction of its masonry walls was
outpaced by the development of new and better cannons.

For the best reenactment, visit on the first
weekend of each month and take a nighttime
candlelight tour that conjures up images of the
Union and Confederate soldiers who battled
on these very grounds. During the summer,
candlelight tours also are held on the second
and third weekends of the month (call for
reservations). In May, a special full-garrison
reenactment by Union soldiers takes place,
then the fort is turned over to the Confederates in October.

For a special side trip, cross the St. Marys
River to get to the Cumberland Island National Seashore in Georgia. Wild horses roam the
northern stretches of the island, and a couple
of old mansions can still be viewed along its
beaches. An eerie island attraction is the ruins
of Dungeness, the stately home of the Carn-
egie family. "It sort of reminds you of Tara
from *Gone with the Wind*—after it burned
down," says a friend.

To get to Cumberland Island, use your own
boat to cross the St. Marys River. An alternative is to drive 40 miles to the town of St.
Marys, Georgia, and catch a ferry from there.
To do this, head west on Highway A1A from
Fort Clinch's campground through Fernandina Beach to northbound I-95. Cross the Flor-
ida/Georgia border. At the first exit, Highway
40, go east to the town of St. Marys. There,
catch a ferry to Cumberland Island, which is

just across the Cumberland Sound from Fort Clinch State Park. For more information, call the national seashore at 912/882-4335.

Campsites, facilities: Sixty-two sites of varying sizes are available for tents and RVs in two sections, all offering water and 30-amp electric hookups and campfire rings. RVs up to 40 feet long and slide-outs can be accommodated at some sites. Restrooms, showers, a dump station, laundry facilities, firewood, and a playground are available. Groceries, LP gas, restaurants, and bait are available within five miles. The bathhouse, fishing pier, and store are wheelchair-accessible. Children are welcome. Leashed pets are permitted with proof of current rabies vaccination.

Reservations, fees: Reservations are highly recommended; contact ReserveAmerica at 800/336-3521 or reserveamerica.com. Sites are $24 per night for up to eight people. You should also call the park to see if a site is available that is large enough to accommodate your RV. Credit cards are accepted. Stays are limited to 14 days.

Directions: From I-95 north of Jacksonville, take Exit 373 and go 15 miles east on Highway A1A, passing through the town of Fernandina Beach along the way. Turn right at Atlantic Avenue. Proceed two miles to the park, on the left.

Contact: Fort Clinch State Park, 2601 Atlantic Avenue, Fernandina Beach, FL 32034, 904/277-7274, www.floridastateparks.org.

3 BOW AND ARROW CAMPGROUND

Scenic rating: 3

on U.S. 17, south of Yulee

Back before I-95 was built, the road in front of this five-acre park, U.S. 17, was the region's main route into Florida. But today, that highway is much less used, although still fairly busy. The sites—some sandy, some grassy—are set back from it quite a ways. So, this park is quiet, and it's shady with oaks and pines. Most people here are stopping through or visiting local relatives.

Campsites, facilities: The park offers 56 full-hookup RV campsites, 24 of them pull-through, and 10 with 50-amp electrical service. Each site has a picnic table and 30-amp electricity. A laundry room, restrooms, showers, propane gas, a pool, cable TV, and telephone hookups are available. Children are permitted for overnight visits. Leashed pets are allowed.

Reservations, fees: Reservations are recommended. Sites are $25 per night for two people, plus $3 per extra person. Credit cards are accepted. Long-term stays are OK.

Directions: From I-95 north of Yulee at Exit 373, drive three miles east on Highway A1A to U.S. 17. Turn right and go south for two miles to the campground.

Contact: Bow and Arrow Campground, 598 U.S. 17, Yulee, FL 32097, 904/225-5577, fax 904/225-9233.

4 FLAMINGO LAKE RV RESORT

Scenic rating: 5

off I-295, northwest of downtown Jacksonville

Visitors at this family-oriented campground, located a quick hop off I-295, have two places to swim: the pool at the park's eastern end, or the 17-acre lake on the western end. Much of the action is at the lake, which has a nice beach with lounging chairs. Gas grills, a pavilion, picnic tables, and a deck are near the shore, where some anglers wet a line. Kids will prefer heading to the east side, though, for the basketball courts, volleyball nets, playground, and pool.

Campsites, facilities: All 152 RV sites (33 pull-through) have full hookups with 30-amp or 50-amp electrical service and cable TV. Paved roads with a speed limit of five miles per hour pass the well-tended campsites. For the best lake views, ask about sites 10–22. Sites 78–98 form a semicircle around the playground, pool, some shaded tables, and a volleyball net on the opposite side of the park. No bicycles are allowed on the beach or sidewalks. Facilities include a pool, a game room, a playground, volleyball, basketball, a bonfire area, a fishing lake, an adult recreation room, a beach, a pavilion with gas grills, and nature trails. Showers, restrooms, a dump station, pay phones, cable TV, LP gas, and a laundry room are also available. A wireless Internet connection is available in the park. Alcoholic beverages must be contained in cups. Parents need to supervise their children at all times. Leashed dogs under 30 pounds are permitted, but they must use the two dog-walk areas and refrain from barking.

Reservations, fees: Reservations are recommended. Sites are $35 per night for two people, plus $3 for each additional person. Credit cards are accepted. Long-term rates are available.

Directions: From Jacksonville, take I-95 north to I-295 (Exit 362B). Head west to the first exit (Exit 32, Lem Turner Road), then drive north a short distance to Newcomb Road. Turn left. You'll soon see the campground.

Contact: Flamingo Lake RV Resort, 3540 Newcomb Road, Jacksonville, FL 32218, 904/766-0672, www.flamingolake.com.

5 LITTLE TALBOT ISLAND STATE PARK

Scenic rating: 10

in Fort George, on the Atlantic Ocean east of Jacksonville

BEST (

Ideal for nature-lovers and beachgoers, sun-washed Little Talbot Island is the only place you can camp in the sprawling complex of natural areas known as the Talbot Islands State Parks. At Little Talbot, you can hike and bike through maritime forests or boat through salt-marsh areas (rental canoes are available from an outfitter one mile north of the park; call 904/251-0016). You also can cross the dunes that protect the island from the Atlantic Ocean to swim or fish for flounder, redfish, bluefish, striped bass, and sheepshead.

The packed-dirt campsites are fairly close together. Some are screened from neighbors by at least limited brush. Still, the island is remote, so it's not difficult to find solitude. Little Talbot's hiking trails span more than four miles and reward walkers with more privacy than found at many state parks. Try to spot otters, rabbits, or bobcats as you explore. Bird-watchers admire the bald eagles and songbirds, which are among the nearly 200 species of birds identified here.

Be sure to explore other portions of the five-square-mile Talbot Islands State Parks. At Big Talbot Island State Park, huge, bleached fallen tree trunks have become improbably large pieces of driftwood that give the shore a surreal, almost spooky feel. Look for birds along the five marked hiking trails that crisscross the sprawling 2,000-acre day-use area. Also nearby are the George Crady Bridge Fishing Pier, the equestrian-oriented Pumpkin Hill Creek Preserve State Park, and the newly restored historic Ribault Club at Fort George Island Cultural State Park.

A little farther north, Amelia Island State Park also offers a taste of "The Real Florida," resembling as closely as possible the Florida that European explorers found when they arrived some 500 years ago. It's a fishing spot, but some people hike along the beach or birdwatch. You can also rent horses to explore the beach. For $45 (age 13 and up only; weight limit 230 pounds), you can saddle up at the Kelly Seahorse Ranch concession in the park. Hourly rides leave at 10 A.M., noon, 2 P.M., and 4 P.M. Check in 30 minutes prior to your ride. For information, call 904/491-5166.

Finally, don't miss a visit to Florida's oldest plantation—nearby Kingsley Plantation, the former home of cotton and sugar planter

Zephaniah Kingsley. The plantation is part of the National Park Service's 46,000-acre Timucuan Ecological and Historic Preserve; call 904/251-3537 for more information. Also nearby is the Fort George State Cultural Center (see *Huguenot Memorial Park* in this chapter).

Campsites, facilities: These 40 water-and-30-amp electric sites are for tents and RVs; about one-third can fit rigs up to 30 feet long. Two sites are pull-through, and two spots are wheelchair-accessible. Each site has a picnic table, a grill, and a fire ring. Canoe rentals, a playground, a nature trail, bike rentals, guided interpretive programs (usually Saturday afternoons), and volleyball entertain campers. Showers, restrooms, a dump station, a small boat ramp, and a laundry room are available. A bird sanctuary is located on nearby Fort George Island. Groceries, restaurants, and bait are located within five miles. Children are allowed. Leashed pets with rabies tags are permitted; no pets may go on the beach.

Reservations, fees: Reservations are recommended; contact ReserveAmerica at 800/336-3521 or reserveamerica.com. Fees are $19 per night for up to eight people. The maximum length of stay is 14 days.

Directions: From I-95 in Jacksonville, take Exit 358A and go east on Heckscher Drive/State Road 105 for 22 miles to the park entrance at right.

Contact: Little Talbot Island State Park, 12157 Heckscher Drive, Jacksonville, FL 32226, 904/251-2320, fax 904/251-2325, www.floridastateparks.org.

6 HUGUENOT MEMORIAL PARK

🚶 🚴 🏊 ⛵ 🎣 🏕 ♿ 🚐 ⛰

Scenic rating: 8

on the Atlantic Ocean, east of Jacksonville

Broad beaches seem to span as far as the eye can see at this 450-acre park surrounded by three bodies of water: Fort George Inlet, the St. Johns River, and the Atlantic Ocean, stretching to 26,000 feet of beachfront. These sandy campsites have no shade, but they're great for passing a few days if you like beach settings. There's a magical quality—although the view from many Florida beaches inevitably includes high-rises or houses, here you'll see just sand and the Atlantic Ocean in the easternmost reaches of the park. Vehicles are permitted on the beach. Bring your own gear to snorkel or windsurf.

Although lacking water and electric hookups, these campsites have the advantage of being reasonably close to some Jacksonville-area highlights. The nearest is the worthwhile Talbot Islands State Parks (see *Little Talbot Island State Park* in this chapter). The campground is also 10 miles from the Jacksonville Zoo and just down the road from the Fort George State Cultural Center, where you can take a 4.4-mile self-guided history tour by foot or car. Moss-draped oaks shade much of the route. Fort George Island has been continuously inhabited for some 5,000 years. Early Indian occupants shucked oysters and tossed them into piles, which today are up to 65 feet tall and are covered by sand and dirt, making this the highest coastal elevation south of North Carolina's Outer Banks.

Campsites, facilities: There are 40 RV sites and 30 tent-only sites, each with a picnic table, a fire ring, and a grill. Water and electricity are not available. Restrooms, showers, a dump station, and a store are on the premises. The restrooms and store are wheelchair-accessible. Boat rentals and charter fishing are in the park. Two waterfront shelters with picnic tables and grills can be rented for $21 per day. Personal watercraft riding, windsurfing, and kite surfing are allowed. Laundry facilities are located eight miles away. Restaurants and bait are available within three miles. Children must be supervised by adults. Two leashed pets are allowed per campsite.

Reservations, fees: Reservations are accepted. Sites are $8 per night for up to six people.

Credit cards are accepted. Stays are limited to 15 days out of any given 45 days.

Directions: From I-95 in Jacksonville, take Exit 358A and go east on Heckscher Drive/ State Road 105 for 20 miles. The park is on the right side of the road, one mile past the ferry slip.

Contact: Huguenot Memorial Park, 10980 Heckscher Drive, Jacksonville, FL 32226, 904/251-3335, fax 904/251-3019, www.coj .net/Departments/Parks+and+Recreation.

7 CARY STATE FOREST

Scenic rating: 7

north of Baldwin

The three campsites here—set amid pine flat woods that provide only moderate shade—are used mostly by Boy Scouts and people who like to ride their horses through these 3,400 wooded acres. A network of nature trails leads through the flat woods and connects with a boardwalk that winds through a dark cypress swamp. Horseback riders and long-distance hikers may wish to range along a network of forest roads and trails stretching eight miles. There's also a 1.2-mile nature trail. Over a few weekends in fall and winter, the forest is open to archers and hunters bearing muzzle-loading guns. A picnic pavilion sits near the camping area (campers must call ahead for a permit), along with a wildlife-observation tower and interpretive signs. Look for deer, wild turkeys, bobcats, and elusive black bears.

Campsites, facilities: An indeterminate number of campers can be accommodated at a single camping area of three primitive sites located in the forest. Drinking water, restrooms, and showers are available. Supplies and other conveniences can be obtained one mile away in Bryceville or seven miles south in Baldwin. Children are allowed. Leashed pets are permitted.

Reservations, fees: Reservations are required.

Camping is $5 per night; you must obtain a permit by calling 904/266-5021. Day visitors are on the honor system and pay $2 per car.

Directions: From Baldwin, drive north on U.S. 301 for about seven miles. Look for the forest on your right, 0.25 mile north of the Bryceville Fire Station. The campsites are on the forest's main entrance road. From the town of Callahan, drive south on U.S. 301 for 15 miles. The entrance is 1.5 miles south of the forestr district office.

Contact: Cary State Forest, Florida Division of Forestry, 7465 Pavilion Drive, Bryceville, FL 32009, forest district office: 904/266-5022, Cary State Forester/camping permits 904/266-5021, www.fl-dof.com/state_ forests/cary.html.

8 KATHRYN ABBEY HANNA PARK

Scenic rating: 8

on the Atlantic Ocean, in Atlantic Beach east of Jacksonville

BEST (

This oceanfront gem—named for a historian who served on the Florida Board of Parks and Historical Places in the 1940s—is one of Jacksonville's most popular parks, and for good reason. These 450 acres offer something for almost everyone. The more adventurous may want to trek through 15 miles of off-road trails on mountain bikes tailored for beginners or advanced riders. Hikers and bicyclists (helmets are required) each enjoy their own narrow, woodsy nature trails that encircle a 60-acre freshwater lake, where anglers can try their luck for catfish. If you prefer saltwater fish, head to the county-run park's 1.5-mile-long beach of grayish-tan sand. Lifeguards watch over ocean swimmers from Memorial Day to Labor Day. From the beach, you're likely to see huge ships headed to nearby May-port Naval Air Station, where ship tours are available most weekends; call 904/270-NAVY

(904/270-6289). Hanna Park is about seven miles from Adventure Landing, a pirate-themed family entertainment center with go-carts, laser tag, a water park, and other activities.

For nature lovers and history buffs, this is the closest campground to the National Park Service's Fort Caroline National Memorial. There, approximately 140 French colonists were killed when Spanish soldiers swept down on their fort just after dawn in September 1565. It was the first decisive battle fought by Europeans for American soil and set into motion a chain of events that left Florida in Spanish hands for years to come. Today, a replica of the fort, with French flags flying above cannons, stands on the banks of the St. Johns River. You can also hike the pretty Old French Trail, which runs through a remnant of the maritime hammock forest that once covered most riversides in northeast Florida. Just down the road from Fort Caroline is the National Park Service's Theodore Roosevelt Area of the Timucuan Ecological and Historic Preserve. There, you can hike the Willie Browne Trail (named for the former landowner, who bequeathed these woods to the public), passing underneath mossy trees and a Confederate soldier's grave en route to the old Willie Browne homestead.

Campsites, facilities: Several loops of campsites are set on either side of a crooked main campground road. The sandy/gravel campsites are irregularly spaced, so don't expect the manicured feel of a modern private campground. Fifteen tent sites are set apart from 278 full-hookup RV sites, which have water and 30-amp electrical service. For recreation, there's a hiking trail, 15 miles of single-track bicycle trails, a playground, and a fishing lake. Showers, restrooms, picnic areas, a dump station, log cabins (for rent), and a laundry room are available. Groceries and restaurants are located within a 0.5 mile-drive in the town of Atlantic Beach, which surrounds Hanna Park. The beach, lake, and six campsites are wheelchair-accessible. Children under the age of eight must be supervised by adults while swimming. Two leashed pets are permitted per campsite.

Reservations, fees: Reservations are recommended but are usually not necessary. Sites are $34 per night for six people. Credit cards are accepted. The maximum stay is 15 days within a 45-day period.

Directions: From I-95 in Jacksonville, take Exit 344 and drive east for about five miles on J. T. Butler Boulevard. Turn left at St. Johns Bluff Road and head north. In about six miles, turn right at Atlantic Boulevard/Highway 10. Continue seven miles, crossing the Intracoastal Waterway. Turn left at Mayport Road/Highway A1A. Turn right on Wonderwood Drive to enter the park, which is just south of the Mayport Naval Air Station.

Contact: Kathryn Abbey Hanna Park, 500 Wonderwood Drive, Jacksonville, FL 32233, 904/249-4700, fax 904/247-8688, www.coj .net/Departments/Parks+and+Recreation.

9 EAST TOWER

🚶 🚴 ⛺ 🐴 🚙 ⛺

Scenic rating: 7

within Osceola National Forest

At East Tower, you'll camp amid some of the most wildlife-rich acreage in the state. It's not uncommon to come across deer and turkeys, or even to hear the rat-a-tat-tat of an endangered red-cockaded woodpecker. In drier sandy areas, look for gopher tortoises lumbering home to their sandy burrows.

This campground primarily is designed for hunters, as evidenced by the sign on a caged pen here: "Lost dogs." Sometimes, people in pursuit of big hairy beasts with the aid of their own smaller hairy beasts notice that their four-legged helpers have vanished. But the dogs usually come back, and fellow hunters place the pooches in these cages to await their masters' return. East Tower is on the middle prong of the St. Marys River (which leads eventually to Jacksonville and splits Georgia from Florida), offering freshwater anglers a place to fish. Mountain bikers will enjoy the backcountry roads in these parts.

Campsites, facilities: About 50 RVs and tents can be accommodated at this primitive camping area. Flush toilets and drinking water are provided, but no electricity. Children are welcome. Leashed pets are permitted.

Reservations, fees: Reservations are not accepted. Camping is free. Stays are limited to 14 days in any 30-day period, except during hunting season.

Directions: From Lake City, take U.S. 441 north to County Road 250 and turn right. Head east about 23 miles. Make a right onto Forest Service Road 202 and continue a short distance to the camp.

Contact: Osceola National Forest, U.S. 90, P.O. Box 70, Olustee, FL 32072, 386/752-2577, www.fs.fed.us/r8/florida/recreation/index_osc.shtml.

under the pines at Osceola National Forest

10 FLORIDA NATIONAL SCENIC TRAIL/OSCEOLA NATIONAL FOREST

Scenic rating: 7

runs southeast to northwest across the southern part of Osceola National Forest

Here's your chance to enjoy totally primitive camping, with only a few places along the trail where you can get water and use backwoods privies. There are basically two kinds of terrain: wet and dry. In the swampy lower areas, you'll hike through bay and gum trees, cypress, ferns, and mosses. Other areas, elevated just a few feet, are known as ridges and have sun-dappled pines and wispy wire grass, along with the fan-shaped leaves of saw palmetto or perhaps wax myrtle. Prepare to get your feet wet if it's been raining heavily; call the Forest Service a week to a few days before your visit to check on conditions.

The trail is marked by orange blazes, or short stripes, painted on trees. To prevent getting lost, look ahead to locate the next painted marking. If you see a double blaze, or two stripes painted next to each other, it indicates that the trail is about to make a turn. Keep a careful eye out around these double blazes to stay on course.

The trail starts at the historic site where the Battle of Olustee was fought during the Civil War. In just four hours on February 20, 1864, some 3,000 soldiers lost their lives in Florida's only major battle during the war. Stop by the worthwhile museum and walk the outdoor interpretive trail to learn how outnumbered Confederates headed off a Sherman-style invasion of Florida, which had for years provided a big chunk of the Confederacy's beef and other staples. Each February, on the second weekend of the month, hundreds of reenactors dressed in Union and Confederate garb come here to light cannons, ride cavalry horses, and the like.

From the interpretive center, it's about 3.5 miles to the Cobb Hunt Camp, at Forest Service Road 235. Look for several small ponds and sinkholes along the trail on the way to Cobb. About 1.5 miles farther along, the orange-blazed Florida Trail crosses a blue-blazed trail that leads to the developed Ocean Pond Campground (see campground in this chapter). In another mile, the trail crosses under I-10 and follows a jeep road for about one mile. Soon, it crosses Forest Service Road 263B, and 1.3 miles later, State Road 250A. Another 1.8 miles brings you to a primitive campsite (10 miles total from the trailhead). A half-mile north, the trail crosses State Road 250. Parking is available here, so this is one place where you could terminate your hike. (You'll need two cars.)

If you decide to forge ahead, the trail hooks up about 3.5 miles later with an old tram road, where ties of cypress and heart pine elevate the trail and make for generally easy hiking. A half-mile later, a boardwalk picks up; and in 1.5 miles, you'll come to the West Tower campsite (see next listing). About 2.5 miles later, the trail crosses Forest Service Road 237, following a jeep road for 1.2 miles to the Osceola National Forest boundary at State Road 262.

During hunting season, generally mid-November–early January, camping is prohibited except at Ocean Pond Campground and designated hunt camps. To prevent assaults of another kind, bring bug repellent for warding off ticks and mosquitoes.

Campsites, facilities: Hikers can camp anywhere in the national forest as long as they pitch a tent more than 100 yards from a road during nonhunting months. That means there are virtually unlimited places to camp along the Florida National Scenic Trail's 20-mile section inside the forest. There also are two primitive backpacking campsites along the trail—one with a chemical toilet and shelter, and one near West Tower, which has a flush toilet and water. For more niceties, the trail passes the developed Ocean Pond Campground. But facilities are basically nonexistent. Campfires may be made using downed wood found on the ground. Pack out trash, and bury human waste in a six-inch hole. Children and leashed pets are permitted.

Reservations, fees: Reservations are not accepted. Camping is free. Stays are limited to 14 days in a 30-day period.

Directions: From Lake City, drive about 10 miles east on U.S. 90, then turn left (north) onto Forest Service Road 241. To reach the north end of the trail, head north from Lake City on U.S. 441 about five miles and turn right onto State Road 262. The trailhead is less than a mile ahead.

Contact: Osceola National Forest, U.S. 90, P.O. Box 70, Olustee, FL 32072, 386/752-2577, www.fs.fed.us/r8/florida/recreation/index_osc.shtml. For trail details, I recommend contacting the Florida Trail Association, which maintains the trail, at 5415 Southwest 13th Street, Gainesville, FL 32608, 352/378-8823 or 877/HIKE-FLA (877-445-3352), www.florida-trail.org.

11 WEST TOWER

Scenic rating: 8

western Osceola National Forest

The national forest system of horseback-riding and bicycling trails is centered on this rustic, no-frills crash pad for outdoorsy types. It's also the main place to camp with your horse. The idea isn't to while away time at the dirt-road camping area in the shadow of a forest lookout tower—instead, you should get out and explore.

From here, you can traverse some 50 miles of horse trails, which also are open to backcountry mountain bikers. For beginning riders, the Green Trail is a quick five-mile jaunt on mostly main roads (be on the lookout for vehicles). If you're riding after heavy rains, stick to the Red Trail, a 20-miler through pine flat woods and a few cypress sloughs. A cutoff allows you to reduce the Red Trail to just 10 miles.

Another 20-mile route is the Blue Trail, which offers the added enticement of the western border of the Big Gum Swamp Wilderness, a 13,640-acre area with no roads at the heart of the national forest, where it is least disturbed by humans. The Gold Trail, which is approximately 16 miles long, passes through two bay swamps. Avoid this route in wetter periods, particularly if you are an inexperienced rider. Check the bulletin board near the stables at West Tower for further information.

Hunters tend to use these campsites mid-November–mid-January. Wear bright-orange clothing while hiking to avoid being mistaken for game.

Campsites, facilities: Up to 75 people can be accommodated at this primitive camping area. The only facilities are drinking water, flush toilets, and horse stalls. There is no electricity. Children are welcome. Leashed pets are permitted.

Reservations, fees: Reservations are not accepted. Camping is free. Stays are limited to 14 days in any 30-day period, except during hunting season.

Directions: From Lake City, take U.S. 441 north about four miles. Turn right onto Forest Service Road 233 and go about 5.5 miles east until you see the camp.

Contact: Osceola National Forest, U.S. 90, P.O. Box 70, Olustee, FL 32072, 386/752-2577, www.fs.fed.us/r8/florida/recreation/index_osc.shtml.

12 OCEAN POND CAMP-GROUND

🚶 🏊 🎣 🛶 🐴 🚐 ⛺

Scenic rating: 9

on the northeast end of Ocean Pond, in Osceola National Forest

This shady, placid campground sits right beside Ocean Pond, which, at 1,760 acres, is quite a large "pond." It's one of the most popular

within Florida's national forests, and the scenery partly explains why. Among other reasons are the sandy beach and the fact that you can keep your boat at your site if you get lucky.

The sites are mostly screened from each other by brushy vegetation, so you're likely to enjoy some privacy. Many sites—most of them under tall, moss-draped pines—face the pretty, round pond. You can swim in a roped-off area in front of the campground.

Boating, fishing, canoeing, and waterskiing are popular at Ocean Pond. If you're into a nice day hike, follow the Florida National Scenic Trail, which passes by the campground, through the outback. Head south for 5.6 miles, passing some smaller, sinkhole-like ponds along the way until you reach the trailhead at the Olustee Battlefield historic site. There, approximately 5,000 Johnny Rebs held off a larger force of Federals during the Civil War, preventing a Sherman-style invasion of Florida, which served as the Confederacy's breadbasket. Hunting in the forest also is popular, although it is restricted in the area immediately around Ocean Pond. Most hunters camp nearby in the far more primitive Hog Pen Landing site (see next campground) and nine primitive hunt camps. During hunting season, camping is allowed only at Ocean Pond and at the designated hunt camps.

Campsites, facilities: There are 66 sites for tents and RVs, including 19 lots with water and 30-amp electricity, 27 sites with water only, and 20 primitive sites for self-contained RVs. The non-primitive sites are placed on paved roads; the primitive sites are on gravel spurs. Each has a lantern post, a picnic table, and a fire ring. Big RVs can be accommodated at most sites. Facilities include a boat ramp, a swimming area, restrooms, a dump station, and showers. Sites 32–45 are closest to the swimming beach. Sites 1–19 are the most developed. There's a convenience store five miles away in Olustee, but you'll have to drive to Lake City for major supply refills and restaurants. Children and leashed pets are permitted.

Reservations, fees: Reservations are not accepted. Sites are $8–18 per night for up to five people. Stays are limited to 14 days between May 1 and September 30, and to 30 days between October 1 and April 30.

Directions: From Lake City, drive east on U.S. 90 for 14 miles. After you pass the ranger's office and the convenience store in the town of Olustee, turn left onto County Road 250A. Follow this road north for about four miles to the campground.

Contact: Osceola National Forest, U.S. 90, P.O. Box 70, Olustee, FL 32072, 386/752-2577, www.fs.fed.us/r8/florida/recreation/index_osc.shtml.

13 HOG PEN LANDING

Scenic rating: 6

north of Ocean Pond, in Osceola National Forest

Here is a tranquil, rustic retreat on the north side of Ocean Pond, with sites set underneath pines and a few oaks. In late fall and early winter, you're likely to share the place with hunters in search of deer, wild hogs, bobcats, and other game. In spring, turkey hunters turn up. It's possible to fish in the freshwater lake from the shore, but you'll do better if you have a boat.

Olustee Beach is worth a visit for a picnic and a walk down an interpretive boardwalk to the site of the long-gone, turn-of-the-20th-century Russell Eppinger sawmill. The trail follows an old tram road that was used to carry trees from the forest to the sawmill. Back then, workers made about $2 per day for cutting 15 cross ties. Not far away is the Olustee Battlefield historic site. The Florida National Scenic Trail passes near here for plentiful hiking opportunities.

Campsites, facilities: This primitive camping area accommodates up to 30 people. Chemical toilets and a boat ramp are available. You won't find drinking water or any other facili-

ties. Water can be obtained four miles away at the developed Ocean Pond Campground. Children are welcome. Leashed pets are permitted.

Reservations, fees: Reservations are not accepted. The cost is $2 per vehicle. Stays are limited to 14 days in any 30-day period, except during hunting season.

Directions: From Lake City, head east on U.S. 90 about 10 miles. Turn left onto Forest Service Road 241, go about three miles north to Forest Service Road 241A, and turn right into the campground.

Contact: Osceola National Forest, U.S. 90, P.O. Box 70, Olustee, FL 32072, 386/752-2577, www.fs.fed.us/r8/florida/recreation/index_osc.shtml.

14 HIDDEN RIVER RESORT

Scenic rating: 8

north of Macclenny, just across the state line

BEST (

Although technically located in Georgia, this 88-acre nature-oriented, nudist park on the St. Marys River is just across the water from Florida. Bring your own horse and ride on the trails that meander through the woods and along the river. The wooded campsites offer privacy. Family groups are welcome; a 60- by 30-foot pavilion provides gathering space. The "Nudie Blues" music festival is held each year on the last weekend in April.

Campsites, facilities: This nudist resort brags there is absolutely no pavement to be seen, so "you can take off your shoes and wiggle your toes." Absolutely prohibited are any kind of glass containers in the park. There an unlimited number of primitive tent sites, plus 26 drive-through RV sites with full hookups (half with 30-amp service, half with 50-amp). Picnic tables, restrooms, showers, and a dump station are available. On the premises are a pool, a hot tub, horseback-riding and hiking trails, and a pavilion. The bathhouse is wheelchair-accessible. Children are welcome. Leashed pets are allowed, as are horses.

Reservations, fees: Reservations are recommended. Sites are $45 per night for two people, plus $15 per extra person and $5 for 50-amp electricity. Credit cards are not accepted. Stay as long as you wish.

Directions: From I-10, take Exit 335 at Macclenny northbound on State Road 121 and drive seven miles. Cross three bridges at the St. Marys River and the Georgia state line and immediately turn left on State Road 185. Drive 8.5 miles to Reynolds Bridge Road and turn left (this is the only paved road). The park entrance is ahead about 2,000 feet on the left.

Contact: Hidden River Resort, 9988 County Road 120, Sanderson, FL 32087, 912/843-2603, www.hiddenriverresort.com.

15 WHITEY'S FISH CAMP

Scenic rating: 4

on Swimming Pen Creek, south of Orange Park

Diners have pulled up in everything from little boats to limousines to eat the alligator-tail appetizers and secret-recipe fried catfish at Whitey's restaurant overlooking Swimming Pen Creek. The popularity of the all-you-can-eat catfish spread is credited with spawning this three-acre campground. Here, oaks shade RV sites and campers launch boats for free to try for snook (particularly in winter) on the St. Johns River. Brackish Swimming Pen Creek meanders into Doctors Lake and the St. Johns. Dogs occasionally accompany their masters at the restaurant deck, and female diners have arrived in swimsuits. Don't try the latter; although Whitey's is casual, sunbathers must slip on shirts. About 25 percent of the park is occupied year-round. Historic St. Augustine is about 35 miles away.

Campsites, facilities: All 40 RV sites have full hookups and 20/30/50-amp electrical outlets. RVs up to 40 feet long and slide-outs can be accommodated. Boat rentals, a boat ramp, charter fishing, a restaurant, and a snack bar are available. Showers, restrooms, picnic tables, a dump station, bait, tackle, and a laundry room are on-site. An 18-hole golf course and grocery stores are located two miles away. Children are welcome. Leashed pets are permitted.

Reservations, fees: Reservations are not necessary. Sites are $28 per night for two people, plus $1 per extra person. Credit cards are accepted. Long-term rates are available.

Directions: From I-295 in Orange Park, take Exit 10 and go south on U.S. 17/Roosevelt Boulevard for about five miles. Turn west (right) at County Road 220. Proceed about two miles to the campground entrance.

Contact: Whitey's Fish Camp, 2032 County Road 220, Orange Park, FL 32073, 904/269-4198, www.whiteysfishcamp.com.

ST. AUGUSTINE

© ST. AUGUSTINE, PONTE VEDRA & THE BEACHES VISITORS AND CONVENTION BUREAU

BEST CAMPGROUNDS

❰ **Beachfront Campgrounds**
Anastasia State Park, page 182

❰ **Most Unusual**
Mike Roess Gold Head Branch State Park, **page 178**

The main attraction in St. Augustine is its historic

heritage, but surrounding this ancient city are large tracts of forest waiting to be explored. Hikers, bicyclists, anglers, and boaters will find much to their liking, and the beaches are lovely.

You won't be the first to focus your attention on this area. It's hard to believe, but Spanish soldiers and missionaries set up housekeeping in St. Augustine two generations before famished Pilgrims landed at Plymouth Rock. It was founded in 1565 and served as Spain's capital for its Florida colony. Today, the biggest reminders of Florida's first conquerors are the massive walls of the nearby Castillo de San Marcos fort, which is still standing and open to visitors. (Similar in style to fortresses built by the Spaniards in their conquest of the Caribbean, the fort was completed 100 years after St. Augustine's founding.) The nation's oldest city, St. Augustine charms visitors with its colorful heritage, amazing beaches, and nature-oriented retreats.

St. Augustine is a supremely pedestrian-friendly city, with restaurants, shops, and quaint watering holes. In fact, the city's cobblestoned historic district may have more tourist attractions than any other place outside of the Orlando/Disney area: sightseeing trains, Ripley's Believe It or Not!, Potter's Wax Museum, the "oldest store" museum, the oldest wooden schoolhouse, an old jail, the purported Fountain of Youth, ghost tours, an alligator farm, Florida's first lighthouse, the "oldest house," and horseback carriage rides. The World Golf Hall of Fame is a duffer's dream, with exhibits about great players and the history of the game. And yes, there are two golf courses, both 18-hole championship and par-72, with five sets of tees. Each golf cart has a global positioning system.

The magnificent Bridge of Lions leads from downtown St. Augustine to Anastasia Island. On the island is Anastasia State Park, popular for its coastal camping at the edge of the Atlantic Ocean. It also gets rave reviews for its beach, windsurfing, fishing, and swimming. For a short walk, hit the 0.25-mile quarry trail just inside Anastasia park's entrance to see where Spaniards mined the Castillo de San Marcos' walls.

Southwest of St. Augustine are vast acres of unspoiled woods on both sides of the St. Johns River as it flows southward into 100-acre Lake George. The fishing is great here, particularly if you're looking for bass.

Inland from the coast are loads of fresh waters competing for anglers' fish tales. The natural eco-systems that offer havens for fish are preserved for back-country camping and hikers. The state of Florida and other public agencies have set aside many acres for natural pursuits, with many more acres being added each year. The St. Augustine area begs for exploration by nature lovers.

Most campers, though, will focus on the coast. It's always a surprising experience to drive your car on the hard-packed sands with the Atlantic Ocean surf nearby. You can even ride your bike. That makes it fun for kids or adults alike. Just be sure to rinse the salt water off all metal parts as soon as you can. It can be corrosive.

St. Augustine's laid-back lifestyle and vacation atmosphere are a plus for anyone's Florida vacation. Experiencing it while camping only allows you to amplify your adventure.

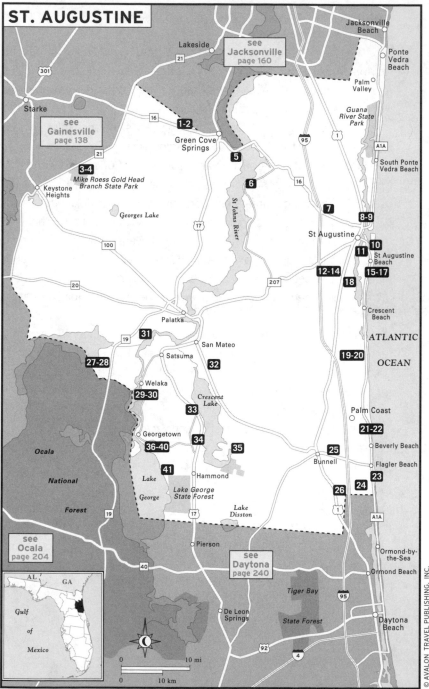

ST. AUGUSTINE

1 BLACK CREEK RAVINES CONSERVATION AREA

🏃 ≈ 🛶 🚤 🐕 ⛰

Scenic rating: 6

northwest of Green Cove Springs

Steep ravines and hills distinguish this remote woodland, with two primitive camping areas popular with hikers and equestrians. Elevations range from 5 to 90 feet above sea level—remarkable for Florida. You can canoe, fish, or boat on adjoining Black Creek on the eastern edge of the preserve. Bicyclists are forbidden, and climbing in the ravines is prohibited because of their sensitive nature. One camping area overlooks Black Creek and is accessible only by foot or boat; the other is inland at the main access point east of Middleburg.

Campsites, facilities: Only tents are permitted at the two primitive campsites. There are no facilities: Bring water, supplies, mosquito repellent, and everything you'll need. Children are welcome. Leashed pets are permitted.

Reservations, fees: Sites are first-come, first-served. Camping is free. Each site accommodates up to six people. If your party has at least seven people, get a free permit and reserve at least one week ahead at 904/329-4410. Maximum stay for all campers is seven days.

Directions: The main access point is on Green Road on the southwest corner of this preserve. From Green Cove Springs, drive west on Highway 16 for five miles. Turn northwest onto County Road 218 and drive approximately one mile. At Green Road, go right two-thirds of a mile to the access point. From the town of Middleburg, drive east one mile on Highway 218. Turn north on Green Road and drive about two-thirds of a mile to the parking lot.

Contact: St. Johns River Water Management District, Division of Land Management, P.O. Box 1429, Palatka, FL 32178-1429, 386/329-4500 or 904/529-2380, www.sjrwmd.com.

2 JENNINGS STATE FOREST

🏃 ≈ 🛶 🚤 🐕 ⛰

Scenic rating: 6

west of Orange Park, near Middleburg

When it's not hunting season, this 20,885-acre state forest is a marvelous place for canoeing, hiking, bicycling, and horseback riding. Public access is restricted during hunts, so be sure to call ahead. The forest encompasses the headwaters of Black Creek and its tributaries. Ecologically speaking, forestry experts say, the area is in remarkably good condition. What this means for you is that you'll see a vast array of wildlife, such as the green tree frog, hawks, foxes, deer, and rare Black Creek crayfish. There are four canoe launches, but you'll have to carry your boat over some rough terrain or use four-wheel drive. In the forest are several small historic cemeteries.

Campsites, facilities: Only tents are permitted at the three primitive campsites. There are no facilities: Bring water, supplies, mosquito repellent, and everything you'll need. Children are welcome. Leashed pets are permitted.

Reservations, fees: Sites are first-come, first-served. Camping is free. Each site accommodates up to six people. If your party has at least seven people, get a free permit and reserve at least one week ahead at 904/329-4410. Maximum stay for all campers is seven days.

Directions: There are five access points; download a map from www.sjrwmd.com before making your plans. Two parking areas are on Live Oak Lane. From Middleburg, drive west on State Road 218.

Contact: Florida State Division of Forestry, 904/291-5530; or the St. Johns River Water Management District, Division of Land Management, P.O. Box 1429, Palatka, FL 32178-1429, 386/329-4500 or 800/451-7106, www.sjrwmd.com.

❸ MIKE ROESS GOLD HEAD BRANCH STATE PARK

🏃 🚴 🏊 ⛴ 🐕 🚐 ⛺

Scenic rating: 10

northeast of Keystone Heights

BEST (

You'll walk along rolling, sandy hills where plants are somewhat sparse and the sun can get hot. But then the remote, three-square-mile park delivers its surprise: a wet mini-canyon, Florida-style. Water pours freely from a ridge, carving a ribbon of lush greenery. It slices the wilderness lengthwise and cools hikers hugging the ravine-bottom stream. It's an unusual sight for mostly griddle-flat Florida.

Among the park's three camping areas, the pine-dotted, open expanse of Sandhill Camp is the sunniest. The soft hills are ancient sand dunes—that's right, the sea was much higher back then. To the south, the gnarly branches of deep-ridged oaks provide some shade at Turkey Oak Camp. Picnic tables and a public parking area for day-use visitors are near Turkey Oak. The southernmost part of the park, Lakeview Camp, has a campfire circle at the edge of the park's largest lake, Big Lake Johnson, where anglers try for bass, speckled perch, and bream.

Five miles of hiking trails wind through this gem of a park, which was built by the Civilian Conservation Corps. The circular Loblolly Trail passes beneath the sparse branches of the park's largest loblolly pines and ends at a mill site. The shortest trail, Fern Loop, starts at the precipitous ravine stairway and passes the headspring of the Gold Head Branch stream. Long ago, the Downing and Burlington narrow-gauge railroad transported logs through the current park. Today, you can hike or ride a bike along the former railroad route. Take a dip at the swimming beach in Little Lake Johnson. On some nights, the park offers stargazing and moonlit walks. Camp Blanding, which once was a training ground for the U.S. Army, is a sprawling presence across the street; its museum is about eight miles from the park.

Campsites, facilities: The 73 tent and RV sites have water, and all but 11 have 30-amp electric hookups. Four have 50-amp electrical service. RVs as long as 40 feet can be accommodated; four sites are drive-through. You'll find plenty of elbow room. Each campsite has a picnic table, a grill, and a fire ring. Recreational offerings include canoe and bicycle rentals, volleyball, and four hiking trails. Showers, restrooms, lakefront cabins, and a dump station are available. Laundry facilities, restaurants, groceries, and bait are available within 6–8 miles. Children are welcome. Leashed pets are permitted with proof of vaccination.

Reservations, fees: Reservations are recommended; contact ReserveAmerica at 800/336-3521 or reserveamerica.com. Sites are $16 per night for up to eight people. Credit cards are accepted. Length of stay is limited to 14 days.

Directions: From I-295 at Jacksonville, take Exit 12 and drive south for about 30 miles on Blanding Boulevard/State Road 21 to the park on the left.

Contact: Mike Roess Gold Head Branch State Park, 6239 State Road 21, Keystone Heights, FL 32656, 352/473-4701, www.florida stateparks.org.

❹ MIKE ROESS GOLD HEAD BRANCH STATE PARK PRIMITIVE CAMPING

🏃 🐕 ⛺

Scenic rating: 6

northeast of Keystone Heights, on the Florida National Scenic Trail

Look skyward for woodpeckers landing on the pointy tips of the bleached-white dead trees along the Florida National Scenic Trail. You'll pitch your tent along this car-width path. A primitive camping area with no bathrooms or other amenities is found a short walk north of Little Lake Johnson. Essentially a clearing immediately west of the pine-shaded Florida Trail, the campsite is disappointingly close to the park's established campgrounds. Although the primitive campsite requires a very short hike, you may wonder: What's the point? Why not stay in a developed campground where toilets and water are readily available? The answers are solitude and the chance to awake closer to the fern-bordered ravine for a morning walk. You're likely to see birds in an area of burned-out pines up the trail from the campsite. The clearing and the dead trees help attract wildlife, hence the occasional soft clatter of white-tailed deer darting into the mossy woods.

Campsites, facilities: Up to 12 people can be accommodated at two primitive hike-in camping sites on the Florida National Scenic Trail. Canoe rentals, volleyball, bicycle rentals, four hiking trails, showers, restrooms, and lakefront cabins are available within the developed portion of the park. Laundry facilities, restaurants, groceries, and bait are available within six to eight miles. Children are allowed. Pets are permitted with proof of vaccination.

Reservations, fees: Reservations are recommended; call up to 60 days ahead to reserve a site. The fee is $3 per night per adult, $2 per child.

Directions: From I-295 at Jacksonville, take Exit 12 and drive south for about 30 miles on Blanding Boulevard/State Road 21 to the park on the left.

Contact: Mike Roess Gold Head Branch State Park, 6239 State Road 21, Keystone Heights, FL 32656, 352/473-4701.

5 BAYARD CONSERVATION AREA

Scenic rating: 6

near Reynolds Airpark, southeast of Green Cove Springs

Overlooking the St. Johns River, these 9,898 acres of pines and riverine bottomland hardwoods harbor turkeys, deer, gopher tortoises, and the rat-a-tat-tat of woodpeckers, yet these woods are close to metropolitan Jacksonville.

One campsite, at Davis Landing, overlooks the river. Indeed, this public land offers seven miles of riverfront, providing the chance to fish from the bank, paddle a canoe (if you bring one), and spy for herons before walking inland to follow crisscrossing trails in search of warblers. One of the three campsites, reached by foot by passing a gate with a walk-through west of Highway 209 and south of Highway 226, is open to anyone most of the year, but is restricted to hunters during hunting season. The popular Pearl's Trail and Lindsey Lane found farther north are off-limits to hunters at any time, and both end near an on-site security station next to a parking area.

Campsites, facilities: Only tents are permitted at the three primitive campsites, which must be reached by boat, canoe, bicycle, hiking, or horseback. There are no facilities: Bring water, supplies, mosquito repellent, and everything you'll need. A boat launch is found north of Highway 16 and west of Shands Bridge. Children are welcome. Pets must be leashed.

Reservations, fees: Sites are first-come, first-served. Camping is free. Each site accommodates up to six people. If your party has at least seven people, get a free permit and reserve at least one week ahead at 904/329-4410. Maximum stay for all campers is seven days.

Directions: From Green Cove Springs, take Highway 16 east; the conservation area is about 0.5 mile west of the Shands Bridge, which spans the St. Johns River.

Contact: St. Johns River Water Management District, Division of Land Management, P.O. Box 1429, Palatka, FL 32178-1429, 386/329-4500 or 904/529-2380, www.sjrwmd.com.

6 PACETTI'S MARINA RV PARK AND FISHING RESORT

Scenic rating: 7

on the St. Johns River, west of St. Augustine

This historic wooded campground on the St. Johns River has lots of huge oak trees and is great for freshwater-fishing enthusiasts who would like to spend a few days relaxing. A tackle shop, gas docks, a boat ramp, a marina, and live bait are among the 25-acre campground's most prominent amenities, but there's plenty to do onshore. The World Golf Village and PGA Tours, Jacksonville, and St. Augustine are nearby, and the ocean is just 20 minutes away. Owners Pinkham and Linda Pacetti also offer square dances, bingo, and campfires. A 200-seat restaurant has inside and outside dining and live entertainment on weekends. A recreation hall offers TV and video games, and there are motel units for the non-campers in your party. The Pacettis are the third generation of their family to own this park, which was established in 1929.

Campsites, facilities: This park has 147 gravel-surface, full-hookup RV campsites (30 pull-through), and 25 tent sites. Some sites have picnic tables; all have 30/50-amp electrical service. RVs as large as 45 feet are welcome. Recreational offerings include a rec room, a playground, a game room, shuffleboard, fishing guide services, a bait and tackle shop, and horseshoes. On the premises are showers, restrooms, a dump station, rental cabins, a motel, a boat ramp and dock, groceries, a restaurant, a camp store, a large pavilion, and laundry facilities. Restrooms are wheelchair-accessible. Children are welcome. Leashed pets are permitted.

Reservations, fees: Reservations are recommended. Sites are $28–32 per night for four people, plus $2 for each extra person over age four. Credit cards are accepted. Long-term stays are OK.

Directions: From I-95 near St. Augustine, take Exit 318 and proceed west along State Road 16 for 12 miles to the campground.

Contact: Pacetti's Marina RV Park and Fishing Resort, 6550 State Road 13 North, St. Augustine, FL 32092, 904/284-5356, fax 904/284-2369, www.pacettirv.com.

7 STAGECOACH RV PARK

Scenic rating: 2

just off I-95, west of St. Augustine

This might make a good stopover for people flying by on I-95, and there's even a small

Take a break from cooking at one of St. Augustine's many waterfront restaurants.

playground with swings and a basketball court to burn off some steam. It's also convenient to downtown St. Augustine attractions, seven miles away. Most of the people staying here are tourists. Campsites are grassy, measuring 45 by 60 feet, and each site has some trees.

Campsites, facilities: This park offers 80 full-hookup RV sites (60 pull-through) with 30/50-amp electrical service. Roads are paved. RVs as long as 60 feet can be accommodated. A recreation room, a small playground, a basketball court, a camp store, restrooms, showers, picnic tables, a dump station, and a laundry room are available. Internet access is available in the office. A cluster of fast-food places and convenience stores are within 0.1 mile, and two outlet malls are about 0.5 mile away. Management says most of the facilities are wheelchair-accessible. Well-behaved children and small, leashed pets are permitted.

Reservations, fees: Reservations are recommended. Sites are $28–30 per night for two people, plus $2 per extra person age four and older. Credit cards are accepted. Long-term stays are OK.

Directions: From I-95 and State Road 16 at Exit 318, turn left at the Denny's onto County Road 208. Drive west for 0.3 mile and look for the campground on your left.

Contact: Stagecoach RV Park, 2711 County Road 208, St. Augustine, FL 32092, 904/824-2319.

🎱 NORTH BEACH CAMP RESORT

🚶 🏊 📷 🚴 ♿ 🚐 ⛺

Scenic rating: 8

on Highway A1A, north of St. Augustine

"Sunrise on the ocean, sunset on the river, and a bit of Olde Florida in between" is the slogan of this 60-acre RV park, which extends from the ocean to the Intracoastal Waterway. Large oaks and myrtle trees add to the park's appeal. Aside from the ocean

access, the location is great: North Beach is just about as close to the downtown historic section of St. Augustine as the Beachcomber Outdoor Resort and Anastasia State Park campgrounds (see listings in this chapter). Trees separate campsites, but campers will appreciate the pool and hot tub. Rent a boat here, or fish off a dock. The park has 1,000 feet of riverfront. Only 10 percent of the sites are occupied by year-round residents. In summer, activities center on the beach, pool, and fishing; in winter, visitors fill their days with potluck dinners, bingo, and typical snowbird entertainment.

Campsites, facilities: Besides 10 tent sites, this park has about 130 level, gravel sites with full hookups. Each site has a picnic table. Most sites have 30-amp hookups, and the rest have 50-amp service. Although the trees provide shade at most sites, privacy varies depending on location. A pool, a hot tub, a recreation room, a playground, boat rentals, horseshoes, shuffleboard, volleyball, basketball, limited winter activities, and a camp circle for gatherings entertain campers. Firewood is available for use in the fire circle. Showers, restrooms, limited groceries, a boat ramp, a dock, a restaurant, a dump station, telephone hookups, bait, cable TV, and a laundry room are available. Internet access is available in the office. Improvements planned at this writing include a wireless network for the entire campground, as well as 100-amp electrical service. The restroom, office, ocean deck, lobby, and pool are wheelchair-accessible. Children and leashed pets are welcome.

Reservations, fees: Reservations are recommended. Sites are $43 per night for two people, plus $3 for each additional person. Credit cards are accepted.

Directions: From downtown St. Augustine, drive about five miles north on Highway A1A.

Contact: North Beach Camp Resort, 4125 Coastal Highway, St. Augustine, FL 32095, 904/824-1806 or 800/542-8316, fax 904/826-0897, www.northbeachcamp.com.

9 BEACHCOMBER OUTDOOR RESORT

🏊 🛶 🐕 👣 🕺 ♿ 🚐

Scenic rating: 7

across from the Atlantic Ocean, in Vilano Beach

An ultra-civilized RV park, this whirlpool tub–equipped resort is across the street from the Atlantic Ocean. A 1,015-foot pier stretches west into the Intracoastal Waterway, making it a fine place to watch a sunset and wet a fishing line. Across the street, the white-capped ocean waves lap onto the beach. There, campers swim, surf-cast, and snorkel. The campground boasts "private ocean beach access," though, legally speaking, all beaches in Florida are public up to the high-tide line.

Campsites, facilities: Beachcomber features 140 full-hookup RV sites (12 are drive-through) with 30-amp electrical service. RVs up to 40 feet long and pullout units can be accommodated. Palm trees provide a bit of shade. About 65 percent of the park is leased to year-round residents. Restrooms, a pool, a hot tub, a shuffleboard, a playground, a barbecue area, a pier, two laundry rooms, two bathhouses, a clubhouse with Internet connection, and a dump station are available. Bait, tackle, and charter fishing services are available nearby. Laundries, restrooms, and the recreation pavilion have wheelchair-access. Children under 12 must be adult-supervised at the pool. At the pier, kids under 14 must be supervised. Pets must be leashed.

Reservations, fees: Reservations are required. Sites are $32 per night. Credit cards are accepted for transactions of $100 or more. It's a private membership resort, so nonmembers may stay a few days as "guests." Monthly leases and RV storage are available.

Directions: From downtown St. Augustine, head north on San Marco Avenue, following it about one mile before the road turns right to become the San Marco Bridge. Turn left onto Highway A1A. The campground is about one mile up the road, on the left.

Contact: Beachcomber Outdoor Resort, 3455 Coastal Highway, St. Augustine, FL 32095, 904/824-9157, fax 904/829-9252.

10 ANASTASIA STATE PARK

🥾 🚴 🏊 🛶 🚣 🐕 👣 ♿ 🚐 ⛺

Scenic rating: 10

in St. Augustine

BEST (

By far a favorite campground for many visitors, this 1,500-acre, state-run heaven seems to send just about everyone home raving about the beach, coastal camping, and windsurfing, fishing, and swimming in the Atlantic Ocean. The sunny park has one of the nicest and least developed stretches of beachfront around. All of that aside, the main reason many campers stay here is found outside the park: St. Augustine's historic district.

Moss-draped oaks help shade the camping area, which is separated from the ocean by a central park road, the slowly flowing Salt Run Lagoon (often dotted with windsurfers riding the surface), a marsh, and a barrier island. Although the campground isn't located directly on the beach, you can still be lulled to sleep by the sounds of the ocean. Campfire-circle programs are offered in summer. A self-guided nature loop trail links two camping areas and leads through sand dunes covered by oaks, magnolias, and red bay trees.

You can rent a canoe or sailboard for a leisurely ride on Salt Run Lagoon. While bicycling on the sun-washed park roads in summer, remember to wear sunscreen. Look for the ruby-throated hummingbird (a summer resident) and the awkwardly beautiful and endangered wood stork (which lives here year-round), among many other birds known to use the park.

Campsites, facilities: Each of the 104 RV sites and 35 tent sites has a picnic table, a grill, a fire ring, water. The RV spots (which can also be used for tents) have 30-amp electricity. All spots require backing up. Privacy is good, with 10-foot to 40-foot spacing between campers. Several campsites are wheelchair-accessible. Canoe rentals, windsurfing lessons and rentals, a playground, a 1.5-mile interpretive nature trail, horseshoes, and a camp circle for gatherings entertain campers. Showers, restrooms, a dump station, bait, beach chair and umbrella rentals, and a laundry room are available. Groceries and restaurants are located within 1.5 miles. Children are welcome. Pets are allowed with proof of vaccination; they are not permitted on the beach.

Reservations, fees: Reservations are recommended; contact ReserveAmerica at 800/336-3521 or reserveamerica.com. Sites are $23 per night for eight people. Credit cards are accepted. Stays are limited to 14 days.

Directions: From I-95 at Exit 311, go east on State Road 207, then turn right onto County Road 312. Turn north on Highway A1A. The park is 1.5 miles ahead on the right.

Contact: Anastasia State Park, 1340-A Highway A1A South, St. Augustine, FL 32084, 904/461-2033, fax 904/461-2006, www.floridastateparks.org.

11 ST. AUGUSTINE BEACH KOA

Scenic rating: 6

in St. Augustine Beach

Stroll just 0.75 mile along a walking/biking path, and you'll be enjoying the sound of ocean waves lapping the sands of St. Augustine's beaches. Fishing without a license for bass and bream is allowed in the campground's three-acre lake, but only with artificial lures, and only for catch-and-release. Many a camper is more interested in hopping the KOA's daily shuttle to St. Augustine's historic district than in hanging out here to swim in the campground pool. Some campsites are sunny, others are shaded. The sites on Shark Fin Drive back up to a shopping plaza. The sites on Fisher-

man's Way are probably the most pleasant, because they face the freshwater lake.

Campsites, facilities: Twenty tent campsites are set apart from 92 paved RV sites (60 pull-through). All RV sites have full hookups; more than half have 50-amp electrical service, and the rest have 30-amp. Each site has a picnic table. A walking/biking path, a fishing lake, a pool, paddleboats, a playground, horseshoes, winter activities, and daily shuttle service to the city's historic area are among the amenities. Showers, restrooms, a dump station, 22 rental cabins, snacks, limited groceries, firewood, cable TV, and a laundry room are available. Propane gas is available at the front entrance. You can walk to restaurants, a shopping center, and tennis courts. Most areas of the park are wheelchair-accessible. Kids and leashed pets are welcome. Stay as long as you like.

Reservations, fees: Reservations are recommended. Sites are $40–48 per night for two adults, plus $5 for each additional adult. Children up to 17 are not charged. Credit cards are accepted. Long-term stays are OK.

Directions: From I-95 at Exit 311, drive three miles north on State Road 207 to State Road 312. Turn right and go four miles east to Highway A1A, then turn right, heading south. Stay in the right lane for one block. Turn right on Pope Road.

Contact: St. Augustine Beach KOA, 525 West Pope Road, St. Augustine, FL 32080, 904/471-3113 or 800/562-4022, fax 904/471-1715, www.staugustinekoa.com.

12 INDIAN FOREST CAMPGROUND

Scenic rating: 5

in St. Augustine

Shaded by oak and maple trees, this park also boasts good sight lines for satellite TV dishes.

It's only 3.75 miles from the St. Augustine city limits. In spite of its proximity to the city, the campground is sometimes visited by deer at the half-acre pond, where you can try your luck catching bass and bream. Some campsites are grassy, others are gravel. The ocean is six miles east. St. Augustine's historic district is a little closer.

Campsites, facilities: There are 105 RV sites (39 are pull-through) with 30/50-amp electrical service and picnic tables. Rigs up to 40 feet long can be accommodated. Pick from shady or sunny sites; most have full hookups. About 30 percent of the park is occupied by year-round residents, and many seasonal visitors return every winter. Horseshoes, a dump station, cable TV at 58 sites, wheelchair-accessible restrooms, propane gas, and laundry rooms are available. A modem is available in the office if you want to check your email or surf the Web. RVs can be stored here in the off-season. Groceries and restaurants are within 0.25 mile. Tents, weapons, firearms, and fireworks are prohibited. Children are welcome; however they must be under supervision at all times. Leashed pets are permitted, but aggressive breeds (defined by management as Rottweilers, pit bulls, Dobermans, and wolf hybrids) are verboten.

Reservations, fees: Reservations are essential in winter and for evening arrivals in summer. Sites are $27–31 per night for two people, plus $2 for each additional person. Fifty-amp electrical service and cable TV are each $2 extra. Credit cards are accepted.

Directions: From I-95 at Exit 311, drive two miles east on State Road 207 to the campground entrance.

Contact: Indian Forest Campground, 1505 State Road 207, St. Augustine, FL 32086, 904/824-3574 or 800/233-4324.

13 SHAMROCK CAMPGROUND

Scenic rating: 2

south of St. Augustine, on U.S. 1

Almost all of your neighbors will be retirees and local workers who stay at Shamrock's grassy, level sites year-round. Shaded by magnolias, oaks, and sabal palms, the campground nonetheless isn't far from urban life. A Wal-Mart is just 1.5 miles away, and a trip to the convenience store simply requires walking to the front of the campground and crossing busy U.S. 1. The inland park is located some five miles from the beach and from St. Augustine's downtown historic district.

Campsites, facilities: Shamrock has 38 full-hookup sites (three are pull-through) with 30-amp electrical service. Showers, restrooms, a laundry room, rental trailers, propane sales, cable TV, and telephone service are available. Limited groceries are across the street; restaurants are one mile away. Children are permitted for short stays. Leashed pets under 30 pounds are allowed.

Reservations, fees: Reservations are advised since most sites are leased. Sites are $30 per night. Credit cards are not accepted. Adults may stay long-term.

Directions: From I-95 at Exit 318, go east on State Road 16 to U.S. 1, then drive seven miles south to the campground entrance at right.

Contact: Shamrock Campground, 3575 U.S. 1 South, St. Augustine, FL 32086, 904/797-2270.

14 ST. JOHNS RV PARK

Scenic rating: 2

just east of I-95, south of St. Augustine

Weekend afternoons can be a noisy affair here, because this campground shares 77 acres with a flea market located next door. Still, it's an easy detour off I-95. The park is split in two: One section is for campers; the other, dotted with pine trees, is for residents living in 50 trailers. At the park's 10-acre lake, some people fish from a gazebo. Beaches and St. Augustine's historic district are about five miles away.

Campsites, facilities: Fifteen pull-through RV sites are available for overnighters and snowbirds; the rest are for full-timers over age 50 or local residents. Seven sites have full-hookups, three have 50-amp service, and the rest have 30-amp. Restrooms, showers, a dump station, a laundry room, a fishing lake, and limited RV supplies are available. Management says showers and laundry facilities are wheelchair-accessible. A golf course, restaurants, and groceries are located within three miles. RV storage is available. Children must be attended at all times; this is primarily a retiree-oriented destination. Leashed pets are permitted.

Reservations, fees: Reservations are recommended. RV sites are $21–29 per night. Add $2 per extra person. Credit cards are accepted. Long-term rates are available.

Directions: From I-95 at Exit 311, head east for 200 feet on State Road 207. The campground is next to a flea market.

Contact: St. Johns RV Park, 2493 State Road 207, St. Augustine, FL 32086, 904/824-9840.

15 OCEAN GROVE RV RESORT

Scenic rating: 8

near the Atlantic Ocean, south of St. Augustine

"Pleasantly windy" describes this barrier island campground, which backs onto the Intracoastal Waterway. On the other side, the Atlantic Ocean is just a 400-yard walk away, presenting opportunities for swimming, fishing, and snorkeling. The 20-acre resort appeals to families pining for a fun beach vacation, as well as snowbirds and visitors from Canada. But there's plenty to do in the park as well. The owners also have an RV sales and service center next door.

A generous three-quarters of the park are shaded by laurels and live oaks. Anglers can launch their watercraft from the campground's boat ramp leading into the Intracoastal Waterway, also known in these parts as the Matanzas River. Downtown St. Augustine's historic district is about six miles away.

Campsites, facilities: The 198 full-hookup RV sites (about 40 pull-through) have picnic tables, and a few sites have fire rings. Thirty sites have 50-amp service, the rest are 30-amp. Tents are permitted in the park on the same sites as the RVs. Two pools, a hot tub, an exercise room, horseshoes, shuffleboard, a kiddie pool, a playground, a game room, cabins and park model rentals, and winter activities including basketball entertain campers. Showers, a recreation room, an outdoor pavilion, a laundry room, bait and tackle, firewood, cable TV, a boat ramp, and wheelchair-accessible restrooms are available. Internet access is available in the office; the owners plan to put in a wireless network throughout the park. About 10 percent of the park is occupied by year-round residents, and some park models are already rented. Groceries and a restaurant are within 0.25 mile. Children are welcome. Leashed pets are permitted.

Reservations, fees: Reservations are recommended. Sites are $45 per night for six people, plus $2 for each additional person and $2 for cable TV. Credit cards are accepted. Long-term stays are OK.

Directions: Take Highway A1A south from St. Augustine for nearly seven miles to the campground.

Contact: Ocean Grove RV Resort, 4225 Highway A1A South, St. Augustine, FL 32084, 904/471-3414 or 800/342-4007, fax 904/471-3590, www.oceangroveresort.com.

16 BRYN MAWR OCEAN RESORT

🏊 🎣 🐕 �️ ♿ 🚐

Scenic rating: 7

on the Atlantic Ocean, south of St. Augustine

It's billed as the only RV park directly on 700 feet of beach in St. Augustine, and a sandy beach is indeed what you get. These 20 or so sun-drenched acres are geared toward RVers who want to camp near the ocean with many of the comforts of home. You'll walk across the sand dunes on one of four wheelchair-accessible boardwalks to get to the water. A security gate controls access to the well-maintained ownership park, where roads subject to a 5 mph speed limit have names like Sea Otter (closest to the beach) and Sea Nettle. If you get tired of fishing, swimming, bodysurfing, and snorkeling in the Atlantic Ocean, you can plunge into the park pool. Don't expect a beach party: Alcoholic beverages are not allowed on the shore.

In park lingo, "beachfront" campers enjoy the best view, beating out "oceanfront" (second-best) and "oceanside" (third-best) campsites. Other campers will see neighboring RVs, but will still feel a sea breeze. If you don't want to camp near the entrance, avoid sites 67–69 and 239–241. All lots are individually owned, but can be rented when not occupied. Some units in the resort are park models. The campground is about eight miles south of the downtown historic district of St. Augustine (see *Anastasia State Park* in this chapter).

Campsites, facilities: All 135 paved RV sites have full hookups; about half have 50-amp electrical service, and 65 are pull-through. The sites closest to the beach are 219–238. In return for sleeping near the beach dunes, though, you'll also be next to all the pedestrian traffic to the ocean, which passes near those sites and across the four boardwalks. RVs up to 45 feet long and pullouts can be accommodated. Shade and elbow room between sites is minimal. A pool, an activity center, an adult center, shuffleboard, horseshoes, a playground, basketball courts,

lighted tennis courts, restrooms, cable TV, snacks, ice, rental trailers, and a laundry room are available. Children are welcome, but parents are responsible for their conduct. Leashed pets are permitted and should use the dog walk north of the propane tank.

Reservations, fees: Reservations are strongly recommended, particularly in winter. Call two months ahead to reserve a park-owned trailer ($91–94 nightly). Regular campsites vary seasonally $46–56 per night for four people, plus $5 for each additional guest or visitor, and $1 per pet. Credit cards are accepted. Long-term stays are OK.

Directions: From I-95 at Exit 305, go east on State Road 206 for six miles to Highway A1A. Turn left, heading north. The campground is three miles ahead to the right. From St. Augustine, take Highway A1A south about eight miles to the campground on the left.

Contact: Bryn Mawr Ocean Resort, 4850 A1A South, St. Augustine, FL 32080, 904/471-3353, fax 904/471-8730, www.brynmawr-oceanresort.com.

17 PEPPERTREE BEACH CLUB RESORT

🏊 🎣 🐕 ♿ 🚐

Scenic rating: 6

on Highway A1A, south of St. Augustine

PepperTree is as much a village as it is an RV resort. Streets are paved and lighted. Lawn maintenance and cable TV are available for long-term visitors. It's reminiscent of many of Florida's established retirement communities. Along with shuffleboard and horseshoes, visitors can take advantage of darts, a big-screen TV, and a fireplace, found in the clubhouse.

The wee grass lawns separating: the well-tended, 30- by 80-foot campsites are sunny and open. Catch-and-release fishing for bass and bream is available at a park lake, where you might even see otters. You can walk two blocks to the beach and will find tennis courts about one mile away. St. Augustine's historic district is about seven miles north.

Campsites, facilities: PepperTree offers 12 sites for RVs, as well as rentals of park-owned homes known as "park units" and sales of lots. About 25 percent of the park is occupied by year-round residents. Each site has a concrete patio and picnic table, full hookups, and 50-amp electrical service. A pool, a fishing deck, shuffleboard, horseshoes, basketball, darts, two fishing ponds, and a clubhouse entertain campers. Showers, restrooms, a dump station, cable TV, and a laundry room are available. Many areas, including a ramp at the pool, are wheelchair-accessible. Kids must be supervised when swimming or fishing; tents are prohibited. RV storage is minimal, due to the sale of an adjacent property. Leashed pets are allowed.

Reservations, fees: Reservations are recommended, particularly in February and March. Sites are $42 per night for two people, plus $3 per additional person and $1.50 for cable TV. Credit cards are accepted. Long-term rates are available.

Directions: From I-95 at Exit 305, go east on State Road 206 for six miles to Highway A1A. Turn left, heading north. The campground is about 1.25 miles ahead on the left. From St. Augustine, take Highway A1A south about seven miles to the campground on the right.

Contact: PepperTree Beach Club Resort, 4825 Highway A1A South, St. Augustine, FL 32084, 904/471-5263 or 800/325-2267, www.sabeachrentals.com.

18 MOSES CREEK CONSERVATION AREA

🥾 🚲 🏊 🛶 🐾 ⛰️

Scenic rating: 6

at Moses Creek, off U.S. 1 south of St. Augustine

The concerns of campers understandably come second to the efforts to help protect the area's water supply and wildlife—the very reason this creekside wilderness was purchased by the St. Johns River Water Management District. Best left to outdoorsy types, this place is Rustic with a capital R. Hiking trails run throughout the property and eventually lead to the crazily crooked Moses Creek or to the much broader stream to which the creek is linked—the Matanzas River.

The trails actually are old jeep routes that became overgrown, then were cleared again, so they may be soggy in wetter months. Bicyclists can use these pathways, but there are strict rules against going off-trail. Canoeing, kayaking, and fishing are possible in Moses Creek, as long as you bring your own gear. Campers can swim in the Atlantic Ocean, a short drive away at Crescent Beach. The group camping area is cool enough that staffers from the water district have been known to spend their Christmastime holidays here.

Campsites, facilities: Primitive hike-in or boat-in camping is allowed at two sites on the north side of the creek; expect no facilities. A group camp—by permit only—is found on the south side of the creek at Braddock's Point and offers a fire grill, picnic tables, and a vista overlooking the marsh and Intracoastal Waterway. Bring everything you need to either place, including food, water, camping supplies, and mosquito repellent. Pack out trash. Children are permitted. Leashed pets are allowed.

Reservations, fees: Sites are first-come, first-served. Camping is free. Each site accommodates up to six people. If your party has at least seven people, get a free permit and reserve at least one week ahead at 386/329-4410. Maximum stay for all campers is seven days.

Directions: Take U.S. 1 south from St. Augustine for about six miles to the St. Augustine Shores subdivision, which will be on your left about one mile before you cross Moses Creek. Turn left onto Shores Boulevard and work your way back to the subdivision's tennis courts. You can park there and hike in from the trailhead a short distance away.

Contact: St. Johns River Water Management

District, Division of Land Management, P.O. Box 1429, Palatka, FL 32178-1429, 386/329-4500 or 800/451-7106, www.sjrwmd.com.

19 FAVER-DYKES STATE PARK

🚶 🛶 � 🚜 ♿ 🚐 ⛺

Scenic rating: 10

on Pellicer Creek, off U.S. 1 south of St. Augustine

At this canoeist's delight, you will discover aquatic trails leading through a landscape that has changed little since Spanish explorers first set foot here. In fact, the main body of water in the 1,608-acre park, Pellicer Creek, is named for Francisco Pellicer, who received a land grant from the king of Spain when the Spanish flag still flew over Florida.

A four-mile canoe trail, which is easy enough for beginners, can be traversed against the weak current. That way, you can make it a loop trip instead of leaving your car at one end of the creek and arranging for a ride back to camp. Call ahead to reserve a park canoe, which rents for $8 for the first two hours, plus $3 for each hour thereafter. Daily rentals are $20.

The sandy/grassy campsites aren't as picturesque as the surroundings. Landlubbers can use the short hiking trail along Pellicer Creek and Rootan Branch. A second, short nature trail leads through the high, dry pinelands near the creek. Swamps, marshes, and elevated pinelands are among the mosaic of natural Florida habitats that enrich this park with such wildlife as otters, alligators, deer, wild turkey, and a variety of birds. Look for bald eagles, which aren't uncommon.

Anglers can launch into the creek and try their luck with trout, flounder, or redfish (live shrimp are the best bait, as is true in most coastal fishing locations). The creek contains both saltwater and freshwater habitats, depending on how far you travel. Currents are mild to medium, changing with the tides.

Campsites, facilities: The 30 sites for RVs or tents have water and 30-amp electricity, but no sewer hookups. Each site has a picnic table, a grill, and a fire ring. One site is paved for wheelchair access. Most of the grassy or sandy sites can accommodate rigs up to 35 feet long; call the park if your unit is larger. All sites require the driver to back in. A primitive youth camping area provides simple facilities for up to 100 people. Canoe rentals, a playground, a nature trail, a boat ramp, a dump station, showers, and wheelchair-accessible restrooms are available. Children are welcome. Pets are not allowed.

Reservations, fees: Reservations are recommended; contact ReserveAmerica at 800/336-3521 or reserveamerica.com. Sites are $15 per night for eight people. Credit cards are accepted. The maximum stay is 14 consecutive days, or 42 days during a six-month period.

Directions: From I-95 at Exit 298, go north on U.S. 1. On the right side of the road, you will see BP and Texaco gasoline stations. Turn right and follow the signs to the park.

Contact: Faver-Dykes State Park, 1000 Faver-Dykes Road, St. Augustine, FL 32086, 904/794-0997, fax 904/794-1378, www.floridastateparks.org.

20 PRINCESS PLACE PRESERVE

🚲 🛶 🚐 🐎 ⛺

Scenic rating: 6

northwest of Palm Coast

This is the "crown jewel" of Flagler County Parks, featuring the oldest structure in the county—a lodge built in 1887—and 1,500 acres located at the confluence of Pellicer Creek, the Matanzas River, and Moody Creek. You'll find canoeing, horseback riding, and bicycle riding. Only primitive tent camping is allowed, and you must get a permit in person from the parks department in Bunnell. Plan accordingly. Campers are not allowed to swim in the lodge pool.

This park is part of the Pellicer Creek Corridor Conservation Area. You might spy rare species in these 3,830 acres of scattered marshes and, in four-fifths of the place, densely forested pines, shrubs, and hardwoods. Look for the Southeastern American kestrel, the cinnamon fern, and a starch-producing plant called the East Coast coontie. The primitive camping area is near the parking lot, restrooms, the lodge house, and a loop trail of at least five miles for bicycling, hiking, or horseback riding (bring your own horse).

Locals know this place for its catfish-stocked, 20-acre Pellicer Pond, which offers new fishing platforms at its opposite sides. Not just any fishing piers, these aluminum platforms are sheltered to protect anglers from the sun. The pond also has an informational kiosk, an educational display, and fish feeders for the catfish. Prefer eating them to feeding them? There's a six catfish-per-day catch limit. Bring a freshwater fishing license.

Campsites, facilities: Tents can be placed overlooking the water or in the pine woods. Most sites have picnic tables and fire rings. Alcohol is prohibited, as are firearms. The gates to the campground are closed at 5 P.M., and campers may not leave or enter the park after that time. Children are welcome. Leashed pets are permitted.

Reservations, fees: Sites are free. However, you must obtain a camping permit—in person—from the Parks and Recreation office, 1200 East Moody Boulevard, Bunnell, FL 32110, 386/437-7474. Office hours are weekdays 8:30 A.M.–5 P.M. The preserve is closed on Monday and Tuesday.

Directions: From I-95, take the exit for U.S. 1 and go east about 1.5 miles. At Old Kings Road, an unpaved but well-marked highway, turn left. Drive 1.5 miles to Princess Place Road and to the park.

Contact: Flagler County Parks and Recreation office, 1200 East Moody Boulevard, Bunnell, FL 32110, 386/437-7474, www.flaglerparks.com.

21 FLAGLER BY THE SEA

Scenic rating: 7

on the Atlantic Ocean, north of Flagler Beach

If you're looking for a relaxing beach experience with easy access to tourist attractions in St. Augustine (about 22 miles) or Daytona Beach (25 miles), this oceanside campground may do the trick. These few acres of beach are also near the residential community of Palm Coast, a place designed mostly for upscale retirees. Some campers swim and fish at the beach. For the best views, consider "oceanfront deluxe" sites, but the other sites are a short hop to steps that lead across the sand dunes and to the beach.

Campsites, facilities: There are 31 full-hookup campsites (15 pull-through) with 30-amp electrical service. Showers, restrooms, and cable TV are available. Groceries, restaurants, and shops are within walking distance. Children are allowed. Leashed pets are permitted and should use a pet walk along Highway A1A. Tents are prohibited.

Reservations, fees: Reservations are recommended. Sites are $30–50 per night for two people, plus $5 for each additional person. Rates are higher on holiday weekends. Credit cards are accepted. Long-term stays are OK.

Directions: From I-95 near Flagler Beach, take Exit 284 and go three miles east on State Road 100. Turn left onto Highway A1A. The campground is four miles ahead.

Contact: Flagler by the Sea, 2982 North Oceanshore Boulevard, Flagler Beach, FL 32136, 386/439-2124, fax 386/439-1666.

22 BEVERLY BEACH CAMPTOWN

🏊 ⛵ 🎣 🚶 ♿ 🚐 ⛺

Scenic rating: 7

on the Atlantic Ocean, in Beverly Beach

Sun worshippers, this 1,500-foot stretch of oceanfront is for you. One of few campgrounds directly overlooking the sand, Beverly Beach Camptown is located in along a relatively uncrowded beach, although some home subdivisions are crowding in around it. The RVs actually sit on top of the seawall above the ocean, and the most choice sites are numbered 1–67. Other RVers who keep their windows open certainly can fall asleep to the sound of rolling waves. But outdoors, "beach-view" campers are likely to be surrounded on three sides by RVs; Highway A1A is the western border.

Head north a few miles past the hamlet of Painter's Hill if you want to enjoy deserted oceanfront. Early-morning beach walks at the campground are popular with patrons enjoying the burnt-orange and purple of the sun breaking over the Atlantic. Some campers wet a fishing line in the surf. Drunkenness is forbidden, and quiet time starts at 10 P.M. For day trips to area historic sites, St. Augustine is about a 30-minute drive away. Closer to home are the Bulow Plantation (see *Bulow Plantation Resort* in this chapter) and Washington Oaks State Gardens (see *Gamble Rogers Memorial State Recreation Area* in this chapter).

Campsites, facilities: All 130 RV sites have full hookups; none are drive-through. About two-thirds have 50-amp service; the rest are 30-amp. Rigs up to 45 feet long and slide-out units can be accommodated. Although sites are plenty long, elbow room is more scarce. A few tent sites are tucked between a home and the clubhouse. A cafe, showers, restrooms, bait, tackle, a gift shop, a convenience store, cable TV, and a laundry room are available. Shopping is available within four miles. Most of the campground is wheelchair-accessible, except for the beach steps. Children are welcome but must be supervised by adults. Pets must be leashed.

Reservations, fees: Reservations are recommended. Sites vary seasonally $48–66. Rates are for two people, plus $5 per extra person age 12 and older. Credit cards are accepted. Long-term rates are available.

Directions: From I-95 near Flagler Beach, take Exit 284 and go three miles east on State Road 100. Turn left onto Highway A1A. Look for the campground three miles ahead to your right, on the beach.

Contact: Beverly Beach Camptown, 2816 North Oceanshore Boulevard, Beverly Beach, FL 32136, 386/439-3111 or 800/255-2706, www.beverlybeachcamptown.com.

23 GAMBLE ROGERS MEMORIAL STATE RECREATION AREA

🚶 🚲 🏊 ⛵ 🎣 🚗 🚐 🎣 🚶 ♿ 🚐 ⛺

Scenic rating: 10

on the Atlantic Ocean, south of Flagler Beach

A seemingly endless breeze wafts through the beachfront campsites of this 145-acre state park named for the late Gamble Rogers, the "Florida Troubadour" who chronicled the state's history and lore in folk songs before drowning in the ocean. The sun-washed campsites, composed of compressed coquina rock, overlook the beach where Rogers died.

For respite from the sun at this pretty picnic spot, a 20-minute nature trail near the park's entrance leads through a coastal scrub habitat of low-lying magnolia, oak, cedar, and sabal palms on the west side of the highway. Pick up an interpretive brochure at the entrance station to recognize the plants.

Bring your own boat or canoe to use the boat launch. Anglers go after trout, redfish, and flounder at the Intracoastal Waterway, located on the park's west side. Surfcasting at the beach may yield pompano, whiting, drum, or, at certain times of year, bluefish.

For a pleasant day trip, the landscaped grounds of Washington Oaks State Gardens are about 13 miles north on Highway A1A. For my money, its nature trails outshine the gardens. You may be alone—or nearly so—on the Bella Vista and Mala Compra Trails, which take in a section of increasingly rare mature coastal hammock, as well as dense canopied coastal scrub and an estuarine tidal marsh. Bicyclists may join hikers on two other trails: the now abandoned Old Highway A1A and the Jungle Road portion of the Bella Vista Trail. Call 386/446-6780 for information. Nearby sites of interest include St. Augustine's historic district, within a 30-minute drive of Gamble Rogers. Nine miles away is the Bulow Plantation State Historic Site (see next listing).

Campsites, facilities: Thirty-four campsites have water and electrical service; call to see if 50-amp sites are available. The hard-packed sandy sites vary in size, but are generally 20–30 feet wide with shrubs between them. If you have a larger unit, call the park to see if a site is available. Each spot has a picnic table, a grill, and a fire ring. The beachfront sites are numbered 1–23, plus 25, 27, 29, 31, 33, and 34. A nature trail, a boat launch, showers, restrooms, and a dump station are available. Three accessible campsites, the restrooms, the picnic pavilion, a grill, a picnic table, and a beach ramp are wheelchair-accessible. A public golf course is less than 0.5 mile away. Children are welcome. Leashed pets are permitted with proof of current rabies vaccination.

Reservations, fees: Reservations are recommended; contact ReserveAmerica at 800/336-3521 or reserveamerica.com. Sites are $25 per night for eight people. Credit cards are accepted. The maximum stay is 14 days.

Directions: From I-95 near Flagler Beach, take Exit 284 and go three miles east on State Road 100. Turn right at Highway A1A and look for the campground about three miles south of Flagler Beach.

Contact: Gamble Rogers Memorial State Recreation Area, 3100 Highway A1A, Flagler Beach, FL 32136, 386/517-2086, www.floridastateparks.org.

24 BULOW PLANTATION RESORT

🏃 🏊 🐾 ♿ 🚐 ⛺

Scenic rating: 8

east of I-95 and west of Flagler Beach

Although parts of this sprawling, 90-acre RV and park model community are sunny, much of it is shaded by the huge old oaks that define Florida's most beautiful woodlands. Visitors fish from canals, while others explore via rented canoes or bicycles. This park has become popular for rallies and gatherings during Daytona's Bike Week in March, as well as other festivals. About half the park is occupied by park models and year-round residents.

The full-service park is practically next door to the ruins of a worthwhile yet little-visited attraction: Bulow Plantation Ruins State Historic Site. Once one of Florida's most prosperous sugar plantations, the place was destroyed during the Seminole Indian Wars. Now all that is left of the gracious mansion and plantation are the towering coquina-rock ruins of the sugar mill, several wells, a springhouse, and the crumbling foundation of the mansion. It looks sort of like a medieval castle in ruins (albeit a small one). Interpretive signs explain how the 1830s plantation functioned, and some mill machinery can be seen.

For a six-mile (one-way) day hike, follow the Florida National Scenic Trail from the plantation to Bulow Creek State Park in Ormond Beach. The route will take you through jungly forest, salt marsh, and pine flat woods. It's real Old Florida, which is increasingly difficult for modern-day vacationers to experience. Bring mosquito repellent. Consider skipping a hike in summer.

Campsites, facilities: All 326 RV campsites (most pull-through) have full hookups with 30/50-amp service; 30 grassy tent sites also are provided; 15 have water, the rest are primitive. Tenters may stay no longer than seven days. RVs as long as 60 feet can be accommodated, as can slide-out units. A pool, horseshoes, shuffleboard, and a 6,000-square-foot recreation hall with raised stage entertain campers. Showers, restrooms, a dump station, a restaurant/pub, rental cabins, cable TV, a convenience store, and a laundry room are available. Most areas of the park are wheelchair-accessible. Children and pets are permitted.

Reservations, fees: Reservations are recommended. They are required during special events ($50 nightly, plus $25 per extra person). Sites normally are $39–45 per night for two people, plus $5 for each additional person. Credit cards are accepted. Long-term stays are OK.

Directions: From I-95 near Flagler Beach, take Exit 284 and go east on State Road 100 to the traffic light. Turn right onto Old Kings Road. Proceed three miles to the campground entrance.

Contact: Bulow Plantation Resort, 3345 Old Kings Road South, Flagler Beach, FL 32136, 386/439-9200 or 800/782-8569, fax 386/439-6757, www.mhchomes.com.

25 GRAHAM SWAMP CONSERVATION AREA
🏃‍♂️🏊‍♂️🛶🚣‍♂️🐕🏕️

Scenic rating: 6

west of Flagler Beach

Conditions here are sometimes too wet for hiking, but there is a primitive campsite near the headwaters of Bulow Creek. This 3,084-acre conservation area is meant to preserve the ecology of an area surrounded by civilized development. You can fish, and the bird-watching is great. Almost two-thirds of the land are wetland hardwood swamp; the fringes are drier.

Campsites, facilities: Tents only are permitted. There are no facilities: Bring water, supplies, mosquito repellent, and everything you'll need. Children are welcome. Leashed pets are permitted.

Reservations, fees: Sites are first-come, first-served. Camping is free. Each site accommodates up to six people. If your party has at least seven people, get a free permit and reserve at least one week ahead at 904/329-4410. Maximum stay for all campers is seven days.

Directions: From I-95, take exit 289 east on State Road 100. Turn south on Colbert Lane and go 4.5 miles to the main access point on the east side of the road.

Contact: St. Johns River Water Management District, Division of Land Management, P.O. Box 1429, Palatka, FL 32178-1429, 386/329-4500 or 800/451-7106, www.sjrwmd.com.

26 HOLIDAY TRAVEL PARK
🏊‍♂️🛶🐕🎣♿🚐🏕️

Scenic rating: 5

off I-95, southwest of Flagler Beach

You're right next to I-95, which is great if you just want a quick place to stop for the night. If you like to fish, you might ask for a spot on Marco Polo Road, which is right across from the campground lake. The busiest area of the park is near the pool, tennis courts, and bathhouse. Three spots are right next to the pool: sites 117, 118, and 119. For longer-term stays, you could find comparably priced campgrounds nearby in woodsier settings or directly on the beach. What you're mainly buying here is convenience, although there is a bulletin of planned activities hanging in the office to help keep campers entertained. The campground is close to the Bulow Plantation Ruins State Historic Site (see *Bulow Plantation Resort* in this chapter). The nation's oldest city, St. Augustine, is within a half-hour drive.

Campsites, facilities: This co-op park has 65 RV sites, seven of which offer full hookups; the rest have water and 20-amp or 30-amp electricity. Ten spots are pull-through. Some of the RV owners leave their rigs on-site year-round; others allow their lots to be rented out. About 40 percent of the park is occupied throughout the year. The roomy sites vary in size, accommodating rigs up to 50 feet long. One site is wheelchair-accessible. Recreational offerings include adult and kiddie heated pools, a playground, tennis courts, a recreation hall, shuffleboard, and fire rings. Showers, restrooms, a dump station, picnic tables, and a laundry room are available. Campers 18 and younger are welcome, but must be accompanied by an adult at the pool. Leashed pets are permitted.

Reservations, fees: Reservations are advised. Nightly fee for two people is normally $22–28 for RV sites, but will be higher during special events. Add $6 per extra person over age 12; $3 for kids ages 6–12. Credit cards are accepted.

Directions: From I-95 at Exit 278, go west on Old Dixie Highway. Make an immediate right turn into the gas station. Follow its road to the back to enter the campground.

Contact: Holiday Travel Park, 2261 South Old Dixie Highway, Bunnell, FL 32110, 386/672-8122, fax 386/437-8432.

27 KENWOOD RECREATION AREA

🚶 🚴 🎣 🚗 🏕 ⛺

Scenic rating: 5

on the Rodman Reservoir, south of Palatka

This campground was closed when the state acquired the land; it is now open only as a day-use area with a boat ramp. When it reopens sometime before 2011, improvements will include modern niceties. Call to check the status. A Cross-Florida Greenways visitors center remains open 9 A.M.–5 P.M. daily except Wednesday (386/312-2273).

Like the Rodman Reservoir, this rustic place owes its existence to the ill-considered damming of the Ocklawaha River during the 1960s. Fishing is the big activity here, with most anglers going after bass and some speckled perch.

Nearby are Palatka's Ravine State Gardens (386/329-3721). The gardens are beautiful, particularly in March and April, when azaleas are in bloom. But the most interesting feature of the park is the steep ravine formed when water flowed through the sandy ridges on the west side of the St. Johns River. Created by the Depression-era Works Progress Administration, the gardens today are a favorite of joggers and bicyclists. Nature trails also are popular. Bicyclists will enjoy the ride from the Kenwood campground to the gardens and back.

Campsites, facilities: The campground may be closed through 2011. Call to see if it has reopened.

Directions: From Palatka, take State Road 19 south about 10 miles. Turn west onto County Road 310. Turn south when it dead-ends into County Road 315. Head south one mile or less and turn left onto Park Access Road, which leads to the campground at 300 Kenwood Boat Ramp Road.

Contact: Florida Greenways and Trails, Department of Environmental Protection, 8282 Southeast Highway 314, Ocala, FL 34470, 352/236-7143, www.dep.state.fl.us/gwt.

28 RODMAN RESERVOIR

🚶 🎣 🚗 🏕 ♿ 🚐 ⛺

Scenic rating: 8

on the Rodman Reservoir, south of Palatka

Once the domain of only primitive campers, this spot has seen significant improvements that make it a good place to stay. The Rodman Reservoir is considered one of the better fishing spots around, and it is a stopping point on the Marjorie Harris Carr Cross Florida Greenway bicycle trail, which stretches from the Gulf of Mexico to the St. Johns River. However, the campground here is also popular with snowbirds in the know during the winter.

You're likely to see bald eagles soar overhead, and you'll definitely have great access to excellent bass fishing. Probably the most popular activity is fishing; there is no shortage of places to wet a line. The boat dock connects to a small island in the reservoir.

The campsites are sandy, semi-shaded, and

set amid pine trees. Good side trips are Ravine State Gardens or the open-air farmers market in Palatka. For waterfront views of the barge canal, choose from sites 59–68.

Campsites, facilities: There are 69 sites. Eight are drive-through. Forty-two sites have water and electricity, including 30/50-amp service, and 26 sites are primitive. Grills, 12 picnic tables, eight picnic shelters, a dump station, a boat dock, a boat ramp, and wheelchair-accessible restrooms with showers are available. Grocery stores, laundry, and other supplies are less than 10 miles away in Palatka. Firearms and alcohol are prohibited. Children under 15 must be accompanied by an adult. Leashed pets are permitted.

Reservations, fees: Reservations are accepted; call 386/326-2846. Sites with water and electricity are $17 per night; primitive sites are $10 per night. Credit cards are not accepted. The maximum stay is 14 days within a 30-day period but can be extended at the discretion of the gate-tender or park ranger. Campers can use the boat launch free; others pay $3.

Directions: From Palatka, take State Road 19 south about 12 miles, crossing the bridge over the Cross Florida Barge Canal, then turn right to head west for three miles on Rodman Dam Road. Turn right onto Rodman Dam Access Road, which leads to the campground.

Contact: Florida Greenways and Trails, Department of Environmental Protection, 8282 Southeast Highway 314, Ocala, FL 34470, 352/236-7143 or 386/326-2846 (campground office), www.dep.state.fl.us/gwt.

29 SHELL HARBOUR RESORT

Scenic rating: 6

on the St. Johns River, in Satsuma

Part of a resort complex that includes a motel, cabins, a restaurant, and a bar, this park is set on 15 wooded acres along the St. Johns River.

Don't be surprised to see at least two dozen peacocks running around the property. With an 800-foot-long dock and 1,600 feet of river shoreline, the campground can accommodate a huge number of anglers. The waterfront restaurant has banquet facilities and makes for a great spot to watch the sun set.

Campsites, facilities: Ten tent sites are set apart from 28 RV sites (some full-hookup). On the premises are restrooms, showers, a dump station, a heated pool, a boat ramp, a dock, horseshoes, volleyball, a restaurant, snacks, a rental cabin, motel-style rooms, a laundry room, and a bar with a pool table, darts, and a big-screen TV. Groceries are about two miles away. Children and leashed pets are welcome.

Reservations, fees: Reservations are recommended. Sites are $10–15 per night. Credit cards are accepted. Long-term stays are OK.

Directions: From Palatka, take U.S. 17 south about 15 miles into Satsuma. Head west (right) on County Road 309 for about two miles until you see Shell Harbour Road. Turn right. The campground is just ahead.

Contact: Shell Harbour Resort, 140 Shell Harbour Road, Satsuma, FL 32189, 386/467-2330.

30 ACOSTA CREEK HARBOR

Scenic rating: 7

north of Welaka

Majestic oak trees and fragrant citrus trees shade this lovely riverfront location on the St. Johns. Popular with anglers and boaters, the four RV sites are part of a large-boat marina with 40 slips and rental cottage complex built on the grounds of a turn-of-the-20th-century home. A boat ramp is one mile away. What to do here? Fish and relax, with the view of the river.

Campsites, facilities: There are four full-hookup sites available for RVs with concrete patios and 30/50-amp electrical hookups. Each has picnic tables, cable TV, and concrete pads. Restrooms, showers, and laundry facilities are available. On the premises are a pool, boat docks, cabins, cottages, a ship store with ice, and efficiencies. The restrooms and pool are wheelchair-accessible. Restaurants are three miles away, and groceries 15 miles. Children are welcome, but most campers are adults, and about half the park is occupied by year-round residents. Leashed pets are permitted.

Reservations, fees: Reservations are recommended. Sites are $25 per night. Credit cards are accepted. Long-term rates are available.

Directions: From the north, take U.S. 17 south to Satsuma. Turn right on County Road 309 and drive 3.5 miles to Acosta Creek Drive. Turn right and go to the end of the road. From Crescent City on U.S. 17, turn left on County Road 308 to Fruitland. Turn on County Road 309 and proceed to Welaka. Drive two more miles and turn left on Acosta Creek Drive.

Contact: Acosta Creek Harbor, 124 Acosta Creek Drive, Satsuma, FL 32189, 386/467-2229, www.acostacreek.com.

31 CARAVELLE RANCH WILDLIFE MANAGEMENT AREA

Scenic rating: 6

south of Palatka

Bald eagles love this place, seeking out hammock islands for nesting sites. You'll also see alligators, a wide variety of birds, and maybe even a Florida black bear. Stretching across 13,383 state-managed acres, Caravelle Ranch Wildlife Conservation Area is distinguished by its location at the confluence of the Ocklawaha and St. Johns Rivers. The Cross-Florida Greenway runs east–west on the northern edge. During hunting season, public access is restricted.

Campsites, facilities: Only tents are permitted at the two primitive campsites. One is on the St. Johns River and accessible only by boat.

The other is inland on the Camp Branch Creek. There are no facilities: Bring water, supplies, mosquito repellent, and everything you'll need. Children are welcome. Leashed pets are permitted.

Reservations, fees: Sites are first-come, first-served. Camping is free. Each site accommodates up to six people. If your party has at least seven people, get a free permit and reserve at least one week ahead at 904/329-4410. Maximum stay for all campers is seven days.

Directions: The main access point by car is the parking lot on State Route 19, six miles south of Palatka. From there, bicyclists and hikers can strike out to the nearest camping area. A boat ramp to the Ocklawaha River is just south of the main entrance on State Route 19.

Contact: Call the Florida Fish and Wildlife Conservation Commission at 352/732-1225. Additional information is available from the St. Johns River Water Management District, Division of Land Management, P.O. Box 1429, Palatka, FL 32178-1429, 386/329-4500 or 800/451-7106, www.sjrwmd.com.

32 DUNNS CREEK CONSERVATION AREA

Scenic rating: 5

south of Palatka

Known mainly by locals and seasonal hunters, this is a very marshy area where people comfortable with primitive backcountry camping may be rewarded with spectacular opportunities to view wildlife, particularly at dusk and dawn. You might see deer, fox, yellow-crowned night herons, red-shouldered hawks, barred owls, and more. But you'll pay for it with comfort, because this 3,182-acre tract of land—purchased by the St. Johns River Water Management District for water conservation purposes—is sparsely developed, with a few dirt roads. Hikers might share a tram road with horseback riders or bicyclists; another dry trail leads through Long Swamp. Bring a hat and sunscreen; occasional pines provide scant shade, but this is mainly floodplain swamp bordering five miles of Dunns Creek.

Campsites, facilities: Only tents are permitted at the two primitive campsites, which must be reached on foot, bicycle, or horseback. There are no facilities: Bring water, supplies, mosquito repellent, and everything you'll need. Children are welcome. Pets must be leashed. During hunting season, the area is closed to other activities.

Reservations, fees: Sites are first-come, first-served. Camping is free. Each site accommodates up to six people. If your party has at least seven people, get a free permit and reserve at least one week ahead at 904/329-4410. Maximum stay for all campers is seven days.

Directions: From Palatka, go south on U.S. 17 eight miles, turn east at Highway 100, and go about three miles to Tram Road. Turn right. Take Tram Road about 0.5 mile to the entrance.

Contact: St. Johns River Water Management District, Division of Land Management, P.O. Box 1429, Palatka, FL 32178-1429, 386/329-4500 or 800/451-7106, www.sjrwmd.com.

33 CRESCENT CITY CAMPGROUND
🏕🏊🐎🚲♿🚐⛺

Scenic rating: 6

near Lake George, on U.S. 17 south of Palatka

Several oaks lend shade to this 10-acre country campground located near the bass-fishing waters of Crescent Lake and Lake George. A small creek runs through the park, where some campsites have concrete pads, while others are gravelly or grassy. All sites have concrete patios. Although overnighters use the park, it's more likely to be filled with vacationers who stay longer and participate in potluck suppers and other planned activities.

Campsites, facilities: Ten tent sites are set apart from the 82 full-hookup RV sites (20 pull-through) with 20-amp, 30-amp, and 50-amp electrical service and cable TV. Park models are available for rent year-round or short-term. Restrooms, showers, a dump station, a laundry room, a recreation room, a pool, a playground, a hiking trail, lighted shuffleboard courts, horseshoes, telephone hookups, fire rings, LP gas sales, and campsite picnic tables are available. Groceries, a restaurant, and bait are about one mile away. Most areas are wheelchair-accessible. Children and leashed pets are permitted.

Reservations, fees: Reservations are recommended in season. Sites are $24–29 per night for two people, plus $3 per extra person. Rates are $5 higher during Race Week (February) and Bike Week (March). Credit cards are accepted. Long-term stays are OK.

Directions: From Palatka, take U.S. 17 south about 20 miles. Look for the campground about one mile north of Crescent City.

Contact: Crescent City Campground, Route 2, P.O. Box 25, Crescent City, FL 32112, 386/698-2020 or 800/634-3968, www.crescentcitycampground.com.

34 LEONARD'S LANDING LAKE CRESCENT RESORT
🏊🚣🚐🐎🚐⛺

Scenic rating: 6

in Crescent City

Lake Crescent is famed for bass and crappie fishing, so most visitors here are focused on angling. At 16,000 acres, the lake is one of the largest in the state and is 13 miles long and two miles wide. This campground (part of the Lake Crescent Motel and Resort) claims to offer the best lake access, with an on-site boat ramp, a dock, and a bait and tackle shop. Sites are sunny and have lake views; about half are occupied by long-term residents.

Campsites, facilities: This 27-unit park has five sites for overnighters in tents or RVs and 21 for seasonal visitors; tents are allowed. All sites have water and electricity (22 have full hookups), picnic tables, grills, cable TV, and optional phone service. Restrooms, showers, a dump station, a heated pool, a recreation room, a boat ramp, a dock, bait and tackle, a restaurant and pub, a snack bar, and a motel are on the premises. A grocery store is across the street. Children are welcome. Small leashed pets are permitted.

Reservations, fees: Reservations are recommended. Sites are $25 per night for two people, plus $3 per extra person. Credit cards are accepted. Stay as long as you like.

Directions: From U.S. 17 in Crescent City, drive east on Grove Avenue when you see the sign for Lake Crescent Motel and Resort, across the street from Miller's Supervalue grocery store.

Contact: Leonard's Landing Lake Crescent Resort, 100 Grove Avenue, Crescent City, FL 32112, 386/698-2485, www.lakecrescent.com.

35 BULL CREEK CAMPGROUND

Scenic rating: 5

at Dead Lake, west of Flagler Beach

Anglers arrive by boat, car, or seaplane to sleep at these waterfront sites that offer easy access to two lakes—Dead Lake and Crescent Lake. The focus of the rustic six-acre campground is water: A guide service helps anglers track down crappie and bass. Waterskiing and a protected cove for boaters round out the water-oriented amenities, including a marina and boat docks.

Campsites, facilities: There are 50 campsites for tents or RVs up to 36 feet long, each with a picnic table and full hookups (but no cable TV). A boat ramp, boat rentals, a restaurant, showers, restrooms, cottages, cabins, horseshoes, bait and tackle, firewood, limited groceries, and a laundry room are available. Quiet time is enforced at 9 P.M., and "rowdiness" and profanity will not be tolerated. Management says most of the park is wheelchair-accessible.

Children and leashed pets are permitted (inside RVs only).

Reservations, fees: Reservations are recommended. Sites are $27 per night for two people, plus $5 for each additional person over age 12. Credit cards are accepted. Long-term rates are offered.

Directions: From I-95 near Flagler Beach, take Exit 284 and drive about six miles west on State Road 100. Turn left at State Road 305. Proceed about four miles south to State Road 2006, turn right, and continue four miles to the campground where the road dead-ends at Dead Lake.

Contact: Bull Creek Campground, 3861 County Road 2006, Bunnell, FL 32110, 386/437-3451.

36 GEORGETOWN MARINA AND LODGE

Scenic rating: 5

on Lake George, in Georgetown

The lure here is fishing for the big bass that inhabit 11-mile-long Lake George. In fact, this quiet, out-of-the-way campground/marina/fish camp boasts, "See what a fish camp should be!" It's located on the St. Johns River at the mouth of Lake George. Largemouth bass are the main game fish, yet some anglers also go after striped bass, bream, shellcracker, catfish, or speckled perch. Efficiency apartments are available, in case you have guests. Retirees are the main patrons of these semi-shaded camping sites, which are set among pines. Other parts of the park are shaded by large oaks.

Campsites, facilities: All 33 full-hookup sites are for RVs, and 8 are pull-through. Each site has a concrete patio. Electrical service is rated 20-amp, 30-amp, and 50-amp. Slideouts and rigs as long as 60 feet can be accommodated. About 65 percent of the park is occupied by permanent residents. Restrooms, showers, a dump station, a boat ramp, boat slips, charter fishing, horseshoes, cable TV, a laundry room, and a wheelchair-accessible fishing dock are available. Planned activities include potluck dinners, cookouts, bingo, and car trips to local malls. Groceries and a restaurant are located within one mile. Children and leashed pets are permitted.

Reservations, fees: Reservations are recommended. Sites are $25 per night for two people, plus $2 for each extra person. Credit cards are accepted. Long-term stays are OK.

Directions: From Palatka, take U.S. 17 south about 15 miles into Satsuma. Turn right on County Road 309 and proceed about 16 miles into Georgetown. When you pass the only yield sign in Georgetown, continue about one mile. The marina and lodge are on the right.

Contact: Georgetown Marina and Lodge, P.O. Box 171, 1533 County Road 309, Georgetown, FL 32139, 386/467-2002 or 866/325-2003, georgetownmarina@gbso.net.

37 PORT COVE RV PARK & MARINA

Scenic rating: 4

near Georgetown

This brand-new water-oriented park on the St. Johns River is still being improved, but as of early 2007, a boat dock and 74 sites were available on wooded sites.

Campsites, facilities: There are 74 RV sites with full hookups and concrete pads. Restrooms, showers, laundry facilities, and cable TV are available. A pool, store, and restaurants are planned. Children are welcome, but adults over age 35 are preferred. Leashed pets under 20 pounds are permitted.

Reservations, fees: Reservations are recommended. Sites are $27 per night for two people, plus $7.50 per extra person. All areas are said to be wheelchair-accessible. Credit cards are not accepted. Long-term rates are available.

Directions: From Palatka, take U.S.17 south

about 15 miles into Satsuma. Turn right on County Road 309 and proceed about 16 miles into Georgetown.

Contact: Port Cove RV Park & Marina, 110 Georgetown Landing Road, Georgetown, FL 32139, 386/467-2880, rkoger@bellsouth .net.

38 LAKE GEORGE CONSERVATION AREA

Scenic rating: 6

west of Seville, near Lake George

Several primitive sites are found in the Lake George Conservation Area, including one described here. It's ideal for a large party of horseback riders who want to camp out together. These 19,831 acres offer virtually unlimited opportunities for exploration along a network of dirt roads. It's about a 10-mile ride to the Jumping Gully campsite (see campground in this chapter), mostly through pine woods, if you'd like to make it a two-night affair. Look for deer and bobcats along the way.

You don't have to be saddle-bound to camp here. Mountain bikers and hikers might wish to use the forest roads in the conservation area, home to threatened and endangered species, including the Florida black bear and Sherman's fox squirrel. Skip swimming, though, because nearby Lake George is quite shallow around the edges and contains a plentiful population of alligators. Bring your own gear to canoe, boat, or fish for bass.

Campsites, facilities: This oak-shaded tent camping area is generally reserved for groups of seven or more people; if your party is smaller, check with the water district to see if it is available. A fire ring is provided, as is a hand-cranked well, but its water technically is not drinkable. It can be used for washing up, watering horses, and the like, and some people do drink from wells like this one, because they're so far removed from civilization that they're considered unlikely to be polluted. Two boat ramps are nearby. Laundry facilities and groceries are about 15 miles away in Crescent City. Children and leashed pets are permitted.

Reservations, fees: Permits are required for groups of seven or more and should be applied for at least one week in advance. Camping is free. The maximum stay is seven days. Camping is forbidden during the general gun season for hunters (typically in November).

Directions: Drive north on U.S. 17 from Barberville. When you reach the hamlet of Seville, head west on County Road 305/Lake George Road. The entrance to the tract is about two miles ahead and is known as Truck Trail No. 2. That's where you'll see the group camping area. For a map, check the website listed below.

Contact: St. Johns River Water Management District, Division of Land Management, P.O. Box 1429, Palatka, FL 32178-1429, 386/329-4883, www.sjrwmd.com. Additional information is available from Volusia County's Department of Environmental Management at 386/804-0439.

39 BARRS LANDING
🏃 🚲 ⛵ 🛶 🐕 ⛺

Scenic rating: 5

near Seville on Lake George, in the Lake George Conservation Area

The Barrs Landing campsite might look like the nicest around if you're perusing a map of the conservation area, because it's the only one right on Lake George. But don't be fooled. This is basically a low-lying clearing in the brush at the water's edge. It's often mosquito-infested and occasionally wet. A better choice is Jumping Gully (see listing in this chapter). Or, if you're camping with a group and have a permit, try the Lake George Conservation Area Group Camping site (see listing in this chapter).

Still, there are virtually unlimited opportunities for horseback riding, biking, and hiking along a network of dirt roads in these 25,000-plus remote acres jointly owned by the water management district, Volusia County, and the state. Bring your own boat or canoe to fish at Lake George. Forget swimming, though. For one thing, the lake is quite shallow at the edge; and for another, it boasts a fairly large population of alligators.

Look for otters, deer, bobcats, and gopher tortoises during your walks. If you're willing to do without such niceties as showers, you'll be rewarded by sleeping in woods that also are home to the Florida black bear (a threatened species), Sherman's fox squirrel (an endangered species), and a large concentration of bald eagles.

Campsites, facilities: Four rustic tent sites accommodate up to 24 people during non-hunting season, but are closed during the general gun season (typically November). No facilities are available. For a vault toilet, you'll need to go to the Lake George Conservation Area group camping site. Laundry facilities and groceries are about 15 miles away in Crescent City. Children and leashed pets are permitted.

Reservations, fees: Reservations are not accepted, but permits are required for groups of seven or more. Camping is free. The maximum stay is seven days.

Directions: Drive north on U.S. 17 from Barberville. When you reach the hamlet of Seville, head west on County Road 305/Lake George Road. The entrance to the tract is about two miles ahead. Just inside the entrance, head north (right) about two miles on Truck Trail No. 2, a dirt road. Turn left onto another dirt road known as Barrs Road, which will take you to the lakeside camping area.

Contact: St. Johns River Water Management District, Division of Land Management, P.O. Box 1429, Palatka, FL 32178-1429, 386/329-4500 or 800/451-7106, www.sjrwmd.com.

40 JUMPING GULLY

Scenic rating: 7

south of Palatka, in the Lake George
Conservation Area

These 39 square miles of remote land near
Lake George are jointly owned by the water
management district, Volusia County, and
the state. If you're willing to do without such
niceties as showers (you *could* rinse off in the
lake), you'll be amply rewarded. You'll camp
in the domain of endangered Sherman's fox
squirrels, a large concentration of bald eagles,
and Florida black bears, a threatened species.
Look for alligators, otters, bobcats, deer, and
gopher tortoises.

Campers sleep in a clearing set in a picturesque oak hammock with a little creek running
through. There are virtually unlimited opportunities for horseback riding, biking, and hiking
along a network of dirt roads. The bass haven
of 11-mile-long Lake George attracts anglers,
boaters, and, at times, canoeists and kayakers.

Camping isn't allowed during periods when
the general gun season is in effect for hunters.
The dates change slightly from year to year,
but normally span mid- to late November.

Campsites, facilities: Four primitive tent
sites accommodate up to 24 people. No facilities are available, other than an artesian-
well spigot for cleanup water. Bring drinking
water, food, mosquito repellent, and all other
supplies. Laundry and groceries are about 10
to 15 miles away in Crescent City. Children
and leashed pets are permitted.

Reservations, fees: Reservations are not accepted, but permits are required for groups of
seven or more. Camping is free. The maximum stay is seven days.

Directions: From Barberville, head north
on U.S. 17. When you reach the hamlet of
Seville, go west on County Road 305/Lake
George Drive. The entrance to the tract is
about two miles ahead. Turn right (north) on
Truck Trail No. 2, a dirt road. Continue for
about five miles, where Denver Road cuts off

to the right. The camping area is off to the
left in a wooded area.

Contact: St. Johns River Water Management
District, Division of Land Management, P.O.
Box 1429, Palatka, FL 32178-1429, 386/329-
4500 or 800/451-7106, www.sjrwmd.com.

41 PINE ISLAND CAMP-GROUND AND MARINA

Scenic rating: 3

on Lake George, west of Seville

If you like fishing, you'll like these four rustic
acres on the shores of 100-square-mile Lake
George. The grassy campsites and cabins are
most popular among anglers seeking bass in
the 72°F lake waters and with hunters hot
on the trail of deer, turkey, hogs, and ducks.
Much of the park is occupied by full-timers.

Campsites, facilities: The 29 campsites are for
RVs up to 32 feet long. Sixteen have full hookups; the rest have water and 30-amp electricity.
On the premises are showers, restrooms, cabin
rentals, a boat ramp, a marina, boat slips,
fishing guide services, a game room, a nature
trail, horseshoes, a snack bar with ice, bait and
tackle, a recreation room, propane gas tank
exchange, and laundry facilities. Most of the
park is wheelchair-accessible. A convenience
store is located within four miles. Children
and leashed pets are allowed.

Reservations, fees: Reservations are recommended. Sites are $9.50–12 per night for two
people, plus $1 for each additional person.
Credit cards are not accepted. Long-term stays
are OK.

Directions: Drive north on U.S. 17 from Barberville. When you reach the hamlet of Seville,
head west on County Road 305/Lake George
Road, passing through the Lake George Conservation Area. The road ends at Pine Island
Marina.

Contact: Pine Island Campground and Marina, 1600 Lake George Road, Seville, FL
32190, 386/749-2818.

OCALA

© MARILYN MOORE

BEST CAMPGROUNDS

◖ **Natural Springs**
Salt Springs Recreation Area, **page 208**
Rainbow Springs State Park, **page 225**

◖ **Most Luxurious**
Grand Lake RV and Golf Resort, **page 205**

◖ **Most Unusual**
Rock Crusher Canyon RV and Music Park,
  page 233

The Ocala area is horse country. You'll see gently rolling hills of green grass, white rail fences, and glossy-coated thorough-breds frolicking in the pastures. But it's probably even better known for being home to the Ocala National Forest, a huge swath of timberland perfect for camping out.

The Silver Springs theme park is a tourist attraction with a long history. Famed for its glass-bottom boat rides that allow you to peer into crystal-clear water, it's a mix of environmental attractions and more traditional theme-park fare, such as concerts, boat and auto shows, festivals, and a gondola ride 80 feet above the springs. Henry Ford, Thomas Edison, and thousands of others have visited the theme park, which today includes animals from six continents, a petting zoo, and picnic areas on its 350 acres. Even Tarzan swung around here long ago – actually, it was actor Johnny Weissmuller shooting a 1939 Tarzan film across the street at the 780-square-foot cavern of Silver Springs. Also across the street is Wild Waters, a six-acre water park.

One of Florida's newest full-service, publicly owned camping parks is at Silver River State Park, practically next door to Silver Springs. With gravel-pad RV sites and paved roads, this is a state park with private-park class. A bonus: Look for otters in the early morning along the Silver River, reached via a short walking trail. Anglers, hikers, mountain bikers, and seasonal hunters can drive a short distance east from the campground to popular Ocala National Forest, one of three federally run forests in Florida.

Alexander Springs, where there's a canoe run, picnic area, and nature trails, hosts another popular campground. The surrounding Ocala National Forest is one of the state's last bastions of the Florida black bear, although you're more likely to glimpse a wild turkey or a deer scampering away in the distance. Farther south is Mount Dora, a quaint historic town set on a big lake, with a historic inn, lots of great restaurants, art galleries, and antiques shops.

If you're in the mood to see more natural art, head west to the Gulf of Mexico, where you can see a manatee up close. At Homosassa Springs State Wildlife Park, a rehabilitation center for manatees born in captivity or orphaned or injured in the wild, an underwater observatory lets visitors observe them eye-to-eye. The manatees share the grounds with wood ducks, flamingos, birds of prey, herons, egrets, alligators, snakes, hippopotamuses, black bears, white-tailed deer, and river otters.

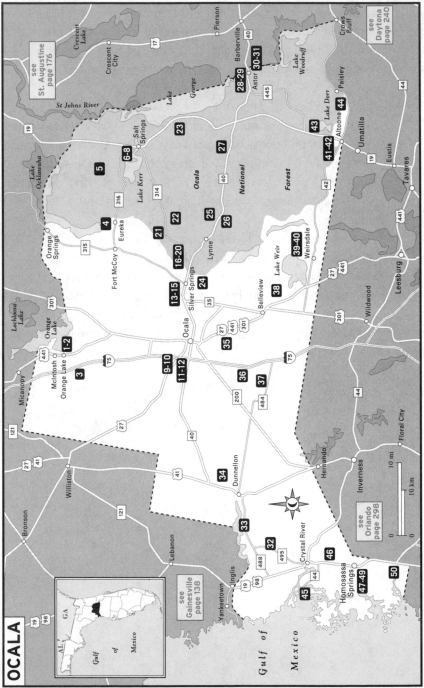

© AVALON TRAVEL PUBLISHING, INC.

1 SPORTSMAN'S COVE ON ORANGE LAKE

Scenic rating: 4

at Orange Lake, in McIntosh

As its name suggests, this campground is used by anglers as a launch pad for a day of snagging panfish and bass at Orange Lake and Lake Lochloosa. But it's also convenient to the interstate for overnighters, and serves as a good base camp for visiting Gainesville or Silver Springs. Oak trees and lake views are the reward for staying here, as well as the quiet. Instead of a monotonous blue sea that stretches hypnotically to the horizon, this scene is broken up by islands—Redbird Island is up ahead, and to the right are Hixon, Bird, and McCormick Islands. Lake levels have varied in recent years; as of this writing, the lake is "beautiful and the crappie are jumping in the boat. You'll have no problem reaching the limit," says the manager. Under new ownership since 2005, this retiree-oriented community of grassy canalside campsites also has wintertime activities to keep campers entertained. Some of the sites are occupied by year-round residents, but most visitors come for three- to six-month stays.

Campsites, facilities: All 49 full-hookup campsites have 30-amp or 50-amp electrical service. Cabins, cable TV, showers, restrooms, a dump station, a boat ramp, boat slips, a recreation room, and laundry facilities are available. Children are welcome. Leashed pets are permitted, but must use the dog walk on the park's east side.

Reservations, fees: Reservations are recommended. Sites are $18 per night for two people, plus $1.50 for each additional person. Long-term rates are available. Credit cards are not accepted.

Directions: From I-75 at Exit 368, take County Road 318 east for two miles to U.S. 441. Turn left. Continue three more miles north, passing State Road 320, and turn right at Avenue F, which is at the second blinking light. The campground entrance is ahead.

Contact: Sportsman's Cove on Orange Lake, 5423 Avenue F (mailing address: P.O. Box 107), McIntosh, FL 32664, 352/591-1435.

2 GRAND LAKE RV AND GOLF RESORT

Scenic rating: 8

on Orange Lake, in the town of Orange Lake

BEST (

A nine-hole championship golf course greets RVers as they drive into this super-manicured resort, which sprawls on a hill overlooking Orange Lake. If golf isn't your game, you'll find world-class bass fishing in the lake and three separate gathering places for socializing; parimutuel betting is available at the jai alai fronton (arena) next door. The management boasts that this is one of the top-rated RV parks in the nation; however, as of this writing, a park-model community was being developed, and lots are for sale. Shade is minimal in most of the park, but some sites have panoramic views of the lake. Be careful with children around the lake; they are not allowed near it, because of alligators.

Campsites, facilities: These 239 full-hookup RV sites overlook Orange Lake and have 30/50-amp electrical service. Some sites are grassy; "super" sites have concrete patios. Large RVs and slideouts can be accommodated, and many sites are pull-through. A nine-hole golf course, a driving range, a pool, a clubhouse, a TV room, shuffleboard, exercise trails, golf lessons, and fishing lessons entertain campers. Showers, restrooms, a dump station, a boat dock, a pier, a barbecue pit, park models, and laundry facilities are available. All areas are wheelchair-accessible. Children must be adult-supervised when at the pool, fishing, or near the pier. Leashed pets must walk in the open field or on the edge of the road.

Reservations, fees: Reservations are

recommended. Sites are $31–35 per night. Credit cards are accepted. Long-term rates are available.

Directions: From I-75 at Exit 368, take County Road 318 east for about two miles, crossing U.S. 441. Turn left (north) on the road next to Ocala Jai Alai to get to the campground.

Contact: Grand Lake RV and Golf Resort, P.O. Box 370/4555 West Highway 318, Orange Lake, FL 32681, 352/591-3474 or 800/435-2291, www.grandlakeresort.com.

3 ENCORE RV PARK–OCALA

Scenic rating: 9

off I-75, between Gainesville and Ocala

Set amid the sprawling ranches of horse country, this immaculate RV resort with a heated pool is surprisingly wooded and parklike. Paved roads wind past concrete-pad campsites with patios. Many campers stay for the season, but the park's location near the interstate makes it a good option for overnight travelers as well. The pool is an impressive sight for a campground swimming hole: The blue waters and encircling patio are surrounded by towering moss-draped oaks that provide some shade. Within a short drive is Orange Lake, famed for bass fishing, and the historic towns of McIntosh and Micanopy, which have quaint antiques shops.

Campsites, facilities: There are 140 full-hookup RV sites (45 pull-through) with 30/50-amp electrical service. The park describes itself as modem-friendly. A pool, horseshoes, shuffleboard, showers, restrooms, a dump station, firewood, cable TV, telephone hookups, laundry facilities, and two recreation halls with kitchens are available. Planned activities include tai chi, aerobics, and fishing outings, plus the usual array of card games, potlucks, movies, and so forth. Supermarkets and restaurants are within six miles. Children are welcome. Leashed pets are permitted, but they must use the wooded dog walk on the park's east side.

Reservations, fees: Reservations are recommended. Sites are $28 per night. Credit cards are accepted. Long-term rates are available.

Directions: From I-75 at Exit 368, turn west onto County Road 318. Go 200 yards, turn left (south) on Highway 225, and continue 0.5 mile to the entrance on the left.

Contact: Encore RV Park—Ocala, 16905 Northwest Highway 225, Reddick, FL 32686, 352/591-1723 or 877/267-8737, fax 352/591-2842, www.rvonthego.com.

4 OCKLAWAHA RV PARK AND CANOE OUTPOST

Scenic rating: 8

on the Ocklawaha River, near Ocala National Forest

Canoeing beneath the moss-draped trees flanking the 110-mile-long Ocklawaha River is something bored office workers might daydream about as they wait for five o'clock to roll around. Paddlers in spring and fall wind through narrow waterways lined with gnarly cypress, swamp maple, and sabal palm—the fan-leafed state tree. Along the way, an early morning mist rises over spring-fed streams. The river widens into lily-pad-filled ponds in some places. Bobcats, deer, and Florida black bears live in the surrounding forest.

Adventure-seekers tend to be drawn to this seven-acre campground, where canoes rent for $35 daily and campsites fill up fast, except in summer. Some seasonal campers have stayed here at least three consecutive winters. Anglers can launch at the boat ramp to go after some 100 species of fish in the Ocklawaha, or take advantage of the park's catch-and-release fishing pond. RV sites are shady or sunny. Proprietor Larry Reiche contends there are no mosquitoes to speak of, and the canopy of trees makes riverfront canoe-in camping comfortably cooler in summer. Hikers and cyclists may see deer or wild turkeys along the nearby Cross Florida Greenway, which long ago was meant to become a barge canal gouged through the belly of Florida, almost like the Panama Canal, linking the Atlantic Ocean and the Gulf of Mexico. A welcome center for the Cross Florida Greenway and Ocala National Forest is at the corner of County Road 316 and Highway 40.

Campsites, facilities: There are 12 full-hookup RV sites with electricity. A catch-and-release fishing pond, a small playground, a recreation room, showers, restrooms, snacks, a boat ramp, limited camping and fishing supplies, a dump station, cabin rentals, and canoe and kayak rentals are available. Children are welcome. Dogs may chase a ball in a large field but must be leashed elsewhere, including along the park's dog walk.

Reservations, fees: Reservations are recommended for canoeing or camping. Nightly fee is $21 for four people. Add $3 for each additional person. A pet deposit of $50 is required. Overnight primitive canoe/camping trips are $95 per rental canoe per day, plus transportation ($20–45). Or bring your own canoe and just pay for the shuttle. Credit cards are accepted. Long-term stays are OK.

Directions: From I-75 at Exit 352, take State Road 40 east about 10 miles through Ocala and Silver Springs. Turn left at County Road 315 and proceed 12 miles north to County Road 316. Turn right. The campground is about four miles ahead at the Ocklawaha River. Turn left before the bridge, and follow to the camp store, located near where the road's pavement ends.

Contact: Ocklawaha RV Park and Canoe Outpost, 15260 Northeast 152nd Place, Fort McCoy, FL 32134, 352/236-4606, www.outpostresort.com.

5 LAKE DELANCY EAST CAMPGROUND

Scenic rating: 3

in northern Ocala National Forest

The Florida National Scenic Trail passes through this rustic, no-frills campground, offering you an opportunity to scale the rolling, sandy, pine-studded hills that dominate the sunny northern part of the forest. You also can try your hand at fishing in the shallow freshwater lake next to the campground, which is little more than a clearing in the woods and is dominated by hunters during prescribed seasons. The campground is closed during the summer. Please note: The Lake Delancy West Campground nearby is designated for motorcyclists, horseback riders, and all-terrain vehicle camping.

Campsites, facilities: This primitive camping area can accommodate up to 30 self-contained RVs and 80 tents. Vault toilets, hand-pumped drinking water, fire rings, grills, and several picnic tables are available. There are no showers. Children are welcome. Leashed pets are permitted.

Reservations, fees: Reservations are not accepted, nor are credit cards. Sites are $6 per night. The maximum stay is 14 days in any 30-day period. The campground is open October 1–June 1 only.

Directions: From Ocala, take State Road 40 east about 12 miles. Turn left onto County Road 314 and continue northeast about 15 miles. Turn left (north) onto Forest Service Road 88 and go about nine miles, then turn right (east) onto Forest Service Road 75 and look for the campground on the right. If you reach State Road 19, you've gone too far.

Contact: Ocala National Forest, Lake George Ranger District, 17147 East State Road 40, Silver Springs, FL 34488, 352/236-0288 or 352/625-2520, www.fs.fed.us/r8/florida/recreation/index_oca.shtml.

6 SALT SPRINGS RECREATION AREA

🏕️ 🏊 🛶 🚤 〰️ 🎣 ♿ 🚐 ⛺

Scenic rating: 9

in northeastern Ocala National Forest

BEST (

The big attraction here is the natural spring, called Salt Springs—but not salty like ocean water. Instead, it's tinged with calcium, sodium, potassium, and other minerals, yet is still clear enough to make swimming or snorkeling pleasant. Flowing at a speedy rate of 53 million gallons per day, the spring was treasured by Native Americans and was said to have medicinal value, with each of the five boils supposedly curing different ailments. It's even been said that these waters were the legendary Fountain of Youth. When President Roosevelt designated the Ocala National Forest in 1908, hardy travelers braved difficult roads to take a dip.

Canoeists follow the spring's run to Lake George (rental canoes are available nearby), while anglers snag bass at Florida's second-largest lake. Motorboats can be rented at Salt Springs Marina and Landing (352/685-2255).

There's good hiking nearby along the Salt Springs Trail, a three-foot-wide dirt path that cuts a two-mile loop through sand-pine scrub, slash-pine flat woods, bayheads, cypress, and clusters of oak trees. The trail leads to an observation platform on the Salt Springs Run, a nice place to picnic in cooler months. For a longer hiking challenge, try the sandier, more open portion of the Florida National Scenic Trail that runs nearby. The Bear Swamp Trail boardwalk winds for 1.5 miles past some huge cypress trees.

The campground itself is sort of bowl-shaped, leading down to the springs. Big shady oaks, as well as some sand pine and longleaf pine, dot the grounds. The RV sites are grassy, and primitive sites are sandy. If you bring horseshoes or a basketball, you can use them at facilities here. Salt Springs

is actually a small town in the woods where you can get pizza, seafood, or a square meal at various restaurants, or mail a postcard at the local post office. Campers are a mix of locals, anglers, families, and tourists from as far away as Germany, the United Kingdom, and Alaska. Planned activities such as bingo, potluck dinners, and day trips to local attractions are available in the winter months (October–April).

Campsites, facilities: There are 103 full-hookup RV sites (back-in only) with full hookups and 20/30/50-amp electrical service. In addition, there are 54 primitive sites for tents or self-contained campers. Rigs as large as 40 feet and slide-outs can be accommodated. Each site has a picnic table, a grill, and a fire ring. On the premises are restrooms, showers, a dump station, a small store, a recreation barn, and a picnic area. You can swim in the springs. The bathhouse, office, and store are wheelchair-accessible. Streets are paved. A camp store offers ice, camping supplies, snacks, and souvenirs. Groceries and restaurants are within one mile. Malls and hospitals are 24–30 miles away. Children and leashed pets are welcome. Pets are not allowed in the day-use area (the spring). Note that checkout time is 1 p.m.; if you stay longer, you will be charged a day-use fee. The campground gate is locked around sunset.

Reservations, fees: Reservations are recommended; call 877/444-6777 or visit www.reserveusa.com. Full-hookup sites are $20 per night for five people and two vehicles, plus $5 for electricity; primitive sites are $14 for five people and two vehicles. The charge for an extra person is $4. Credit cards are accepted. Maximum stay is two weeks during summer (April–October) and six months in winter.

Directions: From Ocala, take State Road 40 east 11 miles. At County Road 314, turn northeast and drive 16 miles. At State Route 19, drive 0.25 mile and look for the campground on the right.

Contact: Salt Springs Recreation Area, Ocala National Forest, 14152 State Road 19 North,

Salt Springs, FL, 32134. Mailing address: c/o American Land and Leisure, P.O. Box 5358, Salt Springs, FL 32134, 352/685-2048 or 352/685-2674.

☑ ELITE RESORTS AT SALT SPRINGS
🚲 🏊 🛶 🚤 🏕 🐕 ♿ 🚐

Scenic rating: 9

in northeastern Ocala National Forest

This wooded 70-acre campground fronts onto Little Lake Kerr, where you can fish or rent pontoon boats from the park. It's one of the more deluxe RV-oriented parks in the Ocala National Forest and is located 300 yards from the Salt Springs. In the recreation hall, you'll find bingo twice weekly, dances on Saturday nights, and myriad other activities. A modem is accessible, if you need to check your email. Vacation homes and lots are for sale.

Campsites, facilities: There are 470 RV sites available for overnighters, of which 50 can be used for seasonal stays. All have full hookups, picnic tables, and cable TV. RVs as large as 45 feet can be accommodated, and eight sites have 50-amp electrical service. Restrooms, showers, a dump station, laundry facilities, and telephone service are available. On the premises are a pool, a sandy beach, a boat ramp, a dock, a clubhouse, propane gas sales, horseshoe pits, volleyball and shuffleboard courts, tennis courts, a dog-walk area, a shopping center with two restaurants, 40 cottages for rent, nature trails, and miniature golf. Most areas are wheelchair-accessible; all roads are paved. Children are welcome. Leashed pets are permitted.

Reservations, fees: Reservations are recommended but usually are not necessary. Sites are $32 per night, plus $3 for 50-amp electricity, $5 for each additional person, and $5 for pull-through sites. Credit cards are accepted. Long-term rates are available.

Directions: From Ocala, take State Road 40 east about 12 miles to County Road 314. Turn left and drive 18 miles north to the campground. At State Road 19, turn north and go one mile to the park. From I-95 in Daytona, take Exit 88 westbound 25 miles on State Road 40 to State Road 19. Turn north and drive 17 miles to the park.

Contact: Elite Resorts at Salt Springs, 25250 East County Road 316, Salt Springs, FL 32134, 352/685-1900, fax 352/685-0557, www.eliteresorts.com.

☑ GORE'S LANDING RECREATION SITE
🛶 🚤 ⛺

Scenic rating: 3

on the Ocklawaha River

You might want to take a look at this little-frequented former hunting camp before deciding, sight unseen, to stop at this county park. Lacking electricity, water, and showers, Gore's Landing won't satisfy big-city sensibilities. But canoeists and anglers in pursuit of any of 100 species of fish can think of this primitive camping area as a crash pad that allows them to get on the Ocklawaha River bright and early, thanks to the on-site boat ramp. If you don't have a canoe, rentals are available at Ocklawaha Outpost on County Road 316 at the river; call 352/236-4606. The 118-acre park is a pleasant enough place to eat a picnic lunch at the no-frills concrete picnic tables shaded somewhat by trees.

Campsites, facilities: Twelve primitive camp sites are here. A restroom, picnic tables, a boat ramp, and barbecue grills are available. Children are welcome. Pets are prohibited.

Reservations, fees: Reservations are not taken. Sites are $5 per night. Credit cards are not accepted.

Directions: From I-75 at Exit 352, take State Road 40 east about 10 miles through Ocala and Silver Springs. Turn left at County Road 315. Turn right at Northeast 105th Street (a sign marks the turn). The park is ahead.

Contact: Marion County Parks and Recreation, 8282 Southeast County Road 314, Ocala, FL 34470, 352/236-7111. The park is located at 13750 Northeast 80th Street, 352/671-8560.

9 OAK TREE VILLAGE CAMPGROUND

Scenic rating: 5

west of Ocala

This park, a quick hop off I-75, feels almost like a subdivision, albeit a tree-shaded one. Row after row, street after street, campers are lined up 14 abreast, all parked diagonally on paved, 10-mph streets that are straight as arrows. When the pool is crowded, floats and tubes are forbidden. Most campsites at the 40-acre park are shaded (hence the park's name). Campsites 7–14 are closest to the laundry facilities, pool, and playground. Sites 104 and 105 flank the showers. Anglers, hikers, mountain bikers, and hunters can head about 15 miles east to Ocala National Forest. For a joyride, head west from the campground on U.S. 27.

In about one mile, you'll begin to see would-be champion horses grazing on the pretty rolling hills of some of the area's fabled horse farms. Double Diamond Farm is one of several in the region that permits visitors (1 P.M.–4 P.M. weekdays, call 352/237-3834).

Campsites, facilities: There are 137 pull-through RV sites (70 with full hookups with 30-amp electrical service). About 68 sites are available for overnight visitors. A pool, a playground, horseshoes, shuffleboard, racquetball, a party room, tennis, and winter social programs entertain campers. Showers, restrooms, picnic tables, a dump station, and laundry facilities are available. Management says restrooms and the recreation room are wheelchair-accessible. Groceries are within one mile, and a restaurant is 0.25 mile away. Children under 12 must be adult-supervised at the pool and recreation area. All pets—even cats—must be leashed.

Reservations, fees: Reservations are not necessary. Sites are $22–25 per night for two people, plus $2 for each additional person. Major credit cards are accepted. Long-term stays are OK.

Directions: From I-75 at Ocala, take Exit 354 onto U.S. 27 heading west and turn right

horses grazing in Ocala

almost immediately at Blitchton Road. Proceed 0.25 mile to the campground.

Contact: Oak Tree Village Campground, 4039 Northwest Blitchton Road, Ocala, FL 34482, 352/629-1569.

10 ARROWHEAD CAMPSITES AND MOBILE HOME PARK

Scenic rating: 4

west of Ocala

This campground is a quick detour from I-75 for weary travelers on the road to Disney, and certainly the park borrows from that proximity in describing itself as a "convenient good neighborly park." About 40 percent of the park is occupied by year-round residents. Most seasonal visitors are from the Midwest and New York. They stay here in the winter months to play shuffleboard and partake in such planned activities as bingo, coffee klatches, dinners, and dances.

Campsites, facilities: Most of the 128 RV sites have full hookups, picnic tables, and drive-through access. A separate tent section in front of the campground office offers four sandy spots with water and electricity. Thirty-three sites have 50-amp service, the rest are 30-amp. The shady, level sites average 20 by 50 feet in size. They can accommodate 40-foot-long RVs and slideouts. About 40 sites are available for overnight visitors. Dial-up Internet service is available in the office. A pool, a playground, an exercise room, horseshoes, shuffleboard, a recreation room, a camp circle, and a wintertime activity schedule entertain campers. Showers, restrooms, firewood, cable TV, and laundry facilities are available. A camp store sells snacks, camping supplies, and propane gas. Most areas are wheelchair-accessible. Roads are paved. Groceries and a restaurant are within 300 feet. Children are permitted. Leashed pets are accepted.

Reservations, fees: Reservations are recommended in winter. Nightly fee for two people in an RV is $21–25. Add $1 per extra person. Major credit cards are accepted. Long-term rates are available.

Directions: From I-75 at Ocala, take Exit 354 onto U.S. 27 heading west, then turn left onto Northwest 38th Avenue. The campground is 250 feet ahead.

Contact: Arrowhead Campsites and Mobile Home Park, 1720 Northwest 38th Avenue, Ocala, FL 34482, 352/622-5627, shan1234@earthlink.net.

11 HOLIDAY TRAV-L-PARK

Scenic rating: 2

off I-75, in Ocala

Snowbirds fleeing blustery northern temperatures like to park big rigs at this 9.5-acre park, but it's also a convenient stop from I-75. Long-term visitors spend many a winter hour engaged in park activities such as bingo, suppers, and group barbecues, or visiting the Silver Springs theme park or nearby flea markets. Row after row, 12 to 13 campers are parked diagonally along ruler-straight streets. Oaks shade some grassy/sandy sites, but others are sunny. About half the lots are occupied year-round, and your neighbors will include families, seasonal vacationers, and working people, as well as repeat visitors who return year after year.

For a pleasant ride, go west along the rolling terrain of U.S. 27 to pass would-be champion thoroughbreds at some of the region's horse farms. To watch equestrian training activity at Ocala Breeders' Sales Company and Training Center, show up before 10 A.M. (352/237-2154). Some anglers, hikers, mountain bikers, and seasonal hunters come here to be just 20 miles from Ocala National Forest.

Campsites, facilities: Four tent sites and 111 full-hookup RV sites are available. All have 30-amp electrical service and picnic tables, and 102 are pull-through. More than 50 sites have 50-amp service. The grassy, mostly shady, level sites are 30–35 feet wide and 65 feet long. Some sites allow for satellite dish setup; cable TV is included in the nightly fee. A wireless network for accessing the Internet is available in the clubhouse. A pool, a playground, a horseshoe pit, shuffleboard, a recreation room, and winter activities entertain campers. Showers, restrooms, picnic tables, a dump station, a store with ice, snacks, propane and camping supplies, cable TV, telephone hookups, and laundry facilities are available. Restaurants, groceries, malls, and hospitals are within three miles. All areas of the park are wheelchair-accessible. Children must be accompanied by an adult at the pool. Leashed dogs should use the dog walk or fenced dog run near the 100 row. The management is super-strict about cleaning up after your dog; in fact, you must carry a visible pickup bag or other device whenever you walk your dog.

Reservations, fees: Reservations are recommended, particularly in winter. Sites are $25 per night for two people, plus $2 for each additional person. Credit cards are accepted. Long-term rates are available, and the maximum length of stay is indefinite.

Directions: From I-75 at Exit 352, take State Road 40 west 0.25 mile to the park on the right.

Contact: Holiday Trav-L-Park, 4001 West Silver Springs Boulevard, Ocala, FL 34482, 352/622-5330 or 800/833-2164.

12 MOTOR INNS MOTEL AND RV PARK
≋ 🐾 ♿ 🚐

Scenic rating: 2

off I-75, in Ocala

Convenience is the main attraction here, though the park prides itself on being clean and quiet. RVs are somewhat surrounded, with a handful of mobile homes to the north and two motel buildings and a fruit stand to the south. I-75, which leads vacationers to Disney World, Tampa, or even Michigan, is just one block west. A paved road with a 10-mph speed limit passes the partially shaded sites. About 15 percent of the park is occupied by year-round residents in mobile homes. Most visitors are over 55, though families are welcome. Free coffee is available in the office.

Campsites, facilities: Most of the 80 sites available for RVs have full hookups, with a choice of 30-amp or 50-amp electrical service. Sites are grassy and level, measuring about 30 feet wide by 60 feet deep, and they can accommodate the largest RVs (up to 50 feet long) and slide-outs. Sunny sites allow for setup of satellite dishes. A pool, showers, restrooms, a dump station, ice, cable TV, and laundry facilities are available. Groceries, malls, and restaurants are within three miles. All areas are wheelchair-accessible. Kids must be supervised at all times. Small leashed animals are permitted, but pooches must use the park's dog walk.

Reservations, fees: Reservations are recommended, particularly in winter. Sites are $26 per night. Credit cards are accepted. Long-term rates are available.

Directions: From I-75 at Exit 352, take State Road 40 east for one block to the campground.

Contact: Motor Inns Motel and RV Park, 3601 West Silver Springs Boulevard, Ocala, FL 34475, 352/629-6902, fax 352/629-2530.

13 THE SPRINGS RV RESORT
≋ 🐾 ♿ 🚐

Scenic rating: 5

near the Silver Springs nature theme park, in Silver Springs

Although you certainly may lounge around the sunny Olympic-sized pool or in the 17,000-square-foot clubhouse, at least some campers prefer spending daylight hours three blocks away at Silver Springs, a 350-acre nature theme park with animal shows and picnic areas. Also within blocks is Wild Waters, a six-acre water park. The 52-acre campground bills itself as "the land of sunshine." Stay at one of these open, unshaded concrete-pad and grassy sites, and you'll probably agree.

Campsites, facilities: All 618 pull-through RV sites have full hookups with 30/50-amp electrical service. For recreation, there's a pool, horseshoes, tennis, shuffleboard, social programs, a wheelchair-accessible clubhouse, a card room, and a poolroom. Showers, restrooms, cable TV, some telephone hookups, and laundry facilities are available. Restaurants are located within blocks of here. Children are welcome. You must walk leashed pets outside the park.

Reservations, fees: Reservations are recommended. Sites are $25 per night for two people, plus $2.50 for each additional person. Credit cards are accepted. Long-term rates are available.

Directions: From I-75 at Exit 352, take State Road 40 east for about eight miles to 52nd Court. Turn left. The campground is ahead.

Contact: The Springs RV Resort, 2950 Northeast 52nd Court, Silver Springs, FL 34488, 352/236-5250, www.rvresorts.com.

14 SILVER SPRINGS CAMPERS GARDEN

Scenic rating: 5

opposite the Silver Springs theme park, in Silver Springs

Tarzan swung through this neighborhood long ago. Actually, it was actor Johnny Weissmuller, shooting the 1939 film *Tarzan Finds a Son!* across the street at the 780-square-foot cavern of Silver Springs—Florida's original tourist attraction. Henry Ford, Thomas Edison, and thousands of others have visited the theme park, which today offers glass-bottom boats, animals from six continents, a petting zoo, and picnic areas on its 350 acres. Also across

the street is Wild Waters, a six-acre water park. The proximity of these attractions makes the campground popular with families, seasonal visitors over age 55, and repeat customers. About 60 percent of the sites are occupied by full-time residents. In the wintertime, visitors play bingo and shuffleboard, and they go to parties, Silver Springs, and concerts nearby.

The bent branches of deep-furled oaks help shade some campsites at the 15.5-acre campground, but others are sunny and open. Just downstream at Silver River State Park, a hiking trail winds beneath fan-leafed sabal palms and shiny-leaf magnolias. If you go, look for otters in early morning along the Silver River, reached via the trail. Anglers, hikers, mountain bikers, and seasonal hunters can drive a short distance east from the campground to Ocala National Forest.

Campsites, facilities: Nearly all the 199 full-hookup RV sites are pull-through. All have 30-amp electrical service, and 75 have 50-amp hookups. Rigs up to 45 feet long and slide-outs can be accommodated. About 75 sites are available for overnight visitors. Dial-up Internet access (via pay phone) is available in the clubhouse. A pool, a playground, a horseshoe pit, a shuffleboard court, a wintertime activity schedule, and a clubhouse entertain campers. Showers, restrooms, a dump station, picnic tables, cable TV, telephone hookups, laundry facilities, and a small store with propane, ice, and camping supplies are available. Most areas of the park are wheelchair-accessible. A restaurant is located next door, and groceries are within two blocks. Children are welcome, but not for long-term stays. Leashed pets are permitted.

Reservations, fees: Reservations are recommended in winter. Sites are $28 per night for two people, plus $2.50 for each additional person, $2.50 for cable TV, and $2.50 when using air conditioners or heaters. Credit cards are not accepted. Long-term rates are available.

Directions: From I-75 at Exit 352, take State Road 40 east for about eight miles. The campground is opposite the Silver Springs nature theme park.

Contact: Silver Springs Campers Garden, 3151 Northeast 56th Avenue, Silver Springs, FL 34488, 352/236-3700 or 800/640-3733, www.campersgarden.com.

15 SILVER RIVER STATE PARK
🥾🚴🚗🐕♿🚐⛺

Scenic rating: 10

east of Ocala and south of Silver Springs

Wow! Dozens of springs, 14 distinct plant communities, and 10 miles of river frontage dot these 5,000 breathtaking acres. "People rave about this place," says one of the park rangers. Canoe or kayak on the Silver River; there are two launching points. One is outside the park at the foot of the Ocklawaha Bridge on State Road 40; the other is in the park at the end of the River Trail (you'll have to portage your canoe 0.6 mile from the parking lot). A concessionaire rents kayaks.

Opened in 1995, this park is popular with families, seasonal visitors, and locals. Bicyclists zip around on a 5.6-mile trail or meander around on the paved roads. Hiking trails lead to a sinkhole and to the river. There's also a museum focusing on nature and Native American culture, as well as a "Cracker village" with houses, a church/school, a cane-syrup boiler, and a blacksmith's shop. The park is also a hot spot for stargazing, bird walks, and annual festivals, such as the Country Cracker Days, held the second week of November. The Silver Springs theme park is next door to the park; a Wal-Mart is about a mile away.

Campsites, facilities: The campsites are divided into two loops, the Sharpe's Ferry camping area (near the museum and closest to the trail heads) and the Fort King camping area. There are 59 gravel, level sites with picnic tables, water and electricity, grills, and fire rings. Big rigs and slideouts are welcome. Six sites have 50-amp electrical service; the rest have 15/30-amp hookups. Sites are spacious, and there is a mix of sunny and shady spots. Drive-through spots can be found at 22 sites. Restrooms, showers, a dump station, laundry facilities, and cabin rentals are available. Restaurants and groceries are within one mile. The park office, bathhouses, museum, and playground are wheelchair-accessible. Children are welcome. Leashed pets are permitted.

Reservations, fees: Reservations are recommended; contact ReserveAmerica at 800/336-3521 or reserveamerica.com. Sites are $21 per night for six people. Major credit cards are accepted. The maximum length of stay is 14 days.

Directions: From the intersection of State Road 40 and State Road 35 in Silver Springs, drive south on State Road 35 one mile.

Contact: Silver River State Park, 1425 Northeast 58th Avenue, Ocala, FL 34470, 352/236-7148, www.floridastateparks.org.

16 WILDERNESS RV PARK ESTATES
🏊🛶🚗🐕🚶♿🚐⛺

Scenic rating: 6

at the western edge of Ocala National Forest

The meandering, tree-flanked Ocklawaha River is only steps from this 39.5-acre wooded campground, so it's no wonder that bass anglers launch boats at the nearby county boat ramp to try their luck in the sun-dappled waters. Canoeists on the lookout for deer and turkey peer into the passing woods as they paddle along the river. Of the paved or gravelly/grassy sites, some are shady, but others are sunny. The park's wintertime activities include bingo, cards, dances, and crafts, and favorite pastimes are walking, biking, boating, and playing horseshoes and shuffleboard. RV sites are laid out along roads like city blocks, and about 25 percent of the park is occupied by year-round residents. Most visitors are from Canada, Illinois, and Wisconsin. Kayaks and canoes are for rent. Under new ownership in 2005, the park now offers lots for sale.

Campsites, facilities: This park has 390 full-hookup RV sites (of which half have 30-amp electrical service, and the rest have 50 amp). Each site has a picnic table and a concrete patio. Slideouts and rigs longer than 40 feet are welcome. Tents are permitted in a large grassy area separate from the RVs; the 11 tent sites have water and electricity. A pool, a hot tub, a playground, a nature trail, a tennis court, a horseshoe pit, shuffleboard, a game room, a camp circle, volleyball, and winter activities entertain campers. Showers, restrooms, a dump station, cabins, laundry facilities, and canoe rentals are available. Internet access is available in the clubhouse. Streets are paved, and the bathhouse, clubhouse, office, and pool area are wheelchair-accessible. A camp store sells ice and propane, and there is a restaurant on the premises. Within 0.5 mile are a boat ramp, a restaurant, bait, and firewood. Groceries can be purchased four miles away. Children are welcome. Leashed pets should use the dog walk in back.

Reservations, fees: Reservations are recommended in winter. Sites are $25 per night for two people, plus $3 for each extra person, $2 for cable TV, and $1 for pets. Credit cards are not accepted.

Directions: From I-75 at Exit 352, take State Road 40 east for about 12 miles. The park is on the left, just beyond the Ocklawaha River Bridge.

Contact: Wilderness RV Park Estates, 10313 East State Road 40, Silver Springs, FL 34488, 352/625-1122, www.wildernessrvparkestates.com.

17 WHISPERING PINES RV PARK

Scenic rating: 6

in western Ocala National Forest

This nine-acre, pine-dotted campground (formerly Forest Cove Campground) offers sun-dappled campsites near several lakes in the surrounding national forest. Under new ownership since March 2003, the neatly kept park has 80 percent of its sites available for seasonal visitors; the rest are occupied year-round. Overnighters will find the park full most of the time from November through March. Most visitors are families and tourists from the Northeast and Canada. Juniper Springs Recreation Area, a popular picnic spot, is about 13 miles east. From November through April, visitors enjoy planned activities such as bingo, potluck dinners, shuffleboard, horseshoes, campfires, games, and casino outings. Favorite activities include playing cards and visiting nearby flea markets. The Silver Springs nature theme park is about five miles west. The Atlantic Ocean and Gulf of Mexico are about an hour's drive in either direction.

Campsites, facilities: RVers camp at the 65 grassy full-hookup sites (19 pull-through). About half the sites have 50-amp electrical service; the rest are 30-amp. Each site has a picnic table. Average site size is 30 by 70 feet, and rigs as long as 45 feet or slideouts are welcome. Sites 22–36 are pull-through. Most sites have cement patios. You can hook up to the Internet in the office; long-term visitors can arrange for DSL service at their site by contacting the local provider. A group barbecue/campfire area, a recreation hall, horseshoes, and shuffleboard entertain campers. Showers, restrooms, two dump stations, laundry facilities, a car wash area, and tire-air machine are available. Propane delivery to your site can be arranged. A convenience store is about one mile away; a supermarket is within five miles. Children are allowed for two-week stays. Leashed pets are permitted.

Reservations, fees: Reservations are accepted. Sites are $20 per night for two people, plus $2 per extra person, $2 for 50-amp electricity, and $1 per night for cable TV. Rates are subject to change. Credit cards are not accepted. Long-term rates are available.

Directions: From I-75 at Exit 352, take State Road 40 east for 14 miles to Piney Path Road/

Northeast 118th Avenue. Turn right. At 19th Street, turn right. When you reach 115th Avenue, turn left (south).

Contact: Whispering Pines RV Park, 1700 Northeast 115th Avenue, Silver Springs, FL 34488, 352/625-1295, whisperingpinesrvpark@yahoo.com.

18 BEN'S HITCHING POST

Scenic rating: 4

in western Ocala National Forest

This adults-only park is the closest private campground to the Ocala National Forest Visitor Center Northeast. Some campsites are open and grassy, but trees help shade others. As much as picnickers like to relax at Juniper Springs Recreation Area, about 13 miles west, or spend the day at the Silver Springs nature theme park, 4–6 miles to the east, this campground makes sure its guests stay busy: Potluck dinners, bingo, and campfires are among the activities on the schedule.

Campsites, facilities: The park offers 46 full-hookup RV campsites (some pull-through) with 30-amp electricity, plus 10 for tents. For recreation, there's a pool, a hot tub, shuffleboard, horseshoes, wintertime planned activities, a recreation hall with a fireplace, game tables, and exercise equipment. Showers, wheelchair-accessible restrooms, picnic tables, telephone hookups, firewood, and laundry facilities are available. Restaurants are within one mile. Children are not permitted. Pets are allowed.

Reservations, fees: Reservations are recommended. Sites are $20 per night for two people, plus $3 per extra person. Credit cards are accepted. Long-term rates are available.

Directions: From I-75 at Exit 69, take State Road 40 east for 14 miles to Piney Path Road/Northeast 115th Avenue. Turn right. The campground is 50 feet ahead.

Contact: Ben's Hitching Post, 2440 North-east 115th Avenue, Silver Springs, FL 34488, 352/625-4213, fax 352/625-0020.

19 LAKE WALDENA RESORT

Scenic rating: 8

in western Ocala National Forest

Check out the wintertime activities posted on the bulletin board: exercise at 9 A.M., bowling at 10 A.M., and bingo at 7 P.M.—and that's just one day. Activities vary daily at this 35-acre campground and may include singing hymns on Sunday or going to a potluck dinner on Saturday. Campers' birthdays and anniversaries are also noted, so you can pass along your best wishes.

The park is surrounded by the Ocala National Forest. Paved roads lead to several tree-shaded campsites that border nature preserves or Lake Waldena, where anglers, boaters, and swimmers head. Don't fish in the lake's roped-off area, though, because that's for swimmers. To sleep closest to Lake Waldena, try sites 2–13. A semitropical environment—unusual for national forests—is located 13 miles east at Juniper Springs Recreation Area. The Silver Springs nature theme park is eight miles west of the campground. About 20 percent of the sites are occupied year-round.

Campsites, facilities: All 105 campsites have full hookups with electricity, a concrete slab, and a picnic table. Tents are accommodated on the same full-hookup sites as the RVs, except for two spots that have water and electricity only. About 70 sites are available for overnight visitors. There are 82 sites with 30-amp service and 23 sites with 50-amp. Some sites are pull-through. Shuffleboard, horseshoes, pool tables, a television, winter activities, a playground, boat rentals, a swimming lake, and a recreation hall entertain campers. Showers, restrooms, firewood, telephone hookups, park model sites, and laundry facilities are available. A wireless Internet connection is available in the park and in the office. Groceries and the nearest restaurant are about three miles away. The bathhouse and clubhouse are wheelchair-accessible. Streets are paved. Kids under 12 must be accompanied by an adult in common areas. Pets should be tied up within your campsite and leashed during walks.

Reservations, fees: Reservations are advised. Sites are $22 per night for two people, plus $2 for each additional person. Credit cards are not accepted. Long-term rates are available.

Directions: From I-75 at Exit 352, take State Road 40 east for about 17 miles through Ocala. (Lake Waldena Resort is eight miles east of the Silver Springs theme park.)

Contact: Lake Waldena Resort, 13582 East Highway 40, Silver Springs, FL 34488, 352/625-2851 or 800/748-7898, fax 352/625-7069, www.lakewaldena.com.

20 ROBIN'S NEST RV PARK

Scenic rating: 4

in western Ocala National Forest

This sunny, over-55 campground at the western edge of the Ocala National Forest attracts retirees who pay by the year or month and enjoy wintertime activities such as ice-cream socials and darts. Most come from New England and Canada, with the same folks visiting year after year. The Silver Springs nature theme park is a short drive to the east. The national forest's popular Juniper Springs Recreation Area is about 10 miles east. About 25 percent of the park is occupied year-round. Although there is an abundance of planned activities in the clubhouse, the favorite thing to do is talking to other visitors. "We have a very friendly group of people," says the manager.

Campsites, facilities: Only self-contained rigs are accepted at these 36 level, grassy, full-hookup sites, which are split between 30-amp and 50-amp electrical service. Sites are open to the sky. Big rigs are welcome. No showers

or restrooms are provided. An exercise room, wintertime planned activities (bingo, potlucks, dances, day trips, crafting), laundry facilities, and a ramp for airboats are available. An Internet connection is available in the office. Groceries and restaurants are within two miles. Snacks and bait are within 0.25 mile. Children are not allowed. Leashed pets are permitted.

Reservations, fees: Reservations are recommended. Sites are $16 per night for two people, plus $2 per extra person. Credit cards are not accepted. Long-term rates are available.

Directions: From I-75 at Exit 352, take State Road 40 east about 20 miles to enter Ocala National Forest and the town of Lynne. Turn right at the campground sign. Proceed to the hilltop and turn right. Go one block, then turn left into the park.

Contact: Robin's Nest RV Park, 13400 Northeast 1st Street Road, Silver Springs, FL 34488, 352/625-3090, www.robinsnestrvpark.com.

21 FORE LAKE CAMPGROUND

Scenic rating: 8

on Fore Lake, in western Ocala National Forest

If you don't mind the lack of electricity, you'll while away the time amid picturesque live-oak hammocks and pines beside a pretty freshwater lake. Fishing and swimming in 77-acre Fore Lake are popular pursuits here at one of the forest's most popular lake-area campgrounds (Juniper Springs, Salt Springs, and Alexander Springs are more popular). You may also launch a canoe, if you bring one. The green, pleasant campground is only a 15-minute drive from the Silver Springs nature theme park (see *Silver Springs Campers Garden* listing in this chapter), and just minutes away from fine nature trails at Lake Eaton.

Campsites, facilities: All seven RV sites have picnic tables, grills, and concrete patios, but no electricity. One site is drive-through. RVs up to

30 feet long can be accommodated. Restrooms with flush toilets, hot showers, and drinking water are available, as are a picnic shelter and pay phone. There are no showers, dump stations, or other facilities. Campfires are permitted inside fire rings. The bathhouse is wheelchair-accessible. Children and leashed pets are welcome.

Reservations, fees: Reservations are not taken. Sites are $10 per night for five people. Credit cards are not accepted. The maximum stay is 30 days.

Directions: From Ocala, take State Road 40 east about 12 miles. Turn left onto County Road 314 and continue northeast about six miles until you see the entrance on the left.

Contact: Ocala National Forest, Lake George Ranger District, 17147 East State Road 40, Silver Springs, FL 34488, 352/236-0288 or 352/625-2520, www.fs.fed.us/r8/florida/recreation/index_oca.shtml.

22 LAKE EATON CAMPGROUND

Scenic rating: 5

on Lake Eaton, in western Ocala National Forest

Oaks and pines tower over this small campground at the southern end of idyllic Lake Eaton. The fishing pier and boat launch are pluses for those who want to stick close to camp; however, you should not miss the opportunity to explore some really interesting hiking terrain nearby. Head back out to County Road 314A and continue north approximately two miles to County Road 314. Turn right (heading east), then make another right onto the dirt road that comes up next, Forest Service Road 86. When that curves around to the left, turn right (south) onto Forest Service Road 79. Whew! All the maneuvering is worth it, though, because you will find two first-class hiking trails that are accessible, short, and interesting enough even for people who aren't into hiking for the sheer pleasure of it.

One favorite is the Lake Eaton Sinkhole Trail, which is actually a network of trails totaling 2.2 miles. The big feature, as you might imagine, is the sinkhole. A mere half-mile hike brings you to an observation deck that allows you to peer into this dark, cool hole spanning 450 feet across and reaching a depth of 80 feet. By all means, take the last few steps and follow the boardwalk and stairs leading down into the sinkhole.

The other trail is the Lake Eaton Loop Trail. It provides access through a slightly inclined forest slope to the lake's northeast shore. Passing over mulch and yellow-red sand, you'll walk through an area where you will encounter odd, dwarflike oaks and the pointy fronds of saw palmetto. Altogether, you can see more than a half dozen natural communities ranging from the dry xeric hammocks filled with sand to the lake itself. Animals of note include the osprey, deer, wild turkey, and scrub jay. People who are interested in rare plants should keep an eye out for the scrub milkwort, scrub buckwheat, and scrub morning glory.

Campsites, facilities: Thirteen primitive campsites are provided for tents or small RVs. Four of the sites can accommodate rigs up to 30 feet long and slideouts. There is no electricity. On the premises are picnic tables, vault toilets, hand-pumped drinking water, a boat ramp, fire rings, and a fishing pier. A few spaces will accommodate RVs up to 35 feet. Children are welcome. Leashed pets are permitted.

Reservations, fees: Reservations are not accepted, nor are credit cards. Sites are $6–8 per night for up to five people. The maximum stay is 14 days in any 30-day period.

Directions: From Ocala, take State Road 40 east for approximately 17 miles, turning left onto County Road 314A about 5 miles after entering the forest. Head north for five miles, then turn right (east) onto Forest Service Road 95. After just 0.5 mile or so, turn left onto Forest Service Road 96A. Drive about one mile north to the campsites.

Contact: Ocala National Forest, Lake George Ranger District, 17147 East State Road 40, Silver Springs, FL 34488, 352/236-0288 or 352/625-2520, www.fs.fed.us/r8/florida/recreation/index_oca.shtml.

23 HOPKINS PRAIRIE

Scenic rating: 4

in central Ocala National Forest

Camp in an oak hammock next to a wet prairie and a shallow lake. You can try your luck fishing there. If you decide to boat, bring a canoe or craft with a motor of no more than 10 horsepower. The Florida National Scenic Trail passes near here.

Campsites, facilities: The camping area has 21 sites with fire rings, lantern posts, and picnic tables, plus some undeveloped sites. Drinking water is available from a hand pump. Vault toilets are provided. Children and leashed pets are permitted.

Reservations, fees: Reservations and credit cards are not accepted. Sites are $6 per night for up to five people. The maximum stay is 14 days in a 30-day period.

Directions: From Ocala, take State Road 40 east about 32 miles. Turn left on State Route 19 and go about eight miles north to the campground entrance on the left.

Contact: Ocala National Forest, Lake George Ranger District, 17147 East State Road 40, Silver Springs, FL 34488, 352/236-0288 or 352/625-2520, www.fs.fed.us/r8/florida/recreation/index_oca.shtml.

24 OCKLAWAHA PRAIRIE RESTORATION AREA

Scenic rating: 6

south of Silver Springs

These 6,077 acres opened to the public when the St. Johns River Water Management District acquired the land for the purpose of restoring the Upper Ocklawaha River Basin. Previously a farm, the homestead and structures have been restored as an eco-tourism retreat renamed The Refuge at Ocklawaha. Local astronomy clubs sometimes gather here to take advantage of the dark skies overhead. Canoes and cabins are for rent at The Refuge.

For the adventurous, the area has appeal for mountain biking, backpacking, canoeing, and horseback riding. The Kyle Young Canal (C-212) is the manmade leg of the Ocklawaha River, and its restoration is intended to restore the surrounding flood plain. Canoeists can paddle the canal or the Ocklawaha River Channel to the west; the more natural channel rejoins the canal at the southeastern end of the property. A boat ramp is at Moss Bluff near the intersection of Country Road 464C and County Road 314A. About six miles of trails are available for biking and hiking.

Campsites, facilities: There are two primitive campsites. One is a short hike northward from The Refuge parking lot. The other is in the southern section of the area called the Chernobyl Memorial Forest. Tents only are permitted. There are no facilities: Bring water, supplies, mosquito repellent, and everything you'll need. Children are welcome. Leashed pets are permitted.

Reservations, fees: Sites are first-come, first-served. Camping is free. Each site accommodates up to six people. If your party has at least seven people, get a free permit and reserve at least one week ahead at 386/329-4410. Maximum stay for all campers is seven days.

Directions: From Ocala, drive south on State Road 40 six miles to County Road 314A. Turn north on 137th Avenue/Old River Road and drive a short distance to The Refuge. For access to the Chernobyl Memorial Forest area, turn south on Country Road 314A and turn right on County Road 464C about two miles to the parking area.

Contact: St. Johns River Water Management District, Division of Land Management, P.O. Box 1429, Palatka, FL 32178-1429, 386/329-4500 or 800/451-7106, www.sjrwmd.com. For information about The Refuge at Ocklawaha, write to 14835 South East 85th Street, Ocklawaha, FL 32179, or call 352/288-2233.

25 MILL DAM LAKE RESORT

🏊 � 🐕 🚐

Scenic rating: 7

in Ocala National Forest

Under new ownership since 2005, this sunny mobile-home/camping community on Mill Dam Lake is popular with boaters, all-terrain vehicle enthusiasts, families, and seasonal visitors. Only self-contained RVs are welcome. Bring your own small boat and launch it at the lake. Anglers try for largemouth bass, bream, catfish, perch, and specks at this huge lake, which is at least 200 acres in size. Or they cross State Road 40 to fish at Halfmoon Lake. Mill Dam Beach is within walking distance. The surrounding national forest is one of the state's last bastions of the Florida black bear, although you're unlikely to see one of the nocturnal creatures. Instead, while hiking any of the 68 miles of the Florida National Scenic Trail that span the national forest, you might glimpse a wild turkey or a deer scampering away in the distance.

Campsites, facilities: All 16 gravel or grassy campsites have water and 50-amp electrical hookups; 7 sites are drive-through. RVs up to 40 feet long and slide-outs can be accommodated. Adjacent but separate is a mobile-home park with 138 lots. Cabins, a screened pavilion, shuffleboard, horseshoes, laundry facilities, showers, restrooms, picnic tables, a snack bar, and a restaurant are available. The camp store also sells groceries, propane, fishing tackle, and bait. Shopping is 12 miles away. Children are welcome. Pets must stay out of the lake and be leashed at all times. The maximum stay is six months.

Reservations, fees: Reservations are advised; there is a 25 percent nonrefundable deposit. Sites are $18 per night for two people, plus

$2 per additional adult. Pets are accepted by prior arrangement; the one-time pet fee is $30. Major credit cards are accepted. Long-term rates are available.

Directions: From I-75 at Exit 352, take State Road 40 east about 21 miles through Ocala and past the Silver Springs nature theme park to the campground entrance. The campground is four miles east of County Road 314A.

Contact: Mill Dam Lake Resort, 18975 East State Road 40, Silver Springs, FL 34488, 352/625-4500, fax 352/625-4506, www.milldamlake.com.

26 LAKE BRYANT PARK

🏊 🎣 � 🐕 🚐 ⛺

Scenic rating: 4

on Lake Bryant in Ocklawaha

Dirt roads lead through this wooded campground/mobile-home park, where launching at the boat ramp for a day of fishing on Lake Bryant is the focus for anglers. It's the only public boat launch in the area, the owners say. Some rustic campsites are fairly sunny, although most have at least a little shade. Forty-five mobile homes share the property, and some long-term campers spend the year here. It's primarily an adult park.

Campsites, facilities: The 84 campsites (some pull-through) have sewer hookups and 30/50-amp electrical service. About 20 tents can be accommodated in a grassy area with no hookups. Trailer rentals, a boat ramp, bait, a general store, showers, restrooms, and cable TV (long-term campers only) are available. A wireless Internet connection is available in the clubhouse and at some campsites. Kids and small leashed pets are permitted.

Reservations, fees: Reservations are recommended. Sites are $24 per night for two people, plus $2 per extra person. Credit cards are accepted. Long-term rates are available.

Directions: From I-75 at Exit 352, take State Road 40 east about 24 miles, passing the Silver

Springs nature theme park, a high bridge, and County Road 314A. Approximately 2.5 miles past County Road 314A, turn right between the church and convenience store. The campground is 2.5 miles ahead.

Contact: Lake Bryant Park, 5000 Southeast 183rd Avenue Road, Ocklawaha, FL 32179, 352/625-2376 or 888/807-4858, fax 352/625-5676, www.lakebryant.com.

27 JUNIPER SPRINGS RECREATION AREA

Scenic rating: 9

near Juniper Springs, in central Ocala National Forest

Situated beside two springs that pour forth 13 million gallons of crystal-blue water each day, this site is a contender for the most popular campground in the forest. Of course, the presence of warm showers and other amenities, such as concession-stand food, doesn't hurt either. This campground has been highly rated by several organizations, so be sure to make reservations.

The campsites are sufficiently sheltered from one another by generous shrubs and a campground setup that utilizes paved, curving roads to help provide privacy. Hiking is available on the Florida National Scenic Trail, which runs through the campground and north into the Juniper Prairie Wilderness. A short interpretive nature trail also wends its way along the creek. Canoeing is popular. There is a security gate that is closed at night.

Campsites, facilities: Juniper Springs has three campground loops with 79 campsites, about half of them pull-through. Sites have picnic tables, grills, fire rings, and lantern posts. There are no hookups. Hot showers, restrooms, a concession stand, hiking trails, canoe rentals, laundry facilities, a modem hookup at a pay phone, a convenience store, and a dump station are available. The day-use buildings are

wheelchair-accessible. Restaurants and shopping are within 10 miles. Children, leashed pets, and campfires are allowed.

Reservations, fees: Reservations are recommended; contact ReserveAmerica at 800/336-3521 or reserveamerica.com. They must be made at least four days in advance of your stay. Sites are $19 per night for five people. Credit cards are accepted. The maximum stay is 14 days in any 30-day period.

Directions: From Ocala, take State Road 40 east about 28 miles. Look for the entrance road on your left.

Contact: Juniper Springs Recreation Area, 26701 East State Road 40, Silver Springs, FL 34488, 352/625-0546, www.camprrm.com.

28 ST. JOHNS RIVER CAMPGROUND

Scenic rating: 6

west of Astor Park

Large, shaded sites and centralized location make this new park a gem. Clean and modern facilities, huge oak trees, and nearby access to fishing on the St. Johns River are just part of the attraction; the campground is also fairly close to Daytona Beach. Marinas and restaurants are 200 yards away.

Campsites, facilities: Fifteen primitive tent sites are set apart from the RVs. Of a total of 60 developed sites, 30 are available for overnighters and seasonal visitors. All RV sites have full hookups and picnic tables; some have grills and cable TV. Restrooms, showers, laundry facilities, a clubhouse, cabin rentals, and shuffleboard courts are available. Children are welcome. Small, leashed pets are permitted.

Reservations, fees: Reservations are recommended. Sites are $20 per night for two people, plus $3 per extra person. Credit cards are accepted. Long-term rates are available.

Directions: From I-95, drive west on State

Road 40 for 28 miles. The park is on the right side, 0.25 mile from the St. Johns River Bridge.

Contact: St. Johns River Campground, 1520 State Road 40, Astor, FL 32102, 352/749-3995, fax 352/759-3419, www.stjohnsriver campground.com.

29 PARRAMORE'S FANTASTIC FISH CAMP AND FAMILY RESORT

Scenic rating: 6

on the St. Johns River, south of Lake George

As the campground's largemouth bass logo suggests, probably the biggest draw here is the lure of good fishing, followed closely by the chance to see wild animals such as deer and, if you're lucky, bobcats. A fishing guide and boat rentals are available, as are docks, a boat ramp, and bait and tackle. The sunny, grassy campsites provide a decent base of operations for those who want easy access to various pursuits in this slow-paced part of the state. About half the 33-acre, semi-shady resort is occupied by year-round residents. It is located across the river from Ocala National Forest and, should you tire of the campground pool, it is quite close to the swimming and hiking opportunities at Alexander Springs (see listing in this chapter). The park is only about six miles from the Pioneer Arts Settlement, where reenactors of pioneer life produce arts and crafts. Festivals are held at the arts settlement twice a year in fall and spring. At nearby Spring Garden Ranch, restaurant patrons can look through windows to watch trotter horses train every morning during winter.

Campsites, facilities: There are 93 full-hook-up sites for RVs with 30-amp electrical service; 45 have 50-amp. A few sites are available for tents; they are located in the same section as the RVs. Each site has a picnic table and fire ring, and some have grills. Rigs up to 45 feet long and slideouts can be accommodated. Wireless Internet service is available in the clubhouse. A pool, boat and canoe rentals, a playground, snorkeling, paddleboats, an exercise room, a game room, tennis, and volleyball entertain campers. On the premises are restrooms, showers, a boat ramp, a dock, a dump station, groceries, bait, tackle, cabin rentals, and laundry facilities. Cable TV, phone service, and firewood are available. The camp store sells ice, camping supplies, groceries, snacks, and souvenirs. All areas are wheelchair-accessible, and streets are paved. A restaurant is about two miles away. Children and leashed pets are welcome.

Reservations, fees: Reservations are recommended. Sites are $32–35 per night for two adults, plus $2 for each additional adult and $1 for each child. Credit cards are accepted. Long-term rates are available.

Directions: From I-95 at Exit 268, go west on State Road 40. About two blocks short of the St. Johns River, turn right (north) onto Riley Pridgeon's Road. After one mile, turn left onto South Moon Road, which leads west to the park entrance.

Contact: Parramore's Fantastic Fish Camp and Family Resort, 1675 South Moon Road, Astor, FL 32102, 386/749-2721 or 800/516-2386, fax 386/749-9744, www.parramores.com.

30 ASTOR LANDING CAMPGROUND AND MARINA

Scenic rating: 7

on the St. Johns River, south of Astor

People arrive by boat and car to camp at these 11 rustic acres on the west bank of the St. Johns River and Lake Dexter, where the owners recently invested in a boat ramp and other amenities. Outdoorsy folks use the tree-shaded spot as a base for hunting, swimming, hiking, and bicycling at Ocala National Forest, the park's neighbor across the street. Anglers fish for bass and specks at the St. Johns River. It's a good location for all sorts of outdoor activities, and the park welcomes family reunions and other groups. Houseboats are for rent (call 352/759-3300), but there's lots to do in this decidedly marine-oriented park.

Campsites, facilities: All 50 sites have full hookups with electricity. An indeterminate number of tents can also be accommodated. Boat slips with 30-amp and 50-amp shore power and water hookups, dockside sewage pump-out, a boat ramp, canoe rentals, a fishing pond, showers, restrooms, a picnic area, a general store, laundry facilities, and a dump station are available. Groceries and a restaurant are about five miles away in Astor. Children and pets are permitted.

Reservations, fees: Reservations are suggested. Sites are $28 per night for a family of four. Credit cards are accepted. Long-term rates are available.

Directions: From I-75 at Exit 352, drive about 40 miles east on State Road 40 through Ocala, Silver Springs, and Ocala National Forest. Turn right at Alco Road, one mile west of the St. Johns River. Continue four miles as the road veers left to the riverside camp.

Contact: Astor Landing Campground and Marina, 25934 Holmar Drive, Astor, FL 32102, 352/759-2121, www.astorlanding.com.

31 WILDWOODS CAMPGROUND

🛥️ 🚤 🏕️ ♿ 🚗 ⛺

Scenic rating: 6

near Astor, in the Ocala National Forest

All travelers are welcome at this fishing-oriented park near the St. Johns River and Lake George, a sleepy area that has not changed much in recent years. Practice your casting in the fishing pond on the premises. You'll find both sunny and shady spots here. About 75 percent of the park is occupied year-round.

Your neighbors will be a mix of seasonal tourists, families, anglers, and working people. Top on the list to do are fishing and boating.

Campsites, facilities: There are 82 large campsites with full hookups for tents or RVs up to 45 feet long and slideouts. Twelve sites are usually available for overnight visitors. Most sites have 30-amp electrical service; a few have 50-amp. Tenters are placed in a grassy shaded area; most are primitive, although five have water and electricity. Dial-up Internet access is available in the clubhouse. Restrooms, showers, laundry facilities, cable TV, telephone service, and propane are available. On the premises are a clubhouse with planned activities, shuffleboard courts, and a dog-walk area. The bathhouse, clubhouse, and office are wheelchair-accessible, and streets are paved. Groceries and restaurants are within 2 miles; malls and hospitals are 25 miles away. Children are welcome. Leashed pets are permitted.

Reservations, fees: Reservations are recommended. Sites are $21 per night for two people, plus $1.50 per extra person. Credit cards are not accepted. Long-term rates are available. Stay as long as you wish.

Directions: From I-95 in Ormond Beach, take Exit 268 and go west 30 miles on State Road 40 the park. From I-75 at Exit 352, go east on State Road 40 for 30 miles.

Contact: Wildwoods Campground, 22113 State Road 40, Astor, FL 32102, 352/759-3538.

32 QUAIL ROOST RV CAMPGROUND

🏊 ♿ 🚗

Scenic rating: 4

north of Crystal River

For retired snowbirds who like conveniences in a more natural setting, this well-maintained

© MARILYN MOORE

Campers settle in for the winter months at an Ocala park.

park may fit the bill: Some sites are set under trees, and some are out in the open. The main roads are paved. Visitors tend to be repeat customers over 55 who come from all over the United States. Social programs in winter include bingo, cards, games, campfires, dinners, and darts. Asked what the favorite thing to do, the owners answered, "Talk!" Pick up major supplies in Crystal River or Dunnellon, both 7.5 miles away. Only 1 percent of the park is occupied year-round.

Campsites, facilities: This adults-preferred park has 72 full-hookup sites with picnic tables and telephone and cable TV access. The level, grassy, or gravel lots measure about 32–40 feet wide by 40 feet deep. More than 40 sites have 50-amp electrical service; the rest have 30-amp. Half are pull-through and can accommodate the largest RVs, even triple slideouts. Swim in the heated pool, or set up your satellite dish. Internet access is available at some sites and in the clubhouse. Restrooms, showers, laundry facilities,

picnic tables, shuffleboard, horseshoes, bocce ball (lawn bowling), basketball, a pool table, wintertime social programs, and a recreation room are available. Two restaurants are within walking distance. The clubhouse, bathhouse, and office are wheelchair-accessible. Streets are paved. There are no facilities for children, however they are allowed for short visits. No dogs are allowed November–April.

Reservations, fees: Reservations are recommended. Sites are $29 per night for two people, plus $1 for each additional person. Credit cards are not accepted. Long-term stays are allowed.

Directions: In downtown Crystal River, from the intersection of U.S. 19 and County Road 495, drive northwest on the county road for 7.5 miles to the park, at right.

Contact: Quail Roost RV Campground, 9835 North Citrus Avenue, Crystal River, FL 34428, 352/563-0404, www.quailroost campground.com.

33 LAKE ROUSSEAU RV AND FISHING RESORT

🏊 🎣 � 🐕 ♿ 🚐

Scenic rating: 6

between Crystal River and Dunnellon

Bass fishing is primo on Lake Rousseau, and a fishing guide is on-site. Land-bound campers will also enjoy views of its sparkling waters. Nestled amid oaks draped with Spanish moss, the campground is home to a mix of year-round residents in mobile homes, travelers in all manner of rigs, and anglers. Some sites are on the water; you may share your bit of lakefront with the ducks. The park is out in the countryside, but not prohibitively far from attractions such as Homosassa Springs State Wildlife Park, golf courses, beaches, Silver Springs, and Weeki Wachee Spring. About 10 percent of the park is occupied year-round. Most visitors come from Ohio, Indiana, and Michigan, but you'll also find locals making this their base camp. Planned activities include bingo, potluck dinners, luaus, day trips, and fishing tournaments.

Campsites, facilities: Park your RV on one of 125 grassy sites with full hookups, concrete patios, and picnic tables. Wireless Internet access, telephone service, and cable TV are available at your site. About 80 sites are available for overnighters. Rigs up to 40 feet long and slideouts can be accommodated. Two sites are pull-through. Restrooms, showers, laundry facilities, a pool, a recreation room with planned activities during the winter season, boat docks, a boat ramp, boat rentals, rental cabins, a store, propane gas, and horseshoes are on-site. The restrooms, office, and recreation hall are wheelchair-accessible. Streets are paved. Groceries and restaurants are five miles away. The park store sells ice, camping supplies, snacks, fishing tackle, and bait. Adults are preferred. Children are allowed for stays up to one month. Leashed pets (no attack dogs) are welcome.

Reservations, fees: Reservations are recommended. Sites are $28 per night for four people. Boat launches are free for campers. Boat dockage is available for an extra charge. Credit cards are accepted. Long-term rates are available.

Directions: From the town of Crystal River, drive north on U.S. 19 for six miles. Turn east on State Road 488 and continue four miles. Turn north on Northcut Avenue (watch for the campground sign) and proceed 1.3 miles until the road dead-ends at the campground. From Dunnellon, at the intersection of U.S. 41 and State Road 488, drive five miles west on State Road 488 to Northcut Avenue and proceed as above.

Contact: Lake Rousseau RV and Fishing Resort, 10811 North Coveview Terrace, Crystal River, FL 34428, 352/795-6336 or 800/561-CAMP (800/561-2267), fax 352/564-4287, www.lakerousseaurvpark.com.

34 RAINBOW SPRINGS STATE PARK

🏊 🎣 🚤 ⛷ 🐕 🚶 ♿ 🚐 ⛺

Scenic rating: 9

near Dunnellon

BEST (

Rainbow Springs is the state's third-largest spring, pumping 600 million gallons of sparkling water a day. The surroundings are so breathtaking that a hotel was built near the spring in the 1890s. In the 1930s, private developers made it a tourist attraction that operated for four decades. The state, in conjunction with the Marion County parks department, acquired the park in 1989, and later acquired the previously privately operated campground (ergo, a swimming pool). Today, the main part of the park has azalea gardens, an amphitheater, and picnic grounds that are popular for group events. Avoid holidays, when the park gets crowded. You can rent canoes and kayaks to drift downstream; note that there is no shuttle service to bring you back to the campground. Strap on a snorkel mask and explore the crystalline waters near the swimming area in the campground.

The campground and the main part of the park are on opposite sides of the river; to reach the main part, you'll have to paddle up the river or drive several miles. As you paddle, you'll be able to peer deep into the water and even see boils where the water bubbles up below you from the sandy floor. Dark green water plants wave in the stream. It's a hypnotic experience. The campground is divided into two areas: a more wooded loop near the picturesque Rainbow River and a sprawling sunny field without trees near the office. You may think you're in two different parks. Each has its pros and cons. The wooded section is prettier but can be crowded and noisy on weekends; the field accommodates large RVs and is near the swimming pool.

Campsites, facilities: The 105 campsites have water and 30-amp electricity; 40 have sewer hookups. Sites vary in size, but some will accommodate slide-outs and bigger rigs. Restrooms, showers, picnic tables, fire rings, grills, laundry facilities, a dump station, a playground, a pool, canoe rentals, and a recreation hall are provided. Also for rent are inner tubes and diver-down flags; however, shuttle service is not provided for those who float too far down the river. Some groceries are available in the camp store, along with ice, firewood, and souvenirs. The restrooms, pool area, office, and store are wheelchair-accessible; some streets are paved. Children are welcome. Pets are permitted in the campground with proof of vaccination.

Reservations, fees: Reservations are recommended; contact ReserveAmerica at 800/336-3521 or reserveamerica.com. Sites are $19 per night for eight people. Credit cards are accepted. Stays are limited to 14 days.

Directions: From I-75 south of Ocala, take Exit 341 onto State Road 484 west for 19 miles. At Southwest 180th Avenue Street (west of the airport), turn north and drive past a high school. Drive 2.5 miles to the entrance, on the west side.

Contact: Rainbow Springs State Park, 18185 Southwest 94th Street, Dunnellon, FL 34432, 352/489-5201, fax 352/465-7209, www .floridastateparks.org.

35 CAMPER VILLAGE OF AMERICA

Scenic rating: 3

off I-75, south of Ocala

With four shopping plazas, a mall, and two movie theaters within one mile of here, you have all the comforts of home. Still, on the other side of the campground, horse farms dominate. This over-55, family-run campground aims to create a small-town, familiar feel by scheduling numerous wintertime activities, including dancing, musical performances, bus trips to nearby attractions, and potluck dinners. The managers call it a "full-scale entertainment program." Each morning, free coffee is brewed at the office of this lighted park with paved roads. There's not a lot of landscaping, so campsites tend to be open and sunny.

Campsites, facilities: The park offers 250 full-hookup RV sites (several pull-through), of which 75 percent have 30-amp electrical service and the rest 50-amp. About 150 sites are filled by park models or permanent residents. Just 20 sites are available for overnight visitors. For recreation, there are shuffleboard courts, horseshoe pits, winter activities, and a 400-person-capacity recreation hall. Showers, restrooms, a dump station, telephone hookups, laundry facilities, and free cable TV are available. Within one mile you'll find four supermarkets, a hospital, and nearly 40 restaurants. The recreation hall, restrooms, and office are wheelchair-accessible. Children are permitted for short stays. Leashed pets are accepted.

Reservations, fees: Reservations are recom-

mended in winter. Sites are $22 per night for two people, plus $2 per additional person. Use of air conditioners or electric heaters costs $2.25 each night. Credit cards are not accepted. Long-term stays are OK.

Directions: From I-75 at Exit 350, take State Road 200 west for 1,000 feet to the campground.

Contact: Camper Village of America, 3931 Southwest College Road, Ocala, FL 34474, 352/237-3236, campervill@aol.com.

36 OCALA RV CAMP RESORT

Scenic rating: 8

off I-75, south of Ocala

Ducks flapping their wings at the two park ponds and the graceful springtime sight of blooming magnolias lend atmosphere to this 20-acre wooded retreat just off I-75. The oak- and magnolia-shaded grassy/sandy campsites tend to fill up pretty quickly in winter, so call ahead. The attractions for couples and families are plunging into the pool or heading to the game room after a long day of interstate driving or taking in area attractions. The Silver Springs nature theme park is less than half an hour east. Ocala National Forest is farther east. For a joyride, head west on U.S. 27 to pass would-be champion horses grazing on the rolling hills of some of the region's more than 1,000 horse farms.

Campsites, facilities: Under new ownership since 2005, this was formerly a KOA. The new owners have expanded the number of sites to 200, added landscaping, and upgraded electrical service and the overall look of the park. The 200 RV sites have full hookups with 30/50-amp electrical services available. Each site has a picnic table. For recreation, there's a pool, a hot tub, a sauna, a kiddie pool, a game room, a playground, a TV lounge, a

Ocala horse farm

© VISIT FLORIDA

horseshoe pit, a shuffleboard court, a volleyball net, a recreation room, a basketball court, and wintertime social activities. Facilities include showers, restrooms, a convenience store, a dump station, cabins, cable TV, and a laundry room. Twenty-five restaurants are within two miles. Children are welcome. Leashed pets are permitted.

Reservations, fees: Reservations are recommended. Sites are $30–35 per night for two people. Add $8 for each additional adult, $4 per extra child age four and older. Credit cards are accepted. Long-term stays are OK, but there are no mobile homes on-site.

Directions: From I-75 at Exit 350, take State Road 200 west to 38th Avenue. Turn right. The campground is 0.5 mile ahead at left, next to the Disney Information Center.

Contact: Ocala RV Camp Resort, 3200 Southwest 38th Avenue, Ocala, FL 34474, 352/237-2138 or 866/858-3400, fax 352/237-9894, www.ocalarvcampresort.com.

37 OCALA RANCH RV PARK

Scenic rating: 6

off I-75, south of Ocala

Winter campers and overnight travelers flock to this renovated park, where amenities include a "doggie bath" and a pool for your pet, a "free-range Doggie Corral," and pet-sitting services. The park boasts that it is one of the few RV parks in the nation with a cardiac defibrillator on-site. There's a 24-hour security patrol, and wireless Internet service is available throughout the park. Visitors tend to be snowbirds from the Midwest and Canada, as well as families. The park is also convenient to the interstate. Favorite things to do include visiting local horse farms.

Campsites, facilities: Among the 171 RV sites, 60 are pull-through. All have full hookups and telephone availability. There are 54 sites with 30-amp electrical service and 100 with 50-amp hookups; each has a picnic table. Big rigs can be accommodated, and sites are as large as 40 by 50 feet. Facilities include a heated pool, a spa, walking paths, and a community center building. Showers, restrooms, and laundry facilities are available. During the winter season, you'll find the usual planned activities such as bingo, boccie ball (lawn bowling), and horseshoes, but also monthly CPR classes. Shopping, restaurants and the Florida Horse Park are within five miles. All areas are said to be wheelchair-accessible. Children are welcome. Pets are allowed.

Reservations, fees: Reservations are recommended. Sites are $20–48 per night for two people, plus $2 for each additional person. Major credit cards are accepted. Long-term stays are OK.

Directions: From I-75 at Exit 341, take County Road 484 west for 0.5 mile to the park on the right.

Contact: Ocala Ranch RV Park, 2559 Southwest Highway 484, Ocala, FL 34473, 352/347-4008 or 877/809-1100, www.ocalaranchrv.com.

38 SOUTHERN SUN RV AND MOBILE HOME PARK

Scenic rating: 3

just south of Belleview

Call early if you want a spot at this sunny, sleepy 10-acre RV park. When contacted one November, the place already was booked up until March and had a waiting list of six parties. Retirees tend to dominate the clientele, and they come back year after year. These grassy lots are sizable: 30 by 50 feet. They're set back from cars zipping by on U.S. 441 and County Road 25, and the park can't be seen from the highway.

Campsites, facilities: All 45 RV sites have full hookups with 30-amp or 50-amp electrical service and a picnic table; an additional 18 mobile homes are on-site. Internet connection is available in the office. Horseshoes, showers, restrooms, a recreation room, cable TV, telephone hookups, and laundry facilities are available. Management says the clubhouse, showers, and laundry room are wheelchair-accessible. Children are allowed for short visits. Small, leashed pets under 15 pounds are permitted.

Reservations, fees: Reservations are recommended. Sites are $20 per night for two people, plus $2 for each additional person. Credit cards are not accepted. Long-term rates are available.

Directions: From Belleview, go south on U.S. 441 a short distance to County Road 25A. Turn left at Southeast 69th Terrace, the first driveway on your left.

Contact: Southern Sun RV and Mobile Home Park, 11665 Southeast 69th Terrace, Belleview, FL 34420, 352/245-8070, fax 352/245-8070.

39 SUNNYHILL RESTORATION AREA

Scenic rating: 6

east of Weirsdale and west of Ocala National Forest

Just south of the Ocklawaha Prairie Restoration Area and covering a nine-mile stretch of the river lies the Sunnyhill Restoration Area, a 4,357-acre public wilderness area managed by the St. Johns River Water Management District. Like the Ocklawaha tract, this was acquired to restore the old straightened river and return water to the wetlands. You'll see lots of wading birds, and sandhill cranes like to spend the winter here. The Blue House, once a farmhouse on the property, has been converted to an exhibit center and offers nature tours. Canoeists can launch at the Moss Bluff boat ramp at the corner of Country Road 314A and County Road 464. Paddle south nine miles to The Blue House. Stretching along the canoe route is a levee trail suitable for biking and hiking. There are three primitive campsites, including one at The Blue House. Access to this area may be restricted while restoration work is being done. Get up-to-date information from the water management district before heading out.

Campsites, facilities: Only tents are permitted. There are no facilities: Bring water, supplies, mosquito repellent, and everything you'll need. Children are welcome. Leashed pets are permitted.

Reservations, fees: Sites are first-come, first-served. Camping is free. Each site accommodates up to six people. If your party has at least seven people, get a free permit and reserve at least one week ahead at 386/329-4410. Maximum stay for all campers is seven days.

Directions: From Weirsdale at the intersection of County Road 42 and County Road 25, drive east six miles to The Blue House. Parking areas for the two other primitive sites are on Southeast 182nd Avenue Road/Forest Road 8, a north–south forest road accessible from the north from County Road 314A just east of Moss Bluff.

Contact: St. Johns River Water Management District, Division of Land Management, P.O. Box 1429, Palatka, FL 32178-1429, 386/329-4500 or 800/451-7106, www.sjrwmd.com.

40 EMERALDA MARSH CONSERVATION AREA

Scenic rating: 6

east of Weirsdale

Migrating birds, ducks ,and rare species such as the bald eagle may be spotted in this 7,089 tract about four miles south of the Sunnyhill Restoration Area. Threaded with small lakes, this area allows hunting, so call ahead to be sure hiking, canoeing, and bird-watching are safe. There are three boat ramps. One primitive site is in the northern section of the property.

Campsites, facilities: Only are permitted. There are no facilities: Bring water, supplies, mosquito repellent, and everything you'll need. Children are welcome. Leashed pets are permitted.

Reservations, fees: Sites are first-come, first-served. Camping is free. Each site accommodates up to six people. If your party has at least seven people, get a free permit and reserve at least one week ahead at 386/329-4410. Maximum stay for all campers is seven days.

Directions: To reach the campsite, hike in from the parking area on Emeralda Island Road. From Weirsdale, drive east past the Sunnyhill Restoration Area on County Road 42 and turn south on County Road 452. Drive about 1.5 miles and turn west on Emeralda Island Road, which continues about four miles, heading west and veering 90 degrees south to the parking area.

Contact: St. Johns River Water Management District, Division of Land Management, P.O.

Box 1429, Palatka, FL 32178-1429, 386/329-4500 or 800/451-7106, www.sjrwmd.com.

41 ALEXANDER SPRINGS CAMPGROUND

🚶 🚲 ⛵ 🛶 🗠 🐕 ♿ 🚐 ⛺

Scenic rating: 9

in southeastern Ocala National Forest

The clear, 72°F water flowing out of this spring at the rate of 80 million gallons daily makes this a very pleasant place to spend a hot summer day. Swimming and snorkeling are popular pursuits (equipment can be rented here), and certified divers may scuba dive. The sandy beach sets it apart from the forest's other popular springs: Juniper Springs. Canoe rentals are available, and many campers make the seven-mile trip down the spring's run. Archaeologists say the area around the springs has been inhabited for more than 1,000 years. You can hike about one mile along an interpretive trail that explains how early inhabitants, the Timucuan Indians, used native plants. A spur trail leads to a nearby section of the Florida National Scenic Trail, which leads over sandy, pine-covered hills. I spotted a baby wild hog, just one of the wildlife species, including deer and black bear, said to abound here.

Look for otters along the spring's run and gopher tortoises in the sandy hills nearby. The campground is open, covered mostly with pines. It offers less privacy than many spots in the national forest, but it's still pleasant. Mountain bikers enjoy the Paisley Woods biking trail, a 22-mile loop that connects Alexander Springs with the Clearwater Lake campground, passing mostly through pine-dotted hills. Visitors here are a mix of seasonal tourists, anglers, and families who enjoy swimming and canoeing.

Campsites, facilities: There are 67 level, paved sites for self-contained campers in slideouts or RVs up to 40 feet long. Tents are also welcome.

No electrical hookups are available. Sites are shady and have picnic tables, fire rings, and grills. On the premises are restrooms, showers, a dump station, a concession stand, a swimming area, hiking trails, and an amphitheater. A camp store sells ice, camping supplies, some groceries, snacks, and souvenirs. Canoes are for rent. Most areas are wheelchair-accessible. Children and leashed pets are permitted.

Reservations, fees: Reservations are taken; call 877/444-6777. Sites are $17 per night for five people. Major credit cards are accepted. Stays are limited to 14 days in summer and six months in winter.

Directions: From Ocala, take State Road 40 east about 26 miles to State Road 19. Turn right and continue about eight miles south. Make a left, heading east, on County Road 445 (not 445A). Look for the entrance to the campground about five miles ahead on the left.

Contact: Alexander Springs Campground, Ocala National Forest, 49525 County Road 445, Altoona, FL 32702, 352/669-3522, www.fs.fed.us/r8/florida/recreation/index_oca.shtml; or write to RRM Regional Office, 26701 East Highway 40, Silver Springs, FL 34488, 352/625-0546, fax 352/625-0712, www.camprrm.com.

42 OCALA FOREST CAMPGROUND

🚲 ⛵ 🛶 🚣 🐕 ♿ 🚐 ⛺

Scenic rating: 9

in southeastern Ocala National Forest

It would be hard to accidentally stumble upon the Skorski family's out-of-the-way private campground within Ocala National Forest. Area attractions include canoeing at the forest's Juniper Springs Recreation Area 12 miles away, and the antiques shops of Mount Dora, 17 miles away. But there's also lots to do in the park, from boating and bicycling to bingo, card games, shuffleboard, dances, parties, and potluck dinners. The owners say it's quiet and relaxing. About 10 percent of the park is occupied by year-round residents, but park models are for sale in an area set apart from the RV section. Most seasonal visitors come from the north, but the customer mix varies from locals to working people, families, and retirees. A long oval island of RVs forms the center of this thumb-shaped campground. To sleep closest to the pool (and dog walk), try sites 1–11. To border stands of trees, ask about sites 69–95.

Campsites, facilities: There are 125 campsites (about half are pull-through) with 30-amp service. Lots are 30 by 50 feet, with concrete patios and picnic tables. Sewer hookups are available at sites 1–68 and sites A–H. Slide-outs and rigs as long as 45 feet can be accommodated. A pool, horseshoes, shuffleboard, a recreation hall, bike rentals, winter activities, a game room, a playground, and a pool table entertain campers. There are showers, restrooms, a dump station, a camp store with ice, snacks, propane, and souvenirs, a park model section, and laundry facilities are available. Wheelchair-accessible areas are the clubhouse, office, store, and pool area, and some of the streets are paved. The park also has a boat ramp and docks. Groceries, restaurants, shopping, and hospitals are about 15 miles away. Young children must be adult-supervised. Leashed pets must use the eastern-border dog walk.

Reservations, fees: Reservations are recommended. Sites are $17 per night for two people, plus $3 for each additional person and $2 for use of air conditioners or electric heaters. Credit cards are accepted. Long-term rates are available.

Directions: From Umatilla, go north on State Road 19, then turn left at County Road 42. The campground is ahead to your right.

Contact: Ocala Forest Campground, 26301 Southeast Highway 42, Umatilla, FL 32784, 352/669-3888.

43 LAKE DORR CAMPGROUND

Scenic rating: 4

in southern Ocala National Forest

Extremely tall, straight pines provide reasonable shade from the sun for these sandy campsites, which are set within a forest where fire has beaten back much of the understory of saw palmetto. This means you won't enjoy a whole lot of privacy. The following could apply to many areas of the forest, but it should be reiterated: Stay away from the clusters of saw palmetto, because they can harbor rattlesnakes. Fishing and waterskiing are popular at nearby Lake Dorr, where you also can swim at a sandy beach. Canoes share the lake with buzzing motorboats—after all, this is one lake where there is no limit on how much horsepower your boat can pack. Hikers can pick up the Florida National Scenic Trail a few miles up State Road 19 at Alexander Springs.

Campsites, facilities: All 34 campsites have picnic tables, fire rings, and grills. No hookups or pull-through sites are available. RVs up to 34 feet long can be accommodated; a few sites will allow slideouts. Drinking water, restrooms, hot showers, picnic tables, boat docks, and two boat ramps are provided. Groceries and restaurants are within three miles. Children and leashed pets are welcome.

Reservations, fees: Reservations are not taken. Sites are $8 per night for five people. Credit cards are not accepted. Stays are limited to 14 days.

Directions: From Deland, go west on County Road 42 for 24 miles. Turn right and head north on State Road 19 about three miles. Look for the entrance to your right.

Contact: Ocala National Forest, Seminole Ranger District, 40929 State Road 19, Umatilla, FL 32784, 352/669-3153, www.fs.fed.us/r8/florida/recreation/index_oca.shtml.

44 CLEARWATER LAKE RECREATION AREA

🏃 🚴 🏊 🛶 🐾 🚐 ⛺

Scenic rating: 8

in southeastern Ocala National Forest

Set in an oak hammock on the shores of Clearwater Lake, this beautiful campground is one of the few National Forest campgrounds that accepts reservations. Swimming, fishing, and canoeing are possible in the lake, but motorboats are banned. Mountain bikers can follow the Paisley Woods biking trail, a 22-mile loop that connects Alexander Springs with the Clearwater Lake campground, passing mostly through pine-dotted hills. Canoes are for rent in the campground. Visitors here come from all over the world.

Hikers can stay busy for quite a while here. Consider the Florida National Scenic Trail, which passes through a section of woods that was burned out a few years ago but is now regenerating. By all means, though, don't miss the nearby St. Francis Interpretive Trail, which passes through riverine swamp, pine flat woods, oak hammock, bayhead swamp, and open flat woods. Keep your eye out for red-tailed hawks and pileated woodpeckers. If you're up to a seven-mile round-trip hike, consider trekking to the former town of St. Francis, once a bustling citrus and timber port on the St. Johns River. After steamboats were replaced by railroads as the main form of transport, St. Francis faded away and eventually was overtaken by the forest. With the aid of a pamphlet available at the trailhead, you can pick out markers of the onetime civilization, including an old levee built to flood a field so rice could be grown. To reach the trailhead, take County Road 42 east a few miles from the campground, turn left (north) on Forest Service Road 542, and look for signs.

Access to the forest's hiking and biking trails is restricted during hunting season, which generally runs mid-November–early January. Check with the Forest Service for exact dates.

Campsites, facilities: The campground is laid out in two loops, with sites 1–23 closest to the beach and lake. Keep in mind that this is also near the day-use area, so it may be busy at times. All 42 campsites have picnic tables, fire rings, and grills. Water is available, but there's no sewer or electric service. On the premises are flush toilets, showers, a dump station, a swimming beach, and hiking trails. Firewood is for sale in the park. Children and leashed pets are permitted.

Reservations, fees: Reservations are accepted; call 877/444-6777. Sites are $14 per night for five people. Credit cards are accepted. Stays are limited to 14 days.

Directions: From DeLand, take County Road 42 west about 15 miles to the hamlet of Paisley. Look for the campground entrance ahead on the left.

Contact: Ocala National Forest, Seminole Ranger District, 40929 State Road 19, Umatilla, FL 32784, 352/669-3153, www.fs.fed.us/r8/florida/recreation/index_oca.shtml.

45 CRYSTAL ISLE RV RESORT

🛶 🚤 🐾 🎾 ♿ 🚐

Scenic rating: 10

west of Crystal River

Located on a canal with access to the Crystal River, this resort owned by the Encore chain offers lots to do, including fishing, boating, social activities, sports, and even tennis. But the location makes it ideal as a base camp for those who want to explore local sights. Manatees are a top tourist draw, with several local tours offering trips to see the 200 lumbering sea cows that spend their winters in the spring-fed, 72°F waters of the Crystal River. Spectacular diving springs, famous around the world for their purity and clarity, are within four miles. King Spring, near the Plantation Inn and Golf Resort (352/795-4211) down the road from the RV resort, is 75 feet across and drops 30 feet to a cavern. If you didn't bring your diving gear, you can rent snorkel or scuba equipment from many local dive shops.

Campsites, facilities: This 30-acre RV resort has 250 full-hookup sites (6 pull-through) with 30/50-amp electrical service and cable TV. Restrooms, showers, picnic tables, grills, fire rings, laundry facilities, a heated pool, a hot tub, a dump station, a recreation room, a playground, horseshoes, shuffleboard, tennis, basketball, volleyball, a boat ramp, boat docks, fishing lake, and a store are on the premises. Children and leashed pets are welcome.

Reservations, fees: Reservations are recommended. Sites are $28–32 per night. Major credit cards are accepted. Long-term stays are OK.

Directions: From U.S. 19 in Crystal River, drive four miles west on State Road 44/Fort Island Trail to the park, on the right.

Contact: Crystal Isle RV Resort, 11419 West Fort Island Trail, Crystal River, FL 34429, 352/795-3774 or 888/783-6763, fax 352/795-4897, www.rvonthego.com.

46 ROCK CRUSHER CANYON RV AND MUSIC PARK

🏞️ 🏊 🐕 🚐 ⛺

Scenic rating: 10

east of Crystal River

BEST (

Want to see headline artists like Willie Nelson, Pat Boone, the Oak Ridge Boys, Three Dog Night, and Faith Hill? This 60-acre RV park is part campground, part concert venue. There's live entertainment every weekend in a garden pavilion, plus outdoor concerts in an amphitheater that seats 7,000. For show information, call 352/795-1313 or visit www.rockcrushercanyon.com. The RV park itself has much to recommend, set in a wooded area

not far from the Withlacoochee State Forest. Rallies and caravans are welcome. The park was opened in 2001, and the grounds are kept immaculate, even to the point of reseeding the RV sites when the grass gets eroded. Don't worry about noise from the concerts; they are usually over by 10 P.M.

Campsites, facilities: There are 398 full-hookup RV sites with 50-amp electrical service, cable TV, instant phone service, and grassy pads. Forty tent sites with water and electricity are also available in an area separated from the recreational vehicles. Sites are wooded. Restrooms, showers, laundry facilities, a heated pool, a whirlpool tub, a fitness station, a restaurant, and a recreation hall are provided. The concert area is set apart from the RV park. Children are welcome. Leashed pets are permitted.

Reservations, fees: Reservations are recommended. Sites are $35 per night for two people, plus $2 per extra person. Credit cards are accepted. Long-term rates are available.

Directions: In Crystal River, from State Road 44 and U.S. 19, drive south on U.S. 19 about two miles to the Home Depot and intersection with Venable Road. Turn left on Venable Road and go west about 3.5 miles. At Rock Crusher Road, turn south and drive 0.5 mile to the park.

Contact: Rock Crusher Canyon RV and Music Park, 275 South Rock Crusher Road, Crystal River, FL 34429, 352/795-3870, www.rccrvpark.com.

47 CAMP 'N' WATER OUTDOOR RESORT

🚲 🏊 🎣 🚐 🐕 🚶 ♿ 🚌

Scenic rating: 7

south of Homosassa Springs

Secluded but not isolated, this 13-acre, well-shaded park is on the banks of the Homosassa River. The resort is oriented to boaters, as well as campers: There are 28 boat slips in the marina, and the fishing grounds of the Gulf of Mexico are just five miles away. Anglers from all over the world flock to the Crystal River area for sport fishing. Sea trout and redfish are plentiful in near-shore waters, and the magnificent silver tarpon is abundant farther out. Don't miss a visit to nearby Homosassa Springs State Wildlife Park (352/628-2311), where you can see a manatee up close. The park, previously a private zoo and tourist attraction, is a rehabilitation center for manatees who were orphaned or injured in the wild, and for those born in captivity. It claims to be the only center in the world where you can view these gentle creatures every day of the year. An underwater observatory lets visitors observe them eye-to-eye. You can also see wood ducks, flamingos, birds of prey, herons, and egrets on the grounds. Alligators, snakes, hippopotamuses, black bears, white-tailed deer, and river otters are among the other residents.

Campsites, facilities: There are 76 RV sites with full hookups, 30/50-amp electrical service, and cable TV; some have telephone access. Most sites are pull-through and have concrete patios. Restrooms, showers, picnic tables, grills, a dump station, laundry facilities, a dining area, rental cabins, and an adult TV room are available. You'll also find a playground, a pool, basketball and shuffleboard courts, horseshoes, a boat ramp, a fish-cleaning station, park model rentals, canoes for rent, and a marina. The bathrooms and clubhouse are wheelchair-accessible. A supermarket is five miles away. Children and leashed pets are welcome.

Reservations, fees: Reservations are advised. Sites are $28 per night for four people, plus $2.50 for each additional person up to a party of six. Credit cards are accepted. Long-term rates are available.

Directions: From Crystal River, drive south on U.S. 19 for 7.3 miles to County Road 490A/West Halls River Road and turn west. Drive 0.5 mile, turn south (left) on Fishbowl Drive, and follow to Mason Creek Road. Turn left. Go one mile to Garcia Road, turn right onto Garcia. Continue four blocks to Priest Lane. Turn right and follow signs to the park.

Contact: Camp 'N' Water Outdoor Resort, 11465 West Priest Lane, Homosassa, FL 34448, 352/628-2000, fax 352/628-0066, campnwater@mindspring.com.

48 TURTLE CREEK RV RESORT

Scenic rating: 7

south of Homosassa Springs

You can cast your line into Turtle Creek from the bank of this campground, but the wintertime action tends to take place indoors. Planned seasonal activities run the gamut, from ladies' luncheons, holiday dinners, and potluck feasts to crafts, exercise classes, card tournaments, and boat tours. There's even a bowling league, plus line dancing and country music shows performed by campers (bring your instrument). A short distance upriver is the Homosassa Springs State Wildlife Park (described in previous campground); six miles downriver is the Gulf of Mexico. Sites are oversized, big enough for large RVs. Folks are friendly; a nice widow brought me home-baked cookies one night.

Campsites, facilities: All 225 sites have full hookups, cable TV, 30-amp electrical service, and picnic tables. Some have 50-amp electricity, and around 10 sites are pull-through. Internet connection is available in the office. Restrooms, showers, laundry facilities, a dump station, a pool, a recreation pavilion, pool tables, fishing from the bank, horseshoes, shuffleboards, and rental units are available. The restrooms, office, recreation hall, and laundry are wheelchair-accessible. Children are welcome. Leashed pets are permitted.

Reservations, fees: Reservations are recommended. Sites are $25 per night for two people, plus $2 per additional adult and $2 for children. Credit cards are accepted. Long-term rates are available.

Directions: From Crystal River, drive south on U.S. 19 for 7.3 miles to County Road 490A/West Halls River Road and turn west. Drive 0.5 mile to Fishbowl Drive, turn south, and go 1.5 miles.

Contact: Turtle Creek Campground, 10200 West Fishbowl Drive, Homosassa Springs, FL 34448, 352/628-2928 or 800/471-3722, fax 352/628-6964, turtlecreek@gowebco.com.

49 NATURES RESORT RV PARK

Scenic rating: 8

south of Homosassa Springs

A full-service marina is the focus of this boating-oriented resort. Pontoon boats, canoes, kayaks, and john boats are available for rent, and most visitors are here to go fishing, boating or watch the wildlife. Some sites are waterfront, with a place to tie up your vessel.

Campsites, facilities: Tents are allowed in a specially designated grassy area set apart from the RV units. Tent sites have water and electricity. The RV section has 305 sites, with 250 available for overnighters. Restrooms, showers, laundry facilities, a dump station, boat rentals, a marina, dock, a pool, a clubhouse with a game arcade and pool tables, basketball court, playground, volleyball, horseshoes, restaurant, store, and rental units are available. Most areas are wheelchair-accessible. Children are welcome. Leashed pets are permitted.

Reservations, fees: Reservations are recommended. Sites are $30–40 per night for four

people, plus $5 per extra person. Credit cards are accepted. Long-term rates are available.

Directions: From Crystal River, drive south on U.S. 19 for 7.3 miles to County Road 490A/West Halls River Road and turn west. The park is located just across the Halls River bridge.

Contact: Natures Resort RV Park, 10359 West Halls River Road, Homosassa Springs, FL 34448, 352/628-9544 or 800/471-3722, fax 352/628-6964, www.naturesresortfla.com.

50 CHASSAHOWITZKA RIVER CAMPGROUND AND RECREATION AREA

Scenic rating: 8

south of Homosassa Springs

This shady campground gets hard use during holidays and weekends, but the location can't be beat, and it's well worth a visit. Campers can launch their boats or canoes from the boat ramp near Chassahowitzka Spring. The waterway flows southwest to the Gulf of Mexico, with dozens of creeks and crystal-clear springs offering tempting side trips along the way. Be sure to rinse your boat motor and trailer thoroughly afterward to remove all weed fragments, and to prevent the spread of weeds to other bodies of water. Canoes and small flat-bottomed boats can be rented at the campground. Nearby is the Chassahowitzka National Wildlife Refuge, a swampy coastal area popular among local anglers for both freshwater and saltwater fishing.

Campsites, facilities: There are 88 campsites for RVs, tents, and pop-up campers in this county-run campground. Forty sites have sewer hookups and 30/50-amp electricity, 16 have electricity and water only, and the rest are primitive. Restrooms, showers, laundry facilities, a camp store, and a boat ramp are available. Canoes and johnboats are for rent. Alcoholic beverages are prohibited. Children are welcome. Leashed pets are permitted with proof of rabies vaccination.

Reservations, fees: Reservations are accepted. Sites are $18–20 per night for two people, plus $3 for each additional person above age six. Credit cards are accepted. Maximum stay is six months.

Directions: From the intersection of U.S. 19 and County Road 480 south of Homosassa Springs and Crystal River, drive west on County Road 480/Miss Maggie Drive for 1.7 miles until the road ends at the campground.

Contact: Chassahowitzka River Campground and Recreation Area, 8600 West Miss Maggie Drive, Homosassa, FL 34448, 352/382-2200. Citrus County Parks and Recreation Office, P.O. Box 1439, Crystal River, FL 34423-1439, 352/795-2202, http://bocc.citrus.fl.us/parks/parks_recreation.htm.

DAYTONA

© PETER TRITLEY

BEST CAMPGROUNDS

◖ Families
Sunshine Holiday Daytona RV Resort, **page 241**

◖ Island Retreats
Hontoon Island State Park, **page 246**

◖ Most Unusual
Sunny Sands Nudist Resort, **page 241**

Daytona offers lots to do for all ages. Though
some RVers spend the winter months here escaping the chilly North, Daytona tends to be a family-oriented and destination vacation spot that is friendly to tent campers and outdoors enthusiasts.

Daytona's claim to fame is racing, and it revels in its celebration of the automobile. The beaches are made of hard-packed sand – hard enough to support the weight of a car – which auto-racing enthusiasts found ideal for setting land-speed records as early as 1903. Auto pioneers Ford, Chevrolet, Olds, and Packard were all here to test their inventions. NASCAR, the sanctioning body for stock-car racing, set up shop in 1947. The Daytona International Speedway provided a track where spectators could watch their favorite drivers compete, and events are still held here, most famously the "great American race" known as the Daytona 500.

Aside from car fans, motorcyclists flock to Daytona for special events, such as Bike Week (a 10-day festival and race, usually held in March), and Biketoberfest in the fall.

If you tire of all things automotive, the area is home to many places where you can get close to nature. Bulow Creek State Park hosts the

Fairchild Oak, which sprang up from an acorn about 800 years ago. Several hiking trails lead through the gorgeous Florida backcountry.

Inland fishing is excellent throughout the area, whether you choose lakes, rivers, or salt marshes. Brackish-water catches include snook, redfish, flounder, and speckled trout. Anglers with freshwater-fishing licenses can find bass, bluegill, shellcrackers, and specks.

Don't leave the area without heading west to visit DeLeon Springs State Park, where you can swim in the springs. Nineteen million gallons of water bubble out of the earth here every day.

Be sure to check out the manatees at Blue Spring State Park, near Orange City. When it's cold, you may spot 60 or so at a time in the 72°F waters flowing from the park's namesake spring. These endangered sea cows congregate generally November–March.

If you're visiting Daytona Beach in the winter months or during special events, reservations are highly recommended at any campground. This area is also popular during spring break, and space near the beach is at a premium.

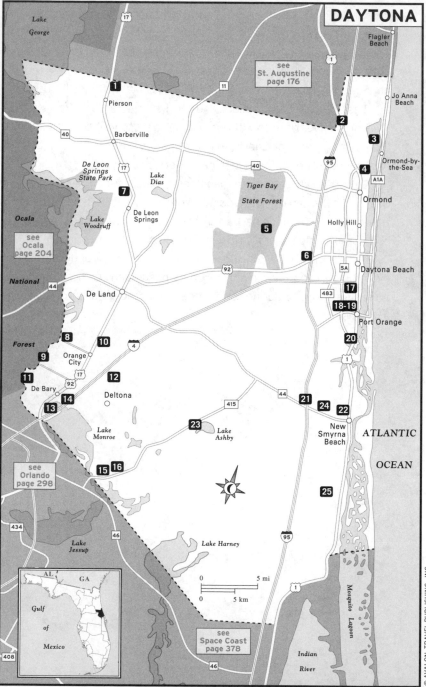

1 SUNNY SANDS NUDIST RESORT

Scenic rating: 3

east of Pierson

BEST (

You're way out in the boondocks here. As if that weren't enough to ensure privacy, the place is fenced and gated. The park should rightfully be called a "clothing-optional" rather than "nudist" resort. You can wear clothes anywhere you'd like except the swimming pool and hot tub, and on cold days, you'll find almost everyone has a stitch of clothing on somewhere. The 45-acre park is heavily shaded with live oaks and, according to the management, features a laid-back lifestyle targeted at families. About 60 couples and families live here permanently in mobile homes. Bring your own canoe to paddle on the small lake, or head a few miles away to catch bass in Lake George. Sites along Lakeshore Drive overlook tiny Crystal Lake. At Sunny Sands, nights are generally quiet, but there are some social events such as bingo, dances, happy hours, and spaghetti and chili cookoffs.

Campsites, facilities: This clothing-optional resort has 14 sites for RVs, 13 with full hookups with 30-amp electrical service; one site has 50-amp. RVs up to 45 feet long and slideouts can be accommodated. A large area is set aside for an indeterminate number of tents. Four tent sites have electricity. On the premises are restrooms, showers, laundry facilities, a nine-hole chipping course, basketball, volleyball, horseshoes, a pool, a hot tub, a one-mile-long walking trail, a restaurant and bar (open on weekends only), and a *pétanque* court (French-style bowling). Cable TV and telephone service are available in the rental trailers. Restaurants and limited groceries are about two miles away; a grocery store is within 15 miles. Malls and hospitals are 30 miles away. The bathhouse, clubhouse, office, and pool area are wheelchair-accessible. Children are welcome. One leashed cat or dog is allowed per site.

Reservations, fees: Reservations are highly recommended, particularly in the winter months. Sites are $28–45 per night for two people, plus $14 per extra person. Single adult campers are asked to phone before visiting. Credit cards are accepted. Long-term rates are available.

Directions: From I-95 at Exit 268, head west on State Road 40 for about 18 miles. In Barberville, turn right onto U.S. 17 and go about five miles north to the town of Pierson. Turn east (right) onto Washington Avenue. Follow it 1.25 miles to Turner Road, where you'll turn left. When the road curves to the right, you'll be within one block of the resort's gate. Continue, then look to the left for the resort gate and telephone.

Contact: Sunny Sands Nudist Resort, 502 Central Boulevard, Pierson, FL 32180, 386/749-2233, fax 386/749-0240, www.sunnysands.com.

2 SUNSHINE HOLIDAY DAYTONA RV RESORT

Scenic rating: 9

in Ormond Beach

BEST (

Set in an area of pine flat woods nine miles from the ocean, this park is ideal if you want a clean, resort-style camping experience far removed from the spring-break atmosphere of Daytona Beach. Many sites are at least partially shaded, thanks to a towering forest of ruler-straight pine trees. If you're just passing through, this is an excellent choice: It's just off the highway, and you'll probably find what you need right at the resort, which has 351 RV sites and several dozen rustic tent sites. In winter, there are planned activities geared toward retirees fleeing cold winters: bingo, dances, exercise classes, coffee klatches, and card parties. But bikers do show up during Daytona's famed Bike Week. A perky staff aims to adhere to the park's "fun and friendly service" mantra, and an example is their name for those giant umbrellas you see scattered around the park—they're "fun-brellas." It's convenient to Tomoka Basin GeoPark (see listing in this chapter) and the Bulow Plantation Ruins State Historic Site (see *Bulow Plantation Resort* in the *St. Augustine* chapter).

Campsites, facilities: There are 335 RV sites (250 full-hookup, 219 pull-through). The tent sites are primitive, with no hookups. For entertainment, try the golf driving nets, *pétanque* (French-style bowling), horseshoes, miniature golf, racquetball, basketball, shuffleboard, sand volleyball, bocce ball (lawn bowling), tennis courts, the playground, the pool, or winter activities. Facilities include restrooms, showers, picnic tables, a convenience store, a dump station, cable TV hookups, and laundry facilities. A wireless Internet network is available throughout the park. Restaurants are within one mile, and groceries are about five miles away. The 80-acre park is broken into two circles of campsites, one devoted to overnight guests, the other mainly for permanent residents and overflow campers. At the center of the camper-oriented circle is a swimming pool, a store, a laundry room, and a campground office. To sleep around this hub of activity (and its parking area), try sites 1–12. You'll pay the highest fee for these "super sites," as they're called. For canal-side spots, request sites 384–390. Children and leashed pets are permitted.

Reservations, fees: Reservations are necessary January–March and are recommended at other times of the year. Sites are $32–38 per night for two people, plus $2 daily if you want to hook up to cable TV. Credit cards are accepted. Long-term rates are available.

Directions: From I-95 at Exit 273, head north on U.S. 1 for 0.5 mile to the park entrance on the right.

Contact: Sunshine Holiday Daytona RV Resort, 1701 North U.S. 1, Ormond Beach, FL 32174, 386/672-3045 or 877/277-8737, fax 386/672-3026, www.rvonthego.com.

❸ TOMOKA BASIN GEOPARK

Scenic rating: 10

Set at the confluence of the Tomoka and Halifax Rivers, this 10,000-acre state park started out as a simple sandbar between the two rivers, but today is a lush forest of large oaks, shady hammocks, and saltwater marshes. Here, Timucuan Indians built a village they dubbed Nocorroco long before a wealthy Scotsman named Richard Oswald transformed it into the Mount Oswald Plantation. Oswald arrived after the American Revolution and proceeded to grow sugar, rice, and indigo, a plant used to make a blue dye popular at the time. (Visit the park museum to learn more about the history of the place.)

A 0.25-mile nature trail leads from the park museum through a shady coastal hammock to a picnic area. Rental canoes allow visitors to explore the rivers and salt marshes, which still teem with the fish that originally attracted the Timucuans. Brackish-water catches include snook, redfish, flounder, and speckled trout. Rangers say the best bait is live shrimp.

The park is a short drive from the Atlantic Ocean and is close to Bulow Creek State Park, a little-used, out-of-the-way slice of natural Florida open for day visits. At Bulow Creek, you'll find the Fairchild Oak, which sprang up from an acorn about 800 years ago. Today, its heavy, gnarly branches, covered in resurrection ferns, dip all the way to the ground. (Don't climb on them, please.) The oak is named for David Fairchild, a botanist who loomed large in Florida's history around the turn of the 20th century. Several hiking trails lead through the gorgeous Florida backcountry, including a six-mile hike along the Florida National Scenic Trail from Bulow Creek State Park to the Bulow Plantation Ruins State Historic Site (see *Bulow Resort Campground* in the *St. Augustine* chapter).

Campsites, facilities: The sandy, landlocked campsites are set along three circles. You'll enjoy at least some privacy from neighbors, thanks to the oaks and palms that help divide camping spots. There are 100 sites with water and 30-amp electricity for tents or RVs (up to 34 feet long and 11 feet high). Five sites have 50-amp service. Each site has a picnic table, a grill, and a fire ring. On the premises are restrooms, showers, a dump station, a recreation room, a boat ramp, firewood, canoe and kayak rentals, and a playground. A camp store sells ice, camping supplies, snacks, souvenirs, bait, and tackle. Groceries, restaurants, and laundry facilities are within six miles. The park's museum, docks, bathhouse, office, store, and picnic shelters are wheelchair-accessible, as are four campsites. Children are welcome. Pets are permitted with proof of rabies vaccination.

Reservations, fees: Reservations are recommended; contact ReserveAmerica at 800/336-3521 or reserveamerica.com. Rates are $20 per night for up to eight people. Credit cards are accepted. The maximum stay is 14 days.

Directions: From I-95 at Exit 268, go east on State Road 40 to North Beach Street. Turn left and drive 3.5 miles north to the park entrance.

Contact: Tomoka Basin GeoPark, 2099 North Beach Street, Ormond Beach, FL 32174, 386/676-4050, www.floridastateparks.org.

4 HARRIS VILLAGE AND RV PARK

Scenic rating: 6

in Ormond Beach

Open October–April, this sunny, over-55 park has a preference for motor homes and describes itself as "a nice little place for quiet people." Still, things can get busy during special events in the Daytona area, such as Bike Week, Speed

Weeks, and Biketoberfest ("bikes" meaning motorcycles), so be sure to call ahead. Daytona Beach's International Speedway is 20 minutes away. About 10 percent of the sites are occupied year-round.

Campsites, facilities: There are 20 RV sites of varying sizes that can accommodate rigs up to 40 feet long. Each site has full hookups, 30/50-amp electrical service, picnic tables, concrete patios, and cable TV. A dialup Internet connection is available in the office. Restrooms, showers, laundry facilities, and rental cabins are available. The office is wheelchair-accessible. Streets are paved. RV supplies, stores, and restaurants are within 0.5 mile. Children are not welcome. One small leashed pet is permitted; barking dogs will not be tolerated, and the management must preapprove all pets.

Reservations, fees: Reservations are required. Sites are $38–70 per night for two people, plus $5–15 per extra person. Rates are higher during special events. Credit cards are accepted. Long-term rates are available.

Directions: From I-95, take Exit 273 southeast four miles on U.S. 1 to the park.

Contact: Harris Village and RV Park, 1080 North U.S. 1, Ormond Beach, FL 32174, 386/673-0494, fax 386/672-5716, www.harrisvillage.com.

5 TIGER BAY STATE FOREST

Scenic rating: 6

west of Daytona beach

More than 11,000 acres of public land suitable for hiking, cycling, horseback riding and backpacking comprise Tiger Bay State Forest, which is under joint management with the St. Johns River Water Management District. Horses and mountain bikes are allowed on forest roads only. Backpackers can access a primitive campsite on Indian Lake, and trails crisscross the tract, which stretches from U.S. 40 in the north to U.S. 92 in the south. Most of the land is wetland forest, marked by "pine islands" of trees and a pine ridge; the habitat is home to black bears and bald eagles. Call ahead to avoid hunting season, usually in the fall and winter months. Much of the forest was burned in 1998, and you may still see damage from the wildfires. Some areas may be closed.

Campsites, facilities: Only tents are permitted. There are no facilities: Bring water, supplies, mosquito repellent, and everything you'll need. Children are welcome. Leashed pets are permitted.

Reservations, fees: Permits are required; call the state forest office at 386/226-0250 for instructions and fees.

Directions: From I-95, take Exit 261 westbound on U.S. 92 for four miles. At Indian Lake Road, turn north. This will bring you to the main access point. The campsite is two miles from here. Other access points are on the north side off U.S. 40, seven miles west of I-95.

Contact: Tiger Bay State Forest, 4316 West International Speedway Boulevard, Daytona Beach, FL 32124, 386/226-0250, fax 386/226-0251, www.fl-dof.com/state_forests/tiger_bay.html. Additional information is available from the St. Johns River Water Management District, 386/329-4404, www.sjrwmd.com.

6 INTERNATIONAL RV PARK AND CAMPGROUND
🏊 🐕 ♿ 🚐 ⛺

Scenic rating: 6

in Daytona Beach

Opened in 2001, this park built on what was once vacant land is convenient to beaches, Daytona's International Speedway, and other tourist attractions. It attracts people of all ages—from snowbirds to race fans. Sites are extra large, accommodating rigs up to 40 feet long, and there's room for 600 tents. Favorite things to do are relaxing, fishing, and going to the beach.

Campsites, facilities: Tenters can set up in a grassy area, where 200 sites have electrical service and 400 are primitive. The 200 RV sites have full hookups, 30/50-amp electrical service, concrete patios, and picnic tables. At 35 by 90 feet, these are some of the largest sites I've seen in a developed campground, and they were planned that way. Other sites are 30 by 45 feet, and 14 are drive-through. Restrooms, showers, laundry facilities, a 20-by-40-foot pool, a clubhouse, horseshoe pits, shuffleboard courts, a dog-walk area, and a putting green are available. All areas are wheelchair-accessible. Streets are paved. A camp store sells ice, camping supplies, and snacks. Groceries, restaurants, malls, and hospitals are within five miles. Children are welcome. Leashed pets are permitted.

Reservations, fees: Reservations are recommended. Sites are $30 per night for two people, plus $2 per extra person. Rates are higher during special events. Credit cards are accepted. Long-term rates are available. The maximum length of stay is six months.

Directions: From I-95, take Exit 261 onto U.S. 92 and travel west 1.1 miles to the park.

Contact: International RV Park and Campground, 3175 West International Speedway Blvd., Daytona Beach, FL 32124, 386/239-0249, www.internationalrvdaytona.com.

7 HIGHLAND PARK FISH CAMP
🚵 🚤 🚐 🐕 🚐 ⛺

Scenic rating: 8

northwest of DeLand, by the Lake Woodruff National Wildlife Refuge

This rustic place is a great location for nature lovers, but the real focus in bass fishing. The oak-shaded and sunny campsites at this 33-acre fish camp give anglers access to the St. Johns River and Lake Woodruff (and the surrounding wildlife refuge) via the Norris Dead River. For hikers, these grassy campsites also are the closest available to two sets of trails, one at Lake Woodruff National Wildlife Refuge and another at DeLeon Springs State Park.

At the wildlife refuge next door, there are three short nature trails and a much longer circuit of about 6.5 miles that leads bicyclists and hikers through woods and atop dikes built to hold in manmade freshwater lakes. Anglers can buy tackle and live bait at the fish camp to try their hand here. Visit in fall or winter to see abundant waterfowl and wading birds. At any time of year, keep an eye out for otters, bobcats, deer, and other wild animals, particularly early or late in the day. Florida black bears live in the refuge, but are rarely seen. To get to the refuge, head north on Grand Avenue to Mud Lake Road, where you will see refuge headquarters (386/985-4673). Proceed down Mud Lake Road to a parking area to find the hiking trails.

Campsites, facilities: There are 59 full-hookup sites, of which 20 are available for overnighters in tents or RVs. All sites have water and 30-amp electricity. On the premises are showers, restrooms, a dump station, firewood (at times), cabin and mobile home rentals, horseshoes, a boat ramp, charter fishing services, fishing guides, motorboat and rowboat rentals, a limited store, bait, tackle, and a dock. Restaurants and a grocery store are located within three miles. Children and leashed pets are welcome.

Reservations, fees: Reservations are recommended but are not always necessary. Sites are $16–20 per night for two people, plus $2 per additional adult. If you want to turn on your air conditioner, a $2 daily fee applies. Credit cards are accepted. Long-term stays are OK.

Directions: From central DeLand, take State Road 44/New York Avenue west to Grand Avenue. Turn right, heading north. Grand Avenue will dogleg, merging for a time with Minnesota Avenue to head west and then turn

north again. Stay on Grand Avenue as you pass the landfill and Humane Society Road on the right. Not far past that, turn left onto Highland Park Road. Follow it 1.5 miles to the fish camp.

Contact: Highland Park Fish Camp, 2640 West Highland Park Road, DeLand, FL 32720, 386/734-2334 or 800/525-3477, fax 386/943-9681, www.hpfishcamp.com.

8 BLUE SPRING STATE PARK

Scenic rating: 9

west of Orange City

At any time of year, this well-used picnic spot is worth a visit, but show up when it's cold for a better chance of seeing lots of manatees—maybe 60 of them, like on the day I visited. These endangered sea cows congregate generally November–March in the 72°F waters flowing from the spring for which the park is named. From the boardwalk above the clear blue waters, it's easy to see their whiskers and the outlines of their dark, blubbery bodies.

You can't take motorboats up the Blue Spring Run, but you can swim there. Canoeing, swimming, and scuba diving may be restricted in certain areas if manatees are present, but you always can enjoy these activities somewhere in the vicinity. Rental canoes give visitors access to the St. Johns River and Lake Beresford, where anglers with freshwater-fishing licenses find bass, bluegill, shellcrackers, and specks.

Regular campsites are in a sun-dappled pine forest not far from the spring. Hikers and backpackers traverse a four-mile trail that tends to flood in summer and fall (bring hiking boots). The trail straddles pine flat woods and marsh, ending in a lush oak hammock where four primitive campsites tend to be dry even when the trail is under water.

History-minded campers should check out the park's waterfront Thursby House, a two-story wooden structure with double verandas and a real Old South feel. The pioneer Thursby family built it in 1872 atop a mound of snail shells deposited by Timucuan Indians, who had made snails a staple of their diet hundreds of years before. Union gunboat crews and U.S. presidents are among the visitors who have arrived at Thursby House over the years.

Campsites, facilities: This state park offers 51 gravel sites for tents and RVs, all with 30/50-amp electricity, water, picnic tables, and grills. Sites are on the small side; RVs up to 30 feet long can be accommodated. On the premises are restrooms, showers, picnic tables, a dump station, rental cabins, a fishing pier, covered pavilions, and canoe rentals. A boat ramp for small boats is nearby. A park concession stand sells snacks and some groceries. Restaurants, groceries, and laundry facilities are about two miles away. Groceries and restaurants are within five miles. Children are welcome. Leashed pets are permitted with proof of current rabies vaccination.

Reservations, fees: Reservations are recommended; contact ReserveAmerica at 800/336-3521 or reserveamerica.com. Sites are $20 per night for up to eight people. Credit cards are accepted. Maximum stay is 14 days.

Directions: From I-4, take Exit 114 and follow the signs south on 17-92 to Orange City, about 2.5 miles. Make a right onto West French Avenue and drive until it ends at the campground. The park is about two miles west of City Hall.

Contact: Blue Spring State Park, 2100 West French Avenue, Orange City, FL 32763, 386/775-3663, fax 386/775-7794.

🔟 HONTOON ISLAND STATE PARK

🚶 🚴 🛶 🚗 🧺 ⛺

Scenic rating: 10

west of Orange City

BEST (

This island between the St. Johns and Hunt-oon Dead Rivers holds special appeal because it is not accessible by car; you must take a boat or the free passenger ferry to get here. Of course, that means RV campers are out of luck. But if you have a tent or a boat big enough to sleep in, you can look forward to a unique experience.

At 2.5 square miles, the island is large enough to allow some hiking or canoeing, but not so big that you'll get lost. A nature trail winds past mounds built hundreds of years ago by Timucuan Indians. In the picnic area, you'll see a replica of a 14th-century owl totem carved by the Native Americans and discovered here in 1955. You're virtually sure to see Florida's ubiquitous turkey vultures and seagulls, and perhaps deer, armadillo, otters, and wild turkeys. Before the state bought the island in 1967, the land served as a pioneer homestead, cattle ranch, and boatyard. Today, much of it has been restored to a more-natural condition.

Seventy-three species of fish have been identified in the St. Johns River, although around here, most anglers use live shiners or artificial bait to lure bass. Other popular targets include shellcrackers, catfish, and bluegill. To add adventure to your visit, consider renting a canoe at Blue Spring State Park (see listing in this chapter) and paddling to a campsite on Hontoon Island. Winter is the best time to avoid mosquitoes, because campsites sit where marsh and hammock meet (no sites are on the water). In summer, says a ranger, "we definitely got the market cornered on mosquitoes." Swimming is out of the question anytime, because of alligators.

Campsites, facilities: Twelve primitive tent sites and 52 slips for boat campers are available. Each tent site has a picnic table, a grill suitable for cooking or a small campfire, and nearby access to communal water spigots. Facilities in the park include restrooms, showers, boat docks, picnic tables, canoe rentals, bicycle trails, an enclosed pavilion, six rustic cabins, and a playground. Access is restricted to boats, so bring all the supplies you will need. Children are permitted. Pets are not allowed. Bring your own firewood; it's against the rules to gather wood within the park.

Reservations, fees: Reservations are required; call ReserveAmerica at 800/326-3521. On weekends and holidays, there is a two-night minimum. Boat slips are first-come, first-served. Rental cabins may be reserved (and often are, particularly at busy times like Thanksgiving and Christmas) up to 11 months in advance. Sites are $8 per night for camping for four people, plus $2 per extra person, $10 for a boat slip, and $2 for electricity. Major credit cards are accepted.

Directions: From DeLand, head west on State Road 44/New York Avenue, veering left on Old Route 44. Follow the well-marked route to the dock where you'll catch the free ferry, which runs on demand 8 A.M.–sunset. Overnight campers may arrive not later than 7 P.M. Blue Spring State Park is a good place to launch your own boat.

Contact: Hontoon Island State Park, 2309 River Ridge Road, DeLand, FL 32720, 386/736-5309, www.hontooncso.com.

10 DELAND/ORANGE CITY KOA

🏊 🛶 🎣 🦮 🚙 ⛺

Scenic rating: 4

in Orange City

Birders might spy hawks, woodpeckers, or other birds in the oaks dotting this family-run park, where sandy interior roads lead to shady, sandy sites, most of them with patios. Children's activities are sometimes scheduled on holiday weekends. There's also a swimming pool, a game room, a playground, and the like. Leave the campground by day to enjoy area highlights such as nearby Blue Spring State Park, Hontoon Island State Park, and DeLeon Springs State Park. It's also close to the St. Francis Interpretive Trail.

Campsites, facilities: All 100 tent sites are separated from the RVs, and they are set in either an open, grassy area or under tall pines, with water and electricity. There are 150 RV sites (70 pull-through) with picnic tables, water, and 30-amp electricity hookups; 130 have full hookups. Some sites have 50-amp service. On the premises are showers, restrooms, a dump station, a recreation room, a pool, a playground, a game room, horseshoes, volleyball, basketball, limited groceries, a restaurant, and laundry facilities. Firewood is available. A grocery store is a five-minute drive away. Children and leashed pets are welcome.

Reservations, fees: Reservations are necessary in February and March. Sites are $23–45 per night for two people, plus $2.50 for each additional adult. For electricity, the fee is $3; add sewer for $2 more. Credit cards are accepted. Long-term stays are OK.

Directions: From I-4 at Exit 114, travel west on State Road 472 for 1.5 miles to Minnesota Avenue. Turn left. The campground is about 0.25 mile ahead.

Contact: DeLand/Orange City KOA, 1440 East Minnesota Avenue, Orange City, FL 32763, 386/775-3996 or 800/KOA-7857 (800/562-7857), www.koa.com.

11 HIGHBANKS MARINA AND CAMP RESORT

🚲 🏊 🛶 🛳 🦮 🎣 ♿ 🚙 ⛺

Scenic rating: 7

on the St. Johns River, in DeBary

Like most campgrounds along the St. Johns River, this one is geared toward anglers who go after bass, shellcracker, catfish, and other freshwater prizes. Big oaks, interspersed with magnolias, shade parts of these 25 acres. The management employs a full-time recreation director year-round, so don't be surprised to find an ice-cream social on Saturday evening or bingo on weekends. Kids can fish at the park's small-fry fishing pond and take a two-hour nature cruise on the park's tour boats to see alligators and other wildlife. Half of the campers live permanently at the grassy/ concrete-pad sites. They enjoy a huge (30-by-60-foot) pool for swimming and 0.5 mile of riverfront for strolling. Hiking trails are nearby. This campground is only a few miles from Blue Spring State Park and, by boat, Hontoon Island State Park. It's also pretty close to DeLeon Springs State Park and Ocala National Forest.

Campsites, facilities: All 221 full-hookup sites are for RVs up to 40 feet long. Six sites are pull-through. Tents are allowed on 20 sites May 1–October 31 only, and tenters may stay only for seven nights. To camp nearest to the St. Johns River, ask about Cypress Lane sites 107–130. To stay beside the fishpond, request sites 38–64 on Hickory and Live Oak Drives. Charter fishing services, wildlife boat tours, rental boats, billiards, a playground, a game room, horseshoes, shuffleboard, a recreation room, and a full-time recreation director entertain campers. On the premises are showers, restrooms, firewood, a 72-slip marina, a boat ramp, bait and tackle, limited groceries, picnic tables, a dump station, rental RV cabins, a snack bar, laundry facilities, and a restaurant. Management says the main bathhouse and clubhouse are wheelchair-accessible. Children are welcome but may stay only two weeks. Two small- to medium-size pets are allowed per RV site, except for the tent sites, where all pets are prohibited.

Reservations, fees: Reservations are recommended and are accepted up to two months in advance. Sites are $25–40 per night for two people, plus $5 for each additional adult. Credit cards are accepted. Adult RVers are welcome for long-term stays. Tenters are limited to a maximum stay of seven nights.

Directions: From I-4 at Exit 104, head north on U.S. 17/92 into DeBary. At the second light, turn left onto Highbanks Road. Go 2.5 miles west to the campground and marina.

Contact: Highbanks Marina and Camp Resort, 488 West Highbanks Road, DeBary, FL 32713, 386/668-4491, fax 386/668-5072, www.campresort.com.

12 ORANGE CITY RV RESORT

Scenic rating: 7

off I-4, in Orange City

This is part of a much larger complex of manufactured homes with suburban-style carports on mowed lots. Most of the sites are snagged by people over age 55 who live here year-round (20 percent) or for the winter season, taking advantage of the park's arts-and-crafts classes, dances, parties, and special outings. Many guests spend time across the street sipping coffee at a diner, frequenting a shopping center, or taking in movies at a theater. Guests also have access to an 18-hole wooded golf course, which surrounds the RV parks. Park models are for sale.

Campsites, facilities: All 525 full-hookup spots have 30-amp electrical service (125 have 50-amp). Twenty sites are pull-through. Tents are allowed at 100 spots in the RV area. A wireless Internet network is available in the park. For entertainment, there's golf, miniature golf, a billiards room, a picnic pavilion, horseshoes, bocce ball (lawn bowling), a large heated pool, a whirlpool tub, a kiddie pool, planned activities, and a game room. Facilities include restrooms, showers, picnic tables, laundry facilities, and a convenience store. The clubhouse and pool area are wheelchair-accessible. Streets are paved. Groceries are within two miles. Children are welcome. Leashed pets are allowed.

Reservations, fees: Reservations are recommended. Sites are $28–34 per night. Credit cards are accepted. Long-terms stays are OK.

Directions: From I-4 at Exit 114, head west on State Route 472 (Howland Avenue) to the traffic light. Turn left on Route 4101 and drive one mile. At Graves Avenue, turn left and drive one block to the park.

Contact: Orange City RV Resort, 2300 East Graves Avenue, Orange City, FL 32763, 386/775-2545 or 866/786-0139, fax 386/775-1517, www.orangecityrvresort.com.

13 LAKE MONROE PARK AND CAMPGROUND

🛶 🚐 🐕 ♿ 🚑 ⛺

Scenic rating: 8

on the St. Johns River, south of DeBary

Renovated in 2004, this small, oak-shaded campground is in a county-run park where Lake Monroe runs into the St. Johns River, a habitat for alligators (don't feed them). It's shady, and you'll often get a breeze off the lake. Saw palmettos between the sites help provide some privacy. Your neighbors may be snowbirds or construction workers who toil up the road a little ways; because it's just off the interstate, this campground may make a convenient stop in a pretty spot. Although anglers catch bluegill and speckled perch from the pier, most guests use this campground as an inexpensive springboard for trips to Orlando, Disney World, Daytona Beach, or Ocala National Forest. Even closer are Blue Spring State Park and Hontoon Island State Park, as well as DeLeon Springs State Park.

Campsites, facilities: This park, just 0.5 mile off the interstate, offers 44 spots for RVs and 26 for tents, all with water and electricity. On the premises are restrooms, showers, a dump station, picnic tables, grills, fire rings, two boat ramps, a playground, a picnic pavilion, and a wheelchair-accessible floating dock and fishing pier. A restaurant and grocery store are about one mile away. Children and leashed pets are permitted.

Reservations, fees: Reservations are recommended. April 1–August 31, rates are $10 per night for two people, plus $2 for each additional person and $2 for electricity. September 1–March 31, the rate rises to $15. During special events, rates are higher. Credit cards are not accepted. Stays are limited to two weeks, or three weeks if no one is waiting for a site.

Directions: From I-4 at Exit 104, head north on U.S. 17/92. Cross the St. Johns River and you'll see the park on your right. If traveling eastbound on I-4, take Exit 52; at the end of the ramp, turn left and proceed to U.S. 17/92, then turn north (left) on U.S. 17/92.

Contact: Lake Monroe Park and Campground, 975 South U.S. 17/92, DeBary, FL 32713, 386/668-3825; or write to Volusia County Leisure Services, 202 North Florida Avenue, DeLand, FL 32720, 386/736-5953, www.volusia.org/parks/camping.htm.

14 GEMINI SPRINGS

🚴 🏊 🛶 🛶 🎿 🐕 ♿ ⛺

Scenic rating: 10

east of DeBary

This 200-acre park was opened by the county in 1996 after it acquired the site from private owners. The biggest attraction is Gemini Springs itself, a natural spring with waters at 72°F year-round, but the pristine woods and surroundings are also a draw. You can swim in the spring's 200-by-60-foot swimming hole, which is about eight feet deep, and kids can amuse themselves by jumping in from a dock. Canoes are available for rent. The park offers interpretive programs and a 1.5-mile-long nature trail. It's frequented mostly by locals or their tourist friends looking for a quiet getaway with no RV traffic.

Campsites, facilities: Only tents are allowed on these 40-plus sites (no hookups). Water is available near the campsites, all of which rest on elevated pads and have picnic tables and grills. Restrooms and showers are available. On the premises are a natural spring with swimming, nature trails, a playground, and a camp circle. Part of the park is wheelchair-accessible, but not the campsites. Children are welcome. Leashed pets are permitted.

Reservations, fees: Reservations are recommended. April 1–August 31, rates are $10 per night for two people, plus $2 for each additional person. September 1–March 31, the rate rises to $15. During special events, rates are higher. The park has a $3.50 admission per car. Credit cards are not accepted. The maximum stay is two weeks.

Directions: From I-4, take Exit 108 onto Dirksen Drive westbound toward DeBary one mile. The park entrance will be on your left.

Contact: Gemini Springs, 37 Dirksen Drive, DeBary, FL 32713, 407/668-3810, fax 386/668-3812; or contact the Volusia County Leisure Services Department, 202 North Florida Avenue, DeLand, FL 32720-4618, 386/736-5953, www.volusia.org/parks/camping.htm.

15 PARADISE LAKES TRAVEL TRAILER PARK

🎣 🛖 🐕 🚶 🚐 ⛺

Scenic rating: 4

south of Deltona

This family-run campground is set in an oak forest, next to a small lake with a swimming beach where anglers try to catch bass. Most campsites are sandy, although a few are grassy. If you want to canoe or go out in a johnboat, bring your own; no motorized watercraft are allowed on the lake. Most campers are senior citizens who stay only during the winter months. Some weekend regulars leave their trailers on-site and pay $50 per month for the privilege. Although campsites 1–40 are termed "lakeside," sunbathers may prefer sites 11–20 to be closest to the beach.

Campsites, facilities: The park offers 170 full-hookup sites with 30-amp electrical service and picnic tables. Seven sites are pull-through. Tents are permitted at the same sites, but they are limited to a maximum of two nights' stay. On the premises are restrooms, showers, a dump station, laundry facilities, a playground, horseshoes, and a limited convenience store that sells ice and camping supplies. Groceries and restaurants are about two miles away. Children are permitted for one-week stays only. Leashed pets are allowed in the camping area but are forbidden at the beach and the grassy beachfront.

Reservations, fees: Reservations are recommended October–April, but are not necessary at other times. Sites are $22 per night for two people, plus $2 for each additional person and $2 for electricity. Credit cards are not accepted. Long-term rates are available.

Directions: From I-4 at Exit 53, head east on DeBary Avenue/Doyle Road for about four miles. You'll see the park on the right.

Contact: Paradise Lakes Travel Trailer Park, 1571 Doyle Road, Deltona, FL 32725, 386/574-2371.

16 LAKE MONROE CONSERVATION AREA

🚶 🚲 🎣 🚐 ⛺

Scenic rating: 6

east of Sanford

Long ago, Native Americans hunted and fished on these marshy 7,390 acres. Now, anglers and boaters travel down this stretch of the St. Johns River and canoeists sometimes paddle on Lake Monroe. In all, this retreat offers more than three miles of shoreline on the lake or river. The rustic, no-frills campsites are on the northern bank of the St. Johns and are well-separated from each other. More than five miles of hiking trails start at the parking area off Reed Ellis Road and make three loops as they wind through floodplain marsh, swamp, and forest. Look for wood storks, sandhill cranes, turkeys, deer, and plentiful alligators. About 94 percent of this land is wetlands, so much of it is not accessible by foot. Bring a hat and sunscreen—it's an open, sunny place. American Forests' Global ReLeaf program is working to add more trees to the place, formerly known as the Kratzert Tract (named for one-time owner Minnie Beck Kratzert).

Campsites, facilities: Only tents are permitted at six primitive campsites, which are reached by boat or hiking. There are no restrooms or other facilities. Bring food, supplies, mosquito repellent, and everything else you'll need. A

An alligator ignores a bird nearby.

nearby boat ramp providing access to the conservation area's portion of the St. Johns River is on State Road 46, a little more than two miles east of County Road 415. Children are welcome. Pets must be leashed.

Reservations, fees: Sites are first-come, first-served. Camping is free. Each site accommodates up to six people. If your party has at least seven people, get a free permit and reserve at least one week ahead at 386/329-4404. Maximum stay for all campers is seven days.

Directions: From Sanford, go east about four miles on State Road 46 to County Road 415, where you'll turn north (left). Travel about three miles on the county road, crossing the St. Johns River, then turn into a parking area, at right. Another parking area—for better hiking, bird-watching, and horseback riding—is farther east. To get there, continue on County Road 415 about one mile, turn left onto Reed Ellis Road, and continue nine-tenths of a mile to the parking area, at left. For more details, get a map and booklet from the water district before your trip.

Contact: St. Johns River Water Management District, Division of Land Management, P.O.

Box 1429, Palatka, FL 32178-1429, 407/893-3127, www.sjrwmd.com.

17 ORANGE ISLES CAMPGROUND

Scenic rating: 6

in Port Orange

One big plus in winter is that you can pick oranges and grapefruit from the trees growing in this renovated 17-acre campground, although some visitors are more interested in jumping into the 50-foot-long swimming pool. The large, shaded campsites are about 2.5 miles from the Atlantic Ocean and just around the corner from the Port Orange Sugar Mill Ruins (see next listing). It's close to Daytona's International Speedway and popular during Bike Week and other festivities.

Campsites, facilities: There are 280 full-hookup sites, with 200 available for overnight RVs. Fifty-amp electrical service is available. A separate grassy, shaded section has room for 70 tents; they do not have water or electricity. Tenters are restricted to a maximum of seven nights and are not permitted in the RV section. Each site has a picnic table. On the premises are showers, restrooms, a dump station, a log cabin recreation room, a 50-foot-long pool, a playground, shuffleboard, horseshoes, and laundry facilities. Restrooms and showers are wheelchair-accessible, according to management. Groceries and restaurants are within one mile. Children are permitted. Leashed pets are allowed.

Reservations, fees: Reservations are recommended. For two people, sites are $28 per night April–September and $34 per night October–January. Rates are higher during special events and in February and March. Each additional adult pays $5–15 per night. All rates are subject to change. Credit cards are accepted. Long-term stays are OK.

Directions: From I-95 at Exit 256, go east on State Route 421/Dunlawton Avenue about three miles to Nova Road. Turn north and look for the park on the left.

Contact: Orange Isles Campground, 3520 South Nova Road, Port Orange, FL 32119, 386/767-9170, www.orangeislescampground.com.

18 NOVA FAMILY CAMPGROUND

Scenic rating: 5

in Port Orange

Amid the big oaks shrouded in Spanish moss, you'll occasionally hear owls hooting at night. Weddings and family reunions are sometimes held in the log cabin recreation hall, and special events include hayrides, pig roasts, canoe trips, and karaoke nights. About 10 percent of the park is occupied year-round. This is an adult park, but families are welcome for short-term stays. Log cabins are for sale.

Campsites, facilities: There are 269 grassy sites with full hookups, cable TV, and 30/50-amp electrical service. RVs up to 35 feet long and slideouts can be accommodated. Ten sites are pull-through. Tents are permitted at 50 grassy, shady sites, but they are limited to a maximum stay of seven nights. Picnic tables and grills are available at some sites. An Internet connection is available in the office. On the premises are showers, restrooms, fire rings, a dump station, a recreation room, a pool, horseshoes, shuffleboard, a game room, rental cabins, limited groceries, snacks, and laundry facilities. Children are welcome for stays of less than 21 days. Pets are permitted, with a daily fee.

Reservations, fees: Reservations are recommended. Sites are $30 per night for two people, plus $3 for each additional person over age 10, $2 for pets, and $2 for electricity. Rates increase during special events such as Bike Week. Credit cards are accepted. Long-term rates are available.

Directions: From I-95 at Exit 256, go east on State Route 421/Dunlawton Avenue through two stoplights to Clyde Morris Boulevard and turn left. Continue north through two more lights to Herbert Street, then turn right. The park is 0.25 mile ahead.

Contact: Nova Family Campground, 1190 Herbert Street, Port Orange, FL 32119, 386/767-0095, fax 386/767-1666, www.novacamp.com.

19 DAYTONA BEACH CAMPGROUND

Scenic rating: 6

in Port Orange

Although it is dubbed Daytona Beach Campground, this 17-acre park is actually in the quieter neighboring city of Port Orange. The sunny campsites are set in a neighborhood located just a few miles from the Daytona Beach Regional Airport and the Daytona International Speedway. Although overnighters appreciate that proximity, patrons also include seasonal residents who enjoy holding bingo games, potluck dinners, and dances away from the bustling throng of oceanside Daytona Beach. Like all campgrounds in the area, this place is extremely popular during certain times February–April, starting with Bike Week and lasting through spring break. For day trips, drive about six miles to swim in the Atlantic Ocean instead of the park's pool. About 10 percent of the park is occupied year-round.

Campsites, facilities: Twenty of the 180 sites are drive-through. All have 30-amp electrical service, and 24 have 50-amp. Each site has a picnic table and a concrete patio. RVs up to 45 feet long and slideouts can be accommodated on lots averaging 30 by 80 feet. On the premises are restrooms, showers, a dump station, a recreation room, a pool, a playground, shuffleboard, horseshoes, basketball, and laundry facilities. Cable TV is available. Management says all areas are wheelchair-accessible. Streets are paved. Groceries, snacks, and a restaurant are within walking distance. Children and leashed, attended pets are welcome.

Reservations, fees: Reservations are required. Sites are $27–30 per night for two people, plus $5–10 for each additional person, including children. Credit cards are accepted. Long-term rates are available.

Directions: From I-95 at Exit 260A, proceed east on State Road 400 for about 2.5 miles to Clyde Morris Boulevard. Turn right and continue about three miles south to the campground on the left.

Contact: Daytona Beach Campground, 4601 South Clyde Morris Boulevard, Daytona Beach, FL 32119, 386/761-2663, fax 386/761-9187, www.rvdaytona.com.

20 ROSE BAY TRAVEL PARK

Scenic rating: 5

at Rose Bay, in Port Orange

Popular with Canadians and Northerners who escape frigid temperatures by spending winters on Rose Bay, inland from the Atlantic beach, this 37-acre park gets crowded with all manner of folks during Bike Week in spring and Race Week in winter. Besides bingo and potluck dinners, some winter residents enjoy fishing in the park's small brackish lake. About 40 percent of the park is occupied year-round.

Campsites, facilities: All 307 full-hookup sites can accommodate RVs up to 40 feet long and slideouts. Ten sites have 50-amp electrical service, and 290 have 30-amp. To sleep closest to the waterfront recreation area at the tip of this long, narrow RV park, ask about campsites 300–305. To be closest to the boat launch and dock, try sites 283–289 or 227–231. The pool and recreation room are at the opposite end of the park near campsite 78. On the premises are restrooms, showers, a dump station, laundry facilities, picnic tables, a pool, shuffleboard and *pétanque* courts, a dock, a boat ramp, and a recreation room. Cable TV and telephone service are available. Groceries and restaurants are within 0.2 mile. All areas are wheelchair-accessible. Children are allowed on a short-term basis. Pets must be kept on three-foot leashes.

Reservations, fees: Reservations are recommended. Sites are $30 per night for two people, plus $5 for each additional person. Credit cards are accepted. Adults are welcome for long-term stays.

Directions: From I-95 at Exit 256, take State Road 421 east for three miles to Nova Road. Turn right and head south. The campground is about five miles ahead on the right, 0.5 mile west of U.S. 1.

Contact: Rose Bay Travel Park, 5200 South

Nova Road, Port Orange, FL 32127, 386/767-4308, fax 386/767-7060.

21 NEW SMYRNA BEACH RV PARK AND CAMPGROUND

🏊 🐕 ♿ 🏕

Scenic rating: 6

west of New Smyrna Beach

Swimmers have their choice of aquatic venues: the campground pool or the Atlantic Ocean five miles away, where you can drive on the hard-packed sand (except when the nests of endangered sea turtles are present). Some shell-rock or grassy sites are sunny, while others enjoy shade from magnolias, oaks, or palms. Indeed, 25 acres of this 30-acre park are dotted with trees, and sites are scattered throughout. Expect little privacy, though, because sites are right next to each other with little or no brush to separate them. During some holiday periods, children's activities are organized here, but retirees dominate November–April, when activities trend toward bingo, potluck dinners, and dances. It's about 20 miles to the Merritt Island National Wildlife Refuge, heading south. Daytona International Speedway is about 20 miles north.

Campsites, facilities: There are 208 sites with full hookups and 30-amp or 50-amp electrical service, cable TV, Internet access, and picnic tables. On the premises are showers, restrooms, a dump station, a recreation room, cabin rentals, a pool, a playground, a game room, miniature golf, horseshoes, shuffleboard, limited groceries, and laundry facilities. Restaurants and bait are within five miles. The showers and store are wheelchair-accessible, according to management. Children and leashed pets are welcome.

Reservations, fees: Reservations are recommended. Sites are $24–27 per night (higher during special events) for two people, plus $3 for each additional adult. Credit cards are accepted. Long-term stays are OK.

Directions: From I-95 at Exit 249, go east on State Road 44 to Old Mission Road. Turn right and continue 1.5 miles south to the campground on your right.

Contact: New Smyrna Beach RV Park and Campground, 1300 Old Mission Road, New Smyrna Beach, FL 32168, 386/427-3581 or 800/928-9962, beachcamp@beachcamp.net.

22 SUGAR MILL RUINS TRAVEL PARK

🏊 🛶 🐕 🏕 🚐 ⛺

Scenic rating: 5

west of U.S. 1, in New Smyrna Beach

At this shady campground, where anglers catch mullet and catfish from the banks of the brackish fishing hole, the owners have taken some pains to preserve native Florida vegetation. The grassy, full-hookup campsites along Quail Hollow Drive tend to enjoy the most shade from palms, pines, and oaks. Camping spots farther from the center of the park can be quite sunny, because they're in the garden section, where small hibiscus bushes dominate. Don't expect to see a sugar mill. The park gets its name from the nearby Sugar Mill Ruins Historic Site, a small, sleepy, wooded, Volusia County–run park. It serves as a reminder of the Second Seminole War, when Indians clashed with settlers who moved into the area to grow sugar and indigo, a plant valued for its role in making a then popular blue dye. You can picnic at tables near the decaying stone walls of the mill, now being overcome by sabal palms and other native vegetation. Elsewhere, the quaint commercial district of New Smyrna Beach is sort of a quiet cousin of Daytona Beach. For now, at least, it's far enough removed from Daytona that it doesn't get the same crowds, except for spillover business during the festivals in Daytona Beach.

Campsites, facilities: There are 117 RV full-hookup sites with 30/50-amp electrical service; many are pull-through. Sites are lined up, as many as 21–25 abreast, along straight, 5-mph roads whose names conjure up natural images—Jack Rabbit Run, Raccoon Road, Armadillo Drive. A primitive area for tent sites is adjacent to the RVs. To sleep nearest to the pool (and the entrance-area laundry room), ask about full-hookup sites 47–50. On the premises are showers, restrooms, a dump station, laundry facilities, a recreation room, a convenience store, a pool, volleyball, basketball, a playground, horseshoes, and canoe rentals. Children must be supervised by adults at the pool. Leashed pets must use the designated dog walk.

Reservations, fees: Reservations are recommended, except in summer. Sites typically run $25–33 per night for two people, plus $5 for each additional person over the age of 13. Credit cards are accepted. Long-term rates are available.

Directions: From I-95 at Exit 249, head east on State Road 44. Turn right onto Old Mission Road. In about 0.25 mile, look for the faux waterwheel marking the campground entrance on the right.

Contact: Sugar Mill Ruins Travel Park, 1050 Old Mission Road, New Smyrna Beach, FL 32168, 386/427-2284, fax 386/428-8521, www.sugarmilltravelpark.com.

23 LAKE ASHBY PARK

Scenic rating: 8

southwest of New Smyrna Beach

Located on 3,200-acre Lake Ashby, this county-run park is set in a beautiful hardwood and softwood hammock. No RVs are permitted, which is a bonus for tenters who want to get away from it all. Note that the showers are cold. The wooded park has a fishing pier and boardwalk near the lake, and there's a prehistoric archaeological site. As always around Florida lakes, be careful of alligators.

Campsites, facilities: Ten tent sites are available. Restrooms and cold showers are provided, but there's no water or electricity hookups. A boardwalk, a pavilion, and a fishing pier are wheelchair-accessible. Children are welcome. Leashed pets are permitted.

Reservations, fees: Reservations are recommended. Sites are $10 to $15 per night for up to six people. Credit cards are not accepted. Campers may stay as long as two weeks.

Directions: From I-95, take Exit 249 west on State Road 44 about five miles. At State Road 415, turn south and drive 4.5 miles to an orange TV tower. Turn east onto Lake Ashby Road and follow the signs to Boy Scout Camp Road. The park is about 0.5 mile ahead on the right.

Contact: Lake Ashby Park, 4150 Boy Scout Camp Road, New Smyrna Beach, FL 32764, 386/428-4589, fax 386/424-2970; or contact the Volusia County Leisure Services Department, 202 North Florida Avenue, DeLand, FL 32720-4618, 386/736-5953, www.volusia .org/parks/camping.htm.

24 SPRUCE CREEK PARK

Scenic rating: 7

south of Port Orange

Spruce Creek Park spells r-e-l-i-e-f for tenters weary of sharing campgrounds with trailers or motorhomes. RVs are not welcome in this county-run park, which is primarily a picnic and daytime recreation spot for locals. At this location just off busy U.S. 1, you can launch your canoe onto Spruce Creek or cast a line from the fishing pier. The surroundings are wooded.

Campsites, facilities: Only tents are allowed at this 17-site campground. Each has a picnic table and grill; water is available, but not electricity. Restrooms, showers, and firewood are available. On the premises are a campground pavilion, a fishing pier, a canoe launch, a playground, and a nature trail. The pavilion and pier are wheelchair-accessible. Children are welcome. Leashed pets are permitted.

Reservations, fees: Reservations are recommended. April 1–August 31, rates are $10 per night for two people, plus $2 for each additional person. September 1–March 31, the rate rises to $15. During special events, rates are higher. Credit cards are not accepted. The maximum stay is two weeks.

Directions: From I-95, take Exit 249 east on State Road 44 for five miles. Turn north on U.S. 1 and drive 5.5 miles. The park is located on the west side, just north of the three bridges crossing Spruce Creek.

Contact: Spruce Creek Park, 6250 South Ridgewood Avenue, Port Orange, FL 32127, 386/322-5133, fax 386/304-5515; or contact the Volusia County Leisure Services, 202 North Florida Avenue, DeLand, FL 32720-4618, 386/736-5953, www.volusia.org/parks/camping.htm.

25 RIVER BREEZE PARK

Scenic rating: 7

south of New Smyrna Beach

No RVs are allowed into this nicely wooded county-run campground, which makes a peaceful and relaxing stay for tenters. The campground is located on the Intracoastal Waterway, where you'll see dolphins at play and sometimes manatees lolling in the shallows. A big draw at the park is the boat ramp, but you can also fish from the dock nearby. Bird-watching is also a favorite activity.

Campsites, facilities: Seventeen tent sites are available. Each has a picnic table and grill but no water or electricity hookups. Restrooms and showers are in the campground. Two campsites, the boat ramp, dock, and restrooms are wheelchair-accessible. Children are welcome. Leashed pets are permitted.

Reservations, fees: Reservations are recommended. April 1–August 31, rates are $10 per night for two people, plus $2 for each additional person. September 1–March 31, the rate rises to $15. During special events, rates are higher. Credit cards are not accepted. Campers can stay up to two weeks.

Directions: If traveling northbound on I-95, take Exit 231 east one mile to U.S. 1. Turn north on U.S. 1 and drive about eight miles to H.H. Burch Road. If traveling southbound, take Exit 244 and drive east to U.S. 1. Turn south on U.S. 1 and drive to Oak Hill and H.H. Burch Road.

Contact: River Breeze Park, 250 H.H. Burch Road, Oak Hill, FL, 386/345-5525, fax 386/345-5526; or contact Volusia County Leisure Services, 202 North Florida Avenue, DeLand, FL 32720, 386/736-5953, www.volusia.org/parks/camping.htm.

LAKELAND AND SEBRING

© MARILYN MOORE

BEST CAMPGROUNDS

⟨ Families
River Ranch RV Resort, **page 281**
Peace River Preserve, **page 286**

⟨ Most Luxurious
River Ranch RV Resort, **page 281**

As its name suggests, this region of Florida is characterized by a plethora of lakes – hundreds of them. This natural beauty has attracted scores of retirees and housing developments, but a rural atmosphere prevails. Driving down the highway, you're as likely to share the road with huge trucks loaded down with fresh oranges just picked from the grove as with suburbanites headed for the local shopping center.

Lakeland doesn't usually jump to mind when you consider Florida's prime tourism spots, but this way station of a city hosts the Detroit Tigers for spring-training games in March. It's also a good home base for the Florida Aquarium or pier in St. Petersburg, as well as Disney World and Historic Bok Sanctuary in Lake Wales.

Golf, fishing, and boating are the names of the game for most vacationers, who tend to be snowbirds staying for the winter either at a typical retirement-oriented RV park or a more rustic fish camp. Most are in search of bass, that elusive trophy fish.

For more hardy campers, several wildlife management areas are hot spots for backpacking, hiking, and bird-watching. The marshy fringes of some lakes harbor alligators and all sorts of birds. Airboat tours offered at some of the area's fish camps can bring you up close and personal with the wildlife.

Two places worth mentioning are the Peace River, whose tannin waters are considered among the best canoeing spots in the state; and

1930s-era Highlands Hammock State Park, a perfect showcase for what Florida would look like if no one had logged the cypress swamps.

Several great places are worth mentioning. Canoeing on the Peace River, whose tannin waters are considered among the best spots in the state, is amazing. Although other rivers farther north in Florida may be prettier, wilder or more adventurous, the Peace River is often remembered as the life-changing trip that introduces a Florida-bred urban kid to the pleasures of nature. The Peace River also is the seminal moment in some marriages, introducing the less hardy mate to backpack-style camping. The Peace River is readily accessible from city areas from Orlando down south, so it's a proving ground for many. During droughts, the water levels fluctuate with the seasons, so it's best to call local outfitters to check conditions.

My personal all-time favorite is camping at Highlands Hammock State Park. The 1930s era park is a perfect showcase for what Florida would look like if no one had logged the cypress swamps. The towering trees, lush foliage, wooden boardwalks over the swamp are awe-inspiring. Plus, the Sebring area has great bicycling, both in the park and in the surrounding hills.

If you make the Lakeland and Sebring area a base camp, it's close to tourist attractions with the addition of its own unique offerings.

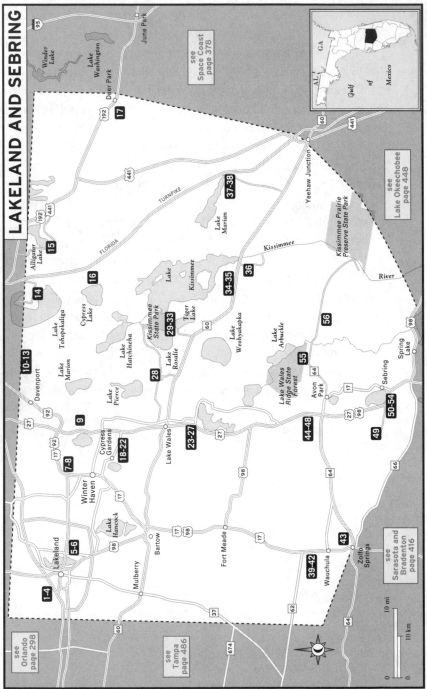

LAKELAND AND SEBRING

see Space Coast page 378

see Lake Okeechobee page 448

see Orlando page 298

see Tampa page 486

see Sarasota and Bradenton page 416

© AVALON TRAVEL PUBLISHING, INC.

❶ LAKELAND RV RESORT

Scenic rating: 7

off I-4, in Lakeland

This manicured 24-acre resort is a convenient stop off I-4. It's near little Lake Deeson, which is stocked with bass, catfish, and bluegill. A heated pool and wintertime activities such as bingo, card nights, and arts classes entertain campers. The park's paved interior roads with streetlights are also used for in-line skating, walking, and bicycling. About 30 percent of the park is occupied by year-round residents, and park models are for sale. Theme parks in Tampa and Orlando are about 30 minutes from the grassy and paved sites (most with patios). A sound wall along I-4 shields the park from highway noise. The Detroit Tigers play spring-training games down the road off State Road 33; call 863/686-8075 for information.

Campsites, facilities: There are 230 full-hookup sites (100 pull-through) for RVs as large as they come. All have 30-amp electrical service; 190 have 50-amp. Each has a picnic table, a concrete patio, and a fire ring. The roomy lots are typically 33 feet wide by 80 feet deep. "Super-size" sites are 100 feet deep. If you travel with a satellite dish, ask for a less shady site. A wireless Internet network is available at each lot, as well as in the office. For recreation, there's a pool, a spa, a kiddie pool, a clubhouse, free paddleboats, rental boats, a stocked lake, a playground, horseshoes, miniature golf, table tennis, basketball, seasonal activities, shuffleboard, and a children's playroom. Also on the premises are showers, restrooms, LP gas sales, a dump station, rental cabins, a camp store, an on-site video/book library, a 3,000-square-foot screened pavilion, two kitchens, laundry facilities, and a dog-washing station (you do the washing). Management says most areas are wheelchair-accessible. Streets are paved. Groceries, a restaurant, and bait are available within a five-minute drive. Children are welcome. Leashed pets are permitted.

Reservations, fees: Reservations are accepted, except January–March, when sites are first-come, first-served. Sites are $32 per night for two people, plus $2.50 for each additional person and $2 for 50-amp electrical service. Credit cards are accepted. Long-term stays are OK.

Directions: From I-4, take Exit 33 and drive about one mile northeast on State Road 33/County Road 582 (Socrum Loop) to Old Combee Road. Turn right and proceed 0.25 mile to the campground, on the right.

Contact: Lakeland RV Resort, 900 Old Combee Road, Lakeland, FL 33805, 863/687-6146 or 888/622-4115, http://carefreeresorts.com/.

❷ TIKI VILLAGE CAMPGROUND

Scenic rating: 5

off I-4, in Lakeland

An RV dealer and one of Florida's largest malls (Lakeland Mall) are within walking distance when you stay at Tiki Village, a fast stop off I-4. Still, you may see tigers—as in the Detroit Tigers, who play spring-training games nearby at Joker Marchant Stadium (2301 Lakeland Hills Blvd., 863/686-8075). Despite the winter social programs and the swimming pool, you're really getting convenience here: Tampa and Orlando theme parks are only about 30 minutes away by car. The two fishponds are a plus, especially for families with kids in tow (though they are limited to short-term stays). The park is favored by adults, repeat visitors, and working people.

Campsites, facilities: All 203 full-hookup, 30/50-amp sites are for RVs up to 45 feet long and slideouts. Twenty are pull-through. Some lots have concrete patios. A pool, a recreation room, a play area, horseshoes, shuffleboard, and winter activities entertain campers. On the premises are showers, restrooms, snacks, LP gas sales, and laundry facilities. A camp store sells snacks, camping supplies, and souvenirs. A wireless Internet network is available throughout the park. Streets are crushed blacktop asphalt. The bathhouse, clubhouse, office, and pool area are wheelchair-accessible. Groceries, restaurants, malls, and hospitals are within two miles. Children are welcome to visit for short-term stays. Two small pets are permitted per site.

Reservations, fees: Reservations are recommended. Sites are $35 per night for two people, plus $5 for each additional person. Credit cards are accepted. Yearly rates are available.

Directions: From I-4, take Exit 32 and drive one block north on U.S. 98 to Crevasse Street. Turn right and proceed about 0.25 mile to the entrance, on the left.

Contact: Tiki Village Campground, 905 Crevasse Street, Lakeland, FL 33809, 863/858-5364 or 863/858-8217, fax 863/853-9446, www.tikivillagecampground.com.

❸ LELYNN RV RESORT
🏊 🎣 🚗 🐕 ♿ 🚐

Scenic rating: 3

in Polk City

Although children are allowed, this RV park is decidedly retiree- and snowbird-oriented, with planned activities during the winter months, such as bingo, potluck dinners, crafts, dancing, games, and exercise. The park boasts of a quiet setting, where campers can watch the sun set over Lake Agnes. Fishing and boating are options, too. About 40 percent of the park is occupied by year-round residents, including working people.

Campsites, facilities: Of the 368 sites, most are available for seasonal visitors; nine are pull-through. All have full hookups, 50-amp service, concrete patios, and picnic tables. A wireless Internet connection is available in the office. Restrooms, showers, a dump station, laundry facilities, and, for long-termers,

telephone service are available. On the premises are a pool, a boat ramp, a dock, propane gas sales, shuffleboard courts, a dog-walk area, and a recreation room. All areas are wheelchair-accessible. Children and small pets are permitted.

Reservations, fees: Reservations are recommended. Sites are $30 per night for two people, plus $4 per extra person. Credit cards are not accepted. Long-term or seasonal stays are allowed.

Directions: From I-4, take Exit 44 and drive north on State Road 559 for one block to the park.

Contact: LeLynn RV Resort, 1513 State Road 559, Polk City, FL 33868, 863/984-1495, fax 863/984-0257.

❹ LAKE JULIANA BOATING AND LODGING
🏊 🎣 🚗 🐕 🏃 ♿ 🚐

Scenic rating: 4

at Lake Juliana, north of Auburndale

In a region normally focused on retirees, families can take solace in knowing that this five-acre fish camp has a swimming beach, pool, volleyball net, and toddler-oriented play center. Bass fishing nonetheless remains the key attraction for campers at these grassy/concrete-pad sites. A canal links nearly two-mile-long Lake Juliana with smaller Lake Mattie, giving anglers and water-skiers 2,100 watery acres to explore. This area is still relatively undeveloped, so you'll find a countryside setting. This being Florida, that could change at any time, but the park prides itself on its natural setting.

Campers are somewhat outnumbered by mobile-home residents at this small complex, where the family atmosphere comes with rules that Mom and Dad would approve of: Eat in the picnic area, not at the pool; and no foul language, please. Disney World, Sea World, and Busch Gardens are within 45 miles. Park models are for sale.

Campsites, facilities: All 10 full-hookup, grassy, sunny sites are for RVs up to 40 feet long. They have 50-amp electrical service and cable TV. On the premises are a pool, an adult swing, a wheelchair-accessible recreation room, a volleyball net, a playground, restrooms (no showers), a dump station, rental cottages, cabins, a boat ramp, covered boat slips, boat rentals, a tanning bed, a toddler play area, limited groceries, a picnic area, bait, tackle, cable TV, and laundry facilities. Restaurants are three miles away. Children must be adult-supervised at the pool and pier. Leashed, attended pets are permitted.

Reservations, fees: Reservations are recommended. Sites are $27 per night for two people, and $5 per extra person. Credit cards are accepted. Long-term rates are available.

Directions: From I-4, take Exit 44 and drive south less than one mile on State Route 559. Turn right onto Lundy Road and proceed to the complex at Lake Juliana.

Contact: Lake Juliana Boating and Lodging, 600 Lundy Road, Auburndale, FL 33823, 863/984-1144, http://lakejuliana.tripod.com.

5 VALENCIA ESTATES

Scenic rating: 2

on U.S. 98, south of Lakeland

Palm trees dot this age-55-and-older park, where residents of the 86 mobile homes outnumber RVers at the 30 grassy/concrete-pad campsites. The full schedule of winter activities includes Bible study, crafts, card nights, bingo, bowling, golf, and pool leagues, as well as weekly coffees, monthly potlucks, and twice-monthly pancake-and-sausage breakfasts. Most visitors hail from Michigan, Indiana, New York, and Canada. Favorite things to do? Walk and talk.

For a pretty walk, park four miles away at Florida Southern College, whose buildings at Ingraham Avenue and Lake Hollingsworth Drive were designed by Frank Lloyd Wright. Then circle Lake Hollingsworth, which fronts the college. You'll pass the Lakeland Yacht and Country Club along the way.

Campsites, facilities: At this age-55-plus park, all 30 full-hookup sites will accommodate RVs up to 39 feet long. Electrical service is 30-amp. A dump station and laundry facilities are provided. Showers and restrooms are available in the clubhouse. A pool, three lighted shuffleboard courts, winter programs, and a clubhouse entertain campers. Cable TV and telephone hookups are available. The bathhouse, clubhouse, and pool area are wheelchair-accessible. Streets are paved. A restaurant and groceries are within two miles. Children are prohibited. Leashed pets up to 45 pounds are allowed.

Reservations, fees: Reservations are recommended, and they are a must for the winter season, because most tenants return year after year. Sites are $23 per night for two people, plus $10 per extra person. Credit cards are not accepted. Long-term rates are available.

Directions: From East Main Street in Lakeland, drive 3.5 miles south on U.S. 98. The park entrance is on the right. From I-4, take Exit 27 to State Road 570 (Polk Parkway) west. Exit on U.S. 98 at Bartow and drive 0.5 mile north to the first left turn.

Contact: Valencia Estates, 3325 Bartow Road/U.S. 98, Lakeland, FL 33803, 863/665-1611 or 800/645-9033, fax 863/667-3698, mfeldm3402@aol.com.

6 SANLAN RANCH CAMPGROUND

Scenic rating: 10

on U.S. 98, south of Lakeland

More than 90 types of birds have been spotted at this notable private recreation area, which covers more than one square mile. Still, golfers tend to prefer walking from their grassy campsites to the adjacent Bramble Ridge Golf Course, where the driving range was voted "Best in the County" by locals. A private camper entrance leads to the par-72, 18-hole course, where Sanlan guests receive a discount. The adjacent wooded 600 acres were once a phosphate mine, resulting in an abundance of trails and wildlife.

Look for alligators and ducks while paddling along the park's canoe trails or walking along three wooded hiking trails (a total of seven miles). A cacophony of bird chatter in winter enlivens a pensive stop along the two-mile-long Rookery Trail, near Banana Lake. A boat ramp provides access to Banana Lake, one of three park lakes. The park isn't only about wilderness activities, though; bingo games and potluck dinners are held in winter at the 200-person-capacity recreation hall, and aquacize sessions are sometimes offered at one of the three solar-heated pools. Joggers follow a three-mile shady trail around the golf course.

Lakefront campsites have no utilities, just tables. At sites along the camping circle, there are no sewer hookups. If you prefer big sites, note that the "ranch-view" sites are smaller than regular full-hookup sites. Park models are for sale.

Campsites, facilities: More than 500 sites and a primitive group camping area are for RVs up to 50 feet long or for tents. Three pools, a wading pool, 18 lighted shuffleboard courts, a lighted golf driving range, a playground, horseshoes, two recreation halls, three nature trails, and winter activities entertain campers. Facilities include restrooms, showers, a dump station, a modem hookup to check email, and laundry facilities. Children are permitted. Two pets are allowed per site.

Reservations, fees: Reservations are recommended. Sites are $21.50–40 per night for two people, plus $2.50 for each additional person. No more than five people are permitted per site. Families with children are limited to 14-day stays. The pet fee is $0.50 daily. Credit cards are accepted. Long-term rates are available.

Directions: From East Main Street in Lakeland, drive 3.5 miles south on U.S. 98 to the park, which is on the right side of the road. Or, from the Polk County Parkway (State Road 520), take Exit 10 southbound on U.S. 98. Drive 0.25 mile to the park on the west side of U.S. 98.

Contact: Sanlan Ranch Campground, 3929 U.S. 98 South, Lakeland, FL 33813, 863/665-1726 or 800/524-5044, www.sanlan.com.

7 OAK HARBOR

Scenic rating: 7

on Lake Lowery, west of Haines City

You'll pass citrus groves—and perhaps the aroma of sweet blossoms—on the approach to this off-the-beaten-path lakefront park, where clumps of tall, lanky palms and brushy oaks lend a woodsy feel. Bass anglers, water-skiers, and swimmers share the calm blue waters of nearly two-mile-long Lake Lowery here. Many campers spend entire winters at these grassy campsites with concrete patios, while other folks live in the 65-acre park's 70 mobile homes and park models. Although the private park enjoys admirable shade from its overstory of trees, there is comparatively little eye-level brush separating camping spots. This is a gathering spot for seaplane and floatplane rallies.

Campsites, facilities: There are 110 RV sites with full hookups and 30/50-amp electrical service. A recreation room, winter social programs, showers, restrooms, picnic tables, a dump station, a boat ramp, and laundry facilities are available. A restaurant and a bait shop are three miles away. Groceries are within five miles. Children and leashed pets under 40 pounds are permitted.

Reservations, fees: Reservations are recommended. Sites are $22 per night for two people, plus $2 for each additional person. Prices include your own boat dock. Credit cards are not accepted. Long-term stays are OK.

Directions: From U.S. 27 in Haines City, drive 4.5 miles west on U.S. 17/92. Turn right at Experiment Station Road. Cross the railroad tracks, then turn right at Old Haines City/Lake Alfred Road. Continue 1.5 miles. Turn left on Lake Lowery Road. The park is ahead at right.

Contact: Oak Harbor, 100 Oak Harbor, Haines City, FL 33844, 863/956-1341 or 877/956-1341, fax 863/956-1341, www.oakharbor-rv.com.

8 CENTRAL PARK OF HAINES CITY

Scenic rating: 7

off U.S. 27, in Haines City

With morning newspaper delivery and daily garbage pickup service, snowbirds don't escape civilization—in this rapidly developing region of the state, they embrace it. Many retirees from the Northeast and Canada spend entire winters here, some taking advantage of cards, darts, bingo, exercises, and Sunday church services in the park's recreation hall. Often, the same visitors come every year. Oaks shade some campsites, which are set block-style in single and double rows. Some sites are at waterfront. This is an over-age-55 park where most people stay for the winter season. Park models are for sale.

Campsites, facilities: The 351 full-hookup sites at this over-55 park are for RVs up to 50 feet long and slideouts. One hundred sites have 50-amp electrical service; the rest have 30-amp. All have a picnic table and a concrete patio. Lots average 30 feet wide by 60 feet deep, and 11 are pull-through. Around 140 sites are usually available for overnight visitors. Ten grassy tent sites have water and electricity. A wireless Internet connection is available. For recreation, there's a pool, a recreation hall, horseshoes, shuffleboard, boccie ball (lawn bowling) courts, and winter activities. Show-

ers, restrooms, laundry facilities, rental cabins, propane, and camping supplies are available. All areas are wheelchair-accessible. A shopping center is 0.25 mile away. An 18-hole golf course is one mile away. Children are permitted. Leashed pets must use two pet walks at park boundaries.

Reservations, fees: Reservations are not necessary. Sites are $30 per night for two people, plus $2 for each additional person and $3 for cable TV. Rates are subject to change. Credit cards are not accepted. Long-term stays are OK.

Directions: From I-4 at Exit 55, go south about 12 miles on U.S. 27. Turn right at Commerce Avenue, which is the second stoplight in Haines City (if you hit U.S. 17/92, you've gone too far). The park is ahead on the left.

Contact: Central Park of Haines City, 1501 Commerce Avenue, Haines City, FL 33844, 863/422-5322, www.centralparkofhainescity.com.

9 GREENFIELD VILLAGE RV PARK

Scenic rating: 3

off U.S. 27, in Dundee

In this region of rolling, citrus-dotted hills, the bigger towns of Lake Wales and Winter Haven (with their antiques shops) are better known than Dundee, a sleepy, wide spot in the road where these 104 concrete-pad RV sites are set. Swimming in the heated pool is a highlight at the grassy, flat park, which is kept neat as a pin. Oaks and palms provide some shade for campers, who often stay at least three months. Park models are for sale. An 18-hole golf course is 0.2 mile away, and locals fish at area lakes. The boat ramp to the biggest nearby body of water, Lake Hamilton, is up U.S. 27 about 3.5 miles northwest of the park. Historic Bok Sanctuary, an estate and gardens where 45-minute carillon recitals are held daily at 3 P.M., is in Lake Wales (863/676-1408).

Campsites, facilities: This age-55-and-up park has 92 sites with full hookups, 30/50-amp electrical service, picnic tables for long-staying RVs or park models, and 12 sites with full hookups for overnighters. Rigs up to 45 feet in length can be accommodated. A pool, shuffleboard, a recreation hall, winter social programs, showers, restrooms, and free local calls are available. Management says the pool, laundry facilities, bathhouse, and recreation hall are wheelchair-accessible. Groceries, a restaurant, and laundry facilities are within 0.25 mile. Children are not allowed. Aggressive dog breeds like Rottweilers, pit bulls, and Doberman pinschers are prohibited; otherwise, pets are permitted.

Reservations, fees: Reservations are recommended. Sites are $45 per night, plus $4 per extra person and $2.50 for electricity. Credit cards are not accepted. Long-term rates are available.

Directions: From U.S. 27 at Dundee, drive west 0.1 mile on State Road 542. Turn left almost immediately into the park.

Contact: Greenfield Village RV Park, 1015 State Road 542 West, Dundee, FL 33838, 863/439-7409.

10 MERRY D RV SANCTUARY

Scenic rating: 6

southeast of Disney World

This 54-acre rural park bills itself as a "back-to-nature" campground where most people stay long-term. Paved interior roads lead to large sites—at least 50 by 80 feet for pull-through spots. In the busy winter season, campers can enjoy arts-and-crafts classes, card games, ice-cream socials, Bible study nights, and periodic group trips to casinos and other places. Fishing is possible in a small lake, but you'll have to travel about eight miles to get bait and tackle. The park is within a few miles of the main gate to Walt Disney World.

Campsites, facilities: Nine tents can be ac-

commodated in an area with no utilities. Only two people may camp in each tent. In the RV section, there are 121 full-hookup sites with 50-amp electricity and cable TV. Forty-two sites are pull-through, and normally just 10 are available for overnight visitors. Each site has a picnic table. On the premises are restrooms, showers, a dump station, rental trailers, a recreation room, a playground, a nature trail, horseshoes, laundry facilities, and a long, narrow field that some campers have used as a golf driving range. Management says the restrooms and showers are wheelchair-accessible. Groceries and restaurants are within two miles. Children and pets are permitted.

Reservations, fees: Reservations are required. Sites are $28 per night for two people, plus $2 for each additional person. Credit cards are accepted. Long-term stays are OK.

Directions: From U.S. 192 in Kissimmee, go south on U.S. 17/92 about three miles. Turn left at County Road 531/Pleasant Hill Road. Continue seven miles to the campground on the left.

Contact: Merry D RV Sanctuary, 4261 Pleasant Hill Road, Kissimmee, FL 34746-2933, 407/870-0719 or 800/208-3434, fax 407/870-0198, www.merryd.com.

11 ALOHA RV PARK

Scenic rating: 1

southwest of Kissimmee

In winter, you can pick oranges at this adults-preferred park, located within 15 miles of Disney World. Anglers may want to head about five miles east to fish for bass, specks, or catfish in 11-mile-long Lake Tohopekaliga. A good number of these paved campsites are taken by full-time or seasonal residents. Park rules tend to be geared toward full-time residents. Also, campers are asked to use the restrooms in their rigs. Winter residents take part in bingo games, shuffleboard, pancake breakfasts, and spaghetti dinners. About 55 percent of the sites are occupied year-round.

Campsites, facilities: Self-contained rigs are accepted. There are 90 full-hookup, grassy RV sites (27 pull-through); 60 sites have 30-amp electrical service, and the rest have 50-amp. RVs up to 40 feet long and slideouts can be accommodated. About 20 sites are usually open for overnighters. Each lot has a picnic table and a concrete patio. A dialup Internet connection is available in the clubhouse. On the premises are restrooms, showers, laundry facilities, a pool, and a game room. Groceries and restaurants are about five miles away. The clubhouse and pool area are wheelchair-accessible. Streets are paved. Children may camp on a short-term basis. Pets under 25 pounds are welcome.

Reservations, fees: Reservations are recommended. Sites are $29 per night for two people, plus $2 per extra person. Credit cards are not accepted. Long-term rates are available.

Directions: From Kissimmee, take U.S. 17/92 south about seven miles.

Contact: Aloha RV Park, 4648 South Orange Blossom Trail, Kissimmee, FL 34746, 407/933-5730.

12 RICHARDSON'S FISH CAMP

🛶 🚗 🐕 ♿ 🚐 ⛺

Scenic rating: 5

on Lake Tohopekaliga, south of Kissimmee

The main reason to stay at this six-acre camp is to venture out onto 23,000-acre Lake Tohopekaliga to fish for trophy bass, specks, and panfish. A fishing guide is available, as are boat docks, a boat ramp, and bait and tackle. This off-the-beaten-path spot on the lake's northeast shore emphasizes a laid-back lifestyle in a quiet setting shaded by large oak trees. Many patrons stay in air-conditioned rental cabins. A plus: One boat slip is included in the price of the campsites, which are sandy or grassy with concrete pads. The park also offers airboat rides. Most visitors are families, locals, and anglers.

Campsites, facilities: There are 16 full-hookup sites (12 pull-through) with 30-amp electrical service. Big rigs and slideouts can be accommodated. The grassy sites are a mix of sunny and shady, and some have concrete patios. Six tent sites with water and electricity are placed under a tree canopy on a grassy/dirt surface. On the premises are restrooms, showers, a dump station, a boat ramp, charter fishing services, a dock, covered slips, and laundry facilities. A camp store sells ice, snacks, and bait and tackle. Management says the dock behind the bait shop and office are wheelchair-accessible. Children and pets are permitted.

Reservations, fees: Reservations are recommended. Sites are $28 per night for two people, plus $5 for each additional person and $1 for pets. Rates are subject to change. Credit cards are not accepted. The maximum length of stay is six months.

Directions: From Kissimmee, take State Road 525/Neptune Road east for one mile. Turn right (south) onto King's Highway and travel 1.5 miles. Turn right onto Pine Island Road and drive 0.5 mile, then right again onto Scotty's Road. You'll be heading north at this point. Follow signs and take the road to the end about 0.25 mile.

Contact: Richardson's Fish Camp, 1550 Scotty's Road, Kissimmee, FL 34744, 407/846-6540.

13 SOUTHPORT RV PARK, CAMPGROUND, AND MARINA

🛶 🚗 🐕 ♿ 🚐 ⛺

Scenic rating: 7

south of Kissimmee, on West Lake Tohopekaliga

Although this 25-acre park is plenty close to Disney World, most folks here are more

fishing in the Lakeland area

© MARILYN MOORE

interested in the boating, fishing, and wooded atmosphere on West Lake Tohopekaliga, known for world-class bass fishing. You get a free boat slip with each campsite. The clientele is a mix of families, anglers, and retirees.

Campsites, facilities: There are 53 full-hookup RV sites with electricity, picnic tables, and grills. Ten tent sites with water and electricity are set apart from the RV area. Sites 28–37 overlook the lake, and two sites are wheelchair-accessible. The campers' fishing area is separated from the boat slips, so you're not apt to snag your line or tangle with a neighbor's boat lines. Restrooms, showers, a dump site, and laundry facilities are available. On the premises are a boat ramp, a dock, a fish-cleaning station, a clubhouse with planned activities in season, bait and tackle, a store, a snack bar, a horseshoe pit, a volleyball net, and a pavilion. Airboat tours leave every 30 minutes, and fishing guide service is available. Children are welcome. Leashed pets are permitted.

Reservations, fees: Reservations are recommended. Sites are $19–24 per night for two people, plus $2 per extra person. Credit cards are not accepted. Long-term rates are available.

Directions: From I-4, take Exit 64A east onto U.S. 192 about six miles. Turn south on Poinciana Boulevard between mile markers 10 and 11. Follow Poinciana Boulevard 18.5 miles until it crosses Pleasant Hill Road and dead-ends at Southport Park.

Contact: Southport RV Park, Campground and Marina, 2001 East Southport Road, Kissimmee, FL 34746, 407/933-5822, www .southportpark.com.

14 LAKE TOHO RV AND MOBILE HOME PARK

Scenic rating: 2

on Lake Tohopekaliga, south of Kissimmee

This place was once known as Red's Fish Camp, which is why they sometimes answer the phone, "Red's!" Lacking amenities such as a pool or other diversions for children, Lake Toho Resort is favored mostly by a crowd interested in fishing or taking airboat rides on the lake. About half the residents live here year-round. Sites are grassy, and shade is fairly sparse unless you manage to get a site in the back row. You can fish from the bank of 11-mile-long Lake Tohopekaliga, but you'll probably have better luck if you bring your own boat (no rentals are available) and use the park boat ramp.

Campsites, facilities: This park has 250 full-hookup RV sites. Each site has a picnic table. Facilities include restrooms, showers, a dump station, laundry facilities, a boat ramp, and a restaurant that serves breakfast, lunch, and dinner. Management says all public areas are wheelchair-accessible. Groceries are seven miles away. Children are welcome. Pets must be leashed.

Reservations, fees: Reservations are recommended in winter. Sites are $20 for two people, plus $2 per extra person. Credit cards are not accepted. Long-term stays are OK.

Directions: From I-4 at Exit 64A, head east on U.S. 192/Irlo Bronson Highway. Turn right at Kissimmee Park Road, at the first stoplight on the east side of town. The road dead-ends into the campground at Lake Tohopekaliga.

Contact: Lake Toho RV and Mobile Home Park, 4715 Kissimmee Park Road, St. Cloud, FL 34772, 407/892-8795.

15 CANOE CREEK CAMPGROUND

Scenic rating: 5

south of St. Cloud

Although it's called Canoe Creek Campground, there is no creek and no place to canoe in this rapidly developing area. You can stay here as long as you like, though. Some sites are grassy; others have concrete patios. For the most part, the place (and its four-foot-deep screened and heated pool) attracts senior citizens. As for the puzzling name, Canoe Creek simply is the name of a creek that connects two nearby lakes—Cypress and Gentry. Disney-area attractions are about 25 miles away.

About 20 percent of the park is occupied year-round. Wintertime activities include golf outings, karaoke, country music, pokeno, and church services.

Campsites, facilities: These 240 full-hookup sites with picnic tables are for RVs only. About 25 are available for overnight camping. Most have 30-amp electrical service; 85 have 50-amp. Thirty-seven sites are pull-through. Big rigs and slideouts can be accommodated. A therapy exercise pool, horseshoes, shuffleboard, and winter social programs entertain campers. On the premises are restrooms, showers, a dump station, trailer rentals, and laundry facilities. The recreation hall, pool area, and laundry facilities are accessible to wheelchairs. Streets are paved. Groceries are within two miles. Children and pets are permitted.

Reservations, fees: Reservations are recommended. Sites are $30 per night for two people, plus $3 for each extra person. Credit cards are not accepted. Long-term rates are available.

Directions: From St. Cloud, drive about six miles south on State Road 523 to the campground.

Contact: Canoe Creek Campground, 4101 Canoe Creek Road, St. Cloud, FL 34772, 407/892-7010 or 800/453-5268.

16 CYPRESS LAKE FISH CAMP AND RV

Scenic rating: 7

on Lake Cypress, south of St. Cloud

Lake Cypress makes this remote RV park a picturesque place to stay. You're sure to see some interesting wildlife, including sandhill cranes, otters, and bald eagles. The main things to do here are ride airboats or fish for bass; some people also go after specks or bream. You don't have to be an angler to appreciate the place—just gazing out at the pretty blue waters of Lake Cypress is a treat.

The park came under new ownership since mid-2005—the proprietors will give you an airboat tour of the lake, where you're likely to see bald eagles, alligators, and other wildlife. A boat launched here can make its way all the way to Lake Okeechobee and back, but not in one day. The sites are grassy and right near the lake's edge; most are sunny, but some are shaded by giant cypress trees. Disney World is about 30 miles north. About 10 percent of the park is occupied year-round.

Campsites, facilities: All 52 RV spaces have full hookups with a choice of 30-amp or 50-amp electrical service, concrete patios, picnic tables, and fire rings. On the premises are restrooms, showers, laundry facilities, a playground, a recreation room, rental cabins, a boat ramp, bait and tackle, snacks, gasoline sales, seven cabins, and basketball. Aviation fuel is also available for seaplanes. Management says the sites and restrooms are wheelchair-accessible. You'll find groceries and restaurants within 10 miles. Kids and small pets are permitted.

Reservations, fees: Reservations are recommended, particularly in winter. Sites are $30. Credit cards are accepted.

Directions: From St. Cloud, take Highway 523/Canoe Creek Road south about 10 miles. Just after you pass under Florida's Turnpike, turn right onto Lake Cypress Road. Follow it to the end, where you'll find the campground.

Contact: Cypress Lake Fish Camp and RV, 3301 Lake Cypress Road, Kenansville, FL 34739, 407/957-3135, fax 407/892-3978.

17 BULL CREEK WILDLIFE MANAGEMENT AREA

🚶 🚴 🛶 🐕 ⛺

Scenic rating: 6

east of Holopaw, on Bull Creek and Billy Lake

Marsh rabbits hop about and sandhill cranes nest in spring in the wet prairies of this 23,504-acre wilderness. Look for deer at dawn or dusk while exploring the oak hammocks, or while following the 8.6-mile loop trail that encircles the heart of these varied woods of sun-dappled pine flatwoods, cypress hardwoods, and wetlands of seasonal lilies and pitcher plants. More than 17 miles of the Florida National Scenic Trail run the length of the area and connect to the Three Lakes Wildlife Management Area to the southwest (see listing in the *Orlando* chapter). The three camping areas could hardly be farther apart from each other. One, near the northern boundary, is at Crabgrass Creek; reach it by walking about one mile from the parking area located immediately south of U.S. 192, about two miles west of Highway 419. Another campsite is along a spur of the loop trail, near the hunt-check station and informational kiosk at the western entrance of the conservation area. Pick up a brochure at this entrance for a self-guided tour whose stops include a historic railroad tram. The third campsite is at the southwestern boundary near the canoeing waters of Billy Lake.

Campsites, facilities: Three primitive camping areas are reached by foot. Two are one mile or less from parking areas. Camping is allowed at the designated campground only during hunting season and throughout the year at designated campsites on the Florida National Scenic Trail (as long as you hike to the site via the trail). A well with a pitcher pump providing nonpotable water is available at each camping area, but there are no other facilities. Bring food, drinking water, supplies, and mosquito repellent. Pack out trash. Children are permitted. Pets must be leashed.

Reservations, fees: Sites are first-come, first-served. Camping is free. Each site accommodates up to six people. If your party has at least seven people, get a free permit and reserve at least one week ahead at 386/329-4410. Maximum stay for all campers is seven days. For ground conditions and hunting dates, contact the Florida Fish and Wildlife Conservation Commission at 352/732-1225.

Directions: From I-95 at Exit 180 (Melbourne), go west on U.S. Highway 192. Drive 21.6 miles west to Crabgrass Road. Turn left. Proceed six miles south to the entrance.

Contact: St. Johns River Water Management District, Division of Land Management, P.O. Box 1429, Palatka, FL 32178-1429, 386/329-4500 or 800/451-7106, www.sjrwmd.com.

18 GOOD LIFE RV RESORT

Scenic rating: 5

at Lake Garfield, east of Bartow

Located along a divided highway east of the phosphate-mining town of Bartow, this sunny, retiree-oriented park is set on mile-wide Lake Garfield. Locals often use a boat ramp off Highway 60 to fish for bass and bream; however, visitors to this park are more interested in the planned activities, day trips, and theme-park visits. There's a nine-hole chipping course between the RV section and the lake, but no beach; swimmers use a heated pool instead. The lakeview sites are taken by full-timers.

Mobile homes and long-term residents nearly dominate the 397 sites (about 125 are for RVs). Ruler-straight streets are laid out in a grid pattern and are named after states that are close to retirees' hearts: Ohio, North Carolina, New York, and so on. To avoid sleeping nearest to State Road 60, skip sites 101–199 and 140–150.

Campsites, facilities: This retiree-oriented park offers 125 RV sites with full hookups, 50-amp electrical service, and concrete patios measuring 20 by 35 feet. The lot size is 35 by 67 feet. A pool, a recreation hall, a golf course, shuffleboard, horseshoes, and winter activities entertain campers. Showers, restrooms, a dump station, and laundry facilities are available. The bathhouse, clubhouse, office, and pool area are wheelchair-accessible. Streets are paved. Groceries and restaurants are within seven miles. Adults are preferred. Children

under 17 must be adult-supervised at the pool, and their length of stay may be restricted. Pets are prohibited.

Reservations, fees: Reservations are recommended. Sites are $25 per night for two people, plus $1.50 per extra person. Credit cards are not accepted. Long-term rates are available.

Directions: From U.S. 98 in Bartow, drive east six miles on State Road 60, passing U.S. 17 and the Peace River. The park is ahead on the right.

Contact: Good Life RV Resort, 6815 State Road 60 East, Bartow, FL 33830, 863/537-1971, fax 863/537-2687.

19 CYPRESS GARDENS MOBILE HOME AND RV PARK

Scenic rating: 5

east of Winter Haven

"Lots of trees and wonderful people" is how the owners describe their adults-preferred park in this lake-dotted region west of Walt Disney World. Most visitors are snowbirds here for the winter months. Shopping and restaurants are close by. About two-thirds of the lots are taken year-round, and there are 143 mobile homes in a separate section. Repeat visitors are the rule, but openings do arise.

Campsites, facilities: There are 126 oversized RV sites with full hookups and picnic tables. About 80 percent have 30-amp electrical service, the rest have 50-amp. Big RVs can be accommodated, and many of the seasonal visitors build carports, awnings, or screen rooms onto their units. Restrooms, showers, laundry facilities, and telephone service are available. On the premises are a pool, a recreation hall with planned activities during the winter, shuffleboard courts, and a dog-walk area. A dial-up connection to the Internet is available in the recreation hall. Most areas are wheelchair-accessible. Children are welcome to visit for short stays. Leashed pets are permitted (no attack breeds).

Reservations, fees: Reservations are recommended. Sites are $30 per night for two people, plus $2 per extra person. Credit cards are not accepted. Long-term rates are available.

Directions: From the intersection of U.S. 17 and State Road 542 in Winter Haven, go east on State Road 542 about 5.5 miles. When you reach the burg of Eastwood, turn right on Lake Daisy Road and go about one mile to the park.

Contact: Cypress Gardens Mobile Home and RV Park, 1951 Lake Daisy Road, Winter Haven, FL 33884, 863/324-3136, fax 863/318-9806.

20 HOLIDAY TRAVEL PARK

Scenic rating: 7

south of Winter Haven

Scrub oaks shade some sites at this 22-acre park, where half the campers stay short-term, and the rest spend the entire winter. All campsites have 8-by-10-foot patios and are set diagonally along paved, ruler-straight, 5-mph roads. At the heart of the park are recreation halls for potluck dinners and arts and crafts, and there's a 25-by-50-foot pool near the entrance. Each Friday night, the park hosts a country music concert and line dancing. The Cypress Gardens theme park is close by.

Campsites, facilities: Ninety RV sites for overnighters and 120 for seasonal visitors are available. Many are pull-through, and all have full hookups, 50-amp electricity, concrete pads, patios, and picnic tables. Twelve tent sites with water and electricity are set apart from RVs. A heated pool, a game room, miniature golf, a playground, horseshoes, tennis, boccie ball (lawn bowling), shuffleboard, a recreation hall, and winter social programs entertain campers. Showers, restrooms, a dump station,

firewood, a limited store, cable TV access, a kitchen, and laundry facilities are available. A restaurant is across the street, and groceries are one mile away. Children are welcome. Leashed pets under 20 pounds are OK.

Reservations, fees: Reservations are recommended. Sites are $24–36 per night, plus $4 for each additional person and $4 for pets. Credit cards are accepted. The maximum stay is six months.

Directions: From U.S. 27, drive one mile west on State Road 540 to the park entrance.

Contact: Holiday Travel Park, 7400 Cypress Gardens Boulevard, Winter Haven, FL 33884, 863/324-7400 or 800/858-7275 (for reservations), www.holidaytravelpark.com.

21 A-OK CAMPGROUND

Scenic rating: 2

near Eagle Lake south of Winter Haven

A citrus grove abuts this three-acre adults-only park, where permanent residents live in 11 mobile homes and at some of the grassy RV sites equipped with concrete patios. Across the street to the north, Eagle Lake stretches about 1.5 miles. Not far south from the sun-dappled park is 0.5-mile-wide Millsite Lake. You can fish for bass in this lake-dotted region. Favorite things to do include going to nearby theme parks, boating, and fishing. Most visitors come from Ohio and Michigan.

Campsites, facilities: Three sites are available for overnight visitors. All 21 full-hookup sites can accommodate RVs up to 40 feet long. Sites have either 30-amp or 50-amp electrical service. Lots are 35 feet wide by 45 feet deep. Showers, restrooms, and a dump station are available. All areas are wheelchair-accessible, according to management. One mile away are groceries, a restaurant, and laundry facilities. Children are not permitted, but they can visit campers here. Leashed pets are allowed.

Reservations, fees: Reservations are

recommended in winter. Sites are $21 per night for two people, plus $2 for each additional person. Credit cards are not accepted. Long-term stays are OK for adults.

Directions: From Winter Haven, go south on U.S. 17, passing Highway 559. At Bartow Municipal Airport, turn right onto Spirit Lake Road. Continue less than two miles to Thornhill Road. Turn right. The campground is on the right at the junction with Crystal Beach Road.

Contact: A-OK Campground, 6925 Thornhill Road, Winter Haven, FL 33880, 863/294-9091.

22 LAKESHORE PALMS TRAVEL PARK

🚲 🏊 ⛺ 🐕 🚐 ⛰️

Scenic rating: 2

south of Winter Haven

Lakeshore Palms claims to be the closest RV park to the Cypress Gardens adventure theme park, famed for its water-ski shows and beautiful gardens. Indeed, from Lakeshore Palms, you can see the distant, towering spindle of the "Island in the Sky" sightseeing ride about 1.4 miles south. This all-ages park offers 40 grassy campsites fitted onto about two acres. A fence and hedges enclose the property, which overlooks 100-acre Lake Grass. Bass anglers and water-skiers find fun in the region's lakes. Bicyclists pedal past orange groves and lakes east of the park on County Road 540A. Disney World is 33 miles north.

Campsites, facilities: There are 40 sites (32 full-hookup) and eight with water and electricity. All have 30-amp electrical service. Fifteen sites are occupied year-round. In 2005, new owners began renovations to the property, which offers two boat docks, a screened pavilion, showers, restrooms, picnic tables, a dump station, a boat ramp, boat rentals, telephone hookups, and laundry facilities. Cable TV is reserved for monthly campers. A wireless In-

ternet network is available in the recreation hall and in some areas of the park. Groceries and a restaurant are two miles away. Children are welcome. Quiet, leashed pets under 25 pounds are allowed.

Reservations, fees: Reservations are recommended. Sites are $22–26 per night for two people, plus $2 for each additional person. Credit cards are not accepted. Long-term stays are OK for adults.

Directions: Follow highway signs to Cypress Gardens; the campground is about two miles north of the park entrance. Or, from Winter Haven, take U.S. 17 south over the bridge past the Cleveland Indians spring-training ballpark and go to the next stoplight. Turn left onto County Road 655. Travel about two miles to the next stoplight. Turn left by the convenience store onto Eagle Lake Loop Road, which becomes Eloise Loop Road/County Road 540A. The campground is about two miles ahead on your right.

Contact: Lakeshore Palms Travel Park, 4800 Eloise Loop Road, Winter Haven, FL 33884, 863/324-1339, www.lakeshorepalms.com.

23 PARAKEET PARK

🏊 🐕 ♿ 🚐

Scenic rating: 2

on South Scenic Highway (State Road 17), south of Lake Wales

On your approach to this 20-acre adults-preferred park, don't be surprised if you need to slow down to follow a truck laden with oranges. You're in the northern portion of Florida's fabled citrus belt. Nonetheless, the park has a residential feel—campers are outnumbered by residents of the 103 mobile homes.

Campsites, facilities: All 25 full-hookup sites are for RVs up to 36 feet long and have picnic tables. Both 30-amp and 50-amp electrical service is available. A pool, a game room, shuffleboard, and winter activities in the wheelchair-accessible clubhouse entertain campers. Showers, restrooms, a dump station, cable TV, telephone hookups, and laundry facilities are available. Groceries and a restaurant are within two miles. Children may camp only on a short-term basis. Small pets are permitted.

Reservations, fees: Reservations are recommended. Sites are $20 per night for two people, plus $1 for each additional person and $2 for using electric heaters or air-conditioning. Credit cards are not accepted. Long-term rates are available.

Directions: From Lake Wales, drive 2.4 miles south on South Scenic Highway/State Road 17 to the park.

Contact: Parakeet Park, 2400 Parakeet Park Boulevard, Lake Wales, FL 33859, 863/676-2812.

24 LAKE WALES CAMPGROUND

Scenic rating: 6

south of Lake Wales

Oaks and the sparse needles of pine trees lend shade to some grassy campsites at this busy winter spot, but other sites are sunny. A shaded walkway leads through a flower garden, and a small natural pond adds to the scenery of the 14-acre, renovated park, which also features an indoor shuffleboard court and indoor, heated pool. Nearby are the Historic Bok Sanctuary, a hilly garden spot perfect for picnics at its 3 P.M. carillon recitals; and Le Chalet Suzanne, a noted gourmet restaurant. More than a few diners have landed private planes at the on-site airstrip to feast by candlelight on six-course dinners. Favorite things to do in the park are "eat, talk, and shuffle," the managers say. Visitors come from all over the United States to participate in planned activities, including bingo, dances, potluck dinners, and day trips. They also enjoy the gym and listening to bands.

Campsites, facilities: There are 114 RV sites (50 pull-through) with full hookups, a choice of 30-amp or 50-amp electrical service, concrete patios, and picnic tables. A wireless Internet connection is available in the park. Shuffleboard courts, wintertime activities, and a wheelchair accessible recreation room entertain campers. The recreation hall has a raised stage, a dance floor, a kitchen, and an entertainment center. Coffee is served every morning, and there are church services on Sundays. Showers, restrooms, and laundry facilities are provided on the grounds. The recreation room is also wheelchair-accessible, and the park's roads are paved. Groceries and restaurants are within three miles. Children may camp for up to two weeks. Leashed pets are permitted.

Reservations, fees: Reservations are recommended. Sites are $24–26 per night for two people, plus $2 for each additional person. If you have more than one pet, another $1 fee is charged. Credit cards are accepted. Long-term stays are OK.

Directions: From State Road 60 at Lake Wales, drive three miles south on U.S. 27 to the park entrance.

Contact: Lake Wales Campground, 15898 U.S. 27, Lake Wales, FL 33859, 863/638-9011, fax 863/638-2873, www.lakewalescampground rvresort.com.

25 LAKEMONT RIDGE HOME AND RV PARK

Scenic rating: 4

in Frostproof

Retirees flock here each year from all over the United States and Canada to partake of a very busy social schedule planned by an activities director, such as exercises, dances, dinners, crafts, live entertainment, bingo, and seasonal events like holiday parties. There are also Sunday-morning church services. Favorite things to do include catch-and-release fishing, bike riding, playing billiards, and throwing horseshoes. A computer with Internet access is available in the recreation hall. About 35 percent of the park is occupied year-round, and there are two sections with park models and mobile homes. Additional land is set aside for future development.

Campsites, facilities: Among 265 full hookup RV sites, 142 have 30-amp electrical service and 110 have 50-amp. In 2005, 100-amp service was added to 100 sites. All have concrete patios and are paved. Big rigs can be accommodated on lots that are 35 feet wide and 78 feet long. An Internet connection is available in the clubhouse. Restrooms, showers, laundry facilities, a pool, a recreation hall, shuffleboard courts, cabin rentals, and a large fenced dog-walk area are on-site. All areas are wheelchair-accessible. Groceries and restaurants are within 3 miles; malls and hospitals are 15 miles away. This tends to be an over-age-55 park. Leashed pets are permitted.

Reservations, fees: Reservations are recommended. Sites are $50 per night for two people, plus $5 for each extra person. Credit cards are not accepted. Long-term rates are available.

Directions: From the intersection of County Road 630 and U.S. 27 in Frostproof, drive east on County Road 630 about 0.5 mile to the park on the right.

Contact: Lakemont Ridge Home and RV Park, 2000 Maine Street, Frostproof, FL 33843, 863/635-4472, fax 863/635-1627, lakemontridge@aol.com.

26 LILY LAKE GOLF RESORT

🚲 🏊 🛶 🚤 🐴 ♿ 🚐

Scenic rating: 6

south of Frostproof

This manufactured-home community really can't be considered an RV park, per se. RVers are welcome to rent a limited number of sites from owners of existing lots. The emphasis is on selling park models and "RV ports," which are manufactured homes with attached two-

story garages for parking your RV. Of course, the amenities are spectacular. Campers can fish on Lily Lake, and guests have free use of boats. The golf course is a major draw for the mostly retirement-age clientele.

Campsites, facilities: A limited number of RV sites (around 15) are available for rent from owners of lots at this sprawling manufactured-home community. Full hookups, 50-amp electrical service, cable TV, full security, and a clubhouse are available. (Pop-up campers and truck campers are prohibited.) On the premises are a heated pool, a golf course, a fishing lake, billiards, a dog-walk area, tennis and shuffleboard courts, and a recreation hall. All areas are wheelchair-accessible. Children are not welcome. Leashed pets are permitted (limit of two).

Reservations, fees: Reservations are recommended. Sites are $30 per night for two people. Credit cards are accepted. Long-term stays are available.

Directions: From the intersection of U.S. 98 and U.S. 27, drive south one mile on U.S. 27. The resort is on the east side.

Contact: Lily Lake Golf Resort, 500 U.S. 27 South, Frostproof, FL 33843, 863/635-3685 or 800/654-5177, www.lilylake.com.

27 CAMP INN RESORTS

🏊 🐴 ♿ 🚐 ⛺

Scenic rating: 7

in Frostproof

Located down the road from the small Lake Wales Municipal Airport, an RV dealer, and other commercial establishments, this 85-acre park is big: 45 campsites line up side by side at its widest point (Evergreen Circle). And the place has not one, but *three*, laundry rooms. Paved roads pass the grassy RV sites where some campers spend months, or even years.

Near the entrance on busy U.S. 27 are a handful of water- and electricity-equipped sites, as well as two pools—one heated. Beyond that, a section of pull-through camping spots leads to eight shuffleboard courts and an 8,000-square-foot recreation hall at the park's center. Farther back, you'll find the bulk of the campsites—meaning most RVs are insulated from U.S. 27. To overlook an oval meadow, ask about sites on Laurel or Seagrape. For pull-through spots closest to a small lake (across a park road), consider sites B1, C1, D1, E5, E6, or E7.

Campsites, facilities: The 796 RV sites have full hookups with 30/50-amp electrical service; 190 are pull-through. Tenters can make camp at 23 sites. There are picnic tables at each site. Two pools, a whirlpool, a game room, a recreation hall, shuffleboard, horseshoes, and winter social programs entertain campers. Showers, restrooms, a dump station, LP gas sales, and laundry facilities are available. Management says all areas are wheelchair-accessible. A restaurant and groceries are within two miles. Children may camp on a short-term basis. Leashed pets should use the entrance-area dog walk.

Reservations, fees: Reservations are recommended. Sites are $22 per night for two people, plus $1 for each additional adult and $2 for cable TV. Credit cards are accepted. Long-term stays are OK for adults, preferably age 50 and up.

Directions: From State Road 60 in Lake Wales, turn south onto U.S. 27. The campground is eight miles ahead on the right side of the road.

Contact: Camp Inn Resorts, 10400 Highway 27, Frostproof, FL 33843, 863/635-2500 or 877/622-6746, fax 863/635-4822.

28 LAKE PIERCE ECO RESORT

Scenic rating: 10

between Haines City and Lake Wales, on the north side of Lake Pierce

Fed up with big-city life, Frank Wezyk sold his assets in 1999 to create this 20-acre paradise

boats safe at dockside

© MARILYN MOORE

on the north side of 4,000-acre Lake Pierce. Once a dilapidated trailer park, the place is now a jewel. You can see wildlife close at hand (Wezyk's feeding of the birds and fish—but not the alligators, of course—is something to see, and visitors are invited to join in), and just enjoy the outdoors. That's the kind of traveler Wezyk wants to host, and he's worked hard to create an "ecological park." For example, a series of lights and mirrors under the 200-foot dock illuminate the fish and watery denizens. You can canoe, fish, hike, and bike around the area. The only thing you can't do is bring pets, since they'll scare away the wildlife. A Vietnam veteran, Wezyk offers special rates for veterans' groups, car clubs, and Harley-Davidson clubs.

Campsites, facilities: There are 15 RV sites with full hookups, and 50 tent sites. Ten tent sites have water and electricity. All developed sites have picnic tables, grills, and cable TV. Restrooms, showers, laundry facilities, a nature trail, a fishing dock, canoe rentals, and shuffleboard courts are on the premises. Most areas are wheelchair-accessible. Children are welcome. No pets, please.

Reservations, fees: Reservations are

recommended. Sites are $20–25 per night for two people, plus $3 per extra person. Credit cards are not accepted. Long-term rates are available.

Directions: From the intersection of State Road 60 and U.S. 27 in Lake Wales, drive east on State Road 60 one mile. Turn north on U.S. Alternate 27/U.S. 17 and proceed 15 miles. Turn right on Tindel Camp Road and go one mile. At Lake Mabel Road, turn left and proceed to Canal Road one mile.

Contact: Lake Pierce Eco Resort, 3500 Canal Road, Lake Pierce, FL 33898, 863/439-2023, fax 863/439-6166, www.lakepierce.com.

29 LAKE KISSIMMEE STATE PARK

🚶 🚲 🛶 🚗 ⛺ ♿ 🚐 ⛺

Scenic rating: 10

at Lake Kissimmee, east of Lake Wales

This nearly-eight-square-mile state park is famous for its weekend living-history demonstrations of an 1876 "cow camp." Just walk 50 yards from the parking lot to the 200-acre pen of scrub cows to swap stories around a campfire with a costumed ranger posing as a "cow hunter." Don't make reference to modern-day things such as MP3 players or cell phones, though, because the cowpoke will claim not to understand you. Instead, he'll hearken back to simpler days—when frontier cowboys herded cattle and, even earlier, provided the Confederacy with much of its beef.

Campers relax north of the cow camp along two loops near an observation tower, where visitors climb three landings to gaze onto an expanse of prairie-like pasture. Each shell-rock campsite is equipped with a grill, a picnic table, and a fire ring handy for building campfires to roast marshmallows by. Plentiful picnic tables sit creekside or beneath the twisted branches of oaks elsewhere in the park.

Look for turkeys, bald eagles, deer, and a sea of pickerelweed stretching toward the horizon during walks along 13 miles of hiking trails. A short nature loop and two long loop trails that encompass much of the park—one north of Zipper Canal, the other south of it—are reachable from the marina-area concession stand north of the cow camp. Notice the park's varied landscape: wide-open wet prairies, sun-dappled pine flatlands, and shady hammocks with orchids and mosses. Bring mosquito repellent for a more pleasant walk.

A launch ramp leads boaters a short distance east to the park's namesake, Lake Kissimmee, where anglers try for specks, bass, and shellcrackers in Florida's third-largest lake. Canoeists who bring their own craft can paddle five to seven miles along a pretty loop starting at Zipper Canal and heading west (counterclockwise) to Lake Rosalie, Rosalie Creek, Tiger Lake, Tiger Creek, and the eastern corner of 47-square-mile Lake Kissimmee, before returning to the boat ramp. The placid waters you'll see here eventually flow south down the Kissimmee River to the Everglades and Florida Bay at the state's southern tip, some 200 miles distant. At night, you'll listen to the croaking of frogs, but on busy fishing weekends, the roar of far-off boat engines can also be heard. Development is beginning to move in to this once remote area.

Campsites, facilities: All 60 sites have water, 30-amp electricity, a picnic table, a grill, and a fire ring. A playground, nature trails, showers, restrooms, a dump station, and a 50-person-capacity youth camping area are available. Two campsites, the fishing pier, and restrooms are wheelchair-accessible. Laundry facilities, a restaurant, snacks, and bait are within 5 miles, and groceries are 15 miles away. Kids are welcome.

Reservations, fees: Reservations are recommended; contact ReserveAmerica at 800/336-3521 or reserveamerica.com. Sites are $17 per night for up to eight people. Credit cards are accepted. The maximum stay is 14 days.

Directions: From U.S. 27 at Lake Wales, travel about nine miles east on State Road 60. Turn left at Boy Scout Road. After three miles, turn right at Camp Mack Road. The park is five miles ahead.

Contact: Lake Kissimmee State Park, 14248 Camp Mack Road, Lake Wales, FL 33853, 863/696-1112, www.floridastateparks.org.

30 FALLEN OAK PRIMITIVE CAMPGROUND

🚶 🚴 🛶 🚤 ⛺

Scenic rating: 6

in Kissimmee State Park

The name of this campground is your first clue that these primitive sites are at the edge of an old oak hammock. One of the biggest oak trees has fallen over, providing food and shelter for lots of small critters. The approximately six-mile loop trail on which these campsites are located is part of a 13-mile stretch of the Florida National Scenic Trail that runs through the state park. Be forewarned that the trail may be very muddy during the June–September rainy season; be sure to check with park rangers ahead of time. This campsite is not too far from the main camp road, but is still far removed from the most used parts of the park, where you'll find plenty of recreation opportunities, including canoeing, fishing, boating, and bicycling. On cooler weekends, expect to have some company here. If you wind up alone, consider yourself lucky.

Campsites, facilities: Primitive camping areas accommodate about 12 people, but you must hike 3–3.5 miles to reach your tent site. A picnic table and campfire area are provided. There is no piped water, no toilet, and no other facilities. Bring water, food, mosquito repellent, and all other supplies. Children are welcome. Pets, firearms, and alcoholic beverages are prohibited.

Reservations, fees: Reservations are recommended. Camping costs $6 per night for two people and $3 per extra person. Major credit cards are accepted. Stays are limited to two weeks.

Directions: From U.S. 27 at Lake Wales, travel approximately nine miles east on State Road 60, then turn left onto Boy Scout Road. In three miles, turn right at Camp Mack Road. The park entrance is five miles ahead.

Contact: Lake Kissimmee State Park, 14248 Camp Mack Road, Lake Wales, FL 33853, 863/696-1112.

31 BUSTER ISLAND PRIMITIVE CAMPGROUND

🚶 🚴 🛶 🚤 🐎 ⛺

Scenic rating: 6

in Kissimmee State Park

Secluded Buster Island is surrounded on six sides by water, including Lakes Tiger, Kissimmee, and Rosalie. But you'd be hard-pressed to know you're on an island, because creeks, not lakes, border three of its six sides. The campsites are part of a six-mile loop on the Florida National Scenic Trail. You'll pass through oak hammocks and scrubby flatwoods of pine and oak. The trail may be very muddy during the June–September rainy season, so check with park rangers ahead of time. If you want to take advantage of the canoeing, boating, fishing, and biking opportunities here, do so before or after your hike, because they are accessible only at the main portion of the park.

Campsites, facilities: Primitive camping areas accommodate about 12 people, but you must hike 3–3.5 miles to reach your tent site. A picnic table and campfire area are provided. There is no piped water and no other facilities. Bring water, food, mosquito repellent, and all other supplies. Children and pets are welcome.

Reservations, fees: Reservations are recommended. Camping costs $6 per night for two people, plus $3 per extra person. Major credit cards are accepted. Stays are limited to two weeks.

Directions: From U.S. 27 at Lake Wales, travel about nine miles east on State Road 60. Turn left at Boy Scout Road. In three miles, turn right at Camp Mack Road. The park is five miles ahead.

Contact: Lake Kissimmee State Park, 14248 Camp Mack Road, Lake Wales, FL 33853, 863/696-1112.

32 CAMP MACK'S RIVER RESORT

Scenic rating: 8

at Lake Kissimmee, east of Lake Wales

Fish camps are not usually known for their amenities, but this one is deluxe—and getting more so every year to fit "a fisherman's dream," as the managers put it. A pool, motel, and a clubhouse were built in the early 2000s, and the park added large sites for big rigs while retaining a wooded atmosphere. But the main deal is fishing, airboat riding, and boating on Lake Kissimmee and other nearby waters famed for bass. Lake Kissimmee State Park is nearby. About 8 percent of the park is occupied year-round.

Campsites, facilities: There are 213 sites with 30/50-amp electrical service, sewer hookups, concrete pads, and picnic tables for tenters and RVers. About 175 sites are available for overnighters. None of the sites is pull-through. Park models are being sold on the property, and cabins are for rent. Restrooms, showers, laundry facilities, a pool, a boat ramp, a fish-cleaning station, a clubhouse, bait and tackle, a store, and boat rentals are available. Most areas are wheelchair-accessible. Streets are paved. Children are welcome. Leashed pets are permitted.

Reservations, fees: Reservations are recommended. Sites are $33 per night for four people, plus $2 per extra person. Additional fees are $2 for 30-amp electrical service, $3 for 50-amp, and $5 for cable TV. Credit cards are accepted. Year-round rates are available for visitors over 55 only.

Directions: From U.S. 27 at Lake Wales, travel about nine miles east on State Road 60. Turn left at Boy Scout Road. After three miles, turn right at Camp Mack Road. The park is six miles ahead.

Contact: Camp Mack's River Resort, 14900 Camp Mack Road, Lake Wales, FL 33898, 863/696-1108 or 800/243-8013, fax 863/696-1500, www.campmack.com.

33 THE HARBOR RV RESORT AND MARINA

Scenic rating: 6

on Lake Rosalie, east of Lake Wales

If the boat ramp on seven-square-mile Lake Rosalie isn't enough to convince you, then the bass logo makes it clear: Fishing is popular at this 13-acre marina and RV park set in a relaxed, lake-dotted region. Many campers enjoy the park's tranquility and the bright glow of the sun rising over the lake. For a lakeside camping spot, request sites 37, 54, 55, or 56. Lots 99–104 are secluded spots near the woods. About 8 percent of the park is occupied by full-timers.

Paved, 5-mph streets pass the grassy/concrete-pad sites, most of which are shaded by oaks. Outside the park, much of the land bordering the lake is undeveloped, making it easy on the eyes. Three miles away is the 1800s-style cow camp at Lake Kissimmee State Park (see listing in this chapter). Orlando-area theme parks are about 45 minutes north.

Campsites, facilities: RVs and tents can be accommodated at 45 grassy or gravel full-hookup sites (10 pull-through). Seventeen sites have 50-amp electrical service; the rest have 30-amp. A wireless Internet connection is available in the clubhouse and in the office. The park caters to a mix of seasonal visitors, baby boomers, and families. A pool, shuffleboard, and a recreation hall entertain campers. Showers, restrooms, laundry facilities, a marina, propane, rental cabins, a fishing guide, boat docks, a boat ramp, and boat rentals are available. Planned activities get started in November, with fishing and shuffleboard tournaments, dinners, art classes, church services, and day tours, to name just a few. Children are welcome. Pets are permitted.

Reservations, fees: Reservations are recommended in winter. Sites are $36 per night for two people, plus $3 for each additional person, $3 for using heaters or air conditioners, and $3 for cable TV. Credit cards are accepted. Long-term rates are available.

Directions: From U.S. 27 at Lake Wales, travel about 9.9 miles east on State Road 60. Turn left at Boy Scout Road. In 3.5 miles, turn right at Camp Mack Road. Continue 1.7 miles to the park entrance.

Contact: The Harbor RV Resort and Marina, 10511 Monroe Court, Lake Wales, FL 33898, 863/696-1194, fax 863/696-4000, www .harbor-rv-marina.com.

34 GRAPE HAMMOCK RV PARK AND MARINA

🛶 🎣 🚤 🐕 🎒 ♿ 🚍 ⛰️

Scenic rating: 6

on the Kissimmee River, east of Lake Wales

Fishing and bicycling are the lure at this relaxed spot on the Kissimmee River. In inclement weather, die-hard anglers can cast lines from the riverbanks, but the usual routine is to head a short distance to the broad waters of Florida's third-largest lake—Lake Kissimmee. Campers have been known to bring back some big bass. In addition to fishing guides and boat rentals, you can arrange to take part in an alligator hunt in September (dates may change, since hunts are regulated by the state of Florida); call 863/676-3173. Also known as Grape Hammock Fish Park, these 21 acres are

rustic and family-owned since 1950. Cabins sit beneath a canopy of oaks. Campsites are sandy or grassy, with some situated near the canal. Three-wheelers may ride slowly through the park to get to the main road. The owners report that the state of Florida purchased three surrounding fish camps in 2005, so the land surrounding it is being preserved from development.

Professional guide Johnny Doub says the odds of catching a 10-pound bass are best from January until summer's end; call 800/826-0621. Campground motorboats rent for $90.

Campsites, facilities: There are 70 grassy, full-hookup RV sites, of which 25 are available for overnighters. Some offer 50-amp electrical service. Sites have concrete patios, picnic tables, and grills. A few are waterfront. Seven primitive sites in a secluded wooded area are available for tents; they have a water source nearby. Unusually, the tent sites are permitted to have fires and pets. A pool, shuffleboard, a recreation room, showers, restrooms, a dump station, cabin rentals, a boat ramp, a dock, boat rentals, airboat tours, houseboat moorings, bait, tackle, and laundry facilities are on the premises. Management says the recreation room and restrooms are wheelchair-accessible. Groceries are 24 miles away; restaurants are within 12 miles. Children under 12 must be adult-supervised at the pool. Pets are welcome, but disruptive animals should be leashed.

Reservations, fees: Reservations are recommended. Sites are $12 to $22 per night for two people, plus $1 per extra person. Credit cards are accepted. Long-term rates are available.

Directions: From Lake Wales, travel 22 miles east on State Road 60. Turn left at Grape Hammock Road. The entrance is 1.25 miles ahead.

Contact: Grape Hammock RV Park and Marina, 1400 Grape Hammock Road, Lake Wales, FL 33853, 863/692-1500, www.grape hammock.com.

35 RIVER RANCH RV RESORT

Scenic rating: 10

on the Kissimmee River, between Lake Wales and Yeehaw Junction

BEST (

Families like this deluxe spot. The buffet is a popular choice at this spectacular resort's restaurant, which is located across the driveway from the on-site airstrip. Kids stop to buy candy at the snack bar between bouts of combat in the game room, and a guard stands posted at the resort's long entranceway. It's a special spot. The setting is rustic and woodsy, right next to the Kissimmee River in a rural section of Florida, but don't even think about roughing it. Choose from a campsite in a shady Old Florida oak hammock or a sunny site next to the canal where you can dock your boat. Fish from a riverbank, or try for bass from your own johnboat or canoe. Fishing guide services are available nearby; inquire at the registration desk. On-site are a catch-and-release pond, a nine-hole golf course, a petting zoo, mini golf, and horseback riding. Try a short hike down the Florida National Scenic Trail next door at KICCO Wildlife Management Area; or take a drive over to Lake Kissimmee State Park and check out the historic cow camp.

Campsites, facilities: All 367 paved RV sites have 30/50-amp electricity, water, cable TV, wireless Internet access, concrete patios, fire rings, and picnic tables. Lots are 40–65 feet wide and 70–85 feet long, accommodating the largest RVs on the market. Facilities include restrooms, showers, a dump station, an airstrip, a restaurant, laundry facilities, a boat dock, hiking trails, a game room, a snack bar, limited bait and tackle sales, guided horseback rides on weekends, golf, tennis courts, and meeting rooms. Other entertainment includes rodeos, "gunslinger" shows, trap and skeet shooting and a gun range, a petting zoo, boat tours, airboat rides, and more. Many areas are wheelchair-accessible. Streets are paved. Children and pets are permitted in the camping area but not in the resort's motel rooms.

Reservations, fees: Reservations are recommended. Sites are $43–53 per night for four people, plus $2 for each extra person. Credit cards are accepted. Long-term rates are available.

Directions: From Florida's Turnpike at Yeehaw Junction, take Exit 193 and travel west on State Road 60 about 25 miles, crossing the Kissimmee River, and look for the entrance ahead on the left. From Lake Wales, head east on State Road 60 about 25 miles; look for the entrance on the right before you reach the Kissimmee River.

Contact: River Ranch RV Resort, 24700 State Road 60/P.O. Box 30421, River Ranch, FL 33867, 863/692-1321, fax 863/692-9707, www.riverranchrv.com.

36 KICCO WILDLIFE MANAGEMENT AREA

Scenic rating: 8

on the Kissimmee River, between Lake Wales and Yeehaw Junction

Three remote and little-used camping spots along the Florida National Scenic Trail are just right for backpackers who want to get away from it all—yet you're within an easy walk of showers, hot food, running water, and the rest of the amenities offered at the River Ranch RV Resort complex, located at the northern end of this wildlife management area.

The hiking trail stretches about eight miles along the length of this mile-wide green ribbon. The 12-square-mile area features deep, dark hammocks of oak trees covered with moss and resurrection ferns, as well as pine flatwoods, scrub, and some marshy areas and stands of cypress. The hiking trail runs parallel to the Kissimmee River. The U.S. Army

Corps of Engineers straightened the gently meandering stream into a big, angular ditch in the 1960s. Now the Corps is working with the South Florida Water Management District, owner of the KICCO property, on a restoration plan for the river.

The name KICCO (pronounced KISS-oh) comes from the 1920s-era Kissimmee Island Cattle Company, which grazed cattle here. Now the tract is managed jointly by the water district and the Florida Fish and Wildlife Conservation Commission. Check with the game commission's Lakeland office (863/648-3203) for hunt dates. Be sure to wear orange-blaze clothing if you camp during those times, generally around Thanksgiving and in the spring turkey season.

The first campsite is within one mile of the trailhead. Another is about three miles farther along, and the third is another three miles past that. None of the sites is actually on the riverbank, but all three are very close to it.

Bicycling is allowed along the hiking trails only. You also can launch a canoe or boat at River Ranch RV Resort and travel downstream, although you might have a rough time finding a place to dock. To explore, hiking is your best bet.

Campsites, facilities: An indeterminate number of tenters can be accommodated at three sites along the Florida National Scenic Trail. No facilities are available. Bring water, food, mosquito repellent, and supplies. Pack out trash, and bury human waste in a six-inch hole. Children and pets are permitted.

Reservations, fees: Reservations are not required to backpack and camp on the Florida National Scenic Trail, although you are advised to call the water management district ahead of time to check on conditions. Camping is free. (As for camping anywhere except on the trail, camping is allowed at designated sites only during hunting season.)

Directions: From Florida's Turnpike at Yeehaw Junction, take Exit 193 and travel west on State Road 60 about 25 miles, crossing the Kissimmee River, and look for the River

Ranch RV Resort entrance ahead on the left. From Lake Wales, head east on State Road 60 about 25 miles; look for the resort entrance on the right before you reach the Kissimmee River. When you reach the security kiosk at River Ranch RV Resort, tell the guard you're headed to the Florida National Scenic Trail to hike.

Contact: Florida Trail Association, 5415 Southwest 13th Street, Gainesville, FL 32608, 352/378-8823 or 877/HIKE-FLA, www.florida-trail.org. For hunting or general information, try Florida Fish and Wildlife Conservation Commission, 941/648-3205.

37 LAKE MARIAN PARADISE

Scenic rating: 3

on Lake Marian, south of St. Cloud

Under new ownership since 2005, this fish-camp-turned-nature-resort values its natural setting, as well as the state's policy of preserving the acreage nearby in its pristine glory. Some retirees and a number of working people live at these sunny and shady sites full-time, or at least long-term (about 70 percent of the park is occupied year-round). Visitors tend to be anglers, families, and repeat customers. The camp is set on Lake Marian, a 5,800-acre unspoiled lake. Besides fishing, you can hike in the wildlife management area, which seems to burst at the seams with critters compared with nearby urban Florida. There's also a par-27 golf course overlooking the lake. A restaurant is located in the nearby hamlet of Kenansville one mile away.

Campsites, facilities: All 57 full-hookup sites have full hookups, 30 or 50-amp electrical service, and picnic tables. A boat dock is included with your camping fee, and the waterfront sites are just steps away from the marina. Rigs up to 40 feet long and slideouts can be accommodated. On the premises are restrooms, showers, a dump station, picnic tables, a boat ramp, efficiency motel rentals, laundry facilities, bait and tackle, a general store, and boat rentals. Planned activities are low-key bingo and potluck dinners; the favorite thing to do is fishing. Groceries are within three miles. The clubhouse and store are wheelchair-accessible. Children may stay short-term. Pets are permitted, although management reserves the right to turn away pets that are troublesome.

Reservations, fees: Reservations are advised. Sites are $32–37 per night for two people, plus $3 for each additional person. Credit cards are accepted. Adults interested in long stays should inquire about monthly rates.

Directions: From St. Cloud, take Highway 523/Canoe Creek Road south about 32 miles. When you see Arnold Road, turn right, heading southwest for 0.5 mile. It leads to the fish camp. If you reach the point where Highway 523 passes under Florida's Turnpike west of Kenansville, you've gone too far. If you're coming from southern Florida, take Florida's Turnpike to the Yeehaw Junction exit. Head north on U.S. 441 about 14 miles to Highway 523, turn left (west), and go about three miles to Arnold Road, where you'll turn left.

Contact: Lake Marian Paradise, 901 Arnold Road, Kenansville, FL 34739, 407/436-1464, www.lakemarian.com.

38 THREE LAKES WILDLIFE MANAGEMENT AREA
🏃 🚲 ➖ 🐕 🚐 ⛺

Scenic rating: 7

south of St. Cloud, near Kenansville

Turkeys scared by the sound of footsteps rush into tall grasses for camouflage at this relatively wildlife-packed 53,000-acre tract. Improbably located within a reasonable drive from the big-city lights of Disney World, this haven of hunters and hikers requires some pre-planning by getting all the current maps and regulations. The area is called Three Lakes because it sits between Lakes Kissimmee,

Jackson, and Marian. After a rain, muddy trails are likely to sport more deer tracks and turkey prints than signs of humans. Look for bobcats or deer darting from a wooded area into the prairies.

You may camp only at hunter-designated campsites during hunting season, which varies from year to year. The rest of the time, you can camp at all designated backpacking campsites on the Florida Trail (352/378-8823, www .florida-trail.org). These various backpacking sites include one that's a 1.5-mile walk from Parker House to Dry Pond, and a more remote camping area that is about 75 yards across and features a little more underbrush. The hiking trail winds through dry pine flatwoods and scrub communities, as well as more lush hardwood hammocks.

It helps to have a four-wheel-drive vehicle in Three Lakes, and I would consider it more or less mandatory if you're hauling an RV when it's been raining. For day use, the roads are well suited for horseback riding and mountain biking. Anglers can head to the end of Road 16 to launch onto Lake Jackson.

Campsites, facilities: Three primitive camping areas accommodate an indeterminate number of RVs or tents during hunting season only. Three other primitive camping areas are accessible only to hikers on the Florida Trail. There are no facilities, so bring drinking water. You will find water pumps in a few places, but the water is not certified as safe for human consumption—although it is usable for washing off, watering animals, and so forth. Children and pets are permitted.

Reservations, fees: Sites are first-come, first-served and require a free permit from the Florida Fish and Wildlife Conservation Commission. When requesting a permit, ask for a map.

Directions: From St. Cloud, take Highway 523/Canoe Creek Road south about 25 miles. The wildlife management area sprawls over nearly 80 square miles. One entrance to the Florida Trail is on State Road 60, 14.5 miles west of the town of Yeehaw Junction.

Others are 25 miles south of St. Cloud on Canoe Creek Road, off County Road 523 west off U.S. 441 near Kenansville, off U.S. 441 13.5 miles south of Holopaw.

Contact: Florida Fish and Wildlife Conservation Commission, Ocala Regional Office, 1239 Southwest 10th Street, Ocala, FL 34474, 352/732-1225, www.floridaconservation .org.

39 PIONEER CREEK RV PARK

Scenic rating: 7

off U.S. 17, south of Bowling Green

You'll find a socially active lifestyle here at Pioneer Creek RV Park, which offers paved, lighted streets and clean RV sites where outdoor clotheslines are forbidden. From golf at 8:30 A.M. to pinochle in the smoke-free clubhouse at 7 P.M., the rotating schedule of winter activities can keep visitors busy in case the heated pool, stained-glass shop, and woodworking shop aren't enough. Small mowed lawns and, in some cases, attached screen rooms lend a residential feel to the park. The favorite thing to do is socializing. RVs on Drum Drive and the northern portion of Arrowhead Loop back onto a conservation area that divides the park. Nearby is the Payne's Creek State Historic Site, where a Seminole Indian trading post once stood. Life in this region of Florida is slow-paced, but you'll find auto dealerships, shopping, and other businesses a ways down U.S. 17 in Wauchula. Most visitors here are from the Midwest and New York.

Campsites, facilities: This park offers 377 full-hookup sites with 50-amp electrical service, concrete patios, and wireless Internet access. Of these sites, 120 are available for overnighters. RVs up to 40 feet and slideouts are welcome. A pool, a clubhouse, a woodworking shop, shuffleboard, horseshoes, pool tables, boccie ball (lawn bowling) courts, and planned wintertime activities entertain campers.

Showers, restrooms, a dump station, picnic areas, winter church services, cable TV (long-term campers only), propane, and laundry facilities are available. All areas are wheelchair-accessible. Groceries and restaurants are within three miles. Children are not allowed. Campers with pets sleep in a designated section; one leashed pet is permitted per site.

Reservations, fees: Reservations are suggested. Sites are $25 per night for two people, plus $2.50 per extra person. Credit cards are accepted. Long-term rates are available. The park's office is closed in summer.

Directions: From Main Street/State Road 64A in Wauchula, go north about six miles on U.S. 17 to Broward Street (just south of the Polk County line) to the park on the right.

Contact: Pioneer Creek RV Park, 138 East Broward Street, Bowling Green, FL 33834, 863/375-4343, www.rvresorts.com.

40 WAGON WHEEL RV PARK

Scenic rating: 5

off U.S. 17, north of Wauchula

Located 50 miles from the beach in a citrus-dotted portion of the state often overlooked by tourists, the 20-acre, adults-only park is 0.5 mile off the main drag, U.S. 17. Retirees take part in wintertime social programs before retiring to their grassy RV sites with concrete patios. About half the park is occupied by full-time residents.

Campsites, facilities: This adults-only park has 265 full-hookup, 50-amp sites for RVs up to 40 feet long. Showers, restrooms, laundry facilities, a recreation room, horseshoes, shuffleboard, and winter social programs are available. A 0.5-acre lake is available for fishing. Management says all facilities are wheelchair-accessible. Children are only permitted to visit park residents; campers must be at least 18. Leashed pets under 30 pounds are allowed; management must preapprove the breed.

Reservations, fees: Reservations are not necessary. Sites are $20 per night for two adults, plus $5 per extra person. Credit cards are not accepted. Long-term stays are encouraged.

Directions: From the junction of U.S. 17 and State Road 62 north of Wauchula, travel 0.5 mile north on U.S. 17 to Bostick Road. Turn left and continue 0.5 mile west to the park, on the right.

Contact: Wagon Wheel RV Park, 2908 Red Barn Lane, Bowling Green, FL 33834, 863/773-3157.

41 CRYSTAL LAKE VILLAGE RV AND MOBILE HOME PARK

Scenic rating: 7

off U.S. 17, north of Wauchula

Orange groves flank three sides of this 37-acre community, set in the sleepy inland region of Florida. Retirees escape cold northern winters by spending six months here, passing the time with square dances, arts and crafts, trips on the park's 29-passenger bus, and fishing at a three-acre stocked lake. Lighted streets and paved driveways lead up to the plentiful park models and the RV sites, some of which are shaded. If the 18-hole golf course located about 1.25 miles away doesn't fit the bill, try another course six miles distant. Disney World is a long day trip to the northeast. More than 70 percent of the park is occupied year-round.

Campsites, facilities: Open to campers age 55 and over, this 360-site mobile-home/RV park offers more than 50 full-hookup sites, with paved driveways and patios for RVs up to 48 feet long. All sites have 30/50-amp electrical service. Internet access is available in the clubhouse. Showers, restrooms, a pool, a hot tub, trailer rentals, horseshoes, shuffleboard, a recreation hall, billiards, planned activities, a fishing lake, and laundry facilities are

provided. Management says all facilities are wheelchair-accessible. A restaurant, groceries, and an 18-hole golf course are within 1.5 miles. Leashed pets are permitted.

Reservations, fees: Reservations are recommended. Sites are $25–28 per night for two people, plus $3 for each additional person and an additional charge for cable TV. Credit cards are accepted. Long-term rates are available.

Directions: From Wauchula, travel three miles north on U.S. 17 to Maxwell Drive, which is 0.25 mile south of State Road 62. Turn right onto Maxwell and continue east to the park.

Contact: Crystal Lake Village RV and Mobile Home Park, 237 Maxwell Drive, Wauchula, FL 33873, 863/773-3582 or 800/661-3582, fax 863/773-0410, www.crystallake-village .com.

42 LITTLE CHARLIE CREEK RV PARK

Scenic rating: 5

at the Peace River, north of Wauchula

Household garbage must be placed in dark-colored bags and recyclables in clear or white bags for the twice-weekly curbside pickup—a hint that this adult park prizes cleanliness and neatness. The park's main attraction is mixing with your neighbors at potluck dinners and organized games of pokeno, bingo, shuffleboard, and pool. For anglers, the lure is the Peace River, located just west of the RV park. Little Charlie Creek passes by here also, eventually intersecting with the Peace River. Keeping the peace is a good idea at the RV park, set in a sleepy section of Florida. Among the 31 park rules: Anything hung on a clothesline must be removed by 4 P.M., and lawn watering must be done early in the morning or late in the evening, and in moderation. Most people stay for winter, though there are a few full-timers. About 40 percent of the lots are occupied year-round.

Campsites, facilities: The adult-oriented park has 190 full-hookup sites with 50-amp electrical service and concrete patios. Six sites are drive-through and around 100 are available for overnight visitors. Showers, restrooms, laundry facilities, shuffleboard, horseshoes, planned activities, and a recreation hall are provided. Internet connections are available in the clubhouse. Visiting children must be accompanied by an adult while in the recreation center or other common areas. Leashed, immunized pets are permitted.

Reservations, fees: Overnighters are welcome, but reservations are suggested. Sites are $30 per night for two people. Credit cards are accepted. Long-term rates are available.

Directions: From the intersection of U.S. 17 and Main Street in Wauchula, drive north on U.S. 17 about one mile. Turn right at REA Road at the Wal-Mart. Soon after, turn left onto Heard Bridge Road. Travel north about two miles, crossing the Peace River. The campground is to your right.

Contact: Little Charlie Creek RV Park, 1850 Heard Bridge Road, Wauchula, FL 33873, 863/773-0088, fax 863/773-2274.

43 PEACE RIVER PRESERVE
🚲 🏊 🎣 ⛵ 🐕 🚶 ♿ 🚐 ⛺

Scenic rating: 10

south of Wauchula

BEST (

With the Peace River running alongside, plus a campground boat ramp, anglers and boaters find this resort (formerly River Valley RV Resort) just their style—so will families and campers with pets. This park is part of the Thousand Trails campground membership club, but trial offers are available to nonmembers. Part of the park has a wooded canopy, and children are welcome year-round. A playground, sand and grass volleyball areas, and a basketball court were added in 2005. A separate area of the park is set aside for older snowbirds. This park has much to offer for

the camper who likes a nature-oriented setting with civilized amenities and lots of sports.

Campsites, facilities: This sprawling, 73-acre, all-ages resort has 454 sites laid out in neat suburb style. About 226 tents can be accommodated in a large field, as well. RV sites have full hookups and picnic tables; big rigs can be accommodated. Restrooms, showers, a dump station, laundry facilities, a heated pool, a snack bar, an activity center/lodge, a boat ramp, shuffleboard courts, propane gas sales, and a nature trail are on the premises. Many areas are wheelchair-accessible. Children are welcome. Leashed pets are permitted.

Reservations, fees: Reservations are recommended. Trial memberships are available. Credit cards are accepted. Stay as long as you wish.

Directions: From Wauchula, drive two miles south on U.S. 17 to the resort, which is on the east side.

Contact: Peace River Preserve, 2555 U.S. 17 South, Wauchula, FL 33873, 863/735-8888, www.1000trails.com.

44 ADELAIDE SHORES RV RESORT
🏊 🎣 ⛵ 🐕 ♿ 🚐

Scenic rating: 7

north of Avon Park

Under new ownership since 2005, this sunny lakeside retirement community offers social programs for residents and guests; they enjoy bingo, cards, parties, shows, trips, and cruises. Many campers are seasonal; Avon Park's population swells from 9,000 to 13,000 in winter. The RV resort is on a 96-acre lake, affording opportunities for fishing. The heated swimming pool and tennis courts are also popular. In the area, numerous golf courses are located within a 10-minute drive. About 25 percent of the sites are occupied year-round.

Campsites, facilities: This adults-only park offers 399 full-hookup sites; some have been sold for RVs or park models. Lots are 45 by 67 feet, and all have 30/50-amp electrical service. Three sites are drive-through. A wireless Internet connection is available in the clubhouse. On the premises are restrooms, showers, a dump station, two laundry facilities, a 5,000-square-foot clubhouse, trailer rentals, an Olympic-sized pool with a tiki bar, a dock with boat slips, an exercise room, a dance floor, tennis courts, boccie ball (lawn bowling) courts, shuffleboard, horseshoes, a pool table, and a putting green. Cable TV (free) and telephone service are available. All areas are said to be wheelchair-accessible. Groceries and restaurants are within one mile. Children are allowed for short visits. Pets are permitted.

Reservations, fees: Reservations are recommended. Sites are $28 per night for two people, plus $3 per extra person. Credit cards are not accepted. Stay as long as you like.

Directions: From Avon Park, travel north four miles on U.S. 27 to the park.

Contact: Adelaide Shores RV Resort, 2881 U.S. 27 North, Avon Park, FL 33826, 863/453-2226 or 800/848-1924, www .adelaideshores.com.

45 ORANGE BLOSSOM RV PARK

Scenic rating: 2

in Avon Park

The RV sites are an adjunct to the more permanent mobile homes. Some residents like to fish at a small on-site lake. Campers have a choice of sandy, concrete-pad, and grassy sites. Shade is sparse. Most people stay two to three months in winter, but 20 percent of the sites are occupied year-round. Says the management: "We are an adult RV park, not a campground."

Campsites, facilities: Among the 173 total sites, overnighters are placed at one of 20 full-hookup sites with 50-amp electrical

service, concrete patios. Rigs up to 45 feet long can be accommodated. On the premises are restrooms, showers, shuffleboard, and a recreation room. The bathhouse and clubhouse are wheelchair-accessible. Streets are paved. Groceries, a restaurant, and laundry facilities are about two miles away. Children are not permitted, except for short stays. Leashed pets under 30 pounds are allowed.

Reservations, fees: Reservations are recommended. Sites are $19 per night for two people, plus $1 for each additional person. Credit cards are not accepted. Long-term rates are available.

Directions: From U.S. 27, take State Road 64/Main Street east through the town of Avon Park. After about two miles, turn left onto County Road 17A. drive about three miles and look for the park ahead on the left.

Contact: Orange Blossom RV Park, 1400 County Road 17A North, Avon Park, FL 33825, 863/453-6052, fax 863/453-0301.

46 STEWARTS MOBILE VILLAGE

Scenic rating: 1

on U.S. 27, in Avon Park

For most visitors, this location's appeal is its proximity to the RV repairs and service center on-site. RVs are outnumbered by mobile homes at this small roadside park, located down the street from Avon Park Municipal Airport. It's within walking distance of a shopping center. You also can cross the street to fish from the piers at 0.25-mile-wide Lake Onaka.

Campsites, facilities: There are seven full-hookup sites with 50-amp electricity. Slideout RVs can be accommodated. On the premises are restrooms, showers, a dump station, picnic tables, laundry facilities, rental trailers, and horseshoes. The restrooms and office are wheelchair-accessible. Streets are paved. Children and pets are welcome.

Reservations, fees: Reservations are recommended. Sites are $20 per night for two people, plus $2.50 for each extra person. Credit cards are accepted.

Directions: Take U.S. 27 south from Avon Park one mile to the campground.

Contact: Stewarts Mobile Village, 1116 U.S. 27 South, Avon Park, FL 33825, 863/453-3849 or 800/724-7502, www.stewartsmobile village.com.

47 REFLECTIONS ON SILVER LAKE
🏊 🛶 🚐 🦌 🎣 ♿ 🚍

Scenic rating: 6

south of Avon Park

A "winter destination community" for the over-age-55 crowd, this family-owned park is divided into three areas: RVs, park models, and mobile homes. A full-time activities coordinator fills the hours for RVers, who come from all over the Midwest and Canada to spend the season here. The park fronts onto Silver Lake for pretty views and fishing.

Campsites, facilities: There are 338 RV sites, of which 20 are available for overnighters. The majority of sites are occupied year-round or rented to tourists on an annual contract. All have full hookups and 30-amp electricity; 10 sites have 50-amp. None are drive-through, but 40-foot-long RVs and slideouts can be accommodated. Sites are gravel, grassy, or paved, with concrete patios. Restrooms, showers, laundry facilities, a heated pool, fishing lake, a boat dock, two recreation halls, shuffleboard, *pétanque* (French-style bowling) and boccie ball (lawn bowling) courts, propane sales, and a dog-walk area are on-site. All areas of the park are wheelchair-accessible. Groceries and hospitals are within 0.5 mile; restaurants and malls are 5 miles away. Children are allowed as guests visiting campers. Leashed pets are permitted.

Reservations, fees: Reservations are recommended. Sites are $25 per night for two people, plus $2 per extra person. Credit cards are accepted. Long-term rates are available.

Directions: From the intersection of U.S. 27 and State Road 64, drive south on U.S. 27 1.5 miles. The park entrance is across the street from South Florida Community College.

Contact: Reflections on Silver Lake, 1850 U.S. 27 South, Avon Park, FL 33825, 863/453-5756, fax 863/453-9468, www.reflections onsilverlake.com.

48 LAKE BONNET VILLAGE
🏊 🛶 🚐 🦌 🎣 ♿ 🚍

Scenic rating: 7

at Lake Bonnet, south of Avon Park

This combination campground and mobile-home park is in a quiet, woodsy setting overlooking spring-fed 260-acre Lake Bonnet. Many sites are shady, and the view of the lake is pretty. Favored by retirees, this is a nice option for those who prefer a more nature-oriented spot. The RV sites have concrete pads. Nearly half the sites are occupied by people who live here year-round, and a good portion of the rest stay here on a long-term basis. Lot purchases are encouraged. You can swim in the heated pool, relax in a hot tub, or go boating, fishing, or waterskiing on Lake Bonnet. Highlands Hammock State Park is about 15 miles away (see next listing). If you're feeling adventurous, check out the secluded hiking trails at the 106,000-acre Avon Park Air Force Range (call 863/452-4254), approximately 12 miles away.

Campsites, facilities: The 209 full-hookup RV sites have 30/50-amp electrical service and can accommodate vehicles up to 40 feet long. Five RV sites are pull-through. On the premises are restrooms, showers, a dump station, laundry facilities, picnic tables, a wheelchair-accessible recreation room, a pool, a hot tub, a boat ramp, a dock, boat and canoe rentals, a playground, horseshoes, shuffleboard, volleyball, and limited groceries. Children are welcome for up to one month. Pets are permitted.

Reservations, fees: Reservations are recommended. Sites are $30–35 per night for two people, plus $2 for each extra person and $1.50 for electricity. Credit cards are accepted. Long-term rates are available.

Directions: From Avon Park, take State Road 17 south about four miles to Lake Bonnet Road. Turn left and go about one mile east to the park.

Contact: Lake Bonnet Village, 2900 East Lake Bonnet Road, Avon Park, FL 33825, 863/385-7010, fax 863/402-0430, www.lakebonnet village.com.

49 HIGHLANDS HAMMOCK STATE PARK

🚶 🚴 🐴 👪 ♿ 🚐 ⛺

Scenic rating: 10

west of Sebring

An occasional white-tailed deer may be seen munching in open fields at dusk here in one of Florida's oldest state parks—one of my favorite campgrounds in the state. During the winter, you're nearly guaranteed to see large groups of deer at the historic homestead/grove area snacking on the still-producing citrus trees! The scenery is worth the somewhat cramped official camping spots. This park offers nearly 10,000 acres of virgin hardwood forest with a cypress swamp, pine flat woods, sand pine scrub, scrubby flat woods, and marsh.

You're almost certain to see an alligator during your stay, and lucky campers could encounter more elusive wildlife, such as bobcats, otters, and owls. Opened in 1931, this gem was one of the four original parks in the state parks system, which was organized in 1935. A museum on-site recounts how the Civilian Conservation Corps helped build Florida's park system during the Great Depression.

Guided walks and tram tours offered by rangers are your best bet for viewing wildlife, but you can also choose from eight nature and mountain-biking trails that cover 11 miles. Horseback-riding trails are available, too. Riding rented bikes along a loop road is popular. Some nature trails traverse boardwalks in a

© PETER TRITLEY

getting ready for the evening at Highlands Hammock State Park

gorgeous old cypress swamp and other wet areas, and dirt paths elsewhere lead through woods. RVs and tents in the regular campground are pretty much squeezed together.

Campsites, facilities: The main campground has 138 sunny and shady sites with water, 30-amp electric hookups, picnic tables, and grills. Most of the sites are grassy or gravel. On the premises are restrooms, showers, a dump station, laundry facilities, grills, a camp store with ice, snacks, souvenirs and camping supplies, a recreation hall, playgrounds, nature trails, horseshoes, shuffleboard, bicycle rentals, and mountain-bike trails. To help avoid seeing a neighbor eye-to-eye, ask about a few of the 16 drive-up primitive camping spots located in pine flatwoods. RVs and tents in the regular campground are pretty much squeezed together.

The Hammock Inn, run by a concessionaire, offers breakfast, lunch, and dinner. Try the locally famous "wild orange" pies and milk shakes. In the winter months, campground hosts provide morning coffee socials, potluck dinners, and music around the campfire. There's also a tram tour. Management says the museum, restrooms, and some trails have wheelchair access. Groceries and restaurants are about five miles away. Children and groups are welcome. Pets are allowed with proof of vaccination.

Reservations, fees: Reservations are recommended; contact ReserveAmerica at 800/336-3521 or reserveamerica.com. Sites are $20 per night for eight people. Credit cards are accepted. Stays are restricted to two weeks.

Directions: From U.S. 27 near Sebring, drive four miles west on County Road 634/Hammock Road to the park.

Contact: Highlands Hammock State Park, 5931 Hammock Road, Sebring, FL 33872, 863/386-6094, fax 863/386-6095, www.floridastateparks.org.

50 HIGHLAND WHEEL ESTATES RV/MOBILE HOME PARK

🏊 🛶 🚤 ♿ 🚙 ⛺

Scenic rating: 3

near Lake Jackson, in Sebring

These shady oak- and pine-dotted lots are located across from 3,000-acre Lake Jackson, where locals scuba dive, snorkel, windsurf, fish, water-ski, and swim. The lake is a spectacular sight as you drive through Sebring, and on windy days, you'll see whitecaps whipping up across the waters. Catering to snowbirds age 50 and older, many of whom have been visiting the park for more than a decade, the park is close to historic downtown Sebring. There, you'll find a small community theater, an arts complex, a library, a civic center, and a YMCA. The campground is about one mile from a mall, and not much farther from Highlands Hammock State Park.

Campsites, facilities: This adult-oriented park has 100 full-hookup RV sites with picnic tables. A heated swimming pool with therapy jets, clubhouse, horseshoes, billiards, a computer room, and winter social programs entertain campers. On the premises are restrooms, showers, a dump station, laundry facilities, and trailer rentals. Be sure to bring your own spoon and dish for the Sunday ice-cream socials. Other activities are water aerobics, arts and crafts, Bible study and church services, bunco, ladies billiards, and more. Management says the clubhouse is wheelchair-accessible. Groceries are one mile away, and a restaurant is within walking distance. Visiting children are welcome. Pets are not allowed.

Reservations, fees: Reservations are recommended. Sites are $23 per night for two people, plus $2 for each additional person. Credit cards are not accepted. Long-term rates are available.

Directions: From the corner of U.S. 27 and Hammock Road in the center of Sebring, travel west on Hammock Road for a short distance.

Contact: Highland Wheel Estates RV/Mobile Home Park, 1004 Hammock Road, Sebring, FL 33872, 863/385-6232, www.hwepark.com.

51 LAKESIDE STABLES

Scenic rating: 3

in Sebring, on Arbuckle Creek

Equestrians will like this campground, which is part of a horse stable operation. It's located on Arbuckle Creek, where you can fish or launch a canoe. But the emphasis is on horses, with breaking and training available, and mounts for sale.

Campsites, facilities: There are 10 RV sites with full hookups and a primitive tenting area. Restrooms, showers, horse stables, canoe rentals, and a dog-walk area are available. Children are welcome. Leashed pets are permitted.

Reservations, fees: Reservations are recommended. Sites are $25 per night for two people, plus $5 per extra person. Credit cards are not accepted.

Directions: From the intersection of U.S. 27 and U.S. 98 in Sebring, drive east on U.S. 98 to the park.

Contact: Lakeside Stables, 5000 U.S. 98, Sebring, FL 33876, 863/655-2252, fax 863/655-9525, www.horserentals.com/lakesidestables.html.

52 SEBRING GROVE RV RESORT

Scenic rating: 5

south of Sebring

Just 0.5 mile from Lake Jackson's swimming, fishing, and boating activities, Sebring Grove is convenient to shopping and restaurants. Planned activities, such as bingo, dinners, trips, and parties, keep guests busy. Sebring is a flourishing retirement community with one of the finest state parks in Florida nearby, Highlands Hammock State Park (see listing in this chapter). About 5 percent of the lots are occupied year-round, and the majority are rented to repeat visitors on a seasonal basis. Most people staying here are from Indiana, Michigan, Ohio, and New York.

Campsites, facilities: There are 20 full-hookup sites with 50-amp electrical service and concrete patios for overnighters in this 115-unit park. Six sites are pull-through. RVs up to 38 feet in length and slideouts can be accommodated. Lots range in size 15–32 feet wide by 38 feet deep. Restrooms, showers, laundry facilities, telephone hookups, a pool, a clubhouse, shuffleboard courts, and a dog-walk area are available. The clubhouse is wheelchair-accessible. Streets are paved. Groceries are within two miles; shops and restaurants are within one mile. Children may stay for short visits. Leashed pets are permitted; only one pet per lot.

Reservations, fees: Reservations are recommended. Sites are $25 per night for two people, plus $2 per extra person. Credit cards are not accepted. Long-term (up to six months) or seasonal stays are preferred.

Directions: From Sebring, drive south on U.S. 27 about two miles. If you pass U.S. 98, you've gone too far.

Contact: Sebring Grove RV Resort, 4105 U.S. 27 South, Sebring, FL 33870-5599, 863/382-1660, fax 863/382-2565.

53 WHISPERING PINES VILLAGE

Scenic rating: 5

in Sebring

This place is one-third mobile homes and two-thirds RV sites, but the feeling is more residential than campground. Shaded by some palms and pines, it is one of the closest places to stay near notable Highlands Hammock State Park (see listing in this chapter). The park tends to attract people for the winter, with just 55 sites available for overnighters. Some lots are occupied year-round. Most visitors hail from Indiana, Ohio, Pennsylvania, and Michigan, and they like each other so much that they hold an annual summer reunion in the northern states. Boating and fishing are possible one mile away at 3,000-acre Lake Jackson, but favorite things to do are boccie ball (lawn bowling) and shuffleboard. Many activities are planned in the recreation hall, such as professional entertainment, trips, potluck dinners, and seminars. A mall and theaters are nearby, and downtown Sebring is three miles away.

Campsites, facilities: This retiree-oriented park has 155 full-hookup RV sites with 30-amp or 50-amp electricity. About 100 have picnic tables, and 112 are drive-through. Lots range in size from 24 to 25 feet wide and 35 to 40 feet deep, accommodating a few 40-foot RVs. On the premises are restrooms, showers, laundry facilities, a wheelchair-accessible recreation room, trailer rentals, and horseshoes. Streets are paved. You will find groceries, malls, and restaurants within one mile. Children are allowed, but the park is geared toward retirees. Pets are prohibited, unless you are an overnight visitor staying with friends camped in the park.

Reservations, fees: Reservations are recommended. Sites are $30 per night for two people, plus $4 daily for each additional person. Credit cards are not accepted. Long-term rates are available.

Directions: From U.S. 27 near Sebring, drive west on County Road 634/Hammock Road for one mile to Brunn's Road. Turn right, heading north, and look for the campground 0.5 mile ahead on the left.

Contact: Whispering Pines Village, 2323 Brunn's Road, Sebring, FL 33872, 863/385-8806, www.campingfriend.com/whisperingpinesrvresort.

54 HIGHLAND OAKS RV RESORT

Scenic rating: 5

off U.S. 27 south of Sebring

Winter visitors from Canada and the United States flock to this RV park and mobile-home community in Central Florida to thaw out in the sun and get to know each other and the surrounding area. The resort doesn't have a pool, but it does have shuffleboard courts and a horseshoe pit. Fishing and waterskiing are possible at area lakes, and Highlands Hammock State Park is a short drive away—but the favorite thing to do is relax with neighbors in the sun.

Campsites, facilities: This adults-only park has 106 grassy, full-hookup RV sites with picnic tables, concrete patios, and 30-amp or 50-amp electrical service. The average site is 34 feet wide by 72 feet deep, accommodating large RVs and slideouts. Sites are a mix of shade and sunshine. Connect to the Internet in the office. On the premises are restrooms, showers, laundry facilities, a recreation room, horseshoes, and shuffleboard. There is no dump station. Management says all facilities are wheelchair-accessible. Cable TV and telephone service are available. Groceries can be purchased within five miles. One restaurant is across the road, and others are about seven miles away in town. Children are welcome only to visit park residents. Pets are permitted.

Reservations, fees: Reservations are recommended. Sites are $20.50 per night for two people, plus $2 for each extra person. Credit cards are not accepted. The maximum length of stay is six months; however, 10 percent of the resort is occupied year-round.

Directions: From the intersection of U.S. 27 and U.S. 98/State Road 66, turn onto U.S. 98 and drive about 0.25 mile. Turn left on County Road 17 North and drive about 0.5

mile. Turn left on 6th Street South and follow the paved road to the park entrance.
Contact: Highland Oaks RV Resort, 7001 Seventh Avenue West, Sebring, FL 33876, 863/655-1685, daveandsherrye@yahoo.com.

55 AVON PARK AIR FORCE RANGE

🏃🚴🛶🎣🐾⛺

Scenic rating: 9

northeast of Avon Park

Yes, this is a bombing range and training area for Air Force pilots, with 82,000 acres open for public access. That may sound like an odd destination for those who seek to escape their worries, but this remote, wooded domain of bobcats, deer, squirrels, and wild turkeys makes a pretty retreat for outdoorsy types who don't mind Port-O-Lets and cold showers. Day or night, you may see jets flying overhead as they head back and forth to the restricted areas for strafing runs and bomb practice. The size of a small county, the range encompasses everything from deep, dark forests to desert-like scrub areas subject to occasional flooding. Gnarly oaks shade the camping areas, which are big enough for most campers to find a sleeping spot away from strangers. You'll like the privacy.

Hunting season is the exception, when about 2,000 people descend on these lands for weekend hunts, collectively bagging a gaggle of turkeys (110 of them, for instance, from mid-March to mid-April 2002). The park is closed to campers during the main hunting season, principally for deer and hogs. These dates typically fall between mid-September and January, so be sure to call ahead.

Hikers can pad along a 27-mile-long section of the Florida National Scenic Trail from here. Head north, and you'll eventually reach the KICCO Wildlife Management Area (see listing in this chapter). Head south, and you'll eventually pass through South Florida Water

Management District lands to reach Bluff Hammock Road, which, on detailed maps, can be found at the Kissimmee River and S-65B Access Road. The Lake Arbuckle National Recreation Trail (16 miles long) originates at Willingham Campground, one of the three camping areas. From the Outdoor Recreation Office, a 1.2-mile boardwalk nature trail leads to the edge of Lake Arbuckle and a 30-foot observation tower. Starting at Austin Hammock Campground, the Sandy Point Wildlife Refuge Trail makes several loops adding up to 6.2 miles so you can adjust your hike to your energies and abilities. All hikers must get a permit.

Bring your own boat to fish for bass, bream, and catfish in the Kissimmee River or stocked catfish ponds. Some day-visitors simply take joyrides on designated roads through the 128 square miles that are open to the public. They just want to get a taste of a real bombing range. Don't get too excited—all you'll really see is woods, since 24,000 military-sensitive acres are off-limits to the public. Undetonated bombs have occasionally been found over the years, although today, the area has been thoroughly cleaned. Still, you are warned not to touch anything that resembles ordnance.

Campsites, facilities: Three primitive camping areas are open to the public some Friday and Saturday nights; two of the three also are open on some Sunday nights. Camping areas also are open to hunters chosen through a lottery process during limited hunting seasons. Facilities include Port-O-Lets and hand pumps to provide water for cleaning up; bring your own drinking water. All three camping areas have cold showers. Most sites have picnic tables. There are no other amenities, so bring food and all other supplies. A convenience store is two miles from the main entrance. Laundries and a restaurant are seven miles away. Children are permitted. Pets must be leashed.

Reservations, fees: Very important: Call Thursday afternoon before your weekend trip to see whether the bombing range will be open to campers that weekend; it's closed when military activities are ongoing. Hunters need to obtain a highly coveted permit by calling during February for an application. Camping costs $5 per person per weekend, or $7 per family per weekend. Credit cards are not accepted.

Directions: From the Orlando area, drive south for about one hour on U.S. 27 to the town of Avon Park, then head left (east) on Highway 64 for about 10 miles. The road dead-ends at the bombing range. A guard will direct you to the Outdoor Recreation Office, where you must purchase a permit and sign a waiver releasing the federal government from liability, should you fall into a shell hole or gun emplacement.

Contact: Outdoor Recreation, 347 RQW, DET1, OLA/CEVN, 29 South Boulevard, Avon Park Air Force Range, FL 33825-5700, 863/452-4254; or listen to a recorded message at 863/452-4119, ext. 5.

56 LAKE GLENADA RV PARK

🐟 ⇌ 🐕 🚐

Scenic rating: 3

south of Avon Park

Adults are preferred at this lakeside RV park in citrus and cattle country. You'll see huge trucks loaded with oranges driving past the park on their way to the citrus processing plants. The park has a boat ramp and access to fishing and boating on Lake Glenada. Favorite things to do are swimming in the heated pool, which has a hot tub, and participating in planned activities.

Campsites, facilities: Out of a total of 212 RV sites with full hookups, about 90 are available for overnighters. Rigs up to 36 feet long can be accommodated. Sites have concrete pads, picnic tables, and cable TV. Restrooms, showers, laundry facilities, a pool, a boat ramp, dock, recreation hall with planned activities, shuffleboard courts, and a dog-walk area are available. Children are not welcome. Small, leashed pets are permitted.

Reservations, fees: Reservations are recommended. Sites are $30–32 per night for two people, plus $4 per extra person. Credit cards are not accepted. Long-term rates are available.

Directions: From the intersection of State Road 64 and U.S. 27 in Avon Park, drive south on U.S. 27 about three miles to the park, on the east side.

Contact: Lake Glenada RV Park, 2525 U.S. 27 South, Avon Park, FL 33825, 863/453-7007, lgrv@strato.net.

ORLANDO

© MARILYN MOORE

BEST CAMPGROUNDS

❰ Biking
Trimble Park, **page 313**
Silver Lake Campground, **page 332**

❰ Families
Disney's Fort Wilderness Campground, **page 363**

❰ Best Natural Springs
Kelly Park, **page 318**
Wekiwa Springs State Park, **page 320**

❰ Most Luxurious
Disney's Fort Wilderness Campground, **page 363**
Deer Creek RV Golf Resort, **page 371**

❰ Most Unusual
Buttgenbach Mine Campground, **page 331**
Lake Como Club, **page 353**
Wallaby Ranch Flight Park, **page 369**

If you think the Orlando area is only about Walt
Disney World, think again. Florida's most popular tourist area has an abundance of outdoor things to do, and not just standing in line for the rides
at the Magic Kingdom.

Metropolitan Orlando is partly encircled by rolling hills, pretty lakes and
rivers saved from suburbia's relentless crawl. The Withlacoochee River has
miles of undeveloped cypress-lined riverbank to canoe or fish. Bicyclists
rave about the 46-mile Withlacoochee State Trail, a paved route that follows an old railroad bed through the state forest of the same name.

At Wekiwa Springs State Park, a natural spring delights swimmers,
snorkelers, and paddlers. Its run to the Wekiva River is a wonderful route to
canoe or kayak in a bit of natural Florida. Backpackers, cyclists, and hikers in
the know can find adventure at wilderness parks, state forests, and nature
preserves. There are several equestrian parks and horse trails, too.

Campgrounds in the Orlando area can be roughly divided into three
types: the Disney-oriented family destinations, the "snowbird" communities where winter visitors congregate for months at a time, and the
nature-focused campgrounds, usually state or county parks.

Most ubiquitous are the adult-preferred parks that cater to Northerners looking to get out of the cold. Here, RVers stay for six months, availing
themselves of the popular "6/6" plan, which allows them to leave their
rig on-site half the year to avoid paying high lodging taxes. Many visitors
return year after year to the same park, making life-long friendships
that they renew each autumn. It's a great lifestyle that allows retirees to
manage two "hometowns" at once.

The other easily-characterized kind of campground are those that cater to theme-park vacationers. For families bound for Disney World, camping out is a great way to save money on hotel rooms and airline tickets, particularly when there's a crowd. And it's not like they're going to miss any holiday perks. Orlando RV parks and campgrounds may have the same amenities as a resort hotel and more: Swimming pools, playgrounds, arcade rooms, fitness clubs, miniature golf courses, basketball courts and volleyball fields. If you're lucky, as my family was a few years ago, you might see a space shuttle or rocket launch from your campsite, even this far inland.

This being Orlando, you can expect local parks to turn on the family fun, with lots of things to do after you're done with Disney or Universal Studios. Dinner theaters, water sports parks, aquarium shows, and even "medieval" jousting exhibitions compete to be sure you are entertained day and night.

However, if you prefer your excitement to come from efforts made under your own power, there are several great hiking, backpacking, canoeing and kayaking areas near Orlando. Notably, in the hills around the town of Mount Dora is the highest bicycling climb in Florida. The so-called Sugar Loaf "mountain" has been ranked by "Bicycling" magazine as one of the top 100 road bike climbs in the United States, and tackling the summit of this and other nearby hills provides training to many bike clubs and racing groups.

Sooner or later, every camper has to pass through Orlando, either as a destination or on the road to somewhere else. If all you are expecting is the touristy side of Orlando, don't miss exploring all the options. You'll be surprised.

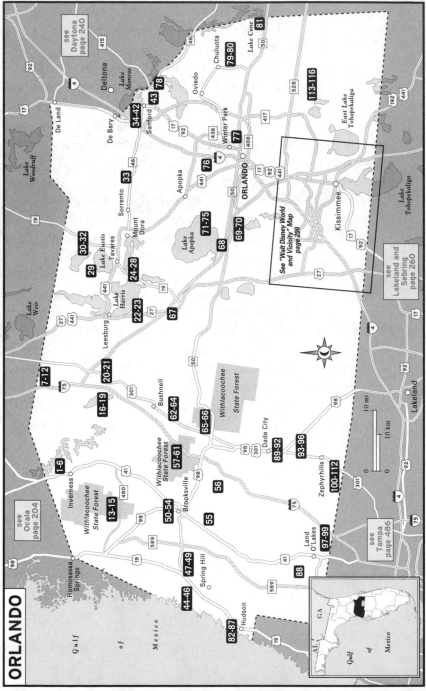

ORLANDO

see Daytona page 240

See "Walt Disney World and Vicinity" Map page 299

see Lakeland and Sebring page 260

see Ocala page 204

see Tampa page 486

© AVALON TRAVEL PUBLISHING, INC.

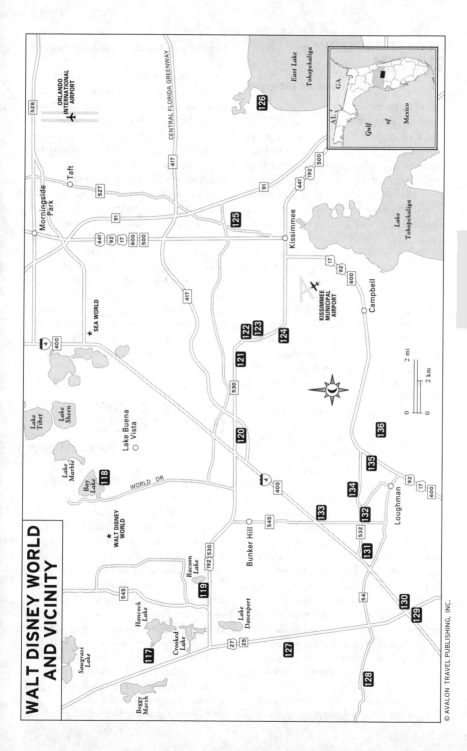

WALT DISNEY WORLD
AND VICINITY

1 POTTS PRESERVE

🚶🚴🛶⛺

Scenic rating: 9

east of Inverness

See map, page 298

When you approach this 8,500-acre property, keep an eye on the left side of the road, where you may see swallow-tailed kites soaring overhead as they search for food. Endangered scrub jays may also be found in the pockets of sandhill scrub interspersed throughout this beautiful land, with riverine swamp, freshwater marsh, Florida flatwoods, and other habitats, including former pasturelands. Other wildlife seen here includes fox squirrels, deer, turkeys, and gopher tortoises.

Hikers can use 30 miles of trails—a four-mile walk along the Withlacoochee River and a 16-mile backcountry loop. There are 12 miles of roads for horseback riders and bicycling. Formerly a ranch, this land was acquired by the state to preserve the wetlands that are so important to Florida's water purity. Canoeists and anglers can enjoy the river and paddle up to the River campsite, described below.

Three campsites are accessible by car: Oak Hammock, Equestrian, and River. Oak Hammock is probably the prettiest, set amid a cluster of the old moss-draped oaks that define backwoods Florida. The Equestrian and Oak Hammock sites have wells, but you'll need to boil or purify the water before drinking. Chemical toilets can be found at the River and Equestrian sites. Additionally, there are two backpacking camps: the Holly Tree site in the northeast portion of the property, and the Far Point site in the northwest corner.

Campsites, facilities: There are several camping areas in this 8,500-acre preserve of forest, freshwater marshes, and oak hammocks. A few sites are near the equestrian staging area, which offers a limited number of horse stalls; water is available. The other two camping areas—one near the banks of the Withlacoochee River and one in an oak hammock—do not have water. Bring water, food, and camping supplies, and pack out trash. Children are allowed, but dogs are not.

Reservations, fees: Permits are required. Contact the district by phone, or download the application from the Southwest Florida Water Management District website (www.swfwmd.state.fl.us/recguide/permitsapps.htm) and mail or fax it back. Allow 10 working days for application processing. Camping is free.

Directions: From Inverness, drive west on U.S. 41 to the intersection with State Road 44. Immediately after the intersection, continue as U.S. 41 curves around. Turn right on Turner Camp Road/County Road 581. Drive about five miles to the entrance on Dee River Road. A boat ramp at Hooty Point, where the county road dead-ends at the water, gives access to the river hiking trail and the canoe route.

Contact: Southwest Florida Water Management District, 2379 Broad Street, Brooksville, FL 34609-6899, 352/796-7211, ext. 4470 or 800/423-1476, ext. 4470, fax 352/754-6877, www.swfwmd.state.fl.us.

2 RIVERSIDE LODGE

🛶🚗🐕🏕♿🚐⛺

Scenic rating: 6

east of Inverness

See map, page 298

Want to stay in a pretty wooded setting with great fishing? Sites are nestled under tall oaks and palms next to the Withlacoochee River and near the Withlacoochee State Trail, a good route for bicycling. Bass anglers and canoeists think this area is paradise. About 10 percent of the park is occupied by year-round residents, a figure that will soon increase, since park models are for sale. Karen and Hardy van Niersen bought the park in 2003 and have been steadily converting this vintage fish camp into a resort. A small island is visible from the campground. Explorers are welcome, but cautioned against feeding the alligators—good advice anywhere you find fresh water.

Campsites, facilities: This 49-unit park has

20 RV sites with full hookups and 30/50-amp electrical service. Two sites are drive-through. Rigs up to 40 feet can be accommodated. Sites 29–33 overlook the river, and several other sites overlook a creek. Nine tents can be accommodated in a grassy area set across from the RVs. Tent site #9 is on the tip of a peninsula near a dock and fronting on the water. On the property are a bathhouse with showers (added in 2005), laundry facilities, a wheelchair-accessible recreation lodge, cabin and boat rentals, a picnic and party pavilion, a swing set, a fishing pier, and a boat ramp. You can connect to the Internet via dialup modem in the clubhouse. Planned activities are not available. A restaurant is across the street, and grocery stores are four miles away. Children are welcome. Leashed pets under 20 pounds are permitted.

Reservations, fees: Reservations are recommended. Sites are $35 per night for two people, plus $5 per extra person. Credit cards are accepted. Long-term stays are OK.

Directions: From Exit 329 on I-75, take State Road 44 west 8.5 miles toward Inverness.

Contact: Riverside Lodge, 12561 East Gulf to Lake Highway, Inverness, FL 34450, 352/726-2002, www.riversidelodgerv.com.

3 FORT COOPER STATE PARK

Scenic rating: 6

midway along the Withlacoochee Trail
See map, page 298

Set in lush hardwood hammocks, these primitive, out-in-the-woods campsites are accessible to touring bicyclists. They're not right on Lake Holathlikaha, but overlook a marsh that leads to the water. The swimming beach is on the opposite side of the lake. About 10 miles of hiking trails wind mostly through shady oak hammocks and sandhill areas. Horseback riders can't use these paths, but the Rails-to-Trails network is open to them just outside park boundaries.

This is the only campground midway along the Withlacoochee Trail bicycle and horse path; call ahead to reserve your site. The sites actually are also accessible by car; however, only organized groups are allowed to enter by motor vehicle.

Campsites, facilities: About 15 tents can be accommodated at three primitive camping areas. Each site has a picnic table, a grill, and a fire ring. The only facilities are vault toilets and running water. The park has canoe and paddleboat rentals and hiking trails. Groceries and restaurants are within three miles. Children are welcome. Pets are prohibited.

Reservations, fees: Reservations are required. Sites are $3 per night per adult, $2 per child. Credit cards are not accepted. Stays are limited to two weeks.

Directions: From Inverness, take U.S. 41 south to the city limits and follow the signs to the park.

Contact: Fort Cooper State Park, 3100 South Old Floral City, Inverness, FL 34450, 352/726-0315, fax 352/726-5959.

4 TRAIL'S END CAMP

Scenic rating: 6

near Floral City
See map, page 298

If you're lucky enough to get a campsite at this heavily wooded mobile-home park on the Withlacoochee River, you'll have views of miles of undeveloped cypress-lined riverbank. "Once you're in the campground, you are in the woods," says the management. Paddle your canoe, or fish from the dock. You're pretty much surrounded by wilderness. The river's headwaters are in northern Polk County at Green Swamp, the same place that gives rise to the Hillsborough, Ocklawaha, and Peace Rivers. The waters are colored dark by the tannins and organic acids seeping from surrounding cypress swamps and pinewoods. Within 10 minutes of the park is the

46-mile Withlacoochee bike trail, but the real attraction is access to several lakes by boat. The park tends to be favored by retirees, hunters, and anglers, many of whom leave their trailers year-round. About half the sites are available for overnighters.

Campsites, facilities: This 65-acre campground has 20 full-hookup RV sites for overnighters; one is drive-through. Ten of the sites have 30-amp electrical service, and the rest have 50-amp. The roads are not paved, and the sites are grassy. About 100 primitive tent sites are separated from the RVs, and a water source is nearby. Restrooms, showers, picnic tables, fire rings, a playground, a fishing pier, boat docks, a gun range, rental cabins, an archery range, rental canoes and rowboats, and horseshoe pits are available. A camp store sells beer, wine, and groceries. Children and leashed pets are welcome.

Reservations, fees: Reservations are not necessary. RV sites are $16 per night for four people. Credit cards are accepted. Stay as long as you wish.

Directions: From I-75, take Exit 314 and drive west on State Road 48 for 10 miles to Trail's End Road. Turn north and go four miles to the river.

Contact: Trail's End Camp, 12900 Trail's End Road, Floral City, FL 34436, 352/726-3699.

5 FLYING EAGLE
🚶 🚵 🛶 ⛺

Scenic rating: 7

along the Withlacoochee River, southeast of Inverness

See map, page 298

It's hard to believe as you look out over the mosaic of small lakes, marshes, and swamps with scattered forest uplands, but this was once a working ranch. The man who built the Flying Eagle ranch heard about a breed of cattle from England, known as Essex cattle, that were adapted to living in swamps. So, during wet periods back in the old days, you could look out over this terrain and see a bunch of cow heads sticking out above the water.

The land, managed by the water management district, is part of the Tsala Apopka chain of lakes. It's an ideal setting for hiking or horseback riding; mountain bikers can follow 13 miles of forest roads, but are strictly prohibited from off-trail use of the property. Some biking may be slow-going; while the scenery is beautiful, some sections of the unpaved roads are sugar-fine sand. Hikers will find more than 16 miles of foot trails. Fishing is best at the Mocassin Slough Bridge.

The most picturesque route is the Loop Road Trail. Turn right off the main road through the property about one-quarter mile past the entrance station. It's a serpentine road that connects a series of small "islands" that lie in the middle of a large swath of marsh. Check ahead of time if you intend to connect back with the main road and continue on toward the backpackers' campsite; the district has removed about a 100-yard section of the road near the end to improve natural water flows on the property. The best months to avoid high water and hunters are January and February. An alternative in wetter times is to stick to the main road, but it runs along a fence line, and the arrow-straight road does not foster quite the same feeling of being "out there."

Campsites, facilities: There are four primitive camping areas on this 10,720-acre preserve. Two areas, one of which is reserved for equestrian camping, are accessible by car from the front gate to the preserve. A third site is accessible only to backpackers. The fourth is for canoeists traversing the Withlacoochee River. Vehicles are prohibited, except when driving to the two sites by the front gate to offload gear. No water is available. Bring water, food, and camping supplies. Pack out trash. Camping is not allowed during hunting season. (Hunting season is scattered throughout the year and changes by a day or two each year, but generally runs September 28–October 5,

October 25–27, November 9–17, November 22–December 15, and March 15–23.) No generators, RVs, or loud music are permitted. Dogs are forbidden.

Reservations, fees: Permits are required. Contact the district by phone, or download the application from the Southwest Florida Water Management District website (www. swfwmd.state.fl.us/recguide/permitsapps. htm) and mail or fax it back. Allow 10 working days for application processing. Camping is free.

Directions: From the intersection of U.S. 41 and State Road 44 in Inverness, go one mile south on U.S. 41. Turn east on Lakeview Drive and go one block to Old Floral City Road. Drive one block south and turn left on Eden Drive. Proceed four miles east to the gate.

Contact: Southwest Florida Water Management District, 2379 Broad Street, Brooksville, FL 34609-6899, 352/796-7211, ext. 4470 or 800/423-1476, ext. 4470, fax 352/754-6877, www.swfwmd.state.fl.us.

6 MOONRISE RESORT

Scenic rating: 6

between Floral City and Inverness

See map, page 298

This campground is part of a quiet five-acre community of rental cabins and mobile homes on the shores of Tsala Apopka Lake. You can rent a boat or canoe and explore the 9,000-acre body of water, which is actually a chain of connected lakes. The park rents johnboats, larger motorboats, canoes, and paddleboats by the hour, day, or week. Cast your line from the dock, or sit on the benches and watch the water. Throughout the park are cypress trees and oaks hung with frilly Spanish moss that trails down from the branches. Pick up supplies in Floral City or in Inverness, five miles north. The Withlacoochee State Trail is nearby—the northern terminus of this 46-mile bicycling, horseback-riding, and walking trail begins in Citrus County, near Dunnellon, and travels south through Hernando County and the Withlacoochee State Forest, ending in northern Pasco County. Access points are scattered throughout the route, which parallels U.S. 41 along the northern half and the Withlacoochee River in the southern half. The trail, formerly a railroad right-of-way, is paved; equestrians use a parallel sandy path.

Campsites, facilities: The park has 14 RV sites with full hookups and 30-amp electrical service. RVs up to 30 feet long can be accommodated; note that there are no drive-through sites. Each site has a patio, and elbow room between sites averages 15 feet on either side. Nearly the entire park is occupied by year-round residents. Restrooms, showers, picnic tables, a dump station, a recreation room, laundry facilities, shuffleboard courts, horseshoe pits, a boat ramp, fishing docks, and rental cottages are on the property. Children and leashed pets are welcome.

Reservations, fees: Reservations are recommended. Sites are $25 per night for two people, plus $1 for each additional person. Credit cards are not accepted. Long-term rates are available. The minimum stay is two nights; on holiday weekends, it's three nights.

Directions: From I-75, take Exit 314 and drive west on State Road 48 for approximately 12 miles until you reach Floral City. One block before you arrive at the big intersection with U.S. 41, turn north on Old Floral City Road, which parallels U.S. 41. Drive 1.5 miles, turn east on Moonrise Lane, and continue 0.25 mile to the park entrance. Or, from the intersection of U.S. 41 and County Road 39A/ Gobbler Road, drive east for one block to Old Floral City Road, then turn south and drive one mile to Moonrise Lane.

Contact: Moonrise Resort, 8801 East Moonrise Lane, Lot 18, Floral City, FL 34436, 352/726-2553 or 800/665-6701, www .moonriseresort.com.

7 RECREATION PLANTATION RV RESORT

Scenic rating: 8

in Lady Lake

See map, page 298

As the name suggests, an active social lifestyle is what campers get in this country setting designed for adults. Events noted on the clubhouse bulletin board may range from 8:30 A.M. exercises to 7 P.M. card games or bingo in winter, so you may need your alarm clock to keep up. Some sort of activity is scheduled for most hours by the full-time winter-activities director. A trio of 18-hole golf courses is located within three miles.

About half of the campsites form concentric circles around the park's central attractions—a clubhouse, a heated pool, a spa, and sports courts. The minimum 65-by-35-foot lots tend to be sunny with token, well-kept bushes and lawns that give the park a residential atmosphere. Kids may feel out of place around the middle-aged and retiree crowd, if only because rules forbid them from using the hot tub, exercise equipment, and pool tables. Full-time residents live at about 300 lots sprinkled throughout the park.

Campsites, facilities: These 850 full-hookup sites are grassy and average 35 by 65 feet in size. All have sewer hookups, 30/50-amp electrical service, picnic tables, and Internet access. Another Internet connection is available in the clubhouse. Recreational offerings include a pool, a spa, two clubhouses (one is wheelchair-accessible), an exercise room, billiards, planned activities, shuffleboard, bocce ball (lawn bowling), tennis, horseshoes, and table tennis. Showers, restrooms, a post office, cable TV access, telephone hookups, and laundry facilities are available. Children may camp for up to two weeks at this otherwise adult-oriented park. Leashed pets are permitted but should be walked around the retention pond and attended at all times.

Reservations, fees: Reservations are suggested. Sites are $33 per night for two people, plus $4 for each additional person. Credit cards are accepted. Long-term rates are available.

Directions: From Leesburg, drive about seven miles north on U.S. 27. Turn left on County Road 466. The park is on the right, 0.5 mile west of the turnoff.

Contact: Recreation Plantation RV Resort, 609 County Road 466, Lady Lake, FL 32159, 352/753-7222 or 800/448-5646, www.recreationplantation.com.

8 BLUE PARROT CAMPING PARK

Scenic rating: 5

in Lady Lake

See map, page 298

Convenience and relaxation are the standout features at this park. Besides teeing off for free at the park's par-3, nine-hole golf course, visitors can swim in the heated pool, share potluck dinners, attend Bible studies, play bingo (in winter), learn to quilt and sew, and take part in other activities organized by a resident association.

La Plaza Grande shopping center and an RV hand-wash business are nearby, so expect a suburban experience. Most of the concrete-pad or grassy sites along the lighted, paved streets are devoted to retirees who spend months at the 80-plus-acre park. Overnighters are relegated to a small area close to County Road 25. Located in sleepy Lake County, which is marked by rolling hills and 1,400 named lakes, the camp could serve as a crash pad for bass anglers.

Campsites, facilities: All 452 full-hookup sites (17 pull-through) at this retiree-oriented park are for RVs up to 44 feet long. A golf course, a pool, billiards, a recreation room, horseshoes, shuffleboard, and social programs entertain campers. Showers, restrooms, a convenience store, a Sunday chapel, cable TV, telephone service, and laundry facilities are available. Children may stay short-term. Leashed pets must use the designated dog walks.

Reservations, fees: Reservations are recommended. Sites are $27 per night for two people, plus $2.50 for each additional person. Credit cards are accepted. Long-term rates are available.

Directions: From County Road 466/Lemon Street in Lady Lake, drive a short distance northwest on U.S. 27/441 to the cutoff for County Road 25. Take County Road 25 north to the park entrance on your right.

Contact: Blue Parrot Camping Park, 40840 County Road 25, Lady Lake, FL 32159, 352/753-2026, fax 352/753-8383, www .rvresorts.com.

⑨ SUNSHINE MOBILE HOME PARK

Scenic rating: 2

south of Lady Lake

See map, page 298

Visitors are outnumbered by residents of the 70 mobile homes at this age-55-plus park, but overnighters can join in winter activities or take a dip in the pool all the same. Activities include breakfasts, potluck dinners, card games, and Bible study. The grassy/concrete-pad RV sites are set on 11 acres about three miles due north of Lake Griffin State Park. Paddlers and bass anglers launch into 14-square-mile Lake Griffin. This growing region of Florida is characterized by lake-dotted countryside surrounded by grassy, rolling hills that were citrus groves before freezes drove the industry to warmer climes. Disney World and other Orlando-area attractions are about one hour south.

Campsites, facilities: This age-55-and-older park has 20 full-hookup RV sites (two pull-through) with picnic tables and 50-amp electric service. Lots have concrete pads set under oak trees and vary in size, but average around

20 by 70 feet. About 15 sites are available for overnight visitors. Also inside the park are 70 mobile homes. A pool, an exercise room, horseshoes, shuffleboard, winter social programs, and a wheelchair-accessible recreation hall entertain campers. Showers, restrooms, and laundry facilities are available. Children are not allowed. Leashed pets are permitted.

Reservations, fees: Reservations are suggested. Sites are $20 per night for two people, plus $2 for each additional person and $1 if you use air conditioners or electric heaters. Credit cards are not accepted. Long-term stays are OK.

Directions: From County Road 466 in the town of Lady Lake, drive south on U.S. 27/441 to Griffin View Drive. Turn left (east). The park is 0.5 mile ahead at Sunshine Boulevard.

Contact: Sunshine Mobile Home Park, 401 Sunshine Boulevard, Lady Lake, FL 32159, 352/753-2415, fax 352/753-2415.

⑩ LAKE GRIFFIN STATE PARK

Scenic rating: 8

in Fruitland Park

See map, page 298

Largemouth bass are the goal of anglers at 14-square-mile Lake Griffin, although bluegill and specks make respectable consolation prizes. Bird-watchers, on the other hand, remark that the rookery, which resounds with a cacophony of bird chatter, is their favorite part of the 500-acre park. Actually, the most unusual facet of this park may be the "floating islands." See the marsh between Lake Griffin and its uplands? Sometimes chunks break off from that marshy mat of soil and roots, and they float like icebergs toward the lake.

Traffic getting to the park can be congested. Campers sleep under oaks, and the sites are lovely. Bring mosquito repellent in summer. All sites—most sandy, some with pads—have a picnic table, a grill, and a fire ring for roasting marshmallows. As at most other state parks, campers are set apart from day-use areas, such as the 0.75-mile nature trail. Look for otters, rabbits, and raccoons during your stay. Canoeists and boaters use a ramp at the head of a 0.25-mile canal leading to Lake Griffin. Ocala National Forest is nearby.

Campsites, facilities: The 40 sites have water and 30-amp electric hookups. Ten spots have 50-amp power, and eight sites are pull-through. Each site has a picnic table, a grill, and a fire ring. On the premises are showers, restrooms, a dump station, a boat ramp, a dock, canoe rentals, a playground, a nature trail, horseshoe and volleyball areas, and laundry facilities. Three campsites, the pavilion, the restrooms, and fishing dock have wheelchair access. A restaurant, bait, and groceries are available within one mile. Children are welcome. Leashed pets are allowed.

Reservations, fees: Reservations are recommended; contact ReserveAmerica at 800/336-3521 or reserveamerica.com. Sites are $17 per night for four people. Credit cards are accepted. The maximum stay is 14 days.

Directions: From Leesburg, drive about two miles north on U.S. 441/27. The park is on the right side of the road.

Contact: Lake Griffin State Park, 3089 U.S. 441/27, Fruitland Park, FL 34731, 352/360-6760, fax 352/360-6762, www.floridastateparks.org.

11 PINE ISLAND CAMPGROUND AND FISH CAMP

Scenic rating: 3

at Lake Griffin, east of Lady Lake

See map, page 298

Bass is king at this remote retreat near the mouth of the Ocklawaha River, at the northwestern end of Lake Griffin. Bream, catfish, and crappie also lurk in the sizable lake. Owner Len Garner and Captain Joe Hammond have more than 25 years of experience

to help anglers seek out the prize that some people mount on their walls—bass. If you don't like to fish or motor around in a boat, look elsewhere for a spot to set up camp. Oaks shade each rustic campsite. About a third of the lots are occupied year-round. The park came under new ownership in mid-2005, and the park has received a facelift with paint and good cleaning.

Campsites, facilities: Thirty-three sites have full hookups, 30/50-amp electricity, and picnic tables. Ten sites are pull-through. RVs up to 45 feet long can be accommodated. The sites vary in size; Average site size is 20 by 40 feet, but some are larger. For recreation, there's a fishing guide, boat rentals, 57 covered boat stalls, a boat ramp, and campfire areas. You can even rent a pontoon boat that accommodates parties of 20. The fish-cleaning station is enclosed. No pool, shuffleboard, or other activities are offered. Boat and trailer storage is on-site. Showers, restrooms, a dump station, laundry facilities, and a camp store that sells the basics, plus bait and tackle, are available. Children are welcome. Pets must be leashed.

Reservations, fees: Reservations are not taken. Sites are $35 per night. Credit cards are accepted. Long-term rates are available.

Directions: From U.S. 27 in Lady Lake, drive east on County Road 466/Lemon Street to the stop sign. Turn left and follow Lake Griffin Road about five miles to the campground entrance.

Contact: Pine Island Campground and Fish Camp, 6808 Lake Griffin Road, Lady Lake, FL 32159, 352/753-2972.

12 MORGAN'S MOBILE HOME PARK AND FISH CAMP

Scenic rating: 2

on Lake Griffin, in eastern Fruitland Park

See map, page 298

At this 15-acre, laid-back RV park and fish camp on Lake Griffin, anglers of all ages

© MARILYN MOORE

RV parked by a lake

launch their boats to pursue bass and bream or to spot alligators, herons, and the occasional otter. Many visitors here are locals who rent by the week, or out-of-towners who have relatives in the immediate area.

Campsites, facilities: All 58 full-hookup sites have 30-amp electrical service. Six spots are drive-through. About 20 percent are occupied by year-round residents. Recreation options include a boat ramp and dock, sightseeing boat tours, and a recreation room. It's one of the few marinas on the lake that sell gasoline, the owners say. Showers, restrooms, a dump station, bait and tackle, and laundry facilities are available. You can access the Internet on a limited basis in the office. A camp store sells snacks and many varieties of alligator souvenirs. Groceries can be purchased one block from here. A restaurant is one mile away. Children are permitted, but the park is geared toward retirees. Small, leashed pets are allowed.

Reservations, fees: Reservations are not nec-

essary. Sites are $18 per night for two people, plus $3 for each additional person. Credit cards are not accepted. Long-term rates are available.

Directions: From the intersection of U.S. 27 and U.S. 441 in Leesburg, drive north on U.S. 27. At the third stoplight, turn right. The park entrance is 1.5 miles ahead on Picciola Road.

Contact: Morgan's Mobile Home Park and Fish Camp, 04056 Picciola Road, Fruitland Park, FL 34731, 352/787-4916.

13 TILLIS HILL

Scenic rating: 9

in the Withlacoochee State Forest Citrus Tract, south of Inverness

See map, page 298

Both families and organized equestrian groups enjoy this campground, which serves as a base camp for dozens of miles of horseback-riding trails through the sandy, rolling terrain of the state forest. Ride for the day on forest roads or on trails weaving through the pinewoods, which sprawl over 41,000 acres. (The Citrus Tract is the largest of the five sections of the Withlacoochee State Forest.) There's also a two-day horseback trail with a primitive camping zone, called Perryman Place, that can accommodate 100 people. Be sure to bring water, because there are no facilities. Organized groups must have a permit for all activities in the forest.

Campsites, facilities: Targeted to horseback riders, this state forest campground has 37 sites with water, 50-amp electricity, picnic tables, grills, and fire rings. There's also a 20-stall horse stable, a dining hall with a kitchen, a large open-air picnic shelter, and a barbecue pit. Restrooms, showers, and a dump station are provided. The bathhouse is wheelchair-accessible. Groceries are 20 miles away; gas and convenience stores are within 13 miles. Children are welcome, but pets are prohibited.

Reservations, fees: Reservations are required.

Sites are $13 per night for five people, plus $3 for each horse stall. The dining hall can be rented for a fee, depending on the size of the group. Credit cards are not accepted.

Directions: From Inverness, drive 10 miles south on U.S. 41 to County Road 480. Turn right and drive eight miles west. Turn north on Forest Road 13 and drive three miles to the campground.

Contact: Withlacoochee State Forest Recreation Visitors Center, 15003 Broad Street, Brooksville, FL 34601, 352/754-6896, 352/344-4238 (reservations), or 352/754-6777 (fire dispatch), www.fl-dof.com.

14 HOLDER MINE

Scenic rating: 9

in the Withlacoochee State Forest Citrus Tract, south of Inverness

See map, page 298

Holder Mine is so named because there were once phosphate mines in the area—a pit created by the mining operation remains near the campground, which offers oversized sites in a pine forest. There's deep water at the bottom of the pit, and curious anglers have been known to catch fish here, although swimming is prohibited and probably not a good idea. This is also a staging area for hikers on the Florida National Scenic Trail (46 miles long) and for horseback riders exploring the forest. A watering area for horses is provided, as is a place to tie them up while riders use the restrooms. The forest roads are also available for bicyclists, though some routes tend to be sandy.

Campsites, facilities: You'll find 27 campsites with water, 50-amp electrical service, picnic tables, grills, and fire rings. Rigs up to 40 feet long are welcome. Wheelchair-accessible restrooms, showers, and a dump station are available. Groceries are within seven miles. Children are welcome. Leashed pets are allowed.

Reservations, fees: Reservations are not taken. Sites are $13 per night for five people. Credit cards are not accepted. This campground is open only on weekends (noon Friday–noon Monday) and holidays.

Directions: From the junction of State Road 44 and State Road 581 on the west side of Inverness, drive five miles south on State Road 581 to the campground entrance.

Contact: Withlacoochee State Forest Recreation Visitors Center, 15003 Broad Street, Brooksville, FL 34601, 352/754-6896 or 352/754-6777 (fire dispatch), www.fl-dof.com.

15 MUTUAL MINE RECREATION AREA

Scenic rating: 9

in the Withlacoochee State Forest Citrus Tract, south of Inverness

See map, page 298

Self-contained campers are well-separated from their neighbors in this secluded pine flatwood forest that's remote enough for escaping urban traffic and noise. The Florida National Scenic Trail can be accessed by walking 1.5 miles west of the campground. An abandoned mining pit is nearby; most of the water has leached out, and it's only about 10 feet deep. Nonetheless, swimming is prohibited. You'll have to pick up supplies in Inverness, because there's not much in the way of civilization around here.

Campsites, facilities: There are 13 sites with water, picnic tables, grills, and fire rings. Flush toilets are available, but there are neither showers nor electricity. The sites are gravel or grassy; none are drive-through. Rigs up to 40 feet long can be accommodated. A dump station and a youth camping group are also on-site. Children are welcome. Pets and alcohol are prohibited.

Reservations, fees: Reservations are not taken. Sites are $10 per night for five people. Credit cards are not accepted. This campground is open only on weekends (noon Friday–noon Monday) and holidays.

Directions: From the junction of State Road 44 and State Road 581 on the west side of Inverness, drive eight miles south on State Road 581 to the campground entrance on the west side of the highway.

Contact: Withlacoochee State Forest Recreation Visitors Center, 15003 Broad Street, Brooksville, FL 34601, 352/754-6896 or 352/754-6777 (fire dispatch), www.fl-dof .com.

16 IDLEWILD LODGE

Scenic rating: 5

at Lake Panasoffkee, southwest of Wildwood

See map, page 298

A four-acre, lakeside campground, Idlewild Lodge has lots of trees and borders a wooded area. The main activity here is fishing on Lake Panasoffkee. The whole region is pretty laid-back, and this small campground is located at the even quieter north end of the lake. The RV sites, with 12-by-30-foot concrete pads, are set behind 10 cottages that front the solar heated pool. Don't forget to pack your swimsuit; park rules forbid swimmers to wear shorts or cutoffs.

Campsites, facilities: Ten sites are available for RVs and tents; around five are usually available for overnighters. Hookups include sewer and 30/50-amp electrical service. Park on concrete pads under the oaks. On the premises are restrooms, showers, laundry facilities, a dump station, some picnic tables, rental efficiencies, bait, tackle, a boat ramp, a pool, horseshoes, basketball, shuffleboard, a camp store with snacks, and boat rentals. Groceries and restaurants are about two miles away. Children and small leashed pets are permitted.

Reservations, fees: Reservations are recommended. Sites are $23 per night for two people, plus $5 for each extra person. Credit

cards are not accepted for overnight stays. Long-term stays are OK.

Directions: From I-75 at Exit 321, head west on County Road 470 for about five miles. Turn right onto County Road 400. The campground is one mile ahead.

Contact: Idlewild Lodge, 4110 County Road 400, Lake Panasoffkee, FL 33538, 352/793-7057, www.idlewildlodge.com.

17 PANA VISTA LODGE

Scenic rating: 5

at the Outlet River, southwest of Wildwood

See map, page 298

You'll find this charmingly rustic park at the mouth of what's known as the Outlet River, a stream that connects the popular boating and bass-fishing waters of Lake Panasoffkee to the Withlacoochee River. The park sees all kinds of visitors: overnighters, snowbirds, and Floridians who leave their rigs on-site to use on the weekends. About half the park is occupied by year-round residents. Fishing for bass, perch, and shellcrackers is the favorite occupation, and competitive types can participate in the occasional fishing contest.

Campsites, facilities: Twenty primitive tent sites are set apart from the 70 full-hookup RV sites, which have picnic tables and 30/50-amp service. Six sites are drive-through. On the premises are restrooms, showers, a dump station, grills, fire rings, rental cabins, mobile homes, a bait and tackle shop, a boat ramp, and boat and canoe rentals. Groceries and restaurants are within two miles. Children are welcome. Small leashed pets are permitted.

Reservations, fees: Reservations are recommended. Sites are $20 per night for two people, plus $1 for each additional person. Credit cards are accepted. Long-term stays are OK.

Directions: From I-75 at Exit 321, drive almost five miles west on County Road 470. Turn right at County Road 421 (you'll see a sign for the lodge).

Contact: Pana Vista Lodge, 3417 County Road 421, Lake Panasoffkee, FL 33538, 352/793-2061, fax 352/793-5683, www .panavista.qsy.com.

18 TURTLEBACK RV RESORT
🏊 ⛴ 🚣 🐕 🎣 👤 ♿ 🚐 ⛺

Scenic rating: 6

off I-75, southwest of Wildwood

See map, page 298

Set on a creek that leads to the popular bass-fishing waters of 27-square-mile Lake Panasoffkee, this wooded park offers campsites that are grassy and mostly shaded for its clientele, which tends to stay for winter. Fish from the dock or from a boat. If you don't own a boat or a canoe, you can rent one here. For visitors who couldn't care less about fishing, try the heated pool or year-round planned activities, such as bingo games, dancing, and potluck dinners. Most folks are over 55 and repeat visitors from places like Michigan and Indiana.

Campsites, facilities: There are 138 RV sites (100 full-hookup, 15 pull-through) in this park, which is 70 percent occupied year-round. Fifteen sites have 50-amp service. Sites vary in size and are laid out irregularly in the woods, not subdivision-style in a row. There is room for about 20 tents in a separate primitive area. Each developed site has a picnic table. A pool, boat and canoe rentals, a playground, a recreation hall, pool tables, horseshoes, two shuffleboard courts, and a nature trail are on the premises. Restrooms, showers, a dump station, laundry facilities, LP gas sales, rental cabins, a boat ramp, telephone service, cable TV, and social activities are available. There's a wireless Internet connection available near the office. Management says all facilities are wheelchair-accessible. Groceries and restaurants are within one mile. Children and pets are permitted.

Reservations, fees: Reservations are recommended. Sites are $28 per night for two people, plus $5 for each additional person.

Credit cards are not accepted. Long-term stays are OK.

Directions: From I-75 at Exit 321, head west for 0.75 mile to the campground on the left.

Contact: Turtleback RV Resort, 190 County Road 488, Lake Panasoffkee, FL 33538, 352/793-2501 or 800/887-8525.

19 COUNTRYSIDE RV PARK
🐕 ♿ 🚐 ⛺

Scenic rating: 5

off I-75, southwest of Wildwood

See map, page 298

This park in a quiet, rural area is good for a quick stopover if you're traveling on I-75. It's also not far from the local focus of interest: Lake Panasoffkee, or any of the creeks leading to the watery domain of anglers and boaters. To paddle a 10-mile stretch of the nearby Withlacoochee River, try renting a canoe from Nobleton Boat Rentals (352/796-7176 or 800/783-5284). During the winter, park activities include bingo, potluck dinners, cards, music around the bonfire, horseshoes, shuffleboard, and a coffeehouse. Oak trees provide some shade and atmosphere. About half the sites are occupied year-round. Most visitors are retirees from the Midwest and Canada.

Campsites, facilities: The camp has 64 full-hookup sites, of which 15 are pull-through (more if the park is not crowded). Almost all have 30/50-amp electrical outlets; five have just 30-amp. Five grassy, level spots are available for tents. On the premises are restrooms, showers, a dump station, a laundry room, a recreation hall, and a game room. Firewood is available, and a boat ramp accessing the Withlacoochee River and Lake Panasoffkee is just three miles away. Management says all buildings are wheelchair-accessible. Campground roads are black-topped. Groceries and restaurants are about two miles away. Children are welcome on a short-term basis. Pets are allowed.

Reservations, fees: Reservations are recommended. Sites are $25 per night for two people, plus $2 for each additional person and $2 for electricity. Credit cards are not accepted. Long-term stays are OK for adults.

Directions: From I-75 at Exit 321, drive west on County Road 470. In less than one mile, bear left on County Road 489, which leads to the park.

Contact: Countryside RV Park, 741 County Road 489, Lake Panasoffkee, FL 33538, 352/793-8103, countrysidervpark@cfl.rr.com.

20 WILDWOOD KOA

Scenic rating: 6

off I-75, in Wildwood

See map, page 298

Perhaps the best thing about this KOA is that it's right off the interstate, making it easier to get to Disney-area attractions, Ocala National Forest, or the Withlacoochee State Forest. If you're tired of the pool, try the miniature golf course or hot tub. Only 2 percent of the occupants stay here year-round; the rest are through-travelers and seasonal visitors.

Campsites, facilities: There are 108 full-hookup sites (76 pull-through, 20 with 50-amp service). Each site has a picnic table. RVs up to 45 feet long can be accommodated on sites that average 52 by 21 feet. Tent sites are set in a big area with no hookups. On the premises are restrooms, showers, a dump station, a pool, a hot tub, a playground, miniature golf, horseshoes, shuffleboard, a camp store with limited groceries, and laundry facilities. Firewood is available. Restrooms and the recreation hall are wheelchair-accessible. Restaurants are located within walking distance; a grocery store is three miles away. Pets and children are allowed.

Reservations, fees: Reservations are recommended. Sites are $33–48 per night for two people, plus $3 for each additional person. Credit cards are accepted. Long-term stays are OK.

Directions: From I-75 at Exit 329, drive 300 yards east on State Road 44.

Contact: Wildwood KOA, 882 East State Road 44, Wildwood, FL 34785, 352/748-2774 or 800/562-3272 (reservations only), fax 352/748-6832, www.floridawildwoodkoa.com.

21 LAKE DEATON RV PARK

Scenic rating: 3

at Lake Deaton, east of Wildwood

See map, page 298

At this wooded adult park, some campers fish in 1.5-mile-wide Lake Deaton or head for three major golf courses nearby. Others like to bicycle down the backroads to Wildwood. If you don't have any fishing luck at Lake Deaton, try a more noted bass-fishing spot—Lake Okahumpka—on the other side of State Road 44. This campground is favored by snowbirds looking for a quiet, out-of-the-way RV park, somewhat isolated from The Villages, a huge retirement community that is being built nearby. About a fourth of the campground is open to overnight visitors.

Campsites, facilities: This retiree-oriented park offers 81 full-hookup RV sites (two pull-through). Lots are 20 by 45 feet and vary from grassy to paved surfaces. On the premises are restrooms, showers, a dump station, a boat ramp, a dock, a clubhouse, horseshoes, laundry facilities, and wireless Internet access. Restrooms and the clubhouse have wheelchair-accessible ramps. Groceries and restaurants are within six miles. Children are permitted only for two weeks. Two small pets are allowed.

Reservations, fees: Reservations are recommended. Sites are $22 per night for two people, plus $2 for each additional person. Credit cards are not accepted. Long-term stays are OK.

Directions: From I-75 at Exit 329, drive eight miles east on State Road 44. Turn left onto State Road 44A and then make an immediate right turn onto County Road 146 and proceed about two miles to the park.

Contact: Lake Deaton RV Park, 4855 County Road 146, Wildwood, FL 34785, 352/748-2397, www.lakedeatonrvpark.com.

22 HOLIDAY TRAVEL RESORT

Scenic rating: 9

in Leesburg

See map, page 298

Indoor pools are rare at Florida camping parks, but here adult swimmers can float on their backs and gaze up at a blue sky through a row of skylights in a modern, bright-white building, or peer out the broad glass doors to see RVs parked in the distance. Outdoors, another pool is open to kids, as well as adults. This 200-plus-acre park is massive: Beyond a security gate, the paved park roads lead to a sprawling resort with 935 sites, of which 185 sites are for short-term campers. The rest are for RVs planning to stay a while. A social director plans activities for not one, but four, recreational buildings. Boaters can access Lake Harris from here.

A retired and semi-retired crowd is targeted by management, but kids can take advantage of the miniature golf course and other amenities by camping short-term. Bring your own boat to launch from a campground ramp into a canal leading to the bass-fishing waters of Lake Harris. A nine-hole chip-and-putt golf course has artificial turf. Palms, native pines, and other trees lend shade to portions of the park, but several gravel or grassy RV sites bear the brunt of the sun's forceful rays. Only 16 percent of occupants live here year-round, though the park has committed about 80 percent of its space to long-term seasonal visitors.

Campsites, facilities: Tenters may only use the park June 1–October 31. There are 185 full-hookup, pull-through sites with 30-amp electrical service for RVs up to 40 feet long. All sites have picnic tables. Another 750 sites are set aside for long-term or seasonal stays, and these have 30/50-amp service. RV storage is available in the off-season. A chip-and-putt golf course, a miniature golf course, two pools, four recreation rooms, a playground, a hot tub, billiards, a softball field, eight horseshoe pits, 14 shuffleboard courts, four lighted tennis courts, two volleyball courts, and winter social programs entertain campers. Showers, restrooms, a marina, a boat ramp, 210 boat slips, a dock, a dump station, groceries, bait and tackle, laundry facilities, propane gas, and a poolside restaurant are available. A wireless Internet connection is available in one of the rec halls. Groceries are within one mile in Leesburg. An activities director organizes live music, the wood shop, ceramics, and T-shirt painting. Church services and a post office are also on-site. The recreation buildings and showers are wheelchair-accessible. Children may camp up to two weeks at this otherwise adult-oriented park. Leashed pets must use the designated dog walk.

Reservations, fees: Reservations are recommended. Sites are $34 per night for two people, plus $3 per extra person and $2 for cable TV. Credit cards are accepted. Long-term rates are available.

Directions: From Leesburg, drive south on U.S. 27 for three miles. Turn west at County Road 33 and proceed one mile to the park.

Contact: Holiday Travel Resort, 28229 County Road 33, Leesburg, FL 34748, 352/787-5151 or 800/428-5334, fax 352/787-1052, www.holidaytravelresort.com.

23 RIDGECREST RV RESORT

Scenic rating: 6

south of Leesburg

See map, page 298

Half of 30-acre Ridgecrest RV Park is devoted to retirees in mobile homes, and the other half is set up for RV campers age 55 and up. The result is a residential feel at this park, located about two miles from the bass-fishing waters of Lake Harris. Some campsites are grassy, and others have concrete pads. A January antiques fair and a March art festival entertain folks in the city of Leesburg, but some overnighters may be more interested in Disney World, which is 36 miles away. Most visitors are repeat campers who come back year after year.

Campsites, facilities: There are 155 full-hookup RV sites (10 pull-through), of which 145 have 50-amp electrical service. Some sites have picnic tables. Lots average 25 by 40 feet, with a mix of grassy and concrete slab surfaces. A heated pool, a hot tub, a recreation hall, shuffleboard, a library, a camp circle for gatherings, winter social programs, a game room, and an exercise room entertain campers. Showers, restrooms, a dump station, rental park models, telephone hookups, propane, and laundry facilities are available. You'll find groceries one mile away and a restaurant within five miles. A golf course is next door. Children are allowed but not encouraged. Pets under 20 pounds are permitted.

Reservations, fees: Reservations are recommended. Sites are $25 per night for two people, plus $2 for each additional person. Credit cards are not accepted. Long-term stays are OK.

Directions: From Leesburg, travel five miles south on U.S. 27 to the park entrance.

Contact: Ridgecrest RV Resort, 26125 U.S. 27 South, Leesburg, FL 34748, 352/787-1504.

24 TRIMBLE PARK

Scenic rating: 6

by Lake Beauclaire, near Mount Dora

See map, page 298   **BEST (**

Set beside serene Beauclaire and Carlton Lakes, this 71-acre, county-run park is well-removed from the hustle and bustle of Orlando. Technically located in the town of Tangerine (despite the Mount Dora address), it's geared toward locals, but vacationers passing through are welcome to set up camp at the grassy sites

shaded by oak trees. Bird-watching and picnicking are popular pursuits, and fishing is possible from lakeside docks. A short nature trail provides about 15 minutes of diversion for hikers, threading through a forest studded with moss-covered oaks. Birds you may see include bald eagles, osprey, woodpeckers and hawks. The hills around Mount Dora area are well-known for road biking and feature several steep climbs.

Campsites, facilities: All 15 sites have 30-amp electricity, picnic tables, grills, and fire rings. Two sites are drive-through. Trees and plants separate the sites from each other. Big rigs are welcome. There are no sewer hookups. On the premises are restrooms, showers, a dump station, a boat ramp, and a playground. The bathhouses are wheelchair-accessible. Groceries, restaurants, and laundry facilities are a three-mile drive away in Mount Dora. Children are welcome. Pets and alcohol are prohibited.

Reservations, fees: Reservations are recommended. Telephone reservations are not accepted; you must make them in person at the park. Sites are $8–18 per night. Credit cards are not accepted. Stays are limited to 14 days.

Directions: From Apopka, head north on U.S. 441 about seven miles. Turn left onto Earl Wood Road, which will turn into Trimble Park Road. The campground is two miles ahead.

Contact: Trimble Park, 5802 Trimble Park Road, Mount Dora, FL 32757, 352/383-1993, http://parks.orangecountyfl.net.

25 LAKE HARRIS RESORT

Scenic rating: 7

near Lake Harris south of Tavares

See map, page 298

This park bills itself as a luxury golf, marina, and RV resort community. About half the campsites back onto a par-3, nine-hole golf course that overlooks tree-lined Lake Harris.

The lake provides both a pretty backdrop for golfers and fertile fishing grounds for anglers seeking bass and catfish. The blue waters are reachable by boat via a canal from the campground boat ramp. Other amenities include a 120-slip marina and dry storage for 160 boats, a six-unit hotel, villa rentals, park models, and a post office. About 10 percent of the park is occupied by full-time residents. Most visitors are over 55, though in the summertime, you may find some children staying here.

Expect plenty of sunshine, although there are a few palm and oak trees to frame the view of the lake. Some of the pricier sites overlook the golf course and Lake Harris. West of the golf course are the heated pool and recreation hall, where volunteers organize potluck dinners, worship services, coffee klatches, and other entertainment. Nearby is historic Mount Dora, home to antiques shops and good restaurants. Disney World is about 45 miles away.

Campsites, facilities: All 330 full-hookup sites are for RVs up to 40 feet long. Forty-five sites have 50-amp service. Some sites are grassy; others have concrete pads. Recreation options include a nine-hole, par-3 golf course, a pool, horseshoes, shuffleboard, two activity lodges, and organized events. Showers, restrooms, a boat ramp, a 120-slip marina, park-model rentals, a small motel, a dump station, propane gas, and laundry facilities are available. Internet access is available in the library/mail-room building near the pool. Most of the park is accessible to wheelchairs, and streets are paved. Children under age 16 must be adult-supervised at the pool. Leashed, attended pets are permitted.

Reservations, fees: Reservations are recommended. Sites are $32–40 per night for two people, plus $10 per extra person. Credit cards are accepted. Long-term rates are available.

Directions: From Tavares, drive 2.5 miles south on State Road 19/Duncan Drive to the campground entrance on your right.

Contact: Lake Harris Resort, 29115 Eichelberger Road, Tavares, FL 32778, 352/343-1233 or 800/254-9993, www.lakeharris resort.com.

26 HOLIDAY MOBILE PARK

Scenic rating: 2

at Lake Eustis, in Tavares

See map, page 298

Campers are outnumbered by residents living in the 40 RV spaces and 159 mobile homes, leaving a handful of sunny, gravel lots for short-term stays. At least in winter, boat slips are hard to come by at the marina. Nearly the entire park is filled with full-timers or repeat visitors who have been coming here for two decades.

Campsites, facilities: This age-55-and-up park has full-hookup sites with 30-amp electrical service for RVs up to 35 feet long; three are drive-through. A pool, a clubhouse, shuffleboard, a lakeside picnic area, and a jam-packed activity schedule entertain campers. Showers, restrooms, a marina, a dump station, and laundry facilities are available. Shopping and restaurants are within walking distance, though many visitors ride their bikes. Children are allowed to visit. Pets are prohibited.

Reservations, fees: Reservations are recommended. Sites are $20 per night for two people. Credit cards are not accepted. Long-term rates are available.

Directions: From the intersection of State Road 19/Duncan Drive and U.S. 441/Burleigh Boulevard in Tavares, continue northeast on U.S. 441 for about one mile to the RV park.

Contact: Holiday Mobile Park, 561 East Burleigh Boulevard, Tavares, FL 32778, 352/343-2300.

27 PALM GARDENS

Scenic rating: 4

at the Dead River, north of Tavares

See map, page 298

Boating and fishing are the pursuits at this tree-dotted, over-55 mobile-home and marina community on the Dead River, linking you to a chain of lakes. If you don't bring your own watercraft, rent one here ($50 and up per half-day for a 14-footer, or $100 per half-day for a 21-foot pontoon boat). Tour the Dead River, which flows for about two miles before joining seven-mile-long Lake Eustis, and check out the bigger fishing waters of Lake Harris. Indeed, boaters and anglers who stay at these paved RV spots can explore thousands of acres of water, including Little Lake Harris and the Dora Canal, which leads to Lake Dora. Mount Dora's antiques shops, boutiques, and many restaurants are close by. Disney World is about 45 miles away. About 20 percent of the park is occupied year-round, and about 100 lots are taken by mobile homes.

Campsites, facilities: The park offers 20 pull-through RV sites with full hookups and 30-amp electrical service. Lots vary in size, but some can accommodate RVs up to 40 feet long. A camp circle for gatherings, showers, a dump station, restrooms, 14 rental cottages, bait, tackle, laundry facilities, snacks, a boat dock, boat rentals, a restaurant, and a lounge are available. The recreation room is available only to mobile-home owners, not RV visitors. Children are welcome. Leashed pets are permitted in the camping area but not the rental cottages.

Reservations, fees: Reservations are advised. Sites are $20 per night for two people, plus $5 for each additional person. Credit cards are accepted. Long-term rates are available.

Directions: From Tavares, drive one mile north on U.S. 441 to the park entrance on the right.

Contact: Palm Gardens, 11801 U.S. 441, Tavares, FL 32778, 352/343-2024, fax 352/342-5516, www.palmgardensmarina.com.

28 WOODS-N-WATER TRAILS RV COMMUNITY

Scenic rating: 4

on Lake Saunders, west of Mount Dora

See map, page 298

A gazebo sits at a point stretching into tree-lined Lake Saunders, where boaters from the 17-acre adult park can tool around. From another nearby point, picnickers can look onto the calm, one-square-mile lake. Campers tend to spend months at this country-atmosphere community, so it may be difficult to get a reservation if you wait to call November 1–March 15. About half the park is occupied year-round. Although Disney World and other Orlando-area attractions are about one hour to the south, Floridians familiar with this region and the February Mount Dora Art Festival think of two other words whenever Mount Dora is mentioned: "antiques" and "art."

Campsites, facilities: This adults-only park has 140 grassy, full-hookup RV sites with concrete patios and driveways. Both 30-amp and 50-amp sites are offered. RVs up to 40 feet long and slideouts can be accommodated at the roomy 40- by 60-foot lots. Twenty-five sites are available for overnighters. For recreation, there's a pool, horseshoes, shuffleboard and boccie ball (lawn bowling) courts, volleyball, a nature walk, a boat ramp, and an activities hall with volunteer-organized activities such as line dancing, dinners, quilting, and craft-making for charities. Once a month, all the men cook breakfast for everyone. Showers, restrooms, a dump station, and laundry facilities are available. The clubhouse and restrooms are wheelchair-accessible. Children are permitted with overnight campers or those staying less than two weeks. Kids should be supervised at all times. Leashed pets are permitted at designated campsites at the park's northern end and must use the bordering dog walk.

Reservations, fees: Reservations are required. Sites are $25 per night, plus $2 for each extra person. Credit cards are not accepted. Long-term rates are available.

Directions: From Eustis, exit on U.S. 441 south to State Road 19A. At Bay Road, turn right and drive 0.25 mile to the park.

Contact: Woods-n-Water Trails RV Community, 1325 North Bay Road, Mount Dora, FL 32757, 352/735-1009, www.woods-n-water-trails.com.

29 HAINES CREEK RV VILLAGE

Scenic rating: 5

on Haines Creek, east of Leesburg

See map, page 298

A campground gazebo and boardwalk overlook Haines Creek, and boaters can tie up at a 650-foot dock. On the banks, anglers try to snag bream and other fish—as do a few long-legged wading birds at creekside. Paved, lighted streets curve past gravel and grassy campsites, a few sporting RVs with attached screen patios. Although you technically could take day trips to Disney World or other Orlando-area attractions farther south, that isn't the focus of this relaxed lake region, where the action revolves around boating, fishing, and, to a lesser extent, canoeing. Tree-lined Haines Creek leads west to Lake Griffin and east to Lake Eustis, and anglers can take advantage of the camp's private docks and boat ramp to get to bass country. About half the park is occupied long-term. Guests run the clubhouse, and they have decided on "lights off" at 9 P.M.

Campsites, facilities: RVers can choose from 40 of 86 full-hookup sites (one is pull-through). The rest of the lots have park models on them. Each RV site is spacious enough to park an extra car or boat, and has a picnic table. Almost all spots have 50-amp service. The facility includes a boat ramp, private docks, horseshoes, and a recreation hall. Showers, restrooms, a dump station, and laundry facilities are available. The restrooms, recreation hall, and laundry room are accessible to wheelchairs. Groceries and bait can be purchased across the street. Restaurants are three miles away. Most areas of the park are wheelchair-accessible. Roads are paved. Children and guests are welcome for up to one month. Leashed pets are permitted.

Reservations, fees: Reservations are recommended. Sites are $22–25 per night for two people, plus $1 for each additional person and $1 for pets. Credit cards are not accepted. Senior citizens are welcome to stay long-term.

Directions: From U.S. 27 in Leesburg, drive south on U.S. 441 about four miles. At the traffic signal, turn left onto County Road 44. Drive five miles and turn left into the campground before you reach the Haines Creek bridge.

Contact: Haines Creek RV Village, 10121 County Road 44 East, Leesburg, FL 34788, 352/728-5939, fax 352/728-5798.

30 SOUTHERN PALMS RV RESORT

Scenic rating: 7

in northern Eustis

See map, page 298

In summer, families stake out the grassy campsites and two swimming pools at this 100-plus-acre park, part of the Manufactured Homes Communities chain. In winter, retired Northerners predominate, attracted by bingo, pancake breakfasts, and other entertainment. Lighted, paved streets lead past the quite sunny RV sites, where mowed lawns and, in some cases, trailer skirts lend a residential touch. A handful of camping spots are near a pond where visitors catch minnows to use for bait at bass lakes found 10 minutes away in Tavares. Disney World and other Orlando-area attractions are about one hour south. Bring an umbrella or hat. Although pines and palms are scattered around the park, they provide relatively little shade. The park also has 320 park model homes.

Campsites, facilities: All 952 full-hookup sites have 30-amp or 50-amp electrical services. RVs up to 42 feet long can be accommodated. Sites are level and grassy, ranging in size from 20 by 40 feet to 40 by 60 feet. Three clubhouses, two pools, two hot tubs, shuffleboard, horseshoes, boccie ball (lawn bowling), a wireless Internet network, and winter social programs provide recreation. An activities director organizes shows, painting classes, choirs, and many other things to do. Showers, restrooms, a dump station, cable TV, telephone hookups, exercise rooms, and three laundry facilities are available. Within one mile are groceries, bait, and restaurants. Most areas are wheelchair-accessible. Children are welcome. Leashed pets are permitted.

Reservations, fees: Reservations are recommended. Sites are $34 per night for two people, plus $5 for each additional person. Credit cards are accepted. Long-term stays are the norm.

Directions: From State Road 44/Orange Avenue in Eustis, turn north on State Road 19/Grove Street. In about 0.5 mile, veer left onto County Road 44 and follow it nearly 0.5 mile. The park is on the right before the intersection with County Road 452.

Contact: Southern Palms RV Resort, 1 Avocado Lane, Eustis, FL 32726, 352/357-8882 or 800/277-9131, fax 352/357-2155, www.southernpalmsrv.com.

31 LAKESIDE RV PARK

Scenic rating: 6

on Lake Smith, south of Umatilla

See map, page 298

Although Lake Smith isn't large enough to appear on a state map, the bass anglers who set up camp here (mainly retirees) don't seem to mind. About 60 percent of the sites in this park are occupied year-round. Visitors hail from Florida and the Northeast, and their favorite activities are boating, fishing, and shopping at local flea markets. To the south, Eustis hosts a folk festival in December, a jazz festival in March, and a Lake County Fair in April. Disney World and other Orlando-area attractions are about an hour's drive south.

Campsites, facilities: This age-55-plus park offers 50 full-hookup RV sites (20 pull-through). Each site has a picnic table. Half the roomy sites (40 by 60 feet) have 50-amp electrical service; the rest have 30-amp. About half the park is taken up with park models and full-timers. A pool, a hot tub, a recreation hall, and winter social programs entertain campers. Showers, restrooms, a dock, a boat ramp, a dump station, firewood, and laundry facilities are available. Management says all areas are wheelchair-accessible. Streets are paved. Groceries, bait, and a restaurant are located within 1.5 miles. Children are allowed to visit. Pets are prohibited.

Reservations, fees: Reservations are recommended. Sites are $20 per night for two people, plus $5 for each additional person. Credit cards are not accepted. Long-term rates are available.

Directions: From the intersection of State Road 44/Lakewood Avenue and State Road 19 in Eustis, drive about 2.5 miles north on State Road 19 to the park entrance. The campground is halfway between Eustis and Umatilla.

Contact: Lakeside RV Park, 38000 State Road 19, Umatilla, FL 32784, 352/669-4418, fax 352/669-5113, bonniemccain4@cs.com.

32 OLDE MILL STREAM RV RESORT

Scenic rating: 7

on Lake Pearl, in Umatilla

See map, page 298

This spotlessly clean and manicured RV park is set on 127 acres on Lake Pearl, and the owners say it's "Florida's best-kept secret." A curving, heated pool overlooks the blue waters of the 100-acre lake, where boaters search for bass. The sizable, sunny sites (40 by 60 feet) are big enough that if you have two or three slideouts, you won't feel stuck on top of your neighbor. Around 80 percent of the visitors here stay for six months, so you'll have plenty of time to get to know one another.

Campsites, facilities: This adults-only park offers 303 large RV sites with sewer hookups,

50-amp electrical service, large concrete patios, and telephone access. Each site has a picnic table. Six sites are drive-through. For entertainment, there's a pool, a driving range, miniature golf, a barbecue picnic area, horseshoes, shuffleboard, wintertime social activities, and a wheelchair-accessible, 800-square-foot recreation hall. Showers, restrooms, three dump stations, and laundry facilities are available. Groceries and a restaurant are across the street. You must be at least 25 years old to camp, but children may visit guests. Two pets under 40 pounds are allowed; they must be leashed and walked in the mowed field.

Reservations, fees: Reservations are recommended. Sites are $31 per night for two people, plus $3 for each additional person. Credit cards are accepted. Long-term rates are available. The maximum length of stay is eight months.

Directions: From Orlando, drive northwest on U.S. 441 to State Road 19. Turn right, heading toward Umatilla. Continue about 10 miles to the park entrance on the right, south of State Road 42.

Contact: Olde Mill Stream RV Resort, 1000 North Central Avenue, Umatilla, FL 32784, 352/669-3141 or 800/449-3141, www.oldemillstreamrv.com.

33 KELLY PARK

Scenic rating: 7

at Rock Springs, in Apopka

See map, page 298   BEST (

Every minute, more than 26,000 gallons of cool, crystal-clear water pour out of a cave to form Rock Springs, the main attraction of this 245-acre county park. Swimming, tubing, and snorkeling in the cool, natural spring waters are favored activities. You can rent an inner tube just outside the park for $5 per day, then float nearly a mile downstream. Fishing is not allowed. The picnic pavilions and two miles of hiking trails also are popular. The camping

sites—concrete pad and shell rock—are set in a shady forest.

Campsites, facilities: This county-run park has 21 RV sites (one pull-through) with 30-amp electricity and water hookups, plus three tent sites. There are no sewer hookups. Each shaded site has a picnic table, a fire ring, and a grill. Campsites are mostly shell rock with concrete pads; they vary in length from 35 to 70 feet, accommodating the largest RVs on the road. On the premises are showers, restrooms, a dump station, a playground, a nature trail, volleyball, and snacks. Festivals, environmental displays, and other community activities are held throughout the year. The restrooms, boardwalks, pavilions, and ramp to the swimming area are wheelchair-accessible. Groceries, restaurants, and laundry facilities are within five miles. Children are allowed. Pets and alcoholic beverages are prohibited.

Reservations, fees: Reservations are recommended, but you must make them in person. Sites are $15 per night for up to four people, plus $3 for electricity. The maximum stay is 14 consecutive days.

Directions: From Orlando, take U.S. 441 northwest into Apopka. Turn right (north) on Park Avenue (Rock Springs Road). Proceed six miles to the end, then bear right onto Kelly Park Road. The park is at the end of the road.

Contact: Kelly Park, 400 East Kelly Park Road, Apopka, FL 32712, 407/889-4179, fax 407/889-3523, www.orangecountyparks.net.

34 TWELVE OAKS RV RESORT

Scenic rating: 5

off I-4, west of Sanford

See map, page 298

The crooked branches of oaks and bristly pines help shade some of the campsites at this nearly 30-acre park that's a quick hop off I-4 but primarily caters to longer-term RVers. Other campsites are sunny. Despite the heated swimming pool and shuffleboard court, some visitors are more interested in other things: nearby shopping malls and Disney World, about 30 miles south. The park has a few sites available for overnighters or new snowbirds staying for the season. About half the park is occupied by RVers living here year-round, including retirees, snowbirds, and local workers.

Campsites, facilities: Of these 247 full-hookup, concrete-pad RV sites (about 35 pull-through), 20 are available for overnighters and 45 are for seasonal stays. Sites have full hookups and 30/50-amp electricity. RVs as large as 42 feet can be accommodated. A pool, two recreation halls with planned activities, shuffleboard, horseshoes, a playground, long-term storage, social programs, a dog walk, and a picnic shelter are available. Showers, restrooms, two dump stations, a small store that sells minimal camping supplies, and two laundry facilities are on the premises. Grocery stores are within 0.5 mile. Internet access is available in the office. The recreation halls, laundry buildings, office, and restrooms are wheelchair-accessible. Children are allowed. Leashed pets under 20 pounds are permitted.

Reservations, fees: Reservations are recommended. Sites are $28 per night for two people, plus $2 for each additional person. Credit cards are accepted. Long-term stays are OK.

Directions: From Orlando, take I-4 north to State Road 46 (Exit 101BC). Drive two miles west to the park.

Contact: Twelve Oaks RV Resort, 6300 State Road 46 West, Sanford, FL 32771, 407/323-0880 or 800/633-9529, fax 407/323-0899.

35 TOWN AND COUNTRY RV RESORT

☆ 🏕 ♿ 🚐

Scenic rating: 4

off I-4, west of Sanford

See map, page 298

Mainly snowbird retirees and motor-home club members pull into this 30-acre community's paved roads to arrive at grassy campsites and concrete patios shaded by oak, palm, and pine trees. Although anglers can head three miles to the St. Johns River or two miles to Lake Monroe, some campers prefer to stay right here on two-lane Orange Boulevard and spend some time socializing. In winter, campers break bread together at numerous organized dinners and take trips to craft shows and flea markets. About half the park is occupied year-round. Nearby are several miles of hiking and canoe trails at Wekiwa Springs State Park. The Sanford Historic District is about 5 miles east, and Disney World is about 30 miles south.

Campsites, facilities: All 300 grassy RV sites have full hookups, 30/50-amp electrical service, concrete pads, and picnic tables. Six sites are pull-through with water and electricity only. Lots average 25 by 40 feet, accommodating rigs up to 45 feet long. Bingo, a swimming pool, a pool table, a recreation room, shuffleboard, horseshoes, and winter activities entertain campers. Showers, restrooms, a dump station, propane gas, and laundry facilities are on the premises. Management says all areas are wheelchair-accessible, with ramps at each building. A mall, restaurants, and bait are available two miles away, and groceries are within one mile. Children are allowed for overnight stays or short vacations, but not long-term. Leashed pets are permitted.

Reservations, fees: Reservations are required in winter. Sites are $30 per night for two people, plus $2 for each additional person. Credit cards are accepted. Long-term rates are available.

Directions: From Orlando, take I-4 north to State Road 46 (Exit 101C). Go west about one mile to Orange Boulevard, then turn right. The park is about one mile ahead on the right.

Contact: Town and Country RV Resort, 5355 Orange Boulevard, Lake Monroe, FL 32747, 407/323-5540, fax 407/321-4495, www.townandcountryrvresort.com.

36 WEKIVA FALLS RESORT

🥾 🏊 🛶 ⛵ 〰️ 🚐 ⛺

Scenic rating: 6

on the Wekiva River, east of Sorrento

See map, page 298

Swimmers plunge into the springs where prehistoric sharks and elephant-like, nine-foot-tall mastodons lived thousands of years ago. It's the kind of place where children can let their imaginations run wild: Cave divers have uncovered shark teeth dating back at least 10 million years from the caverns beneath the swimming-beach area—and a mastodon jawbone with teeth was found here accidentally during a cleanup of the spring boil (the spot where the most water surges out of the ground).

Campsites, facilities: All 786 RV sites offer full hookups and electricity, and 47 tent sites have water and electricity. A fishing pier, sightseeing cruises, rental canoes, and hiking trails entertain campers. On the premises are showers, restrooms, a marina, more than 200 picnic tables, a dump station, limited groceries, and laundry facilities. Children are welcome. Pets are prohibited.

Reservations, fees: Reservations are recommended. Sites are $18 per night for two people, plus $9 for each additional person older than 12 or $6 for campers ages 2–11. Electricity costs $2 extra. Credit cards are not accepted. Long-term rates are available.

Directions: From I-4 at Exit 101C, drive about six miles west on State Road 46 to Wekiva River Road. Turn left and go 1.25 miles south to the campground entrance.

Contact: Wekiva Falls Resort, 30700 Wekiva River Road, Sorrento, FL 32776, 407/830-9828 or 352/383-8055.

37 WEKIWA SPRINGS STATE PARK

🥾 🚴 🏊 🛶 ⛵ 🚐 〰️ 🐕 🎣 ♿ 🚐 ⛺

Scenic rating: 10

at Wekiwa Springs, north of Apopka

See map, page 298   BEST (

This is one of the most popular and well-used Florida state parks, and for good reason. Wekiwa Springs pumps about 42 million gallons of cool, clear water daily, to the delight of

enjoying the beauty of Wekiwa Springs

© MARILYN MOORE

swimmers, snorkelers, and paddlers. Its run to the Wekiva River and ultimately the St. Johns River is a wonderful route to canoe or kayak in a bit of natural Florida that is being rapidly surrounded by the creep of suburbia. Tall oaks lend shade to campsites, which give visitors a good base for seeing natural Florida. Some campers hike on the 13.5-mile Sand Lake Trail or the shadier 5.3-mile Volksmarch Trail. Bicyclists are limited to paved roads within the 10-square-mile park and some of the hiking trails. The equestrian crowd can set out on eight miles of trails set largely along backcountry roads, and stop to water horses at Camp Big Fork (where horse camping is allowed for a fee). The horse trails are divided into two loops and are used by hikers and park staff. Keep your eye out for black bears, because this park, not far south of Ocala National Forest, is one of the bruins' southernmost outposts in the region. Periodically, the shy, nocturnal mammals turn up in the backyards of suburbanites whose homes are quickly clogging this once peaceful swath of the Sunshine State.

Campsites, facilities: Sixty shell-pad sites with 30-amp electricity and water are offered. Each site has a picnic table, a grill, and a fire ring. Like most state parks, these sites vary in size to fit into the natural environment. These range from 25 by 55 feet to 30 by 60 feet. On the premises are restrooms, showers, a dump station, snacks, and canoe and kayak rentals. The rentals are handled by a concessionaire (407/880-4110 or 407/884-4311); two-hour fees range from $12 for canoes to $15 for a kayak, and shuttle service is available. Horseshoes, a playground, and a volleyball court are in a picnic area. Management says all park buildings and two sites (Numbers 30 and 60) are accessible to wheelchairs. Groceries, restaurants, and laundry facilities are within four miles of the park. Two golf courses are within one mile. Children are welcome. Leashed pets with proof of rabies vaccination are permitted. Firearms and alcohol are prohibited.

Reservations, fees: Reservations are recommended; contact ReserveAmerica at 800/336-

3521 or reserveamerica.com. Sites are $20 per night for eight people. Pet fee is $2 daily. Credit cards are accepted. Maximum stay is 14 days.

Directions: From Orlando, take I-4 northeast to Exit 94. Head west on State Road 434 for about one mile to Wekiwa Springs Road. Turn right and continue 5.5 miles to the campground.

Contact: Wekiwa Springs State Park, 1800 Wekiwa Circle, Apopka, FL 32712, 407/884-2008, fax 407/884-2014, www.floridastate parks.org.

38 LIVE OAK BACKPACKING SITE

Scenic rating: 7

in Wekiwa Springs State Park

See map, page 298

As you might gather from the name, this campsite is located in an oak hammock. It's probably the least popular primitive camping area in the 10-square-mile state park, and it is used mostly for overflow when others are full. There's a good side to that, though: You're likely to have to yourself thousands of acres of native Florida woodlands that look much as they did in Ponce de Leon's day. Or nearly so. The campsite is one of two along a 13-mile trail. You'll hike through open pine flatwoods and dark oak hammocks. The trail can be pretty soggy after heavy rains, so check with park rangers ahead of time.

Campsites, facilities: Up to 10 backpackers can be accommodated at this primitive campsite, which requires a five-mile round-trip hike. The only facility is an in-ground fire circle. You must carry in water, food, firewood, and all supplies and pack out trash. Fires are allowed in the provided ground grill. Children are permitted. Pets, firearms, and alcohol are prohibited.

Reservations, fees: Reservations are required; call the park office at 407/884-2008. Fees are

$3 per night for each person age 16 or older, $2 for younger children. At least one member of your camping party must be at least age 18. Major credit cards are accepted.

Directions: From Orlando, take I-4 northeast to Exit 94. Head west on Highway 434 for about one mile to Wekiwa Springs Road. Turn right, continue 5.5 miles to the campground parking lot, and start hiking at the trailhead near the park's popular spring area. Talk to a ranger for instructions on finding the site.

Contact: Wekiwa Springs State Park, 1800 Wekiwa Circle, Apopka, FL 32712, 407/884-2008.

39 CAMP COZY CANOE/ BACKPACKING SITE

Scenic rating: 8

in Wekiwa Springs State Park

See map, page 298

Although set aside primarily for hikers, this primitive campsite, located about 100 yards off Rock Springs Run, is sometimes opened to canoeists as well. It's an old hunting camp from a time before this area was a state park. Hence the spigot, which provides water that is OK for cleaning up, but technically not designated for drinking. The campsite is on the edge of an oak hammock, so you can take your pick between a shady spot under the arching branches of oaks or a sunnier sleeping spot in the bordering pine flatwoods. Rock Springs Run, which forms the border between the state park and Rock Springs Run State Reserve, spans eight miles downstream and is covered in an easy four-mile canoe trip. The run is the headwaters of the Wekiva River. (About the two spellings: Wekiva is Indian for Flowing Water, and Wekiwa means Spring of Water.")

Campsites, facilities: This primitive site can accommodate 10 backpackers or canoeists. Hikers trek about five miles round-trip. The only facilities are a fire ring and a spigot that

produces non-potable water. You must carry in drinking water, food, firewood, and all other supplies and pack out trash. Children are permitted. Pets, firearms, and alcohol are prohibited.

Reservations, fees: Reservations are required; call the park office at 407/884-2008. Fees are $3 per night for each person age 16 or older, $2 for younger children. Major credit cards are accepted.

Directions: From Orlando, take I-4 northeast to Exit 94. Head west on Highway 434 for about one mile to Wekiwa Springs Road. Turn right and continue 5.5 miles to the campground parking lot and trailhead. Talk to a ranger to get instructions on finding the site and where to launch a canoe.

Contact: Wekiwa Springs State Park, 1800 Wekiwa Circle, Apopka, FL 32712, 407/884-2008. Canoes are rented out by the park's concessionaire; call 407/880-4110 for rates, or try local canoe liveries such as King's Landing, 5714 Baptist Camp Road, 407/886-0859.

40 BIG BUCK CANOE SITE

Scenic rating: 8

in Wekiwa Springs State Park

See map, page 298

This is the last of three primitive campsites along the popular Rock Springs Run canoe route between Wekiwa Springs and the Wekiva River. All are an easy half-day paddle—maybe two to three hours, traveling with the current. Big Buck is in a riverine swamp studded by sweet gum and cypress trees, and the campsite itself is shaded by a big live oak tree. Pitch your tent on mowed native grasses. There are a couple of benches and a ground grill. Other than that, you're on your own. You may see other canoeists go by, but you won't hear the rumble of motorboats; they're not allowed on this part of the run.

Some canoeists opt instead for the two other primitive campsites on this run. Indian Mound is preferred by most paddlers because it's right on the river, whereas Big Buck is about 50 yards inland. The park's newest canoe-in site, called Otter Camp, is a little smaller than the rest. Yet, it may please some tentative campers because it's the newest (hence, least known) and, as the first site reached from the trailhead, it's the easiest to reach.

Campsites, facilities: Up to 10 people can sleep at this small primitive campsite, reached by canoe in 2.5–3 hours. Besides a ground grill, a couple of benches, and a spigot with non-potable water, there are no facilities. Bring drinking water, food, firewood, and all the supplies you will need. Pack out trash. Children are allowed. Pets, firearms, and alcohol are prohibited.

Reservations, fees: Reservations are required; call the park office at 407/884-2008. Fees are $3 per night for each person age 16 or older, $2 for younger children. At least one member of your camping party must be age 18 or older. Major credit cards are accepted. Stays are limited to a few days.

Directions: From Orlando, drive northeast on I-4 to Exit 94. Head west on Highway 434 for about one mile to Wekiwa Springs Road. Turn right and continue 5.5 miles to the campground parking lot and trailhead. Talk to a ranger for instructions on finding the site and where to launch a canoe.

Contact: Wekiwa Springs State Park, 1800 Wekiwa Circle, Apopka, FL 32712, 407/884-2008. Canoes can be rented from the park; call 407/880-4110 for rates.

41 INDIAN MOUND CANOE SITE

🏊 🛶 ⛺

Scenic rating: 9

in Wekiwa Springs State Park

See map, page 298

If you've read the canoe magazines carefully or looked at the material available online, this is likely the campsite you hear about whenever Wekiwa Springs State Park is mentioned. Indian Mound is on an S-turn on Rock Springs Run by a nice white-sand beach, right by the water, on a little raised bank overhung with huge live oaks. Notice the "hill" overgrown with palmettos next door—that's an old Indian "midden," or mound, built up by Native Americans who piled their garbage; sort of like a prehistoric landfill, but cleaner than today's version. Like the Big Buck site, this is no more than a three-hour paddle, and you'll be running with the current. Here, as at Buffalo Tram, look for deer, river otters, wild turkeys, bobcats, and the secretive black bear.

Campsites, facilities: Up to 10 canoeists can sleep at this primitive campsite, reached in 2.5–3 hours. A fire ring is provided, but there are no other facilities. Bring drinking water, food, firewood, and all the supplies you will need. Pack out trash. Children are allowed. Pets, alcohol, and firearms are prohibited.

Reservations, fees: Reservations are required; call the park office at 407/884-2008. Fees are $3 per night for each person in your party age 16 or older, $2 for younger children. Major credit cards are accepted. Stays are limited to a few days. Canoes can be rented at the park.

Directions: From Orlando, take I-4 northeast to Exit 94. Head west on Highway 434 for about one mile to Wekiwa Springs Road. Turn right and continue 5.5 miles to the campground parking lot. Talk to a ranger to get instructions on finding the site and where to launch a canoe.

Contact: Wekiwa Springs State Park, 1800 Wekiwa Circle, Apopka, FL 32712, 407/884-2008.

42 BUFFALO TRAM BOAT/CANOE SITE

🏊 🛶 🚤 ⛺

Scenic rating: 7

in Wekiwa Springs State Park

See map, page 298

Here, you'll camp next to remnants of the old cypress-logging operations that used to provide jobs when there weren't many to be found in this part of Florida. The pilings you see in the Wekiva River are from old mechanical logging equipment used to move logs around. They were known as "buffaloes"—hence the name of this camping site. The fairly small, mostly sunny site is considered by some to be less pretty than Indian Mound, which is located farther south on Rock Springs Run. And you'll also chance hearing the occasional motor of a small passing skiff, whereas you won't hear motors on Rock Springs Run, where they are prohibited. This spot is set up relatively high, perhaps six feet above the water, so you're in a kind of blind: Canoeists can go past and you can see them, but they likely won't see you.

Campsites, facilities: Up to 10 people can sleep at this primitive campsite. A fire ring is provided, but there are no other facilities. Bring drinking water, food, firewood, and all other camping supplies. Pack out trash. Children are permitted. Pets, alcohol, and firearms are prohibited. Canoes can be rented from the state park.

Reservations, fees: Reservations are required; call the park office at 407/884-2008. Fees are $3 per night for each person age 16 or older, $2 for younger children. At least one member of your camping party must be age 18 or older. Major credit cards are accepted. Stays are limited to a few days.

Directions: From Orlando, take I-4 northeast to Exit 94. Head west on Highway 434 for about one mile to Wekiwa Springs Road. Turn right and continue 5.5 miles to the campground parking lot. Talk to a ranger for instructions on finding the site and where to launch.

Contact: Wekiwa Springs State Park, 1800 Wekiwa Circle, Apopka, FL 32712, 407/884-2008.

43 LAKE JESUP CONSERVATION AREA

Scenic rating: 6

Lake Jesup, south of Sanford

See map, page 298

Here on the north bank of the boating and fishing waters of Lake Jesup, you'll sleep within a nearly two-square-mile area that offers trails for hiking and horseback riding through wet prairie grasslands. Look for eagles, hawks, and alligators along the lakeshore. The conservation area is actually bigger than the tract in which you'll camp—it comprises three distinct areas totaling 3,432 acres around Lake Jesup. Bird-watching is good in Marl Beds Flats tract, to the southwest, which is reached by car by following Sanford Avenue south from State Road 46 to the road's dead-end at the lake. A lakeview observation tower is at the East Lake Jesup Tract, on the southern bank of Lake Jesup at the northern dead-end of Elm Street, north of Oviedo. The point of the conservation area is to protect Lake Jesup, so expect a frills-free existence. It's mostly wet prairie grasslands that extend back from the lakeshore to the marl beds and thickly wooded hammocks found at Caldwell's Field, at the Marl Beds Flats tract.

Campsites, facilities: A primitive camping area in the North Lake Jesup tract and is reachable via a short walk. Three nearby boat ramps provide access to Lake Jesup, but there are no facilities in the camping area. Bring food, supplies, drinking water, and mosquito repellent. Children are permitted. Pets must be leashed.

Reservations, fees: Sites are first-come, first-served. Camping is free. Each site accommodates up to six people. If your party has at least seven people, get a free permit and reserve at least one week ahead by calling 386/329-4410. Maximum stay for all campers is seven days.

Directions: From U.S. 17/92 in Sanford, go east about 3.5 miles, passing Sanford Airport. Turn right (south) onto Cameron Avenue, and proceed about two miles until the road dead-ends at the conservation area's North Lake Jesup tract.

Contact: St. Johns River Water Management District, Division of Land Management, P.O. Box 1429, Palatka, FL 32178-1429, 386/329-4500 or 800/451-7106, www.sjrwmd.com.

44 HOLIDAY SPRINGS RV RESORT

Scenic rating: 2

southwest of Brooksville

See map, page 298

This clean park has an eight-acre lake for fishing and boating and an unusual 100-by-200-foot spring-fed natural swimming pool whose temperature stays at about 75°F year-round. A short nature trail leads from the lake to the spring. Management works extra hard at security, parking patrol cars with dummies near the entrance and keeping doors to common areas locked at times. The park, "a semi-retirement community," caters to the 55-plus age group, and about 35 percent of the sites are occupied year-round. In winter, you'll find the traditional planned activities, such as bingo and cards.

Campsites, facilities: There are 20 RV sites in this 248-unit mobile-home community that accommodates rigs up to 40 feet long. Sewer hookups, 30/50-amp electrical service, cable TV and telephone access, picnic tables, laundry facilities, a dump station, recreation rooms, a 40-by-80-foot dance hall, shuffleboard courts, a boat dock, and rental trailers are available. Roads are paved, and sites have cement slabs. Twelve sites are drive-through. The park may allow families with small children for overnight stays, but management is primarily interested in people age 55 and over who drive newer RVs. One small pet is permitted per site.

Reservations, fees: Reservations are not necessary. Sites are $35 per night for two people, plus $2 for each additional person. Credit cards are not accepted. Long-term rates are available.

Directions: From the junction of U.S. 19 and State Road 50, drive seven miles south on U.S. 19. The park is on the northwest side of the intersection of U.S. 19 and County Road 578/County Line Road.

Contact: Holiday Springs RV Resort, 138 Travel Park Drive, Spring Hill, FL 34607, 352/683-0034, www.holidayspringsrvresort.com.

45 MARY'S FISH CAMP

Scenic rating: 3

on the Mud River, west of Weeki Wachee

See map, page 298

You'll find this quiet, secluded park tucked into an almost jungle-like thicket of trees on the Mud River, a tidal watercourse that joins the scenic Weeki Wachee River 2.5 miles away. It's ideal for canoeists, anglers, and boaters (the river has gulf access); a few brave sailors have even been known to come up the river when the water is high. A boat ramp is nearby at Bayport. You can also fish from the campground docks. Mullet is a particular delicacy, and there is a lot of pride and discussion on how to cook it properly. To keep a "nice, quiet, family atmosphere," management does not permit alcohol or use of foul language in the park. About half the sites are occupied year-round. Some visitors (mostly from Michigan) have been coming here every winter for 15 years or more. Activities are not formally organized; rather, the occasional cookout or potluck dinner breaks up the fishing.

Campsites, facilities: There are 27 sites with full hookups and 30-amp electrical service. Nine sites are available for overnighters. Restrooms, showers, picnic tables, three rental cabins, and boat docks on the Mud River are available. The restroom is wheelchair-accessible. Absolutely no alcohol or profanity are allowed. Restaurants and shopping are within four miles. Children are welcome. Leashed pets are permitted.

Reservations, fees: Reservations are recommended. Nightly fee for two people is $18. Add $1.50–2.50 for each additional person. Credit cards are not accepted.

Directions: From U.S. 19 and State Road 50 in Weeki Wachee, drive four miles west on Cortez Boulevard (Highway 550). Look for the park sign at Mary's Fish Camp Road and drive 0.25 mile south.

Contact: Mary's Fish Camp, 8092 Mary's Fish Camp Road, Weeki Wachee, FL 34607, 352/596-2359, fax 352/596-5562.

46 CHIEF ARIPEKA TRAVEL PARK

Scenic rating: 2

west of Spring Hill

See map, page 298

Close to shopping and restaurants, the RV park is nonetheless secluded and far from noise and traffic. Oversized lots of crushed white rock accommodate big rigs. There's not much to do in the park, but within a couple of miles are the deep-sea fishing charters and marinas of Hernando Beach. The community of Aripeka is a fishing village today, but in the 1920s, it was quite the fashionable vacation resort.

Campsites, facilities: All 28 RV sites have sewer hookups. Ten sites have 50-amp service; the rest have 30-amp. Restrooms, showers, and a dump station are provided. A wheelchair-accessible ramp leads to the bathhouse. The park is oriented toward retirees and snowbirds. Children may visit adult campers. Pets are permitted.

Reservations, fees: Reservations are recommended. Sites are $23 per night for two people, plus $1 for each additional person. Fifty-amp electrical service costs $2 per night extra. Credit cards are not accepted. Long-term stays are permitted.

Directions: From U.S. 19 and County Road 595 in Spring Hill, drive west on County Road 595 for two miles. The park is on the south side of the road.

Contact: Chief Aripeka Travel Park, 1582 Osowaw Boulevard, Spring Hill, FL 34607, 352/686-3329.

47 CAMPER'S HOLIDAY TRAVEL PARK

Scenic rating: 6

southeast of Brooksville

See map, page 298

This countryside park with a 13-acre fishing lake offers large sites set in a grid-like fashion. The RV section adjoins the park's 300 retirement-camper condominium lots, and campers may use all of the common areas. Don't feed or approach the alligators you may see on Sparkman Lake. Note that boat motors are limited to three horsepower. A convenience store is next door to the park, and a gatehouse keeps out curiosity seekers. It's too remote from the interstate for overnight campers who don't plan ahead, and reservations are absolutely required for winter stays. About 75 percent of the visitors stay 3–6 months; no year-round residents are located in the RV section. Popular activities include card games, shuffleboard, and horseshoes, as well as visiting area tourist attractions.

Campsites, facilities: All 66 RV sites have full hookups and cable TV and telephone access. They are black-topped with grassy sides. Twelve sites have 50-amp service; the rest have 30-amp. RVs as long as 45 feet are welcome. Restrooms, showers, picnic tables, laundry facilities, a dump station, a pool, a recreation room, shuffleboard courts, and a playground are on the premises. Roads are paved. Most common areas are wheelchair-accessible. Shopping and restaurants are within 15 miles. Children are allowed. One leashed pet is permitted per site.

Reservations, fees: Reservations are recommended. Sites are $24 to $28 per night for two people, plus $2 for each additional person. Add $2.50 for using 50-amp electricity. Credit cards are not accepted. Campers must be vacationers or retired snowbirds.

Directions: If driving south on I-75, take Exit 301 and drive west on State Road 50 into Brooksville. At the intersection with Emerson Road/County Road 581, turn south for 5.5 miles. Stay on that road all the way to the park; it winds around. Look for the park sign at left. If driving north on I-75, take Exit 285 onto County Road 52 and drive west. Turn north on County Road 581 and drive five miles. The park is just past the intersection with Hayman Road/County Road 576.

Contact: Camper's Holiday Travel Park, 2092 Culbreath Road, Brooksville, FL 34602, 352/796-3707, fax 352/796-6232.

48 TOPICS RV COMMUNITY

Scenic rating: 4

south of Brooksville

See map, page 298

Set on a hill in the open countryside, the Topics RV and park-model community has unusually large sites at 40 by 100 feet. Loads of social activities are planned during the winter months, including golf leagues (ending the season with a competition), monthly ladies' and men's luncheons at local restaurants, a mixed bowling league, and a year-end festival with free food and drink. The Blue Tees driving range is across the street, and many golf courses are nearby. About half the sites are occupied by year-round residents, and park models are for sale. Only 35 of the 231 sites are available for overnighters.

Campsites, facilities: The 40-acre, 231-unit, adults-only park has large RV sites with sewer hookups, cable TV, and telephone access. Internet connectivity is available at the campsites. Twenty-one sites have 50-amp electrical service; the rest have 30 amps. Restrooms, showers, laundry facilities, a clubhouse with kitchen facilities, shuffleboard courts, a dump station, and a heated pool are available. All areas are wheelchair-accessible. Children are not allowed. Two leashed pets are permitted per site.

Reservations, fees: Reservations are required. Sites are $33 per night for two people, plus $5 for each additional person. Credit cards are accepted. Seasonal visitors are preferred.

Directions: From U.S. 41, drive two miles west on County Road 578/County Line Road. Or, from U.S. 19, drive eight miles east on County Road 578/County Line Road.

Contact: Topics RV Community, 13063 County Line Road, Spring Hill, FL 34609, 352/796-0625, fax 352/796-0282, topics@mhchomes.com.

49 GULF COAST RESORT

Scenic rating: 5

east of Hudson

See map, page 298

Nudists will find a relaxed, friendly, rustic setting with lots of trees, say the managers of this eight-acre, clothing-optional park. RVs up to 45 feet in length are welcome. About 15 percent of the sites are occupied year-round. Dominoes, bingo, tennis, shuffleboard, and card games are popular in the wintertime. Most visitors are snowbirds here to soak up the rays.

Campsites, facilities: There are 178 grassy RV sites with sewer hookups; 20 sites are pull-through. Thirty-amp electrical service is provided at 60 sites, and 50-amp at 18 sites. A grassy area accommodates six tents; some of the tent sites have water and electricity. Picnic tables, restrooms, showers, laundry facilities, a dump station, a pool, a recreation hall, tennis courts, horseshoes, shuffleboard, *pétanque* (French-style bowling) courts, a camp circle, a small restaurant, and rental trailers are on-site.

The restaurant and clubhouse are wheelchair-accessible. Children are welcome. Leashed pets are permitted; they must be cleared by management when making your reservation.

Reservations, fees: Reservations are required; you'll have to make a $25 non-refundable deposit. Sites are $20–60 per night for two people, plus half the camping fee for each additional person. Credit cards are accepted. Long-term stays are OK.

Directions: From U.S. 19 in Hudson, drive two miles east on County Road 578/County Line Road. At East Road, turn south and continue two miles. Look for the campground's six-foot sign on a fence.

Contact: Gulf Coast Nudist Resort, 13220 Houston Avenue, Hudson, FL 34667, 727/868-1061, www.gulfcoastresort.com.

50 FRONTIER CAMPGROUND

Scenic rating: 3

west of Brooksville

See map, page 298

Near the campground office is a small, open-air gathering place called "Liar's Corner," presumably reserved for anglers bragging about their catch of the day. With little screening between the sites, however, neighbors will know the real truth. Populated by snowbirds and permanent residents, this fenced park is close to doctors' offices, auto-repair outfits, and a Wal-Mart. About 40 percent of the sites are occupied year-round, and visitors tend to return year after year. Motorbikes are allowed in the park only for registered camper transportation to their sites.

Campsites, facilities: There are 110 full-hookup RV sites in this community of 66 mobile homes. Since most of the campers here are repeat visitors from Canada and the Northeast, space is limited. Around 20 sites are available for overnighters. Half the sites have 50-amp electrical service; the rest have

30-amp. Seventy sites are drive-through. Each spot has a patio and a picnic table. Restrooms, showers, laundry facilities, a dump station, an adult recreation hall, a pool, horseshoe pits, shuffleboard courts, and a playground are provided. Roads are paved. Most of the park is wheelchair-accessible. Shopping and groceries are within three miles. Children are welcome. One small dog or cat is permitted on each lot; pets must not be kept outside.

Reservations, fees: Reservations are accepted, but credit cards are not. Sites are $25 per night for two people, plus $1 for each additional person. Long-term stays are allowed.

Directions: From Brooksville, drive west on State Road 50 for five miles.

Contact: Frontier Campground, 15549 Cortez Boulevard, Brooksville, FL 34613, 352/796-9988.

51 BRENTWOOD LAKE CAMPING

Scenic rating: 2

north of Brooksville

See map, page 298

Secluded from the highway on a wooded hill, this camping spot is perched on high ground overlooking a private lake stocked with bass, catfish, and bream. Tall oaks provide shade and atmosphere. In the center is a grassy field for outdoor games. Grocery stores, restaurants, and a golf course are within two miles. Children are welcome, although most people staying here are retirees. "Spend a little time or a lifetime," say the owners, Laine and Elaine Brayko. "People of all ages are welcome." During the winter months, activities are planned for each day. Favorites are cards, crafts, Bible study, horseshoes, shuffleboard, potluck dinners, and pancake breakfasts.

Campsites, facilities: There are 64 RV sites with water and 30-amp electricity; 60 have sewer hookups. Eight sites are drive-through. RVs as long as 40 feet can be accommodated.

Restrooms, showers, picnic tables, a dump station, laundry facilities, a recreation room, shuffleboard courts, and horseshoe pits are available. The restrooms and recreation hall are wheelchair-accessible, as is the office. Children are allowed. Small leashed pets are permitted.

Reservations, fees: Reservations are not necessary. Sites are $17 per night for two people, plus $2 for each additional person. If you use air-conditioning or electric heaters, there is an additional charge of $2 per unit. Credit cards are not accepted. Long-term rates are available.

Directions: From Brooksville, drive north on U.S. 41 for 3.2 miles. Turn west onto Ancient Trail, a gravel road, and go 0.2 mile to the campground.

Contact: Brentwood Lake Camping, 11089 Ancient Trail, Brooksville, FL 34601, 352/796-5760, www.brentwoodlake camping.com.

52 CLOVER LEAF FOREST RV PARK

Scenic rating: 6

in Brooksville

See map, page 298

A sign at the entrance states: "Welcome back, winter residents. We missed you." What are they coming back to? A shaded, wooded setting of slash pines and leafy oak trees and neatly kept campsites with concrete patios. Other unusual features include the indoor swimming pool, whirlpool tub, and sauna. Believe it or not, it can easily get too cold for outdoor swimming in upper Florida—although, of course, everything's relative. The RV park is next door to a mobile-home community, and many campers stay for the season or year-round. Only 5 percent of visitors make this their home for less than a month. Favorite activities in the winter season are arts and crafts, carving, bingo, sewing, horseshoes, and swimming.

Campsites, facilities: All 277 RV sites have

sewer hookups and 20/30/50-amp electrical outlets. Restrooms, showers, laundry facilities, picnic tables, an indoor and an outdoor pool, a recreation room, shuffleboard, a billiards and card room, horseshoe pits, cable TV access, and telephone service are available. Most areas are wheelchair-accessible; in fact, there is a lift in and out of the pool, plus ramps to the clubhouse, bathhouse, and office. You can access the Internet in the office. Propane can be delivered to your site on a weekly basis. Children may stay up to two weeks as guests of their grandparents. Leashed pets are permitted.

Reservations, fees: Reservations are recommended. Sites are $28–32 per night for two people, plus $1 per extra person. Credit cards are accepted. Long-term rates are available.

Directions: From I-75 at Exit 301, go west 10 miles on State Road 50, which merges into State Road 50A. Turn right (north) onto State Road 41. Look for the park one mile ahead, across the street from an elementary school.

Contact: Clover Leaf Forest RV Park, 910 North Broad Street, Brooksville, FL 34601, 352/796-8016 or 877/796-5381, fax 352/796-5381, cnichols@hometownamerica.net.

53 HIDDEN VALLEY CAMPGROUND

Scenic rating: 4

east of Brooksville

See map, page 298

Enormous live-oak trees provide a pretty, leafy canopy over this rustic, family-friendly campground, a longtime family operation where the owner raised his children. About 40 percent of the occupants live here year-round. Most of the folks here are snowbirds and retirees. One attraction nearby in Brooksville is Roger's Christmas House Village, a garden complex of five historic houses where various vendors sell gifts. Also in Brooksville, you'll find grocery stores and plenty of fast-food restaurants.

Campsites, facilities: All 64 RV sites have full hookups and cable TV access. Eight sites earmarked for long-term visitors have 50-amp electrical service; the rest have 30 amps. Rigs up to 40 feet can be accommodated. Two spots are large enough for 45-foot RVs. Most sites are shaded with picnic tables and concrete pads. About 30 sites are available for overnighters. Restrooms, showers, picnic tables, laundry facilities, a communal fire pit, a playground, a recreation hall, horseshoe pits, and shuffleboard courts are provided on the property. Groceries are within four miles. Families with children are welcome. Leashed pets are allowed.

Reservations, fees: Reservations are not necessary. Sites are $22 per night for two people, plus $2 for each additional person and $2 for cable TV. A surcharge of $2 per day applies if you use air-conditioning or an electric heater. Credit cards are accepted. Long-term stays are permitted.

Directions: From I-75, take Exit 301 and drive west for approximately seven miles on State Road 50 to the campground entrance. Or, from Brooksville, drive 2.5 miles east on State Road 50.

Contact: Hidden Valley Campground, 22329 Cortez Boulevard, Brooksville, FL 34601, 352/796-8710.

54 LAKESIDE MOBILE MANOR

Scenic rating: 2

in Brooksville

See map, page 298

Coffee and doughnuts are served to guests at this RV park on Saturday mornings, but if that's not enough to get you going, cast your line in a four-acre fishing lake and try your luck. Most campers here are snowbirds staying for six months, availing themselves of the popular "6/6" plan, which allows you to leave your RV on-site after you head back north.

Popular activities are birding, fishing, bingo, crafts, horseshoes, and dominoes. A wooded area nearby is home to a pair of eagles and a flock of wood storks.

Campsites, facilities: Targeting snowbirds, this 14-acre lakefront mobile-home park has 73 spaces, with 35 available for RVs. Sewer hookups, 30-amp electrical service, cable TV and telephone access, and picnic tables are provided at each site. There are no showers. Campers under age 55 are not welcome. The recreation hall is wheelchair-accessible. One leashed pet weighing less than 30 pounds is permitted per site.

Reservations, fees: Reservations are recommended. Sites are $22 per night for two people, plus $3 per extra person. Credit cards are not accepted. Long-term stays are OK; stay for six months and leave the RV for the rest of the year for free.

Directions: From downtown Brooksville, travel one mile north on U.S. 41. The park entrance is at the intersection of the highway and Croom Road.

Contact: Lakeside Mobile Manor, 1020 Lakeside Drive, Brooksville, FL 34601, 352/796-4600.

55 BIG OAKS RV PARK

Scenic rating: 3

south of Brooksville

See map, page 298

Set in the countryside, this adult park caters to overnighters, as well as snowbirds. It's within an hour's drive of Busch Gardens, Weeki Wachee Spring, Sea World, Disney World, the Gulf of Mexico, and Roger's Christmas House Village. The latter is a fanciful Victorian year-round place where six houses are each decorated with their own Christmas theme. Golf, fishing, bowling, shopping, restaurants, and flea markets are within 10–15 minutes. Sites are large and grassy. They're also shady, except for the two treeless sections of pull-through spaces.

Campsites, facilities: The park has 110 sites with full hookups and concrete pads. Sixty sites are drive-through. Restrooms, showers, laundry facilities, a pool, a clubhouse, shuffleboard courts, horseshoes, and a dump station are on the premises. Rental trailers are available. Children are permitted for visits only. One small leashed pet per site is permitted.

Reservations, fees: Reservations are recommended. Sites are $25 per night for two people, plus $2 for each additional person. Credit cards are not accepted. Long-term stays are OK.

Directions: From Brooksville at State Road 50, drive south on U.S. 41 for eight miles. Or, from I-75, take Exit 285 onto County Road 52 and drive west. Turn north on U.S. 41 and drive five miles.

Contact: Big Oaks RV Park, 16654 U.S. 41, Spring Hill, FL 34610, 352/799-5533, www.bigoakspark.com.

56 TRAVELERS REST RESORT

Scenic rating: 7

off I-75, west of Dade City

See map, page 298

Long-legged egrets and blue herons swoop into the three lakes of this wooded "retirement playground" resort, set in the rolling hills of Florida's citrus and cattle ranching country. But it's no shrinking violet of a place—not with wood carving, a gardening club, a motorcycle club, mini-sailboat races, a restaurant, a post office, a library, a fire department, and an active "teaching staff" of volunteers who help visitors master hobbies, crafts, and the like. And let's not forget the USGA-rated nine-hole golf course, two tennis courts, a shuffleboard "plaza," and an auditorium that seats 600. You'll likely be parked on a hill, where there's room for 60 rigs. This age-55-plus community is near the

Pioneer Museum and antique malls and just three miles off of I-75.

Campsites, facilities: The mobile-home/RV-park community has 647 sites, of which about 80 spots with full hookups are for RVs staying overnight. Only self-contained, hard-sided, factory-made RVs are allowed. All sites have 20/30/50-amp plugs. A heated pool, a spa, a nine-hole golf course, three recreation buildings, two tennis courts, table tennis, shuffleboard, and boccie ball (lawn bowling) are on-site. Cable TV, telephone access, restrooms, showers, laundry facilities, limited supplies, propane, a dump station, and wireless Internet access are available. Groceries and restaurants are within 12 miles. Children are welcome to visit for no more than 30 days. Pets must be leashed.

Reservations, fees: Reservations are recommended. Sites are $27 per night. Credit cards are accepted. Long-term stays are OK for adults.

Directions: From I-75, take Exit 293 and drive 0.24 mile west. Turn south on County Road 577 and continue one mile. At Johnston Road, turn west and go one mile to the park.

Contact: Travelers Rest Resort, 29129 Johnston Road, Dade City, FL 33523, 352/588-2013, fax 352/588-3462, www.travelersrestresort.com.

57 BUTTGENBACH MINE CAMPGROUND

Scenic rating: 7

in the Croom Tract of Withlacoochee State Forest

See map, page 298   **BEST**

Nearby is the Croom Motorcycle Area—nirvana for motorcyclists, dirt bikers, and all-terrain cycle fans. The motorcycle area sets aside 2,600 acres for cyclists to rev their engines and roar around the forest. The result is a kind of dusty moonscape of denuded trails, lonely trees with all the soil eroded around their roots, and a noise level to rival the Grand Prix. Decades ago, the terrain had been damaged already by phosphate mining operations, borrow pits dug to build the interstate highway, and cyclists during a time when their activities were not regulated, and they were free to roam. By setting aside this land, the state confines motorcycles to one area. Bikers from as far north as Canada come to use the "training pit," a crater-sized sandy valley with plenty of bumps for getting airborne. An "inexperienced rider area" is near the campground. There's also a day-use area with picnic tables, water, restrooms, and parking. Bikers must purchase permits in person at the entrance gate; credit cards are not accepted. All cycles must be trailered in; however, you are allowed to ride your vehicle in low gear from the campground to the riding area. No bicycling is allowed. If the campground is full, then try the nearby Silver Lake Recreation Complex or Tall Pines RV Park.

Campsites, facilities: All 50 sites in this state forest campground have 50-amp electricity. RVs up to 40 feet long can be accommodated. Water, restrooms, showers, grills, fire rings, picnic tables, and a dump station are available. The bathhouse is wheelchair-accessible. Children are welcome. Pets are prohibited. Alcoholic beverages are not allowed.

Reservations, fees: Reservations are not accepted. Sites are $13 per night for five people. Up to five people, using one RV, are permitted per site. Larger groups need to get a permit. Credit cards are not accepted.

Directions: From I-75, take Exit 301 westbound on State Road 50 and drive 0.1 mile. Turn north onto Western Way; the forest entrance is just ahead. Buttgenbach Mine Campground is four miles north of the entrance. Be sure your gear is tied securely because the dirt road is pitted and bumpy.

Contact: Withlacoochee State Forest Recreation Visitors Center, 15003 Broad Street, Brooksville, FL 34601, 352/754-6896 or 352/754-6777 (fire dispatch), www.fl-dof.com.

58 SILVER LAKE CAMPGROUND

🥾 🚲 🛶 ⛴ 🏕 ♿ 🚐 ⛺

Scenic rating: 9

in the Croom Tract of Withlacoochee State Forest, at Silver Lake Recreation Complex

See map, page 298   BEST (

Silver Lake gets much use from locals and savvy folks during the summer, but it can be nearly deserted weekdays in winter. It's also convenient to I-75, a fact that campers on the road may not realize. Interstate noise is the only drawback; otherwise, the campground would be nearly perfect. It overlooks Silver Lake, which is really a broad area on the Withlacoochee River; your neighbors in the campground may be canoeists passing through, or bicyclists. The woods are thick and shady, and cypress trees with peculiar-looking root knobs erupting from the ground line the bottomlands near the lake. More than 30 miles of hiking trails are in the surrounding forest. The wonderful paved bicycle trail called the Withlacoochee State Trail is just a few minutes away from the campground access road. The trailhead at Ridge Manor is about three miles north. Note that mountain bikes are restricted to forest roads and the approved off-road trails; hiking trails are for foot traffic only. The local health department has banned swimming in the river as a potential health hazard because of bacteria, but the truth is that people do go for dips at will.

Campsites, facilities: Twenty-three campsites have water, 50-amp electricity, grills, fire rings, and picnic tables. Restrooms, showers, a dump station, and a boat ramp are available. RVs up to 44 feet can be accommodated. The bathhouses are wheelchair-accessible, but the roads are not paved. Children are welcome. Pets are allowed. Alcohol is prohibited.

Reservations, fees: Reservations are not taken. Sites are $13 per night for five people. Up to five people, using two tents or one RV, are permitted per site. Groups require a permit. Credit cards are not accepted.

Directions: From I-75, take Exit 309 eastbound on State Road 50 for 0.75 mile. Turn north at the traffic light; the highway is marked as Croom Rital Road on the north side and Kettering Road on the south side, but just follow the signs for the Withlacoochee State Trail. Drive 3.5 miles. Just before the interstate overpass, turn east into the Silver Lake complex. This is the first campground on your left.

Contact: Withlacoochee State Forest Recreation Visitors Center, 15003 Broad Street, Brooksville, FL 34601, 352/754-6896 or 352/754-6777 (fire dispatch), www.fl-dof .com.

59 CYPRESS GLEN CAMPGROUND

Scenic rating: 9

in the Croom Tract of Withlacoochee State Forest, at Silver Lake Recreation Complex

See map, page 298

Set in a mixed forest of pines and hardwoods, the campground slopes toward Silver Lake, where there's a small beach and a far-off view of the interstate bridge. Sites are generously spaced, and the forest creates lush shade. The hiking trails begin at Silver Lake Campground down the road; bicycles are allowed on forest roads. Just north of the Silver Lake area is a canoe outfitter: Nobleton Boat and Canoe Rental (352/796-7176). Anglers regularly catch all kinds of bass, panfish, and catfish in the river.

Campsites, facilities: The largest of the three campgrounds in this state forest complex, Cypress Glen has 43 sites with piped water and 50-amp electricity. Large RVs (as long as 44 feet) are welcome, but the roads are not paved. Restrooms, showers, picnic tables, grills, and fire rings are provided. The bathhouse is wheelchair-accessible. Children and pets are welcome; no alcohol, please.

Reservations, fees: Reservations are not taken. Sites are $13 per night for five people. Up to

five people, using one RV, are permitted per site. Groups need a permit. Credit cards are not accepted. This campground is open only on weekends (noon Friday–noon Monday) and holidays.

Directions: From I-75, take Exit 309 eastbound on State Road 50 for 0.75 mile. Turn north at the traffic light; the highway is marked as Croom Rital Road on the north side and Kettering Road on the south side, but just follow the signs for the Withlacoochee State Trail. Drive 3.5 miles. Just before the interstate overpass, turn east into the Silver Lake complex. This is the second campground on your left, about 0.8 mile from the turn.

Contact: Withlacoochee State Forest Recreation Visitors Center, 15003 Broad Street, Brooksville, FL 34601, 352/754-6896 or 352/754-6777 (fire dispatch), www.fl-dof .com.

60 CROOKED RIVER CAMPGROUND

Scenic rating: 9

in the Croom Tract of Withlacoochee State Forest, at Silver Lake Recreation Complex

See map, page 298

You'll find more level, open sites here than in the other campgrounds in this forest complex, making it a better choice for self-contained RVs. Many sites overlook the Withlacoochee River, which at this point becomes a narrow, winding course with coffee-colored waters. Steps lead down to the river's edge.

Campsites, facilities: All 26 sites have water, picnic tables, grills, and fire rings but no electricity. Restrooms and showers, which are wheelchair-accessible, are available. Roads are not paved. Children are welcome, but pets and alcoholic beverages are prohibited.

Reservations, fees: Reservations are not taken. Sites are $10 per night for five people. Up to five people, using two tents or one RV, are permitted per site. Groups need a permit. Credit cards are not accepted.

Directions: From I-75, take Exit 309 east-bound on State Road 50 for 0.75 mile. Turn north at the traffic light; the highway is marked as Croom Rital Road on the north side and Kettering Road on the south side, but just follow the signs for the Withlacoochee State Trail. Drive 3.5 miles. Just before the interstate overpass, turn east into the Silver Lake complex. This is the third campground on your left, about 1.2 miles from the main entrance.

Contact: Withlacoochee State Forest Recreation Visitors Center, 15003 Broad Street, Brooksville, FL 34601, 352/754-6896 or 352/754-6777 (fire dispatch), www.fl-dof .com.

61 TALL PINES RV PARK

Scenic rating: 3

near Brooksville

See map, page 298

This 5.5-acre park is right off I-75 and gets overflow use from the all-terrain vehicle and motorbike users of the Croom Motorcycle Area, located in the state forest less than a mile away. Don't be concerned about the motorcyclists; they're more Nickelodeon types than Hell's Angels, with brightly colored racing silks, expensive gear, and miniature motorbikes for their kids. Nearby are all the usual interstate stops: restaurants, fast food, gas stations, and even tourist information; a big grocery store and a shopping center are within walking distance. You can stay as long as you like—60 percent of guests here are year-round residents.

Campsites, facilities: Fifty sites have full hookups and electrical service (18 have 50-amp plugs). A few sites can accommodate large RVs. Restrooms, showers, laundry facilities, a dump station, and a wheelchair-accessible recreation hall are provided. Shopping and groceries are within two blocks. Children are welcome. Leashed pets are permitted.

Reservations, fees: Reservations are not necessary. Sites are $22 per night for two people, plus $3 per extra person. Credit cards are accepted. Long-term stays are OK.

Directions: From I-75, take Exit 301 east-bound on State Road 50 for 0.1 mile. Watch for the park driveway on the north side of the road, between the Waffle House and the RaceTrac station.

Contact: Tall Pines RV Park, 30455 Cortez Boulevard, Brooksville, FL 34602, 352/799-5587, tallpinesrvpark@yahoo.com.

62 THE OAKS CAMPGROUND

Scenic rating: 4

in Bushnell

See map, page 298

Most folks come for the season, enjoying all manner of dancing, bingo, exercise programs, bus tours, craft and quilting classes, and non-denominational Sunday school and Bible study. But the theme here is music. "There's always something musical going on," the owners say. Jam sessions and choir practices are held each week; a piano bar offers crooners the chance to entertain. Indoors or out, you might find a spontaneous sing-along. Tastes are eclectic, from country music and Broadway tunes to swing. Tampa, Walt Disney World, and other Central Florida attractions are within a one-hour drive. The park is for visitors ages 55 and up. There's a Wal-Mart across the street.

Campsites, facilities: This 530-unit community is laid out subdivision-style and features 100 sites for overnighters. Fifty sites are pull-through. Big rigs can be accommodated. All sites have full hookups with 30/50-amp electrical service, picnic tables, cable TV, and wireless Internet access. Park models are for sale. Restrooms, showers, a dump station, laundry facilities, a pool, spa, a recreation and entertainment hall, meeting rooms, horseshoe pits, and bocce ball (lawn bowling) and shuffleboard courts are on the premises. Most areas are wheelchair-accessible, and streets are paved. Children are permitted for short visits only. Leashed pets are allowed.

Reservations, fees: Reservations are recommended. Sites are $27 per night, plus $2 for cable TV. Credit cards are accepted. Stay as long as you wish. Long-term rates are available.

Directions: From I-75, take Exit 314 and drive east 0.25 mile on State Road 48.

Contact: The Oaks Campground, 5551 Southwest 18th Terrace, Bushnell, FL 33513, 352/793-7117, fax 352/793-7792, www.oaksrv.com.

63 SUMTER OAKS RV PARK

Scenic rating: 3

south of Bushnell

See map, page 298

With planned activities keeping visitors busy November–March, this Escapees RV Club membership park is only open to nonmembers when space is available.

Campsites, facilities: There are 99 RV sites that have concrete patios, 30/50-amp electrical service, and sewer hookups. Fifteen are pull-through. Restrooms, showers, laundry facilities, a pool, a clubhouse, shuffleboard courts, a snack bar, propane gas, and a store are on the premises. All areas are wheelchair-accessible. Children are permitted for short visits. Pets are permitted.

Reservations, fees: Reservations are recommended. Sites are $25 per night for two people, plus $1 per extra person. Credit cards are accepted.

Directions: From I-75, take Exit 309 and drive east 1.5 miles on County Road 673.

Contact: Sumter Oaks RV Park, 4602 County Road 673, Bushnell, FL 33513, 352/793-1333.

64 RED BARN RV RESORT

Scenic rating: 5

off I-75, in Bushnell

See map, page 298

Under new ownership since 2005, the park is big-rig-friendly and near shopping; there's a Wal-Mart across the street. This is the closest campground to the Dade Battlefield Historic Site, where Major Francis Dade and his troops were massacred three days after Christmas in 1835 by Seminole Indians dead-set against being moved to Oklahoma. "Have a good heart. Our difficulties and dangers are over now," Dade said shortly before the battle, believing his soldiers had passed the most likely spots for an Indian ambush. "And as soon as we arrive at Fort King, you'll have three days to rest and keep Christmas gaily." You can walk along the old Fort King Military Road, the route the soldiers took from Fort Brooke (now Tampa) to Fort King (now Ocala). Make sure to stop at the visitors center that dissects the battle's action. The battle is re-enacted during one weekend each December.

Campsites, facilities: This retiree-oriented community has 397 full-hookup RV sites. Most sites are pull-through, and some have picnic tables. A pool, a recreation room, horseshoes, shuffleboard, and winter social programs entertain campers. On the premises are restrooms, showers, a recreation room, and laundry facilities. Shopping is available within two miles. Management says all areas are wheelchair-accessible. Children are permitted. Pets are allowed.

Reservations, fees: Reservations are recommended. Sites are $36 per night for two people, plus $2 per extra person and $2 for cable TV. If you're a first-time visitor, ask for a special daily rate of $30. Credit cards are accepted. Long-term stays are OK.

Directions: From I-75 at Exit 314, drive east on State Road 48. You will see the park almost immediately.

Contact: Red Barn RV Resort, 5923 Southwest 20th Drive, Bushnell, FL 33513, 352/793-6065 or 352/793-6220.

65 SEVEN ACRES RV PARK

Scenic rating: 1

north of Dade City, on U.S. 301

See map, page 298

Although it's located on busy U.S. 301, this park is quiet and favored by long-term RVers, snowbirds, and people living in manufactured homes. During the winter season, planned activities include potlucks, bingo, and picnics.

Campsites, facilities: There are 160 grassy RV sites with full hookups, 30/50-amp electrical service, and telephone access. Five sites are pull-through (these are usually designated for overnighters; the rest are seasonal or long-term). RVs up to 40 feet long and slideouts can be accommodated on sites that average 30 feet wide by 65 feet long. The recreation hall, laundry, and bathrooms are wheelchair-accessible. About 80 percent of the sites are occupied by full-timers. Groceries are within four miles. Children and small pets are permitted.

Reservations, fees: Reservations are not necessary. Sites are $15 per night for two people, plus $1 for each additional person and $2 for electricity. Credit cards are not accepted. Long-term stays are OK.

Directions: From Dade City, drive three miles north on U.S. 301 to the park on the west side of the road.

Contact: Seven Acres RV Park, 16731 U.S. 301, Dade City, FL 33525, 352/567-3510, 7acresrv@wmconnect.com.

66 WITHLACOOCHEE RIVER PARK

Scenic rating: 9

east of Dade City

See map, page 298

As one of the few areas in Pasco County that has not been developed for farming or commercial use, this park is a gem. You may see bald and golden eagles, owls, deer, wild hogs, alligators, blue indigo snakes, armadillos, and more. The campground makes a good base for hiking the 13 miles of nature trails here, or for canoe trips on the Withlacoochee River. There's also a two-mile bike path. Fish off the dock on the river, not on the riverbank; it's adjacent to the canoe launch. Note that you'll have to carry your canoe 100 feet from the parking area to the launch.

The park also offers a 40-foot observation tower, picnic shelters, playground, a recreation field, and a taste of life from the 19th century—you'll see a reconstructed 1800s fort, a primitive log cabin, and Indian villages. The campground is part of a 260-acre county-run park in the larger wilderness area operated by the Southwest Florida Water Management District.

Campsites, facilities: Twenty-four RV sites with electricity and water are planned for some point in the future. As of this writing, there was a small primitive campground for tenters only. You'll have to hike 0.5 mile to the campground in this 260-acre wilderness park. There are 10 primitive sites with picnic tables and fire rings; there's a compost toilet in the camping area. Wheelchair-accessible flush toilets and running water are 0.5 mile from the camping area; no showers are available. The nearest groceries are five miles away in Dade City. Children are welcome. Leashed pets are permitted.

Reservations, fees: Call for the latest information.

Directions: From Dade City, take State Road 533 to River Road and turn right (east). Follow the road about five miles to Auton Road, then turn right (south) and go to the park entrance.

Contact: Withlacoochee River Park, 12929 Withlacoochee Boulevard, Dade City, FL 33525, 352/567-0264 or 352/521-4104, fax 352/521-4104. Information is also available from the East Pasco Parks and Recreation Department, 36620 State Road 52, Dade City, FL 33525, 352/521-4182.

67 CLERBROOK RESORT

🚲 🏊 🎣 🚣 🐕 🛶 ♿ 🚐

Scenic rating: 9

in Clermont

See map, page 298

You can't do this place justice by calling it an RV park, not with its library, post office, beauty salon, barbershop, country-club amenities, and, oh yes, obvious devotion to golf. Osprey and long-legged wading birds sometimes look onto the 18-hole, par-67 golf course from surrounding wetlands and lakes. If golfers somehow lose a club, they can order a customized replacement from the park's pro shop and ask the golf pro for tips to try out at the putting green or driving range.

Clearly, the idea is to leave your grassy, sunny RV site at this 287-acre resort each morning and take part in everything else it offers: 13 shuffleboard courts, three pools, four hot tubs, and more. Anglers try for bass and catfish at ponds and any of the region's chain of 17 lakes, including Lake Harris, a boating and waterskiing spot. A full-time activities director also keeps campers moving with square dancing lessons, bingo, and a host of other events in the three clubhouses. For a day trip, try Disney World, Sea World, or other Orlando-area attractions. The park is so huge that it's laid out like a town, with several subdivisions or neighborhoods. About 430 sites have park models.

Campsites, facilities: There are 1,257 sites, of which 850 full-hookup sites are for RVs up to 40 feet long. All have 50-amp electrical service. Six sites are drive-through. Each site has a picnic table. Internet access is available at the clubhouse in the "Lifestyles" and "Cross Roads" areas. For recreation, there's a golf course, three pools, three hot tubs, a playground, an exercise room, a driving range, a putting range, horseshoes, lighted shuffleboard courts, a softball field, a game room, tournament pool tables, and winter social programs. In the wintertime, BYOB (Bring Your Own Bottle) for happy hour in the clubhouse every Wednesday. For rallies or group retreats, the resort offers a reception and meeting rooms. Showers, restrooms, villa rentals, a dump station, cable TV, and three laundry facilities are available. The golf pro shop sells coffee, snacks, and candy, but there's also a major grocery store and restaurants within one mile or so. Management says all areas are wheelchair-accessible. Children are welcome, though it's primarily an over-55 group. Leashed pets are permitted.

Reservations, fees: Reservations are required. Sites are $31 per night. Credit cards are accepted. Long-term rates are available.

Directions: From Florida's Turnpike west of Winter Garden, take Exit 289 and drive south on U.S. 27 for about two miles. The park is on the east side.

Contact: Clerbrook Resort, 20005 U.S. 27, Clermont, FL 34711, 352/394-5513 or 800/440-3801, fax 352/394-8251.

68 TORCHLITE RV AND MOBILE HOME PARK

🐕 ♿ 🚐

Scenic rating: 2

south of Clermont

See map, page 298

Thirty-nine grassy/concrete-pad RV sites are set on 13 shaded acres near department stores, groceries, and shopping centers. Fifty-four mobile homes are also in this park, and space for travelers is scarce; 85 percent of the lots are taken by year-round residents. Local bass anglers head west to Lake Louisa, one of 13 lakes linked together by an officially designated Outstanding Florida Water: the Palatlakaha River. To swim, fish, or canoe, try the lake's namesake state park (352/394-3969) at Louisa's southwestern corner off U.S. 27, seven miles south of State Road 50.

Campsites, facilities: There are 30 sites with 30-amp electrical service and nine with 50-amp, for RVs up to 40 feet long. Each site has a picnic table and full hookups. Shuffleboard and a recreation room entertain campers. Showers, restrooms, a dump station, and laundry facilities are available. Groceries are 4.5 miles. Bathhouses, laundry facilities, and the recreation hall are wheelchair-accessible. Children and people of all ages are welcome to camp but may not reside in mobile homes. Leashed pets are permitted.

Reservations, fees: Reservations are recommended. Sites are $15–20 per night for two people, plus $1 for each additional person. Credit cards are not accepted. Long-term rates are available.

Directions: From State Road 50 in Clermont, drive 3.5 miles south on U.S. 27. You'll see the park entrance on the right.

Contact: Torchlite RV and Mobile Home Park, 10201 U.S. 27 South, Clermont, FL 34711, 352/394-3716.

69 LAKE LOUISA STATE PARK

Scenic rating: 8

south of Clermont

See map, page 298

One of the newer additions to the Florida State Park system, this campground opened in 2003 with fanfare that called it a "world-class" park. Indeed, it offers spectacular recreation, with six lakes and rolling hills for horseback riding and hiking (although you may have to wait a few years for the planted landscape to grow to full regalia). Swim or catch some rays on the sandy beach at Lake Louisa, or canoe and kayak on Dixie Lake; the park has a small ramp there and on Lake Hammond. Campers can fish in four of the lakes, but gas-powered engines are not allowed. A public boat ramp is outside the park on the west side of Lake Louisa on Hull Road. There are 15 miles of equestrian trails and 20 miles of hiking paths. The park is a popular site for marathons, triathlons, and equestrian events held by Orlando area clubs.

Campsites, facilities: The camping areas are arranged in three loops. The 60 sites have water and 30/50-amp electrical service; 15 have sewer hookups. Each site has a picnic table, a grill, and a fire ring. On the premises are showers, restrooms, a dump station, two fishing piers, three docks, a pavilion, an amphitheater, and rental cabins. The restrooms and three campsites have wheelchair access. Groceries are within three miles. Children are welcome. Leashed pets are allowed.

Reservations, fees: Reservations are recommended; contact ReserveAmerica at 800/336-3521 or reserveamerica.com. Sites are $21 per night for four people. Credit cards are accepted. The maximum stay is 14 days.

Directions: From Clermont, drive south seven miles on State Road 50.

Contact: Lake Louisa State Park, 7305 U.S. 27, Clermont, FL 34714, 352/394-3969, www.floridastateparks.org.

70 THOUSAND TRAILS ORLANDO

Scenic rating: 8

south of Clermont

See map, page 298

Part of the Thousand Trails national campground membership club, this 255-acre resort (or "preserve," as the marketing folks call it) targets Disney World and theme-park-destination campers, families, and full-timers. Disney World is just nine miles away, but there's plenty to do in the campground, too. On the premises is a 60-acre, spring-fed lake with fishing, rowboats, and canoeing options. Teens can play video games in the game room, and playgrounds occupy the younger set. Entertainment is presented weekly in the recreation hall. Activities directors lead campers in arts and crafts, line dancing, and the like; they also plan children's activities. If you invite friends or family who don't camp, they can rent one of the 30 on-site trailers to round out your party.

Campsites, facilities: In this membership park, RVs and tents can be accommodated on 734 sites, all of which have picnic tables and grills. Restrooms, showers, a dump station, and laundry facilities are available. Amenities include a pool and spa, a boat ramp and dock, canoe rentals, miniature golf, a recreation hall, playgrounds, nature trails, shuffleboard and tennis courts, a video and game room, horseshoe pits, a campground store, rental trailers, and propane gas sales. Most areas are wheelchair-accessible. Children are welcome. Leashed pets are permitted.

Reservations, fees: Reservations are recommended, especially during the busy season (December 19–March 31). Call 90 days in advance for reservations during this high-demand period. Trial memberships are available for one weekend. Credit cards are accepted.

Directions: From Clermont, drive 13 miles south on U.S. 27. From Kissimmee, drive west on State Road 192 eight miles to U.S. 27; turn north on U.S. 27 and drive two miles.

Contact: Thousand Trails Orlando, 2110 U.S. 27 South, Clermont, FL 34711, 352/394-7575 or 800/723-1217, www.1000trails.com.

71 ORLANDO WINTER GARDEN RV RESORT

Scenic rating: 5

in Winter Garden

See map, page 298

All the streets in this 30-acre community are paved, and about 85 percent are shaded by oaks and many orange trees. There are four bathhouses, two laundry rooms, and an adult lounge. When guests aren't busy driving the 30 minutes to Disney World or other theme parks (backroads near the park get you there with less traffic), they enjoy swimming in the two heated pools and biking around the park. For other outdoor adventures, head to a nearby favorite of bicyclists, joggers, and inline skaters—the West Orange Trail, two miles west of Florida's Turnpike at the Lake/Orange County line. The trail links Apopka, Clarcona, Winter Garden, and other points; for details, call West Orange Trail (407/654-1108). About a third of the park is occupied by year-round residents.

Campsites, facilities: The 376 sites for RVs have full hookups, 50-amp electrical service, cable TV, and picnic tables. Sites 1–26 and 57–85 are drive-through. RVs as large as 45 feet and slideouts can be accommodated. About 100 sites are available for overnight visitors. Internet access is available in the clubhouse. Two pools, a playground, a recreation room, horseshoes, shuffleboard, an adult lounge, cable TV, and winter social programs entertain campers. On the premises are restrooms, showers, a dump station, dog run area, and laundry facilities. Management says the pool, laundry room, and restrooms are wheelchair-accessible. A restaurant and groceries are across the street. Children and leashed pets are permitted.

Reservations, fees: Reservations are recommended. Sites are $34 per night for two people, plus $3.50 for each additional person. Credit cards are accepted. Long-term rates are available.

Directions: From Florida's Turnpike at Exit 267, take Colonial Drive/State Road 50 west for two miles to the campground at right.

Contact: Orlando Winter Garden RV Resort, 13905 West Colonial Drive, Winter Garden, FL 34787, 407/656-1415, fax 407/656-0858, www.wintergardenrv.com.

72 STAGE STOP CAMPGROUND

Scenic rating: 6

in Winter Garden

See map, page 298

These 22 acres of grassy sites are set alongside a major highway 10 miles west of Orlando, where about 20 percent of the land is occupied by year-round residents. Some sites overlook a small lake and pinewoods, but shopping centers are across the street and next door. Most visitors are retirees. One unusual feature is the Olympic-sized swimming pool, although guests also can take advantage of horseshoes, shuffleboard, and badminton. Disney-area attractions are about 30 minutes away.

Campsites, facilities: Fifty-amp electrical service is available at 80 of the 248 full-hookup sites; the rest have 30-amp. Each has a concrete patio and picnic table. About 30 sites are pull-through, and big rigs are welcome. Streets are paved. Sites are 25 feet wide, varying in depth from 50 to 60 feet. A pool, horseshoes, shuffleboard, a playground, badminton, winter activities, restrooms, showers, a convenience store with RV supplies, and laundry facilities are available. Management says the clubhouse and restrooms are wheelchair-accessible. Children and pets are permitted.

Reservations, fees: Reservations are recommended in winter. Sites are $25 per night for two people, plus $4 for each additional person. May 1–September 30, there is an additional electricity fee of $1.50 per day. Credit cards are accepted. Long-term stays are OK.

Directions: From Florida's Turnpike (northbound), take Exit 267 and travel 2.5 miles west on State Road 50 to the campground. If you're traveling southbound on the turnpike, get off at Exit 272 and drive 2.5 miles east on State Road 50 to the campground.

Contact: Stage Stop Campground, 14400 West Colonial Drive, Winter Garden, FL 34787, 407/656-8000, fax 407/656-3840.

73 MAGNOLIA PARK

🐟 🚤 🐕 🚵 🚐 ⛺

Scenic rating: 4

on Lake Apopka, west of Apopka

See map, page 298

Orange County promotes this 56-acre park/campground as a place that features spectacular sunsets on the county's largest lake (33,000 acres). That much is true—the sunsets over Lake Apopka are simply gorgeous. What they don't tell you is that Lake Apopka was once fouled by runoff from nearby vegetable farms. Years of work are still ongoing to bring the lake back to a healthful state, and the water quality is said to have improved to the point where you can even fish in it. The state has purchased 33,000 acres on the north side as a kind of huge water filter, which also protects it from development. The park is shaded by oak, magnolia, and hickory trees. Anglers who bring a boat can make a run down toward Winter Garden and try their luck, or work their way up into the canals on the lake's north side to fish for specks or catfish before returning to the gravel campsites.

Campsites, facilities: All 18 sites at this county-run park have 30-amp electricity, cement pads, water, picnic tables, and fire rings. Sewer hookups are not available. RVs as long as 40 feet can be accommodated on wood sites that vary in size from 30 to 40 feet wide by 60 to 80 feet deep. On the premises are restrooms, showers, a dump station, a boat ramp, and a playground. The restrooms and sites 15 and 16 are wheelchair-accessible. Groceries, restaurants, and laundry facilities are within five miles. Children are welcome. Pets are permitted in the camping area, but not in the general park or playground. Alcohol is prohibited.

Reservations, fees: Reservations are recommended; they must be made in person. Sites are $13–18 per night, depending on your age and county residency. Credit cards are not accepted. Maximum stay is 14 days.

Directions: From Apopka, head south on County Road 437/Ocoee-Apopka Road. Turn right onto Binion Road, which leads to the campground.

Contact: Magnolia Park, 2929 Binion Road, Apopka, FL 32703, 407/886-4231, www.orangecountyparks.net.

7.4 SUN RESORTS

🏊 🐕 🚶 ♿ 🚐 ⛺

Scenic rating: 8

west of Apopka

See map, page 298

Targeting families and adult visitors, this park does a nice job of separating overnighters and seasonal vacationers from permanent residents in a 110-acre wooded condominium park. It also emphasizes a balance of shaded areas and tree-limb clearance in the RV area. The Y-shaped pool is one of the largest I've heard of in an RV park, with 100,000 gallons of water, Olympic-sized swimming lanes, and a poolside stage for entertainment. A kiddie pool is next to the big pool. A park model area with about 800 manufactured homes is set apart from the overnighters, so it has more of an RV park feel. Shopping and restaurants are nearby, and Walt Disney World is a 25-mile ride away—you can make a day trip of it. Manufactured homes and lots are for sale or rent.

Campsites, facilities: There are 108 RV sites (45 pull-through), and most have 30-amp electrical service. Six sites have 50-amp service, for an additional fee. Sewer hookups can be found at 74 sites, while 34 have just water and electricity. Rigs up to 40 feet can be accommodated on lots varying in size from 35 or 40 feet wide and 60 feet deep. All sites have picnic tables; some have cable TV. The tent sites are located in a grassy, wooded area. A wireless Internet network is available at the trading post and at campsites near it. Restrooms, showers, laundry facilities, a pool, a trading post/store with limited groceries, a snack bar, miniature golf, propane gas sales, a recreation hall with planned activities, a dog-walk area, and shuffleboard courts are on the premises. Entertainment includes volleyball, basketball, billiards, bingo, holiday events, water aerobics, a kiddie pool, and a playground. Five RV sites, the bathhouses, the office, the recreation hall, and laundry and trading post areas are wheelchair-accessible. Grocery stores and shopping are within five miles. Children are welcome, though wintertime guests tend to be snowbirds, while summertime visitors are families. Leashed pets are permitted.

Reservations, fees: Reservations are recommended. Sites are $28 per night for two adults and three children, plus $5 per additional person and $2 for 50-amp electrical sites. First-time visitors should ask about special rate offers. Credit cards are accepted. Long-term rates are available. Tenters are limited to 14-day stays.

Directions: From the Florida Turnpike, take Exit 267A to 429 North. Turn right on West Road (Exit 26). At Clarcona-Ocoee Road, turn left and go 3.2 miles. Turn north on Apopka Vineland Road and drive 1.8 miles to the park on the left. From I-4, take Exit 92 onto Semoran Boulevard and drive west 6.5 miles. Turn south on Sheeler Road and proceed 2.8 miles. At Clarcona-Ocoee Road, turn left and drive 0.2 mile to the resort.

Contact: Sun Resorts, 3000 Clarcona Road, Apopka, FL 32703, 407/889-3048, fax 407/889-0887, www.sunrvresorts.net.

7.5 CLARCONA HORSEMAN'S PARK

🐕 🚐 ⛺

Scenic rating: 6

in Apopka

See map, page 298

Saddle up! This 40-acre park, with access to the 22-mile West Orange Trail equestrian path, was created for horseback riders, but anyone can camp here if space is available. The campground primarily accommodates equestrians participating in myriad competitions and shows, or those who want to take their mounts on the adjoining trail. Operated by Orange County, the park also has a go-cart track for Quarter Midget Racing. A manager lives on the property; office hours are 7 A.M.–6 P.M. daily, but the park is open 24 hours. Since it's on the show circuit, you may hear your neighbors leaving at 3 A.M. to get to the next stop.

Campsites, facilities: There are 28 campsites for RVs or tents; each has water and electricity. Restrooms, showers, horse barns, bleacher seating, judging towers, and dressage show rings are on the premises. Children are welcome. Leashed pets are permitted.

Reservations, fees: All sites are first-come, first-served. Sites are $15 per night for two people, plus $3 for electrical service. Credit cards are not accepted. The maximum stay is two weeks.

Directions: From I-4, take Exit 80B onto U.S. 441/Orange Blossom Trail and drive northbound to Apopka, about 13 miles. Turn west on Apopka-Vineland Road/County Road 435 and drive four miles. Turn right on McCormick Road and proceed 0.5 mile. Turn right on Damon Road to the park.

Contact: Clarcona Horseman's Park, 3535 Damon Road, Apopka, FL 32703, 407/886-6255 or 407/886-9761 (if horse shows are in progress), fax 407/886-2142, www.orange countyparks.net.

76 BILL FREDERICK PARK AND POOL AT TURKEY LAKE

🏃 🚴 🏊 🎣 🐎 🎠 ♿ 🚐 ⛺

Scenic rating: 7

in west Orlando

See map, page 298

A very unusual addition to this popular, shady, wooded city-run park is the Children's Farm, which re-creates a nostalgic look at Florida's rural life. Seven miles of nature trails meander through the live-oak hammock and cattail marshes, and bicyclists can cover three miles of trails before returning to their asphalt camp-. Picturesque enough to be used for the

occasional wedding, the park is a local favorite for weekend picnics, as families stake out the 125 picnic tables, 77 barbecue grills, and 15 picnic shelters. Swimmers plunge into a pool overlooking Turkey Lake. A 200-foot-long fishing pier aids freshwater anglers. What's remarkable is that this little nature spot is just about 1 mile from Universal Studios, 5 miles from International Drive, and 15 miles from Disney-area attractions.

Campsites, facilities: There are 36 full-hookup campsites with 30/50-amp electrical outlets. Each site has a picnic table and a grill. A pool, three playgrounds, a nature trail, disc golf, volleyball, cabins, restrooms, showers, a dump station, and laundry facilities are on the premises. Groceries and restaurants are about one mile away. The restrooms, laundry, and picnic areas are wheelchair-accessible. Children are welcome. Leashed pets are permitted.

Reservations, fees: Reservations are recommended on weekends and holidays; the camping area is full almost every weekend. Nightly fee for four people is $18 (full hookups), plus $2.50 for each additional person. Credit cards are accepted. Stays are limited to 29 days.

Directions: Head west from downtown Orlando on the East–West Expressway/State Road 408. Exit at Hiawassee Road. Go south 3.5 miles to the campground.

Contact: Bill Frederick Park and Pool at Turkey Lake, 3401 South Hiawassee Road, Orlando, FL 32835, 407/299-5594 or 407/299-5581, www.cityoforlando.net.

77 HAL SCOTT REGIONAL PRESERVE AND PARK

🏃 🚴 🎣 🐎 ⛺

Scenic rating: 6

on the Econlockhatchee River, southeast of Orlando

See map, page 298

The Econlockhatchee River divides these 8,427 acres of untamed country preserved by the county and the St. Johns River Water Management District, to the benefit of resident bald eagles, gopher tortoises, bobcats, and river otters. Look up—maybe you'll see a sandhill crane while following several miles of trails available for hiking, bicycling, birdwatching, or horseback riding. Trails crisscross the property, leading past the old Yates Homestead to a creek called Cowpen Branch, as well as more distant points in the sun-dappled prairie and flatwoods. Anglers have a short walk from the parking lot to reach a 17-acre lake named for Hal Scott. Campsites, found farther into the preserve, are on the river and well-separated from each other.

Campsites, facilities: The park offers four primitive backpacking tent sites. From the parking area, the nearest campsite requires about a one-mile hike. Bring drinking water, food, mosquito repellent, and all supplies that you'll need. Pack out trash. Children are welcome. Pets must be leashed.

Reservations, fees: Sites are first-come, first-served. Camping is free. Each site accommodates up to six people. If your party has at least seven people, get a free permit and reserve at least one week ahead at 386/329-4410. Maximum stay for all campers is seven days.

Directions: From Orlando, go east on State Road 50 to State Road 520. Turn right (south). A few miles down, turn right again into the Wedgefield subdivision on Maxim Parkway. Turn left at Bancroft Street, right at Meredith Avenue, and left onto Dallas Boulevard, then follow signs. The park entrance is 1.6 miles from the intersection of Meredith and Dallas, on the right. There is also an exit for Dallas Boulevard from the Bee-Line Expressway eastbound.

Contact: St. Johns River Water Management District, Division of Land Management, P.O. Box 1429, Palatka, FL 32178-1429, 386/329-4500 or 800/451-7106, www.sjrwmd.com. Or, contact Orange County Parks and Recreation, 407/836-6200; http://parks.orange countyfl.net.

78 MULLET LAKE PARK

Scenic rating: 3

east of Sanford, on Mullet Lake

See map, page 298

The blue waters of Mullet Lake beckon anglers and boaters who stay at this 151-acre, county-operated campground. Access to the St. Johns River is the main attraction, but you can camp here (with a permit) to overlook the 631-acre lake, or enjoy the picnicking area for day use. Swimming is not allowed. There is no staff on-site.

Campsites, facilities: There are no designated campsites, and camping is primitive. However, restrooms, showers, grills, water, a boat ramp, and a picnic pavilion are available. Children are welcome. Pets are not allowed.

Reservations, fees: A camping permit is required; call the Seminole County Parks and Recreation Department for details. The park is open 24 hours a day. Sites are $5 per night for four people. Credit cards are not accepted. The maximum stay is seven days.

Directions: From Sanford, drive south on U.S. 17/U.S. 92 for nearly one mile. Turn east onto State Road 46 and drive 6.3 miles. Turn left onto West Osceola Road and proceed 1.5 miles. Turn left onto Mullet Lake Park Road. The park is ahead 1.7 miles.

Contact: Mullet Lake Park, 2368 Mullet Lake Road, Geneva, FL 32732; or contact the Seminole County Parks and Recreation Department, 1101 E. First Street, Sanford, FL 32771, 407/788-0405, www.co.seminole .fl.us/parks/mullet.asp.

79 FLORIDA NATIONAL SCENIC TRAIL/CHULUOTA

Scenic rating: 7

in Chuluota

See map, page 298

You'll need to hike in with a tent, water, and other supplies strapped to your back, because no facilities are available at this campsite on a woodsy stretch of the Florida Trail. It's simply a wild retreat from urban Orlando. Amy Gagnon, a dog trainer in Oviedo, Florida, says she likes to take her Yorkie and three Labrador retrievers camping in the remote wilderness here.

Campsites, facilities: Primitive camping for backpackers is permitted along the trail. There are no facilities, so bring food, water, a tent, and other camping gear. Bury all human waste, and pack out garbage. Children are allowed. Leashed pets are tolerated.

Reservations, fees: No permission is needed to camp, and sites are taken on a first-come, first-served basis. Camping is free.

Directions: From Highway 419 in Chuluota, turn left at Langford Drive. After about 0.25 mile, look to the right for a wide dirt road with no houses; it leads to the marked Florida National Scenic Trail entrance. The trailhead is off Langford Drive and Washington Avenue.

Contact: Florida Trail Association, 5415 Southwest 13th Street, Gainesville, FL 32608, 352/378-8823 or 877/HIKE-FLA, www .florida-trail.org. For help with directions, call the Greater Sanford Chamber of Commerce, 407/322-2212.

80 LAKE MILLS PARK

Scenic rating: 6

east of Casselberry, near Chuluota

See map, page 298

No large RVs can be accommodated at this rural nature park—just small trailers or pop-up campers that set up in a grassy clearing. Towering oak trees said to be 150 years old, pine forests, and a mixed hardwood swamp are reminiscent of how Florida used to look. Carry-in boats or canoes can head out on the lake, but fishing and motorized vessels are prohibited. This pretty 50-acre county park also has a day-use area, with volleyball, a playground, and a jogging trail, but camp-

ers tend to be families or Scouts in a walk-in group campsite.

Campsites, facilities: There are 12 primitive sites (no water, no electricity, no dump station) with picnic tables. Restrooms and showers are provided. In the park are a boardwalk, playground, a jogging and fitness trail, sand volleyball courts, an amphitheater, and picnic pavilions. Children are welcome. Pets are not allowed.

Reservations, fees: A camping permit is required; call the park at 407/788-0609 for details. The fee is $5 per person, or $20 for the park's single group site. Credit cards are not accepted. The maximum stay is seven days.

Directions: From County Road 415/Chuluota Road in the town of Chuluota, drive east on Lake Mills Road about 0.25 mile. Turn north on Tropical Avenue and proceed a short distance to the park.

Contact: Lake Mills Park, 1301 Tropical Avenue, Chuluota, FL 32766, 407/788-0609; or contact the Seminole County Parks and Recreation Department, 1101 East 1st Street, Sanford, FL 32771, 407/788-0405, www .co.seminole.fl.gov.

81 CHRISTMAS AIRSTREAM PARK

Scenic rating: 5

in Christmas east of Orlando

See map, page 298

Although the name might mislead you, you don't have to arrive in an Airstream to camp at the concrete pad/gravel sites in this 18-acre park popular with snowbirds staying for the season. Any RV will do. The flat, wooded park is about 20 miles from the Kennedy Space Center, and about 50 miles from Disney-area attractions. Generally speaking, this sleepy part of Florida is skipped by most out-of-towners except at Christmastime when people travel for hours to the post office here to have their greeting cards postmarked "Christmas, FL." About

10 percent of the lots in this park are occupied year-round. Overnight sites are limited.

Campsites, facilities: All of the 165 grassy RV sites have full hookups and 30-amp electrical service, and a few have 50-amp. More than 120 sites are pull-through, and RVs as long as 45 feet can be accommodated. However, rigs with slideouts must be approved by the management in advance, and pop-up campers are prohibited. Roads are crushed shell and dirt; some sites have concrete pads. Picnic tables are provided. Internet connections are available in the clubhouse. A pool, a playground, three recreation rooms, a camp circle for gatherings, winter recreation programs organized by volunteers, restrooms, showers, dump stations, telephone service, and laundry facilities are available. Two meeting halls are offered for camper rallies. Shopping is eight miles away in Titusville or 15 miles away in Orlando. Management says the rec halls and restrooms are wheelchair-accessible. Children are welcome, though most visitors are snowbirds. Two leashed pets are permitted per site; aggressive breeds are prohibited.

Reservations, fees: Reservations are necessary in winter. Sites are $25 per night for four people, plus $5 for each additional person. Credit cards are accepted. Long-term rates are available.

Directions: From I-95, take Exit 215 and drive eight miles west on State Road 50 to the park. If you're traveling on I-4, use Exit 83B and drive 18 miles east on State Road 50 to the park.

Contact: Christmas Airstream Park, 25525 East Colonial Drive, Christmas, FL 32709, 407/568-5207, www.christmasairstream rvpark.com.

82 WINTER PARADISE RV PARK
🏊 🐕 ♿ 🚐

Scenic rating: 3

north of Hudson Beach

See map, page 298

Whether for golfing, boating, fishing, visiting the beach, shopping, or relaxing by the pool, this park is centrally located, just three miles from the Gulf of Mexico in a busy suburb with plenty of entertainment. The area has many seafood and ethnic restaurants, as well as chain-operated eateries. Favorite things to do include water aerobics in the pool, bingo, and other fun pastimes organized by the year-round activities director.

Campsites, facilities: Most sites at this 302-unit RV park have full hookups and 30-amp electrical service; a few are drive-through. Forty sites have 50-amp service. RVs as long as 45 feet can be accommodated. Heavier units can be parked on gravel sites. Other spots are grassy, with concrete patio slabs. Restrooms, showers, laundry facilities, a dump station, shuffleboard courts, horseshoe pits, a pool, and a recreation building with billiard tables and a library are provided. Propane delivery is available. The clubhouse, office, and laundry room are wheelchair-accessible. Roads are paved. Shopping and restaurants are within three miles. Children are welcome. Pets are allowed; dog walks are on two sides of the park.

Reservations, fees: Reservations are recommended. Sites are $35 per night. Credit cards are accepted. Long-term stays are OK.

Directions: From Hudson, drive 2.5 miles north on U.S. 19 to the park, at the corner with Denton Avenue.

Contact: Winter Paradise RV Park, 16108 U.S. 19, Hudson, FL 34667, 727/868-2285 or 800/328-0775.

83 SEVEN OAKS TRAVEL PARK
🏊 🐕 ♿ 🚐 ⛺

Scenic rating: 3

in Hudson

See map, page 298

Although located smack-dab in the middle of the urbanized Gulf Coast, this 297-unit adult park has a semi-rural setting among rolling hills. It's just east of the major thoroughfare at

17 feet above sea level, which means it's probably secure from high water if you leave your RV parked here long-term. Beaches and golf courses are within three miles. Two-thirds of residents stay here year-round. Planned activities in the wintertime include cruises, swimming, playing pool, potluck dinners, bingo, and shuffleboard.

Campsites, facilities: This adults-only park has 297 sites, of which 100 are available for overnights. Sites have full hookups to accommodate rigs up to 40 feet long. Half the available sites have 30-amp service; the rest have 50-amp. Most sites have concrete patios or are paved. Restrooms, showers, laundry facilities, a heated pool, shuffleboard courts, a recreation hall, horseshoe pits, and propane gas are available. The clubhouse, pool, office, and bathhouse are wheelchair-accessible. Children are welcome to stay two weeks at a time. Leashed pets are permitted.

Reservations, fees: Reservations are recommended. Sites are $25 per night for two people, plus $3 for each additional person. Credit cards are not accepted. Long-term stays are OK.

Directions: From Hudson, drive 1.5 miles north on U.S. 19. Turn east on Bolton Avenue in town and continue 0.7 mile to the park on the north side.

Contact: Seven Oaks Travel Park, 9207 Bolton Avenue, Hudson, FL 34667, 727/862-3016, www.7oakstravelpark.com.

84 SHADY ACRES MOBILE HOME AND RV PARK

Scenic rating: 3

north of Hudson

See map, page 298

About 20 percent of sites are occupied year-round at this mobile-home park located off a six-lane highway. Head to the recreation hall for bingo, coffee, doughnuts, cookouts, and potluck dinners. The beach is one mile away.

Supermarkets, doctors' offices, and a hospital are conveniently close.

Campsites, facilities: This 72-unit urban mobile-home community with a recreation hall, laundry facilities, and restrooms has 25 roomy full-hookup RV sites, of which 9 are drive-through. Twenty sites have 30-amp electrical service, and four have 50-amp. RVs up to 37 feet long can be accommodated. Cable TV and telephone access are available, and the rec hall and restrooms are wheelchair-accessible. Picnic tables and a fire ring round out the picture. supermarkets, doctors' offices, and a hospital are within 0.4 mile. Children are welcome. Small pets are allowed.

Reservations, fees: Reservations are recommended. Sites are $20 per night. Overnighters must check out by 10 A.M. Credit cards are accepted. Long-term rates are available.

Directions: From the junction of State Road 52 and U.S. 19, drive two miles north on U.S. 19.

Contact: Shady Acres Mobile Home and RV Park, 14417 U.S. 19 North, Hudson, FL 34667, 727/868-9589.

85 GULFBREEZE RV PARK

Scenic rating: 2

north of Hudson

See map, page 298

The park targets long-term visitors for, as management says, "a week, a month, forever." It's set on a hill in a quiet residential area with plenty of trees, yet is still close to shops and restaurants. About half the occupants live here year-round. In winter, snowbirds and retirees enjoy pancake breakfasts, spaghetti dinners, crafts, golf and bowling leagues, deep-sea fishing charters, and line dancing. A "get acquainted" coffee is held every Wednesday.

Campsites, facilities: There are 147 RV sites with full hookups, 50-amp electrical service, and telephone and cable TV access. Most sites are grassy and average 30 by 50 feet in size.

RVs up to 40 feet long and slideouts can be accommodated. Restrooms, showers, laundry facilities, picnic tables, a dump station, a pool, a recreation hall with Internet access, horseshoe pits, and shuffleboard courts are on the premises. Streets are paved, and the clubhouse and bathhouse are wheelchair-accessible. Children are welcome. Leashed pets are permitted.

Reservations, fees: Reservations are not necessary. Sites are $20 per night for two people, plus $3 for each additional person. Credit cards are accepted. Long-term RVers are preferred.

Directions: From the junction of State Road 52 and U.S. 19, drive five miles north on U.S. 19. Turn east at Bolton Avenue (look for the Chevron sign) and go two blocks.

Contact: Gulfbreeze RV Park, 9014 Bolton Avenue, Hudson, FL 34667, 727/862-6826.

86 LAKEWOOD TRAVEL PARK

Scenic rating: 2

in Hudson

See map, page 298

Backing up to a country meadow and overlooking a pond, this suburban park contains a mix of sunny and shady spots. The atmosphere is friendly and homey, with some 70 percent of the residents living here year-round. It may be hard to find a spot in winter, when many campers opt for the $295 monthly rate. Within a few miles are gulf beaches, Tarpon Springs, Weeki Wachee, nature parks, and golf courses.

Campsites, facilities: Of the 88 lots, about 40 RV sites are available to visitors. They have 30-amp electrical service, full hookups, and optional cable TV and telephone service. Restrooms, showers, laundry facilities, and an activities building are provided. The park caters to retirees staying one month at a time. Children are welcome for short-term visits. Pets are allowed.

Reservations, fees: Reservations are not necessary. Sites are $20 per night for two people, plus $2 for each additional person and $1 for pets. Credit cards are not accepted.

Directions: From U.S. 19 in Hudson, drive east on State Road 52 for 4.5 miles.

Contact: Lakewood Travel Park, 11517 State Road 52, Hudson, FL 34669, 727/856-1306.

87 BARRINGTON HILLS RV RESORT

Scenic rating: 7

in Hudson

See map, page 298

Targeting active retirees, this RV park is centrally located near shopping and the Gulf of Mexico. Sometimes known as Sunburst, the park is part of the Equity Lifestyle Properties chain, which also owns the Encore parks. During the winter, a full schedule of planned activities helps seasonal visitors socialize and get to know each other.

Campsites, facilities: There are 390 RV sites, of 20 are pull-through. Rigs up to 45 feet long can be accommodated. All sites have full hookups, 50-amp service, picnic tables, cable TV, and telephone service available. Wireless Internet access is available at two-thirds of the resort; if you want one of these spots, be sure to ask. Restrooms, showers, a dump station, laundry facilities, a pool, a clubhouse, horseshoe pits, shuffleboard courts, a billiards room, and a golf net are on the premises. Children are welcome. Leashed pets are permitted.

Reservations, fees: Reservations are recommended. Sites are $26 per night. Credit cards are accepted. Long-term rates are available.

Directions: From the intersection of U.S. 19 and State Road 52 in Hudson, drive north on U.S. 19 for 2.5 miles. Turn east on New York Avenue and drive 1.4 miles to the park.

Contact: Barrington Hills RV Resort, 9412

New York Avenue, Hudson, FL 34667, 727/868-3586 or 877/287-2757, fax 727/863-7259, www.rvonthego.com.

88 CREWS LAKE PARK

Scenic rating: 8

on Crews Lake, off U.S. 41

See map, page 298

Here's another area the bulldozers haven't touched. Operated by Pasco County, this 111-acre park is heavily wooded with large live oak trees overlooking 750-acre Crews Lake. Urban-dwellers can seek respite from city life, but the park gets little use because so few people know about it. Take a quiet walk along 2.5 miles of trails through the palmetto and pine forest. A specially planted garden is replete with flowers and plants that draw butterflies and birds. A paved bike path winds one mile through the woods; it's popular with inline skaters. However, fishing and boating are not possible; a drought has severely affected Crews Lake, and weeds have taken over much of the lakebed. The campground was originally built for Scout use but has been opened to the public because it wasn't being used during the week.

Campsites, facilities: The park has 10 primitive tent-only sites with picnic tables, grills, and one community water source; there is a chemical toilet, but no restrooms on the campground. An outdoor cold-water shower is available. Elsewhere in the park are restrooms, nature trails, horseshoe pits, a boat ramp, a pier, a volleyball field, two playgrounds, picnic pavilions, and an observation tower. Children are welcome. Leashed pets are allowed.

Reservations, fees: Reservations are not necessary, but call in advance to see if there are vacancies. Scout groups take priority. Camping is free. The maximum stay is seven days.

Directions: From I-75, take Exit 285 and drive 10 miles west on State Road 52 past U.S. 41. Continue two more miles, then turn north on Shady Hills Road and drive 3.5 miles to Crews Lake Road.

Contact: Crews Lake Park, 16739 Crews Lake Drive, Shady Hills, FL 34610, 727/861-3038. Reserve a pavilion at 727/861-3052. Information is also available from the Pasco County Parks and Recreation Department, 4111 Land O' Lakes Boulevard, Suite 202, Land O' Lakes, FL 34639, 352/521-4182.

89 GROVE RIDGE ESTATES

Scenic rating: 3

south of Dade City, on U.S. 98

See map, page 298

Horses graze near this neatly kept park, located adjacent to an orange grove—unless the bulldozers get to it. The country setting offers plenty of wide-open spaces for those who crave the outdoors, but stores and other conveniences are nearby in Dade City. About half the sites are occupied year-round. Park models are for sale.

Campsites, facilities: This adults-only RV resort accepts self-contained rigs at least 20 feet long at 256 full-hookup sites with 50-amp electrical service. Sites are 30 by 50 feet, and rigs up to 42 feet long can be accommodated. Laundry facilities, shuffleboard courts, horseshoe pits, a recreation hall, a pool, telephone service, and rental trailers are available. There is no bathhouse. The clubhouse is wheelchair-accessible and has an Internet connection. Children are not allowed except for brief visits. One pet under 25 pounds is permitted per site.

Reservations, fees: Reservations are recommended. Sites are $25 per night for two people, plus $2 for each additional person. Credit cards are not accepted. Most campers are retirees staying for the winter season.

Directions: From I-75, take Exit 285 eastbound 10 miles on State Road 52 to Dade City. Turn south on U.S. 301/U.S. 98 and go through town. At the point where U.S. 98 veers off toward Lakeland, keep traveling on U.S. 98. Drive 0.5 mile southeast to the park.

Contact: Grove Ridge Estates, 10721 U.S. 98, Dade City, FL 33525, 352/523-2277, www .bel-aireresorts.com.

90 COUNTRY AIRE ESTATES

Scenic rating: 4

south of Dade City

See map, page 298

Groceries and restaurants are nearby, and antiques hounds will find plenty of shops to browse in Dade City. Social activities are held year-round at this park, where the vast majority of the 68 lots are owned by residents, leaving about 18 sites open to people passing through in winter. There's a two-acre pond for anglers inclined to try their luck. Most people here hail from Michigan, Ohio, Pennsylvania, New York, New Jersey, and Canada.

Campsites, facilities: Catering to RVers age 55 and older, this hillside park, with a total of 68 units, has about 18 sites with sewer hookups, 30/50-amp electrical service, and picnic tables available for short-term visitors. The maximum RV that can be accommodated is 38 feet. Some sites are waterfront. Restrooms, showers, picnic tables, laundry facilities, a heated pool, a clubhouse, horseshoe pits, shuffleboard courts, telephone service, and cable TV are available. Groceries and restaurants are within one mile. All areas are wheelchair-accessible. Families with children are permitted to stay a couple of nights in summer; children are not accepted at other times. Pets under 15 pounds are permitted.

Reservations, fees: Reservations are recommended. Sites are $25 per night for two people. Credit cards are not accepted. Long-term rates are available.

Directions: From downtown Dade City, drive south on U.S. 301 for three miles, turn east

on McDonald Road near the city limits, just before the Wal-Mart shopping center, and go 0.2 mile.

Contact: Country Aire Estates, 38130 McDonald Road, Dade City, FL 33525, 352/567-3630.

91 MORNINGSIDE RV ESTATES

Scenic rating: 4

on the south side of Dade City

See map, page 298

This snowbird-oriented resort with a gated entrance is within walking distance of two large shopping centers. Shade in the RV park is minimal. About 25 percent of the residents stay here year-round. Favorite activities include euchre (a card game) and ice-cream socials.

Campsites, facilities: This 55-and-older park has 399 sites with full hookups, 50-amp electrical service, free cable TV, and telephone access. Restrooms, showers, a dump station, a heated indoor pool, two clubhouses, two laundry facilities, horseshoe pits, and shuffleboard courts are provided. Lots are 36 by 60 feet, and a few have concrete slabs. The recreation hall, pool, and pool hall are wheelchair-accessible. Groceries and shopping are within 0.25 mile. Pets are prohibited.

Reservations, fees: Reservations are recommended. Sites are $30 per night for two people, plus $1 for each additional person. Credit cards are not accepted. Long-term rates are available.

Directions: From downtown Dade City, drive south on U.S. 301 for three miles, turn east on McDonald Road near the city limits, just before the Wal-Mart shopping center, and go 0.2 mile.

Contact: Morningside RV Estates, 12645 Morning Drive, Dade City, FL 33525, 352/523-1922, morningrv@aol.com.

92 MANY MANSIONS RV PARK

🐕 ♿ 🚐

Scenic rating: 3

south of Dade City

See map, page 298

Surrounded by dwindling citrus groves and open pastureland, this park is located in the country, yet is just five minutes from shopping, dining, and downtown Dade City. Planned activities include bingo, cards, pokeno, and cookouts, as well as weekly evening church services. Sites are laid out neatly in subdivision style, with straight roads; most spots are not back-to-back. About half the units are occupied year-round.

Campsites, facilities: This adults-oriented RV park has 235 grassy, full-hookup sites (of which around 50 are available for overnighters). RVs up to 40 feet long can be accommodated. Sites average 30 by 50 feet. Restrooms, showers, laundry facilities, a dump station, a camp circle, and a clubhouse with Internet access are available. The clubhouse, bathhouse, and laundry facilities are wheelchair-accessible. Streets are paved. Some trailers are available for rent. Children may camp short-term only. Small pets are permitted on a leash.

Reservations, fees: Reservations are recommended. Sites are $32 per night for two people, plus $3 for each additional person. Credit cards are not accepted. Long-term rates are available.

Directions: From Dade City, drive south on U.S. 301/98. When U.S. 98 forks south on the edge of town, continue on U.S. 98 for three miles. Take the Richland exit to County Road 35A, turn right and go one mile to Stewart Road. Turn left (east) at the park entrance.

Contact: Many Mansions RV Park, 40703 Stewart Road, Dade City, FL 33525, 352/567-8667 or 800/359-0135.

93 CITRUS HILL PARK AND SALES

🐕 ♿ 🚐

Scenic rating: 3

between Dade City and Zephyrhills

See map, page 298

As the name implies, the trailer park is on a hill in what used to be orange grove country, before freezes forced the citrus industry to look south to warmer points. Activities within the park include a golf league, bingo, crafts, bunco, euchre, church services, special dinners and socials, and a weekly coffee hour. Grocery stores, restaurants, and five golf courses are within five miles. There are no facilities for children. About 15 percent of the occupants stay here all year long, and most visitors return year after year from places like Canada, Indiana, and Michigan.

Campsites, facilities: This retiree-oriented park has 183 spots with full hookups and telephone and cable TV access, of which 45 are for RVs up to 40 feet long. Restrooms, showers, picnic tables, laundry facilities, a recreation hall, horseshoe pits, shuffleboard courts, a post office, and planned social activities are provided. The clubhouse is wheelchair-accessible. Children are welcome to visit their grandparents for two weeks. Leashed pets are allowed.

Reservations, fees: Reservations are required. Sites are $24 per night for two people, plus $2 for each additional person. Credit cards are not accepted. Stays of up to seven months are OK. Long-term rates are available.

Directions: From Dade City, drive six miles south on U.S. 98. The park is on the east side of the road.

Contact: Citrus Hill Park and Sales, 9267 U.S. 98, Dade City, FL 33525, 352/567-6045, fax 352/567-3119, www.bel-aireresorts.com.

94 FOREST LAKE RV RESORT

Scenic rating: 5

north of Zephyrhills

See map, page 298

This sparkling-clean park maintains it is "your year-round vacation home," and fewer than half of the sites are open for seasonal campers. Interior street names attest to the park's affinity for Canadian campers: Bruins Drive, Maple Leaf Drive, and Canadiens Drive, for example. The location is close to Gulf of Mexico beaches and Central Florida attractions, including baseball spring training, dog and horse racing, and Seminole bingo. Planned activities, such as ice-cream socials, make sure the residents have fun if they care to stay on-site most of the time. It's also a popular spot for camping rallies.

Campsites, facilities: The RV resort/mobile-home park has 124 sunny lots with concrete slabs for RVers (out of a total of 274). Sites have sewer hookups, 30/50-amp electrical service, and telephone and cable TV access. Lots are 30 by 50 feet, on average, and they can accommodate RVs up to 40 feet long. Restrooms, showers, laundry facilities, a dump station, six shuffleboard courts, four lighted horseshoe pits, a recreation hall, a pool, and a spa are on the premises. The pool area and clubhouse are wheelchair-accessible. Shopping and golf courses are within eight miles. Children are not welcome except when visiting residents for less than two weeks. Small pets are permitted on a leash.

Reservations, fees: Reservations are recommended. Sites are $24 per night. Credit cards are accepted.

Directions: From I-75, take Exit 279 and drive 12 miles east on State Road 54 to the intersection with U.S. 301. The park is on the south side of the highway, east of the intersection.

Contact: Forest Lake RV Resort, 41219 Hockey Drive, Zephyrhills, FL 33540, 813/782-1058 or 800/283-9715, fax 813/788-5246, www.forestlake-estates.com.

95 WATERS EDGE RV RESORT

Scenic rating: 4

north of Zephyrhills

See map, page 298

Set on 20 acres among tall oak trees, Waters Edge is located far enough away from town to enjoy a rural neighborhood setting, but still within a few minutes of shopping, restaurants, and a hospital. Paved interior roads lead to grassy back-in sites; few are shady. Social activities in winter include bingo, billiards, card games, and exercises in the pool. About 20 percent of the park is occupied year-round.

Campsites, facilities: This adult park has 70 RV sites with full hookups and cable TV and telephone access. Sites average 25 by 50 feet. Restrooms, showers, laundry facilities, a dump station, a pool, a clubhouse, horseshoe pits, and shuffleboard courts are on-site. The park caters to retirees who stay seven months out of the year and store their RVs on-site the rest of the time. Children may visit park residents for up to two weeks. Leashed pets are permitted.

Reservations, fees: Reservations are recommended. Sites are $25 per night for two people, plus $2 for each additional person. Credit cards are not accepted.

Directions: From Zephyrhills, drive one mile north on U.S. 301. Turn east onto Pretty Pond Road and go 0.5 mile to the stop sign at Wire Road. Head north on Wire Road for 0.25 mile to Otis Allen Road, then turn east and continue 0.5 mile to the entrance.

Contact: Waters Edge RV Resort, 39146 Otis Allen Road, Zephyrhills, FL 33540, 813/783-2708 or 800/471-7875, www.bel-aireresorts.com.

96 BAKER ACRES RV RANCH

Scenic rating: 4

on the north side of Zephyrhills

See map, page 298

Nondenominational church services are held each Sunday in the recreation hall. Other activities include dances, a singles club, exercise classes, ceramics, crafts, sewing, wood carving, quilting, bowling, cards, bingo, and field trips. The pool is heated. In the card room, residents play cribbage, euchre, pinochle, and more. The park is part of the Bel-Aire Resorts group. More than half the park is occupied year-round.

Campsites, facilities: Among 355 sites, 60 are available for RVs. They have sewer hookups, 50-amp electricity, telephone service and cable TV available. About half have concrete pads. The average site size is 30 by 40 feet, and RVs up to 40 feet long can be accommodated. Restrooms (but no showers), laundry facilities, shuffleboard and boccie ball (lawn bowling) courts, horseshoe pits, a recreation hall, a card room, and a pool are on the premises. RVs must be at least 20 feet long (up to a maximum of 35 feet) and must be less than 10 years old. Management says all areas of the park are wheelchair-accessible. Shopping, groceries, and restaurants are within one mile. Children are not welcome except for short visits. Leashed pets under 25 pounds are permitted.

Reservations, fees: Reservations are recommended. Sites are $25 per night for two people, plus $2 for each additional person. Credit cards are not accepted. Long-term rates are available.

Directions: From Zephyrhills, drive one mile north on U.S. 301. Turn east onto Pretty Pond Road and go 0.5 mile to the stop sign at Wire Road. Head north on Wire Road to the park entrance.

Contact: Baker Acres RV Ranch, 7820 Wire Road, Zephyrhills, FL 33540, 813/782-3950 or 800/741-7875, fax 813/783-3406, www.bel-aireresorts.com.

97 QUAIL RUN RV PARK

Scenic rating: 6

west of Zephyrhills, in Wesley Chapel

See map, page 298

"No rig is too big," brag the managers. Tall oaks shade this gated RV park, which is close enough to I-75 to be a practical overnight refuge. You might spot a flock of sandhill cranes on the rolling hills nearby, or even in the park. A golf course, tennis courts, and a driving range are within one mile, and the park is a nice stopping place for interstate drivers. About a third of the park is occupied by year-round residents.

Campsites, facilities: All 145 grassy RV sites have sewer hookups, 30/50-amp electrical service, and telephone access. Lots vary in size, but the average is 20 by 50 feet. Some have cement patios and are pull-through. A pool, a playground, a volleyball field, horseshoes, shuffleboard, restrooms, showers, a computer room, picnic tables, propane gas, and a dump station are provided. Internet access via wireless network is available in the park. The camp store sells ice, some groceries, snacks, and beer. Management says the bathhouse, recreation hall, laundry, and office are wheelchair-accessible. Families with children are welcome for short stays, although the park tends to attract full-time RVers and retirees. Leashed pets under 35 pounds are permitted. Only two pets are allowed per site, and attack breeds are prohibited.

Reservations, fees: Reservations are recommended. Sites are $32 per night for two people, plus $5 for each additional person. Credit cards are accepted. Long-term stays are allowed.

Directions: From I-75, take Exit 279 westbound on State Road 54 0.5 mile. At Old Pasco Road, turn north and drive two miles.

Contact: Quail Run RV Park, 6946 Old Pasco Road, Wesley Chapel, FL 33544, 813/973-0999 or 800/582-7084, www.quailrunrv.com.

98 ENCORE RV PARK–TAMPA NORTH

🏊 🚣 🚐 🏕 ♿ 🚍

Scenic rating: 6

north of Lutz

See map, page 298

In winter, snowbirds thaw out in the solar-heated hot tub and swimming pool and catch some rays on the pool deck. Set on 28 acres across from a Wal-Mart and near other shopping, the community offers comfortable amenities for those who like this style of vacation. Park models are for sale as well. A 17-acre fishing lake keeps anglers busy; a gazebo overlooks it. This is a bustling place in winter, when the park population swells to 550 and an activities director arranges special events, parties, tournaments, and dances. About 25 percent of guests live here year-round, conveniently close to Busch Gardens, numerous Disney-area attractions, Crystal Springs, the Hillsborough River, several lakes, and Gulf Coast beaches. Big-rig sites are available.

Campsites, facilities: All 256 grassy sites have sewer hookups, 50-amp electrical service, paved patios, wireless Internet access, and telephone availability. Sites vary in size, but some will accommodate RVs up to 40 feet long and slideouts. None are drive-through. A heated pool, a whirlpool tub, a recreation center, horseshoes, shuffleboard, billiards, a game room, restrooms, showers, a dump station, picnic tables, propane, park model sales, and laundry facilities are on the premises. An activities director organizes dances, dinners, games, and crafts October–April. Across the street is a shopping center with a supermarket, restaurants, a pharmacy, a Wal-Mart, and hair salons. Most areas are wheelchair-accessible with ramps. Children are permitted. Pets must be leashed.

Reservations, fees: Reservations are recommended. Sites are $31 for two people. Add $5 for each additional person. Credit cards are accepted. Monthly rates are available.

Directions: From I-75, take Exit 279 and drive 8.2 miles west on State Road 54. The resort is at left, near the corner of U.S. 41.

Contact: Encore RV Park—Tampa North, 21632 State Road 54, Lutz, FL 33549, 813/949-6551 or 800/879-2131, fax 813/949-4921, www.rvonthego.com.

99 LAKE COMO CLUB

🚶 🏊 🚣 🛶 🚐 🏕 🎣 ♿ 🚍 ⛺

Scenic rating: 5

on U.S. 41, north of Tampa

See map, page 298   **BEST (**

Lake Como Club has all of the amenities of a fancy RV park: three clay tennis courts, a heated swimming pool, a hot tub, a sauna, a golf driving range, an archery range, planned activities in the recreation hall, and fishing and boating on a 35-acre lake with a sandy beach. The major difference? This has been a nude recreation community since 1940. In fact, Pasco County claims to have more nudist resorts than any other place in Florida—there's even a nudist housing development.

Campsites, facilities: This family nudist resort has 75 RV sites and 20 tent-only sites separate from the RV section. All have water and 30-amp electricity. Two sites have 50-amp service, and 38 have sewer hookups. A couple of sites are drive-through. About a third of the park is occupied year-round. On the premises are restrooms, showers, a dump station, a pool, a boat ramp, a dock, a playground, a volleyball field, laundry facilities, and motel rooms. Most of the visitors are from Canada or the local nudist club. Planned activities include karaoke, *pétanque* (French-style bowling), boccie ball (lawn bowling), bingo, and pot-luck dinners. Internet access is available in the library. The RV sites, restrooms, and showers are wheelchair-accessible. Children are welcome. Leashed pets are permitted.

Reservations, fees: Reservations are required. Sites are $30–36 per night for two people, plus one half the camping fee for each additional person. For 50-amp electrical service, the fee is $2.50 per night. Credit cards are accepted.

Directions: From I-75, take Exit 275 and drive west on State Road 56 for one mile. At State Road 54, bear west five more miles. At the intersection with U.S. 41, turn south and drive one block to Leonard Road, where you will turn west. Drive 0.5 mile to the park.

Contact: Lake Como Club, 20500 Cot Road, Lutz, FL 33549, 813/949-1810 or 877 RY-LAKE (877/879-5253), fax 813/949-4937, www.lakecomoresort.com.

100 SWEETWATER RV PARK

Scenic rating: 4

south of Zephyrhills

See map, page 298

Like most Zephyrhills parks, this one caters to retired RVers who like to spend several months at a time in Florida. It's part of a chain of nine parks in this area, including Baker Acres, Blue Jay, Citrus Hill, Glen Haven, Grove Ridge, Rainbow Village, Southern Charm, Water's Edge, and Big Tree. Yearly rates ($1,380) are for seven months' occupancy and five months' storage, allowing residents to avoid paying sales tax on their rent. The park is surrounded by a wooden fence. About 10 percent of the lots are occupied year-round.

Campsites, facilities: This 289-unit, snowbird-oriented mobile home and RV park offers full hookups, restrooms, showers, telephone availability, cable TV, and laundry facilities. Two hundred sites have 30-amp electrical service; the rest are 50-amp. Your RV must be self-contained. Lots average 30 feet wide by 50 feet deep, and RVs up to 40 feet long and slideouts can be accommodated. None of the sites are drive-through. A recreation hall, shuffleboard and boccie ball (lawn bowling) courts, horseshoe pits, and table tennis and pool tables are provided. Most areas are wheelchair-accessible. Streets are paved. Campers age 50 and up are preferred, although children

may stay for up to two weeks. Pets are permitted in the designated pet section.

Reservations, fees: Reservations are recommended. Sites are $24 per night for two people, plus $2 for each additional person. Credit cards are not accepted. Long-term rates are available.

Directions: From U.S. 301 just south of Zephyrhills, turn west on Chancey Road and drive 0.25 mile.

Contact: Sweetwater RV Park, 37647 Chancey Road, Zephyrhills, FL 33541, 813/788-7513, www.bel-aireresorts.com.

101 SETTLER'S REST RV PARK

Scenic rating: 3

south of Zephyrhills

See map, page 298

Seasonal visitors flock here each winter to escape the chilly North, and most of them return year after year to this 350-unit adult community. Just 14 sites are available for overnighters. About 15 percent of the units are occupied year-round. Also on the premises are park models, which are for sale. This family-owned park has a homey atmosphere. The visitors have their own form of government and raise funds each year to make improvements to the park; for example, they bought an organ for their church services. The church has a Methodist affiliation.

Campsites, facilities: RVs as long as 40 feet can be accommodated at the 14 RV sites open for overnighters. The rest of the sites are for long-term visits. Sites are split evenly between 30-amp and 50-amp electrical service. Sites are shady and average 30 by 60 feet. All have sewer hookups, picnic tables, cable TV, and phone service available. Restrooms, showers, a dump station, laundry facilities, and a recreation hall are in the park. The clubhouse and showers are wheelchair-accessible. Children are welcome as visitors only. Leashed pets are permitted.

Reservations, fees: Reservations are advised. Sites are $32 a night for two people, plus $2 per extra person. Credit cards are not accepted. Long-term (up to six months) or seasonal stays are encouraged.

Directions: From U.S. 301 just south of Zephyrhills, turn west on Chancey Road and drive about 0.25 mile.

Contact: Settler's Rest RV Park, 37549 Chancey Road, Zephyrhills, FL 33541, 813/782-2003.

102 SOUTHERN CHARM RV RESORT

Scenic rating: 5

south of Zephyrhills

See map, page 298

Most sites are occupied by RVs parked year-round in this 48-acre, super-manicured mobile-home resort with a total of 500 spaces. Trees are sparse, although some sites overlook a lake. Lighted, paved roads lead to sites, some with trees. If you like golf, many challenging courses are located within an easy drive. Unusual wintertime activities include pool exercises, wood carving, and a kitchen band.

Campsites, facilities: At this adults-only park, 200 RV lots have full hookups, 30/50-amp electrical service, optional telephone service, and cable TV access. None of the sites are drive-through. Sites are 35 by 50 feet. Maximum vehicle length is 40 feet, and slideouts are permitted. An Internet connection is available in the office and the clubhouse. Facilities include a recreation hall with a large stone fireplace, shuffleboard courts, horseshoes, planned activities, laundry facilities, a post office, a pool room, a whirlpool tub, and a heated pool. RVs must be in excellent condition and at least 20 feet long. Small pets are permitted in the designated pet section.

Reservations, fees: Reservations are recommended. Sites are $25 per night for two people, plus $2 for each additional person.

Credit cards are not accepted. Long-term rates are available.

Directions: From U.S. 301 just south of Zephyrhills, turn west on Chancey Road and drive 0.5 mile to Autumn Palm. The resort is just ahead, at right.

Contact: Southern Charm RV Resort, 37811 Chancey Road, Zephyrhills, FL 33541, 813/783-3477 or 800/471-7875, fax 813/783-3406, www.bel-aire resorts.com.

103 GLEN HAVEN RV AND MOBILE PARK

Scenic rating: 4

south of Zephyrhills

See map, page 298

Glen Haven is one of several retirement-oriented parks along this road. Grocery stores and restaurants are three miles away in Zephyrhills. About 70 percent of this park is populated with park models, though just a few are occupied year-round.

Campsites, facilities: This mobile-home community/RV park has 218 concrete-pad sites with full hookups, 30/50-amp electricity, optional telephone service, cable TV access, and cement slabs. RVs up to 40 feet long can be accommodated. Average lot size is 35 by 50 feet. Restrooms, showers, a whirlpool tub, a pool, horseshoe pits, shuffleboard courts, an exercise room, a clubhouse with Internet connection, propane gas, and laundry facilities are provided. Activities include the usual pancake breakfasts, dances, and ice-cream socials, but also a computer club with software classes. Most areas are wheelchair-accessible. Campers must be 55 or older, though children may visit for a short time. Leashed pets under 25 pounds are permitted.

Reservations, fees: Reservations are recommended. Sites are $35 per night for two people, plus $2 for each additional person. Credit cards are not accepted. Long-term stays are OK.

Directions: From the south side of Zephyrhills, drive south on U.S 301/County Road 41 to the intersection with Chancey Road. Turn west on Chancey Road and go one mile.

Contact: Glen Haven RV and Mobile Park, 37251 Chancey Road, Zephyrhills, FL 33541, 813/782-1856 or 800/362-5181, fax 813/783-3132, www.bel-aireresorts.com.

104 WHITE'S RV PARK

Scenic rating: 4

south of Zephyrhills

See map, page 298

Set on 18 acres, this family-owned and -operated park offers lots of planned activities for its retired clientele, which hails from the northeast and central United States. A golf course, grocery stores, and restaurants are close. Favorite things to do include bingo, cards, euchre, potluck dinners and breakfasts, dances, church activities, crafts, and off-site trips.

Campsites, facilities: This 55-and-older park has 270 concrete-pad RV sites with full hookups, 30/50-amp electrical plugs, picnic tables, and telephone service available. Lots range in size from 30 to 32 feet wide by 50 feet deep. None of the sites are drive-through. An Internet connection is available in the clubhouse. Restrooms, showers, a dump station, laundry facilities, a pool, a recreation room, billiard tables, and shuffleboard courts are on the premises. A golf course, grocery stores, and restaurants are within three miles. Management says all areas are wheelchair-accessible. Children are permitted for short visits only. Pets are allowed.

Reservations, fees: Reservations are recommended. Sites are $18 per night for two people, plus $1 for each additional person. Credit cards are not accepted. Long-term stays are OK.

Directions: From U.S. 301 just south of Zephyrhills, turn west on Chancey Road and

drive 0.5 mile. The park is on the south side of the road.

Contact: White's RV Park, 37400 Chancey Road, Zephyrhills, FL 33541, 813/783-1644, whiterv374@aol.com.

105 HUNTER'S RUN RV RESORT

Scenic rating: 4

south of Zephyrhills

See map, page 298

This community offers retirees a relaxing winter, with lots of opportunities to make friends. Of the 309 sites, many are occupied by park models. Planned social activities are held during the winter in the recreation hall, including live bands every Saturday, line dancing, church services on Sunday, ice-cream socials, bingo, potluck dinners, breakfasts, cruises, and casino trips. The owners say their park is different because it's in the countryside, yet close to everything.

Campsites, facilities: All 309 sites have sewer hookups, 30-amp electricity, telephone service and cable TV access. About 40 sites have 50-amp service. RVs up to 35 feet long can be accommodated. Restrooms, showers, a dump station, laundry facilities, shuffleboard and boccie ball (lawn bowling) courts, horseshoe pits, a recreation hall with Internet connection, a pool, a spa, a sauna, and an exercise room are on the premises. Shopping and groceries are within two miles. Most areas are wheelchair-accessible, and streets are paved. Campers must be 55 or older, although children are allowed to visit for up to two weeks. Small pets are permitted on a leash.

Reservations, fees: Reservations are recommended. Sites are $24 per night for two people, plus $2 for each additional person. Credit cards are not accepted.

Directions: From the south side of Zephyrhills, drive south on U.S 301/County Road 41 to the intersection with Chancey Road. Turn west and go 1.2 miles to the park, near the corner of South Allen Road.

Contact: Hunter's Run RV Resort, 37041 Chancey Road, Zephyrhills, FL 33541, 813/783-1133.

106 PALM VIEW GARDENS

Scenic rating: 4

south of Zephyrhills

See map, page 298

This sprawling, well-manicured park on a corner of a major highway is somewhat exposed to the road. Trees are minimal, but most RVers in Zephyrhills don't seem to mind, and about two-thirds of the park are occupied year-round. Bench seating overlooks the stocked fishing lake, and the paved, lighted interior roads lend themselves to bicycling. Social activities are held during the season in two spacious recreation halls. The oversized pool is heated during the cooler months.

Campsites, facilities: This adults-only park has 525 sites with full hookups, 30-amp electrical service, concrete patios, and telephone and cable TV access. Sites are a roomy 30 by 90 feet, with 10 feet of buffering between neighbors. The management creates a directory of its visitors, so they can stay in touch with each other when they go back home to places like Michigan, New York, and Canada. Restrooms, showers, laundry facilities, a dump station, a pool, two recreation halls with kitchens, horseshoes, championship shuffleboard courts, and a fishing lake are provided. Most areas are wheelchair-accessible, and streets are paved. Children may visit tenants for no longer than two weeks. Leashed pets are permitted.

Reservations, fees: Reservations are recommended. Sites are $23 per night for two people, plus $2.50 for each additional person. Credit cards are accepted. Long-term stays are preferred.

Directions: From State Road 54 and U.S. 301

in Zephyrhills, turn south on U.S. 301 and drive two miles to the park. Gall Boulevard is the same as U.S. 301.

Contact: Palm View Gardens, 3331 Gall Boulevard, Zephyrhills, FL 33541, 813/782-8685, www.rvresorts.com.

107 HAPPY DAYS RV PARK

Scenic rating: 5

west of Zephyrhills

See map, page 298

Churches, a shopping center, and other points of interest are close to this park. There's even a bus stop nearby. Planned activities, such as exercise and crafts classes, fashion shows, games, bingo, and Sunday church services, are held in winter. The recreation hall has a dance floor, a stage, and an electronic bingo scoreboard; the smaller lodge has a workshop area for hobbies. About half the park is occupied by park models.

Campsites, facilities: All 300 lots have sewer hookups and 20/30-amp electrical outlets; 150 sites are available for RVs. Rigs up to 40 feet in length can be accommodated. Restrooms, showers, laundry facilities, a dump station, shuffleboard courts, horseshoe pits, a recreation hall, two pool tables, cable TV, and a heated pool are available. The streets are paved, and the laundry and clubhouse are wheelchair-accessible. This is an age-55-and-over park; children are not permitted, except for short visits. Leashed pets under 20 pounds are allowed in one area of the park.

Reservations, fees: Reservations are recommended. Sites are $22 per night for two people, plus $2 for each additional person. Credit cards are accepted. Long-term stays are permitted.

Directions: From State Road 54 and U.S. 301 in Zephyrhills, drive west on State Road 54 for about 0.5 mile. Turn south on Allen Road by the convenience store. The park is

ahead within 0.5 mile, just past the shopping center.
Contact: Happy Days RV Park, 4603 Allen Road, Zephyrhills, FL 33541, 813/788-4858.

108 ANDY'S TRAVEL TRAILER PARK

Scenic rating: 2

west of Zephyrhills

See map, page 298

Ready for a Saturday-night bonfire? This retirement-oriented snowbird park boasts a very active social schedule, with barbecues, coffee hours, potluck dinners, bingo, cards, video nights, and more. About 10 percent of the park is occupied by year-round residents. Favorite things to do? "Walk, talk, and enjoy life."
Campsites, facilities: Designed for the winter visitor, the park has 75 full-hookup sites for snowbirds, and six spots for overnighters. All have picnic tables, 30-amp electrical service, and concrete patios. Lots vary in size; in fact, all are different, the owners say. Some sites can handle large rigs and slideouts. An Internet connection is available in the office. Restrooms, showers, a wheelchair-accessible clubhouse, shuffleboard courts, and a dog-walk area are on-site. The bathhouse and clubhouse are wheelchair-accessible. Streets are paved. Groceries and restaurants are within 0.5 mile. Adults over 55 are preferred; children are not allowed. Leashed pets under 12 pounds are permitted.
Reservations, fees: Reservations are recommended. Sites are $20 per night for two people, plus $2 per extra person. Credit cards are not accepted. Long-term rates are available.
Directions: From I-75, take Exit 279 and drive east on State Road 54 for 10 miles.
Contact: Andy's Travel Trailer Park, 37707 State Road 54, Zephyrhills, FL 33541, 813/782-3843, jodyr@3oaks.com.

109 JIM'S RV PARK

Scenic rating: 3

west of Zephyrhills

See map, page 298

Catering to retired snowbirds who like to stay put for the season, this park has a volunteer committee that organizes a full array of winter activities, such as bingo, crafts, potluck suppers, dances, bowling parties, and golf outings. Within one mile are shops, restaurants, a library, banks, and video rentals. Flea markets abound in the area.
Campsites, facilities: The adults-only park has 151 sites with sewer hookups—more than 60 percent are occupied year-round. Sixty sites are available for overnight visitors, half with 30-amp electrical service and the other half with 50-amp. Slideouts and 45-foot-long RVs can be accommodated on lots that average 30 by 60 feet. Sites are sunny and paved. Restrooms, showers, laundry facilities, a dump station, shuffleboard and horseshoe courts, a recreation hall, and a pool are on the premises. The bathhouse, pool area, and recreation hall are wheelchair-accessible. Children may visit campers for up to two weeks. One small, leashed pet is permitted per unit.
Reservations, fees: Reservations are recommended. Sites are $22 per night for two people, plus $1 for each additional person. Credit cards are not accepted. Long-term stays are OK.
Directions: From I-75, take Exit 279 and drive east on State Road 54 for nine miles.
Contact: Jim's RV Park, 35120 State Road 54 West, Zephyrhills, FL 33541, 813/782-5610.

110 RALPH'S TRAVEL PARK

Scenic rating: 4

west of Zephyrhills

See map, page 298

Canadians get a warm welcome at this sprawling wooded park, which has full-service amenities, plus a carwash area. Gas and food stores are located next door. Owners claim it has the largest swimming pool in the Zephyrhills area.

Campsites, facilities: There are 100 RV sites available with full hookups and 30/50-amp electrical service in this 404-lot snowbird retreat, where folks return year after year. About half the units are occupied year-round. Restrooms, showers, laundry facilities, a pool, shuffleboard courts, horseshoe pits, two recreation halls, and a workshop are available. The recreation halls, laundry room, and restrooms are accessible to wheelchairs. Campers must be 50 or older. Pets under 25 pounds are allowed, but aggressive breeds are prohibited.

Reservations, fees: Reservations are recommended. Sites are $21 per night for two people, plus $2 for each additional person. Credit cards are not accepted. Long-term stays are the norm.

Directions: From I-75, take Exit 279 and go six miles east on State Road 54 to the park, which is on the corner of Morris Bridge Road, across the street from the Home Depot.

Contact: Ralph's Travel Park, 34408 State Road 54 West, Zephyrhills, FL 33543, 813/782-8223 or 866/234-2056.

111 HILLCREST RV RESORT

Scenic rating: 4

on the west side of Zephyrhills

See map, page 298

Extra-large lots accommodate residents in this sunny park-model/RV retreat, which caters to seasonal visitors and retirees, about half of whom live here year-round. The management of this 40-acre resort prides itself on keeping the premises neat and orderly. RVs must be modern and well-maintained; rules are strict regarding maintenance of the lots. In the wintertime, popular activities are bingo, golf, game nights, men's and women's billiards, a jam session every Wednesday, aerobics in the pool, and Crime Watch meetings once a month.

Campsites, facilities: There are 497 full-hookup sites with 30/50-amp electrical service and telephone availability, of which 200 are available for overnighting RVs. Restrooms, showers, two laundries, a dump station, a pool, and two clubhouses are provided; many areas are wheelchair-accessible. Internet access is available in the clubhouse. Grocery stores and restaurants are within one mile. Children are not welcome, except for brief visits. Leashed pets are permitted.

Reservations, fees: Reservations are recommended. Sites are $28 per night for two people, plus $2 for each additional person.

Directions: From I-75, take Exit 279 eastbound on State Road 54 for 10 miles. After passing the Winn-Dixie, go 0.5 mile farther, turn south on Lane Road, and proceed to the park.

Contact: Hillcrest RV Resort, 4421 Lane Road, Zephyrhills, FL 33541, 813/782-1947 or 800/992-8735, hillcrestrv@verizon.net.

112 LEISURE DAYS RV RESORT

Scenic rating: 3

west of Zephyrhills

See map, page 298

Staying at this sunny, landscaped, retiree-oriented park puts you close to fishing waters, tennis courts, golf courses, shopping, and Central Florida attractions. Social programs are held November–mid-April; among them are planned campfires, bingo, crafts, card parties, pancake breakfasts, and dances. The pool is heated.

Campsites, facilities: This park has 41 RV

sites with full hookups for overnighters, cable TV, and telephone access. They accommodate rigs up to 37 feet in length. Restrooms, showers, laundry facilities, a pool, an activity center, horseshoe pits, and shuffleboard courts are available. All units must be self-contained. There are 200 additional sites for long-termers. All areas are wheelchair-accessible. An age-55-and-older park, Leisure Days permits children as visitors and for short periods only. Leashed pets under 25 pounds are allowed.

Reservations, fees: Reservations are recommended. Sites are $14.50 per night. Credit cards are not accepted. Long-term stays are OK.

Directions: From I-75, take Exit 279 and drive east on State Road 54 for six miles. Turn south on Morris Bridge Road and drive one block.

Contact: Leisure Days RV Resort, 34533 Leisure Days Drive, Zephyrhills, FL 33541, 813/788-2631, fax 813/715-7617.

113 ORLANDO SOUTHEAST/ LAKE WHIPPOORWILL KOA

Scenic rating: 7

on Lake Whippoorwill, east of Orlando

See map, page 298

These mostly grassy sites are set amid palm trees alongside fishable, spring-fed 355-acre Lake Whippoorwill, in the rural eastern section of Orange County. A hairdresser is available in winter, when the place fills up with snowbirds who enjoy pancake breakfasts, potluck dinners, bingo, and the hot tub at this 40-acre park. Swimming, boating, fishing, and waterskiing are popular. The management says it's about a 20-minute drive to Disney-area attractions and 35 minutes to Cape Canaveral. Many people live here on a semi-permanent basis.

Campsites, facilities: Nine grassy tent sites are set apart from 120 RV sites (all full-hookup with 30/50-amp electrical service; 22 are pull-through). Each site has a picnic table. Rigs up to 45 feet long and slideouts can be accommodated. Sites vary in size from 15 feet wide and 25–45 feet deep. Three developed tent sites are located next to a canal; six are in a field and more suited for group camping. Cable TV and telephone service are available. A pool, a recreation hall, a hot tub, canoe rentals, a playground, horseshoes, shuffleboard, and volleyball entertain campers. On the premises are restrooms, showers, a boat ramp, a dock, a dump station, cabin rentals, laundry facilities, limited bait and tackle, and a gift shop and store. The recreation hall, pool, and convenience store are wheelchair-accessible. Restaurants and groceries are within two miles. Children and leashed pets are welcome.

Reservations, fees: Reservations are recommended. Sites are $37–47 per night for two people, plus $2–3 for each additional person. Credit cards are accepted. Long-term stays are OK.

Directions: From Orlando, take State Road 528/the Bee Line Expressway east about 10 miles to State Road 15/Narcoossee Road, then go south for five miles to the park.

Contact: Orlando Southeast/Lake Whippoorwill KOA, 12345 Narcoossee Road, Orlando, FL 32827, 407/277-5075 or 800/999-5267, www.orlandokoa.com.

114 MOSS PARK

Scenic rating: 7

near Lake Hart, southeast of Orlando

See map, page 298

Boating, hiking, and wildlife observation are the most popular activities at this 2.5-square-mile county campground, which is favored by locals. The heavily wooded shell-rock sites, each with a picnic table, a grill, and a fire ring, are nestled between Lake Hart and Lake Mary Jane, both of which are popular for swimming and fishing. It's adjacent to the 1,800-acre Split Oak Forest Mitigation Park, where you'll

Many anglers come to Central Florida for freshwater fishing.

find several hiking trails. Hurricanes in 2004 blew away more than 400 trees, so the park is less shady these days.

Look for sandhill cranes, deer, wild turkeys, wood storks, and fox squirrels—a remarkable array, when you consider how close you are to Orlando. When the Moss family donated the land to Orange County in 1930, it was known as Bear Island, but you won't see any bears today. Canoeing, kayaking, waterskiing, and windsurfing are possible on the lakes, if you bring your own equipment. A three-mile nature trail and several more miles of hiking trails will please day hikers. This park is 25 miles from Disney-area attractions. Park rangers live on-site.

Campsites, facilities: The county-run campground offers 54 hard-shell sites with 30/50-amp electric service and piped water. Sites 1–4, also designated as multifamily sites for a maximum of 12 people per site, are pull-through. Sites 5 and 6 are wheelchair-accessible. Each site has a picnic table, a grill, and a fire ring. Facilities include restrooms, showers, two dump stations, two boat ramps, a beach, hiking trails, playgrounds, pavilion rentals, softball field, and volleyball. Management says the restrooms are wheelchair-accessible. Children are welcome. Pets are prohibited. Absolutely no alcohol is allowed; the rule is enforced with a $500 fine and/or six months in jail.

Reservations, fees: Reservations must be made in person. Pay by cash or check when you make the reservation 45 days in advance, and you must stay a minimum of two nights. Telephone reservations are not accepted. Sites are $14–19 per night. Credit cards are not accepted. Stays are limited to 14 days.

Directions: Take State Road 528/Bee Line Expressway east from Orlando International Airport about three miles. At Exit 22, head south on Narcoossee Road/State Road 15 for 2.5 miles, then turn left onto Moss Park Road. From State Road 417/Greenway Expressway, take Exit 22 onto Narcoossee Road and go north one mile to Moss Park Road.

Contact: Moss Park, 12901 Moss Park Road, Orlando, FL 32812, 407/273-2327, fax 407/249-4498, www.orangecountyparks .net.

115 EAST LAKE FISH CAMP

Scenic rating: 3

on East Lake Tohopekaliga, south of Orlando

See map, page 298

The main road through the park isn't known as Big Bass Road for nothing. This place on four-mile-wide East Lake Tohopekaliga is designed for anglers, but the airboat rides are also a big attraction. You'll find a kidney-shaped pool and a barnyard with donkeys, geese, and ducks. Some families camp here even if they're not after bass, specks, or shellcrackers, but the majority of visitors are snowbirds. You may be able to get a shady spot, but about a third of the sites are sunny. Permanent residents take up about 40 percent of the spots, and there's a restaurant on-site with all-you-can eat buffets on weekend nights.

Campsites, facilities: There are 263 grassy full-hookup campsites (about 35 pull-through) with concrete pads. Fifty lots have 50-amp electrical service; the rest have 30-amp. RVs up to 40 feet long and slideouts can be accommodated at the grassy sites, which vary in size. Facilities include restrooms, showers, a dump station, gasoline and LP gas sales, laundry facilities, picnic tables, cabin rentals, a pool, a restaurant, boat rentals, fishing guide services, bait and tackle sales, a boat ramp, and tennis courts. The camp store sells beer, ice, and fishing tackle. Management says the bathhouse and camp store are wheelchair-accessible. Children and pets are permitted.

Reservations, fees: Reservations are not accepted. Nightly fee for two people is $20 for an RV site. Add $1 per extra person. Credit cards are accepted. Long-term rates are available.

Directions: From the Central Florida Greenway/Highway 417, take Exit 17 and drive south on Boggy Creek Road for about five miles. Turn right onto Fish Camp Road and continue south to Big Bass Road, which leads through the park.

Contact: East Lake Fish Camp, 3705 Big Bass Road, Kissimmee, FL 34744, 407/348-2040, fax 407/348-7797, eastlake@concentric.net.

116 THE FLORIDIAN RV RESORT

Scenic rating: 7

south of Orlando, on the Orange/Osceola County line

See map, page 298

This large, 140-acre gated park is next to a mobile-home park run by the same folks who manage the campground. Some college students live on the campground; the rest are retirees staying year-round or those who park their RVs under the "6/6" plan, which allows them to leave their rigs in the park during hot months. During the busy winter season, campers enjoy dances, play bingo and card games, organize tennis teams, and attend periodic on-site health fairs. If you bring a boat or canoe, you can launch from the park into Fells Cove, which leads to East Lake Tohopekaliga. Bathrooms are within easy walking distance on lighted paths from the water-and-electric sites. The campground is about 20 miles from Walt Disney World.

Campsites, facilities: The campground offers 457 grassy RV sites (about 350 full-hookup) with concrete slabs. RVs up the 40 feet long can be accommodated. Tenters can use 70 RV sites in an area with water and electric hookups only. On the premises are restrooms, showers, a dump station, laundry facilities, picnic tables, a playground, a recreation hall, a hot tub, a boat ramp and dock, volleyball, shuffleboard, and tennis courts. The clubhouse has an atrium seating area where you can access the Internet, TV and card rooms, and billiards. Many areas have wheelchair access. Streets are paved. Children and small pets are allowed.

Reservations, fees: Reservations are recommended in January, February, and March. Sites are $18 to $28 per night for two people, plus $1 for each additional person age six and older. Credit cards are accepted. Long-term rates are available.

Directions: From Orlando, take State Road 15/Narcoossee Road south 150 miles to State Road 530. The campground is at the intersection of State Roads 530 and 15.

Contact: The Floridian RV Resort, 5150 Boggy Creek Road, St. Cloud, FL 34771, 407/892-5171, www.florida-rv-parks.com.

117 ELITE RESORTS AT CITRUS VALLEY

Scenic rating: 5

in Clermont, within 10 miles of Disney World

See map, page 299

Proximity to Disney World—less than 10 miles away—may be the biggest selling point of this place. New owners in 2005 converted the campground to a condominium RV park, and lots are for sale. Still, management says that most sites are available for overnighters. Anglers can head to little Hancock Lake, perhaps the closest of the region's plentiful (mostly small) lakes. Local bass anglers prefer 3,634-acre Lake Louisa, located about six miles north of the park as the crow flies. Picnicking and swimming at Lake Louisa State Park (352/394-3969) requires a longer drive, yet you may get to see alligators and deer at the 1,790-acre parcel of land, which is home to 10 types of biological communities, including scrubland, a blackwater stream, and upland hardwoods.

Campsites, facilities: Of the 378 sites, most have full hookups, 30/50-amp electrical service, and wireless Internet access. A pool, a playground, horseshoes, shuffleboard, a pool table, a recreation hall, and seasonal planned activities entertain campers. Showers, restrooms, a dump station, trailer rentals, cable TV, telephone hookups, and laundry facilities are available. All areas are said to be wheelchair-accessible. Shopping, groceries, and restaurants are within two miles. Children are welcome. Pets must be leashed.

Reservations, fees: Reservations are recommended. Sites are $24–38 per night for two people, plus $3 for each additional person. Credit cards are accepted.

Directions: From I-4 at Exit 64B in Kissimmee, take U.S. 192 west. Turn north onto U.S. 27 and continue 2.5 miles to the park on your right.

Contact: Elite Resorts at Citrus Valley, 2500 U.S. 27 South, Clermont, FL 34714, 352/394-4051 or 877/369-0004, www.eliteresorts.com.

118 DISNEY'S FORT WILDERNESS CAMPGROUND

Scenic rating: 10

on the grounds of Walt Disney World

See map, page 299   **BEST (**

At this gem of a park, 700 acres of lush wilderness stand out as the sole campground located on the Disney resort property, with full access to Disney World by land, water, or monorail. Guests enjoy complimentary transportation throughout the Walt Disney World Resort. For a campground, the recreational opportunities are mind-boggling: Swimming, fishing, waterskiing, and canoeing are popular at lakes on the property, and golf courses are nearby. Biking, tennis, horseback riding, and hiking on a two-mile nature trail are available. Children's activities include a nightly campfire visit by Disney characters, Disney movies, a petting farm, and pony rides.

The park, which has paved sites with separate gravel sitting areas, is highly recommended to parents. This is camping with a very polished feel, including air-conditioned bathrooms and heated swimming pools. Of course, you pay for the amenities. Still, the price is no more than you'd expect to pay to stay in most of the mid- to low-priced motels in the area. Plan on waiting quite awhile if you're checking in at a busy time. An hour-long wait is not unusual, but arriving early in the day helps. The busy times of year are generally in summer and around major holidays, although things can get busy at any time.

Campsites, facilities: The 694 full-hookup RV sites have 30/50-amp service, picnic tables, and grills. The RV area is set apart from the 90 tent sites. A pool, charter fishing, boat and canoe rentals, paddleboats, a playground, game rooms, a nature trail, golf and miniature golf, a driving range, horseshoes, shuffleboard, tennis, volleyball, hayrides, horseback riding, a petting farm, dinner shows, and pony rides entertain guests. On the premises are restrooms, showers, a dump station, groceries, laundry facilities, and restaurants. Management says the restrooms and transportation to other facilities on the Disney property are wheelchair-accessible. Cable TV is available at some RV sites. Children are welcome. Leashed pets are restricted to full-hookup sites.

Reservations, fees: Reservations are recommended. Site fees are $39–92 per night, depending on the time of year. Credit cards are accepted. Long-term stays are OK.

Directions: From I-4, take Exit 67 onto State Road 536 westbound and follow signs to the campground entrance.

Contact: Disney's Fort Wilderness Campground, 4510 North Fort Wilderness Trail, Lake Buena Vista, FL 32830, 407/824-2900 or 407/939-6244 (reservations), fax 407/824-3508, www.disney.com.

119 LAKE MAGIC RV RESORT

Scenic rating: 10

four miles west of Disney World

See map, page 299

Just four miles from Walt Disney Resort, this park (formerly known as Encore) is convenient to shopping and restaurants. You won't have to leave the park to enjoy yourself; it's a self-contained recreation place for all ages. Pools, tennis courts, planned activities, and views

of 160-acre Lake Davenport offer relaxation after a day in the theme parks. It's all done in the first-class manner this chain of parks is known for. About 10 percent of the park is occupied by year-round residents.

Campsites, facilities: There are 467 sunny RV sites (70 pull-through). RVers have picnic tables, paved pads, and patios with 30/50-amp electrical hookups available, plus cable TV and telephone service. Rigs up to 45 feet long can be accommodated. Internet connection is available at the clubhouse. Restrooms, showers, laundry facilities, two heated pools, a whirlpool tub, a playground, tennis courts, sand volleyball, a basketball court, horseshoe pits, shuffleboard courts, a recreation center, a fitness center, a mail center, and golf nets are on the premises. Groceries and shopping are within 0.2 mile. Most areas are wheelchair-accessible. Children are welcome. Leashed pets are permitted.

Reservations, fees: Reservations are recommended. Sites are $39–46 per night for two people, plus $5 for each extra person. Credit cards are accepted. Long-term rates are available.

Directions: From I-4 westbound, take Exit 64B, drive west about five miles on U.S. 192/Irlo Bronson Highway to the park entrance on the left. Eastbound from I-4, take U.S. 27 north to U.S. 192; turn east and go 0.25 mile. The resort will be on the right.

Contact: Lake Magic RV Resort, 9600 Irlo Bronson Highway, Clermont, FL 34714, 863/420-1300 or 888/558-5777, fax 863/420-1400, www.rvonthego.com.

120 TROPICAL PALMS FUNRESORT

Scenic rating: 8

off U.S. 192, near Disney World

See map, page 299

A fair supply of palms, pines, and other trees shade the sites at this resort, but you can get a sunny spot if that's what you're after. The

60 acres located behind a Days Inn motel are shared by campers and people renting cottages, but no year-round residents. A full-sized, somewhat Y-shaped heated pool is open 24 hours, and sunbathers lounging around its patio can gaze at a pleasant green backdrop. But the main benefit of staying here is that you're within a few minutes of major Central Florida attractions. You can even walk to the Old Town entertainment district, which has 80 shops, restaurants, and rides. Two championship golf courses and Pirate's Cove adventure golf are nearby.

Campsites, facilities: Twenty-five tent sites are set apart from 525 roomy RV sites (425 full-hookup, 200 pull-through) large enough to accommodate huge rigs and slide-outs. Both 30-amp and 50-amp electrical service are provided. Each site has a picnic table. The office has an Internet connection. A pool, a kiddie pool, a playground, a cafe, basketball hoops, a game room, shuffleboard, a recreation room, horseshoes, and a sand volleyball court entertain campers. A shuttle bus, store with camping supplies, snacks, laundry facilities, restrooms, showers, a dump station, cable TV, telephone hookups, a business center, discounted attraction tickets, rental cottages, rental suites, rental park models, and a poolside café are available. The bathhouse and one of the cottages are wheelchair-accessible. Restaurants and shops are located within walking distance. Children and leashed pets are welcome.

Reservations, fees: Reservations are recommended. Sites are $25–49 per night. Credit cards are accepted. Stays are limited to 30 days.

Directions: From I-4 at Exit 64A, head east one mile on U.S. 192/Irlo Bronson Highway, then turn right on Holiday Trail. Follow it south to the campground, which is located behind Old Town.

Contact: Tropical Palms Fun Resort, 2650 Holiday Trail, Kissimmee, FL 34746, 407/396-4595 or 800/64-PALMS (800/647-2567), fax 407/396-8938, www.tropical palmsrv.com.

121 SHERWOOD FOREST RV RESORT

🏊 🐕 👶 ♿ 🚐 ⛺

Scenic rating: 7

on U.S. 192, near Disney World

See map, page 299

Like numerous campgrounds in the area, the big attraction of Sherwood Forest is its proximity to the many Disney-area attractions. Staying here puts you about four miles from the main gate to Disney World. Parts of the sprawling, manicured community have oaks and pines. Paved roads lead from the security gate to the campsites—most grassy, some sunny. Parents are welcome to bring the kids, who can enjoy the playground while their folks head to the small on-site lake (no fishing) or heated pool. About half the park is occupied year-round by park models. The clubhouse is big enough to seat at least 200.

Campsites, facilities: All 512 full-hookup sites (375 pull-through) have 30-amp or 50-amp electrical service; about half are available for tourists. Most sites have a picnic table. Sites 31–40 overlook the lake. A pool, a hot tub, putt-putt golf, a fitness room, a library, a post office, a financial center, horseshoes, tennis, shuffleboard, a clubhouse, and winter social programs are on the premises. Volunteers organize activities such as bingo, potluck dinners, and casino trips. On the premises are restrooms, showers, a dump station, laundry facilities, trailer rentals, and limited groceries. The office has an Internet connection. Restaurants and shopping are within 0.2 mile. Management says the restrooms and camp store are wheelchair-accessible. Children are welcome. Two pets under 30 pounds each are permitted per site.

Reservations, fees: Reservations are recommended. Sites are $38–43 per night for two people, plus $1.50 for each extra person.

Credit cards are accepted. Long-term rates are available.

Directions: From I-4 at Exit 64A, head east on U.S. 192/Irlo Bronson Highway nearly three miles to the campground.

Contact: Sherwood Forest RV Resort, 5300 West Irlo Bronson Highway, Kissimmee, FL 34746, 407/396-7431 or 800/548-9981, fax 407/396-7239, www.mhchomes.com.

122 KISSIMMEE/ORLANDO KOA

Scenic rating: 6

off U.S. 192 in Kissimmee, east of Disney World

See map, page 299

This KOA is tucked just off the busy main drag—U.S. 192—about five miles from Walt Disney World. The eight-acre park has a pool and grassy or gravel sites with shade. Some sites designated as "deluxe" have patio furniture (not just picnic tables) and come with a bundle of firewood for the chiminea firepot; they are also pull-through, and you park your rig on a concrete pad, instead of gravel or grass. It's a real RV park; there are no full-time occupants.

Campsites, facilities: The camp has 96 full-hookup sites with 20/30/50-amp electrical outlets and cable TV. Each has a picnic table and campfire. Sites vary in size; some are as deep as 80 feet and can accommodate huge RVs or slideouts. On the premises are restrooms, showers, a dump station, a pool, a playground, a basketball court, rental bikes, a convenience store with firewood and s'mores ingredients for your campfire, propane, and laundry facilities. An Internet connection is available via wireless network throughout the park, and there's also a stand-alone Internet room. Roads are paved, and most areas of the park are said to be wheelchair-accessible. You can select your own site before settling in; the park management will drive you through to inspect the sites first.

Groceries and restaurants are within one mile. Children and pets are welcome.

Reservations, fees: Sites are $45–79 for two people, $6 for each additional adult, and $3 for children. Credit cards are accepted. Stays are limited to six months.

Directions: The campground is off U.S. 192, between mile markers 12 and 13. Coming from the west on I-4, take Exit 192 five miles east on U.S. 192/Irlo Bronson Highway, passing Highway 535. Turn left at Seven Dwarfs Lane, then right on Happy Camper Place. If coming from the east on I-4, take Highway 535 to U.S. 192, and follow the directions starting with Seven Dwarfs Lane.

Contact: Kissimmee/Orlando KOA, 2644 Happy Camper Place, Kissimmee, FL 34746, 407/396-2400 or 800/562-7791, fax 407/396-7577, www.koa.com.

123 ORANGE GROVE CAMPGROUND

Scenic rating: 6

off U.S. 192 in Kissimmee, east of Disney World

See map, page 299

Imagine waking up on a brisk winter morning, walking a few feet from your paved or grassy campsite, and plucking fresh oranges off a tree for breakfast. You can do it at this former orange grove, where campers can savor tangerines, grapefruits, lemons, and oranges for free. Onetime grove or not, trees—and therefore shade—are sparse. Play miniature golf on the premises, or drive a short distance to get in a round of the real thing. Most visitors are snowbirds, although a few families find their way here.

The 14-acre park is behind the Value Outlet Shops in the heart of Disney-area shopping and entertainment attractions. It's essentially around the corner from the Medieval Times dinner show and about five miles from the main gate to Disney World.

This is not camping in the get-back-to-nature sense. Your eyes will be assaulted whenever you venture far from the campground by the electric signs of T-shirt shops, restaurants, and the rest of the tourist traps packed chockablock along U.S. 192. But it is one of the more convenient spots to camp if you're making the rounds at Disney World.

Campsites, facilities: The park offers 177 full-hookup RV sites (four drive-through) and 30 grassy tent sites with water and electricity. Thirty spots have 50-amp electrical service; 137 have 30-amp. Each site has a picnic table. The office has an Internet connection and a wireless network has been installed. A pool, miniature golf, a playground, horseshoes, shuffleboard, and winter social programs organized by volunteers entertain campers. On the premises are restrooms, showers, a dump station, laundry facilities, propane sales, and limited groceries (no bread or milk). Golf and restaurants are within one mile; groceries are two miles away. Most areas are wheelchair-accessible. Children are welcome. Leashed, attended pets are permitted.

Reservations, fees: Reservations are recommended in winter. Sites are $30–35 per night for two people, plus $1 for each additional person over the age of three. Credit cards are accepted. The maximum length of stay for new visitors is six months, though about 25 percent of the sites are occupied by year-round residents.

Directions: From I-4 at Exit 68, head east on State Road 535 for 2.5 miles. Turn south on U.S. 192/Irlo Bronson Highway and drive 3.5 miles to the stoplight with the Wal-Mart. Turn west on Old Vineland Road and proceed one mile to the campground on the right, behind the Kissimmee Manufacturers Outlet Mall. From Florida's Turnpike, take Exit 244 westbound to U.S. 192 for 6.75 miles. Turn right at Old Vineland Road and drive one mile to the park on the right side.

Contact: Orange Grove Campground, 2425 Old Vineland Road, Kissimmee, FL 34746, 407/396-6655.

124 GREAT OAK RV RESORT

Scenic rating: 6

in Kissimmee, six miles east of Disney World

See map, page 299

If you want to sleep closest to the well-used swimming pool or the restrooms, ask for a spot in section C. Although some families vacation here, typical campers at Great Oak RV Resort are snowbird couples who might like to take part in bingo, potluck suppers, or trips to the bowling alley during the winter months. About 20 percent of the sites are occupied year-round. Disney World is about six miles from these grassy campsites with concrete patios—some with shade and others in the sunshine. About four miles away is a Kissimmee city park on 11-mile-long Lake Tohopekaliga, where fishing, boating, and picnicking are popular pursuits.

Campsites, facilities: The gated park offers 196 grassy full-hookup sites (10 pull-through) suitable for tents or RVs. Each site has a picnic table and a concrete patio. Shade is minimal. Rigs up to 38 feet long can be accommodated; lots are 26 feet wide by 28–40 feet deep. All sites have 30/50-amp electrical outlets. On the premises are restrooms, showers, a dump station, a heated pool, horseshoes, shuffleboard, a playground, and laundry facilities. In season (November–April 1), planned activities include group meals, trips, bingo, and a "senior Olympics" sports contest in March. Management says the office, showers, and recreation hall are wheelchair-accessible. Groceries and restaurants are within two miles. Children are welcome, but not pets.

Reservations, fees: Reservations are recommended. Sites are $28 per night for two people, plus $2 for each additional person. Credit cards are accepted. Long-term rates are available.

Directions: From I-4, take Exit 68 and proceed east on U.S. 192/Irlo Bronson Highway for five miles. Turn right on Bass Road (the first street past the Wal-Mart). Continue about

0.75 mile to Yowell Road. Turn right. You'll soon see the campground.

Contact: Great Oak RV Resort, 4440 Yowell Road, Kissimmee, FL 32741, 407/396-9092, fax 407/396-9093.

125 MILL CREEK RV RESORT

Scenic rating: 1

in Kissimmee, east of Disney World

See map, page 299

This may not be the ideal vacation spot, with 75 percent of its occupants being full-time campers, families, and students attending the Motorcycle and Marine Institute of Orlando. But if you needed a place to stay, it's about 13 miles from the entrance to Disney World and about three miles from the bass-fishing waters of 11-mile-long Lake Tohopekaliga. In spring, the Houston Astros play exhibition games a short drive away at 5,130-capacity Osceola County Stadium (1000 Bill Beck Boulevard, 407/839-3900 for tickets).

Campsites, facilities: This park offers 157 full-hookup RV sites (three pull-through). Twelve have 50-amp electrical service; the rest have 30-amp. Rigs up to 45 feet long can be accommodated on some of the larger sites. Restrooms, showers, laundry facilities, a pool, a recreation hall, shuffleboard, horseshoes, cable TV, propane, and telephone service are available. Management says restrooms, the clubhouse, and laundry facilities are wheelchair-accessible. Groceries and restaurants are within one mile. Children are allowed. Small pets under 20 pounds are OK.

Reservations, fees: Reservations are recommended. Sites are $30 per night for two people, plus $1 for each additional person. Credit cards are accepted. Long-term rates are available.

Directions: From I-4 at Exit 68, head east on U.S. 192/Irlo Bronson Highway about 10 miles to Michigan Avenue/Highway 531. At

the bowling alley, turn left (north). Proceed about two miles to the park.

Contact: Mill Creek RV Resort, 2775 Michigan Avenue, Kissimmee, FL 34744, 407/847-6288.

126 PONDEROSA RV PARK

Scenic rating: 5

off U.S. 192, east of Kissimmee

See map, page 299

The Houston Astros' spring training home and Osceola Heritage Park rodeo arena and expo center are across the street from this snowbird- and family-oriented park, where the sparse needles of pine trees partially shade some camping spots (other sites are sunny). The 15-acre park is about three miles northeast of a Kissimmee city park, where you can fish, boat, and picnic, at the north end of 11-mile-long Lake Tohopekaliga. It's also close to the four-mile-wide bass-fishing waters of East Lake Tohopekaliga. But to answer the kids' question, the campground is about 15 miles northeast of Disney World. About 65 percent of the park is occupied by year-round residents, and most winter months are sold out far in advance. To secure a reservation during the season, you'll have to call before June. In summer, it's easier to get a site.

Campsites, facilities: Ten tent sites with water and electricity are set somewhat apart from the RV section. Of the 200 shady or sunny RV sites, all have full hookups and 30-amp or 50-amp electrical service, 2 are pull-through, and most have concrete pads. For recreation, there's a heated pool, a recreation room, a playground, horseshoes, shuffleboard, basketball, and winter social programs planned by a paid activities director. Restrooms, showers, a dump station, laundry facilities, and a wireless Internet network are available. Management says the restrooms, recreation hall, and other buildings are wheelchair-accessible. Streets are paved. Groceries are within one mile. Children and pets (no pit bulls) are permitted. Campfires are forbidden.

Reservations, fees: Reservations are highly recommended for winter stays. Sites are $29 per night for two adults, plus $2 for each additional person. Credit cards are accepted. Stay as long as you like.

Directions: From I-4 at Exit 64A, head east on U.S. 192/Irlo Bronson Highway to Boggy Creek Road. Turn left and proceed about one mile north to the park.

Contact: Ponderosa RV Park, 1983 Boggy Creek Road, Kissimmee, FL 34744, 407/847-6002, fax 407/847-2400, www.ponderosarvpark.com.

127 FLORIDA CAMP INN

Scenic rating: 6

southwest of Disney World on U.S. 27, north of Davenport

See map, page 299

Bring sunscreen if you plan to lounge around the patio of the heated pool or spend a lot of time outdoors at this sun-drenched community, located about a 12-mile drive from Disney World. A few bushes and trees separate the grassy campsites. You'll be certain to meet your neighbors, even if you don't attend the organized winter dances and sing-alongs. About two-thirds of the park are occupied by year-round residents, and a mobile-home section is on the north side of the park. Pet sites are grouped together near the entrance and on the eastern border.

From the air, this grid-pattern park appears to be a sea of white RVs with clumps of shade trees at the center. Beyond its borders, broad expanses of dirt fields are broken up by green dots of citrus trees planted in straight rows. Campers tend to spend months here and are asked to follow the 33 park rules. Among them: Follow the 9.75-mph speed limit on park roads, use power tools between 10 A.M.

and 3 P.M. only, and ride your bike only during daylight hours.

Campsites, facilities: There are 503 full-hookup sites, most with 30-amp electrical service. Sixteen have 50-amp hookups. RVs up to 40 feet long can be accommodated at the sites, which average 40 by 60 feet in size. Sites are grassy with cement pads. Some lots are drive-through, though availability varies seasonally. A pool, a recreation hall, shuffleboard, a dump station, grills, four bathhouses, cable TV, ice cream, ice, snacks, and laundry facilities are available. The bathhouses and clubhouse are wheelchair-accessible. Children are permitted. Leashed pets are permitted for overnight, but not monthly, stays and must use the dog walk between the fence and the highway.

Reservations, fees: Reservations are recommended. Monthly and seasonal campsites are first-come, first-served, although reservations may be made for stays of four months or more. Sites are $19 per night for two people, plus $2 for each additional person. Credit cards are not accepted. Long-term rates are available.

Directions: From I-4 at Exit 55, drive 4.5 miles north on U.S. 27 to the park on your left.

Contact: Florida Camp Inn, 9725 U.S. 27 North, Davenport, FL 33837, 863/424-2494, fax 863/424-3599.

128 WALLABY RANCH FLIGHT PARK

Scenic rating: 6

southwest of Disney World

See map, page 299   **BEST (**

This hang-glider park is included as an inducement for the free spirits out there who might want to try something completely new while camping their way across Florida. "The Best Place on Earth to Fly Hang Gliders" is how the 200-acre former cattle ranch bills itself. And darned if it doesn't attract hang gliders from all over. RVs should be self-contained, as there are no hookups.

The focus of the ranch is a 120-acre, level field of green grass, which is free of debris and power lines. With six "aerotugs" available, veteran hang gliders won't have to wait long to get in the air. Novices are welcome, too. The park promises a safe, enjoyable training session. Back on the ground, members of your party who are not interested in hang gliding can swim in a pool, enjoy woodsy hiking or mountain biking trails, or scale the climbing wall.

Campsites, facilities: An indeterminate number of campsites are available; you do not have to be a hang glider to stay here. The owners welcome curious adventurers who wander in now and then (and discover a new hobby along the way).

Reservations, fees: Reservations are not accepted, nor are they necessary for hang gliders using the park's facilities. Camping is $5 (subject to change). Hang-gliding rides are $20 each. Novices can go up with an instructor in a tandem flight and learn to hang glide for $95 a flight.

Directions: From Kissimmee, take I-4 south to U.S. 27 (Exit 55). Head north for 1.5 miles. Turn left at Dean Still Road. Look for the ranch 1.7 miles ahead on the left.

Contact: Wallaby Ranch Flight Park, 1805 Dean Still Road, Wallaby Ranch, FL 33837-9358, 863/424-0070, www.wallaby.com.

129 FORT SUMMIT KOA CAMPING RESORT

Scenic rating: 8

off I-4, south of Disney World

See map, page 299

Don't be confused by the name. This is not Disney World's famed Fort Wilderness Campground, but Disney World is definitely the focus for staying here. Set behind a Best Western motel that shares ownership with the RV park, this sunny, palm-dotted campground nonetheless caters to the theme-park crowd by offering free shuttle rides to Disney World, which is seven miles northeast. The grassy sites with concrete patios are large. Expect to have a good view of neighboring RVs (which is par for the course this close to Disney). Scattered native palms provide token shade. Grass, not privacy hedges, is the preferred landscaping.

In a region often dominated by retirees, parents may breathe a sigh of relief here. A fenced low-impact playground, video games, a wading pool, and a heated pool with plenty of lounge furniture keep young campers entertained. So can the park's car rentals, if you want to drive the family to Sea World or Universal Studios, about 20 minutes away.

Campsites, facilities: Thirty-eight tent sites have water and electricity. They are set apart from 249 full-hookup RV sites (80 pull-through) with 30/50-amp electrical service, concrete pads, picnic tables, brick campfire pits, and grills. A large heated pool, a wading pool, a sundeck, a recreation room, a playground, a game room, an exercise room, basketball, volleyball, pool tables, and social programs entertain campers. Wireless Internet connections are available near the store and in the pool area. Showers, restrooms, rental cabins, a dump station, a fully stocked convenience store with beer, wine, supplies, souvenirs and groceries, snacks, laundry facilities, car rentals, cabins, cable TV, telephone hookups, and free Disney World shuttles are available. Planned activities are on tap in the winter months. The store and restrooms are wheelchair-accessible. A restaurant is within walking distance. Children are welcome. Leashed pets are permitted.

Reservations, fees: Reservations are not necessary. Sites are $34–66 per night for two people, plus $4 for each additional person. Credit cards are accepted. Long-term rates are available.

Directions: From I-4 at Exit 55, go south on U.S. 27 about .1 mile; turn right on Frontage Road and go two blocks. The park is behind the Best Western Motel.

Contact: Fort Summit KOA Camping Resort,

2525 Frontage Road, Davenport, FL 33837, 863/424-1880 or 800/424-1880, fax 863/420-8831, www.fortsummit.com.

130 DEER CREEK RV GOLF RESORT

Scenic rating: 8

off I-4 south of Disney World

See map, page 299   BEST

With names like Arnold Palmer Drive and Jack Nicklaus Lane in one of the park's lot-ownership sections, it's clear that the most un-usual amenities aren't the two-story poolside clubhouse or the five heated pools. Instead, golf is king. It would be hard to find a Florida RV destination more focused on golf than this one, with a lighted driving range, a pro shop, a putting green, and a hilly, 18-hole course.

The RV portion of this manicured, 200-acre, residential-style retirement community welcomes families, while the huge park-model sections are for people over age 55. The mostly sunny RV campsites sit about 35–40 feet apart on what is known as the Lake Wales Ridge (elevation 150 feet above sea level, once a long island in a much deeper ancient sea). As you drive through this complex of park models and RVs to get to your paved campsite, you'll go up one major hill to approach the RV section. Some sites are on one side of the hill; others are on the descent. Disney World is about 10 miles north.

Campsites, facilities: One hundred of the 861 lots are for RVs and have picnic tables, full hookups, and 30/50-amp electrical outlets. RVs must be self-contained and use sewer hookups. Rigs up to 45 feet can be accommodated on sites varying in size but averaging 40 by 80 feet. A golf course, a driving range, a pro shop, pools, a spa, a playground, a game room, horseshoes, shuffleboard, basketball, tennis, volleyball, billiards, and organized activities (usually in winter) entertain camp-ers. Two hired activities directors organize

casino trips, cruises, golf tournaments, bingo, dances, and crafts classes. Showers, restrooms, park-model rentals, a snack bar, a restaurant/lounge, cable TV, LP gas sales, and laundry facilities are available. Groceries are within 0.5 mile. The clubhouse and bathhouse are wheelchair-accessible. Children are welcome. Pets are permitted.

Reservations, fees: Reservations are recom-mended in winter. The rate is $40–45 per night for two people, plus $10 per extra per-son. Credit cards are accepted. Long-term stays are OK.

Directions: From I-4 at Exit 55, drive one mile south on U.S. 27 to the park on your left.

Contact: Deer Creek RV Golf Resort, 42049 U.S. 27 North, Davenport, FL 33837, 863/424-2839 or 800/424-2931, fax 836/424-3336, www.deercreekrv.com.

131 MOUSE MOUNTAIN RV AND MOBILE HOME RESORT

Scenic rating: 7

south of Disney World

See map, page 299

Some campers here plan to go to Disney World, located a mere six-mile drive north past citrus groves and tiny Reedy Lake (on the left). The sunny or somewhat shaded, grassy campsites and accompanying paved patios are set on a hill, which in flat Florida passes for a mountain (hence the park's name). A plus: The family-managed spot is set a respectable dis-tance from the neon signs and multiple lanes of U.S. 192, where many bargain-hunting, Disney-bound motel guests end up. About a third of the park is occupied by year-round residents in mobile homes. In winter, you'll find mostly snowbirds; and in summer, the park is popular with families.

Campsites, facilities: Seven grassy, primitive tent sites are set apart from 299 full-hookup sites with 30/50-amp electrical service and concrete patios. Rigs up to 40 feet long can be accommodated (12 pull-through). Sites are a mix of gravel and grass. Twelve are available for overnight RVers. A heated pool, a playground, horseshoes, shuffleboard, practice putting greens, a recreation hall, and winter activities entertain campers. Restrooms, showers, a dump station, snacks, propane, cable TV, laundry facilities, and a pet walk are available. You can hook up your laptop in the office to pick up your email. Groceries are within one mile. The bathhouse, recreation hall, laundry area, and office are wheelchair-accessible. Children and leashed pets are permitted.

Reservations, fees: Reservations are recommended. Sites are $30–36 per night for two people, plus $2 for each additional person and $2 for cable TV. Credit cards are accepted. Long-term rates are available.

Directions: From I-4, take Exit 58 onto State Road 532/Osceola Polk Line Road. Drive east 1.6 miles just past the light. The park is on the right.

Contact: Mouse Mountain RV and Mobile Home Resort, 7500 State Road 532/Osceola-Polk Line Road, Davenport, FL 33896, 863/424-2791 or 800/347-6388, fax 863/420-9104, www.mousemountainrv.com.

near the pool, ask for a site in the lower end of the alphabet; section R is farthest away, at the back of the park. Overnight spaces during the winter months are limited and do not accommodate RVs more than 33 feet long.

Campsites, facilities: There are 175 full-hookup sites (many pull-through) with 30-amp electrical service. For recreation, there's a pool, a playground, horseshoes, shuffleboard, a recreation hall, and wintertime planned activities. Restrooms, showers, a dump station, and laundry facilities are available. Children under 12 must be adult-supervised at the pool. Leashed, attended pets under 30 pounds are permitted and must use the designated dog walk.

Reservations, fees: Reservations are recommended. Sites are $29–38 per night for two people, plus $2 for each additional person. Credit cards are not accepted. Long-term rates are available.

Directions: From I-4 at Exit 58, go east on State Road 532/Osceola/Polk Line Road less than one mile to the park on the right side. The park is just beyond a traffic light.

Contact: Lakewood RV Resort, 7700 Osceola/Polk Line Road, Davenport, FL 33896, 863/424-2669, fax 863/424-6229, lakewood-fl@earthlink.net.

132 LAKEWOOD RV RESORT

Scenic rating: 6

south of Disney World

See map, page 299

Many campers leave their rigs on-site when they head home for spring and summer, and on about half the sites are mobile homes. The grounds support 482 sunny or shady sites—221 in a park-model section and most others used by long-term residents accustomed to the routine of 3 P.M. daily garbage pickups (except Sundays). The 30-by-40-foot pool sits closest to campsites A6–A8 in the grid-pattern portion of the park, where every street is accorded an alphabetical letter. So, to sleep

133 PARADISE RV RESORT

Scenic rating: 4

four miles west of Disney World

See map, page 299

This park has an unusual amenity for its denizens: an underground shelter in case of tornadoes or threatening weather. Many campers stay for extended periods in winter, and some live at the nine-acre park year-round, congregating at the TV and card room to socialize.

Campsites, facilities: There are 115 sunny full-hookup sites (5 pull-through) with 50-amp electrical service, concrete patios, and picnic tables. RV sites are set diagonally on 20- by 40-foot concrete pads separated by grass. For recreation, there's a rec room, horseshoes, a campfire area, a playground, and basketball hoops. Restrooms, showers, a dump station, LP gas sales, limited groceries, a laundry room, cable TV, telephone hookups, and an underground storm shelter are available. Management says the restrooms and showers are wheelchair-accessible. Restaurants are about four miles away. Children and leashed pets are welcome.

Reservations, fees: Reservations are recommended. Sites are $20 per night for two people, plus $1.50 for each additional person over age three. Credit cards are not accepted. Long-term stays are allowed.

Directions: From I-4 at Exit 64B, head west on U.S. 192/Irlo Bronson Highway. Turn left onto County Road 545/Old Lake Wilson Road and proceed 3.5 miles south, passing under I-4. The campground is on the left.

Contact: Paradise RV Resort, 725 South Old Lake Wilson Road, Kissimmee, FL 34747, 407/396-7711, fax 407/396-2506, www.snowfresh.com/page26.html.

134 21 PALMS RV RESORT

Scenic rating: 6

seven miles south of Disney World

See map, page 299

A small alligator in the fishpond certainly intrigues out-of-state visitors, but the even bigger attraction of these 30 secluded acres is the short seven-mile drive to Disney World. This park isn't only for campers who want to lounge around a solar-heated pool—offerings include a free Nautilus fitness center with an unusual pitch: "Take a healthy break. Relax and enjoy our facilities while you strengthen, firm, and tone your body." Paved roads lead to the level RV sites and concrete patios. A few palm trees dot the lots, although the surrounding land is woodsy. About a third of the park is occupied year-round. In winter, the park plays host to snowbirds. Summer visitors include families and temporary workers.

Campsites, facilities: This all-ages park has 160 paved sites with full hookups, 50-amp electrical service, and concrete patios. About half are pull-through, and 45 are available for overnight visitors. RVs up to 45 feet long can be accommodated. A pool, a fitness center, horseshoes, shuffleboard, a pool table, a recreation hall, and activities planned by volunteers keep campers entertained. Restrooms, showers, a dump station, picnic tables, TV hookups, propane, rental park models, propane, and air-conditioned laundry facilities are available. The office, laundry room, and bathhouse are wheelchair-accessible, and the streets are paved. Children are welcome. Inquire about pet restrictions.

Reservations, fees: Reservations are recommended. Sites are $20 to $25 per night. Credit cards are accepted.

Directions: From Orlando, take I-4 to U.S. 192 (Exit 64B). Go west nearly three miles, passing the Disney World entrance, to State Road 545. Turn left. Continue five miles to Polk County Road. Turn left. The park is two miles ahead. From Tampa, take I-4 to Polk County Road (Exit 58) and go about two miles east to the park.

Contact: 21 Palms RV Resort, 6951 Polk County Road, Davenport, FL 33837, 407/397-9110.

135 RV CORRAL

Scenic rating: 2

south of Disney World, on U.S. 17/92

See map, page 299

All ages are welcome at this 25-acre park, where about 70 percent of the sites are occupied year-round. It's located about 11 miles south of Disney World in a rapidly developing area. Most visitors hail from Florida or the Midwest.

Campsites, facilities: There are 29 full-hookup RV sites (four pull-through) with concrete patios; most have picnic tables and

30-amp electrical service. Eight lots have 50-amp service. Wheelchair-accessible showers, restrooms, and laundry facilities are available. Streets are paved. A supermarket and restaurant are about four miles away, but you can pick up snacks in the park. Adults are preferred. Leashed, attended pets are allowed.

Reservations, fees: Reservations are recommended. Sites are $20 per night for two people, plus $2 for each additional person. Credit cards are not accepted. Long-term rates are available.

Directions: From I-4 at Exit 58, go left on Osceola Polk Line Road. Turn right on U.S. 17/92 and drive four miles south. The park is ahead at right.

Contact: RV Corral, 4141 U.S. 17/92 North, Davenport, FL 33837, 863/420-2181, conrad20015@cs.com.

136 THREE WORLDS RV AND MOBILE HOME RESORT

🚲 🏊 🛶 🐕 ♿ 🚐

Scenic rating: 6

on U.S. 17/92, south of Disney World

See map, page 299

"Country living" is the catchphrase at this 120-acre rural home of preserved wooded areas and three small fishing lakes, yet the park is not far from two major tourist attractions: Sea World is about 18 miles away, while the I-4 exit to Disney World is 11 miles off. (Also about 18 miles away is Cypress Gardens, a 70-year-old park best known for its water-ski exhibitions, beautiful grounds, and "Southern belle" hostesses dressed in long gowns.) Many retirees treat the place like a second home and spend entire winters at the grassy/concrete-pad sites.

The typically sunny campsites sit along curvy roads in an amoeba-shaped section dotted with pines and sabal palms. To sleep apart from most RVs, ask for one of the 12 lake-view spots at the northwest corner of the RV recreational area. Farther east, sites east of the heated pool also enjoy the relative seclusion of having no neighbors to the back. You'll just need to walk a couple of blocks to attend dances and other activities at the 5,000-square-foot lakeside clubhouse, shared with residents of the park's 64 mobile homes (situated to the east of RVs) and 66 park models (set to the west).

Campsites, facilities: This park has 247 full-hookup sites for RVs (five pull-through). A pool, a recreation hall, shuffleboard, horseshoes, social programs, billiards, and a miniature golf course provide entertainment. Showers, restrooms, a dump station, trailer rentals, cable TV, a country store, and laundry facilities are available. Management says the showers, bathhouse, recreation hall, and pool area are wheelchair-accessible. A supermarket and restaurant are about seven miles away in Haines City. Families with small children may camp up to two weeks. Leashed pets under 30 pounds are permitted.

Reservations, fees: Reservations are not necessary. Sites are $28 nightly for two people, plus $2 for each additional person. Credit cards are accepted. Adults may stay long-term.

Directions: From I-4 at Exit 58, drive east to U.S. 17/92. Turn south and proceed 4.5 miles. The park is ahead at left.

Contact: Three Worlds RV and Mobile Home Resort, 3700 U.S. 17/92 North, Davenport, FL 33837, 863/424-1286 or 888/293-3020, fax 863/424-3877.

SPACE COAST

© VISIT FLORIDA

BEST CAMPGROUNDS

❰ Island Retreats
Canaveral National Seashore Beach, **page 379**
Long Point Park, **page 394**

❰ Most Luxurious
Seasons in the Sun Motorcoach Resort, **page 381**
Outdoor Resorts Melbourne Beach, **page 391**

❰ Most Unusual
Manatee Hammock, **page 384**

A roughly 72-mile sliver of territory stretching from Titusville to Melbourne, the Space Coast encompasses pristine Atlantic beaches, unparalleled boating and fishing, and opportunities to view wildlife.

The atmosphere is definitely laid-back, as this area has not been under quite as much pressure from developers as other parts of the east coast of Florida. And the waxing and waning of the fortunes of the nation's space program means that the most consistent economic engine is tourism.

If you're fortunate, you may find yourself along Florida's Space Coast during a NASA space shuttle launch, which can be seen at various spots throughout the area. Several campgrounds boast they are close to good viewing spots and will give campers specific directions. At Jetty Park, for example, campers can watch from a 500-foot-long fishing pier as the rockets rumble into the heavens. Other days, you can spot Disney and Carnival cruise ships sail in on the jetty from Cape Canaveral.

The space center abuts Merritt Island National Wildlife Refuge, 219 square miles of mostly unspoiled Florida backcountry that will please casual hikers and thrill birders — at least 310 species of winged creatures have been spotted. Show up in January or February to watch tens of thousands of ducks and coots stopping to dine. Great bird-watching can also be found on the isolated beaches of the Canaveral National Seashore. Park rangers say 1,045 species of plants can also be found on the barrier island.

Sebastian Inlet State Park is popular with surfers and boasts three miles of natural beaches and an inlet connecting the ocean and Indian River Lagoon. It's also paradise for anglers who take out their own boats, rent them from the park, or use the jetties to catch any of a vast array of fish. If summer, sign up for a ranger-guided nighttime turtle walk to watch sea turtles lumber onto the beach to dig holes in which they'll lay more than 100 eggs each. The park's Sebastian Fishing Museum highlights the area's history of commercial fishing.

So, how convenient is the Space Coast to Orlando? Theoretically, you could head 55 miles west for day trips to the theme parks, but it would be a long day. Best to save the Space Coast for when you can devote more time to its unique pleasures.

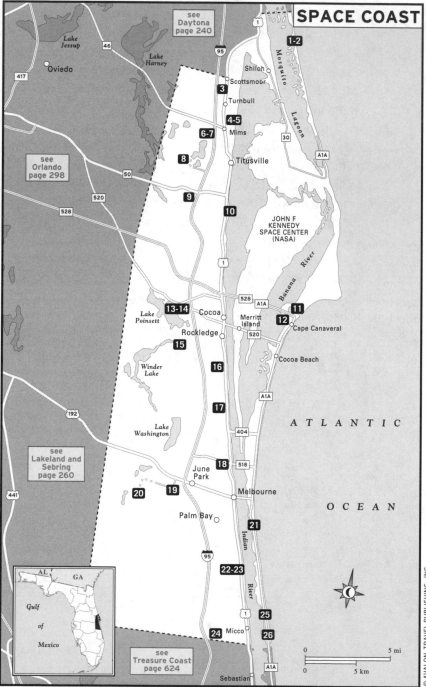

SPACE COAST

see
Daytona
page 240

1-2

Shiloh

Scottsmoor

3

Turnbull

4-5

6-7 Mims

8

Titusville

see
Orlando
page 298

9

10

JOHN F
KENNEDY
SPACE CENTER
(NASA)

Banana River

Mosquito Lagoon

13-14 Cocoa

Lake
Poinsett

Merritt
Island

11

12

Cape Canaveral

Rockledge

15

Winder
Lake

16

Cocoa Beach

17

Lake
Washington

ATLANTIC

18

June
Park

20 19

Melbourne

OCEAN

Palm Bay

21

see
Lakeland and
Sebring
page 260

22-23

25

24 Micco

26

Sebastian

see
Treasure Coast
page 624

AL

GA

Gulf

of

Mexico

0   5 mi

0   5 km

© AVALON TRAVEL PUBLISHING, INC.

1 CANAVERAL NATIONAL SEASHORE BEACH

🏊 🎣 ⛺

Scenic rating: 9

between Cape Canaveral and New Smyrna Beach

BEST (

Wow. If you're lucky enough to snag one of these sites during the six months a year they're open, consider yourself blessed. This is the largest stretch of undeveloped beach left between Miami and Daytona Beach. Don't think of this as car camping, because you may have to slog three-quarters of a mile to reach the farthest site. Think of it as a backpacking trip, and you'll be there in no time. Your reward is awakening to the sight of the sun coming up over the Atlantic as you listen to the waves lapping at the shore. Bring plenty of sunscreen, even in the winter.

Campsites, facilities: Two beach sites accommodate as many people as you like. No facilities are provided. You must bring everything, including water and stove. A chemical toilet is located at the parking lot. Trash must be packed out. Children are OK. No pets are allowed. The camping area is closed April 30–October 31.

Reservations, fees: Reservations and a permit are required in advance of your trip. Get a backcountry permit from the visitors information center at 7611 South Atlantic Avenue, New Smyrna Beach, FL 32169, or call 386/428-3384 to see if a site is available. Fees are $10 per night for the first six people, plus another $10 if your party exceeds six people. Permits are issued, in person only, at the visitors center before 4 P.M. on the day before your camping trip begins. The visitors center is open 9 A.M.–4:30 P.M.

Directions: From Exit 249 on I-95, head east on State Road 44 to A1A. Turn south. The visitors center is about 10 miles ahead.

Contact: Canaveral National Seashore, 308 Julia Street, Titusville, FL 32796, 386/428-3384, ext. 10, www.nps.gov/cana/index.htm.

2 CANAVERAL NATIONAL SEASHORE ISLAND

🚣 🚤 🎣 ⛺

Scenic rating: 9

between Cape Canaveral and New Smyrna Beach

If you love backcountry camping by boat, you have to try this. You get your own island in an area known for great fishing and bird-watching. You'll want to obtain a detailed nautical chart, a compass, and knowledge of how to use them. Some of the sites require you to navigate fairly intricate waterways. Because of the lack of development along its edges, the Mosquito Lagoon is one of the most productive estuaries in Florida, and the fishing is nearly always good—but there's a good reason this is called the Mosquito Lagoon. Even in the winter, you'll want to bring along plenty of bug dope.

Campsites, facilities: Eleven sites accommodate 6–40 people. The only facilities are a picnic table at each site, plus fire containers of some form at most sites. You must bring everything, including water, a stove, and firewood. No bathroom facilities are provided; you must dig a cathole or pack out waste. Trash must also be packed out. Download a small map of the island campsites at the website listed below (not useful for navigation). Children and pets are OK.

Reservations, fees: Reservations are required. Get a backcountry permit from the visitors information center at 7611 South Atlantic Avenue, New Smyrna Beach, FL 32169, or call 386/428-3384 to see if a site is available. Permits are issued up to seven days in advance for lagoon camping. Fees are $10 per night for the first six people, plus $10 if your party exceeds six people.

Directions: From Exit 249 on I-95, head east on State Road 44 to A1A. Turn south. The visitors center is about 10 miles ahead. There are several options for putting in your watercraft; these are explained to you when you pick up your permit.

Contact: Canaveral National Seashore, 308 Julia Street, Titusville, FL 32796, 386/428-3384, ext. 10, www.nps.gov/cana/index .htm.

❸ CRYSTAL LAKE RV PARK
🏊 🎣 🐕 🚐 ⛺

Scenic rating: 4

off I-95, in Scottsmoor

A quick hop off I-95, this family-owned park offers the main attraction of looking skyward to watch NASA's thunderous space-shuttle liftoffs. At other times, the key on-site entertainment is fishing at a three-acre lake, where you can catch bass and catfish, although you may also want to wet a line for saltwater species in the Indian River, three miles away. This is probably the closest private campground to the isolated beaches of the Canaveral National Seashore. During special events at Daytona Beach, such as Bike Week and Speed Weeks, the management says there's room here for a quiet night's sleep. (Bike Week is usually held in March; Speed Weeks vary from year to year, but tend to fall in the early part of the year and in the summer.) It's also fairly close to the Merritt Island National Wildlife Refuge (see *Cape Kennedy KOA* in this chapter). Kennedy Space Center (321/452-2121) is about 30 miles from these grassy campsites, which are surrounded by a few maples, palms, and cedar trees. About 15 percent of the park is occupied by year-round residents.

Campsites, facilities: This park offers 60 full-hookup RV sites (44 pull-through), most with 30-amp electricity. Ten sites have 50-amp. RVs up to 45 feet long and slideouts can be accommodated. Tents may use RV sites, or camp in a separate small primitive area. The park has a wireless Internet network. On the premises are restrooms, showers, laundry facilities, picnic tables, a pool, a recreation hall, horseshoes, and shuffleboard. A convenience store is 1.5 miles away; groceries and restaurants are seven miles away. Children and leashed pets are welcome.

Reservations, fees: Reservations are recommended in winter. Sites are $26–32 per night for two people, plus $3 for each additional person. Credit cards are not accepted. Long-term rates are available.

Directions: From I-95, take Exit 231 and drive east 1,000 feet on State Road 5A/Stuckway Road. Look for the campground on the left behind Stuckey's.

Contact: Crystal Lake RV Park, 4240 Stuckway Road (or P.O. Box 362), Scottsmoor, FL 32775, 321/268-8555 or 888/501-7007, www.nbbd.com/crystallake.

❹ BUCK LAKE CONSERVATION AREA
🥾 🚵 🎣 🛶 🐕 ⛺

Scenic rating: 5

west of Mims, on Buck Lake in northwestern Brevard County

Bring binoculars, because this wilderness area is home to otters, foxes, gopher tortoises, turkey, and deer. Also bring skeeter repellent; the campsite overlooking Buck Lake is basically in marshy floodplain, as is a nearby camping spot. Formerly used for grazing cattle and harvesting timber, these 9,291 acres of backcountry are found on the opposite side of State Road 46 from another woodsy alternative—Seminole Ranch Conservation Area (see listing in this chapter). A small ridge in the eastern part of the Buck Lake property provides conditions dry enough that you might see a rare scrub jay. Two campsites, in the middle of the conservation area, are near a freshwater-fishing lake and require a bit of a trek from either of the two provided parking areas; some campers might prefer to bicycle the three-plus miles.

Boaters can use a ramp on State Road 46 at Six Mile Creek, then travel up the creek to explore a small part of the conservation area or travel south to Salt Lake and the fishing waters of Loughman Lake, both in the Seminole Ranch Conservation Area, and continue to the St. Johns River. Camping is prohibited during hunting season.

Campsites, facilities: Only tents are permitted at the five primitive campsites, reached by foot, bicycle, or horseback. Two sites are within 0.75 mile of a parking area; the next closest spot requires a trek twice as long. There are no restrooms, showers, or supplies. Bring water, food, mosquito repellent, and everything you'll need. A boat ramp is nearby. Children are permitted. Pets must be leashed.

Reservations, fees: Sites are first-come, first-served. Camping is free. Each site accommodates up to six people. If your party has at least seven people, get a free permit and reserve at least one week ahead at 386/329-4410. Maximum stay for all campers is seven days.

Directions: From I-95 at Exit 223, go west on State Road 46 about one mile. To explore the eastern end of the tract, continue about 4.5 miles and look for the western entrance, which leads to the closest parking area for campsites by Buck Lake.

Contact: St. Johns River Water Management District, Division of Land Management, P.O. Box 1429, Palatka, FL 32178-1429, 386/329-4500 or 800/451-7106, www.sjrwmd.com.

5 WILLOW LAKES RV AND GOLF RESORT

🏊 🎣 🚐 🐕 🚙

Scenic rating: 6

in Titusville

Willow Lakes is a deluxe ownership park that targets 55-plus RVers. It offers RV lots for overnighters, but many have already been sold for park models or seasonal visitors. Once built

out, it may have more than 400 sites. Some lots are waterfront or golf-view, and you can watch space launches from the park. Your RV must be at least 22 feet long. As of this writing, a nine-hole golf course is scheduled to be expanded to 18 holes. All facilities are new; the park looks more like a fancy housing development than a campground.

Campsites, facilities: There are two areas, one for Class A motor homes only and one for Class C vehicles and fifth-wheels. All sites are full-hookup, with 30/50-amp electrical service, cable TV, and concrete pads. Restrooms, showers, a dump station, laundry facilities, and telephone service are available. On the premises are a heated pool, a recreation hall, a golf course, shuffleboard courts, and *pétanque* and boccie ball (lawn bowling) courts. Park models are for rent. This is an adults-only park, but children are allowed to visit. Leashed pets are permitted.

Reservations, fees: Reservations are recommended. Sites are $35 per night. Credit cards are accepted. Long-term rates are available.

Directions: From I-95, take Exit 223 eastbound on State Road 46 to U.S. 1. Turn south and drive 0.5 mile to the park.

Contact: Willow Lakes RV and Golf Resort, 2199 North U.S. 1, Titusville, FL 32796, 321/269-7440 or 877/787-2751, www.willowlakes.com.

6 SEASONS IN THE SUN MOTORCOACH RESORT

🏊 🐕 ♿ 🚐

Scenic rating: 8

in Mims

BEST (

Opened in 2002, this big-rig resort has 232 sites in a sunny, landscaped area of citrus trees and shady old oak hammocks. The owners say you can see space-shuttle launches from within the park, and most tourist attractions are within easy driving distance.

Campsites, facilities: All 232 sites have full hookups with 20/30/50-amp electrical service, picnic tables, grills, cable TV, and telephone service connections. Restrooms, showers, a dump station, and laundry facilities are available. On the premises are a heated pool, a lap-swimming pool, whirlpools, lakes, a recreation hall with a fully equipped kitchen, exercise equipment, tennis and boccie ball (lawn bowling) courts, a reading library, shuffleboard courts, a dog-walk area, and a nature trail. A wireless Internet network is available throughout the RV section, plus a dialup modem in the bathhouse. Most areas are wheelchair-accessible. Children are welcome. Leashed pets are permitted.

Reservations, fees: Reservations are recommended. Sites are $33 per night for two people, plus $1.50 per extra person and $1.50 for electrical service. Rates are subject to change. Credit cards are accepted. Long-term rates are available.

Directions: From I-95, take Exit 223 westbound on State Road 46 for 0.5 mile to the park.

Contact: Seasons in the Sun Motorcoach Resort, 2400 Seasons in the Sun Boulevard, Titusville, FL 32754, 877/687-7275, fax 321/385-0450, www.seasonsinthesunrvresort.com.

▼ TITUSVILLE/KENNEDY SPACE CENTER KOA

🏊 🏕 🐎 🚐 ⛺

Scenic rating: 5

off I-95, west of Mims

The names of the paved streets—Michigan Avenue, Iowa Avenue, and Ontario Boulevard, for example—at this 14-acre park are a clue that the place is popular among snowbirds. These mostly shady, grassy spots, about 5 percent of which are occupied by permanent residents, are within one mile of an 18-hole golf course. Temperatures can dip to an average low of 48°F in winter, which explains the fireplace in the adult recreation room, where potluck dinners and bingo entertain visitors during the busy winter.

The campground is less than 20 miles from Kennedy Space Center, so periodically, you'll hear the roar of NASA launches. But another big draw is that this is one of the closest parks to the Merritt Island National Wildlife Refuge—219 square miles of mostly unspoiled Florida backcountry that will please hikers or vacationers who prefer a casual walk in the woods. Try the 0.5-mile Oak Hammock Interpretive Trail, the two-mile Palm Hammock Loop Trail, or the five-mile Allan D. Cruickshank Loop Trail, which features an observation tower and leads to the Indian River. For a self-guided driving tour, pick up a pamphlet at the visitors center. Keep your eye out for birds—at least 310 species of winged creatures have been spotted. If you show up in January or February, you're likely to see tens of thousands of ducks and coots stopping to dine. Call the refuge at 321/861-0667.

Campsites, facilities: Twenty grassy tent sites are set slightly apart from the RV section; they have water and electricity. The 150 RV sites have full hookups and picnic tables. Half the sites have 30-amp electrical service; the other half have 50-amp. Big RVs are welcome; lots are up to 60 feet long. Forty sites are drive-through. A free wireless Internet network is available throughout the park. A pool, a playground, a game room, shuffleboard, horseshoes, a pool table, video games, and wintertime social programs entertain campers. On the premises are restrooms, showers, a dump station, laundry facilities, LP gas sales, a camp store, a picnic pavilion, rental cabins, and a lodge where functions are held. The bathhouse, clubhouse, store, and pool area are wheelchair-accessible. Streets are paved. Children must be adult-supervised at the pool and play in designated areas. Leashed, attended, vaccinated pets are permitted and must use the perimeter dog walk.

Reservations, fees: Reservations are recommended. Sites are $30–32 per night for two people, plus $2 for each additional child and $3 per adult. Add $3.25 nightly for cable TV. Credit cards are accepted. Long-term rates are available.

Directions: From I-95, take Exit 223 and drive west on State Road 46 for 0.25 mile to the campground, on your left.

Contact: Titusville/Kennedy Space Center KOA, 4513 West Main Street, Mims, FL 32754, 321/269-7361 or 800/KOA-3365 (800/562-3365), fax 321/267-2417, www .koa.com.

🔟 SEMINOLE RANCH CONSERVATION AREA

🧍🚴🛶🚗🐎⛺

Scenic rating: 6

east of Orlando, at the convergence of Orange, Brevard, Volusia, and Seminole Counties

Set along 12 miles of the St. Johns River, there are 28,785 acres of marshy wilderness best left to fans of primitive camping, horseback riders, bird watchers, and canoeists. There's also a mountain bike trail. This land was the first purchase made under the state's Save Our Rivers land acquisition program, intended to protect water quality by preserving the land from development. Except for two boat ramps, there are no facilities. The rewards are occasional sightings of roseate spoonbills, white pelicans, and sandhill cranes, and hiking along 4.3 miles of the Florida National Scenic Trail. Seasonal hunting is permitted in a nearly 6,000-acre southern section, which is not near the campsites. One campsite overlooks little Silver Lake; another, right off Hatbill Road, is near the fishing grounds of Loughman Lake. A fairly convenient parking area is between the two sites. A camping spot overlooking the St. Johns River is within a short walk of the park's information kiosk

and another parking area. You've certainly left city life behind—neighbors of this wilderness include the Tosahatchee State Reserve, Little-Big Econ State Forest, and the St. Johns National Wildlife Refuge.

Campsites, facilities: Only tents are permitted at the four primitive campsites, which require a short walk or trip by bicycle, horseback, boat, or canoe. The only facilities are two boat launches. There are no restrooms or showers. Bring water, food, mosquito repellent, and everything you'll need. Children are permitted. Pets must be leashed.

Reservations, fees: Sites are first-come, first-served. Camping is free. Each site accommodates up to six people. If your party has at least seven people, get a free permit and reserve at least one week ahead at 386/329-4410. Maximum stay for all campers is seven days.

Directions: From I-95 at Exit 223, go west on State Road 46. Before you reach the Brevard/Volusia county line, turn left (south) onto Hatbill Road to enter the conservation area. Drive about three miles to the parking area. If you arrive by boat, there is boat access at the junction of State Road 50 and the St. Johns River (Midway Fish Camp) and an Orange County public boat ramp. Follow the river north to the Hatbill Park boat ramp, which is near the campsites at the center of the conservation area. For more detailed directions, contact the water district.

Contact: St. Johns River Water Management District, Division of Land Management, P.O. Box 1429, Palatka, FL 32178-1429, 386/329-4500 or 800/451-7106, www.sjrwmd.com.

🔟 THE GREAT OUTDOORS RESORT

🧍🚴🏊🛶🐎🧑‍🦽🚐

Scenic rating: 10

off I-95, west of Titusville

To call this a campground is a major understatement. Actually, it's a sprawling retirement community, complete with a post office, a beauty shop, and a golf-cart showroom. Lots are for sale. It's also one of the few RV parks I know that markets itself through a videotape and CD-ROM.

Located across the street from the St. Johns National Wildlife Refuge, the complex is huge—about 4.5 square miles. Facilities range from back-in RV sites to a full-scale retirement home for the non-RVer. An interesting innovation between those two extremes is the RV "port," or "executive suite," which looks sort of like a garage or carport. You can park your RV under its roof and feel more or less like you're in a regular home. Some have decks and screened porches. Others have three-bedroom homes with full kitchens built around them. Instead of adding a garage to the home, these folks have added homes to the garage.

The range of available activities is astounding: golfing at a par-71 course, tennis at four lighted courts, swimming in two pools, getting in a game of darts or billiards, and participating in year-round organized activities such as arts-and-crafts classes, bicycling around the park, relaxing at the restaurant and lounge, exercising at the health club, or hiking on nature trails. You can even rent a golf cart. Anglers try for catfish, bass, and panfish in at least 20 stocked freshwater lakes on the property. The park emphasizes its array of resident wildlife, including deer, wild turkeys, bald eagles, quail, rabbits, and waterfowl. Kennedy Space Center is about 12 miles away.

Campsites, facilities: Out of a total of 600, the campground has 125 full-hookup RV sites available for overnighters. Sites have 30/50-amp electrical service, a wireless Internet network, and picnic tables. All are for self-contained rigs at least 18 feet long. Conversion vans, pop-tops, and truck campers are banned. Sites vary in size, but most are 40 by 80 feet and require backing in. On the premises are restrooms, showers, a dump station, laundry facilities, two pools, two hot tubs, a recreation room, an exercise room, shuffleboard, a golf course, tennis courts,

groceries, and a restaurant. A camp store sells limited groceries, souvenirs, and camping supplies. Grocery stores and restaurants are within 0.5 mile. All areas are wheelchair-accessible. This park permits children, but it targets older campers. Two dogs per site are allowed.

Reservations, fees: Reservations are recommended. Sites are $35–45 per night for two adults, plus $3 for each additional adult. To rent an RV port, add $10. Credit cards are accepted.

Directions: From I-95, take Exit 215 and head west on State Road 50 for 0.5 mile.

Contact: The Great Outdoors Resort, 125 Plantation Drive, Titusville, FL 32780, 321/269-5004 or 800/621-2267, fax 321/269-0694, www.tgoresort.com.

10 MANATEE HAMMOCK

Scenic rating: 9

on the Indian River, in Titusville

BEST (

This lovely 26-acre spot on the Indian River is probably the closest, most nature-oriented campground from which to feel the ground rumble beneath your feet as you look skyward at the space shuttle blasting off from Kennedy Space Center, less than 10 miles away. It's a wooded park, a pleasant piece of Old Florida preserved by the county government. The grassy or compacted-dirt campsites sit along narrow 5-mph roads marked by occasional tight turns that can challenge big rigs. Near the park's center sit many of its entertainment options: shuffleboard, a pool, and horseshoe pits. To the northeast, windsurfing and fishing are possible in the Indian River. You also can canoe or kayak (bring your own watercraft). Campfires are forbidden at individual campsites, unless you rent a portable fire ring at $10 per stay. You can also use the public fire ring across the road from the east bathhouse if you're up for telling ghost stories late at night.

Nearby is the Enchanted Forest Nature Center (321/264-5192).

Campsites, facilities: There are 30 tent sites and 147 full-hookup RV sites (12 pull-through) and 35 sites with water and electricity only. Rigs up to 40 feet long can be accommodated. Each site has a picnic table. On the premises are restrooms, showers, a dump station, laundry facilities, a grill area, a pool, a small boat ramp, horseshoes, shuffleboard, volleyball, and a recreation hall. Management says the restrooms are wheelchair-accessible. Children are welcome but must be adult-supervised. Two leashed, attended pets are permitted per RV.

Reservations, fees: Reservations are taken up to one year in advance but are not accepted for some spots. A two-night minimum payment is required before your reservation can be confirmed. Sites are $20–22 per night for six people. Credit cards are accepted. Long-term stays are OK.

Directions: From I-95, take Exit 215 and drive east on State Road 50 for three miles to U.S. 1. Turn right, heading south. Look for the park on your left, four miles beyond the turnoff.

Contact: Manatee Hammock, 7275 U.S. 1 South, Titusville, FL 32780, 321/264-5083, fax 321/264-6468, www.campingspacecoast .com.

🚩 JETTY PARK CAMPGROUND

🏊 🚣 🚴 🐴 ♿ 🚐 ⛺

Scenic rating: 10

in Cape Canaveral

For spectacular views, check out Jetty Park. This 30-acre publicly owned park is best known as one of the great places to stand at a 500-foot-long fishing pier to watch NASA's space shuttle rumble into the heavens from Kennedy Space Center, about 10 miles away. Other days, campers can watch Disney and Carnival cruise ships sail in on the jetty from Cape Canaveral; in fact, the park is operated by the Canaveral Port Authority. In 2001, seaport officials began undertaking improvements to Jetty Park, one of the most popular in this area, including upgrades to the roads, utilities, and other niceties (it's a 20-year project and still ongoing). Dolphins and manatees travel the waterway at times. In summer, you might notice sea turtles lumbering onto the beach to dig holes and plop as many as 200 eggs in their earthen "nests" at night.

The campsites—mostly sandy and grassy, with precious little shade—are set back from the beach alongside the channel into Port Canaveral. Most spots are along two loops; restrooms, showers, and laundry facilities are at the center of each loop. To be closest to the beach, ask for sites 87–117.

Campsites, facilities: The camp has 150 sites (32 full-hookup with electricity), plus an overflow area. Each site has a grill and picnic table. On the premises are restrooms, showers, laundry facilities, a playground, a fishing pier, horseshoes, volleyball, bait and tackle, snacks, picnic pavilions, a dump station, and limited groceries. Management says the jetties and fishing pier are accessible to wheelchairs. A restaurant is within three miles. Children are welcome. Pets under 35 pounds are permitted in the campsites only.

Reservations, fees: Reservations are recommended; a two-day minimum stay is required for reserved sites. Sites are $25–31 per night for six people, plus $2 for pets. It costs $2 to make the reservation. Credit cards are accepted. The maximum stay is 21 days.

Directions: From I-95, take Exit 205 and follow the Bee Line Expressway/State Road 528 east. Exit at mile marker 54, enter Port Canaveral's South Cruise Terminal, then turn right onto George King Boulevard. Follow the signs to the campground at 400 East Jetty Park Road.

Contact: Jetty Park Campground, 400 East Jetty Road, Cape Canaveral, FL 32920, 321/783-7111, fax 321/783-5005, www .portcanaveral.org.

12 MANGO MANOR

Scenic rating: 2

in Cape Canaveral

This is a quiet, no-frills place in an industrial area not particularly geared toward recreation. About half of the 20-acre facility is occupied by people (many of them retirees) who live year-round in mobile homes or stay for the winter season. Kennedy Space Center is about 10 miles from the sites—most paved, some grassy.

Campsites, facilities: All 51 full-hookup sites in this park are for self-contained RV units up to 40 feet long. Most sites have 20/30/50-amp electrical hookups and concrete patios. There are no restrooms, showers, or cable TV; however, wheelchair-accessible laundry facilities and a dump station are provided. Children are welcome. One leashed pet per site is permitted.

Reservations, fees: Reservations are recommended; the park fills up early in winter. Sites are $45 per night for two people, plus $5 per extra person. Credit cards are not accepted. Long-term rates are available.

Directions: From I-95, take Exit 205 and follow the Bee Line Expressway/State Road 528 east to Port Canaveral. At the port, go right (south) on Highway A1A over the bridge to the traffic light. Turn left onto Central Avenue. Look for the park to your left, just past the lumberyard, at 8705 North Atlantic Avenue.

Contact: Mango Manor, 190 Oak Manor Drive, Cape Canaveral, FL 32920, 321/799-0741, fax 321/783-8671.

13 SON RISE PALMS

Scenic rating: 5

off I-95, west of Cocoa

This sunny and open park is a convenient place to pull off the highway for a night's rest. Geared to all ages, the campsites are close to restaurants. About 1 percent of the park is occupied year-round. Favorite things to do in winter inlcude golf, fishing, flea-market shopping, and playing cards.

Campsites, facilities: The 83 full-hookup RV sites have a mix of 30-amp and 50-amp electrical service, concrete patios, and picnic tables. Sites vary in size, but a few sites will accommodate 40-foot rigs. Six sites are available for overnight visitors. On the premises are restrooms, showers, laundry facilities, a nature trail, horseshoes, rental units, and a pool. Management says the bathhouse and pool area are wheelchair-accessible. Streets are paved. A supermarket is two miles away; restaurants are within three miles. Children are welcome. Non-aggressive, leashed pets under 35 pounds are permitted.

Reservations, fees: Reservations are recommended, particularly in winter. Sites are $40 per night for two people, plus $2 per additional adult, $1 per extra child. Credit cards are accepted. Maximum stay is unlimited.

Directions: From I-95, take Exit 201 and head west one short block on State Road 520 to Tucker Lane. Turn left, heading south for about 0.7 mile. The park is just ahead.

Contact: Son Rise Palms, 660 Tucker Lane, Cocoa, FL 32926, 321/633-4335, www.sonrisepalmsrvpark.com.

14 F. BURTON SMITH REGIONAL PARK

Scenic rating: 7

west of Cocoa and Titusville

Only tents are permitted at this 1,360-acre county park, which is primarily a day-use area for nature walks, canoeing, picnicking, and fishing in a small lake (no swimming is allowed). There's also a large pavilion that seats 600 people for group outings. The campground, which overlooks a pond, is used mostly by Scout groups, but anyone can camp here with a permit if there's room.

Campsites, facilities: There's a 0.5-acre primitive tent area with a fire ring. Restrooms and showers are provided, and water is available. On the premises are two lakes for fishing and canoeing, a playground, nature trail, picnic pavilions, and group pavilion. Children are welcome. Pets are prohibited.

Reservations, fees: Camping is by reservation only, and a permit is required. You can download a permit from the website or obtain one in person from the parks and recreation department, which is open weekdays 8 A.M.–5 P.M.

Directions: From I-95, take Exit 201 and head west on State Road 520 for five miles to the park.

Contact: F. Burton Smith Regional Park, 7575 West State Road 50, Cocoa, FL. For information, contact the Brevard County Parks and Recreation Department, 8400 Forrest Avenue, Cocoa, FL 32922, 321/633-1874, fax 321/633-1850, www.brevardparks.com.

15 RIVER LAKES CONSERVATION AREA

Scenic rating: 6

west of Rockledge, on the St. Johns River

An isolated getaway within easy driving distance for Space Coast boaters and canoeists, this 19,536-acre conservation area straddles a stretch of the St. Johns River. The stretch is dotted by a few lakes, making it like a short strand of pearls—the northernmost pearl is Lake Poinsett, Lake Winder is at the center, and southernmost are the fishing waters of Lake Washington. The conservation area is a prized spot for boaters, anglers, seasonal hunters, and bird-watchers. The latter are on the lookout for rare Florida sandhill cranes and endangered wood storks. Bald eagles and river otters may be seen in this floodplain, where saw grass, maidencane, and arrowhead are among the telltale wetland plants. Wetlands mean airboat country in these parts, so don't

be surprised if an airboat rumbles past your campsite. You'll sleep around Lake Winder, which is near the center of this elbow-shaped conservation area. A fixed-crest weir, which helps ensure Melbourne's water supply, is just north of Lake Washington.

Campsites, facilities: Only tents are permitted at the 11 boat-in or canoe-in, primitive campsites, all scattered around Lake Winder and a bit south of the lake. The nearest campsite is about four miles from the Lake Florence trailhead. There are no facilities. Bring water, food, mosquito repellent, and everything you'll need. Five boat ramps provide access to the conservation area. Two shelters have been built on the east side of the river, to be used for daytime recreation or weather protection. Children are permitted. Pets must be leashed.

Reservations, fees: Sites are first-come, first-served. Camping is free. Each site accommodates up to six people. If your party has at least seven people, get a free permit and reserve at least one week ahead at 386/329-4410. Maximum stay for all campers is seven days.

Directions: From I-95 in Cocoa, take Exit 201 west less than one mile on State Road 520, turn left (south) onto Tucker Lane, and follow the road about two miles to a parking area and boat/canoe launch at Lake Florence. Alternatively, you could enter the conservation area via four other boat ramps. For detailed directions and a map showing all campsites, contact the water district before your trip.

Contact: St. Johns River Water Management District, Division of Land Management, P.O. Box 1429, Palatka, FL 32178-1429, 386/329-4500 or 800/451-7106, www.sjrwmd.com.

16 SPACE COAST RV RESORT

Scenic rating: 7

off I-95, south of Rockledge

Convenient to I-95, this 22-acre park benefits from its location, if you happen to be passing through and need a place to spend the night, or want to stay somewhat near a space launch. Fishing is possible in two small on-site ponds and in the nearby Indian River. If you're too pooped to drive nine miles to the Atlantic Ocean, you can swim in the park's heated pool or walk across the street to a golf course. To stay nearest to a long pond, ask for full-hookup sites E15–E24. Kennedy Space Center is about 15 miles away. Most visitors are from the eastern seaboard and northern states. Favorite things to do in the park are socializing, walking, shopping, and sightseeing.

Campsites, facilities: There are 259 full-hookup RV sites (88 pull-through) with concrete patios and picnic tables. One hundred sites have 30-amp electrical service, and 124 have 50-amp. A few have 100-amp service. RVs up to 45 feet long and slideouts can be accommodated on sites that average 40 by 55 feet. There are two tents sites in a separate grassy area with water and electricity. On the premises are restrooms, showers, a dump station, wireless Internet network, LP gas sales, laundry facilities, rental cabins, a pool, a unisex beauty shop, a TV lounge, and shuffleboard. A camp store sells ice, camping supplies, and snacks. All areas of the park are wheelchair-accessible. Children are welcome. Small, leashed, attended pets are permitted but must be transported to and from the designated pet-walk area.

Reservations, fees: Reservations are recommended in winter. Sites are $40 per night, plus $3 per extra person. Credit cards are accepted. Long-term rates are available.

Directions: From I-95, take Exit 195 and head north on Fiske Boulevard to Barnes Boulevard. Turn right (east). The campground is about 0.5 mile ahead.

Contact: Space Coast RV Resort, 820 Barnes Boulevard, Rockledge, FL 32955, 321/636-2873 or 800/982-4233, fax 321/636-0275, www.spacecoastrv.net.

17 CASA LOMA ESTATES

Scenic rating: 2

at the Indian River, north of Melbourne

At this 55-plus mobile-home park located 300 yards from the Indian River, retirees count bingo, exercise classes, and potluck dinners among the highlights of a wintertime visit. Many visitors stay for winter or are retired military personnel who want to be near the base exchange and social milieu of Patrick Air Force Base. The grassy sites have concrete patios and asphalt driveways. The 21-acre park is on busy U.S. 1 and is a good 35-minute drive from the Kennedy Space Center. The ocean is about four miles away, across the nearby Pineda Causeway. About 10 percent of the park is occupied year-round.

Campsites, facilities: This adults-only park has 24 full-hookup RV sites, each with a picnic table and a concrete patio; all have 50-amp electricity. On the premises are restrooms, showers, a dump station, a recreation hall, a pool table, an indoor shuffleboard table, table tennis, horseshoes, shuffleboard, and laundry facilities. Management says the recreation room is wheelchair-accessible. Streets are paved. A convenience store is next door. Groceries and restaurants are within two miles. Children are prohibited, except when visiting older family members. Pets are permitted.

Reservations, fees: Reservations are advised in winter. Sites are $30 per night. Credit cards are not accepted. Long-term rates are available.

Directions: From I-95, take Exit 191 and head east on Highway 509/Wickham Road. As soon as the road angles right to head south, turn left onto Suntree Boulevard. At U.S. 1, turn right and proceed less than one mile to the park, on the right.

Contact: Casa Loma Estates, 6560 North Harbor City Boulevard/U.S. 1, Melbourne, FL 32940, 321/254-2656.

18 WICKHAM PARK

Scenic rating: 7

west of U.S. 1, in Melbourne

Not only can you horse around at Wickham Park, but you also likely see horses in the stalls or along horse trails at the 400-acre local landmark. In far-flung Brevard County, this popular county-run picnic spot stands out because of its size and all that it offers, including archery, disc golf, a horse exercise area, and a 20-station, 1.5-mile-long workout trail. Visitors can jump into two sand-bottomed fishing lakes for a swim, or hike through a honeycomb of nature trails on the park's east side or ride their own horses along trails on the west side. Bicyclists and in-line skaters take advantage of the wide, paved streets that circle the open, airy park. In the wintertime, planned activities are held, such as dances and potluck dinners. Favorite things to do in the park are exercise, Frisbee, golf, and letting the dogs frolic in the dog park.

The 88 grassy campsites are not too far removed from major streets, giving the place a suburban feel. The water- and 30-amp-electricity-equipped grassy sites are set along two loops—Campground A (with about 55 sites) and smaller Campground B. If you want to roast marshmallows around a campfire, head to the fire pit in Campground A. Brush screens some of the 35-by-35-foot sites from neighboring campsites. All have picnic tables, and some are waterfront. The campground is busy in winter; the park's separate day-use areas are most popular in summer. The fishing waters of the Indian River are five miles away. Kennedy Space Center is about 35 miles distant.

Campsites, facilities: All 88 RV sites have water and electricity and are set apart from 22 primitive tent sites. Two manmade swimming lakes, a nature trail, an archery range, horseshoes, volleyball, a horse trail, ball fields, disc golf, a playground, restrooms, showers, a dump station, an amphitheater, picnic pavilions, horse stalls, a horse show ring, grills, picnic tables, and laundry facilities are available. Campground A has a fire pit. Management says the office and restrooms are wheelchair-accessible. Streets are paved. Groceries and restaurants are within one mile. Children must be adult-supervised. Two leashed pets are permitted per site.

Reservations, fees: Reservations are accepted with a two-night minimum stay. Sites are $20 per night. Credit cards are accepted. The maximum stay is six months (for RVs).

Directions: From I-95, take Exit 183 and head east on State Road 516/Eau Gallie-Sarno Road to the third traffic light. Turn left on Wickham Road. Travel about 2.5 miles north to Parkway Drive, then turn right. The entrance is ahead on the left.

Contact: Wickham Park, 2500 Parkway Drive, Melbourne, FL 32935, 321/255-4307, fax 321/255-4343; or contact the Brevard County Parks and Recreation Department, 8400 Forrest Avenue, Cocoa, FL 32922, 321/633-1874, fax 321/633-1850, www.campingspacecoast .com.

19 LAND YACHT HARBOR

Scenic rating: 4

west of Melbourne

Mainly an owners' park for Airstream trailers, these 20 acres are geared to people who like to vacation near shops, a flea market, restaurants, or the beach—not within remote woods. With few trees and precious little shade, it's a quiet place for retired people. Most residents own their lots; they stay at these paved sites and the accompanying patios full-time or at least long-term. Campsites are lined up 16 to 28 abreast along paved, palm-lined streets. The Brevard Zoo is within two miles, and Kennedy Space Center is about 30 miles away. Although restrooms are in the recreation building, practically speaking, this is a residential park with some room set aside for self-contained RVs. In the winter, campers take part in bingo, band events, card games, and three kinds of dancing: ballroom, line, and square.

Campsites, facilities: This adults-only park offers 304 full-hookup sites for self-contained units up to 36 feet long. A few sites are available for overnighters regardless of the brand of their RV. On the premises are restrooms, a recreation hall, game rooms, horseshoes, and shuffleboard. A wireless Internet network is available in most of the park. There is no dump station for overnighters. Management says the recreation hall is wheelchair-accessible. Groceries, restaurants, shops, and laundry facilities are about a mile away. Children and pets are prohibited.

Reservations, fees: Reservations are recommended. Sites are $29 a night. Credit cards are not accepted.

Directions: From I-95, take Exit 180 and head east on U.S. 192 0.3 mile to John Rodes Boulevard at the first traffic light. Turn left. The park is about two miles ahead.

Contact: Land Yacht Harbor, 201 North John Rodes Boulevard, Melbourne, FL 32934, 321/254-6398, www.landyachtharbor melbourne.com.

20 THREE FORKS MARSH CONSERVATION AREA

Scenic rating: 5

west of Melbourne, in southwestern Brevard County

Alligators sun themselves along the banks of this floodplain, and river otters, wading birds, and shorebirds are the expected beneficiaries of an ongoing restoration effort. These 52,000 acres had been severely impacted by diking and draining for farms, so the water management district bought the land to ultimately help the St. Johns River; here, the channels of the St. Johns arise in the marsh south of Lake Hell 'n' Blazes. You'll traverse those channels—called Three Forks Run—to get to the rustic campsite at Lake Hell 'n' Blazes. Anglers and canoeists favor the narrow waters that connect that lake to Sawgrass Lake, about four miles northeast, where another campsite is found. It's a rustic experience; some visitors opt for day visits, following the looped rectangular hiking trail found far from the campsites and southeast of the parking area (south of Malabar Road), or riding their own airboats up the C-40 canal, which runs down the middle of the long conservation area. Hiking also is possible at the southern boundary along the C-54 canal, which doubles as the Brevard/Indian River county line, and at the eastern neighbor, T.M. Goodwin Waterfowl Management Area. If that's not enough, just across the C-54 canal is the Blue Cypress Conservation Area (see listing in the *Treasure Coast* chapter).

Campsites, facilities: Only tents are permitted at the two boat-in or canoe-in primitive campsites, which are about two to four miles from the nearest boat ramps. There are no facilities at the campsites, but there are restrooms and picnic tables by the recreation area's parking lot. Bring water, food, mosquito repellent, and all other necessities. Three boat ramps provide access to the conservation area. Children are permitted. Pets must be leashed.

Reservations, fees: Sites are first-come, first-served. Camping is free. Each site accommodates up to six people. If your party has at least seven people, get a free permit and reserve at least one week ahead by calling 386/329-4410. Maximum stay for all campers is seven days.

Directions: From I-95 in Melbourne at Exit 173, go west about eight miles on Malabar Road/State Road 514 to the Thomas O. Lawton Recreation Area, the main entry point into the Three Forks Marsh Recreation Area. A boat ramp/canoe launch is at a man-made lake near the parking lot, picnic tables, and restrooms. From here, the nearest campsite (at Lake Hell 'n' Blazes) is about four miles beyond the water retention area, up Three Forks Run. Two boat ramps are located off of Kenansville Road on the southern side of the conservation area; enter from Kenansville Road/Fellsmere Grade. For detailed directions and a map, contact the water district before your trip.

Contact: St. Johns River Water Management District, Division of Land Management, P.O. Box 1429, Palatka, FL 32178-1429, 386/329-4500 or 800/451-7106, www.sjrwmd.com.

21 OUTDOOR RESORTS MELBOURNE BEACH

🚴 🏊 🐟 🛶 🐕 ♿ 🚐

Scenic rating: 10

on Highway A1A, in Melbourne Beach

BEST (

One of the best things about this luxury RV resort is its proximity to the ocean and beach, which are just across Highway A1A, and to the Indian River nearby. You'll often feel a sea breeze here. The paved RV sites—with patios and a few sabal palms—are across the highway from a nicely landscaped beachside recreation complex that includes a 3,000-square-foot activity center and a palm-flanked oceanview pool.

The 40-acre park isn't exactly a place for shrinking violets. You can swim in the ocean or in one of three pools, choose from six tennis courts or eight lighted shuffleboard courts, use the boat ramp to access the Indian River for boating or fishing, or drop a line off the 300-foot fishing pier. Bicyclists tool around the park or on a path that runs along Highway A1A. On summer nights, some guests watch sea turtles nest on the nearby beach. Kennedy Space Center is within a 45-minute drive.

Campsites, facilities: Amid this 576-unit community, there's a varying number of full-hookup sites available for overnight or seasonal RVs. Each site has a picnic table. On the premises are restrooms, showers, three pools, lighted tennis courts, a hot tub,

beach scene near Melbourne

an activities center, a health club, two clubhouses, a boat ramp, a dock, shuffleboard, and a laundry room. Planned activities are held during the winter months. A wireless Internet network is available in some parts of the park. Management says the buildings, bathhouse, and pool areas are wheelchair-accessible. Children are welcome. Leashed, attended pets are permitted.

Reservations, fees: Reservations are recommended. Sites are $38–49 per night for four people, plus $2 for each additional person. Credit cards are accepted. Long-term stays are OK.

Directions: From I-95, take Exit 180 and travel east on State Road 192 to Highway A1A. Turn right (south). Look for the campground on the right in four miles.

Contact: Outdoor Resorts Melbourne Beach, 3000 Highway A1A South, Melbourne Beach, FL 32951, 321/724-2600 or 800/752-4052, fax 321/727-0175, www.outdoorresorts melbournebeach.com.

22 ENCHANTED LAKES ESTATES
🏊 ⛵ 🐕 ♿ 🚐

Scenic rating: 3

in Malabar

Mention the obscure town of Malabar, and many Floridians will scratch their heads. But bring up the nearby Indian River, and they'll certainly know what you're talking about. A popular boating and fishing destination, the river is two miles east of the grassy/concrete-pad sites at this 28-acre park. The ocean is just two miles farther east as the crow flies, but you should expect to drive six miles north to a Melbourne causeway first to get there. This neatly kept, sunny RV park's "enchanted lake" has fountains and lush tropical landscaping. About 45 percent of the park is occupied year-round. Visitors

come primarily from Canada, New York, Maine, and Massachusetts.

Campsites, facilities: Of the 75 full-hookup RV sites, 65 are pull-through. Each site has 30/50-amp electricity, a concrete patio, and a picnic table. RVs up to 50 feet long and slideouts can be accommodated. Only a few sites are available for overnighters. On the premises are showers, restrooms, a recreation hall, a heated pool, an exercise room, a pool table, laundry facilities, and planned activities. Cable TV and telephone service are available. Management says the recreation hall and office are wheelchair-accessible. Streets are paved. A restaurant, groceries, and bait are available within two miles. Children are allowed. Leashed pets are permitted.

Reservations, fees: Reservations are recommended. Sites are $30 per night for two people, plus $5 for each additional person. Credit cards are not accepted. Long-term rates are available.

Directions: From I-95, take Exit 173 and travel east on State Road 514/Malabar Road for two miles. The park is next to Palm Bay Hospital.

Contact: Enchanted Lakes Estates, 750 Malabar Road, Malabar, FL 32950, 321/723-8847, fax 321/724-1102, www.enchantedlakes .net.

23 CAMELOT RV PARK
🎣 🚤 🐕 ♿ 🚐

Scenic rating: 6

on U.S. 1, in Malabar

Finding out what activities are scheduled to take place at the recreation hall is as simple as turning on the free 40-channel cable TV service and tuning to Channel 5, the park's information station. Why would you need a TV channel to tell you what's happening? Because as many as 75 volunteers organize things to do, that's why. Beyond the entrance gates of the family-run park, paved roads lead to sunny spots equipped with concrete patios and picnic tables. Anglers and boaters can cross the street—well-traveled U.S. 1—to get to a dock on the Indian River. Many of the usual RV-park rules apply at this 20-acre RV/mobile-home destination, with two perhaps welcome exceptions: You may wash your RV or car; and two vehicles, not one, may be parked at each site. Channel 15 on the cable TV service delivers information about NASA, so you can monitor space launches at the Kennedy Space Center, about a 45-minute drive northeast. The park overlooks the Indian River Lagoon.

Campsites, facilities: Many of the 130 full-hookup sites with concrete pads are available for overnighting RVs, and two or three are taken by seasonal visitors. Thirty-amp and 50-amp electrical service, cable TV, and telephone service are available. Rigs up to 45 feet long can be accommodated. A recreation hall, a craft center, a fishing dock, shuffleboard, basketball, and winter activities entertain campers. Restrooms, showers, picnic tables, laundry facilities, and a dog-walk area are on-site. Most areas are wheelchair-accessible. Children are allowed to visit, but this is primarily a 50-plus-age park. Leashed, attended pets are permitted.

Reservations, fees: Reservations are recommended. Sites are $31–35 per night for two people, plus $5 for each additional adult. Credit cards are accepted. Long-term rates are available.

Directions: From I-95, take Exit 173 and travel 4.5 miles east on State Road 514/Malabar Road to U.S. 1. Turn right. The park entrance is about two blocks ahead at right.

Contact: Camelot RV Park, 1600 U.S. 1, Malabar, FL 32950, 321/724-5396, fax 321/724-9022, www.camelotrvpark.com.

24 ST. SEBASTIAN STATE BUFFER PRESERVE

Scenic rating: 7

between Fellsmere and Sebastian, on the C-54 Canal

Bring a camera to preserve memories of seeing turkey, deer, bald eagles, and otters, among other critters, at this 21,951-acre preserve. Wildlife is abundant. Indeed, a wheelchair-accessible platform serves as a manatee viewing area. This place aims to protect manatees, red-cockaded woodpeckers, and Florida scrub jays by providing an upland buffer to the creek (hence the park's "buffer" name). You'll sleep near a hiking trail north of the C-54 Canal, which divides the preserve in two. Look for white pelicans along the canal. Hikers, bicyclists, and horseback riders can follow more than seven miles of trails that ribbon the preserve and are named by color—Blue Trail, Red Trail, Yellow Trail, Green Trail. Two short spur trails (less than one mile each) lead to the north prong of the St. Sebastian River. If that's not enough, a looped walking path is behind the visitors center. Bring sunscreen and a hat; it's an open and sunny place with seasonal wetlands, hardwood swamp, and pines, which provide little in the way of sun protection. Get maps from the St. Johns River Water Management District before heading out.

Campsites, facilities: Only tents are permitted at the five primitive hike-in campsites. You'll walk 0.1 mile to Storytelling Camp or 0.5 mile to the other site, called Horseman's Headquarters. There are no facilities in the camping area, except for the paddock and water for horses at Horseman's Headquarters. On the opposite end of the preserve, there are restrooms at the wheelchair-accessible Visitors Center, which is open weekdays only. Bring water, food, and supplies. Children are permitted. Pets must be leashed.

Reservations, fees: Reservations are advised at least three days ahead, preferably earlier. Camping is free. Each site accommodates about 15 people.

Directions: From I-95 at Exit 173, go west on Malabar Road/State Road 514, then south (right) onto Babcock Road/County Road 507. Continue 11.5 miles and turn east onto Buffer Preserve Drive. The south entrance can be reach by driving 1.8 miles east of I-95 on Fellsmere Road/County Road 512.

Contact: St. Sebastian River State Buffer Preserve, 1000 Buffer Preserve Drive, Fellsmere, FL 32948, 321/953-5004 or 321/676-6614. Additional information and maps are available from the St. Johns River Water Management District, Division of Land Management, P.O. Box 1429, Palatka, FL 32178-1429, 386/329-4500 or 800/451-7106, www.sjrwmd.com.

25 LONG POINT PARK

Scenic rating: 7

at the Indian River, in Melbourne Beach

BEST (

Long Point is actually on an island, not a point, but that probably makes it all the more popular. Surrounded by the Indian River, this 60-acre, county-run camping park draws boaters, anglers, canoeists, and kayakers bound for the Indian River. Most of the grassy campsites are set around the park perimeter. Full-hookup sites are located at the center. As a brochure puts it, this place has two little lakes—one for swimming, and one for wildlife. To be closest to the swimming lake, ask about the water- and electricity-equipped sites numbered 14–22. Full-hookup sites are near the other lake. Tenters who want to get away from it all may want to get away from the on-site bait and tackle sales, located near tent sites 30 to 40; ask for a camping spot in the other two rustic areas instead. The park is on the Indian River, just 1.5 miles

from the quiet, slow-paced Sebastian Inlet State Park.

Campsites, facilities: Many tents can be accommodated in a primitive tenting overflow area set apart from 170 RV sites. Fifteen sites have full hookups; 113 have water and electricity only. On the premises are showers, restrooms, a dump station, picnic tables, grills, fire rings (at waterfront sites), a one-lane boat ramp, a fishing pier, a playground, horseshoes, volleyball, and a laundry room. Management says the restrooms, pavilions, swimming pond, and playground are wheelchair-accessible. Children are welcome. Two leashed, well-attended pets are permitted per site.

Reservations, fees: Reservations are accepted; but if you make a reservation, you are required to stay for at least two nights. There is a $12.50 cancellation charge if you change your mind 72 hours prior to check-in date. No refunds are given if you cancel within 72 hours. Sites are $23–25 per night, depending on the campsite services you need. Credit cards are accepted. The maximum stay is 180 days.

Directions: From U.S. 192 in Melbourne, go south approximately 17 miles on Highway A1A. Look for the turnoff to the park on the right, about 1.5 miles north of Sebastian Inlet State Park.

Contact: Long Point Park, 700 Long Point Road, Melbourne Beach, FL 32951, 321/952-4532, www.campingspacecoast.com.

26 SEBASTIAN INLET STATE PARK

Scenic rating: 10

on the Indian River, in Melbourne Beach

Surfers are fond of this popular state-run park, which boasts three miles of natural beaches and an inlet connecting the ocean and Indian River Lagoon. And it's paradise for anglers who take out their own boats, rent them from

a campsite at Sebastian Inlet

the park, or use the jetties to catch any of a vast array of fish attracted to the inlet.

This 379-acre park has much to offer beyond surfing. Sunbathers favor a dip in the ocean. Picnickers stake out their favorite sun-washed spots (bring caps and sunscreen). Bicyclists who desire something more challenging than the park roads can head north for 14 miles along Highway A1A, stopping to enjoy numerous access points to the ocean. Snorkeling is also possible, but you should avoid the inlet itself, which has wicked currents. Instead, rangers recommend heading to the southern portion of the park to snorkel in the ocean; reefs are about 50 feet offshore.

Campsites overlook the Sebastian Inlet. You will enjoy relative peace away from the madding daytime crowds because you'll camp at the Indian River side of the park, not near the concession stand, ocean swimmers, surfers, or showers on the Atlantic side across Highway A1A.

Don't neglect the park's Sebastian Fishing Museum, which highlights the area's history of commercial fishing, or the McLarty Treasure Museum, recollecting the days hundreds of years ago when treasure-laden Spanish galleons would crash along this coast. The museum commemorates a Spanish fleet that was wrecked near here by a hurricane in 1715 while carrying gold and silver from Peru to Spain.

If you arrive in summer, sign up for a ranger-guided nighttime turtle walk to watch sea turtles lumber onto the beach to dig holes and lay as many as 200 eggs each. This park is one of my favorite campgrounds in Brevard County, but it's *way* down at the southeastern corner. Expect at least a 30-minute drive to Kennedy Space Center and Cocoa Beach. Still, if you want to see a slice of southern oceanside Brevard in a more or less natural state, this is probably your best bet.

Campsites, facilities: All 51 sites are for RVs and tents, and all have water and 30-amp electricity. Each site has a picnic table, a grill, a fire ring, and a pad made of stabilized fill. Three sites have 50-amp electrical service. RVs up to 40 feet and slideouts can be accommodated. On the premises are restrooms, showers, a dump station, a boat ramp, kayak and canoe rentals, a nature trail, a breakfast-and-lunch snack bar, and laundry facilities. Management says that restrooms, parking lots, docks, store, both museums and jetties, and the concession area are wheelchair-accessible. A camp store sells ice, snacks, souvenirs, bait, and tackle. Groceries are 12 miles away. Children are welcome. Pets are allowed in designated areas.

Reservations, fees: Reservations are recommended; contact ReserveAmerica at 800/336-3521 or reserveamerica.com. Sites are $23 per night for eight people. Credit cards are accepted. The maximum stay is 14 days.

Directions: From U.S. 192 in Melbourne, travel approximately 22 miles south on Highway A1A. Look for the park about 1.5 miles south of Long Point Park. If you're traveling from Vero Beach, drive about 12 miles north on Highway A1A to the park entrance.

Contact: Sebastian Inlet State Park, 9700 Highway A1A South, Melbourne Beach, FL 32951, 321/984-4852, www.floridastateparks.org.

ST. PETERSBURG

© MARILYN MOORE

BEST CAMPGROUNDS

€ **Beachfront Campgrounds**
Fort de Soto Park Campground, **page 412**

€ **Island Retreats**
Anclote Key State Preserve Boat-In Sites,
   page 404
Fort de Soto Park Campground, **page 412**

Three "Bs" are the watchwords for the

St. Petersburg-Clearwater area: beaches, boating, and bicycling. All are top-notch activities for visitors drawn to this area bounded on the west by the Gulf of Mexico and on the east by Tampa Bay. This popular tourist destination offers 35 miles of first-rate beaches of white sand and gentle waters, plus even a few waterfront campgrounds.

First, the beaches. The two top-rated beaches in Florida are located here, but even the ones that don't make the official ratings are pretty spectacular. The sparkling gulf waters are calm and tranquil most of the year, gently lapping the shoreline. Sea kayaking, kite sailing, canoeing, and hunting for seashells are popular activities.

Fort de Soto, a county-run park and campground, offers the officially designated number one beach in America. Almost all 235 sites are waterfront, and some have good views of St. Petersburg and the Gulf of Mexico. For day use, Honeymoon Island State Park, north of Dunedin, is another excellent beach with four miles of sand and a dog park.

If you brought your boat, don't miss Anclote Key State Preserve. You'll have to anchor offshore and wade in or beach your boat on the sand. The effort is worthwhile, though. On the southern shore is a lighthouse built in 1887 that once guided shipping traffic with its 101-foot-high beacon. The island is a bird-watcher's delight; more than 43 species have been spotted, including the bald eagle.

Slightly more accessible is Caladesi Island State Park, with 650 dry acres and 1,800 acres of mangrove flats and submerged lands. The beach is so beautiful that it's been graded as one of the top 10 in the United States for nearly a decade. Walk the four miles of unspoiled beach in search of the perfect seashell or hike the island's nature trails. Those without access to a boat can use the ferry from Honeymoon Island to make a day trip out of it.

For bicycling, the Pinellas Trail is a 42-mile, paved biking and walking path converted from an old railway. It runs mostly parallel to the main highway; besides being a great place to train, you can also use it to get from point A to point B with a minimum of danger.

St. Petersburg is an easy 30-minute drive to most Tampa attractions, so it makes a great base camp for visiting Busch Gardens. On the northern edge of the peninsula is quaint Tarpon Springs, famed for its fishing, sponge docks, and numerous restaurants serving great seafood and Greek dishes.

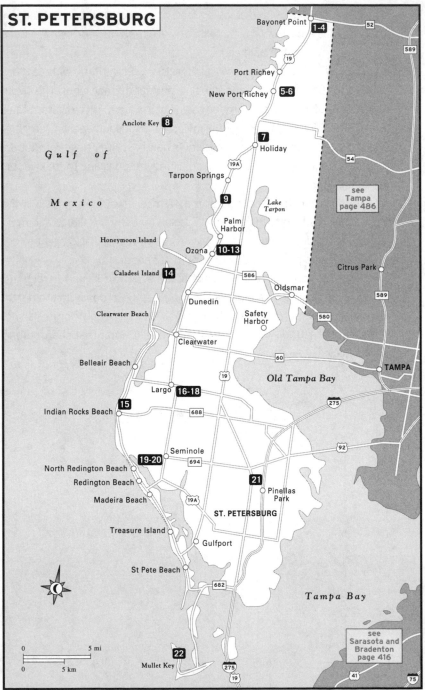

ST. PETERSBURG

◼ SUNDANCE LAKES RV RESORT

Scenic rating: 3

in Port Richey

This sunny and neatly kept community, which can accommodate rigs up to 40 feet long, is set back one block from a busy six-lane highway, but boasts four fishing lakes. Shopping centers are within walking distance and a flea market is next door. Five major golf courses are a short drive away. Tarpon Springs, Busch Gardens, Weeki Wachee Spring, Disney World, Epcot, the Salvador Dalí Museum, and Homosassa Springs are easy day trips from the park. Hudson Beach is two miles away, and the beach at Green Key is four miles away. Complete medical facilities and churches are close by. With an 11,000-square-foot recreation hall to enjoy, many visitors stay on-site for planned activities.

Campsites, facilities: Perfectly manicured, the park has a total of 523 concrete-pad sites with full hookups, 30/50-amp electrical service, and telephone access. Restrooms, showers, laundry facilities, a heated pool, tennis, a pool hall, a huge recreation hall with a sitting porch, shuffleboard, horseshoes, and four lakes are on the premises. Children are welcome for short stays, but there is no playground, and management prefers campers age 55 and older. Leashed pets under 25 pounds are permitted.

Reservations, fees: Reservations are recommended. Sites are $25 per night for two people, plus $2.50 for each additional person. Credit cards are accepted. Long-term rates are available. The resort targets Northerners age 55 and over who stay for the season, although overnighters are welcome.

Directions: From the junction of U.S. 19 and State Road 52, drive 300 yards south on U.S. 19. Turn west on Hachem Drive and continue into the park.

Contact: Sundance Lakes RV Resort, 6848 Hachem Drive, Port Richey, FL 34668, 727/862-3565, www.rvresorts.com.

◼ SUNCOAST RV RESORT

Scenic rating: 4

north of New Port Richey

With tall pines casting sun-dappled shadows, you can hardly tell this RV resort is next to a mall and on a major highway. The managers guarantee in writing that restrooms will be clean, staff will be courteous, and the pool will be sparkling. It's near shopping, restaurants, and fishing and boating on the Gulf of Mexico. Planned activities are held in the winter months, with everyone pitching in to offer ideas and help. Choose between sunny and shady sites. About 25 percent of the park is occupied year-round.

Campsites, facilities: There are 154 RV sites with full hookups, 30/50-amp electrical service, and wireless Internet access throughout the park. A pool, shuffleboard courts, horseshoe pits, a recreation hall, a pavilion with a fireplace, and laundry facilities are available. Shops and restaurants are within 0.2 mile. The laundry room and pavilion are wheelchair-accessible. Children and leashed pets are welcome.

Reservations, fees: Reservations are recommended. Sites are $25 to $28 per night for two people, plus $3 for each additional person and $3 for using electrical service. Credit cards are accepted.

Directions: From the junction of U.S. 19 and State Road 52, drive 1.8 miles south on U.S. 19 to the park, on the east side of the road.

Contact: Suncoast RV Resort, 9029 U.S. 19, Port Richey, FL 34668, 727/842-9324 or 888/922-5603, www.suncoastrvresort.com.

3 OAK SPRINGS TRAVEL PARK

Scenic rating: 3

north of New Port Richey

Several small lakes are scattered throughout this huge adult travel resort, which is so big it has bicycle parking near the recreation hall to accommodate guests who want to cover a lot of ground on wheels. In winter, snowbirds pass the time with social activities such as line dancing, potluck dinners, ice-cream socials, exercise classes, parties, arts-and-crafts classes, and bingo. Church services are held here, too.

Campsites, facilities: For adults only, this 528-unit park has 200 RV sites with full hookups and 30-amp electrical service. Facilities include restrooms, showers, a pool, a horseshoe pit, a game room, shuffleboard courts, and a laundry room. Children are not welcome. Leashed pets are allowed.

Reservations, fees: Reservations are recommended. Sites are $25 per night for two people, plus $2.50 for each additional person. Credit cards are accepted. Long-term rates are available.

Directions: From the junction of U.S. 19 and State Road 52 in New Port Richey, drive two miles south on U.S. 19. At Jasmine Boulevard, turn west and go one block to the park entrance on Scenic Drive.

Contact: Oak Springs Travel Park, 10521 Scenic Drive, Port Richey, FL 34668, 727/863-5888, www.rvresorts.com.

4 JA-MAR TRAVEL PARK

Scenic rating: 3

in Port Richey

Actually two resorts located 1,800 feet apart, this mobile-home/RV park welcomes overnighters, even though most people here are seasonal visitors. Planned activities—as many as 10 daily—include everything from Bible study to line dancing and euchre games. Bus trips are arranged to nearby attractions. Stores and restaurants are close by. Two ponds line the entrance drive; be careful when entering the park at night. One of the lakes is stocked for fishing.

Campsites, facilities: There are 400 lots with full hookups and 30/50-amp electrical service, with about half available for overnighters. Rigs up to 38 feet in length can be accommodated. Restrooms, showers, laundry facilities, a recreation hall, shuffleboard courts, lakes, and a pool are on the premises. All areas are wheelchair-accessible. This is a 55-and-older park, but children may stay short-term. Leashed pets are permitted.

Reservations, fees: Reservations are recommended. Sites are $26 per night for two people, plus $2 for each additional person, $2 for 30-amp electrical service, and $3.50 for 50-amp service. Credit cards are not accepted. Long-term stays are allowed.

Directions: From U.S. 19 near Hudson, drive south to State Road 52. The park is on the west side of the road, just south of the intersection.

Contact: Ja-Mar Travel Park, 11203 U.S. 19, Port Richey, FL 34668, 727/863-2040, fax 727/862-8882, www.ja-mar-travelpark.com.

5 JAY B. STARKEY WILDERNESS PARK

Scenic rating: 10

on the east side of New Port Richey

Pop-up campers can get even here. Well, at least two of them. Sometimes pop-ups are not allowed in the more snooty RV parks, but in this beautiful nature park, they are the only trailers permitted. Set on the edge of an urban area and upscale housing developments, this 8,700-acre public preserve is part of a wilderness tract originally owned by Jay B. Starkey, who bought the land in 1937 for cattle-grazing. An environmental education center was built for meetings, exhibits, and nature training. Almost all the sites are for tents; only two can accommodate pop-up trailers. Picnic areas, pavilions, shelters, a paved bike trail, and 13 miles of hiking trails are in the park. Limited freshwater fishing is available along the Anclote and Pithlachasotee Rivers. The following are not allowed: alcoholic beverages, guns or trapping devices, collecting or removing plants or animals, swimming, canoeing or boating, digging, motorcycles, and all-terrain vehicles. The park has 10 miles of marked bridle paths designated for equestrian use. Horses must be trailered into the park, and each rider must carry proof of a current negative Coggins test.

Campsites, facilities: The main campground has 16 primitive sites for tents, including two for pop-up campers. Larger RVs and generators are not allowed. Facilities include restrooms, showers, picnic tables, grills, and fire rings. A backcountry camping area has been designated for equestrian use. Supplies and provisions must be packed into those sites because vehicles are not allowed. All ground fires must be contained. Three backpacking campsites are located near the foot trails; each has a picnic table, a grill, and a fire ring. Large cabins are available for rent for $15 per night for eight persons; smaller cabins are $10 per night for four people. One cabin and the environmental education center are wheelchair-accessible. Children are welcome. Pets are prohibited in the campground, though you may walk a dog on a six-foot leash elsewhere in the park.

Reservations, fees: Reservations are required for the main campground; they may be made up to 30 days in advance in person. Pop-up camper sites in the main area are $5 per night (a site accommodates up to eight people). For backpacking, sites may be reserved up to 90 days in advance, and campers must register at the kiosk in person for their own safety. Tent sites in the main area are $5 per night (a site

accommodates up to eight people and two tents). Credit cards are not accepted. Camping is free for backpacking and equestrian sites. Credit cards are not accepted. Stays are limited to seven days, with an extension available for a maximum of 14 days.

Directions: From I-75, take Exit 285 and drive west on State Road 52 for 21 miles. At Little Road, turn south and go six miles. Turn east onto River Crossing Boulevard and drive three miles to the park entrance. The drive winds through a residential development until it dead-ends at Wilderness Road. When coming from U.S. 19 in New Port Richey, take State Road 54 east for 2.5 miles to Little Road, then head north to River Crossing Boulevard. Drive three miles east to the park entrance.

Contact: Jay B. Starkey Wilderness Park, 10500 Wilderness Road, New Port Richey, FL 34656, 727/834-3247 or 727/834-3262, fax 727/834-3277; or write to Pasco County Parks and Recreation Department, 7750 North Congress Street, New Port Richey, FL 34653.

❻ ORCHID LAKE TRAVEL PARK

🏊 🎣 🐕 ♿ 🚐

Scenic rating: 3

in New Port Richey

This quiet park is located on Orchid Lake near orange groves, upscale homes, shopping, and many golf courses. Social programs are held in the winter months.

Campsites, facilities: The 55-and-older, retiree-oriented park has 406 RV sites with full hookups, 30-amp and 50-amp electrical service, concrete patios, and telephone and cable TV access. Lots are 30 by 50 feet, accommodating RVs up to 40 feet long and slideouts. None of the sites are drive-through. An Internet connection is available in the clubhouse. Restrooms, showers, a recreation hall, a card room, laundry facilities, a pool, horseshoe pits, and shuffleboard courts are provided. The clubhouse, office, and pool are wheelchair-accessible. Streets are paved. Visiting grandchildren are welcome. Indoor cats are permitted; no dogs are allowed.

Reservations, fees: Reservations are recommended. Sites are $30 per night for two people, plus $2 for each additional person. Credit cards are not accepted. Long-term rates are available.

Directions: From I-75, take the exit to State Route 52 and go west to Little Road and proceed one mile to Arevee Drive. Turn west; the park is near the corner.

Contact: Orchid Lake Travel Park, 8225 Arevee Drive, New Port Richey, FL 34653, 727/847-1925.

◻ HOLIDAY TRAVEL PARK

Scenic rating: 3

in Holiday, north of Tarpon Springs

This is a convenient base for exploring Gulf Coast attractions, such as the sponge docks of Tarpon Springs, four miles south. Rigs up to 40 feet long can be accommodated. At 7,000 square feet, the clubhouse has a seating capacity of 400, a poolroom, a card room, and a library. For those cool winter days, the pool is heated.

Campsites, facilities: The 613-unit park has 60 full-hookup RV sites with 50-amp electrical service (some pull-through). Wheelchair-accessible restrooms, plus showers, laundry facilities, a dump station, a pool, pet areas, and a recreation hall are provided. Rental trailers are available. There is a dial-up Internet connection in the clubhouse. The resort caters to 50-and-older travelers, but all ages are welcome. Leashed pets are permitted.

Reservations, fees: Reservations are not necessary. Sites are $30 per night for two people, plus $2 for each additional person. Credit cards are not accepted. Long-term rates are available.

Directions: From the intersection of U.S. 19 and State Road 54, drive 3.5 miles south on U.S. 19. The park is on the east side of the junction of U.S. 19 and Alternate U.S. 19.

Contact: Holiday Travel Park, 1622 Aires Drive, Holiday, FL 34690, 727/934-6782.

◻ ANCLOTE KEY STATE PRESERVE BOAT-IN SITES

Scenic rating: 10

on Anclote Key, three miles west of Tarpon Springs

BEST (

The deserted white sand beach is an amazing four miles long, and camping here is a real Robinson Crusoe experience. No ferry service is available; you'll have to come in your own boat. Furthermore, there are no docks, so you'll have to anchor offshore and wade in or beach your boat on the sand. The effort is worthwhile, though. On the southern shore is a lighthouse built in 1887 that once guided shipping traffic with its 101-foot-high beacon. The island is a bird-watcher's delight; more than 43 species have been spotted, including the bald eagle. Rangers say the swimming is great, but they advise using caution, because of boat traffic.

Campsites, facilities: Primitive camping is permitted on the north side of the island. A chemical toilet is available, but there are no other facilities. Bring everything you need, including water. There are several picnic shelters on the island for day use. All litter must be carried out. Children are welcome. Pets are forbidden.

Reservations, fees: Reservations are not necessary. Camping is free; you must check in by calling 727/469-5942 and providing your boat registration number, number of campers, arrival and departure dates, and an emergency contact phone number.

Directions: Boaters will need to use nautical chart 11411.

Contact: Anclote Key State Preserve,

c/o Honeymoon Island State Preserve, #1 Causeway Boulevard, Dunedin, FL 34698, 727/469-5942.

9 PALM HARBOR RESORT

Scenic rating: 3

in Palm Harbor

With just a few spots for overnighters, this trailer park and fish camp overlooks the Sutherland Bayou. Most folks here are anglers, and the park fills up fast for the entire winter. About a third of this tiny park is occupied by year-round residents.

Campsites, facilities: There are 22 RV sites available with full hookups, 30/50-amp electrical service, and picnic tables. About half have concrete pads. Restrooms, showers, laundry facilities, and telephone service are available. On the premises are a pool, a boat ramp, a fish-cleaning station, a clubhouse, and a bait and tackle store. Children are welcome. Leashed pets are permitted.

Reservations, fees: Reservations are recommended. Sites are $30 per night for two people. Credit cards are accepted. Long-term rates are available.

Directions: From Palm Harbor, drive north on Alternate 19 North to the Crystal Beach area. Look for the park on the big curve between Tampa Road and Alderman Road.

Contact: Palm Harbor Resort, 2119 Alternate 19 North, Palm Harbor, FL 34683, 727/785-3402.

10 BAY AIRE RV PARK

Scenic rating: 5

in Palm Harbor

Like most Florida RV campgrounds, this park wears two coats: In the wintertime, retirees migrate south to renew old acquaintances and participate in planned activities in the recreation hall. In the off-season, the demographics are more mixed, and the place is less crowded. At either time, the grassy park has a friendly, homey feel, with a blend of Australian pines, palm trees, tropical shrubs, and grass lawns, plus a gate for security. Across the street is the Pinellas Trail, a 42-mile paved biking and walking path converted from an old railway. This park also makes a good stopover for those who want to explore Tarpon Springs and its Greek village. Beach-lovers will appreciate the park's proximity to Caladesi Island State Park and Honeymoon Island State Park. Ferry service is available to Caladesi Island from Honeymoon Island. The ferry leaves from the Honeymoon Island State Park Marina on the hour 10 A.M.–4 P.M. For ferry information, call 727/442-7433 or visit www.dolphin encounter.org.

Campsites, facilities: This park has 167 campsites, all with full hookups, 30-amp and 50-amp electricity, and cable TV. Tents are allowed only May–October; they are placed on the regular RV sites. A limited number of sites are available for 40-foot rigs and slide-out trailers. On the premises are restrooms, showers, a recreation hall, a pool, shuffleboard courts, horseshoe pits, and laundry facilities. The recreation hall and restrooms are wheelchair-accessible. This is primarily an adult park. Children are welcome only in the summer months, up to October 1; after that, they can visit campers. Leashed pets are welcome.

Reservations, fees: Reservations are recommended November–April. Sites are $28–38 per night for two people, plus $1.50 for each additional person over the age of three and $1.50 for 50-amp electrical service. Credit cards are accepted. RVers can stay as long as they like. Long-term rates are available.

Directions: From the intersection of Alternate U.S. 19 and State Road 584/Tampa Road, drive 1.4 miles north on Alternate U.S. 19. The park is on the east side of the road.

Contact: Bay Aire RV Park, 2242 Alternate U.S. 19, Palm Harbor, FL 34683, 727/784-4082, fax 727/784-9698 or 888/241-9090.

11 SHERWOOD FOREST RV RESORT

🏊 🚤 � 🏕 ♿ 🚐 ⛺

Scenic rating: 4

in Palm Harbor

About 70 percent of the sites are occupied by year-round residents. The park was to be sold in May 2007; check to see if it is still open for camping.

Campsites, facilities: As of early 2007, the park had four primitive tent sites and 104 grassy RV sites with full hookups, electricity, concrete patios, and picnic tables. Sites up to 45 feet long and slideouts can be accommodated. One site is drive-through; the rest are back-in. On the premises are restrooms, showers, a clubhouse, a pool, and laundry facilities; all areas are said to be wheelchair-accessible. Streets are paved. An Internet connection is available in the clubhouse. Children are welcome. Cats and dogs under 35 pounds are permitted in a separate section.

Reservations, fees: Reservations are recommended. All sites are $45 per night for two people, plus $2.50 for each additional person. Credit cards are accepted. Long-term stays are OK.

Directions: From the intersection of Alternate U.S. 19 and State Road 586/Curlew Road, drive 0.8 mile north on Alternate U.S. 19 to the park on the west side of the road.

Contact: Sherwood Forest RV Resort, 175 Alternate U.S. 19 North, Palm Harbor, FL 34683, 727/784-4582, www.meetrobinhood.com.

12 CLEARWATER-TARPON SPRINGS KOA

🏊 🏕 � ♿ 🚐 ⛺

Scenic rating: 6

in Palm Harbor

If you like KOA-style convenience and plan on doing a lot of sightseeing, then this vacation-oriented park may be for you. It's on a busy six-lane highway convenient to Tarpon Springs, the beaches at Dunedin, and Central Florida attractions, such as Busch Gardens, Weeki Wachee, St. Petersburg museums and aquariums, and Ybor City. The pool is heated. Only two percent of the sites are occupied by year-round residents.

Campsites, facilities: There are 116 back-in RV sites with full hookups, 30-amp and 50-amp electrical service, wireless Internet access, concrete patios, and picnic tables. RVs up to 42 feet long and slideouts can be accommodated. Sites vary in size. A separate area with water and electricity hookups is for about 24 tents. Restrooms, showers, laundry facilities, a dump station, a pool, and a recreation hall (with planned activities) are on the property. A separate wheelchair-accessible restroom is provided, and all other areas of the park, including the pool area, office, and store, are navigable for wheelchairs. Streets are paved. A camp store sells ice, camping supplies, snacks, and souvenirs. Groceries and restaurants are within one mile. Children are welcome. Leashed pets are permitted.

Reservations, fees: Reservations are recommended. Sites are $33–38 per night for two people, plus $1.50 for extra children under 17 and $5 for each additional adult. Use of air conditioners and electric heaters costs $4 per day. Credit cards are accepted. Long-term stays are OK.

Directions: From U.S. 19 and State Road 584/Tampa Road, drive 2.9 miles north on U.S. 19 to the park on the east side of the road.

Contact: Clearwater–Tarpon Springs KOA, 37061 U.S. 19 North, Palm Harbor, FL

34684, 727/937-8412 or 800/KOA-8743 (800/562-8743), www.koa.com.

13 DUNEDIN RV RESORT

Scenic rating: 7

in Dunedin

Targeted to the "active and adventurous," this immaculate park is near everything civilized, as well as the ocean and beaches. For guests who enjoy biking and walking, the Pinellas Trail passes right by the park, where about 10 percent of the sites are occupied year-round. You're just three miles from the Caladesi Island ferry and Honeymoon Island State Park, the Toronto Blue Jays spring training facilities, Tarpon Springs sponge docks, antiques shops, flea markets, deep-sea fishing, and restaurants. Planned activities are held November 1–May 1. Visitors come from all over the United States, Canada, Germany, and the Netherlands.

Campsites, facilities: This 233-unit park has 81 RV sites available with full hookups, 30-amp and 50-amp electrical service, wireless Internet, concrete patios and picnic tables; 18 are pull-through. Lots vary in size, but some are 30 by 60 feet and can accommodate RVs up to 45 feet long and slideouts. Some 75 sites are available for overnighters. Tenters are welcome April–November only; they are accommodated on the same sites as the RVs. Restrooms, showers, a dump station, a recreation hall with big-screen TV and wireless Internet hookup, a heated pool, a playground, laundry facilities, and a clubhouse are provided. You'll also find shuffleboard courts, table tennis, foosball, volleyball, boccie ball (lawn bowling), and a playground. The mobile homes are separated from the RV area. All sites, one bathhouse, the laundry room, and the recreation room are wheelchair-accessible. Streets are paved. Groceries and restaurants are within 0.5 mile. Children and leashed pets are welcome.

Reservations, fees: Reservations are recommended. Sites are $39–47 per night for two people, plus $4 for each additional person. Credit cards are accepted. Long-term rates are available.

Directions: From the intersection of Alternate U.S. 19 and State Road 586/Curlew Road in Dunedin, drive 0.5 mile north on Alternate U.S. 19 to the park.

Contact: Dunedin RV Resort, 2920 Alternate U.S. 19 North, Dunedin, FL 34698, 727/784-3719 or 800/345-7504, www.dunedinrv.com.

14 CALADESI ISLAND STATE PARK

Scenic rating: 9

On Caladesi Island, west of Dunedin

You can't really camp here in the official sense of the word because you have to sleep on your boat. But since the island is accessible only by boat, we assume you'll love the 650 dry acres and 1,800 acres of mangrove flats and submerged lands—walk the four miles of unspoiled beach in search of the perfect seashell or hike the island's nature trails. The beach is so beautiful that it's been ranked as one of the top 10 in the United States for nearly a decade. A new floating concrete dock that is wheelchair-accessible and a marine pump-out station were built a couple of years ago. In addition, the marina, seawalls, and boardwalk system were overhauled. If you don't have access to a boat, you can make a day trip out of it by boarding the ferry that leaves from the Honeymoon Island State Recreation Area Marina on the hour 10 A.M.–4 P.M. For ferry information, call 727/442-7433 or visit www.dolphinencounter.org.

Campsites, facilities: Boaters are welcome for overnight stays on this barrier island, although camping on the shore is not allowed. There are 100 boat slips at a dock located on the bay side of the island; electricity and water are available. Restrooms, cold-water showers, a picnic area with grills, and a concession stand are on the island. The marina, floating dock, concession stand, restrooms, and boardwalk to the beach are wheelchair-accessible. Children are welcome, as are pets.

Reservations, fees: Reservations are recommended; call ReserveAmerica at 800/326-3521. Major credit cards are accepted. The fee is $9 per night for four people, plus $2 per extra person, $2 for electricity, and $2 for pets with proof of rabies vaccination.

Directions: Boaters should use nautical chart 11411. Day visitors taking the ferry should drive west from U.S. 19 in Dunedin on State Road 586/Curlew Road until it ends at Honeymoon Island State Recreation Area. The ferry leaves from the state park's marina. It costs $4 to enter the park; ferry fees are $7 for adults and $3.50 for children (round-trip).

Contact: Caladesi Island State Park, c/o Gulf Islands GEOPark, 1 Causeway Boulevard, Dunedin, FL 34698, 727/469-5918 or 727/469-5942, www.floridastateparks.org.

15 INDIAN ROCKS TRAVEL PARK

Scenic rating: 2

in Largo

An 18-hole golf course is within walking distance. Best of all, though, this open and sunny park is just 1.5 miles east of the beach. The place is oriented to retirees who spend winter in Florida, so expect organized activities. About 80 percent of the park is occupied year-round.

Campsites, facilities: There are 40 RV sites with full hookups, 30-amp electrical service, and access to cable TV and telephone service in this 175-unit retirement trailer park. Lots are 25 by 50 feet, and rigs up to 40 feet long can be accommodated. On the premises are

restrooms, showers, a dump station, a pool, a recreation room, shuffleboard courts, and laundry facilities. An Internet connection is available in the clubhouse. The office, clubhouse, and pool area are wheelchair-accessible. Streets are paved. Families with small children may stay only for short visits. Pets are prohibited.

Reservations, fees: Reservations are recommended. Sites are $30 per night for two people, plus $3 for each additional person. Credit cards are accepted. Long-term stays are OK.

Directions: From the intersection of U.S. 19 and State Road 688/Ulmerton Road, drive west on State Road 688 for 11 miles. At Vonn Road, turn right and continue 0.3 mile north to the park at right.

Contact: Indian Rocks Travel Park, 12121 Vonn Road, Largo, FL 33774, 727/595-2228.

16 YANKEE TRAVELER RV PARK

Scenic rating: 7

in Largo

A maintenance crew works daily to keep up the park's neat appearance, and the managers live on-site to ensure that older RVers have everything they need for a relaxing vacation. The pool is heated, and social programs are held in winter. Dances, bingo, potluck suppers, day trips, cards, art classes, pancake breakfasts, Bible study, swimming in the pool, and going to the beach are favorite activities. Under family ownership for more than two decades, this park intends to stay in the big leagues of snowbird destinations. About 90 percent of the lots are occupied year-round. As the owners say, "Luxury at your front door—the best of Florida in your backyard." Lake Seminole is three miles away for the anglers in your group.

Campsites, facilities: There are about 30 RV sites with full hookups for overnighters in this 210-unit park. All sites have 30/50-amp electrical service (renovated in 2006), sewer hookups, concrete patios, and picnic tables. Rigs up to 40 feet and slideouts can be accommodated on lots averaging 30 by 60 feet. An Internet connection is available in the clubhouse. On the premises are restrooms, showers, a dump station, a pool, a whirlpool tub, a wheelchair-accessible recreation hall, horseshoe pits, shuffleboard courts, a dog-walk area, and laundry facilities. Streets are paved. Public parks, malls, and restaurants are within 0.1 mile. Campers must be over 55; children may visit them for short periods. Pets under 15 pounds are permitted.

Reservations, fees: Reservations are recommended. Sites are $25–31 per night for two people, plus $2 for each additional person. Credit cards are accepted. Long-term rates are available.

Directions: From I-275 southbound, take Exit 31B on Ulmerton Road west for 6.6 miles. The campground is on the left. Northbound, take Exit 30. Drive 1.5 miles northwest on State Road 686/Roosevelt Boulevard. At State Road 688/Ulmerton Road, turn west and drive 5.1 miles to the park on the south side of the road.

Contact: Yankee Traveler RV Park, 8500 Ulmerton Road, Largo, FL 33771, 727/531-7998, fax 727/373-0084, www.yankeetraveler.net.

17 VACATION VILLAGE/ SUNBURST

Scenic rating: 6

in Largo

Bingo, billiards, card games, and trips to the dog track entertain RVers at this park, part of the Encore chain. Stores, hair salons, an 18-hole golf course, restaurants, and shopping are within 0.5 mile.

Campsites, facilities: There are 288 full-hookup RV sites with cable TV. Rigs up to 45 feet long can be accommodated. Restrooms, showers, a dump station, laundry facilities, and telephone service are available. On the premises are a pool, a recreation hall with planned activities, horseshoe pits, shuffleboard courts, a billiards room, and a golf net. Children are welcome. Leashed pets are permitted.

Reservations, fees: Reservations are recommended. Sites are $20 and up per night. Credit cards are accepted. Long-term rates are available.

Directions: From I-275 southbound, take Exit 31B on Ulmerton Road West. The park is just past Roosevelt Road on the left.

Contact: Vacation Village, 6900 Ulmerton Road, Largo, FL 33771, 727/531-5589 or 877/297-2757, fax 727/531-0160, www.rvonthego.com.

18 BRIARWOOD TRAVEL VILLA

Scenic rating: 5

in Largo

You may forget you're in the city—when I was here, I was stunned to find such a pretty RV spot in an urban setting. Even though there's a bus stop at the front, this peaceful community is heavily wooded with hundreds of tall oak trees and winding paved roads that encircle little Lake Kathleen. "Sometimes I feel like I have my own little cabin out in the woods," says one resident, whose remarks are printed in the park brochure, and I concur. Some lots overlook the one-acre lake, and all sites have shade trees. Golf courses, groceries, a mall, and laundry facilities are nearby; the Pinellas Trail bike path is 0.5 mile away. RV and boat storage is available. About 85 percent of the park is occupied year-round.

Campsites, facilities: This adults-only park has 138 RV sites, most with full hookups and

30/50-amp electrical service. Overnighters are accommodated on a first-come, first-served basis. Twelve grassy sites near the park pavilion are available for tenters; they do not have water or electricity. On the premises are a dump station, a picnic shelter, horseshoe pits, shuffleboard courts, and a restaurant. Campers must be self-contained; there are no showers or restrooms. The nearest grocery store is 0.25 mile away. Children are permitted for short stays only; the park prefers campers who are over 55. Cats are welcome, but dogs are not allowed.

Reservations, fees: Reservations are not taken. Sites are $30 per night. Credit cards are not accepted. Long-term rates are available.

Directions: From the intersection of State Road 688/Ulmerton Road and Alternate U.S. 19/Seminole Boulevard in Largo, drive two blocks north on Seminole Boulevard. The park is on the west side.

Contact: Briarwood Travel Villa, 2098 Seminole Boulevard, Largo, FL 33778, 727/581-6694.

19 BICKLEY PARK

Scenic rating: 3

in Seminole

Concrete-pad sites accommodate rigs up to 35 feet long at this park set beside a busy highway. It's 1.5 miles from the beach and near golf courses, fishing, shopping, and churches. Bay Pines Veterans Hospital is one mile away. But what really keeps the same folks coming back winter after winter are the planned activities, such as potluck dinners, bingo, crafts, and parties. "We're just a friendly mom-and-pop place," says the manager. Most of the park is occupied by year-round residents in park models or other units.

Campsites, facilities: The 186-unit adults-only park has 150 paved RV sites available, with full hookups, 30/50-amp electrical ser-

vice, and concrete patios. Twenty-five sites are generally available for overnighters. Lots are 38 or 40 feet wide by 30 feet long, accommodating RVs up to 35 feet long and slideouts. Restrooms, showers, shuffleboard courts, a clubhouse, and laundry facilities are provided. A wireless Internet connection is available in the clubhouse. Shopping is within 1.2 miles. All areas are wheelchair-accessible. Children are not welcome. Leashed pets under 35 pounds are permitted.

Reservations, fees: Reservations are recommended. Sites are $40 per night for two people, plus $2 per extra person. Credit cards are accepted. Long-term rates are available.

Directions: From I-275, take Exit 28 and drive nine miles west on County Road 694 (Gandy Boulevard/Park Boulevard) to Alternate U.S. 19 (Seminole Boulevard). Turn south and drive 1.5 miles to the park, which is on the west side between 54th and 57th Streets.

Contact: Bickley Park, 5640 Seminole Boulevard, Seminole, FL 33772, 727/392-3807, www.bickleypark.com.

20 ST. PETERSBURG RESORT KOA

Scenic rating: 6

in St. Petersburg

A secluded family resort, this KOA offers large sites in a quiet oak- and palm-shaded setting adjacent to Boca Ciega Bay and two miles from Gulf of Mexico beaches. The bay provides boat access to the gulf waters. Among the activities for kids are video games, bike rentals, and miniature golf. Sites of interest nearby include the Pinellas Trail bike path, Busch Gardens, Sunken Gardens, the municipal pier, John's Pass Boardwalk, the Great Explorations Hands-on Museum, and the Florida Aquarium. Of special note is the Salvador Dalí Museum (727/823-3767), which holds the world's largest collection of

© MARILYN MOORE

A beachgoer parks his bike.

the artist's surrealist works, including several huge "masterwork" canvases.

Campsites, facilities: The park has nine tent-only sites, with no hookups, and 379 RV sites (87 pull-through) with full hookups, 30/50-amp electricity, and picnic tables. "Deluxe water's edge" sites have 50-amp service and overlook a mangrove-fringed bayou. Restrooms, showers, a dump station, a pool, a whirlpool tub, a boat ramp, docks, a playground, a game room, walking trails, horseshoe pits, shuffleboard and volleyball courts, laundry facilities, and a store are on the property. The stores, restrooms, recreation hall, pool, and pier are wheelchair-accessible. Rental cabins are available. Children and leashed pets are welcome.

Reservations, fees: Reservations are recommended. Sites are $36–67 per night for two people, plus $6 for each additional adult and $4 for children ages 4–17. The deluxe sites are $64–80 per night. Credit cards are accepted. RV campers can stay as long as they like. Long-term rates are available.

Directions: From I-275, take Exit 25 and drive 5.5 miles west on 38th Avenue North. Veer right onto Tyrone Boulevard/Bay Pines Boulevard and drive 1.5 miles to 95th Street, then turn north and continue 0.5 mile.

Contact: St. Petersburg Resort KOA, 5400 95th Street North, St. Petersburg, FL 33708, 727/392-2233 or 800/562-7714, fax 727/398-6081, www.koa.com.

21 ROBERT'S MOBILE HOME AND RV RESORT

Scenic rating: 4

in **St. Petersburg**

This 624-unit, neatly manicured mobile-home park draws older campers who appreciate the large RV sites shaded by oaks and pines. Social programs are held in winter; you can also play tennis or relax in the pool's spa. A mall and restaurants are nearby.

Campsites, facilities: There are 427 RV sites with full hookups, 30/50-amp electrical service, cable TV, and available telephone service. On the premises are restrooms, showers, a dump station, a recreation room, a pool, a whirlpool tub, horseshoe pits, shuffleboard, volleyball and tennis courts, and laundry facilities. All areas are wheelchair-accessible, and streets are paved. Older travelers are preferred, but children are allowed to visit for short periods. Pets under 40 pounds are permitted.

Reservations, fees: Reservations are recommended. Sites are $25–30 per night for two people, plus $3 for each additional person. Credit cards are accepted. Long-term rates are available.

Directions: From I-275, take Exit 28 and drive 1.3 miles west on County Road 694 (Gandy Boulevard/Park Boulevard) to the park.

Contact: Robert's Mobile Home and RV Resort, 3390 Gandy Boulevard North, St. Petersburg, FL 33702, 727/577-6820, www.robertsrv.com.

22 FORT DE SOTO PARK CAMPGROUND

Scenic rating: 10

on Pinellas Bayway South in Tampa Bay

BEST (

Not only is this park wooded and shady, but it also has great water views and abundant foliage screening campers from their neighbors. Guests are not allowed to swim in the waters off the campground, but there are two swimming beaches within the park. Like most great parks so close to a city, Fort De Soto draws a crowd on weekends, so consider making a reservation.

Campsites, facilities: This 235-site county campground is divided into two areas: one along a spit of land surrounded by water, the other fronting on the bay. Among them are 149 RV sites and 86 tent sites. Almost all sites are waterfront, and some have good views of St. Petersburg and the Gulf of Mexico. Most areas are wheelchair-accessible. Sites 1–85 are designated for tent, van, and pop-up campers; the good news is that these are beautifully situated on the waterfront. The RV sites (86–233) are excellent, too. Water, 30-amp electricity, picnic tables, grills, restrooms, showers, a dump station, laundry facilities, a store, and two play areas are provided. A boat ramp is in the park. Alcoholic beverages are prohibited. Children are welcome. Previously prohibited, pets are now allowed on a trial basis in certain campsites only.

Reservations, fees: Reservations are recommended, though a number of sites are set aside for first-come, first-served campers. You can make reservations at the campground, by telephone, or online. Sites are $28 per night for six people. Credit cards are not accepted. The maximum stay is 14 days during any 30-day period January–April; the rest of the year, you may extend your visit by 14 days depending on availability of campsites.

Directions: From I-275, take Exit 17 and drive two miles west on State Road 682, also known as U.S. 19 North/54th Avenue South/Pinellas Bayway. At Pinellas Bayway South, turn south and continue about three miles to the park.

Contact: Fort De Soto Park Campground, 3500 Pinellas Bayway South, Tierra Verde, FL 33715, 727/582-2267, www.pinellascounty.org/park/05_ft_desoto.htm.

SARASOTA AND BRADENTON

© MARILYN MOORE

BEST CAMPGROUNDS

❰ **Beachfront Campgrounds**
Gulf Beach Campground, **page 433**

❰ **Best for Families**
Arcadia's Peace River Campground, **page 429**

On the western fringes of this famous tourist

hot spot are two of the best canoeing rivers in Florida: The Myakka River and the Peace River. Car campers can use several developed parks as a base camp for day trips on the rivers; the more hardy will find remote riverside primitive sites to break up longer paddle trips.

The Myakka, one of only two designated Wild and Scenic rivers in the state, runs through one of Florida's largest state parks. Myakka River State Park is 28,875 acres and noted for its wide variety and number of birds, especially turkeys and hawks, as well as wildlife. Tours are offered by tram and boat; guests may see alligators, deer, bobcats, and cottontail rabbits.

The Peace River Canoe Trail runs 67 miles with swift-flowing narrows and occasional rapids (when water levels are high). Along its banks are dense forests teeming with wild hogs, armadillos, egrets, and the like.

West of the wilderness areas lie the cities of Bradenton and historic Sarasota, the state's cultural center. Its downtown contains an opera house, theaters, and art galleries.

Traveling southward to Punta Gorda, campers will find tranquil beachside destinations along the Gulf of Mexico, such as Anna Maria Island and Longboat Key. The much lauded beaches are renowned for their white, powdery sand. Vacationers can watch pelicans skim above the water's surface, or head down to the beach to tan, build sand castles, or play in the surf. The mostly gentle waves are perfect for kids.

History buffs should note that in 1539, Spanish explorer Hernando de Soto landed with 600 soldiers near what is now Bradenton, with a mandate to colonize Florida for Spain. The effort was the first large-scale European mission into North America, and the National Park Service commemorates this spot at the De Soto National Memorial in Bradenton. Visitors should include a trip to the Gamble Plantation State Historic Site, the last surviving antebellum mansion in the southern half of the state.

Nearly every visitor to the area will get a thrill out of crossing the Sunshine Skyway Bridge (I-275), a spectacular, almost dizzying drive that takes motorists 150 feet above the waters of Tampa Bay.

Aside from nature destinations, most of the parks in this region are RV-oriented campgrounds that cater to family beachgoers or older visitors who come every year to get out of the cold.

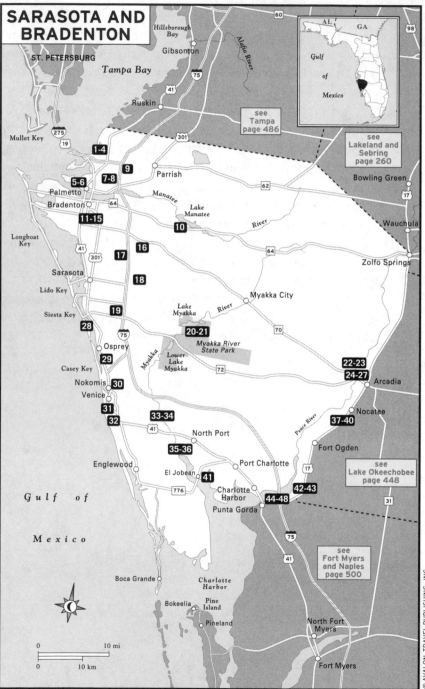

SARASOTA AND BRADENTON

1 FROG CREEK CAMPGROUND AND RV PARK

🏊 🐕 ♿ 🚐

Scenic rating: 6

in Palmetto

Improvements made to this all-ages park since 2000 include a heated pool and a 100- by 100-foot fenced dog-play area. A fishing stream runs through the park, which is a short drive from the beaches, deep-sea fishing, museums, and other attractions. The managers maintain a blog, so visitors can keep in touch with the latest news. Tents are prohibited. About a third of the sites are occupied year-round. The location is near the Sunshine Skyway Bridge (I-275).

Campsites, facilities: RVers can choose from 173 grassy or gravel lots with 30/50-amp electrical service, concrete pads, and picnic tables. A wireless Internet network is available in the clubhouse and at most of the campsites. RVs up to 45 feet long and slideouts can be accommodated. Sixteen sites are pull-through. On the premises are restrooms, showers, laundry facilities, a dump station, shuffleboard courts, horseshoe pits, a dog field, and a recreation hall. All areas are wheelchair-accessible. Groceries, restaurants, and malls are within five miles. A boat ramp is within one mile. Children under 16 are welcome, but they must be supervised by an adult in public areas. Leashed pets are permitted.

Reservations, fees: Reservations are recommended. Sites are $32 per night for two people, plus $5 for each additional person, $3 for electricity, and $1 for pets. Credit cards are accepted. Long-term stays are OK.

Directions: From I-75, take Exit 228 and drive one mile west on I-275. Exit northbound on U.S. 41 and continue 0.5 mile to Bayshore Road. Turn west and drive 0.6 mile.

Contact: Frog Creek Campground and RV Park, 8515 Bayshore Road, Palmetto, FL 34221, 941/722-6154 or 800/771-3764, www.frogcreekrv.com.

2 FIESTA GROVE RV RESORT

🏊 🐕 ♿ 🚐

Scenic rating: 6

in Palmetto

This park, once a citrus grove, is dotted with orange trees, and guests are welcome to pick and eat the fruit. Activities in the recreation hall include aerobics, line dancing, card games, bingo, ice-cream socials, bowling, bicycle rides, bus trips, and coffees.

Campsites, facilities: Most of the 220 lots are taken by park models, but about one-third are RV sites. The RVers have full hookups and cable TV, except in 15 sites that have water and electricity only. Restrooms, showers, laundry facilities, a heated pool, shuffleboard, boccie ball (lawn bowling), a wheelchair-accessible recreation hall, and a dump station are available. Children under 17 must be supervised in public areas. Pets are permitted.

Reservations, fees: Reservations are recommended. Sites are $24 per night for two people, plus $1.50 for each additional person and $1 for cable TV. Credit cards are not accepted. Long-term stays are OK.

Directions: From I-75, take Exit 228 and drive one mile west on I-275. Exit northbound on U.S. 41 and continue 0.5 mile to Bayshore Road. Turn west and drive 0.5 mile.

Contact: Fiesta Grove RV Resort, 8615 Bayshore Road, Palmetto, FL 34221, 941/722-7661.

3 TERRA CEIA VILLAGE RV RESORT

🏊 🎣 🐕 ♿ 🚐

Scenic rating: 4

in Palmetto

Oak trees enhance the park grounds, which also contain a stocked pond for fishing. This adult-oriented, 15-acre resort is 12 miles from the beach and close to golf courses,

Indian Mound Park, and the Sunshine Skyway Bridge. Planned activities are held November–mid-April. About two-thirds of the sites are occupied year-round.

Campsites, facilities: Sixty of the 203 RV lots are available to travelers and offer full hookups, including 30/50-amp electrical service, cable TV, and telephone access. Six sites are pull-through. RVs up to 45 feet long and slide-outs can be accommodated. On the premises are restrooms, showers, laundry facilities, a dump station, a heated pool, a stocked pond, horseshoes, shuffleboard, boccie ball (lawn bowling), wireless Internet network, and a clubhouse. The bathhouse, clubhouse, and pool area are wheelchair-accessible. Streets are paved. A convenience store is at the corner. The nearest restaurant is about two miles away; a supermarket is about five miles away. Children are welcome for short-term visits. Leashed pets are permitted.

Reservations, fees: Reservations are required. Sites are $32 per night for two people, plus $5 for each additional person. Credit cards are accepted. Year-round stays are OK.

Directions: From I-75, take Exit 228 and go west to U.S. 41 (Exit 1). Go north on U.S. 41 for 0.75 mile to the park on the left.

Contact: Terra Ceia Village RV Resort, 9303 Bayshore Road, Palmetto, FL 34221, 941/729-4422, www.rvonthego.com.

4 WINTERSET PARK

Scenic rating: 4

in Palmetto

Frog Creek, a fishing stream, borders the property. Several golf courses and driving ranges are within a few minutes' drive of this over-age-55 manufactured-home and RV community, where park models are for sale. About 15 percent of the sites are occupied year-round. Most visitors come from Canada, Ohio, Michigan, Iowa, Maine, Massachusetts, Kentucky,

Tennessee, and New York. Planned activities during the winter season include bingo, potluck dinners, crafts, wood carving, golf, day trips, cards, Bible study, church services, and games. **Campsites, facilities:** Out of a total of 221 sites, 60 are available for overnighters. They overlook the tennis courts and horseshoes area. Campsites have full hookups, concrete patios, and picnic tables. The lot size is 30 by 40 feet, and RVs up to 40 feet long and slideouts can be accommodated. Facilities include restrooms, showers, laundry facilities, shuffleboard courts, two pools, a wheelchair-accessible recreation room, tennis courts, and a dog-walk area. A wireless Internet connection is available in the clubhouse and a few other places in the park. All areas are wheelchair-accessible. Grocery stores and restaurants are within five miles. This is an adults-only park. Pets under 25 pounds are allowed.

Reservations, fees: Reservations are recommended. Sites are $28 per night for two people, plus $1.50 per additional person. Credit cards are not accepted. Long-term rates are available.

Directions: From I-75, take Exit 228 and drive one mile west on I-275. Exit northbound on U.S. 41 and continue 0.5 mile to the park.

Contact: Winterset Park, 8515 U.S. 41 North, Palmetto, FL 34221, 941/722-4884, fax 941/722-5820, www.wintersetrvresort.com.

5 FISHERMAN'S COVE RESORT

Scenic rating: 4

near Palmetto

Don't forget to pack your racquet, because this is one of the few RV parks in Florida with tennis courts right on the property. If tennis isn't your game, try launching your boat from the campground boat ramp, and you'll be right on Terra Ceia Bay, which has access to Tampa Bay and the Gulf of Mexico.

St. Petersburg is a quick ride away over the spectacular Sunshine Skyway Bridge, which soars 150 feet above the water. Golf courses are within easy driving distance, and groceries and restaurants are within two miles. Social programs are held in the recreation hall year-round. Campsites are grassy, with concrete pads, and are large enough to accommodate even bigger rigs; however, there are no pull-through sites. About two-thirds of the park are occupied by year-round residents. Most visitors come from New England, Michigan, and Florida.

Campsites, facilities: All 78 RV lots have full hookups with 30/50-amp electrical service, cable TV, and telephone access. RVs up to 38 feet long and slideouts can be accommodated. An Internet connection is available in the clubhouse. On the premises are restrooms, showers, a dump station, laundry facilities, a heated pool with a whirlpool tub, a boat ramp, tennis courts, a clubhouse, exercise and game rooms, and a tiki hut for camp gatherings. A full social calendar in the winter season includes arts and crafts and other activities; in the summertime, organized events are more limited. All areas are wheelchair-accessible. Streets are paved. Children may visit for short periods. Pets are permitted.

Reservations, fees: Reservations are recommended. Sites are $50 per night for two people, plus $2 for each additional person. Credit cards are accepted. Long-term rates are available.

Directions: Traveling southbound on the Sunshine Skyway Bridge (I-275/U.S. 19), continue two miles south from the toll plaza to the park, set on the east side of U.S. 19 after you cross Terra Ceia Bay. Traveling northbound on I-275, turn south at U.S. 41 and drive 2.3 miles. At U.S. 19, drive north one mile. The park is just before the Sunshine Skyway Bridge toll plaza.

Contact: Fisherman's Cove Resort, 100 Palmview Road, Palmetto, FL 34221, 941/729-3685, fax 941/721-0614, www .myfishermanscove.com.

6 TROPIC ISLES MOBILE HOME PARK

Scenic rating: 4

in Palmetto

As a visitor at Tropic Isles Mobile Home Park, you automatically earn the privilege of using the permanent boating facilities and marina, just as long-term residents do. Boaters will appreciate the location: Access to the Gulf of Mexico and its fishing grounds is first-rate. The open, sunny park overlooks Terra Ceia Bay, and many sites are waterfront. During the winter, the clubhouse buzzes with activity, with weekly social hours (coffee and doughnuts are served), potluck suppers, game nights, bingo, and card parties. There's even an auditorium with a stage for large functions. The park has a bus that takes residents out for weekly shopping trips; group outings to local attractions are also available. Note that bicycles have the right-of-way on the park's paved roads. About 30 percent of the park is occupied year-round. Most visitors hail from Ohio, Michigan, Wisconsin, and Canada. Lots and mobile homes are for sale; many permanent residents run their own businesses from their homes.

Campsites, facilities: All lots in this adults-only, 362-unit mobile-home park have full hookups and concrete patios. Twenty-four sites are for RVs up to 40 feet long and slideouts; seven are drive-through. RVs must be self-contained; there are no showers or restrooms. On the premises are a heated pool, 12 championship shuffleboard courts, horseshoe pits, a clubhouse, a wheelchair-accessible auditorium and yacht club, a boat ramp, docks, a marina, a grocery store, laundry facilities, and a beauty parlor. For cable TV and telephone service, you must call the proper utility. Only adults age 55 and older are welcome as campers, but children may visit for short periods. Small, leashed pets are permitted but must not be tied outside units.

Reservations, fees: Reservations are recommended. Sites are $40 per night for two people, plus $5 per extra person. Credit cards are not accepted. Stays up to six months are allowed.

Directions: From I-75, take Exit 224 westbound on U.S. 301 and drive 10.5 miles to the park on the right.

Contact: Tropic Isles Mobile Home Park, 3100 10th Street West, Palmetto, FL 34221, 941/721-8888, fax 941/729-0687, www.tropic isles.org.

◻7 ELLENTON GARDENS TRAVEL RESORT

Scenic rating: 3

in Ellenton

For people who like to shop, this 16-acre park is a find. Factory outlets, malls, and all manner of other stores are nearby; and doctors' offices, a hospital, and a library are within one mile. A small fishing lake lies at the center of the park, which is home to many semi-permanent trailers and manufactured homes. Activities held in the recreation hall include exercise and arts-and-crafts classes, line dancing, and bingo. Campsites have concrete pads fronting paved roads.

Campsites, facilities: All 196 sites have full hookups with 30-amp electrical service, optional telephone service, and cable TV. About 76 sites are available for overnight or short visits. RVs must be self-contained. Restrooms, showers, laundry facilities, a heated pool, shuffleboard courts, a lake, a dump station, and a recreation hall are on-site. Grocery stores are within 0.75 mile. All areas are wheelchair-accessible. Children are welcome for short-term visits only. Small dogs and cats are permitted.

Reservations, fees: Reservations are recommended. Sites are $35 per night for two people, plus $2 for each additional person. Credit cards are not accepted. Long-term rates are available.

Directions: From I-75, take Exit 224 and head northeast on U.S. 301 for 1.4 miles to the park entrance on the left side of the road.

Contact: Ellenton Gardens Travel Resort, 7310 U.S. 301 North, Ellenton, FL 34222, 941/722-0341, fax 941/723-6121.

◻8 PALM BAY RV PARK

Scenic rating: 3

north of Bradenton

A private walk provides pedestrian access from this adult-oriented park to a large shopping center. Churches and the Manatee Memorial Hospital are within one mile. This park is geared toward senior citizens staying three–four months at a time.

Campsites, facilities: These 78 full-hookup RV spots are set inside a 164-unit, adult-oriented mobile-home park. Sites have 30-amp electrical service and vary in size. Some lots can accommodate RVs up to 40 feet long. Facilities include restrooms, showers, a laundry room, a pool, a billiard and card room, shuffleboard courts, and a clubhouse. Children may stay a maximum of two weeks. Pets aren't allowed—not even with visitors.

Reservations, fees: Reservations are recommended. Sites are $25 per night for two people, plus $2 for each additional person. Credit cards are not accepted. Long-term stays are OK.

Directions: From I-75, take Exit 224 and drive west on U.S. 301 for 3.1 miles. The park is 0.25 mile west of U.S. 41.

Contact: Palm Bay RV Park, 751 10th Street East, Palmetto, FL 34221, 941/722-7048.

🖸 WINTER QUARTERS MANATEE RV RESORT

🏊 🛶 🚣 🐕 ♿ 🚐 ⛺

Scenic rating: 9

near Bradenton

Spotless sites with concrete pads and patios are arranged in a circle around 17-acre Lake Mohoina, which is stocked with fish. Four spots are pull-through, and unlike many private RV parks in Florida, this 70-acre resort has picnic tables at each site. An activities director keeps campers busy during the winter with games and other recreation in the two-story clubhouse. Stained-glass classes are among the more unusual planned activities. A small boat ramp puts you on the Manatee River, which accesses the Gulf of Mexico. Restaurants, shops, and a golf course are within a couple of miles. Most visitors come from Canada, Michigan, Ohio, New York, Indiana, and West Virginia.

Campsites, facilities: All 200 RV sites have picnic tables and full hookups, with 50-amp electrical service, cable TV, and telephone availability. Another 215 sites are semi-permanent. RVs up to 45 feet long can be accommodated, as well as slideouts. Some sites are waterfront. Lot size averages 25 by 60 feet. Tents are allowed, but they are placed on the same sites as the RVs. A wireless Internet connection is available in the clubhouse and in parts of the park. On the premises are two heated pools, a spa, a clubhouse, picnic area, restrooms, showers, a small boat ramp, an exercise and game room, horseshoes, billiards, limited supplies, a lake, a dump station, and golf nets. All areas are wheelchair-accessible. Children are permitted. Leashed pets are permitted.

Reservations, fees: Reservations are recommended. Sites are $26–60 per night. Credit cards are accepted. Long-term rates are available.

Directions: From I-75, take Exit 220 westbound 0.5 mile on State Road 64 to Kay Road.

Turn northeast and drive 0.9 mile to the park entrance on the left.

Contact: Winter Quarters Manatee RV Resort, 800 Kay Road Northeast, Bradenton, FL 34212, 239/745-2600 or 800/678-2131, fax 239/748-8964, www.rvonthego.com.

🔟 LAKE MANATEE STATE PARK

🥾 🚲 🏊 🛶 🚣 🐕 🧗 ♿ 🚐 ⛺

Scenic rating: 10

on the south shore of Lake Manatee

The thickly landscaped camping area is within walking distance of Lake Manatee's swimming area and a playground. Although the shrubs are not tall enough to provide shade, they form a dense screen between each site, so you'll feel secluded from your neighbors. There are 30 sites on each of two campground loops, further promoting a sense of privacy. Groceries and laundry facilities are nine miles away. The 2,400-acre lake, part of the reservoir that supplies drinking water to Manatee and Sarasota Counties, is ideal for canoeing and fishing. Note that boat motors are limited to 20 horsepower. A grassy beach slopes gently down to the water in the swimming area. Watch out for alligators, the park rangers warn. The gators are monitored, but not fenced—if you see one near the beach, report it to the office and, of course, don't harass it. A one-mile-long nature trail offers a chance to learn more about the park's biological communities: flat woods and sand-pine scrub. Animals regularly seen in the park include cottontail and marsh rabbits, cotton rats, and gray squirrels. Occasionally, you may see bobcats, gray foxes, and deer.

Campsites, facilities: There are 60 sites with water and 30-amp electricity for tents and camping vehicles. RVs up to 40 feet long and slideouts can be accommodated. Restrooms, showers, picnic tables, fire rings, grills, a playground, a boat ramp, a dock, a nature trail, and a dump station are provided. Boats are available for rent. One campsite, the bathhouse, docks, and office are wheelchair-accessible. Groceries and restaurants are five miles away. Children are welcome. Pets are permitted with proof of vaccination.

Reservations, fees: Reservations are recommended; contact ReserveAmerica at 800/336-3521 or reserveamerica.com. Sites are $18 per night for four people. Credit cards are accepted. Stays are limited to two weeks.

Directions: From I-75, take Exit 220 eastbound nine miles on State Road 64 to the park on the left.

Contact: Lake Manatee State Park, 20007 State Road 64, Bradenton, FL 34212, 941/741-3028 (3–5 P.M.), fax 941/741-3486, www .floridastateparks.org.

11 SARASOTA BAY TRAVEL TRAILER PARK

Scenic rating: 4

in Bradenton

This park's Friendship Hall offers pool tables, table tennis, and a full schedule of social activities, including a computer club with classes for new users. Campers can build things in the woodworking shop, tinker with their boats, or work out in the exercise room, which is stocked with Nautilus equipment. A public beach is one mile away, and managers are considering plans to build a pool in the coming years. The park overlooks Sarasota Bay, where pelicans and seagulls wheel and turn in the breeze. Follow the bay by boat, and it leads to the ocean. Most guests leave their rigs here year-round, and many have added carports, porches, and screened rooms to their trailers. Located in a suburban neighborhood on a main road leading to the beach, the neatly kept park is near shops and restaurants. Its roads are paved, and Norfolk pines and queen palms provide a little greenery. If you hail from Michigan or Canada and come to escape the frigid winters, you'll find plenty of fellow campers from your neck of the woods. This park is part of a mobile-home community called Paradise Bay.

Campsites, facilities: There are 241 spots, with about eight full hookup sites available for overnighters and 50 for seasonal visitors. Most folks stay for the winter and leave their rigs on-site during the summer; around 25 people live in the park year-round. All sites have 50-amp electrical service. RVs up to 45 feet long and slideouts can be accommodated. An Internet connection is available in the clubhouse. Restrooms, showers, laundry facilities, a recreation hall, shuffleboard courts, horseshoe pits, boat ramps, a boat repair area, docks, an exercise room, and a woodworking shop are available. The bathhouse, clubhouse, and office are wheelchair-accessible. Streets are paved. Restaurants and groceries are within two miles. Children may visit for up to two weeks for $2 per person per night. Pets are prohibited.

Reservations, fees: Reservations are recommended. Sites are $40 per night for two people, plus $2 for each additional person. Credit cards are not accepted. Long-term rates are available. The maximum length of stay is six months.

Directions: From I-75, take Exit 217 and drive west on State Road 70 for about 11 miles to State Road 684/Cortez Road. Turn left. Drive two miles west to the park entrance, at left.

Contact: Sarasota Bay Travel Trailer Park, 10777 Cortez Road West, Bradenton, FL 34210, 941/794-1200 or 800/247-8361, fax 941/761-0629, www.paradisebay-sarasota bayrvpark.com.

12 HOLIDAY COVE RV RESORT

Scenic rating: 5

in Cortez

Set in a stand of Australian pines and palm trees, this resort has water access to Sarasota

Bay and the Intracoastal Waterway. Boat slips are available, and you can fish from the docks in the park. The long white-sand beaches of Anna Maria Island and Longboat Key are nearby, and you can walk to restaurants, shops, and the beachfront, less than a mile away. Many visitors come for the season and park models are available for rent, but this park is decidedly RV-oriented, with only 1 percent of its sites occupied by year-round residents. Visitors arrive from all over the nation, as well as the United Kingdom, Germany, and the Netherlands.

Campsites, facilities: All 112 sites have full hookups with electricity and cable TV. Lots vary in size, but rigs up to 42 feet and slideouts can be accommodated. There's a wireless Internet connection in the clubhouse and at the sites. Restrooms, showers, picnic tables, a heated pool, shuffleboard courts, horseshoe pits, laundry facilities, a recreation hall, and a boat ramp are provided. A small camp store sells ice, camping supplies, and souvenirs. All areas are wheelchair-accessible. Groceries and a restaurant are across the street. Children are welcome. Pets are permitted.

Reservations, fees: Reservations are recommended. Sites are $36–69 per night for two people, plus $5 for each additional person. Credit cards are accepted. Long-term rates are available. The maximum length of stay is six months.

Directions: From I-75, take Exit 217 and drive west on State Road 70 for 13 miles to Cortez Road. Turn left and drive five miles. The park entrance is on the north side.

Contact: Holiday Cove RV Resort, 11900 Cortez Road West/P.O. Box 713, Cortez, FL 34215, 941/792-1111 or 800/346-9224, fax 941/761-4662, www.holidaycoverv.com.

13 PLEASANT LAKE RV RESORT

Scenic rating: 4

in Bradenton

In the center of this sunny, manicured park is a rectangular manmade lake stocked for bass fishing, with grassy slopes where campers pull their johnboats ashore. You'll have to confine your swimming to the pool, however—like most bodies of freshwater in Florida, there's always a possibility that an alligator may be lurking nearby. Suitable for big RVs, the park has large sites with concrete pads and few trees to get in the way. A guardhouse and golf-cart patrol provide a feeling of security. Park models are for sale, and about 20 percent of the park is occupied year-round. Visitors hail from New York, Ohio, Michigan, New Hampshire, and Maine. Down the street is a large shopping plaza with a grocery store, restaurants, banks, and a gas station. Area tourist attractions include gulf beaches, the Ringling Museum of Art, the Gamble Plantation Historic Site, the Lionel Train Museum, Jungle Gardens, a dog-racing track, Sunken Gardens, and Busch Gardens.

Campsites, facilities: All 120 sites have full hookups with 30/50-amp electrical outlets. Telephone and cable TV service are available. A wireless Internet connection is available in the clubhouse. Lots are 40 by 50 feet, accommodating RVs up to 42 feet long and slideouts. On the premises are restrooms, showers, laundry facilities, a pool, shuffleboard courts, horseshoe pits, boccie ball (lawn bowling) courts, a fishing lake, and a recreation room. The restrooms, laundry, and recreation room are wheelchair-accessible. This is an over-age-55 park, but families with children may stay for up to two weeks. Leashed pets are permitted.

Reservations, fees: Reservations are recommended. Sites are $45 per night for two people, plus $2 for each additional person.

Credit cards are accepted. Long-term rates are available.

Directions: From I-75, take Exit 217 and drive west on State Road 70 for 0.3 mile to the park, on the north side of the road.

Contact: Pleasant Lake RV Resort, 6633 State Road 70 East, Bradenton, FL 34203, 941/756-5076 or 800/283-5076, www.pleasantlakerv.com.

14 TROPICAL GARDENS RV PARK

Scenic rating: 2

in Bradenton

Although many of the units in this suburban park are permanent, 48 spaces are available for overnighters. Sites are small, with concrete pads. During the winter, planned social activities in the clubhouse keep residents entertained, and church services are held on Sundays. The security gate is locked at night. About 60 percent of the park is occupied year-round. The location is convenient for exploring nearby tourist attractions, such as the Gamble Plantation Historic Site. Sea World, Disney World, and Silver Springs are within two hours' drive.

Campsites, facilities: This park's 136 grassy, sunny, full-hookup sites have 30/50-amp electrical service and concrete patios. Telephone and cable TV access are available by arrangement with the local utilities. Lot sizes vary, but RVs up to 40 feet long and slideouts can be accommodated. Twenty-five sites are drive-through. On the premises are restrooms, showers, a screened pool, shuffleboard, a dump station, laundry facilities, and a recreation hall. All areas are wheelchair-accessible. Within two blocks are a supermarket, a drugstore, a medical center, and a restaurant. Adults are preferred, but children are allowed to visit. Leashed pets under 20 pounds are permitted.

Reservations, fees: Reservations are recommended. Sites are $30 per night for two people, plus $3 for each additional person. Credit cards are not accepted. Long-term rates are available.

Directions: From I-75, take Exit 217 (traveling southbound) or 217B (traveling northbound) and drive west on State Road 70 for about six miles to the park on the south side of the road, just past 15th Street East/Old 301 Boulevard.

Contact: Tropical Gardens RV Park, 1120 53rd Avenue East, Bradenton, FL 34203, 941/756-1135, www.tropicalgardensrv.com.

15 HORSESHOE COVE RESORT

Scenic rating: 7

in Bradenton

At the heart of this all-ages park is a lovely 12-acre island with a nature trail, picnic areas with barbecue grills, lighted fishing docks, boating facilities, and a gazebo. During the winter, there's plenty to do in the 2,000-square-foot recreation hall, including a music program, square dancing, quilting, wood carving, billiards, bingo, and social activities. In summer, kids can catch fish off the docks, swim in the pool, or ride bikes on the paved road. Some sites overlook the Braden River. Unlike many parks with security gates, this park's gate is secured 24 hours a day, not just at night. About 75 percent of the park is occupied by year-round residents.

Campsites, facilities: The park has 476 full-hookup sites, with 150 or so available for overnighters (no tents permitted). Each site has 50-amp electrical service, a concrete patio, and a picnic table. A wireless Internet connection is available in the clubhouse and other parts of the park. For cable TV and telephone service, call the appropriate utility company. RVs up to 40 feet long and slideouts can be accommodated. Restrooms, showers, laundry facilities, a recreation hall, a game room, a pool, a spa, shuffleboard, horseshoes, two fishing docks, boat docks, a picnic shelter and separate picnic area, and a nature trail are on the property. The bathhouse, clubhouse, office, pool area, and docks are wheelchair-accessible. Streets are paved. Groceries are within two miles. Children are welcome for up to 30 days per year. Leashed pets are allowed if you get an RV spot in the pet section.

Reservations, fees: Reservations are recommended in winter. Sites are $30–45 per night for two people, plus $3 for each additional person. Credit cards are accepted. Long-term rates are available.

Directions: From I-75, take Exit 217 westbound on State Road 70 for 1.1 miles to the first traffic light at Caruso Road/60th Street East. Turn north and proceed to the park on the west side of the road.

Contact: Horseshoe Cove Resort, 5100 60th Street East, Bradenton, FL 34203, 941/758-5335 or 800/291-3446, www.horseshoecove.net.

16 LINGER LODGE RV RESORT

Scenic rating: 7

near Bradenton

Linger Lodge borders the Braden River, a peaceful stream where you'll see blue herons wading on the banks and other birds roosting in low overhanging branches. Anglers regularly hook bass, bluegill, crappie, and catfish. A few campsites are near the river, but travelers passing through tend to sleep at upland sites with standard views of other trailers and park models. About 75 percent of the park is occupied year-round. Fried "local farm-raised" alligator is the big seller at the lodge's unusual restaurant, which was named by a national TV personality as "one of the top five weirdest restaurants in the country." The rustic decor features stuffed wildlife, such as an alligator with a mannequin's leg in its mouth. It's a popular place, offering seafood and sandwiches at indoor and screened outdoor seating overlooking the river. It draws crowds on weekends, and you'll hear cars coming and going from 11 A.M. until closing time at 9 P.M. (8 P.M. on Sundays; the restaurant is closed on Mondays). The 10-acre park also contains a small aviary, home to peacocks and other exotic birds. The showers, restrooms, and laundry facilities are toward the back of the building that houses the restaurant. Also on display is a stuffed "short-horned deer," which has a story behind it: In 1992, a hurricane picked up a Florida deer and swept it off to Texas, where it bred with a long-horned steer. A Texas tornado then allegedly blew the rare offspring back to Linger Lodge.

Campsites, facilities: Of the 104 sites, five are available for overnighters. All have full hookups with 30-amp electrical service, concrete pads, and picnic tables. Five sites have 50-amp electricity. Rigs up to 40 feet can be accommodated. Restrooms, showers, laundry facilities, a dump station, a boat ramp, boat docks, a restaurant, and a store that sells ice, propane, and souvenirs are on the premises. The bathhouse and docks are wheelchair-accessible. Groceries are within two miles. This is an adults-only park, but children are allowed to stay 15 days up to twice per year. Small, leashed pets are permitted in one section.

Reservations, fees: Reservations are recommended. Sites are $26 per night for two people, plus $13 for each extra person. Credit cards are accepted. Long-term rates are available.

Directions: From I-75, take Exit 217 and drive west on State Road 70 for 0.2 mile to Tara Boulevard. Turn south and drive four miles. Note that the road name changes to Linger Lodge Road, then turns sharply east and crosses I-75. At the stop sign at Oak Hammock Road, turn south and drive 0.3 mile into the park.

Contact: Linger Lodge RV Resort, 7205 Linger Lodge Road, Bradenton, FL 34202, 941/755-2757, fax 941/758-0718, www.lingerlodgeresort.com.

17 ARBOR TERRACE RV RESORT

🏊 🐾 🚐 ⛺

Scenic rating: 4

in Bradenton

Located between Bradenton and Sarasota, this park offers easy access to local attractions. Groceries and restaurants are within 0.5 mile. Road warriors can relax: Lots of spaces are pull-through. You'll also find some well-shaded spots. Mobile homes and park models are for sale.

Campsites, facilities: Set on 40 acres, the 402-unit resort has 189 available RV sites with full hookups; telephone service is available at most spots. On the premises are restrooms, showers, a dump station, horseshoe pits, shuffleboard courts, a pool, two recreation rooms, and laundry facilities. Campers of all ages are welcome. Pets are accepted.

Reservations, fees: Reservations are recommended. The fee for two people is $39 per night. Add $4 for each additional person. Credit cards are accepted. Long-term rates are available.

Directions: From I-75, take Exit 217 and drive west on State Road 70 for 10 miles. Turn south on U.S. 41 and continue one mile. At 57th Avenue West, turn left by the Red Lobster and drive east for about 0.25 mile.

Contact: Arbor Terrace RV Resort, 405 57th Avenue West, Bradenton, FL 34207, 941/755-6494 or 800/828-6992, fax 941/755-8177, www.suncommunities.com.

18 SUN-N-FUN RV RESORT

🏊 🚤 🐾 🚐

Scenic rating: 7

in Sarasota

As the name implies, the emphasis here is on fun. A full-time activities director coordinates dozens of programs each day for guests, most of whom are snowbirds and retirees from all over the United States, Canada, and England. They have plenty to choose from, including swimming in a heated Olympic-sized pool with two whirlpool tubs, exercising in the fitness center, fishing in the private lake, playing the nine-hole miniature golf course, or lobbing tennis balls on three lighted courts. Also offered are crafts classes, theme parties and dances, variety shows, and boccie (lawn bowling). The park has a total of 1,600 sites, many of them shaded by oaks, and is close to some RV service centers. Beaches are eight miles to the west, and shopping and outlet malls are within a 15-minute drive.

Campsites, facilities: This 1,600-unit resort park with park models and rental units has about 600 RV sites with full hookups, concrete patios, and picnic tables. A wireless Internet network is available throughout the park. Restrooms, showers, laundry facilities, a dump station, several recreation rooms, rental units, a lake, two whirlpool tubs, a pool, an exercise room, horseshoe pits, rental trailers, The Sandbar Grill restaurant (open during the season), and courts for shuffleboard, volleyball, boccie ball (lawn bowling), and tennis, are on-site. Snacks, souvenirs, and propane are for sale. The clubhouse, office, and pool area are wheelchair-accessible. Streets are paved. Groceries and restaurants are within two miles. All ages are welcome. Pets are allowed.

Reservations, fees: Reservations are recommended. Sites are $29–69 per night. Credit cards are accepted. The maximum stay is nine months. Long-term rates are available.

Directions: From I-75, take Exit 210 eastbound on Fruitville Road and drive one mile. The park is on the north side.

Contact: Sun-n-Fun RV Resort, 7125 Fruitville Road, Sarasota, FL 34240, 941/377-8250 or 800/843-2421, fax 941/378-4810, www.sunnfunfl.com.

19 WINDWARD ISLE RV PARK

Scenic rating: 2

in Sarasota

This open, sunny park is convenient to the interstate for overnighters, but note that no bathhouse or dump station are available. Next door is a Waffle House, plus three fast-food joints. A golf course is across the street. A supermarket is about 0.25 mile away.

Campsites, facilities: This mobile-home park has 99 grassy, full-hookup sites with 50-amp electrical service for self-contained RVs. Just 30 sites are available for overnighters; the rest are taken by people who stay year-round or choose to leave their rigs during the hot summer months. There are no showers or restroom facilities. A pool, horseshoe pits, shuffleboard courts, laundry facilities, picnic tables, putting green, social programs, and a recreation room are available. Children may stay a maximum of 15 days, twice a year. Pets are prohibited.

Reservations, fees: Reservations are recommended. Sites are $30–40 per night for two people, plus $2 for each additional person. Credit cards are not accepted. Long-term stays are OK.

Directions: From I-75, take Exit 205 westbound on State Road 72. Drive 0.1 mile to the park on the north side of the road.

Contact: Windward Isle RV Park, 1 Catamaran Drive, Sarasota, FL 34233, 941/922-3090.

20 MYAKKA RIVER STATE PARK

Scenic rating: 10

outside of Sarasota, on the Myakka River

One of only two rivers in Florida designated as Wild and Scenic, the Myakka River is the centerpiece of this 28,875-acre state park,

one of Florida's largest. Bird-watchers, canoeists, anglers, hikers, backpackers, horseback riders, and tourists flock here year-round to experience nature close at hand. The park is especially noted for its large variety and number of birds, especially turkeys and hawks, although many other forms of wildlife abound, including alligators, deer, bobcats, and cottontail rabbits—a fourth of the park is a wilderness preserve open to a limited number of users.

Because the park is so popular, its two main campgrounds seem to squeeze everyone together—but there's fast, easy access to canoeing, mountain-biking and hiking trails, the boat basin, tram tours of the hammocks and river floodplain, and airboat tours. An elevated, 125-foot walkway allows for a good view of the forest tree canopy. The river flows 34 miles through the park and widens into two large lakes. Don't think about taking a dip, though, because no swimming is permitted anywhere. You'll understand why when you realize that the "log" right next to your canoe is actually a huge alligator.

Anglers routinely catch bass, bream, and catfish. There's a boat ramp on Upper Myakka Lake, but the water is shallow, and you'll need a boat with minimum keel. A fishing pier is wheelchair-accessible. It's best to pick up supplies before you arrive; a snack bar operates within the park, but groceries and restaurants are 10–15 miles away. Wildlife tours are offered by tram and boat.

Campsites, facilities: The two campgrounds have a total of 76 sites for RVs. Sites have 30-amp electricity and water; they vary in size, but RVs up to 35 feet long can be accommodated. The Old Prairie Campground, the smallest of the two with 25 sites, also has five cabins for rent. The other campground, Big Flats, is about three miles from the main gate. Each campsite has a picnic table and a grill or fire ring/grill combination. Restrooms, showers, laundry facilities, a dump station, a playground, boat rentals,

© VISIT FLORIDA

campsite near the Myakka River

a boat ramp, and rental cabins are available. There are too many trees at most sites for a camper to use a satellite dish. The visitors center, restrooms, fishing pier, nature trail, picnic areas, and concession building are wheelchair-accessible. A camp store sells ice, camping supplies, snacks, and souvenirs. Groceries are 15 miles away; restaurants are within nine miles. Children are welcome, but pets are prohibited.

Reservations, fees: Reservations are recommended; contact ReserveAmerica at 800/336-3521 or reserveamerica.com. Sites are $22 for up to eight people. Electricity costs $2 per night. Credit cards are accepted. The maximum stay is 14 days.

Directions: From I-75, take Exit 205 eastbound on State Road 72 and drive nine miles to the park.

Contact: Myakka River State Park, 13207 State Road 72, Sarasota, FL 34241, 941/361-6511, fax 941/361-6501, www.floridastate parks.org.

21 MYAKKA RIVER TRAIL PRIMITIVE BACKPACKING SITES

Scenic rating: 9

in Myakka River State Park

You'll likely see deer, turkey, wild hogs, otters (if you're lucky), armadillos, a bobcat, or even a bald eagle while hiking along the 39-mile Myakka River Trail, which meanders in four loops through oak and palm hammocks, pine flatwoods, and dry prairies. With lots of small marshes on the trail, too, rangers say you can expect to have wet feet during the rainy summer months. Driest conditions are from late fall through early spring. Always carry water with you; although pitcher-pump wells are available at each campsite, they may be dry in the spring. The Mossy Hammock camping area is the closest to the parking area, 2.2 miles away on the Bee Island loop. Continue hiking south and west to the Bee Island site, about 2.9 miles away. You can complete the loop and end at the parking area—but if you're not ready to return to civilization, the Honore, Deer Prairie, and East loops continue farther east.

Four other primitive campgrounds, each with three campsites, are also available. Distance from the trailhead varies, with Panther Point 8.6 miles away; Honore, 8.7 miles; Oak Grove, 9.5 miles; and the Prairie site, 14.1 miles. The path, maintained by the Florida Trail Association, is marked with orange and blue blazes. You may encounter day hikers and horseback riders at various points. Bicycles are not permitted on the hiking trails, but are allowed on most of the dirt roads crisscrossing the park. Hikers and backpackers visiting the park in the summertime will find themselves almost completely alone—their reward for braving the heat.

Campsites, facilities: There are six primitive camping zones, each suitable for a maximum of 12 backpackers. Bring your own water—a well pump is available at each area, but all water should be purified by boiling or chemical means, and the well may run dry during the spring. Bury human waste six inches deep, away from the campsite and water supply. Use camp stoves, if possible. Pets are not allowed.

Reservations, fees: Reservations are recommended; call ReserveAmerica at 800/326-3521. Camping costs $3 per night per adult and $2 for anyone aged 6 to 17. All backpackers must register at the ranger station and obtain instructions.

Directions: From I-75, take Exit 205 eastbound on State Road 72 and drive nine miles to the park.

Contact: Myakka River State Park, 13207 State Road 72, Sarasota, FL 34241, 941/361-6511, fax 941/361-6501.

22 ARCADIA'S PEACE RIVER CAMPGROUND

Scenic rating: 10

in Arcadia

BEST (

Ready for something amazing? You get the best of both worlds at this 151-acre private campground: the conveniences of full-service RV camping, and vast acres of wild beauty along the Peace River. In addition to the RV section, which has a selection of shady and sunny sites, a whopping two-thirds of the park are left wild. At the center of the park are the mysterious-looking ruins of a chautauqua, an open-air stadium that burned down in the 1930s. The park is also laced with nature trails and dirt roads for walking and biking, and there's a dock on the river that offers a scenic overlook. Other recreational amenities include fishing, paddleboat rentals, and an 18-hole miniature golf course. One unusual feature: You can go fossil-hunting in the wilderness. Planned activities include the usual bingo and potlucks, plus dog parades and kids' games.

For the adventurous, canoe outfitters provide shuttle transportation and equipment for exploring and camping expeditions along the Peace River Canoe Trail, a popular 67-mile waterway that once marked the boundary between Indian territory to the east and pioneer settlements to the west. The river trail has swift-flowing narrows and occasional rapids, and is bordered by dense forests teeming with wildlife: wild hogs, armadillos, egrets, and the like. For more information and reservations, call Canoe Outpost (863/494-1215) or Canoe Safari (863/494-7865).

Campsites, facilities: The campground has 182 RV sites with full hookups, 30-amp electrical service, and picnic tables. Six sites have 50-amp service, and some sites have concrete patios. RVs up to 45 feet long and slideouts can be accommodated in the park. On the premises are restrooms, showers, laundry facilities, a dump station, a convenience store, a pool, a playground, a fishing pond, a miniature golf course, a recreation room, horseshoe pits, shuffleboard courts, and two paintball fields. There's also a large number of wilderness sites without water, electricity, or other facilities (RVs are not allowed on these sites). The office, store, recreation hall, and restrooms are wheelchair-accessible; in addition, you can rent golf carts to drive anywhere in the 150 acres. A wireless Internet network is available in the clubhouse and at most of the campsites. Children are welcome. Leashed pets are permitted.

Reservations, fees: Reservations are recommended. Sites are $29–39 per night for two people, plus $5 for each additional person. Credit cards are accepted. Long-term stays are OK.

Directions: From southbound I-75, take Exit 217 onto State Road 70 and drive 38 miles east to the park, at the junction of State Road 72. From northbound I-75, take Exit 164 onto U.S. 17 and drive north for 24 miles to State Road 70 in Arcadia. Turn west and drive two miles to the park at the State Road 72 junction.

Contact: Arcadia's Peace River Campground, 2998 Northwest Highway 70, Arcadia, FL 33821, 863/494-9693 or 800/559-4011, fax 863/494-9110, www.peacerivercampground .com.

23 PEACE RIVER PRIMITIVE CANOE SITES

Scenic rating: 10

on the Peace River

The slow-moving Peace River winds past cattle farms and walls of moss-draped oaks near the west-central Florida town of Arcadia. Once in a while, a cow, normally hidden within the green backdrop, can be spotted munching grass at the water's edge. You may also see alligators and wading birds. Your mission:

Fritter away a morning by paddling a canoe to a primitive camping spot. Start staking out a secluded place on the west side of the river after passing the cabins about eight miles into the 23-mile, two-day trip. You'll probably enjoy more privacy the farther south you go; besides, the sunnier, open clearings that make obvious camping spots farther north tend to be snagged early. Choose a camping spot before you pass the main recognizable landmark—a bridge at mile 13. Otherwise, your canoe trip the next day may seem too short.

Paddling nine hours during a long weekend on the Peace River belies the waterway's warring history; many Seminole War battles occurred on its banks. Nowadays, you may occasionally hear gunfire—from hunters stalking wild hogs and deer in winter. Normally, the river lives up to its peaceful name, and it's a favorite getaway for Floridians from all over the state.

Campsites, facilities: Campers may pitch tents at various primitive locations on the right side of the river. You can download a map of permitted campsites at www.dep.state.fl.us/gwt/ guide/regions/westcentral/trails/peace_riv. htm. There are no facilities, so bring water, tents, a food-packed cooler, and camping supplies. Piped water is not available. Children and pets are permitted.

Reservations, fees: Making reservations through a canoe outfitter is recommended. Fees for two people run around $65 overnight, including canoe rental and a ride to the canoe launch; you'll essentially paddle back to your parked car. Camping is free if you have your own canoe and can arrange for a friend to pick you up downriver.

Directions: From Arcadia, drive west on State Road 70, then turn right at County Road 661 to get to Canoe Outpost or Canoe Safari. If you own a canoe, you can have an outfitter drive you to the canoe launch; or you can launch on your own from Pioneer Park at the intersection of U.S. 17 and State Road 64 in Zolfo Springs, then have someone pick you up downriver.

Contact: Canoe Outpost, 2816 Northwest County Road 661, Arcadia, FL 34266, 863/494-1215, fax 863/494-4391, www.canoeoutpost.com. Canoe Safari, 3020 Northwest County Road 661, Arcadia, FL 34266, 863/494-7865, www.canoesafari.com. If you own a canoe and have questions about launching from Pioneer Park, call the park at 863/735-0330. Additional information about canoeing on the Peace River can be obtained from the Office of Greenways & Trails, 3900 Commonwealth Boulevard, MS 795, Tallahassee, FL 32399, 850/488-3701 or 877/822-5208.

24 BIG TREE RV RESORT
🚲 🏊 🐕 🚐

Scenic rating: 4

east of Arcadia

Big Tree attracts active senior citizens by offering a busy schedule of social activities and crafts sessions. In addition to a pool and a huge spa, this largely open and sunny park has pool tables. There's a bowling alley one mile down the street and a Wal-Mart shopping center practically next door; it's connected to the park by a paved bicycle path. Down the road is historic Arcadia, with its bounty of antiques shops and restaurants. About 10 percent of the park is occupied year-round.

Campsites, facilities: All 409 full-hookup RV sites are for people age 55 and older; 45 are available for overnighters. Sites are 40 by 55 feet, accommodating RVs up to 40 feet long and slideouts. None are drive-through. On the premises are restrooms, showers, laundry facilities, a recreation hall, a heated pool and spa, a billiards hall, shuffleboard courts, and horseshoes. Children may visit for a few days but not camp. Dogs are not allowed; cats are permitted, but they must be confined.

Reservations, fees: Reservations are recommended. Sites are $37 per night for two people, plus $5 per extra person. Credit cards are not accepted. Long-term rates are available.

Directions: From southbound I-75, take Exit 217 onto State Road 70 and drive 42 miles east to the intersection of U.S. 17 in Arcadia. Continue 1.8 miles on State Road 70 to the park. From northbound I-75, take Exit 164 onto U.S. 17 and drive north for 24 miles to State Road 70. Turn right and drive 1.8 miles east to the park, at left.

Contact: Big Tree RV Park, 2626 Northeast Highway 70, Arcadia, FL 34266, 863/494-7247 or 800/741-7875.

25 TOBY'S RV RESORT
🚲 🏊 🚣 🏕 🦽 🚐 ⛺

Scenic rating: 6

on the east side of Arcadia

Targeted to retirees seeking a "home away from home," this park is within bicycling distance of Wal-Mart and a grocery store. Much of the infrastructure was built in the early 2000s, so everything feels new and well-maintained. In the clubhouse, campers can socialize and take part in all kinds of planned activities, including computer classes, arts and crafts, bingo, and line dancing. "We have any activity under the sun," say the managers. Campers can use the park's wireless network to get online. Sites are large enough to fit any size RV, and they're nice and sunny, all the better to thaw out snowbirds weary from the cold up north. The area is still somewhat rural.

Campsites, facilities: Of 407 total sites at this age-50-and-older park, 60 are available for overnighters and the rest for seasonal guests. Sites have full hookups and 50-amp service; all have concrete pads, picnic tables, and phone service availability. Tenters are welcome to stay for a maximum of seven days; they are accommodated on the same grassy sites with concrete patios as the RVs. On the premises are restrooms, showers, a dump station, laundry facilities, a heated pool and spa, a driving range, miniature golf, a nature trail, a lake with a dock, propane gas sales, a dog-walk area, and courts for *pétanque* (French-style bowling), boccie (lawn bowling), shuffleboard, and horseshoes. All areas are wheelchair-accessible. Children are not welcome. Leashed pets under 35 pounds are permitted.

Reservations, fees: Reservations are recommended. Sites are $37 per night for two people, plus $1 per extra person. Credit cards are not accepted. Long-term stays are permitted.

Directions: From I-75, take Exit 217 eastbound on State Road 70 for 45 miles through Arcadia. The park is one mile east of the Wal-Mart on the north side of the road.

Contact: Toby's RV Resort, 3550 Northeast Highway 70, Arcadia, FL 34266, 800/307-0768 (reservations only) or 863/494-1744, fax 863/494-2944, www.rvonthego.com.

26 LITTLE WILLIE'S RV RESORT

Scenic rating: 3

north of Arcadia

This adults-only park overlooks wide-open farm country and is convenient for passersby on U.S. 17. Most sites are on an open field. There's not a whole lot to do beyond swimming in the heated pool, but canoeing, boating, and golf are nearby.

Campsites, facilities: All 331 RV sites have full hookups and concrete patios. Facilities include restrooms, showers, laundry facilities, a clubhouse, a heated pool, horseshoes, and shuffleboard. A convenience store is across the street. Children are not welcome as campers but may visit short-term. Leashed pets are allowed; no aggressive breeds.

Reservations, fees: Reservations are recommended. Sites are $30 per night for two people, plus $3 for electricity. Credit cards are not accepted. The park is usually closed May 15–September 15.

Directions: From southbound I-75, take Exit 217 onto State Road 70 and drive 42 miles east to the intersection of U.S. 17 in Arcadia. Turn north and drive five miles to the park. From northbound I-75, take Exit 164 onto U.S. 17 and drive north for 24 miles into Arcadia at State Road 70. Continue north on U.S. 17 for five miles to the park.

Contact: Little Willie's RV Resort, 5905 Northeast Cubitis Avenue, Arcadia, FL 34266, 863/494-2717.

27 CRAIG'S RV PARK

Scenic rating: 4

north of Arcadia

This 65-acre park caters to snowbirds and bluegrass-lovers, offering bus tours of the area, daily exercise programs, weekend socials, church services, bingo, golf putting greens, and a driving range. It's near the Peace River, a good spot for fishing and boating. Close by is the historic village of Arcadia, whose downtown is dotted with restored turn-of-the-20th-century buildings and antiques stores. This is also cowboy country: Rodeos are a highlight in March and July. The park is host to several bluegrass festivals.

Campsites, facilities: The park has 357 RV sites with full hookups; overnighters can camp at around half of them. Most have 50-amp electrical service and concrete patios. RVs up to 40 feet long can be accommodated. A wireless Internet network is available in the office. On the premises are restrooms, showers, laundry facilities, a dump station, a pool, a recreation hall, a golf driving range, horseshoe pits, and shuffleboard courts. All areas are wheelchair-accessible. Streets are paved. Children are allowed to visit during the winter. Pets are not allowed.

Reservations, fees: Reservations are required in winter. Sites are $25 per night for two people, plus $1 for each additional person.

Credit cards are accepted. Long-term stays are OK.

Directions: From southbound I-75, take Exit 205 onto State Road 72 and drive 40 miles east to Arcadia, then travel 7 miles north on U.S. 17 to the park. From northbound I-75, take Exit 164 onto U.S. 17 and drive north. The park is seven miles north of Arcadia.

Contact: Craig's RV Park, 7895 Northeast Cubitis Avenue, Arcadia, FL 34266, 863/494-1820 or 877/750-5129, fax 863/494-1079, www.craigsrv.com.

28 GULF BEACH CAMPGROUND

Scenic rating: 10

on Siesta Key

BEST (

At these prices, you should expect something special, and Gulf Beach Campground delivers. This park is on the much lauded beaches of Siesta Key on the Gulf of Mexico. Siesta Key's sand is considered among the whitest and most powdery stuff in the world. From a bench at the edge of the campground, you can watch the pelicans skim inches above the surface of the water. Down on the beach, you can play in the surf, build a sand castle, or work on your tan. The campground is next to a county park, so at least on one side, you're not hemmed in by buildings. Waves are gentle most of the time, perfect for little kids, but don't bring your surfboard. Australian pines provide relief from the sun. Sites are a bit close together, laid out in two long rows stretching perpendicular from the street to the beach, with a driveway in the middle. Nearby is a bike path; you'll find restaurants, stores, and beach supplies two miles north in Siesta Village.

Campsites, facilities: RVs and tents can be accommodated on 48 campsites with full hookups, 30/50-amp electrical service, cable TV, and picnic tables. Sites vary in length; if you have a big rig, you should call first to see if a large site is available. All sites are back-in. Restrooms, showers, and laundry facilities are available. A dial-up Internet connection is available in the laundry room. Children are welcome. Call for the current pet policy; it varies by season and by location in the park.

Reservations, fees: Reservations are recommended. The fee for two people varies seasonally from $28 nightly in summer to a high of $61 nightly in winter. Rates vary according to how close you are to the beach. There's a $2 fee for each additional person, plus a $2 surcharge each for use of cable TV, air conditioners, and electric heaters. Credit cards are accepted. Seasonal rates are available.

Directions: From I-75, take Exit 205 west for about seven miles to the dead end at Midnight Pass Road. Turn left (south) and travel 2.3 miles to the park, on the right.

Contact: Gulf Beach Campground, 8862 Midnight Pass Road, Sarasota, FL 34242, 941/349-3839.

29 OSCAR SCHERER STATE PARK

Scenic rating: 10

in Osprey, midway between Sarasota and Venice

The seclusion and natural beauty of this park will surprise you. After battling traffic on busy U.S. 41, which is lined with strip shopping centers, auto dealerships, and commercial chaos, you'll enter 1,384 acres of woods and tranquility. Home to many endangered animals, notably the Florida scrub jay, the park has a freshwater swimming lake and a tidal creek for canoeing. Canoes are available for rent at the ranger station ($5/hour or $25/day); you are not permitted to pull boats or canoes on the creek bank, because they cause erosion. Here's a paradox: You may catch bass, bream, or catfish above the dam on South Creek if you have a freshwater fishing license; however, if you fish below the dam for snook, redfish, or snapper, then a saltwater license is a must. Two nature trails run along the creek. Got a hankering for beaches on the Gulf of Mexico? They're three miles west of the park. You'll just have to face that traffic again.

Campsites, facilities: There are 104 campsites with water, 30-amp electricity, picnic tables, grills, and fire rings; among these, 6 have 50-amp service. Six sites are drive-through; RVs up to 35 feet long and slideouts can be accommodated. Restrooms, showers, a dump station, a playground, a lake, and canoe and kayak rentals are available. Wheelchair-accessible areas include some sites, the docks, the office, the bathhouse, and the picnic areas. Children are welcome. Pets are permitted with proof of vaccination.

Reservations, fees: Reservations are recommended; contact ReserveAmerica at 800/336-3521 or reserveamerica.com. Sites are $24 per night for up to eight people. Credit cards are accepted. The maximum stay is 14 days.

Directions: From I-75 traveling north, take Exit 195 westbound on Laurel Road for two miles. At U.S. 41, turn north and drive two miles. The park is on the east side. If you're traveling south, use Exit 200.

Contact: Oscar Scherer State Park, 1843 South Tamiami Trail, Osprey, FL 34229, 941/483-5956.

30 ROYAL COACHMAN RV RESORT

Scenic rating: 9

east of Nokomis

This deluxe park on Dona Bay is a huge hit with retired snowbirds who spend the cooler months in Florida, but it has plenty of things to keep people of all ages occupied, including golf, two pro sand volleyball courts, four tennis courts, and basketball. The heated, 120,000-gallon pool is big enough for laps and water aerobics. But it's not all about sports—

opportunities to socialize run the gamut from theme parties (Germanfest, lobster feasts, country-and-western dinner shows) to bingo, card games, arts and crafts, and auctions. Professional shows and concerts are held in an outdoor amphitheater. There's even a business center with fax, copier, Internet access, and computers. "We're kind of like a small town all to ourselves," say the managers.

Campsites, facilities: There are 167 sites for RVs. Full hookups, 30/50-amp electrical service, cable TV, telephone service, and picnic tables are available. Also on-site are restrooms, showers, laundry facilities, a dump station, a pool, a recreation hall, an outdoor amphitheater, a model train room, a nature walk, a clubhouse, a game arcade, four tennis courts, a golf practice complex, a miniature golf course, a volleyball area, a fitness center, a kid's pirate ship play fort, a library with children's room, a basketball court, horseshoe pits, shuffleboard courts, a tool and craft shop, boat storage, and a boccie ball (lawn bowling) park. Most areas are wheelchair-accessible. Children are welcome. Leashed pets are permitted.

Reservations, fees: Reservations are recommended. Sites are $48 per night for two people, plus $2 for each additional person. Credit cards are accepted. Long-term rates are available.

Directions: From I-75, take Exit 195 westbound on Laurel Road for one mile. Look for the park to your left.

Contact: Royal Coachman RV Resort, 1070 Laurel Road East, Nokomis, FL 34275, 941/488-9674 or 800/548-8678, fax 941/485-5678, www.rvonthego.com.

31 COUNTRY CLUB ESTATES

Scenic rating: 2

in Venice

The Intracoastal Waterway borders this community on the east, and Gulf of Mexico beaches are less than one mile to the west. Shopping centers, restaurants, banks, doctors' offices, and a hospital are all within two blocks. There's even a golf course nearby, which is fitting, because the park itself is a former golf course, as hinted by street names like Bogie and Turf. Dock your boat for an additional fee; a lagoon in the park provides access to the Intracoastal Waterway. RVers have access to the common areas of the mobile-home park, including a heated pool and a recreation hall with an auditorium, a stage, a card room, and a ceramics room. The place also has a bowling league, tennis groups, and golf leagues for men and women.

Campsites, facilities: A 509-unit mobile-home community for adults only, Country Club Estates has 10 RV sites for travelers with full hookups and cable TV. Restrooms, showers, a pool with a spa, boat docks, shuffleboard courts, boccie (lawn bowling) courts, and a recreation hall are available. You must be 55 or older to camp. Pets are prohibited in the RV section.

Reservations, fees: Reservations are recommended. Sites are $35–45 per night. Credit cards are not accepted. Six-month stays are permitted.

Directions: From the intersection of U.S. 41 and Business Route 41 on the north side of Venice, drive south on the business route for 1.5 miles and turn into the park, which is behind the Publix supermarket. The park entrance is located directly off the main highway.

Contact: Country Club Estates, 700 Waterway, Venice, FL 34285, 941/488-2111, fax 941/483-4958.

32 FLORIDA PINES MOBILE HOME COURT

Scenic rating: 2

in Venice

Social programs are held for residents October 15–April 15 in this clean, well-landscaped mobile-home and RV community for retirement living near the Gulf of Mexico. Shopping, restaurants, and supplies are available 0.25 mile away.

Campsites, facilities: There are 30 paved RV sites with cement patios in this mobile-home community for retirees. Full hookups, cable TV, restrooms, showers, laundry facilities, a dump station, horseshoe pits, shuffleboard courts, and a wheelchair-accessible recreation room are available. Big rigs can be accommodated. You must be 55 or older to stay here. Pets are prohibited.

Reservations, fees: Reservations are recommended. Sites are $32 per night for two people, plus $1.50 for each additional person and for air-conditioning use, and $2.50 for using electrical heaters. Credit cards are not accepted.

Directions: From I-75, take Exit 193 southwest for 6.5 miles. At State Road 776, turn right and drive two blocks.

Contact: Florida Pines Mobile Home Court, 150 Satulah Circle, Venice, FL 34293, 941/493-0019.

33 VENICE CAMPGROUND

Scenic rating: 8

east of Venice

Want to get out of the sun? Set on the scenic Myakka River, Venice Campground is tucked into an old-growth oak hammock that casts shady relief. Some RV sites overlook an inlet off the river. Three miles of nature trails offer views of the river, which is popular with canoeists and anglers. A restaurant is next door, but there's not much else in the way of development; the park has a secluded, back-to-nature ambience. A security gate keeps out the curious. The campground sells some groceries—ice, soda, and even a few RV supplies—but you'll have to drive into Venice, three miles west, for most items. Venice, like its Italian namesake, is laced with canals and waterways, but it's best known for an unusual beachcombing sport: Instead of shells, people look for fossilized shark teeth. North of Venice is a popular surfing spot at North Jetty Park.

Campsites, facilities: This 25-acre campground has 104 RV sites with full hookups and 30-amp electrical service. Picnic tables, restrooms, showers, laundry facilities, a dump station, a pool, a boat ramp, boat and canoe rentals, cabin rentals, a playground, a game room, horseshoe pits, shuffleboard courts, a volleyball field, and a limited store are available. A supermarket is about 3.5 miles away. Children are welcome. Leashed pets are permitted at RV sites only.

Reservations, fees: Reservations are recommended. RV sites are $45. Prices are for four people; add $2.75 for each additional person over age six. Credit cards are accepted. The maximum stay is nine months.

Directions: From I-75, take Exit 191 southbound on River Road and drive one mile. Turn left on Venice Avenue (a gravel road) and continue 0.5 mile east to the campground.

Contact: Venice Campground, 4085 East Venice Avenue, Venice, FL 34292, 941/488-0850, fax 941/485-1666, www.campvenice.com.

34 RAMBLERS REST RESORT CAMPGROUND

🏊 🛶 🎣 🐕 🧗 ♿ 🚐 ⛺

Scenic rating: 6

east of Venice

Towering slash pines welcome campers to this 100-acre park on the Myakka River in an area little touched by development. Many of the sites are occupied by retirees in park models. Bingo, arts and crafts, choir singing, wood carving, and square dancing are among the activities held in the recreation hall. Fish from the riverfront dock, or launch your boat and head south for the Gulf of Mexico. The

swimming pool is heated. Sarasota-area tourist attractions are within 20 miles.

Campsites, facilities: There are 589 RV sites, 563 of which have full hookups and 30-amp or 50-amp electricity. Water and electricity are available at the remaining spots, which can accommodate 18 tenters. On the premises are picnic tables, restrooms, showers, a dump station, a clubroom, a pool with a whirlpool tub, a boat ramp, a dock, a playground, an exercise room, horseshoe pits, shuffleboard courts, a convenience store, and laundry facilities. Most areas are wheelchair-accessible. Children are welcome. Pets under 20 pounds are allowed; they may be walked in remote areas only.

Reservations, fees: Reservations are recommended. Sites are $33–38 per night for two people, plus $2 for each additional person. Credit cards are not accepted. Long-term rates are available for seasonal visitors.

Directions: From I-75, take Exit 191 southbound on River Road and drive three miles. The campground is on the east side.

Contact: Ramblers Rest Resort Campground, 1300 North River Road, Venice, FL 34293, 941/493-4354, fax 941/496-9520, www.rvinthesun.com.

35 MYAKKA STATE FOREST

🥾 🚴 🛶 🐕 ⛺

Scenic rating: 6

southeast of Venice and west of Port Charlotte

At nearly 8,600 acres, this state forest preserves a swatch of undeveloped marsh and pinelands under Florida's forward-thinking state land acquisition program. More than two miles front along the Myakka River, a popular canoeing tributary and fishing spot. There are two loops of hiking/equestrian trails stretching 13 miles. Off-road bicycling is popular.

Campsites, facilities: Primitive campers in tents and small RVs can set up camp at five designated spots along two unpaved roads that encircle the interior of the tract; none has water or electricity, and only one is near the river. Download a map of the forest at www. fl-dof.com/state_forests/sf_pdf/myakka.pdf. Children and leashed pets are welcome.

Reservations, fees: Campsites are $5 per night; you must obtain a permit from the state forest office.

Directions: From I-75, take Exit 191 southbound on River Road and drive 11 miles too the forest entrance.

Contact: Myakka State Forest, 2000 South River Road, Englewood, FL 34223, 941/460-1333, www.fl-dof.com/state_forests/myakka .html.

36 MYAKKA RV RESORT

Scenic rating: 6

west of North Port

This quiet park is located at the delta of the Myakka River, in an area overlooking the river floodplain. The location is good for bird-watching, if you can get a site on the south side of the 40-acre park. The sites are big enough for 40-foot rigs; two sites even accommodate 48-footers. About two-thirds of the park are taken up by park models. Nearby is North Port, which has seen less development than many of the fast-growing cities on Florida's west coast. The town is home to Warm Mineral Springs (941/426-1692), a health spa that calls itself a "fountain of youth." The water stays at 87°F year-round. You can swim there for $16 a day.

Campsites, facilities: You'll find 38 grassy sites with full hookups, 30/50-amp electrical service, picnic tables, and concrete patios, as well as 56 park-model sites. Sites vary in size. A wireless Internet network is available in the clubhouse, at the campsites, and in the office. Restrooms, showers, laundry facilities, shuffleboard, a pool, rental units, picnic tables, a patio with a barbecue, a clubhouse,

and a canoe launch are available. The bathhouse and clubhouse are wheelchair-accessible. Streets are paved. A public boat ramp for bigger vessels is three miles away. Two supermarkets are within two miles. Children are welcome. Leashed pets are permitted.

Reservations, fees: Reservations are recommended. Sites are $29–43 per night for two people, plus $3 for each extra person; they are subject to change. Credit cards are accepted. Long-term rates are available.

Directions: From I-75, take Exit 191 southbound on River Road and drive six miles to U.S. 41. Turn left and drive 0.5 mile. The park is on the right side of the road, just beyond the bridge.

Contact: Myakka RV Resort, 10400 Tamiami Trail, Venice, FL 34287, 941/426-5040, fax 941/426-5712.

37 RIVERSIDE RV RESORT AND CAMPGROUND

Scenic rating: 10

south of Arcadia

More than 70 acres in size, this park is convenient for I-75 travelers. It caters to young families—some weekend activities are specifically for children—but also offers river canoeing, kayaking, and fishing for teenagers and adults. There's a video arcade, and the proximity of the playground to the swimming pools—one designed for water volleyball—was established with parental supervision in mind. These oak-shaded and sunny sites are large, buffered by a wildlife area and the Peace River, near its mouth on the Gulf of Mexico. It's a true RV park; the only sites occupied year-round are those of park employees. The park attracts families April 20–December 15, and older snowbirds from the Midwest during the winter season, roughly December 15–April 20.

Campsites, facilities: This park offers 356 full-hookup sites with picnic tables, fire

Boating is a way of life on the west coast of Florida.

rings, and concrete patios, as well as a small primitive tent camping area. Thirty-amp electrical service is available at 120 sites; 236 have 50-amp. A wireless Internet network is available in the clubhouse. Some sites are waterfront. RVs as long as 40 feet or more and slideouts can be accommodated. Lots vary in size, with the largest "premium" sites measuring 40 by 70 feet. There are restrooms, showers, laundry facilities, a dump station, a canoe launch, a boat ramp, and rentals, a recreation hall, a playground, horseshoes, shuffleboard, a volleyball field, two pools (one heated), a spa, a limited store with propane, ice, snacks, souvenirs, fishing tackle, and RV supplies, and a boat dock on the Peace River. All areas are said to be wheelchair-accessible. Groceries and restaurants are within 4.5 miles. Children are welcome. Leashed cats and dogs are permitted; a pet-walking area is provided.

Reservations, fees: Reservations are recommended. Fee for two people is $34–47. Add

$2.50 for each extra person. Credit cards are accepted. Long-term rates are available.

Directions: From I-75, take Exit 170 onto Kings Highway/County Road 769 and drive five miles east to the park.

Contact: Riverside RV Resort and Campground, 9770 Southwest County Road 769, Arcadia, FL 34266, 863/993-2111 or 800/795-9733, fax 863/993-2021, www.riversiderv resort.com.

38 LETTUCE LAKE TRAVEL RESORT

Scenic rating: 5

near Fort Ogden

Greeted by Canadian flags, campers at this manicured park tend to stay for winter or even longer in their RVs or park models, some of which are for sale or rent. The big attraction is a county boat ramp that gives anglers and boaters access to Lettuce Lake, a wide spot on the Peace River as it flows into the Gulf of Mexico. The campground has a dock on the "lake" and a pretty wooded area on the banks, where you can sit at picnic tables with a drink in hand and while away the hours. It's a rural spot, out there with the orange groves and cattle, and it has shell-rock roads, as well as oaks, palms, and hibiscus. This rural flavor is part of its appeal.

Campsites, facilities: There are 252 sites with full hookups, 30-amp electrical service, and picnic tables; about half the sites have concrete pads. RVs up to 40 feet long can be accommodated. About 38 sites are available for overnighters. Restrooms, showers, laundry facilities, a pool, a recreation center, a lakefront dock, horseshoes, and shuffleboard courts are available. A public boat ramp is next door. A supermarket is 7.5 miles away. Children are permitted if they are well supervised. Leashed, supervised pets under 20 pounds are allowed.

Reservations, fees: Reservations are recommended. Sites are $34 per night for two people, plus $3 for each additional person. Credit cards are not accepted. Long-term stays are OK.

Directions: From southbound I-75, take Exit 170 onto Kings Highway/County Road 769 and drive northeast for six miles to County Road 761. Turn southeast, go two miles, then take Lettuce Lake Avenue to the park. From northbound I-75, take Exit 164 onto U.S. 17 and drive north 10 miles to County Road 761. Turn west, go two miles, then take Lettuce Lake Avenue to the park, which is right next to Oak Haven Park.

Contact: Lettuce Lake Travel Resort, 8644 Southwest Reese Street, Arcadia, FL 34269, 863/494-6057, fax 863/494-4254, www.lettucelake.com.

39 OAK HAVEN PARK

🏊 🚣 � 🏠 🚐

Scenic rating: 4

near Fort Ogden

Oak Haven Park is adjacent to Lettuce Lake Park, which has a public boat ramp. A small golf course is down the block. The park is on the same street as Lettuce Lake Travel Resort (see previous listing). Says the management: "We are country. You come here to rest."

Campsites, facilities: All 119 RV sites have full hookups with 30/50-amp electrical service; about 20 are available for overnighters and new seasonal visitors. On the premises are restrooms, showers, laundry facilities, a pool and spa, shuffleboard, horseshoes, a wireless Internet network, and a small library for guests. A supermarket and restaurants are eight miles away. The park is senior-oriented, but children may visit. Leashed pets under 45 pounds are permitted in a separate section.

Reservations, fees: Reservations are recommended. Sites are $25 per night for two people, plus $3 per extra person. Credit cards are not accepted. Long-term stays are the norm.

Directions: From southbound I-75, take Exit 170 onto County Road 769 and drive northeast for six miles to County Road 761. Turn southeast, go two miles, then take Lettuce Lake Avenue to the park. From northbound I-75, take Exit 164 onto U.S. 17 and drive north for 10 miles to County Road 761. Turn west, go two miles, then take Lettuce Lake Avenue to the park.

Contact: Oak Haven Park, 10307 Southwest Lettuce Lake Avenue, Arcadia, FL 34269, 863/494-4578.

40 LIVE OAK RV RESORT

🏊 🏠 🚐

Scenic rating: 6

south of Arcadia, off I-75

This 80-acre park with a security gate is nestled in an area of horse ranches, farms, and fruit groves along the Peace River near historic Punta Gorda. The park caters to upscale retirees, with an executive golf course on the property and plenty of recreational activities. During the winter season, the park hosts dances, dinners, other social events, choir singing, and religious services, but golf is really the focus.

Campsites, facilities: The resort has 399 RV sites, most with full hookups, 30/50-amp electrical service, and concrete pads. Pop-up trailers, pickup-truck campers, and tenters will be turned away; RVs must be at least 23 feet long. On the premises are showers, restrooms, laundry facilities, a pool and a whirlpool tub, two recreation halls, an exercise room, a game room, a golf putting and chipping green, horseshoe pits, shuffleboard courts, and boccie ball (lawn bowling) courts. A supermarket and restaurants are eight miles away. Children may visit but not camp. Leashed pets are permitted.

Reservations, fees: Reservations are taken.

Sites are $35 per night. Credit cards are accepted. Long-term stays are OK.

Directions: From I-75, take Exit 164 onto U.S. 17 and drive 10 miles north to the entrance.

Contact: Live Oak RV Resort, 12865 Southwest Highway 17, Arcadia, FL 34266, 863/993-4014 or 800/833-4236, fax 863/993-0940.

41 HARBOR LAKES RV RESORT

Scenic rating: 8

in the community of El Jobean, near the Myakka River

About half of the 528 concrete-pad sites in this well-manicured mobile-home community are available for RVs, although none are pull-through. Lots are roomy, measuring 30 by 80 feet. You won't find much shade in the camping area, but there is a view of pine trees near the lakes. A path winding through the complex has mile markers, so joggers and bicyclists can keep track of their progress. The park is minutes from the Texas Rangers' winter training camp, the Charlotte Towne Center mall, Englewood Beach, Gasparilla Island State Park, the Thomas Edison Home, and the Ringling Brothers and Barnum and Bailey Circus and Museum.

Campsites, facilities: This adults-only resort has 268 RV sites with full hookups and telephone access. The property contains four spring-fed lakes, shuffleboard courts, a pool, horseshoe pits, laundry, and a recreation hall used for dances, exercise classes, and other activities. Leashed pets are allowed.

Reservations, fees: Reservations are recommended. Sites are $32–37 per night for two people, plus $3 for each additional person. Credit cards are accepted. Long-term stays are permitted.

Directions: From I-75, take Exit 179 onto Toledo Blade Boulevard heading southwest. Go 6.5 miles to State Road 776/El Jobean Road and turn south. The park is 3.3 miles ahead on the right.

Contact: Harbor Lakes RV Resort, 3737 El Jobean Road, Port Charlotte, FL 33953, 941/624-4511 or 800/468-5022, fax 941/624-5238, www.rvonthego.com.

42 PALMS AND PINES RIVERSIDE RESORT

Scenic rating: 2

on the south side of the Peace River, east of Punta Gorda

Palms and Pines Riverside Resort, primarily a residential trailer park, faces the scenic Peace River. Some lots have boat docks, but swimming is not permitted, because of the presence of alligators. Close by are boat ramps, fishing piers, a golf course, and shopping. Life in Charlotte County revolves around boating, so you'll find plenty of marinas and boating supply stores nearby. In the wintertime, manatees are commonly seen along the Peace River and in the harbor.

Campsites, facilities: Overlooking the Peace River, this 114-unit mobile-home park offers overnighters 40 concrete-pad RV sites with full hookups, 50-amp electrical service, picnic tables, cable TV, and telephone access. RVs up to 39 feet long can be accommodated. On the premises are a boat ramp, fishing paddleboats, a wheelchair-accessible recreation room, horseshoe pits, and shuffleboard courts. There are no restrooms, so rigs must be self-contained. Children are allowed. Pets are welcome.

Reservations, fees: Reservations are recommended in winter. Sites are $26 per night for two people, plus $5 for each additional person. Rates are subject to change. Credit cards are not accepted. Long-term stays are encouraged.

Directions: From I-75, take Exit 164 and drive 1.8 miles north on U.S. 17 to Cleveland

Avenue. Turn west and drive 0.3 mile to Riverside Drive, then head north for half a block. **Contact:** Palms and Pines Riverside Resort, 5400 Riverside Drive, Punta Gorda, FL 33982, 941/639-5461, www.palmsand pinesinc.com.

43 SHELL CREEK RESORT

Scenic rating: 6

east of Punta Gorda

Set far from urban sights, this open and sunny park overlooks scenic Shell Creek, a tributary of the Peace River. Also nearby is the Fred C. Babcock/Cecil M. Webb Wildlife Management Area, a 65,000-acre hunting park famous for its doves, quail, deer, and wild hogs, as well as for freshwater fishing and frog gigging. But frankly, this adult-oriented park welcomes visitors for more civilized fun. During the winter months, visitors can keep in shape with an aquacise program in the heated pool,

and anglers will delight in the great fishing. Bands entertain at holiday dances held five times a year.

Campsites, facilities: RVers over age 55 are welcome at the 185 full-hookup RV spots and 30-amp electrical service. Cable TV access, wheelchair-accessible restrooms, showers, laundry facilities, a pool and spa, a billiards room, tournament shuffleboard courts, a boat ramp, a marina, and a store are on the grounds. A supermarket and pizza parlor are within seven miles. Children can visit for up to 30 days. Leashed pets are permitted and must use the designated dog-walk area.

Reservations, fees: Reservations are recommended. Sites are $35 per night for two people, plus $4 per extra person. Credit cards are accepted. Long-term stays are OK.

Directions: From I-75, take Exit 164 northbound on U.S. 17 and go four miles. At County Road 764, turn east and drive 4.5 miles to the park.

Contact: Shell Creek Resort, 35711 Washington Loop Road, Punta Gorda, FL 33982, 941/639-4234, fax 941/639-2801.

© MARILYN MOORE

Waterfront cafés are plentiful in this area.

44 PUNTA GORDA RV RESORT

Scenic rating: 6

off U.S. 41, in Punta Gorda

This palm-dotted 30-acre park and mobile-home community is set on a canal offering direct access to Alligator Creek and the Gulf of Mexico for fishing; even sailboats can cruise right out to the open water without encountering bridges. A bait and tackle store is next door. A par-three golf course is across the street, and a restaurant is within walking distance. A monthly activity calendar and newsletter keep campers apprised of the on-site social programs. About 80 percent of the park is occupied year-round.

Campsites, facilities: This adult-oriented community has 80 campsites available, out of a total of 223 sites with full hookups, cable TV, and telephone access. Most spots are waterfront. An Internet connection is available in the office. Restrooms, showers, picnic tables, a clubhouse, two spas, a boat ramp, an exercise room, horseshoes, shuffleboard, a convenience store, a beauty salon/barbershop, laundry facilities, and both city water and well water are available. There's also a pool with a tiki hut. The recreation hall, bathhouse, and pool area are accessible to wheelchairs. Streets are paved. Groceries are within 0.5 mile. Children are not welcome as campers, but grandkids can visit for short stays. Small, leashed pets (one per site) are permitted.

Reservations, fees: Reservations are recommended in summer and required in the winter season. Sites are $34 per night for two people, plus $4.50 for each additional person. Credit cards are not accepted. Long-term rates are available.

Directions: From I-75, take Exit 164 and drive 2.3 miles west on U.S. 17 to U.S. 41. Go south for two miles, turn west onto Rio Villa Drive, and take the second left at the sign.

Contact: Punta Gorda RV Resort, 3701 Baynard Drive, Punta Gorda, FL 33950, 941/639-2010, fax 941/637-4931, www.pgrvresort.com.

45 ALLIGATOR MOBILE HOME AND RV PARK

Scenic rating: 3

south of Punta Gorda

In the cool of the evening, you'll see a few tenants gather outside their trailers to exchange news, but the center of activity is a large two-story recreation hall in the middle of the grounds. Catering to retirees who stay for the season, this ownership and site-share park is on a quiet side road five miles south of downtown Punta Gorda, with good access to local attractions. A golf course, restaurants, and groceries are within two miles. Although the park is age-restricted (one person must be at least 55, the spouse at least 45).

Campsites, facilities: This mobile-home park has 166 sites available for RVs, offering full hookups, 30/50-amp electrical service, cable TV, and telephone access. On the premises are restrooms, showers, a dump station, a wheelchair-accessible clubhouse, a pool, shuffleboard courts, a pool table, and laundry facilities. An Internet connection is available in the clubhouse. Families with children are not allowed, but grandchildren may visit. Leashed pets are permitted.

Reservations, fees: Reservations are recommended. Sites are $35 per night for two people, plus $3 for each additional person. Credit cards are accepted. Long-term rates are available.

Directions: From I-75, take Exit 161 onto Jones Loop Road and drive 0.5 mile west. Turn south onto County Road 765A/Taylor Road and drive one mile to the park.

Contact: Alligator Mobile Home and RV Park, 6400 Taylor Road, Lot 112, Punta Gorda, FL

33950, 941/639-7000 or 941/639-7916, www
.alligatorpark.com.

46 WATER'S EDGE RV RESORT

Scenic rating: 5

east of Punta Gorda

A 1,500-square-foot recreation room adjacent
to the pool is the hub of activity, hosting pancake breakfasts, potlucks, wine-and-cheese
parties, ice-cream socials, and crafts classes.
The campsites, which are big enough to accommodate RVs up to 45 feet long, form a half
circle around a 20-acre fishing lake. Canoes
and paddleboats are available for rent. A few
pine trees provide a touch of greenery, but
there isn't much shade. At this 55-plus park,
sites are offered for sale or rent.

Campsites, facilities: This resort has 175
roomy sites for RVs up to 45 feet long, slideouts, trailers, and campers. About 75 are available for overnighters. The sunny sites are 45 by
70 feet; some have concrete patios and picnic
tables. Thirty spots are drive-through. An Internet connection is available in the clubhouse.
Restrooms, showers, picnic tables, a dump
station, laundry facilities, a pool with a spa,
a playground, horseshoes, a volleyball field,
a small camp store, and paddleboat rentals
are available. All areas are wheelchair-accessible. This is an over-55 park. Leashed pets
are permitted.

Reservations, fees: Reservations are recommended. RV sites are $35–45 per night for
two people, plus $4 for each additional adult.
Credit cards are accepted. Maximum stay is
six months.

Directions: From I-75, take Exit 161 onto
Jones Loop Road and drive east for 500 feet.
Turn north onto Piper Road and drive 2.7
miles. Piper Road becomes Golf Course Boulevard; the campground is just 0.5 mile past
the four-way stop sign at Airport Road.

Contact: Water's Edge RV Resort, 6800 Golf
Course Boulevard, Punta Gorda, FL 33982,
941/637-4677 or 941/637-1188 or 800/637-
9224, fax 941/637-9543, www.watersedge
rvresort.com.

47 GULFVIEW RV RESORT

Scenic rating: 8

south of Punta Gorda

Brown pelicans rest atop dock posts here,
taking a break after their latest round of fishing. Campers, too, can fish at this well-kept,
boating-oriented resort with a stream running past. That is, if they're not busy with the
golf outings, movies, dancing, potlucks, and
weekly bingo games offered in winter. The
campground is screened from the road by lots
of greenery, and the sites are a cut above those
at most RV parks.

Campsites, facilities: All 206 RV sites have full
hookups and 30/50-amp electrical service; about
150 are available for overnight use. RVs up to
40 feet long can be accommodated. Restrooms,
showers, picnic tables, laundry facilities, a boat
ramp, a heated pool with a spa, a game room,
shuffleboard courts, horseshoes, and propane
are available. For cable and telephone service,
call the appropriate utility company. Children
may stay a few days or visit; the typical camper
at this retiree-oriented park is around age 70, a
staffer says. Leashed pets are permitted.

Reservations, fees: Reservations are recommended. Sites are $35 and up per night for two
people, plus $5 for each extra person. Credit
cards are accepted. Long-term stays are OK.

Directions: From I-75, take Exit 161 onto
Jones Loop Road and drive west for 0.75 mile
to U.S. 41. Cross U.S. 41 and continue 0.5
mile to the park, at right.

Contact: Gulfview RV Resort, 10205 Burnt
Store Road, Punta Gorda, FL 33950, 941/639-
3978 or 877/237-2757, fax 941/639-8073,
www.rvonthego.com.

48 SUN-N-SHADE CAMPGROUND

Scenic rating: 6

south of Punta Gorda

This mostly sunny campground is favored by retirees and snowbirds seeking to escape the long, cold winter up north. A few trees provide shade and landscaping. Planned activities keep folks busy in the recreation hall.

Campsites, facilities: Of 191 total full-hookup RV sites, 25 are available for overnighters. All sites have concrete pads and phone service availability. Restrooms, showers, a dump station, and two laundry facilities round out the basic facilities. Amenities include a pool, a recreation hall, shuffleboard courts, two dog-walk areas, and a nature trail. In season, planned activities include bingo, games, cards, parties, dinners, and breakfasts. The clubhouse, pool area, and restrooms are wheelchair-accessible. Children are not allowed. Leashed pets are permitted, but not aggressive breeds.

Reservations, fees: Reservations are recommended. Sites are $33 per night for two people, plus $3.50 per extra person. Credit cards are accepted. Long-term or seasonal stays are preferred.

Directions: From I-75, take Exit 158 and drive one mile west on Tucker's Grade/State Road 762. At U.S. 41, turn south and go 3.5 miles.

Contact: Sun-n-Shade Campground, 14880 Tamiami Trail, Punta Gorda, FL 33955, 941/639-5388, fax 941/639-0368, www .sunnshade.com.

LAKE OKEECHOBEE

BEST CAMPGROUNDS

◖ **Most Unusual**
Pioneer Park of Hardee County, **page 449**
Kissimmee Billie Swamp Safari, **page 482**

Forgotten by many but the most hard-core

anglers and boaters, the Lake Okeechobee area has the taste of "Old Florida" that is lost by the glitzy tourist developments, beachside resorts, and hip urbanism that swamps most of the state south of Orlando. This area retains a rural charm.

Driving around Lake Okeechobee is a favorite route for motorcyclists and curious drivers. The more adventurous way is to circumnavigate the lake 148 miles on a mountain bike or in hiking boots atop a mostly gravel, sunbaked levee, camping along the way.

Lake O (Okeechobee means "big water" in the Seminole Indian language) is the second-largest inland lake in the United States, and the largest in Florida – 730 square miles. With an average depth of 10 feet, the lake and the Kissimmee River on the north shore were once the headwaters to the Everglades, allowing water to seep southward through the "river of grass." After devastating hurricanes flooded waterside communities in the 1930s, the U.S. Army Corps of Engineers reined in the lake with a towering 34-foot dike and a series of drainage canals. These control flooding and allowed development of the cities on the Atlantic Coast.

The lake provides ocean-like views on the northeast and south side; on the west side, the shore is thick marshland. The waters teem with bass and many other kinds of fish. In the hunting season, camo-clad adventurers line up at boat ramps to head out in small open-water skiffs. Snowbirds and retirees flock here in the winter months, many staying the entire season and returning to the same RV park year after year. Asked what there is to do at one RV park, the manager summed it up easily: "Fish, fish, fish."

For the boater, Lake Okeechobee is a watery path that cuts 152 miles across the state from the Atlantic Ocean on the east to the Gulf of Mexico on the west, passing through several locks that equalize the water level. For landlubbers, the paradox is that you can't see the water unless you get above the levee, which is also part of the Lake Okeechobee Scenic Trail and the Great Florida Birding Trail. About 60 miles of the old gravel levee road were paved in 2004 and 2005 (from the town of Okeechobee past Port Mayaca).

If you have the time and interest, this area is worth including on your to-do list.

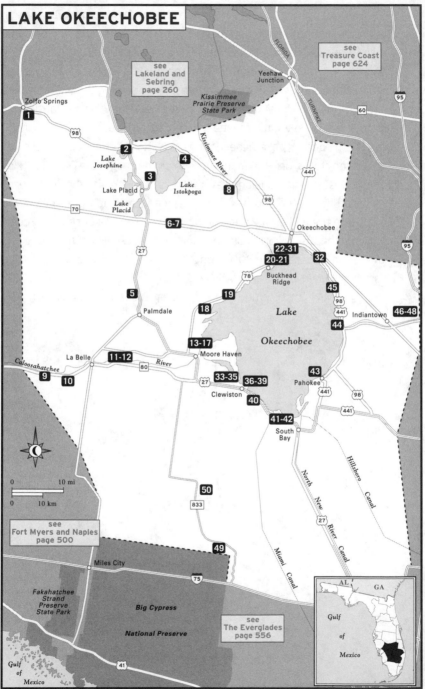

LAKE OKEECHOBEE

see Lakeland and Sebring page 260

see Treasure Coast page 624

Zolfo Springs **1**

Kissimmee Prairie Preserve State Park

Yeehaw Junction

Lake Josephine **2**

4

3

Lake Placid

Lake Istokpoga

Lake Placid

8

6-7

5

Palmdale

Okeechobee

22-31
20-21
32

Buckhead Ridge

45

19

18

Lake

Okeechobee

Indiantown **46-48**

44

13-17

Moore Haven

La Belle

11-12

9 **10**

Coloosahatchee River

33-35 **36-39**

Clewiston

40

43

Pahokee

41-42

South Bay

50

North New River Canal

Hillsboro Canal

see Fort Myers and Naples page 500

49

Miles City

Miami Canal

Fakahatchee Strand Preserve State Park

Big Cypress

National Preserve

see The Everglades page 556

Gulf of Mexico

0   10 mi
0   10 km

© AVALON TRAVEL PUBLISHING, INC.

AL   GA

Gulf of Mexico

1 PIONEER PARK OF HARDEE COUNTY

Scenic rating: 7

on the Peace River, in Zolfo Springs

BEST (

You won't soon forget this focal point of Hardee County, if only for its wildlife refuge near the campground in Pioneer Park, and its museum celebrating the early settlers of this agricultural region. In the refuge, animals move freely in a natural habitat, while visitors watch from an elevated boardwalk. The animals include cougars and two black bears. All the denizens of this refuge cannot be returned to the wild for one reason or another, and previously they were kept in a caged, zoo-like environment here. One of the bears is a retired professional wrestler (declawed). The cougar was given up by its owners when the pet—once fist-sized—grew too big. Each has its own personality, and of course, a name. The refuge is open daily 10 A.M.–4 P.M., except Wednesdays, Thanksgiving, and Christmas Day. Admission of $1–2 per person helps contribute to support the animals and their habitat.

The campground offers grassy sites in this 115-acre county-owned park, which is favored by retirees, snowbirds, and family campers. A dike and a handful of short walking trails are by the Peace River, where anglers try for panfish. This sleepy region also attracts weekend canoeists, who launch here and paddle past cattle farms and woods on the slow-moving river, ending the overnight journey 23 miles downstream in Arcadia, or closer to home for half-day trips. Among the area canoe outfitters is Canoe Outpost (2816 Northwest County Road 661 in Arcadia, 863/494-1215). If your dog will be joining you, try Canoe Safari (3020 Northwest County Road 661 in Arcadia, 800/262-1119). Other outfitters typically nix pets.

The big event here is Pioneer Park Days, a five-day festival usually held around the first weekend in March (call 863/773-2161 for exact dates). The festival gets off to a rousing start with an old-fashioned parade through downtown Wauchula, and continues with displays of antique farm equipment, entertainers, and a 500-booth flea market in the park. Year-round, visitors can tour the Pioneer Park Museum, which has an 1879 cabin and blacksmith display, demonstrations of how cane syrup is made, and an exhibit depicting mastodon bones found in the area by Boy Scouts several years ago. The original bones were sent to the Smithsonian for study. The museum is open Monday–Saturday 9 A.M.–5:30 P.M.

Campsites, facilities: There are 62 campsites for RVs. Most sites have water and electricity, but not sewer hookups. Showers, restrooms, a small museum, a playground, nature trails, fishing ponds, an entertainment pavilion, a picnic area, and a dump station are available. A restaurant, a convenience store, a bank, and bait are within 0.25 mile. Children and leashed pets are permitted. Pets must be kept under control at all times; pet "disturbances" will not be tolerated "at any time." Alcohol is forbidden.

Reservations, fees: Reservations are not accepted. Sites are $7 per night for two people, plus $2 per extra person and $4 for electricity. Credit cards are not accepted. Stays are limited to 150 days per year.

Directions: The park is at the intersection of U.S. 17 and State Road 64 in Zolfo Springs.

Contact: Pioneer Park of Hardee County, c/o Hardee County Public Works Department, 205 Hanchey Road, Wauchula, FL 33873, 863/735-0330. Contact the wildlife refuge and museum at 650 Animal Way, Zolfo Springs, FL 33890, 863/735-0119.

2 BUTTONWOOD BAY

Scenic rating: 9

on Lake Josephine, south of Sebring

"A great place to live" and "your fun-filled winter home" are two of the ways this deluxe

130-acre resort describes itself. Geared to the retired set (but you can stay if you are 19 or older), the park is set in the middle of orange groves on 1,300-acre Lake Josephine. A small stream runs through the property as well.

Paved, lighted streets lead to two pools and two recreation centers, where bingo, cards, and dancing entertain snowbirds from more than half of the United States. Golf aficionados can warm up at an on-site driving range before heading to any of the 15 golf courses within 15 miles. If the 1.5-mile-long nature trail gets to be old hat, try the trails at Highlands Hammock State Park.

Campsites, facilities: This adults-only park has 151 full-hookup RV sites, and 850 manufactured homes with year-round residents. The sites are quite large at 40 by 50 feet, and many have paved patios. Two recreation centers, two heated pools, an exercise room, a nature trail, miniature golf, a driving range, horseshoes, lighted tennis courts, a boccie ball (lawn bowling) court, snacks (in winter), a woodworking shop, pool tables, shuffleboard, and organized activities entertain campers. On the premises are restrooms, showers, a dump station, laundry facilities, a boat ramp, and a dock. Management says the buildings and common areas are wheelchair-accessible. Hook up to the Wi-Fi Internet network in the clubhouse. You can store your RV or boat on-site. Groceries are 5–10 minutes away. Restaurants are about two miles away. Children may visit only for short stays. Pets are welcome.

Reservations, fees: Reservations are recommended. Sites are $36 per night for two people, plus $4 for each additional person. Credit cards are accepted. Long-term stays are OK.

Directions: From Sebring, take U.S. 27 five miles south and look for the RV resort on the right.

Contact: Buttonwood Bay, 10001 U.S. 27 South, Sebring, FL 33870, 866/655-5565 or 863/655-1122, www.buttonwoodbay.com.

🟦 CYPRESS ISLE RV PARK AND MARINA

🏊 🦢 🛥️ 🏠 🚐 ⛺

Scenic rating: 5

on Lake Istokpoga, in Lake Placid

This is a fishing hot spot. Wild shiners and lake access are the amenities the proprietors mention first when asked about their park. Eleven-mile-long Lake Istokpoga is well-known for its bass, bream, and crappie fishing. Boating is a popular pursuit, and each campsite has a covered boat slip. A fair number of cypress trees shade the grassy sites.

Campsites, facilities: Of the 30 sites for RVs or tents, seven have full hookups. All sites have water and 30-amp electricity. Some of the campsites have the lake at their back doors. RVs up to 35 feet long can be accommodated; none of the sites are drive-through. On the premises are restrooms, showers, a dump station, laundry facilities, a recreation room, rental cabins, trailer rentals, a boat ramp, boat rentals, charter fishing services, covered boat slips, a convenience store, and bait and tackle. Groceries and stores are about seven miles away. RV storage is available. Children are welcome. Pets are prohibited.

Reservations, fees: Reservations are recommended, but drive-ins are usually available. Sites are $15–30 per night for two people, plus $7 for each additional person. Credit cards are not accepted. Maximum stay is six months.

Directions: From U.S. 27 in Lake Placid, take East County Road 621 for 7.5 miles east to Cypress Isle Road. Turn left. Go to the end of the road and turn right.

Contact: Cypress Isle RV Park and Marina, East County Road 621, Lake Placid, FL 33852, 863/465-5241.

4 MOSSY COVE FISH CAMP AND RV RESORT

Scenic rating: 7

east of Lake Istokpoga

These seven acres are on the quiet, scenic, little-used eastern side of cypress-ringed Lake Istokpoga. You may spot wildlife along the shore, although most visitors turn their attention toward the fish in the 43-square-mile lake, going after crappies, bass, and bluegill. Several bass fishing tournaments are organized here. You can also charter an airboat ride.

Campsites, facilities: In 2006, new owners modernized and enlarged this fish camp to 48 full-hookup RV spots, plus 11 cabins. Sites have crushed-shell surfaces, and all have 30-amp electrical service. About 80 percent of the occupants live here year-round. On the premises are restrooms, showers, a dump station, laundry facilities, rental cottages, a boat ramp, a wheelchair-accessible dock, a convenience store, and bait and tackle. Activities include the usual holiday dinners and recreation center, with the added twist of "clogging" (sort of like Irish step-dancing) and airboat tours. The open-air clubhouse has been enclosed and is now known as the "Tree House," because it is surrounded by woods. RV storage is available. Children and pets are welcome.

Reservations, fees: Reservations are recommended. Sites are $28 per night for two people, plus $3 for each additional person. Lakeside lots are more expensive, varying by season and availability. Credit cards are not accepted. Long-term stays are OK.

Directions: From Lorida, drive about three miles east on U.S. 98. Turn right (south) on County Road 621. In about five miles, turn right (west) on Godwin Road and proceed to the fish camp.

Contact: Mossy Cove Fish Camp and RV Resort, 3 Mossy Cove Drive, Lorida, FL 33857, 863/655-0119 or 800/833-2683, www.mossy-cove.us.

5 FISHEATING CREEK CAMPGROUND

Scenic rating: 10

on Fisheating Creek, in Palmdale

Fisheating Creek is one of Florida's prettiest natural areas and has attracted generations of picnickers, swimmers, and canoeists. Bring or rent a canoe at the campground, and you can paddle through marshes and past raised banks, where you'll sometimes see rope swings that kids once used to jump into the water (be on the lookout for alligators). Enjoy a picnic on riverbanks fringed by moss-draped oaks and cypress trees. Wildlife abounds along the creek, particularly wading birds, alligators, otters, and turtles. Back in the woods, you'll sometimes see deer, wild hogs, and armadillos. The swimming beach is a delight, located on a normally breezy, oak-shaded, five-acre, spring-fed lake. Astronomy buffs come here because it is one of the few places where city lights won't blot out the stars. The park is part of 18,000 acres of wilderness.

Campsites, facilities: About 60 primitive sites with fire rings and picnic tables are available along the creek and near the swimming lake. Another 50 full-hookup RV sites have 30/50-amp electrical service. Restrooms, showers, laundry facilities, a boat ramp, canoe and kayak rentals, and a campground store are available. A supermarket is located within 15 miles. Swim in the lake, but it's against the rules to swim in the creek. If you plan an overnight canoe trip, call the park first to determine if the water is high enough. Transportation is available to your starting point, and you can leave your car at the campground. Primitive sites are available along the river for trips as long as two days. Children are permitted. Leashed pets are allowed, but must be kept under control at all times.

Reservations, fees: Reservations are recommended. Sites with full hookups are $25. Credit cards are accepted. Long-term rates are available.

Directions: From Moore Haven, go north on U.S. 27 for 16 miles to the entrance. The wildlife management area is one mile north of State Road 29 at Fisheating Creek.

Contact: Fisheating Creek Campground, 7555 North U.S. 27, Palmdale, FL 33944, 863/675-5999, www.fisheatingcreek.com. Or contact the Florida Fish and Wildlife Conservation Commission, 3900 Drane Field Road, Lakeland, FL 33811-1299, 863/648-3203.

6 SUNSHINE RV RESORT

🚴 🏊 🛶 🐕 ♿ 🚐

Scenic rating: 6

south of Lake Placid

Formerly known as Sunburst RV Resort, this home of wintertime dances, crafts, bingo, pot-lucks, gospel music, a "kitchen" band, west-ern/country music jams, and special events is geared toward retirees who spend months or years at these RV sites and mobile homes. An activities director runs these activities in season, and lots of RV rally clubs gather here for fun. Campers who want to go it alone can bicycle past surrounding orange groves. Of the 27 area lakes, perhaps two are most famous for fishing and waterskiing—Lake Placid, about three miles northwest, and 43-square-mile Lake Istokpoga, farther northeast.

Campsites, facilities: At this 300-site mobile-home/RV park, about 125 sites are available for RVs; the rest are occupied by year-round residents. The majority have 30-amp electrical service; 50-amp service is available at 10 sites. Between 15 and 20 sites are considered drive-through. A recreation hall, a heated pool, boccie ball (lawn bowling) courts, billiards, horseshoes, shuffleboard, tennis, and winter social programs entertain campers. Restrooms, showers, a dump station, laundry facilities, park-model rentals, cable TV hookups, and telephone service are available. Groceries are within walking distance. One bathhouse, the laundry, clubhouse, and recreation hall are

wheelchair-accessible. Restaurants and shopping are about three miles away. RV storage is available. Children are permitted and leashed pets under 40 pounds are accepted.

Reservations, fees: Reservations are recommended. Sites are $25–28 per night for two people, plus $5 per extra person and $2 for cable TV. Credit cards are accepted. Long-term stays are OK.

Directions: From Lake Placid, drive south on U.S. 27 for 6.5 miles to State Road 70. Turn left. The park is 0.5 mile ahead, on the right.

Contact: Sunshine RV Resort, 303 State Road 70 East, Lake Placid, FL 33852, 863/465-4815 or 877/317-2757, fax 863/465-1077, www.sunshinervresorts.com.

7 CAMP FLORIDA RESORT

🏊 🛶 🚤 🐕 🚐

Scenic rating: 8

south of Lake Placid

This resort employs an unusual circular lay-out—a nice change from the rectangular same-ness of other RV parks. Set on Lake Grassy, everything is spotless—from the landscaping to the infrastructure. Lots are sort of pie-shaped, giving you breathing space from your neighbors, and each circle is separated from the next one by a road. Nearby are 27 lakes for fishing and boating, 12 golf courses, and historical attractions, but there's more than enough to do in the park, including tennis, a nature trail, a marina, and docks. Park models are for rent.

Campsites, facilities: There are 180 full-hookup RV sites, all available for overnighters and seasonal visitors. Most sites have concrete pads and picnic tables. Restrooms, showers, laundry facilities, and telephone service are available. On the premises are a pool, a boat ramp, a clubhouse, shuffleboard courts, a dog-walk area, and miniature golf. A grocery store and many restaurants are within 0.5 mile.

Children are welcome, though retirees are more frequent than families. Leashed pets under 20 pounds are permitted.

Reservations, fees: Reservations are recommended. Sites are $28 per night. Credit cards are accepted. Long-term rates are available.

Directions: From Lake Placid, drive south on U.S. 27 about five miles to the park. From the intersection of U.S. 27 and State Road 70, drive north on U.S. 27 about six miles.

Contact: Camp Florida Resort, 100 Shoreline Drive, Lake Placid, FL 33852, 863/699-1991 or 800/226-5188, fax 863/699-1995, www.campfla.com.

8 NINE MILE GRADE CAMPGROUND

Scenic rating: 8

east of Lorida, on the Kissimmee River

In exchange for the longer trips you'll have to make for such conveniences as groceries, you'll get a secluded, quiet campground alongside the Kissimmee River. It's the kind of place where you can roast marshmallows at campfire rings for a relaxing, old-style camping experience. Many visitors rave about it (though they'd understandably like to keep its location secret). You can fish along 1,500 feet of riverfront shoreline to catch bass, bluegill, peacock bass, and oscars.

The campground is set in one of the old oak hammocks that mark the edge of the historic floodplain of the Kissimmee River, where fishing, boating, and canoeing are popular. The once meandering stream has been straitjacketed by federal engineers into a big, angular ditch. But the U.S. Army Corps of Engineers and the South Florida Water Management District are working to restore the river to its natural state, in which it overflows and drenches the marshy areas along its banks, providing a home for waterfowl and other creatures. However, the restoration project will not cause changes at Nine Mile Grade, since it does not reach this far past the Lake Okeechobee locks, which control water flow.

Canoeists in particular might enjoy exploring some of the river's old oxbows, which are set to be reinvigorated during the restoration. Bring your own watercraft, or make plans to rent a boat in the area. Near the campground are eight miles of hiking and biking trails. You also can cross the river north of here to hike along the Florida National Scenic Trail.

Campsites, facilities: This campground offers eight RV sites with water and electricity (two are drive-through), and eight primitive sites for tents or self-contained units. Each site, which measures 20 by 30 feet, has a picnic table, a fire ring, and a grill. On the premises are restrooms, showers, a dump station, a boat ramp, a playground, basketball courts, and baseball and soccer fields. All areas are wheelchair-accessible. Groceries and restaurants are six miles away. The nearest laundry facilities are eight miles away. Children and pets are permitted.

Reservations, fees: Reservations are not accepted. Sites are $10 per night for six people. Credit cards are not accepted. Long-term stays are OK.

Directions: From Okeechobee, take State Road 70 west 16 miles to County Road 721 north. Turn right and go 4.5 miles to Butlers Bluff Road (on the right). Turn left. Proceed to the end of the road.

Contact: Nine Mile Grade Campground, 992 Butlers Bluff Road, Lorida, FL 33857, 863/763-3113.

9 WHISPER CREEK RV RESORT

Scenic rating: 4

near the Caloosahatchee River, in La Belle

Besides a little lake and the surrounding woods, this 57-acre park has the advantage of being just one mile north of the Caloosa-hatchee River, which is a plus for some anglers. If that won't do, head 30 minutes east to the bass haven of Lake Okeechobee. Don't worry if fishing is not your only interest: The owners say this is a "destination" park, where 75 percent of guests are snowbirds, and there are plenty of scheduled activities for landlubbers. Sunny sites will warm your bones in winter.

Campsites, facilities: All 473 sites in this wheel-chair-accessible, adults-only park have full hook-ups, including telephone and cable TV, plus 30/50-amp electrical service. About 30 sites are available for overnight stays. Lots are 40 by 50 feet, with 10-by-30-foot concrete patios. None are drive-through, but they can accommodate rigs up to 40 feet long. About 80 percent of the sites are occupied by year-round residents. Pop-up campers are discouraged. Facilities include a solar-heated pool, horseshoes, shuffleboard, and a 5,000-square-foot clubhouse, which has a large auditorium with an elevated stage, a community kitchen, a game room with pool tables, and a library. Socialize with fellow age-55-plus campers at Saturday-night dances, bingo, exercise classes, potluck suppers, arts and crafts, shuffleboard tournaments, Bible study, and nondenominational church services on Sunday mornings. Showers, restrooms, a dump station, laundry facilities, and propane delivery also are available. Internet access is available in the office. Grocery stores, a restaurant, bait, and tackle are located one mile away. All the public areas, including the pool, laundry, recreation hall, and restrooms, are readily accessible to the physically challenged—an amenity in which the owners take pride. Children are permitted for short visits. Two leashed pets per household are permitted.

Reservations, fees: Reservations are recommended. Sites are $30 per night. Credit cards are not accepted. Long-term stays are encouraged.

Directions: From State Road 80 in the town of La Belle, turn north onto State Road 29. Continue for about one mile to the park entrance.

Contact: Whisper Creek RV Resort, 1980 Hickory Drive/State Road 29 North, La Belle, FL 33975, 863/675-6888, fax 863/675-2323, www.whispercreek.com.

10 GRANDMA'S GROVE RV PARK

🏃 🏊 🎣 ⛺ 🐕 ♿ 🚐

Scenic rating: 4

near the Caloosahatchee River, in La Belle

Guests can pluck free fruit off orange trees in the surrounding 40-acre grove during the citrus season, where fragrant orange blossoms peak in March and April. A walking trail passes by the grove and circles much of the 18-acre, adults-only RV park. This campground has been in business more than 25 years under the same ownership; most visitors are repeat customers and people who hear about the park by word of mouth. Anglers tend to strike out for the nearby Caloosahatchee River or farther east for Lake Okeechobee, about 30 minutes away. Potluck dinners and street names like Grandma's Boulevard and Feather Bed Lane lend a folksy air. Groceries and restaurants are within two miles. Like other grandmothers, this Grandma lays down some strict rules: No converted school buses are permitted, clotheslines must be hung at the rear of units, and quiet hours begin at 10 P.M.

Campsites, facilities: All 208 RV sites at this wheelchair-accessible, age-55-plus park offer full hookups with 30-amp electrical service. Each site has a picnic table and a concrete patio with gravel driveway. Most sites are roomy at 50 by 75 feet, and elbow room between neighbors is easily 20 feet. About 25 percent of the occupants are year-round residents. A pool, dances, arts and crafts, exercises, shuffleboard, horseshoe pits, a social club, fitness classes, bingo, potluck dinners, dances, and a walking trail entertain guests. Showers, restrooms, a campfire ring, a barbecue grill, laundry facilities, propane delivery, and on-site cable TV and telephone service (for long-term campers) are available. The restrooms and recreation hall are wheelchair-accessible. This is an adults-only park. Pets should use the designated dog walk near an orange grove.

Reservations, fees: Reservations are recommended. Sites are $25 per night for two people. Credit cards are not accepted. Long-term rates are available.

Directions: From Fort Myers, drive 22 miles east on State Road 80 to the campground on the left.

Contact: Grandma's Grove RV Park, 2250 State Road 80 West, La Belle, FL 33935, 863/675-2567.

11 ORTONA SOUTH CAMPGROUND

Scenic rating: 9

on the Caloosahatchee River, east of La Belle

Visitors tend to fall into one of two groups: The first set adores this remote and peaceful 25-acre recreation area, with a view of cow pastures and the off-chance of hearing a distant rooster crow. The other likes the quick access to boating and fishing from this U.S. Army Corps of Engineers campground on the Caloosahatchee River. Ortona's faithful fans (many of them retirees) normally keep the 51 sites filled through winter. Don't count on finding an open spot in time to hear blue-grass music at the one-day Ortona Cane Grinding Festival, held each February. The sunwashed campsites are lined up in rows, creating sort of a parking-lot feel; however, all areas are wheelchair-accessible to federal standards. Tenters need free-standing tents; all sites have concrete pads. A pair of bald eagles nests nearby, to the delight of birders. Don't miss the drama of walking across the narrow, steel-grate footbridge directly over the rushing waters of the Caloosahatchee River lock and dam. An ongoing project is the planting of magnolia, red maple, cypress, and cocoplum trees to replace nonnative plants; this work

is being carried out by Scout troops and the local Civil Air Patrol.

Campsites, facilities: All 51 sites have water and 30/50-amp electrical hookups, picnic tables, grills, fire rings, and concrete pads surrounded by gravel. If you're using a tent, note that you will not be able to use ground stakes. None of the sites is drive-through. Besides two fishing piers and a boat ramp, the campground offers showers, restrooms, a dump station, and laundry facilities. Three wheelchair-accessible campsites are near restrooms; other accessible areas are the laundry room and one fishing pier. Groceries are available nine miles away in La Belle; convenience stores are within five miles. Children are allowed. Leashed pets are permitted.

Reservations, fees: Reservations are accepted (877/444-6777, www.reserveusa.com/nrrs/fl/orto). The fee is $16 per night during the season and $12 May 1–September 30. Credit cards are accepted. Stays are limited to 14 days in a 30-day period.

Directions: From La Belle, go east on State Road 80 for 10 miles to Dalton Lane. Turn north and follow the signs to the campground. From Clewiston, drive nine miles north on U.S. 27. At State Road 80, turn west and drive 14 miles to Dalton Lane.

Contact: Ortona South Campground, 4330 Dalton Lane SW, Moore Haven, FL 33471, 863/675-8400, www.saj.usace.army.mil/recreation/ortonas/orindex.htm. For more information, contact the U.S. Army Corps of Engineers, South Florida Operations Office, 525 Ridgelawn Road, Clewiston, FL 33440-5399, 863/983-8101.

12 MEADOWLARK CAMPGROUND

Scenic rating: 4

on the Caloosahatchee River, in Moore Haven

Regulars escape the snowy Midwest, Canada, and the Northeast to winter at this neatly laid-out park, one of the few set on the Caloosahatchee River. This relaxed place allows boats to be parked on the oversized lots. In the summertime, locals and families play here. Under owner Dan Short, 32 boat docks and two boat ramps were improved in 2005, and Internet connectivity was added.

Campsites, facilities: This adults-only park has 160 full-hookup sites (two pull-through) for RVs up to 42 feet long; about two-thirds are available for overnighters and seasonal visitors. All sites have 30-amp electrical service. Half have cement pads. A game room, horseshoes, shuffleboard, quilting classes, and wintertime activities entertain campers. Showers, restrooms, picnic tables, cable TV, a dump station, a pool, propane gas sales, and laundry facilities are available. Most of the facilities are wheelchair-accessible. RV storage is available. Groceries can be purchased 12 miles away. Children are permitted to visit. Leashed pets are permitted but may not be tied up outside.

Reservations, fees: Reservations are recommended. Sites are $28 per night for two people, plus $3 for each additional person. Credit cards are not accepted. Long-term rates are available, and you can stay as long as you like.

Directions: From La Belle, take State Road 29 north. Turn right (east) at State Road 78. Turn right at Ortona Road. The campground is two miles ahead (stay straight at the fork in the road).

Contact: Meadowlark Campground, 12525 Williams Road Southwest, Moore Haven, FL 33471, 863/675-2243 or 800/889-5636.

13 LAKE OKEECHOBEE SCENIC TRAIL-CULVERT 5A

Scenic rating: 7

on southwestern Lake Okeechobee, near Moore Haven

You're virtually certain to see alligators, birds, and furry critters while hiking or bicycling along this remote stretch of the 110-mile-long Herbert Hoover Dike. You'll sleep in marsh country. The site is on the rim canal, easily accessible by boat. To the east, a broad expanse of reeds leads to the far-off open waters of Lake Okeechobee. To the west, you should be able to make out the fuzzy outlines of Nicodemus Slough, a meandering waterway working its way slowly through lots of marsh.

Mosquitoes may drive you crazy in summer here. But officials say that the birds, fish, and animals that lure thousands of people to the Big O each year wouldn't be so numerous if it weren't for the three- to eight-mile-wide littoral zone bordering the lake's southern and western shores. Just bring your DEET. Some consider western Lake Okeechobee the prettiest part of the Southeast's largest lake. If you're continuing to the next rustic campsite by foot or bicycle, travel 12 miles southeast to Lake Okeechobee Scenic Trail-Liberty Point. If you're traveling northbound, it's about six miles to Lake Okeechobee Scenic Trail-Lakeport.

Campsites, facilities: This primitive tent-camping area is accessible by foot, boat, and bicycle. A fire ring and a shelter with a picnic table are provided. There are no toilets, piped water, or other facilities. Bring water, food, camping supplies, sunscreen, and mosquito repellent. Children and leashed pets are permitted.

Reservations, fees: Camping is first-come, first-served. There is no fee.

Directions: The campsite is on the rim canal on the lakeside of the levee, two miles south of the intersection of Highway 78 and the Herbert Hoover Dike. For detailed directions and a map, contact the U.S. Army Corps of Engineers. You can also download a map of the trail at www.saj.usace.army.mil/sfoo/images/maps/lostmap.pdf.

Contact: U.S. Army Corps of Engineers, South Florida Operations Office, 525 Ridgelawn Road, Clewiston, FL 33440, 941/983-8101, www.saj.usace.army.mil.

14 LAKEPORT RV RESORT

Scenic rating: 5

near Lake Okeechobee, in Lakeport

This over-55 park has sunny spots overlooking the Rim Canal; some lots are on the waterfront. The park's claim to fame: Really big (70- by 40-foot) sites. Visitors (mostly retirees) escape blustery winters in Michigan, New York, Ohio, and other snowy parts of the country here, and about 90 percent of the sites are occupied or reserved year-round. Bass anglers can head out of the canal to get to Florida's largest lake—Okeechobee. Hike or cycle on the dike above the lake, but the managers strongly suggest: "Fish! Fish!" Groceries and restaurants are within one mile. The famous Gatorama tourist attraction is about eight miles away (see the listing for *Clewiston/Lake Okeechobee KOA* in this chapter).

Campsites, facilities: There are 86 sunny full-hookup RV sites, 10 of which are available for overnight stays. Most spots have cement pads, and the 12-acre park has paved roads. Two tents are permitted to be set up on a large field with no hookups. Facilities include showers, restrooms, a laundry, a boat ramp, a dock, and a recreation building where bingo, cards, a quilting club, and organized dinners are on tap. The restrooms and recreation hall are wheelchair-accessible. Children may stay no longer than one month. Leashed pets with good dispositions are permitted. Bring proof of up-to-date rabies shots.

Reservations, fees: Reservations are recommended. Sites are $25–30 per night for up to four people. Credit cards are not accepted. Long-term rates are available.

Directions: From Moore Haven, drive about nine miles north on State Road 78 to Lakeport. Turn left at State Road 74. In 0.5 mile, turn left by the water tower onto Ted Beck Road, which curves into Milum Drive. The campground is the first RV park on Milum Drive.

Contact: Lakeport RV Resort, 2800 Milum Drive, Moore Haven, FL 33471, 863/946-1415, lakeportrvresort@direcway.com.

15 ARUBA RV PARK

Scenic rating: 4

near Lake Okeechobee, in Lakeport

Fishing is popular here. A boat launch and moorings, plus two fish-cleaning areas, make this obvious. Anglers hoping for bass and speckled perch use the campground boat ramp for access to Lake Okeechobee, but you can also fish from a bank. Like most RV parks circling Lake Okeechobee, this place is mostly flat and sunny, with a relatively sparse sprinkling of palms, oaks, and towering Australian pines. A nearby trailhead leads hikers and bicyclists to the top of the Herbert Hoover Dike encircling the lake. The views are often rewarding: Boaters are said to have spotted as many as 32 types of birds during an outing on the lake. If you tire of roughing it, drive about 15 minutes to use the video games and poker tables at Brighton Seminole Bingo (863/467-9998), located at the Indian tribe's reservation off Highway 721, west of Lake Okeechobee.

Campsites, facilities: All 137 RV sites have full hookups and picnic tables. Sites are exceptionally large at 40 by 52 feet. Some are grassy and have shade; most have concrete slabs. Park models are for sale. A heated pool and exercise room, fishing guide services, bank fishing, pontoon-boat fishing or sightseeing, a dance floor, shuffleboard, a clubhouse, horseshoes, and a community fire ring entertain campers. Moorings are available for most boats. Showers, restrooms, a boat ramp, on-water fuel pumps, tackle, bait, a dump station, and laundry facilities are on the premises. A small grocery store is across the street. Children are permitted. Dogs should use the pet walk next to the dump station.

Reservations, fees: Reservations are recommended. Sites are $30–35 per night for two people, plus $5 for each additional adult and $3 per child. Credit cards are accepted. Long-term stays are OK.

Directions: From Okeechobee, take Highway 78 west about 25 miles to County Road 74 in Lakeport, then turn right. The park is ahead at left.

Contact: Aruba RV Park, 1825 Old Lakeport Road, Lakeport, FL 33471, 863/946-1324, fax 863/946-1270, www.okeedirect.com.

16 NORTH LAKE ESTATES RV RESORT

Scenic rating: 6

near Lake Okeechobee, in Lakeport

The paved, lighted streets at this 36-acre RV community have names like Mallard Drive and Perch Lane—a reflection of its visitors' interest in fishing and duck hunting on nearby Lake Okeechobee. Boaters launch from North Lake Marina adjacent to the park. Don't expect to rough it. This may be the neatest, cleanest, most manicured RV park on this side of the lake. With trash pickup, a $325,000 clubhouse, resident managers, and concrete pads that extend to the streets, the RV park feels like a residential community. Many people stay at least two months. Nearly all campers are retirees. For a view of the park's ornamental lake, request a waterfront site on Bass Drive or Widgeon Lane. Alternatively, most Pintail Lane sites back onto a canal. Campers on Mallard Drive and Widgeon Lane have the shortest walk to the pool.

Campsites, facilities: This 300-unit, adult-oriented park accepts RVs at all 100 full-hookup sites, each with a 700-square-foot concrete pad. All sites have 30/50-amp electrical service. RVs up to 40 feet long can be accommodated. A boat ramp, clubhouse (with a deck and pool), horseshoes, shuffleboard, a game room, an exercise room, a crafts room, and wintertime activities entertain guests. Showers, restrooms, picnic tables, on-site park-model sales, and laundry facilities are available. Management says buildings are wheelchair-accessible. Streets are paved. Convenience stores, restaurants, groceries, and a public boat ramp are within two miles. This is an over-age-55 park; children tend to visit long-term campers for a week or so, then leave. Leashed pets are permitted.

Reservations, fees: Reservations are recommended. Sites are $30 per night for two people, plus $3 per extra person. Credit cards are not accepted. Long-term rates are available.

Directions: From Moore Haven, go north for nine miles on State Road 78 to the campground, at right.

Contact: North Lake Estates RV Resort, 765 East State Road 78, Moore Haven, FL 33471, 863/946-0700.

17 GATOR'S RV

Scenic rating: 2

near Lake Okeechobee, in Lakeport

Devoted to this casual spot, retirees and snowbirds come to snag easy-to-catch speckled perch at Lake Okeechobee and fry up dinners of the flaky white meat. Boaters launch from Harney Pond Canal one block from the campground to fish or hunt ducks at the nation's second-largest natural lake. About two-thirds of the park are occupied by year-round residents. Visitors tend to come from Ohio, Illinois, and Kentucky.

Campsites, facilities: Thirteen full-hookup sites (three pull-through) are for RVs as long as 26 feet. Thirty-amp electrical service, showers, restrooms, a dump station, cable TV access, and limited laundry facilities are available. Most campers use a laundry business one block away. Boat launches, a convenience store, restaurants, and bait are also one block away. There's a supermarket within five miles. Children are permitted, although there is little for them to do; management says kids usually visit long-term campers for a week or so, then leave. Leashed pets are permitted.

Reservations, fees: Reservations are recommended in winter, but are not necessary in summer. Sites are $20 per night. Credit cards are not accepted. Long-term rates are available.

Directions: From Okeechobee, go south on U.S. 441. Turn right at State Road 78 and continue about 27 miles to the entrance. The campground is one block west of Harney Pond Canal.

Contact: Gator's RV, 900 East State Road 78, Lakeport, FL 33471, 863/983-9155. Mailing address: P.O. Box 974, Moore Haven, FL 33471.

18 LAKE OKEECHOBEE SCENIC TRAIL-LAKEPORT

Scenic rating: 7

on the western bank of Lake Okeechobee

Awakening to a pastel sun rising over Florida's largest lake is an experience you're unlikely to get at a motel room or an established campground, no matter what you pay. Here you can get it for free.

The Herbert Hoover Dike rises an average of 34 feet to hold in Lake Okeechobee and avoid a repeat of the massive hurricane-spawned floods that killed nearly 2,000 people in 1928. Although the dike irritatingly blocks views of the lake for anyone driving around it, hikers and mountain bikers making their way along the top of the sun-washed dike will see the lake all day long and sleep at the water's edge on somewhat uneven ground (bring an air mattress). This western side of Lake Okeechobee is the most scenic. Look for ducks and long-legged wading birds. If you continue your trek around the lake, it's about six miles south to the next rustic campsite, Lake Okeeechobee Scenic Trail-Culvert 5A. To the north, it's 12.2 miles to Indian Prairie.

Campsites, facilities: This primitive tent-camping area is reached by foot or bicycle; boats can access the area from the lake by going through the lock at Lakeport. A fire ring and a shelter with a picnic table are provided. There is no restroom or piped water. Bring water, food, a hat, sunscreen, camping supplies, and mosquito repellent. Children and leashed pets are OK.

Reservations, fees: Camping is first-come, first-served. There is no fee.

Directions: The campsite is 0.75 mile north of the intersection of Highway 78 and the Herbert Hoover Dike at Lakeport. The camping spot is on the borrow canal, on the land side of the levee. For detailed directions and a map, contact the U.S. Army Corps of Engineers. You can also download a map of the trail at www.saj.usace.army.mil/sfoo/images/maps/lostmap.pdf.

Contact: U.S. Army Corps of Engineers, South Florida Operations Office, 525 Ridgelawn Road, Clewiston, FL 33440-5399, 863/983-8101, www.saj.usace.army.mil.

19 INDIAN PRAIRIE CANAL PRIMITIVE SITES

🚶 🚴 🎣 🐕 🚐 ⛺

Scenic rating: 6

on the northern side of Lake Okeechobee

Duck hunters flock to this primitive campground in one of the prettiest regions of Lake Okeechobee, so don't count on solitude. What you will get is a campground host and no-frills campsites with shell-rock pads. Look for birds commonly found in the Everglades—for instance, the black-headed, white-feathered, gawky-looking wood stork, and the brown, goose-sized, white-spotted limpkin, whose eerie wail may give you a start the first time you hear it. The camping area is part of the Lake Okeechobee Scenic Trail (LOST), which allows hikers or bicyclists with a few days to spare to encircle the huge lake by camping at nine rustic camping areas and four more developed campgrounds located no more than 10 miles apart. If you're fishing, bring a fishing license and check current regulations. The LOST trail is one of Florida's jewels and one of the more unusual trails in the nation. The trail is on top of the berm around the lake, and it's possible to hike or bike the complete circle of 110 miles, or access the trail at various points around the lake. Three trailhead information shelters are at the Clewiston office of the U.S. Army Corps of Engineers, adjacent to the Okee-Tantie Campground, and at Nubbins Slough Access Area. You can also download the map of shelters and access points at www.sfwmd.gov.com. In addition to the campsites, about 30 shade shelters have been built around the lake; each is about 2–3 miles apart. The gates at the top of the levee have been replaced to allow a two-foot gap for bikers, and much exotic, non-native vegetation has been removed to allow vistas of the pretty lake.

Campsites, facilities: Ten primitive campsites and a group camping area are available for tents and RVs. There are no hookups and no shade. Facilities include a vault toilet, a fire ring, a boat ramp, a trash receptacle, and picnic tables. There is no piped water, so bring plenty of your own, plus food and camping supplies. Pack out trash. Children and leashed pets are permitted. If you crave shade and are hardy, hike to the LOST campsite about 0.5 mile south of here. There's a shade shelter, fire ring, and mowed area to set up one tent.

Reservations, fees: Sites are first-come, first-served. Camping is free.

Directions: The campsite is 0.5 mile south of the Indian Prairie Canal, on the land side of the levee. From the town of Okeechobee, go south on State Road 78. Cross over the Kissimmee River and pass through the settlement of Buckhead Ridge. The Indian Prairie Canal is the next major canal. Go over the bridge to the canal, then turn left into the campground. You can also download a map of the trail at www.saj.usace.army.mil/sfoo/images/maps/lostmap.pdf.

Contact: U.S. Army Corps of Engineers, South Florida Operations Office, 525 Ridgelawn Road, Clewiston, FL 33440, 863/983-8101, www.saj.usace.army.mil.

20 BUCKHEAD RIDGE MARINA

🎣 🎣 🚐 🏠 🐕 ♿ 🚐

Scenic rating: 4

at Lake Okeechobee, in Buckhead Ridge

Some down-home anglers cotton to Buckhead Ridge, a small, backwoods town that hasn't been ruined yet by overdevelopment. At sunny Buckhead Ridge Marina, everyone fishes. The flat campground has a smattering of palms and other native trees. About 90 sites overlook a canal and have water views. A few sites are occupied by year-round residents; annual leases and mobile-home spots are available.

Folks tend to be here for one thing: to go out onto the lake, found beyond a set of locks farther down the canal rimming the campground. Veteran bass guide Captain Mac Russell (863/467-4516) can tell you whether you should use a junebug worm for bass, or if bluegills are biting at the mouth of the campground-area canal. Pontoon boats, johnboats, and canoes are available for rent.

Campsites, facilities: All 120 full-hookup campsites are paved; most have 30-amp electrical service. Ten tents can be set up in a grassy area. Each site has a picnic table. Recreational offerings include a pool, fishing guide services, a recreation hall, and boat rentals. You'll also find a restaurant, a snack bar, a boat ramp, boat storage, waterfront mobile-home rentals, a dump station, and laundry facilities. Most areas are wheelchair-accessible. Children are welcome. Pets are permitted.

Reservations, fees: Reservations are recommended. Sites are $15–25 per night. Credit cards are accepted. Long-term stays are OK.

Directions: From Okeechobee, turn right onto State Road 78 and continue about 10 miles. Turn left on State Road 78B and drive 1.5 miles to the marina/campground on the left. The campground is one mile past the Kissimmee River.

Contact: Buckhead Ridge Marina, 670 State Road 78B, Okeechobee, FL 34974, 863/763-2826 or 800/367-1358, www.buckhead ridgerv.com.

21 LAKE OKEECHOBEE SCENIC TRAIL-KISSIMMEE RIVER

🚶 🚴 🐴 ⛺

Scenic rating: 7

on the northern bank of Lake Okeechobee

You'll sleep near the Kissimmee River, which, along with Lake Okeechobee and the Everglades, is part of an ecosystem that stretches north to Disney World and south to the tip of Florida. The Kissimmee, a ruler-straight river-turned-canal, once was a shallow, meandering stream about 100 miles long. Now straightened and deepened by dozens of feet, its course runs only about 50 miles. Ecologically speaking, this alteration has meant trouble. All of the perimeter marsh that needs to be flooded with fresh, clean water—once provided by the river—now doesn't get flushed out. So where you used to see tens of thousands of ducks and wading birds along the Kissimmee, you'll see fewer today in the slow-moving and impeded waterway. Federal engineers and state biologists are working to return the Kissimmee to a more natural state. Many more birds have returned since, and the river now counts as part of a great birding trail.

Look for wading birds and other creatures as you hike along the levee that holds in "the liquid heart of South Florida," as the lake is known. Indeed, birders consider the northwestern lake region one of the best birding areas in Florida. If you're making the trip around the entire lake by foot or bicycle, the next rustic camp spot is 9.9 miles southwest at Indian Prairie. Heading east, it's nine miles to Lake Okeechobee Scenic Trail-Nubbin Slough.

Campsites, facilities: This primitive tent-camping area is reached by foot or bicycle. A fire ring and a shelter with a picnic table are provided. There is no restroom or piped water. Bring water, food, a hat, sunscreen, camping supplies, and mosquito repellent. Children and leashed pets are OK.

Reservations, fees: Camping is first-come, first-served. There is no fee.

Directions: The campsite is off Highway 78, just southwest of the Kissimmee River. Specifically, the campsite is one-half mile south of Highway 78 on the lakeside of the levee. For detailed directions, a map, and a brochure, contact the U.S. Army Corps of Engineers before your trip. You can also download a map of the trail at www.saj.usace.army.mil/sfoo/images/maps/lostmap.pdf.

Contact: U.S. Army Corps of Engineers, South Florida Operations Office, 525 Ridgelawn Road, Clewiston, FL 33440-5399, 863/983-8101, www.saj.usace.army.mil.

22 OKEE-TANTIE CAMPGROUND AND MARINA

Scenic rating: 5

at Lake Okeechobee and the Kissimmee River, west of Highway 441

This county-owned, peninsular park is a local landmark on the north shore of Lake Okeechobee at the mouth of the Kissimmee River, with boat ramps providing direct access to both bodies of water. It could be a good base camp for fishing, as well as a chance to enjoy the outdoors and view wildlife. Hikers and bicyclists can get a rare view of Lake Okeechobee from atop the 34-foot-high, 107-mile-long Herbert Hoover Dike, which is also part of the Lake Okeechobee Scenic Trail and the Great Florida Birding Trail. Campsites are very sunny, and a hat and sunscreen are always recommended. Paved roads lead to the gravel/grassy sites. The park has a restaurant and serves as tournament headquarters for various bass-fishing contests.

Campsites, facilities: There are 280 large RV sites (164 full-hookup, with 20 pull-through, and 107 with water and electricity). More than half the sites have 50-amp electrical service, the rest have 30-amp. Six sites are accessible by wheelchair, as are the docks, boat ramp, and store. Additionally, 38 primitive tent sites are available. All sites have a picnic table and a grill. You'll find showers, restrooms, laundry facilities, a day-use picnic area and playground, public boat ramps and fish-cleaning stations, boat rentals, a marina and fuel dock, bait and tackle, limited groceries and firewood, and a seafood restaurant. Propane can be delivered to your site once a week. The nearest full grocery store is about four miles away. Children are welcome. Leashed pets are permitted.

Reservations, fees: Reservations are recommended. May 1–October 31, sites are $18 per night for two people (base rate), plus $5 for each additional adult and $3 per child (under age six is free). The base rate November 1–April 30 is $31. Credit cards are accepted. Long-term rates are available.

Directions: From State Road 70 and U.S. 441/Parrott Avenue in the town of Okeechobee, go south on U.S. 441/Parrott Avenue. Turn right on State Road 78 West and continue about 4.5 miles to the campground entrance on the left, just before the Kissimmee River bridge.

Contact: Okee-Tantie Campground and Marina, 10430 Highway 78 West, Okeechobee, FL 34974, 863/763-2622, fax 863/763-8136, okeetantie@yahoo.com.

23 BIG "O" RV RESORT

Scenic rating: 6

southwest of Okeechobee

With lake access, a boat ramp, and a fish-cleaning station, this 55-plus condominium park is all about fishing—but when they aren't biting, there are plenty of other things to do. October–April, the park's activities director plans live entertainment, special dinners, bingo, line dancing, and more. On Sundays, church services are held. Some sites overlook the Rim Canal. Shopping and golf courses are nearby in the town of Okeechobee.

Campsites, facilities: This 55-and-older, wheelchair-accessible park has 324 full-hookup RV or park model spots with picnic tables and concrete pads; many sites have been sold for condominium ownership. About 50 overnight spots are available. Restrooms, showers, a dump station, laundry facilities, and a wireless Internet network. On the premises are a heated pool, a boat ramp, a fish-cleaning station, a clubhouse, horseshoe pits, shuffleboard courts, a dog-walk area, and a putting green. Children are not welcome. Leashed pets are permitted.

Reservations, fees: Reservations are recommended. Sites are $36 per night for two people during the winter, and $25 April 1–November 1. Major credit cards are accepted. Long-term (up to six months) or seasonal stays are preferred.

Directions: From the intersection of U.S. Highway 441 and State Road 78, continue southwest on State Road 78 for about 3.5 miles. The resort will be on your left. From Moore Haven, drive toward the town of Okeechobee on State Road 78 for about 35 miles; the park will be on your right.

Contact: Big "O" RV Resort, 7950 Southwest Highway 78, Okeechobee, FL 34974, 863/467-5515, fax 863/467-1183.

24 BIG LAKE LODGE AND RV PARK

Scenic rating: 7

southwest of Okeechobee

Want to keep your boat close by? This well-maintained, all-ages fish camp has a boat dock at almost every campsite, making it easy to carry out those cleaning, loading, and maintenance chores. You'll overlook the wide blue waters of the rim canal leading to Lake Okeechobee and catch glimpses of the fantastic variety of birds that make this area their home. The park attracts anglers and birdwatchers and brags that it's only 40 miles east of the Atlantic Ocean, making it convenient for snowbirds visiting the Fort Pierce or West Palm Beach area. Owner Betty Arrington describes the fish camp as "down to earth, in a country atmosphere . ... We don't compete with Holiday Inn or the Joneses." Stores are nine miles away. Only about 10 percent of the park is occupied by year-round residents.

Campsites, facilities: There are 37 roomy RV sites for rigs up to 45 feet long; eight sites are pull-through. Each has concrete pads, full hookups with 50-amp electrical service, grills, and cable TV, and 32 are waterfront with boat docks. Internet service is available at the sites.

Four tents can be accommodated in an area separate from the RVs; these sites have water and electricity. Restrooms, showers, laundry facilities, and telephone service are available. On the premises are a boat ramp, a fish-cleaning station, rental units, and planned activities, such as fish fries, barbecues, and potluck suppers. Children are welcome. Leashed pets under 20 pounds are permitted, but they are not encouraged and should stay in the RV most of the time.

Reservations, fees: Reservations are recommended. Sites are $25 per night. Credit cards are not accepted. Long-term rates are available, and you can stay as long as you like.

Directions: From the town of Okeechobee, drive south on U.S. 441 to the park at the intersection with County Road 15A.

Contact: Big Lake Lodge and RV Park, 8680 Highway 441 Southeast, Okeechobee, FL 34974, 863/763-4638 or 866/256-5566.

25 LAKEVIEW MANOR RV PARK (FORMERLY WINDSOR)

Scenic rating: 2

southwest of Okeechobee

Open October 15–May 1, this sunny park attracts boaters and anglers who sign year-long or seasonal leases. They leave their rigs on the premises year-round to avoid the hassle of hauling them back home at the end of the season. A boat ramp leading to Lake Okeechobee is across from the park entrance, and plenty of boat trailer storage is available.

Campsites, facilities: There are 42 sites for RVs, two of them pull-through. All have full hookups, 50-amp electrical service, grills, picnic tables, and concrete patios. Restrooms, showers, a dump station, laundry facilities, and telephone service are available. On the premises are a fish-cleaning station, a recreation hall, horseshoe pits, shuffleboard courts, a gazebo, and planned social activities. Campers must be 55 years and older. Pets are not welcome.

Reservations, fees: Reservations are recommended. Sites are $20 per night for two people. Only two people per site are permitted. Credit cards are not accepted. Long-term rates are available.

Directions: From Okeechobee, head south on Highway 78 West for six miles to the park.

Contact: Lakeview Manor RV Park, 10000 Highway 78 West, Okeechobee, FL 34974, 863/467-1833, fax 863/384-1241.

26 LAKE OKEECHOBEE RESORT KOA

Scenic rating: 7

in Okeechobee

Beyond the security gate sits the continent's largest KOA, covering 117 acres. You won't find a simple recreation hall here, but a 20,000-square-foot convention center and RV rally site where dances, bingo, meetings, and the clatter of table-tennis balls bring the place alive. And there's not just a pool. Instead, one heated pool serves families, and a separate adults-only pool has a tiki-style bar set in a fountain-filled pond.

The horseshoe-shaped park is built around the putting greens and fairways of a nine-hole golf course. From the big windows of the park's fitness center (formerly a restaurant), you can overlook the golf course from behind the first tee. Wintertime campers have been known to show up from every state east of the Mississippi River to camp at the grassy or paved sites. Some coastal urbanites use the place as a weekend fishing or boating getaway. Lake Okeechobee, where several largemouth bass tournaments are held each year, is 0.25 mile south. Disney World is less than two hours north.

Campsites, facilities: About half of the 748 full-hookup sites are for RVs up to 45 feet long; the rest are for permanent residents. Tents stay in the same sites as the RVs. Recreational facilities include two pools, a hot tub, a nine-hole golf course, golf car rentals, a game room, a playground, horseshoes, tennis courts, volleyball, shuffleboard, pool tables, a recreation hall, and wintertime social programs. Showers, restrooms, a fitness center, cable TV, boat rentals, limited groceries, park-model sites, and laundry facilities are available. Wireless Internet access is available at most sites. Management says bathhouses, pools, the recreation center, and laundry facilities are wheelchair-accessible. RV storage is available. Children are welcome. Leashed pets are permitted. Stay as long as you like.

Reservations, fees: Reservations are recommended. Sites are $38–75 per night for two people, plus $6 per extra person. Cable TV costs $3 per day. Credit cards are accepted.

Directions: If you're traveling south on Florida's Turnpike, exit at Yeehaw Junction. Follow U.S. 441 south for 33 miles to the park. If you're traveling north on Florida's Turnpike, exit at PGA Boulevard. Go west to the Beeline Highway/State Road 710. Turn right and follow this road to the town of Okeechobee. Turn left (west) onto State Road 70, then turn left (south) on U.S. 441. The park is ahead, near the junction with State Road 78.

Contact: Lake Okeechobee Resort KOA, 4276 U.S. 441 South, Okeechobee, FL 34974, 863/763-0231 or 800/562-7748, fax 863/763-0531, www.koa.com.

27 LAKESIDE RV PARK

Scenic rating: 3

southwest of Okeechobee

Year after year, seasonal visitors return to this small park south of Okeechobee for "great fishing and even better fishing stories." The town of Okeechobee has dozens of these semi-permanent RV parks, set jowl-to-jowl on U.S. 441. This park, for example, also competes with a Veterans of Foreign Wars (VFW) clubhouse nearby that allows its members to stay for free. But those folks won't have the chance to fish from Lakeside RV Park's shoreline. "Bigger fish are caught right around the fish-cleaning station than were ever caught in a boat," says manager Gary Rupert. Five miles from the park is downtown Okeechobee, with shopping and supplies. A Labor Day rodeo is held there, and the Brighton Seminole Indian reservation casino is nearby.

Campsites, facilities: Anglers and outdoorslovers occupy these 72 grassy sites with concrete pads and 30-amp electrical service. Sites vary in size, but rigs up to 40 feet in length can be accommodated at some. All have full hookups. Restrooms, showers, laundry facilities, and telephone service are available. Nearly half the park is occupied by year-round residents. The park is partially shaded and restaurants, boating supply stores, and other conveniences are within two miles. Planned activities are held in winter, such as dinners and chili cook-offs on Super Bowl Sunday. Children are OK, though there is no playground or other facilities for them. Leashed pets are permitted.

Reservations, fees: Reservations are recommended. Sites are $15 per night for two people, plus $2 per extra person. Credit cards are not accepted. Long-term rates are available.

Directions: From the intersection of State Road 70 and U.S. 441, head south to the park.

Contact: Lakeside RV Park, 4074 U.S. Highway 441 Southeast, Okeechobee, FL 34974, 863/467-1530.

28 ZACHARY TAYLOR CAMPING RESORT

Scenic rating: 6

south of Okeechobee

This green place offers more shade than many Lake Okeechobee–area campgrounds, which may explain why it can't guarantee a site preference at reservation time. In fact, the park now encourages year-long lot leases, rather than overnight stays or short-term vacations.

Cypress trees and native palms shade these 20 acres set along 1,500 feet of lazy Taylor Creek, and some campers end up becoming equity owners. Although a heated pool and planned activities at the waterfront recreation hall are provided, fishing remains the god of all activities here in the shadow of the nation's second-largest inland freshwater lake. An onsite concrete boat ramp leads to the Big O.

Campsites, facilities: There are 250 full-hookup sites with 30/50-amp electrical service. For recreation, there's a pool, a recreation hall, horseshoes, shuffleboard, and planned activities. Showers, a boat ramp, a dock, rental units, picnic tables, bait, and laundry facilities are available. Trips with fishing guides can be arranged. Cable TV and phone service are available if you stay at least one month. The recreation hall and restrooms are wheelchair-accessible. Children are permitted for short stays. Leashed pets are accepted for $2 daily.

Reservations, fees: Reservations are preferred. Sites are $35 per night for two people, plus $3 per extra person, $2 for electricity, and $1 or pets. Credit cards are not accepted. Long-term stays are preferred.

Directions: From State Road 70 and U.S. 441/Parrott Avenue in the town of Okeechobee, go south on U.S. 441/Parrott Avenue to Lake Okeechobee. Turn left to continue east on U.S. 441. Turn left at Southeast 30th Terrace. The campground is ahead.

Contact: Zachary Taylor Camping Resort, 2995 U.S. 441 Southeast, Okeechobee, FL

34974, 863/763-3377 or 888/282-6523, fax 863/763-6301.

29 TAYLOR CREEK RESORT RV PARK

Scenic rating: 6

south of Okeechobee

The driving ambition of visitors here is catching speckled perch, bass, bluegill, and catfish at Taylor Creek and nearby Lake Okeechobee. Its location is ideal: just a few feet from the Taylor Creek lock, the only one on the lake with no restrictions on boat height. Other angler-oriented amenities are covered boat slips (remodeled in 2005), a fish-cleaning station, bait, tackle, and a nearby fishing guide service. Some sites have water views, but most are inland. Many water-view sites are reserved for residents of the park's 48 mobile homes, which are squeezed together. Under new ownership since 2005, the campsites and docks were renovated in 2006.

Campsites, facilities: All 96 sites have sewer, water, and 30-amp electricity; two sites have 50-amp service. Restrooms, showers, cabins, rental boat slips, and bait and tackle are available. The bathhouse, office, and docks are wheelchair-accessible. Streets are paved. Children are welcome, but not for permanent stays. Small pets are permitted, but must be approved by the management.

Reservations, fees: Reservations are advised. Sites are $35–45 per night for two people, plus $5 for each additional person. Credit cards are not accepted.

Directions: From State Road 70 and U.S. 441/ Parrott Avenue in the town of Okeechobee, go south on U.S. 441/Parrott Avenue to Lake Okeechobee. Turn left to continue east on U.S. 441 and proceed about four miles to the campground.

Contact: Taylor Creek Resort RV Park, 2730 U.S. 441 Southeast, Okeechobee, FL 34974,

863/763-4417, fax 863/763-8517, www .taylorcreekresort.com. Mailing address: P.O. Box 1796, Okeechobee, FL 34973-1796.

30 LAKE OKEECHOBEE SCENIC TRAIL-NUBBIN SLOUGH

Scenic rating: 6

on the northeastern bank of Lake Okeechobee, east of Okeechobee

Beautiful sunsets and good access by powerboat from the lake are what set this rustic campsite apart. This part of Lake Okeechobee doesn't get as many visitors as areas that are more convenient to modern facilities, but that's why I like it. You can still find some increasingly rare xeric hammocks on this end of the lake, although you may have to go afar to see them. If you're spending several days hiking or bicycling along the Herbert Hoover Dike, the next campsite south is 10.3 miles away at Lake Okeechobee Scenic Trail-Chancy Bay. To the west, travel about nine miles, just passing the Kissimmee River, to reach Lake Okeechobee Scenic Trail-Kissimmee River.

Until not that long ago, Nubbin Slough was one of the traditional routes for cow poop to get into Lake Okeechobee. Now, the South Florida Water Management District has launched a cleanup of the dairies to the north, which has included paying dairy farmers to move their herds north into other drainage basins.

Campsites, facilities: This primitive tent-camping area is accessible by foot or bicycle; powerboats also have good access from the lake. A fire ring and a shelter with a picnic table are provided. There is no toilet, no water, and no other facilities. Bring water, food, sunscreen, a hat, camping supplies, and mosquito repellent. Children and leashed pets are permitted.

Reservations, fees: Camping is first-come, first-served. There is no fee.

Directions: The campsite is 0.5 mile north of the Nubbins Slough recreation area on the lakeshore, east of the town of Okeechobee and off U.S.98/441. For detailed directions, a map, and a brochure, contact the U.S. Army Corps of Engineers before your trip. You can also download a map of the trail at www.saj.usace.army.mil/sfoo/images/maps/lostmap.pdf.

Contact: U.S. Army Corps of Engineers, South Florida Operations Office, 525 Ridgelawn Road, Clewiston, FL 33440-5399, 863/983-8101, www.saj.usace.army.mil.

31 PRIMROSE RV PARK

Scenic rating: 4

south of Okeechobee

One of a dozen or so adults-preferred RV parks on the northern side of Lake Okeechobee, Primrose RV Park overlooks the rim canal leading to the lake, and tends to attract anglers and snowbirds staying for the mild Florida winter. Waterfront sites are available; others are set under tall oak trees. New owners arrived in 2003, and they upgraded the electrical service and added a seawall to the 1,180-foot waterfront. Additional work is to be carried out through the next few years. Most of the visitors are into fishing (on the canal, lake, or creek), and many are repeat customers from Missouri, Illinois, and Virginia. About half the sites are occupied year-round.

Campsites, facilities: Of the 59 sites in this community, about half are available for overnighters and seasonal visitors in rigs up to 40 feet and slideout units. Two sites are pull-through, and all but 13 have concrete pads. All RV sites have full hookups and picnic tables. Restrooms, showers, a dump station, laundry facilities, propane service, cable TV, and telephone service are available. On the premises are a boat ramp, 38 boat docks, a fish-cleaning station, and a wheelchair-accessible clubhouse, where planned activities include potluck suppers, "ladies' day out," craft days, charter fishing, boat trips, and bingo. RV storage is available for a monthly fee. Children are welcome, but this is primarily an adults-oriented park. Small, leashed pets are permitted.

Reservations, fees: Reservations are recommended. Sites are $20 to $30 a night, plus $2 for electricity. Credit cards are not accepted. Long-term stays are the norm.

Directions: From the intersection of U.S. 98 and U.S. 441 with State Road 78 in Okeechobee, drive 4.3 miles south to the park.

Contact: Primrose RV Park, 6070 Highway 441 Southeast, Okeechobee, FL 34974, 863/763-8711.

32 FIJIAN RV PARK

Scenic rating: 4

south of Okeechobee

Under new ownership since July 2005, this "fisherman's park" is now open year-round. Sitting on the northern end of 740-square-mile Lake Okeechobee, this 3.5-acre park has an understandable focus—the lake. Campers (mostly retirees) launch boats from a park ramp to follow a canal to the watery home of bass and specks. Some campers fish from the bank; the open and sunny park has 850 feet of waterfront. With no swimming pool, playground, or shuffleboard, these grassy sites with concrete patios are best left to grown-up anglers and boaters. In the wintertime, live entertainment in the 5,000-square-foot recreation building provides another way to pass time. Activities include bingo, potluck dinners, dancing, holiday parties, and bus trips to historical sites, amusement parks, and dining. Shopping and supplies are within eight miles.

Campsites, facilities: Campers age 55 and older are welcome at the 40 full-hookup grassy RV sites in this 77-unit park; half the park is occupied by year-round residents. Sites are about 20 feet wide by 35 feet deep. Winter social programs, a game room, a recreation room, showers, restrooms, a dump station, a boat ramp, a dock, cable TV, telephone hookups, and laundry facilities are available. RV storage is available in the summer season. Children are permitted for short-term stays or to visit long-term campers. Small, leashed pets are accepted; use the designated dog walk.

Reservations, fees: Reservations are recommended. Sites are $30 per night for two people, plus $5 per extra person. Credit cards are not accepted. Long-term rates are available.

Directions: From State Road 70 and U.S. 441/Parrott Avenue in the town of Okeechobee, go south on U.S. 441/Parrott Avenue to Lake Okeechobee. Turn left to continue east on U.S. 441. Proceed about five miles, passing Nubbin Slough, to the park entrance at right.

Contact: Fijian RV Park, 6500 U.S. 441 Southeast, Okeechobee, FL 34974, 863/763-6200.

33 UNCLE JOE'S FISH CAMP

Scenic rating: 5

south of Moore Haven

If you love fishing for bass or hunting for ducks at Lake Okeechobee, then you'll like these grassy or concrete-pad campsites. (You can also use this as an access point for bicycling and hiking on the dike.) This family-owned fish camp is just what the name implies—a place to sleep, so you can rise early the next day to catch fish. Forget swimming pools or shuffleboard; you won't find such amenities here, though that's not really the point. During the season, planned activities include weekly fish fries, and a pub serves up beer and jukebox music. Boaters will be glad that the boat ramp has direct access to Lake Okeechobee, meaning they won't face the hassle of waiting to get past a lock. I happened to stop by on the first day of duck-hunting season, and the boat ramp was a beehive of activity.

Hunters clad in green camouflage waited in line to launch their watercraft, some of which were edged with frilly dried plant matter—the better to fool the ducks.

Some folks stay at this five-acre camp for months, earning a free, reserved boat dock after a four-month stay. Says manager Ed Massey: "This is the best place in the world to live from November through May. From June to September, it's one of the worst—because of the high humidity and heat." Nonetheless, he says he's happy to be home "in a little country town along the lake." Maybe that's why about 75 percent of the occupants live here year-round.

Motorboats rent for $60 daily. If someone in your party is dying for a hot meal in front of a TV after so much solitude on the lake, then the cabins with kitchenettes (renting for $42 and up) will provide a little extra comfort. The real Uncle Joe arrived in the early 1940s and built a few cabins, and the park still has that "Old Florida" feel. Joe has passed away, but his legacy continues.

Campsites, facilities: All 18 full-hookup sites are for RVs up to 38 feet long. The occasional tenter who comes through can set up across the street on 10 primitive sites in a field. Fishing guides and boat rentals are available. Showers, restrooms, a dump station, cabin rentals, a boat ramp, limited groceries, snacks, sandwiches, firewood, bait, boat gas, dock space, and laundry facilities are on the premises. Most areas are wheelchair-accessible. Restaurants and a supermarket are 10 minutes away. Families with small children and pets are welcome.

Reservations, fees: Reservations are not necessary. Sites are $20 per night, plus $5 if your party has more than two people. Credit cards are not accepted. Stay as long as you like.

Directions: From Clewiston, take U.S. 27 west to State Road 720 and turn right. Continue four miles, then turn right at the Uncle Joe's sign.

Contact: Uncle Joe's Fish Camp, 2005 Griffin Road Southeast, Moore Haven, FL 33471, 863/983-9421, unclejoefishcamp@aol.com.

© MARILYN MOORE

Fishing is popular on Lake Okeechobee.

34 LAKE OKEECHOBEE SCENIC TRAIL- LIBERTY POINT

Scenic rating: 7

on the land-side canal bordering the dike along Lake Okeechobee

At dawn, a gorgeous burnt-orange and purple glow rises over the 740-square-mile expanse of Lake Okeechobee. The view is your reward for skipping conveniences like showers and toilets.

People who take the trouble of following the tire ruts along the sunwashed, shell-rock Herbert Hoover Dike tend to rave about the experience. Wading birds stand like statues in the shallow marsh to the east before pouncing on meals of fish. Otters sometimes scurry into the lake early in the morning. And you're almost certain to see some alligators. Places to fish from shore are hard to find here, because of the plentiful water plants sticking up from the surface of Florida's largest lake; fishing lines are bound to get caught in the weeds.

If this stop is part of a bicycle or hiking trip along the entire 110-mile-long levee, then the next rustic campsite to the southeast is 10.8 miles away (Lake Okeechobee Scenic Trail-Lake Harbor). It's a 12-mile trek northwest to Lake Okeechobee Scenic Trail-Culvert 5A.

Campsites, facilities: This primitive tent-camping area is accessible by foot; long-distance trekkers circling the lake might arrive by bicycle or foot. Boaters can dock nearby at Uncle Joe's Fish Camp. A fire ring and a shelter with a picnic table are provided. There are no toilets or piped water. Bring plenty of water, food, camping supplies, and mosquito repellent. Children and leashed pets are OK.

Reservations, fees: Camping is first-come, first-served. There is no fee.

Directions: The campsite is just east of Uncle Joe's Fish Camp (see previous listing), so park at Uncle Joe's; you may be asked to pay $3. To get there from Clewiston, take U.S. 27 to State Road 720, turn right, then go to the Uncle Joe's entrance. From Uncle Joe's levee gate, hike atop the dike in a southeastern direction about 0.5 mile to the Florida Trail campsite. You can also download a map of the trail at

www.saj.usace.army.mil/sfoo/images/maps/
lostmap.pdf.

Contact: U.S. Army Corps of Engineers, South
Florida Operations Office, 525 Ridgelawn
Road, Clewiston, FL 33440-5300, 863/983-
8101, www.saj.usace.army.mil.

35 THE MARINA RV RESORT

Scenic rating: 7

southwest of Okeechobee

This renovated park is on federal lands adjacent to the Moore Haven Lock that connects
eastern Lake Okeechobee to the Caloosahatchee River, which leads to Fort Myers and
the Gulf Coast; management leases the land
from the U.S. Army Corps of Engineers. The
campground is popular with boaters, anglers,
hunters, and locals, but also offers access to
the dike for bicycling and hiking. Renovations
include a swimming pool, recreation buildings, and wireless Internet access. There is a
gated security entrance and plenty of parking
for boat trailers. Managers live on-site. Most
sites have views of the water—not the lake, but
the wooded canals that lead to the lake. Palms
dot the park, but shade is not significant on
these 40 acres. About 20 percent of the park
is occupied by year-round residents.

Campsites, facilities: Among 151 paved or
gravel sites, 59 have full hookups and the rest
have water and 30/50-amp electric service.
For the best sites along the water, ask for lots
82–98 on Fisherman's Lane. Tent sites are
available along Duck Hunter's Circle near
the clubhouse. Restrooms, showers, a dump
station, laundry facilities, and rental units are
available. On the premises are a swimming
pool, a boat ramp, a fish-cleaning station, a
clubhouse, a gazebo, horseshoe pits, shuffleboard courts, a bait house with fishing supplies, and gas pumps. A large kitchen area is
available, where community breakfasts and

dinners are prepared (bring your own utensils,
unless you don't mind using plastic forks and
paper plates). Other activities include dancing,
gospel music, and jam sessions, plus the usual
bingo and crafts. The laundry, bathhouse,
and clubhouse are wheelchair-accessible. You
can store your RV in the off-season summer
months. Children are welcome. Leashed pets
are permitted.

Reservations, fees: Reservations are recommended. Sites are $18 per night. Credit cards
are accepted. Long-term rates are available.

Directions: From the intersection of U.S. 27
and State Road 78, go north on 78 for about
a mile. Turn right on Canal Road and drive
through a residential area until the road ends
at the park.

Contact: The Marina RV Resort, 900 County
Road 720, Moore Haven, FL 33471, 863/946-
2255 or 904/824-7063 (reservations).

36 CLEWISTON/ LAKE OKEECHOBEE KOA

Scenic rating: 5

west of Clewiston

This family-friendly campground is much
more than a convenient place to sleep if you
want to walk, cycle, or take your boat out to
fish for largemouth bass. Within three miles of
the campground are a golf course, tennis and
racquetball facilities, a Lake Okeechobee boat
launch, shopping, tours of local sugar mills,
and a hospital in Clewiston. Inside the park
is a massive playground area erected in 2006
and featuring a huge chess set with pieces that
are the size of a small child. There's also a
kid-friendly game room with arcade games,
a volleyball area, and funny-shaped bicycles
to ride around the campground.

The park boasts a smattering of exotic fruit
trees, such as loquats, and offers large (35- by
55-foot), grassy, level sites. Although part of

the park is occupied by year-round residents, the managers emphasize this is a campground, not a trailer park, welcoming snowbirds and family campers.

Favorite things to do include visits to Gatorama. Just 15 miles north on U.S. 27, Gatorama (863/675-0623, www.gatorama.com), is a fascinating tourist attraction and working alligator farm. One of Florida's earliest alligator parks, it typifies the classic roadside attraction of the mid-1950s. These days, it has been modernized and is a commercial success, as well as a tourist destination that will stay in your mind forever. It houses 2,000 gators and crocodiles by age and size in open-air pens, as well as a variety of other animals. The really big gators swim freely in the adjacent ponds. Walk on the shaded boardwalk all the way to the end, or you'll miss seeing Goliath. He's known as the "serial killer" American crocodile, who had to be segregated in his own pen because he killed so many of his neighbors in territorial battles. Gatorama's breeding operation also harvests 1,000 alligators a year for meat and hide.

Campsites, facilities: There are 124 RV sites, of which 100 have full hookups, plus a separate area with 10 tent sites that have water and electricity. Almost all the sites are pull-through, and RVs up to 40 feet long can be accommodated. Both 30-amp and 50-amp electrical service are offered, and 12 sites are set aside for pop-up campers that need just water and electricity. Propane gas can be delivered to your site. Connect to the Internet via wireless connection right from your RV. Although cable TV hookups are not available, broadcast reception is good, with approximately 15 TV channels. Facilities include restrooms, showers, a dump station, a store, cabin rentals, and laundry facilities. There's also a hot tub, a pool, a horseshoe pit, a game room, a playground, a shuffleboard court, and an adult activity room. Fishing tournaments, movies, bingo, potluck suppers, card games, and crafts also keep guests entertained. All

areas are wheelchair-accessible. Children are permitted; parents are responsible for the safety of their kids at the pool. Leashed dogs must use a pet walk at the back of the park. You can store your RV here during the off-season.

Reservations, fees: Reservations are required December–March. Sites are $34 per night for two people, plus $5 for each additional adult. Credit cards are accepted. Six-month stays are permitted for new visitors.

Directions: From Clewiston, travel about two miles west on U.S. 27 and then turn right at County Road 720. The campground entrance is located about 700 feet ahead on the right.

Contact: Clewiston/Lake Okeechobee KOA, 194 County Road 720, Clewiston, FL 33440, 863/983-7078 or 800/562-2174, www.clokoa.com.

37 ROBIN'S NEST RV RESORT

Scenic rating: 3

north of Moore Haven

This family-owned park targets seasonal visitors looking for a convenient base for Lake Okeechobee's charms, but also proximity to city-like amenities (Wal-Mart, restaurants, and other shopping). Open year-round, the park lies neatly under the sun along U.S. 27, accommodating even the biggest rigs. This park has affiliations with The Marina RV Resort on Lake Okeechobee (see listing in this chapter) and membership privileges with several private RV time-share clubs, though nonmembers are very welcome. About 5 percent of the park is occupied by year-round residents, but that number seems to be increasing. Music is a big selling point here: You'll find everything from karaoke and square dancing to jam sessions and live gospel singing. A pastor lives on the premises and holds nondenominational Sunday services.

Campsites, facilities: There are 248 large RV sites (30 by 50 feet) with full hookups, concrete pads, and picnic tables on 87 acres; 25 of those acres are not developed. Overnight sites may be scarce during the Christmas holidays and February–March. Restrooms, showers, laundry facilities, cable TV, telephone service, a dump station, and propane gas are available. Wireless Internet access is planned for the future. All sites have 50-amp service, and asphalt roads lead to the paved RV sites. On the premises are a heated pool, two clubhouses, a four-hole golf course, shuffleboard courts, and a snack bar. Live music is scheduled every weekend from December through the end of March. Planned activities include music, games, group meals, and church services. Restaurants and grocery shops are located seven miles away in Moore Haven and 18 miles away in Clewiston. Management says the bath, laundry, and clubhouse have wheelchair access. RV storage is available. Children are welcome for short stays only at this age-50-plus-preferred park. Leashed pets are permitted. Stay here and get full-day use of the owners' boat and recreational facilities at The Marina RV Resort on Lake Okeechobee.

Reservations, fees: Reservations are recommended. Sites are $20 per night for two people, plus $5 per extra person. Credit cards are accepted. Long-term rates are available.

Directions: From Moore Haven, drive nine miles north on U.S. 27 to the park, which is on the west side.

Contact: Robin's Nest RV Resort, 2365 North U.S. 27, Moore Haven, Fl 33471, 863/946-3782, fax 863/946-3883.

38 OKEECHOBEE LANDINGS

Scenic rating: 4

in Clewiston

Purchasers of park models, trailer lots, and seasonal visitors in big RVs people this 27-acre community, which attracts anglers and retirees from Canada and the Midwestern states. Big ,grassy sites are the park's crowning glory, promising "peace and quiet" for campers, according to management. Speckled perch, bluegill, largemouth bass, and catfish tempt them from nearby Lake Okeechobee. This park is a member of several private timeshare RV clubs. You won't be able to see the "Big O" from here or, for that matter, from most places around the lake, because the levee is so high. If you'd like a water view, request a campsite near the park's seven-acre lake.

Campsites, facilities: All 270 large RV sites are set on paved streets with lots 30 by 50 feet in size, accommodating rigs up to 44 feet long. They have full hookups, including cable TV; 249 sites have 30-amp electrical service, and 26 have 50-amp. Tenters are usually placed on grassy sites near the bathhouses; the sites have water and electricity. A pool, a whirlpool tub, shuffleboard, horseshoes, a tennis court, a game room, bingo, and special events entertain guests. Showers, restrooms, picnic tables, a dump station, and laundry facilities are available. Internet access is available from the park office. Propane is delivered to your site once a week during the winter season. Campers can store a boat, car, or RV for $60 a month. Groceries can be purchased one mile away; a restaurant and bait shop are within 0.5 mile. Management says the office, bathhouse, and clubhouse are wheelchair-accessible. Children are welcome. Leashed pets are permitted if they weigh less than 40 pounds, and aggressive breeds are verboten.

Reservations, fees: Reservations are recommended. Sites are $30 per night for two people and $2 per extra person. Campers who stay for six months or more must pay additional charges for electricity. Credit cards are accepted. Long-term stays are OK.

Directions: From downtown Clewiston, go east on U.S. 27 to the park entrance. Signs on the highway mark the turnoff to the park, which is at the eastern end of town.

Contact: Okeechobee Landings, 420 Holiday Boulevard, Clewiston, FL 33440, 863/983-4144, www.okeechobeelandingsrv.com.

39 LAKE OKEECHOBEE SCENIC TRAIL-LAKE HARBOR

Scenic rating: 6

on Lake Okeechobee, east of Clewiston

Look for bald eagles, turkeys, deer, bobcats, and hawk-like ospreys as you hike along this portion of the 107-mile-long semi-grassy berm that holds in Lake Okeechobee. Former park ranger Tambour Eller once counted about 10 types of birds while strolling the short distance from the U.S. Army Corps of Engineers office to the lake. "I see more wildlife and birds here than I actually have at the Everglades," Eller says.

Most South Floridians aren't aware that they can hike, bicycle, and camp along the sunwashed, shell-rock hiking trail atop the Herbert Hoover Dike. It's one of the few ways to see Florida's largest lake, which, for motorists, is hidden from view by the 34-foot-high dike. For the squeamish, this campsite may present a good introduction to experiencing the lake. It is fairly close to amenities in Clewiston as well as the Army Corps office that oversees the trail. If you're going the distance around the lake, it's 10.8 miles northwest to the next rustic campsite, Lake Okeechobee Scenic Trail-Liberty Point. Need a hot shower? It's about nine miles southeast to tent-permissible South Bay RV Park.

Campsites, facilities: This primitive tent-camping area is accessible by foot or bicycle. A fire ring and a shelter with a picnic table are provided. There is no toilet, water, or other facilities. Bring water, food, sunscreen, a hat, camping supplies, and mosquito repellent. Children and leashed pets are permitted.

Reservations, fees: Camping is first-come, first-served. There is no fee.

Directions: The campsite is on the lakeside of the Herbert Hoover Dike, about four miles east of Clewiston. You could park at the U.S. Army Corps of Engineers (with permission), or at the nearby Clewiston city boat ramp, then hike about 5.2 miles south. A better bet is to ask for a shortcut, as well as a map and a brochure, from the U.S. Army Corps of Engineers before your trip. You can also download a map of the trail at www.saj.usace.army.mil/sfoo/images/maps/lostmap.pdf.

Contact: U.S. Army Corps of Engineers, South Florida Operations Office, 525 Ridgelawn Road, Clewiston, FL 33440-5399, 863/983-8101, www.saj.usace.army.mil.

40 CROOKED HOOK RV RESORT

Scenic rating: 6

east of Clewiston

One of the cleanest private parks around Lake Okeechobee, Crooked Hook is sought out by anglers for its proximity to the bass haven. But seasonal visitors fill up the park fast in the wintertime for line dancing, bowling outings, or other daily activities, and it is close to shopping and restaurants in Clewiston. In a region where sunbaked RV sites tend to be the norm, this 30-acre, retiree-oriented place offers something different: It has shaded campsites and greenery that make it feel tropical and relaxing. Because it was developed long ago, the sites are irregular in size (ranging from 25 by 25 feet to 30 by 40 feet). The cookie-cutter feel of parks plotted out on cleared land is a nice absence. More than 200 fruit trees are on the property, many of which grow edibles, including mango. The levee is across the highway, hiding the big blue waters of the lake—not that it makes any difference to the folks who come here year after year.

Owners Dan and Laurel Darlington indicate the park has more of a neighborhood feel, with so many planned activities that the "chief complaint is there are too many things to do." Visitors have to be selective with their time, whether it's focused on golf, fishing, poker tournaments, casino nights, poker, card games, or the crafts room. In season (meaning the winter months), cookouts are held every weekend. "There is something to do every day," visitors say. One unusual activity is the park's "holey board" field, where eight competitors toss items called "washers" at boards with holes in them, for points. The Darlingtons have upgraded many sites to 50-amp service to accommodate visitors. About 35 percent of the park is occupied by year-round residents, because housing choices in this area are scarce. Park models are available for sale.

Campsites, facilities: Three of the 200 full-hookup RV sites are pull-through. A heated pool, a recreation room, a playground, an exercise room, horseshoes, shuffleboard, *pétanque* (French-style bowling), and wintertime daily activities entertain campers. Showers, restrooms, picnic tables, and laundry facilities are available. Three miles away are restaurants, groceries, an 18-hole golf course, and bait. Wal-Mart (called "Wally Mart" by park visitors) is the biggest store for miles around, and it's just six miles north. Some visitors leave their RVs or boats on-site during the hot summer months; the park will store them for six months for $30 per month. Children are welcome, although the park mainly attracts retirees. Small, leashed pets are permitted.

Reservations, fees: Reservations are required. Sites are $30 per night for two people, plus $3 per extra person. Credit cards are accepted. Long-term stays are the norm, though a few sites are available for overnighters in winter. Stay as long as you wish.

Directions: From Clewiston, go three miles east on U.S. 27 to the campground entrance.

Contact: Crooked Hook RV Resort, 51700 U.S. Highway 27, Clewiston, FL 33440, 863/983-7112, www.crookedhookrv.biz.

41 SOUTH BAY RV CAMPGROUND

Scenic rating: 10

in South Bay

This is one of the cleanest, best-managed campgrounds on the lakeshore, with particular appeal to RVers. It's just on the edge of the town of South Bay, and across the levee from fishing, hiking, cycling, and bird-watching on the lake. If you have a boat, you'll appreciate the city boat ramp/day-use picnic area across from the park; please note that the approach to the ramp is up and over a steep one-way drive over the 34-foot levee. A 24-hour on-site manager lives within footsteps of the county-run campground's office. The large paved campsites are sunny and are set along two elongated loops named Shellcracker Circle and Bluegill Circle. Plenty of elbow room exists between the sites, and the landscaping is well-maintained. Most of the sites have views overlooking a mowed field and Shiner Lake, which has a short walking trail on the shoreline. There's also a screened-in picnic area with large grills for gatherings, and an air-conditioned recreational hall with a pool table, card tables, and a color TV. A campfire ring offers socializing opportunities. Swimming is not allowed, and other rules are enforced (no loud music or disruptive behavior, no barking dogs, for example). A security gate is kept closed 9 P.M.–7 A.M.

One visitor tells the story of a favorite jacket left outside during a storm. Imagine her surprise when the campground manager returned it to her by courier a week after she got home. Someone had found it hanging in a tree on the other side of the park.

Campsites, facilities: The 72 campsites have water, electricity, and cable TV. Both 30-amp and 50-amp electrical service is available. Showers, restrooms, a playground, a game room, a dump station, laundry facilities, horseshoes, and pool tables are in the park. A boat ramp is nearby. Nearly 20 campsites are wheelchair-accessible. Children are welcome. Leashed, attended pets (no pit bulls) are permitted; no more than two pets per site.

Reservations, fees: The park is being used by FEMA as a shelter for hurricane victims and is not open to the public; call to check the status. Sites are $17–18 per night for five people, plus $2 for each additional person. Credit cards are accepted. Monthly rates are available; however, stays are limited to 100 days within a 12-month period.

Directions: From U.S. 27 and State Road 80 in South Bay, follow U.S. 27 northwest about 2.5 miles. Turn right at Levee Road, then turn right into the campground.

Contact: South Bay RV Campground, 100 Levee Road, South Bay, FL 33493, 561/992-9045 or 877/992-9915. Additional information: Palm Beach County Parks and Recreation Department, 561/966-6600, www.pbcgov.com/parks.

42 BELLE GLADE MARINA CAMPGROUND

🛶 🚐 🐕 🚙 ⛺

Scenic rating: 5

on Lake Okeechobee's Torry Island

If you're coming from eastern Palm Beach County, this is probably the closest place to hook up a rig at Lake Okeechobee, particularly if you want a golf course practically on the premises. The Belle Glade Country Club is across from the campground, which is popular with bass anglers and boaters who seek to experience the nation's second-largest inland freshwater lake. This park was closed in 2005 due to hurricane damage, but in early 2007, it was completely rebuilt from the ground up. Belle Glade is a farming community and the largest city on Lake Okeechobee.

Campsites, facilities: All facilities were newly built in late 2006 and early 2007. There are 350 concrete-pad campsites with picnic tables. All have 50-amp electricity, water, and sewer hookups. None of the sites are drive-through, and many sites are arranged on waterfront loops that overlook reedy, pond-like waters. Tents are allowed in a separate primitive area with no hookups. Boat ramps, showers, restrooms, barbecue/picnic areas, and laundry facilities are available. Within walking distance are a golf course, boat rentals, a restaurant, bait, and tackle. Children and pets are permitted.

Reservations, fees: Camping is first-come, first-served. Sites are $93 per week; rates are subject to change. Long-term stays are allowed.

Directions: From U.S. 27 and State Road 80 in South Bay, go east nearly two miles on State Road 80. Turn left at State Road 715 and proceed about 2.25 miles. Turn left at West Canal Street North/State Road 717. Continue about two miles west to the campground entrance on Torry Island. (On Torry Island, State Road 717 is known as Chosen–Torry Island Road.)

Contact: Belle Glade Marina Campground, 110 Southwest Avenue E, Belle Glade, FL 33430, 561/996-6322. Or contact the City of Belle Glade Office of Parks and Recreation, Municipal Complex, Belle Glade, FL 33430, 561/996-0100.

43 EVERGLADES ADVENTURES RV AND SAILING RESORT

Scenic rating: 10

at Lake Okeechobee

Formerly known as Pahokee Marina and Campground, this park has a unique setting: It boasts the only developed lakefront campsites on the eastern shore of Lake Okeechobee. The grassy campsites are directly on the banks of the lake, providing unrivaled water views. From this point, the lake shimmers blue like an ocean, and you can gaze into the unobstructed horizon to see sailboats and other vessels under way. The shoreline is rocky (not a beach). The steep berm that surrounds the lake is behind the park, so you'll actually drive up and over the dike, then down to the park. It's also convenient to groceries and the small shops of Pahokee, a farming community. Although the park has some trees, expect plenty of sunshine. Fishing and boating are the main attractions, but access to the hiking and bicycling options on the dike is excellent. All ages are welcome. Part of the park has cabins for rent or sale.

Campsites, facilities: There are 109 level, grassy sites with full hookups. None of the sites are drive-through, but the access road is paved. The sites vary in size from 20 to 24 feet wide and 60 to 75 feet long. About 10 percent of the sites are used by year-round residents, but most visitors here are anglers. Shuffleboard, horseshoes, a playground, restrooms, showers, cabin rentals, a dump station, a honey wagon, a boat ramp, bait, tackle, and limited groceries are available. The park has 86 deep-water slips in its marina, two fishing piers, three boat ramps, and trailer storage. If you didn't bring your boat, you can rent pontoon boats and Boston whalers fully equipped for fishing. Bicycle, canoe, and kayak rentals are on-site. Groceries are available within one mile. All areas are wheelchair-accessible. Children and pets are permitted.

Reservations, fees: Reservations are

Parts of the levee road that encircles Lake Okeechobee have been paved, making it ideal for roadies.

© MARILYN MOORE

recommended. Sites are $39 per night January 1–April 30, and $29 per night the rest of the year. The rates apply to two campers; additional people are charged $8 each. Credit cards are accepted. Stay as long as you like.

Directions: The park is on Lake Okeechobee in the heart of Pahokee. Head west over the levee from the intersection of U.S. 441 and State Road 715.

Contact: Everglades Adventures RV and Sailing Resort, 190 North Lake Avenue, Pahokee, FL 33476, 561/924-7832 or 800/335-6560, fax 561/924-7271, www.everglades adventuresresort.com.

44 LAKE OKEECHOBEE SCENIC TRAIL- SOUTH PORT MAYACA

Scenic rating: 8

on the eastern bank of Lake Okeechobee

This part of the trail is a lot more scenic since the removal of vegetation, allowing first-rate views of the lake from atop 34-foot-high Herbert Hoover Dike. Still, so few people hike along the shell-rock road atop the dike that you'll feel like you're getting away from it all. You'll see miles of water stretching ahead of you like an ocean; to the land side are marshy areas and tiny farms of banana groves or ranches. Listen to the waves lapping against the rough shoreline—on windy days, they may sound more like a roar. Birds are plentiful. Stop for a picnic on the swath of mowed grass along the dike during your hike or bike ride. Bicyclists have been known to circle the sunwashed, 110-mile-long dike in as little as two days, seeing first hand why the Seminole tribe dubbed the lake Big Water (Okeechobee). If you're going the distance along the entire lake, the next rustic campsite is seven miles north at Lake Okeechobee Scenic Trail-Chancy Bay. Want a shower

and civilization? Go to Everglades Adventure RV and Sailing Resort (formerly Pahokee Campground), about 10.3 miles south in Pahokee.

Campsites, facilities: This primitive tent-camping area is accessible by foot or bicycle. A fire ring/grill and a newly built shelter with a picnic table are provided. There is no toilet or other facilities. Bring water, food, sunscreen, a hat, camping supplies, and mosquito repellent. Children and leashed pets are OK.

Reservations, fees: Camping is first-come, first-served. There is no fee.

Directions: The campsite is on the lakeside of the levee, about two miles south of the Port Mayaca lock, at the base of the berm overlooking the water. The lock is on U.S. 441/U.S. 98 at the Okeechobee Waterway and the intersection with State Road 76. You'll park at the Port Mayaca levee gate, then hike or bike two miles south to the campsite. You can also access this site from the Canal Point picnic area on U.S. 441/98, approximately 3.4 miles north of the town of Pahokee. It's a seven-mile trek to the site. For detailed directions and a map, contact the U.S. Army Corps of Engineers. You can also download a map of the trail at www.saj.usace. army.mil/sfoo/images/maps/lostmap.pdf.

Contact: U.S. Army Corps of Engineers, South Florida Operations Office, 525 Ridgelawn Road, Clewiston, FL 33440, 941/983-8101, www.saj.usace.army.mil.

45 LAKE OKEECHOBEE SCENIC TRAIL- CHANCY BAY CAMPSITE

Scenic rating: 8

on Lake Okeechobee

Creamy pastels light the sky above Lake Okeechobee at dusk. This lakeshore campsite has a beautiful westward view over the lake.

Ranger Jerre Killingbeck planted the cluster of palm trees and dragged a picnic table to this spot, as he did at the eight other Lake Okeechobee Scenic Trail (LOST) sites he developed around the lake. Expect to walk about 0.5 mile from the boat ramp to the site. That's not too far, by design. "This would allow even folks with small kids to 'hike' and 'camp' away from developed parks," says Killingbeck. If you're going the distance around the lake, the next rustic campsite to the north—Nubbin Slough—is 10.3 miles away. If you're traveling southbound, it's nine miles to the next sleeping spot, Lake Okeechobee Scenic Trail-South Nubbin Slough.

Campsites, facilities: This primitive tent-camping area accommodates several tents and is accessible by foot; long-distance trekkers circling the lake might arrive by bicycle. A fire ring and a shelter with a picnic table are provided. There are no toilets and no piped water. Bring plenty of water, food, camping supplies, and mosquito repellent. Children and leashed pets are OK.

Reservations, fees: Sites are first-come, first-served. Camping is free. Stays are limited to five consecutive days.

Directions: From the junction of Highway 76 and U.S. 98/441 at Port Mayaca, go north on U.S. 98/441 about seven miles to the Chancy Bay boat ramp, at left. Park your car. Walk to the campsite, which is just over the levee and maybe 0.5 mile north, on the lake side of the Herbert Hoover Dike. The area is hidden in a tree canopy and isn't visible from the trail. Look for the Scenic Trail sign and follow the path to the campsite. For detailed information, contact the U.S. Army Corps of Engineers before your trip or study the website. You can also download a map of the trail at www.saj.usace.army.mil/sfoo/images/maps/lostmap.pdf.

Contact: U.S. Army Corps of Engineers, South Florida Operations Office, 525 Ridgelawn Road, Clewiston, FL 33440-5399, 863/983-8101, www.saj.usace.army.mil.

46 DUPUIS MANAGEMENT AREA

Scenic rating: 8

east of Port Mayaca

Before it was purchased by the South Florida Water Management District to help conserve some of the cleanest water remaining in this part of the world, this remote spot was known as the White Belt Ranch. Why? It was cattle country, and the moo-heads who grazed here were black, with a big white stripe down their sides. The 21,875 acres of oaks, pines, and marshes has an equestrian camping area and a separate family camping area. Set in pine flatwoods, the general campground is a getaway—here, you're two miles east of angler haven Lake Okeechobee, and the armadillos scurrying through the palm thickets are a reminder that you're many miles west of urban South Florida. The campsites encircle a little pond, and if you're well-prepared for roughing it, this is a nice place to stay.

Backpackers hike a little more than two miles to reach the first primitive, cleared camping area, with fire rings. If the site has been taken, hikers are expected to continue another four miles or so to get to the next rustic camping area.

This is great country for hiking and mountain biking in South Florida. It's especially pleasant if you arrive in winter, when the weather's cool and bugs are bearable. Don't be surprised to spot deer, turkey, wild hogs, and small mammals at dawn or dusk. Bald eagles nest here. Wood storks and white ibis, in search of food, stalk the marshes close to the road during the rainy season. More than 35 miles of the Florida Trail wind through the forest. Four loop trails—measuring 4.3 miles, 6.8 miles, 11.5 miles, and 15.6 miles—were developed by the Florida Trail Association, and begin in pine flatwoods. The terrain varies throughout the reserve and includes wet prairie, lots of cypress domes, and some scrub. A connector trail leads to J.W. Corbett Wildlife Management Area (see listing in this chapter). Together, Corbett and the Dupuis Management Area offer the biggest swath of pine flatwoods remaining in Palm Beach County. In some places, you'll notice little ponds; they're former watering holes for the cattle that lived here when the late John Dupuis, Jr., owned this land.

Fat-tired bicycles are permitted only on named and numbered forest roads. Camping is permitted during hunting season, but this is a time to be careful and wear orange or other bright colors. Hunters are warned to watch out for hikers and horseback riders. They tend to be a hospitable bunch; one friendly hunter freely offered us his orange vests when we expressed concern about mountain biking on the property during bird-hunting season. But he also noted that it would not be such a great idea to bike around here during ground hunts, when people are shooting low to the surface. Although season dates change from year to year, hunting for deer and small game tends to occur most weekends in September, October, November, most of December, and early January. March weekends are reserved for turkey hunters. Another warning is in order about the wild hogs on the property. They can be dangerous, particularly if they feel cornered. The hogs are pests—the only animal hunted here with no bag limit. Remember also that the place was bought by the government because it helps store clean water. Some of that water may make the trails impassable, if you're not up to getting your feet wet.

Campsites, facilities: A drive-up, primitive family camping area of 20 sites with picnic tables is provided, as well as three hike-in backcountry campsites along portions of the Florida National Scenic Trail. A portable toilet and a fire ring are offered in the family camping area. No facilities are provided in the backcountry. Bring plenty of water, plus food, camping gear, and mosquito repellent. Children are welcome, but not dogs. At the family campground, only tents and pop-top campers are allowed. Generators are prohibited. Call 561/924-5310, ext. 3333, to check on conditions before you head out.

Reservations, fees: Sites are first-come, first-served. A day-use fee of $3 per person per day is included in the camping fees. Camping is $4 per person at backcountry sites, $5 per person at the family campground, and $7 at the equestrian site. Registration is on the honor system.

Directions: From I-95, take Exit 101 west on State Road 76 for about 20 miles. For the drive-up family camping area, enter Gate 1, which is the main entrance, and drive about one mile on the dirt road to the campground. For backcountry camping, enter the reserve at Gate 2 and park. Follow the hiking trail to the backcountry campsites. For more details and a map, contact the water management district.

Contact: South Florida Water Management District DuPuis Reserve Field Office, 23500 Southwest Kanner Highway, Canal Point, FL 33438, 561/924-5310. Additional information is available from the headquarters office of the South Florida Water Management District, 3301 Gun Club Road, West Palm Beach, FL 33406, 561/686-8800 or 800/432-2045, www.sfwmd.gov.

47 DUPUIS MANAGEMENT AREA EQUESTRIAN CENTER AND CAMPGROUND

Scenic rating: 8

east of Port Mayaca

Horses are limited to this equestrian campsite, roads, and designated horse trails developed by the Dupuis Horsemen's Association. Still, you'll find plenty of places to ride in this 34-square-mile forest of oaks, pines, and marsh. Four looped horseback-riding trails range from 7.2 to 17.5 miles. Be aware of the presence of some wild hogs on the property. You can see the gouged terrain where they have rooted around in the ground for grubs and such; make sure to steer your steed away from those potentially injuring holes.

Campsites, facilities: A countless number of primitive sites accommodate tenters on horseback. Restrooms, about 20 horse stalls, and a fenced exercise area for horses are provided. There is no drinkable water, so bring plenty of water, plus food, camping gear, mosquito repellent, and other supplies. Children are welcome. Dogs are prohibited.

Reservations, fees: Sites are first-come, first-served. Camping is $7 per person per night without a horse, or $9 per night for one person and one horse housed in a stall.

Directions: From I-95, take Exit 101. Go west on State Road 76 for a little over 20 miles to the forest, at left. Enter at Gate 3, which is the equestrian center entrance.

Contact: South Florida Water Management District DuPuis Reserve Field Office, 23500 Southwest Kanner Highway, Canal Point, FL 33438, 561/924-5310. South Florida Water Management District, 3301 Gun Club Road, West Palm Beach, FL 33406, 561/686-8800 or 800/432-2045, www.sfwmd.gov.

48 J. W. CORBETT WILDLIFE MANAGEMENT AREA

Scenic rating: 7

west of West Palm Beach

At 94 square miles, this chunk of backwoods stands out for outdoorsy types in largely suburban and agricultural Palm Beach County. At certain wet times of year, the muddy roads tend to be fresh with the tracks of resident creatures, such as deer, turkeys, bobcats, raccoons, and, occasionally, ill-tempered wild hogs. No wonder that a portion of the Florida National Scenic Trail slices east–west

through the southern portion of these 60,224 acres, from Seminole Pratt Whitney Road to northwest of Big Gopher Canal, crossing abandoned tomato fields (east of the canal) along the way.

You can drive into this mosaic of wetlands, pines, and hardwoods for a somewhat rough-and-tumble windshield tour down dirt roads. It's best to use a four-wheel-drive vehicle. Most campsites are found alongside canals. Two others are near the northern entrance on either side of the main dirt road, called North Grade. Even near the entrance you may see endangered wood storks—black-headed, white-bodied, goose-sized birds—fishing for dinner. You're certainly out in the woods here. Twenty-five miles to the east, West Palm Beach, the nearest major city, seems light years away. Yet the power lines crossing diagonally through parts of this wilderness are reminders that the place isn't untouched.

Campsites, facilities: These 16 primitive camping areas for tents, trailers, and RVs are open during hunting season (generally winter and spring) and on Fridays, Saturdays, and Sundays from the close of the wintertime hunting season until the Sunday two weeks prior to the next hunting season in spring. There is no piped water, so bring plenty of your own. Bring food and camping supplies, including mosquito repellent. There are no toilets or other facilities. Children and pets are allowed.

Reservations, fees: Sites are first-come, first-served. Backpacking requires a permit, so contact the Florida Fish and Wildlife Conservation Commission. Camping is free.

Directions: From I-95 (Exit 77), go west on Northlake Boulevard. Turn right at State Road 710/Beeline Highway and continue about 20 miles. Look for the entrance to your left after passing the Pratt Whitney/United Technologies plant. If you reach the Martin County line, you've gone too far.

Contact: Florida Fish and Wildlife Conservation Commission, South Regional Office,

8535 Northlake Boulevard, West Palm Beach, FL 33412, 561/625-5122. Or contact its state headquarters at 850/488-4676, www.florida conservation.org.

49 BIG CYPRESS RV RESORT

Scenic rating: 7

in the Everglades, on the Big Cypress Seminole Indian Reservation

Back when Native American tribes were forced to follow the Trail of Tears to reservations out west, the resistant Seminoles had the distinction of never surrendering to federal troops. Eventually, three wars with United States soldiers forced the Seminoles southward through the length of Florida to vanish into the mysterious Everglades. There they lived for decades, until they struck peace—but did not sign a treaty—with the federal government. The Seminoles today say they remain "unconquered." To underline the point, the Big Cypress Seminole Indian Reservation welcomes tourists with many more attractions than a casino. The 54-acre RV park is a citified choice in what was once wilderness. The well-tended lawn encircling the basketball and shuffleboard courts could be mistaken for suburban parkland, if it weren't for the park's native thatched-roof shelters (called "chickees"), which shade some of the picnic tables.

Oaks and cabbage palms dot the landscape and help separate RV campsites, although trees don't totally block views of neighbors. Free buses will take you to one of the tribe's gambling casinos, and there are ice-cream socials, potluck dinners, and other planned activities in the recreation room. A new casino is planned across the street from the RV resort. A motocross track, popular with families, is being expanded to 85 acres, making it the largest lighted course in the United States.

Open since late 2003, the track hosts races and practice sessions throughout the year.

Within one mile, the tribe's Kissimmee Billie Swamp Safari Wildlife Park offers airboat rides and swamp-buggy eco-tours. Frog legs and alligator-tail nuggets are served at the safari's Swamp Water Cafe. Hunters can track such animals as trophy boars and red stag deer year-round at the tribe's 3,000-acre Big Cypress Hunting Adventures hunting preserve; call 800/689-2378 for reservations. Also nearby is the Ah-Tah-Thi-Ki Museum, which tells the story of the tribe's history and culture. The museum (863/902-1113) is worth the trip: It has perhaps the prettiest and longest nature boardwalks in Florida, winding more than a mile through bald cypress and native trees. Incredible carpentry went into the construction of the boardwalk, which is also completely wheelchair-accessible.

Special note: The speed limit of 25 mph inside the reservation is strictly enforced by police.

Campsites, facilities: There are 60 roomy RV campsites, of which 9 are pull-through. Streets are paved, making access easy for even the largest RVs. Some sites are shady. RV sites have concrete pads and full hookups. Primitive tenters can set up camp in their own area far from the rumble of RV generators. Facilities include a clubhouse, a pool, a hot tub for adults only, miniature golf, basketball courts, shuffleboard, horseshoes, a playground, and a weight room. Showers, restrooms, cabins, and laundry facilities are available. Telephone service and Internet access are available at each site, but not cable TV. A small store offers ice and snacks. All areas are wheelchair-accessible. Children are welcome. Leashed pets are permitted. You can leave your RV in storage for a monthly fee.

Reservations, fees: Reservations are suggested. Sites are $25 per night for two adults and two children, plus $5 for each extra person. Credit cards are accepted. Maximum length of stay is six months.

Directions: From Fort Lauderdale, take I-75 west to Exit 49, then head north for about 19 miles to the campground. From Naples, take I-75 east for 52 miles to Exit 49, then go north to the campground.

Contact: Big Cypress RV Resort, HC 61, P.O. Box 54-A, Clewiston, FL 33440, 863/983-1330 or 800/437-4102, www.bigcypress rvresort.com.

50 KISSIMMEE BILLIE SWAMP SAFARI

Scenic rating: 6

in the Everglades, on Seminole Indian land

BEST (

Today's Seminole Indians sleep in modern houses, instead of the thatched-roof chickee huts of yore, but visitors can still get a taste of the past. You won't actually be camping in a traditional sense: Beds surrounded by mosquito netting are provided in these waterfront huts, which look like tiny wood cabins with plentiful slatted, screened windows. Still, this qualifies as roughing it for most people, because there is no electricity, no air-conditioning, no sink, and no in-hut bathroom. Lanterns provide light. Outside, torches light pathways. In short, campers can imagine time-traveling back to the days when the tribe settled in this remote land to escape federal troops in the Seminole War.

What attracts Miami regulars, foreigners, and other curious visitors to this remote wilderness is the overall experience. Campers can sit around a fire and hear Indian folklore after

gliding across the grassy Everglades waters in an airboat. They can kick back on a porch rocking chair at the park's Swamp Water Cafe after trying Indian fry bread and frog legs, or explore the surrounding wilderness by horse. Guided hiking tours are $20 per person. Rides in a swamp buggy—a pickup truck with massive wheels—are $20 for adults, $10 for ages 6–12. At the Gum Slough, panthers, American bison, antelopes, and hogs may be seen. Hunters with at least $285 to spare can take home a hog or other game at the tribe's 3,000-acre Big Cypress Hunting Adventures preserve (800/689-2378), accessed here.

Campsites, facilities: Thirty thatched-roof native Indian shelters called chickees sleep two people each, and the nine dormitory-style chickees sleep 8–12 people each. Indian gift shops, a restaurant, guided hiking tours, airboat rides, swamp buggy eco-tours, safari hunting trips, alligator pits, and reptile shows entertain visitors. Showers, restrooms, and laundry facilities are provided. Chickees have no electricity or plumbing. Children are permitted. No pets, please.

Reservations, fees: Reservations are suggested. Two-person chickees are $35 per night; dorm-style chickees are $65 per night. Major credit cards are accepted. Long-term stays are allowed.

Directions: From Fort Lauderdale, take I-75 west to Exit 49. Go north for about 22 miles to the park entrance.

Contact: Kissimmee Billie Swamp Safari, HC 61, Box 46, Clewiston, FL 33440, 863/983-6101 or 800/949-6101, www.seminoletribe .com/safari.

TAMPA

© MARILYN MOORE

BEST CAMPGROUND

Biking
Alafia River State Park, **page 493**

The prettiest camping around Tampa, a thriving

city built in a rough half circle around Tampa Bay, centers on three rivers – the Hillsborough, the Alafia, and the Little Manatee.

While Tampa is a tourist destination in its own right, with plenty of interesting historical and entertainment options, look beyond its big-city skyline. The sparkling waters of Tampa Bay offer great boating and fishing.

Most of the RV parks in the Tampa area are inland along the rivers. One of the most attractive is lushly forested Hillsborough River State Park, farther northeast. Developed by the Civilian Conservation Corps during the 1930s, the park features eight miles of nature trails, a huge spring-fed swimming pool, and canoeing on one of the few rivers in the state with Class II rapids.

Also worthy of note for mountain bikers and equestrians is Alafia River State Park, which fronts 12 miles of the Alafia River's south prong. The canoeing is good, but this park's real attraction is 14 miles of off-road biking for users of various skill levels. Horseback riders can meander around on 16 miles of trails, and there are four miles of hiking paths and even a horse corral area in the campground.

The Tampa area has the usual snowbird-oriented RV parks where retirees gather during the winter months, most of them on the outskirts of the city. But you'll also find families on vacation campouts, because of Busch Gardens. The enormous safari-style theme park is the area's major citified tourist attraction, with eight roller coasters, children's educational activities, more than 2,700 animals, and a petting zoo.

RV Overnighters and rally groups are welcome at Rally Park, northeast of Tampa. Part of a 104-acre RV-oriented shopping center, the park includes the Lazy Days Super Center and a Camping World store. There's a full-time coordinator to help plan group events, and a banquet kitchen that can serve as many as 600 people. Of course, if you want to kick the tires of a new RV, this is the place.

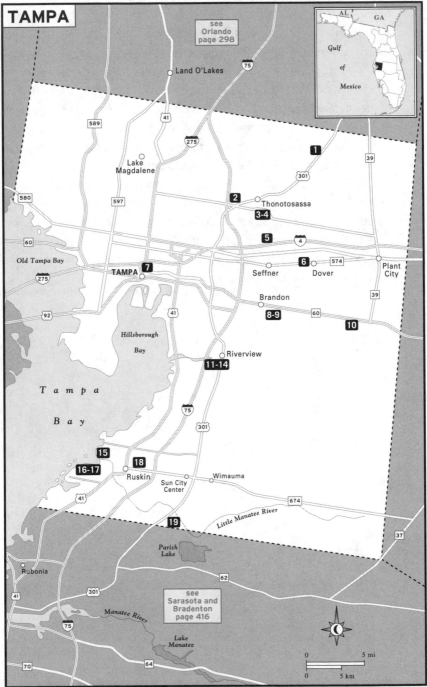

1 HILLSBOROUGH RIVER STATE PARK

Scenic rating: 10

north of Thonotosassa and south of Zephyrhills

Like most of the Florida parks developed by the Civilian Conservation Corps during the 1930s, Hillsborough River State Park is a jewel. The river flows through a lush forest of pines and oaks, its waters dark with tannin. Canoeing is great, because this is one of the few rivers in the state with Class II rapids. There are eight miles of nature trails, and a huge, manmade, spring-fed swimming pool draws crowds of bathers on hot summer days. You can also tour Fort Foster (by reservation only); sometimes, volunteers clad in period dress enact what life was like in the fort in the 1830s, when to the fort protected a military road during the Indian wars. Bicycles and canoes are available for rent, but you're not allowed to take rental canoes on the rapids. The campground is thoughtfully arranged in three loops, so there's a feeling of privacy and seclusion. Visitors come from all over the United States, as well as Germany and England. Pick up supplies in Thonotosassa or Zephyrhills, 6–8 miles away.

Campsites, facilities: There are 114 sites with water and electricity (no sewer hookups), suitable for tents or RVs. Seventy-one sites have 30-amp service, and 43 have 50-amp. RVs up to 40 feet long and slideouts can be accommodated. Picnic tables, grills, fire rings, restrooms, showers, a dump station, a pool, canoe rentals, hiking trails, a historic fort, horseshoe pits, a snack bar, and laundry facilities are available. A camp store sells ice, snacks, and souvenirs. Campsites, picnic areas, and the pool are wheelchair-accessible. Streets are paved. Children are welcome. Leashed pets are permitted in the Hammock Circle camping area with proof of vaccination.

Reservations, fees: Reservations are recommended; contact ReserveAmerica at 800/336-3521 or reserveamerica.com. Sites are $22.40 per night for up to eight people. Credit cards are accepted. The maximum stay is 14 days.

Directions: From I-75, take Exit 265 and drive east on State Road 582/Fowler Avenue for 1.2 miles. At U.S. 301, turn north and drive 12 miles to the park. From I-4, take Exit 7 onto U.S. 301 and drive 13 miles north to the park.

Contact: Hillsborough River State Park, 15402 U.S. 301 North, Thonotosassa, FL 33592, 813/987-6771, fax 813/987-6773, www.floridastateparks.org.

2 HAPPY TRAVELER RV PARK

Scenic rating: 6

east of I-75, in Thonotosassa

Leafy trees shadow many of the sites in this 28-acre, all-ages, RV-oriented park, which claims to be the closest campground to Busch Gardens, the zoo-and-roller-coaster attraction. The Big Top Flea Market is across the street, and plenty of shops and restaurants are nearby. Paved interior roads lead to sites that are grass or dirt; a few are concrete. About 25 percent of the park is occupied year-round. Favorite things to do include "making friends," which is made easier through the planned activities (bingo, day trips, and shows) held in the park during the winter season. Visitors come from all over the world.

Campsites, facilities: This adult park has 220 full-hookup sites with 30/50-amp electrical service. A wireless Internet network is available in the clubhouse and in other parts of the park. On the premises are restrooms, showers, a dump station, a pool, a clubhouse, tennis, shuffleboard, horseshoes, table tennis, and laundry facilities. Restaurants are within 0.2 mile. The clubhouse, bathhouse, and store are wheelchair-accessible. All ages are welcome, but no one under age 21 can stay longer than two weeks. Leashed, non-aggressive pets are allowed.

Reservations, fees: Reservations are recommended. Sites are $22–29 per night for two people, plus $1 for each additional person, $2 for electricity, and $2 for cable TV. Credit cards are accepted. Long-term rates are available.

Directions: From I-75, take Exit 265 onto Fowler Avenue and go 0.5 mile east to the park, at the corner of Walker Road.

Contact: Happy Traveler RV Park, 9401 East Fowler Avenue, Thonotosassa, FL 33592, 813/986-3094 or 800/758-2795, fax 813/986-9077, www.happytravelerrvpark.com.

❸ CAMP LEMORA RV PARK

Scenic rating: 6

in Thonotosassa

Much of the park is open to the sun, with plenty of space for big RVs, and a little creek runs down the back of the property. The owners describe the place as a quiet, relaxing nature park close to springs, a river, and a lake, with an area for hiking nearby. In the winter months, this park is often fully booked by seasonal visitors. Favorite things to do are "getting together and having fun." Planned activities are held late October–late April, and most visitors come from all over the United States and Canada.

Campsites, facilities: This 302-slot RV park has 150 sites available for overnight campers; the rest are occupied by winter residents. Full hookups, 30-amp electrical service, and picnic tables are available. Some sites have concrete patios. Sites average 40 by 50 feet, accommodating RVs up to 40 feet long and slideouts. On the premises are restrooms, showers, a dump station, a pool, horseshoe pits, shuffleboard courts, a general store, and laundry facilities. A camp store sells ice, camping supplies, and limited groceries. Restaurants, grocery stores, and other shops are within 11 miles. Most areas are wheelchair-accessible, and streets are paved. Children are welcome. Leashed pets are allowed.

Reservations, fees: Reservations are recommended. Sites are $24 per night for two people, plus $2 for each additional person. Credit cards are not accepted. Long-term rates are available.

Directions: From I-75, take Exit 265 and drive east on State Road 582/Fowler Avenue for 1.2 miles. At U.S. 301, turn north and drive eight miles to the park. From I-4, take Exit 7 onto U.S. 301 and drive north for 1.5 miles. Or, from I-4 at Exit 6, drive north on U.S. 301 for 12.5 miles.

Contact: Camp Lemora RV Park, 14910 Dead River Road, Thonotosassa, FL 33592, 813/986-4456.

❹ SOUTHERN AIRE

Scenic rating: 6

in Thonotosassa

Rigs up to 40 feet long can be accommodated on the manicured grounds of this countryside park. A sunny, Olympic-sized, heated pool, neatly tended shuffleboard courts, and a large private lake keep snowbirds busy during the winter. Park models are for sale.

Campsites, facilities: This park has 450 sites with full hookups, 30/50-amp electricity, plus cable TV, picnic tables, and telephone service. On the premises are restrooms, showers, a recreation hall, a pool, a whirlpool tub, horseshoe pits, shuffleboard courts, and laundry facilities. Children and pets are permitted.

Reservations, fees: Reservations are not necessary. Sites are $24 per night for two people, plus $2.50 for each additional person. Credit cards are accepted. Long-term rates are available.

Directions: From I-4, take Exit 10 and drive

north on County Road 579 for four miles. Turn right on Florence Avenue and drive 0.1 mile east to the park.

Contact: Southern Aire, 10511 Florence Avenue, Thonotosassa, FL 33592, 813/986-1596, www.rvresorts.com.

5 RALLY PARK

Scenic rating: 4

northeast of Tampa

This is part of a 104-acre RV-oriented shopping center, the Lazy Days Super Center (formerly Lazy Days RV Resort), with more than 1,100 new and used rigs on display, plus a Camping World store where you can pick up needed supplies. Overnighters and rally groups are welcome, and there's a full-time coordinator to help plan group events. The banquet kitchen can serve as many as 600 people. Favorite things to do include sitting in the hot tub and lounging in the pool. This is not one of those parks where you spend the winter season.

Campsites, facilities: There are 299 RV sites with full hookups, 50-amp electricity, high-speed Internet access, concrete pads, and picnic tables. Rigs up to 45 feet long can be accommodated, and all sites are available to overnighters. Restrooms, showers, laundry facilities, a dump station, a screened and heated pool, a 12,000-square-foot recreation hall, a computer room with Internet access, tennis courts, and horseshoe and shuffleboard courts are on the premises. A Cracker Barrel restaurant is part of the complex. All areas are wheelchair-accessible. Included with the price of your site are breakfast and lunch Monday–Saturday, cable TV, and the morning newspaper. Children are welcome. Leashed pets are permitted.

Reservations, fees: Reservations are recommended. Sites are $20–35 per night. Credit cards are accepted. The maximum stay is two weeks.

Directions: From I-4 north of Tampa, take Exit 10 northbound on County Road 579 for 0.2 mile to the Lazy Days Super Center.

Contact: Rally Park, 6210 County Road 579, Seffner, FL 33584, 813/246-4777 or 800/905-6627, fax 813/246-5504, www.lazydays.com/rallypark.html.

6 TAMPA EAST RV RESORT

Scenic rating: 8

near Dover

Convenient to the interstate and Tampa attractions, 12 miles west, this enormous park (actually two parks combined into one) attracts retirees and families on vacation. Some visitors head to Busch Gardens theme park, one of the nation's largest zoos. In winter, the RV park largely becomes a site for snowbirds, and social programs include music jamborees, dances, line dancing, potlucks, and parties. RVs up to 45 feet long can be accommodated. This is a good place to stay when attending RV shows nearby. Interior paved roads lead to a mixture of sites, some grassy and sunny, others shell-carpeted and shaded by palms. Some sites have patios.

Campsites, facilities: All sites are full-hookup, with 30/50-amp electrical service, wireless Internet access, and concrete patios. Picnic tables, restrooms, showers, laundry facilities, a dump station, three swimming pools, a heated spa, a playground, horseshoes, two recreation halls, fishing ponds, propane, a camp store, and shuffleboard are available. Restaurants and shops are a 10-minute drive away. Children are welcome. Leashed pets are permitted.

Reservations, fees: Reservations are recommended. Sites are $27–43 per night, higher during special events. Credit cards are accepted. Long-term stays are OK.

Directions: From I-4, take Exit 14. Drive south about 0.1 mile to the park at right.

Contact: Tampa East RV Resort, 4630 Mc-Intosh Road, Dover, FL 33527, 813/659-2504 or 866/786-6298, fax 813/659-2171, www .tamparvresort.com.

7 BAY BAYOU RV RESORT

Scenic rating: 5

west side of Tampa

Free coffee and snacks are served each morning to wintertime campers, who also enjoy a full menu of planned activities in the 6,000-square-foot recreation hall, including ice-cream socials, potluck dinners, bingo, card games, poker, and special outings. Sites are grassy, oversized, and shady, with paved access roads. Some overlook a creek. The modern, free-form pool is heated during the cooler months, and the whirlpool tub is kept at the same temperature as the pool. About 25 percent of the park is occupied year-round.

Campsites, facilities: All 241 RV sites in this adult-oriented park have full hookups and 30-amp electrical service; 166 have 50-amp. Concrete patios and picnic tables are on hand. RVs up to 45 feet long and slideouts can be accommodated on sites averaging 40 by 50 feet. A wireless Internet connection is available in the clubhouse and the park. On the premises are restrooms, showers, a dump station, a pool, a whirlpool tub, shuffleboard courts, and laundry facilities. A camp store sells ice, camping supplies, and snacks. Kayaks are available for rent. Groceries and restaurants are within one mile; malls and hospitals are within four miles. All areas are wheelchair-accessible. Children are permitted for a maximum of 30 days. One leashed dog under 30 pounds is allowed per site.

Reservations, fees: Reservations are recommended. Sites are $39 per night for two people, plus $4 for each extra person. Credit cards are accepted. Long-term rates are available.

Directions: From I-275, take Exit 50 and drive west on Busch Boulevard for 0.1 mile. At Florida Avenue, turn left and drive 0.5 mile south. At Waters Avenue, turn and travel west for 10 miles to Country Way Boulevard. Turn south and drive 0.25 mile. Turn west on Memorial Highway and drive 0.8 mile to the park. From I-4 going west, take Exit 7 onto Hillsborough Avenue (U.S. 92). Drive west through Tampa for 17 miles. At County Way Boulevard, turn north and drive 0.5 mile to Memorial Highway. Turn west on Memorial Highway 0.8 mile to the park.

Contact: Bay Bayou RV Resort, 12622 Memorial Highway, Tampa, FL 33635, 813/855-1000, fax 813/925-0815, www.baybayou .com.

8 CITRUS HILLS RV PARK

Scenic rating: 3

east of Brandon

This quiet, shady park is family-owned and has a relaxing atmosphere. About half the sites are sunny; oaks lend shade to the rest. It's a retiree magnet in winter, when bingo and potluck dinners are among activities. The park is close to several Tampa attractions, including Ybor City, a worthwhile stop with entertainment and restaurants.

Campsites, facilities: All 220 RV sites have full hookups, 30/50-amp electrical service, and cable TV. More than half are permanent residents. No sites are pull-through. On the premises are picnic tables, restrooms, showers, and a 6,000-square-foot recreation hall with planned activities, such as bingo and cards. Restaurants and a supermarket are one mile away. The park targets retired travelers, but there are no age restrictions. Small pets are allowed.

Reservations, fees: Reservations are not necessary. Sites are $18 per night for two people, plus $3 for each additional person. Credit cards are not accepted. Long-term rates are available.

Directions: From I-75, take Exit 257 and drive east on State Road 60 about two miles to the park on the east side of Brandon.
Contact: Citrus Hills RV Park, 5311 State Road 60 East, Dover, FL 33527, 813/737-4770.

9 LITHIA SPRINGS PARK

Scenic rating: 8

southeast of Brandon

This park has plenty of scenic beauty, but some of the facilities need modernization. Still, camping is a first-come, first-served deal at this popular 160-acre Hillsborough County park, so you'll have to register early on holiday weekends. The oversized sites are shaded by a jungle of scrub oak trees. Each year, some 200,000 people come from all over to swim in the 72°F spring, which has been fenced off and resembles a municipal pool. A lifeguard is on duty on winter weekends, and everyone is ordered out of the water every hour or two for safety checks. You can canoe and fish in the Alafia River, but swimming is banned by the health department.

Campsites, facilities: There are 40 campsites with water, 30-amp electricity (six with 50-amp), picnic tables, grills, and fire rings. Some sites will not fit RVs because of low-hanging trees; others can accommodate rigs up to 38 feet long. Restrooms, showers, a dump station, horseshoe pits, a canoe launch, and a playground are on the property. Groceries and restaurants are within two miles. Children are welcome. Leashed pets are permitted.

Reservations, fees: Reservations are not taken. Campsites are $16 per night for eight people. Credit cards are not accepted. The maximum stay is 14 days at a time, or 90 days in a year.

Directions: From I-75, take Exit 257 and drive east on State Road 60 for two miles. At County Road 640/Lithia Road, turn right and drive south to the park.

Contact: Lithia Springs Park, 3932 Lithia Springs Road, Lithia, FL 33547, 813/744-5572. Hillsborough County Parks and Recreation Administrative Office: 1101 East River Cove Street, Tampa, FL 33604, 813/975-2160, www.hillsboroughcounty.org/parks.

10 EDWARD MEDARD PARK AND RESERVOIR

Scenic rating: 9

east of Brandon

Once a phosphate mine, this 1,284-acre tract near the Alafia River includes a 700-acre reservoir with a white-sand swimming beach. The emphasis is on fishing. Bream, speckled perch, and catfish are plentiful, but officials are trying hard to increase the population of the coveted largemouth bass. Paradoxically, to encourage bigger, better bass, anglers are urged to harvest those under 14 inches; that's so the older fish can mature and grow. To really get the frenzy going, two fish feeders have been placed in the lake near the Burnt Stump dock and a footbridge. You're invited to bring commercial fish food, dry dog food, oatmeal, and even bread to use as chum. Boaters are instructed to anchor away from four fish attractors in deeper water and to cast toward them. The state's regulations on largemouth bass don't apply here, where it's a whole different ball game. For more angling tips, get a copy of the park's fishing brochure.

The heavily wooded campsites are arranged in two loops near the lake, and horseback-riding trails wind through the park. Allow four hours for a round-trip ride on the bridle paths. (You can rent horses by the hour at the stable just north of the park.) Because no reservations are accepted and the park receives about 500,000 visitors a year, try to time your visit for the middle of the week or a non-holiday weekend.

Phosphate, used to manufacture

agricultural fertilizer, is dug from enormous earth-scarring pits, and it's interesting to see how land used for such a purpose can be reclaimed for public recreation. The soil around the so-called Sacred Hills play and picnic area was dug from the mine.

Campsites, facilities: This Hillsborough County park has 40 sites with water, electricity, picnic tables, and grills. Restrooms, showers, a dump station, a boat ramp, a fishing pier, a playground, nature trails, horseshoe pits, and horseback-riding trails are available. Groceries, restaurants, and laundry facilities are within 0.8 mile. Children and pets are welcome.

Reservations, fees: Reservations are not accepted. Sites are $16 per night. Credit cards are not accepted. Campers must register 30 minutes before sunset. If the sign says the campground is full, drive through and check, then go back and tell the ranger about any empty spots. The maximum stay is 14 days.

Directions: From I-75, take Exit 257 and drive east on State Road 60 through Brandon. Continue six miles farther. At Turkey Creek Road, turn and drive one mile south to the park.

Contact: Edward Medard Park and Reservoir, 5276 Panther Loop, Plant City, FL 33567, 813/757-3802, fax 813/757-3939. Hillsborough County Parks and Recreation Administrative Office: 1101 East River Cove Street, Tampa, FL 33604, 813/975-2160, www.hillsboroughcounty.org/parks.

November–April, and about half the park is occupied year-round. Favorite things to do are lounging by the pool, biking, walking, and working out in the exercise room.

Campsites, facilities: All 350 RV sites have full hookups, 30-amp electrical service, and concrete patios. There are 150 sites with 50-amp service. Ten sites are drive-through. Lot sizes are variable, but RVs up to 40 feet long and slideouts can be accommodated. An Internet connection is available in the clubhouse. On the premises are picnic tables, restrooms, showers, laundry facilities, a dump station, a pool, a boat ramp, boat docks, a playground, a nature trail, a small golf course, horseshoe pits, a volleyball area, a game room, rental trailers, a camp circle, and a one-acre lake. The common areas are wheelchair-accessible. Adults are preferred, but children are welcome for short stays. Pets are permitted. Annual residents are especially welcome.

Reservations, fees: Reservations are recommended. Sites are $30 per night for two people, plus $2 for each additional person. Credit cards are not accepted. Long-term rates are available.

Directions: From I-75, take Exit 250 and drive east on Gibsonton Drive/Boyette Road for 2.5 miles. At McMullen Loop Road, turn north and drive 0.8 mile to the park.

Contact: Hidden River Travel Resort, 12500 McMullen Loop Road, Riverview, FL 33569, 813/677-1515, www.hiddenriverrv.com.

11 HIDDEN RIVER TRAVEL RESORT

🥾 ⛵ 🏊 ⛲ 🏠 🚶 ♿ 🚐

Scenic rating: 7

in Riverview

The quiet, peaceful Alafia River runs the length of this resort. Fish from the docks on the river, swim in the heated pool, relax by the one-acre lake, or drive a few golf balls on the three-hole course. There's also a 2.5-mile nature trail. Planned activities are held

12 ALAFIA RIVER RV RESORT

🏊 ⛵ ⛲ 🏠 ♿ 🚐

Scenic rating: 7

in Riverview

Swim in the heated pool or launch your fishing boat from the boat ramp on the Alafia River. Shade trees and river views give this park a natural atmosphere, even though it's conveniently close to the interstate.

Campsites, facilities: All 203 RV sites (four pull-through) have full hookups and 30-amp electricity; cable TV and telephone service are available for long-term visitors. A wireless Internet network is available in the park. Restrooms, showers, laundry facilities, a dump station, a pool, a clubhouse, horseshoe pits, shuffleboard courts, and a boat ramp are provided. The restrooms and clubhouse are wheelchair-accessible. Children are welcome. Leashed pets under 25 pounds are permitted.

Reservations, fees: Reservations are recommended. Sites are $32–36 per night for two people, plus $2.50 for each extra person. Credit cards are accepted. Long-term rates are available.

Directions: From I-75, take Exit 250 east and drive 0.25 mile to the park.

Contact: Alafia River RV Resort, 9812 Gibsonton Drive, Riverview, FL 33569, 813/677-1997 or 800/555-4384, www.alafia riverrvresort.com.

13 RICE CREEK RV RESORT
🏊 🐕 🚐

Scenic rating: 7

in Riverview

The park attracts snowbirds with its paved, lighted streets, a mix of sunny and shady sites with concrete patios, and a tree canopy of massive oaks. All sorts of recreational facilities are available, including craft and pool rooms and a lounge. Entertainers are booked into the 15,000-square-foot clubhouse. Groceries, restaurants, and golf courses are nearby.

Campsites, facilities: The RV resort has 573 full-hookup sites. Restrooms, showers, laundry facilities, a heated pool, a whirlpool tub, a clubhouse with wireless Internet access, an exercise room, a library, horseshoe pits, and shuffleboard courts are available. Campers over age 55 are preferred; children are allowed for short visits. Leashed pets are permitted.

Reservations, fees: Reservations are required

in winter and recommended the rest of the year. Sites are $27 per night for two people, plus $2.50 for each additional person. Credit cards are accepted. Long-term rates are available.

Directions: From I-75, take Exit 250 and drive east on Gibsonton Drive/Boyette Road for one mile to U.S. 301. Turn south and drive 0.25 mile to the park on the left.

Contact: Rice Creek RV Resort, 10714 U.S. 301 South, Riverview, FL 33569, 813/677-6640, fax 813/677-1373, www.rvresorts .com.

14 ALAFIA RIVER STATE PARK
🏃 🚲 🛶 🎣 🏊 🚤 🐕 🚐 ⛰️

Scenic rating: 10

east of Riverview

BEST (

These 6,879 acres were once a phosphate mine. Today, this land is becoming famous as the site of some of the best mountain-bike trails in Florida. But the news for non-bikers is that campers, equestrians, and canoeists will find a home here, too. The park originally opened for day use only in 1998, but a campground was completed in 2003. There is a ranger station on-site and a picnic area. The park has 14 miles of off-road biking for users of different skill levels (as one biker said, the red markers for advanced users really do mean "advanced"). Horseback riders can meander along 16 miles of trails, and there are four miles of hiking paths. The park fronts onto 12 miles of the Alafia River's south prong, and the canoeing is considered quite good.

Campsites, facilities: Thirty campsites with water and 30/50-amp electricity also have grills, fire rings, and picnic tables. RVs up to 55 feet long and slideouts can be accommodated. Fifteen sites are drive-through. Some sites can be used by equestrians, with an area nearby set aside for portable horse corrals. Facilities include restrooms, showers, and paved roads.

The bathhouse and office are wheelchair-accessible. Groceries and restaurants are within eight miles. Children are welcome. Leashed pets are permitted.

Reservations, fees: Reservations are recommended; contact ReserveAmerica at 800/336-3521 or reserveamerica.com. Sites are $18 per night for up to eight people. Credit cards are accepted. The maximum length of stay is 14 days.

Directions: From southbound I-75, take Exit 246 east on Big Bend Road for one mile. At U.S. 301, turn south for 1.5 miles. Turn east onto County Road 672 and drive 12 miles. Turn north onto County Road 39 and proceed 1.5 miles to the park on the right side. If traveling north, take I-75 Exit 240 and drive east on State Road 674 for 15 miles. At County Road 39, turn north and drive five miles to the park. From the east, take I-45 westbound to Exit 22. Turn left onto Park Road and proceed 2.5 miles. Bear right onto 39B. Turn left onto State Road 39 (also known as James Redman Parkway) and drive 15 miles to the park on the left side.

Contact: Alafia River State Park, 14502 South County Road 39, Lithia, FL 33547, 813/672-5132, www.floridastateparks.org.

15 E. G. SIMMONS PARK

Scenic rating: 8

west of Ruskin

Views of sparkling-blue Tampa Bay are marvelous from several places in this 469-acre park, but the camping areas are set in mangroves and overlook a bayou. There's a swimming beach about one mile away from the campsites. Fish from the piers or launch your boat at the ramp. Like many Florida parks so close to urban areas, the spot gets a lot of use on weekends and holidays. You can camp in two separate loops. Shade and privacy are minimal.

Campsites, facilities: All 88 sites in this Hill-

sborough County park have water; 70 have electricity. Picnic tables, grills, fire rings, restrooms, showers, a dump station, a boat ramp, and a playground are provided. Children are welcome. Leashed pets are permitted.

Reservations, fees: Reservations are not accepted. Sites are $16 per night. Credit cards are not accepted. The maximum stay is 14 days.

Directions: From I-75, take Exit 240 and drive west on State Road 674 for three miles. At U.S. 41, turn north and go one mile. Head west on 19th Avenue Northeast about two miles to the park.

Contact: E. G. Simmons Park, 2401 19th Avenue Northwest, Ruskin, FL 33570, 813/671-7655. Hillsborough County Parks and Recreation Administrative Office: 1101 East River Cove Street, Tampa, FL 33604, 813/975-2160, www.hillsboroughcounty .org/parks.

16 RIVER OAKS RV RESORT

Scenic rating: 7

south of Ruskin

Campers over 55 and retirees are welcome at this small, quiet park on the pristine Little Manatee River. "It's like being in the country, away from traffic and noise," says the manager. Bingo, fish fries, and community dinners in the recreation hall are counterpoints to fishing in the river and boating. Trees shade the park, and waterfront sites are available. A county boat ramp is nearby.

Campsites, facilities: Thirty-two RV sites are available for overnighters, plus 68 for seasonal visitors. None are pull-through, and rigs must be no longer than 30 feet. All have 30/50-amp electricity, concrete pads, full hookups, picnic tables, and grills. Restrooms, showers, laundry facilities, a recreation hall, horseshoe pits, shuffleboard courts, and a dog-walk area are on site. Streets are paved. Children are not welcome. Small, leashed pets are permitted.

Reservations, fees: Reservations are recommended. Sites are $28 per night for two people, plus $2 per extra person and $2 for using 50-amp electricity. Credit cards are not accepted. Long-term stays are permitted.

Directions: From I-75, take Exit 240 and drive west on State Road 674 for three miles. At U.S. 41, turn south and drive six miles to Stephens Road. Turn left on Stephens Road and take the first right. Follow the drive to the end; the park will be on your left.

Contact: River Oaks RV Resort, 201 Stephens Road, Ruskin, FL 33570, 813/645-2439 or 800/645-6311, www.riveroaksrv.com.

17 HAWAIIAN ISLES

Scenic rating: 7

outside of Ruskin, on Bay Road

Hawaiian mystique sells, even in tropical Florida. The lighted, paved roads in this RV park boast names like Aloha Boulevard, Waikiki Way, and Leilani Lane, but don't look too closely for hula girls, except on the park brochure. The Wilder Resort Parks chain understands its market—snowbirds who want a resort experience combined with cruise-ship-style luxuries. Hawaiian Isles scores with an Olympic-sized swimming pool (heated, of course), a two-story "sky lounge" cabana overlooking the pool, a whopping 33-unit laundry room, two huge recreation halls with card and billiard rooms, a one-mile nature trail, 16 championship shuffleboard courts, and many waterfront campsites. The park overlooks Cockroach Bay and canals. Golf courses and tennis courts are a short distance away. Reserve early, because campers tend to reserve for next winter before they leave at season's end.

Campsites, facilities: This mobile-home/RV park has 1,000 full-hookup sites with 30/50-amp electrical service. Cable TV, telephone service, restrooms, showers, two enormous recreation halls, a pool, a whirlpool, horseshoe pits, shuffleboard courts, and laundry facilities are available. Adult campers are preferred; children are allowed for short visits. Pets under 25 pounds are permitted.

Reservations, fees: Reservations are recommended. Sites are $26 per night for two people, plus $2.50 for each additional person. Credit cards are accepted. Long-term stays are OK.

Directions: From I-75, take Exit 240 and drive west on State Road 674 for three miles. Turn south on U.S. 41 and drive two miles to the park.

Contact: Hawaiian Isles, 4120 Cockroach Bay Road, Ruskin, FL 33570, 813/645-1098, www.rvresorts.com.

18 HIDE-A-WAY RV RESORT

Scenic rating: 7

In Ruskin

Set on the Little Manatee River, this park is laid out lengthwise to take maximum advantage of the waterfront. At the heart of the park are a pool, a recreation room, a fishing pier, and a campfire circle. About 25 percent of the park is occupied year-round. There's room for 34 boats to tie up at the docks, and the river offers access to Tampa Bay and the Gulf of Mexico. Golfing, flea markets, and Sun City Center are nearby.

Campsites, facilities: All 307 RV sites have full hookups; 257 have 30-amp electrical service, and 50 have 50-amp. Sites vary in size. They can accommodate rigs up to 40 feet long and slideouts. A wireless Internet connection is available in the library. On the premises are picnic tables, restrooms, showers, a dump station, recreation hall, a boat ramp, docks, a pool, a whirlpool tub, horseshoe pits, shuffleboard courts, a fishing pier, and laundry facilities (most areas are wheelchair-accessible). Streets are paved. Groceries and restaurants are seven miles away. Children are welcome. A maximum of two pets are permitted, provided they stand no taller than 18 inches at the shoulder.

Reservations, fees: Reservations are required. Sites are $28 per night for two people, plus $2 for each additional person and $2 if you use air-conditioning. Credit cards are accepted. Long-term rates are available.

Directions: From I-75, take Exit 240 and drive west on State Road 674 for three miles. Turn south on U.S. 41 and drive 2.5 miles to Chaney Road, then go east on Chaney to the park.

Contact: Hide-A-Way RV Resort, 2206 Chaney Road, Ruskin, FL 33570, 813/645-6037 or 800/607-2532, www.hideawayrv resort.com.

tent camping in the Florida woods

19 LITTLE MANATEE RIVER STATE PARK

Scenic rating: 10

south of Wimauma

This state park fronts on the Little Manatee River, a narrow, tannin-stained tributary that widens as it flows southwest to the Gulf of Mexico. Rent canoes from Canoe Outpost just north of the park on U.S. 301, or bring your own. The campsites are nestled in a sand pine scrub forest, with lush screening from your neighbors. There's plenty to do here: In addition to canoeing, check out the 6.5-mile hiking trail (part of the Florida National Trail), which skirts the park's northern wilderness area, or explore on horseback. Ten miles of horseback trails wind through the rest of the park. You might see bobcats roaming remote areas in the 2,416-acre park.

Campsites, facilities: This park has 34 tent and RV sites with water, electricity, picnic tables, grills, and fire rings. Ten sites have 50-amp electrical service; the rest have 30-amp. Sites average 24–50 feet wide, and some can accommodate RVs up to 50 feet long and slideouts. None of the sites are drive-through. Restrooms, showers, a dump station, a canoe ramp, canoe rentals, a playground, a nature trail, and horse stalls are available. The campground, picnic area, and restrooms are wheelchair-accessible. Groceries are within five miles. Children are welcome. Pets are permitted with proof of vaccination. A primitive backpacking site is also available; hikers must obtain a permit at the ranger station. In addition, four campsites are set aside for equestrians.

Reservations, fees: Reservations are recommended; contact ReserveAmerica at 800/336-3521 or reserveamerica.com. Sites are $18 per night for up to eight people. Credit cards are accepted. The maximum stay is 14 days.

Directions: From I-75, take Exit 240 and drive east on State Road 674 for six miles. In Wimauma, turn south on U.S. 301 and drive five miles. At Lightfoot Road, turn west and go 0.2 mile to the park.

Contact: Little Manatee River State Park, 215 Lightfoot Road, Wimauma, FL 33598, 813/671-5005, fax 813/671-5009, www .floridastateparks.org.

FORT MYERS AND NAPLES

© MARILYN MOORE

BEST CAMPGROUND

◀ **Island Retreats**
Cayo Costa State Park Boat-In Sites, **page 507**

The Fort Myers and Naples area is a popular

vacation spot, tending to draw retirees staying for the winter in RV parks that range from the most basic to ultra-luxurious. There are more Class A motorhome parks here than in many other parts of Florida. However, for those who want a more nature-oriented experience, this is an excellent base for exploring the Everglades and Big Cypress National Preserve.

In addition, nature sanctuaries in this area include the J. N. "Ding" Darling National Wildlife Refuge, Six-Mile Cypress Slough Preserve, and the National Audubon Society's Corkscrew Swamp Sanctuary, a unique forest of towering 500-year-old bald cypress bisected by a two-mile boardwalk. The refuge teems with nearly 200 species of birds, including nesting wood storks, plus alligators, deer, and bobcats.

Hiking and off-road bicycling are possible year-round, though it's most pleasant in the winter months when there are fewer mosquitoes. Many people bring canoes or kayaks to explore mangrove-shaded creeks that run down to the Gulf of Mexico. Fish are abundant both inland and in the gulf, which yields the coveted snook and the more commonly caught snapper and sheepshead.

Even if you're not a beach-lover, it would be a shame to miss the sugar-white sands found here. Many of the barrier island beaches are open for day use. For example, Lover's Key State Park between Fort Myers and Naples is a 434-acre collection of islands, canals, tidal lagoons, and mangroves, accessible by road or by water for fishing, boating, canoeing, and swimming. A footbridge connects some of these little islands, so you'll have more of an opportunity to spot wildlife, including several species of woodpeckers and shorebirds such as roseate spoonbills and egrets. You may also see porpoises and manatees near shore.

A favorite beach activity is hunting for shells, particularly on Sanibel Island, Captiva Island, and Marco Island. When you find one, try soaking it in a bucket of water with bleach to remove algae and make it look nearly as perfect as those for sale in souvenir shops. Another method for cleaning shells is to leave them outside in the Florida rain and sun for a few days.

Traffic is noticeably heavier when tourists are in town. (The "high season" runs roughly November 15 through April 15, peaking January through Easter.)

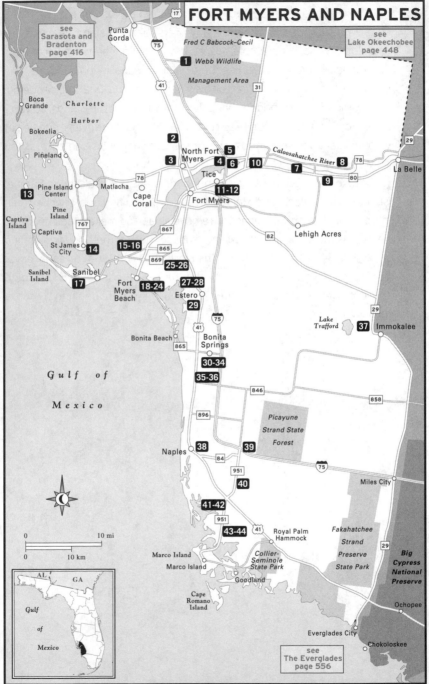

FORT MYERS AND NAPLES

1 FRED C. BABCOCK/ CECIL M. WEBB WILDLIFE MANAGEMENT AREA

🚶 🚴 🎣 ⛴ 🐕 🚐 ⛺

Scenic rating: 8

overlooking Webb Lake

Hunters from as far away as Jacksonville show up to participate in frenetic nine-day deer and three-day hog hunts, taking home 65 deer and 139 hogs one winter. But this 103-square-mile pine-dotted wilderness is better known among locals for its quail hunting, with about 2,500 birds snagged yearly. Regulars also fish for the bluegill, catfish, and bass stocked in the 5.25-mile-long lake, or ride their horses or mountain bikes through the mostly sunny wilderness (all-terrain vehicles are prohibited). There are no official campsites—just head to Loop A or Loop B on the west side of Webb Lake to stake out your own primitive spot. A thick stand of pines shades the camping area. Hikers won't find official trails. Instead, walk along the many elevated or unimproved roads that slice the landscape; wear orange during hunting season. After hunting season, only about 15,000 acres of the wildlife management area are freely accessible, but you may climb fences to continue walking or riding a bike around the entire 65,770 acres during open hours after hunting season.

Campsites, facilities: Forty-one tents, trailers, or self-propelled campers can be accommodated at this primitive camping area daily during the hunting season, which generally runs mid-October–mid-January. At other times, camping is permitted 5 P.M. Friday–9 P.M. Sunday, as well as Memorial Day, Independence Day, Martin Luther King Jr. Day, and Labor Day. There are no hookups and no piped water, so bring all the water you'll need. A portable toilet is available during hunting season only; bury human waste six inches deep at other times. Small campfires are permitted, as long as you ring your fire with rocks. A boat ramp and a lake for fishing are available. Children are welcome. Dogs should be caged or leashed in the camping area.

Reservations, fees: Camping is first-come, first-served. If you are not hunting, a recreational use permit is $3 daily per person or $6 per carload; keep it in your possession. Alternatively, camping is free if you buy a $27 annual hunting permit (also known as a wildlife management area stamp) at any county tax collector's office around Florida or from the sporting goods department at stores such as Wal-Mart and Kmart. You can also order a license by phone by calling 888/347-4356 (fishing) or 888/486-8356 (hunting).

Directions: From I-75, take Exit 158 and drive east for 0.5 mile on Tuckers Grade to the entrance on the right.

Contact: Fred C. Babcock/Cecil M. Webb Wildlife Management Area, 239/575-5768; Florida Fish & Wildlife Conservation Commission, 863/648-3203.

2 TAMIAMI RV PARK

🏊 🐕 ♿ 🚐 ⛺

Scenic rating: 3

north of Fort Myers

With its fitness classes on land and in the pool, this park is perhaps the epitome of the "active" retirement lifestyle people seek in Florida. The idea is to experience the RV park first, then decide to stay longer. On a serious note, the community has established a veteran's memorial garden to commemorate those who have served the United States in wartime. Across the street from this sun-drenched park is the Shell Factory, a 70,000-square-foot store that claims to have the largest collection of seashells and coral in the world (for sale, of course). Next door is an enormous mobile-home community (a sister park, Tamiami Village, with 700 sites) and a barbershop.

Campsites, facilities: This park has a total of 243 full-hookup RV sites with cable TV and telephone service available. About half are taken by visitors who stay six months and then store their trailers, and a third house permanent residents. The rest are available for shorter-term visitors. Big rigs up to 45 feet long and slideouts can be accommodated. Forty sites have 50-amp electrical service; the rest have 30-amp. Tents are permitted at 15 sites; they are grassy with concrete patios and have water and electricity. A wireless Internet network is available in the park. Restrooms, showers, laundry facilities, three shuffleboard courts, three recreation halls, three swimming pools, horseshoe pits, and two pool tables are on-site. The restrooms, laundry room, and recreation hall are wheelchair-accessible. Groceries and restaurants are within two miles; malls and hospitals are eight miles away. Streets are paved. Children are welcome for short visits. Two pets under 25 pounds are allowed.

Reservations, fees: Reservations are recommended. Sites are $23–27 per night for two people, plus $3 for each additional person. Credit cards are accepted. Long-term rates are available.

Directions: From I-75, take Exit 158 westbound eight miles to new U.S. 41. Turn north at Cleveland Avenue. Don't be fooled into turning north on Business Route 41, one mile before you reach U.S. 41.

Contact: Tamiami RV Park, 16555-A North Cleveland Avenue, North Fort Myers, FL 33903, 239/995-7747, 239/997-2697, or 888/609-9697, www.tamiamirvpark.com.

3 SWAN LAKE VILLAGE AND RV RESORT
♨ 🛶 🐕 🚐

Scenic rating: 5

in North Fort Myers

Snowbirds who patronize this park are so devoted that one woman even wrote a poem about the place. What sets Swan Lake apart is that, unlike many campgrounds married to a mobile-home park, here the RV area is removed from high-

way noise and separate from the manufactured homes. It even has its own clubhouse with an adjacent pool. Slash pines and palm trees shade the 60-acre park, which has two fishing lakes and a citrus grove. Shopping, the Shell Factory, and Fort Myers attractions are close by.

Campsites, facilities: This 156-unit mobile-home community has an attached RV park with 104 full-hookup sites that accommodate RVs up to 40 feet long. Each site has a picnic table and 30-amp electrical service. Restrooms, showers, laundry facilities, a pool, a clubhouse with wireless Internet access, two lakes, a recreation room, horseshoes, shuffleboard, daily wintertime activities, and an open field (where some campers hit golf balls) are available. For cable TV and telephone service, you must call the utility companies. A supermarket is one mile away. Adults over 50 are preferred; children are not permitted. Leashed pets that weigh under 20 pounds are permitted, and you can walk your dog in a special pooches area.

Reservations, fees: Reservations are recommended. Sites are $28 per night for two people, plus $3 per extra person. Credit cards are not accepted. Long-term stays are OK.

Directions: Take I-75 to Exit 143 and go west on State Road 78 for 5.2 miles to Business Route 41. Turn north (right) and drive a little over one mile to the park, on the right.

Contact: Swan Lake Village and RV Resort, 2400 North Tamiami Trail, North Fort Myers, FL 33903, 239/995-3397, fax 239/995-7879, www.swanlakevillage.com.

4 PIONEER VILLAGE
♨ 🐕 🚐

Scenic rating: 7

in North Fort Myers

RVers may not want to leave if they stay overnight in this 80-acre deluxe snowbird resort, where more than half the sites go to visitors who stay for the season. It's close to the local attractions, but so many sports facilities and other activities are available on-site that you may want to stay a month or more. Under the direction of an activities director during the high season (November 15–April 15), residents can compete in tennis, horseshoe, and shuffleboard tournaments, and the recreation hall is Action Central for arts-and-crafts classes, bingo, card games, square dancing, quilting, ice-cream socials, and potluck dinners. A few mature oaks shade some sites, but many spots are sunny. Not too far away is the Edison Winter Home and Laboratory (239/334-3614), where inventor Thomas A. Edison—who gave us, among other things, the light bulb and the phonograph—spent his winters. Next door is the home of auto magnate Henry Ford, which is also open to the public and reached at the same phone number. Six-Mile Cypress Slough Preserve (239/432-2004) is a 2,000-acre wetland northeast of Fort Myers. It features a self-guided nature boardwalk and an opportunity to see alligators in the wild.

Campsites, facilities: This community has 470 RV sites (no size restrictions, and most are pull-through) with full hookups and 30/50-amp electrical service; 200 are available for overnighters. A heated, oversized swimming pool with whirlpool and cabana, an 8,700-square-foot clubhouse, and a putting-and-chipping green are available. Volleyball, billiards, tennis, shuffleboard, basketball, horseshoes, a library, laundry facilities, showers, and restrooms also are on the premises. The park is oriented to active retirees, but families with children are permitted for short-term stays. Leashed animals are permitted, and there's a dog-walk area.

Reservations, fees: Reservations are recommended. Sites are $30 and up per night for two people, plus $2.50 for each extra person. Credit cards are accepted. Long-term stays are the norm.

Directions: From I-75, take Exit 143 westbound on Bayshore Road for one mile. At Samville Road, turn south and go 0.2 mile.

Contact: Pioneer Village, 7974 Samville Road, North Fort Myers, FL 33917, 239/543-3303 or 877/897-2757, fax 239/543-3498, www.rvonthego.com.

5 SEMINOLE CAMPGROUND

Scenic rating: 1

near North Fort Myers

Set on 20 acres, this rustic campground is convenient for overnighters. You may request an adults-only or family-only area. Take a look around before you decide; the clientele varies.

Campsites, facilities: The park has 129 sites with full hookups, 30-amp electrical service, cable TV, restrooms, showers, picnic tables, a dump station, a pool, a playground, a game room, laundry facilities, and rental trailers are on-site. Tenters have a community water source, but no electricity. Children are welcome, but not pets.

Reservations, fees: Reservations are not necessary. Sites are $11–15 per night for two people, plus $1 to $2 for each additional person. Credit cards are not accepted. Long-term stays are OK.

Directions: From I-75, take Exit 143 eastbound on State Road 78/Bayshore Road for 0.25 mile. Turn north on Wells Road and go 0.25 mile. At Triplett Road, turn west and proceed to the park.

Contact: Seminole Campground, 8991 Triplett Road, North Fort Myers, FL 33917, 239/543-2919, fax 239/731-2598.

6 UPRIVER CAMPGROUND RV RESORT

Scenic rating: 8

in North Fort Myers, on the Caloosahatchee River

Some sites overlook a short inlet leading to the Caloosahatchee River, so you can feed pelicans from your own private dock or look for a manatee trying to stay warm in the river during the cooler months. A full-time activities director makes sure campers are entertained in winter. This self-described "luxury" campground has an unusual setting: back from the road, with a huge open golf chipping range in front. Shade is minimal. The surrounding area is somewhat rural. Still, there's plenty to do (fishing and boating on the river, swimming in the pool), and the park is a popular destination for snowbirds and retirees. Park models are for sale.

Campsites, facilities: Catering to RVers 55 and older, the park has 350 sites with full hookups, 30/50-amp electrical service, large concrete patios, cable TV, and telephone availability. Fifty sites are pull-through. Half of the sites are available for overnights. A high-speed Internet connection is available in the clubhouse. Restrooms, showers, picnic tables, a boat ramp, an exercise-and-game room, a golf chipping course, three laundry facilities, a pool, and tennis courts are provided. The restrooms, laundry room, and recreation hall are wheelchair-accessible. Children are welcome for short periods in summer. One small pet is allowed per site.

Reservations, fees: Reservations are recommended. Sites are $34–55 per night for two people, plus $4 for each additional person. Credit cards are accepted. Long-term rates are available.

Directions: From I-75, take Exit 143 eastbound on State Road 78 for 1.5 miles. The campground is on the south side.

Contact: Upriver Campground RV Resort, 17021 Upriver Drive, North Fort Myers, FL 33917, 239/543-3330 or 800/848-1652, fax 239/543-6663, www.upriver.com.

⑦ W. P. FRANKLIN LOCK AND DAM CAMPGROUND
🛶 ⛴ 🐕 🚗 ⛺

Scenic rating: 8

east of Fort Myers

This is the westernmost campground run by the U.S. Army Corps of Engineers on the 152-mile Okeechobee Waterway, which crosses Lake Okeechobee and ends on the east coast of Florida near Stuart. This section on the Caloosahatchee River is the most scenic, because it still has the old river oxbows outside of the main boating channel. You can ski in the channel, but at that speed, you'll likely miss seeing wildlife, such as alligators, river otters, bobcats, eagles, ospreys, hawks, and black vultures. The endangered West Indian manatee swims upstream to warmer waters in winter; sometimes manatees get penned in with boats going through the locks and hitch a ride farther upstream. Campsites are paved and shade is minimal, although all sites overlook the river and a small inlet, where boat campers can tie up their craft.

Campsites, facilities: There are 30 sites for RVs, tents, and drive-in campers, as well as eight boat-in spots. Sites have water and 30-amp electrical service. Showers, restrooms, laundry facilities, a dump station, and a boat ramp are provided. A supermarket is 12 miles away. Children and leashed pets are welcome.

Reservations, fees: Reservations are recommended; contact ReserveAmerica at 800/336-3521 or reserveamerica.com. Sites are $20 per night. Credit cards are accepted. Maximum stay is 14 days in a 30-day period.

Directions: From I-75, take Exit 141 eastbound on State Road 80 for 10 miles. While driving, you will come to a stop sign after five miles; turn north and continue on State Road 78 as it winds around south again and west. The campground is on the south side of the road.

Contact: W. P. Franklin Lock and Dam Campground, 17850 North Franklin Lock Road, Alva, FL 33920, 239/694-8770 or 239/694-2582 (visitors center); or call the U.S. Army Corps of Engineers headquarters, 863/983-8101 (weekdays).

8 CALOOSAHATCHEE REGIONAL PARK

Scenic rating: 8

east of North Fort Myers, on the
Caloosahatchee River

Tent campers, rejoice. This 768-acre park is
for you—and also mountain bikers, horseback riders, hikers, and nature-lovers. And
let's not forget canoeists and kayakers. Run
by Lee County, the park has palmetto prairies
and cypress domes, as well as three other kinds
of habitats to explore. Five miles of dedicated
hiking trails let you get back to the wilderness, while 10 additional miles of shared hiking, mountain biking, and equestrian trails
offer another option. The first weekend in
December, this is the site of a reenactment
of the Battle of Fort Myers, and rangers hold
campfire programs periodically throughout
the year. There's a fishing dock and kayak
rentals on the river.

Campsites, facilities: There are 27 tent sites
with picnic tables and grills. Water is available
at eight sites, and two are wheelchair-accessible. Restrooms and showers are provided,
but no electricity. Children are welcome. Pets
are prohibited.

Reservations, fees: Reservations are recommended (www.leeparks.org). Sites are $10 per
night, $15 for group sites of six tents, and $20
for horse camping. Major credit cards are accepted. Maximum stay is two weeks.

Directions: From I-75, take Exit 143 onto
State Road 78 and drive northeast 3.2 miles.
At State Road 31, turn left and drive one mile.
Turn right on County Road 78/North River
Road and proceed eight miles to the park.

Contact: Caloosahatchee Regional Park,
19130 North River Road, Alva, FL 33920,
239/693-2689, fax 239/693-8248, www
.leeparks.org.

9 RIVERBEND MOTORCOACH RESORT

Scenic rating: 9

north of Fort Myers, on the Caloosahatchee
River

This luxury resort, which opened in 2003,
welcomes Class A motorcoaches only. About
50 of the sites are available for rent; the rest are
condominium lots. Ten percent of the park is
occupied by year-round residents, and visitors
come from as far away as Canada, Australia, and Germany. The park has 1,000 feet
of frontage on the Caloosahatchee River's
northern shore, and 25 acres are preserved
as nature areas. Favorite things to do include
group campfires, talent nights, karaoke, happy
hours, breakfasts, swimming, massages, and
planned activities. East of here, in the town
of Alva, is the Eden Vineyards Winery, one
of only a few wineries in Florida.

Campsites, facilities: All 315 sites have full
hookups with 50-amp electrical service, wireless Internet connection, concrete patios, and
phone service available. Lots are landscaped,
and the developers have kept some natural
preserve areas on the site, including an oak
grove along the river. About half the sites
are drive-through. During the winter tourist
season, only as many as five sites are open for
overnighters; the rest of the year, spots are
plentiful. A bar and restaurant are open during the winter. Restrooms, showers, laundry
facilities, a pool, a boat ramp, a dock, pontoon boat rentals, three clubhouses, horseshoe pits, shuffleboard courts, a snack bar, a
store, and nature trails are available. All areas
are wheelchair-accessible. The store sells ice,
food, camping supplies, snacks, and souvenirs. Groceries and restaurants are within five
miles. Malls are 20 miles away, and hospitals
are 12 miles. Children are welcome, but no
more than four people are allowed per coach.
Leashed pets are permitted.

Reservations, fees: Reservations are recommended. Only Class A motorhomes are permitted. Sites are $55–85 per night for two people. Credit cards are accepted. Stay as long as you like.

Directions: From I-75, take Exit 141 and go east on State Road 80 for 17 miles. The park will be on your left.

Contact: RiverBend Motorcoach Resort, 5800 West State Road 80, Alva, FL, 33920, 866/568-7368 or 863/674-0085, fax 863/674-0089, www.riverbendflorida.com.

10 ORANGE HARBOR MOBILE HOME AND RV PARK

Scenic rating: 4

in Fort Myers

As you cross the soaring bridge over the Caloosahatchee River, you can see this sprawling mobile-home and RV park on the south bank. It's near a manatee haven and bird sanctuary on the Caloosahatchee and Orange Rivers. The open and sunny RV area is separate from the 364-unit mobile-home community, where there seems to be a golf cart parked in every driveway; campers may use the pool and common areas there. Near this park is Manatee World (239/694-4042), where you can book a river cruise through one of the state's most populated manatee sanctuaries. The endangered manatees (or sea cows, as these gentle animals are sometimes called) are often injured or killed by speeding boats; many bear the scars of past encounters with propellers, because they stay close to the surface to breathe. On this cruise, the captain shuts off the engines so you can float quietly among the creatures. Reservations are recommended.

Campsites, facilities: Overnighters are not allowed. Long-term visiting senior citizens are the preferred campers at this park, which offers 130 full-hookup sites for RVs. Restrooms, showers, a pool, laundry facilities, a boat ramp, boat docks, and a recreation room are provided. A supermarket is 0.5 mile away. Children are not permitted, except to visit campers. Pets are forbidden.

Reservations, fees: Reservations are recommended. Sites are $1,100 for two months or $1,585 for three months, plus the cost of electricity. Add $50 per month for 50-amp service. Big rigs may be charged an additional fee. Credit cards are not accepted. Minimum stay is two months.

Directions: From I-75, take Exit 141 eastbound on State Road 80/Palm Beach Boulevard for 0.5 mile, then turn north into the park.

Contact: Orange Harbor Mobile Home and RV Park, 5749 Palm Beach Boulevard, Fort Myers, FL 33905, 239/694-3707, www.orangeharbor.com.

11 TICE MOBILE HOME COURT

Scenic rating: 3

near Fort Myers

This older mobile home park is in a working-class neighborhood planted with some of Fort Myers' famous royal palms; they once lined major streets downtown, but are now dwindling. Campers use the screened pool in the backyard of the owner's house. Social activities include swimming, shuffleboard, bicycling, and taking walks.

Campsites, facilities: All 34 sites in this 107-unit mobile home community have full hookups. Three sites are pull-through; size restrictions are 20 by 40 feet. On the premises are restrooms, showers, a pool, a dump station, a game room, horseshoe pits, shuffleboard courts, laundry facilities, and a recreation room. Campers must be over age 55. Pets are not allowed.

Reservations, fees: Reservations are recommended. Sites are $24 a night for two people, plus $1 per extra person. Credit cards are not accepted. Long-term stays are OK.

Directions: From I-75, take Exit 141 westbound on State Road 80/Palm Beach Boulevard for 1.2 miles, then turn south at New York Drive. The park entrance is immediately past the corner.

Contact: Tice Mobile Home Court, 541 New York Drive, Tice, FL 33905, 941/694-3545, www.ticemobilehomecourt.com.

12 CYPRESS WOODS RV RESORT

Scenic rating: 8

east of Fort Myers

This park was among the first of a new breed of Florida luxury resorts targeted to motorcoaches, fifth-wheels, and travel trailers—"one of the most beautiful and private outdoor resorts ever created," according to the color brochure. Sites have space for two cars, 50-foot concrete pads, and a patio. The 12,000-square-foot recreation hall has a $30,000 sound system. The property is architecturally planned to incorporate nature preserves and open spaces. Besides RV spots, lots are being sold for homes. In 2007, the developers were also selling lots at a new mega-luxury motorcoach resort east of Fort Myers called Golden Palms Motorcoach Estates, which will feature two-story "casitas" with kitchens, bathrooms and two-car garages.

Campsites, facilities: This luxury campground has 290 RV sites large enough to accommodate the biggest rigs. Each site has concrete pads, full hookups, and cable TV; telephone service is available. Restrooms, showers, and laundry facilities are available. On the premises are a heated pool and spa, a lake, a recreation hall, and a dog-walk area. All areas are wheelchair-accessible. Children are allowed for stays up to 30 days. Leashed pets are permitted; limit of two per site.

Reservations, fees: Reservations are recommended, and require a 25 percent deposit. No refunds are allowed if you cancel within 30 days of your arrival date, nor are they permitted for early checkouts. Sites are $36 per night May 1–September 30. October 1–April 30, the fee is $60 per night for two people, plus $5 for each additional person; lakefront lots are $75. Rates are subject to change. Credit cards are accepted. Long-term stays are OK.

Directions: From I-75, take Exit 139 eastbound about 0.5 mile to the resort entrance on the left.

Contact: Cypress Woods RV Resort, 5551 Luckett Road, Fort Myers, FL 33905, 239/694-2191, fax 239/694-4969, www.cypresswoodsrv.com.

13 CAYO COSTA STATE PARK BOAT-IN SITES

Scenic rating: 10

On Cayo Costa Island, 12 miles west of Pine Island

BEST (

Play Robinson Crusoe on this nearly deserted island, which is accessible only by boat. At 2,300 acres, Cayo Costa State Park is one of the state's largest unspoiled barrier islands, with extensive dunes and white-sand beaches on the Gulf side and protected waters and mangroves on the east side. In the middle are pine flatwoods and oak hammocks; the island is big enough to accommodate six miles of hiking trails. If you don't have your own boat, the *Tropic Star* shuttle boat (239/283-0015, www.tropicstarcruises.com) runs from Pineland Marina in Bokeelia. Reservations are required, and the fare is $25 round-trip for adults and $20 for children. The ferry leaves Bokeelia at 9:30 A.M. daily and at 2 P.M. on some days, with return trips departing from

Cayo Costa at 3 P.M. A park ranger meets the ferry on the island with a tram, so you can load your camping gear. The tram (50 cents per person) takes you one mile west to the camping area and the cabins. Of course, you can hike it, too.

As you walk across the island from the boat docks to the Gulf of Mexico, you'll see a tiny pioneer cemetery, a legacy of the small settlement that was here through the 1950s. Earlier, the Calusa Indians lived on this land. The north end of the island at Boca Grande Pass is acclaimed for its tarpon fishing, but you may also catch the much-prized snook, flounder, redfish, trout, and sheepshead.

Campsites, facilities: There are 25 primitive tent sites and 12 rustic cabins with bunks. Bring all supplies. No water or electricity are available at the boat docks. The campground is one mile west of the docks on the Gulf side; restrooms, water, cold showers, picnic tables, and grills are provided. Although drinking water is available on the island, you may want to carry in better-tasting stuff. The really big luxury here? Once a day, the park ranger sells ice made with a generator. Pets are prohibited.

Reservations, fees: Reservations are recommended; call ReserveAmerica at 800/326-3521. Sites are $13 per night for four people. Reservations are required for cabins, which are $20 per night for six people. Boaters who want to tie up at the dock and sleep overnight pay the regular camping fee. Major credit cards are accepted.

Directions: From I-75, take Exit 143 westbound on State Road 78 for 20 miles. When you reach the dead end at Pine Island Center, turn north on Stringfellow Road/State Road 767 and drive 10 miles to Four Winds Marina in Bokeelia. By boat, use nautical chart 25E.

Contact: Cayo Costa State Park, P.O. Box 1150, Boca Grande, FL 33921, 239/964-0375, fax 239/964-1154, www.floridastateparks.org.

14 FORT MYERS/ PINE ISLAND KOA

Scenic rating: 7

on the southern end of Pine Island

Lapped by the warm waters of the Gulf of Mexico, Pine Island has a climate so tropical that fruit is grown here commercially. The island has seen little development until recently. Nearby is the Matlacha fishing village, site of the "fishing-est bridge" in the United States—but the fishing is great in all the waters nearby. The two-wheeled set can take their bikes for a spin around the quiet town of St. James City.

If you don't have a boat, call one of the many local marinas to rent one so you can see all the interesting islands around Bokeelia. Among them, Cabbage Key is home to a little restaurant and inn where patrons over the decades have made wallpaper out of dollar bills. Supposedly, this is where Jimmy Buffett was inspired to write "Cheeseburger in Paradise," although his former neighbors in Key West would surely dispute that claim. Or cruise by Useppa Island, where wealthy people from all over the world have constructed the kind of fabulous getaways we all would build (in even better taste, of course) if we ever won the lottery.

Campsites, facilities: This 370-unit KOA offers RV sites with full hookups, 50-amp electrical service, cable TV, and telephone service. Restrooms, showers, picnic tables, a playground, shuffleboard courts, a pool, a spa, tennis courts, three fishing lakes, horseshoe pits, a pool table, a clubhouse with a kitchen and a stage, saunas, laundry facilities, a store, and a gift shop are available. Children and leashed pets are welcome.

Reservations, fees: Reservations are recommended. Sites are $28–60 per night for two adults. Kids camp free; the charge for extra adults is $5. Major credit cards are accepted.

Directions: From I-75, take Exit 143

westbound on State Road 78 for 20 miles to Pine Island. When you reach the dead end at Pine Island Center, turn south on Stringfellow Road/State Road 767 and drive 10 miles to the park.

Contact: Fort Myers/Pine Island KOA, 5120 Stringfellow Road, St. James City, FL 33956, 239/283-2415 or 800/562-8505, www.koa.com or www.pineislandkoa.com.

15 THE GROVES RV RESORT

Scenic rating: 7

in Fort Myers

The Groves boasts that it's the closest RV park to Sanibel Island, which is saying something, since the fabled isle houses only one campground and hundreds of luxury condos and homes. Social activities are planned during winter. The Sanibel Factory Shops outlet mall is nearby. To get to Sanibel Island beaches, located just across the causeway, you'll have to pay a toll of $3. Many people park their RVs or cars just off the causeway and go fishing, swimming, or windsurfing; they don't beat the toll, but these wide spots in the road have Australian pines, a modicum of privacy, and vistas of water, water everywhere.

Campsites, facilities: All 306 grassy RV sites have full hookups, picnic tables, cable TV, and telephone availability. Lots are for sale. Restrooms, showers, picnic tables, concrete patios, laundry facilities, a pool, a library, a game room, shuffleboard, horseshoes, boccie ball (lawn bowling), an exercise room, wintertime social programs, and a dump station are available. Management says the clubhouse is wheelchair-accessible. An 18-hole golf course is nearby; a supermarket is about five miles away. Children are welcome. Leashed pets under 35 pounds are permitted.

Reservations, fees: Reservations are recommended. Sites are $42 per night for two people, plus $4 for each additional person.

Credit cards are accepted. Long-term rates are available.

Directions: From I-75, take Exit 131 west on Daniels Parkway for 5.5 miles to State Road 869/Summerlin Road. Turn southwest on State Road 869 and drive 6.6 miles to John Morris Boulevard. Turn north and go 0.8 mile to the park.

Contact: The Groves RV Resort, 16175 John Morris Road, Fort Myers, FL 33908, 239/466-5909, 239/466-4300, or 800/828-6992, fax 239/466-6310, www.suncommunities.com.

16 SIESTA BAY RV RESORT

Scenic rating: 5

east of Sanibel Island, on the mainland

Favored by busy, busy wintering retirees who like lots of activity, this sparkling-clean park is three miles from the beach on Sanibel Island. There are more double-wide mobile homes here than RVs, and a sense of permanence and community holds forth—at least in the wintertime, when everyone is here. Sabal palms and two lakes give a touch of greenery. Don't feed the swans on the lake, although you are welcome to watch them float lazily on the water. The broad, smooth concrete roadways are perfect for bicycling; plenty of residents have adult tricycles parked in front of their units.

Campsites, facilities: The sprawling mobile-home/RV park has 162 RV sites with full hookups and concrete pads available for overnighters and seasonal visitors. Lots are for sale. Restrooms, showers, two pools, a whirlpool tub, horseshoe pits, shuffleboard and three lighted tennis courts, volleyball, a putting green and driving range, laundry facilities, fishing lakes, two recreation halls, a library, a card room, and a fitness center are available. Tours, field trips, theme parties, dances, clubs, classes, music groups, and competitive sports keep visitors more than occupied. Management says all buildings are wheelchair-accessible. Golf is two miles away. Children are permitted for short visits only. Pets are forbidden.

Reservations, fees: Reservations are required. Sites are $46 per night for two people, plus $4 for each additional person. Credit cards are accepted. Long-term rates are available.

Directions: From I-75, take Exit 131 west on Daniels Parkway for 5.5 miles to State Road 869/Summerlin Road. Turn southwest on State Road 869 and drive 6.5 miles to the park.

Contact: Siesta Bay RV Resort, 19333 Summerlin Road, Fort Myers, FL 33908, 239/466-8988 or 800/828-6992, www .suncommunities.com.

17 PERIWINKLE PARK
🚲 🚐 ⛺

Scenic rating: 8

on Sanibel Island

Periwinkle Park is the only campground on Sanibel Island, famous worldwide for its wonderful shelling beaches. If you camp here instead of on the mainland, you'll at least avoid paying the $6 toll each time you cross the causeway to experience Sanibel. The island has expensive vacation homes, fancy resort hotels, and quaint boutiques selling pastel-colored vacation clothing and knickknacks made of shells, but it retains much of its jungle-like lushness and small-town atmosphere. A two-lane road winds north to the J. N. "Ding" Darling National Wildlife Refuge, where camping is not permitted. Hike the nature trails in this 5,030-acre sanctuary (closed on Fridays) or paddle your canoe; less-adventurous types or those in a hurry can see much of the refuge on the five-mile road that winds through it.

Also on Sanibel is a historic village and museum, a lighthouse built in 1884, and several shell and marine-life attractions. More great beaches are farther north on Captiva Island,

so named because the pirate Jose Gasparilla had a camp there and kept captives on it. The campground stays in island character with shady trees and roads built of crushed shells and gravel. It's 0.5 mile from the beach; from the back of the campground, you can ride a fat-tired bike on an unpaved access road or walk to the Gulf of Mexico. Some sites overlook a little pond next to an aviary filled with exotic birds.

Campsites, facilities: Eighty RVs can be accommodated on tropical wooded sites with full hookups in this 326-unit park; 50 sites have telephone access. Seven sites are pull-through. Tenters can choose from among 11 sites set apart from the RV area. Restrooms, showers, a dump station, laundry facilities, and a recreation room are on the premises. Children are allowed. Dogs are forbidden.

Reservations, fees: Reservations are recommended January–March and on holiday weekends. Sites are $32–40 per night for two people, plus $2 for each additional person. Credit cards are not accepted. Long-term rates are available.

Directions: From I-75, take Exit 131 west on Daniels Parkway for 5.5 miles to State Road 869/Summerlin Road. Turn left on State Road 869 and drive 9.5 miles to the Sanibel Island Causeway. Continue over the causeway to the four-way intersection, then turn north on Periwinkle Way and go 0.25 mile. The park is on the left.

Contact: Periwinkle Park, 1119 Periwinkle Way, Sanibel, FL 33957, 239/472-1433, www .sanibelcamping.com.

18 RED COCONUT RV RESORT
🏊 🐕 🚐 ⛺

Scenic rating: 9

on Estero Island, at Fort Myers Beach

How close do you want to be to the beach? This is the only Fort Myers campground directly on the Gulf of Mexico. The best (and most expensive) sites are on the beach side and enjoy shade from tall Australian pines. Less pricey sites are across the street; they're also less crowded and shaded by Norfolk pines and coconut trees, and they put you within walking distance of the beach. Nine-hole golf courses and boat/canoe rentals are close by. When you tire of beachside fun, ride your bike north to the Times Square area clustered around the bridge to the mainland. It's great for people-watching, even if you're not interested in the honky-tonk T-shirt shops, pizzerias, and ice-cream parlors.

Campsites, facilities: All 176 full-hookup sites have electricity, cable TV, and wireless Internet access. Tents are allowed on the same spots as the RVs. Restrooms, showers, picnic tables, a dump station, horseshoe pits, shuffleboard courts, laundry facilities, and a recreation room featuring a six-foot TV screen and movies are on the premises. Rental trailers are available. Children are welcome. Leashed pets are permitted.

Reservations, fees: Reservations are recommended. Sites are $31–60 per night for two people, depending on location of the site and time of year, plus $6 for each additional person in your party. Credit cards are accepted. The minimum stay is three nights, and long-term rates are available. The pet fee is $3; you must provide proof of inoculation and a photograph of the animal.

Directions: From I-75, take Exit 131 west on Daniels Parkway for 5.5 miles to State Road 869/Summerlin Road. Turn southwest on State Road 869 and drive 5.5 miles to San Carlos Boulevard. Turn south (left) on that road and go one mile until it ends on Estero Island. Turn left on Estero Boulevard and drive 1.5 miles.

Contact: Red Coconut RV Resort, 3001 Estero Boulevard, Fort Myers Beach, FL 33931, 239/463-7200, ext. 200, or 888/262-6226, fax 239/463-2609, www.redcoconut.com.

19 EBB TIDE RV PARK

🏊 🎣 � 🐕 🚐

Scenic rating: 2

in Fort Myers Beach

This over-55 mobile home and RV park, open October–April only, shares the street with the big local commercial fishing fleet. Boats rigged with enormous nets trawl the Gulf of Mexico for their catch, returning with loads of shrimp, lobster, and fish. If you want fish, you probably can't buy it any fresher than from their seafood markets, some of which sell retail. The streets in the little park are narrow, so be careful with big trailers. Nearby is another seasonally open retirement-oriented RV park named Oyster Bay, at 1711 Main Street (239/463-2171); it has 101 sites for snowbirds and three for overnighters.

Campsites, facilities: The park has 148 RV-only sites with full hookups and seven sites for overnighters. Restrooms, showers, laundry facilities, a pool, a boat ramp, shuffleboard courts, and a recreation room are on the premises. The recreation hall is wheelchair-accessible. Most campers are retired, but small children are welcome. Leashed pets are permitted.

Reservations, fees: Reservations are advised as early as one year ahead. The camping fee is $45 per night for two people, plus $2 per extra person. Credit cards are not accepted. Long-term stays are permitted.

Directions: From I-75, take Exit 131 west on Daniels Parkway for 5.5 miles to State Road 869/Summerlin Road. Turn southwest on State Road 869 and drive 5.5 miles to San Carlos Boulevard. Turn south on that road and go three miles to Main Street, just before the bridge, then turn left. The park is 0.25 mile ahead on the left.

Contact: Ebb Tide RV Park, 1725 Main Street, Fort Myers Beach, FL 33931, 239/463-5444.

20 GULF WATERS RV RESORT

Scenic rating: 9

in Fort Myers Beach

Just minutes from the beach, this park is so manicured it looks more like a hotel property. It's usually booked solid November–April. A security gate keeps the park secluded, though it is close to bicycle paths, and shopping is within one mile. Lots are for sale, but management says no one lives here year-round. Tennis courts and shuttle service to the beach complement the busy planned activities schedule. If you drive a fancy, newer RV, you will feel at home: All motor homes, fifth-wheels, and travel trailers must be 26 feet or longer, and any unit 10 years old or more must be approved.

Campsites, facilities: There are 319 full-hookup RV sites, all with 50-amp electrical service, picnic tables, cable TV, and telephone service availability. Rigs up to 45 feet long and slideouts can be accommodated on huge lots measuring 30 by 100 feet. Restrooms, showers, laundry facilities, a computer room with wireless Internet network, a heated pool, a spa, a poolside tiki bar, a 5,000-square-foot clubhouse with wireless Internet access, horseshoe pits, shuffleboard courts, basketball, and a dog-walk area are available. All areas are wheelchair-accessible. Streets are paved. Children are welcome. Leashed pets are permitted.

Reservations, fees: Reservations are recommended during winter. Sites are $60 per night, and rates are subject to change. Credit cards are accepted. Long-term rates are available.

Directions: From I-75, take Exit 131 west on Daniels Parkway for 5.5 miles to State Road 869/Summerlin Road. Turn southwest on Summerlin Road and drive 5.5 miles to Pine Ridge Road. Turn left, then make an immediate right on Summerlin Square Drive. The park will be on your left.

Contact: Gulf Waters RV Resort, 11301 Summerlin Square Drive, Fort Myers Beach, FL 33931, 239/437-5888, fax 239/437-5922, www.gulfwatersrv.com.

21 FORT MYERS BEACH RV RESORT

Scenic rating: 5

in Fort Myers Beach

This 15-acre park is centrally located near gulf beaches, the Thomas Edison and Henry Ford homes, Sanibel Island, and Fort Myers Beach. Paved interior roads lead to grassy sites with concrete patios.

Campsites, facilities: RVs up to 40 feet in length and tents are accommodated at the 305 full-hookup sites with cable TV and telephone access. Sites have 30/50-amp electrical service. Restrooms, showers, picnic tables, a dump station, a pool, a whirlpool tub, an exercise room, wireless Internet access, shuffleboard courts, laundry facilities, rental trailers, and winter entertainment are available. Families with children are welcome. Leashed pets are permitted.

Reservations, fees: Reservations are required. Sites are $45 per night for two people, plus $5 for each additional person. Credit cards are accepted. Campers can stay as long as seven months.

Directions: From I-75, take Exit 131 west on Daniels Parkway for 5.5 miles to State Road 869/Summerlin Road. Turn southwest on State Road 869 and drive 5.5 miles to San Carlos Boulevard. Turn north (right) on that road and go 0.7 mile to the park on the right.

Contact: Fort Myers Beach RV Resort, 16299 San Carlos Boulevard, Fort Myers, FL 33908, 239/466-7171 or 800/553-7484, fax 239/466-6544.

22 GULF AIR RV PARK

Scenic rating: 7

in Fort Myers Beach

A nest for snowbirds, this mobile-home/RV park dotted with queen palms hosts coffee hours for its campers, along with many other social activities, including bingo, potluck dinners, dances, and arts and crafts. The park is central to the Minnesota Twins spring training camp, golf courses, dog racing, shelling, a bird sanctuary, marinas, deep-sea fishing charters, and miles of white-sand beaches. A shopping center is located next door.

Campsites, facilities: This adult-oriented park has 55 full-hookup sites with 50-amp electrical service. Restrooms, showers, picnic tables, laundry facilities, wireless Internet network, shuffleboard courts, a recreation hall, a pool, a dump station, and horseshoe pits are available. Activity programs run November 15–April 15. Children are welcome for short-term stays only. Leashed pets are allowed.

Reservations, fees: Reservations are recommended. Sites are $29 per night for two people. Credit cards are accepted. Long-term stays are OK.

Directions: From I-75, take Exit 131 west on Daniels Parkway for 5.5 miles to State Road 869/Summerlin Road. Turn southwest on State Road 869 and drive 5.5 miles to San Carlos Boulevard. Turn south and go 0.5 mile to the park on the left.

Contact: Gulf Air RV Park-Fort Myers Beach, 17279 San Carlos Boulevard Southwest, Fort Myers Beach, FL 33931, 239/466-8100 or 877/937-2757, fax 239/466-4044, www .rvonthego.com.

23 SAN CARLOS RV PARK AND ISLANDS

Scenic rating: 8

near Fort Myers Beach

Fish from some of the campsites at this seven-acre, boating-oriented campground, which extends off a causeway onto a peninsula surrounded by mangroves. You may see porpoises, manatees, mullets, and numerous tropical birds. If you're into deep-sea fishing, this is a great location: Charter boats are within walking distance, and you can tie up your own boat at the docks. There's a one-mile bicycling and walking path to the beach; restaurants are close by. The campground, which is shaded by Australian pines and surrounded by water on three sides, lies at the base of the busy Matanzas Pass Bridge, the only access road to the Gulf of Mexico and Estero Island. Sometimes traffic backs up at this spot in front of the park.

Campsites, facilities: Tent campers and RVs up to 40 feet long can stay at the 120 full-hookup sites, which have 30/50-amp electrical service and concrete pads. Tenters are allowed for up to two weeks; they camp at eight sites that have picnic tables. Some of the tent sites are waterfront and are shady. Only one tent is permitted per site. Restrooms, showers, picnic tables, a dump station, a pool, a whirlpool tub, a boat ramp, kayak rentals, shuffleboard and horseshoe areas, laundry facilities, a marina with boat dockage, fish cleaning station, and a recreation room are on-site. Management also rents out 19 mobile homes to vacationers. The office and recreation hall are wheelchair-accessible. Children and leashed pets are welcome.

Reservations, fees: Reservations are recommended. Sites are $34–50 per night for two people, plus $2 for each additional person. Credit cards are accepted.

Directions: From I-75, take Exit 131 west on Daniels Parkway for 5.5 miles to State Road 869/Summerlin Road. Turn southwest on State Road 869 and drive 5.5 miles to San Carlos Boulevard. Turn south and go two miles.

Contact: San Carlos RV Park and Islands, 18701 San Carlos Boulevard, Fort Myers Beach, FL 33931, 239/466-3133 or 800/525-7275, www.sancarlosrv.com.

24 INDIAN CREEK RV RESORT

Scenic rating: 6

in Fort Myers Beach

In winter, people from Michigan, Ohio, New York, Massachusetts, and Quebec flock to this sprawling but immaculate park, which is one of the largest in Florida if you count the number of sites. Many visitors leave their rigs here year-round; they've built Florida rooms (typically with windows on all sides) onto their trailers and added utility sheds. Park models are for sale. On the scale of a small city's recreation department, the park offers three swimming pools, 16 shuffleboard courts, three tennis courts, a year-round recreation director, and a tournament-sized pool hall. Nineteen small lakes dot the park, which is two miles from the beach and next door to a miniature golf course. Social activities, needless to say, are ubiquitous.

Campsites, facilities: Set on 200 acres, this senior-oriented park has a whopping 1,140 RV sites (plus another 300 mobile-home sites) with full hookups, 30/50-amp electrical service, cable TV, wireless Internet access, telephone service, concrete patios, and picnic tables. Overnighters can be accommodated at 232 sites. Lots are 30 feet wide by 55 feet deep. Rigs as long as 40 feet and slideouts can be accommodated. On the premises are restrooms, showers, a dump station, three pools, whirlpool tubs, 19 lakes, three clubhouses with Internet access, horseshoe pits, shuffleboard, three tennis courts, a wireless Internet network in the clubhouse, and laundry facilities. An 18-hole golf course is two miles away. The clubhouses and bathhouses are wheelchair-accessible. Streets are paved. Groceries and restaurants are within 0.5 mile; malls and hospitals are within three miles. Children are welcome for stays no longer than 30 days. Small pets are permitted at certain sites only.

Reservations, fees: Reservations are required. Sites are $45 per night for two people, plus $4 for each additional person. Credit cards are accepted. Long-term rates are available.

Directions: From I-75, take Exit 131 west on Daniels Parkway for 5.5 miles to State Road 869/Summerlin Road. Turn southwest (left) on State Road 869 and drive 5.5 miles to San Carlos Boulevard. Turn left onto San Carlos Boulevard. The park is 0.2 mile ahead.

Contact: Indian Creek RV Resort, 17340 San Carlos Boulevard, Fort Myers Beach, FL 33931, 239/466-6060 or 800/828-6992, fax 239/466-7475, www.sunrvresorts.com.

25 FORT MYERS RV RESORT

Scenic rating: 6

in Fort Myers

"We pamper the camper," insist the owners of neatly kept Fort Myers RV Resort, and they've certainly included nearly every amenity seen in an RV park, from an 18-hole miniature golf course to a post office and beer sales. What you won't find is a beach, so drive about eight miles to Sanibel Island or Fort Myers Beach if you pine for sand. Although part of the park fronts on busy U.S. 41, the place is so large that campers toward the back won't be conscious of much noise. Some spots are on a creek where you can fish. Greenery includes slash pine, queen palms, and Australian pines. Shopping centers are close by.

Campsites, facilities: All 345 grassy RV sites offer full hookups with a mix of 30-amp and 50-amp electrical service. Restrooms, showers, some picnic tables, a dump station, a playground, a pool, wireless Internet network, a boat ramp, a dock, horseshoes, shuffleboard, a miniature golf course, a recreation hall, a pool table, a volleyball field, a store, and laundry facilities are on-site. Children and pets are welcome.

Reservations, fees: Reservations are required October–April. Sites are $32 per night for two people, plus $2.50 for each additional person. Credit cards are accepted. Long-term stays are OK.

Directions: From I-75, take Exit 128 westbound on Alico Road for three miles. Turn north (right) on U.S. 41. Drive 0.6 mile to the park on the west side of the highway.

Contact: Fort Myers RV Resort, 16800 South Tamiami Trail, Fort Myers, FL 33908, 239/267-2141 or 239/267-2211.

26 WOODSMOKE CAMPING RESORT

Scenic rating: 7

south of Fort Myers

Slash pines, melaleucas, and lakeside cypress trees cast shade throughout the park. Resist the temptation to feed the ducks, but feel free to watch their antics. Hike on a short boardwalk nature trail. Two miles away is the Koreshan State Historic Site (see listing in this chapter). Woodsmoke is within easy driving distance of beaches, deep-sea fishing charters, Sanibel Island and nature preserves, the Henry Ford and Thomas Edison homes, the Shell Factory, and the Corkscrew Swamp Sanctuary. Most visitors stay here for the season.

Campsites, facilities: You'll find 300 sites, all with full hookups and 30/50-amp elec-

trical service. Seventy-five are pull-through. For cable TV and telephone, you must call the appropriate utility company. Restrooms, showers, a heated pool, a spa, a recreation hall, three lakes, a large pavilion, shuffleboard, horseshoes, dial-up modem, and laundry facilities are available. Children are welcome. Leashed pets are permitted, except for Doberman pinschers, pit bulls, German shepherds, and Rottweilers.

Reservations, fees: Reservations are recommended, particularly in winter. Sites are $30–50 per night for two people, plus $3.50 for each additional adult. Credit cards are accepted. Long-term stays are OK.

Directions: From I-75, take Exit 123 westbound on Corkscrew Road for two miles. Turn north on U.S. 41 and drive two miles. The park is between Hickory Street and Sanibel Boulevard.

Contact: Woodsmoke Camping Resort, 19551 U.S. 41 South, Fort Myers, FL 33908, 239/267-3456 or 800/231-5053, fax 239/267-6719, http://woodsmokecampingresort.com.

27 SHADY ACRES RV PARK

Scenic rating: 7

south of Fort Myers

On cool nights, folks gather around the community campfire for socializing in this well-shaded, lushly landscaped park. Orange-colored flame vine and purple bougainvillea add color. Watch squirrels scramble up the sabal palms. In winter, a restaurant and snack bar are open on the grounds, and social activities, such as crafts, bingo, dances, pool parties with live entertainment, exercise classes, and singing, are available. A golf course is within two miles. Some sites overlook a pond and a creek. Although U.S. 41 is a congested highway, this park is nicely secluded from the road. Shopping centers and tourist attractions are nearby. About 30 percent of the sites are occupied year-round.

Campsites, facilities: The retiree-oriented

park has 356 full-hookup RV sites with 30-amp and 50-amp electrical service, wireless Internet access, concrete patios, and picnic tables. Approximately 217 sites are available for overnighters. Three sites are pull-through. RVs up to 50 feet long and slideouts can be accommodated. Tents are permitted on 17 grassy sites with water and electricity. Restrooms, showers, picnic tables, a dump station, a pool, laundry facilities, cable TV, a playground, horseshoe pits (tournaments during winter), shuffleboard courts, propane sales, and a recreation room with a wireless Internet network, pool tables, and table tennis are provided. Grocery stores are within two miles. Streets are paved, and most areas are wheelchair-accessible. Children may camp for two weeks only. Leashed pets are permitted, except for Rottweilers, pit bulls, German shepherds, and Doberman pinschers.

Reservations, fees: Reservations are recommended. Sites are $34 per night for two people, plus $3 for each additional person. Credit cards are accepted. Long-term rates are available.

Directions: From I-75, take Exit 128 westbound for three miles on Alico Road. Turn south on U.S. 41 and go three miles. At the campground sign, turn west and drive 0.25 mile to the park.

Contact: Shady Acres RV Park, 19370 South Tamiami Trail, Fort Myers, FL 33908, 239/267-8448, fax 239/267-7026, www.shadyacresfl.com.

28 SUNSEEKERS RV PARK

Scenic rating: 7

south of Fort Myers

This park claims to have the lowest rates in Fort Myers and is open to tents and RVs of all sizes, not just the big ones. Sites are shaded by pine trees and palms. Among the activities offered here is a "senior prom."

Campsites, facilities: There are 224 full-hookup RV sites with 30-amp electrical service and concrete patios; 35 sites are available for overnighters. Twenty tent sites are set aside in a separate area. They have water and electricity and concrete patios. Restrooms, showers, a pool, laundry facilities, and a recreation room are on site. Grocery stores are within two miles. Streets are paved, and most areas are wheelchair-accessible. Children and leashed pets are permitted.

Reservations, fees: Reservations are recommended. Sites are $30 per night for two people, plus $2 for each additional person. RVs less than 22 feet long may get a discount. Credit cards are accepted. Long-term rates are available.

Directions: From I-75, take Exit 128 westbound for three miles on Alico Road. Turn south on U.S. 41 and go three miles. At the campground sign, turn west and drive 0.25 mile to the park.

Contact: Sunseekers RV Park, 19701 North Tamiami Trail, Fort Myers, FL 33903, 239/731-1303, www.sunseekersrvpark.com.

29 KORESHAN STATE HISTORIC SITE

Scenic rating: 10

in Estero

Adjoining the Estero River, the campground is part of a state historic site that memorializes a utopian communal religious settlement founded in 1870 by a New York doctor who planned to construct a "New Jerusalem" here, to follow the religion of "Koreshanity." Cyrus Teed was inspired by the Bible to take the name Koresh, a Hebrew transliteration of Cyrus, which was the name of the Persian king who allowed the Jews held captive in Babylon to return to Israel.

Tours of the Koreshan communal settlement are held regularly, including views of the founder's house, the bakery, outbuildings, and the "planetary court." Followers believed that Earth was a hollow sphere, with the planets inside. The governing council consisted of seven women who ran the day-to-day operations of the settlement; leaders of the religion were celibate. Many of the followers came from Chicago with all their furnishings, much of which still can be seen. Teed thought he was immortal, but he died in 1908. Even his tomb has not lasted; it was destroyed in a hurricane in the 1920s. When the settlement dwindled to four members, they donated this land in 1961 to the state; however, the Koreshan Unity Foundation still runs a library and museum near the state park. Don't miss touring the historic site while you're camped here, and imagine what it would be like if Teed's plans for settling 8–10 million people had come to fruition. The campground is shady and cool—a real treat in itself. Swimming is not permitted in the Estero River; canoeing, cycling, boating, and fishing are the things to do. Canoes are for rent on the river, which is part of a state-designated canoe trail.

Campsites, facilities: The 156-acre state park has 48 sites with water and 30-amp electricity. Restrooms, showers, picnic tables, grills, a dump station, laundry facilities, a playground, rental canoes, a camp circle, and a boat ramp are available. Some campsites, the tour areas, and the restrooms are wheelchair-accessible, and the shell roads are wide and level. Most areas and four campsites are wheelchair-accessible. Children are welcome. Pets are allowed with proof of vaccination.

Reservations, fees: Reservations are recommended; contact ReserveAmerica at 800/336-3521 or reserveamerica.com. Sites vary seasonally from $22 per night. Credit cards are accepted. The maximum stay is 14 days.

Directions: From I-75, take Exit 123 westbound on Corkscrew Road for two miles. Cross U.S. 41 and continue 0.25 mile west to the park.

Contact: Koreshan State Historic Site, P.O. Box 7, Estero, FL 33928, 239/992-0311, fax 239/992-1607, www.floridastateparks.org and http://koreshan.mwweb.org.

30 BONITA BEACH TRAILER PARK

🐕 ♿ 🚐

Scenic rating: 4

in Bonita Springs

Tall slash pines, scarlet bougainvillea blossoms, and perfectly formed Norfolk pines give visitors a sense of being sheltered from the busy road that leads to the beach nearby. You'll find pool tables and—in winter—dances, bingo, and card games in the recreation hall. About 80 percent of the park is occupied year-round. A miniature-golf course is across the street. Ride your bicycle to Barefoot Beach Preserve two miles west or take a free trolley. The Gulf of Mexico is 1.25 miles away, and Lover's Key State Park (239/463-4588) is seven miles distant.

Campsites, facilities: The 12.5-acre park has 20 RV sites with full hookups, 30-amp electrical service, and cable TV. Four sites can accept rigs up to 40 feet long. There is an Internet connection in the clubhouse. Restrooms, showers, picnic tables, a dump station, a clubhouse, shuffleboard, a pool, winter activities, and telephone service are available. A supermarket is two blocks away. Children are allowed. Only one leashed pet under 20 pounds is permitted per site.

Reservations, fees: Reservations are recommended. Sites are $37 per night for two people, plus $3 for each additional person. Credit cards are not accepted. Long-term rates are available.

Directions: From I-75, take Exit 116 westbound on Bonita Beach Road for five miles. The park is two blocks west of U.S. 41. Turn north on Meadowlark Lane, and go one block to the park entrance.

Contact: Bonita Beach Trailer Park, 27800 Meadowlark Lane, Bonita Springs, FL 34134,

239/498-1605 or 800/654-9907, bbtpcoop@
aol.com.

31 IMPERIAL BONITA ESTATES

🏊 🎣 🚤 🐕 🏇 ♿ 🚐

Scenic rating: 4

in Bonita Springs

Located on the Imperial River, this resident-owned manufactured-home community and RV park has social activities year-round, although winter is the more active season. Typical things to do are pancake breakfasts, bingo, shuffleboard, fishing, card games and shopping. Grocery stores and restaurants are within three miles, and beaches are close by.

Campsites, facilities: There are 140 RV sites with full hookups and 30/50/100-amp electrical service available for transient travelers. The RV section includes 312 lots, of which about half have units that are tied down permanently. The rest of the park is a 247-unit manufactured-home community, which is wheelchair-accessible. Restrooms, showers, picnic tables, a dump station, two laundry facilities, a large heated pool, horseshoe pits, shuffleboard courts, a recreation room, and a computer room with both dial-up and high-speed Internet access are on-site. There is a boat ramp with access to the Imperial River. Visitors should be age 55 or older, but children may visit, and those under 10 must be accompanied outside the RV. House pets are permitted; be sure to clean up after them and keep them leashed.

Reservations, fees: Reservations are recommended. Sites are $40–50 per night January–March, and $35–40 April–December. Credit cards are accepted. Long-term visits are OK.

Directions: From I-75, take Exit 116 westbound on Bonita Beach Road for 1.1 miles. Turn north on Imperial Street and drive 0.3 mile. At Dean Street, turn east and go two blocks. The park is on the left.

Contact: Imperial Bonita Estates, 27700

Bourbonniere Drive, Bonita Springs, FL 34135, 239/992-0511 or 800/690-6619, fax 239/992-6126, www.imperialbonitaestates.com.

32 CITRUS PARK

🏊 🐕 ♿ 🚐

Scenic rating: 5

in Bonita Springs

This RV resort and manufactured-home community offers 968 sites for vacationers, seasonal visitors, and full-timers. Its claim to fame: more activities than you can shake a stick at. The motto seems to be, "Be active!" The roster of things to do fills four pages of the park's monthly newsletter. For example: a theater troupe, softball, a driving range, tennis, exercise classes, film screenings, choral groups, square dancing, and the usual trips, potlucks, bingo, cards, and so forth. About 20 percent of the occupants live here year-round; others leave their rigs on-site after their vacations are over.

Campsites, facilities: All 968 sites have full hookups, 50-amp electrical service, and cable TV. Picnic tables are available upon request. Twenty-five sites are pull-through. A wireless Internet network is available. Restrooms, showers, laundry facilities, and telephone service are available. On the premises are two pools, a recreation hall, several lakes, horseshoe pits, shuffleboard courts, a driving range, two softball fields, a dog-walk area, and *pétanque* and boccie (lawn bowling) courts. All areas are wheelchair-accessible. This is an age-55-plus park; children are allowed for short visits only. Leashed pets are permitted.

Reservations, fees: Reservations are recommended. Sites are $25 per night for two people, plus $5 per extra person. Credit cards are not accepted. Long-term rates are available.

Directions: From I-75, take Exit 116 eastbound on Bonita Beach Road .5 miles. Turn north on Bonita Grande Road and proceed one mile to East Terry Drive. Turn left on East Terry Drive and drive 0.5 mile to Trost Boulevard. Turn north on Trost Boulevard and drive one mile to the park.

Contact: Citrus Park, 25501 Trost Boulevard, Bonita Springs, FL 34135, 239/992-3030, fax 239/992-4130, www.citrusparkrvmobile.com.

33 GULF COAST CAMPING RESORT

Scenic rating: 3

in Bonita Springs

At Christmastime, at least one camping couple has been known to set out baskets of grapefruit for their neighbors to take—a sign of both friendliness and the abundance of winter citrus yields among the slowly dwindling fruit trees. Set in a neighborhood of small, warehouse-based businesses, this park has a little pond and tends to attract boaters and snowbirds. As more people buy lots here, the number of spots for overnighters shrinks, but most sites still cater to people passing through or looking to spend a few winter months in a warm retreat. About a third of the park is occupied by mobile homes.

Campsites, facilities: Catering to people age 55 and older, this 260-unit park offers about 196 full-hookup grassy sites for RVs up to 37 feet long. Sites have 30/50-amp electrical service. Restrooms, showers, a pool, a recreation hall, shuffleboard courts, horseshoe pits, a wireless Internet network, and wintertime social programs are available. Children may visit campers. Small, leashed dogs are allowed.

Reservations, fees: Reservations are recommended in winter, or anytime for stays of three months or longer. Sites are $29 per night for two people, plus $3 for each additional person. Credit cards are not accepted. Long-term rates are available.

Directions: From the intersection of Old U.S. 41 and U.S. 41 in North Bonita Springs, drive 0.25 mile north on U.S. 41. Turn east at the sign and go two blocks.

Contact: Gulf Coast Camping Resort, 24020 Production Circle, Bonita Springs, FL 34135, 239/992-3808.

34 BONITA LAKE RV RESORT

Scenic rating: 5

in Bonita Springs

Most campers here are retired folks spending winter in the sunshine, and there's plenty of that. A few fruit trees offer greenery; the pool is heated in winter, and the whirlpool is open year-round for soothing weary muscles. A fishing lake might yield hours of relaxation. Some people eat lunch at what is considered a small picnic island. Everglades Wonder Gardens, an old-time tourist attraction with birds, alligators, otters, snakes, and other wildlife, is nearby.

Campsites, facilities: The 167 grassy sites at this 10-acre park have full hookups with 30-amp and 50-amp electrical service and are for RVs up to 40 feet long. There are 50 sites where tents are allowed; they have water and electricity. All sites have picnic tables and concrete patios. Telephone service and a wireless Internet network are available. Restrooms, showers, a dump station, a pool, a whirlpool tub, horseshoe pits, shuffleboard courts, laundry facilities, a recreation hall, and wintertime social programs are available. An 18-hole golf course is five miles away. Children are allowed. Small, leashed pets are permitted.

Reservations, fees: Reservations are recommended. Sites are $39 per night for two people, plus $4 for each additional person. Credit cards are accepted. Long-term stays are permitted.

Directions: From I-75, take Exit 116 westbound on County Road 865/Bonita Beach

Boulevard for two miles. At County Road 887/Old U.S. 41, turn north and drive 1.7 miles to the park.

Contact: Bonita Lake RV Resort, 26325 Old U.S. 41, Bonita Springs, FL 34135, 239/992-2481 or 800/828-6992, fax 239/992-2357, www.bonitalake.com.

35 LAKE SAN MARINO RV PARK

Scenic rating: 6

north of Naples

Visitors to this over-age-55 park keep a keen edge: Shuffleboard is so competitive that the courts are surrounded by bleachers for spectator seating. The pastime seems to be taken as seriously as a Wimbledon tennis match. Campsites are grassy, with adjoining concrete patios. Lake San Marino RV Park is strategically poised for enjoying Greater Naples, close to shopping, restaurants, and several golf courses, and two miles from the spectacular beachfront Delnor-Wiggins Pass State Park (239/597-6196). The state park, south from here on U.S. 41, then east on County Road 846, is open for day use only. There's gulf-front swimming and shelling, fishing, a boat ramp, and an observation tower.

Campsites, facilities: The 35-acre park has 415 sites with full hookups, 30/50-amp electrical service, wireless Internet network, and picnic tables. About half are available for new seasonal visitors; the rest are taken by folks who leave their units on-site in summer. Restrooms, showers, laundry facilities, a pool, horseshoe pits, shuffleboard courts, a clubhouse, telephone service, wintertime social programs, a camp circle for gatherings, and a small fishing lake with a pier are available. Management says the pool area and bathhouse are wheelchair-accessible. Two miles away are groceries, a restaurant, bait, and LP gas. Children are permitted, but in winter the park is predominantly retiree oriented. One leashed pet under 35 pounds is permitted per site.

Reservations, fees: Reservations are required. Sites are $29–42 per night for two people, plus $4 for each additional person. Credit cards are accepted. Long-term stays are OK.

Directions: From I-75 Exit 111, go west to U.S. 41, then north (right) to Wiggins Pass Road. Turn right onto Wiggins Pass. The park is 0.25 mile ahead at right. Alternatively, from U.S. 41 in Bonita Springs, drive two miles south to Wiggins Pass Road. Turn east and go 0.25 mile.

Contact: Lake San Marino RV Park, 1000 Wiggins Pass Road, Naples, FL 34110, 239/597-4202 or 800/828-6992, fax 239/592-0790, www.suncommunities.com.

36 PALM RIVER MOBILE HOME PARK

Scenic rating: 2

north of Naples

Set on the Cocohatchee River, this senior-oriented park hosts potluck dinners, pancake breakfasts, cards, bingo, and crafts during the winter season. Campers can fish from the docks, which accommodate boats up to 20 feet long for an extra charge. Paved, lighted roads lead to concrete sites at this open and sunny park. Shopping, medical facilities, churches, and restaurants are nearby. At least one camper in your party must be over age 55.

Campsites, facilities: This 68-unit condominium mobile-home park is targeted to people over age 55. There are 10 RV sites with full hookups, a clubhouse, and boat docks. Groceries are 0.5 mile away. Children and pets are not allowed.

Reservations, fees: Reservations are recommended. Sites are $25 per night. Credit cards are not accepted. Long-term stays are OK.

Directions: From U.S. 41 in Bonita Springs, drive three miles south to Walker Bilt Road, which intersects with the highway on the south side of the Cocohatchee River. Turn west on Walker Bilt Road and drive a short distance to the park.

Contact: Palm River Mobile Home Park, 793 Walker Bilt Road, Naples, FL 34110, 239/597-3639.

37 LAKE TRAFFORD MARINA AND CAMPGROUND

Scenic rating: 3

in Immokalee

Immokalee—meaning "my home" in the Seminole Indian tongue—is home to sprawling cattle ranches, citrus and vegetable farms, and anglers, which makes it an offbeat destination for campers. This fish camp is nestled on the shores of Lake Trafford, a 1,600-acre basin described as "infested" with largemouth bass, as well as crappie, bluegill, and shellcracker. Children are welcome, although parents should be sure to keep an eye on them: "Too many alligators!" warns the camp's

management. The park also offers boat tours, fishing guides, and airboat rides.

Campsites, facilities: There are 63 sites with full hookups and 30-amp electrical service. Internet connection is available. On the premises are restrooms, showers, a dump station, a boat ramp, a lakeside pier, and a marina with a bait and tackle store, boat rentals, and fishing guides. The office is wheelchair-accessible. Groceries and restaurants are within three miles. Children and pets are welcome.

Reservations, fees: Reservations are taken. Sites are $24 per night for two people, plus $2 for each additional person. Credit cards are accepted. Long-term rates are available. The maximum length of stay is six months.

Directions: From I-75, take Exit 111 east onto County Road 846 and drive 30 miles to Immokalee. Turn west on State Road 29 and drive about two miles to County Road 890/Lake Trafford Road. Continue three miles west to the campground.

Contact: Lake Trafford Marina and Campground, 6001 Lake Trafford Road, Immokalee, FL 34142, 239/657-2214, fax 239/658-2401, laketraffordmarina@earthlink.net.

© MARILYN MOORE

relaxing on the beach in Naples

38 ROCK CREEK RV RESORT AND CAMPGROUND

♨ 🎣 � 🚐

Scenic rating: 6

in Naples

Overnight visitors need luck to get into this suburban park, but it's worth a try to sleep so close to Naples attractions. Despite being in the heart of the city, the place is shady and jungly, with sabal palms, bougainvillea, oaks, and flowering hibiscus. The 17-acre park sits on the banks of pretty Rock Creek, which flows into the Gulf of Mexico. Seasonal guests don't seem to mind the noise of traffic from the small airport next door. A short 2.5-mile drive away are downtown Naples' quaint but pricey marketplaces, such as Tin City, a trendy enclave of restaurants and shops on the city's old fishing wharves. From there, charter boats wait to embark on gulf fishing excursions. Tour boats are available, as well. Also near the park are a big regional shopping mall and the Caribbean Gardens zoo (239/262-5409).

Campsites, facilities: The 225-unit park has lots with picnic tables, full hookups, 30-amp electrical service, and cable TV. Park models are for sale, and many older units are being removed and replaced. Restrooms, showers, laundry facilities, a dump station, a large heated pool, two recreation halls, a boat ramp, horseshoe pits, shuffleboard courts, wintertime planned activities, and a chickee hut (Seminole-style thatched-roof dwelling) for gatherings are available. Children and overnighters are welcome only in summer for short periods; in the winter months, this is an adults-only park. Call for current pet policy.

Reservations, fees: Reservations are required for the few campsites available in the winter season; they are not necessary in summer. Sites are $45–56 per night for two people, plus $3 for each additional person. Credit cards are not accepted. Long-term stays are OK.

Directions: From I-75, take Exit 107 and turn right onto Pine Ridge Road. Drive two miles, then turn left onto Airport Pulling Road. Continue south for 4.5 miles, then turn right onto North Road. The park entrance sign is 100 yards ahead. The park is just south of Naples Municipal Airport.

Contact: Rock Creek RV Resort and Campground, 3100 North Road, Naples, FL 34104, 239/643-3100, fax 239/643-3101, www.rockcreekrv.com.

39 CLUB NAPLES RV RESORT

♨ 🐕 ♿ 🚐 ⛺

Scenic rating: 5

southeast of Naples

To eastbound travelers on I-75, Exit 101 is the last opportunity for easy-on, easy-off camping before reaching Greater Fort Lauderdale or Miami, which typically takes two hours. Popular with campers age 55 and up, this well-kept campground has paved roads and grassy sites set on 20 acres. The first of several campgrounds near the interstate along Collier Boulevard (County Road 951), it is also convenient to fast-food restaurants, gas stations, and Naples-area tourist attractions. South on Collier Boulevard, about a 20-minute drive, is Marco Island, a resort town with plenty of golfing, fishing, boating, fine dining, and shopping options, plus Tigertail Beach on the Gulf of Mexico, which is open to the public. This is also the way to reach U.S. 41/Tamiami Trail, the eastbound route to Big Cypress National Preserve and Everglades National Park.

Campsites, facilities: There are 307 sites with full hookups, cable TV, and picnic tables. About 65 percent of the lots have 30-amp electrical service; the rest have 50-amp. RVs up to 40 feet long can be accommodated. Tenters are permitted to stay at the same sites as the RVs. On the premises are restrooms, showers,

© MARILYN MOORE

a stand of cypress trees east of Naples

laundry facilities, a dump station, propane supply, a small general store, a swimming pool and whirlpool, a playground, activity rooms, rental park models, a miniature golf course, volleyball, *pétanque,* basketball, horseshoe pits, shuffleboard courts, and modem hookup for computers. The restrooms, clubhouse, pool area, store, and office are wheelchair-accessible. Children are welcome. Leashed pets are permitted.

Reservations, fees: Reservations are recommended. Sites are $40–45 per night for two people, plus $2.50 for each extra person. Credit cards are accepted. Long-term stays are OK.

Directions: From I-75, take Exit 101 south on Collier Boulevard (County Road 951). Turn east on Beck Boulevard and drive one mile to the resort.

Contact: Club Naples RV Resort, 3180 Beck Boulevard, Naples, FL 34114, 239/455-7275 or 888/795-2780, fax 239/455-7271, www.clubnaplesrv.com.

40 KOUNTREE KAMPINN RV RESORT

Scenic rating: 6

south of Naples

A tropical forest canopy of pines and palms envelops this campground near Everglades National Park, Marco Island, the Ten Thousand Islands, and Naples. A gun range and golf courses are nearby. Pick up supplies three miles away at shopping centers on the corner of County Road 951/Collier Boulevard and U.S. 41/Tamiami Trail. About 10 percent of the park is occupied by year-round residents. Within a short hike from the park, you'll find a flea market and a rustic county-owned sports complex that has a go-cart track and spectator bleachers for swamp-buggy races.

Campsites, facilities: All 161 RV sites have full hookups (most with 30-amp electrical service; 36 with 50-amp), concrete patios, picnic tables, cable TV, and telephone availability. Lots are 25 by 50 feet, on average. RVs up to 45 feet long and slideouts can be accommodated. You can access a wireless Internet network in the office and the clubhouse, as well as a few other areas of the park. Restrooms, showers, picnic tables, laundry facilities, a pool, horseshoe pits, a recreation room, boccie ball (lawn bowling), shuffleboard courts, and wintertime social programs are available. A camp store sells ice, snacks, propane, and camping supplies. All areas are wheelchair-accessible. Children are welcome. Leashed pets under 30 pounds are permitted.

Reservations, fees: Reservations are recommended. Sites are $45 per night for two people, plus $3 per extra person. Children under 12 are free. Cable TV is free, but a $2 fee applies if you need to hook up to 50-amp electrical service. Credit cards are accepted. Long-term rates are available.

Directions: From I-75, take Exit 101 and head

south on County Road 951/Collier Boulevard for five miles to the park. To enter the park, you must pass the campground and make a U-turn 0.25 mile past Edison College. From U.S. 41/Tamiami Trail, turn north on County Road 951 and drive three miles.

Contact: Kountree Kampinn RV Resort, 8230 Collier Boulevard, Naples, FL 34114, 239/775-4340, fax 239/775-2269, www.kountreekampinn.com.

41 MARCO-NAPLES HITCHING POST TRAVEL TRAILER RESORT

Scenic rating: 4

south of Naples

These sun-drenched pull-through sites measure a roomy 30 by 60 feet, with 8-by-20-foot concrete patios. The park is within seven miles of two beaches and close to "U-pick" vegetable and fruit farms, shopping centers, bowling alleys, golf courses, grocery stores, and restaurants. But the park's recreation hall activities may keep campers close to home, with an action-packed schedule that includes blood-pressure checks every other week, Jazzercise, water aerobics in the pool, a library, square dances, cookouts, and outings such as cruises. There's even a ladies' horseshoe-throwing group.

Campsites, facilities: This wheelchair-accessible park has 300 sites with full hookups, 30-amp electrical service, and picnic tables. About 236 are available for seasonal visitors, and 30 for overnighters. Sites are about 30 feet wide by 50 feet deep, accommodating RVs up to 40 feet long and slideouts. A wireless Internet network is available. Restrooms, showers, laundry facilities, a dump station, a recreation building, a pool, shuffleboard and handball courts, and horseshoe pits are available. All areas are wheelchair-accessible. Children are permitted for short stays only. Leashed pets are allowed.

Reservations, fees: Reservations are recommended. Sites are $33 per night for two people, plus $3 for each additional person. Credit cards are not accepted. The maximum stay is seven months. The park is open October 1–April 30.

Directions: From I-75, take Exit 101 and head south on County Road 951 for 6.8 miles. Turn north at U.S. 41/Tamiami Trail and drive 1.3 miles to Barefoot Williams Road. Turn south and continue to the park entrance.

Contact: Marco-Naples Hitching Post Travel Trailer Resort, 100 Barefoot Williams Road, Naples, FL 34113, 239/774-1259 or 800/362-8968, fax 239/774-9552, www.hitchingpostrv.com.

42 NAPLES/MARCO ISLAND KOA KAMPGROUND

Scenic rating: 6

south of Naples

This KOA and the Silver Lakes RV Resort (see listing in this chapter) are best situated for campers who want all the amenities of a developed park, plus convenient access to Marco Island. For tenters and those with pop-tops, this is the only close option, because most parks won't open their gates to them. The sites are fairly crowded but designed for easy parking, and planned activities entertain folks during the season. The boat ramp provides access to the Gulf of Mexico and for canoeing in Henderson Creek and the Audubon Society's Rookery Bay Wildlife Sanctuary, which is a short paddle downstream. The mangroves offer good saltwater fishing grounds for snapper, sheepshead, redfish, and—albeit rarely—snook. A license is required, and you must be sure to follow the rules and season restrictions, as well as boating speed limits, because Florida Marine Patrol enforcement is strict.

Campsites, facilities: There are 172 sites with full hookups, 30-amp and 50-amp electrical service, cable TV, and picnic tables. RVs can pull through half the sites. On the premises are restrooms, showers, laundry facilities, a dump station, a pool and hot tub, a playground, wireless Internet network, a game room, shuffleboard and boccie ball (lawn bowling) courts, canoe and banana bike rentals, a boat ramp, cabin rentals, and two pet walks. The restrooms, recreation hall, and some campsites are wheelchair-accessible. Children are welcome. Leashed pets are permitted.

Reservations, fees: Reservations are recommended. Sites are $62–72 per night for two people, plus $4 for each additional child and $6 per extra adult. Credit cards are accepted. Long-term stays are OK.

Directions: From I-75, take Exit 101 and drive eight miles south on County Road 951. At the intersection with U.S. 41/Tamiami Trail, continue south on County Road 951 for 0.5 mile. Turn west on Tower Road, then drive one more mile to the park entrance.

Contact: Naples/Marco Island KOA Kampground, 1700 Barefoot Williams Road, Naples, FL 33962, 239/774-5455.

43 SILVER LAKES RV RESORT AND GOLF CLUB

🏊 🛶 🐕 ♿ 🚐

Scenic rating: 8

north of Marco Island

Its slogan: An Invitation to the Good Life! The emphasis is on "the good life" because this park is marketed to older adults who've made significant investments in their RVs and are willing to spend as much as $80 a night—among the higher prices I've seen. Of course, you get what you pay for: The gated park has spent awesome bucks on amenities, from a pristinely maintained nine-hole executive golf course to two swimming pools. Lots (measuring 45 by 90 feet, with 24- by 40-foot concrete pads) are for sale for those who want to return each winter, but owners are permitted to rent them

to overnighters. Worried about the lawn in your absence? Automatic sprinklers make sure the grass stays green. The park, which is close to Marco Island, is two miles from a public boat ramp with direct access to the Gulf of Mexico and the Ten Thousand Islands. A factory outlet shopping mall is next door, and department and grocery stores are within five minutes' drive. About two miles south on County Road 951 at Shell Island Road is the Stephen F. Briggs Memorial Nature Center at Rookery Bay (239/775-8569), a nature exhibit and interpretive boardwalk through a mangrove estuary ecosystem. Here's where you can see how Southwest Florida looked before development: low-lying foliage that's home to an array of birds, lizards, snakes, and the almost-extinct Florida panther.

Campsites, facilities: This ultra-deluxe, adult-oriented condominium RV resort has 560 full-hookup lots with 30/50-amp electrical service, telephone service, cable TV, restrooms, showers, and laundry facilities available. About 200 sites are available for overnight visitors. Three stocked freshwater fishing lakes, a nine-hole golf course, two heated swimming pools, two spas, three tennis courts, six shuffleboard courts, six regulation horseshoe pits, a fitness center, two clubhouses with dialup Internet access, pool tables, and a pro shop are on-site. The Diamond Club House has banquet facilities, a dance floor, a library, and a TV room. RV and boat storage is available so you can leave your stuff in spring. All areas are wheelchair-accessible. Converted trailers, pop-up campers, and truck campers are prohibited. Children are welcome for short stays. Two pets are permitted per site.

Reservations, fees: Reservations are recommended. Sites are $35 to $80 per night for up to six people. Credit cards are accepted. Long-term stays are OK.

Directions: From I-75, take Exit 101 southbound on County Road 951 for seven miles to the intersection with U.S. 41/Tamiami Trail. Continue on County Road 951 for 1.5 miles to the park entrance on the south side.

Contact: Silver Lakes RV Resort and Golf Club, 1001 Silver Lakes Boulevard, Naples, FL 33114, 239/775-2575 or 800/843-2836, fax 239/775-9989.

44 PARADISE POINTE RV RESORT

🏊 🎣 ⛵ 🐕 🚐

Scenic rating: 8

north of Marco Island

Paradise Pointe targets the upscale RV crowd: RVs must be at least 24 feet long, and pop-up campers and camping vans are not welcome. The sites have huge concrete pads for easy parking. The relatively young landscaping is growing in, adding an increasing lushness to the grounds. The park, built around five lakes, has a luxurious air-conditioned clubhouse with pool tables, a TV room, and a large gathering hall for parties. The other amenities are resort-class: tennis courts, a large swimming pool and whirlpool tub, and a fully equipped health spa.

Campsites, facilities: The 56-acre park offers 383 full-hookup sites with 30-amp and 50-amp electrical service, cable TV, wireless Internet network, and telephone access. Restrooms, showers, a pool, a spa, tennis and shuffleboard courts, horseshoe pits, a clubhouse with a kitchen, a TV room, a game room, laundry facilities, a small putting green, and a health spa with a massage therapist and weights are on the premises. A supermarket and restaurants are two miles away. Children are allowed for two weeks. Pets are permitted.

Reservations, fees: Reservations are recommended. Sites are $45 per night. Credit cards are accepted. Long-term stays are allowed.

Directions: From the intersection of U.S. 41/ Tamiami Trail and County Road 951, drive east on U.S. 41 for 2.5 miles.

Contact: Paradise Pointe RV Resort, 14500 East Tamiami Trail, Naples, FL 34114, 239/793-6886 or 877/4-NAPLES (877/462-7537).

GOLD COAST

© MARILYN MOORE

BEST CAMPGROUNDS

◖ Families
Lion Country Safari KOA, **page 534**
Markham Park, **page 543**

◖ Island Retreats
Peanut Island, **page 532**
Boca Chita Key Boat-In Sites, **page 549**

◖ Most Unusual
Sunsport Gardens, **page 533**
Lion Country Safari KOA, **page 534**
Quiet Waters Park, **page 536**
Seminole Health Club, **page 544**

The traffic, continuous construction projects,

and parking problems make the eastern part of the Gold Coast unfriendly to campers. Yet many out-of-town visitors use it as a jumping-off point to the Florida Keys and Central Florida, both of which are easy drives. For other campers, the Gold Coast can be a gateway to the sawgrass wilds of the Everglades.

Stretching from Palm Beach in the north, through Fort Lauderdale in the middle, to Miami on the south, the eastern half of what is also called South Florida is knit together by office towers and condominiums that bump up against the Atlantic Ocean. On the west side, sprawling bedroom suburbs end abruptly at the levees that define the edge of the Everglades, the legendary "river of grass."

Palm Beach County is home to 1,100 tennis courts and 160 golf courses – including the famous PGA National Resort and Spa. Fishing charters are available along the Atlantic coast, and the waters off Palm Beach County offer first-rate scuba diving. Palm Beach is among several Florida East Coast resorts put on the map by pioneer developer Henry Flagler, who planned them in the 1920s as refuges for well-heeled travelers in search of tropical climates. Nearby are quaint Jupiter, which boasts a historic lighthouse, and Lake Okeechobee, the second-largest freshwater lake in the United States.

Fort Lauderdale is often referred to as the "Venice of America" because of its network of artificial canals that wind through neighborhoods and past boatyards. The water theme doesn't end there: Sailboats and pleasure craft are parked along nearly every foot of waterfront, and the beaches star in many a family vacation. The New River leads to the fishing grounds of the Gulf Stream; other waterways access backcountry fishing spots.

I-75 is the easiest Everglades access point from Fort Lauderdale. While no camping is allowed on the high-speed thoroughfare that stretches from Fort Lauderdale to Naples, recreation areas and rest stops have boat ramps and covered picnic tables. Several camping parks are nestled along the urban/Everglades boundary.

Miami-Dade County is probably the most famous spot on the Gold Coast, known as the gateway to Latin America and the Caribbean, the cruise ship capital of the world, and the Manhattan of the South for attracting the ultra-hip from all over the globe. To the east lies the city of Miami Beach, which is what most visitors think of when they hear "Miami." The beaches are almost beside the point. There is so much else to do: late-night clubs, pedestrian-friendly Lincoln Road, and a burgeoning arts and music scene.

South of Miami are the main entrances to two national parks: Everglades and Biscayne, both located near the farmlands and horticultural fields of Homestead. Biscayne National Park has no camping – in fact, you'll need a boat to experience most of it. The main entrance to Everglades National Park is on the west side of Homestead.

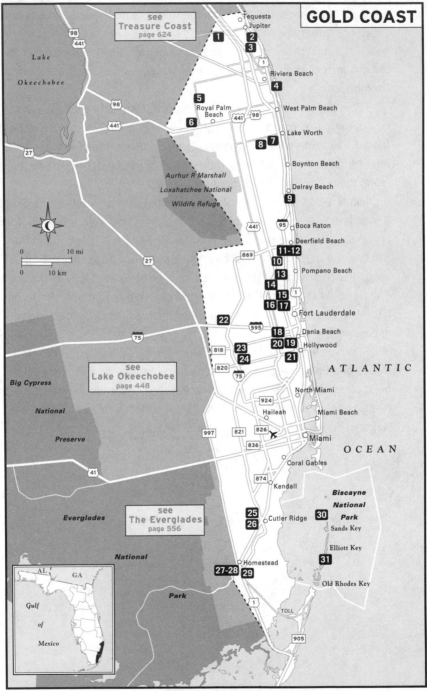

1 WEST JUPITER CAMPING RESORT

Scenic rating: 6

west of Jupiter

Fan-shaped palm fronds shade portions of this improved 10-acre campground, but odds are the paved roads will lead you to a sunny RV campsite. Video games are found in a large tiki hut, and monthly entertainment may bring a band, a magician, or a disc jockey to the campground. Favorite thing to do? "Have fun!" say the owners. The beach is about a 10-minute drive east, and the St. Louis Cardinals play spring-training games one highway exit south at Roger Dean Stadium (4751 Main Street, Jupiter, 561/775-1818). Within a 30-minute drive are Lion Country Safari and fishing charters at Lake Okeechobee. In Jupiter, the oldest lighthouse in Palm Beach County is open for tours Sunday–Wednesday and has a small museum at its base (561/747-6639).

Campsites, facilities: The 74 full-hookup RV-only sites have 30-amp (22 sites) and 50-amp (52 sites) electrical hookups; a few sites are pull-through (available in summer only). Lots are 25 by 45 feet and can accommodate RVs up to 45 feet long and slideouts. A pool, a playground, tennis, volleyball, horseshoes, shuffleboard, monthly entertainment, a basketball court, a catch-and-release fishing pond, and a game room with video games and pool tables entertain campers. Showers, restrooms, picnic tables, concrete pads and patios, a convenience store, deli foods, cable TV, telephone hookups, rental RVs, LP gas, and laundry facilities are available. Nearby are canoe rentals, a golf course, and a theater. Most areas are wheelchair-accessible. Streets are paved. Groceries are within three miles. Children are permitted. Pets are allowed, but small dogs are preferred.

Reservations, fees: Reservations are recommended. Fees for two people are $27–30 per night for RVs. Add $3 per additional adult and $4 for cable TV. Credit cards are accepted.

Long-term stays are OK, but the maximum stay is six months and one day.

Directions: From I-95, take Exit 87B and go west about five miles on State Road 706/Indiantown Road. Turn left (south) at 130th Avenue North and proceed to the campground entrance at the first right.

Contact: West Jupiter Camping Resort, 17801 130th Avenue North, Jupiter, FL 33478, 561/746-6073 or 888/746-6073, fax 561/743-3738, www.westjupitercampingresort.com.

2 JUNO BEACH RV PARK

Scenic rating: 6

off U.S. 1, in Juno Beach

The lapping waves of the Atlantic Ocean are within walking distance of this sunny 25-acre park, where paved streets (maximum speed of 10 mph) pass two rectangular fishing lakes, a playground, and a heated pool with a hot tub. If the place feels like a residential community, the park's condominium concept explains why: A monthly maintenance fee for condo owners includes niceties such as lawn upkeep and underground sprinklers, and some campers opt to buy their concrete-pad RV sites at about half the cost of monthly rental rates. (The fee does not apply for overnighters or seasonal visitors.)

Campsites, facilities: Among the 246 sites in this condominium resort, 100 full-hookup spots are for transient RVs up to 45 feet long and have a picnic table and a fire ring. A pool with a sundeck and a hot tub, a recreation room, a playground, horseshoes, shuffleboard, two fishing lakes, and social programs keep campers busy. Restrooms, a dump station, rental trailers, and two laundry facilities are available. Groceries and restaurants are within 1.1 miles. Management says most areas are wheelchair-accessible. Young children must be adult-supervised, and everyone under 18 is subject to a 10 P.M. curfew. Leashed pets (a maximum of two are allowed per site) must walk in designated areas.

Reservations, fees: Reservations are recommended. If you arrive after office hours, the park posts available sites on the office door. Sites are $44–79 per night for two people, plus $3 for each additional person or pet. Add $3 for electrical service; cable TV is included in the base rate. Credit cards are accepted. Long-term stays are OK.

Directions: From I-95, take Exit 87A and go east a little over four miles on Indiantown Road to U.S. 1. Turn right (south). In about three miles, you'll see a shopping center called The Bluffs on the left side. Turn right at the corner of SunTrust Bank. The RV park is one block ahead to your right.

Contact: Juno Beach RV Park, 900 Juno Ocean Walk, Juno Beach, FL 33408, 561/622-7500, fax 561/627-6595.

❸ PALM BEACH GARDENS RV PARK

🏊 🐕 🚐

Scenic rating: 4

in Palm Beach Gardens

Plunging into the heated pool, tossing horseshoes, or playing a wintertime game of bingo at the recreation room are the main activities for folks at these grassy and gravel RV sites—but they may wish to venture out of the 10-acre park for more action. Within 2.5 miles are the PGA National Resort and Spa, as well as the full-service yacht harbor of Soverel Harbour. For more down-to-earth activities, the big rolling dunes and fairly wide stretch of sand at Juno Beach are about three miles east of this former KOA. In spring, the St. Louis Cardinals play practice games at nearby Roger Dean Stadium (4751 Main Street, Jupiter, 561/775-1818). Farther west, drag racers and racing-school students attend more than 150 events per year at the 200-acre Moroso Motorsports Park (561/622-1400). Most visi-

tors to this park stay for a month or two, or the entire winter.

Campsites, facilities: All 106 full-hookup RV sites (most of them pull-through) have picnic tables with 30-amp electricity. A pool, a recreation room, horseshoes, propane gas sales, showers, restrooms, limited RV parts, and a dump station are available. A supermarket, restaurants, and Palm Beach Gardens Mall are about one mile away. Children are allowed for short-term stays, and leashed pets are permitted.

Reservations, fees: Reservations are recommended. Sites are $30–32 per night for two people, plus $5 for each additional adult. Credit cards are not accepted. Long-term stays are allowed.

Directions: From I-95, take Exit 83 and go east about 1.5 miles on Donald Ross Road to Military Trail. Turn right. Proceed less than 1.5 miles to Hood Road. Turn left (east). The park is about 0.25 mile ahead.

Contact: Palm Beach Gardens RV Park, 4063 Hood Road, Palm Beach Gardens, FL 33410, 561/622-8212.

❹ PEANUT ISLAND

🏊 🏊 🚤 🐕 🎣 ♿ 🚐 ⛺

Scenic rating: 10

near Riviera Beach, between Singer Island and Palm Beach

BEST (

Can it get much better than this? You have (almost) your own wooded private island, accessible only by boat, yet so close to civilization—plus there's a fascinating historic hook. Peanut Island is a Palm Beach County park with 20 primitive tent sites, but you can only get there by ferry or private boat. Just east of the island is the Port of Palm Beach, where cruise and cargo ships sail past to their docks; on the west side is the barrier island protecting this lovely spot from Atlantic Ocean waves. All around you are waterways and sailboat anchorages. You'll have to make an effort, and definitely reservations, but it's worthwhile.

This 86-acre "spoil island," formed from sand dredged from the ocean in 1919, when developer Henry Flagler decided he needed ocean access for his yachting customers, became a historical hot spot in 1961 during the Cuban Missile Crisis. The U.S. Navy Seabees secretly built an emergency fallout shelter here for President John F. Kennedy, who often spent winter weekends nearby at the Kennedy compound, in the ritzy town of Palm Beach. Today, the bunker—and what would have been a command center for the president in case of a nuclear attack—are part of the tour offered by the Palm Beach Maritime Museum onsite (561/842-8202). The island also served as a Coast Guard station, and the ecology-oriented park service plans to reforest the island with native vegetation. Australian pines are pretty, but they are a non-Florida-native tree and considered a nuisance, because of their brittleness in high winds. Meantime, kayakers and boaters use the island during the day, either beaching their craft on the shore or anchoring nearby and swimming to or walking on the shallow sandbars to the island. A paved path of pretty blocks encircles the isle, so you can have a panoramic experience.

Campsites, facilities: There are 20 primitive tent sites set on this oval-shaped island wooded with Australian pines and palm trees. You can also camp on some of the beaches on the east side of the island with prior permission. Wheelchair-accessible restrooms, showers, picnic tables and a communal fire ring are available. The island is closed after dark for campers' use only. Children are welcome. Leashed pets are permitted. A 170-foot fishing pier, boat dock and slips for 19 boats are provided.

Reservations, fees: You must have reservations. Camping is $16.50 per night. Check-in is 1 P.M., and checkout is 11 A.M. Only six people are allowed per site. Call the park office at 561/845-4445 or 561/966-6600 for information. The campground/dock office also monitors VHF channel 16. For ferry ser-

vice, call 561/339-2504 or stop by Phil Foster Park, across from the island on Blue Heron Boulevard.

Directions: From I-95, take Exit 76 eastbound onto Blue Heron Island Boulevard. Drive 3.5 miles east to Phil Foster Park for the ferry service. Marinas and boat services are nearby for private boaters, including the Riviera Beach Marina on Blue Heron Boulevard.

Contact: Palm Beach County Parks and Recreation Department, 2700 Sixth Avenue South, Lake Worth, FL 33461, 561/582-7992, fax 561/588-5469, www.pbcgov.com/parks/peanutisland/.

5 SUNSPORT GARDENS

Scenic rating: 7

in Loxahatchee, west of West Palm Beach

BEST (

At this family-targeted nudist retreat located in rural Loxahatchee, everyone is expected to be in the altogether while swimming in the pool or the hot tub, although exceptions are made in other areas of the 42-acre resort. For afternoon shade, duck into the screened pavilion for a game of darts or cards. The restaurant serves breakfast, lunch, and dinner; and every February, this park is the home of the Midwinter Naturist Festival. Lion Country Safari, golf courses, and shopping are close at hand. Prince Charles has climbed onto polo ponies at the nearby 125-acre Palm Beach Polo and Country Club (561/798-7000), where matches are held in winter.

Campsites, facilities: This 42-acre family nudist retreat has 100 RV sites; 50 sites with 30-amp service, and 20 with 50-amp electricity. Sewer hookup sites are available. Tenters may set up primitive campsites wherever they'd like. A heated pool, a hot tub, a sauna, a playground, a Kidz Club, a game room, two lighted tennis courts, regulation volleyball courts, two *pétanque* (French-style bowling) courts, paddleboats, horseshoe pits, a game room with table-tennis and pool tables, a sundeck, and a 0.25-mile nature trail keep campers busy. Dances are held Saturday nights in the pavilion. Showers, restrooms, two dump stations, rental trailers and cabins, firewood, laundry facilities, snacks, and a restaurant are on the premises. All areas are wheelchair-accessible. Groceries are six miles away. Children are welcome. Leashed pets are OK.

Reservations, fees: Reservations are required. Sites are $18–35 per night. Additionally, you will be charged a $25 daily grounds fee for each person in your party. Credit cards are accepted. Long-term rates are available.

Directions: From I-95, take Exit 70B and go west on Okeechobee Boulevard about 14 miles, passing through Royal Palm Beach. At D Road, turn right. Continue 2.5 miles until it dead-ends into North Road. Turn right, then take the first left to enter the campground.

Contact: Sunsport Gardens, 14125 North Road, Loxahatchee, FL 33470, 561/793-0423 or 800/551-7217, fax 561/793-6370, www.sunsportgarden.com.

6 LION COUNTRY SAFARI KOA

Scenic rating: 7

in Loxahatchee, west of West Palm Beach

BEST (

Wake to the roar of lions. No kidding. The kings of the jungle tend to express their opinions around their 6:30 A.M. feeding time, next door at the 500-acre Lion Country Safari wildlife park, where tourists drive within inches of the freely roaming cats, 2.5-ton white rhinos, and more than 1,000 other creatures. In the afternoon, monkeys get into the verbal act. You'll hear them from your partially shaded or sunny shell-rock campsite.

Although a heated pool and social activities can keep campers busy, sleeping next to the nation's first drive-through zoo (opened in 1967) is the prime reason to stay at this remote 20-acre campground. There is precious little else to do in this fairly rural region, where roadside vegetable stands sometimes can be found along State Road 80. So ,campers understandably head next door to the safari's amusement park rides and drive-through zoo, where they stop to let elephants cross in front of their cars.

Elsewhere, hikers who travel about four miles west of the KOA can see the northern Everglades by visiting one of the largest water-pumping stations in the world—the S5-A, which is bigger than most houses. Walk down the little-explored levee separating sugarcane fields from the Everglades. To your left, you'll probably see alligators, wading birds, and waterfowl, such as ducks and coots. Within the first mile, you'll see an experimental project aimed at cleaning dirty sugarcane water before it reaches the Everglades, and maybe get a glimpse of more wildlife. To get to the S5-A pump station, turn right from the KOA onto State Road 80/Southern Boulevard. Head west about four miles to where the road bends (called 20 Mile Bend). Instead of taking the main road to the right, make a left across the metal bridge crossing the canal, then immediately turn left. Take that road east to the dead end by a picnic area and then park. Look to the southwest and you'll see a gate preventing vehicular access to the levee. Just walk around the gate and hike as far south as you'd like; you could also ride a mountain bike.

Campsites, facilities: Twenty-two tent sites are set apart from the 211 full-hookup RV sites (158 pull-through) with 30-amp and 50-amp electricity. For recreation, there's a pool, a playground, a game room, volleyball, basketball, shuffleboard, horseshoes, miniature golf, winter and summer social programs, rental cabins, and a recreation room. Showers, restrooms, a dump station, picnic tables, limited groceries, LP gas sales, and laundry facilities are on the premises. Management says wheelchairs have access to the store, showers, restrooms, pool, and laundry room. Children are welcome. Leashed pets are OK.

Reservations, fees: Reservations are recom-

mended. Sites are $38–47 per night for two people, plus $8 for each additional person over age two, and $2–3.50 for electricity. Credit cards are accepted. The maximum stay is three months.

Directions: From I-95, take Exit 68 and go west on U.S. 98/Southern Boulevard for 15 miles to the campground on the right.

Contact: Lion Country Safari KOA, P.O. Box 16066, 2000 Lion Country Safari Road, Loxahatchee FL 33470, 561/793-9797 or 800/562-9115, fax 561/763-9603, www .lioncountrysafari.com.

7 JOHN PRINCE PARK CAMPGROUND

Scenic rating: 6

on Lake Osborne, west of Lake Worth

The placid waters of Lake Osborne provide a pleasant backdrop for joggers and bicyclists following the five-mile exercise path that winds through 726-acre John Prince Park, a county-run recreation complex big enough to merit three entrances. The 48-acre campground is set in the southern portion of the sunny park. Golfers can take their pick of a driving range, an 18-hole miniature golf, or a par-3 golf course. At the park's focal point— Lake Osborne—you can boat, water-ski, or fish for bass (just bring the gear). Tennis courts and volleyball areas are also in the park.

Inquire about waterview sites on Explorer Lane or Allegro Road, if you don't plan to camp for more than two weeks (the limit at those sites). For the best lakeview spots on a loop drive with a central community campfire circle, try sites 38–41. Fifty-three sites are paved; the rest have a shell-rock surface. Swimming is not allowed in the lake; rules clearly state that alligators and snakes are considered residents who should be respected and left alone. A security gate is closed 24 hours a day.

Campsites, facilities: All 265 campsites have water, 30-amp electricity, and picnic tables. RVs up to 45 feet long and slideouts can be accommodated. Six sites are drive-through. Restrooms, fire rings, a boat ramp, a dump station, and four playgrounds are on-site. At the park beyond the entrance gate are a fitness trail, a golf course, a driving range, tennis courts, a nature area, and picnic areas. The bathhouse, office, and docks are wheelchair-accessible. Streets are paved. Children are welcome. Leashed, attended pets (no pit bulls) are permitted.

Reservations, fees: Reservations are recommended for holiday weekends and in the wintertime. You can reserve by phone between three and 90 days before arrival. Sites are $20 per night for five people, plus $2 for each additional person. Credit cards are accepted. Long-term rates are available, but camping is limited to 100 days per year. The maximum stay at waterfront sites with the best views is 14 days.

Directions: From I-95, take Exit 63 and go west on Sixth Avenue South to Congress Avenue. Turn left. The campground entrance is about 0.5 mile ahead on the left. From the Florida Turnpike, take the Lake Worth Road exit and turn left. Drive 5.2 miles to Congress Avenue and turn right. Drive 0.9 mile to the park.

Contact: John Prince Park Campground, 4759 South Congress Avenue, Lake Worth, Florida 33461; or contact the Palm Beach County Parks and Recreation Department, 2700 Sixth Avenue South, Lake Worth, FL 33461, 561/582-7992 or 877/992-9925, fax 561/588-5469, www.pbcgov.com/parks.

8 PALM BEACH TRAVELER PARK

Scenic rating: 1

in Lantana

This 7.5-acre suburban home of wintertime bingo games and potluck dinners attracts a

50/50 mix of permanent residents and travelers. The paved park roads, which have a 10-mph speed limit, form a rough figure eight through the grounds, passing staggered, instead of rigidly side-by-side, sleeping spots. Atlantic Ocean beaches are four miles east. A few minutes away is Lake Worth, which is ignored by many tourists. Still, head that way for some bright spots: a 1,000-foot ocean fishing pier, a beach where early birds get the best parking spots, and free concerts at the Bryant Park band shell on the Intracoastal Waterway.

Campsites, facilities: This adult-oriented park has 100 full-hookup sites for RVs, some with 20/30-amp service and some with 50-amp. A pool, shuffleboard, a clubhouse, horseshoes, rental trailers, laundry facilities, and volunteer wintertime social programs are available. The pool and clubhouse are wheelchair-accessible. Children may visit a registered camper for no more than two weeks per year. Pets are forbidden.

Reservations, fees: Reservations are recommended. Sites are $50 per night for two people, plus $5 per additional person. Credit cards are accepted. Long-term stays are OK.

Directions: From I-95, take Exit 61 and go west a little more than two miles on Lantana Road/County Road 812. Turn left at Lawrence Road. The park is 0.5 mile ahead on the right.

Contact: Palm Beach Traveler Park, 6159 Lawrence Road, Lantana, FL 33462, 561/967-3139, jerryrv@msn.com.

9 DEL-RATON TRAVEL TRAILER PARK

Scenic rating: 4

on U.S. 1, in Delray Beach

If you want to sleep in your RV near the beach in southern Palm Beach County, this is pretty much your only choice. Tourists are sometimes astounded by the seemingly endless stream of condominiums and shopping centers spanning almost the length of U.S. 1 in South Florida, and this neck of the woods is no exception. Car dealerships, shops, eateries, and other hubs of commerce line the street on the approach to the five-acre park. Once you pass the security gate, the straight, paved roads (with 5-mph speed limits) pass tree-dotted yet largely sunny concrete-pad campsites separated from each other by grassy lawns. The park is the closest to the tony shops at Mizner Park in Boca Raton. The Atlantic Ocean is a short drive east.

Campsites, facilities: The park has 60 full-hookup sites (25 pull-through) for RVs up to 36 feet long, with 30/50-amp service. Only a handful of overnight spaces are available, usually in an overflow area where rigs are limited to 30 feet long. Showers, restrooms, a dump station, a recreation room, LP gas sales, and laundry facilities are available. Groceries and a restaurant are across the street. Children are welcome short-term but not as monthly residents. Pets are forbidden.

Reservations, fees: Reservations are recommended, except in summer. Sites are $32–36 per night for two people, plus $1 per extra person. Credit cards are not accepted. Long-term stays are permitted for adults.

Directions: From I-95, take Exit 51 and go east one mile on Linton Boulevard to U.S. 1/South Federal Highway. Turn right. Proceed one mile to the trailer park.

Contact: Del-Raton Travel Trailer Park, 2998 South Federal Highway, Delray Beach, FL 33483, 561/278-4633, delraton@aol.com.

10 QUIET WATERS PARK

Scenic rating: 8

in Pompano Beach

BEST (

Tall Australian pines shade the campsites, which overlook a fjord-like lake. You almost could forget you're in the city, if it weren't for the park's noisy public beach and nearby water playground. (Swimming at the campsites is prohibited.) If you're camping with friends who don't have their own equipment, tell them about "rent a camp," a package deal that includes a sleeping pad for each person, a cooler, and use of a canoe. On weekends, the park tends to be chaotic, so try to arrange your stay during quieter times. Site 23 is the most secluded, although it's also farthest from the bathhouse. An unusual feature of the park is a "cable skiing" concession near the swimming beach: Instead of a boat, a mechanized cable pulls you across the water on skis. You can also try your luck in the fishing lake, paddle a canoe, catch a breeze on a sailboard, or ride your bike. This park has one of South Florida's few mountain bike trails. Ten minutes from the park is Butterfly World, a tourist attraction where thousands of butterflies flutter freely.

Campsites, facilities: This 430-acre county park offers 16 "rent-a-camp" sites with permanent canvas tents mounted on 8-by-10-foot wooden platforms. Seven additional tent-only sites accommodate campers with their own gear. Restrooms, showers, picnic tables, grills, and fire rings are provided; water is available only at a central source. The park has a camp store, an 18-hole miniature golf course, two lakes, a swimming area, and a playground. The campsites, water playground and walking paths are wheelchair-accessible. Children and one leashed pet are welcome.

Reservations, fees: Prepaid reservations are required. Sites are $25 per night for two people, plus $2 for each extra person up to a group of six. Two pets are permitted; the extra fee is $1 per pet. Major credit cards are accepted. The maximum stay is two weeks.

Directions: From I-95, take Exit 42B and drive 2.8 miles west on Hillsboro Boulevard. Turn south at Powerline Road and continue 0.5 mile to the park entrance on the west.

Contact: Quiet Waters Park, 6601 North Powerline Road, Pompano Beach, FL 33073, 954/360-1315, www.broward.org/parks.

11 BREEZY HILL RV RESORT

Scenic rating: 3

in Pompano Beach

Security gates and a concrete-block wall guards the entry to this neatly kept RV park and mobile-home community dotted by palm trees and Norfolk pines. It's preferred by French Canadians, many of whom leave their rigs here year-round. During the winter, campers keep busy by taking English classes, reading a newsletter in French, bowling, playing boccie ball (lawn bowling), *pétanque* (French-style bowling), or shuffleboard, and participating in other activities. All sites have concrete pads and accommodate RVs up to 40 feet long. This is one of three well-established snowbird refuges within two blocks of each other.

Campsites, facilities: Among the 594 full-hookup sites, about 250 are designated for overnighters and the rest are available for seasonal RVs or prefabricated homes. About 33 percent of the park is occupied by permanent residents. Telephone and cable TV are available for long-term visitors. Restrooms, showers, laundry facilities, a billiard hall, horseshoes, and shuffleboard are available. There are two pools (one heated) and two recreation halls. Most facilities are wheelchair-accessible. A convenience store is one block away. A supermarket and the ocean are three miles away. Propane can be delivered to your site during the winter months. You must be 55 or older to stay here, and pop-up campers are not allowed. Children and pets are prohibited.

Reservations, fees: Reservations are recommended. Sites are $29–37 per night for two people, plus $5 per additional person. Credit cards are accepted. Long-term stays are permitted.

Directions: From I-95, take Exit 39 east on Sample Road and drive 0.25 mile. At Northeast 3rd Avenue, turn north and go 1.5 miles to Northeast 48th Street. Turn east and use the second park entrance.

Contact: Breezy Hill RV Resort, 800 Northeast 48th Street, Pompano Beach, FL 33064, 954/942-8688, www.mhchomes.com.

12 HIGHLAND WOODS RV RESORT
🏊 🐕 ♿ 🚐

Scenic rating: 2

in Pompano Beach

If you have business in the area or are visiting relatives, then this place might do, although it is transitioning to manufacturing homes. The quiet park is "age-qualified," meaning it is geared to people over 55. Paved interior roads lead to the concrete sites, each offering a grassy area in back and to the side. This park is selling home sites, reducing the number of RV spots available to 68, with 30/50-amp electrical service. Fort Lauderdale's famous sandy beaches are four miles away.

Campsites, facilities: This 148-site, adult-oriented mobile-home park offers full hookups, restrooms, showers, a swimming pool, a recreation room, *pétanque* (French-style bowling), horseshoes, shuffleboard, pool tables, two laundry rooms, and wintertime activities such as bingo and darts. About 100 sites are available for overnighters. Groceries, restaurants, movies, and a flea market require about a five-minute drive. Children are allowed to visit. Pets are permitted in a designated area.

Reservations, fees: Reservations are recommended. Sites are $29–37 per night for two people, plus $5 per extra person. Credit cards are accepted. Long-term stays are OK.

Directions: From I-95, take Exit 39 east on Sample Road and drive 0.25 mile. At Northeast 3rd Avenue, turn north and go 1.5 miles to Northeast 48th Street. Turn east; the park is on the south side of the road.

Contact: Highland Woods RV Resort, 900 Northeast 48th Street, Pompano Beach, FL 33064, 954/942-6254, www.mhchomes .com.

13 GOLF VIEW ESTATES
🏊 ♿ 🚐

Scenic rating: 3

in Pompano Beach

An immaculate, walled manufactured-home community wedged between a busy highway and a warehouse area, this resort has the feel of a permanent neighborhood. Many big RVs are parked here year-round, and their owners have built on Florida rooms (screened porches). An adult tricycle is parked in almost every well-tended driveway. Nightly security patrols, a heated swimming pool with a whirlpool tub, saunas for men and women, and a sundeck complete the picture. About 90 percent of the visitors and residents are from Canada.

Campsites, facilities: Open to campers 55 and older, this RV park/mobile-home community offers 129 RV sites with full hookups. About half have 30-amp service; the other have 50-amp. Paved lots vary from 32 to 45 feet in length; they are 12 feet wide. A third of the community is occupied by full-timers. Mobile homes are for sale. Shuffleboard courts, a heated pool, a whirlpool tub, saunas, a dump station, and two wheelchair-accessible clubhouses are provided. Favorite things to do are cards, parties, exercise classes, and cruises. Groceries and shopping are within 0.5 mile. RV storage is available in the off-season. Children and pets are prohibited.

Reservations, fees: Reservations are recommended. Sites are $30–55 per night for two people. Credit cards are accepted. Long-term rates are available.

Directions: From I-95, take Exit 36 and drive 2.5 miles west on Atlantic Boulevard to Northwest 31st Avenue. Turn north; the entrance to the park is on the west side. From Florida's Turnpike, take Exit 67 and go 0.5 mile south on Northwest 31st Avenue.

Contact: Golf View Estates, 901 Northwest 31st Avenue, Pompano Beach, FL 33069, 954/972-4140, fax 954/972-3041, www .golfviewestates.com.

14 KOZY KAMPERS RV PARK

Scenic rating: 2

in Fort Lauderdale

Despite its urban locale, this pine-needle-blanketed park is notable for its forest of 100-foot-tall Australian pines. You can park even the biggest rig under towering trees that shelter many of the concrete-pad or grassy sites. Shopping centers and restaurants are nearby, and the location offers good access to local attractions, such as the *Jungle Queen* riverboat cruise, the Sawgrass Mills outlet mall, Pompano Harness Racing, and Dania Jai Alai. Although kids are permitted, parents are warned that they must assume financial responsibility for any damage or injury caused by their children, "regardless of age." About half the park is occupied by year-round residents.

Campsites, facilities: All 104 sites have full hookups with 30/50-amp service, cable TV, and telephone availability. Thirteen are pull-through. During busy times, an overflow area with water and electricity only is opened for additional campers. Sites vary in size from 30 by 40 feet to 25 by 50 feet. Dialup Internet service is available in the clubhouse. Restrooms, showers, a laundry room, a dump station, a small store, and a recreation hall are provided. All areas are said to be wheelchair-accessible. RV and boat storage is available for a monthly fee. Shopping centers and restaurants are within 0.2 mile. Children are welcome but must be supervised by an adult in all areas of the park. Leashed dogs are permitted; a small dog-walk area has been set aside.

Reservations, fees: Reservations are recommended. Sites are $28–38 per night for two people, plus $3 for each additional person over the age of 12. Major credit cards are accepted. Long-term stays are OK.

Directions: From I-95, take Exit 32 on Commercial Boulevard and drive west three miles to the park, which is on the north side. From Florida's Turnpike, take Exit 62 and go east on Commercial Boulevard 0.5 mile.

Contact: Kozy Kampers RV Park, 3631 West Commercial Boulevard, Fort Lauderdale, FL 33309, 954/731-8570, fax 954/731-3140, www.kozykampers.com.

15 JOHN D. EASTERLIN PARK

Scenic rating: 7

in Oakland Park

It's hard to believe you're still in urban Fort Lauderdale. Some cypress trees are more than 200 years old and stand 100 feet tall. A magnificent canopy of cypress, cabbage palms, and oaks shades the grassy sites. Don't miss the winding nature trail, where you'll see ferns, wild-coffee bushes, red maple trees, and cabbage palms in a 0.75-mile walk. This Designated Urban Wilderness Area was acquired by the county in 1944 by foreclosure and originally named Cypress Park; it was renamed after a county commissioner in 1965. You can fish in the lake, but you're encouraged to release your catch; swimming is not allowed. The winding paved road is good for leisurely cycling. During the winter season, you'll find visitors from Europe and Canada, as well as Floridians year-round.

Campsites, facilities: The 46-acre county park has 46 shady, paved RV sites, and seven tent sites with electricity, water, restrooms, showers, picnic tables, and grills. The biggest RVs on the road can be accommodated. All sites have 20/30/50-amp service and full hookups. Also in the park are a dump station, a lake, a one-mile nature trail, two playgrounds, horseshoe pits, shuffleboard courts, and a volleyball field. Limited Internet access is available by dialup in the office. Five campsites and the bathhouse are wheelchair-accessible. Groceries and shopping are within two miles. No alcohol or firearms are permitted. Children are welcome. Pets are permitted with proof of vaccination.

Reservations, fees: Reservations are recommended. Sites are $19–23 per night for four people, plus $2–2.50 for each additional person. Credit cards are accepted. The maximum stay is 14 days; if you pay by the month, you can stay up to six months.

Directions: From I-95 southbound, take Exit 32 and head west on Commercial Boulevard for 0.1 mile. Turn south at Powerline Road and go 0.9 mile. Turn west at Northwest 38th Street; you'll see the park entrance on the south side of the road. From I-95 northbound, take Exit 31 and go east to Powerline Road. Go north on Powerline Road to Northwest 38th Street. Turn west and drive under the interstate and across the railroad tracks. The entrance is just past the tracks.

Contact: John D. Easterlin Park, 1000 Northwest 38th Street, Oakland Park, FL 33309, 954/938-0610, fax 954/938-0625, www.broward.org/parks.

16 SUNSHINE HOLIDAY RV RESORT

🏊 🐕 🚐

Scenic rating: 2

in Fort Lauderdale

Only self-contained RVs are allowed in this family-friendly park, where about a third of the tenants stay year-round. It has a security gate that requires you to punch in an entrance code. Some sites on the east side are shaded by mature oaks, but much of the park is sunny. A shopping center is across the street. A majority of the visitors and mobile-home residents are from Quebec; you'll hear plenty of French spoken here.

Campsites, facilities: There are 100 full-hookup RV sites set apart from the 300-unit mobile-home park for families. The campsites are 22 by 60 feet, including a paved patio area 11 feet long, and they have 30/50-amp electri-

cal service. There is no bathhouse, but you'll find a pool, laundry facilities, a 33-acre lake, a clubhouse with dialup Internet access, and shuffleboard courts. A social committee comprised of campers organize activities in winter. Children are welcome. Pets are permitted.

Reservations, fees: Reservations are recommended. Sites are $28–37 per night. Major credit cards are accepted. Long-term stays are permitted.

Directions: From I-95, take Exit 31B and drive 1.5 miles west on Oakland Park Boulevard. The park entrance is on the south side.

Contact: Sunshine Holiday RV Resort, 2802 West Oakland Park Boulevard, Fort Lauderdale, FL 33311, 954/731-1722 or 877/327-2757, fax 954/731-0451, www.rvonthego.com.

17 PARADISE ISLAND RV RESORT

🏊 🐕 🚶 🚐

Scenic rating: 4

in Fort Lauderdale

This is a homey kind of place where campers grow potted geraniums in their front yards and hang little wooden signs with their names on their rigs. A high ficus hedge surrounds the clean, manicured RV resort, cutting it off from city sights. Mature oaks and palm trees shade some campsites. A security gate offers peace of mind. About half the folks here are permanent residents. Most visitors are snowbirds, and the managers say that there's not a lot for kids to do except swim in the pool.

Campsites, facilities: There are 150 RV sites with full hookups and 50-amp electrical service in this 232-unit park, with 18 drive-through spots. RVs up to 45 feet long can be accommodated. The park has paved streets and some oaks and palm trees. Sites are grassy or paved, varying in size up to 45 feet long and 25 feet wide. Many have concrete pads. Wireless Internet connection is available at each campsite, but not cable TV. Restrooms, showers, laundry facilities, a pool, a recreation hall, two adults-only lounges, a barbecue pavilion, and shuffleboard, boccie ball (lawn bowling), and *pétanque* (French-style bowling) courts are available. In winter, dinner dances, breakfasts, and card games also entertain. A small store offers RV supplies, but not food. Grocery stores are about three miles away. Children under 16 must be accompanied by an adult in the clubhouse, pool, bathrooms, and laundry. Two leashed pets per site are permitted.

Reservations, fees: Reservations are recommended. Sites are $31–38 per night for two people, plus $3 for each additional person. Credit cards are accepted. Long-term stays are OK.

Directions: From I-95, take Exit 31B and drive 0.25 mile west on Oakland Park Boulevard. Turn south onto Northwest 21st Avenue; the park entrance is on the west side of the street.

Contact: Paradise Island RV Resort, 2121 Northwest 29th Court, Fort Lauderdale, FL 33311, 954/485-1150 or 800/487-7395, fax 954/485-5701, www.paradiserv.com.

18 TWIN LAKES TRAVEL PARK

Scenic rating: 3

in Fort Lauderdale

Tucked into an industrial neighborhood in a web of major highways, Twin Lakes is a peaceful, sunny campground dotted with tabebuia and mature shade trees. A sign at the entrance announces *"Il est impossible de parquer ici"* ("It is impossible to park here"), evidence of the French-Canadian clientele. About 95 percent of the visitors here are from Canada; 10 percent live here year-round. Besides being a good base from which to explore the Everglades, it's convenient to Sawgrass Mills, the world's largest outlet mall; Blockbuster Golf and Games

entertainment park; and the Old West–theme town of Davie, where even the McDonald's has hitching posts.

Campsites, facilities: All 374 sites have full hookups; almost all drive-through and 70 feet long, "like having your own little yard." Rigs as long as 45 feet can be accommodated. Cable TV is available, and you can access the Internet in the laundry room by the pool. Restrooms, showers, a pool, wading pool for tots, laundry facilities, *pétanque* (French-style bowling) and shuffleboard courts, horseshoe pits, a recreation hall, a dump station, and propane delivery are on-site. A small store sells beer and soda; groceries are within one mile. All buildings have wheelchair-ramps. Children are welcome. Small leashed pets are permitted.

Reservations, fees: Reservations are recommended. Sites are $35–45 per night for two people, plus $5 per additional person. Major credit cards are accepted. Long-term stays are allowed.

Directions: From I-595, or Florida's Turnpike, exit onto U.S. 441 and go 0.4 mile south. Turn west (right) on Southwest 36th Court/Oakes Road and drive two blocks, then turn north on Burris Road. Continue 0.5 mile to the park.

Contact: Twin Lakes Travel Park, 3055 Burris Road, Fort Lauderdale, FL 33314, 954/587-0101 or 800/327-8182, fax 954/587-9512.

19 SEMINOLE PARK

Scenic rating: 3

in Hollywood

This private campground on land leased from the Seminole Indian tribe welcomes older travelers, 95 percent of whom return year after year from Canada and the north. You'll have to reserve as much as a year in advance to get a spot here in the winter season. Bingo, potluck dinners, and dances keep people busy, but the real attraction is the Seminole Hard

Rock Hotel and Casino (866/502-7529), located within 0.5 mile. Some sites are paved, others are grassy. Stores are within walking distance, but be careful because the highway carries heavy traffic.

Campsites, facilities: All 102 RV sites have full hookups, plus cable TV and telephone access for long-term visitors. Amenities include restrooms, showers, a pool, two recreation halls, and *pétanque* (French-style bowling) and shuffleboard courts. Most of the sites have 30-amp electrical service; a few have 50-amp. A volunteer group of park guests organizes planned activities, such as cards, dances, and bicycle outings. The office, recreation halls, laundry, bathhouses, and pool are wheelchair-accessible. RV storage is available. Adult campers are preferred, but children are allowed for short visits. Only pets under 10 pounds are permitted.

Reservations, fees: Reservations are recommended. Sites are $32 per night for two people, plus $2 per extra person. Credit cards are not accepted. Long-term rates are available.

Directions: From I-95, take Exit 25 westbound for 2.8 miles on Stirling Road. Turn south at U.S. 441/State Road 7 and drive 0.2 mile to the park, on the east side of the road.

Contact: Seminole Park, 3301 North State Road 7, Hollywood, FL 33021, 954/987-6961.

20 T. Y. PARK

Scenic rating: 5

in Hollywood

Bring a fishing pole to try your luck in the well-stocked lake that is the centerpiece of this 150-acre, oak-shaded county park in the middle of the metropolitan area. (You'll also need a Florida fishing license.) A two-mile path around the lake is a favorite with joggers and bicyclists. On weekends, the park is jammed with local kids and families picnicking on the grounds and swimming in the lake. In winter, many Canadians use this campground as their vacation base. Art fairs and community festivals are sometimes held here, too, adding to the crowds. What does T. Y. stand for? "Topeekeegee Yugnee" means the Gathering Place" in the Seminole language.

Campsites, facilities: There are 48 campsites, including 40 that are drive-through. While six-month stays are allowed if sites are available, no visitors live here year-round, and the normal limit is 14 days. Water, electricity, grills, picnic tables, and patios are provided at RV sites. Restrooms, showers, laundry facilities, a dump station, a trading post, bicycle and boat rentals, a swimming lagoon with a waterslide, and basketball and volleyball courts are available. One campsite, the bathhouse, and laundry are wheelchair-accessible. Children are welcome. Leashed pets are permitted at campsites and in the park ,but may not be taken on the beach; they must be preregistered at the park office. Twenty-four-hour security is provided.

Reservations, fees: Reservations are recommended. Sites are $18–25 per night for four people, plus $2 for each additional person. Credit cards are accepted. The maximum stay is six months if paid each month in advance. Long-term rates are available.

Directions: From I-95 in Hollywood, take Exit 21 west on Sheridan Street for 0.7 mile. Turn north at Park Road and drive 0.2 mile to the entrance.

Contact: T. Y. Park, 3300 North Park Road, Hollywood, FL 33021, 954/985-1980, fax 954/961-5950, www.broward.org/parks.

21 LAKE TRINITY ESTATES

Scenic rating: 4

in Pembroke Park

This 61-acre park is ingeniously slipped underneath a Christian TV station's towering antenna and studios, which broadcasts live religious programming and screens movies in a state-of-the-art surround-sound theater. On the south side of the property is a lake with a golf driving range on the shore. Putt-putt golf is available, if you want to try your hand. The sites are well-landscaped. Each winter, campers, many of them French-Canadians, compete in *pétanque* (French-style bowling) and shuffleboard contests. About 80 percent of the inhabitants live here year-round, and park models are for sale. The beach is about six miles east, and the Miami Dolphins play pro football about a 10-minute drive west (305/620-2578).

Campsites, facilities: This 284-unit community hosts 117 RV-only sites with 30-amp electrical service and full hookups. For over-nighters, six full-hookup sites and 29 partial-hookup spots are available. Most sites fit rigs up to 40 feet and have concrete patios and 10 feet of space of elbow room. Restrooms, showers, laundry facilities, a swimming pool, a dump station, a gift shop, shuffleboard, and *pétanque* (French-style bowling) are available. Some areas are wheelchair-accessible. Groceries, shopping, and tourist attractions are within two miles. Children are welcome. Dogs are not permitted, but cats and birds are allowed. The park requires sites to be kept neat, clean and quiet; profanity, fighting, and drunkenness can result in eviction.

Reservations, fees: Reservations are recommended in winter. Sites are $27–39 per night for two people, plus $1 for each additional person. Major credit cards are accepted. Long-term stays are OK.

Directions: From I-95, take Exit 19 westbound on Pembroke Road for 0.5 mile to the park, which is on the south side.

Contact: Lake Trinity Estates, 3300 Pembroke Road, 1 Lake Trinity Estates, Pembroke Park, FL 33021, 954/962-7400, laketrinityestates@tbn.org.

22 MARKHAM PARK

Scenic rating: 8

near the Everglades

BEST (

You'd have to spend weeks at this 665-acre county park before you could sample everything to do here. For one, there's a mountain-biking trail with sharp turns and what passes for altitude in flat South Florida. (The other

Markham Park near Fort Lauderdale

© MARILYN MOORE

two popular mountain-biking parks are Oleta State Park in North Miami and Amelia Earhart Park in Hialeah, both in Miami-Dade County, south of here. Markham Park is said to be the most technical, requiring more skill than the others.) You can also bicycle on paved roads that wind through the park and in the campground clusters. If your tastes run to the cosmic, there's stargazing in the observatory every Saturday. Gun enthusiasts come from all over to take aim on the 50-yard and 100-meter target ranges, said to be Florida's best. There are two dog parks—one for pets under 25 pounds, and one for heavier canines—where you can let your friend off-leash. Water scooters are allowed to buzz around in a lake on weekends.

From the concrete boat ramps, you can launch your craft into the L-35A Canal, which stretches along the eastern edge of the Everglades, or the New River Canal, which runs east to west. Hike through the Australian pine forest to the levee that separates the vast watery prairie of the Everglades from civilization; from atop the levee, you can see for miles. When you get hot, cool down in the oversized pool (swimming is not allowed in the lake or the canals). The pool is open from spring break to Labor Day. On weekends, the campground fills up fast, so be sure to make reservations. During the week, you can relax at your large, wooded RV site in peace and quiet.

Campsites, facilities: Split among 12 campground clusters are 88 spots with water and electricity. Each cluster has a paved site for wheelchair access. Eight drive-through sites have full hookups. An additional 10 tent sites have no water or electricity. The campground lost a lot of trees in the 2006 hurricane season, so landscaping is new, and shade is minimal. All have picnic tables, grills, and fire rings. Restrooms, showers, and a dump station are available. For fun, take your pick from the pool, the lake, two boat ramps, boat rentals, racquetball and tennis courts, mountain-biking trails, playgrounds, gun ranges, horseshoe pits, volleyball courts, an observatory, a personal-watercraft lake, a biking/jogging path, a 0.5-mile nature trail, a one-mile-long equestrian trail, and a model airplane field. With two miles are grocery stores, restaurants, and upscale shopping. Most areas are wheelchair-accessible, including some paved campsites. Children and leashed dogs are welcome.

Reservations, fees: Reservations are recommended, especially on weekends, and are accepted up to one year in advance. Sites are $19–23 per night for four people, plus $2 for each additional person. Major credit cards are accepted. Most overnighters stay 14 days. Maximum length of stay is six months if paid in advance month to month.

Directions: From Fort Lauderdale, take I-595 west eight miles to Exit 1A at State Road 84. Continue on State Road 84 west to the second traffic light (Weston Road), then turn north into the park entrance.

Contact: Markham Park, 16001 State Road 84, Sunrise, FL 33326, 954/389-2000, www .broward.org/parks.

23 SEMINOLE HEALTH CLUB

Scenic rating: 3

in Davie

BEST (

Coconut palms, orchids, and banana and mango trees give this wooded, 11-acre naturist park a tropical feel, even though it's rapidly being surrounded by housing subdivisions. Horses and a goat or pig (or two) on the premises will make you think of the farm. In the center of the park's pond is Monkee Island, where real primates run loose—a treat for children. As at most nudist campgrounds, the managers are careful to screen out curiosity-seekers and to protect the privacy of their guests. If you pass muster, you'll get the ultimate tan. A plus for those who travel with their pets: There's also a free-roaming area for dogs.

Campsites, facilities: This nudist resort offers 50 RV slots and five tent sites with water and 30-amp electricity hookups. Restrooms, showers, two laundry rooms, a dump station, an outdoor gym, a game room, a dance floor, a restaurant, motel rooms with color TVs (but no bathrooms), a large swimming pool, and courts for tennis, shuffleboard, horseback-riding lessons, and *pétanque* (French-style bowling) are available. Internet access is available in the office. Most areas are wheelchair-accessible. Visitors are asked to spend the day here before camping, to make sure everyone is comfortable with each other. Families with children are welcome. Leashed pets are permitted.

Reservations, fees: Reservations are required. Sites are $40 per night for two people or a family. Beyond that, add $10 per extra person. Credit cards are not accepted. Long-term stays are OK.

Directions: From Fort Lauderdale, take I-595 west for seven miles to Southwest 136th Avenue. Drive three miles south to Southwest 26th Street. Turn west and continue 1.6 miles to Southwest 142nd Avenue, then turn left. At 37th Court, turn left, then immediately turn right onto a paved road that leads to the park entrance. From I-75, take the Griffin Road exit eastbound about three miles to the first traffic light that allows you to cross the canal to Orange Drive, which parallels Griffin Road. On Orange Drive, turn west and drive to Southwest 142nd Avenue. Go north past the mountain-like county park (it used to be a dump), and the RV place will be on your right.

Contact: Seminole Health Club, 3800 Southwest 142nd Avenue, Davie, FL 33330, 954/473-0231, fax 954/476-7042, sonshiners@aol.com.

24 C. B. SMITH PARK
🏊 🛶 🚣 🐕 🚵 🚐 ⛺

Scenic rating: 7

in Pembroke Pines

Kids flop down a waterslide on inner tubes at this 320-acre county park, but you won't be able to hear their gleeful shouts from the sunny, palm-dotted campground on the park's other side. The lake is the focus of attention. For fun, try the waterslide, sunbathe at the beach, tool around in a paddleboat, play racquetball, tennis, or volleyball, visit the playground, or toss a few horseshoes at the horseshoe pits.

Campsites, facilities: Sixty full-hookup RV sites (30 pull-through) and 12 tent sites overlook an 80-acre lake. Restrooms, showers, picnic tables, grills, and laundry facilities are available. Children are welcome. Leashed pets are permitted.

Reservations, fees: Reservations are recommended. Sites are $19 per night for four people, plus $2 for each additional person. Major credit cards are accepted. Unlike most public parks, this one permits long-term stays of up to six months.

Directions: From I-75, take Exit 9A east on Pines Boulevard for one mile to Flamingo Road. Turn north and go to the park at 900 North Flamingo Road.

Contact: C. B. Smith Park, 900 North Flamingo Road, Pembroke Pines, FL 33028, 954/437-2650, www.broward.org/parks.

25 LARRY AND PENNY THOMPSON MEMORIAL PARK AND CAMPGROUND
🚴 🏊 🛶 🐕 🚵 ♿ 🚐 ⛺

Scenic rating: 7

west of Perrine, near Metrozoo

This is likely the best base camp for exploring the Miami area. It's a bit far from Miami Beach, but it's close to tourist attractions like Coral Castle, Monkey Jungle, Miami Metrozoo, and Biscayne Bay. With 240 RV sites and 30 tent spots, this urban campground ought to have a more crowded feel, but the sites are thoughtfully laid out in spoke-and-wheel groups of 15–20 spots each. Trees are plentiful in the campground, with mango

© MARILYN MOORE

sailboarding off of Key Biscayne, near Miami

and avocado orchards nearby (no picking allowed).

The secret is out, too. While traveling in Canada a couple of years ago, I met Canadians who have come to this county park to catch some winter sunshine and the ambience of 275 acres of woodlands. They couldn't always remember the name of the park, but they recalled the details of their good times here.

The fishing lake and swimming beach get crowded on weekends with day-trippers and locals using the picnic shelters for birthday parties and other festivities. When Miami's only county-run waterslides reopen for summer here (Memorial Day–Halloween), platoons of kids each weekend climb up a wooden platform to reach the top of a rocky palm-dotted hill, then plunge down three slides into the 72–75°F clear waters of a well-fed lake. Wednesday is the slowest day at the slides. The Florida Keys are one hour away.

Campsites, facilities: All 240 sites have full hookups and 30/50-amp electrical service.

Twenty sites are pull-through. Restrooms, showers, picnic tables, laundry facilities, a dump station, and ice are available. Within the county park are a lake, a swimming beach, three waterslides, a fishing pier, a concession stand, bridle trails, and picnic pavilions. A supermarket is one mile away. The laundry, restrooms, and playground are wheelchair-accessible. Rules requiring neatness and quiet hours are enforced. Internet access is available in the office. Children are welcome. Leashed pets may camp, but are forbidden in the rest of the county park. All pets must be properly licensed and are welcome if kept under control and quiet. Pets may not be tied to trees or left unattended.

Reservations, fees: Reservations are taken, but you cannot reserve specific sites. Sites are $22 per night for four people, plus $2–5 for each extra person over age four. Credit cards are accepted. Stays are limited to three months, but an extension is available for another three months, and weekly and monthly rates are available.

Directions: From Florida's Turnpike, exit west on Eureka Drive/Southwest 184th Street. Continue one mile to the park entrance at 12451 Southwest 184th Street on the north side of the road.

Contact: Larry and Penny Thompson Memorial Park and Campground, 12451 Southwest 184th Street, Miami, FL 33177, 305/232-1049, fax 305/293-4529, www.miamidade.gov/parks/parks/larry_penny.asp.

26 MIAMI EVERGLADES CAMPGROUND

Scenic rating: 7

in southern Dade County, on Southwest 162nd Avenue between Quail Roost Drive and Hainlin Mill Road

Pick free avocados and mangoes right off the trees at this farm country campground, which is convenient to such attractions as Monkey Jungle, Metrozoo, Parrot Jungle, the Everglades, and the Florida Keys. Nearby is the Redland, Dade County's agricultural area, where many of the nation's limes are grown, as well as tropical crops, including yucca and malanga. These tubers are often cooked like potatoes and served with "mojo," a mixture of vinegar, spices, and olive oil. Staples of the Cuban-American diet, yucca and malanga have become trendy with chefs of the "New World" cooking school. In these parts, you'll see acres and acres of palm trees at tree fams, soon to be planted outdoors in Florida subdivisions and inside Midwestern shopping malls. The real plus of this park is its rural feel, yet it is close to restaurants and shopping.

Campsites, facilities: This former KOA has 330 RV sites (140 are pull-through) and 20 tent spots. About 15 percent of the sites are occupied by year-round residents. The park offers full hookups; 50-amp service at a third of the sites, and 30-amp service at the rest. Facilities include picnic tables, restrooms, showers, laundry facilities, a circular pool with hot tub, horseshoe pits, paved biking trail, restaurant, shuffleboard, volleyball, and basketball courts, an adult lounge, rental cabins, a dump station, propane, and a convenience store. The bathhouses, store, and recreation hall are wheelchair-accessible. Wireless Internet service is available in some of the common areas; there are phone jacks and two computers in the lounge. Slideout RVs and rigs up to 45 feet can be accommodated. Grocery shops and restaurants are within one mile. Children under 14 must be accompanied by a responsible adult at all times. Leashed pets are welcome.

Reservations, fees: Reservations are recommended—a $30 deposit is required, and the park requires seven days' notice for cancellations. Sites are $34–65 per night for two people, plus $3 for each additional person. Rates are higher during special events. Holiday weekends require a three-night stay. Credit cards are accepted. Long-term stays are permitted.

Directions: From Florida's Turnpike, exit west on Quail Roost Drive and proceed five miles to Southwest 162nd Avenue, then turn south. The park entrance is 0.5 mile ahead on the east side of the road. From U.S. 1, drive 4.5 miles west on Southwest 216th Street to Southwest 162nd Avenue, then turn north and continue to the park.

Contact: Miami Everglades Campground, 20675 Southwest 162nd Avenue, Homestead, FL 33187, 305/233-5300 or 800/917-4923, www.miamicamp.com.

27 THE BOARDWALK

Scenic rating: 5

in Homestead

This mobile-home and RV park is a gated community close to city amenities, Everglades National Park, the Florida Keys, and Biscayne Bay. About 75 percent of the land is dedicated to manufactured homes, but you'll also find RV spaces available for overnighters and seasonal visitors in their own section. Everything is neat and spotlessly maintained—from the swimming pool and suburban-style landscaping to the fitness center, clubhouse, and social areas. A concrete wall surrounds the park, and a security gate keeps out curiosity seekers. A speed limit of 15 mph is enforced.

Campsites, facilities: There are 108 RV sites with concrete pads and full hookups. The entire park is laid out in checkerboard fashion, with the RV section confined to one corner; some RV spots are up against the property line. The rest of the park is occupied by mobile homes. About 25 percent of the RV sites have 50-amp electrical service; the rest are 30-amp. Most sites have concrete patios, and rigs up to 44 feet can be accommodated. Restrooms, showers, and laundry facilities are available. On the premises are a heated pool, a clubhouse with billiards and card room, a fitness center, planned activities in winter, lighted shuffleboard courts, horseshoe pits, propane, and a barbecue area. The office has an Internet connection. Children are welcome. Leashed pets of small and medium size are permitted. Visitors must register in the office and should be off-premises by 10 P.M.

Reservations, fees: Reservations are recommended; however, a $150 deposit is required. Sites are $35–65 per night for two people, plus $6 per extra person. Credit cards are accepted. Long-term rates are available.

Directions: From the Florida Turnpike, take Exit 2 west on Campbell Drive and proceed to U.S. 1. Turn left on U.S. 1 and drive 0.3 mile to Northeast 6th Avenue.

Contact: The Boardwalk, 100 Northeast 6th Avenue, Homestead, FL 33030, 305/248-2487 or 888/233-9255, fax 305/248-2075, www .boardwalkcommunity.com.

28 GOLDCOASTER MOBILE HOME AND RV PARK

🚴 ⛵ 🐕 ♿ 🚐

Scenic rating: 3

in Homestead

Part of the Sun Communities mobile-home and RV park chain that owns dozens of parks across the nation, Goldcoaster Mobile Home and RV Park is a squeaky-clean, professionally landscaped and managed destination for snowbirds, retirees, and local workers, about half of whom live here year-round. A concrete wall encircles the park, and there's a security gate. Four miles of paved roads are ideal for bicycling and strolling. Big rigs are welcome, and a full-time recreation director is in charge of the social program. It's convenient to the Florida Keys and Biscayne Bay, and 15 minutes from the main entrance to Everglades National Park. Nearby is a large outlet mall, as well as the Homestead motor-sports racing complex. Surrounding this area is the South Dade farming area, where vegetables—including tomatoes, green beans, and more—flourish

in the winter sun. For a fun and different experience, drive to one of the "you-pick" strawberry fields and gather your own harvest of sweet berries.

Campsites, facilities: This 548-site manufactured-home community offers around 150 full-hookup sites for travelers, who can use the restrooms, showers, craft and card room, laundry facilities, deluxe shuffleboard courts, heated pool, and whirlpool tub. Most sites have 30/50-amp electrical service; 20 have 50-amp service. The pool, clubhouse, bathhouse, and laundry are wheelchair-accessible. In the wintertime, bingo, dances, pancake breakfasts, crafting classes, water aerobics, and bicycle trips are held to entertain visitors. Children and leashed pets are welcome.

Reservations, fees: Reservations are taken. Sites are $30–43 per night for two people, plus $3 for each additional person. Credit cards are accepted.

Directions: From U.S. 1 in Florida City, turn west at Palm Drive/Southwest 344th Street and proceed 1.5 miles to Southwest 187th Avenue/Redland Road, then turn south. The park entrance is on the west side.

Contact: Goldcoaster Mobile Home and RV Park, 34850 Southwest 187th Avenue, Homestead, FL 33034, 305/248-5462 or 800/828-6992, fax 305/248-5467, www .suncommunities.com.

29 SOUTHERN COMFORT RV RESORT

⛵ 🐕 🚐 ⛺

Scenic rating: 7

in Florida City

With its swaying royal palms, fruit trees, and a rainbow of hibiscus flowers, this park displays a Caribbean mood. It's convenient to the Florida Keys, national parks, and other attractions; a discount shopping mall, the Florida Keys Factory Shops, is across the street. If you're driving to the Florida Keys, this is the last resort-style overnight campground near U.S. 1—something to note if there's an accident on the highway between Florida City and Key Largo. Often, the road is completely shut down in both directions, and you're stuck for hours. Traffic may be rerouted on Card Sound Road, but that can be slow-going in a crowd.

Campsites, facilities: There are 338 full-hookup RV sites (50 pull-through), and 10 tent-only sites with water and electricity. Picnic tables, restrooms, showers, laundry facilities, a pool, a recreation room, shuffleboard, and a tiki bar are on the premises. Organized activities are offered, including aerobic exercises, bingo, and dances in winter. Rigs up to 40 feet long can be accommodated. You can connect to the Internet in the recreation hall. Children are welcome. Leashed pets, except Rottweilers and pit bulls, are permitted.

Reservations, fees: Reservations are recommended. Sites are $30–38 per night for two people, plus $5 for each additional person. Rates may be higher during special events. Credit cards are accepted. Long-term stays up to six months are OK.

Directions: From U.S. 1 in Florida City, turn east at Palm Drive and proceed one block to the park entrance on the south side.

Contact: Southern Comfort RV Resort, 345 East Palm Drive, Florida City, FL 33034, 305/248-6909, fax 305/245-1345.

30 BOCA CHITA KEY BOAT-IN SITES

Scenic rating: 10

in Biscayne National Park, east of Homestead

BEST (

For a taste of Robinson Crusoe–style living, camping on Boca Chita can't be beat. The only way to get here is by boat, canoe, or kayak (and that's a nine-mile paddle from the visitor center). If you don't have any of those, call the park concessionaire to see if boat transportation to the island is available. The company also rents canoes and kayaks and conducts glass-bottom boat, snorkeling, and diving trips. All trips depend on weather conditions. The camping area overlooks a small harbor and an ornamental lighthouse, and a hiking trail encircles the island. Be prepared for mosquitoes and other insects throughout the year. The best time to camp here is January–April.

Campsites, facilities: There are 30 primitive campsites with picnic tables and grills. Saltwater flush toilets are available, but there is no freshwater on the island, so bring your own. Pack out all trash, and lock anything edible in a hard-sided cooler to foil raccoons. Children are welcome. Pets are prohibited. The mainland park areas and restroom on the island are wheelchair-accessible.

Reservations, fees: Reservations are not accepted. The fee is $15 per boat, covering six people and two tents. The maximum stay is 14 days. If a boat drops you off for camping only, the fee is $10 per site for two tents.

Directions: To reach the island in your own boat, you must use nautical chart 11451, which includes all of Biscayne National Park. Charts can be ordered from the Florida National Parks and Monument Association (10 Parachute Key, #15, Homestead, FL 33034, 305/247-1216, www.nps.gov/ever), or may be purchased at the visitors center or local bait and marine stores. To get to the Dante Fascell Visitor Center and the park concessionaire, drive south on Florida's Turnpike to Homestead. Take Exit 6 onto Speedway Boulevard and drive 4.5 miles south. At Southwest 328th Street, turn east and drive five miles to the entrance. From U.S.1, drive south toward Homestead and turn east on Southwest 328th Street, also called North Canal Drive. Drive nine miles to the entrance.

Contact: Biscayne National Park, 9700 SW 328th Street, Homestead, FL 33033, 305/230-7275, www.nps.gov/bisc. For information about boat service to the island, contact the park concessionaire, Biscayne National

Underwater Park, Inc., 9710 SW 328th Street, Homestead, FL 33033, 305/230-1100, fax 305/230-1120; dive970@aol.com.

31 ELLIOTT KEY BOAT-IN SITES

Scenic rating: 10

in Biscayne National Park, east of Homestead

On weekends, Elliott Key is a popular destination for local boaters, most of whom sleep aboard their craft tied up at the dock or anchored just offshore, leaving the campground to tougher folks. The raccoons are even hardier; park rangers advise you to bring hard-sided coolers that you can lock tight. Those raccoons have even been known to open water jugs. Resist the temptation to string a hammock, because they're not permitted. There's a large fire pit for group campers, but ground fires are prohibited elsewhere. Backcountry camping is not permitted. The park concessionaire sometimes provides boat service to Elliott Key for campers. By canoe or kayak, expect a seven-mile paddle. January–April is the best time to camp and avoid bugs.

Campsites, facilities: Accessible only by boat, this island harbors a 40-site campground with saltwater flush toilets, cold showers, grills, picnic tables, boat slips, and a nature trail. Drinking water is available. Pack out your trash. Children are welcome. Pets are permitted on a six-foot leash.

Reservations, fees: Reservations are accepted. The fee is $15 per boat, covering six people and two tents. The maximum stay is 14 days. The fee for campers being dropped off by a boat is $10.

Directions: To reach the island in your own boat, you must use nautical chart 11451 (for details, see *Boca Chita* in this chapter). To get to the Dante Fascell Visitor Center and the park concessionaire, drive south on Florida's Turnpike to Homestead. Take Exit 6 onto Speedway Boulevard and drive 4.5 miles south. At Southwest 328th Street, turn east and drive five miles to the entrance. From U.S. 1, drive south toward Homestead and turn east on Southwest 328th Street, also called North Canal Drive. Drive nine miles to the entrance.

Contact: Biscayne National Park, 9700 SW 328th Street, Homestead, FL 33033, 305/230-7275, www.nps.gov/bisc. For information about boat service to the island, contact the park concessionaire, Biscayne National Underwater Park, Inc., 9710 SW 328th Street, Homestead, FL 33033, 305/230-1100, fax 305/230-1120, dive970@aol.com.

THE EVERGLADES

© MARILYN MOORE

BEST CAMPGROUNDS

⟨ Biking
Collier Seminole State Park, **page 558**
Long Pine Key Campground, **page 566**

More than any other natural feature, the

Everglades define south Florida. They are, in the true sense of the word, unique. Author Marjory Stoneman Douglas recognized this in her 1947 classic, *The Everglades: River of Grass*, when she penned these famous words: "There are no other Everglades in the world."

The river of grass is the 50-mile-wide band of wispy saw grass that looks from afar like a dry prairie, until your boots sink knee-deep in the watery bottom. The broad expanse is punctuated by small rises covered with trees (known as "hammocks"). It stretches from Lake Okeechobee nearly to Florida Bay, and from the area east of Naples to the western suburbs of Fort Lauderdale and Miami. Water levels fluctuate from ankle- to chest-deep. Modern drainage efforts have thrown that hydrologic equilibrium out of whack, but much of the Everglades' appeal still can be enjoyed. Meanwhile, the state and federal governments are working overtime to restore the original wilderness.

Winter is the best time to visit, because you'll have less trouble with the 40-odd types of resident mosquitoes. From muggy May to November, temperatures reach the high 80s°F to high 90s°F. Lightning storms and torrential downpours are common. From January to mid-March, the temperature moderates and skies tend to be clear.

Almost anywhere, you'll see an alligator sunning itself on a canal bank as you drive by, or laying across a hiking or biking trail on a levee. A note of caution about alligators: Do not feed them. Also, don't throw your fish-cleaning remains into the water. First of all, it's against the law. Second, alligators that become acclimated to humans may expect food and could eventually chomp off someone's hand or foot. If an alligator approaches you, get out of its way. In the wild, most alligators will run from you; you'll hear a big splash. Others that are more tame will lollygag around in the sun.

The place that most tourists visit is Everglades National Park, considered by the United Nations to be as significant as the Egyptian pyramids and Australia's Great Barrier Reef. It is twice the size of Rhode Island and offers 2,356 square miles to explore.

The Big Cypress Preserve adjoins Everglades National Park on the northwestern side. The trees are indeed bald cypress, but most of the big ones were felled for lumber decades ago. This is a different view of the prairie, and prettier in many ways.

Fishing is excellent throughout Everglades National Park and the Big Cypress Preserve. Be aware that even though you're on national land, you'll still need a Florida fishing license.

Two main east-west roads cross the Everglades and the Big Cypress: I-75, which connects Naples and Fort Lauderdale; and U.S. 41, also called Tamiami Trail. U.S. 41 is a pretty drive; however, keep in mind that it is a two-lane highway. You should drive with your headlights on. Gasoline is limited on both roads. For the best views of wildlife, choose Tamiami Trail and take a detour on Loop Road. This 26-mile stretch is only partially paved. It may take more than an hour to drive this part-gravel road, but it's a terrific experience with plenty of places to gaze into the woods.

Most of the national park is underwater, so many of the following campsites can be reached only by boat, canoe, or kayak, and a few others only by trail. But overland, there are several sites where you can see what makes the Everglades special. You can also camp in places that offer the standard comforts, where you can bring a mountain bike and your hiking boots.

For the total Everglades experience, camping in backcountry areas requires special preparation and precautions. First, bring all the water you'll need, generally one gallon per person per day. Also, be wary of raccoons, which will make their way into your food and drinking water if possible. Carry a hard-bodied cooler, put your food inside, and tie it shut. In brackish and saltwater areas, raccoons seem perpetually thirsty and will go after your freshwater. They're crafty, so take some time to figure out how you're going to preserve your sustenance. Discuss other precautions with backcountry rangers when you pick up a camping permit. Know your capabilities, and watch the weather carefully. If you can afford one, a global positioning system (GPS) will help keep you from getting lost – but it's no substitute for a good grasp of orienteering. If you're canoeing or kayaking, consider transporting some of your dry clothes and other valuables in a waterproof bag. Dry Bag is one well-known brand name.

There are three types of backcountry campsites in the park. At a ground site, you pitch your tent on the ground. An equal number of sites are on so-called chickees. Although named after the thatched-roof huts of the Seminole Indians, chickee campsites in the park are 10- by 12-foot wooden platforms raised above the water and covered by a flat roof. At chickee sites, you'll need a free-standing tent; no stakes can be driven into the platform. Chickees are equipped with chemical toilets. The third type is the beach site. The shelly beaches of the Everglades won't remind you of Miami Beach, but they have a beauty all their own. Most beach sites and a few ground sites do not have toilets. You'll have to dig a hole at least six inches deep to bury waste or, better yet, pack out waste.

Raccoons and bugs are worst at ground and beach sites. Many beach sites also have biting gnats known as no-see-ums. This is another reason to come when it's cold, or at least cool – meaning in the winter. Do not underestimate the mosquitoes or other biting bugs: Bring lots of repellent and mosquito netting, even in the winter. These items are not optional. For all practical purposes, the skeeters make camping in the Everglades backcountry impossible from about April to October.

Some campers prefer beach sites if they want to build a campfire, which is not allowed at chickee or ground sites but is permitted at most beach sites.

Die-hard adventurers can paddle a canoe or kayak 99 miles through the western length of Everglades National Park to sample many campsites on a trail called the Wilderness Waterway. It takes a lot of planning – and supplies – to make the 7- to 10-day trip. Some people rave about the trek's solitude and the challenge of maneuvering through a monotonous maze of red mangroves.

Don't expect an Amazonian jungle alive with critters and adventure at every turn. You really have to like the solitude, so rangers tell most visitors to try loop trails instead. Consult a ranger about which overnight camping trips are best for you.

Something to consider if you're taking a backcountry trip: Occasionally, a canoeing party will show up at a backcountry site when their permit is technically for another site. Perhaps they fell behind, got held up by weather, or encountered some other unfortunate circumstances. Perhaps they simply prefer a particular site and show up there, even though they have a permit for another destination. If they're traveling under muscle power and it's late in the day, or if the weather is turning bad, there's little you can do but smile and tolerate the crowding. But if it's relatively early in the day, or they're in a powerboat, and the weather is OK, you may want to call their bluff and ask them to produce a permit. If they're in the wrong place, you are within your rights to ask interlopers to go to the correct campsite. Use your judgment. Whatever you decide to do, make it a point to report such invaders to backcountry rangers.

The national park entrance fees are $10 at the main entrance in Homestead and free at Everglades City; camping costs extra. Visit www.nps.gov/ever for more information.

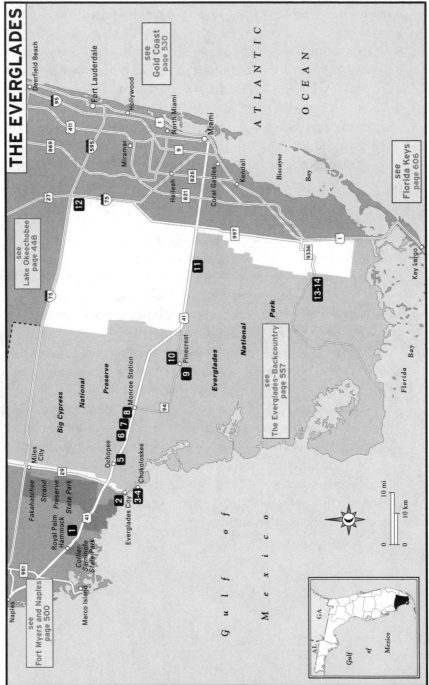

THE EVERGLADES

see
Gold Coast
page 530

see
Lake Okeechobee
page 448

see
Florida Keys
page 606

see
Fort Myers and Naples
page 500

see
The Everglades–Backcountry
page 557

ATLANTIC OCEAN

Gulf of Mexico

Florida Bay

Biscayne Bay

Deerfield Beach

Fort Lauderdale

Hollywood

North Miami

Miami

Miramar

Hialeah

Coral Gables

Kendall

Key Largo

Naples

Marco Island

Miles City

Ochopee

Everglades City

Chokoloskee

Monroe Station

Pinecrest

Big Cypress National Preserve

Fakahatchee Strand Preserve State Park

Collier Seminole State Park

Royal Palm Hammock

Everglades National Park

95

411

869

595

27

75

1

9

826

821

997

9336

41

94

29

951

75

1

1
2
3-4
5
6 7 8
9
10
11
12
13-14

10 mi
10 km
0

AL GA
Gulf of Mexico

© AVALON TRAVEL PUBLISHING, INC.

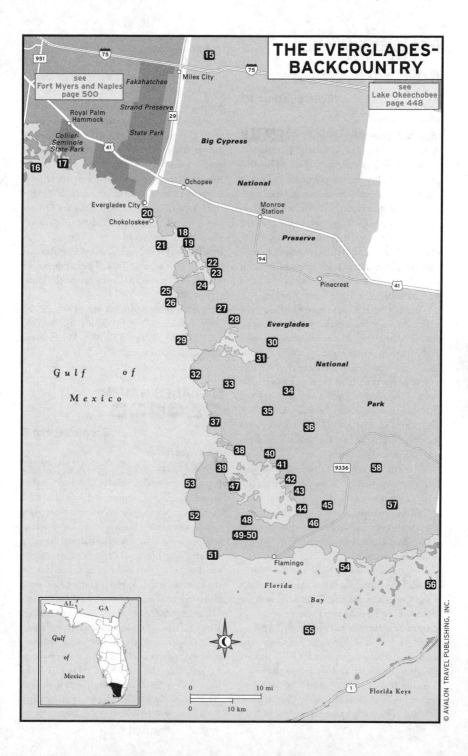

THE EVERGLADES-
BACKCOUNTRY

1 COLLIER SEMINOLE STATE PARK

Scenic rating: 10

south of Naples

See map, page 556   BEST (

A gateway to the Ten Thousand Islands and the western side of the Everglades and Big Cypress National Parks, this popular state park is a showcase for South Florida's unique landscape of mangrove and cypress swamps, salt marshes, and pine flatwoods. Common to the park are royal palms, tropical hammock trees typical of the West Indies; and wildlife ranging from pelicans, wood storks, and bald eagles to American crocodiles and black bears. Mosquitoes tend to be less bothersome in the cooler months.

Think of what it must have been like here before the advent of mosquito repellent. When the Tamiami Trail (the road linking Tampa and Miami, hence the name) was built in the 1920s, crews labored in chest-deep water under nearly impossible conditions. An enormous piece of their equipment, known as a "walking dredge," is on display in the state park, which was named for Barron Collier (the developer of much of Naples) and for the Seminole Indians who lived on these lands.

Adventurers can get a taste of those difficult days (as well as a sense of the abundant birds and other wildlife also present back then, including the wood stork, brown pelican, osprey, and roseate spoonbill) by canoeing the 13.6-mile tidal creek into the park's 4,760-acre wilderness preserve.

Pick up supplies in Naples or on Marco Island. From here, you can explore Everglades City, Corkscrew Swamp Sanctuary, and the Fakahatchee Strand State Preserve.

Campsites, facilities: Part of a 6,243-acre state park and wilderness preserve, the campground offers 118 sites for RVs; all have 30-amp electricity and water; 45 sites have 50-amp service. Sites tend to be 20 by 40 feet in size, and some are shady. One unusual feature: The park has a screen room with an Internet connection available during the winter. Restrooms, showers, fire rings with grills, picnic tables, a dump station, laundry facilities, two playgrounds, a boat ramp, and hiking trails are within the park, which is mostly wheelchair-accessible. Call ahead to see if canoes are available for rent. Children are welcome. Pets are allowed with proof of vaccination.

Reservations, fees: Reservations are recommended; contact ReserveAmerica at 800/336-3521 or reserveamerica.com. Sites are $18 per night for eight people. Credit cards are accepted. The maximum stay is 14 days.

Directions: From Naples, travel 14 miles east on U.S. 41/Tamiami Trail. The campground entrance is just east of the junction with County Road 92.

Contact: Collier Seminole State Park, 20200 East Tamiami Trail, Naples, FL 34114, 239/394-3397, fax 239/394-5113, www.floridastateparks.org.

2 GLADES HAVEN

Scenic rating: 7

in Everglades City

See map, page 556

Nestled between Everglades City and Chokoloskee Island, this campground is an ideal base camp for exploring the Wilderness Waterway, a backwater route flush with fish and feathered wildlife, that meanders along the edge of Everglades National Park. From the causeway bridge, it takes 2–5 hours, depending on the tide and wind, to reach Comer Key, once home to hermit/mangrove philosopher Robert Osmer. He holed up here a half-century ago with his favorite books and a coffeepot, ready for strangers and friends who were welcome to drop by for a cup and some conversation. For information, call Kitty Hawk Kayaks (800/948-0759). Everglades National Park Boat Tours (239/695-2591) rents canoes and conducts nearly two-hour scenic boat rides for the less adventuresome. Boats leave the center every 30 minutes.

Campsites, facilities: All 51 sites have full hookups and picnic tables. On the premises are restrooms, showers, laundry facilities, a dump station, a boat ramp, a full-service marina, boat and canoe rentals, a restaurant, a delicatessen, cabins, a chickee (thatched-roof) bar, and a general store. Children are welcome. Leashed pets are permitted.

Reservations, fees: Reservations are recommended October–April. Sites are $20–30 per night for two people, plus $5 for each additional person. Credit cards are accepted. Long-term stays are OK.

Directions: From Naples, take U.S. 41/ Tamiami Trail east to State Road 29. Turn south and drive about three miles to Everglades City. The park is on the south side of town, across from the Everglades National Park Gulf Coast Visitor Center.

Contact: Glades Haven, P.O. Box 580 (or 800 Copeland Avenue), Everglades City, FL 34139, 239/695-2746, fax 239/695-2091, www .gladeshaven.com.

❸ CHOKOLOSKEE ISLAND PARK
🚲 🛥 🚐 🐾 ♿ 🚙 ⛺

Scenic rating: 4

on Chokoloskee Island, south of Everglades City

See map, page 556

Fishing is the name of the game at this waterfront mobile-home and RV park. It has the rustic charm of an old seaside motor court, although it's a bit cluttered with boat trailers and the like. The setting is right on the water, with boat and canoe rentals available, as well as charter fishing services. There's a busy social schedule during the winter, including potluck dinners, bingo, and crafts. You'll find a full-service marina selling cold drinks, bait, ice, oil, and gas, as well as sheltered docks with 67 boat slips. Park rules say that quiet times

are enforced and that drunkenness, profanity, and offensive conduct will not be tolerated.

One interesting place in Chokoloskee is Smallwood's store museum. This is the site where turn-of-the-20th-century murder suspect Ed Watson was shot to death in 1910. A hulking, bearded man, Watson supposedly moved to the Everglades to flee pursuers who believed he had killed, among others, the famous female outlaw Belle Star. Soon, Watson's hired hands began to disappear—funny, right around payday. Nervous neighbors suspected the boss had killed them. After the body of Hannah Smith was seen floating nearby in 1910, frightened townsfolk took matters into their own hands and killed him. To add dimension to your stay, bring along Peter Matthiessen's book *Killing Mr. Watson,* a fictionalized yet largely historical account of the secretive man's exploits.

Campsites, facilities: The 87-unit park has 20 grassy sites with 30-amp electrical service available for RVs; the rest are occupied by year-round residents. Full hookups, wheelchair-accessible restrooms, showers, picnic tables, a dump station, a boat ramp, horseshoe pits, shuffleboard courts, and laundry facilities are available. RVs up to 27 feet long can be accommodated. Sites vary in size up to 20 by 45 feet, and the park has palms and other landscaping. A few sites are drive-through. Internet access is available in the office. Children are welcome. Leashed pets are permitted.

Reservations, fees: Reservations are recommended. Sites are $38 per night for two people, plus $2 for each additional person and $1.50 for electricity during summer months. Cable TV is included in the camping fee. Credit cards are accepted. Long-term stays are OK.

Directions: From Naples, take U.S. 41/Tamiami Trail east to State Road 29. Turn south and drive about three miles to Everglades City, then continue about three miles to Chokoloskee Island. Turn west (right) at the post office and follow the signs to the park at 1175 Hamilton Lane.

Contact: Chokoloskee Island Park, P.O. Box 430, Chokoloskee, FL 34138, 239/695-2414, http://chokoloskee.com.

4 OUTDOOR RESORTS OF CHOKOLOSKEE ISLAND

🏊 🛶 � 🦌 ♿ 🚐

Scenic rating: 9

on Chokoloskee Island, south of Everglades City

See map, page 556

Tiny, secluded Chokoloskee Island, linked to the mainland by a causeway, is the snook-fishing capital of the world. It's within one hour's drive of most Naples and Everglades attractions, but the focus is on canoeing, boating, and fishing—and with good reason. These waters are great for teaching little ones to fish; just about any persistent kid or novice can pick up enough skills in a few hours to hook a small snapper or sheepshead right from the dock. Bigger anglers in search of game fish, such as snook, should venture into the mangroves or to the fishing holes a short distance offshore. There's nothing like heading toward a spot where you see the gulls circling. Pop your line into the middle of a school of blue runner or amberjack; they're fun to catch, practically jumping into the boat, although not great to eat. Nearby is Everglades City, famous for its stone crab and seafood festival, held the first full weekend in February. Boat and canoe rentals are available in the park, and many fishing guides and charter boats can be hired close by. More than 160 campsites have docks available; 86 are on canals or gulfside. Shade is minimal, but, hey, you're on the water, which is presumably what you came for. Spring for a waterfront site if your budget permits. It's strictly a vacation spot; no full-timers are allowed.

Campsites, facilities: This condominium park has 283 full-hookup RV sites with cable TV and 30/50-amp outlets. All sites are back-in, but rigs as long as 45 feet can be accommodated. Restrooms, showers, laundry facilities, and groceries are on the premises. In addition, the park has three recreation centers, three pools, three hot tubs, a health club, shuffleboard courts, lighted tennis courts, a marina, boat docks, motel rooms, bait, tackle, canoe and kayak rentals, and wintertime activities.

The restrooms and laundry are wheelchair-accessible. Internet access is available in the marina office. Children are welcome. Two leashed pets are permitted per site, as long as they do not annoy other guests. You must provide proof of rabies vaccination. Pop-up campers, vans, and are prohibited.

Reservations, fees: Reservations are recommended. Sites are $79–99 per night for two people; these rates are subject to change. The maximum number of people per site is four. Some lots are available for resale, but overnighters can rent sites from the park. Credit cards are accepted.

Directions: From Naples, take U.S. 41/Tamiami Trail east to State Road 29. Turn south and drive about three miles to Everglades City, then continue about three miles to Chokoloskee Island. Look for the park at left.

Contact: Outdoor Resorts of Chokoloskee Island, P.O. Box 39, Chokoloskee Island, FL 34138, 239/695-3788, fax 239/695-3338, www.outdoor-resorts.com.

5 BIG CYPRESS TRAIL LAKES CAMPGROUND

🚶 🛶 🦌 ♿ 🚐 ⛺

Scenic rating: 5

on the Tamiami Trail, in Big Cypress National Preserve

See map, page 556

Keep an eye out for the giant concrete panther sitting out front, along with a sign that says: Alligators, Snakes, Ice Cream. For Big Cypress campers in search of full hookups, this is one of only two fully developed campgrounds in the area. The sunny campsites surround two ponds, and the place is a bit rustic. The world's smallest post office—a tiny little building about the size of a parking lot attendant's booth—is just down the road in Ochopee and draws the occasional tour bus. Owner David Shealy says the campground land has been in the family since the 1800s, which is practically an epoch in Florida historical terms. An animal exhibit sits in front of the campground office, which also serves as a gift shop. Most visitors are hunters, anglers, and international travelers. Occasionally, concerts are held here. A stage accommodates bands and other events.

Campsites, facilities: There are 100 gravel RV sites with full hookups, 30-amp electrical service, and picnic tables. About 30 percent of the occupants live here year-round. On the premises are restrooms, showers, a dump station, laundry facilities, and a store for groceries and souvenirs. An activities house and the restrooms are wheelchair-accessible. Children are welcome. Leashed pets are permitted.

Reservations, fees: Reservations are recommended. Sites are $14–16 per night for two people, plus $5 for each additional person. Children under 10 are not charged extra. Credit cards are accepted. Long-term stays are OK.

Directions: From Naples, drive east on U.S. 41/Tamiami Trail to the intersection of State Road 29. Continue on U.S. 41 for six miles to the campground, on the south side of the highway. From Florida's Turnpike in Miami, exit at U.S. 41 and drive west for 53 miles.

Contact: Big Cypress Trail Lakes Campground, U.S. 41, Ochopee, FL 33943, 239/695-2275 or 239/695-3063, traillakes@netscape.net.

6 BURNS LAKE CAMPGROUND

Scenic rating: 3

on the Tamiami Trail, in Big Cypress National Preserve

See map, page 556

This free campground is open only during hunting season, basically September 1–January 6. Aside from hunting, it's a base for exploring 728,000-acre Big Cypress National Preserve, and you will find hardy snowbirds here soaking up the sunshine. Sunny, rustic campsites surround a small lake, which is off-limits to swimmers. No sites are marked; just stake out a spot in the clearing. Bring everything, including drinking water. Camping is no-frills—the only comforts are a couple of portable toilets. The reward is getting away from it all: The croaks of frogs, the chirps of cicadas, and panther-crossing signs are reminders that you're far from the city.

Campsites, facilities: At this clearing set around a lake, there is room for about 40 RVs or tents. There are no hookups. Rigs as large as 45 feet can find a home here. The campground has two chemical toilets, but the nearest source of drinking water is Dona Drive, four miles west on U.S. 41. Bring mosquito repellent, food, water, and any supplies you'll need. Children are welcome. Pets must be on a six-foot leash and restrained at all times.

Reservations, fees: Reservations are not accepted, and there is no fee. Stays are limited to 10 days.

Directions: From Naples, drive east on U.S. 41/Tamiami Trail to the intersection of State Road 29. Continue on U.S. 41 for seven miles, then turn north on Burns Road. Drive one mile on gravel to the campground. From Florida's Turnpike in Miami, exit at U.S. 41 and drive west for 52 miles. Turn north on Burns Road.

Contact: Big Cypress National Preserve, 33100 Tamiami Trail East, Ochopee, FL 34141, 239/695-1201 or 239/695-2000, www.nps.gov/bicy. For hunting information, call 239/695-2040.

7 MONUMENT LAKE CAMPGROUND

Scenic rating: 6

on the Tamiami Trail, in Big Cypress National Preserve

See map, page 556

The preserve's managers have upgraded this site to offer niceties you won't find at most public camping spots within 728,000-acre

Big Cypress National Preserve. Here, you'll find actual restrooms with running water and an outdoor cold-water shower (but not electricity). Otherwise, Monument Lake is a rustic, bare-bones place where sunny sites surround a lake. Swimming is prohibited, lest you encounter an alligator. Winter is the best time to camp: Mosquitoes are bearable, the weather is cool, and the ground is unlikely to be sodden by rain. One of my favorite things about Big Cypress is listening to the building crescendo of sounds at night—the croaking frogs, the maracas music of cicadas. It feels a world away from urban Miami, yet it's within easy reach for a quick weekend getaway. The campground is used primarily by retirees, anglers, and Scout groups. It's closed during the warmer parts of the year.

Near the campground is Monroe Station, a roadhouse dating back to the building of U.S. 41, or the Tamiami Trail. This Herculean effort was launched in 1917 and took 11 years to finish, with progress stymied by labor shortages during World War I, as well as difficulties encountered when dynamiting limestone for the roadbed. Cranes on giant barges dredged up the rock, creating the canal as they built up the roadbed.

Behind Monroe Station is the Loop Road Scenic Drive, a 26-mile single-lane road leading deep into the preserve's southern reaches. Watch out for potholes and flooding. Along the road is the Tree Snail Hammock Nature Trail, with signs explaining the preserve's plants and animals. The loop leads to two more campgrounds, Pinecrest and Mitchell's Landing (see listings in this chapter), before connecting with U.S. 41 at Forty Mile Bend.

Campsites, facilities: At this clearing set around a lake, there is room for 26 RVs and 10 tents. There are no electrical or water hookups. Wheelchair-accessible restrooms with running water and sinks, plus an outdoor shower that can be used if you wear a bathing suit, are provided. Rigs as long as 45 feet can be accommodated. Some sites have fire rings or grills. Registered campers may use the dump station

at Dona Drive for free. The Oasis Visitor Center is five miles east on U.S. 41/Tamiami Trail. Bring water, food, mosquito repellent, and any supplies you'll need. Children are welcome. Pets must be on a six-foot leash and restrained at all times.

Reservations, fees: Reservations are not accepted. The fee is $16 per site per night and is charged December 15–April 15 only. The campground is open September 15–April 15, and it often fills up on weekends in January and February. Stays are limited to 10 days.

Directions: From Florida's Turnpike in Miami, exit on U.S. 41/Tamiami Trail and drive 46 miles west to the campground on the north side of the highway. From Naples, drive east on U.S. 41 to the intersection of State Road 29, then continue east on the same road for 13 miles.

Contact: Big Cypress National Preserve, 33100 Tamiami Trail East, Ochopee, FL 34141, 239/695-1201 or 239/695-2000, www.nps.gov/bicy. For hunting information, call 239/695-2040.

8 MIDWAY CAMPGROUND

🏕️ 🛶 🎣 🐕 ♿ 🚐 ⛺

Scenic rating: 5

on the Tamiami Trail, in Big Cypress National Preserve

See map, page 556

Finally, you'll find an Everglades campground with electricity, which was added in December 2005. Other improvements at Midway include flush toilets, cement pads, picnic tables, fire rings, and grills—welcome additions for RVers accustomed to more primitive setups at other campgrounds in the Big Cypress preserve. Midway is closest to the Oasis Visitor Center. From here, hikers can pick up the Florida National Scenic Trail and walk deep into the preserve. The sometimes flooded path meanders for 31 miles. Oasis is a nerve center for activities in the preserve: ranger-led bicycling, hiking, and canoe trips; group campfires; and nature talks. Inside the center are films and exhibits detailing the preserve's rich environment. For program information, call 239/695-1201. Lots of alligators tend to hang out near the visitors center.

Campsites, facilities: At this clearing around a lake, 26 campsites with water hookups are available for RVs, and 10 sites are for tents. Electrical service is 20/30/50-amp. There is a wheelchair-accessible restroom with flush toilets. Children are welcome. Pets must be on a six-foot leash and restrained at all times.

Reservations, fees: Reservations are not accepted. The fee is $16–19 per night per campsite. The campground often is filled on weekends in January and February. Stays are limited to 10 days.

Directions: From Florida's Turnpike in Miami, exit on U.S. 41/Tamiami Trail and drive 41 miles west to the park on the north side of the highway. From Naples, drive east on U.S. 41 to the intersection of State Road 29. Proceed east on U.S. 41 for about 22 miles, then turn north into the campground.

Contact: Big Cypress National Preserve, 33100 Tamiami Trail East, Ochopee, FL 34141, 239/695-1201 or 239/695-2000, www .nps.gov/bicy. For hunting information, call 239/695-2040.

⑨ MITCHELL'S LANDING

🚶 🚴 🎣 🛶 🐕 🚐 ⛺

Scenic rating: 5

off Loop Road, in Big Cypress National Preserve

See map, page 556

Airboats launch from this part of 1,138-square-mile Big Cypress National Preserve, so you may hear the rumble of their engines as the craft roar off into the distance. The road leading to this remote clearing is not paved. For some tastes, campers here may seem rougher than normal, and no park volunteer is stationed nearby to keep an eye on things. On weekdays, you may have the place to yourself; on weekends, you may share it with Boy Scout

troops or groups of frog-hunters. Winter is the best time to camp anywhere in otherwise buggy Big Cypress, which offers many miles of hiking trails, seasonal hunting, and fishing in scattered areas. Bring a mountain bike to follow trails in the northern part of the preserve. You're virtually certain to see an alligator during your visit.

Campsites, facilities: At this clearing outfitted with two portable toilets, about 20 sites are available. A few have improvised fire rings. There are no hookups or picnic tables. A paved boat ramp is provided, but there are no other facilities. Bring water, food, mosquito repellent, a hat, and everything else you'll need. Children are welcome. Pets must be on a six-foot leash and restrained at all times.

Reservations, fees: Reservations are not accepted, and there is no fee. Stays are limited to 10 days.

Directions: From Florida's Turnpike in Miami, exit on U.S. 41/Tamiami Trail and drive about 28 miles west, passing the Shark Valley entrance to Everglades National Park and the

A deer stops to check out tourists at Shark Valley in Everglades National Park.

Miccosukee tribe cultural center. Don't veer right when the road jogs north. Instead, bear a tad left onto a little road called Loop Road; it's marked by a sign that reads Hunters Must Check In. Follow Loop Road a little more than 10 miles to the Mitchell's Landing primitive camping area on the south side of the road. You'll see a brown tent sign instead of the posted name of the site; drive onto a rough-grade road to reach the camping area.

Contact: Big Cypress National Preserve, 33100 Tamiami Trail East, Ochopee, FL 34141, 239/695-1201 or 239/695-2000, www .nps.gov/bicy. For hunting information, call 239/695-2040.

10 PINECREST CAMPGROUND

Scenic rating: 7

off Loop Road, in Big Cypress National Preserve

See map, page 556

Peace. Quiet. Remoteness. That's what you get at this open and sunny clearing in 1,138-square-mile Big Cypress National Preserve. Daytime visitors to the preserve travel slowly down Loop Road by car, motorcycle, or bicycle, in the hope of glimpsing deer, alligators, birds, and the occasional bobcat or bear. Very rarely, you may catch sight of an endangered Florida panther hurrying across Loop Road. Many miles of hiking trails can be accessed from here. Trails suitable for mountain bikes are found in the northern part of Big Cypress; get a map from a ranger. Fishing is possible in the canals along Tamiami Trail, Turner River Road, and other spots. This campground is favored by RV campers over Mitchell's Landing (see listing in this chapter). You might bring a canoe if you want to paddle the Turner River and Halfway Creek south to Chokoloskee Bay. The Turner River is just west of H. P. Williams Roadside Park, which is at U.S. 41 and

Highway 839. Halfway Creek is about five miles west, just beyond the intersection of U.S. 41 and Highway 841.

Campsites, facilities: At this clearing outfitted with portable toilets, about 20 RVs can be accommodated. There are no hookups. Bring water, food, mosquito repellent, a hat, and everything else you'll need. Children are welcome. Pets must be on a six-foot leash and restrained at all times.

Reservations, fees: Reservations are not accepted, and there is no fee. Stays are limited to 10 days.

Directions: From Florida's Turnpike in Miami, exit on U.S. 41/Tamiami Trail and drive about 28 miles west, passing the Shark Valley entrance to Everglades National Park and the Miccosukee tribe cultural center. Don't veer right when the road jogs north. Instead, bear a tad left onto a little road called Loop Road; it's marked by a sign that reads "Hunters Must Check In." Follow Loop Road about five to six miles to the Pinecrest primitive camping area on the north side of the road. You'll see a brown tent sign instead of the posted name of the site; drive into that driveway and follow it to a clearing that serves as the camping area.

Contact: Big Cypress National Preserve, 33100 Tamiami Trail East, Ochopee, FL 34141, 239/695-1201 or 239/695-2000, www .nps.gov/bicy. For hunting information, call 239/695-2040.

11 GATOR PARK

Scenic rating: 4

on the Tamiami Trail, west of Coopertown

See map, page 556

Gator Park is a tourist stop with a campground out back and a gator pen, offering airboat tours of the Everglades. This is a popular spot for tour buses that come from Miami loaded with international travelers. About 25–40 percent of the park is occupied year-round. The last chance for groceries and gas is six miles east at Dade Corners, the intersection of U.S. 41 and State Road 997, also known as Krome Avenue. Also at this intersection is the popular Miccosukee Indian casino and hotel. Drive very carefully; I've seen a lot of car accidents at this intersection.

Campsites, facilities: Self-contained rigs are accepted at these 21 sites, with water and 30-amp electric hookups. Usually, about eight sites are available for traveling RVs. On the premises are a dump station, cooking grills, chickee (thatched-roof) huts, an airboat concession, a souvenir shop, and a restaurant. The park has palms, black olive trees, and a small pond. Children are welcome. Leashed pets are permitted.

Reservations, fees: Reservations are not necessary. Sites are $30 per night; dry camping is allowed for $10 per night. Credit cards are accepted. Long-term stays are OK.

Directions: From Florida's Turnpike in Miami, exit on U.S. 41/Tamiami Trail and drive west for 12 miles. The park is on the south side of the road, behind a tourist shop.

Contact: Gator Park, 24050 Southwest 8th Street, Miami, FL 33187, 305/559-2255 or 800/559-2205, www.gatorpark.com.

12 EVERGLADES HOLIDAY PARK

Scenic rating: 6

west of Fort Lauderdale, in the Everglades

See map, page 556

Favored by locals for weekend getaways, this rustic bass-fishing haven and gateway to the Everglades is known by tourists for its narrated one-hour-long airboat rides. International visitors arrive by the busload for the airboats. It's also popular with motorcycle riders, who make a pit stop here to relax on the covered deck with a refreshment or two. But fishing is a big thing here—you can be out on the water at daybreak if you use this 30-acre park as your base camp. You can rent fishing rods and boats, or hike or cycle atop the levee for miles. You're sure to see an alligator or two, plus some long-legged wading birds hunting for their dinner. The mosquitoes aren't as plentiful in the cooler winter months, but they'll eat you alive in summer if you're not prepared. Pick up groceries and other items in Fort Lauderdale, because there's nothing much around here. Some supplies are sold 24 hours a day at the

dry camping at an Everglades National Park campground off of Tamiami Trail general store, souvenir shop, and bait shop. There's also a restaurant that serves takeout hamburgers and sandwiches.

Campsites, facilities: There are 90 RV sites with 30-amp electrical service and sewer hookups. RVs up to 40 feet long can be accommodated. Most of the sites have concrete slabs and are shaded by palms, oaks, and palmettos. Twenty sites are drive-through. About 75 percent of the park is occupied by year-round residents. Restrooms, showers, and picnic tables are provided. Airboat tours, fishing charters, a two-acre lake, a tackle shop, and boat rentals are available. You can also rent a rod and reel. The bathhouses and laundry are wheelchair-accessible. All ages are welcome. Pets must be on handheld leashes, which is wise, because alligators live in the nearby saw grass and canals.

Reservations, fees: Reservations are recommended November–May (reserve no later than August). Sites are $22 per night for two people, plus $5 per extra person. Credit cards are accepted. Long-term stays are OK.

Directions: From I-95 in Fort Lauderdale, drive west on I-595 for eight miles until the road becomes I-75. Continue six miles, following the signs for northbound traffic on I-75. At the exit for U.S. 27, turn south and drive 6.5 miles. Turn west on Griffin Road and drive 0.5 mile to the park.

Contact: Everglades Holiday Park, 21940 Griffin Road, Fort Lauderdale, FL 33332, 954/434-8111 or 800/226-2244, www.evergladesholidaypark.com.

13 LONG PINE KEY CAMPGROUND
🚶 🚵 🎣 🐕 🚐 ⛺

Scenic rating: 10

in Everglades National Park

See map, page 556   BEST (

The pine-dotted campground is the closest to the most popular walking trails and the main park entrance. It's ideal for self-contained RVs.

You can view plentiful birds along the nearby Anhinga Trail boardwalk in winter, and you will still see a few pine trunks snapped in two by 1992's Hurricane Andrew along the Long Pine Key Trail leading west from the campground. Rangers speak at the amphitheater in winter and answer questions year-round at the visitors center to the east. There's a great six-mile, one-way bike trail just across the road from the campground, leading fat-tire bikes through a double-track dirt road in a winding pine forest and more. You can make it a 12-mile loop by exiting the trail onto the main highway, turning north, and heading back on the road to the campground. Another little-used biking trail is the Old Ingraham Highway, built in the 1920s; it's a 21-mile trip out and back on an old rutted road where alligators will flee your approach, and you'll spook blue herons and other birds from their hiding places.

For a woodsy walk, drive west along the sole road to reach the thicker canopy of Mahogany Hammock (bring mosquito repellent). Its parking area is at the first turnoff after Pa-hay-okee Overlook, one of several stops along the 38-mile park road leading to Flamingo. Although the beauty of Pa-hay-okee's sea of saw grass is typically described as subtle, even a first-time visitor might notice the huge white clouds—sometimes described as "Florida's mountains"—building over the pancake-flat prairie.

Campsites, facilities: The 108 campsites have no water or electricity, but the roads are paved. You will find restrooms (but no showers), picnic tables, grills, a pay phone, a dump station, an amphitheater for winter programs, several nearby hiking trails, and a fishing pond. Children and leashed pets are permitted.

Reservations, fees: Reservations are accepted up to five months in advance at 301/722-1257 or 800/365-CAMP (800/365-2267). Sites are $14 per night for up to eight people. Group sites are $28 for up to 15 people. Campers must pay a $10 entrance fee, which is good for one week. Credit cards are accepted. The maximum stay is 14 days November 1–April 30, or 30 days per year.

Directions: From Miami, take Florida's Turnpike to its southern terminus at U.S. 1. In about one block, turn right at Palm Drive. Cross the railroad tracks and pass the Circle K. At the traffic light at 192nd Avenue/State Road 9336, turn left by the Robert Is Here fruit stand. Proceed south about two miles. When State Road 9336 veers right, follow it to the right instead of going straight toward the alligator farm. The park entrance is four miles ahead. The campground is on the left about four miles beyond the entrance.

Contact: Everglades National Park, 40001 State Road 9336, Homestead, FL 33034, 305/242-7700, www.nps.gov/ever.

14 FLAMINGO CAMPGROUND

Scenic rating: 10

on Florida Bay, in Everglades National Park

See map, page 556

If you want to see a manatee, the goose-sized limpkin bird, and other Everglades animals all in one day, try Flamingo Marina, east of this campground in Everglades National Park. You're sure to spot some sort of wildlife there—maybe alligators, wading birds, or the occasional American crocodile. Flamingo is at the end of the 38-mile main park road and is one of the prettiest spots reachable by car. You'll find visitors here from all over the world. Hurricanes have destroyed some of the shade, the adjacent hotel, and other buildings. However, fuel, limited groceries, and freshwater became available in 2006.

The campground overlooks the smooth, blue-green waters of Florida Bay and far-off mangrove islands. Campers drag canoes to their campsites or tie them near the water in anticipation of a morning launch to sightsee or fish for snook, snapper, jacks, trout, redfish, and sheepshead. Motorboaters launch to the east at the marina to fish for big-game tarpon or cross the bay to the Florida Keys.

Canoes, single-person kayaks, motorized skiffs, and bicycles are available for rent at the marina. Tickets to a tram tour and the worthwhile Bald Eagle and Pelican sightseeing boats also are sold there. A 12-hour advance reservation is required for the Cape Sable beach and birding cruise; call 239/695-3101.

Campsites, facilities: This is the biggest campground in Everglades National Park. It offers 234 drive-up campsites for tents, trailers, or RVs and 64 walk-up tent sites. There are no electrical hookups or showers, but you will find restrooms, picnic tables, grills, a pay phone, two dump stations, an amphitheater for winter programs, and two hiking trails. RVs up to 45 feet can be accommodated. The restrooms are wheelchair-accessible. Several mountain biking trails can be started from here; ask the park office for maps. Children and leashed pets are permitted.

Reservations, fees: Reservations are accepted up to five months in advance at 301/722-1257 or 800/365-CAMP (800/365-2267). Sites are $14 per night for up to eight people. Group sites are $28 nightly for up to 15 people. Campers pay a $10 park entrance fee, which is good for seven days. Credit cards are accepted. The maximum stay is 14 days November 1–April 30, or 30 days per year.

Directions: From Miami, take Florida's Turnpike to its southern terminus at U.S. 1. In about one block, turn west at Palm Drive. Cross the railroad tracks and pass the Circle K. At the traffic light at Southwest 192nd Avenue/State Road 9336, turn left by the Robert Is Here fruit stand. Proceed south about two miles. When State Road 9336 veers right, follow it to the right instead of going straight toward the alligator farm. The park entrance is four miles ahead. Follow the main park road about 38 miles to the campground on the left, beyond the marina.

Contact: Everglades National Park, 40001 State Road 9336, Homestead, FL 33034, 305/242-7700, www.nps.gov/ever. For questions about Flamingo, contact the Flamingo Visitor Center, 239/695-2945.

15 BEAR ISLAND

🏕️ 🚵 🐕 ⛺

Scenic rating: 4

Backcountry, north of I-75, in Big Cypress
National Preserve

See map, page 557

In winter, hunters flock to this northern part of 1,138-square-mile Big Cypress National Preserve. Located way out in the boonies, Bear Island tends to be lively in winter—with campers using swamp buggies, all-terrain vehicles, and any sort of off-road vehicle—and it's growing popular with mountain bikers and hikers. The most accessible camping area, called Bear Island, is little more than a dirt road with 40 campsites on either side. A campground host may reside here at certain points in the year. Also in the Bear Island section are two other primitive campgrounds with nine sites each; they are reachable only by foot, bicycle, or off-road vehicle.

Campsites, facilities: Only tent campers may sleep at these primitive camping areas. There are no hookups. A portable toilet is provided, but there are no other facilities. Bring mosquito repellent, food, water, and any supplies you'll need. Children are welcome. Pets must be on a six-foot leash and restrained at all times.

Reservations, fees: Reservations are not accepted, and there is no fee to camp. A $35 off-road-vehicle annual permit is required for the Pink Jeep and Gator Pit sites. Get it at the Big Cypress Visitor Center.

Directions: From Naples, drive east on U.S. 41/Tamiami Trail to the intersection of State Road 29. Continue on U.S. 41 for about six miles, then turn left (north) onto Highway 839, which borders the little H. P. Williams Roadside Park. Continue north on this gravel road 22 miles, passing under I-75, to the Bear Island camping area. Bicycle campers and hikers can access the Pink Jeep and Gator Pit campgrounds through a locked gate from State Road 29, six miles north of I-75. Download a trail map at www.nps.gov/bicy/planyourvisit/upload/bear_island_map.pdf.

Contact: Big Cypress National Preserve, 33100 Tamiami Trail East, Ochopee, FL 34141, 239/695-1201 or 239/695-1205, www.nps.gov/bicy. For hunting information, call 239/695-2040.

16 TIGER KEY BOAT/CANOE SITES

🐟 🚤 ⛺

Scenic rating: 10

Backcountry, on the Gulf of Mexico, in the Ten Thousand Islands

See map, page 557

Great sunsets reward campers at this quiet, breezy, secluded beach, which features a broad, unobstructed view of the Gulf of Mexico. Thumbnail-sized horseshoe crabs scamper on the beach at low tide, and the clicking sound you hear may be from the shrimp spending their youth in the gulf. Sleeping at the beach instead of deep within the national park's woodsy bowels is the best alternative for anyone who likes campfires (permitted only at beach campsites), or anyone averse to the park's 40-odd types of mosquitoes. Even so, bring DEET for insurance, and try to visit in winter. "Of course, that's when the people are here," notes a park ranger. Tip: To try to beat other winter visitors to the punch, show up as early as 7:30 A.M. (or before the ranger station opens; check current hours) the day before your intended campout to obtain the necessary permit.

Occasionally, raccoons make an appearance, so keep water in locked coolers to protect it from masked marauders. Be aware of shallow water and limited access at low tides. The place is accessible only by canoe, kayak, or small powerboat (at low tide, the three-foot beach waters present trouble for some boats). Although the official campsite is on the west side of the island, some friends of mine have bent the rules and slept on the spit of land at the north end of the island. They say a channel running in front of this spit of land provides good fishing when the tides run. No-see-ums may bug you at dusk; if you retreat to your tent to escape them, be sure to return outside when they subside an hour or two later. That way, you'll enjoy a black sky filled with stars.

Campsites, facilities: Three beach tent sites accommodate a total of 12 people. You must use a canoe or kayak to travel eight miles from the Gulf Coast Ranger Station in Everglades City. You can use a motorboat to reach the northwest side, although you might have a problem at dead low tide if your boat has a deep draft. No piped water is available, so bring plenty. There is no toilet; bury human waste six inches deep. Dead and downed wood may be used for campfires below the high-tide line. Trash must be packed out. Children are OK. No pets, please. If you're under human power, it's best to plan this trip far ahead, so you can ride out to the site on an outgoing tide and ride the incoming tide back in another day. Trying to paddle against the tide is virtually pointless.

Reservations, fees: Get a backcountry permit in person up to 24 hours before the day of your intended campout at the Gulf Coast Visitor Center. They are not issued by phone or mail. Camping costs $10 for the permit, plus $2 nightly per person. Major credit cards are accepted. There's a three-night stay limit.

Directions: From the intersection of U.S. 41/Tamiami Trail and State Road 29 east of Naples, drive south on State Road 29 for three miles into Everglades City and follow signs to Everglades National Park Gulf Coast Visitor Center, which will be on your right by Chokoloskee Bay. A ranger will explain the Tiger Key route. To avoid getting lost, obtain nautical chart 11430 at area bait stores, the ranger station or downstairs from the ranger station at Everglades National Park Boat Tours.

Contact: Everglades National Park, 40001 State Road 9336, Homestead, FL 33034, 305/242-7700, www.nps.gov/ever. For backcountry questions, contact the Gulf Coast Visitor Center, 239/695-3311.

17 PICNIC KEY BOAT/CANOE SITES

Scenic rating: 10

Backcountry, on the Gulf of Mexico, in the Ten Thousand Islands

See map, page 557

People once headed to the long white-sand beach of Picnic Key in the Ten Thousand Islands for big picnic dinners. The unobstructed view of the Gulf of Mexico and the long, thin beach of this mangrove-covered island continue to win fans. For Sandee and David Harraden, it was the perfect place to marry. In 1996, they brought inflatables for floating lazily on the water and set up a volleyball net and a campfire to entertain their wedding guests, who arrived by powerboat. With the westward view at sunset, the fiery disc of the sun "sits onto the water," says Sandee, who, along with her husband, rents canoes and arranges trips from the local outfitter North American Canoe Tours. "It's a really pretty sunset."

In addition to a fishing pole and bait for surfcasting, bring bug repellent. Mosquitoes and no-see-ums have a field day here when winds subside. Camp well above the high-tide line of the narrow beach. In storms, westerly winds can pummel the shore. As some of my party learned on one stormy night here, make sure you stake down your tent well. Beach your boat securely; the deep offshore channel is swift, and the sharp underwater oyster bars aren't kind to feet. The camping area on the southwest side of Picnic Key—just east of the small mangrove island in the channel between Picnic and Tiger Keys—is accessible to canoes and small boats at all tides. Only the northern beach has water deep enough to accommodate powerboats.

Campsites, facilities: Three beach tent sites accommodate a total of 16 people. You must use a kayak, canoe, or powerboat to travel seven to eight miles from the Gulf Coast Visitor Center in Everglades City. No piped water is available, so bring plenty. A vault toilet is provided. Dead and downed wood may be used for campfires below the high-tide line. Trash must be packed out. Children are OK. No pets are allowed.

Reservations, fees: Get a backcountry permit in person up to 24 hours before the day of your intended campout at the Gulf Coast Visitor Center. They are not issued by phone or mail. Camping costs $10 for the permit, plus $2 nightly per person. Major credit cards are accepted. There's a three-night stay limit.

Directions: From the intersection of U.S. 41/Tamiami Trail and State Road 29 east of Naples, drive five miles south on State Road 29 to the Everglades National Park Gulf Coast Visitor Center, located on your right by Chokoloskee Bay. A ranger will explain the Picnic Key route. To avoid getting lost, obtain nautical chart 11430 at area bait stores, the ranger station, or downstairs from the ranger station at Everglades National Park Boat Tours. If you're under human power, it's best to plan this trip far ahead, so you can ride out to the campsite on an outgoing tide, then ride the incoming tide back in another day. Paddling against the tide is arduous.

Contact: Everglades National Park, 40001 State Road 9336, Homestead, FL 33034, 305/242-7700, www.nps.gov/ever. For backcountry questions, contact the Flamingo Visitor Center, 239/695-2945; or the Gulf Coast Visitor Center, 239/695-3311.

18 SUNDAY BAY BOAT/CANOE SITES

🛶 🚤 ⛺

Scenic rating: 7

Backcountry, on Sunday Bay, in Everglades National Park

See map, page 557

Look for dolphins as you paddle or motor to this roof-covered chickee, set in a shallow bay and tucked behind a little mangrove-covered island. Other than Lopez River (see listing below), this is the closest site on the Wilderness

Waterway to the outpost of civilization you'll find at Chokoloskee and nearby Everglades City. It's a decent first stop if you're planning a three- or four-day canoe or kayak loop, say to Watson's Place and Rabbit or Pavilion Key, then back to Chokoloskee. You'll get your arms limbered up without paddling all that far.

Canoeists and kayakers will also find this spot to be a good choice for an overnighter if the wind kicks up and makes a trip across Chokoloskee Bay or "outside" in the Gulf of Mexico difficult. Of course, bugs are likely to be worse if it's the least bit warm, so try to come in winter. Sunday Bay can get kicked up by a decent wind. The fishing here is usually excellent. Snook travel the backwater creeks during winter. This attracts anglers who arrive by boat, so occasional buzz of motors may annoy paddlers who want absolute solitude.

Campsites, facilities: Two tent sites on elevated wooden platforms accommodate up to six people each. You must use a kayak, canoe, or powerboat to travel 11.5–12 miles from the Gulf Coast Visitor Center in Everglades City or 8.5–9 miles from Chokoloskee. No piped water is available, so bring plenty. Bring a portable stove because campfires are prohibited. Pack out trash. A dock and a vault toilet are provided. Children are OK. No pets, please.

Reservations, fees: Get a backcountry permit in person up to 24 hours before the day of your intended campout at the Flamingo Visitor Center or Gulf Coast Visitor Center. They are not issued by phone or mail. Camping costs $10 for the permit, plus $2 nightly per person. Major credit cards are accepted. There's a one-night stay limit.

Directions: From the intersection of U.S. 41/Tamiami Trail and State Road 29 east of Naples, drive five miles south on State Road 29 to the Everglades National Park Gulf Coast Visitor Center, on your right by Chokoloskee Bay. A ranger will explain the route to Sunday Bay. Obtain nautical chart 11430.

Contact: Everglades National Park, 40001 State Road 9336, Homestead, FL 33034, 305/242-7700, www.nps.gov/ever. For backcountry questions, contact the Flamingo Visitor Center, 239/695-2945; or the Gulf Coast Visitor Center, 239/695-3311.

19 LOPEZ RIVER BOAT/CANOE SITES

Scenic rating: 7

Backcountry, on the Lopez River, along the Wilderness Waterway, in Everglades National Park

See map, page 557

If you want to admire stars in an ebony sky, but have only enough time or energy for the shortest possible overnight trip from the Chokoloskee boat ramp, this is it. These ground sites on the southern bank of the Lopez River sit five miles from the Chokoloskee boat ramp and eight miles from Everglades City, making this the closest camping option on the fabled Wilderness Waterway—an inland water route and adventurist's dream spanning 99 miles from Everglades City to Flamingo. Because these shady campsites are near civilization, you may hear the buzz of powerboat motors; vessels pass closely to avoid oyster bars in the river. The Lopez family lived here for two generations up until the 1940s, and as you approach from the tea-colored river, you can't miss the tree-shaded concrete cistern that marks their turn-of-the-20th-century family homestead. For Marie Lopez and her beau, Walter Alderman, it was a pretty and unusual setting for tying the knot.

The downside of the thick tangle of buttonwood trees and mangroves is mosquitoes, which can be ravenous even in winter. Meanwhile, hungry raccoons can rip into Styrofoam coolers and plastic gallon water jugs. They also can get into backpacks of food hanging in trees. Tip: Wrap rope several times around a locked plastic cooler containing your edibles and water, then tie the rope to keep critters out. Because of these drawbacks, some people prefer to stop at this campsite only to picnic or stretch their legs, then spend the night elsewhere.

Campsites, facilities: Three ground tent sites accommodate a total of 12 people. You must use a kayak, canoe, or powerboat to travel five miles from the Chokoloskee boat ramp or eight miles from the Gulf Coast Visitor Center in Everglades City. No piped water is available, so bring plenty. Bring a portable stove because campfires are prohibited. Pack out trash. A vault toilet and tables are provided. Children are OK. No pets are allowed.

Reservations, fees: Get a backcountry permit in person up to 24 hours before the day of your intended campout at the Flamingo Visitor Center or Gulf Coast Visitor Center. They are not issued by phone or mail. Camping costs $10 for the permit, plus $2 nightly per person. Major credit cards are accepted. There's a two-night stay limit.

Directions: From the intersection of U.S. 41/Tamiami Trail and State Road 29 east of Naples, drive five miles south on State Road 29 to the Everglades National Park Gulf Coast Visitor Center, on your right by Chokoloskee Bay. A ranger will explain the Lopez River route. Use nautical chart 11430.

Contact: Everglades National Park, 40001 State Road 9336, Homestead, FL 33034, 305/242-7700, www.nps.gov/ever. For backcountry questions, contact the Flamingo Visitor Center, 239/695-2945; or the Gulf Coast Visitor Center, 239/695-3311.

20 RABBIT KEY BOAT/CANOE SITES

Scenic rating: 8

Backcountry, on the Gulf of Mexico, in the Ten Thousand Islands, in Everglades National Park

See map, page 557

This beach is a favorite because it's one of the closest sandy sleepover spot to Chokoloskee and nearby Everglades City. If you're in a motorboat, getting here is a cinch—just nine miles from Everglades City, six from Cho-koloskee. And if you fish, you'll have your choice of the oyster bars in Chokoloskee Bay, the tide-influenced comings and goings of redfish and the like in Chokoloskee Pass, and, of course, the Gulf of Mexico.

Dolphins may occasionally swim by. Shore-birds flutter along the sandy strip. You'll sleep on the western end of the island at the mouth of Rabbit Key Pass. Unlike ground or chickee campsites within the park, here you can enjoy a campfire. Some people know this beach as the place where early 20th-century murder suspect Ed Watson was buried for a short time; outraged Chokoloskee residents shot him and dragged his body here to ensure he no longer hurt anyone (see the listing for *Watson's Place* in this chapter for a fuller story).

For paddlers, the key to getting here is care-ful timing. One paddler scours the tide charts for weeks ahead to prepare for this trip. (It's worth it, though, to get a beach where you can watch a fabulous Everglades sunset alone, or virtually so.) Here's the thing: Pick a day when the tide is going out at the time you want to head out for the site, and will come back in the next day about when you want to. For example, if the high tide is at, say, 6 A.M. on Saturday, you can start going out any time after that (there will be an hour or so of slack time). The next day, wait until low tide about midday, then start paddling in. It makes for a good, quick, fun overnighter with plenty of time for fishing. If you ignore the tides, you do so at your own peril. Trying to paddle against the tide through one of the passes in the Ten Thousand Islands is misery.

The island has a fairly narrow beach. Be-ware of prickly pear near the toilet, and pitch your tent up on the grasses off the beach.

Campsites, facilities: Two beach tent sites accommodate a total of eight people. You must use a kayak, canoe, or powerboat to travel six miles from Chokoloskee or nine miles from the Gulf Coast Visitor Center in Everglades City. No piped water is available, so bring plenty in raccoon-proof containers. A vault toilet is provided. Dead and downed wood may be used for campfires below the high-tide line. Trash must be packed out. Children are OK. No pets, please. Reservations, fees: Get a backcountry permit in person up to 24 hours before the day of your intended campout at the Flamingo Visitor Center or Gulf Coast Visitor Center. They are not issued by phone or mail. Camping costs $10 for the permit, plus $2 nightly per person. Major credit cards are accepted. There's a two-night stay limit.

Directions: From the intersection of U.S. 41/Tamiami Trail and State Road 29 east of Naples, drive five miles south on State Road 29 to the Everglades National Park Gulf Coast Visitor Center, on your right by Chokoloskee Bay. A ranger will explain the Rabbit Key route. To avoid getting lost, obtain nautical chart 11430.

Contact: Everglades National Park, 40001 State Road 9336, Homestead, FL 33034, 305/242-7700, www.nps.gov/ever. For back-country questions, contact the Flamingo Visitor Center, 239/695-2945; or the Gulf Coast Visitor Center, 239/695-3311.

21 PAVILION KEY BOAT/CANOE SITES

Scenic rating: 8

Backcountry, on the Gulf of Mexico, in Everglades National Park

See map, page 557

Walk ashore this cacti-dotted island and see nary a footprint in the sand. "You are alone," says Joe Podgor, a Miami Springs environmental activist. Bird-watching, fishing, and collecting seashells are popular, as is watching the orange glow of the sunset on the horizon. Stake out a private shoreline campsite at the northern end of the island (the southern end is closed to landings). Legend has it that pirates once camped along this long, sandy beach and their tents resembled a pavilion—hence the island's name. Pirates are said to have captured prisoners from a schooner, including one young woman who died tragically and still walks the beach at night. Today, raccoons, not pirates, resemble of a platoon of flag-waving soldiers as they approach docked canoes and boats in search of water and food. Store water and edibles in locked, thick-plastic coolers, and wrap and tie rope tightly around them. Raccoons have been known to bite through plastic water jugs. If you're planning to spend several days in the Everglades, you may reach Pavilion Key from such places as Rabbit Key (4 miles), Watson's Place (8 miles), Lopez River (10 miles), or the Chokoloskee boat ramp (10 miles).

Campsites, facilities: Four beach tent sites accommodate six people each. You must use a kayak, canoe, or powerboat to get here from other campsites or to travel 13 miles here from the Gulf Coast Visitor Center in Everglades City. Boats must land on the northernmost sand spit only, not elsewhere, per park rules. No piped water is available, so bring plenty. Pack out trash. A vault toilet is provided. Dead and downed wood may be used for campfires below the high-tide line. Children are OK. No pets, please.

Reservations, fees: Get a backcountry permit in person up to 24 hours before the day of your intended campout at the Flamingo Visitor Center or Gulf Coast Visitor Center. They are not issued by phone or mail. Camping costs $10 for the permit, plus $2 nightly per person. Major credit cards are accepted. There's a three-night stay limit.

Directions: From the intersection of U.S. 41/Tamiami Trail and State Road 29 east of Naples, drive about five miles south on State Road 29 to the Everglades National Park Gulf Coast Visitor Center, on your right by Chokoloskee Bay. A ranger will explain the Pavilion Key route. To avoid getting lost, obtain nautical chart 11430 at area bait stores, the ranger station, or downstairs from the ranger station at Everglades National Park Boat Tours.

Contact: Everglades National Park, 40001 State Road 9336, Homestead, FL 33034, 305/242-7700, www.nps.gov/ever. For backcountry questions, contact the Flamingo Visitor Center, 239/695-2945; or the Gulf Coast Visitor Center, 239/695-3311.

22 DARWIN'S PLACE BOAT/CANOE SITES

Scenic rating: 8

Backcountry, on the Wilderness Waterway, in Everglades National Park

See map, page 557

Basically a clearing found at water's edge along the Wilderness Waterway, Darwin's Place is preferred over more famous Watson's Place by some campers. That's because it's a smaller site—odds are you'll share it with fewer people. Also, picnic tables are provided, which makes mealtime more pleasant.

A man named Arthur Darwin moved to this island between Chevalier and Cannon Bays just as World War II was ending. Some old nautical charts still refer to it as Opossum Key, yet by the time Darwin left his homestead in 1971 (park officials let him stay on after the park was established in 1947), everyone knew it as Darwin's Place. Like the famous Charles Darwin who wrote *The Origin of Species,* the grandfatherly Arthur Darwin was a naturalist. But he was self-taught and got lots of practice living on his Everglades homestead.

Today, you can see the shell-and-concrete foundation of Darwin's cistern at this elevated, partly shady campsite. Walk inland a bit, and you also may notice mounds as tall as five feet; they're oyster-shell middens created by earlier residents, the Calusa Indians. Mosquitoes can be atrocious (as at any ground site), so bring DEET, mosquito coils, and, if possible, a hat with mosquito netting. Darwin's Place is accessible to powerboats as well as canoes—hence the frequent buzz of boats passing by on the Wilderness Waterway. Tie your craft securely; there's no dock.

Campsites, facilities: Two ground tent sites

accommodate a total of eight people. You must use a kayak, canoe, or powerboat to travel to this location, which sits 20.5 miles from Everglades City's Gulf Coast Visitor Center. No piped water is available, so bring plenty. Pack out trash. Bring a portable stove because campfires are prohibited. A vault toilet and two picnic tables are provided. Children are OK. No pets, please.

Reservations, fees: Get a backcountry permit in person up to 24 hours before the day of your intended campout at the Flamingo Visitor Center or Gulf Coast Visitor Center. They are not issued by phone or mail. Camping costs $10 for the permit, plus $2 nightly per person. Major credit cards are accepted. There's a three-night stay limit.

Directions: From the intersection of U.S. 41/Tamiami Trail and State Road 29 east of Naples, drive five miles south on State Road 29 to the Everglades National Park Gulf Coast Visitor Center, on your right by Chokoloskee Bay. A ranger will explain the route to Darwin's Place. To avoid getting lost, obtain nautical chart 11430 at area bait stores, the ranger station, or downstairs from the ranger station at Everglades National Park Boat Tours.

Contact: Everglades National Park, 40001 State Road 9336, Homestead, FL 33034, 305/242-7700, www.nps.gov/ever. For backcountry questions, contact the Flamingo Visitor Center, 239/695-2945; or the Gulf Coast Visitor Center, 239/695-3311.

23 WATSON'S PLACE BOAT/CANOE SITES

Scenic rating: 9

Backcountry, on the Chatham River, in Everglades National Park

See map, page 557

If you bring plenty of DEET and a vivid imagination to this large wooded campsite on the north side of the Chatham River, hiking around the stomping grounds of turn-of-the-20th-century murder suspect Ed Watson will be a treat. A hulking, bearded man, Watson settled here in a two-story house built on a native shell mound (the house's concrete cistern still stands). He supposedly moved here to flee pursuers who believed he had killed, among others, the famous female outlaw Belle Star. Soon, Watson's hired hands began to disappear—funny, right around payday. Nervous neighbors suspected the boss had killed them. After the body of Hannah Smith was seen floating nearby in 1910, frightened townsfolk took matters into their own hands and shot Watson to death at postmaster Ted Smallwood's store (now a museum), 16 miles away in Chokoloskee.

Today, hikers still may see the ruins of Watson's sugarcane syrup cauldron and farm machinery, as well as several exotic plants (picking them is prohibited). To add dimension to your stay, bring along Peter Matthiessen's book *Killing Mr. Watson,* a fictionalized yet largely historical account of the secretive man's exploits. The family of alligator hunter and marijuana smuggler Loren "Totch" Brown moved to this same outpost in the 1930s, inspiring his autobiography, *Totch: A Life in the Everglades.*

You'll likely share this site with others, since it can accommodate far more tents than most Everglades backcountry spots. The long distance from Everglades City makes popular Watson's Place impractical for many weekend kayakers and canoeists. Consider spending at least three nights in the national park, camping at Lopez River (8 miles from Everglades City), then Watson's Place (19 miles from Everglades City), before doubling back for a campout at Sunday Bay (8.5 miles from Watson's Place) and waking to an 11.5-mile paddle back to Everglades City. To get to Watson's Place from the Wilderness Waterway, leave the well-marked water route at marker 99 and head 1.5 miles down the Chatham River. The campsite is accessible to paddlers and powerboats at all tides.

Campsites, facilities: Five ground tent sites

accommodate a total of 20 people. You must use a kayak, canoe, or powerboat to travel 16 miles from the Chokoloskee boat ramp or 19 miles from the Gulf Coast Visitor Center in Everglades City. No piped water is available, so bring plenty in raccoon-proof containers. Pack out trash. Bring a portable stove, because campfires are prohibited. A vault toilet, long dock, and canoe ramp are provided. Children are OK. No pets.

Reservations, fees: Get a backcountry permit in person up to 24 hours before the day of your intended campout at the Flamingo Visitor Center or Gulf Coast Visitor Center. They are not issued by phone or mail. Camping costs $10 for the permit, plus $2 nightly per person. Major credit cards are accepted. There's a two-night stay limit.

Directions: From the intersection of U.S. 41/Tamiami Trail and State Road 29 east of Naples, drive five miles south on State Road 29 to the Everglades National Park Gulf Coast Visitor Center, on your right by Chokoloskee Bay. A ranger will explain the route to Watson's Place. To avoid getting lost, obtain nautical chart 11430.

Contact: Everglades National Park, 40001 State Road 9336, Homestead, FL 33034, 305/242-7700, www.nps.gov/ever. For backcountry questions, contact the Flamingo Visitor Center, 239/695-2945; or the Gulf Coast Visitor Center, 239/695-3311.

24 SWEETWATER BOAT/CANOE SITES

Scenic rating: 7

Backcountry, on Sweetwater Creek, in Everglades National Park

See map, page 557

Relatively few people take the two-mile detour from 99-mile-long Wilderness Waterway (spanning Everglades City to Flamingo) to sleep on this double chickee set off the north end of a small island on Sweetwater Creek.

Solitude is your reward. "Sweetwater" is the colloquial term for the fresh, drinkable water that falls from the sky. You must bring your own drinking water on the long trip here, so every drop you conserve may very well seem sweet.

The buckets of water that fall during the summer rainy season help explain the site's name. The campsite also is near the transition zone between brackish and fresh water.

Look for alligators. The bordering mangroves are alive with herons and other birds. Fish splash in the shallow water. If you're paddling, set aside about three nights to get to and from Everglades City, making two sleepover stops at Lopez River (8 miles from Everglades City) or at other sites suggested by a ranger. Only low-profile powerboats under 18 feet in length and with shallow draft should attempt docking at Sweetwater. Bring extra rope to tie a free-standing tent to the wooden, roof-covered platform that will serve as your campsite. No stakes or nails may be used.

Campsites, facilities: Two parties of up to six people each may stay at this elevated roof-covered wooden platform; a vault toilet separates the two sites. You must use a kayak, canoe, or powerboat to travel 16.5 miles from the Chokoloskee boat ramp or 19.5 miles from the Gulf Coast Visitor Center in Everglades City. No water is available. Pack out trash. Bring a portable stove because campfires are prohibited. A dock is provided. Children are OK. Pets are prohibited.

Reservations, fees: Get a backcountry permit in person up to 24 hours before the day of your intended campout at the Flamingo Visitor Center or Gulf Coast Visitor Center. They are not issued by phone or mail. Camping costs $10 for the permit, plus $2 nightly per person. Major credit cards are accepted. There's a one-night stay limit.

Directions: From the intersection of U.S. 41/Tamiami Trail and State Road 29 east of Naples, drive five miles south on State Road 29 to the Everglades National Park Gulf Coast Visitor Center, on your right by Chokoloskee

Bay. A ranger will explain the route to Sweetwater. To avoid getting lost, obtain nautical chart 11430.

Contact: Everglades National Park, 40001 State Road 9336, Homestead, FL 33034, 305/242-7700, www.nps.gov/ever. For backcountry questions, contact the Flamingo Visitor Center, 239/695-2945; or the Gulf Coast Visitor Center, 239/695-3311.

25 MORMON KEY BOAT/CANOE SITES

Scenic rating: 8

Backcountry, on the Gulf of Mexico, in Everglades National Park

See map, page 557

This is one of those odd pieces of real estate in the national park to which individual landowners laid claim for years. Even a half-century after the park was dedicated in 1947, some persistent souls continued to cite problems with the deed transfers. However, none of that will interfere with your enjoyment of a long, shelly beach, where you can sit around a campfire or collect a handful of seashells (look for old conchs).

The beach is low, but long—more than 100 yards, a rarity here. This affords pretty views of the sun setting on the Gulf of Mexico's broad horizon, but the sun can bear down hard on this open beach at high noon, making it uncomfortably hot. Beyond the beach, you'll find the area's ubiquitous vegetation: mangroves. Bring a fishing rod; you'll be close to good angling spots near the mouth of the Huston and Chatham Rivers. Canoes can access Mormon Key at all tides. Powerboats, cautiously driven, should also be able to get close to the beach; check with rangers for tide information. It's best to land on the west side, facing Chatham Bend. The key is a miserable place to land during a storm, when northnorthwest winds pummel it.

Campsites, facilities: Two beach tent sites

accommodate a total of 12 people. You must use a canoe, kayak, or powerboat to get here. Travel distances vary by your chosen route; the sites are 14.5–20 miles from the Chokoloskee boat ramp or 17.5–20.5 miles from the Gulf Coast Visitor Center in Everglades City. No piped water is available, so bring plenty in raccoon-proof containers. There is no toilet, electricity, table, or dock. Human waste must be buried at least six inches deep or packed out with the trash. Dead and downed wood may be used for campfires below the high-tide line. Children are welcome, but not pets.

Reservations, fees: Get a backcountry permit in person up to 24 hours before the day of your intended campout at the Flamingo Visitor Center or Gulf Coast Visitor Center. They are not issued by phone or mail. Camping costs $10 for the permit, plus $2 nightly per person. Major credit cards are accepted. There's a three-night stay limit.

Directions: From the intersection of U.S. 41/Tamiami Trail and State Road 29 east of Naples, drive five miles south on State Road 29 to the Everglades National Park Gulf Coast Visitor Center, on your right by Chokoloskee Bay. A ranger will explain the route to Mormon Key. Use nautical chart 11430.

Contact: Everglades National Park, 40001 State Road 9336, Homestead, FL 33034, 305/242-7700, www.nps.gov/ever. For backcountry questions, contact the Flamingo Visitor Center, 239/695-2945; or the Gulf Coast Visitor Center, 239/695-3311.

26 NEW TURKEY KEY BOAT/CANOE SITES

Scenic rating: 7

Backcountry, on the Gulf of Mexico, in Everglades National Park

See map, page 557

Secluded New Turkey Key and its sister campsite, Turkey Key, feature small beaches facing the fine sunsets over the Gulf of Mexico. The beach sand is actually a shelly mix, but it's the best you'll see in these parts. There's a large, open, grassy area, perhaps 75 feet by 50 feet, where you can pitch a tent in the middle of the key.

Campsites, facilities: Two beach tent sites accommodate 10 people. You must use a canoe, kayak, or powerboat. Travel distance varies by the route you choose; expect to travel 16.5 miles to 22 miles from the Chokoloskee boat ramp or 19.5 miles to 25 miles from the Gulf Coast Visitor Center in Everglades City. No piped water is available, so bring plenty in raccoon-proof containers. Pack out trash. A vault toilet is provided. Dead and downed wood may be used for campfires below the high-tide line. Children are allowed, but not pets.

Reservations, fees: Get a backcountry permit in person up to 24 hours before the day of your intended campout at the Flamingo Visitor Center or Gulf Coast Visitor Center. They are not issued by phone or mail. Camping costs $10 for the permit, plus $2 nightly per person. Major credit cards are accepted. There's a two-night stay limit.

Directions: From the intersection of U.S. 41/Tamiami Trail and State Road 29 east of Naples, drive about five miles south on State Road 29 to the Everglades National Park Gulf Coast Visitor Center, on your right by Chokoloskee Bay. A ranger will explain the route to New Turkey Key. Use nautical chart 11430.

Contact: Everglades National Park, 40001 State Road 9336, Homestead, FL 33034, 305/242-7700, www.nps.gov/ever. For backcountry questions, contact the Flamingo Visitor Center, 239/695-2945; or the Gulf Coast Visitor Center, 239/695-3311.

27 PLATE CREEK BAY BOAT/CANOE SITE

Scenic rating: 8

Backcountry, on Plate Creek Bay, along the Wilderness Waterway, in Everglades National Park

See map, page 557

If you want a camping retreat all to yourself, you're certain to get it here. This single tent site, which was built before the national park

© MARILYN MOORE

mangroves taking root in a tidal flat

was established in 1947, is nirvana to adventurists tired of "wilderness" outings that pack strangers' tents together like sardines. At this former base camp for Joseph Cotton's real estate sales operations and his hunting/fishing parties, breezes and a southeastern exposure help make insects less of a problem. Fans love the clear water, pretty sunsets and sunrises, and the star-filled sky. On the downside, weekend boat traffic tends to be heavy. You'll be sleeping along the sole inland route between Chokoloskee and the good fishing holes down south. Bring extra rope to tie a free-standing tent to the chickee hut that serves as a tent site. No stakes or nails may be used.

Anyone relying on muscle power to get here should set aside five days or so to paddle a canoe or kayak to and from Everglades City, making sleepover stops at perhaps Lopez River (8 miles from Everglades City) and Sweetwater (19.5 miles from Everglades City) along the way. Outdoors enthusiasts also stop here during trips along the Wilderness Waterway, a well-marked inland water route that runs from Everglades City to Flamingo. Tides aren't a big issue at Plate Creek; it's accessible to canoes and powerboats up to 21 feet in length at all tides. But overhanging branches of mangroves may snag boats with T-tops.

Campsites, facilities: One tent site on an elevated wooden platform accommodates up to six people. You must use a kayak, canoe, or powerboat to travel 23 miles from the Chokoloskee boat ramp or 26 miles from the Gulf Coast Visitor Center in Everglades City. No water is available. Pack out trash. Bring a portable stove. Campfires are prohibited. A vault toilet and a dock are provided. Children are allowed, but no pets.

Reservations, fees: Get a backcountry permit in person up to 24 hours before the day of your intended campout at the Flamingo Visitor Center or Gulf Coast Visitor Center. They are not issued by phone or mail. Camping costs $10 for the permit, plus $2 nightly per person. Major credit cards are accepted. There's a one-night stay limit.

Directions: From the intersection of U.S. 41/Tamiami Trail and State Road 29 east of Naples, drive five miles south on State Road 29 to the Everglades National Park Gulf Coast Visitor Center, on your right by Chokoloskee Bay. A ranger will explain the route to Plate Creek Bay. To avoid getting lost, obtain nautical chart 11430 at area bait stores, the ranger station, or downstairs from the ranger station at Everglades National Park Boat Tours.

Contact: Everglades National Park, 40001 State Road 9336, Homestead, FL 33034, 305/242-7700, www.nps.gov/ever. For backcountry questions, contact the Flamingo Visitor Center, 239/695-2945; or the Gulf Coast Visitor Center, 239/695-3311.

28 LOSTMAN'S FIVE BAY BOAT/CANOE SITES

Scenic rating: 5

Backcountry, on Lostman's Five Bay, in Everglades National Park

See map, page 557

Because this camping area involves a two-to-three-day paddle from Everglades City and can accommodate a large number of campers, it gets a fair amount of use by people completing the Wilderness Waterway, a 99-mile route from Everglades City to Flamingo. But it can be buggy. Among other drawbacks: It tends to flood during extreme high tides or heavy rains, and is usually windy and sun-baked. For a more pleasant night's sleep, opt instead for Broad River or the nearby Plate Creek Bay chickee, if you can.

Campsites, facilities: Two tent sites accommodate a total of 10 people. You must use a canoe, kayak, or powerboat to travel 24 miles from the Chokoloskee boat ramp or 27 miles from the Gulf Coast Visitor Center in Everglades City. No piped water is available, so bring plenty. Bring a portable stove because campfires are prohibited. A toilet is provided, as is a large dock that can fit several medium-sized boats. Trash must be packed out. Children are OK. No pets, please.

Reservations, fees: Get a backcountry permit in person up to 24 hours before the day of your intended campout at the Flamingo Visitor Center or Gulf Coast Visitor Center. They are not issued by phone or mail. Camping costs $10 for the permit, plus $2 nightly per person. Major credit cards are accepted. There's a two-night stay limit.

Directions: From the intersection of U.S. 41/Tamiami Trail and State Road 29 east of Naples, drive five miles south on State Road 29 to the Everglades National Park Gulf Coast Visitor Center, on your right by Chokoloskee Bay. A ranger will explain the route to Lostmans Five. To avoid getting lost, obtain nautical charts 11430 and 11432 at area bait stores, the ranger station, or downstairs from the ranger station at Everglades National Park Boat Tours.

Contact: Everglades National Park, 40001 State Road 9336, Homestead, FL 33034, 305/242-7700, www.nps.gov/ever. For backcountry questions, contact the Flamingo Visitor Center, 239/695-2945; or the Gulf Coast Visitor Center, 239/695-3311.

29 HOG KEY CANOE/KAYAK SITES

Scenic rating: 7

Backcountry, on the Gulf of Mexico, in Everglades National Park

See map, page 557

Powerboats can't approach this remote getaway, because the water surrounding the island is quite shallow—and a history of strong winds and rough seas makes landing dicey (if you must, use two anchors). Even canoeists and kayakers may have to anchor a good distance from the island and wade across shallow mudflats to the campsite. Although small, this site is well-liked by many paddlers because it's right on the Gulf of Mexico. Bring a fishing pole; prime spots are minutes away to the north and south. This is also a good way station for kayakers and canoeists to camp and shorten their paddling days because seas usually are rough between Turkey Key and Lostman's River. Downsides include a northern view—lousy for taking in sunsets or sunrises—and the fact that no signs mark the campsite, making it all the more difficult to find. Look for the campsite's namesake; resident wild hogs occasionally make appearances.

Campsites, facilities: Two beach tent sites accommodate a total of eight people. You must use a canoe or kayak. Travel distance varies; the shortest distance is 22.5 miles from the Chokoloskee boat ramp and 25.5 miles from the Gulf Coast Visitor Center in Everglades City. Powerboats are no use, as you can't dock here. No piped water is available, so bring plenty. There is no toilet; bury human waste or pack it out with the trash. Dead and downed wood may be used for campfires below the high-tide line. Children are OK. No pets are allowed.

Reservations, fees: Get a backcountry permit in person up to 24 hours before the day of your intended campout at the Flamingo Visitor Center or Gulf Coast Visitor Center. They are not issued by phone or mail. Camping costs $10 for the permit, plus $2 nightly per person. Major credit cards are accepted. There's a two-night stay limit.

Directions: From the intersection of U.S. 41/Tamiami Trail and State Road 29 east of Naples, drive five miles south on State Road 29 to the Everglades National Park Gulf Coast Visitor Center, on your right by Chokoloskee Bay. A ranger will explain the route to Hog Key. To avoid getting lost, obtain nautical charts 11430 and 11432.

Contact: Everglades National Park, 40001 State Road 9336, Homestead, FL 33034, 305/242-7700, www.nps.gov/ever. For backcountry questions, contact the Flamingo Visitor Center, 239/695-2945; or the Gulf Coast Visitor Center, 239/695-3311.

30 WILLY WILLY BOAT/CANOE SITES

Scenic rating: 7

Backcountry, on Rocky Creek Bay, in
Everglades National Park

See map, page 557

Nobody likes mosquitoes, so it's understandable that Calusa Indians hundreds of years ago used the remains of the shellfish they ate to build this ground higher, helping them get away from blood-sucking skeeters (and floods). Today, tropical hardwood trees—not ever-present mangroves—shade tenters just as they did Indians.

This site is favored by serious anglers, who venture into area waters to go after snook and mangrove snapper, then sleep here. The formidable distance makes Willy Willy impractical for weekend kayakers or canoeists. Consider a week-long vacation, with campouts along the way at Lopez River (8 miles from Everglades City), Sweetwater (19.5 miles from Everglades City), and Plate Creek Bay (26 miles from Everglades City). Adventurists sometimes make a two-mile northeastward detour to sleep here during trips along the Wilderness Waterway, a well-marked inland water route that runs from Everglades City to Flamingo. Early settlers are said to have burned smudge pots of dead black mangrove to try to keep bugs away, and were said to have lived entirely in smoke. Tip: Bring mosquito netting and DEET. Also, protect your food and water from raccoons. Fortunately, tides aren't a big issue at Willy Willy; it's accessible to canoes and powerboats at all tides.

Campsites, facilities: Three ground tent sites accommodate a total of 10 people. You must use a kayak, canoe, or powerboat to travel 32.5 miles from the Chokoloskee boat ramp or 35.5 miles from the Gulf Coast Visitor Center in Everglades City. No piped water is available, so bring plenty. Bring a portable stove because campfires are prohibited. A vault toilet, small dock, and picnic table are provided. Trash must be packed out. Children are OK. No pets, please.

Reservations, fees: Get a backcountry permit in person up to 24 hours before the day of your intended campout at the Flamingo Visitor Center or Gulf Coast Visitor Center. They are not issued by phone or mail. Camping costs $10 for the permit, plus $2 nightly per person. Major credit cards are accepted. There's a three-night stay limit.

Directions: From the intersection of U.S. 41/Tamiami Trail and State Road 29 east of Naples, drive about five miles south on State Road 29 to the Everglades National Park Gulf Coast Visitor Center, on your right by Chokoloskee Bay. A ranger will explain the route to Willy Willy. To avoid getting lost, obtain nautical charts 11430 and 11432 at area bait stores, the ranger station, or downstairs from the ranger station at Everglades National Park Boat Tours. It pays to get a new chart 11432; older versions misplace Willy Willy. After going north on Rocky Creek, turn left—not right—on Rocky Creek Bay, then go southwest for one-tenth of a mile, looking for the narrow dock on the uncharted creek flowing north of the bay. A sign marks the campsite.

Contact: Everglades National Park, 40001 State Road 9336, Homestead, FL 33034, 305/242-7700, www.nps.gov/ever. For backcountry questions, contact the Flamingo Visitor Center, 239/695-2945; or the Gulf Coast Visitor Center, 239/695-3311.

31 RODGERS RIVER BAY BOAT/CANOE SITES

Scenic rating: 8

Backcountry, on Rodgers River Bay, in
Everglades National Park

See map, page 557

Tarpon fishing is considered good in the surrounding bays, and bass waters are nearby, so camping at this site set in a small, protected cove is popular. You'll sleep closest to a traditional nesting site for Everglades wading birds, considered an important barometer of the ecosystem's overall health. Consider this description from the 1940s: "The whole scene fairly swamped, seethed and crawled with running, flapping young birds . . . . Overhead, constantly arriving and departing, wheeling, circling, were squadrons of adults, which pitched and dived into the general melee on whistling, rushing wings."

Alas, the birds' numbers have been greatly reduced by disruptions in the natural Everglades water flows caused by development and farming. Still, in some good years when enough water courses through the Everglades, you'll find this nesting site alive with birds, albeit fewer.

From the campsite, you'll notice egrets and herons flying overhead. Look for alligators, and possibly a small crocodile. The site is a typical Everglades National Park backcountry chickee. It is close to the halfway point on the 99-mile-long Wilderness Waterway from Everglades City to Flamingo, which takes about 10 days by canoe or one to two days by motorboat. Bring extra rope to tie a free-standing tent to the chickee hut that serves as a tent site. No stakes or nails may be used.

Campsites, facilities: Two tent sites on elevated wooden platforms accommodate up to six people each. You must use a powerboat, kayak, or canoe to travel 36 miles from the Chokoloskee boat ramp or 39 miles from the Gulf Coast Visitor Center in Everglades City. No piped water is available, so bring plenty. Bring a portable stove because campfires are prohibited. A vault toilet and dock are provided. Trash must be packed out. Children are OK. No pets, please.

Reservations, fees: Get a backcountry permit in person up to 24 hours before the day of your intended campout at the Flamingo Visitor Center or Gulf Coast Visitor Center. They are not issued by phone or mail. Camping costs $10 for the permit, plus $2 nightly per person. Major credit cards are accepted. There's a one-night stay limit.

Directions: From the intersection of U.S. 41/Tamiami Trail and State Road 29 east of Naples, drive about five miles south on State Road 29 to the Everglades National Park Gulf Coast Visitor Center, on your right by Chokoloskee Bay. A ranger will explain the route to Rodgers River. To avoid getting lost, obtain nautical charts 11430 and 11432 at area bait stores, the ranger station, or downstairs from the ranger station at Everglades National Park Boat Tours.

Contact: Everglades National Park, 40001 State Road 9336, Homestead, FL 33034, 305/242-7700, www.nps.gov/ever. For backcountry questions, contact the Flamingo Visitor Center, 239/695-2945; or the Gulf Coast Visitor Center, 239/695-3311.

32 HIGHLAND BEACH BOAT/CANOE SITES

Scenic rating: 7

Backcountry, on the Gulf of Mexico, in Everglades National Park

See map, page 557

This large site is heavily used, despite its remoteness. The reason: It features a beach on the Gulf of Mexico framed by palms. Sunsets can be gorgeous, with the feel of a tropical paradise in this subtropical wilderness. The vegetation, a kind of low brush, is set back about 50 feet from the water, allowing campers a beach that is nice and wide, if a little low-slung. The shoreline's low profile can be a problem when a west wind kicks up, because the tides can rush in fairly fast and far, so check the weather forecast. In any case, pitch your tent a healthy distance from where the waves are breaking.

Birds abound in winter, including ibises, herons, and egrets. Wild boars occasionally make appearances. The sand consists of broken shells and marl mud. Be mindful of tides when approaching camp; if you arrive at low tide, you may be cut off by huge, exposed mudflats. In that case, prepare to wade. And wear old sneakers—you never know when you might step on an oyster shell that can cut you badly. Unless you have a motorboat, you'll need more than one day to make it to Highland Beach. Consult with rangers about other stops to make along the way.

Campsites, facilities: Four beach tent sites accommodate a total of 24 people. You must use a powerboat, kayak, or canoe to travel a minimum of 29.5 miles from the Chokoloskee boat ramp or 32.5–39 miles from the Gulf Coast Visitor Center in Everglades City, depending on your chosen route. There is no piped water, so bring your own. Trash must be packed out. No toilet is available; bury human waste six inches deep. Dead and downed wood may be used for campfires below the high-tide line. Children are OK. No pets, please.

Reservations, fees: Get a backcountry permit in person up to 24 hours before the day of your intended campout at the Flamingo Visitor Center or Gulf Coast Visitor Center. They are not issued by phone or mail. Camping costs $10 for the permit, plus $2 nightly per person. Major credit cards are accepted. There's a three-night stay limit.

Directions: From the intersection of U.S. 41/Tamiami Trail and State Road 29 east of Naples, drive about five miles south on State Road 29 to the Everglades National Park Gulf Coast Visitor Center, on your right by Chokoloskee Bay. A ranger will explain the route to Highland Beach. To avoid getting lost, obtain nautical charts 11430 and 11432 at area bait stores, the ranger station, or downstairs from the ranger station at Everglades National Park Boat Tours.

Contact: Everglades National Park, 40001 State Road 9336, Homestead, FL 33034, 305/242-7700, www.nps.gov/ever. For backcountry questions, contact the Flamingo Visitor Center, 239/695-2945; or the Gulf Coast Visitor Center, 239/695-3311.

33 BROAD RIVER BOAT/CANOE SITES

Scenic rating: 7

Backcountry, on the Broad River, in Everglades National Park

See map, page 557

This is the campsite closest to the halfway point on the Wilderness Waterway, which runs 99 miles from Flamingo to Everglades City. The trip will generally take about 10 days by kayak or canoe, although it's possible to complete it in a day or two by powerboat. If you're trying to save time or avoid the waves of the Gulf of Mexico, you may be able to take a cutoff just south of here known as "The Nightmare." This moniker did not come from nowhere. Although The Nightmare shaves a few miles off your trip, it's also nearly impassable, even for kayaks and canoes, during low tide. Luckily, though, the Broad River campsite is usually accessible at low tide, even to big boats. Just be ready for strong river currents and up to a three-foot tidal differential when mooring at this site on the south bank of the Broad River. Mosquitoes and other bugs can be a big problem in any season. The ground campsite can get quite muddy when it's been raining.

Campsites, facilities: Three ground tent sites accommodate a total of 10 people. You must use a powerboat, kayak, or canoe to get here. Travel distance varies by route chosen; expect to travel a minimum of 33.5 miles from the Chokoloskee boat ramp, 36.5 miles from the Gulf Coast Visitor Center in Everglades City, or 39.5 miles from the Flamingo Visitor Center. No piped water is available, so bring plenty. Bring a portable stove, because campfires are prohibited. A vault toilet, table, small dock, and canoe ramp are provided. Trash must be packed out. Children are OK. No pets, please.

Reservations, fees: Get a backcountry permit in person up to 24 hours before the day of your intended campout at the Flamingo

The Everglades **583**

Visitor Center or Gulf Coast Visitor Center. They are not issued by phone or mail. Camping costs $10 for the permit, plus $2 nightly per person. Major credit cards are accepted. There's a two-night stay limit.

Directions: From the intersection of U.S. 41/Tamiami Trail and State Road 29 east of Naples, drive five miles south on State Road 29 to the Everglades National Park Gulf Coast Visitor Center, on your right by Chokoloskee Bay. A ranger will explain the route to Broad River. To avoid getting lost, obtain nautical charts 11430 and 11432 at area bait stores, at the ranger station, or downstairs from the ranger station at Everglades National Park Boat Tours. If you're approaching from Flamingo, buy charts 11432 and 11433 at the Flamingo Visitor Center.

Contact: Everglades National Park, 40001 State Road 9336, Homestead, FL 33034, 305/242-7700, www.nps.gov/ever. For backcountry questions, contact the Flamingo Visitor Center, 239/695-2945; or the Gulf Coast Visitor Center, 239/695-3311.

34 CAMP LONESOME BOAT/CANOE SITES

Scenic rating: 7

Backcountry, on the Broad River, in Everglades National Park

See map, page 557

They don't call this place Lonesome for nothing. It's about three miles east of the Wilderness Waterway, which itself is sparsely populated. To find the campsite, you have to look for a narrow dock jutting out of thick brush. When you get closer to it, you'll see the campsite sign. This old Calusa Indian mound was built up from oyster shells and other leavings, and is shaded by sabal palms and relatively rare tropical hardwoods, such as red-barked gumbo-limbo.

It is one of the few campsites in the park where you can catch sight of the sawgrass prai-

ries that earned the Everglades its nickname, "River of Grass." Another plus: Picnic tables will make meals easier.

There are, however, lots of mosquitoes, so come during a winter cold snap, if possible. The site is next to a large fork in the Broad River. Look for the dock on the north bank. Camp Lonesome can be done as an overnight trip only if you have a motorboat. Otherwise, plan an outing of several days or even a week.

Campsites, facilities: Three ground tent sites accommodate a total of 10 people. You must use a powerboat, kayak, or canoe to get here. Travel distances vary by route chosen; it's a minimum of 41 miles from the Chokoloskee boat ramp, 44 miles from the Gulf Coast Visitor Center in Everglades City, or 49 miles from the Flamingo Visitor Center. The site is accessible at all tides. No piped water is available, so bring plenty. Bring a portable stove because campfires are prohibited. Pack out trash. A vault toilet, two picnic tables, and a dock are provided. Children are OK. No pets, please.

Reservations, fees: Get a backcountry permit in person up to 24 hours before the day of your intended campout at the Flamingo Visitor Center or Gulf Coast Visitor Center. They are not issued by phone or mail. Camping costs $10 for the permit, plus $2 nightly per person. Major credit cards are accepted. There's a three-night stay limit.

Directions: From the intersection of U.S. 41/Tamiami Trail and State Road 29 east of Naples, drive about five miles south on State Road 29 to the Everglades National Park Gulf Coast Visitor Center, on your right by Chokoloskee Bay. A ranger will explain your route to Camp Lonesome. To avoid getting lost, obtain nautical charts 11430 and 11432 at area bait stores, the ranger station, or downstairs from the ranger station at Everglades National Park Boat Tours. If you're approaching from Flamingo, buy charts 11432 and 11433 at the Flamingo Visitor Center.

Contact: Everglades National Park, 40001 State Road 9336, Homestead, FL 33034,

305/242-7700, www.nps.gov/ever. For back-country questions, contact the Flamingo Visitor Center, 239/695-2945; or the Gulf Coast Visitor Center, 239/695-3311.

35 HARNEY RIVER BOAT/CANOE SITE

Scenic rating: 6

Backcountry, on the Broad River, in Everglades National Park

See map, page 557

For one researcher of this book, the Harney River chickee will forever have a special significance. This is the place where—after coming down the Shark River Slough and unmarked routes through the mangroves, and spending two nights quite lost in the Everglades—Robert McClure and his partner saw the sign Harney River on the chickee. Finally, they knew where they were. Their destination was Flamingo. But if they'd gone just another three or four miles, they would have entered the Gulf of Mexico. It just goes to show how handy a global positioning system can be. The chickee is nothing special by Everglades standards, but it is out in wild country, where the fishing is great.

Lt. Colonel William Harney wasn't looking for a fishing hole when he was said to have discovered the river in 1840. Instead, he was coming back from leading 90 soldiers in 16 canoes on a successful December raid against Seminole leader Chief Chekika's camp to avenge the deaths of seven people. Bring extra rope to tie your free-standing tent to the chickee platform that serves as a tent site. No stakes or nails may be used.

Campsites, facilities: One tent site on an elevated wooden platform accommodates up to six people. You must use a powerboat, kayak, or canoe to travel 31 miles from the Flamingo Visitor Center, a minimum 42 miles from the Chokoloskee boat ramp, or at least 45 miles from the Gulf Coast Visitor Center in Ever-

glades City. No piped water is available, so bring plenty. Bring DEET to combat bugs and any supplies you'll need, including a portable stove (campfires are prohibited). A vault toilet and dock are provided. Trash must be packed out. Children are OK. No pets, please.

Reservations, fees: Get a backcountry permit in person up to 24 hours before the day of your intended campout at the Flamingo Visitor Center or Gulf Coast Visitor Center. They are not issued by phone or mail. Camping costs $10 for the permit, plus $2 nightly per person. Major credit cards are accepted. There's a one-night stay limit.

Directions: To avoid getting lost, obtain nautical charts 11432 and 11433 at the Flamingo Visitor Center or area bait stores. If you're approaching from Everglades City, buy charts 11430 and 11432 downstairs from the Gulf Coast Visitor Center.

Contact: Everglades National Park, 40001 State Road 9336, Homestead, FL 33034, 305/242-7700, www.nps.gov/ever. For back-country questions, contact the Flamingo Visitor Center, 239/695-2945; or the Gulf Coast Visitor Center, 239/695-3311.

36 CANEPATCH BOAT/CANOE SITES

Scenic rating: 8

Backcountry, east of Tarpon Bay, on Squawk Creek, in Everglades National Park

See map, page 557

It's called Canepatch because some misguided soul once tried to eke out a living here raising cane. Sugarcane, that is—the very crop grown across an 1,100-square-mile swath two counties northeast of here that environmentalists say is a threat to the Everglades. This little cane patch never really worked out, though. Today, there's no remnant of it except for an elevated clearing where you can pitch a tent. You may see wild bananas, limes, and papayas. Although remote, this former Seminole

Indian site gets used a fair bit by locals, largely because small motorboats can easily reach the dock leading to it. Expect to see birds and alligators in winter. In summer, mosquitoes make camping here impractical; even in winter, they can swarm mercilessly. Bring mosquito netting and mosquito coils.

These waters are popular among anglers looking for snook in winter; the snook head up into the backcountry to keep warm when cold fronts blow through Florida Bay. If you continue northeast one mile or two from this site, you'll come to Rookery Branch, where freshwater flows into brackish water. It's a spot favored by anglers looking for bass and snook. The formidable distance makes it impractical for weekend kayakers or canoeists. Consider making it a stop on a week-long vacation.

Worthy of note: Canepatch has a lot of poison ivy. Really a lot. Know what it looks like before you come here, or you could end up very uncomfortable. Also, ask a ranger whether any problem alligators frequent these waters now.

Caution to canoeists: Boaters sometimes speed through narrow Avocado Creek, so keep alert while paddling there. Once you reach the Canepatch site, you may want to continue north about one mile so you can look for a small batch of banana trees on the west side of Rookery Branch. They're delicious, sweet, plump little things. There are also banana trees at Canepatch, but they have usually been picked clean by previous campers.

Campsites, facilities: Four ground tent sites accommodate a total of 12 people. You must use a canoe, kayak, or powerboat to travel 29.5 miles from the Flamingo Visitor Center, a minimum of 51.5 miles from the Chokoloskee boat ramp, or at least 54.5 miles from the Gulf Coast Ranger Station in Everglades City. No piped water is available, so bring plenty. Bring a portable stove because campfires are prohibited, although you shouldn't be surprised to find remainders of illicit campfires here. A toilet, table, and dock are provided. Trash must be packed out. Children are OK. No pets, please.

Reservations, fees: Get a backcountry permit in person up to 24 hours before the day of your intended campout at the Flamingo Visitor Center or Gulf Coast Visitor Center. They are not issued by phone or mail. Camping costs $10 for the permit, plus $2 nightly per person. Major credit cards are accepted. There's a three-night stay limit.

Directions: From Miami, take Florida's Turnpike to its southern terminus at U.S. 1. In about one block, turn right at Palm Drive. Cross the railroad tracks and pass the Circle K. At the flashing traffic light at 192nd Avenue/State Road 9336, turn left by the Robert Is Here fruit stand. Proceed south about two miles. When State Road 9336 veers right, follow it to the right instead of going straight toward the alligator farm. The park entrance is four miles ahead. Follow the main park road 38 miles to Flamingo Marina on the left to launch. To avoid getting lost, obtain nautical charts 11432 and 11433 at the Flamingo Visitor Center or area bait stores. If you're approaching from Everglades City, buy charts 11430 and 11432 downstairs from the Gulf Coast Visitor Center.

Contact: Everglades National Park, 40001 State Road 9336, Homestead, FL 33034, 305/242-7700, www.nps.gov/ever. For backcountry questions, contact the Flamingo Visitor Center, 239/695-2945; or the Gulf Coast Visitor Center, 239/695-3311.

37 GRAVEYARD CREEK BOAT/CANOE SITES

Scenic rating: 7

Backcountry, on the Gulf of Mexico, in Everglades National Park

See map, page 557

Once upon a time, there was a graveyard somewhere along this creek, but it has long since been obliterated by hurricanes or covered over by the encroaching mangroves. As legend has it, feuding hunters who were supplying pelts for the popular raccoon coats of the 1920s had it out on this spot.

Spectacular sunsets and fine fishing are the payoff for staying at this ground site, where bugs sometimes swarm thickly—so much so, in fact, that some discouraged campers retreat into their tents at dusk (reminder: Go in winter). If you retreat at dusk, be sure to return outdoors an hour or two later to admire the terrific stars, advises a park ranger. Or you can listen to the nighttime sounds of fish splashing in these waters.

You'll sleep on a somewhat shady sand ridge that is subject to limited southwesterly winds. It's surrounded by red mangroves. Getting to the site, at the mouth of Graveyard Creek, can be a little tricky. You actually go to the east of the main mouth of the creek and circle counterclockwise to find the spot where you can land your boat or canoe. (Use your nautical chart.) What's more, the fast current that lures game fish to this area has also been known to sink boats that weren't moored properly at the dock. Check with rangers about tide conditions, because the flats around here can be left high and dry during a particularly low tide.

Campsites, facilities: Two ground tent sites accommodate a total of eight people. You must use a canoe, kayak, or powerboat to get here. Travel distances vary by route chosen; expect to travel 28 miles from the Flamingo Visitor Center, a minimum of 38.5 miles from the Chokoloskee boat ramp, or a minimum of 41.5 miles from the Gulf Coast Ranger Station in Everglades City. No piped water is available, so bring plenty. Bring a portable stove because campfires are prohibited. Pack out trash. A toilet and table are provided. Children are OK. No pets, please.

Reservations, fees: Get a backcountry permit in person up to 24 hours before the day of your intended campout at the Flamingo Visitor Center or Gulf Coast Visitor Center. They are not issued by phone or mail. Camping costs $10 for the permit, plus $2 nightly per person. Major credit cards are accepted. There's a three-night stay limit.

Directions: To avoid getting lost, obtain nauti-

cal chart 11432 at the Flamingo Visitor Center or area bait stores. If you're approaching from Everglades City, buy charts 11430, 11432, and 11433 downstairs from the Gulf Coast Visitor Center.

Contact: Everglades National Park, 40001 State Road 9336, Homestead, FL 33034, 305/242-7700, www.nps.gov/ever. For backcountry questions, contact the Flamingo Visitor Center, 239/695-2945; or the Gulf Coast Visitor Center, 239/695-3311.

38 SHARK RIVER BOAT/CANOE SITE

Scenic rating: 6

Backcountry, on the Shark River, in Everglades National Park

See map, page 557

The origin of the name Shark River is a little obscure—you're unlikely to see many sharks today. For that, you'd probably have to head out to nearby Ponce de Leon Bay or beyond to the Gulf of Mexico. You're much more likely to spot birds and perhaps a porpoise or two playfully swimming along the mangrove-flanked Shark River. Or maybe you'll see a raccoon trying to get into your water jug. Bring a free-standing tent; no stakes can be pounded into the chickee platform, which sits against a thick stand of mangroves (and, hence, can be buggy). This site is more than a full day's paddle from Flamingo, but it's easily reachable by motorboat. It's best used as a stopover on your way to Canepatch or points farther north on the Wilderness Waterway.

Campsites, facilities: One tent site on an elevated wooden platform accommodates up to six people. You must use a canoe, kayak, or boat to travel 21 miles from the Flamingo Visitor Center or, depending on your chosen route, a minimum of 45 miles from the Chokoloskee boat ramp or 48 miles from the Gulf Coast Ranger Station in Everglades City. No piped water is available, so bring plenty. Bring a portable stove because campfires are prohibited. Pack out trash. A vault toilet and dock are provided. Children are OK. No pets, please.

Reservations, fees: Get a backcountry permit in person up to 24 hours before the day of your intended campout at the Flamingo Visitor Center or Gulf Coast Visitor Center. They are not issued by phone or mail. Camping costs $10 for the permit, plus $2 nightly per person. Major credit cards are accepted. There's a one-night stay limit.

Directions: From Miami, take Florida's Turnpike to its southern terminus at U.S. 1. In about one block, turn right at Palm Drive. Cross the railroad tracks and pass the Circle K. At the flashing traffic light at 192nd Avenue/State Road 9336, turn left by the Robert Is Here fruit stand. Proceed south about two miles. When State Road 9336 veers right, follow it to the right instead of going straight toward the alligator farm. The park entrance is four miles ahead. Follow the main park road 38 miles to Flamingo Marina to launch your vessel. Ask a ranger for directions to Shark River. To avoid getting lost, obtain nautical chart 11433 at the Flamingo Visitor Center or area bait stores. If you're approaching from Everglades City, buy charts 11430, 11432, and 11433 downstairs from the Gulf Coast Visitor Center.

Contact: Everglades National Park, 40001 State Road 9336, Homestead, FL 33034, 305/242-7700, www.nps.gov/ever. For backcountry questions, contact the Flamingo Visitor Center, 239/695-2945; or the Gulf Coast Visitor Center, 239/695-3311.

39 OYSTER BAY BOAT/CANOE SITES

Scenic rating: 7

Backcountry, on Oyster Bay, in Everglades National Park

See map, page 557

If the weather is turning nasty, you should consider staying in this double chickee tucked behind an island. By the same token, you'll have to follow your nautical chart closely to find the place, which is located in a cove about one mile southwest of Wilderness Waterway marker No. 2. This stopover is not obvious from Oyster Bay and has been missed by more than one canoeing party. Two researchers of this book, Robert McClure and Sally Deneen, learned this the hard way one trip, when their canoe was half-swamped in Oyster Bay. Several boats have sunk near here because of the oyster bars—hence the campsite's name. The area is known for good fishing. Bottlenose dolphins sometimes make appearances. Also, look skyward as you paddle; you may see an osprey flying toward its sizable nest atop a snag. Lucky anglers just might pull in a redfish near one of the bay's oyster bars.

Campsites, facilities: Two tent sites on an elevated wooden platform accommodate up to six people each. A vault toilet separates the two sites. You must use a boat, canoe, or kayak to travel 18 miles from the Flamingo Visitor Center or, depending on your chosen route, a minimum of 48.5 miles from the Chokoloskee boat ramp, or a minimum of 51.5 miles from the Gulf Coast Ranger Station in Everglades City. No piped water is available, so bring plenty. Bring a portable stove because campfires are prohibited. Pack out trash. A dock is provided. Children are OK. No pets, please.

Reservations, fees: Get a backcountry permit in person up to 24 hours before the day of your intended campout at the Flamingo Visitor Center or Gulf Coast Visitor Center. They are not issued by phone or mail. Camping costs $10 for the permit, plus $2 nightly per person. Major credit cards are accepted. There's a one-night stay limit.

Directions: To avoid getting lost, obtain nautical chart 11433 at the Flamingo Visitor Center or area bait stores. If you're approaching from Everglades City, buy charts 11430, 11432, and 11433 downstairs from the Gulf Coast Visitor Center.

Contact: Everglades National Park, 40001 State Road 9336, Homestead, FL 33034,

305/242-7700, www.nps.gov/ever. For back-country questions, contact the Flamingo Visitor Center, 239/695-2945; or the Gulf Coast Visitor Center, 239/695-3311.

40 WATSON RIVER BOAT/CANOE SITES

Scenic rating: 7

Backcountry, on the Joe River, in Everglades National Park

See map, page 557

This is a little-used chickee, even though the fishing around here is excellent. Go figure. Despite the name, the site is not actually on the river. As you head north toward the mouth of the river, follow your nautical chart carefully. The chickee is on the northern tip of a big island behind some mangroves, which should help protect you from winds and rough seas. Look for manatees and alligators from your campsite. Only one party of campers per night is allowed, so you'll have privacy.

Campsites, facilities: One tent site on an elevated wooden platform accommodates up to six people. You must use a boat, canoe, or kayak to get here; expect to trek 16 miles from the Flamingo Visitor Center or, depending on your chosen route, a minimum of 56 miles from the Chokoloskee boat ramp or 59 miles from the Gulf Coast Ranger Station in Everglades City. No piped water is available, so bring plenty. Bring a portable stove because campfires are prohibited. Pack out trash. A toilet and dock are provided. Children are OK. No pets, please.

Reservations, fees: Get a backcountry permit in person up to 24 hours before the day of your intended campout at the Flamingo Visitor Center or Gulf Coast Visitor Center. They are not issued by phone or mail. Camping costs $10 for the permit, plus $2 nightly per person. Major credit cards are accepted. There's a one-night stay limit.

Directions: From Miami, take Florida's Turn-pike to its southern terminus at U.S. 1. In about one block, turn right at Palm Drive. Cross the railroad tracks and pass the Circle K. At the flashing traffic light at 192nd Avenue/State Road 9336, turn left by the Robert Is Here fruit stand. Proceed south about two miles. When State Road 9336 veers right, follow it to the right instead of going straight toward the alligator farm. The park entrance is four miles ahead. Follow the main park road 38 miles to Flamingo Marina to launch your vessel. Ask a ranger for directions to Watson River. To avoid getting lost, obtain nautical chart 11433 at the Flamingo Visitor Center or area bait stores. If you're approaching from Everglades City, buy charts 11430, 11432, and 11433 downstairs from the Gulf Coast Visitor Center.

Contact: Everglades National Park, 40001 State Road 9336, Homestead, FL 33034, 305/242-7700, www.nps.gov/ever. For back-country questions, contact the Flamingo Visitor Center, 239/695-294; or the Gulf Coast Visitor Center, 239/695-3311.

41 NORTH RIVER BOAT/CANOE SITE

Scenic rating: 8

Backcountry, on the North River, in Everglades National Park

See map, page 557

There is no marked canoe trail leading here, so you'll need to be extremely handy with a map and compass. The North River chickee is set amid a maze of islands off the north edge of Whitewater Bay. You'll likely head here from the Roberts River or Watson River campsites, both of which are three miles away. It's brackish water, and during the wintertime the snook fishing is quite good. Look for manatees in winter.

Campsites, facilities: One tent site on an elevated wooden platform accommodates up to six people. You must use a boat, canoe, or kayak to travel 17 miles from the Flamingo Visitor Center, a minimum of 59 miles from the Chokoloskee boat ramp or at least 62 miles from the Gulf Coast Ranger Station in Everglades City. No piped water is available, so bring plenty. Bring a portable stove because campfires are prohibited. Pack out trash. A toilet and dock are provided. Children are OK. No pets, please.

Reservations, fees: Get a backcountry permit in person up to 24 hours before the day of your intended campout at the Flamingo Visitor Center or Gulf Coast Visitor Center. They are not issued by phone or mail. Camping costs $10 for the permit, plus $2 nightly per person. Major credit cards are accepted. There's a one-night stay limit.

Directions: Ask a ranger for directions to North River. To avoid getting lost, obtain nautical chart 11433 at the Flamingo Visitor Center or area bait stores. If you're approaching from Everglades City, buy charts 11430, 11432, and 11433 downstairs from the Gulf Coast Visitor Center.

Contact: Everglades National Park, 40001 State Road 9336, Homestead, FL 33034, 305/242-7700, www.nps.gov/ever. For backcountry questions, contact the Flamingo Visitor Center, 239/695-2945; or the Gulf Coast Visitor Center, 239/695-3311.

42 ROBERTS RIVER BOAT/CANOE SITES

Scenic rating: 7

Backcountry, on the Roberts River, in Everglades National Park

See map, page 557

Like the North River and Lane Bay chickees, Roberts River is snuggled way up into the maze of mangrove islands that marks the transition from freshwater to saltwater Everglades northeast of Whitewater Bay. This is a decent choice if you expect a strong wind to be blowing, because it's tucked against the north side of the river in a crook, affording some protection. Be sure to keep a map and compass

handy, and ask a ranger for great directions; it can be easy to get lost on the way here.

Campsites, facilities: Two tent sites on an elevated wooden platform accommodate up to six people each; a vault toilet separates the two sites. You must use a boat, canoe, or kayak to travel 13.5 miles from the Flamingo Visitor Center. If you're arriving from the north, Roberts River is a minimum of 62 miles from the Chokoloskee boat ramp or 65 miles from the Gulf Coast Visitor Center in Everglades City. No piped water is available, so bring plenty. Bring a portable stove because campfires are prohibited. Pack out trash. A dock is provided. Children are OK. No pets, please.

Reservations, fees: Get a backcountry permit in person up to 24 hours before the day of your intended campout at the Flamingo Visitor Center or Gulf Coast Visitor Center. They are not issued by phone or mail. Camping costs $10 for the permit, plus $2 nightly per person. Major credit cards are accepted. There's a one-night stay limit.

Directions: From Miami, take Florida's Turnpike to its southern terminus at U.S. 1. In about one block, turn right at Palm Drive. Cross the railroad tracks and pass the Circle K. At the flashing traffic light at 192nd Avenue/State Road 9336, turn left by the Robert Is Here fruit stand. Proceed south about two miles. When State Road 9336 veers right, follow it to the right instead of going straight toward the alligator farm. The park entrance is four miles ahead. Follow the main park road 38 miles to Flamingo Marina to launch your vessel. Ask a ranger for directions to Roberts River. To avoid getting lost, obtain nautical chart 11433 at the Flamingo Visitor Center or area bait stores. If you're approaching from Everglades City, buy charts 11430, 11432, and 11433 downstairs from the Gulf Coast Visitor Center.

Contact: Everglades National Park, 40001 State Road 9336, Homestead, FL 33034, 305/242-7700, www.nps.gov/ever. For backcountry questions, contact the Flamingo Visitor Center, 239/695-2945; or the Gulf Coast Visitor Center, 239/695-3311.

43 LANE BAY BOAT/CANOE SITE

Scenic rating: 7

Backcountry, on Lane Bay, in Everglades
National Park

See map, page 557

It could be said for almost any of the campsites in the remote Everglades, but it goes doubly so for Lane Bay and, perhaps to a lesser degree, Hell's Bay (see listing in this chapter) and Pearl Bay (see listing in this chapter): Don't attempt this canoe route unless you are at least moderately skilled with a map and compass. The maze of passageways that leads to these campsites is truly mind-boggling, and even experienced canoeists know to watch every twist and turn on the nautical chart to avoid getting lost. A global positioning system, and knowledge of how to use it, can help make up for a lack of experience in the Everglades backcountry but will *not* replace basic orienteering skills.

Now that we've scared the bejesus out of you, there is an upside: You're likely to be alone on the water much of the day, and probably won't have any company at night. Unlike Pearl Bay and Hell's Bay, there is no marked canoe trail leading to Lane Bay. On the other hand, unlike her sisters to the south, Lane Bay features pretty straightforward access by motorboat. You'll feel sun and wind from the south—and itchiness all over, if you don't avoid the abundant poison ivy and poison-wood around the site, which abuts mangroves. Bring extra rope to tie a free-standing tent to the chickee hut that serves as a tent site. No stakes or nails may be used. Try to spot manatees in the wintertime. At night, stars fill an ebony sky.

Campsites, facilities: One tent site on an elevated wooden platform accommodates up to six people. You must use a boat, canoe, or kayak to travel about 13 miles from the Flamingo Visitor Center. If you're arriving from the north, Lane Bay is a minimum of 63 miles from the Chokoloskee boat ramp or 66 miles from the Gulf Coast Ranger Station in Everglades City, depending on which route you choose. No piped water is available, so bring plenty. Bring a portable stove because campfires are prohibited. Pack out trash. A toilet and dock are provided. Children are OK. No pets, please.

Reservations, fees: Get a backcountry permit in person up to 24 hours before the day of your intended campout at the Flamingo Visitor Center or Gulf Coast Visitor Center. They are not issued by phone or mail. Camping costs $10 for the permit, plus $2 nightly per person. Major credit cards are accepted. There's a one-night stay limit.

Directions: From Miami, take Florida's Turnpike to its southern terminus at U.S. 1. In about one block, turn right at Palm Drive. Cross the railroad tracks and pass the Circle K. At the flashing traffic light at 192nd Avenue/State Road 9336, turn left by the Robert Is Here fruit stand. Proceed south about two miles. When State Road 9336 veers right, follow it to the right instead of going straight toward the alligator farm. The park entrance is four miles ahead. Follow the main park road 38 miles to Flamingo Marina to launch your vessel. To avoid getting lost, obtain nautical chart 11433 at the Flamingo Visitor Center or area bait stores.

Contact: Everglades National Park, 40001 State Road 9336, Homestead, FL 33034, 305/242-7700, www.nps.gov/ever. For backcountry questions, contact the Flamingo Visitor Center, 239/695-2945; or the Gulf Coast Visitor Center, 239/695-3311.

44 HELL'S BAY BOAT/CANOE SITES

Scenic rating: 8

Backcountry, on Hell's Bay, in Everglades
National Park

See map, page 557

Wickedly meandering Hell's Bay is a canoeist's delight, or bane, if you don't enjoy bumping periodically into the branches and thick roots of mangrove trees. Like Lane Bay (see listing in this chapter), Hell's Bay and Pearl Bay (see listing in this chapter) should be avoided by those who aren't skilled with a map and compass. The passageways that lead to these sites are a veritable maze. Even experienced canoeists know to watch every twist and turn on the nautical chart to avoid getting lost. A global positioning system, and knowledge of how to use it, can help make up for a lack of experience in the Everglades backcountry but should never be used to replace basic orienteering skills. Still, the journey is worth the effort, because you're likely to be alone—or nearly so—on the water all day and, if you're lucky, won't have any company at night. Anglers make day trips to try for snook and bass, and at times pull out nuisance Mayan cichlids one after another. The trail got its name from a ranger who happened upon a fine fishing hole back here and found it was "hell to get into and hell to get out of" Whitewater Bay, so he built the Hell's Bay Canoe Trail. Bring extra rope to tie a free-standing tent to the chickee hut that serves as a tent site. No stakes or nails may be used.

A saving grace for Hell's Bay and Pearl Bay: Both are on a canoe trail marked by white, numbered PVC pipes sticking up above the water; however, the meandering trail makes sharp turns, and sometimes you'll find that a marker has disappeared for one reason or another.

To use the canoe trail, you'll need to find a way to strap a canoe to the top of your vehicle and head north from Flamingo Marina along the main park road about eight miles to the canoe trailhead. If you're renting a canoe, try to beat the rush by arriving early on winter mornings. I do not recommend trying to reach these sites by motorboat. You can't use a boat on the Hell's Bay Canoe Trail, so you'd have to circle in from Whitewater Bay to get here. Find another spot instead.

Campsites, facilities: Two tent sites on an elevated wooden platform accommodate up to six people each. You must canoe or kayak six miles from the Hell's Bay Canoe Trailhead or take a boat up to 20 feet long via the East River and Whitewater Bay. From Everglades City, Hell's Bay is a minimum of 69.5 miles away. From the Chokoloskee boat ramp, it's at least 66.5 miles. No piped water is available, so bring plenty. Bring a portable stove because campfires are prohibited. Pack out trash. A toilet and dock are provided. Children are OK. No pets, please.

Reservations, fees: Get a backcountry permit in person up to 24 hours before the day of your intended campout at the Flamingo Visitor Center or Gulf Coast Visitor Center. They are not issued by phone or mail. Camping costs $10 for the permit, plus $2 nightly per person. Major credit cards are accepted. There's a one-night stay limit.

Directions: From Miami, take Florida's Turnpike to its southern terminus at U.S. 1. In about one block, turn right at Palm Drive. Cross the railroad tracks and pass the Circle K. At the flashing traffic light at 192nd Avenue/State Road 9336, turn left by the Robert Is Here fruit stand. Proceed south about two miles. When State Road 9336 veers right, follow it to the right instead of going straight toward the alligator farm. The park entrance is four miles ahead. Follow the main park road for 29 miles to the Hell's Bay Canoe Trailhead on the right to launch. To avoid getting lost, obtain nautical chart 11433 at the Flamingo Visitor Center or area bait stores.

Contact: Everglades National Park, 40001 State Road 9336, Homestead, FL 33034, 305/242-7700, www.nps.gov/ever. For backcountry questions, contact the Flamingo Visitor Center, 239/695-2945; or the Gulf Coast Visitor Center, 239/695-3311.

45 PEARL BAY BOAT/CANOE SITES

Scenic rating: 8

Backcountry, on Pearl Bay, in Everglades National Park

See map, page 557

Pearl Bay is a worthwhile destination, a place to sit back and admire the scenery of the mangrove-bordered bay after a morning spent paddling through a meandering route to get here. The paddle is just right for some tastes—not long enough to be overly taxing, yet curvy enough to present some challenge. Don't be too alarmed if you look across the calm bay from your chickee at dusk and see the red, glowing eyes of an alligator. Gators often get a bum rap; more people around the country die from bee stings and encounters with pigs than from alligators. The reptiles rarely attack people. That said, campers have seen an overly friendly alligator here—be sure not to drop remains of fish-cleaning or other odiferous goodies in the water.

The sharply curving canoe route to Pearl Bay is the same as for Hell's Bay; just leave the trail at marker 165. During your paddle, which will take about three hours from the trailhead, look skyward for the snag with the osprey nest along the way. No motorized craft are allowed on this canoe trail, which adds to the wilderness experience. For more on Hell's Bay, see the listing in this chapter.

Campsites, facilities: Two tent sites on an elevated wooden platform accommodate up to six people each. You must canoe or kayak four miles from the Hell's Bay Canoe Trailhead or take a boat up to 20 feet long via the East River and Whitewater Bay. From Everglades City, Pearl Bay is a minimum of 71.5 miles away. From the Chokoloskee boat ramp, it's a minimum of 68.5 miles, depending on your chosen route. No piped water is available, so bring plenty. Bring a portable stove because campfires are prohibited. Pack out trash. Kids are welcome. No pets, please. Management

says the accessible chemical toilet, handrails, and canoe dock make this the park's sole wheelchair-accessible backcountry site.

Reservations, fees: Get a backcountry permit in person up to 24 hours before the day of your intended campout at the Flamingo Visitor Center or Gulf Coast Visitor Center. They are not issued by phone or mail. Camping costs $10 for the permit, plus $2 nightly per person. Major credit cards are accepted. There's a one-night stay limit.

Directions: From Miami, take Florida's Turnpike to its southern terminus at U.S. 1. In about one block, turn right at Palm Drive. Cross the railroad tracks and pass the Circle K. At the flashing traffic light at 192nd Avenue/State Road 9336, turn left by the Robert Is Here fruit stand. Proceed south about two miles. When State Road 9336 veers right, follow it to the right instead of going straight toward the alligator farm. The park entrance is four miles ahead. Follow the main park road 29 miles to the Hell's Bay Canoe Trailhead on the right to launch. To avoid getting lost, obtain nautical chart 11433 at the Flamingo Visitor Center or area bait stores.

Contact: Everglades National Park, 40001 State Road 9336, Homestead, FL 33034, 305/242-7700, www.nps.gov/ever. For backcountry questions, contact the Flamingo Visitor Center, 239/695-2945; or the Gulf Coast Visitor Center, 239/695-3311.

46 LARD CAN BOAT/CANOE SITES

Scenic rating: 4

Backcountry, along the Hell's Bay Canoe Trail, in Everglades National Park

See map, page 557

What sets Lard Can apart from Hell's Bay is that it is somewhat easier to reach—the first stop on the wickedly meandering canoe trail (just depart the trail at marker 156); however, it is a ground site set amid towering mangroves and buttonwoods, so it's easily missed by canoeists not paying close attention to their maps. Also, because it's a low-lying ground site, the ground is often damp, and the bugs are likely to be a lot worse than at a chickee, even in winter. I'd steer clear of the site, except on the coldest days. This is a fitting place to stop for a bathroom break, but try to avoid it as a nighttime respite. It's also not nearly as picturesque as Hell's Bay (three miles away) or Pearl Bay (one mile). For more on Hell's Bay, see the listing in this chapter.

Campsites, facilities: Four ground tent sites accommodate a total of 10 people. You must canoe or kayak three miles from the Hell's Bay Canoe Trailhead or take a boat up to 20 feet long via the East River and Whitewater Bay. From Everglades City, Lard Can is a minimum of 72.5 miles. From the Chokoloskee boat ramp, it's at least 69.5 miles. No piped water is available, so bring plenty. Bring a portable stove because campfires are prohibited. Pack out trash. A toilet is provided. Children are OK. No pets, please.

Reservations, fees: Get a backcountry permit in person up to 24 hours before the day of your intended campout at the Flamingo Visitor Center or Gulf Coast Visitor Center. They are not issued by phone or mail. Camping costs $10 for the permit, plus $2 nightly per person. Major credit cards are accepted. There's a two-night stay limit.

Directions: From Miami, take Florida's Turnpike to its southern terminus at U.S. 1. In about one block, turn right at Palm Drive. Cross the railroad tracks and pass the Circle K. At the flashing traffic light at 192nd Avenue/State Road 9336, turn left by the Robert Is Here fruit stand. Proceed south about two miles. When State Road 9336 veers right, follow it to the right instead of going straight toward the alligator farm. The park entrance is four miles ahead. Follow the main park road 29 miles to the Hell's Bay Canoe Trailhead on the right to launch. To avoid getting lost, obtain nautical chart 11433 at the Flamingo Visitor Center or area bait stores. If you're approaching from Everglades City, buy charts

11430, 11432, and 11433 downstairs from the Gulf Coast Visitor Center.

Contact: Everglades National Park, 40001 State Road 9336, Homestead, FL 33034, 305/242-7700, www.nps.gov/ever. For backcountry questions, contact the Flamingo Visitor Center, 239/695-2945; or the Gulf Coast Visitor Center, 239/695-3311.

47 JOE RIVER BOAT/CANOE SITES

Scenic rating: 7

Backcountry, on the Joe River, in Everglades National Park

See map, page 557

One of this book's researchers, Robert McClure, spent many a happy childhood afternoon fishing for redfish and snapper around here. Like nearby Oyster Bay and South Joe River, this campsite, with a pair of chickee platforms, is one of the most easily accessible from Flamingo by canoe. As such, it's heavily used. Joe River is good for winter canoeists: It's calm back here, compared to the rough waters and gusty winds out on Whitewater Bay. The chickee is tucked back into a crook along the north bank of the Joe River just east of where it empties into Mud Bay. Because of its out-of-the-wind location, it's fairly buggy for a chickee site.

Campsites, facilities: Two tent sites on an elevated wooden platform accommodate up to six people each. You must use a boat, canoe, or kayak to travel a minimum of 17 miles from the Flamingo Visitor Center. If you're arriving from the north, it's a minimum of 52.5 miles from the Chokoloskee boat ramp or at least 55.5 miles from the Gulf Coast Ranger Station in Everglades City, depending on your chosen route. No piped water is available, so bring plenty. Bring a portable stove because campfires are prohibited. Pack out trash. A toilet and dock are provided. Children are OK. No pets, please.

Reservations, fees: Get a backcountry permit in person up to 24 hours before the day of your intended campout at the Flamingo Visitor Center or Gulf Coast Visitor Center. They are not issued by phone or mail. Camping costs $10 for the permit, plus $2 nightly per person. Major credit cards are accepted. There's a one-night stay limit.

Directions: From Miami, take Florida's Turnpike to its southern terminus at U.S. 1. In about one block, turn right at Palm Drive. Cross the railroad tracks and pass the Circle K. At the flashing traffic light at 192nd Avenue/State Road 9336, turn left by the Robert Is Here fruit stand. Proceed south about two miles. When State Road 9336 veers right, follow it to the right instead of going straight toward the alligator farm. The park entrance is four miles ahead. Follow the main park road 38 miles to Flamingo Marina to launch your vessel. Ask a ranger for directions to Joe River. To avoid getting lost, obtain nautical chart 11433 at the Flamingo Visitor Center or area bait stores. If you're approaching from Everglades City, buy charts 11430, 11432, and 11433 downstairs from the Gulf Coast Visitor Center.

Contact: Everglades National Park, 40001 State Road 9336, Homestead, FL 33034, 305/242-7700, www.nps.gov/ever. For backcountry questions, contact the Flamingo Visitor Center, 239/695-2945; or the Gulf Coast Visitor Center, 239/695-3311.

48 SOUTH JOE RIVER BOAT/CANOE SITES

Scenic rating: 7

Backcountry, on the Joe River, in Everglades National Park

See map, page 557

This is the closest backcountry site to Flamingo, and as such, it sees heavy use from canoeists who want to get somewhere in one—albeit long—day and don't want to travel the whole 99-mile-long Wilderness Waterway spanning the watery innards of the national park. Some anglers motor up for snapper, snook, and other game fish. The raised wooden chickee platforms are set in a small bay away from Whitewater Bay, so they afford some protection against bad weather. Bring a free-standing tent; no stakes may be pounded into the wooden platform. Look for manatees in nearby Hidden Lake.

Campsites, facilities: Two tent sites on an elevated wooden platform accommodate up to six people each. You must use a boat, canoe, or kayak to travel about 11.5 miles from the Flamingo Visitor Center. From Everglades City, South Joe River is a minimum of 62 miles, depending on your chosen route. From Chokoloskee, it's at least 59 miles. No piped water is provided, so bring plenty. Bring a portable stove because campfires are prohibited. Pack out trash. A toilet and dock are available. Children are OK. No pets, please.

Reservations, fees: Get a backcountry permit in person up to 24 hours before the day of your intended campout at the Flamingo Visitor Center or Gulf Coast Visitor Center. They are not issued by phone or mail. Camping costs $10 for the permit, plus $2 nightly per person. Major credit cards are accepted. There's a one-night stay limit.

Directions: From Miami, take Florida's Turnpike to its southern terminus at U.S. 1. In about one block, turn right at Palm Drive. Cross the railroad tracks and pass the Circle K. At the flashing traffic light at 192nd Avenue/State Road 9336, turn left by the Robert Is Here fruit stand. Proceed south about two miles. When State Road 9336 veers right, follow it to the right instead of going straight toward the alligator farm. The park entrance is four miles ahead. Follow the main park road 38 miles to Flamingo Marina to launch your vessel. Ask a ranger for directions to South Joe River. To avoid getting lost, obtain nautical chart 11433 at the Flamingo Visitor Center or area bait stores. If you're approaching from Everglades City, buy charts 11430, 11432, and 11433 downstairs from the Gulf Coast Visitor Center.

Contact: Everglades National Park, 40001 State Road 9336, Homestead, FL 33034, 305/242-7700, www.nps.gov/ever. For backcountry questions, contact the Flamingo Visitor Center, 239/695-2945; or the Gulf Coast Visitor Center, 239/695-3311.

49 EAST CLUBHOUSE BEACH HIKE-IN OR BOAT/CANOE SITES

Scenic rating: 8

Backcountry, on Florida Bay, in Everglades National Park

See map, page 557

You're likely to be alone in this vast wilderness, giving you the feeling that you could walk around nude if you wanted (if not for the mosquitoes that come out at dusk and hang around until dawn). If you paddle out for a little fishing, don't be surprised if a spider has spun a web on your cooler by the time you return. The threat of raccoons getting into your cooler is a reminder that this is wilderness. Stars sparkle in a black nighttime sky untouched by city lights. The sand/marl beach camping area is fairly level and backed by mangroves and buttonwoods. East Clubhouse Beach and Clubhouse Beach to the west are the only places on Florida Bay where backpackers can hike for an overnight stay. Forget hiking in wet, muddy, skeeter-happy summer, when six inches of standing water aren't uncommon. Indeed, the sea can rise high enough in winter that it can be difficult to figure out where to stake a single tent to keep it dry, let alone four tents, which this site supposedly accommodates.

Campsites, facilities: Four beach tent sites theoretically accommodate a total of 24 people—but, for practical purposes, this site is best left to one tent party, due to the rising seas that shrink the beach. You must hike or use a boat, canoe, or kayak to travel about four miles from the Flamingo Visitor Center. No piped water is available on site, so bring plenty of your own. There is no dock, nor a toilet; bury human waste six inches deep. Dead and downed wood may be used for campfires below the high-tide line. Pack out trash. Children are allowed. No pets, please.

Reservations, fees: Get a backcountry permit in person up to 24 hours before the day of your intended campout at the Flamingo Visitor Center or Gulf Coast Visitor Center. They are not issued by phone or mail. Camping costs $10 for the permit, plus $2 nightly per person. Major credit cards are accepted. There's a three-night stay limit.

Directions: From Miami, take Florida's Turnpike to its southern terminus at U.S. 1. In about one block, turn right at Palm Drive. Cross the railroad tracks and pass the Circle K. At the flashing traffic light at 192nd Avenue/State Road 9336, turn left by the Robert Is Here fruit stand. Proceed south about two miles. When State Road 9336 veers right, follow it to the right instead of going straight toward the alligator farm. The park entrance is four miles ahead. Follow the main park road 38 miles to Flamingo Marina to launch your vessel. Ask a ranger for directions to East Clubhouse Beach. To avoid getting lost, obtain nautical chart 11433 at the Flamingo Visitor Center or area bait stores.

Contact: Everglades National Park, 40001 State Road 9336, Homestead, FL 33034, 305/242-7700, www.nps.gov/ever. For backcountry questions, contact the Flamingo Visitor Center, 239/695-2945; or the Gulf Coast Visitor Center, 239/695-3311.

50 CLUBHOUSE BEACH HIKE-IN OR BOAT/CANOE SITES

Scenic rating: 8

Backcountry, on Florida Bay, in Everglades National Park

See map, page 557

Clubhouse Beach and East Clubhouse Beach are the only places on Florida Bay where backpackers can hike and camp. The seven-mile Coastal Prairie Trail starts near Flamingo Marina and can be a miserable experience in summer, when six inches of water may be standing in the muddy, buggy trail (try winter instead). Canoeists and kayakers love this place, because it's quite close to Flamingo and easy to reach. You'll sleep on a sand/marl beach backed by mangroves and buttonwoods. Skeeters and sand fleas can be trouble if the wind is coming from the north. When the water is quite low, exposed mudflats may make the place inaccessible to boaters. Check with a ranger on tide and wind conditions beforehand to time your trip so you won't face a tough boat trip or paddle in either direction. It's not as breathtaking as the campsites at nearby Cape Sable, but you'll be in a coastal prairie area, so look for birds.

Campsites, facilities: Four beach tent sites technically accommodate a total of 24 people, but rising seas can make it difficult to figure out where to pitch a tent where it's certain to stay dry during high tide (ask a ranger for pointers). You must hike or use a boat, canoe, or kayak to travel about seven miles from the Flamingo Visitor Center. No piped water is available, so bring plenty. There is no dock, nor toilet; bury human waste six inches deep. Dead and downed wood may be used for campfires below the high-tide line. Pack out trash. Children are OK. No pets, please.

Reservations, fees: Get a backcountry permit in person up to 24 hours before the day of your intended campout at the Flamingo Visitor Center or Gulf Coast Visitor Center. They are not issued by phone or mail. Camping costs $10 for the permit, plus $2 nightly per person. Major credit cards are accepted. There's a three-night stay limit.

Directions: From Miami, take Florida's Turnpike to its southern terminus at U.S. 1. In about one block, turn right at Palm Drive. Cross the railroad tracks and pass the Circle K. At the flashing traffic light at 192nd Avenue/State Road 9336, turn left by the Robert Is Here fruit stand. Proceed south about two miles. When State Road 9336 veers right, follow it to the right instead of going straight toward the alligator farm. The park entrance is four miles ahead. Follow the main park road 38 miles to Flamingo Marina to launch your vessel. Ask a ranger for directions to Clubhouse Beach. To avoid getting lost, obtain nautical chart 11433 at the Flamingo Visitor Center or area bait stores.

Contact: Everglades National Park, 40001 State Road 9336, Homestead, FL 33034, 305/242-7700, www.nps.gov/ever. For backcountry questions, contact the Flamingo Visitor Center, 239/695-2945; or the Gulf Coast Visitor Center, 239/695-3311.

51 EAST CAPE SABLE BOAT/CANOE SITES

Scenic rating: 8

Backcountry, in Everglades National Park

See map, page 557

The Cape Sable sites—East Cape Sable, Middle Cape Sable (see listing in this chapter), and Northwest Cape Sable (see listing in this chapter)—are some of the most beautiful in the park. Set on a high, shelly, sunny, breezy beach some six feet above Florida Bay, the sites mark the place where the Florida Peninsula turns to head north. Fires are allowed below the high-tide line; use only driftwood or limbs that are already dead and down. Try to reach your campsite by midafternoon, so you can sit and contemplate the exceptional sunset. Look for pink flamingos—the real thing, not the plastic lawn ornament.

Cape Sable can be a very long paddle from Flamingo when conditions are not right, so check with rangers ahead of time and keep a close eye on the weather. The short, steep, breaking waves create downright hazardous conditions for canoeists who try to go against the tide and winds. The cape tends to be dominated by motorboaters. In all, the three Cape Sable camping areas can hold a total of 156 people, making them by far the largest backcountry sites in the park. Rangers seem to discourage it, but you can swim here. One of this book's researchers, Robert, was sure to take a dip every time he visited as a boy.

Even in winter, be prepared for an onslaught of mosquitoes. Repellent and netting are a must.

Campsites, facilities: Fifteen beach tent sites accommodate a total of 60 people. You must use a boat, canoe, or kayak to travel about 10 miles from the Flamingo Visitor Center. No piped water is available, so bring plenty. There is no dock, nor toilet; bury human waste six inches deep. Dead and downed wood may be used for campfires below the high-tide line. Pack out trash. Children are permitted. No pets, please.

Reservations, fees: Get a backcountry permit in person up to 24 hours before the day of your intended campout at the Flamingo Visitor Center or Gulf Coast Visitor Center. They are not issued by phone or mail. Camping costs $10 for the permit, plus $2 nightly per person. Major credit cards are accepted. There's a seven-night stay limit.

Directions: From Miami, take Florida's Turnpike to its southern terminus at U.S. 1. In about one block, turn right at Palm Drive. Cross the railroad tracks and pass the Circle K. At the flashing traffic light at 192nd Avenue/State Road 9336, turn left by the Robert Is Here fruit stand. Proceed south about two miles. When State Road 9336 veers right, follow it to the right instead of going straight toward the alligator farm. The park entrance is four miles ahead. Follow the main park road 38 miles to Flamingo Marina to launch your vessel. Ask a ranger for directions to East Cape Sable. The campground can be approached by way of Florida Bay or, when conditions are right, inland through the Bear Lake Canoe Trail. To avoid getting lost, obtain nautical chart 11433 at the Flamingo Visitor Center or area bait stores. If you're approaching from Everglades City, buy charts 11430, 11432, and

11433 downstairs from the Gulf Coast Visitor Center.

Contact: Everglades National Park, 40001 State Road 9336, Homestead, FL 33034, 305/242-7700, www.nps.gov/ever. For backcountry questions, contact the Flamingo Visitor Center, 239/695-2945; or the Gulf Coast Visitor Center, 239/695-3311.

52 MIDDLE CAPE SABLE BOAT/CANOE SITES

Scenic rating: 9

Backcountry, on the Gulf of Mexico, in Everglades National Park

See map, page 557

Sunsets are pretty at this breezy, sunwashed, shelly, sandy beach, but don't expect to have the place to yourself. Nearly five dozen other campers might show up at the popular spot. Tip: Canoeists should hug the protective coastline and try to paddle with the winds and tides between Cape Sable and Flamingo, particularly in windy winter—something easier said than done. If you're lucky, you'll get the winds in your favor both ways as they shift.

Even in winter, be prepared for an onslaught of mosquitoes. Repellent and netting are a must. See the listing for East Cape Sable in this chapter.

Campsites, facilities: Fifteen beach tent sites accommodate a total of 60 people. You must use a boat, canoe, or kayak to travel about 13.5 miles from the Flamingo Visitor Center. No piped water is available, so bring plenty. There is no dock, nor toilet; bury human waste six inches deep. Dead and downed wood may be used for campfires below the high-tide line. Pack out trash. Children are OK. No pets, please.

Reservations, fees: Get a backcountry permit in person up to 24 hours before the day of your intended campout at the Flamingo Visitor Center or Gulf Coast Visitor Center. They are not issued by phone or mail.

Camping costs $10 for the permit, plus $2 nightly per person. Major credit cards are accepted. There's a seven-night stay limit.

Directions: From Flamingo, ask a ranger for directions to Middle Cape Sable. To avoid getting lost, obtain nautical chart 11433 at the Flamingo Visitor Center or from area bait stores. If you're approaching from Everglades City, buy charts 11430, 11432, and 11433 downstairs from the Gulf Coast Visitor Center.

Contact: Everglades National Park, 40001 State Road 9336, Homestead, FL 33034, 305/242-7700, www.nps.gov/ever. For backcountry questions, contact the Flamingo Visitor Center, 239/695-2945; or the Gulf Coast Visitor Center, 239/695-3311.

53 NORTHWEST CAPE SABLE BOAT/CANOE SITES

Scenic rating: 9

Backcountry, on the Gulf of Mexico, in Everglades National Park

See map, page 557

The sun pounds this shelly beach, where a breeze blows from all sides and sunsets are characteristically pretty. The other Cape Sable camping areas are more popular, but this one has the advantage of fewer potential neighbors—eight other parties, tops. Anchor your boat from the bow if the weather is dicey, and pull canoes way up onto the beach, lest they float out to sea. Be prepared for skeeters, sand fleas, and marauding raccoons. See the listing for East Cape Sable in this chapter.

Campsites, facilities: Nine beach tent sites accommodate a total of 36 people. You must use a boat, canoe, or kayak to travel about 18.5 miles from the Flamingo Visitor Center. No piped water is available, so bring plenty. There is no dock, nor toilet; bury human waste six inches deep. Dead and downed wood may be used for campfires below the high-tide line.

Trash must be packed out. Children are permitted. No pets, please.

Reservations, fees: Get a backcountry permit in person up to 24 hours before the day of your intended campout at the Flamingo Visitor Center or Gulf Coast Visitor Center. They are not issued by phone or mail. Camping costs $10 for the permit, plus $2 nightly per person. Major credit cards are accepted. There's a seven-night stay limit.

Directions: From Miami, take Florida's Turnpike to its southern terminus at U.S. 1. In about one block, turn right at Palm Drive. Cross the railroad tracks and pass the Circle K. At the flashing traffic light at 192nd Avenue/State Road 9336, turn left by the Robert Is Here fruit stand. Proceed south about two miles. When State Road 9336 veers right, follow it to the right instead of going straight toward the alligator farm. The park entrance is four miles ahead. Follow the main park road for 38 miles to Flamingo Marina to launch your vessel. Ask a ranger for directions to Northwest Cape Sable. To avoid getting lost, obtain nautical chart 11433 at the Flamingo Visitor Center or from area bait stores. If you're approaching from Everglades City, buy charts 11430, 11432, and 11433 downstairs from the Gulf Coast Visitor Center.

Contact: Everglades National Park, 40001 State Road 9336, Homestead, FL 33034, 305/242-7700, www.nps.gov/ever. For backcountry questions, contact the Flamingo Visitor Center, 239/695-2945; or the Gulf Coast Visitor Center, 239/695-3311.

54 ALLIGATOR CREEK CANOE SITES

Scenic rating: 8

Backcountry, on Alligator Creek, in Everglades National Park

See map, page 557

A backcountry campground set amid huge mangroves awaits paddlers at the end of the meandering West Lake Canoe Trail, which is accessible off the main park road not far north of Flamingo. Despite the easy access, it's relatively remote. Your reward may be seeing Everglades wading birds or crocodiles— North America's only crocs, which are not dangerous.

You'll sleep on slightly higher ground along a canal section of Alligator Creek, but the surrounding, somewhat shady buttonwood forest blocks views (and wind). The place was used as a wilderness camping area long ago, which explains the abandoned, overgrown foot trail and many visible former campsites in the area. Only small boats with motors under 5.5 horsepower can make it to today's official camping area, which is at the junction of Garfield Bite and Alligator Creek. The vegetation in Long Lake at low tide can pose a problem even for small motors. Bring mosquito repellent; skeeters make extreme pests of themselves most times of the year.

Campsites, facilities: Three ground tent sites accommodate a total of eight people. You must canoe or kayak 8.5 miles from the West Lake Canoe Trailhead. No piped water is available, so bring plenty. There is no dock, nor toilet. Dead and downed wood may be used for campfires below the high-tide line. Pack out trash. Children are allowed. No pets, please.

Reservations, fees: Get a backcountry permit in person up to 24 hours before the day of your intended campout at the Flamingo Visitor Center or Gulf Coast Visitor Center. They are not issued by phone or mail. Camping costs $10 for the permit, plus $2 nightly per person. Major credit cards are accepted. There's a two-night stay limit.

Directions: From Miami, take Florida's Turnpike to its southern terminus at U.S. 1. In about one block, turn right at Palm Drive. Cross the railroad tracks and pass the Circle K. At the flashing traffic light at 192nd Avenue/State Road 9336, turn left by the Robert Is Here fruit stand. Proceed south about two miles. When State Road 9336 veers right, follow it to the right instead of going straight

toward the alligator farm. The park entrance is four miles ahead. The West Lake Canoe Trailhead is 31 miles ahead on the left.

Contact: Everglades National Park, 40001 State Road 9336, Homestead, FL 33034, 305/242-7700, www.nps.gov/ever. For backcountry questions, contact the Flamingo Visitor Center, 239/695-2945; or the Gulf Coast Visitor Center, 239/695-3311.

55 LITTLE RABBIT KEY BOAT/CANOE SITES

Scenic rating: 7

Backcountry, on Florida Bay, in Everglades National Park

See map, page 557

Sorry, canoe fans. Realistically, this spot is best reserved for motorboaters and the hardiest of kayakers, because you have to cover so much open water. The beach campsite is situated on the west side, where the sunsets are pretty, but getting there can be a little tricky. Approach the island from the east, keeping your eye out for PVC pipes with orange flags that mark a channel. As you approach the island, watch to see where a moat, perhaps 8–10 feet deep, has been trenched around the north side of the island. Bear right to follow it around to the small dock on the west side.

Campsites, facilities: Four ground tent sites accommodate a total of 12 people. You must use a boat, canoe, or kayak to travel about 11 miles from Flamingo. No piped water is available, so bring plenty. Bring a portable stove because campfires are prohibited. A chemical toilet, picnic table, and dock are provided. Trash must be packed out. Children are OK. No pets, please.

Reservations, fees: Get a backcountry permit in person up to 24 hours before the day of your intended campout at the Flamingo Visitor Center. Or, if you're leaving from the Keys, call the Flamingo Visitor Center for a permit—this is one of the few places for which permits are commonly issued by phone. If you intend to call for a permit, prepare to be insistent, because some park employees are unaware that phone permits are available for remote Florida Bay sites, including this particularly far-off one. Camping costs $10 for the permit, plus $2 nightly per person. Major credit cards are accepted. There's a two-night stay limit.

Directions: From Miami, take Florida's Turnpike to its southern terminus at U.S. 1. In about one block, turn right at Palm Drive. Cross the railroad tracks and pass the Circle K. At the flashing traffic light at 192nd Avenue/State Road 9336, turn left by the Robert Is Here fruit stand. Proceed south about two miles. When State Road 9336 veers right, follow it to the right instead of going straight toward the alligator farm. The park entrance is four miles ahead. Follow the main park road about 38 miles to Flamingo Marina to launch. From there, follow nautical chart 11451. You can also launch from Lower Matecumbe Key in the Florida Keys.

Contact: Everglades National Park, 40001 State Road 9336, Homestead, FL 33034, 305/242-7700, www.nps.gov/ever. For backcountry questions, contact the Flamingo Visitor Center, 239/695-2945.

56 NORTH NEST KEY BOAT/CANOE SITES

Scenic rating: 7

Backcountry, on eastern Florida Bay, in Everglades National Park

See map, page 557

This island, with white beaches surrounded by blue water in northeastern Florida Bay, often has a sort of Caribbean feel—at least when the water stays clear. It's one of only three keys in the Florida Bay section of Everglades National Park where visitors are allowed to land, so it gets a fair amount of day use by motorboaters. They generally come to the crescent-shaped beach on the northwest part of the island. If you're in a canoe (actually, kayaks make more sense, because you'll be covering a lot of open water), opt instead for the southwest side, where there is no dock, and you'll have at least a little more privacy. There is room for seven groups of people, and the place is quite popular, especially on weekends, so count on company.

A note on navigation: Even with a nautical chart, some powerboaters have been known to navigate their way from Blackwater Sound into Florida Bay (through a passage known as "The Boggies"), then cut directly southwest for North Nest Key. Some of these same boaters also have been known to run aground or worse, so avoid the temptation. Look due west, and you'll see Duck Key. Head for that until your chart shows you've cleared the shallows off your port before you turn to head for North Nest Key. Canoeists and kayakers, of course, won't have that problem.

Campsites, facilities: Seven beach tent sites accommodate a total of 25 people. You must use a boat, canoe, or kayak to travel about eight miles from launch sites in the Upper Florida Keys. No piped water is available, so bring plenty. Bring a portable stove because campfires are prohibited. A toilet and dock are provided. Pack out trash. Children are OK. No pets, please.

Reservations, fees: Get a backcountry permit in person up to 24 hours before the day of your intended campout at the Flamingo Visitor Center or Gulf Coast Visitor Center. Or, if you're leaving from the Keys (which makes sense if you're coming here), call the Flamingo Visitor Center for a permit—this is one of the few places for which permits are commonly issued by phone. If you intend to call for a permit, prepare to be insistent, because some park employees are unaware that phone permits are available for remote Florida Bay sites, including this particularly far-off one. Camping costs $10 for the permit, plus $2 nightly per person. Major credit cards are accepted. There's a seven-night stay limit.

Directions: From Miami, take Florida's Turnpike to its southern terminus at U.S. 1 in Florida City. Check there to make sure you have gas, because there will be none until you reach Key Largo, some 20 miles farther south. Once you get to Key Largo, you need to launch your boat on the Florida Bay side. There are several places from which to launch. Probably the most convenient is Florida Bay Outfitters (305/451-3018) at mile marker 104. You can obtain nautical chart 11451 and other supplies there, and they'll probably let you launch and park for free. Also ask Everglades National Park rangers for recommended launch sites in the Upper Florida Keys.

Contact: Everglades National Park, 40001 State Road 9336, Homestead, FL 33034, 305/242-7700, www.nps.gov/ever. For backcountry questions, contact the Flamingo Visitor Center, 239/695-2945.

57 ERNEST COE HIKE-IN/ BICYCLE-IN SITE

🚶 🚲 ⛺

Scenic rating: 3

Backcountry, in Everglades National Park

See map, page 557

This is one of three campsites in Everglades National Park suited for backpackers and two for cyclists. The others are Ingraham (OK for cycling, see listing in this chapter), about six miles down the trail; and Clubhouse Beach (see listing in this chapter), near Flamingo. Do not attempt this trip except in the winter. It's just too buggy and humid otherwise. Unlike most backcountry backpacking and bicycling adventures in national parks, this one follows the remnants of an old road. Decades ago, the now rutted limestone roadbed led to what was then the fishing village of Flamingo, at the south end of the mainland. The road has since been abandoned for vehicle traffic and runs along a canal that angles southwest toward the campsite from the trailhead. You'll rarely have human company when traveling along this road, where the pavement has given way in some places to double-track mud and dirt.

The camp is a tiny, almost imperceptible spot off the road inside a hardwood hammock—the relatively rare collection of thick-trunk gumbo-limbos and tropical mahogany trees that dot the southern Everglades. Before you hit the trail, learn about poisonwood, a cousin of poison ivy and poison oak. You're likely to encounter it out here.

Campsites, facilities: One primitive ground tent site accommodates up to eight people. You must hike or bicycle about five miles to get here from the Royal Palm area; less if you travel from the gate at the park's sole road (ask rangers for directions). No piped water is available, so bring plenty. There is no toilet; bury human waste. Pack out trash. Children are allowed. Sorry, no pets or campfires.

Reservations, fees: Get a backcountry permit in person up to 24 hours before the day of your intended campout from the entrance station at the Homestead main park entrance. They are not issued by phone or mail. Camping costs $10 for the permit, plus $2 nightly per person. Major credit cards are accepted. There's a three-night stay limit.

Directions: From Miami, take Florida's Turnpike to its southern terminus at U.S. 1. In about one block, turn right at Palm Drive. Cross the railroad tracks and pass the Circle K. At the flashing traffic light at 192nd Avenue/State Road 9336, turn left by the Robert Is Here fruit stand. Proceed south about two miles. When State Road 9336 veers right, follow it to the right instead of going straight toward the alligator farm. The park entrance is four miles ahead. Once inside the park, drive toward the Royal Palm Visitor Center. Park at the entrance to Ingraham Highway, near Hidden Lake.

Contact: Everglades National Park, 40001 State Road 9336, Homestead, FL 33034, 305/242-7700, www.nps.gov/ever. For backcountry questions, contact the Flamingo Visitor Center, 239/695-2945; or the Main Visitor Center, 305/242-7700.

58 INGRAHAM HIKE-IN/ BICYCLE-IN SITE

🏃 🚲 ⛰

Scenic rating: 3

Backcountry, in Everglades National Park

See map, page 557

You'll definitely feel like you're in the middle of nowhere. For what to expect, see the listing for Ernest Coe in this chapter. The distinction here is that you will have to hike or bicycle another 5–7 miles through the park's officially designated Pinelands area to sleep at the end of the old roadbed. The feeling of isolation is hard to match in bustling South Florida, with a view of sweeping sawgrass plains dotted by hardwood hammocks. Unless you just like the feeling of carrying a pack on your back, this place is best suited for bicyclists. Backpackers should opt for Ernest Coe, if it's available. It offers more shade, and you won't have to hike as far.

Campsites, facilities: One primitive ground tent site accommodates up to eight people. You must hike 11 miles one-way from the trailhead to get here. No piped water is available, so bring plenty. There is no toilet; bury human waste. Trash must be packed out. Children are allowed. Sorry, no pets or campfires.

Reservations, fees: Get a backcountry permit in person up to 24 hours before the day of your intended campout from the entrance station at the Homestead main park entrance. They are not issued by phone or mail. Camping costs $10 for the permit, plus $2 nightly per person. Major credit cards are accepted. There's a three-night stay limit.

Directions: From Miami, take Florida's Turnpike to its southern terminus at U.S. 1. In about one block, turn right at Palm Drive. Cross the railroad tracks and pass the Circle K. At the flashing traffic light at 192nd Avenue/State Road 9336, turn left by the Robert Is Here fruit stand. Proceed south about two miles. When State Road 9336 veers right, follow it to the right instead of going straight toward the alligator farm. The park entrance is four miles ahead. Once inside, drive toward the Royal Palm Visitor Center. Park at the entrance to Ingraham Highway, near Hidden Lake.

Contact: Everglades National Park, 40001 State Road 9336, Homestead, FL 33034, 305/242-7700, www.nps.gov/ever. For backcountry questions, contact the Flamingo Visitor Center, 239/695-2945; or the Main Visitor Center, 305/242-7700.

FLORIDA KEYS

© MARILYN MOORE

BEST CAMPGROUNDS

❰ Beachfront Campgrounds
Long Key State Park, **page 610**
Curry Hammock State Park, **page 612**
Bahia Honda State Park, **page 614**

❰ Island Retreats
Dry Tortugas National Park/Fort Jefferson
Boat-In or Fly-In Sites, **page 619**

❰ Most Luxurious
Bluewater Key RV Park, **page 617**

Just an hour from fast-paced Miami, the Keys

are a spectacular haven for anyone seeking a laid-back, casual, Caribbean-style atmosphere. Favorite activities are snorkeling, scuba diving, boating, and fishing. You can rent equipment, such as ocean kayaks, canoes, and snorkeling gear, for just about any water sport; there are plenty of dive boats, fishing guides, and paddling tours; and if you don't want to get wet, a glass-bottom boat tour will take you to the beautiful reefs offshore. What you will not find is many beaches – most of the shoreline that is accessible to the public is rocky.

Beginning at Key Largo and ending at Key West, the Keys are actually a string of small islands strung together by one highway, with sparkling crystalline blue waters on either side. Not only is the water incredibly clear, it reflects so many shades of blue and green that you'll be glad to have polarized sunglasses.

At the end of the journey is Key West, a city celebrated by songwriters (Jimmy Buffett's "Margaritaville"), authors (Ernest Hemingway, Tennessee Williams), artists (John James Audubon), and even presidents (Harry S. Truman, who started the Hawaiian-shirt craze here). Today, Key West is so far from the mainland that it's hard to believe this was once a major Florida trading port, bustling with early settlers from the Bahamas, pirates, treasure salvors, and rumrunners. Many of the gingerbread houses that were home to these early residents have been restored.

Campgrounds in the Keys are scarce, but a few stand out as destinations in their own right. John Pennekamp State Park in Key Largo is the first underwater state park in the United States. It's a marvelous place to learn to snorkel, even for small children. At Long Key State Park and at the new Curry Hammock State Park campground, you can snag a campsite on a sandy beach with a gentle shoreline. Bahia Honda State Park also has a lovely beach, though the campsites are not overlooking it. The closest campgrounds to famous Key West – America's southernmost city and just 90 miles from Havana, Cuba, by water – are now on Stock Island, about five miles outside the town.

Wherever you plan to stay, reservations are a must. Camping in parking lots is not an option, and RVs are prohibited from parking along U.S. 1 after 11 P.M.

Anywhere in the Keys, drive carefully. Since U.S. 1 is the only major artery to which all side streets lead, traffic can be a problem, especially on the weekends when Miamians come south to play, or when visitors pile in during the winter tourist season. Speed limits are strictly enforced, as are laws against drunken driving.

Ultimately, the Keys, part resort, part natural paradise, are worth the drive, no matter how far south you venture.

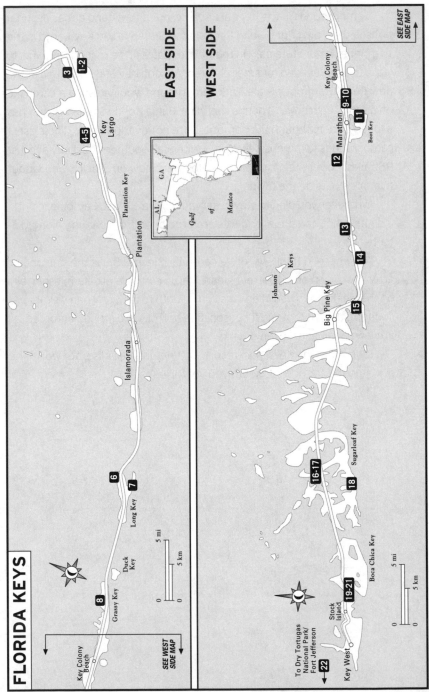

FLORIDA KEYS

EAST SIDE

WEST SIDE

Key Largo

Plantation Key

Plantation

Islamorada

Long Key

Duck Key

Grassy Key

Key Colony Beach

SEE WEST SIDE MAP

1-2

3

4-5

6

7

8

AL. GA.

Gulf of Mexico

Key Colony Beach

Marathon

Boot Key

Johnson Keys

Big Pine Key

Sugarloaf Key

Boca Chica Key

Stock Island

Key West

To Dry Tortugas National Park/ Fort Jefferson

SEE EAST SIDE MAP

9-10

11

12

13

14

15

16-17

18

19-21

22

0   5 mi

0   5 km

© AVALON TRAVEL PUBLISHING, INC.

1 JOHN PENNEKAMP CORAL REEF STATE PARK

🧑‍🦯🏊🎣🛶🚵♿🚐⛺

Scenic rating: 10

in Key Largo, on U.S. 1/Overseas Highway

The first underwater state park in the United States, this is also one of the finest parks in Florida, with a sandy beach and boat service to diving or snorkeling reefs 3–6 miles offshore. Please note that the coral reefs are accessible only by boat; however, you can practice snorkeling or diving skills at the beach, where you'll see colorful fish and sunken cannons. It's a rare setting of tropical hardwood hammocks, mangroves, and crystal-clear water bordering the Key Largo Coral Reef National Marine Sanctuary, which covers 178 nautical square miles. Paddle a canoe or visit the interpretive center. The park gets a lot of traffic from international and United States tourists and locals alike, and the gates often close by midday when crowds reach capacity. It has been called the world's most-traveled-to dive destination, and the cars of daytime visitors may stretch for 200 yards waiting to get into

this home of brain coral and barracuda. Don't forget mosquito repellent in the hot months.

This is the perfect place for novice snorkelers, especially children. The gently sloping swimming beach near the visitors center lets them try out their skills without worries. Once proficient, they can swim farther out. Just 130 feet from the water's edge lies a reconstruction of an early Spanish shipwreck. You'll see 14 cannons, an anchor, and ballast stones recovered from a ship lost in a 1715 hurricane.

Campsites, facilities: This state park has 47 gravel sites with water, 30/50-amp electricity, picnic tables, and grills. None are drive-through; a few are large enough to accommodate rigs larger than 35 feet. Restrooms, showers, and laundry facilities are provided. Three sites are wheelchair-accessible, as are the bathhouses and the laundry. In the main part of the park are two beaches, two nature trails, a playground, a visitors center with a 30,000-gallon saltwater aquarium, a marina, a dive shop, boat and canoe rentals, and a snack shop. Scuba instruction, snorkeling, and glass-bottom boat tours are available. Restaurants and grocery stores are with two miles. Children are welcome. Pets

© MARILYN MOORE

canoeing at John Pennekamp Coral Reef State Park

are not allowed in the campground or on the beach.

Reservations, fees: Reservations are recommended; contact ReserveAmerica at 800/336-3521 or reserveamerica.com. Sites are $32 per night for up to eight people. Major credit cards are accepted. The maximum stay is 14 days. Reservations are advised for snorkeling trips, which cost $25–30 per person, plus $5 to rent a snorkel and mask; reserve at 305/451-1621.

Directions: Follow U.S. 1/Overseas Highway to mile marker 102.5 in Key Largo. The park is on the ocean side.

Contact: John Pennekamp Coral Reef State Park, P.O. Box 487, Key Largo, FL 33037, 305/451-1202, www.floridastateparks.org.

2 KEY LARGO KAMPGROUND AND MARINA

🏊 🛶 ⛴ 🐕 🚐 ⛺

Scenic rating: 9

in Key Largo, south of U.S. 1/Overseas Highway

One of the nicest campgrounds in the Florida Keys, this resort reflects thoughtful planning designed to please nearly everyone. RVs are accommodated under shade trees or on waterview sites with private docks. The sites have been sold as condominium spaces, but are often rented to tourists, usually divers or visitors from Europe. In the winter, understandably, owners tend to be in town, so transient spaces are scarcer then. Spring for a site with your own private dock overlooking the long boat channel. Isolated from the beaten track, the waters don't get as stirred up as they do at other places. You'll see stingrays, tarpon, and snapper when you're snorkeling over the grassy sea bottom off the two beaches. The surrounding woods and uninhabited mangrove islands give this deluxe campground a secluded feeling, even though it's close to shopping and Key Largo attractions.

Campsites, facilities: There are 32 primitive tent sites and 171 full-hookup slots with 50-amp electrical service for RVs up to 40 feet long. About a third are drive-through sites. Facilities include cable TV, restrooms, showers, a dump station, a pool, a boat ramp, two recreation halls, small camp store, chickee huts (Seminole Indian thatched-roof dwellings), horseshoe pits, two sandy beaches, and volleyball, basketball, and shuffleboard courts are available. Some sites have gravel surfaces, while others have concrete pads. The pool and laundry area are wheelchair-accessible. Groceries are within one mile. A gate provides security. Limited RV storage is available. Children are welcome. Leashed pets are permitted.

Reservations, fees: Reservations are recommended. Sites are $46–63 per night for two adults and two children under 12, plus $3 for each additional person. No more than six people are allowed per site. Major credit cards are accepted. Long-term stays are OK.

Directions: From U.S. 1/Overseas Highway at mile marker 101.5 in Key Largo, turn south at Samson Road, which dead-ends at the park entrance, on the ocean side.

Contact: Key Largo Kampground and Marina, 101551 Overseas Highway, Key Largo, FL 33037-4596, 305/451-1431 or 800/526-7688, fax 305/451-8083, www.keylargokampground.com.

3 KING'S KAMP RV PARK MARINA AND MOTEL

🏊 🛶 ⛴ 🐕 🚐 ⛺

Scenic rating: 1

in Key Largo, on U.S. 1/Overseas Highway

A boat ramp and a small swimming beach provide good access to Blackwater Sound and Florida Bay; the pull-up RV sites are said to accommodate rigs as long as 40 feet. Most people are here to stay, rooted nearly as strong as the lush royal poinciana and gumbo-limbo trees that shade the park. But the location is worth the effort to see if a site is available. Sunsets are magnificent. Motel rooms and rental units are also available, and you can dock your boat in the marina for an additional fee of $10 per day. The park is near restaurants and shopping.

Campsites, facilities: The park has 60 sites, of which only 7 are available for RVs and a few for tents. Water, electricity, restrooms, showers, picnic tables, and fire grills are available. There is a boat ramp, a dock, and a jetty. Grocery shops and restaurants are within one mile. Children and leashed pets are permitted.

Reservations, fees: Reservations are highly recommended since space is at a premium. Sites are $40–50 per night for two people, plus $5 for each additional person. Major credit cards are accepted. Long-term stays are permitted.

Directions: Follow U.S. 1/Overseas Highway to mile marker 103.5 in Key Largo. The park is on the bay side.

Contact: King's Kamp RV Park Marina and Motel, 103620 Overseas Highway, Key Largo, FL 33037, 305/451-0010, www.kingskamp.com.

4 THE RIPTIDE RV PARK AND MOTEL

Scenic rating: 5

in Key Largo on U.S. 1/Overseas Highway

This well-kept trailer park has great views of Florida Bay and pretty coconut palms. It's a quiet place that mixes seasonal residents with travelers. Sites line a hairpin drive that leads to Florida Bay, a dock, and picnic tables by the water.

Campsites, facilities: Of the 36 trailer sites, five are set aside for RV travelers in rigs up to 30 feet long (none of the sites are pull-through). Full hookups, 30-amp electrical service, cable TV, picnic tables, restrooms, showers, a dock, and rental units are available; two waterfront sites have water and electricity only (no sewer hookups). The campground

caters primarily to retirees, but children are allowed to visit. Pets are not permitted.

Reservations, fees: Reservations are recommended. Sites are $55 per night for two people, plus $10 for each additional person. Major credit cards are accepted. Long-term stays are OK. The park is open October 1–May 1.

Directions: Follow U.S. 1/Overseas Highway to Key Largo. The park is at mile marker 97.6 on the bay side.

Contact: The Riptide RV Park and Motel, 97680 Overseas Highway, Lot 1, Key Largo, FL 33037, 305/852-8481.

5 BLUE FIN-ROCK HARBOR

Scenic rating: 5

in Key Largo

With just four sites for overnighters and 14 for seasonal visitors, you'll have to reserve ahead to stay at this tiny, sunny park on the ocean side of the highway. You'll park on a spit of land near this park's large marina operation and docks filled with expensive fishing boats. Oceanview sites are naturally in high demand. Big rigs can be accommodated.

Campsites, facilities: There are 18 sites in this boating and fishing-oriented park. Sites have full hookups and cable TV. Restrooms, showers, laundry facilities, a dog walk area, and telephone service are available. On the premises are a restaurant, a boat ramp, docks, cabana rental, and boat slips. Most areas are wheelchair-accessible. Children are welcome. Leashed pets are permitted.

Reservations, fees: Reservations are required. Fees, which are subject to change, are $40 to $65 per night for two people. Credit cards are not accepted. Long-term rates are available.

Directions: Follow U.S. 1/Overseas Highway to Key Largo. When you reach mile marker 97 on the ocean side, turn left at First State Bank onto First Avenue. Look for Second Street on your left.

Contact: Blue Fin-Rock Harbor, P.O. Box 888, 36 East Second Street, Key Largo, FL 33037, 305/852-2025 or 800/350-6572, fax 305/852-0227, www.milemarker97.com.

6 FIESTA KEY RESORT KOA KAMPGROUND AND MOTEL

Scenic rating: 7

near Layton

This 28-acre KOA is a self-contained resort designed to please all ages. Favored by anglers and boaters, the campground gets busy on summer weekends and during the winter. Many Miami residents park their trailers here all summer long, so they can get away quickly for the weekend. The views of Florida Bay are breathtaking, and you can snorkel off the seawall near the swimming beach. Fishing in these parts for the wily bonefish is world-famous. The park organizes parties for special events like New Year's.

Campsites, facilities: There are 300 RV sites (204 full-hookup) and a shaded section for 50 tents. Ninety-six RV sites have water and electricity only. A separate "tent village" has six roofed structures with electricity, a storage compartment, and a grassy area for tents. Picnic tables, grills, restrooms, showers, LP gas, a convenience store, and two laundry rooms are available. Other features include a playground, a game room, a store, an air-conditioned recreation hall, 20 motel units, a heated pool, two hot tubs, a beach, a marina, a boat ramp, boat rentals, bicycle rentals, horseshoes, basketball, beach volleyball, and a waterfront restaurant and bar. Children are welcome. Leashed pets are permitted.

Reservations, fees: Reservations are recommended. Sites are $42–95 per night for two people, plus $7 for each additional child and $9 per extra adult. Major credit cards are accepted. Long-term stays are OK.

Directions: Follow U.S.1/Overseas Highway to the resort at mile marker 70 on the bay side of Fiesta Key.

Contact: Fiesta Key Resort KOA Kampground and Motel, P.O. Box 618, Long Key, FL 33001, 305/664-4922, 800/562-7730, fax 305/664-8741, www.koa.com.

7 LONG KEY STATE PARK

Scenic rating: 10

on Long Key, south of Layton

BEST (

With so few sites, the campground in this 980-acre state park is often filled, but don't let that deter you from trying. The camping area has a gently curving natural shoreline, and all sites are at beachfront. Get up in the morning and walk a few feet right into the water. There's almost always a breeze (sometimes too much of one!). Expect little in the way of natural vegetative buffers; many campsites and even the pedestrians on the park's beloved walking path are fairly visible to cars passing by on U.S. 1. A few campsites are big enough, however, to give the illusion of being far from neighbors. At low tide, kids can look for fiddler crabs and

Long Key State Park campsite

© MARILYN MOORE

minnows in rocky tidal pools at the east end of the campground. The sea level was 20–30 feet higher 100,000 years ago, but today, the water is so shallow that you can wade 0.5 mile out to sea and only get waist deep. This makes it a great place to learn to snorkel, although you won't see dramatic coral formations and big fish unless you go far offshore in a boat. A world-record bonefish was caught on the grassy flats at Long Key, according to park rangers. The Long Key Lakes Canoe Trail winds through mangrove flats and a shallow lagoon. Nearby is the Golden Orb Trail, a 40-minute nature walk. On the bay side (across U.S. 1 and east of the campground) is the Layton Trail, a meandering path through a dark, almost impenetrable tropical hardwood hammock.

Campsites, facilities: This state park has 50 sites for RVs. Water and 30-amp electricity are available at all. Picnic tables, grills, restrooms, and showers are provided. There's a canoe trail, a 1.25-mile nature trail, and an interpretive program. A convenience store is within 0.5 mile; a grocery store is 15 miles away. Children are welcome. Pets are prohibited.

Reservations, fees: Reservations are recommended; contact ReserveAmerica at 800/336-3521 or reserveamerica.com. Sites are $32 per night for up to eight people. Major credit cards are accepted. The maximum stay is 14 days.

Directions: From the town of Layton on Long Key, drive south on U.S. 1/Overseas Highway to mile marker 67. Turn south at the park sign.

Contact: Long Key State Park, P.O. Box 776, Long Key, FL 33001, 305/664-4815, www.floridastateparks.org.

8 JOLLY ROGER TRAVEL PARK

Scenic rating: 7

On Grassy Key

Campers at primitive sites will sleep nearly surrounded by water, if they book one of the six sunny sites on a tiny triangle of land jutting into Florida Bay. Concrete-paved RV sites handle rigs up to 40 feet long; 15 are pull-through. Part of the park houses 100 mobile homes. A convenience store is within walking distance. Wintertime activities include bingo, kayak trips, bus tours to the Wal-Mart in Florida City, dances, ice cream socials, and live music in the recreation pavilion. You can swim or snorkel off the dock. There's little shade at this boating-oriented campground.

Campsites, facilities: Eighty RV sites have full hookups and cable TV, 14 tent sites have water and electricity, and six sites are primitive. Picnic tables, restrooms, showers, horseshoes, and laundry facilities are available. The park is family-oriented, but tends to attract older people. Leashed pets are permitted.

Reservations, fees: Reservations are recommended. Sites are $32 per night for two tent campers and $40–50 for two RVers, plus $5 for each additional person over age 5. Major credit cards are accepted. Long-term stays are OK for RVers. Only four occupants are allowed per tent site, and tenters can stay no more than two weeks. RV occupancy limit is six persons.

Directions: On Grassy Key, follow U.S.1/Overseas Highway to mile marker 59.5. The park is on the bay side.

Contact: Jolly Roger Travel Park, 59275 Overseas Highway, Marathon, FL 33050, 305/289-0404, 800/995-1525, fax 305/743-6913, www.jrtp.com.

9 PELICAN MOTEL AND TRAILER PARK

Scenic rating: 6

on Grassy Key, near Marathon

In wintertime, you'll find senior citizens enjoying boating, fishing, water sports, and activities in the recreation room, and relaxing in the sheltered picnic area next to the water.

This trailer-park/motel complex on the gulf side is next door to a full-service marina and near a dolphin research center.

Campsites, facilities: A varying number of RV sites (usually around 10) are available for overnighters and short-term visitors in this 85-unit trailer park, where 25 percent of the occupants live year-round. All sites have full hookups, 30-amp electrical service, picnic tables, cable TV, and optional telephone service. Restrooms, showers, a dump station, and laundry facilities are available. On the premises are a pool, a boat ramp, a dock, a clubhouse with planned activities during the winter, shuffleboard courts, a dog-walk area, and a picnic area. RV storage is available. Children are welcome, but adults and senior citizens are preferred. Small, leashed pets are permitted.

Reservations, fees: Reservations are recommended. Sites are $25–38 per night for two people, plus $3 per extra person. Major credit cards are accepted. Long-term (up to six months) stays are allowed.

Directions: From Follow Overseas Highway to mile marker 59; the park is on the gulf side.

Contact: Pelican Motel and Trailer Park, 59151 Overseas Highway, Marathon, FL 33050, 305/289-0011.

10 CURRY HAMMOCK STATE PARK
🚲 🏊 🎣 🛥 🏕 🐕 🚶 ♿ 🚐 ⛺

Scenic rating: 10

on Grassy Key, near Marathon

BEST (

This tiny but very special campground opened in 2005 and gets rave reviews from just about everyone lucky enough to book a site. Not only is it located directly on the ocean, all the facilities are newly built. The park features a gorgeous sandy beach with a shallow slope suitable for families, and some sites overlook the water. Sunsets are spectacular. A day-use area is next door, but the campground is sepa-

rated from it by a wooden fence and security gate. What it lacks is privacy between the sites and shade; low scrub and bushes are the only visual separation and trees are scarce. It's only open to campers in the winter and spring, and with this prime waterfront location, it understandably fills up quickly. The day-use area is open year-round.

Campsites, facilities: The 28 gravel sites encircle a paved street with a bathhouse at the center. Each site has a picnic table, 30/50-amp electrical service, and water. Most spots also have a sandbox suitable for pitching a tent (sites 10–19, 21, and 26 do not have a sandbox). If you have an air mattress, the gravel sites should make for comfortable sleeping. Sites 11, 13, 15, 16, 17, 19, and 21 have the best views and are nearest to the beach. Also on the premises are restrooms, showers, a playground, a dumpsite, canoe and kayak mooring, a swimming beach, pavilions, a pet-walk area, and day-use area. Children and pets are welcome.

Reservations, fees: The park is open to camping November 1–May 31 only. Reservations are recommended; contact ReserveAmerica at 800/336-3521 or reserveamerica.com. Sites are $32 per night for up to eight people. Major credit cards are accepted. The maximum stay is 14 days.

Directions: Follow Overseas Highway to mile marker 56; the campground is on the ocean side.

Contact: Curry Hammock State Park, 56200 Overseas Highway, Marathon, FL 33050, 305/289-2690, www.floridastateparks.org.

11 KEY RV PARK
🎣 🛥 🏕 🚐

Scenic rating: 3

in Marathon

This well-kept park caters to boaters who want ocean access near their campsite and visitors who stay for the season. Shade is minimal. A small lighthouse and park benches overlook the water. Sites line a paved road around a narrow boat channel; about half are on the canal. The park is within two blocks of restaurants and shopping, and convenient to an 18-hole, par-3 golf course, public tennis courts, groceries, and miniature golf.

Campsites, facilities: There are 200 RV-only sites, most with full hookups, and some with 50-amp electrical service. About 30 percent of the park is occupied by year-round residents, who also moor their boats at the docks. This makes dockage for transient visitors rather scarce. Sites are gravel and many have concrete slabs. Restrooms, showers, a boat ramp, a boat dock ($4/day charge), picnic tables, three laundry rooms, and a recreation hall are available. Social programs are directed by an activities committee during the winter months. Internet access is available in the clubhouse. Children are allowed. Small, friendly pets are accepted.

Reservations, fees: Reservations are recommended. Sites are $45–75 per night for up to four people, plus $4 for each additional person. Major credit cards are accepted. Long-term rates are available.

Directions: The park is in Marathon, on U.S. 1/Overseas Highway between mile markers 50 and 51, on the ocean side.

Contact: Key RV Park, 6099 Overseas Highway, Marathon, FL 33050, 305/743-5164 or 800/288-5164.

12 KNIGHT'S KEY PARK CAMPGROUND AND MARINA

Scenic rating: 7

on Knight's Key

Mature banyan, olive, and gumbo-limbo trees shade the grassy 19-acre campground (owned by the same family since 1962), which has some nice sites near the water. There's a small swimming beach with picnic tables and tiki huts for shade. A big plus: The old Seven Mile Bridge span, favored by inline skaters and bicyclists, is close by. Sites are oversized, some 30 feet wide and big enough to accommodate slideout trailers. Other sites are as long as 69 feet. The Kyle Inn Restaurant, open December 15–April 1, offers live entertainment.

Campsites, facilities: There are 192 RV sites with water and electricity, and 17 tent sites. Picnic tables, restrooms, showers, laundry facilities, a swimming beach, a marina, a boat ramp, shuffleboard courts, pool tables, and a modem hookup to check email are available. There's also a snack bar and a restaurant. Boat and trailer storage is available. Children are welcome. You may bring pets only if you have an air-conditioned RV.

Reservations, fees: Reservations are recommended, especially on holiday weekends and during lobster season (which changes every year, but generally runs for a week in August, with a "mini" season of three days in late July). Sites are $32–77 per night for two people, plus $8 for each additional person. Major credit cards are accepted. Campers may stay for up to six months.

Directions: The park is on the ocean side of U.S.1/Overseas Highway at mile marker 47 and the last turnoff before the Seven Mile Bridge.

Contact: Knight's Key Park Campground and Marina, P.O. Box 525, Marathon, FL 33050, 305/743-4343, 800/348-2267, fax 305/743-2907, www.keysdirectory.com/knightskeycampground.

13 SUNSHINE KEY RV RESORT

Scenic rating: 8

on Ohio Key

At 75 acres, this is one of the largest campgrounds in the Keys. Surrounded by crystal-clear seas, the park bills itself as a water-sports wonderland, with a 172-slip marina for anglers, and a narrow swimming beach. From the marina, scuba divers, snorkelers, sailors, canoeists, and ocean kayakers have access to both bay and ocean waters. But there are plenty of activities on land, too—even a game arcade for teens who feel they're too grown-up to hang out with their parents. Coconut palms give the campground that tropical island feel. There are walking trails on 35 acres. RVs up to 12 feet wide can be accommodated, and a remarkable 325 sites are pull-through. Although seasonal stays are allowed and RV storage is available, no one lives here year-round.

Campsites, facilities: All 400 grassy or gravel sites are for RVs up to 48 feet long; all sites have full hookups and 30 /50-amp service. The sites are a mix of shady and sunny spots, varying in size from 25 to 30 feet wide and 40 to 50 feet long. Pull your rig through at 325 sites. Picnic tables, restrooms, showers, a pool, a boat ramp, two recreation halls, a horseshoe pit, shuffleboard and basketball courts, tennis, wintertime planned activities, cable TV, propane, a dump station, honeywagon service (a truck pumps out the sewer bilges from your RV), a dive shop, a boat ramp, boat rentals, a fishing pier, and diving and snorkeling trips are on the premises. Planned activities include bingo, dancing, dinners, and fishing tournaments. Also on-site are groceries, a snack bar, bait and tackle, laundry facilities, and rental cottages. Internet service is available in the office. Children are welcome. Leashed pets are permitted; a dog kennel is provided.

Reservations, fees: Reservations are recommended. Sites are $60–105 per night. Major credit cards are accepted. Six-month stays are allowed.

Directions: The park is on Ohio Key, on U.S. 1/Overseas Highway at mile marker 39 on the bay side.

Contact: Sunshine Key RV Resort, 38801 Overseas Highway, Big Pine Key, FL 33043, 305/872-2217 or 800/852-0348, fax 305/872-3801, rvonthego.com. Reserve campsites or dive/snorkel trips at 800/852-0348.

14 BAHIA HONDA STATE PARK

Scenic rating: 10

on Bahia Honda Key

BEST (

This beautiful state park's two swimming beaches, routinely named among the top 10 in the nation, are spectacular. One overlooks the Bahia Honda bridge, and the other is on the ocean. You can spend hours lazing on a raft and imagine yourself floating across the Atlantic, or toss a beach ball around on the shore. Hike up to the old roadbed that once served as Henry Flagler's original rail line to Key West; on the top deck is the old highway. It juts eerily into space because the state removed the central span when the new road was built.

Campsites, facilities: The two camping areas have a total of 80 sites with piped water, electricity, picnic tables, and nearby restrooms and showers. On the south side of the park, smaller sites are tucked into a lush hardwood hammock. On the north side, campers stay on a sun-drenched gravel promontory suitable for RVs. Some sites and the restrooms are wheelchair-accessible. A snack bar, a gift shop, snorkeling tours, ocean-kayak and beach-bike rentals, and diving equipment are provided by a concessionaire. In addition, 19 boat slips (where you can also stay overnight) are available (reservations are recommended). Children are welcome, but pets are not permitted.

Reservations, fees: Reservations are recommended; contact ReserveAmerica at 800/336-3521 or reserveamerica.com. Sites are $26 per night for up to eight people. Boat slips cost $1 per linear foot (minimum charge is $22) and include water, electricity, and use of the park facilities. Major credit cards are accepted. The maximum stay is 14 days.

Directions: The park is on Bahia Honda Key, at mile marker 37 on U.S. 1/Overseas Highway, on the ocean side.

Contact: Bahia Honda State Park, 36850

Overseas Highway, Big Pine Key, FL 33043, 305/872-2353.

15 BIG PINE KEY FISHING LODGE

🏊 🎣 🚗 🐕 ⛹ ♿ 🚐 ⛺

Scenic rating: 8

on Big Pine Key

A sprawling motel/campground resort on 10 acres, Big Pine Key Fishing Lodge is paradise for anglers. The complex has a spectacular location, bordering on Looe Key National Underwater Marine Sanctuary and the ocean. An unusually well-developed canopy of tropical trees (frangipani, gumbo-limbo, and buttonwood, among others) creates a natural ambience even in the interior of the campground. Swimmers can bask in lawn chairs near the coral rock shoreline (not a beach) or at the pool. Kids will find lots of things to keep them busy, and boaters have all the amenities they could need on hand, from fishing guides to a full-service marina. The boat ramp has an immediate drop-off from the seawall edge, however, and you're advised to launch with caution. When you come home with your catch, you must use the fish-cleaning tables near the boat basin. During most of the year (except for September and October), planned activities include dances, parties, card games, "banana split" nights, and trips to golf clubs and theaters in Key West.

Campsites, facilities: There are 94 RV sites with full hookups (accommodating rigs up to 34 feet long), and 58 primitive tent-only sites with community water spigots and grills. Ten of the RV sites have 50-amp electrical service; the rest have 30-amp. Picnic tables, restrooms, showers, laundry facilities, a dump station, honeywagon service, docks, a boat ramp, boat rentals, charter fishing and diving services, a pool, a beach, horseshoe pits, shuffleboard courts, a playground, a recreation room, and a game room are available. A convenience store, a bait and tackle shop, and rental units are on the premises. Most areas are wheelchair-accessible. Internet service is available in the office. Groceries are two miles away; Key West is 28 miles south. Children are welcome. Dogs are prohibited, because they are likely to scare the endangered key deer; other pets are welcome.

Reservations, fees: Reservations are required during holidays and recommended at other times. Sites are $41–45 per night for two people, plus $7 for each person over age seven. Children under seven are free. Major credit cards are accepted. Long-term stays are not permitted.

Directions: From U.S. 1/Overseas Highway at mile marker 33 on Big Pine Key, turn south at the park entrance on the ocean side.

Contact: Big Pine Key Fishing Lodge, 33000 Overseas Highway, P.O. Box 430513, Big Pine Key, FL 33043, 305/872-2351, fax 305/872-3868.

16 SUGARLOAF KEY RESORT KOA KAMPGROUND

🏊 🎣 🚗 🐕 🚐 ⛺

Scenic rating: 8

on Sugarloaf Key

The southernmost KOA in North America has much to offer families who want a resort-style vacation, along with the waterfront necessities that define the Florida Keys experience. Ficus, sea grape, palm trees, and ocean vistas enhance the campsites. Fifteen sites are at waterfront; the tent area is in a large, shady, grassy clearing. There are plenty of amenities, including a private sandy beach with tiki huts for sunning and playing, plus the Crews Nest social pavilion and planned activities. RVs and cabins are available for rent. Boaters and anglers can use the campground's full-service marina, which has 25 boat slips. An inlet leads from the marina to the Atlantic Ocean. Canoes and other boats are available for rent. Like everywhere on the waterfront in the Keys, the waters are crystal-clear for snorkeling. Located just 14 miles from Key West, this is a good base camp for touring the city and its attractions.

Campsites, facilities: There are 200 gravel sites with full hookups, plus 30/50-amp electrical services and picnic tables. A few primitive sites accommodate tents. Slideouts and RVs up to 40 feet long can be accommodated. None of the sites are drive-through. Facilities include restrooms, showers, dump station, honeywagon service, propane, a sandy beach, a heated pool with a hot tub, a restaurant, café, a marina, a boat ramp, a convenience store, a game room, miniature golf, laundry facilities, trailer rentals, basketball, volleyball, horseshoe pits, a bar with wintertime live entertainment, and rentals of bicycles, boats, and canoes are available. Planned activities are held during the winter season, and the park sponsors a dolphin-fishing tournament in June. Internet hookup is available in the office; a wireless connection can be found near the café. The bathrooms and laundry are wheelchair-accessible. Children are welcome. Leashed pets are permitted.

Reservations, fees: Reservations are recommended. Sites are $67–112 per night for two people, plus $9 per extra person. Major credit cards are accepted. Stays are limited to 30 days.

Directions: From U.S. 1/Overseas Highway at mile marker 20 on Sugarloaf Key, turn south and drive 0.2 mile to the park entrance.

Contact: Sugarloaf Key Resort KOA Kampground, 251 County Road 939, Sugarloaf Key, FL 33042, 305/745-3549 or 800/562-7731, fax 305/745-9889, www.koa.com.

17 LAZY LAKES CAMPGROUND

🏊 🛶 🎣 🐕 ♿ 🚐 ⛺

Scenic rating: 6

on Sugarloaf Key

The six-acre artificial lake, an almost perfect rectangle nearly split in two by a promenade that ends in a swim ladder, is the focus of this campground. Snorkeling, swimming, windsurfing, and fishing are popular camper activities. If you get a waterfront site, be careful with children; the lake is 20 feet deep (even at the shoreline, in some places). In fact, children under 14 must be accompanied by an adult when near the lake, the pool, or the bathhouse. Always use a flashlight when walking at night. Scuba divers are welcome, but they're not allowed to use spears or guns in the lake. Motorboats are forbidden. Coconut palms and Australian pines are counterpoints to the rather barren terrain, but many sites have no shade and little vegetation. Cool off in the pool, or work off some calories while line dancing. In the recreation hall, where planned activities take place in the wintertime, you can curl up with a good book or relax in front of the TV.

Campsites, facilities: Full hookups, cable TV, and telephone access are available at 80 RV sites, which accommodate rigs up to 40 feet long. There are 10 tent spots, some primitive, others with water and electricity. Both 50-amp and 30-amp electrical service are available. Picnic tables, restrooms, showers, a dump station, a pool, a lake, boat docks, rental units, laundry facilities, a basketball court, and a recreation hall are available. Most areas are wheelchair-accessible. Children are welcome. Two leashed pets are permitted per site.

Reservations, fees: Reservations are recommended. Sites are $28–51 per night for two people, plus $5 for each additional person and $2 for cable TV. Major credit cards are accepted. Long-term stays are OK.

Directions: From U.S. 1/Overseas Highway at mile marker 19.8 on Sugarloaf Key, turn south on Johnson Road. Drive 0.25 mile to the park.

Contact: Lazy Lakes Campground, 311 Johnson Road, Sugarloaf Key, FL 33042, 305/745-4129 or 800/354-5524, fax 305/745-1680, www.rvonthego.com.

18 BLUEWATER KEY RV PARK

🏊 🎣 ➡️ 🐾 ♿ 🚐

Scenic rating: 10

on Sugarloaf Key

BEST (

You can park your big rig at poolside, on a canal lot, or on the bayfront in this deluxe park, which has a three-story clubhouse and a resort-style pool. The park is set in a quiet, residential neighborhood. Key West is only 10 miles away. Waterfront sites have their own docks and tiki huts.

Campsites, facilities: Rigs up to 47 feet can be accommodated at this 81-site ownership park. Your RV must use full hookups and be at least 26 feet long; tents are not permitted. Electrical service at each site is both 30 amps and 50 amps. Picnic tables, restrooms, showers, and laundry facilities are provided. Waterfront sites have swimming, docks, tiki huts, and coconut palms. There's also a boat ramp, a pool, a clubhouse, and a security gate. The clubroom, laundry, and showers are wheelchair-accessible. Propane deliver service can be scheduled once a week. Internet hookup is available in the clubhouse. Children are welcome. Two leashed pets are permitted per site.

Reservations, fees: Reservations are required. Sites are $110 per night for two people, plus $10 per additional person. Cable TV is included. Telephone service is available at $2 per night. Rates are higher during Fantasy Fest (usually held mid- to late October) and holidays. Major credit cards are accepted. Long-term stays are welcome; however, only a few occupants live here year-round.

Directions: On Sugarloaf Key, from U.S. 1/ Overseas Highway at mile marker 14.5, turn on Bluewater Drive toward the ocean side and proceed to the park entrance.

Contact: Bluewater Key RV Park, 2950 U.S. Highway 1, Key West, FL 33040, 305/745-2494 or 800/237-2266, fax 305/745-2433, www.bluewaterkey.com.

19 LEO'S CAMPGROUND

🐾 🚐 ⛺

Scenic rating: 2

on Stock Island

Set on two wooded acres, this quiet, shady campground is convenient to Key West's historic area, beaches, dive shops, and fishing charters. From here, you could ride your bicycle into town or catch a bus. Parking in Key West is notoriously difficult, and a lot of visitors rent moped scooters to get around. Some sights you shouldn't miss: the buoy marking the southernmost point in the United States, only 90 miles from Cuba; sunset at Mallory Square; the Audubon House and Tropical Gardens; the Hemingway Home and Museum; and the Mel Fisher Maritime Heritage Society Museum. Fisher is a modern-day treasure salvor who discovered the wreck of a gold-laden Spanish galleon and brought his booty ashore.

Campsites, facilities: A separate tent section offers 12 sites overlooking a small lake; two have electricity, six have grills, and all have water. The 34 other grassy, shaded campsites come with picnic tables; seven have 50-amp electrical service, and 27 have 30-amp. RVs up to 40 feet long can be accommodated; none of the sites are drive-through. There is no dump station. Most sites are 24 feet wide. A separate tent section offers 12 sites overlooking a small lake. About 10 percent of the occupants live here year-round. Restrooms, showers, and a laundry facility are available. Internet service is available in the office. A bus stop is on the corner and serves Key West–bound passengers. Restaurants, parasailing, and kayak and water scooter rentals are within two blocks; grocery stores are one mile away. Children are welcome. Leashed pets under 30 pounds are permitted in RVs only.

Reservations, fees: Reservations are recommended. Sites are $49 per night for two people, plus $8 each extra person and $1 per pet. Rates are higher during Fantasy Fest (in October), Christmas, and New Year's. Major credit cards are accepted. Long-term stays are OK.

Directions: On Stock Island, from U.S. 1/ Overseas Highway at mile marker 4.5, turn south at Cross Street and drive one block to the campground on Suncrest Road.

Contact: Leo's Campground, 5236 Suncrest Road, Key West, FL 33040, 305/296-5260.

20 BOYD'S KEY WEST CAMPGROUND

🏊 🎣 🚤 🐕 ♿ 🚐 ⛺

Scenic rating: 5

on Stock Island

Although set in a busy urban area just outside the Key West city limits, this 12-acre campground manages to sustain a tropical ambience, with a swimming beach, water views, and coconut palms. Like Key West, it attracts all kinds of people. Here, you might see a tent cooled by a room air conditioner on concrete blocks, as well as luxury-loving campers parked in $150,000 RVs. The proprietors say most visitors here are "very active" snowbirds in their fifties or sixties, as well as families. This is the largest park close to Key West, a city celebrated by songwriters (Jimmy Buffett's "Margaritaville"), authors (Ernest Hemingway, Tennessee Williams), artists (John James Audubon), and even presidents (Harry S. Truman, who started the Hawaiian-shirt craze here).

Today, Key West is so far from the mainland that it's hard to believe this was once a major Florida trading port, bustling with early settlers from the Bahamas, pirates, treasure salvors, and rumrunners. Many of the gingerbread houses that were home to these early residents have been restored. Modern-day "Conchs" (pronounced "konks"), as Keys natives call themselves, now make their living from art galleries, boutiques, and souvenir and T-shirt shops, or by giving circus-style performances on Mallory Square.

Campsites, facilities: There are 150 full-hook-up RV sites, plus 53 spots set apart for tents. Ninety sites have 50-amp electrical service; 60 have 30-amp. You'll find concrete patios at some sites, and some with scrub bushes to provide a modicum of privacy. Restrooms, showers, picnic tables, laundry facilities, a dump station, a heated pool, a beach, a game room, a boat ramp, telephone service, cable TV, a camp store with limited supplies, and a dock are available. Planned activities including cards, crafting classes, snorkeling, and parties. All areas are wheelchair-accessible. Children are welcome. Pets are permitted on leashes; however Dobermans, pit bulls, Rottweilers, chows, wolf hybrids, German shepherds, and non-domesticated animals are prohibited. RV storage is available only in the summer months.

Reservations, fees: Reservations are recommended. Sites are $45–110 per night for two people, plus $10 for each additional person over the age of 12. Major credit cards are accepted. Long-term stays are OK.

Directions: From U.S. 1/Overseas Highway, turn south at mile marker 5 onto 3rd Street. Drive one block and turn east onto Maloney Avenue/State Road 941. The park is at 6401 Maloney Avenue.

Contact: Boyd's Key West Campground, 6401 Maloney Avenue, Key West, FL 33040, 305/294-1465, fax 305/293-9301, www.boydscampground.com.

21 EL MAR RV RESORT

🏊 🎣 🚤 🐕 🚐

Scenic rating: 6

on Stock Island

Modeling itself as "upscale," El Mar RV Resort has sunny waterfront sites for self-contained RVs that are 26 feet or longer. No tents, truck campers, or pop-ups are allowed. Indeed, expensive motor coaches and fifth-wheelers are the norm at this sparsely landscaped park that

Bridge fishing is both spectacular and rewarding along the Overseas Highway.

offers eastward views of the beautiful Keys waters. Adults are the preferred visitors.

Campsites, facilities: There are five waterfront sites and five inland sites. All have full hook-ups with 30/50-amp service and are available for overnighters or snowbirds. Picnic tables, cable TV, and phone availability are at each site, which measure 30 by 75 feet with concrete patios. Interior roads are paved. RVs must be self-contained; no restrooms or showers are provided. Children are discouraged. Leashed pets under 25 pounds are permitted.

Reservations, fees: Reservations are recommended. Sites are $65–95 per night for two people, plus $10 per extra person. Major credit cards are accepted. Long-term rates are available.

Directions: From U.S. 1/Overseas Highway, turn south at mile marker 5 onto 3rd Street. Drive one block and turn east onto Maloney Avenue/State Road 941. The park is 0.5 mile away at 6700 Maloney Avenue.

Contact: El Mar RV Resort, 6700 Maloney Avenue, Key West, FL 33040, 305/294-0857 or 315/524-8687, fax 603/880-8187, www.elmarrvresort.com.

22 DRY TORTUGAS NATIONAL PARK/ FORT JEFFERSON BOAT-IN OR FLY-IN SITES

Scenic rating: 10

70 miles west of Key West

BEST (

The 13 sunwashed camping sites on Garden Key aren't much—really just open, grassy areas with a little shade from coconut palms, buttonwood trees, and steady, cooling sea breezes. But, wow, just look around you. The most imposing presence is six-sided, brick-walled Fort Jefferson, built beginning in 1846 to enable the United States to protect ship traffic between the mouth of the Mississippi River and the Atlantic Ocean.

Fort Jefferson, including a visitors center with interpretive exhibits detailing the fort's history, is open daily. It served as a Union outpost during the War between the States, and at one time housed four men suspected of trying to help bring about President Lincoln's assassination after the war's conclusion.

Garden Key is one of a cluster of islands known as the Dry Tortugas. The "dry" part of the name comes from the fact that there is no freshwater here; it can't be emphasized enough that you must bring all the water you'll need for your entire stay. "Tortugas" (turtles) dates to 1513, when Spanish explorer Ponce de León, who discovered Florida, spied the green, loggerhead, and hawksbill sea turtles that came ashore to nest. Today the green turtle is endangered, and the loggerhead and hawksbill are classified as threatened. But, if you're lucky, you can still watch them arrive to lay eggs in spring and summer.

Summer and spring are also the time to see the annual spectacle of 100,000 sooty terns nesting on nearby Bush Key. The sooties show up as early as mid-January and begin nesting in March. They stick around until September or so. You're also likely to see brown noddy terns, frigate birds with seven-foot wingspans, masked and brown boobies, roseate terns, double-breasted cormorants, and brown pelicans.

In the aquamarine waters between these spots of land, snorkeling is popular. Divers delight to the sight of schools of vividly colored small fish, such as the neon yellow and sky blue smallmouth grunt, making their way among multicolored sea fans and staghorn coral. Scuba divers also see sharks and barracuda. Anglers make the Dry Tortugas a frequent stop, coming back with amberjack, grouper, wahoo, and snapper, among others. If you tire of the water and Garden Key, you can make a day trip to Loggerhead Key and picnic beneath a towering lighthouse (provided you have your own boat or kayak).

A few words of caution: Watch your step in the fort, because the uneven walkways and loose bricks have been known to trip up more than one visitor. In the water, you'll want to be familiar with—and carefully avoid—sea urchins, fire coral, and jellyfish.

The first-come, first-served policy can be a little intimidating, particularly if you're paying in the neighborhood of $80 per head for boat service or $150 for an air taxi; however, the ferry services will call ahead to make sure there's room for you, and one operator told us he has never seen anyone turned away. The park service also says there is an overflow area available. Things can get a little tight in March and April, when bird-watchers show up. Unofficially, more than 10 parties are usually accommodated. Still, this place is so remote that crowds are rarely an issue.

Rules are strict at Dry Tortugas: Prohibited are water-skiing, personal watercraft, anchoring on or otherwise harming coral, taking lobster or conchs, spearfishing, and possession of more than one day's bag limit of fish, as determined by State of Florida fishing regulations. Firearms must be unloaded and cased at all times and may not be brought ashore. All historic and archaeological material, including such items as bricks, bottles, glass, and metal, must be left undisturbed.

Campsites, facilities: Ten primitive tent sites and three sites in an overflow area are available to boaters or others who arrange to fly or boat to the island. A historic fort, a visitors center, saltwater flush toilets, and some picnic tables and grills are provided. You must bring everything else, including water, fuel, food, and other camping supplies. There is no piped water. A portable grill is recommended. Trash must be packed out. Personal watercraft and water-skiing are prohibited. Leashed pets are permitted. The long list of other rules boils down to this: Take only pictures, leave only footsteps. The campground, visitors center, bookstore, and the lower level of the fort are wheelchair-accessible.

Reservations, fees: Reservations are required for groups of 10 or more. Otherwise, camping is first-come, first-served. Sites are $3 per person per night. Credit cards are not accepted.

Directions: To get to the island, you'll need a ferry boat, an air taxi service, or your own boat (consult nautical chart 11438). Most campers depart from Key West. There, air taxi operators include Seaplanes of Key West (305/294-0709, www.seaplanesofkeywest .com). Ferry boats serve the Dry Tortugas from the Florida Keys, including Yankee Fleet (305/294-7009, www.yankeefleet.com) and Sunny Days (305/296-2042). Ask the ferry operators if they can accommodate your kayak. It's also possible to leave from Naples, Key Largo, Marathon, Fort Myers, or St. Petersburg. Ask the park for details.

Contact: Dry Tortugas National Park, P.O. Box 6208, Key West, FL 33041. Everglades National Park, tel. 305/242-7700, www.nps .gov/drto.

TREASURE COAST

© MARILYN MOORE

BEST CAMPGROUND

◖ **Most Unusual**
Sunnier Palms Nudist Campground, **page 631**

The citizenry of the Treasure Coast have done

a lot of work to control development, which is good for active campers who like canoeing, kayaking, fishing, boating, or just getting back into the woods. For more citified tastes, the Treasure Coast offers beaches and easy access to the ocean, as well as top-notch golfing, boating, and relaxation.

The Atlantic Ocean defines the region on the east, and towns such as Vero Beach, Fort Pierce, and Stuart hug the coast. They are quieter and more relaxed than their southern big-city cousins. Noteworthy are the Los Angeles Dodgers spring-training camp in Vero Beach and the PGA Village in Fort Pierce, home to 72 holes of championship golf and a learning center for duffers who want to perfect their game. Public beachfront parks are plentiful.

Although campgrounds are relatively few in this area, many provide interesting places to explore. The St. Lucie Lock Recreation Area offers a view of how engineers use their skills to control nature. The St. Lucie Canal, built by the U.S. Army Corps of Engineers as part of South Florida's massive drainage system, is the east-west waterway from Lake Okeechobee to the ocean. Visitors can stand above the massive lock system and watch boats travel beneath their feet. At this restful, sunny spot, daytime picnickers and campers alike stop to watch the action.

Head farther south to the always popular Jonathan Dickinson State Park for something that will please almost everyone in your party. Campers can choose from easy, level hiking trails well-suited for a day trip, horseback riding, mountain biking, fishing, nature study, and side trips to nearby beaches. The Loxahatchee, the only federally designated Wild and Scenic River in this part of the state, is worth exploring by canoe or kayak. Paddling seaward, you'll pass through dark, brooding cypress forests to where the freshwater turns salty and mangroves appear on the banks. You're virtually certain to see alligators (and maybe a manatee, if you're lucky); bald eagles and hawk-like osprey are also sighted. The park is populated by deer, Florida sandhill cranes, wading birds, alligators, raccoons, and other wild animals.

Fishing is good, both in the Loxahatchee River and the nearby Indian River. Redfish, trout, and snook are among the favored game fish. Some anglers prefer surfcasting in the nearby Atlantic Ocean for whiting, pompano, and jack. For a side trip, visit the Jupiter Lighthouse and Museum, where Confederate soldiers captured the light and doused it, and Blowing Rocks Preserve, where water jets up through blowholes in an intriguing rock formation.

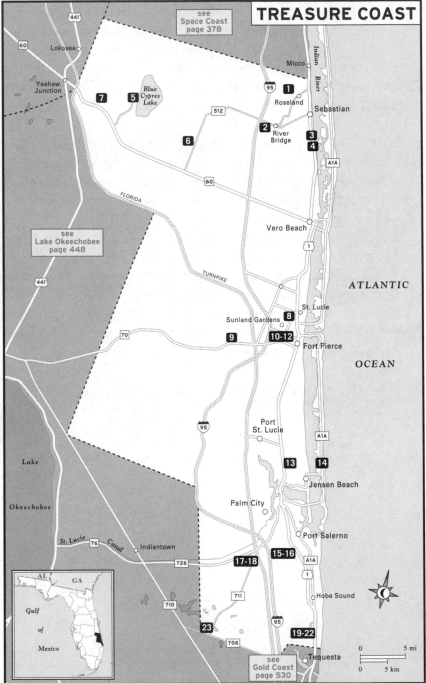

TREASURE COAST

see
Space Coast
page 378

see
Lake Okeechobee
page 448

see
Gold Coast
page 530

© AVALON TRAVEL PUBLISHING, INC.

1 DONALD MACDONALD PARK

🚶 🛶 🚤 🏕 🐕 ♿ 🚐 ⛺

Scenic rating: 8

in Roseland

Tall pines, scraggly oaks, sabal palms, and southern red cedars shield the rustic campsites from each other and give a raw, wild flavor to this primitive, heavily wooded, county-run campground located near civilization. Each camping spot has some shade, a picnic table, and a ground grill. Anglers, canoeists, and boaters use the boat ramp to launch onto the Sebastian River. For a short walk, try the interpretive nature trail and observation boardwalk. The campground is close to the Sebastian Inlet State Recreation Area.

Campsites, facilities: There are 28 primitive tent campsites with no hookups, and one RV site with electricity. Water faucets are located randomly around the campground. The tent sites can also be used for self-contained RVs. Showers, restrooms, a fire pit, a boat ramp, a short nature trail, and an observation boardwalk are available. Site #2 and restrooms are wheelchair-accessible. Children are welcome. Pets are permitted.

Reservations, fees: Sites are first-come, first-served. They cost $15 per night for tent sites, and $20 for the single RV site. Credit cards are not accepted.

Directions: From I-95 at Exit 156, drive east on County Road 512/Fellsmere Road, then turn north (left) on Roseland Road/County Road 505. The entrance is on your left, beyond Dale Wimbrow Park.

Contact: Donald MacDonald Park, 12315 Roseland Road, Roseland, FL 32957, 772/589-0087.

2 SUNSHINE TRAVEL-ENCORE RESORT VERO BEACH

🏊 🏕 🎣 🚐

Scenic rating: 5

off I-95, north of Vero Beach

This 35-acre RV resort is so civilized that garbage is picked up at your campsite, by the concrete-paved road, at 10 A.M. daily, and loud radios are forbidden. It's owned by a chain of manufactured-home communities, so expect professional landscaping and services. The park is designed for RVers looking to spend one month or longer in a resort community, but overnight travelers also show up at the large sites and plunge into the 22-by-36-foot, kidney-shaped heated pool.

King Palm Drive is the closest to nearby I-95. On the other side of the park is a pine forest. The Los Angeles Dodgers have played spring-training baseball games eight miles to the south since 1953 (4001 26th Street, Vero Beach, 772/569-6858).

Campsites, facilities: All 300 sites have full hookups, 30/50-amp electrical service, and cable TV. Some sites are pull-through. For recreation, there's a heated pool, a game room, horseshoes, miniature golf, a playground, shuffleboard, boccie ball (lawn bowling), croquet, table tennis, a lending library, two recreation halls (one with a kitchen), and scheduled winter activities. Showers, restrooms, a general store, picnic tables, rental park models, and laundry facilities are available. Restaurants and grocery stores are within three miles. Children are welcome. Leashed pets are permitted.

Reservations, fees: Reservations are advised. Sites are $22–43 per night for two people, plus $2 per extra person. Credit cards are accepted. Long-term rates are available.

Directions: From I-95 at Exit 156, drive east for one block on County Road 512/Fellsmere Road to the park entrance on your right at 108th Avenue. The park is behind McDonald's.

Contact: Sunshine Travel-Encore Resort Vero Beach, 9455 108th Avenue, Vero Beach, FL 32967, 772/589-7828 or 877/362-6736, fax 772/628-7081.

3 WHISPERING PALMS RV PARK

Scenic rating: 5

on U.S. 1, in Wabasso

Retirees escaping frosty Northern winters are targeted by this sprawling 35-acre home of not one, but two, heated pools and two recreation rooms, located four miles west of Atlantic Ocean beaches. The sunny, concrete-pad RV sites are outnumbered by the 328 mobile homes. The nicely kept park is set in a sleepy area bordered by U.S. 1 and FEC Railroad tracks. Most visitors here are from Canada. Anglers often travel a few miles northeast to the Indian River/Brevard County line to crowd the jetty at the 500-acre Sebastian Inlet State Park.

Campsites, facilities: This adult-oriented park has 257 full-hookup RV sites with 30-amp and 50-amp electrical service. Two pools, horseshoes, shuffleboard, winter social programs, two recreation rooms, and two tennis courts entertain campers. Showers, restrooms, a dump station, and laundry facilities are available. The pull-through sites are wheelchair-accessible. Groceries, snacks, and restaurants are one mile away. Children are allowed for short-term visits only. Leashed pets under 25 pounds are permitted.

Reservations, fees: Reservations are recommended. Sites are $25–35 per night for two people, plus $3 for each additional person. Credit cards are accepted. Long-term stays are OK.

Directions: From I-95 at Exit 156, drive east for six miles on County State Road 512 to U.S. 1. Turn right and continue 2.1 miles south to the campground.

Contact: Whispering Palms RV Park, 10305 U.S. 1, Sebastian, FL 32958, 772/589-3481.

4 VERO BEACH KAMP

Scenic rating: 6

on U.S. 1, north of Vero Beach

A hair salon, a ceramics shop, and other businesses set a commercial tone for the road that fronts this 14-acre campground—U.S. 1. Still, the region focuses on its pretty outdoor attributes, with Atlantic Ocean beaches two miles east, a boat ramp on the Indian River 0.5 mile from the campground, deep-sea fishing at offshore reefs, and shelling and clamming nearby. Visitors come from all over the United States, plus Canada and Germany. Favorite things to do include fishing, golfing, going to museums, surfing, and lolling around at the beach.

Campsites, facilities: Five rows of grassy RV slots line up campers side by side, about 20 sites per row, for a total of 100 sites. Seventy sites have 30-amp electrical service, and 30 have 50-amp. All sites have concrete patios, grills, and picnic tables. Tenters are allowed at two grass sites with water and electricity. For recreation, there's a pool, a playground, shuffleboard, winter social programs, and a recreation room. Showers, grills, fire rings, a dump station, cabins, a convenience store, a deli, a gift shop, cable TV, and laundry facilities are available. Restrooms, the office, and the activity building are wheelchair-accessible. Groceries and restaurants are within two miles. Children are welcome. Leashed, attended pets are permitted.

Reservations, fees: Reservations are required in winter and recommended at other times. Sites are $40 per night for two people, plus $3 for each additional person. Credit cards are accepted. Long-term rates are available.

Directions: From I-95 at Exit 156, drive east for two miles on County Road 512 to County Road 510 and turn right. Continue six miles, following the curve to the left, to U.S. 1. Turn left. The campground is 0.25 mile ahead on the right.

Contact: Vero Beach Kamp, 8850 U.S. 1, Sebastian, FL 32958, 772/589-5665 or 877/589-5643, fax 561/388-5722.

5 MIDDLETON'S FISH CAMP
🚶 🛶 �- 🐴 ♿ 🚌 ⛺

Scenic rating: 8

at Blue Cypress Lake, west of Vero Beach

Even though serious anglers try for speckled perch and bass at 6,500-acre Blue Cypress Lake, this wild region holds promise for birdwatchers, wildlife admirers, duck hunters, and anyone who doesn't mind giving up niceties like electric hookups for a night. Some Midwesterners return to this rustic campground year after year, lured by 80°F-plus winter temperatures and the call of the outdoors. The primitive camp is surrounded by huge, government-owned lands set aside for wildlife.

At dusk, deer cross the five-mile dirt road that leads to cypress-lined Blue Cypress Lake, which is named for the trees' blue appearance at sunrise. Alert campers may see otters, eagles, hawks, alligators, and osprey. Yet, as the name suggests, fishing is the highlight at the only camp on the lake, which is the headwaters to the St. Johns River. Motorboats start at $55 for four hours. You can also rent pontoon boats and kayaks.

Campsites, facilities: This primitive, county-owned camping area offers approximately a dozen or so RV sites and about 20 tent spots. There are no hookups, but showers, restrooms, a boat ramp, boat and canoe rentals, bait and tackle, fishing guides, cabins, and rental trailers are available. Most areas are said to be wheelchair-accessible. Children and leashed pets are permitted.

Reservations, fees: Sites are first-come, first-served, and there is no fee. There is a $10 deposit for pets. Credit cards are accepted for

cabin and boat rentals. The maximum stay is one week.

Directions: From I-95 at Exit 147, drive west for 18 miles on State Road 60, veering around a bend known as 20 Mile Bend, and passing a waterway called Padgett Branch. Signs will instruct you to turn right at Blue Cypress Lake Road. If you pass a microwave tower on State Road 60, then you've missed the turn to the lake. Follow Blue Cypress Lake Road for five miles to its end to reach the fish camp.

Contact: Middleton's Fish Camp, 21704 73rd Manor, Vero Beach, FL 32966, 772/778-0150, www.middletonsfishcamp.com.

6 BLUE CYPRESS CONSERVATION AREA
🚶 🛶 🚐 🐴 ⛺

Scenic rating: 8

at Blue Cypress Lake, west of Fellsmere and Vero Beach

Airboaters thunder through the area in their private craft, and duck hunters sleep here in season, but these 52,671 wild acres also hold allure for hikers and bird-watchers. Look for alligators, bald eagles, osprey, long-legged wading birds, and a few of the nation's 500 to 1,000 endangered snail kites—a dark, hawk-like bird with a tightly curled, reddish-orange beak. They sometimes nest in the conservation area's southeastern portion. There are several access points, so be sure to get a map before planning your trip.

Duck Camp is at the southern end of a four-mile-long, diked, manmade lake. From the camp, marshland stretches about one mile west to the angler haven of Blue Cypress Lake. Watch fiery orange sunsets there. Farther southeast, North Camp abuts marshland that spreads about one mile west to another diked, artificial lake on the west side of County Road 512. Marsh means mosquitoes—so bring repellent, or you'll be sorry.

Hikers can follow a network of about 20 miles

of foot trails. For a casual stroll, an unshaded, car-width hiking path runs west from the parking lot off County Road 512. From atop the levee, you'll see a mosaic of wetland communities dominated by maidencane, saw grass, and willows. The trail can be a little monotonous, but the occasional unexpected squeaks from coots and the roar of approaching airboats (usually on weekends) help enliven the walk. A 10-mile-long hiking trail starts at one of several conservation-area parking lots, this one found on the north side of State Road 60, just west of a short bridge located nine miles west of I-95. The trail goes north along Levee 77, passing a primitive campsite about 2.5 miles down, then west along Levee 76; the last four miles are considered by state staffers to be among the most scenic. You can take a break at two benches before the trail ends at a water control structure. Boating is best at Blue Cypress Lake, which is reached by a ramp west of the lake at Middleton's Fish Camp (see previous listing). You also may fish and paddle your own canoe around a manmade lake that is reachable from the boat ramp just west of County Road 512.

Campsites, facilities: Six primitive camping areas offer no hookups; most require at least a short hike to reach. A boat ramp, restrooms and canoe launch are at the main access point on the north side of State Road 60 at North Camp. Bring water, sunscreen, insect repellent, bright orange clothing during hunting season, and rain gear May–September.

Reservations, fees: Sites are first-come, first-served. Camping is free. Each site accommodates up to six people. If your party has at least seven people, get a free permit and reserve at least one week ahead by calling 386/329-4410. Maximum stay for all campers is seven days.

Directions: To reach the eastern camping area—North Camp—from I-95 (Exit 147), go west on State Road 60, then travel 7.5 miles to County Road 512, where you'll turn right (north). Continue about 3.5 miles, passing a parking area along the way, and turn left into the closest parking area to North Camp. For a map, directions, and other details about campsites, contact the water management district before your trip, or see the website listed below.

Contact: St. Johns River Water Management District, Division of Land Management, P.O. Box 1429, Palatka, FL 32178-1429, 386/329-4500 or 800/451-7106, www.sjrwmd.com.

⁊ FORT DRUM MARCH CONSERVATION AREA
🚶 🛶 🚻 🐕 ⛺

Scenic rating: 8

10 miles east of Yeehaw Junction, west of Vero Beach, between State Road 60 and Florida's Turnpike

Just south of the Blue Cypress March Conservation Area, you'll find 20,862 acres of mostly marshy, impassable wetlands. You can hike or bike three of the perimeter edges of this square-shaped plot as the trail parallels manmade canals. On the west side, where land is higher and drier than the center section, are a couple of little lakes and the Fort Drum Creek. Horseback riding, bird-watching, and boating are favored activities, but avoid hunting season, when camping is closed. The Florida Trail Association has developed the trails and three primitive campsites.

Campsites, facilities: Only tents are permitted. There are no facilities: Bring water, supplies, mosquito repellent, and everything you'll need. Children are welcome. Leashed pets are permitted.

Reservations, fees: Sites are first-come, first-served. Camping is free. Each site accommodates up to six people. If your party has at least seven people, get a free permit and reserve at least one week ahead by calling 386/329-4410. Maximum stay for all campers is seven days.

Directions: From I-95, take Exit 147 westbound on State Road 60 to the "20 Mile Bend." Pass the intersection with County Road 512 and continue west 10.9 miles to the access area on the north side.

© VISIT FLORIDA

sunrise at Vero Beach

Contact: St. Johns River Water Management District, Division of Land Management, P.O. Box 1429, Palatka, FL 32178-1429, 386/329-4500 or 800/451-7106, www.sjrwmd.com.

8 PORT ST. LUCIE RV RESORT

Scenic rating: 6

in Port St. Lucie

Port St. Lucie RV Resort fills a void for campers with large motorhomes and trailers who want to explore the Treasure Coast. Just five miles from the ocean, this well-manicured park opened in 2000 with all-new facilities. Within one block are several shopping centers, two groceries, and many restaurants; visitors can access a Wal-Mart behind the park through a side gate. In wintertime, planned activities include potluck meals, swimming

and exercises in the pool, horseshoes, and group outings.

Campsites, facilities: The park has 117 sites with full hookups, 30/50-amp electrical service, picnic tables, and concrete pads. Four sites are pull-through, and there are no size restrictions. About half the sites have cable TV. Restrooms, showers, laundry facilities, a pool, and a recreation hall with dial-up Internet access are available. All areas are wheelchair-accessible. Children are welcome, but adults are preferred. Leashed pets are permitted.

Reservations, fees: Reservations are recommended. Sites are $37–47 nightly for two people, plus $3 per extra person and $1.80 for cable TV. A onetime fee of $2 is charged for pets. Credit cards are accepted. Seasonal stays are permitted.

Directions: From I-95 southbound, take Exit 121 east to U.S. 1 and follow directions below. From I-95 northbound, use Exit 118 and go east to U.S. 1. From the Florida Turnpike, use Exit 142 and go east to U.S. 1. From the intersection of Port St. Lucie Boulevard and U.S. 1, drive north about 0.5 mile. Turn right on Jennings Road; the park will on your right about 2,000 feet ahead.

Contact: Port St. Lucie RV Resort, 3703 Jennings Road, Port St. Lucie, FL 34952, 772/337-3340 or 877/405-2333, fax 772/337-7347, http://portstluciervresort.com.

9 ROAD RUNNER TRAVEL RESORT

Scenic rating: 6

west of Fort Pierce

This 38-acre blend of citified amenities in a wooded, rural setting lures some people to live here, and others to visit. Besides the campground's heated pool and unusual offerings—such as a *pétanque* (French-style bowling) court, a par-three golf course, and th recreation halls—owners Jim and Marilyn Minix's park rules aim to satisfy urban sensibilities: Keep your campsite neat. Overnighters should place garbage bags at the paved road in front of their campsite before checking out. Long-term campers should rake lawn debris into a pile in front of their lots to be picked up. Still, the park won't soon be mistaken for a suburban subdivision, if only because of its pines and sabal palms. Roads are paved. And how many suburbs boast a fishing pond by a general store? About 40 percent of the park is occupied year-round.

For fun, boaters and anglers can drive 5–6 miles to Atlantic Ocean beaches, the Indian River, or the St. Lucie Inlet. Back at the campground, the packed winter activities schedule keeps visitors busy. A sample day: 7 A.M. walk, 8 A.M. flea market trip, 9 A.M. exercises, 2 P.M. water exercises, 7 P.M. cards. To sleep beside the park's lake, ask about the sunny, nearly treeless campsites on Lincoln Circle. For a canopy of shade trees, ask about campsites on Madison and Eisenhower Drives (although several other streets have at least some shade). The park is near the small St. Lucie County Airport.

Campsites, facilities: These 452 full-hookup campsites for tents or RVs mostly have 50-amp electrical service; 75 have 30-amp. RVs up to 45 feet in length and slideouts can be accommodated. Twelve sites are drive-through. A pool, a tennis court, a *pétanque* court, shuffleboard, horseshoes, winter activities, and three recreation halls keep campers entertained. Showers, restrooms, a restaurant, groceries, a dump station, rental park models, rental villas, the on-site convenience store, and laundry facilities are available. Most areas are wheelchair-accessible. Streets are paved. Children under 12 must be adult-supervised at the pool and other public areas. Leashed pets are permitted.

Reservations, fees: Reservations are advised. Sites are $32 per night for two people, plus $3 for each additional person. Credit cards are accepted. Long-term rates are available.

Directions: From I-95 at Exit 131B, go west on Orange Avenue/State Road 68 a short distance to the first light. Turn right at Kings Highway/State Road 713. Turn right in 2.5 miles at St. Lucie Boulevard. The campground is one mile ahead on your left.

Contact: Road Runner Travel Resort, 5500 St. Lucie Boulevard, Fort Pierce, FL 34946, 772/464-0969 or 800/833-7108, www .roadrunnertravelresort.com.

10 TREASURE COAST RV RESORT

Scenic rating: 7

west of Fort Pierce

This campground is sparkling new from the ground up. It opened in early 2006 in an unusual location where two superhighways, I-95 and Florida's Turnpike, run parallel to each other only one mile apart. This means convenience for two sets of travelers. The main drag between the two expressways is chock full of restaurants, outlet shopping, and auto/truck maintenance businesses. More than just a traveler's way stop, the park is also near Port St. Lucie golf courses, beaches, and other attractions, and many RVers have such high compliments for the pristine, modern facilities that they end up staying more than one night.

Campsites, facilities: Big rigs are easily accommodated on the 164 oversized lots, most of which encircle an artificial lake. All sites have cement pads surrounded by grass, 30/50-amp electricity, sewer hookups, cable TV, and wireless Internet access. Restrooms, showers, laundry facilities, a pool, hot tub, clubhouse with a kitchen, meeting room, covered porch for socializing, wintertime planned activities, and a security gate are provided. Children and leashed pets are welcome.

Reservations, fees: Reservations are recommended. Sites are $35–49 per night.

Directions: If traveling on I-95, take Exit 129 west at Okeechobee Road and drive 0.5 mile to South Kings Highway; turn north and proceed 0.25 mile to the park. From Florida's Turnpike, use Exit 152 and cross Okeechobee Road. Traveling north on South Kings Highway about 0.3 mile from the toll booth.

Contact: Treasure Coast RV Resort, 2550 Crossroads Parkway, Fort Pierce, FL 34945, 772/468-2099 or 866/468-2099.

11 SUNNIER PALMS NUDIST CAMPGROUND

🌊 🚐 ⛺

Scenic rating: 5

off I-95, west of Fort Pierce

BEST (

Everyone at this 24-acre park is expected to participate in the nudist lifestyle and must be nude in the pool or hot tub. There is also a definite nature orientation, and even activism: The park helped save a rare plant and a butterfly species that lost its habitat to development, by allowing the colonies to be moved to the park land. Foot trails lead through a sun-dappled forest of pines and spiky palmettos interspersed with shady oaks. Some campers at this private, flat, fenced park hike or take blankets out to lie naked in the 12 acres or so of woods. You'll get a taste of both worlds here: The reasonably close highway and fast-food joints are reminders of city life. Favorite things to do are sightseeing and fishing, and there's a potluck dinner every Sunday. Most visitors are from the Northeast and Canada.

Campsites, facilities: This nudist resort has 13 full-hookup RV sites with 50-amp electricity and picnic tables. Perhaps 100 tents can be accommodated in a field. Rigs up to 40 feet long and slideouts can be accommodated. A pool, a hot tub, organic gardening, nature trails, a playground, and a butterfly exhibit entertain campers. A certain amount of decorum is expected: "Your behavior is your passport." Part of the park is a 12-acre nature sanctuary. Showers, restrooms, a dump station, a grocery store, rental villas, and laundry facilities are available. The bathhouse is wheelchair-accessible. Groceries and restaurants are within three miles. Children are welcome. Pets are prohibited.

Reservations, fees: Reservations are necessary in winter. Sites are $45 per night, plus $1 for electricity. Credit cards are accepted. Long-term rates are available. The maximum length of stay is six months.

Directions: From I-95 at Exit 129, drive west on Okeechobee Road/State Road 70 for about 1.5 miles to the campground. The park is one mile west of Florida's Turnpike (Exit 152).

Contact: Sunnier Palms Nudist Campground, 8800 Okeechobee Road, Fort Pierce, FL 34945, 772/468-8512, www.sunnier.com.

12 OUTDOOR RESORTS AT ST. LUCIE WEST

🌊 🐕 ♿ 🚐

Scenic rating: 6

west of Port St. Lucie ,between I-95 and Florida's Turnpike

This resort is for Class A motorhomes 25 feet or longer. This should give you an idea of the kinds of amenities to expect: several swimming pools, lighted tennis courts, a golf course, and deluxe paved sites on which to park that expensive rig. It's three miles from the famous PGA Golf Club, but already has nine holes of its own on-site. About 5 percent of the park is occupied by year-round residents, and lots are for sale.

Campsites, facilities: There are 259 campsites, each with 30/50-amp electrical service, cement pads, picnic tables, full hookups, wireless Internet access, and cable TV. Motor coaches 25–45 feet long can be accommodated. On the premises are three pools, two lighted tennis courts, a nine-hole golf course, wireless Internet network, and a large clubhouse. Security and on-site staff are available 24 hours. Restrooms, showers, a dump station, three dog-walk areas, and laundry facilities are also provided. Most areas are wheelchair-accessible. Freestanding satellite dishes are not allowed. Children are welcome. Leashed pets are permitted, but only two are allowed per site.

Reservations, fees: Reservations are recommended. Sites are $45–65 per night for four people, plus $5 per extra person. No more than six people are allowed per site. Credit cards are accepted. Long-term rates are available.

Directions: From I-95, take Exit 121 onto St. Lucie West Boulevard in an eastbound direction. Drive 0.3 mile and turn left on Northwest Peacock Boulevard. Continue 1.3 miles to the park entrance on the left. From Florida's Turnpike, take Exit 152 at Fort Pierce. Follow the signs to I-95 and proceed with the directions above.

Contact: Outdoor Resorts at St. Lucie West, 800 Northwest Peacock Boulevard, Port St. Lucie, FL 34986, 772/336-1136 or 866/456-2303, fax 772/336-1193, www.outdoor-resorts-slw.com.

13 THE SAVANNAS RECREATIONAL AREA

Scenic rating: 8

east of U.S. 1, in southeastern Fort Pierce

Some people rave about the rustic Savannas, a 550-acre county park/camping getaway where boaters snag bass and visitors lazily paddle rental canoes. Inside the gate, in day-use area #2, you can eat a picnic lunch, then walk along the Everglades-like marsh on a hiking trail shaded by shaggy Australian pines. The trail leads to a sort of makeshift observation tower, where you can peer out over the saw grass and cattails. You'll hear frogs croaking—after all, this is a wild retreat. Rent a canoe for $4 hourly for an up-close view of the marsh.

Although the park is large, it feels fairly small if you don't head out into the marsh. The limited dry land is hemmed in by the watery prairie. Expect to see your neighbors from your no-frills, grassy campsite. To help minimize that, spring for a waterview site.

County promoters say the Savannas is Florida's last freshwater lagoon system. The

preserve actually extends outside this campground to take in about eight square miles of marsh and uplands between White City Road/State Road 172 and Jensen Beach Boulevard/State Road 707A. From the campground, Atlantic Ocean beaches are nine miles east, for those who want to swim or sunbathe.

Campsites, facilities: There are 33 campsites for RVs and 13 for tents. All have water and electricity; some also have sewer hookups. Canoe rentals, nature trails, a playground, a dump station, showers, restrooms, a boat ramp, a picnic shelter, and laundry facilities are available. Groceries can be purchased within two miles. A restaurant is within 10 miles. Children are welcome. Leashed dogs are permitted.

Reservations, fees: Reservations are accepted. Sites are $13–20 per night for four people, plus $1–2 for each extra person. There is an additional admission fee of $1 per car. Credit cards are accepted. RVers can stay as long as two months.

Directions: From I-95 at Exit 131A, drive east for about four miles on Orange Avenue/State Road 68. Turn right (south) at South 4th Street/U.S. 1. Continue almost five miles to Midway Road/County Road 712. Turn left and proceed east to the park entrance, about 1.5 miles ahead.

Contact: The Savannas Recreational Area, 1400 East Midway Road, Fort Pierce, FL 34982, 772/464-7855 or 800/789-5776, fax 772/464-1765, www.stlucieco.gov/leisure/savanna.htm.

14 THE VILLAGE AT NETTLES ISLAND

Scenic rating: 6

on the Atlantic Ocean, on Hutchinson Island

This 130-acre, ocean-to-river island resort feels like a residential community. Before you pull into the concrete driveway beside your RV site and personal patio, you'll follow paved roads that pass park models with attached Florida rooms, lots with docks on the Intracoastal Waterway, and maybe even a retirement-ready, double-wide mobile home with a front porch and garden. It seems like every square inch of this sunwashed barrier island is covered with villas, RVs, and park models, although roads and green ribbons of lawn separate sleeping spots. The hub of activity is at the resort's center—a clubhouse, a pool, and sports courts. From the marina (bring your own boat), you can embark on a day of boating or fishing in the Intracoastal Waterway, the Atlantic Ocean, or the Indian River Lagoon.

The Intracoastal Waterway stretches one mile from the wee backyards of western waterfront lots. RV sites are scattered throughout this barrier island off Florida's Treasure Coast. Although the island technically has 1,578 sites, only 50–125 at any given time may be open to campers who bring their own rigs. The other sites at this condominium-concept park are largely devoted to vacation rentals. February is the busiest time of the year, so call early if you'll be coming then.

Campsites, facilities: All 1,578 sites have full hookups, but only 50 or so are available for self-contained RVs staying overnight or for the season. Pop-ups and other small trailers without facilities are not allowed. For recreation, there's a pool, miniature golf, a clubhouse, horseshoes, a playground, tennis, shuffleboard, and volleyball. Showers, restrooms, a café, a dump station, a grocery store, cable TV, park models, a marina, and laundry facilities are available. Children are permitted. Leashed pets are allowed on park streets and in a dog walk in front.

Reservations, fees: Reservations are advised. Sites are $37–64 per night, plus $3 for electricity. Credit cards are accepted. Long-term stays are OK.

Directions: From Stuart, drive north on Highway A1A/Ocean Drive to Hutchinson Island past the county line. Nettles Island is located just ahead, on the left side of the road.

Contact: VNI Realty, 9803 South Ocean Drive, Jensen Beach, FL 34957, 772/229-1300, www.vnirealty.com.

15 SOUTH FORK ST. LUCIE RIVER MANAGEMENT AREA

Scenic rating: 8

west of Stuart

Here's a nice new spot near urban South Florida, but it's only accessible by canoe or on foot. Eventually, these 180 acres may become part of the planned Atlantic Ridge State Park, but until public road access issues are resolved through a neighboring residential area, you'll have to get here under your own steam. A canoe and kayak livery (South River Outfitters) is located near the highway, but the campground and official trailhead are 20 miles south, and there are no public roads to this particular spot. You will need a permit from the South Florida Water Management District to sleep at the campsite. The canoe and kayak livery offers guided trips, as well as boat rentals.

Campsites, facilities: Campsites accommodate 20 persons at a canoe landing at the sound end of the tract. Only tents are permitted. There are no facilities: Bring water, supplies, mosquito repellent, and everything you'll need. Children are welcome. Leashed pets are permitted. Children are welcome. Leashed pets are permitted.

Reservations, fees: Permits are required. Contact the water management district by phone at 561/682-6635 or 561/682-6649, or download the application from www.sfwmd.gov. Camping is free.

Directions: From I-95, take Exit 101 eastbound or a fourth of a mile on State Road 76/Kanner Highway. Turn south on Lost River Road. You'll immediately see South River Outfitters located opposite the Wendy's Restaurant. Do not keep driving toward the Halpatiokee Regional Park, which is a Martin County–operated day-use area for baseball, skating, and soccer.

Contact: For camping permits, contact the South Florida Water Management District, 3301 Gun Club Road, West Palm Beach,

561/686-8800 or toll-free in Florida 800/432-2045, www.sfwmd.gov. For boat launching or rentals, contact South River Outfitters, 7645 Lost River Road, Stuart, FL 34996, 772/223-1500.

16 RONNY'S RV RANCH

Scenic rating: 2

in Stuart

Perhaps the main attraction of this largely residential park is its convenient location—just a hop off I-95—for anyone on a long-distance journey. RVs are outnumbered by 49 mobile homes. Some sites are sunny. Others have some shade. The park is about two miles outside the town of Stuart, so while it's not in the country, neither is it a citified experience.

Campsites, facilities: These 40 RV sites have full hookups, 30-amp electrical service, and access to 80 cable TV channels. A clubhouse, restrooms, showers, and laundry facilities are available, but there's no dump station. Children are OK. Pets are permitted.

Reservations, fees: Reservations are advised. Sites are $35 a night, with long-term rates available. Credit cards are not accepted.

Directions: From I-95, take Exit 101 (Indiantown/Stuart) and go northeast about one mile on State Road 76/Kanner Highway to the campground entrance.

Contact: Ronny's RV Ranch, 5545 State Road 76/South Kanner Highway, Stuart, FL 34994, 561/287-2730.

17 PHIPPS PARK

Scenic rating: 7

on the St. Lucie Canal, west of Stuart

This 57-acre, grassy, county-operated park on the St. Lucie Canal has huge spaces and lots of room for big rigs on its grassy camping spots. Boats under 20 feet can launch from Phipps Park, while campers with bigger boats should opt for the nearby St. Lucie Lock and Dam. Feel free to keep your boat at your site. Locals and out-of-towners alike camp at the park, which is on the saltwater side of the St. Lucie Lock and Dam. Anglers take boats out to try for snook and bass. The park restrooms are not modern, but there's lots of room for everyone in the park, and you won't feel crowded, even in the high winter season. A gate locked nightly and an on-site manager provide a feel of security.

Campsites, facilities: The 54 officially numbered campsites and open field of about 17 overflow sites are for tents or RVs. No hookups are offered. Each site has a picnic table, a grill, and a fire ring. A playground, a nearby boat launch, showers, a dump station, and wheelchair-accessible restrooms are available. Restaurants, laundry facilities, a bank, and a supermarket are five or six miles away. Children are welcome. Pets are forbidden.

Reservations, fees: Reservations are not accepted. Sites are $6 per night. Credit cards are not accepted. You may stay up to 15 days per year.

Directions: From I-95, take Exit 101 and go west on State Road 76. Pass Florida's Turnpike. Turn right at Locks Road. Proceed one mile to the park entrance at right.

Contact: Phipps Park, 2175 Southwest Locks Road, Stuart, FL 34997, 772/287-6565.

18 ST. LUCIE LOCK RECREATION AREA

Scenic rating: 8

on the St. Lucie Canal, west of Stuart

This 154-acre area run by the U.S. Army Corps of Engineers combines the opportunity to commune with nature with the chance to marvel at the ingenuity of the human mind.

The drama of standing above the massive lock system and watching boats travel beneath your feet is one attraction of this restful, sunny spot on the St. Lucie Canal. Daytime picnickers and campers alike stop to watch the action. As boats spend 15–20 minutes passing through the lock, the curious look downward to read the home ports on the boat transoms to get an idea of just how far the vessels have traveled. It's an awesome sight to behold. A one-mile nature trail is available for hikers on the north side of the lock/dam, with an observation area overlooking Hog Creek. You may spot alligators and gopher tortoises near the trail and on Killingbeck Island. To the east of the campground is a 2,500-square-foot visitors center with a free lending library, a movie, and exhibits on the Okeechobee Waterway.

Tall Australian pines provide some shade for the concrete-pad RV sites. Meanwhile, boaters can motor up to this camping area and sleep aboard their vessels at the eight boat campsites. Anglers can launch from the camping area to go up the canal for bass. Others catch mullet and catfish from the lock's pier. Tip: Cross the lock if you want to try for snook. This campground is another example of the U.S. Army Corps of Engineers' taste for precision, from the immaculate sites to the attention to detail.

Campsites, facilities: Eight RV sites with 30-amp electricity and water hookups are offered. Each site has a picnic table, a grill, and a fire ring. The three grassy canal-view tent sites sit just beyond the RVs, with shaded picnic tables and fences around them. Tall Australian pines provide some shade for the remaining concrete-pad RV sites. A playground, a boat ramp, showers, a dump station, and wheelchair-accessible restrooms are available. A convenience store and a deli are two miles away; laundry facilities and a supermarket are six miles away. Children are welcome. Leashed pets are permitted.

Reservations, fees: Reservations are accepted. RVers pay $16 nightly. Credit cards are accepted. You may stay 14 days in a 30-day

period. If you're lucky and plan ahead, you can get a free campsite in exchange for 24–30 hours of weekly volunteer service; these opportunities are limited during the popular winter months.

Directions: From I-95, take Exit 101 and go west on State Road 76 for about two miles, passing Florida's Turnpike. Turn right at Locks Road. Continue 1.5 miles to the end of the road, then turn left at Canal Street and proceed to the campground.

Contact: St. Lucie Lock Recreation Area, 2170 Southwest Canal Street, Stuart, FL 34997, 772/219-4575. For reservations, call 877/444-6777 or see www.reserveamerica.com.

19 JONATHAN DICKINSON STATE PARK

🥾 🚴 🛶 🚤 🐴 👨 ♿ 🚐 ⛺

Scenic rating: 10

near the Atlantic Ocean, in Hobe Sound

This place is excellent for a family outing, because something will please almost everyone in your party. You can hike to the top of piney hills and, if you stand and look toward the Indian River in the distance, you can imagine how these were once huge sand dunes at the edge of Florida—eons ago, when the oceans were much deeper. Much of the hiking here is easy, level, and suited to a day excursion with the kids. Horseback riding is popular, as are canoeing in the Loxahatchee River, fishing, nature study, and side trips to nearby beaches. Mountain-biking trails complete the picture; ask about "Camp Murphy," which served as an Army base for 6,000 troops during World War II. You're likely to see deer, Florida sandhill cranes, wading birds, and other wild animals throughout the park.

The park is named for a Quaker merchant who shipwrecked nearby in 1696, but probably the most colorful of the historic figures is a 20th-century addition to local lor known as Trapper Nelson. Taking a canoe narrated riverboat tour up to the site of Trapper Nelson's old camp on the Loxahatchee River is highly recommend. Nelson was a hermit who came to live on the banks of the beautiful Loxahatchee during the Great Depression, eking out an existence by trapping animals for their fur. Before dying under mysterious circumstances more than three decades later, he built a small zoo at his place and added to his income by charging tourists who were passing by on the river a fee to see the menagerie. After his death the site was preserved, complete with the animal pens, his cabin, a chickee shelter (Seminole-style thatched-roof dwelling), and exotic trees, including wild almond, bamboo, sausage tree, guava, and java plum.

If you're handy with a canoe or kayak, try an all-day paddle down the Loxahatchee, designated by the federal government as the only Wild and Scenic River in this part of the state. From the spot where Indiantown Road crosses the Loxahatchee, you'll paddle seaward, past dark, brooding cypress forests to where the freshwater turns salty and mangroves appear on the banks. Some parts of the trip are achingly beautiful and serene, although you will pass underneath I-95 and Florida's Turnpike at one point. You're virtually certain to see alligators (in fact, one of the few documented cases of an alligator attacking a human occurred here a few years ago, when an old, sick gator attacked and killed a young boy). If you're lucky, you might even see a manatee, that lumbering but lovable endangered mammal also known as the sea cow. Bald eagles, once endangered but now on the upswing, also are sighted sometimes, along with the hawk-like osprey. The park rents canoes, but the area's most popular canoe livery is Canoe Outfitters of Florida (772/746-7053), which charges $50 for three people in a canoe and $40 for a kayak, with shuttle service.

Fishing is good, both in the Loxahatchee River and the nearby Indian River. Redfish, trout, and snook are among the favored game fish. Some anglers prefer surfcasting in the nearby Atlantic Ocean for whiting, pompano, and jack, while other members of the family sunbathe.

Also consider two other side trips: At the Jupiter Lighthouse and Museum, a short drive away, you can learn how Confederate soldiers captured the light and doused it—without firing a shot—to aid ships running the Yankee blockade. Also, don't miss a trip to Blowing Rocks Preserve (772/747-3113), within a 30-minute drive, where water jets up through blowholes in an intriguing rock formation in what's known as Anastasia limestone. The wave action has worn the relatively soft stone into fascinating and beautiful shapes. At high tide, watch water spout through the blowholes. At low tide, explore the caves and tidal pools. Guided nature walks are offered Thursday at 2 P.M. and Sunday at 11 A.M.

Campsites, facilities: All 135 back-in sites have water and 30-amp electrical hookups; 16 also have 50-amp service. Each site has a grill, a fire ring, and a picnic table. None of the sites are pull-through. Boat tours, canoe rentals, a playground, horseback-riding trails, four nature trails, and a bicycling trail entertain campers. Showers, a boat ramp, limited groceries, and rental cabins are available. About two miles away are restaurants, bait, and laundry facilities. Some areas of the park are wheelchair-accessible. Children are welcome. One pet is permitted in the campground with proof of vaccination.

Reservations, fees: Reservations are recommended; contact ReserveAmerica at 800/336-3521 or reserveamerica.com. Sites are $22 per night for up to eight people. Credit cards are accepted. The maximum stay is 14 nights.

Directions: From I-95, take Exit 87A and go east on State Road 706. Turn left at U.S. 1. Look for the park entrance on the left.

Contact: Jonathan Dickinson State Park, 16450 Southeast Federal Highway, Hobe Sound, FL 33455, 772/546-2771, www.floridastateparks.org.

20 KITCHING CREEK BACKCOUNTRY SITE

👫 🎣 ⛺

Scenic rating: 9

In Jonathan Dickinson State Park

This primitive campground on the Florida National Scenic Trail is great if you want to get away from all the trappings of modern society, but there is a price to pay—you have to hike approximately 9.5 miles from the trailhead. The first third or so of the route runs through the ancient beach dunes that once protected this part of Florida from the Atlantic Ocean, back when the Earth was warmer and the seas much higher than today. Now you'll find stunted scrub oaks and pines along these ridges, which will make the early going a little difficult if you're used to Florida flatlands. After about three miles, though, the trail flattens out into the pine woods that mark many a Florida backcountry site and provide the setting for this campground. You'll recognize the place because there's a fire ring on the ground.

You have to show up at least 3.5 hours before sundown, but we recommend a much earlier start, even if you're a fast hiker. That head start will ensure that you get to the site before others do, particularly on fall and winter weekends. Kitching Creek itself is a fairly small freshwater stream at this point. It's way upstream of the Loxahatchee River, but dedicated freshwater anglers may want to try their luck.

Campsites, facilities: No more than eight backpackers may share these three primitive campsites. There is a pit toilet. Water is available, but you'll have to treat it before drinking. You must bring everything you'll need, including extra water, food, mosquito repellent, camping supplies, and bags to pack out trash. Human waste must be packed out as well. Children are welcome. Pets are prohibited.

Reservations, fees: Reservations are not accepted. Campsites are claimed on a first-come, first-served basis at the park entrance station. Fees are $3 per night per adult and $2 per child. Major credit cards are accepted.

Directions: From I-95, take Exit 87A and go east on State Road 706. Turn left at U.S. 1. Look for the park entrance on the left.

Contact: Jonathan Dickinson State Park, 16450 Southeast Federal Highway, Hobe Sound, FL 33455, 772/546-2771.

21 SCRUB JAY BACKCOUNTRY SITE

👫 ⛺

Scenic rating: 9

In Jonathan Dickinson State Park

Of the two backcountry sites reserved for hikers at one of Florida's loveliest state parks, this is the closest to the trailhead. Show up by the mandated deadline of 2 P.M. (preferably much earlier) to begin your 5.6-mile hike. You'll make your way through about three miles of gently rolling ancient beach dunes now covered by stunted scrub oaks and pine trees. Go another two miles or so through pine flatwoods to reach the campsite. It's on the same trail as the Kitching Creek site in this chapter.

Campsites, facilities: No more than eight backpackers may share these three primitive campsites. There are no facilities. Water is available, but you'll have to treat it before drinking. You must bring everything you'll need, including extra water, food, mosquito repellent, camping supplies, and bags to pack out trash. Human waste must be packed out as well. Children are welcome. Pets are prohibited.

Reservations, fees: Reservations are not accepted. Campsites are claimed on a first-come, first-served basis at the park entrance station. Fees are $3 per night per adult and $2 per child. Major credit cards are accepted.

Directions: From I-95, take Exit 87A and go east on State Road 706. Turn left at U.S. Look for the park entrance on the left.

Contact: Jonathan Dickinson State Park, 16450 Southeast Federal Highway, Hobe Sound, FL 33455, 772/546-2771.

22 EAGLE VIEW EQUESTRIAN SITE

Scenic rating: 8

in Jonathan Dickinson State Park

This is a site designed specifically for people with horses. At one time, there was an old stable house here, a remnant of the time when this land was privately owned. Bring some kind of portable fencing to keep your horse contained, although using a system of ground stakes is permissible. The land is part of a multiuse area studded with sabal palmettos, wax myrtles, and tall pines. Some pockets will get muddy at wetter times of the year.

Campsites, facilities: Three equestrian campsites accommodate up to three parties. No facilities are provided, except for fire rings and picnic tables. You must bring everything you'll need, including water, food, mosquito repellent, camping gear, and bags to pack out trash. RVs should be self-contained; there are no toilets. Children are welcome. Pets are prohibited.

Reservations, fees: Call ahead to make arrangements to bring your horse. Fees are $3 per night per adult and $2 per child; additional fees are required for horses. Major credit cards are accepted.

Directions: From I-95, take Exit 87A and go east on State Road 706. Turn left at U.S. 1. Look for the park entrance on the left.

Contact: Jonathan Dickinson State Park, 16450 Southeast Federal Highway, Hobe Sound, FL 33455, 772/546-2771.

23 WEST JUPITER WETLANDS MANAGEMENT AREA

Scenic rating: 2

west of Jupiter

Part of the state's continuing Save Our Rivers (SOR) program of purchasing and preserving wetlands, this 1,922-acre tract provides hiking and canoeing within easy distance of the urban areas of Palm Beach and Martin counties. You can camp anywhere along the south side of the canal that crosses this rectangular shaped property (but not elsewhere). You are allowed to canoe in the interior ponds, but not in the canal. Swimming and boating are prohibited. Eventually, this area (sometimes known as Pal Mar) may be developed and opened to hunting.

Campsites, facilities: There are no facilities, and this area is accessible only on foot from designated access points on State Road 706 (Indiantown Road). Bring water, food, and everything you'll need. Children are welcome. Leashed pets are permitted.

Reservations, fees: Permits are required. Contact the water management district by phone at 561/682-6635 or 561/682-6649, or download the application from www.sfwmd .gov. Camping is free.

Directions: From I-95, drive west from Exit 87A on State Road 706. After the intersection with State Road 711, continue west about two miles. The management area is on your right. If you reach State Road 710, you're gone too far.

Contact: For camping permits, contact the South Florida Water Management District, 3301 Gun Club Road, West Palm Beach, FL, 561/686-8800 or 800/432-2045 (toll-free in Florida only), www.sfwmd.gov.

RESOURCES

© PETER TRITLEY

Resources

U.S. NATIONAL FORESTS

For further information about National Forests in Florida, write, call, or visit the following forest services:

Apalachicola National Forest
www.r8web.com/florida/forests/
apalachicola.htm
Divided into two ranger districts:
Apalachicola Ranger District
P.O. Box 579
Bristol, FL 32321
850/643-2282

Wakulla Ranger District
57 Taft Drive
Crawfordville, FL 32327
850/926-3561

Florida Forest Supervisor's Office
325 John Knox Road, Suite F-100
Tallahassee, FL 32303
850/523-8500
TDD: 850/942-9351

Ocala National Forest
www.r8web.com/florida/forests/ocala.htm
Divided into two ranger districts:
Seminole Ranger District
40929 State Road 19
Umatilla, FL 32784
352/669-3153

Lake George Ranger District
17147 East Highway 40
Silver Springs, FL 34488
352/625-2520

Osceola National Forest
P.O. Box 70
Olustee, FL 32072
386/752-2577
www.r8web.com/florida/forests/osceola.htm

USDA Forest Service
Southern Region
1720 Peachtree Road Northwest
Atlanta, GA 30367
404/347-4177
www.fs.fed.us/r8/index.php

U.S. NATIONAL PARKS

For further information about National Park units in Florida, write, call, or visit the following websites:

Big Cypress National Preserve
33100 Tamiami Trail East
Ochopee, FL 34141
239/695-1201
www.nps.gov/bicy

Biscayne National Park
9700 Southwest 328th Street
Homestead, FL 33033-5634
305/230-1144 or 305/230-7275
www.nps.gov/bisc

Canaveral National Seashore Park Headquarters
308 Julia Street
Titusville, FL 32796
407/267-1110
www.nps.gov/cana

Castillo de San Marcos National Monument
One South Castillo Drive
St. Augustine, FL 32084
904/829-6506
www.nps.gov/casa

De Soto National Memorial
P.O. Box 15390
Bradenton, FL 34280
941/792-0458
fax 941/792-5094
www.nps.gov/deso

Everglades National Park
40001 State Road 9336
Homestead, FL 33034-6733
305/242-7700
www.nps.gov/ever

**Fort Caroline National Memorial/
Timucuan Preserve**
12713 Fort Caroline Road
Jacksonville, FL 32225
904/641-7155
www.nps.gov/foca

Fort Matanzas National Monument
8635 Highway A1A South
St. Augustine, FL 32080
904/471-0116
www.nps.gov/foma

**Gulf Islands National Seashore Florida
District**
1801 Gulf Breeze Parkway
Gulf Breeze, FL 32561
850/934-2600
www.nps.gov/guis

Reservations Service
800/365-CAMP (800/365-2267)
www.recreation.gov

Southeast Region
National Park Service
100 Alabama Street Southwest
1924 Building
Atlanta, GA 30303
404/562-3100
www.nps.gov

**Timucuan Ecological and
Historic Preserve**
13165 Mount Pleasant Road
Jacksonville, FL 32225
(or write to:
12713 Fort Caroline Road
Jacksonville, FL 32225)
904/221-5568
www.nps.gov/timu

U.S. FISH AND WILDLIFE SERVICE

For further information about U.S. Fish and Wildlife Service units, including National Wildlife Refuges in Florida, visit the following websites:

National Wildlife Refuges directory
www.fws.gov/refuges

Southeast Regional Office
www.fws.gov/southeast

U.S. ARMY CORPS OF ENGINEERS

The U.S. Army Corps of Engineers regulates, among other things, recreational activities at several sites in Florida. For more information, contact:

Jacksonville District
P.O. Box 4970
Jacksonville, FL 32232-0019
Public Affairs Office:
904/232-2568
fax 904/232-2237
www.saj.usace.army.mil
Governs Lake Okeechobee and most of Florida

South Florida Operations Office
525 Ridgelawn Road
Clewiston, FL 33440-5399
863/983-8101
www.saj.usace.army.mil/sfoo/index.html

Mobile District
P.O. Box 2288
Mobile, AL 36628-0001
334/471-5966
www.sam.usace.army.mil/op/rec/seminole
Governs Lake Seminole on the Florida-Georgia state border

**Lake Seminole Resource
Management Office**
P.O. Box 96
Chattahoochee, FL 32324
229/662-2001

FLORIDA STATE PARKS

Almost 150 parks are part of the award-winning Florida State Parks system. The *Florida State Parks guide* is available from:

Florida Department of Environmental Protection
Parks Information
Mail Station #535
3900 Commonwealth Boulevard
Tallahassee, FL 32399-3000
850/245-2157
www.floridastateparks.org

Order the guide online or download park information and park maps at www.florida stateparks.org/communications/feedback .cfm?Form=ParkGuide. You can search for individual Florida State Parks at www.florida stateparks.org/FindaPark.cfm.

FLORIDA DIVISION OF FORESTRY

For a trail-walker's guide to exploring Florida's state forests, visit www.fl-dof.com/forest_ recreation/trailwalker_index.html, which lists individual trails throughout the state.

For equestrian trails, see www.fl-dof.com/ forest_recreation/trailtrotter_index.html.

For information about Florida's 30 state forests, contact:

Florida Division of Forestry
3125 Conner Boulevard
Tallahassee, FL 32399-1650
850/488-4274
fax 850/488-0863
www.fl-dof.com

Download state forest maps in Adobe Acrobat format at www.fl-dof.com/state_forests/ index.html.

Florida Division of Forestry Field Unit/District Offices

Blackwater Forestry Center
11650 Munson Highway
Milton, FL 32570
850/957-6140
fax 850/957-6143

Bunnell District Office
5001 U.S. Highway 1
North Bunnell, FL 32110
904/446-6785
fax 904/446-6789

Caloosahatchee District Office
10941 Palm Beach Boulevard
Fort Myers, FL 33905
239/690-3500
fax 239/690-3504

Chipola River Forestry Center
715 West 15th Street
Panama City, FL 32401
850/872-4175
Fax 850/872-4879

Everglades District
3315 Southwest College Avenue
Davie, FL 33314
954/475-4120
fax 954/475-4126

Jacksonville District
7247 Big Oaks Road
Bryceville, FL 32009
904/266-5001
fax 904/266-5018

Lakeland District Office
5745 South Florida Avenue
Lakeland, FL 33813
863/648-3163
fax 863/648-3169

Myakka River District Office
4723 53rd Avenue East
Bradenton, FL 34203
941/751-7627
fax 941/751-7631

Orlando Office
8431 South Orange Blossom Trail
Orlando, FL 32809
407/856-6512
fax 407/856-6514

Perry District Office
618 Plantation Road
Perry, FL 32348
850/838-2299
fax 850/838-2284

Suwannee District Office
Route 7, P.O. Box 369
Lake City, FL 32055
386/758-5700
fax 386/758-5725

Tallahassee District
865 Geddie Road
Tallahassee, FL 32304
850/488-1871
fax 850/922-2107

Waccasassa Forestry Center
1600 Northeast 23rd Avenue
Gainesville, FL 32609
352/955-2005
fax 352/955-2125

Withlacoochee Forestry Center
15019 Broad Street
Brooksville, FL 34601-4201
352/754-6777
fax 352/754-6751

SELECTED INDIVIDUAL STATE FORESTS
Blackwater River State Forest
11650 Munson Highway
Milton, FL 32570
850/957-6140
fax 850/957-6143

Cary State Forest
7465 Pavilion Road
Bryceville, FL 32009
904/266-5021 or 904/266-5022

Etoniah Creek State Forest
390 Holloway Road
Florahome, FL 32140
386/329-2552
fax: 386/329-2554

Goethe State Forest
9110 Southeast County Road 337
Dunnellon, FL 34431
352/465-8585
fax 352/465-8515

Jennings State Forest
1337 Longhorn Road
Middleburg, FL 32068
904/291-5530

Lake George State Forest
5460 North Highway 17
DeLeon Springs, FL 32130
386/985-7822

Lake Talquin State Forest
865 Geddie Road
Tallahassee, FL 32304
850/488-1871
fax 850/922-2107

Lake Wales Ridge State Forest
851 County Road 630 East
Frostproof, FL 33843
865/635-8589

Little Big Econ State Forest
1350 Snow Hill Road
Geneva, FL 32732
407/971-3500

Myakka State Forest
2000 South River Road
Englewood, FL 34223
941/460-1333

Okaloacoochee State Forest
6265 County Road 832
Felda, FL 33930
863/674-4679

Picayune Strand State Forest
2121 52nd Avenue Southeast
Naples, FL 34117
239/348-7557
fax 239/348-7557

Pine Log State Forest
5583-A Longleaf Road
Ebro, Fl 32437
850/535-2888

Point Washington State Forest
5865 East U.S. Highway 98
Santa Rosa Beach, Fl 32459
850/231-5800

Ralph E. Simmons State Forest
Route 3, Box 299
Hillard, FL 32046
904/845-3597

Seminole State Forest
Leesburg Forestry Station, 9610 CR 44
Leesburg, FL 34788
352/360-6675 or 352/360-6667

Tate's Hell State Forest
290 Airport Road
Carrabelle, FL 32322
850/697-3734
fax 850/697-2892

Tiger Bay State Forest
4316 West International Speedway
   Boulevard
Daytona Beach, FL 32124
386/226-0250

Twin Rivers State Forest
7620 133rd Road
Live Oak, FL 32060
386/208-1460

Wakulla State Forest
3674 Bloxham Cutoff Road
Crawfordville, Florida 32327
850421-3101
fax 850421-3100

Welaka State Forest
P.O. Box 174
Welaka, FL 32193-0174
386/467-2388

Withlacoochee State Forest
15003 Broad Street
Brooksville, FL 34601
352/754-6896

FLORIDA FISH AND WILDLIFE CONSERVATION COMMISSION

The Florida Fish and Wildlife Conservation
Commission supervises hunting and fishing
activities, as well as wildlife conservation. For
more information, contact:

**Florida Fish and Wildlife
Conservation Commission**
620 South Meridian Street
Tallahassee, FL 32399-1600
850/488-4676
http://myfwc.com

For recreation use permits, hunting season
information, freshwater and saltwater fishing
licenses, and information about wildlife management area regulations, see http://myfwc
.com/license_permit.

Florida Fish and Wildlife Conservation Commission District Offices

North Central Region
3377 East U.S. Highway 90
Lake City, FL 32055-8713
386/758-0525

Northeast Region
1239 Southwest 10th Street
Ocala, FL 34474-2797
352/732-1225

Northwest Region
3911 Highway 2321
Panama City, FL 32409-1658
850/265-3676

South Region
8535 Northlake Boulevard
West Palm Beach, FL 33412
561/625-5122

Southwest Region
3900 Drane Field Road
Lakeland, FL 33811-1299
863/648-3203

FLORIDA WATER MANAGEMENT DISTRICTS

In addition to managing the quality and quantity of water throughout Florida, five water management districts provide recreational opportunities on lands they control. Contact the following:

Northwest Florida Water Management District
81 Water Management Drive
Havana, FL 32333
850/539-5999
fax 850/539-2777
www.nwfwmd.state.fl.us

Suwannee River Water Management District
9225 County Road 49
Live Oak, FL 32060
386/362-1001
www.srwmd.state.fl.us

St. Johns River Water Management District
4049 Reid Street
Palatka, FL 32177
386/329-4500 or 800/451-7106
http://sjr.state.fl.us

South Florida Water Management District
3301 Gun Club Road
West Palm Beach, FL 33406
561/686-8800
www.sfwmd.gov

Southwest Florida Water Management District
2379 Broad Street
Brooksville, FL 34604
352/796-7211
www.swfwmd.state.fl.us

Florida has a rapidly growing program for the development of new trails. For more information, contact:

Cross Florida Greenway Field Office
8282 Southeast Highway 314
Ocala, FL 34470
352/236-7143

Office of Greenways and Trails
Florida Department of
Environmental Protection
3900 Commonwealth Boulevard, MS 795
Tallahassee, FL 32399-2400
850/245-2052 or 877/822-5208
www.dep.state.fl.us/gwt

ACTIVE VOLUNTEERING

All outdoors-oriented agencies or civic groups need money, but some also want your energy. The following would be glad for volunteer help or hands-on support.

Florida State Parks

If you are interested in volunteering at a particular state park or in becoming a campground host, contact the park directly. Each park screens its own volunteers. An application can be downloaded online or by contacting:

Coordinator of Volunteer Services
Bureau of Operational Services
Division of Recreation and Parks
3900 Commonwealth Boulevard, MS 535
Tallahassee, FL 32399
http://floridastateparks.org/volunteers

Florida Trail Association
5415 Southwest 13th Street
Gainesville, FL 32608
352/378-8823 or
877-HIKE-FLA (877-445-3352)
fta@florida-trail.org
www.florida-trail.org

Friends of Florida State Forests
3125 Conner Boulevard, Suite C-25
Tallahassee, FL 32399-1650
850/414-9852
www.floridastateforests.org

Volunteer Florida

www.volunteerflorida.org
This statewide organization coordinates volunteer efforts for a variety of good causes. Local opportunities are listed online.

Index

Page numbers in **bold**
indicate maps.

A
A Camper's World: 108
Acosta Creek Harbor:
194–195
Adelaide Shores RV Resort:
286–287
Adventures Unlimited
Outdoor Center: 55
Alabama border: **50,** 51
Alafia River RV Resort:
492–493
Alafia River State Park:
493–494
Alexander Springs
Campground: 230
Alligator Creek: 598–599
Alligator Creek Canoe Sites:
598–599
Alligator Mobile Home and
RV Park: 442
Aloha RV Park: 266–267
Anastasia State Park: 182–183
Anclote Key: 404–405
Anclote Key State Preserve
Boat-In Sites: 404–405
Andy's Travel Trailer Park:
358
A-OK Campground:
272–273
Apalachee Bay: 125–126
Apalachicola National
Forest: **98,** 117–121
Apalachicola River: **74,**
92–93
Apalachicola River Water
Management Area: 92–93
Apopka: **298,** 318, 320–321,
340–342
Arbor Terrace RV Resort:
426
Arbuckle Creek: 291
Arcadia: **416,** 429–430,
431–433, 437–438,
439–440

Arcadia's Peace River
Campground: 429–430
Arrowhead Campsites: 81
Arrowhead Campsites and
Mobile Home Park: 211
Aruba RV Park: 457–458
Astor: **204,** 222–223
Astor Landing Campground
and Marina: 222–223
Astor Park: 221–222
Atlantic Beach: **160,**
166–167
Auburndale: 262–263
Avon Park: **260,** 286–289,
293–294
Avon Park Air Force Range:
293

B
Bahia Honda Key: 614
Bahia Honda State Park: 614
Baker: **50,** 53, 54
Baker Acres RV Ranch: 352
Baldwin: **160,** 166
Barrington Hills RV Resort:
347–348
Barrs Landing: 199
Bartow: **260,** 271
Bass Haven Campground:
76
Bay Aire RV Park: 405
Bayard Conservation Area:
179
Bay Bayou RV Resort: 490
Bay Road: 495
Bayview RV Resort: 68
Beachcomber Outdoor
Resort: 182
Bear Creek Tract: 103–104
Bear Island: 568
Bear Lake: 52
Bear Lake Recreation Area:
52–53
Belle Glade Marina
Campground: 475
Belleview: **204,** 228
Ben's Hitching Post: 216

Beverly Beach: **176,** 190
Beverly Beach Camptown:
190
Bickley Park: 410
Big Buck Canoe Site:
322–323
Big Cypress National
Preserve: **556,** 560–564,
568
Big Cypress RV Resort: 481
Big Cypress Seminole Indian
Reservation: 481–482
Big Cypress Trail Lakes
Campground: 560–561
Big Lagoon State Park:
60–61
Big Lake Lodge and RV
Park: 463
Big Oak RV Park: 106
Big Oaks River Resort and
Campground: 155–156
Big Oaks RV Park: 330–331
Big "O" RV Resort: 462
Big Pine Key: **606,** 615
Big Pine Key Fishing Lodge:
615
Big Shoals Conservation
Area: 115
Big Tree RV Resort: 431
Billy Lake: 270
Biscayne National Park:
530, 549–550
Black Creek Ravines
Conservation Area: 177
Blackwater River State
Forest: **50,** 52–54, 55
Blackwater River State Park:
55
Blountstown: **74,** 90–91
Blue Cypress Conservation
Area: 627–628
Blue Cypress Lake: **624,**
627–628
Blue Fin-Rock Harbor:
609–610
Blue Parrot Camping Park:
304–305

Blue Spring State Park:
245–246
Bluewater Key RV Park: 617
Boca Chita Key Boat-In
Sites: 549–550
Bonita Beach Trailer Park:
517–518
Bonita Lake RV Resort:
519–520
Bonita Springs: **500,** 517–520
Bow and Arrow
Campground: 163
Bowling Green: 284
Boyd's Key West Camp-
ground: 618
Bradenton: **416,** 420–421,
422, 423–426
Bradford Motel and
Campground: 146–147
Brandon: **486,** 490–492
Breezy Acres Campground:
152
Breezy Hill RV Resort: 537
Brentwood Lake Camping:
328–329
Brevard County: 380–381,
390–391
Briarwood Travel Villa:
409–410
Bristol: **98,** 99–100, 117
Broad River: 582–584
Broad River Boat/Canoe
Sites: 582–583
Brooksville: **298,** 325,
326–327, 328–331, 334
Bryn Mawr Ocean Resort:
186
B's Marina and
Campground: 156
Buckhead Ridge: 460–461
Buckhead Ridge Marina:
460–461
Buck Lake: 380–481
Buck Lake Conservation
Area: 380–381
Buffalo Tram Boat/Canoe
Site: 323–324
Bull Creek: 270
Bull Creek Campground:
197

Bull Creek Wildlife
Management Area:
270–271
Bulow Plantation Resort:
191–192
Burns Lake Campground:
561
Bushnell: **298,** 334–335
Buster Island Primitive
Campground: 278–279
Buttenbach Mine
Campground: 331–332
Buttonwood Bay: 449–450

C
Caladesi Island: **400,**
407–408
Caladesi Island State Park:
407–408
Caloosahatchee Regional
Park: 505
Caloosahatchee River: **448,**
453–456, **500,** 503–504,
505
Camel Lake: 117
Camelot RV Park: 392–393
Camp Cozy Canoe/
Backpacking Site: 322
Camper's Holiday Travel
Park: 326–327
Camper's Inn: 88–89
Camper Village of America:
226–227
Camp Florida Resort:
452–453
Camp Inn Resorts: 275–276
Camp Lemora RV Park: 488
Camp Lonesome Boat/
Canoe Sites: 583–584
Camp Mack's River Resort:
279
Camp 'N' Water Outdoor
Resort: 233–234
Canaveral National Seashore
Beach Camping: 379
Canaveral National Seashore
Island Camping: 380
Canepatch Boat/Canoe Sites:
584–585

Canoe Creek Campground:
269
Cape Canaveral: **378,**
379–380, 385–386
Caravelle Ranch Wildlife
Management Area: 195
Carrabelle: 122–123
Carrabelle Palms RV Park:
122–123
Cary State Forest: **160,** 166
Caryville: 77–78, 83
Casa Loma Estates: 388
Casey Jones Campground:
141
Casselberry: 344
Cattail Creek RV Park: 156
Cayo Costa Island: 507
Cayo Costa State Park
Boat-In Sites: 507–508
C. B. Smith Park: 545
Cedar Key: **138,** 153–154
Cedar Key Sunset Isle Park:
153–154
Cedar Lakes RV Park and
Campground: 57–58
Cedar Pines Campground:
58–59
Central Park of Haines City:
265
Century: **50,** 51
C-54 Canal: 393–394
Chassahowitzka River
Campground and
Recreation Area: 235
Chatham River: 574–575
Chattahoochee: **98,** 99, 101
Chattahoochee River: **74,** 79
Chattahoochee/ Tallahassee
West KOA: 101
Chief Aripeka Travel Park:
326
Chiefland: 151–152
Chipley: **74,** 78–79
Choctawhatchee East
Rivers: 83
Choctawhatchee River:
77–78
Choctawhatchee River Water
Management Area Boat-In
Sites: 77–78

Choctawhatchee River Water Management Area Hike-In Sites: 78
Choctawhatchee River Water Management Area Southern Boat-In Sites: 83
Chokoloskee Island: 559–560
Chokoloskee Island Park: 559
Christmas: 344
Christmas Airstream Park: 344–345
Chuluota: **298,** 343–344
Citrus Hill Park and Sales: 350
Citrus Hills RV Park: 490–491
Citrus Park: 518–519
Clarcona Horseman's Park: 341–342
Clearwater Lake Recreation Area: 232
Clearwater–Tarpon Springs KOA: 406
Clerbrook Resort: 337
Clermont: 337–339, 363
Clewiston: **448,** 470–474
Clewiston/Lake Okeechobee KOA: 470–471
Clover Leaf Forest RV Park: 329
Clubhouse Beach Hike-In or Boat/Canoe Sites: 595–596
Club Naples RV Resort: 522–523
Cocoa: **378,** 386
Coe's Landing: 105–106
Coldwater Recreation Area: 52
Collier Seminole State Park: 558
Coopertown: 564–565
Cortez: 422–423
Cotton Landing: 117
Country Aire Estates: 349
Country Club Estates: 434–435
Countryside RV Park: 310–311

Craig's RV Park: 432–433
Crescent City: 196–197
Crescent City Campground: 196
Crews Lake: 348
Crews Lake Park: 348
Crooked Hook RV Resort: 473–474
Crooked River Campground: 333–334
Croom Tract Withlacoochee State Forest: 331–334
Cross City: 132–133, 149
Crystal Isle RV Resort: 232–233
Crystal Lake RV Park: 380
Crystal Lake Village RV and Mobile Home Park: 285
Crystal River: 155–156, **204,** 223–224, 225, 232–233
Curry Hammock State Park: 612
Cypress Gardens Mobile Home and RV Park: 271–272
Cypress Glen Campground: 333
Cypress Isle RV Park and Marina: 450
Cypress Lake Fish Camp and RV: 269–270
Cypress Woods RV Resort: 507

D
Dade City: **298,** 331, 336, 348–350
Dade County: 546–547
Darwin's Place Boat/Canoe Sites: 573–574
Davenport: 369
Davie: 544–545
Daytona Beach: **240,** 243–244
Daytona Beach Campground: 252–253
De Funiak Springs: **50,** 66–67, **74,** 75–77
Dead Lake: 197
Dead Lakes Park: 91–92

Dead River: 314–315
DeBary: **240,** 247–248, 249–250
Deer Creek RV Golf Resort: 371
DeLand: **240,** 244–245
DeLand/Orange City KOA: 247
Del-Raton Travel Trailer Park: 536
Delray Beach: **530,** 536
Deltona: **240,** 250
Destin: **50,** 68–70, 85–86
Destin RV Beach Resort: 68–69
Disney's Fort Wilderness Campground: 363–364
Disney World: 266, **299,** 363–368, 369–374
Donald MacDonald Park: 625
Dover: **486,** 489–490
Dove Rest RV Park: 81–81
Dr. Julian G. Bruce St. George Island State Park: 122
Dry Tortugas National Park/Fort Jefferson Boat-In or Fly-In Sites: 619–620
Dundee: 265–266
Dunedin: **400,** 407–408
Dunedin RV Resort: 407
Dunnellon: **204,** 225–226
Dunns Creek Conservation Area: 195–196
DuPuis Management Area: 478–479
DuPuis Management Area Equestrian Center and Campground: 479–480

E
Eagle Lake: 272–273
Eagle's Landing RV Park: 56
Eagle View Equestrian Site: 638
East Bank Campground, Lake Seminole: 99
East Cape Sable Boat/Canoe Sites: 596–597

East Clubhouse Beach Hike-
In or Boat/Canoe Sites: 595
East Lake Fish Camp: 362
East Lake Tohopekaliga: 362
Eastpoint: 121–122
East Tower: 167–168
Ebb Tide RV Park: 511
Ebro: 83–84
Econfina Creek: 84–85
Econfina Creek Water
Management Area: 84–85
Econfina River Resort: 126
Econlockhatchee River:
342–343
Edward Medard Park and
Reservoir: 491–492
Eglin Air Force Base: **50,**
66–67
E. G. Simmons Park: 494
El Governor RV
Campground: 93
Elite Resorts at Citrus
Valley: 363
Elite Resorts at Little Orange
Lake: 149–150
Elite Resorts at Salt Springs:
209
El Jobean: **416,** 440
Ellenton: 420
Ellenton Gardens Travel
Resort: 420
Ellie Ray's River Landing:
142–143
Elliott Key Boat-In Sites:
550
El Mar RV Resort: 618–619
Emeralda Marsh
Conservation Area:
229–230
Emerald Beach RV Park:
63–64
Emerald Coast RV Beach
Resort: 87
Enchanted Lakes Estates:
392
Encore RV Park—Ocala: 206
Encore RV Park—Tampa:
353
Ernest Coe Hike-In/
Bicycle-In Site: 601

Escambia River: **50,** 56–57
Escambia River Water
Management Area: 56–57
Estero: **500,** 516–517
Estero Island: 510
Eustis: 316–317
Everglades: 481–482,
543–544, **556,** 565–566
Everglades Adventures RV
and Sailing Resort: 476
Everglades City: **556,**
558–560
Everglades Holiday Park:
565–567
Everglades National Park:
556, 570–602
E-Z Stop RV Park: 142

F
Fallen Oak Primitive
Campground: 278
Falling Waters State Park:
78–79
Fanning Springs: 152
Faver-Dykes State Park: 188
F. Burton Smith Regional
Park: 386–387
Fellsmere (Space Coast):
393–394
Fellsmere (Treasure Coast):
627–628
Fiesta Grove RV Resort: 417
Fiesta Key Resort KOA
Kampground and Motel:
610
Fijian RV Park: 467–468
Fisheating Creek: 451–452
Fisheating Creek
Campground: 451–452
Fisherman's Cove Resort:
418–419
Flagler Beach: **176,** 189,
190–193, 197
Flagler by the Sea: 189
Flamingo Campground: 567
Flamingo Lake RV Resort:
163–164
Floral City: 301–302, 303
Florida Bay: **556,** 567,
595–596, 599–601

Florida Camp Inn: 369
Florida Caverns State Park:
80–81
Florida City: 548–549
Florida National Scenic
Trail: 178–179
Florida National Scenic
Trail/Chuluota: 343–344
Florida National Scenic
Trail/Osceola National
Forest: 168–169
Florida Pines Mobile Home
Court: 435
Flying Eagle: 302–303
Fore Lake: 217–218
Fore Lake Campground:
217–218
Forest Lake RV Resort: 351
Fort Braden Tract: 104
Fort Clinch State Park:
161–162
Fort Cooper State Park: 301
Fort de Soto Park Camp-
ground: 412
Fort Drum March Conserva-
tion Area: 628
Fort George: 164–165
Fort Lauderdale: **530,** 539,
540–541, 565–566
Fort Myers: **500,** 501–502,
504, 506–507, 509,
514–516
Fort Myers Beach: **500,**
510–514
Fort Myers Beach
RV Resort: 512
Fort Myers/Pine Island
KOA: 508–509
Fort Myers RV Resort:
514–515
Fort Ogden: **416,** 438–439
Fort Pickens Campground:
62
Fort Pierce: **624,** 629–631.
632
Fort Summit KOA Camping
Resort: 370
Fort Walton Beach: **50,**
63–64, 65
Fort White: 143–144

Fountain: 84–85
Fred C. Babcock/
  Cecil M. Webb Wildlife
  Management Area: **500,**
  501
Fred Gannon Rocky Bayou
  State Park: 67–68
Freeport: **50,** 66, **74,** 82
Frog Creek Campground
  and RV Park: 417
Frontier Campground: 328
Frostproof: 274–276
Fruitland Park: 305–306

G
Gainesville: **138,** 147–148,
  149, 206
Gamble Rogers Memorial
  State Recreation Area:
  190–191
Gator Park: 564–565
Gator's RV: 458–459
Gemini Springs: 249–259
Georgetown: **176,** 197–198
Georgetown Marina and
  Lodge: 197–198
Georgia border: 79
Ginnie Springs Resort:
  144–145
Glades Haven: 558–559
Glen Haven RV and Mobile
  Park: 355–356
Goldcoaster Mobile Home
  and RV Park: 548
Golf View Estates: 538
Good Life RV Resort: 271
Gore's Landing Recreation
  Site: 209–210
Gornto Springs Park: 129
Graham Swamp Conserva-
  tion Area: 192
Grand Lake RV and Golf
  Resort: 205–206
Grandma's Grove RV Park:
  454–455
Grape Hammock RV Park
  and Marina: 280
Grassy Key: **606,** 611–612
Graveyard Creek
  Boat/Canoe Sites: 585–586

Grayton Beach State Park:
  85–86
Great Oak RV Resort:
  367–368
Green Cove Springs: **176,**
  177, 179
Greenfield Village RV Park:
  265–266
Grove Ridge Estates: 348
Gulf Air RV Park: 513
Gulf Beach Campground:
  433
Gulfbreeze RV Park:
  346–347
Gulf Coast Camping Resort:
  519
Gulf Coast Resort: 327–328
Gulf Holiday Travel Park:
  69–70
Gulf Islands National
  Seashore: 62
Gulf View Campground:
  121–122
Gulfview RV Resort: 443
Gulf Waters RV Resort: 512

H
Haines City: 264–265, 276
Haines Creek: 316
Haines Creek RV Village:
  316
Hainlin Mill Road: 546–547
Hal Scott Regional Preserve
  and Park: 342–343
Halifax River: 242–243
Hall's Landing: 104–105
Happy Days RV Park:
  357–358
Happy Traveler RV Park:
  487–488
Harbor Lakes RV Resort:
  440
Harney River Boat/Canoe
  Site: 584
Harris Village and RV Park:
  243
Hart Springs Gilchrist
  County Park: 151
Hawaiian Isles: 495
Hawthorne: **138,** 148–150

Hell's Bay: 590–591
Hell's Bay Boat/Canoe Sites:
  590–591
Hell's Bay Canoe Trail:
  592–593
Henderson Beach State
  Park: 69
Hickory Landing: 121
Hidden River Resort:
  171–172
Hidden River Travel Resort:
  492
Hidden Valley Campground:
  329–330
Hide-A-Way RV Resort:
  495–496
Highbanks Marina and
  Camp Resort: 247–248
High Bluff Campground
  (formerly Joe Budd): 103
Highland Beach Boat/Canoe
  Sites: 581–582
Highland Oaks RV Resort:
  292–293
Highland Park Fish Camp:
  244–245
Highlands Hammock State
  Park: 289–290
Highland Wheel Estates
  RV/Mobile Home Park:
  290–291
Highland Woods RV Resort:
  538
High Springs: **138,**
  142–143, 144–146
High Springs Campground:
  146
Highway A1A: **176,** 181,
  186–187, **378,** 391–392
Hillcrest RV Resort: 359
Hilliard: **160,** 161
Hillsborough River State
  Park: 487
Hinton Landing: 130–131
Hitchcock Lake: 118–119
Hobe Sound: **624,** 635–636
Hog Key Canoe/Kayak Sites:
  579
Hog Pen Landing: 171
Ho-Hum RV Park: 123

Holder Mine: 308
Holiday: **400,** 404
Holiday Cove RV Resort:
 422–423
Holiday Mobile Park: 314
Holiday Park and
 Campground: 124
Holiday Springs RV Resort:
 325
Holiday Travel Park
 (Lakeland): 272
Holiday Travel Park (St.
 Augustine): 192–193
Holiday Travel Park (St.
 Petersburg): 404
Holiday Travel Resort: 312
Holiday Trav-L-Park:
 211–212
Hollywood: **530,** 541–542
Holopaw: 270–271
Holt: **50,** 56, 65–66
Holton Creek Conservation
 Area: 112–113
Homestead: **530,** 547–548,
 549–550
Homosassa Springs: **204,**
 233–236
Hontoon Island State Park:
 246–246
Hopkins Prairie: 219
Horseshoe Beach Park:
 132–133
Horseshoe Cove Resort:
 424–425
Hudson: **298,** 327–328,
 345–348
Hudson Beach: 345
Huguenot Memorial Park:
 165–166
Hunter's Run RV Resort:
 356
Hurricane Lake Recreation
 Area: 53
Hutchinson Island: 632–633

I
Ichetucknee Springs
 Campground: 143–144
Idlewild Lodge: 309
I-4: **299,** 371

Immokalee: **500,** 521
Imperial Bonita Estates: 518
Indian Creek RV Resort: 514
Indian Forest Campground:
 183–184
Indian Mound Canoe Site:
 323
Indian Prairie Canal
 Primitive Sites: 460
Indian River: **378,** 384–385,
 388, 394–396
Indian Rocks Travel Park:
 408
Inglis: **138,** 155
Ingraham Hike-In/
 Bicycle-In Site: 602
Ingram's Marina: 102–103
Inn and Out Campground:
 140
International RV Park and
 Campground: 244
Inverness: **298,** 300–301,
 302–303, 307–309

J
Jacksonville: **160,** 163–167
Ja-Mar Travel Park: 402
Jasper: **98,** 112–113
Jay B. Starkey Wilderness
 Park: 402–403
Jennings Outdoor Resort: 110
Jennings State Forest: 177
Jetty Park Campground: 385
Jim's RV Park: 358
Joe River: 588, 593–595
Joe River Boat/Canoe Sites:
 593–594
John D. Easterlin Park:
 539–540
John Pennekamp Coral Reef
 State Park: 607–608
John Prince Park Camp-
 ground: 535
Jolly Roger Travel Park: 611
Jonathan Dickinson State
 Park: 635–638
Jumping Gully: 200
Juniper Lake: 76–77
Juniper Lake Campground:
 76–77

Juniper Springs: 221
Juniper Springs Recreation
 Area: 221
Juno Beach: 531–532
Juno Beach RV Park:
 531–532
Jupiter: **530,** 531, 638
J. W. Corbett Wildlife
 Management Area:
 480–481

K
Karick Lake: 54
Kathryn Abbey Hanna Park:
 166–167
Kelly Park: 318
Kelly's RV Park: 116–117
Kenansville: 283–284
Kenwood Recreation Area:
 193
Key Largo: **556, 606,**
 607–610
Key Largo Kampground and
 Marina: 608
Key RV Park: 612–613
Keystone Heights: **176,**
 178–179
Key West: **606,** 619–620
KICCO Wildlife Manage-
 ment Area: 281–282
King's Kamp RV Park Ma-
 rina and Motel: 608–609
Kings Lake: 75
Kissimmee: 266–269, **299,**
 366–369
Kissimmee Billie Swamp
 Safari: 482
Kissimmee/Orlando KOA:
 366
Kissimmee River: **260,**
 280–282, **448,** 453, 462
Kissimmee State Park:
 278–279
Kitching Creek Backcountry
 Site: 637
Knight's Key: 613
Knight's Key Park Camp-
 ground and Marina: 613
Koreshan State Historic Site:
 516–517

Kountree Kampinn RV
Resort: 523–524
Kozy Kampers RV Park: 539
Krul Recreation Area: 52

L
La Belle: **448,** 453–455
Lady Lake: 304–305, 306
Lafayette Blue Springs State
Park: 128
Lake Apopka: **298,** 340
Lake Ashby Park: 255
Lake Beauclaire: 313
Lake Bonnet: 288–289
Lake Bonnet Village:
288–289
Lake Bryant: 220–221
Lake Bryant Park: 220–221
Lake City: **138,** 139–142
Lake City Campground:
139–140
Lake City RV Park: 142
Lake Como Club: 353
Lake Cypress: **260,** 269–270
Lake Deaton: 311–312
Lake Deaton RV Park:
311–312
Lake Delancy East
Campground: 207
Lake Dorr Campground:
231
Lake Eaton: 218
Lake Eaton Campground:
218
Lake Eustis: **298,** 314
Lake Garfield: 271
Lake George: **176,** 196,
197–200, **204,** 222
Lake George Conservation
Area: 198–200
Lake Glenada RV Park: 294
Lake Griffin: 306–307
Lake Griffin State Park:
305–306
Lake Harris: **298,** 313–314
Lake Harris Resort: 313–314
Lake Hart: 360–361
Lake Istokpoga: **448,** 450,
451
Lake Jackson: 290–291

Lake Jesup: 324–325
Lake Jesup Conservation
Area: 324–325
Lake Josephine: **448,**
449–450
Lake Juliana: 262–263
Lake Juliana Boating and
Lodging: 262–263
Lake Kissimmee: **260,**
277–278, 279
Lake Kissimmee State Park:
260, 277–278
Lakeland: **260,** 261–262,
263
Lakeland RV Resort:
261–262
Lake Louisa State Park: 338
Lake Lowery: 264–265
Lake Magic RV Resort: 364
Lake Manatee: **416,**
421–422
Lake Manatee State Park:
421–422
Lake Marian: **260,** 282–283
Lake Marian Paradise:
282–283
Lake Mills Park: 344
Lake Monroe Conservation
Area: 250–251
Lake Monroe Park and
Campground: 249
Lakemont Ridge Home and
RV Park: 274–275
Lake Okeechobee: **448,**
456–462, 466–467,
469–470, 473, 475–478
Lake Okeechobee Resort
KOA: 464
Lake Okeechobee Scenic
Trail-Chancy Bay
Campsite: 477–478
Lake Okeechobee Scenic
Trail-Culvert 5A: 456–457
Lake Okeechobee Scenic
Trail-Kissimmee River: 461
Lake Okeechobee Scenic
Trail-Lake Harbor: 473
Lake Okeechobee Scenic
Trail-Lakeport: 459
Lake Okeechobee Sce-

nic Trail-Liberty Point:
469–470
Lake Okeechobee Scenic
Trail-Nubbin Slough:
466–467
Lake Okeechobee Scenic
Trail-South Port Mayaca:
477
Lake Osborne: 535
Lake Panasoffkee: 309
Lake Pearl: 317–318
Lake Pierce: **260,** 276
Lake Pierce Eco Resort:
276–277
Lake Placid: **448,** 450,
452–453
Lakeport: 457–459
Lakeport RV Resort: 457
Lake Rosalie: **260,** 279–280
Lake Rousseau RV and
Fishing Resort: 225
Lake San Marino RV Park:
520
Lake Saunders: 315
Lake Seminole: **74,** 99
Lakeshore Palms Travel
Park: 273
Lakeside at Barth: 54
Lakeside Mobile Manor: 330
Lakeside RV Park (Lake
Okeechobee): 464–465
Lakeside RV Park (Orlando):
317
Lakeside Stables: 291
Lakeside Travel Park and
Campground: 106–107
Lake Smith: 317
Lake Stone Campground: 51
Lake Talquin: **98,** 101–103,
104–106
Lake Talquin State Forest:
103–104
Lake Toho RV and Mobile
Home Park: 268–269
Lake Tohopekaliga: **260,**
267–269
Lake Trafford Marina and
Campground: 521
Lake Trinity Estates:
542–543

Lakeview Manor RV Park (formerly Windsor): 463–464
Lake Waldena Resort: 216–217
Lake Wales: **260,** 273–274, 276, 277, 279–282
Lake Wales Campground: 274
Lake Whippoorwill: 360
Lake Woodruff National Wildlife Refuge: 244–245
Lakewood RV Resort: 372
Lakewood Travel Park: 347
Lake Worth: **530,** 535
Lamont: 126
Land Yacht Harbor: 389–390
Lane Bay: 590
Lane Bay Boat/Canoe Site: 590
Lantana: 535–536
Lard Can Boat/Canoe Sites: 592–593
Largo: **400,** 408–410
Larry and Penny Thompson Memorial Park and Campground: 545–546
Layton: 610–611
Lazy Days RV Park: 66
Lazy Lakes Campground: 616
Lee: 109–110
Leesburg: **298,** 312–313, 316
Leisure Days RV Resort: 359–360
LeLynn RV Resort: 262
Leonard's Landing Lake Crescent Resort: 196–197
Leo's Campground: 617–618
Lettuce Lake Travel Resort: 438–439
Lily Lake Golf Resort: 275
Linger Lodge RV Resort: 425
Lion Country Safari KOA: 534–535
Lithia Springs Park: 491
Little Charlie Creek RV Park: 285–286

Little Manatee River State Park: 496
Little Rabbit Key Boat/Canoe Sites: 599–600
Little Talbot Island State Park: 164–165
Little Willie's RV Resort: 431–432
Live Oak: 111–113, **138,** 139
Live Oak Backpacking Site: 321–322
Live Oak RV Resort: 439–440
Lochloosa Harbor RV Park: 148–149
Lochloosa Lake: **138,** 150
Lochloosa Wildlife Conservation Area: 150
Long Key: **606,** 610–611
Long Key State Park: 610–611
Long Leaf RV Park: 75–76
Long Pine Key Campground: 566–567
Long Point Park: 394
Loop Road (Big Cypress National Preserve): 563–564
Lopez River: 571
Lopez River Boat/Canoe Sites: 571
Lorida: 453
Lostman's Five Bay: 578–579
Lostman's Five Bay Boat/Canoe Sites: 578–579
Loxahatchee: 533–534
Lutz: 353

M
Macclenny: 171–172
Mack Landing: 119–120
Madison: **98,** 108–110
Madison Blue Springs State Park: 109–110
Madison Campground: 108–109
Magnolia Beach Campground: 64–65
Magnolia Park: 340
Malabar: 392–393

Manatee Hammock: 384–385
Manatee Springs State Park: 151–152
Mango Manor: 386
Many Mansions RV Park: 350
Marathon: **606,** 611–613
Marco Island: **500,** 525–526
Marco-Naples Hitching Post Travel Trailer Resort: 524
Marianna: **74,** 80–82
Markham Park: 543–544
Mary's Fish Camp: 325–326
Mayfair Motel and RV Park: 60
Mayo: **98,** 128–129
McDavid: 51
McIntosh: **204,** 205
Meadowlark Campground: 455–456
Melbourne: **378,** 388–391
Melbourne Beach: 391–392, 394–396
Merry D RV Sanctuary: 266
Metrozoo: 545–546
Mexico Beach: **74,** 93
Miami Everglades Campground: 546–547
Micanopy: 147–148
Middleburg: 177
Middle Cape Sable Boat/Canoe Sites: 597–598
Middleton's Fish Camp: 627
Midway Campground: 562–563
Mike Roess Gold Head Branch State Park: **176,** 178
Mike Roess Gold Head Branch State Park Primitive Camping: 178–179
Mill Creek RV Resort: 368
Mill Dam Lake Resort: 220
Miller's Marine Campground: 133–134
Milton: **50,** 55, 56, 57–59, 62–63
Milton/Gulf Pines KOA: 58
Mims: **378,** 380–382

Mitchell's Landing: 563–564
Molino: **50,** 51, 54
Monticello: **98,** 108
Monument Lake
   Campground: 561–562
Moonrise Resort: 303
Moore Haven: **448,**
   455–456, 468, 471–472
Morgan's Mobile Home Park
   and Fish Camp: 306–307
Mormon Key Boat/Canoe
   Sites: 576
Morningside RV Estates:
   349
Moses Creek: 187–188
Moses Creek Conservation
   Area: 187–188
Moss Park: 360–361
Mossy Cove Fish Camp and
   RV Resort: 451
Motor Inns Motel and RV
   Park: 212
Mount Dora: **298,** 313, 315
Mouse Mountain RV and
   Mobile Home Resort:
   371–372
Mud River: 325–326
Mullet Lake: 343
Mullet Lake Park: 343
Munson: **50,** 52–53
Mutual Mine Recreation
   Area: 308–309
Myakka River: **416,**
   427–428, 440
Myakka River State Park:
   416, 427–429
Myakka River Trail Primi-
   tive Backpacking Sites:
   428–429
Myakka RV Resort: 437
Myakka State Forest:
   436–437
Mystic Springs Cove
   Airstream Park: 51

N
Naples: **500,** 520–521,
   522–525, 558
Naples/Marco Island KOA
   Kampground: 524–525

Natures Resort RV Park: 235
Navarre: **50,** 64–65
Navarre Beach Camp-
   ground: 64
Neal's Landing: 79
New Pine Landing: 131–132
Newport: **98,** 125
Newport Recreation Park:
   125
New Port Richey: **400,** 401,
   402–404
New Smyrna Beach: **240,**
   254–255, 256, 379–380
New Smyrna Beach RV Park
   and Campground: 254
New Turkey Key Boat/Ca-
   noe Sites: 576–577
Niceville: **50,** 66, 67–68
Nine Mile Grade
   Campground: 453
Nokomis: **416,** 434
North Beach Camp Resort:
   181
North Fort Myers: **500,**
   502–504, 505
North Lake Estates RV
   Resort: 458
North Nest Key Boat/Canoe
   Sites: 600–601
North Port: **416,** 437
North River: 588–589
North River Boat/Canoe
   Site: 588–589
Northwest Cape Sable Boat/
   Canoe Sites: 598
Nova Family Campground:
   252

O
Oak Harbor: 264–265
Oak Haven Park: 439
Oakland Park: 539–540
Oak Springs Travel Park:
   402
Oak Tree Village
   Campground: 210–211
Ocala: 149, **204,** 206,
   210–212, 214, 226–228
Ocala Forest Campground:
   230–231

Ocala National Forest: **204,**
   206–209, 214–219, 220,
   221, 223, 229, 230–232
Ocala Ranch RV Park: 228
Ocala RV Camp Resort: 227
Ocean Grove RV Resort: 185
Ocean Pond: 170–171
Ocean Pond Campground:
   170–171
Ochlockonee River: **98,** 119
Ochlockonee River State
   Park: 123–124
Ocklawaha: 220–221
Ocklawaha Prairie Restora-
   tion Area: 219–220
Ocklawaha River: 206–207,
   209–210
Ocklawaha RV Park and
   Canoe Outpost: 206–207
Ohio Key: 613–614
Okeechobee: **448,** 462–468,
   470
Okeechobee Landings:
   472–473
Okee-Tantie Campground
   and Marina: 462
Olde Mill Stream RV
   Resort: 317–318
Old Town: **98,** 129–132
Old Town Campground 'n'
   Retreat: 130
O'Leno State Park: 145–146
Orange Blossom RV Park:
   287
Orange City: **240,** 245–247,
   248
Orange City RV Resort: 248
Orange Grove Campground:
   366–367
Orange Harbor Mobile
   Home and RV Park: 506
Orange Isles Campground:
   251–252
Orange Lake: **204,** 205
Orange/Osceola County
   line: 362
Orange Park: 172, 177
Orchid Lake Travel Park:
   403–404

Original Suwannee River
Campground: 129–130
Orlando: **298,** 342–345,
360–363, 383
Orlando Southeast/Lake
Whippoorwill KOA: 360
Orlando Winter Garden RV
Resort: 339
Ormond Beach: 241–243
Ortona South Campground:
455
Oscar Scherer State Park:
433–434
Osceola National Forest:
160, 167–171
Osprey: **416,** 433
Otter Creek: **138,** 154–155
Otter Springs RV Resort: 152
Outdoor Resorts at St. Lucie:
631–632
Outdoor Resorts Melbourne
Beach: 391–392
Outdoor Resorts of
Chokoloskee Island: 560
Outlet River: 309–310
Oyster Bay: 587–588
Oyster Bay Boat/Canoe
Sites: 587–588

P
Pace: **50,** 59
Pacetti's Marina RV Park
and Fishing Resort:
179–180
Palatka: **176,** 193–196, 200
Palm Bay RV Park: 420
Palm Beach: 532–533
Palm Beach Gardens: 532
Palm Beach Gardens RV
Park: 532
Palm Beach Traveler Park:
535–536
Palm Coast: **176,** 188–189
Palmdale: **448,** 451–452
Palmetto: **416,** 417–420
Palm Gardens: 314–315
Palm Harbor: **400,** 405–407
Palm Harbor Resort: 405
Palm River Mobile Home
Park: 520–521

Palms and Pines Riverside
Resort: 440–441
Palm View Gardens: 357
Panacea: 124
Pana Vista Lodge: 309–310
Panama City Beach: **74,**
86–90
Panama City Beach RV
Resort: 89
Paradise Island RV Resort:
540–541
Paradise Lakes Travel Trailer
Park: 250
Paradise Pointe RV Resort:
526
Paradise RV Resort:
372–373
Parakeet Park: 273–274
Parker Farm Campground: 91
Parramore's Fantastic Fish
Camp and Family Resort:
222
Pat Thomas Park: 102
Pavilion Key Boat/Canoe
Sites: 572–573
Paynes Prairie Preserve State
Park: 147–148
Peace River: 285–286, **416,**
430–431, 440–441, 449
Peace River Preserve: 286
Peace River Primitive Canoe
Sites: 430–431
Peach Creek RV Park: 86
Peanut Island: 532–533
Pearl Bay: 592
Pearl Bay Boat/Canoe Sites:
592
Pelican Motel and Trailer
Park: 611–612
Pelican Palms RV Park:
62–63
Pellicer Creek: 188
Pembroke Park: 542–543
Pembroke Pines: 545
Pensacola: **50,** 54, 59–61,
63–64, 66–67
Pensacola/Perdido Bay KOA:
61–62
PepperTree Beach Club
Resort: 186–187

Perdido Key: 60–62
Periwinkle Park: 510
Perrine: 545–546
Perry: **98,** 127–128
Perry KOA: 127
Phipps Park: 634
Picnic Key Boat/Canoe Sites:
569–570
Pierson: **240,** 241
Pine Creek Landing: 119
Pinecrest Campground: 564
Pineglen Motorcoach and
RV Park: 86–87
Pine Island: **500,** 507–508
Pine Island Campground
and Fish Camp: 306
Pine Island Campground
and Marina: 200
Pine Lake RV Park: 85
Pinellas Bayway: 412
Pine Log State Forest: 83–84
Pioneer Creek RV Park: 284
Pioneer Park of Hardee
County: 449
Pioneer Village: 502
Plate Creek Bay: 577–578
Plate Creek Bay Boat/Canoe
Site: 577–578
Playa del Rio RV Park: 61
Playground RV Park: 65
Pleasant Lake RV Resort:
423–424
Polk City: 262
Pompano Beach: **530,**
536–538
Ponce de Leon: **74,** 77
Ponderosa RV Park:
368–369
Port Charlotte: 436–437
Port Cove RV Park &
Marina: 198
Porter Lake: 118
Port Mayaca: 478–480
Port Orange: **240,** 251–256
Port Richey: **400,** 401, 402
Port St. Joe: **74,** 93–94
Port St. Lucie: **624,** 629
Port St. Lucie RV Resort:
629

Potts Preserve: 300
Presnell's Bayside Marina and RV Resort: 94
Primrose RV Park: 467
Princess Place Preserve: 188–189
Punta Gorda: **416,** 440–444
Punta Gorda RV Resort: 442

QR
Quail Roost Drive: 546–547
Quail Roost RV Campground: 223–224
Quail Run RV Park: 352
Quiet Waters Park: 536–537
Quincy: **98,** 101–103
Rabbit Key Boat/Canoe Sites: 571–572
Raccoon River Camp Resort: 88
Rainbow RV Campground: 154
Rainbow Springs State Park: 225–226
Rally Park: 489
Ralph E. Simmons Memorial State Forest: **160,** 161
Ralph's Travel Park: 359
Ramblers Rest Resort Campground: 436
Ranch Motel and Campground: 148
Recreation Plantation RV Resort: 304
Red Barn RV Resort: 335
Red Coconut RV Resort: 510–511
Reflections on Silver Lake: 288
Reynolds Airpark: 179
Rice Creek RV Resort: 493
Richardson's Fish Camp: 267
Ridgecrest RV Resort: 312–313
RiverBend Motorcoach Resort: 505–506
River Breeze Park: 256
River Lakes Conservation Area: 387

River Oaks RV Resort: 494–495
River Ranch RV Resort: 281
River's Edge RV Campground: 65–66
Riverside Lodge: 300–301
Riverside RV Resort and Campground: 437–438
Riverview: **486,** 492–494
Riviera Beach: **530,** 532–533
Riviera Naturist Resort: 59
Road Runner Travel Resort: 629–630
Robert's Mobile Home and RV Resort: 411–412
Roberts River: 589–590
Roberts River Boat/Canoe Sites: 589–590
Robin's Nest RV Park: 217
Robin's Nest RV Resort: 471–472
Rock Creek RV Resort and Campground: 522
Rock Crusher Canyon RV and Music Park: 233
Rock Springs: 318
Rockledge: **378,** 387–388
Rocky Creek Bay: 580
Rodgers River Bay: 580–581
Rodgers River Bay Boat/Canoe Sites: 580–581
Rodman Reservoir: 193–194
Ronny's RV Ranch: 634
Rose Bay: 253
Rose Bay Travel Park: 253
Roseland: **624,** 625
Royal Coachman RV Resort: 434
Ruskin: **486,** 494–496
RV Corral: 373–374

S
Salt Springs Recreation Area: 208
San Carlos RV Park and Islands: 513–514
Sanford: 250–251, **298,** 318–320, 324–325, 343
Sanibel Island: **500,** 509–510

Sanlan Ranch Campground: 263–264
Santa Rosa Beach: **50,** 70
Santa Rosa Island: 62
Sarasota: **416,** 426–428, 433
Sarasota Bay Travel Trailer Park: 422
Satsuma: **176,** 194
Scotts Ferry General Store and Campground: 90–91
Scottsmoor: **378,** 380
Scrub Jay Backcountry Site: 637–638
Seasons in the Sun Motorcoach Resort: 381–382
Sebastian: 393–394
Sebastian Inlet State Park: 394–496
Sebring: **260,** 289–293, 449–450
Sebring Grove RV Resort: 291
Seminole: **400,** 410
Seminole Campground: 503
Seminole Health Club: 544–545
Seminole Indian land: 482
Seminole Park: 541–542
Seminole Ranch Conservation Area: 383
Settler's Rest RV Park: 354–355
Seven Acres RV Park: 336
Seven Oaks Travel Park: 345–346
76 Bill Frederick Park and Pool at Turkey Lake: 342
Seville: 198–200
Shady Acres Mobile Home and RV Park: 346
Shady Acres RV Park: 515–516
Shady Oaks Campground: 154–155
Shamrock Campground: 184
Shark River: 586–587
Shark River Boat/Canoe Site: 586–587
Shell Creek Resort: 441
Shell Harbour Resort: 194

Shell Mound County Park: 153

Sherwood Forest RV Resort (Orlando): 365–366

Sherwood Forest RV Resort (St. Petersburg): 406

Shired Island Park: 133

Siesta Bay RV Resort: 509–510

Siesta Key: **416,** 433

Silver Lake Campground: 332–333

Silver Lakes RV Resort and Golf Club: 525–526

Silver River State Park: 214

Silver Springs: **204,** 212–214, 219–220

Silver Springs Campers Garden: 213–214

Silver Springs nature theme park: 212–213

Singer Island: 532–533

Slow and Easy Living RV Park: 141

Sneads: **74,** 82

Son Rise Palms: 386

Sopchoppy: 119–120, 123–124

Sorrento: **298,** 320

South Bay: **448,** 474–475

South Bay RV Campground: 474–475

Southern Aire: 488

Southern Charm RV Resort: 355

Southern Comfort RV Resort: 548–549

Southern Palms RV Resort: 316–317

Southern Sun RV and Mobile Home Park: 228

South Fork St. Lucie River Management Area: 633–634

South Joe River Boat/Canoe Sites: 594

Southport RV Park, Campground, and Marina: 267–268

South Scenic Highway (State Road 17): **260,** 273–274

Space Coast RV Resort: 387–388

Spirit of the Suwannee Music Park: 112

Sportsman's Cove on Orange Lake: 205

Spring Hill: **298,** 326

Spruce Creek Park: 255–256

Squawk Creek: 584–585

Stagecoach RV Park: 180–181

Stage Stop Campground: 339–340

St. Andrews State Park: 90

Starke: **138,** 146–147

Starke KOA: 147

St. Augustine: **176,** 179–188

St. Augustine Beach: 183

St. Augustine Beach KOA: 183

St. Cloud: 269–270, 282–284

Stephen Foster Folk Culture Center State Park: 113–114

Stewarts Mobile Village: 287–288

St. George Island: **98,** 122

St. Johns River: **176,** 179–180, 194, **204,** 222–223, 247–249, 387

St. Johns River Campground: 221–222

St. Johns RV Park: 184–185

St. Lucie Canal: **624,** 634–635

St. Lucie Lock Recreation Area: 634–635

St. Marks National Wildlife Refuge: **98,** 125–126

St. Marys River: 151

Stock Island: **606,** 617–619

St. Petersburg: **400,** 410–412

St. Petersburg Resort KOA: 410–411

St. Sebastian State Buffer Preserve: 393–394

Stuart: 633–635

Sugarloaf Key: **606,** 615–617

Sugarloaf Key Resort KOA Kampground: 615–616

Sugar Mill Ruins Travel Park: 254–255

Sumatra: 117, 120–121

Sumner: 154

Sumter Oaks RV Park: 335

Sun Resorts: 340

Suncoast RV Resort: 401

Sundance Lakes RV Resort: 401

Sunday Bay: 570

Sunday Bay Boat/Canoe Sites: 570

Sun-n-Fun RV Resort: 426

Sunnier Palms Nudist Campground: 631

Sun-n-Shade Campground: 444

Sunny Sands Nudist Resort: 241

Sunnyhill Restoration Area: 229

Sunseekers RV Park: 516

Sunset King Lake Resort: 75

Sunshine Holiday Daytona RV Resort: 241–242

Sunshine Holiday RV Resort: 540

Sunshine Key RV Resort: 613–614

Sunshine Mobile Home Park: 305

Sunshine RV Resort: 452

Sunshine Travel-Encore Resort Vero Beach: 625–626

Sunsport Gardens: 533–534

Suwannee: 133–134

Suwannee River: **98,** 111–116

Suwannee River Hideaway Campground: 131

Suwannee River State Park: 111–112

Suwannee Valley Campground: 114–115

Swan Lake Village and RV Resort: 502

Sweetwater Boat/Canoe Sites: 575–576
Sweetwater Creek: 575–576
Sweetwater RV Park: 354
Swift Creek Conservation Area: 114
Swimming Pen Creek: 172

T
Tallahassee: **98,** 104–107, 125
Tallahassee East KOA: 108
Tallahassee RV Park: 107
Tall Oaks Campground: 59–60
Tall Pines RV Park: 334
Tamiami RV Park: 501–502
Tamiami Trail: 560–565
Tampa: 353, **486,** 489, 490
Tampa Bay: **400,** 412
Tampa East RV Resort: 489–490
Tarpon Bay: 584–585
Tarpon Springs: **400,** 404–405
Tavares: **298,** 313–315
Taylor Creek Resort RV Park: 466
Telogia: 118–119
Ten Thousand Islands: 568–572
Terra Ceia Village RV Resort: 417–418
The Boardwalk (Gold Coast): 547–548
The Floridian RV Resort: 362
The Great Outdoors Resort: 383–384
The Groves RV Resort: 509
The Harbor RV Resort and Marina: 279–280
The Marina RV Resort: 470
The Oaks Campground: 334–335
The Outpost RV Park: 82
The Riptide RV Park and Motel: 609
The River Rendezvous: 128–129

The Savannas Recreational Area: 632
The Springs RV Resort: 212–213
The Village at Nettles Island: 632–633
Thonotosassa: **486,** 487–489
Thousand Trails Orlando: 338–339
Three Forks Marsh Conservation Area: 390–391
Three Lakes Wildlife Management Area: 283–284
Three Rivers State Park: 82
Three Worlds RV and Mobile Home Resort: 374
T. H. Stone Memorial St. Joseph Peninsula State Park: 93–94
Tice Mobile Home Court: 506–507
Tiger Bay State Forest: **240,** 243–244
Tiger Key Boat/Canoe Sites: 568–569
Tiki Village Campground: 261–262
Tillis Hill: 307–308
Titusville: **378,** 381, 383–387
Titusville/Kennedy Space Center KOA: 382–383
Toby's RV Resort: 431
Tomoka Basin GeoPark: 242–243
Topics RV Community: 327
Topsail Hill State Preserve: 70
Torchlite RV and Mobile Home Park: 337–338
Torreya State Park: 99–101
Torreya State Park Backpacking Sites: 100–101
Torry Island: 475
Town and Country Camper Lodge: 127
Town and Country RV Resort: 319–320
Trail's End Camp: 301–302

Travelers Rest Resort: 331
Treasure Coast RV Resort: 630–631
Trenton: 151
Tresca Memorial Park/Advent Christian Village: 139
Trimble Park: 313
Tropical Gardens RV Park: 424
Tropical Palms FunResort: 364–365
Tropic Isles Mobile Home Park: 419–420
Turtleback RV Resort: 310
Turtle Creek RV Resort: 234–235
Twelve Oaks RV Resort: 318–319
21 Palms RV Resort: 373
Twin Lakes Fish Camp: 149
Twin Lakes Travel Park: 541
T. Y. Park: 542

U
Umatilla: 317–318
Uncle Joe's Fish Camp: 468
Upper Chipola River: 79–80
Upper Chipola River Water Management Area: 79–80
Upriver Campground RV Resort: 503–504
U.S. 41: **98,** 113–114, **298,** 353, **416,** 442
U.S. 19/98: **138,** 151–152
U.S. 192: **299,** 364–366, 368–369
U.S. 90: **74,** 81
U.S. 98: **50,** 63–64, **98,** 125–126, **260,** 263–264, **298,** 348
U.S. 1: 184, **240,** 254–255, **378,** 389, 392–393, **530,** 531–532, 536, **624,** 626–627, 632
U.S. 1/Overseas Highway: **557,** 607–609
U.S. 17: **160,** 163, **176,** 196, **260,** 284–285
U.S. 17/92: **299,** 373–374

U.S. 301: **298,** 336
U.S. 29: 54
U.S. 27: **138,** 152–153, **260,**
265–266, 287, 292, 369

VW
Vacation Village/Sunburst:
409
Valencia Estates: 263
Venice: **416,** 433, 434–437
Venice Campground:
435–436
Vero Beach: **624,** 625–627
Vero Beach Kamp: 626–629
Vilano Beach: 182
Village Pines Campground:
155
Vortex Spring RV Park: 77
Wabasso: 626
Wagon Wheel RV Park:
284–285
Wakulla County: 125–126
Wallaby Ranch Flight Park:
369–370
Waters Edge RV Resort
(Orlando): 351
Water's Edge RV Resort
(Sarasota): 443
Watson River Boat/Canoe
Sites: 588
Watson's Place Boat/Canoe
Sites: 574–575
Wauchula: **260,** 284–286
Wayne's RV Resort: 140
Webb Lake: 501
Weeki Wachee: 325–326
Weirsdale: **204,** 229–230
Wekiva Falls Resort: 320
Wekiva River: 320
Wekiwa Springs: 320–321
Wekiwa Springs State Park:
320–324
Welaka: **176,** 194–195

Wesley Chapel: 352
Westgate Motel
Campground: 128
West Jupiter Camping
Resort: 531
West Jupiter Wetlands
Management Area: 638
West Lake Tohopekaliga:
267–268
West Palm Beach: 480–481,
533–534
West Tower: 169–170
Wewahitchka: **74,** 91–92
Whippoorwill Sportsman's
Lodge: 101–102
Whisper Creek RV Resort:
453–454
Whispering Palms RV Park:
626
Whispering Pines RV Park:
215–216
Whispering Pines Village:
291–292
Whitehead Lake: 118
White Springs: 113–117
White's RV Park: 356
Whitey's Fish Camp: 172
Wickham Park: 389
Wilderness RV Park Estates:
214–215
Wilderness Waterway: 571,
573–574, 577–578
Wildwood: 309–312
Wildwood KOA: 311
Wildwoods Campground:
223
William's Landing: 105
Willow Lakes RV and Golf
Resort: 381
Willy Willy Boat/Canoe
Sites: 580
Wimauma: 496
Windward Isle RV Park: 427

Winter Garden: 339–340
Winter Haven: **260,**
271–273
Winter Paradise RV Park:
345
Winter Quarters Manatee
RV Resort: 421
Winterset Park: 418
Withlacoochee River: 109–
110,111–112, 302–303
Withlacoochee River Park:
336
Withlacoochee State Forest
Citrus Tract: 307–309
Wood Lake: 120
Woodsmoke Camping
Resort: 515
Woods-n-Water Trails RV
Community: 315
W. P. Franklin Lock and
Dam Campground: 504
Wright Lake: 120–121

XYZ
Yankeetown: **138,** 156
Yankee Traveler RV Park:
408–409
Yeehaw Junction: **260,**
281–282, **624,** 628
Yellow Jacket Campground:
132
Yellow River: **50,** 63
Yellow River Wildlife
Management Area: 63
Yogi Bear's Jellystone Park
Camp-Resort: 109
Yulee: **160,** 163
Zachary Taylor Camping
Resort: 465–466
Zephyrhills: **298,** 350–352,
354–360, 487
Zolfo Springs: **448,** 449

Acknowledgments

Joanne S. Moore and Sally Deneen provided
valuable assistance in the preparation of this book.

www.moon.com

For helpful advice on planning a trip, visit www.moon.com for the **TRAVEL PLANNER** and get access to useful travel strategies and valuable information about great places to visit. When you travel with Moon, expect an experience that is uncommon and truly unique.

MOON OUTDOORS

"A smart new look provides just one more reason to travel with Moon Outdoors. Well written, thoroughly researched, and packed full of useful information and advice, these guides really do get you into the outdoors."

—GORP.COM

ALSO AVAILABLE AS FOGHORN OUTDOORS ACTIVITY GUIDES:

101 Great Hikes of the
   San Francisco Bay Area
250 Great Hikes in
   California's National Parks
Baja Camping
California Beaches
California Fishing
California Golf
California Hiking
California Recreational
   Lakes & Rivers
California Waterfalls
California Wildlife
Camper's Companion
Easy Biking in Northern
   California

Easy Hiking in Northern
   California
Easy Hiking in Southern
   California
Florida Beaches
Georgia & Alabama Camping
Great Lakes Camping
Maine Hiking
Massachusetts Hiking
Montana, Wyoming & Idaho
   Camping
New England Biking
New England Cabins
   & Cottages
New England Camping
New England Hiking

New Hampshire Hiking
Oregon Hiking
Pacific Northwest Hiking
Southern California
   Cabins & Cottages
Tom Stienstra's Bay Area
   Recreation
Utah Camping
Utah Hiking
Vermont Hiking
Washington Boating
   & Water Sports
Washington Fishing
Washington Hiking
West Coast RV Camping

MOON FLORIDA CAMPING

Avalon Travel Publishing
a member of the Perseus Books group

1400 65th Street, Suite 250
Emeryville, CA 94608, USA
www.moon.com

Editor: Shaharazade Husain
Series Manager: Sabrina Young
Copy Editor: Mia Lipman
Graphics Coordinator: Elizabeth Jang
Production Coordinator: Elizabeth Jang
Cover Designer: Elizabeth Jang
Interior Designer: Darren Alessi
Map Editor: Kevin Anglin
Cartographers: Suzanne Service, Kat Bennett
Proofreader: Valerie Sellers Blanton
Indexer: Rachel Kuhn

ISBN-10: 1-56691-825-1
ISBN-13: 978-1-56691-825-1
ISSN: 1095-1814

Printing History
1st Edition – 1998
4th Edition – September 2007
5 4 3 2 1

Front cover photo: Caladesi Island State Park, © James Randklev, www.jamesrandklev.com
Title page photo: Camping at Long Pine Key in Everglades National Park, © Marilyn Moore
Back cover photo: © Al Valeiro / Getty Images

Printed in the United States of America by Worzalla

KEEPING CURRENT

We are committed to making this book the most accurate and enjoyable camping guide to Florida. You can rest assured that every campground in this book has been carefully reviewed in an effort to keep this book as up-to-date as possible. However, by the time you read this book, some of the fees listed herein may have changed and campgrounds may have closed unexpectedly.

If you have a favorite gem you'd like to see included in the next edition, or see anything that needs updating, clarification, or correction, please drop us a line. Send your comments via email to feedback@moon.com, or use the address above.